THE RISE OF REALISM

AMERICAN LITERATURE: A PERIOD ANTHOLOGY

OSCAR CARGILL, *General Editor*

THE ROOTS OF NATIONAL CULTURE: TO 1830

ROBERT E. SPILLER
Swarthmore College

THE ROMANTIC TRIUMPH: 1830-1860

TREMAINE McDOWELL
University of Minnesota

THE RISE OF REALISM: 1860-1888

LOUIS WANN
University of Southern California

THE SOCIAL REVOLT: 1888-1914

OSCAR CARGILL
New York University

CONTEMPORARY TRENDS: SINCE 1914

JOHN HERBERT NELSON
University of Kansas

THE RISE OF
REALISM

American Literature
FROM 1860 TO 1888

EDITED BY

LOUIS WANN
PROFESSOR OF ENGLISH LANGUAGE
AND LITERATURE
UNIVERSITY OF SOUTHERN CALIFORNIA

NEW YORK
THE MACMILLAN COMPANY

PREFACE

The aim of this volume, *The Rise of Realism*, is to present the essential materials, critical and illustrative, for a study of the literature of America during the generation following the outbreak of the Civil War. In harmony with the common aim of the volumes that constitute this series, this volume stresses the dominant literary phenomenon of the age which it embraces—the genesis of realism.

Recent American criticism has tended more and more to recognize the necessity of studying the social, economic, and political factors in a nation's life if one is to understand its literature which is, after all, but the reflection of that life. For this reason it is essential, in an attempt to study intensively the interplay of those diverse forces which ultimately produced a body of realistic literature in this country, that many forms of writing other than mere *belles lettres* be given recognition. No apology therefore is required for the representation in this volume of the writings and addresses of Lincoln, the songs of the Civil War, the literature of Reconstruction, the varied contributions of the Western Humorists, folk literature (cowboy ballads, mountaineer ballads, Paul Bunyan stories, and Negro songs and rhymes), and the considerable body of local-color stories and poems from various sections of the country. Much of this material may lack high literary value, but all is exceedingly important as basic material for understanding the works of acknowledged literary merit. It is also essential that the literature of decadent romanticism be adequately represented if the full meaning of the struggle between "romanticism" and "realism" is to be appreciated. Hence the inclusion, on a scale somewhat greater than in most anthologies, of writers of the Genteel Tradition and producers of Romance and Sentiment. The real significance of Twain, Howells, and James is apparent only by comparison with the Aldriches, the Stoddards, the Stocktons, and the Rileys. In short, the endeavor has been to avoid the suggestion of special pleading for any one group or movement, but to let the whole literature of the period tell the inevitable story—the rise of realism, with all the accompanying checks and counterchecks. It is to be regretted that copyright restrictions make impossible the adequate or proper representation of some authors, notably John Burroughs, Emily Dickinson, Sidney Lanier, Thomas Nelson Page, and James Whitcomb Riley. It should also be borne in mind that space restrictions have not only necessitated the elimination of much desirable material from the authors here represented but have compelled the entire exclusion of other authors slightly, if at all, less worthy than those included.

A movement such as the development of realism in a literature affects all forms of writing; hence all are here illustrated,—criticism, history, the novel, and the drama,—though the last (reaching on the professional stage its lowest ebb, perhaps, in the past hundred years) is here represented only by one of Howells' farces which, in spite of their unprofessional character, possibly offer a better index to the spirit of the time than the melodramas and sentimental comedies then in vogue. The obvious disadvantages in the use of excerpts, especially in the case of the novel, have been partially overcome by choosing such passages as have an entity in themselves. Moreover, in studying the rise of realism, the method of a novelist like Howells can be perceived almost as clearly from a characteristic chapter as the method of Harte can be from a typical short story. The genuine necessity for including the novel in any study of that literary movement in which it was the dominant form is perfectly apparent.

In the use of texts, preference has been given to the original form of publication, as in the case of the *Atlantic Monthly* texts of *Old Times on the Mississippi, The American,* and *Deephaven Cronies,* and in the use of the original (1855) version of the Preface to *Leaves of Grass.* Those who wish the revised forms of such works as James' *The American* or Stockton's *Rudder Grange* have relatively easy access to them; the present work aims to present the actual text that was read *at the time*—texts which in many cases were of distinct influence on other writers.

The critical section of the volume consists of an Introduction and a body of Notes at the end. The Notes attempt to provide: (1) brief, accurate biographical sketches of all authors represented; (2) bibliographies (works, lives, and criticism); and (3) a select number of explanatory notes covering the text itself.

The date of composition of poems (where known) appears at the left, following the poem. The dates at the right are those of first known publication. Where two such dates appear, as in the case of Whitman, the latter represents first inclusion in a collection and usually represents a revised form of the poem. The same arrangement applies to the prose, except in the case of selections from Lincoln and the letters of Lanier and Emily Dickinson where the date of writing appears at the head of the selection. All titles in brackets are those of the present editor. Omissions for which he is responsible are indicated by asterisks. Ellipses mark either their actual appearance in the author's text or, in the case of a standard editor's preparation of the text, the omissions of that editor.

The indebtedness of the present editor to previous anthologists and critics of American literature is partly but inadequately indicated in the bibliographies at the end of this volume. Special acknowledgment is due to such painstaking and stimulating scholars as the late Professor Vernon L. Parrington, Professor Fred Lewis Pattee, and the writers of the various chapters in the *Cambridge History of American Literature* for invaluable contributions toward a sane and comprehensive view of the nation's literary expression.

For specific assistance, grateful appreciation is accorded the following: Mr. Hamlin Garland, for criticism of the Introduction; Miss Mary Elizabeth Russell, for information regarding the life and work of Irwin Russell; various colleagues, especially Professor Oscar Cargill and the other editors of this series; Professors Lynn Clark, Allison Gaw, and Garland Greever, for helpful criticism of the plan and contents of the volume; the members of various library staffs, especially those of the University of Southern California, the Los Angeles Public Library, and the San Diego Public Library, as well as Mr. Harry S. Wedding, librarian of the Wabash College Library, and Miss Mabel R. Gillis, State Librarian of the California State Library, for generous assistance in procuring texts and furnishing bibliographical help; and Miss Velma Hayden, Miss Esther Kohler, Mrs. Helen Walker Truesdell, Miss Mary Caroline Wann, and Mrs. Ross Wills, for generous assistance in the preparation of the text, the notes, and the index.

For permission to print or reprint certain texts the editor is deeply indebted to the following: Professor John Harrington Cox, for the ballad "The Rowan County Crew"; the Henry E. Huntington Library and Art Gallery, for Bret Harte's "The Work on Red Mountain"; and Professor Homer A. Watt, for "Paul Bunyan Provides for His Crew."

LOUIS WANN

ACKNOWLEDGMENTS

For permission to reprint copyright material, the editor is indebted to the following individuals and publishers:

D. Appleton and Company: for the selection from *Uncle Remus: His Songs and Sayings,* by Joel Chandler Harris.

The Bobbs Merrill Company: for the selections from the poems of James Whitcomb Riley.

The Century Co.: for the selections from the works of John Muir and Irwin Russell.

Professor John Harrington Cox and the Harvard University Press: for the selections from *Folk-Songs of the South,* edited by John Harrington Cox.

Doubleday, Doran and Company, Inc.: for the selections from the works of Walt Whitman.

Harper and Brothers: for the selection from *The Gilded Age,* by Mark Twain and Charles Dudley Warner, for "The Celebrated Jumping Frog of Calaveras County," by Mark Twain, and for the selections from the following works of Mark Twain: *The Innocents Abroad, Roughing It, The Adventures of Huckleberry Finn, The Mysterious Stranger,* and *Mark Twain's Autobiography.*

Houghton Mifflin Company: for all selections from the works of John Burroughs, John Fiske, Richard Watson Gilder, John Hay, Mary Noailles Murfree, Edward Rowland Sill, Edmund Clarence Stedman, and Lew Wallace; for all selections from the poems of Thomas Bailey Aldrich and Bayard Taylor; for the selections from *Creole Sketches*, by Lafcadio Hearn; for the selection from *The American*, by Henry James; and for the selection from *Condensed Novels*, by Bret Harte, all poems by Bret Harte, and "The Luck of Roaring Camp," by Bret Harte.

Mr. Edgar Watson Howe: for the selection from *The Story of a Country Town*.

Miss Mildred Howells and Mr. John Mead Howells: for all selections from the writings of William Dean Howells.

P. J. Kenedy and Sons: for the selections from the poems of Abram J. Ryan.

Little, Brown and Company: for eight poems by Emily Dickinson, and for the chapter from *Ramona*, by Helen Hunt Jackson.

Mrs. Austin Long: for the selections from the poems of Maurice Thompson.

Professor John A. Lomax: for the selections from *Cowboy Songs and other Frontier Ballads*, by John A. Lomax.

The Macmillan Company: for the story "The Upper Berth," by Francis Marion Crawford; for the selection from *Japan: An Attempt at Interpretation*, by Lafcadio Hearn; for the story "The Lesson of the Master" and the selection from *Partial Portraits*, by Henry James; for the story "A Drama of Three," by Grace Elizabeth King; and for the selections from *Negro Folk Rhymes*, by Thomas W. Talley.

Dr. Henry Middleton Michel: for all selections from the poems of Paul Hamilton Hayne.

Mrs. Abbie Leland Miller and the Harr Wagner Publishing Company: for all selections from the "Bear" edition of the poems of Joaquin Miller.

Mrs. V. C. Sanborn: for the selection from *Zury: The Meanest Man in Spring County*, by Joseph Kirkland.

Charles Scribner's Sons: for all selections from the poems of Eugene Field; for the story "Aunt Fountain's Prisoner," by Joel Chandler Harris; for all selections from the poems and the letters of Sidney Lanier; for the story "Unc' Edinburg's Drowndin'," by Thomas Nelson Page; and for all selections from the poems of Richard Henry Stoddard.

CONTENTS

CONTENTS

CONTENTS

THE RISE OF REALISM

THE RISE OF REALISM -
(1860–1888)

The generation of Americans that reached maturity at the beginning of the Civil War was faced with a set of conditions as unpropitious for literature and general culture as the United States had yet seen. In fact, so barren and unlovely have these years seemed to recent critics of our life and letters that most of the epithets used to describe them have a distinct flavor of sneering or hostile criticism. The period has been called "The Gilded Age," "The Brown Decades," "The Wasted Generation," "The Dreadful Decade" (1870–1880), and "The Frontier Period." The first of these terms has had the widest currency and, no doubt, suggests most vividly the actual tone of the age. But each of these terms, except the last, reveals a critical bias, and, partly for this reason, only this last term seems a satisfactory designation. For, in spite of the fact that the frontier had been a dominant factor in American life from the first settlement of this country, it was only in the last third of the nineteenth century that the power of the frontier in all aspects of American life became paramount above all other influences both for good and for evil. With one final, sweeping rush the long-vacant lands of the West were filled up, by 1890 the frontier was gone, and the brief thirty years that preceded had seen such tremendous changes in the face of the country, in its political constitution, and in the standard of living of its inhabitants that we are still feeling the repercussions of many of the movements of that time.

What were the factors that made this Gilded Age, this Frontier Period? First in importance was the frontier itself—that ever-changing, ever-beckoning dividing line between the settled East and the unsettled West. It has seemed worthy of remark that not until the frontier had passed did students of American history fully realize that there had been a frontier, to say nothing of realizing its true significance.* This ever-shifting line had worked its siren charms for more than a century, drawing more and more thousands of the hardy and adventurous from the ease of settled provinces to the uncertainties and dangers of the wilderness, the prairie, the desert, and the mountain range. But following the discovery of gold in California in 1848 the trails were more and more crowded, and the great waves of immigrants from politically disturbed Europe of the mid-century swelled the ranks of those looking for new homes and new wealth.

* Frederick J. Turner's epoch-making paper on "The Significance of the Frontier in American History" appeared in 1893, just after the Oklahoma rush had marked the end of the free land opportunities. A generation later, Professor Turner published *The Frontier in American History* (1920), to be followed by Frederic L. Paxson's *History of the American Frontier* (1924) and *When the West Is Gone* (1930).

This basic factor—the frontier—was in turn productive of other factors. The Civil War itself would certainly not have taken place at the time and in the way it did had it not been for the critical controversy over the exact status of the new states and territories made possible by the extension of the frontier. The anxiety over whether Kansas and Nebraska and the rest of the new domains should be slave or free was more immediately responsible for the dire events of 1860–65 than the somewhat remote abstractions of the rights or wrongs of slavery itself. The event of the War, in turn, had its reaction upon the westward movement, and thus each interacted upon the other.

To these two factors—the frontier and the Civil War—are attributable in large measure most of the remaining factors that make the period, though a third—the progress of science and invention—was responsible in great part, not merely for the new industrialism that followed the War, but for the changed character of the westward movement itself. In fact, the westward movement, the Civil War, and scientific advance may be recognized as intertwined influences, interacting upon one another and in turn producing profound social changes among the people of the nation as a whole.

The most immediate effects produced by these three factors were: the exploitation of the West, the introduction of radical changes in agriculture, and the creation of a new and expansive industrial organization, embracing the inauguration of the great factory system and the building of the great transcontinental railroads. In the wake of these legitimate expressions of the new national life followed those reprehensible effects that have given the odor of scandal to the whole period: political corruption, wild financial speculation, and the degradation of private taste as manifested in domestic life, architecture, and the arts in general. The natural stimulus to science and invention was a corresponding deterrent to poetry, and especially to romantic poetry. The unsettled, hurried temper of the day was inimical to the best in the theatre— the Gilded Age is the most barren of our theatrical periods. But, preoccupation with the soil, the exploitation of the actual resources of the country, the constant contemplation of the American scene—all this was particularly favorable to the gradual, yet sure, growth of the realistic attitude. Hence it is no accident that in this most unlovely of American historic periods, the firmest basis should have been laid for that view of life and art which has dominated American letters for the past forty years and bids fair to dominate it for some time to come. It is in short this very Gilded Age that saw the Rise of Realism.

Against the background of The Gilded Age was enacted the conflict between two literary interpretations of life that had been struggling for mastery in other countries for some time—the "romantic" and the "realistic." * Almost

* At bottom, of course, both "romanticism" and "realism" are merely different manifestations of an interpretation of life that, in its emphasis upon the material, is in direct opposition to the "classical" view of life, that which disregards the external and the material in favor of the ideal, the inner reality. In recent days the opposition between these two philosophies has most clearly come to a head in the conflict between the so-called "New Hu

from the beginning of our national literature, the issue has lain between those who would *idealize* the external world in one of its many aspects, and those who would report that same external world in all its verity. The terms applied by Hamlin Garland to the opposition between two principles in conflict during the Gilded Age—namely "effectism" and "veritism" *—suggest with substantial truth the contrasting spirits of the "romantic" and the "realistic" theories of literary art. Romanticism, which had begun in England early in the eighteenth century and had come to its culmination in the work of the great romantic poets of the Age of Wordsworth, began in America to show its influence as early as the 1770's. By the year 1800 Romanticism was something of a force in American life and letters. By 1830 this movement had come to represent the dominant literary trend in America, and from 1830 to 1860 the romantic view of life and art held full sway. But the demands of the frontier, the crisis of the Civil War, and the rise of the new industrialism put an end to romanticism, not all at once, but step by step. The transition was to be, from a literary point of view, through the middle ground of "local color." From a romantic interest in a wholly foreign or vaguely realized American scene, through the local color concreteness of a specifically localized American scene, even though presented with sentimentality and exaggerated emphasis upon the merely external, to the final stage of emphasis upon character, demanding a veritable portrayal of both the scene and the actors upon the scene—this is the manner in which romanticism gradually changed its character until, in its present manifestation as extreme realism or naturalism, it may seem the very opposite of its old self.

Somewhere, then, between 1860 and 1890, the dominant emphasis in American literature was radically changed. But it is obvious that this change was not necessarily a matter of conscious concern to all writers. In fact, many writers may seem to have been actually unaware of the shifting emphasis. Moreover, it is not possible, as one might like to do, to trace the steady march of the realistic emphasis from its first feeble notes to its dominant trumpet-note of unquestioned leadership. The progress of realism is, to change the figure, rather that of a small stream, receiving accessions from its tributaries at unequal points along its course, its progress now and then balked by the sand-bars of opposition or the diffusing marshes of error and compromise. Again, it is apparent that any attempt to classify rigidly, as romanticists or realists, the great body of major and minor writers of this period is doomed

manists," including Irving Babbitt and Paul Elmer More, and the exponents of present-day Naturalism, such as H. L. Mencken, Van Wyck Brooks, and Henry Hazlitt. To Mr. Babbitt the eighteenth century French romanticist Rousseau is chiefly responsible for that view of life and art which seems most to dominate the world to-day, with its emphasis upon material things; and Mr. More in the Preface to *The Drift of Romanticism* has expressed his opposition to the whole romantic-realistic trend in the following words: "If I had to designate very briefly this underlying principle which gives to historic romance a character radically different from the mystery and wonder of classic art, I should define it as that expansive conceit of the emotions which goes with the illusion of beholding the infinite within the stream of nature itself instead of apart from the stream."

*Cf. Garland's *Crumbling Idols* (1893), based on the veritistic principle: "Strive for truth and leave the effect to take care of itself."

to failure, since it is not by virtue of the writer's conscious espousal of the romantic or realistic creed that he does much of his best work, but by virtue of that writer's sincere surrender to the "atmosphere" of the subject. Mark Twain is thus a realist in *Old Times on the Mississippi* and a romanticist in his *Personal Recollections of Joan of Arc.* Whitman's message has the idealism of the romanticist, but his sympathetic concern for the people and the stuff of the life close at hand allies him with the realists. So true is this that it is the major writers who are most difficult to accept as romanticists or realists. Of the six major writers of the period, Walt Whitman and Emily Dickinson defy classification—they are too distinctive, too personal. Sidney Lanier may more safely be designated as romantic. But when we speak of Mark Twain, William Dean Howells, and Henry James as realists, we must do so with the consciousness that for Twain the badge seems inappropriate on a man who hated classifications, and that the larger significance of Howells and James lies in their transcending the limits of any artistic creed, however much both may have dedicated their services to making that creed known and practiced in the world of letters. Of major importance is the sincerity of the author, and it is as possible for a "romantic" poem of Lanier's to be true to life as it is for a "realistic" novel to be essentially untrue to life. What counted during this transition period was the succession of new discoveries that men were making about America or the relationship of Americans to the world at large, whether in Eggleston's realistic *Hoosier Schoolmaster,* or in the local color sentiment of Harte or Cable, or in the thoughtful study of the international situation in James's *The American,* or in the somewhat Byronic but fresh-blowing verse of the Poet of the Sierras, Joaquin Miller. In short, as more than one critic has insisted, this era saw the "second discovery of America."

In large outline, the course of American letters during this era may be visualized as having four main stages, or rather four focal points of interest: (1) The Decline of Romanticism, embracing the message of Whitman, the literature of Civil Conflict, the work of Lanier, and the product of the Genteel Tradition; (2) the Bases of Realism, embracing the work of the Western Humorists, the varied Literature of the Folk, and the Progress of Realism and Local Color, first in the Far West and soon after in the East and Middle West; (3) the contribution of the three most important realists of the period Twain, Howells, and James, utterly unlike and even mutually antipathetic, yet united in their earnestness to report life aright and in their acknowledged ability to do so, within the limits of the creed of each; and finally (4) the progress toward that Naturalism that was to dominate the next era of American letters, a progress now helped by the work of historian, scientist, and nature writer, now doubtfully sustained by the belated contribution of the South to local color and realism, now hindered by the writers of romance and sentiment in the 1880's, and finally receiving its greatest additions in the work of the new realists, like Howe and Kirkland, who stand on the threshold of the varied naturalism of Garland, Crane, Norris, London, and Dreiser, and in the thoroughly modern and individualistic work of Emily Dickinson, who, like Whitman at the opening of this era, fittingly closes it with an independence that belongs to no age.

In the figure of Walt Whitman, who strides across nineteenth century America with a presence that commands the attention of friend and foe alike, there are easily discernible both the striking defects and the striking merits of romantic idealism. Whitman was the culmination of the Transcendental movement. As such, he was guilty of most of those defects of romanticism that spring from its self-centeredness, its easy optimism, its disregard of class and race lines, its emphasis on the "natural," its uncritical tolerance of departure from the accepted conventions of form—defects which the "classicist" has found particularly repugnant. Most poets who are harshly assailed are attacked on one of two grounds—unacceptable subject-matter or unacceptable form. Whitman displeased on both grounds. His naked exposition of the body seemed bad enough, but it was doubly unacceptable in its free verse medium. Yet as time passed and as Whitman mellowed under the influence of the Civil War, these very defects were seen to constitute his chief claim to recognition as the distinctive poet of "these States." The merits of romanticism were seen in his broad human sympathies, his genuine democracy that put to shame the lip-service of generations, his honest recognition of the facts of life, his determination to publish those facts, and his really artistic recognition of the necessity of new forms to express new concepts. But Whitman transcends the bounds of romanticism by dealing with the "here and now," by concerning himself with a realistic, detailed presentation of the American scene, its actual cities with their wharves and sidewalks, its actual landscape, with fruitful farms and open roads. More and more clearly, as we look back from our later vantage-point, does Whitman seem, in the 1855 *Leaves of Grass* and its notable *Preface,* to have anticipated the views of post Civil War America, with its rough but honest realistic reaction to the trappings and tinsel of a decadent romanticism. Nor was Whitman blind to the grave defects of democracy. The striking note running all through Whitman's important prose utterances, from the 1855 *Preface,* through *Democratic Vistas,* to *A Backward Glance o'er Travelled Roads,* is the denunciation of the American emphasis on "things," with its accompanying political and commercial corruption, its lack of soul, its consequent need for poets. No fitter indictment of the "jazz age" of the 1920's themselves could be found than in *Democratic Vistas.* Compound as he was of good, bad, and indifferent, yet always thoroughly himself, Whitman gave America a message and a form that have proved to be the basic inspiration of all its later literature. As Professor Pattee has well said: "He is the central figure of the later period, the voice in the wilderness that hailed its dim morning and the strong singer of its high noon." *

As Whitman's career was profoundly influenced by the Civil War, so was

* *American Literature since 1870,* pp. 184–185.

the whole course of American thought and creative expression. It was not merely the physical conflict that was important—it was that larger Civil Conflict, that Conflict of Ideas that found merely its most tragic manifestation on the battlefield. Irreconcilable differences of opinion as to the rights of human slavery, long before foreshadowed by Cotton Mather and John Woolman, fundamental differences in the economic life and demands of various sections of the country, chiefly the North and the South, different social structures, different conceptions of the functions of government, especially federalism and states' rights—these contrasts served not only to change the character of American writers and their form of expression but essentially to produce new writers who would not have existed but for this conflict. Chief among this latter group is, of course, Abraham Lincoln, whose late maturity strikingly parallels that of Whitman. The miracle of Lincoln's later prose style, so apparently unheralded by his earlier utterances, is almost as remarkable as the contrast between "When Lilacs Last in the Dooryard Bloomed" and the conventional Whitman poems of the 1840's. The close of the *Second Inaugural* and the *Gettysburg Address* are but the most perfect of Lincoln's many manifestations of that lucidity, that utter rightness of thought and expression, that powerful human sympathy, and that ineffable poetic imagination whose achievement is as much a matter for wonder as was the inscrutable personality of the man himself. The "homely" side of Lincoln suggests such contemporaries of his youth as Augustus B. Longstreet, whose realistic *Georgia Scenes* (1835) presents us with a vivid picture of the rough life of the old Southwest similar to that of the Middle West that Lincoln knew, and David Crockett, whose *Narrative of the Life of David Crockett* (1834) illustrates the Western delight in exaggeration and coarse humor so definitely associated with Lincoln in his life-long fondness for a good "yarn" and his inveterate preference for the homespun.

The Conflict of Ideas left many and varied expressions of its influence among men of different faiths and sectional sympathies. Edward Everett Hale's short-story, *The Man without a Country* (1863), expressed that larger patriotism that grew out of but transcended the North's concern for the Union. The songs and ballads of the Civil War, only a fraction of whose number have survived or deserve to survive, offered an emotional outlet for feelings ranging from the contemplation of a single episode, as in "Little Giffen" and "Sheridan's Ride," to such stirring embodiments of national and sectional enthusiasm as the "John Brown" Song, "Dixie," and the "Battle-Hymn of the Republic." Especially in the South was there a distinctive group of poets of sensitiveness and promise, some of whom would no doubt have accomplished more had not the knife of war cut across their lives: Henry Timrod, Paul Hamilton Hayne, Sidney Lanier, Abram J. Ryan, and John Bannister Tabb. The work of these Southern poets, coupled with the oratory of such men as Henry W. Grady and the treatments of reconstruction problems illustrated by Albion W. Tourgée's *A Fool's Errand* (1879), presents us with that phenomenon that we have come to call The Changing South, the enforced transformation of the section that suffered most from the civil conflict. The general tone of the work of these writers was romantic, though the note of bitterness in Hayne and Timrod and the realistic portrayal of the Ku Klux Klan by Tourgée suggest the power of war to turn men's thoughts from fancies to realities.

Out from the group of war-crushed poets the figure of Sidney Lanier emerges more and more distinct and important. Excessively concerned as he was with an ethical emphasis and a beauty of form that ally him so definitely with the Romantics as to expose him to the charge of softness and sentimentality, Lanier yet contributed to American literature in enough ways to entitle him to the position of a major American writer. He was the only poet of the South, as was Whitman of the North, to rise above sectional prejudice and to display that compassion for the men who had to fight and that denunciation of the fight itself (in *Tiger Lilies*) that Whitman showed in "Reconciliation" and "Beat! Beat! Drums!" Again, Lanier showed, more than any poet of his day, that hatred of commercialism, of the tyranny of Trade which, in poems like "The Symphony," makes him the pleader for the cause of true refinement and humanity. Lanier was, with Poe, the outstanding exemplar among American poets of devotion to beauty and melody, as Thoreau and Whitman are our most striking representatives of reliance upon the earthy, the autochthonous. Lanier contributed an exposition of verse in *The Science of English Verse* that has not yet been superseded. He displayed qualities as a letter-writer that place him high among the ranks of great English epistolary masters. His critical work, though not of first-rate quality, is of no mean value. And he has given us a body of poems, suggestive of comparison with Poe's in their emphasis on beauty and melody, yet different in their ethical emphasis, which enshrines a pure and ethereal romantic idealism. Unmistakable in his verse is the eternal note of the knight errant in the cause of the true refinements of life.

The most distinctive manifestation of the decline of romanticism in America is to be seen in that considerable body of verse and prose (largely the former) produced by the great number of conventional writers, chiefly New Englanders, in defense of what has been named The Genteel Tradition. On the whole these writers showed a direct antipathy to the growing realism of the day, were shocked by the "yawping" of Whitman, turned a delicate shoulder upon the rough laughter and dialect of the West, and in their very striving to keep alive the essentially outworn subject-matter and artificial forms of "refined" writing, marked the decline of New England dominance in the creative leadership of this country. Many of these writers had real ability, many served distinctively in one or another rôle, but with a few exceptions they continued blind to the demands of the new day. In poetry the chief exponent of the Genteel Tradition was perhaps Thomas Bailey Aldrich, a master of form, notably in his sonnets, and one gifted with no small insight into the delicate social differences observable among men, as witnessed by his "Pauline Pavlovna" (1887). Yet it was Aldrich who wrote the unsympathetic "Unguarded Gates" and revealed the conservative stand of his school in the poem called "Realism." Perhaps, as some feel, Aldrich's bid for lasting remembrance may come rather through his prose, in his real contributions to the short-story, as in "Marjory Daw" and in his longer realistic narratives such as *The Story of a Bad Boy*. Of perhaps less importance now seems the work of the critic Edmund Clarence Stedman, remembered for only a few poems but still respected for his service as an anthologist and critic of both English and American verse, and for some distinct, scholarly service in the interpretation of particular writers, notably Edgar Allan Poe. Of much less importance now seem Richard Henry Stoddard, poet of the exotic, and Richard Watson Gilder, who sounded a somewhat individual note in his poems of more forthright thought like "The Passing of Christ" or those of freer form, suggesting poetic prose, like "The Night Pasture." Celia Thaxter and Louise Chandler Moulton are examples of fairly facile versifiers who sprinkled the pages of the magazines in the seventies and eighties with work that was well done, with occasionally a certain amount of freshness, as in the case of the nature descriptions of Mrs. Thaxter, but withal still confined within the limits of the conventional. Of more substance was Edward Rowland Sill, whose introspective doubts sought consolation in the newer clime, California; but in spite of fresh stimulus and serious endeavor, Sill did not fulfill the promise that was in him. His best things, all too few, are those in which he unwittingly reveals the great gulf between the introverted East and the outward-looking West. If travel, experience, and hard work could make a man of letters, they should have made one of Bayard Taylor, the most-travelled American of his day, a trained journalist and an indefatigable devotee of his art. Little remains of the once widely known writings of Taylor except a few snatches of Oriental song, some genuine character sketches in verse like "The Quaker Widow," and some of his travel sketches. Of these last, *El Dorado* (1850) deserves to find its place among the important transcriptions of a bygone time, the stirring gold-rush days in California. Taylor is not merely vivid; he is also accurate in his portrayal of all aspects of the social life of early California. Beginning as a conventional poet but roused to the heights of individuality by the wrongs of her race, Emma Lazarus offers in her social point of view, as illustrated by her sonnet "The New Colossus," a striking contrast to Aldrich in "The Unguarded Gates." She confirms the feeling experienced by the student of this period that the most vital poetry was produced by those detached from the main currents, such as Whitman, Emily Dickinson, and the Roman Catholic poets, John Bannister Tabb, John Boyle O'Reilly, and Louise Imogen Guiney. In the field of the essay the Genteel Tradition is preserved by Donald Grant Mitchell, George William Curtis, Charles Dudley Warner, and their like, men capable of good writing, now and then expressing worthwhile thought, especially in the field of criticism, as did Curtis in the Editor's Chair of *Harper's*, but men for the most part who preferred the comfortable chair before the fire to the joy of combat with the untamed. The fiction that proceeded from the genteel school is mostly forgotten. It was the age of the "dime novel" and its supposed corrective, the novel of sentiment, as exemplified by *The Wide Wide World, Little Lord Fauntleroy, The Opening of a Chestnut Burr,* and their kin. Of this great outpouring, the product of a few writers rose above mere mediocrity, such as the work of Lew Wallace, Helen Hunt Jackson, and Frank R. Stockton. But in general the need for a new art was as manifest in fiction as in poetry and the essay. The state of the drama from 1860 to 1890 was perhaps more unsatisfactory than it has ever been since American plays began to be written. The stage lagged far behind the other arts in meeting the demands of the new day. Sentiment, melodrama, farce, unreality—these dominated the theatre. There were notable actors, such as Edwin Booth and Joseph Jefferson. There were popular playwrights, such as Dion Boucicault. But only in the more realistic work of Steele Mackaye, James A. Herne, and Bronson Howard at the end of the period, and in the social comedies and farces of William Dean Howells (in which both Mrs. Kendall and Ellen Terry appeared) do we see much awareness of the real dignity of the theatre. Herne and Howard especially show distinct progress toward the realistic drama of the next age, and Howells's clever farces and comedies laid in the drawing rooms and apartment houses of the time perhaps reveal contemporary manners with far more truth than do the plays of the stage proper.

The three most important stones in the foundation of American realism were Western Humor, the Literature of the Folk, and the Vogue of Local Color.

What has been called "The Laughter of the West" shook the nation out of its smugness. Its origins have been debated, but it seems fairly certain that this distinctive humor is based upon: first, the hard life of the frontier, with its necessity for an outlet; second, the democratic irreverence of the West; third, the barrenness of social life in the newer communities, making welcome any means of entertainment; and finally, the recognition of humor as one of the most forceful weapons for social criticism, in an age when many things needed the lash. The chief characteristics of this humor were gross exaggeration, sharp common sense, and the element of surprise. The form was of course unconventional, running in many cases to outlandish spelling. Americans had from Puritan times displayed a distinctive liking for humor, but the humor of the New Englander was a canny humor; the later humor of the South and West was broader, looser, more side-shaking. The New England tradition is seen in the Yankee of Royall Tyler's play *The Contrast* (1787), Seba Smith's *Life and Writings of Major Jack Downing* (1833), the Sam Slick of Thomas C. Haliburton's *The Clockmaker* (1837–40), and Benjamin P. Shillaber's Mrs. Partington in *The Life and Sayings of Mrs. Partington* (1854). With the advent of *The Narrative of the Life of David Crockett* (1834), Longstreet's *Georgia Scenes* (1835), J. J. Hooper's *Some Adventures of Captain Simon Suggs* (1845), and J. G. Baldwin's *Flush Times of Alabama and Mississippi* (1853), we get the transition to a distinctly broader type of humor.

With the approach of the Civil War and well beyond it we see the culmination of American humor in the work of George Horatio Derby (*Phoenixiana,* 1855, and *Squibob Papers,* 1859), Charles Henry Smith (*Bill Arp, So Called, a Side Show of the Southern Side of the War,* 1866), George Washington Harris (*Sut Livingood's Yarns,* 1867), Charles Farrar Browne ("Artemus Ward"), David Ross Locke ("Petroleum Volcano Nasby"), and Henry Wheeler Shaw ("Josh Billings"). Of all these later humorists, Derby was the pioneer, but Artemus Ward, Josh Billings, and Nasby made almost equal claims to a more widespread popularity. The influence of several of these men upon Mark Twain is well known—a fact that in itself is testimony to the importance of Western humor in the building of American realism. The tradition of these men was continued in the following generations by M. Quad, Edgar Wilson ("Bill") Nye, Marietta Holley, Finley Peter Dunne, George Ade, John Kendrick Bangs, and the still later Irvin S. Cobb, Stephen Leacock, and Will Rogers.

Of scarcely less importance for the historian but of less tangible influence in the development of realism was the great and varied body of folk material that was unconsciously expressing the lives of cowboys, homesteaders, lumberjacks, negroes, West Virginia mountaineers, and even the roustabouts of the great cities. Of especial significance are four classes of folk material: the songs of the cowboy and frontiersman, such as "The Cowboy's Dream" and "Jesse James," the tall stories of the lumberjack, such as those about Paul Bunyan and Tony Beaver, the ballads commemorating incidents in the lives of mountaineers, such as "The Wreck on the C. and O." and "The Rowan County Crew," and the songs of the negro, both the spirituals, such as "The Coming Day" and "Room in There," and the secular songs, such as "John Henry" and "She Hugged Me and Kissed Me."

To the real but somewhat intangible influence of Western humor and folk material there was now added the vogue of a literary *genre,* whose popularity throughout the sixties and seventies served as a bridge from the decadent romanticism of the Genteel Tradition to the virile realism of the next age. This was the vogue of local color. The distinction between local color and realism is not always easy to make; but, broadly speaking, local color is the result of attention to the physical surroundings in which characters are placed (typical scenery) or the external appearance of those characters (typical costume), or the manner of expression of those characters (typical dialect). When, however, the interest of the writer passes from these mere externals to a portrayal of character, whether typical or individual, local color takes on the hue of realism. In general it is quite true, as most critics of local color have insisted, that its tone is romantic, yet there are many writers whose work is called local color by some and realism by others—writers like Eggleston, Cable, Harte, etc.—in whom the transition from romance to realism is in process. Thus, much as local color may be derided for its sentimentality and mechanical emphasis, yet its very focussing of attention on definite parts of the country and on specific types of character, specific dialects, specific dress, made for that careful scrutiny of the realities of life which constituted the prime demand of the out-and-out realist. Howells said: "Realism is nothing more and nothing less than the truthful presentation of material." To what extent Harte and his local color imitators were also realists is a moot point, but it may be questioned, in fairness to the Harte school, whether the very sentiment and exaggeration of "The Outcasts of Poker Flat" may not be artistically truer to the actual life of the mining camp, with its undoubted sentiment and exaggeration, than could have been a more restrained telling of the story. In other words, the local colorist secured in many cases by his very manner of writing just that effect which is the desideratum of the true realist.

To the Far West must go the chief credit for making local color and eventually realism the ruling influence in American writing. As early as 1860 we have from Bret Harte's pen "The Work on Red Mountain," the first form of "Mliss," not published till ten years later. It was the vogue of "The Luck of Roaring Camp" (1868) that ushered in what was certainly one of the most interesting decades in American literature. Bret Harte and Joaquin Miller, each in his own way, opened up the wonders of the Far West. Harte, of course, was practically a stranger in this land; Miller became a real part of it and stood for it to the end of his days. If Harte is a second Dickens, so is Miller a Western Whitman, whose significance as an exponent of the disappearing frontier is still too lightly valued.

Bret Harte's success fired the train of local colorists in the East and Middle West. Volume after volume testified to the mining of separate claims of local color. Rebecca Harding Davis's "Life in the Iron Mills" (1861), Harriet Beecher Stowe's Sam Lawson stories (1860), Rose Terry Cooke's "Too Late" (1875), and Sarah Orne Jewett's Deephaven stories (1875) represent the offering of the East. From the Middle West came John James Piatt's homely farm poems, Will Carleton's *Farm Ballads* (1873), John Hay's *Pike County Ballads* (1871), Edward Eggleston's *The Hoosier Schoolmaster* (1871), one of the most important documents in the rise of realism in America, and Constance Fenimore Woolson's tales about the Great Lakes region. With a band of writers thus spread from the Far West to the East calling attention to the verities of American life, the time was ripe for the great realists of the seventies and eighties—Howells, Twain, and James. In only one section of the country, the South, was the vogue of local color somewhat delayed and the consequent influence of realism postponed. Hence, also, the longer vogue of sentiment and romance in the South.

The realistic conception of the representation of life that held sway during the seventies and eighties in America had as its most noteworthy exemplars three men very different from one another, both in personality and in predominant interests. Yet these three—Twain, Howells, and James—were alike in insisting upon "veritism" in writing as opposed to "effectism." We have already noted Howells's definition of realism as "nothing more and nothing less than the truthful presentation of material." Mark Twain said in his preface to *The Innocents Abroad* what might be said of all his work: "I am sure I have written at least honestly, whether wisely or not." And one of James's injunctions to the youthful aspirant in "The Art of Fiction" is: "Do not think too much about optimism and pessimism; try and catch the color of life itself." Truthful presentation, honest writing, catching the color of life itself —it is the harmony of these varied emphases of the same matter that unites these masters of prose.

Samuel Langhorne Clemens has been acclaimed the fulfillment of the prophecy of Whitman regarding the great American democrat. This bluff product of the Middle West had perhaps more qualities that Americans like to think of *as* American than any other writer this country has produced. But the stature of Mark Twain is to be recognized, not merely in the way in which he reflected the multiform aspects of American life, but also in the way his nature more and more rebelled against that life—its commercialism, its easy optimism, its essential shallowness. From "The Jumping Frog of Calaveras County" to *The Mysterious Stranger* Mark Twain ran the gamut from droll, innocent laughter to the bitter pessimism of disillusionment. Twain was a curious combination of humorist, romancer, and realist. "The Jumping Frog" and *Innocents Abroad* represent the first; *Roughing It* and *Joan of Arc* the second; and *Huckleberry Finn, Old Times on the Mississippi,* and *The Mysterious Stranger,* each in a different way, the third. But at bottom it is with Twain as with Whitman: we are not concerned whether he was a romanticist or a realist or still something else. His work is simply stamped "Mark Twain."

A much more conscious artist was Twain's mentor, William Dean Howells. Likewise a product of the Middle West, this self-schooled journalist well illustrates the need for the true realist to get away from his material in order to acquire a standard of comparison, to get the right perspective. Just as Twain required time to get the true perspective for *Roughing It* and *Life on the Mississippi,* so was Howells's trip to the East conducive to that comparison between the freshly seen East and the Middle West he had known that stimulated his first realistic sketches, such as *Their Wedding Journey.* Then came Howells's experience abroad (serving as a further standard of comparison) and his careful study of American and foreign masters, whose influence upon the American realist he acknowledges in *My Literary Passions.* But he did not care to go beyond that "genteel realism" which eschewed the seamy side of life, though full acknowledgment is due to the real strength displayed in such novels as *A Hazard of New Fortunes.* A bolder step was needed to produce the advance in realism that was to usher in the naturalists. In this limited field of the "genteel," however, Howells was supreme. His care for detail, his penetration of character, his definite æsthetic position—all this makes him our first conscious realist of major proportions. Of very great significance also, is that considerable body of dramatic work which Howells did in the farce and comedy types—that delicate portrayal through conversation of such social relationships as those of the apartment house, the drawing room, the parlor-car. Finally, the battle fought by Howells from 1886 to 1892 on behalf of realism in America entitles him to the gratitude of all lovers of tolerance and progress in the development of the arts.*

Whether Henry James is to be classed as an American or a British writer is an academic question, of no real concern except to those whose sensitiveness to geographical boundaries is so keen that the whole point of James's internationalism would be lost to them. To many, of course, James is our finest example of the "back trailer," he who has been so overcome by the nostalgia for Old World culture that step by step he moves from his *frontier* home back to the *settled* home of his forefathers. To be sure, James was sincerely desirous of presenting the American in the best possible light, as he does in the novel of that name. Nevertheless, the artist's highly complex nature could not be satisfied by the simplicities and roughnesses of the Western scene and its associations. Moreover, the mere surface of life, even in Paris or London, did not satisfy him. His passion for the delicate gradations of thought and for the nuances of response ultimately led him into a world more remote than that of philosophical abstraction. He is most happy in painting his *Portrait of a Lady,* or in telling such stories as "The Lesson of the Master." But even the devotees of Mr. James confess to weariness and even provocation at the endless spinning of words without action. So far does James's world seem removed from the actual world inhabited by most of us that Americans may perhaps be forgiven if they thought, about 1890, that James did not care to be understood by them and so turned their backs upon him. It is strange that, aside from Mrs. Wharton, this artist should have had no important disciples. The answer may be that, though we may be living in an 'international" age, it is an age too democratic for the sympathetic acceptance of the essentially aristocratic message of this realist of the finer, inner life of the cultured men and women of the world.

Among the various manifestations of the welter of tendencies whose whole upshot was the production of a more virile literature was the contribution of the more purely expository forms of prose to the advance of realism—history, science, and nature writing. The early nineteenth-century historical work of Jared Sparks and George Bancroft was followed by the remarkable contributions of that trio of New England historians, William Hickling Prescott, Francis Parkman, and John Lothrop Motley, who raised American historical writing to a plane of real distinction and dignity. If Prescott revealed the glamour of the South American pageant, and if Parkman disclosed the fascination of the struggle for the possession of the North American continent, with the subsequent thrill of the extension of the frontier, Motley turned to the struggle of a sister republic in Europe and presented, in spite of certain now acknowledged inaccuracies of treatment, a vivid, dramatic account of stirring episodes that indicate the influence which the realistic method was to have on the writing of history—an influence which was in turn to show its repercussion in the field of creative prose as well. A very different quality of history is

* See the papers of "The Editor's Study" in *Harper's Magazine,* 1886–91.

shown in such straightforward accounts as the *Memoirs* of Ulysses S. Grant, whose simple honesty of treatment betrays the rugged Man of the West to whom ornament was alien. The interest in science in the large is hard to separate from that preoccupation with the phenomena of external nature which has given America so many capable nature writers. In John Fiske, both historian and expositor of science, we see more of the pure scientist, one whose voluminous and cogent *Outlines of Cosmic Philosophy* did battle for the Darwinian theory in America, much to the disturbance of religious circles. As intermediary between investigator and public, Fiske rendered much the same service that distinguished Huxley in England; and the influence of the propagation of the true scientific attitude upon realism in creative writing is unquestionable. In John Burroughs one sees perhaps our best example of the combination of the true scientific temper with the imaginative insight into the more poetic aspects of nature, as seen especially in the life of birds, bees, and kindred inhabitants of the external world. Beginning as an Emersonian, as revealed in his early essay on "Expression," and an enthusiast for the poetic interpretation of nature, as revealed in his espousal of Whitman and in his numerous early essays on bird life, Burroughs deepened his philosophic interests steadily until, in *Accepting the Universe*, he showed himself more of an interpreter of the underlying order of things than as a depicter of the concrete manifestations of Nature's ways. Burroughs belongs essentially in the long line of American nature essayists, including Audubon, Thoreau, and William Beebe. Burroughs's interest in the common and less striking aspects of nature is parallelled by John Muir's attention to the mountain range and the glacier, the larger elements in the external world. Not without a distinctly poetic vein, as seen in his charming *Mountains of California*, Muir is nevertheless more the objective scientist than the seer. In all of these expository writings lay that "eye upon the object" emphasis which, aided by the very different manifestation of the same principle in the cult of local color, hastened the advent of the new realism.

Somewhat behind other sections of the country, the South espoused the cause of local color with an ardor unequalled in the other regions. With a greater tendency to sentiment and possessing more colorful contrasts in manners and dialect, Southern writers in the late seventies and eighties made abundant use of the negro, the mountaineer, and the Creole. The negro offered most of the inspiration. Although anticipated by Clifford and Sidney Lanier, Irwin Russell was the first to make extended use of the negro dialect; and no better examples of sympathetic understanding can be found in American dialect poetry than in such poems as his "Christmas Night in the Quarters" and "Nebuchadnezzar." The same may be said for the prose dialect of Joel Chandler Harris, himself a man of rare sweetness of character, whose Uncle Remus stories constitute perhaps the most important salvage of native folklore in this country. But Harris's more serious work has been unduly neglected. His portrayals, not only of the negro but

f the mountaineer, in *Free Joe and Other Georgian Sketches*, show
n understanding of human nature that is far beyond local color—it is true
realism. Regarding the accuracy of the dialect of Thomas Nelson Page there
as been some question, and it is evident that the sentiment pervading "Marse
han" reveals rather the romantic local colorist than the understanding realist.
et the tales in the collection entitled *In Ole Virginia* are an important
ddition to that literature of regionalism upon whose basis is built a sounder
realism. The outstanding portrayer of the mountaineer was Mary Noailles
Iurfree ("Charles Egbert Craddock") whose tales comprising *In the Ten-
essee Mountains* are the best of her somewhat exaggerated depictions of a
cality and a type of people still waiting for a really adequate artist. With
e Creole three names are most frequently associated: George Washington
able, Lafcadio Hearn, and Grace Elizabeth King. It now seems evident
at there is more of romantic local color than realism in the warm tales
the New Orleans Creoles that, originally contributed separately to *Scribner's
onthly,* Cable later published as *Old Creole Days* (1879). The accuracy
his portrayal was disputed by Miss King, who at once undertook to depict
e *true* Creole, in such tales as "Monsieur Motte" (1888) and in such col-
ctions of brief stories as *Balcony Stories* (1893). Lafcadio Hearn has a
uble association, with Creole New Orleans in such exotic tales as "Chita"
d such sketches as those making up the recently published *Creole Sketches,*
d with Japan, the land of his adoption, which he portrayed with rare
timacy and understanding in such works as *Glimpses of Unfamiliar Japan*
d *Japan: An Attempt at Interpretation.* No other American prose has quite
e color and exoticism of Hearn. Still another devotee of Louisiana was Kate
hopin, whose *Bayou Folk* presents trustworthy portraits of the canebrake
vellers of central Louisiana.

Rather different from the more romantic of the local colorists was that
nsiderable band of out-and-out purveyors of romance and sentiment, whose
notional temperament or positive artistic creed either carried the writer to
stant lands and past times or impossible happenings in the here and now,
forced upon the work of one who might have been a realist the sentimental
ne which made a wide appeal to the masses but, except in a few cases,
issed the genuine reality. Such, of course, were Edward Payson Roe and
s kind, Frances Hodgson Burnett, Mary J. Holmes, T. S. Arthur, and a
ore of others who turned out all too facilely the forerunners of the present-
y sentimental best-sellers. On a somewhat higher plane was the work of
eneral Lew Wallace, to whose powers as the writer of *The Fair God* adequate
stice has not been done, and Helen Hunt Jackson, whose *Ramona,* though
work of sentiment, is nevertheless a very moving presentation of a real
oblem—the status of the American Indian in his own home. Avowed
mancers were Frank R. Stockton and Francis Marion Crawford. The
rmer was the delight of the "wasted generation," with the whimsicalities of
s *Rudder Grange* and *Mrs. Lecks and Mrs. Aleshine,* the deft turns of such
ories as "The Lady or the Tiger?," and the ease of telling revealed in his

many ghost stories and stories of mere adventure. Crawford has a more solid basis for claim to serious consideration as an artist, since the skill of his Italian historical romances, notably the Saracinesca series, and the pure entertainment of his shorter tales justify his contention expressed in *The Novel, What It Is* that the fictionist's only function is to entertain—he is not the mentor of his age. Three Middle Westerners, Maurice Thompson, Eugene Field, and James Whitcomb Riley, may well represent that sentiment in verse which still appeals to great numbers in such contemporary versifiers as Edgar Guest. Riley and Field knew children; Riley knew all aspects of the life of the common Hoosier and could make him talk; Thompson, though in his verse showing more classical and conventional interests, anticipated the more distinctive local colorists of the Middle West in his dialect sketches comprising *Hoosier Mosaics* (1875).

In direct opposition to the school of romance and sentiment were a few writers who went beyond the more genteel realism of Howells and James in their portrayal of the less lovely aspects of American life. The chief of these, and both of paramount importance in the trend toward naturalism, were Edward Watson Howe, whose *The Story of a Country Town* (1883) bids fair to enjoy much the same kind of re-birth as has Melville's *Moby Dick*, and Joseph Kirkland, pioneer son of a pioneer mother (Caroline M. Kirkland, author of *Homes in the West: Who'll Follow?*), whose *Zury: the Meanest Man in Spring County* (1887) shares with *The Story of a Country Town* the credit of pointing definitely the way to the new realism of *Main Travelled Roads* and the later *Sister Carrie*. Both Howe and Kirkland seem destined for a more honorable place among recognized contributors to American realism than they have hitherto enjoyed. In the field of criticism, no minor writer of the age shows the changing spirit more clearly than does Brander Matthews, whose essay on "The Philosophy of the Short Story" (1884) marks the beginning of the modern critical appraisal of an important art form, and whose realistic sketches and tales of New York City signal the coming of the new realism in the depiction of city life much as Howe and Kirkland emphasized country and small town life.

The enigma of Emily Dickinson's personality is still too much in the foreground for the critic to make a just appraisal of her work. Whatever may be the exact facts of her love life, however real or imaginary were the experiences that she reflects in her brittle little poems and her fascinating letters, it is certain that the conventions of the material world meant little to her. Romantically idealistic though she was, there is an independence and a self-respect in her every utterance that ally her with the *progressives* of the Gilded Age, not with the conservatives. So it was only just that, except for one or two poems, none of her work appeared during her lifetime, and that the age of the revolting nineties should be the first to see her product. But, though the asserted neglect of her work has been shown to be exaggerated, it was not until the 1920's that both critical and popular attention united in paying her proper consideration. Her poetry is of that distinctive kind that knows no age—it can not be "dated." Moreover, there has never been a writer who so appealingly slipped from prose into verse as did this writer of letters who opened her heart, though ever so guardedly, to both near-by relatives and distant friends. Incongruous as it may seem, there is no artist whose poetic comment closes more fittingly a study of the Gilded Age than this one whose true gold shamed the gilt of that era which had earlier been shocked when Walt Whitman's rough hand held up for thoughtful consideration his fresh and beautiful leaves of grass.

LOUIS WANN

WALT WHITMAN
(1819–1892)

PREFACE TO *LEAVES OF GRASS* *

America does not repel the past or what it has produced under its forms or amid other politics or the idea of castes or the old religions . . . accepts the lesson with calmness . . . is not so impatient as has been supposed that the slough still sticks to opinions and manners and literature while the life which served its requirements has passed into the new life of the new forms . . . perceives that the corpse is slowly borne from the eating and sleeping rooms of the house . . . perceives that it waits a little while in the door . . . that it was fittest for its days . . . that its action has descended to the stalwart and wellshaped heir who approaches . . . and that he shall be fittest for his days.

The Americans of all nations at any time upon the earth have probably the fullest poetical nature. The United States themselves are essentially the greatest poem. In the history of the earth hitherto the largest and most stirring appear tame and orderly to their ampler largeness and

stir. Here at last is something in the doings of man that corresponds with the broadcast doings of the day and night. Here is not merely a nation but a teeming nation of nations. Here is action untied from strings necessarily blind to particulars and details magnificently moving in vast masses. Here is the hospitality which forever indicates heroes. . . . Here are the roughs and beards and space and ruggedness and nonchalance that the soul loves. Here the performance disdaining the trivial unapproached in the tremendous audacity of its crowds and groupings and the push of its perspective spreads with crampless and flowing breadth and showers its prolific and splendid extravagance. One sees it must indeed own the riches of the summer and winter, and need never be bankrupt while corn grows from the ground or the orchards drop apples or the bays contain fish or men beget children upon women.

Other states indicate themselves in their deputies . . . but the genius of the United States is not best or most in its executives or legislatures, nor in its ambassadors or authors or colleges or churches or parlors, nor even in its newspapers or inventors . . . but always most in the common people. Their manners, speech, dress, friendships—the freshness and candor of their physiognomy—the picturesque looseness of their carriage . . . their

* The selections from Whitman are from *Leaves of Grass,* by Walt Whitman, reprinted by permission from Doubleday, Doran & Company, Inc., and from *Complete Prose,* by Walt Whitman, reprinted by permission from Doubleday, Doran & Company, Inc., publishers.

deathless attachment to freedom—
their aversion to anything indecorous
or soft or mean—the practical
acknowledgment of the citizens of one
state by the citizens of all other states
—the fierceness of their roused resentment—their curiosity and susceptibil-
ity to a slight—the air they have of
persons who never knew how it felt
to stand in the presence of superiors 10
—the fluency of their speech—their
delight in music, the sure symptom
of manly tenderness and native elegance of soul . . . their good temper
and openhandedness—the terrible significance of their elections—the President's taking off his hat to them not
they to him—these too are unrhymed
poetry. It awaits the gigantic and
generous treatment worthy of it.   20

The largeness of nature or the nation were monstrous without a corresponding largeness and generosity of
the spirit of the citizen. Not nature
nor swarming states nor streets and
steamships nor prosperous business
nor farms nor capital nor learning may
suffice for the ideal of man . . . nor
suffice the poet. No reminiscences 30
may suffice either. A live nation can
always cut a deep mark and can have
the best authority the cheapest . . .
namely from its own souls. This is
the sum of the profitable uses of individuals or states and of present action and grandeur and of the subjects
of poets.—As if it were necessary to
trot back generation after generation
to the eastern records! As if the 40
beauty and sacredness of the demonstrable must fall behind that of the
mythical! As if men do not make
their mark out of any times! As if
the opening of the western continent

by discovery and what has transpired
since in North and South America
were less than the small theater of
the antique or the aimless sleepwalk-
ing of the middle ages! The pride
of the United States leaves the wealth
and finesse of the cities and all returns of commerce and agriculture
and all the magnitude of geography
or shows of exterior victory to enjoy
the breed of full sized men or one
full sized man unconquerable and
simple.

The American poets are to enclose
old and new for America is the race
of races. Of them a bard is to be
commensurate with a people. To him
the other continents arrive as contributions . . . he gives them reception
for their sake and his own sake. His
spirit responds to his country's spirit
. . . he incarnates its geography and
natural life and rivers and lakes. Mississippi with annual freshets and
changing chutes, Missouri and Columbia and Ohio and Saint Lawrence
with the falls and beautiful masculine
Hudson, do not embouchure where
they spend themselves more than they
embouchure into him. The blue
breadth over the inland sea of Virginia and Maryland and the sea ·off
Massachusetts and Maine and over
Manhattan bay and over Champlain
and Erie and over Ontario and Huron
and Michigan and Superior, and over
the Texan and Mexican and Floridan
and Cuban seas and over the seas off
California and Oregon, is not tallied
by the blue breadth of the waters below more than the breadth of above
and below is tallied by him. When
the long Atlantic coast stretches longer
and the Pacific coast stretches longer
he easily stretches with them north

or south. He spans between them also from east to west and reflects what is between them. On him rise solid growths that offset the growths of pine and cedar and hemlock and live-oak and . locust and chestnut and cypress and hickory and limetree and cottonwood and tuliptree and cactus and wildvine and tamarind and persimmon . . . and tangles as tangled as any canebrake or swamp . . . and forests coated with transparent ice and icicles hanging from the boughs and crackling in the wind . . . and sides and peaks of mountains . . . and pasturage sweet and free as savannah or upland or prairie . . . with flights and songs and screams that answer those of the wildpigeon and highhold and orchard-oriole and coot and surf-duck and red-shouldered-hawk and fish-hawk and white-ibis and indian-hen and cat-owl and water-pheasant and qua-bird and pied sheldrake and blackbird and mockingbird and buzzard and condor and night-heron and eagle. To him the hereditary countenance descends both mother's and father's. To him enter the essences of the real things and past and present events—of the enormous diversity of temperature and agriculture and mines—the tribes of red aborigines—the weatherbeaten vessels entering new ports or making landings on rocky coasts—the first settlements north or south—the rapid stature and muscle—the haughty defiance of '76, and the war and peace and formation of the constitution . . . the union always surrounded by blatherers and always calm and impregnable —the perpetual coming of immigrants —the wharf-hem'd cities and superior marine—the unsurveyed interior—the loghouses and clearings and wild animals and hunters and trappers . . . the free commerce—the fisheries and whaling and gold-digging—the endless gestation of new states—the convening of Congress every December, the members duly coming up from all climates and the uttermost parts . . . the noble character of the young mechanics and of all free American workmen and workwomen . . . the general ardor and friendliness and enterprise —the perfect equality of the female with the male . . . the large amativeness—the fluid movement of the population—the factories and mercantile life and laborsaving machinery—the Yankee swap—the New York firemen and the target excursion—the southern plantation life—the character of the northeast and of the northwest and southwest—slavery and the tremulous spreading of hands to protect it, and the stern opposition to it which shall never cease till it ceases or the speaking of tongues and the moving of lips cease. For such the expression of the American poet is to be transcendant and new. It is to be indirect and not direct or descriptive or epic. Its quality goes through these to much more. Let the age and wars of other nations be chanted and their eras and characters be illustrated and that finish the verse. Not so the great psalm of the republic. Here the theme is creative and has vista. Here comes one among the wellbeloved stonecutters and plans with decision and science and sees the solid and beautiful forms of the future where there are now no solid forms.

Of all nations the United States with veins full of poetical stuff most need poets and will doubtless have the greatest and use them the greatest.

Their Presidents shall not be their common referee so much as their poets shall. Of all mankind the great poet is the equable man. Not in him but off from him things are grotesque or eccentric or fail of their sanity. Nothing out of its place is good and nothing in its place is bad. He bestows on every object or quality its fit proportions neither more nor less. He is the arbiter of the diverse and he is the key. He is the equalizer of his age and land . . . he supplies what wants supplying and checks what wants checking. If peace is the routine out of him speaks the spirit of peace, large, rich, thrifty, building vast and populous cities, encouraging agriculture and the arts and commerce —lighting the study of man, the soul, immortality—federal, state or municipal government, marriage, health, free trade, intertravel by land and sea . . . nothing too close, nothing too far off . . . the stars not too far off. In war he is the most deadly force of the war. Who recruits him recruits horse and foot . . . he fetches parks of artillery the best that engineer ever knew. If the time becomes slothful and heavy he knows how to arouse it . . . he can make every word he speaks draw blood. Whatever stagnates in the flat of custom or obedience or legislation he never stagnates. Obedience does not master him, he masters it. High up out of reach he stands turning a concentrated light . . . he turns the pivot with his finger . . . he baffles the swiftest runners as he stands and easily overtakes and envelopes them. The time straying toward infidelity and confections and persiflage he withholds by his steady faith . . . he spreads out his dishes

. . . he offers the sweet firmfibere[d] meat that grows men and women. Hi[s] brain is the ultimate brain. He is n[o] arguer . . . he is judgment. H[e] judges not as the judge judges but a[s] the sun falling around a helples[s] thing. As he sees the farthest he ha[s] the most faith. His thoughts are the hymns of the praise of things. In the talk on the soul and eternity and Go[d] off of his equal plane he is silent. H[e] sees eternity less like a play with [a] prologue and denouement . . . he see[s] eternity in men and women . . . h[e] does not see men and women a[s] dreams or dots. Faith is the anti[-] septic of the soul . . . it pervades the common people and preserves the[m] . . . they never give up believing an[d] expecting and trusting. There is tha[t] indescribable freshness and uncon[-] sciousness about an illiterate perso[n] that humbles and mocks the power o[f] the noblest expressive genius. The poet sees for a certainty how one no[t] a great artist may be just as sacre[d] as the greatest artist. . . . The power to destroy or remold is freel[y] used by him but never the power o[f] attack. What is past is past. If h[e] does not expose superior models an[d] prove himself by every step he take[s] he is not what is wanted. The pres[-] ence of the greatest poet conquer[s] . . . not parleying o[r] struggling or an[y] prepared attempts. Now he ha[s] passed that way see after him! ther[e] is not left any vestige of despair o[r] misanthropy or cunning or exclusive[-] ness or the ignominy of a nativit[y] or color or delusion of hell or th[e] necessity of hell . . . and no ma[n] thenceforward shall be degraded fo[r] ignorance or weakness or sin.

The greatest poet hardly knows pet[ti-]

tiness or triviality. If he breathes into any thing that was before thought small it dilates with the grandeur and life of the universe. He is a seer . . . he is individual . . . he is complete in himself . . . the others are as good as he, only he sees it and they do not. He is not one of the chorus . . . he does not stop for any regulations . . . he is the president of regulation. What the eyesight does to the rest he does to the rest. Who knows the curious mystery of the eyesight? The other senses corroborate themselves, but this is removed from any proof but its own and foreruns the identities of the spiritual world. A single glance of it mocks all the investigations of man and all the instruments and books of the earth and all reasoning. What is marvelous? what is unlikely? what is impossible or baseless or vague? after you have once just opened the space of a peachpit and given audience to far and near and to the sunset and had all things enter with electric swiftness softly and duly without confusion or jostling or jam.

The land and sea, the animals fishes and birds, the sky of heaven and the orbs, the forests, mountains and rivers, are not small themes . . . but folks expect of the poet to indicate more than the beauty and dignity which always attach to dumb real objects . . . they expect him to indicate the path between reality and their souls. Men and women perceive the beauty well enough . . . probably as well as he. The passionate tenacity of hunters, woodmen, early risers, cultivators of gardens and orchards and fields, the love of healthy women for the manly form, seafaring persons, drivers of horses, the passion for light

and the open air, all is an old varied sign of the unfailing perception of beauty and of a residence of the poetic in outdoor people. They can never be assisted by poets to perceive . . . some may but they never can. The poetic quality is not marshalled in rhyme or uniformity or abstract addresses to things nor in melancholy complaints or good precepts, but is the life of these and much else and is in the soul. The profit of rhyme is that it drops seeds of a sweeter and more luxuriant rhyme, and of uniformity that it conveys itself into its own roots in the ground out of sight. The rhyme and uniformity of perfect poems show the free growth of metrical laws and bud from them as unerringly and loosely as lilacs or roses on a bush, and take shapes as compact as the shapes of chestnuts and oranges and melons and pears, and shed the perfume impalpable to form. The fluency and ornaments of the finest poems or music or orations or recitations are not independent but dependent. All beauty comes from beautiful blood and a beautiful brain. If the greatnesses are in conjunction in a man or woman it is enough . . . the fact will prevail through the universe . . . but the gaggery and gilt of a million years will not prevail. Who troubles himself about his ornaments or fluency is lost. This is what you shall do: Love the earth and sun and the animals, despise riches, give alms to every one that asks, stand up for the stupid and crazy, devote your income and labor to others, hate tyrants, argue not concerning God, have patience and indulgence toward the people, take off your hat to nothing known or unknown or to any man or number of men, go freely with powerful uneducated persons and with the young and with the mothers of families, read these leaves in the open air every season of every year of your life, re-examine all you have been told at school or church or in any book, dismiss whatever insults your own soul, and your very flesh shall be a great poem and have the richest fluency not only in its words but in the silent lines of its lips and face and between the lashes of your eyes and in every motion and joint of your body. . . . The poet shall not spend his time in unneeded work. He shall know that the ground is always ready plowed and manured . . . others may not know it but he shall. He shall go directly to the creation. His trust shall master the trust of everything he touches . . . and shall master all attachment.

The known universe has one complete lover and that is the greatest poet. He consumes an eternal passion and is indifferent which chance happens and which possible contingency of fortune or misfortune and persuades daily and hourly his delicious pay. What balks or breaks others is fuel for his burning progress to contact and amorous joy. Other proportions of the reception of pleasure dwindle to nothing to his proportions. All expected from heaven or from the highest he is rapport with in the sight of the daybreak or a scene of the winterwoods or the presence of children playing or with his arm round the neck of a man or woman. His love above all love has leisure and expanse . . . he leaves room ahead of himself. He is no irresolute or suspicious lover . . . he is sure . . . he scorns intervals. His experience and the showers and thrills are not for nothing. Nothing can jar him . . . suffering and darkness cannot—death and fear cannot. To him complaint and jealousy and envy are corpses buried and rotten in the earth . . . he saw them buried. The sea is not surer of the shore or the shore of the sea than he is of the fruition of his love and of all perfection and beauty.

The fruition of beauty is no chance of hit or miss . . . it is inevitable as life . . . it is exact and plumb as gravitation. From the eyesight proceeds another eyesight and from the hearing proceeds another hearing and from the voice proceeds another voice eternally curious of the harmony of things with man. To these respond perfections not only in the committees that were supposed to stand for the rest but in the rest themselves just the same. These understand the law of perfection in masses and floods . . . that its finish is to each for itself and onward from itself . . . that it is profuse and impartial . . . that there is not a minute of the light or dark nor an acre of the earth or sea without it—nor any direction of the sky nor any trade or employment nor any turn of events. This is the reason that about the proper expression of beauty there is precision and balance . . . one part does not need to be thrust above another. The best singer is not the one who has the most lithe and powerful organ . . . the pleasure of poems is not in them that take the handsomest measure and similes and sound.

Without effort and without exposing in the least how it is done the greatest poet brings the spirit of any or all events and passions and scenes and persons some more and some less to bear on your individual character as you hear or read. To do this well is to compete with the laws that pursue and follow time. What is the purpose must surely be there and the clue of it must be there . . . and the faintest indication is the indication of the best and then becomes the clearest indication. Past and present and future are not disjoined but joined. The greatest poet forms the consistence of what is to be from what has been and is. He drags the dead out of their coffins and stands them again on their feet . . . he says to the past, Rise and walk before me that I may realize you. He learns the lesson . . . he places himself where the future becomes present. The greatest poet does not only dazzle his rays over character and scenes and passions . . . he finally ascends and finishes all . . . he exhibits the pinnacles that no man can tell what they are for or what is beyond . . . he glows a moment on the extremest verge. He is most wonderful in his last half-hidden smile or frown . . . by that flash of the moment of parting the one that sees it shall be encouraged or terrified afterwards for many years. The greatest poet does not moralize or make applications of morals . . . he knows the soul. The soul has that measureless pride which consists in never acknowledging any lessons but its own. But it has sympathy as measureless as its pride and the one balances the other and neither can stretch too far while it stretches in company with the other. The inmost secrets of art sleep with the twain. The greatest poet has lain close betwixt both and they

are vital in his style and thoughts.

The art of art, the glory of expression and the sunshine of the light of letters is simplicity. Nothing is better than simplicity . . . nothing can make up for excess or for the lack of definiteness. To carry on the heave of impulse and pierce intellectual depths and give all subjects their articulations are powers neither common nor very uncommon. But to speak in literature with the perfect rectitude and insousiance of the movements of animals and the unimpeachableness of the sentiment of trees in the woods and grass by the roadside is the flawless triumph of art. If you have looked on him who has achieved it you have looked on one of the masters of the artists of all nations and times. You shall not contemplate the flight of the graygull over the bay or the mettlesome action of the blood horse or the tall leaning of sunflowers on their stalk or the appearance of the sun journeying through heaven or the appearance of the moon afterward with any more satisfaction than you shall contemplate him. The greatest poet has less a marked style and is more the channel of thoughts and things without increase or diminution, and is the free channel of himself. He swears to his art, I will not be meddlesome, I will not have in my writing any elegance or effect or originality to hang in the way between me and the rest like curtains. I will have nothing hang in the way, not the richest curtains. What I tell I tell for precisely what it is. Let who may exalt or startle or fascinate or sooth I will have purposes as health or heat or snow has and be as regardless of observation. What I experience or portray shall go from my composition without a shred of my composition. You shall stand by my side and look in the mirror with me.

The old red blood and stainless gentility of great poets will be proved by their unconstraint. A heroic person walks at his ease through and out of that custom or precedent or authority that suits him not. Of the traits of the brotherhood of writers savans musicians inventors and artists nothing is finer than silent defiance advancing from new free forms. In the need of poems philosophy politics mechanism science behavior, the craft of art, an appropriate native grand-opera, shipcraft, or any craft, he is greatest forever and forever who contributes the greatest original practical example. The cleanest expression is that which finds no sphere worthy of itself and makes one.

The messages of great poets to each man and woman are, Come to us on equal terms, Only then can you understand us, We are no better than you, What we enclose you enclose, What we enjoy you may enjoy. Did you suppose there could be only one Supreme? We affirm there can be unnumbered Supremes, and that one does not countervail another any more than one eyesight countervails another . . . and that men can be good or grand only of the consciousness of their supremacy within them. What do you think is the grandeur of storms and dismemberments and the deadliest battles and wrecks and the wildest fury of the elements and the power of the sea and the motion of nature and of the throes of human desires and dignity and hate and love? It is that something in the soul which says,

Rage on, Whirl on, I tread master here and everywhere, Master of the spasms of the sky and of the shatter of the sea, Master of nature and passion and death, And of all terror and all pain.

The American bards shall be marked for generosity and affection and for encouraging competitors. . . . They shall be kosmos . . . without monopoly or secrecy . . . glad to pass any thing to any one . . . hungry for equals night and day. They shall not be careful of riches and privilege, they shall be riches and privilege . . . they shall perceive who the most affluent man is. The most affluent man is he that confronts all the shows he sees by equivalents out of the stronger wealth of himself. The American bard shall delineate no class of persons nor one or two out of the strata of interests nor love most nor truth nor the soul most nor the body most . . . and not be for the eastern states more than the western or the northern states more than the southern.

Exact science and its practical movements are no checks on the greatest poet but always his encouragement and support. The outset and remembrance are there . . . there are the arms that lifted him first and brace him best . . . there he returns after all his goings and comings. The sailor and traveler . . . the atomist chemist astronomer geologist phrenologist spiritualist mathematician historian and lexicographer are not poets, but they are the lawgivers of poets and their construction underlies the structure of every perfect poem. No matter what rises or is uttered they sent the seed of the conception of it . . . of them and by them stand the visible proofs of souls . . . always of their fatherstuff must be begotten the sinewy races of bards. If there shall be love and content between the father and the son and if the greatness of the son is the exuding of the greatness of the father there shall be love between the poet and the man of demonstrable science. In the beauty of poems are the tuft and final applause of science.

Great is the faith of the flush of knowledge and of the investigation of the depths of qualities and things. Cleaving and circling here swells the soul of the poet yet is president of itself always. The depths are fathomless and therefore calm. The innocence and nakedness are resumed . . . they are neither modest nor immodest. The whole theory of the special and supernatural and all that was twined with it or educed out of it departs as a dream. What has ever happened . . . what happens and whatever may or shall happen, the vital laws enclose all . . . they are sufficient for any case and for all cases . . . none to be hurried or retarded . . . any miracle of affairs or persons inadmissible in the vast clear scheme where every motion and every spear of grass and the frames and spirits of men and women and all that concerns them are unspeakably perfect miracles all referring to all and each distinct and in its place. It is also not consistent with the reality of the soul to admit that there is anything in the known universe more divine than men and women.

Men and women and the earth and all upon it are simply to be taken as they are, and the investigation of their past and present and future shall be unintermitted and shall be done with perfect candor. Upon this basis philosophy speculates ever looking toward the poet, ever regarding the eternal tendencies of all toward happiness never inconsistent with what is clear to the senses and to the soul. For the eternal tendencies of all toward happiness make the only point of sane philosophy. Whatever comprehends less than that . . . whatever is less than the laws of light and of astronomical motion . . . or less than the laws that follow the thief the liar the glutton and the drunkard through this life and doubtless afterward . . . or less than vast stretches of time or the slow formation of density or the patient upheaving of strata—is of no account. Whatever would put God in a poem or system of philosophy as contending against some being or influence, is also of no account. Sanity and ensemble characterize the great master . . . spoilt in one principle all is spoilt. The great master has nothing to do with miracles. He sees health for himself in being one of the mass . . . he sees the hiatus in singular eminence. To the perfect shape comes common ground. To be under the general law is great for that is to correspond with it. The master knows that he is unspeakably great and that all are unspeakably great . . . that nothing for instance is greater than to conceive children and bring them up well . . . that to be is just as great as to perceive or tell.

In the make of the great masters the idea of political liberty is indispensable. Liberty takes the adherence of heroes wherever men and women exist . . . but never takes any adherence or welcome from the rest more than from poets. They are the voice and exposition of liberty. They out of ages are worthy the grand idea . . . to them it is confided and they must sustain it. Nothing has precedence of it and nothing can warp or degrade it. The attitude of great poets is to cheer up slaves and horrify despots. The turn of their necks, the sound of their feet, the motions of their wrists, are full of hazard to the one and hope to the other. Come nigh them awhile and though they neither speak nor advise you shall learn the faithful American lesson. Liberty is poorly served by men whose good intent is quelled from one failure or two failures or any number of failures, or from the casual indifference or ingratitude of the people, or from the sharp show of the tushes of power, or the bringing to bear soldiers and cannon or any penal statutes. Liberty relies upon itself, invites no one, promises nothing, sits in calmness and light, is positive and composed, and knows no discouragement. The battle rages with many a loud alarm and frequent advance and retreat . . . the enemy triumphs . . . the prison, the handcuffs, the iron necklace and anklet, the scaffold, garrote and leadballs do their work . . . the cause is asleep . . . the strong throats are choked with their own blood . . . the young men drop their eyelashes toward the ground when they pass each other . . . and is liberty gone out of that place? No never. When liberty goes it is not the first to go nor the second nor third to go . . . it waits for all the rest to go . . . it is the last. . . . When the memories of the old martyrs are faded utterly away . . . when the large names of patriots are laughed at in the public halls from the lips of the orators . . . when the boys are no more christened after the same but christened after tyrants and traitors instead . . . when the laws of the free are grudgingly permitted and laws for informers and blood-money are sweet to the taste of the people . . . when I and you walk abroad upon the earth stung with compassion at the sight of numberless brothers answering our equal friendship and calling no man master—and when we are elated with noble joy at the sight of slaves . . . when the soul retires in the cool communion of the night and surveys its experience and has much extasy over the word and deed that put back a helpless innocent person into the gripe of the gripers or into any cruel inferiority . . . when those in all parts of these states who could easier realize the true American character but do not yet—when the swarms of cringers, suckers, doughfaces, lice of politics, planners of sly involutions for their own preferment to city offices or state legislatures or the judiciary or congress or the presidency, obtain a response of love and natural deference from the people whether they get the officers or no . . . when it is better to be a bound booby and rogue in office at a high salary than the poorest free mechanic or farmer with his hat unmoved from his head and firm eyes and a candid and generous heart . . . and when servility by town or state or the federal government or any oppression on a large scale or small scale can be tried on without its own punishment following duly after in exact proportion against the smallest chance of escape . . . or rather when all life and all the souls of men and women are discharged from any part of the earth—then only shall the instinct of liberty be discharged from that part of the earth.

As the attributes of the poets of the kosmos concenter in the real body and soul and in the pleasure of things they possess the superiority of genuineness over all fiction and romance. As they emit themselves facts are showered over with light . . . the daylight is lit with more volatile light . . . also the deep between the setting and rising sun goes deeper many fold. Each precise object or condition or combination or process exhibits a beauty . . . the multiplication table its—old age its—the carpenter's trade its—the grand-opera its . . . the hugehulled cleanshaped New-York clipper at sea under steam or full sail gleams with unmatched beauty . . . the American circles and large harmonies of government gleam with theirs . . . and the commonest definite intentions and actions with theirs. The poets of the kosmos advance through all interpositions and coverings and turmoils and stratagems to first principles. They are of use . . . they dissolve poverty from its need and riches from its conceit. You large proprietor they say shall not realize or perceive more than any one else. The owner of the library is not he who holds a legal title to it having bought and paid for it. Any one and every one is owner of the library who can read the same through all the varieties of tongues and subjects and styles, and in whom they enter with ease and take residence and force toward paternity and maternity, and make supple and powerful and rich and large. . . . These American states strong and healthy and accomplished

shall receive no pleasure from violations of natural models and must not permit them. In paintings or moldings or carvings in mineral or wood, or in the illustrations of books or newspapers, or in any comic or tragic prints, or in the patterns of woven stuffs or anything to beautify rooms or furniture or costumes, or to put upon cornices or monuments or on the prows or sterns of ships, or to put anywhere before the human eye indoors or out, that which distorts honest shapes or which creates unearthly beings or places or contingencies is a nuisance and revolt. Of the human form especially it is so great it must never be made ridiculous. Of ornaments to a work nothing outré can be allowed . . . but those ornaments can be allowed to conform to the perfect facts of the open air and that flow out of the nature of the work and come irrepressibly from it and are necessary to the completion of the work. Most works are most beautiful without ornament. . . . Exaggerations will be revenged in human physiology. Clean and vigorous children are jetted and conceived only in those communities where the models of natural forms are public every day. . . . Great genius and the people of these states must never be demeaned to romances. As soon as histories are properly told there is no more need of romances.

The great poets are also to be known by the absence in them of tricks and by the justification of perfect personal candor. Then folks echo a new cheap joy and a divine voice leaping from their brains: How beautiful is candor! All faults may be forgiven of him who has perfect candor.

Henceforth let no man of us lie, for we have seen that openness wins the inner and outer world and that there is no single exception, and that never since our earth gathered itself in a mass have deceit or subterfuge or prevarication attracted its smallest particle or the faintest tinge of a shade —and that through the enveloping wealth and rank of a state or the whole republic of states a sneak or sly person shall be discovered and despised . . . and that the soul has never been once fooled and never can be fooled . . . and thrift without the loving nod of the soul is only a fœtid puff . . . and there never grew up in any of the continents of the globe nor upon any planet or satellite or star, nor upon the asteroids, nor in any part of ethereal space, nor in the midst of density, nor under the fluid wet of the sea, nor in the condition which precedes the birth of babes, nor at any time during the changes of life, nor in that condition that follows what we term death, nor in any stretch of abeyance or action afterward of vitality, nor in any process of formation or reformation anywhere, a being whose instinct hated the truth.

Extreme caution or prudence, the soundest organic health, large hope and comparison and fondness for women and children, large alimentiveness and destructiveness and causality, with a perfect sense of the oneness of nature and the propriety of the same spirit applied to human affairs . . . these are called up of the float of the brain of the world to be parts of the greatest poet from his birth out of his mother's womb and from her birth out of her mother's. Caution seldom goes far enough. It has been thought that the prudent citizen was the citizen who applied himself to solid gains and did well for himself and his family and completed a lawful life without debt or crime. The greatest poet sees and admits these economies as he sees the economies of food and sleep, but has higher notions of prudence than to think he gives much when he gives a few slight attentions at the latch of the gate. The premises of the prudence of life are not the hospitality of it or the ripeness and harvest of it. Beyond the independence of a little sum laid aside for burial-money, and of a few clapboards around and shingles overhead on a lot of American soil owned, and the easy dollars that supply the year's plain clothing and meals, the melancholy prudence of the abandonment of such a great being as a man is to the toss and pallor of years of moneymaking with all their scorching days and icy nights and all their stifling deceits and underhanded dodgings, or infinitesimals of parlors, or shameless stuffing while others starve . . . and all the loss of the bloom and odor of the earth and of the flowers and atmosphere and of the sea and of the true taste of the women and men you pass or have to do with in youth or middle age, and the issuing sickness and desperate revolt at the close of a life without elevation or naïveté, and the ghastly chatter of a death without serenity or majesty, is the great fraud upon modern civilization and forethought, blotching the surface and system which civilization undeniably drafts, and moistening with tears the immense features it spreads and spreads with such velocity before the reached kisses of the soul. . . .

Still the right explanation remains to be made about prudence. The prudence of the mere wealth and respectability of the most esteemed life appears too faint for the eye to observe at all when little and large alike drop quietly aside at the thought of the prudence suitable for immortality. What is wisdom that fills the thinness of a year or seventy or eighty years' to wisdom spaced out by ages and coming back at a certain time with strong reinforcements and rich presents and the clear faces of wedding-guests as far as you can look in every direction running gaily toward you? Only the soul is of itself . . . all else has reference to what ensues. All that a person does or thinks is of consequence. Not a move can a man or woman make that affects him or her in a day or a month or any part of the direct lifetime or the hour of death but the same affects him or her onward afterward through the indirect lifetime. The indirect is always as great and real as the direct. The spirit receives from the body just as much as it gives to the body. Not one name of word or deed . . . not of venereal sores or discolorations . . . not the privacy of the onanist . . . not of the putrid veins of gluttons or rum-drinkers . . . not peculation or cunning or betrayal 'or murder . . . no serpentine poison of those that seduce women . . . not the foolish yielding of women . . . not prostitution . . . not of any depravity of young men . . . not of the attainment of gain by discreditable means . . . not any nastiness of appetite . . . not any harshness of officers to men or judges to prisoners or fathers to sons or sons to fathers or husbands to wives or bosses to their boys . . . not of greedy looks or malignant wishes . . . nor any of the wiles practised by people upon themselves . . . ever is or ever can be stamped on the programme but it is duly realized and returned, and that returned in further performances . . . and they returned again. Nor can the push of charity or personal force ever be any thing else than the profoundest reason, whether it brings arguments to hand or no. No specification is necessary . . . to add or subtract or divide is in vain. Little or big, learned or unlearned, white or black, legal or illegal, sick or well, from the first inspiration down the windpipe to the last expiration out of it, all that a male or female does that is vigorous and benevolent and clean is so much sure profit to him or her in the unshakable order of the universe and through the whole scope of it forever. If the savage or felon is wise it is well . . . if the greatest poet or savan is wise it is simply the same . . . if the President or chief justice is wise it is the same . . . if the young mechanic or farmer is wise it is no more or less . . . if the prostitute is wise it is no more nor less. The interest will come round . . . all will come round. All the best actions of war and peace . . . all help given to relatives and strangers and the poor and old and sorrowful and young children and widows and the sick, and to all shunned persons . . . all furtherance of fugitives and of the escape of slaves . . . all the self-denial that stood steady and aloof on wrecks and saw others take the seats of the boats . . . all offering of substance or life for the good old cause, or for a

friend's sake or opinion's sake . . . all
pains of enthusiasts scoffed at by their
neighbors . . . all the vast sweet love
and precious suffering of mothers . . .
all honest men baffled in strifes recorded or unrecorded . . . all the
grandeur and good of the few ancient
nations whose fragments of annals we
inherit . . . and all the good of the
hundreds of far mightier and more 10
ancient nations unknown to us by
name or date or location . . . all that
was ever manfully begun, whether it
succeeded or not . . . all that has at
any time been well suggested out of
the divine heart of man or by the
divinity of his mouth or by the shaping of his great hands . . . and all
that is well thought or done this day
on any part of the surface of the globe 20
. . . or on any of the wandering stars
or fixed stars by those there as we
are here . . . or that is henceforth to
be well thought or done by you whoever you are, or by any one—these
singly and wholly inure at their time
and inure now and will inure always
to the identities from which they
sprung or shall spring. . . . Did you
guess any of them lived only its mo- 30
ment? The world does not so exist
. . . no parts palpable or impalpable
so exist . . . no result exists now without being from its long antecedent
result, and that from its antecedent,
and so backward without the farthest
mentionable spot coming a bit nearer
to the beginning than any other spot.
. . . Whatever satisfies the soul is
truth. The prudence of the greatest 40
poet answers at last the craving and
glut of the soul, is not contemptuous
of less ways of prudence if they conform to its ways, puts off nothing,
permits no let-up for its own case or

any case, has no particular sabbath o
judgment-day, divides not the livin
from the dead or the righteous from
the unrighteous, is satisfied with th
present, matches every thought or ac
by its correlative, knows no possibl
forgiveness or deputed atonement . .
knows that the young man who com
posedly periled his life and lost it ha
done exceeding well for himself, whil
the man who has not periled his lif
and retains it to old age in riches an
ease has perhaps achieved nothing fo
himself worth mentioning . . . an
that only that person has no grea
prudence to learn who has learnt t
prefer real longlived things, and favor
body and soul the same, and perceive
the indirect assuredly following the d
rect, and what evil or good he doe
leaping onward and waiting to mee
him again—and who in his spirit i
any emergency whatever neither hu
ries or avoids death.

The direct trial of him who woul
be the greatest poet is today. If h
does not flood himself with the im
mediate age as with vast oceanic tid
. . . and if he does not attract b
own land body and soul to himse
and hang on its neck with incompa
rable love and plunge his semitic mu
cle into its merits and demerits . .
and if he be not himself the age tran
figured . . . and if to him is n
opened the eternity which gives simil
tude to all periods and locations ar
processes and animate and inanima
forms, and which is the bond of tim
and rises up from its inconceivab
vagueness and infiniteness in the swir
ming shape of today, and is held b
the ductile anchors of life, and mak
the present spot the passage fro
what was to what shall be, and cor

mits itself to the representation of
this wave of an hour and this one
of the sixty beautiful children of the
wave—let him merge in the general
run and wait his development. . . .
Still the final test of poems or any
character or work remains. The
prescient poet projects himself centuries ahead and judges performer or
performance after the changes of time.
Does it live through them? Does it
still hold on untired? Will the same
style and the direction of genius to
similar points be satisfactory now?
Has no new discovery in science or
arrival at superior planes of thought
and judgment and behavior fixed him
or his so that either can be looked
down upon? Have the marches of
tens and hundreds and thousands of
years made willing detours to the right
hand and and the left hand for his sake?
Is he beloved long and long after
he is buried? Does the young man
think often of him? and the young
woman think often of him? and do
the middle-aged and the old think of
him?

A great poem is for ages and ages
in common and for all degrees and
complexions and all departments and
sects and for a woman as much as a
man and a man as much as a woman.
A great poem is no finish to a man
or woman but rather a beginning. Has
any one fancied he could sit at last
under some due authority and rest
satisfied with explanations and realize
and be content and full? To no such
terminus does the greatest poet bring
. . . he brings neither cessation or
sheltered fatness and ease. The touch
of him tells in action. Whom he takes
with firm sure grasp into live regions
previously unattained . . . thence-

forward is no rest . . . they see the
space and ineffable sheen that turn
the old spots and lights into dead
vacuums. The companion of him beholds the birth and progress of stars
and learns one of the meanings. Now
there shall be a man cohered out of
tumult and chaos . . . the elder en-
courages the younger and shows him
how . . . they two shall launch off
fearlessly together till the new world
fits an orbit for itself and looks unabashed on the lesser orbits of the
stars and sweeps through the ceaseless rings and shall never be quiet
again.

There will soon be no more priests.
Their work is done. They may wait
awhile . . . perhaps a generation or
two . . . dropping off by degrees. A
superior breed shall take their place
. . . the gangs of kosmos and prophets en masse shall take their place. A
new order shall arise and they shall be
the priests of man, and every man
shall be his own priest. The churches
built under their umbrage shall be the
churches of men and women. Through
the divinity of themselves shall the
kosmos and the new breed of poets be
interpreters of men and women and
of all events and things. They shall
find their inspiration in real objects
today, symptoms of the past and future. . . . They shall not deign to
defend immortality or God or the perfection of things or liberty or the
exquisite beauty and reality of the
soul. They shall arise in America and
be responded to from the remainder
of the earth.

The English language befriends the
grand American expression . . . it is
brawny enough and limber and full
enough. On the tough stock of a race

who through all change of circumstances was never without the idea of political liberty, which is the animus of all liberty, it has attracted the terms of daintier and gayer and subtler and more elegant tongues. It is the powerful language of resistance . . . it is the dialect of common sense. It is the speech of the proud and melancholy races and of all who aspire. It is the chosen tongue to express growth faith self-esteem freedom justice equality friendliness amplitude prudence decision and courage. It is the medium that shall well nigh express the inexpressible.

No great literature nor any like style of behavior or oratory or social intercourse or household arrangements or public institutions or the treatment by bosses or employed people, nor executive detail or detail of the army or navy, nor spirit of legislation or courts or police or tuition or architecture or songs or amusements or the costumes of young men, can long elude the jealous and passionate instinct of American standards. Whether or no the sign appears from the mouths of the people, it throbs a live interrogation in every freeman's and freewoman's heart after that which passes by or this built to remain. Is it uniform with my country? Are its disposals without ignominious distinctions? Is it for the evergrowing communes of brothers and lovers, large, well-united, proud beyond the old models, generous beyond all models? Is it something grown fresh out of the fields or drawn from the sea for use to me today here? I know that what answers for me an American must answer for any individual or nation that serves for a part of my materials.

Does this answer? or is it without reference to universal needs? or sprung of the needs of the less developed society of special ranks? or old needs of pleasure overlaid by modern science and forms? Does this acknowledge liberty with audible and absolute acknowledgment, and set slavery at naught for life and death? Will it help breed one goodshaped and well-hung man, and a woman to be his perfect and independent mate? Does it improve manners? Is it for the nursing of the young of the republic? Does it solve readily with the sweet milk of the nipples of the breasts of the mother of many children? Has it too the old ever-fresh forbearance and impartiality? Does it look with the same love on the last born and those hardening toward stature, and on the errant, and on those who disdain all strength of assault outside of their own?

The poems distilled from other poems will probably pass away. The coward will surely pass away. The expectation of the vital and great can only be satisfied by the demeanor of the vital and great. The swarms of the polished deprecating and reflectors and the polite float off and leave no remembrance. America prepares with composure and goodwill for the visitors that have sent word. It is not intellect that is to be their warrant and welcome. The talented, the artist the ingenious, the editor, the statesman, the erudite . . . they are not unappreciated . . . they fall in their place and do their work. The soul of the nation also does its work. No disguise can pass on it . . . no disguise can conceal from it. It rejects none, it permits all. Only toward as

ood as itself and toward the like of
tself will it advance half-way. An in-
lividual is as superb as a nation when
ıe has the qualities which make a
uperb nation. The soul of the largest
nd wealthiest and proudest nation
nay well go half-way to meet that
of its poets. The signs are effectual.
There is no fear of mistake. If the
one is true the other is true. The
proof of a poet is that his country
absorbs him as affectionately as he has
absorbed it.

1855

SONG OF MYSELF

1

celebrate myself, and sing myself,
And what I assume you shall assume,
or every atom belonging to me as good belongs to you.

loafe and invite my soul,
lean and loafe at my ease observing a spear of summer grass.

My tongue, every atom of my blood, formed from this soil, this air,
Born here of parents born here from parents the same, and their parents the
    same,
, now thirty-seven years old in perfect health begin,
Ioping to cease not till death.

Creeds and schools in abeyance,   10
Retiring back a while sufficed at what they are, but never forgotten,
harbor for good or bad, I permit to speak at every hazard,
Iature without check with original energy.

2

Iouses and rooms are full of perfumes, the shelves are crowded with perfumes,
breathe the fragrance myself and know it and like it,
he distillation would intoxicate me also, but I shall not let it.

he atmosphere is not a perfume, it has no taste of the distillation, it is
    odorless,
is for my mouth forever, I am in love with it,
will go to the bank by the wood and become undisguised and naked,
am mad for it to be in contact with me.   20

he smoke of my own breath,
choes, ripples, buzzed whispers, love-root, silk-thread, crotch and vine,
Iy respiration and inspiration, the beating of my heart, the passing of blood
    and air through my lungs,
he sniff of green leaves and dry leaves, and of the shore and dark-colored
    sea-rocks, and of hay in the barn,

The sound of the belched words of my voice loosed to the eddies of the wind
A few light kisses, a few embraces, a reaching around of arms,
The play of shine and shade on the trees as the supple boughs wag,
The delight alone or in the rush of the streets, or along the fields and hill-side
The feeling of health, the full-noon trill, the song of me rising from bed an
     meeting the sun.

Have you reckoned a thousand acres much? have you reckoned the eart
     much?
Have you practiced so long to learn to read?
Have you felt so proud to get at the meaning of poems?

Stop this day and night with me and you shall possess the origin of all poem
You shall possess the good of the earth and sun (there are millions of sun
     left),
You shall no longer take things at second or third hand, nor look through th
     eyes of the dead, nor feed on the spectres in books,
You shall not look through my eyes either, nor take things from me,
You shall listen to all sides and filter them from your self.

3

I have heard what the talkers were talking, the talk of the beginning an
     the end,
But I do not talk of the beginning or the end.

There was never any more inception than there is now,
Nor any more youth or age than there is now,
And will never be any more perfection than there is now,
Nor any more heaven or hell than there is now.

Urge and urge and urge,
Always the procreant urge of the world.
Out of the dimness opposite equals advance, always substance and increas
     always sex,
Always a knit of identity, always distinction, always a breed of life.
To elaborate is no avail, learn'd and unlearn'd feel that it is so.

Sure as the most certain sure, plumb in the uprights, well entretied, braced
     the beams,
Stout as a horse, affectionate, haughty, electrical,
I and this mystery here we stand.

Clear and sweet is my soul, and clear and sweet is all that is not my soul.

Lack one lacks both, and the unseen is proved by the seen,
Till that becomes unseen and receives proof in its turn.

Showing the best and dividing it from the worst age vexes age,
Knowing the perfect fitness and equanimity of things, while they discuss I a
     silent, and go bathe and admire myself.

Welcome is every organ and attribute of me, and of any man hearty and
    clean,
Not an inch nor a particle of an inch is vile, and none shall be less familiar
    than the rest.

I am satisfied—I see, dance, laugh, sing;
As the hugging and loving bed-fellow sleeps at my side through the night, and
    withdraws at the peep of the day with stealthy tread,   60
Leaving me baskets covered with white towels swelling the house with their
    plenty,
Shall I postpone my acceptation and realization and scream at my eyes,
That they turn from gazing after and down the road,
And forthwith cipher and show me to a cent,
Exactly the value of one and exactly the value of two, and which is ahead?

4

Trippers and askers surround me,
People I meet, the effect upon me of my early life or the ward and city I live
    in, or the nation,
The latest dates, discoveries, inventions, societies, authors old and new,
My dinner, dress, associates, looks, compliments, dues,
The real or fancied indifference of some man or woman I love,   70
The sickness of one of my folks or of myself, or ill-doing or loss or lack of
    money, or depressions or exaltations,
Battles, the horrors of fratricidal war, the fever of doubtful news, the fitful
    events;
These come to me days and nights and go from me again,
But they are not the Me myself.

Apart from the pulling and hauling stands what I am,
Stands amused, complacent, compassionating, idle, unitary,
Looks down, is erect, or bends an arm on an impalpable certain rest,
Looking with side-curved head curious what will come next,
Both in and out of the game and watching and wondering at it.

Backward I see in my own days where I sweated through fog with linguists
    and contenders,   80
have no mockings or arguments, I witness and wait.

5

believe in you my soul, the other I am must not abase itself to you,
And you must not be abased to the other.

Loafe with me on the grass, loose the stop from your throat,
Not words, not music or rhyme I want, not custom or lecture, not even
    the best,
Only the lull I like, the hum of your valvèd voice.

mind how once we lay such a transparent summer morning,
How you settled your head athwart my hips and gently turned over upon me,

And parted the shirt from my bosom-bone, and plunged your tongue to my
    bare-stripped heart,
And reached till you felt my beard, and reached till you held my feet.   90

Swiftly arose and spread around me the peace and knowledge that pass all
    the argument of the earth,
And I know that the hand of God is the promise of my own,
And I know that the spirit of God is the brother of my own,
And that all the men ever born are also my brothers, and the women my
    sisters and lovers,
And that a kelson of the creation is love,
And limitless are leaves stiff or drooping in the fields,
And brown ants in the little wells beneath them,
And mossy scabs of the worm fence, heaped stones, elder, mullein and poke-
    weed.

6

A child said *What is the grass?* fetching it to me with full hands,
How could I answer the child? I do not know what it is any more than he.   100

I guess it must be the flag of my disposition, out of hopeful green stuff woven.

Or I guess it is the handkerchief of the Lord,
A scented gift and remembrancer designedly dropped,
Bearing the owner's name someway in the corners, that we may see and
    remark, and say *Whose?*

Or I guess the grass is itself a child, the produced babe of the vegetation.

Or I guess it is a uniform hieroglyphic,
And it means, Sprouting alike in broad zones and narrow zones,
Growing among black folks as among white,
Kanuck, Tuckahoe, Congressman, Cuff, I give them the same, I receive them
    the same.

And now it seems to me the beautiful uncut hair of graves.   110

Tenderly will I use you curling grass,
It may be you transpire from the breasts of young men,
It may be if I had known them I would have loved them,
It may be you are from old people, or from offspring taken soon out of their
    mothers' laps,
And here you are the mothers' laps.

This grass is very dark to be from the white heads of old mothers,
Darker than the colorless beards of old men,
Dark to come from under the faint red roofs of mouths.

O I perceive after all so many uttering tongues,
And I perceive they do not come from the roofs of mouths for nothing.   120

I wish I could translate the hints about the dead young men and women,
And the hints about old men and mothers, and the offspring taken soon out
    of their laps.

What do you think has become of the young and old men?
And what do you think has become of the women and children?

They are alive and well somewhere,
The smallest sprout shows there is really no death,
And if ever there was it led forward life, and does not wait at the end to
    arrest it,
And ceased the moment life appeared.

All goes onward and outward, nothing collapses,
And to die is different from what any one supposed, and luckier.   130

7

Has any one supposed it lucky to be born?
I hasten to inform him or her it is just as lucky to die, and I know it.

I pass death with the dying and birth with the new-washed babe, and am not
    contained between my hat and boots,
And peruse manifold objects, no two alike and every one good,
The earth good and the stars good, and their adjuncts all good.

I am not an earth nor an adjunct of an earth,
I am the mate and companion of people, all just as immortal and fathomless
    as myself
(They do not know how immortal, but I know).

Every kind for itself and its own, for me mine male and female,
For me those that have been boys and that love women,   140
For me the man that is proud and feels how it stings to be slighted,
For me the sweet-heart and the old maid, for me mothers and the mothers of
    mothers,
For me lips that have smiled, eyes that have shed tears,
For me children and the begetters of children.

Undrape! you are not guilty to me, nor stale nor discarded,
I see through the broadcloth and gingham whether or no,
And am around, tenacious, acquisitive, tireless, and cannot be shaken away.

8

The little one sleeps in its cradle,
I lift the gauze and look a long time, and silently brush away flies with my
    hand.

The youngster and the red-faced girl turn aside up the bushy hill,   150
I peeringly view them from the top.

The suicide sprawls on the bloody floor of the bedroom,
I witness the corpse with its dabbled hair, I note where the pistol has fallen.

The blab of the pave, tires of carts, sluff of boot-soles, talk of the prome-
    naders,
The heavy omnibus, the driver with his interrogating thumb, the clank of the
    shod horses on the granite floor,
The snow-sleighs, clinking, shouted jokes, pelts of snow-balls,
The hurrahs for popular favorites, the fury of roused mobs,
The flap of the curtained litter, a sick man inside borne to the hospital,
The meeting of enemies, the sudden oath, the blows and fall,
The excited crowd, the policeman with his star quickly working his passage to
    the center of the crowd,   160
The impassive stones that receive and return so many echoes,
What groans of over-fed or half-starved who fall sunstruck or in fits,
What exclamations of women taken suddenly who hurry home and give birth
    to babes,
What living and buried speech is always vibrating here, what howls restrained
    by decorum,
Arrests of criminals, slights, adulterous offers made, acceptances, rejections
    with convex lips,
I mind them or the show or resonance of them—I come and I depart.

9

The big doors of the country barn stand open and ready,
The dried grass of the harvest-time loads the slow-drawn wagon,
The clear light plays on the brown gray and green intertinged,
The armfuls are packed to the sagging mow.   170

I am there, I help, I came stretched atop of the load,
I felt its soft jolts, one leg reclined on the other,
I jump from the cross-beams and seize the clover and timothy,
And roll head over heels and tangle my hair full of wisps.

10

Alone far in the wilds and mountains I hunt,
Wandering amazed at my own lightness and glee,
In the late afternoon choosing a safe spot to pass the night,
Kindling a fire and broiling the fresh-killed game,
Falling asleep on the gathered leaves with my dog and gun by my side.

The Yankee clipper is under her sky-sails, she cuts the sparkle and scud,   180
My eyes settle the land, I bend at her prow or shout joyously from the deck

The boatmen and clam-diggers arose early and stopped for me,
I tucked my trowser-ends in my boots and went and had a good time;
You should have been with us that day round the chowder-kettle.

I saw the marriage of the trapper in the open air in the far west, the bride
    was a red girl,
Her father and his friends sat near cross-legged and dumbly smoking, they
    had moccasins to their feet and large thick blankets hanging from their
    shoulders,
On a bank lounged the trapper, he was dressed mostly in skins, his luxuriant
    beard and curls protected his neck, he held his bride by the hand,
She had long eyelashes, her head was bare, her coarse straight locks descended
    upon her voluptuous limbs and reached to her feet.

The runaway slave came to my house and stopped outside,
I heard his motions crackling the twigs of the woodpile,   190
Through the swung half-door of the kitchen I saw him limpsy and weak,
And went where he sat on a log and led him in and assured him,
And brought water and filled a tub for his sweated body and bruised feet,
And gave him a room that entered from my own, and gave him some coarse
    clean clothes,
And remember perfectly well his revolving eyes and his awkwardness,
And remember putting plasters on the galls of his neck and ankles;
He stayed with me a week before he was recuperated and passed north,
I had him sit next me at table, my fire-lock leaned in the corner.

11

Twenty-eight young men bathe by the shore,
Twenty-eight young men and all so friendly;   200
Twenty-eight years of womanly life and all so lonesome.

She owns the fine house by the rise of the bank,
She hides handsome and richly dressed aft the blinds of the window.

Which of the young men does she like the best?
Ah the homeliest of them is beautiful to her.

Where are you off to, lady? for I see you,
You splash in the water there, yet stay stock still in your room.

Dancing and laughing along the beach came the twenty-ninth bather,
The rest did not see her, but she saw them and loved them.

The beards of the young men glistened with wet, it ran from their long
    hair,   210
Little streams passed all over their bodies.

An unseen hand also passed over their bodies,
It descended tremblingly from their temples and ribs.

The young men float on their backs, their white bellies bulge to the sun, they
    do not ask who seizes fast to them,
They do not know who puffs and declines with pendant and bending arch,
They do not think whom they souse with spray.

12

The butcher-boy puts off his killing-clothes, or sharpens his knife at the stall in the market,
I loiter enjoying his repartee and his shuffle and break-down.

Blacksmiths with grimed and hairy chests environ the anvil,
Each has his main-sledge, they are all out, there is a great heat in the fire.   220

From the cinder-strewed threshold I follow their movements,
The lithe sheer of their waists plays even with their massive arms,
Overhand the hammers swing, overhand so slow, overhand so sure,
They do not hasten, each man hits in his place.

13

The negro holds firmly the reins of his four horses, the block swags underneath on its tied-over chain,
The negro that drives the long dray of the stone-yard, steady and tall he stands poised on one leg on the string-piece,
His blue shirt exposes his ample neck and breast and loosens over his hip-band,
His glance is calm and commanding, he tosses the slouch of his hat away from his forehead,
The sun falls on his crispy hair and mustache, falls on the black of his polished and perfect limbs.

I behold the picturesque giant and love him, and I do not stop there,   230
I go with the team also.

In me the caresser of life wherever moving, backward as well as forward sluing,
To niches aside and junior bending, not a person or object missing,
Absorbing all to myself and for this song.

Oxen that rattle the yoke and chain or halt in the leafy shade, what is that you express in your eyes?
It seems to me more than all the print I have read in my life.

My tread scares the wood-drake and wood-duck on my distant and day-long ramble,
They rise together, they slowly circle around.

I believe in those wing'd purposes,
And acknowledge red, yellow, white, playing within me,   240
And consider green and violet and the tufted crown intentional,
And do not call the tortoise unworthy because she is not something else,
And the jay in the woods never studied the gamut, yet trills pretty well to me,
And the look of the bay mare shames silliness out of me.

14

The wild gander leads his flock through the cool night,
Va-honk he says, and sounds it down to me like an invitation,
The pert may suppose it meaningless, but I listening close,
Find its purpose and place up there toward the wintry sky.

The sharp-hoofed moose of the north, the cat on the house-sill, the chickadee,
    the prairie-dog,
The litter of the grunting sow as they tug at her teats,   250
The brood of the turkey-hen and she with her half-spread wings,
 see in them and myself the same old law.

The press of my foot to the earth springs a hundred affections,
They scorn the best I can do to relate them.

 am enamored of growing out-doors,
Of men that live among cattle or taste of the ocean or woods,
Of the builders and steerers of ships and the wielders of axes and mauls, and
    the drivers of horses,
 can eat and sleep with them week in and week out.

What is commonest, cheapest, nearest, easiest, is Me,
Me going in for my chances, spending for vast returns,   260
Adorning myself to bestow myself on the first that will take me,
Not asking the sky to come down to my good will,
Scattering it freely forever.

15

The pure contralto sings in the organ loft,
The carpenter dresses his plank, the tongue of his foreplane whistles its wild
    ascending lisp,
The married and unmarried children ride home to their Thanksgiving dinner,
The pilot seizes the king-pin, he heaves down with a strong arm,
The mate stands braced in the whale-boat, lance and harpoon are ready,
The duck-shooter walks by silent and cautious stretches,
The deacons are ordained with crossed hands at the altar,   270
The spinning-girl retreats and advances to the hum of the big wheel,
The farmer stops by the bars as he walks on a First-day loafe and looks at
    the oats and rye,
The lunatic is carried at last to the asylum a confirmed case
(He will never sleep any more as he did in the cot in his mother's bedroom);
The jour printer with gray head and gaunt jaws works at his case,
He turns his quid of tobacco while his eyes blurr with the manuscript;
The malformed limbs are tied to the surgeon's table,
That is removed drops horribly in a pail;
The quadroon girl is sold at the auction-stand, the drunkard nods by the bar-
    room stove,
The machinist rolls up his sleeves, the policeman travels his beat, the gate-
    keeper marks who pass,   280

The young fellow drives the express-wagon (I love him, though I do no
    know him);
The half-breed straps on his light boots to compete in the race,
The western turkey-shooting draws old and young, some lean on their rifles
    some sit on logs,
Out from the crowd steps the marksman, takes his position, levels his piece
The groups of newly-come immigrants cover the wharf or levee,
As the woolly-pates hoe in the sugar-field, the overseer views them from hi
    saddle,
The bugle calls in the ball-room, the gentlemen run for their partners, th
    dancers bow to each other,
The youth lies awake in the cedar-roofed garret and harks to the musical rain
The Wolverine sets traps on the creek that helps fill the Huron,
The squaw wrapped in her yellow-hemmed cloth is offering moccasins an
    bead-bags for sale,   29
The connoisseur peers along the exhibition-gallery with half-shut eyes ben
    sideways,
As the deck-hands make fast the steamboat the plank is thrown for the shore
    going passengers,
The young sister holds out the skein while the elder sister winds it off in
    ball, and stops now and then for the knots,
The one-year wife is recovering and happy having a week ago borne her firs
    child,
The clean-haired Yankee girl works with her sewing-machine or in the factor
    or mill,
The paving-man leans on his two-handed rammer, the reporter's lead flie
    swiftly over the note-book, the sign-painter is lettering with blue an
    gold.
The canal boy trots on the tow-path, the book-keeper counts at his desk, th
    shoemaker waxes his thread,
The conductor beats time for the band and all the performers follow him,
The child is baptized, the convert is making his first professions,
The regatta is spread on the bay, the race is begun (how the white sai'
    sparkle!),   30
The drover watching his drove sings out to them that would stray,
The pedler sweats with his pack on his back (the purchaser higgling abou
    the odd cent);
The bride unrumples her white dress, the minute-hand of the clock move
    slowly,
The opium-eater reclines with rigid head and just-opened lips,
The prostitute draggles her shawl, her bonnet bobs on her tipsy and pimple
    neck,
The crowd laugh at her blackguard oaths, the men jeer and wink to each othe
    (Miserable! I do not laugh at your oaths nor jeer you);
The President holding a cabinet council is surrounded by the great Secretarie
On the piazza walk three matrons stately and friendly with twined arms,
The crew of the fish-smack pack repeated layers of halibut in the hold,   3
The Missourian crosses the plains toting his wares and his cattle,
As the fare-collector goes through the train he gives notice by the jinglir
    of loose change,

The floor-men are laying the floor, the tinners are tinning the roof, the masons
    are calling for mortar,
In single file each shouldering his hod pass onward the laborers;
Seasons pursuing each other the indescribable crowd is gathered, it is the
    fourth of Seventh-month (what salutes of cannon and small arms!),
Seasons pursuing each other the plougher ploughs, the mower mows, and the
    winter-grain falls in the ground;
Off on the lakes the pike-fisher watches and waits by the hole. in the frozen
    surface,
The stumps stand thick round the clearing, the squatter strikes deep with
    his ax,
Flatboatmen make fast towards dusk near the cotton-wood or pecan-trees,
Coon-seekers go through the regions of the Red River or through those
    drained by the Tennessee, or through those of the Arkansas,   320
Torches shine in the dark that hangs on the Chattahooche or Altamahaw,
Patriarchs sit at supper with sons and grandsons and great grandsons around
    them,
In walls of adobie, in canvas tents, rest hunters and trappers after their day's
    sport,
The city sleeps and the country sleeps,
The living sleep for their time, the dead sleep for their time,
The old husband sleeps by his wife and the young husband sleeps by his wife;
And these tend inward to me, and I tend outward to them,
And such as it is to be of these more or less I am,
And of these one and all I weave the song of myself.

16

I am of old and young, of the foolish as much as the wise,   330
Regardless of others, ever regardful of others,
Maternal as well as paternal, a child as well as a man,
Stuffed with the stuff that is coarse and stuffed with the stuff that is fine,
One of the Nation of many nations, the smallest the same and the largest the
    same,
A Southerner soon as a Northerner, a planter nonchalant and hospitable down
    by the Oconee I live,
A Yankee bound my own way ready for trade, my joints the limberest joints
    on earth and the sternest joints on earth,
A Kentuckian walking the vale of the Elkhorn in my deer-skin leggings, a
    Louisianian or Georgian,
A boatman over lakes or bays or along coasts, a Hoosier, Badger, Buckeye;
At home on Kanadian snow-shoes or up in the bush, or with fishermen off
    Newfoundland,
At home in the fleet of ice-boats, sailing with the rest and tacking,   340
At home on the hills of Vermont or in the woods of Maine, or the Texan
    ranch,
Comrade of Californians, comrade of free North-Westerners (loving their big
    proportions),
Comrade of raftsmen and coalmen, comrade of all who shake hands and
    welcome to drink and meat,

A learner with the simplest, a teacher of the thoughtfullest,
A novice beginning yet experient of myriads of seasons,
Of every hue and caste am I, of every rank and religion,
A farmer, mechanic, artist, gentleman, sailor, quaker,
Prisoner, fancy-man, rowdy, lawyer, physician, priest.

I resist any thing better than my own diversity,   350
Breathe the air but leave plenty after me,
And am not stuck up, and am in my place.

(The moth and the fish-eggs are in their place,
The bright suns I see and the dark suns I cannot see are in their place,
The palpable is in its place and the impalpable is in its place.)

17

These are really the thoughts of all men in all ages and lands, they are not
    original with me,
If they are not yours as much as mine they are nothing, or next to nothing,
If they are not the riddle and the untying of the riddle they are nothing,
If they are not just as close as they are distant they are nothing.

This is the grass that grows wherever the land is and the water is,
This the common air that bathes the globe.   360

18

With music strong I come, with my cornets and my drums,
I play not marches for accepted victors only, I play marches for conquered
    and slain persons.

Have you heard that it was good to gain the day?
I also say it is good to fall, battles are lost in the same spirit in which they
    are won.

I beat and pound for the dead,
I blow through my embouchures my loudest and gayest for them.

Vivas to those who have failed!
And to those whose war-vessels sank in the sea!
And to those themselves who sank in the sea!
And to all generals that lost engagements, and all overcome heroes!   370
And the numberless unknown heroes equal to the greatest heroes known!

19

This is the meal equally set, this the meat for natural hunger,
It is for the wicked just the same as the righteous, I make appointments
    with all,
I will not have a single person slighted or left away,

The kept-woman, sponger, thief, are hereby invited,
The heavy-lipped slave is invited, the venerealee is invited;
There shall be no difference between them and the rest.

This is the press of a bashful hand, this the float and odor of hair,
This the touch of my lips to yours, this the murmur of yearning,
This the far-off depth and height reflecting my own face,   380
This the thoughtful merge of myself, and the outlet again.

Do you guess I have some intricate purpose?
Well I have, for the Fourth-month showers have, and the mica on the side
    of a rock has.

Do you take it I would astonish?
Does the daylight astonish? does the early redstart twittering through the
    woods?
Do I astonish more than they?

This hour I tell things in confidence,
I might not tell everybody, but I will tell you.

                          20

Who goes there? hankering, gross, mystical, nude;
How is it I extract strength from the beef I eat?   390

What is a man anyhow? what am I? what are you?

All I mark as my own you shall offset it with your own,
Else it were time lost listening to me.

I do not snivel that snivel the world over,
That months are vacuums and the ground but wallow and filth.

Whimpering and truckling fold with powders for invalids, conformity goes to
    the fourth-removed,
I wear my hat as I please indoors or out.

Why should I pray? why should I venerate and be ceremonious?

Having pried through the strata, analyzed to a hair, counseled with doctors
    and calculated close,
I find no sweeter fat than sticks to my own bones.   400

In all people I see myself, none more and not one a barley-corn less,
And the good or bad I say of myself I say of them.

I know I am solid and sound,
To me the converging objects of the universe perpetually flow,
All are written to me, and I must get what the writing means.

I know I am deathless,
I know this orbit of mine cannot be swept by a carpenter's compass,
I know I shall not pass like a child's carlacue cut with a burnt stick at night

I know I am august,
I do not trouble my spirit to vindicate itself or be understood,   41
I see that the elementary laws never apologize
(I reckon I behave no prouder than the level I plant my house by, after all)

I exist as I am, that is enough,
If no other in the world be aware I sit content,
And if each and all be aware I sit content.

One world is aware and by far the largest to me, and that is myself,
And whether I come to my own to-day or in ten thousand or ten million years
I can cheerfully take it now, or with equal cheerfulness I can wait.

My foothold is tenoned and mortised in granite,
I laugh at what you call dissolution,   42
And I know the amplitude of time.

21

I am the poet of the Body and I am the poet of the Soul,
The pleasures of heaven are with me and the pains of hell are with me,
The first I graft and increase upon myself, the latter I translate into a new
    tongue.

I am the poet of the woman the same as the man,
And I say it is as great to be a woman as to be a man,
And I say there is nothing greater than the mother of men.

I chant the chant of dilation or pride,
We have had ducking and deprecating about enough,
I show that size is only development.   43

Have you outstripped the rest? are you the President?
It is a trifle, they will more than arrive there every one, and still pass on.

I am he that walks with the tender and growing night,
I call to the earth and sea half-held by the night.

Press close bare-bosomed night—press close magnetic nourishing night!
Night of south winds—night of the large few stars!
Still nodding night—mad naked summer night.

Smile O voluptuous cool-breathed earth!
Earth of the slumbering and liquid trees!
Earth of departed sunset—earth of the mountains misty-topped!   44
Earth of the vitreous pour of the full moon just tinged with blue!

Earth of shine and dark mottling the tide of the river!
Earth of the limpid gray of clouds brighter and clearer for my sake!
Far-swooping elbowed earth—rich apple-blossomed earth!
Smile, for your lover comes.

Prodigal, you have given me love—therefore I to you give love!
O unspeakable passionate love.

22

You sea! I resign myself to you also—I guess what you mean,
I behold from the beach your crooked inviting fingers,
I believe you refuse to go back without feeling of me,   450
We must have a turn together, I undress, hurry me out of sight of the land,
Cushion me soft, rock me in billowy drowse,
Dash me with amorous wet, I can repay you.

Sea of stretched ground-swells,
Sea breathing broad and convulsive breaths,
Sea of the brine of life and of unshoveled yet always-ready graves,
Howler and scooper of storms, capricious and dainty sea,
I am integral with you, I too am of one phase and of all phases.

Partaker of influx and efflux, I, extoller of hate and conciliation,
Extoller of a[r]mies and those that sleep in each others' arms,   460

I am he attesting sympathy
(Shall I make my list of things in the house and skip the house that supports them?).

I am not the poet of goodness only, I do not decline to be the poet of wickedness also.

What blurt is this about virtue and about vice?
Evil propels me and reform of evil propels me, I stand indifferent,
My gait is no fault-finder's or rejecter's gait,
I moisten the roots of all that has grown.

Did you fear some scrofula out of the unflagging pregnancy?
Did you guess the celestial laws are yet to be worked over and rectified?

I find one side a balance and the antipodal side a balance,   470
Soft doctrine as steady help as stable doctrine,
Thoughts and deeds of the present our rouse and early start.

This minute that comes to me over the past decillions,
There is no better than it and now.

What behaved well in the past or behaves well to-day is not such a wonder,
The wonder is always and always how there can be a mean man or an infidel.

23

Endless unfolding of words of ages!
And mine a word of the modern, the word En-Masse.

A word of the faith that never balks,
Here or henceforward it is all the same to me, I accept Time absolutely.   480

It alone is without flaw, it alone rounds and completes all,
That mystic baffling wonder alone completes all.

I accept Reality and dare not question it,
Materialism first and last imbuing.

Hurrah for positive science! long live exact demonstration!
Fetch stonecrop mixed with cedar and branches of lilac,
This is the lexicographer, this the chemist, this made a grammar of the old
    cartouches,
These mariners put the ship through dangerous unknown seas,
This is the geologist, this works with the scalpel, and this is a mathematician.

Gentlemen, to you the first honors always!   490
Your facts are useful, and yet they are not my dwelling,
I but enter by them to an area of my dwelling.

Less the reminders of properties told my words,
And more the reminders they of life untold, and of freedom and extrication,
And make short account of neuters and geldings, and favor men and women
    fully equipped,
And beat the gong of revolt, and stop with fugitives and them that plot and
    conspire.

24

Walt Whitman, a kosmos, of Manhattan the son,
Turbulent, fleshy, sensual, eating, drinking and breeding,
No sentimentalist, no stander above men and women or apart from them,
No more modest than immodest.   500

Unscrew the locks from the doors!
Unscrew the doors themselves from their jambs!

Whoever degrades another degrades me,
And whatever is done or said returns at last to me.

Through me the afflatus surging and surging, through me the current and index.

I speak the pass-word primeval, I give the sign of democracy,
By God! I will accept nothing which all cannot have their counterpart of on
    the same terms.

Through me many long dumb voices,
Voices of the interminable generations of prisoners and slaves,
Voices of the diseased and despairing and of thieves and dwarfs,   510
Voices of cycles of preparation and accretion,
And of the threads that connect the stars, and of wombs and of the father-
      stuff,
And of the rights of them the others are down upon,
Of the deformed, trivial, flat, foolish, despised,
Fog in the air, beetles rolling balls of dung.

Through me forbidden voices,
Voices of sexes and lusts, voices veiled and I remove the veil,
Voices indecent by me clarified and transfigured.

I do not press my fingers across my mouth,
I keep as delicate around the bowels as around the head and heart,   520
Copulation is no more rank to me than death is.

I believe in the flesh and the appetites,
Seeing, hearing, feeling, are miracles, and each part and tag of me is a miracle.

Divine am I inside and out, and I make holy whatever I touch or am touched
      from,
The scent of these arm-pits aroma finer than prayer,
This head more than churches, bibles, and all the creeds.

If I worship one thing more than another it shall be the spread of my own
      body, or any part of it,
Translucent mold of me it shall be you!
Shaded ledges and rests it shall be you!
Firm masculine colter it shall be you!   530
Whatever goes to the tilth of me it shall be you!
You my rich blood! your milky stream pale strippings of my life!
Breast that presses against other breasts it shall be you!
My brain it shall be your occult convolutions!
Root of washed sweet-flag! timorous pond-snipe! nest of guarded duplicate
      eggs! it shall be you!
Mixed tussled hay of head, beard, brawn, it shall be you!
Trickling sap of maple, fiber of manly wheat, it shall be you!
Sun so generous it shall be you!
Vapors lighting and shading my face it shall be you!
You sweaty brooks and dews it shall be you!   540
Winds whose soft-tickling genitals rub against me it shall be you!
Broad muscular fields, branches of live oak, loving lounger in my winding
      paths, it shall be you!
Hands I have taken, face I have kissed, mortal I have ever touched, it shall
      be you.

I dote on myself, there is that lot of me and all so luscious,
Each moment and whatever happens thrills me with joy,

I cannot tell how my ankles bend, nor whence the cause of my faintest wish,
Nor the cause of the friendship I emit, nor the cause of the friendship I
    take again.

That I walk up my stoop, I pause to consider if it really be,
A morning-glory at my window satisfies me more than the metaphysics of
    books.

To behold the day-break!   550
The little light fades the immense and diaphanous shadows,
The air tastes good to my palate.

Hefts of the moving world at innocent gambols silently rising, freshly exuding,
Scooting obliquely high and low.

Something I cannot see puts upward libidinous prongs,
Seas of bright juice suffuse heaven.

The earth by the sky stayed with, the daily close of their junction,
The heaved challenge from the east that moment over my head,
The mocking taunt, See then whether you shall be master!

                                25

Dazzling and tremendous how quick the sun-rise would kill me,   560
If I could not now and always send sun-rise out of me.

We also ascend dazzling and tremendous as the sun,
We found our own O my soul in the calm and cool of the daybreak.

My voice goes after what my eyes cannot reach,
With the twirl of my tongue I encompass worlds and volumes of worlds.

Speech is the twin of my vision, it is unequal to measure itself,
It provokes me forever, it says sarcastically,
Walt you contain enough, why don't you let it out then?

Come now I will not be tantalized, you conceive too much of articulation,
Do you not know O speech how the buds beneath you are folded?   570
Waiting in gloom, protected by frost,
The dirt receding before my prophetical screams,
I underlying causes to balance them at last,
My knowledge my live parts, it keeping tally with the meaning of all things,
Happiness (which whoever hears me let him or her set out in search of this
    day).

My final merit I refuse you, I refuse putting from me what I really am,
Encompass worlds, but never try to encompass me,
I crowd your sleekest and best by simply looking toward you.

Writing and talk do not prove me,
I carry the plenum of proof and every thing else in my face,   580
With the hush of my lips I wholly confound the skeptic.

26

Now I will do nothing but listen,
To accrue what I hear into this song, to let sounds contribute toward it.

I hear bravuras of birds, bustle of growing wheat, gossip of flames, clack of
      sticks cooking my meals,
I hear the sound I love, the sound of the human voice,
I hear all sounds running together, combined, fused or following,
Sounds of the city and sounds out of the city, sounds of the day and night,
Talkative young ones to those that like them, the loud laugh of work-people
      at their meals,
The angry base of disjointed friendship, the faint tones of the sick,
The judge with hands tight to the desk, his pallid lips pronouncing a death-
      sentence,   590
The heave'e'yo of stevedores unlading ships by the wharves, the refrain of the
      anchor-lifters,
The ring of alarm-bells, the cry of fire, the whirr of swift-streaking engines
      and hose-carts with premonitory tinkles and colored lights,
The steam-whistle, the solid roll of the train of approaching cars,
The slow march played at the head of the association marching two and two
(They go to guard some corpse, the flag-tops are draped with black muslin).

I hear the violoncello ('tis the young man's heart's complaint),
I hear the keyed cornet, it glides quickly in through my ears,
It shakes mad-sweet pangs through my belly and breast.

I hear the chorus, it is a grand opera,
Ah this indeed is music—this suits me.   600

A tenor large and fresh as the creation fills me,
The orbic flex of his mouth is pouring and filling me full.
I hear the trained soprano (what work with hers is this?)
The orchestra whirls me wider than Uranus flies,
It wrenches such ardors from me I did not know I possessed them,
It sails me, I dab with bare feet, they are licked by the indolent waves,
I am cut by bitter and angry hail, I lose my breath,
Steeped amid honeyed morphine, my windpipe throttled in fakes of death,
At length let up again to feel the puzzle of puzzles,
And that we call Being.   610

27

To be in any form, what is that?
(Round and round we go, all of us, and ever come back thither)
If nothing lay more developed the quahaug in its callous shell were enough.

Mine is no callous shell,
I have instant conductors all over me whether I pass or stop,
They seize every object and lead it harmlessly through me.

I merely stir, press, feel with my fingers, and am happy,
To touch my person to some one else's is about as much as I can stand.

28

Is this then a touch? quivering me to a new identity,
Flames and ether making a rush for my veins,   620
Treacherous tip of me reaching and crowding to help them,
My flesh and blood playing out lightning to strike what is hardly different
    from myself,
On all sides prurient provokers stiffening my limbs,
Straining the udder of my heart for its withheld drip,
Behaving licentious toward me, taking no denial,
Depriving me of my best as for a purpose,
Unbuttoning my clothes, holding me by the bare waist,
Deluding my confusion with the calm of the sunlight and pasture-fields,
Immodestly sliding the fellow-senses away,
They bribed to swap off with touch and go and graze at the edges of me,   630
No consideration, no regard for my draining strength or my anger,
Fetching the rest of the herd around to enjoy them a while,
Then all uniting to stand on a headland and worry me.

The sentries desert every other part of me,
They have left me helpless to a red marauder,
They all come to the headland to witness and assist against me.

I am given up by traitors,
I talk wildly, I have lost my wits, I and nobody else am the greatest traitor,
I went myself first to the headland, my own hands carried me there.

You villain touch! what are you doing! my breath is tight in its throat,   640
Unclench your floodgates, you are too much for me.

29

Blind loving wrestling touch, sheathed hooded sharp-toothed touch!
Did it make you ache so, leaving me?

Parting tracked by arriving, perpetual payment of perpetual loan,
Rich showering rain, and recompense richer afterward.

Sprouts take and accumulate, stand by the curb prolific and vital,
Landscapes projected masculine, full-sized and golden.

30

All truths wait in all things,
They neither hasten their own delivery nor resist it,
They do not need the obstetric forceps of the surgeon,   650

The insignificant is as big to me as any
(What is less or more than a touch?).

Logic and sermons never convince,
The damp of the night drives deeper into my soul.

(Only what proves itself to every man and woman is so,
Only what nobody denies is so.)

A minute and a drop of me settle my brain,
I believe the soggy clods shall become lovers and lamps,
And a compend of compends is the meat of a man or woman,
And a summit and flower there is the feeling they have for each other,   660
And they are to branch boundlessly out of that lesson until it becomes omnific,
And until one and all shall delight us, and we them.

31

I believe a leaf of grass is no less than the journey-work of the stars,
And the pismire is equally perfect, and a grain of sand, and the egg of the
    wren,
And the tree-toad is a chef-d'œuvre for the highest,
And the running blackberry would adorn the parlors of heaven,
And the narrowest hinge in my hand puts to scorn all machinery,
And the cow crunching with depressed head surpasses any statue,
And a mouse is miracle enough to stagger sextillions of infidels.

I find I incorporate gneiss, coal, long-threaded moss, fruits, grains, esculent
    roots,   670
And am stuccoed with quadrupeds and birds all over,
And have distanced what is behind me for good reasons,
But call any thing back again when I desire it.

In vain the speeding or shyness,
In vain the plutonic rocks send their old heat against my approach,
In vain the mastodon retreats beneath its own powdered bones,
In vain objects stand leagues off and assume manifold shapes,
In vain the ocean settling in hollows and the great monsters lying low,
In vain the buzzard houses herself with the sky,
In vain the snake slides through the creepers and logs,   680
In vain the elk takes to the inner passes of the woods,
In vain the razor-billed auk sails far north to Labrador,
I follow quickly, I ascend to the nest in the fissure of the cliff.

32

I think I could turn and live with animals, they're so placid and self-contained,
I stand and look at them long and long.

They do not sweat and whine about their condition,
They do not lie awake in the dark and weep for their sins,
They do not make me sick discussing their duty to God,

Not one is dissatisfied, not one is demented with the mania of owning things,
Not one kneels to another, nor to his kind that lived thousands of years ago, 690
Not one is respectable or unhappy over the whole earth.

So they show their relations to me and I accept them,
They bring me tokens of myself, they evince them plainly in their possession.

I wonder where they get those tokens,
Did I pass that way huge times ago and negligently drop them?

Myself moving forward then and now and forever,
Gathering and showing more always and with velocity,
Infinite and omnigenous, and the like of these among them,
Not too exclusive toward the reachers of my remembrancers,
Picking out here one that I love, and now go with him on brotherly terms. 700

A gigantic beauty of a stallion, fresh and responsive to my caresses,
Head high in the forehead, wide between the ears,
Limbs glossy and supple, tail dusting the ground,
Eyes full of sparkling wickedness, ears finely cut, flexibly moving.

His nostrils dilate as my heels embrace him,
His well-built limbs tremble with pleasure as we race around and return.
I but use you a minute, then I resign you, stallion,
Why do I need your paces when I myself out-gallop them?
Even as I stand or sit passing faster than you.

33

Space and Time! now I see it is true, what I guessed at,   710
What I guessed when I loafed on the grass,
What I guessed while I lay alone in my bed,
And again as I walked the beach under the paling stars of the morning.

My ties and ballasts leave me, my elbows rest in sea-gaps,
I skirt sierras, my palms cover continents,
I am afoot with my vision.

By the city's quadrangular houses—in log huts, camping with lumbermen,
Along the ruts of the turnpike, along the dry gulch and rivulet bed,
Weeding my onion-patch or hoeing rows of carrots and parsnips, crossing
        savannas, trailing in forests,
Prospecting, gold-digging, girdling the trees of a new purchase,   720
Scorched ankle-deep by the hot sand, hauling my boat down the shallow river,
Where the panther walks to and fro on a limb overhead, where the buck turns
        furiously at the hunter,
Where the rattlesnake suns his flabby length on a rock, where the otter is
        feeding on fish,
Where the alligator in his tough pimples sleeps by the bayou,

Where the black bear is searching for roots or honey, where the beaver pats
    the mud with his paddle-shaped tail;
Over the growing sugar, over the yellow-flowered cotton plant, over the rice
    in its low moist field,
Over the sharp-peaked farm house, with its scalloped scum and slender shoots
    from the gutters,
Over the western persimmon, over the long-leaved corn, over the delicate blue-
    flower flax,
Over the white and brown buckwheat, a hummer and buzzer there with the rest,
Over the dusky green of the rye as it ripples and shades in the breeze;   730
Scaling mountains, pulling myself cautiously up, holding on by low scragged
    limbs,
Walking the path worn in the grass and beat through the leaves of the brush,
Where the quail is whistling betwixt the woods and the wheat-lot,
Where the bat flies in the Seventh-month eve, where the great gold-bug drops
    through the dark,
Where the brook puts out of the roots of the old tree and flows to the meadow,
Where cattle stand and shake away flies with the tremulous shuddering of
    their hides,
Where the cheese-cloth hangs in the kitchen, where andirons straddle the
    hearth-slab, where cobwebs fall in festoons from the rafters;
Where trip-hammers crash, where the press is whirling its cylinders,
Where the human heart beats with terrible throes under its ribs,
Where the pear-shaped balloon is floating aloft (floating in it myself and look-
    ing composedly down),   740
Where the life-car is drawn on the slip-noose, where the heat hatches pale-
    green eggs in the dented sand,
Where the she-whale swims with her calf and never forsakes it,
Where the steam-ship trails hind-ways its long pennant of smoke,
Where the fin of the shark cuts like a black chip out of the water,
Where the half-burned brig is riding on unknown currents,
Where shells grow to her slimy deck, where the dead are corrupting below;
Where the dense-starred flag is borne at the head of the regiments,
Approaching Manhattan up by the long-stretching island,
Under Niagara, the cataract falling like a veil over my countenance,
Upon a door-step, upon the horse-block of hard wood outside,   750
Upon the race-course, or enjoying picnics or jigs or a good game of base-ball,
At he-festivals, with blackguard gibes, ironical license, bull-dances, drinking,
    laughter,
At the cider-mill tasting the sweets of the brown mash, sucking the juice
    through a straw,
At apple-peelings wanting kisses for all the red fruit I find,
At musters, beach-parties, friendly bees, huskings, house-raisings;
Where the mocking-bird sounds his delicious gurgles, cackles, screams, weeps,
Where the hay-rick stands in the barn-yard, where the dry-stalks are scattered,
    where the brood-cow waits in the hovel,
Where the bull advances to do his masculine work, where the stud to the
    mare, where the cock is treading the hen,
Where the heifers browse, where geese nip their food with short jerks,
Where sun-down shadows lengthen over the limitless and lonesome prairie,   760

Where herds of buffalo make a crawling spread of the square miles far and
near,
Where the humming-bird shimmers, where the neck of the long-lived swan is
curving and winding,
Where the laughing-gull scoots by the shore, where she laughs her near-human
laugh,
Where bee-hives range on a gray bench in the garden half hid by the high
weeds,
Where band-necked partridges roost in a ring on the ground with their
heads out,
Where burial coaches enter the arched gates of a cemetery,
Where winter wolves bark amid wastes of snow and icicled trees,
Where the yellow-crowned heron comes to the edge of the marsh at night and
feeds upon small crabs,
Where the splash of swimmers and divers cools the warm noon,
Where the katy-did works her chromatic reed on the walnut-tree over the
well,   770
Through patches of citrons and cucumbers with silver-wired leaves,
Through the salt-lick or orange glade, or under conical firs,
Through the gymnasium, through the curtained saloon, through the office or
public hall;
Pleased with the native and pleased with the foreign, pleased with the new
and old,
Pleased with the homely woman as well as the handsome,
Pleased with the quakeress as she puts off her bonnet and talks melodiously,
Pleased with the tune of the choir of the whitewashed church,
Pleased with the earnest words of the sweating Methodist preacher, impressed
seriously at the camp-meeting;
Looking in at the shop-windows of Broadway the whole forenoon, flatting the
flesh of my nose on the thick plate glass,
Wandering the same afternoon with my face turned up to the clouds, or down
a lane or along the beach,   780
My right and left arms round the sides of two friends, and I in the middle;
Coming home with the silent and dark-cheeked bush-boy (behind me he rides
at the drape of the day),
Far from the settlements studying the print of animals' feet, or the moccasin
print,
By the cot in the hospital reaching lemonade to a feverish patient,
Nigh the coffined corpse when all is still, examining with a candle;
Voyaging to every port to dicker and adventure,
Hurrying with the modern crowd as eager and fickle as any,
Hot toward one I hate, ready in my madness to knife him,
Solitary at midnight in my back yard, my thoughts gone from me a long
while,
Walking the old hills of Judæa with the beautiful gentle God by my side,   790
Speeding through space, speeding through heaven and the stars,
Speeding amid the seven satellites and the broad ring, and the diameter of
eighty thousand miles,
Speeding with tailed meteors, throwing fire-balls like the rest,
Carrying the crescent child that carries its own full mother in its belly,

Storming, enjoying, planning, loving, cautioning,
Backing and filling, appearing and disappearing,
I tread day and night such roads.

I visit the orchards of spheres and look at the product,
And look at quintillions ripened and look at quintillions green.

I fly those flights of a fluid and swallowing soul,   800
My course runs below the soundings of plummets.

I help myself to material and immaterial,
No guard can shut me off, no law prevent me.

I anchor my ship for a little while only,
My messengers continually cruise away or bring their returns to me.

I go hunting polar furs and the seal, leaping chasms with a pike-pointed staff,
    clinging to topples of brittle and blue.

I ascend to the foretruck,
I take my place late at night in the crow's-nest,
We sail the arctic sea, it is plenty light enough,
Through the clear atmosphere I stretch around on the wonderful beauty,   810
The enormous masses of ice pass me and I pass them, the scenery is plain in
    all directions,
The white-topped mountains show in the distance, I fling out my fancies toward
    them,
We are approaching some great battle-field in which we are soon to be
    engaged,
We pass the colossal outposts of the encampment, we pass with still feet and
    caution,
Or we are entering by the suburbs some vast and ruined city,
The blocks and fallen architecture more than all the living cities of the globe.

I am a free companion, I bivouac by invading watchfires,
I turn the bridegroom out of bed and stay with the bride myself,
I tighten her all night to my thighs and lips.

My voice is the wife's voice, the screech by the rail of the stairs,   820
They fetch my man's body up dripping and drowned.

I understand the large hearts of heroes,
The courage of present times and all times,
How the skipper saw the crowded and rudderless wreck of the steamship, and
    Death chasing it up and down the storm,
How he knuckled tight and gave not back an inch, and was faithful of days
    and faithful of nights,
And chalked in large letters on a board, *Be of good cheer, we will not desert
    you;*

How he followed with them and tacked with them three days and would not
    give it up,
How he saved the drifting company at last,
How the lank loose-gowned women looked when boated from the side of their
    prepared graves,
How the silent old-faced infants and the lifted sick, and the sharp-lipped un-
    shaved men;   830
All this I swallow, it tastes good, I like it well, it becomes mine,
I am the man, I suffered, I was there.

The disdain and calmness of martyrs,
The mother of old, condemned for a witch, burnt with dry wood, her children
    gazing on,
The hounded slave that flags in the race, leans by the fence, blowing, covered
    with sweat,
The twinges that sting like needles his legs and neck, the murderous buckshot
    and the bullets,
All these I feel or am.

I am the hounded slave, I wince at the bite of the dogs,
Hell and despair are upon me, crack and again crack the marksmen,
I clutch the rails of the fence, my gore dribs, thinned with the ooze of my
    skin,   840
I fall on the weeds and stones,
The riders spur their unwilling horses, haul close,
Taunt my dizzy ears and beat me violently over the head with whip-stocks.

Agonies are one of my changes of garments.
I do not ask the wounded person how he feels, I myself become the wounded
    person,
My hurts turn livid upon me as I lean on a cane and observe.

I am the mashed fireman with breast-bone broken,
Tumbling walls buried me in their debris,
Heat and smoke I inspired, I heard the yelling shouts of my comrades,
I heard the distant click of their picks and shovels,   850
They have cleared the beams away, they tenderly lift me forth.

I lie in the night air in my red shirt, the pervading hush is for my sake,
Painless after all I lie exhausted but not so unhappy,
White and beautiful are the faces around me, the heads are bared of their
    fire-caps,
The kneeling crowd fades with the light of the torches.

Distant and dead resuscitate,
They show as the dial or move as the hands of me, I am the clock myself.

I am an old artillerist, I tell of my fort's bombardment,
I am there again.

Again the long roll of the drummers,   860
Again the attacking cannon, mortars,
Again to my listening ears the cannon responsive.

I take part, I see and hear the whole,
The cries, curses, roar, the plaudits for well-aimed shots,
The ambulanza slowly passing trailing its red drip,
Workmen searching after damages, making indispensable repairs,
The fall of grenades through the rent roof, the fan-shaped explosion,
The whizz of limbs, heads, stone, wood, iron, high in the air.

Again gurgles the mouth of my dying general, he furiously waves with his
    hand,
He gasps through the clot *Mind not me—mind—the entrenchments.*   870

34

Now I tell what I knew in Texas in my early youth
(I tell not the fall of Alamo,
Not one escaped to tell the fall of Alamo,
The hundred and fifty are dumb yet at Alamo),
'Tis the tale of the murder in cold blood of four hundred and twelve young
    men.

Retreating they had formed in a hollow square with their baggage for breast-
    works,
Nine hundred lives out of the surrounding enemy's, nine times their number,
    was the price they took in advance,
Their colonel was wounded and their ammunition gone,
They treated for an honorable capitulation, received writing and seal, gave up
    their arms and marched back prisoners of war.

They were the glory of the race of rangers,   880
Matchless with horse, rifle, song, supper, courtship,
Large, turbulent, generous, handsome, proud, and affectionate,
Bearded, sunburnt, dressed in the free costume of hunters,
Not a single one over thirty years of age.

The second First-day morning they were brought out in squads and massacred,
    it was beautiful early summer,
The work commenced about five o'clock and was over by eight.

None obeyed the command to kneel,
Some made a mad and helpless rush, some stood stark and straight,
A few fell at once, shot in the temple or heart, the living and dead lay together,
The maimed and mangled dug in the dirt, the new-comers saw them there,   890
Some half-killed attempted to crawl away,
These were dispatched with bayonets or battered with the blunts of muskets.
A youth not seventeen years old seized his assassin till two more came to
    release him.
The three were all torn and covered with the boy's blood.

At eleven o'clock began the burning of the bodies;
That is the tale of the murder of the four hundred and twelve young men.

35

Would you hear of an old-time sea-fight?
Would you learn who won by the light of the moon and stars?
List to the yarn, as my grandmother's father the sailor told it to me.

Our foe was no skulk in his ship I tell you (said he),   900
His was the surly English pluck, and there is no tougher or truer, and never
    was, and never will be;
Along the lowered eve he came horribly raking us.

We closed with him, the yards entangled, the cannon touched,
My captain lashed fast with his own hands.

We had received some eighteen pound shots under the water,
On our lower-gun-deck two large pieces had burst at the first fire, killing all
    around and blowing up overhead.

Fighting at sun-down, fighting at dark,
Ten o'clock at night, the full moon well up, our leaks on the gain, and five
    feet of water reported,
The master-at-arms loosing the prisoners confined in the after-hold to give them
    a chance for themselves.

The transit to and from the magazine is now stopped by the sentinels,   910
They see so many strange faces they do not know whom to trust.

Our frigate takes fire,
The other asks if we demand quarter?
If our colors are struck and the fighting done?

Now I laugh content, for I hear the voice of my little captain,
We have not struck, he composedly cries, *we have just begun our part of the
    fighting.*

Only three guns are in use,
One is directed by the captain himself against the enemy's main-mast,
Two well served with grape and canister silence his musketry and clear his
    decks.

The tops alone second the fire of this little battery, especially the main-top,   920
They hold out bravely during the whole of tne action.

Not a moment's cease,
The leaks gain fast on the pumps, the fire eats toward the powder-magazine.

One of the pumps has been shot away, it is generally thought we are sinking.

Serene stands the little captain,
He is not hurried, his voice is neither high nor low,
His eyes give more light to us than our battle-lanterns.

Toward twelve there in the beams of the moon they surrender to us.

36

Stretched and still lies the midnight,
Two great hulls motionless on the breast of the darkness,   930
Our vessel riddled and slowly sinking, preparations to pass to the one we
  have conquered,
The captain on the quarter-deck coldly giving his orders through a counte-
  nance white as a sheet,
Near by the corpse of the child that served in the cabin,
The dead face of an old salt with long white hair and carefully curled whiskers,
The flames spite of all that can be done flickering aloft and below,
The husky voices of the two or three officers yet fit for duty,
Formless stacks of bodies and bodies by themselves, dabs of flesh upon the
  masts and spars,
Cut of cordage, dangle of rigging, slight shock of the soothe of waves,
Black and impassive guns, litter of powder-parcels, strong scent,
A few large stars overhead, silent and mournful shining,   940
Delicate sniffs of sea-breeze, smells of sedgy grass and fields by the shore,
  death-messages given in charge to survivors,
The hiss of the surgeon's knife, the gnawing teeth of his saw,
Wheeze, cluck, swash of falling blood, short wild scream, and long, dull, taper-
  ing groan,
These so, these irretrievable.

37

You laggards there on guard! look to your arms!
In at the conquered doors they crowd! I am possessed!
Embody all presences outlawed or suffering,
See myself in prison shaped like another man,
And feel the dull unintermitted pain.

For me the keepers of convicts shoulder their carbines and keep watch,   950
It is I let out in the morning and barred at night.

Not a mutineer walks handcuffed to jail but I am handcuffed to him and walk
  by his side
(I am less the jolly one there, and more the silent one with sweat on my
  twitching lips).

Not a youngster is taken for larceny but I go up too, and am tried and
  sentenced.

Not a cholera patient lies at the last gasp but I also lie at the last gasp,
My face is ash-colored, my sinews gnarl, away from me people retreat.

Askers embody themselves in me and I am embodied in them,
I project my hat, sit shame-faced, and beg.

38

Enough! enough! enough!
Somehow I have been stunned. Stand back!   96
Give me a little time beyond my cuffed head, slumbers, dreams, gaping.
I discover myself on the verge of a usual mistake.

That I could forget the mockers and insults!
That I could forget the trickling tears and the blows of the bludgeons and
    hammers!
That I could look with a separate look on my own crucifixion and blood
    crowning!

I remember now,
I resume the overstaid fraction,
The grave of rock multiplies what has been confided to it, or to any graves,
Corpses rise, gashes heal, fastenings roll from me.

I troop forth replenished with supreme power, one of an average unending
    procession,   97
Inland and sea-coast we go, and pass all boundary lines,
Our swift ordinances on their way over the whole earth,
The blossoms we wear in our hats the growth of thousands of years.

Eleves, I salute you! come forward!
Continue your annotations, continue your questionings.

39

The friendly and flowing savage, who is he?
Is he waiting for civilization, or past it and mastering it?

Is he some Southwesterner raised outdoors? is he Kanadian?
Is he from the Mississippi country? Iowa, Oregon, California?   9
The mountains? prairie-life, bush-life? or sailor from the sea?

Wherever he goes men and women accept and desire him,
They desire he should like them, touch them, speak to them, stay with them

Behavior lawless as snowflakes, woods simple as grass, uncombed head, laughter
    and naïveté,
Slow-stepping feet, common features, common modes and emanations,
They descend in new forms from the tips of his fingers,
They are wafted with the odor of his body or breath, they fly out of the
    glance of his eyes.

40

Flaunt of the sunshine I need not your bask—lie over!
You light surfaces only, I force surfaces and depths also.

Earth! you seem to look for something at my hands,
Say, old top-knot, what do you want?   990

Man or woman, I might tell how I like you, but cannot,
And might tell what it is in me and what it is in you, but cannot,
And might tell that pining I have, that pulse of my nights and days.

Behold, I do not give lectures or a little charity,
When I give I give myself.

You there, impotent, loose in the knees,
Open your scarfed chops till I blow grit within you,
Spread your palms and lift the flaps of your pockets,
I am not to be denied, I compel, I have stores plenty and to spare,
And any thing I have I bestow.   1000

I do not ask who you are, that is not important to me,
You can do nothing and be nothing but what I will infold you.

To cotton-field drudge or cleaner of privies I lean,
On his right cheek I put the family kiss,
And in my soul I swear I never will deny him.

On women fit for conception I start bigger and nimbler babes
(This day I am jetting the stuff of far more arrogant republics).

To any one dying, thither I speed and twist the knob of the door,
Turn the bed-clothes toward the foot of the bed,
Let the physician and the priest go home.   1010

I seize the descending man and raise him with resistless will,
O despairer, here is my neck,
By God, you shall not go down! hang your whole weight upon me.

I dilate you with tremendous breath, I buoy you up,
Every room of the house do I fill with an armed force,
Lovers of me, bafflers of graves.

Sleep—I and they keep guard all night,
Not doubt, not disease shall dare to lay finger upon you,
I have embraced you, and henceforth possess you to myself,
And when you rise in the morning you will find what I tell you is so.   1020

41

I am he bringing help for the sick as they pant on their backs,
And for strong upright men I bring yet more needed help.

I heard what was said of the universe,
Heard it and heard it of several thousand years;
It is middling well as far as it goes—but is that all?

Magnifying and applying come I,
Outbidding at the start the old cautious hucksters,
Taking myself the exact dimensions of Jehovah,
Lithographing Kronos, Zeus his son, and Hercules his grandson,
Buying drafts of Osiris, Isis, Belus, Brahma, Buddha,   103
In my portfolio placing Manito loose, Allah on a leaf, the crucifix engraved
With Odin and the hideous-faced Mexitli and every idol and image,
Taking them all for what they are worth and not a cent more,
Admitting they were alive and did the work of their days
(They bore mites as for unfledged birds who have now to rise and fly and
    sing for themselves),
Accepting the rough deific sketches to fill out better in myself, bestowing
    them freely on each man and woman I see,
Discovering as much or more in a framer framing a house,
Putting higher claims for him there with his rolled-up sleeves driving the
    mallet and chisel,
Not objecting to special revelations, considering a curl of smoke or a hair on
    the back of my hand just as curious as any revelation,
Lads ahold of fire-engines and hook-and-ladder ropes no less to me than the
    gods of the antique wars,   104
Minding their voices peal through the crash of destruction,
Their brawny limbs passing safe over charred laths, their white foreheads
    whole and unhurt out of the flames;
By the mechanic's wife with her babe at her nipple interceding for every
    person born,
Three scythes at harvest whizzing in a row from three lusty angels with shirts
    bagged out at their waists,
The snag-toothed hostler with red hair redeeming sins past and to come,
Selling all he possesses, traveling on foot to fee lawyers for his brother and
    sit by him while he is tried for forgery;
What was strewn in the amplest strewing the square rod about me, and not
    filling the square rod then,
The bull and the bug never worshiped half enough,
Dung and dirt more admirable than was dreamed,
The supernatural of no account, myself waiting my time to be one of the
    supremes,   105
The day getting ready for me when I shall do as much good as the best, and
    be as prodigious;
By my life-lumps! becoming already a creator,
Putting myself here and now to the ambushed womb of the shadows.

                                    42

A call in the midst of the crowd,
My own voice. orotund sweeping and final.

Come my children,
Come my boys and girls, my women, household and intimates,
Now the performer launches his nerve, he has passed his prelude on the reeds
    within.

Easily written loose-fingered chords—I feel the thrum of your climax and close.

My head slues round on my neck,   1060
Music rolls, but not from the organ,
Folks are around me, but they are no household of mine.

Over the hard unsunk ground,
Over the eaters and drinkers, ever the upward and downward sun, ever the
    air and the ceaseless tides,
Over myself and my neighbors, refreshing, wicked, real,
Over the old inexplicable query, ever that thorned thumb, that breath of itches
    and thirsts,
Over the vexer's *hoot! hoot!* till we find where the sly one hides and bring him
    forth,
Over love, ever the sobbing liquid of life,
Over the bandage under the chin, ever the trestles of death.

Here and there with dimes on the eyes walking,   1070
To feed the greed of the belly the brains liberally spooning,
Tickets buying, taking, selling, but in to the feast never once going,
Many sweating, ploughing, thrashing, and then the chaff for payment receiving,
A few idly owning, and they the wheat continually claiming.

This is the city and I am one of the citizens,
Whatever interests the rest interests me, politics, wars, markets, newspapers,
    schools,
The mayor and councils, banks, tariffs, steamships, factories, stocks, stores,
    real estate and personal estate.

The little plentiful manikins skipping around in collars and tailed coats,
I am aware who they are (they are positively not worms or fleas),
I acknowledge the duplicates of myself, the weakest and shallowest is death-
    less with me,   1080
What I do and say the same waits for them,
Every thought that flounders in me the same flounders in them.

I know perfectly well my own egotism,
Know my omnivorous lines and must not write any less,
And would fetch you whoever you are flush with myself.

Not words of routine this song of mine,
But abruptly to question, to leap beyond yet nearer bring;
This printed and bound book—but the printer and the printing-office boy?
The well-taken photographs—but your wife or friend close and solid in your
    arms?

The black ship mailed with iron, her mighty guns in her turrets—but the
     pluck of the captain and engineers?   109
In the houses the dishes and fare and furniture—but the host and hostess
     and the look out of their eyes?
The sky up there—yet here or next door, or across the way?
The saints and sages in history—but you yourself?
Sermons, creeds, theology—but the fathomless human brain,
And what is reason? and what is love? and what is life?

43

I do not despise you priests, all time, the world over,
My faith is the greatest of faiths and the least of faiths,
Enclosing worship ancient and modern and all between ancient and modern,
Believing I shall come again upon the earth after five thousand years,
Waiting responses from oracles, honoring the gods, saluting the sun,   11
Making a fetich of the first rock or stump, powowing with sticks in the circle
     of obis,
Helping the llama or brahmin as he trims the lamps of the idols,
Dancing yet through the streets in a phallic procession, rapt and austere in
     the woods a gymnosophist,
Drinking mead from the skull-cup, to Shastas and Vedas admirant, minding
     the Koran,
Walking the teokallis, spotted with gore from the stone and knife, beating the
     serpent-skin drum,
Accepting the Gospels, accepting him that was crucified, knowing assuredly
     that he is divine,
To the mass kneeling or the puritan's prayer rising, or sitting patiently in a
     pew,
Ranting and frothing in my insane crisis, or waiting dead-like till my spirit
     arouses me,
Looking forth on pavement and land, or outside of pavement and land,
Belonging to the winders of the circuit of circuits.   11

One of that centripetal and centrifugal gang I turn and talk like a man leaving
     charges before a journey.

Down-hearted doubters dull and excluded,
Frivolous, sullen, moping, angry, affected, disheartened, atheistical,
I know every one of you, I know the sea of torment, doubt, despair and
     unbelief.

How the flukes splash!
How they contort rapid as lightning, with spasms and spouts of blood!

Be at peace bloody flukes of doubters and sullen mopers,
I take my place among you as much as among any,
The past is the push of you, me, all, precisely the same,
And what is yet untried and afterward is for you, me, all precisely the
     same.   1

I do not know what is untried and afterward,
But I know it will in its turn prove sufficient, and cannot fail.

Each who passes is considered, each who stops is considered, not a single one
    can it fail.

It cannot fail the young man who died and was buried,
Nor the young woman who died and was put by his side,
Nor the little child that peeped in at the door, and then drew back and was
    never seen again,
Nor the old man who has lived without purpose, and feels it with bitterness
    worse than gall,
Nor him in the poor house tubercled by rum and the bad disorder,
Nor the numberless slaughtered and wrecked, nor the brutish koboo called
    the ordure of humanity,
Nor the sacs merely floating with open mouths for food to slip in,   1130
Nor any thing in the earth, or down in the oldest graves of the earth,
Nor any thing in the myriads of spheres, nor the myriads of myriads that
    inhabit them,
Nor the present, nor the least wisp that is known.

44

It is time to explain myself—let us stand up.

What is known I strip away,
I launch all men and women forward with me into the Unknown.

The clock indicates the moment—but what does eternity indicate?

We have thus far exhausted trillions of winters and summers,
There are trillions ahead, and trillions ahead of them.

Births have brought us richness and variety,   1140
And other births will bring us richness and variety.

I do not call one greater and one smaller,
That which fills its period and place is equal to any.

Were mankind murderous or jealous upon you, my brother, my sister?
I am sorry for you, they are not murderous or jealous upon me,
All has been gentle with me, I keep no account with lamentation
(What have I to do with lamentation?).

I am an acme of things accomplished, and I an encloser of things to be.

My feet strike an apex of the apices of the stairs,
On every step bunches of ages, and larger bunches between the steps,   1150
All below duly traveled, and still I mount and mount.

Rise after rise bow the phantoms behind me,
Afar down I see the huge first Nothing, I know I was even there,
I waited unseen and always, and slept through the lethargic mist,
And took my time, and took no hurt from the fetid carbon.

Long I was hugged close—long and long.

Immense have been the preparations for me,
Faithful and friendly the arms that have helped me.

Cycles ferried my cradle, rowing and rowing like cheerful boatmen,
For room to me stars kept aside in their own rings,
They sent influences to look after what was to hold me.

116

Before I was born out of my mother generations guided me,
My embryo has never been torpid, nothing could overlay it.

For it the nebula cohered to an orb,
The long slow strata piled to rest it on,
Vast vegetables gave it sustenance,
Monstrous sauroids transported it in their mouths and deposited it with care

All forces have been steadily employed to complete and delight me,
Now on this spot I stand with my robust soul.

45

O span of youth! ever-pushed elasticity.
O manhood, balanced, florid and full.

117

My lovers suffocate me,
Crowding my lips, thick in the pores of my skin,
Jostling me through streets and public halls, coming naked to me at night,
Crying by day *Ahoy!* from the rocks of the river, swinging and chirping ov
　　my head,
Calling my name from flower-beds, vines, tangled underbrush,
Lighting on every moment of my life,
Bussing my body with soft balsamic busses,
Noiselessly passing handfuls out of their hearts and giving them to be min

Old age superbly rising! O welcome, ineffable grace of dying days!　　11

Every condition promulges not only itself, it promulges what grows after a
　　out of itself,
And the dark hush promulges as much as any.

I open my scuttle at night and see the far-sprinkled systems,
And all I see multiplied as high as I can cipher edge but the rim of the farth
　　systems.

Wider and wider they spread, expanding, always expanding,
Outward and outward and forever outward.

My sun has his sun and round him obediently wheels,
He joins with his partners a group of superior circuit,
And greater sets follow, making specks of the greatest inside them.

There is no stoppage and never can be stoppage,   1190
If I, you, and the worlds, and all beneath or upon their surfaces, were this
      moment reduced back to a pallid float, it would not avail in the long run,
We should surely bring up again where we now stand,
And surely go as much farther, and then farther and farther.

A few quadrillions of eras, a few octillions of cubic leagues, do not hazard the
      span or make it impatient,
They are but parts, any thing is but a part.

See ever so far, there is limitless space outside of that,
Count ever so much, there is limitless time around that.

My rendezvous is appointed, it is certain,
The Lord will be there and wait till I come on perfect terms,
The great Camerado, the lover true for whom I pine will be there.   1200

46

know I have the best of time and space, and was never measured and never
      will be measured.

tramp a perpetual journey (come listen all!),
My signs are a rain-proof coat, good shoes, and a staff cut from the woods,
No friend of mine takes his ease in my chair,
have no chair, no church, no philosophy,
  lead no man to a dinner-table, library, exchange,
But each man and each woman of you I lead upon a knoll,
My left hand hooking you round the waist,
My right hand pointing to landscapes of continents and the public road.

Not I, not any one else can travel that road for you,   1210
You must travel it for yourself.

It is not far, it is within reach,
Perhaps you have been on it since you were born and did not know,
Perhaps it is everywhere on water and on land.

Shoulder your duds dear son, and I will mine, and let us hasten forth,
Wonderful cities and free nations we shall fetch as we go.

If you tire, give me both burdens, and rest the chuff of your hand on my hip,
And in due time you shall repay the same service to me,
For after we start we never lie by again.

This day before dawn I ascended a hill and looked at the crowded heaven,   122

And I said to my spirit *When we become the enfolders of those orbs, and th*
  pleasure and knowledge of every thing in them, shall we be filled an
  satisfied then?

And my spirit said *No, we but level that lift to pass and continue beyond.*

You are also asking me questions and I hear you,

I answer that I cannot answer, you must find out for yourself.

Sit a while dear son,

Here are biscuits to eat and here is milk to drink,

But as soon as you sleep and renew yourself in sweet clothes, I kiss you wit
  a good-by kiss and open the gate for your egress hence.

Long enough have you dreamed contemptible dreams,

Now I wash the gum from your eyes,

You must habit yourself to the dazzle of the light and of every moment o
  your life.   123

Long have you timidly waded holding a plank by the shore,

Now I will you to be a bold swimmer,

To jump off in the midst of the sea, rise again, nod to me, shout, and laugh
  ingly dash with your hair.

47

I am the teacher of athletes,

He that by me spreads a wider breast than my own proves the width of m
  own,

He most honors my style who learns under it to destroy the teacher.

The boy I love, the same becomes a man not through derived power, but i
  his own right,

Wicked rather than virtuous out of conformity or fear,

Fond of his sweetheart, relishing well his steak,

Unrequited love or a slight cutting him worse than sharp steel cuts,   124

First-rate to ride, to fight, to hit the bull's eye, to sail a skiff, to sing a sor
  or play on the banjo,

Preferring scars and the beard and faces pitted with small-pox over all latherer

And those well-tanned to those that keep out of the sun.

I teach straying from me, yet who can stray from me?

I follow you whoever you are from the present hour,

My words itch at your ears till you understand them.

I do not say these things for a dollar or to fill up the time while I wait for
  boat

(It is you talking just as much as myself, I act as the tongue of you,

Tied in your mouth, in mine it begins to be loosened).

swear I will never again mention love or death inside a house,   1250
And I swear I will never translate myself at all, only to him or her who
    privately stays with me in the open air.

f you would understand me go to the heights or water-shore,
'he nearest gnat is an explanation, and a drop or motion of waves a key,
'he maul, the oar, the hand-saw, second my words.

Jo shuttered room or school can commune with me,
ut roughs and little children better than they.

'he young mechanic is closest to me, he knows me well,
'he woodman that takes his ax and jug with him shall take me with him
    all day,
'he farm-boy ploughing in the field feels good at the sound of my voice,
n vessels that sail my words sail, I go with fishermen and seamen and love
    them.   1260

'he soldier camped or upon the march is mine,
'n the night ere the pending battle many seek me, and I do not fail them.
'n that solemn night (it may be their last) those that know me seek me.

Iy face rubs to the hunter's face when he lies down alone in his blanket,
he driver thinking of me does not mind the jolt of his wagon,
he young mother and old mother comprehend me,
he girl and the wife rest the needle a moment and forget where they are,
hey and all would resume what I have told them.

                               48

have said that the soul is not more than the body,
nd I have said that the body is not more than the soul,   1270
nd nothing, not God, is greater to one than one's self is,
nd whoever walks a furlong without sympathy walks to his own funeral
    dressed in his shroud,
nd I or you pocketless of a dime may purchase the pick of the earth,
nd to glance with an eye or show a bean in its pod confounds the learning
    of all times,
nd there is no trade or employment but the young man following it may
    become a hero,
nd there is no object so soft but it makes a hub for the wheeled universe,
nd I say to any man or woman, Let your soul stand cool and composed
    before a million universes.

nd I say to mankind, Be not curious about God,
or I who am curious about each am not curious about God
No array of terms can say how much I am at peace about God and about
    death).   1280
hear and behold God in every object, yet understand God not in the least,
or do I understand who there can be more wonderful than myself.

Why should I wish to see God better than this day?
I see something of God each hour of the twenty-four, and each moment then
In the faces of men and women I see God, and in my own face in the glass,
I find letters from God dropped in the street, and every one is signed b
   God's name,
And I leave them where they are, for I know that wheresoe'er I go
Others will punctually come for ever and ever.

49

And as to you Death, and you bitter hug of mortality, it is idle to try t
   alarm me.

To his work without flinching the accoucheur comes,   129
I see the elder-hand pressing receiving supporting,
I recline by the sills of the exquisite flexible doors,
And mark the outlet, and mark the relief and escape.

And as to you Corpse I think you are good manure, but that does not offend m
I smell the white roses sweet-scented and growing,
I reach to the leafy lips, I reach to the polished breasts of melons.

And as to you Life I reckon you are the leavings of many deaths
(No doubt I have died myself ten thousand times before).

I hear you whispering there O stars of heaven,
O suns—O grass of graves—O perpetual transfers and promotions,   130
If you do not say any thing how can I say any thing?

Of the turbid pool that lies in the autumn forest,
Of the moon that descends the steeps of the soughing twilight,
Toss, sparkles of day and dusk—toss on the black stems that decay in th
   muck,
Toss to the moaning gibberish of the dry limbs.

I ascend from the moon, I ascend from the night,
I perceive that the ghastly glimmer is noonday sunbeams reflected,
And debouch to the steady and central from the offspring great or small.

50

There is that in me—I do not know what it is—but I know it is in me.

Wrenched and sweaty—calm and cool then my body becomes,   131
I sleep—I sleep long.

I do not know it—it is without name—it is a word unsaid.
It is not in any dictionary, utterance, symbol.

Something it swings on more than the earth I swing on,
To it the creation is the friend whose embracing awakes me.

'erhaps I might tell more. Outlines! I plead for my brothers and sisters.

)o you see O my brothers and sisters?
t is not chaos or death—it is form, union, plan—it is eternal life—it is
    Happiness.

51

'he past and present wilt—I have filled them, emptied them,
.nd proceed to fill my next fold of the future.   1320

istener up there! what have you to confide to me?
ook in my face while I snuff the sidle of evening
Talk honestly, no one else hears you, and I stay only a minute longer).

•o I contradict myself?
ery well then I contradict myself
I am large, I contain multitudes).

concentrate toward them that are nigh, I wait on the door-slab.

'ho has done his day's work? who will soonest be through with his supper?
/ho wishes to walk with me?

'ill you speak before I am gone? will you prove already too late?   1330

52

ie spotted hawk swoops by and accuses me, he complains of my gab and my
    loitering.
too am not a bit tamed, I too am untranslatable,
sound my barbaric yawp over the roofs of the world.

he last scud of day holds back for me,
flings my likeness after the rest and true as any on the shadowed wilds,
coaxes me to the vapor and the dusk.

depart as air, I shake my white locks at the runaway sun,
effuse my flesh in eddies, and drift it in lacy jags.

bequeath myself to the dirt to grow from the grass I love,
you want me again look for me under your boot-soles.   1340

ou will hardly know who I am or what I mean,
it I shall be good health to you nevertheless,
id filter and fiber your blood.

•iling to fetch me at first keep encouraged,
issing me one place search another,
stop somewhere waiting for you.

                                        1855, 1881

THERE WAS A CHILD WENT FORTH

There was a child went forth every day,
And the first object he look'd upon, that object he became,
And that object became part of him for the day or a certain part of the day
Or for many years or stretching cycles of years.

The early lilacs became part of this child,
And grass and white and red morning-glories, and white and red clover, and
  the song of the phœbe-bird,
And the Third-month lambs and the sow's pink-faint litter, and the mare's
  foal and the cow's calf,
And the noisy brood of the barnyard or by the mire of the pond-side,
And the fish suspending themselves so curiously below there, and the beautiful
  curious liquid,
And the water-plants with their graceful flat heads, all became part of him.

The field-sprouts of Fourth-month and Fifth-month became part of him,
Winter-grain sprouts and those of the light-yellow corn, and the esculent roots
  of the garden,
And the apple-trees cover'd with blossoms and the fruit afterward, and wood-
  berries, and the commonest weeds by the road,
And the old drunkard staggering home from the outhouse of the tavern whence
  he had lately risen,
And the schoolmistress that pass'd on her way to the school,
And the friendly boys that pass'd, and the quarrelsome boys,
And the tidy and fresh-cheek'd girls, and the barefoot negro boy and girl,
And all the changes of city and country wherever he went.

His own parents, he that had father'd him and she that had conceiv'd him in
  her womb and birth'd him,
They gave this child more of themselves than that,
They gave him afterward every day, they became part of him.

The mother at home quietly placing the dishes on the supper-table,
The mother with mild words, clean her cap and gown, a wholesome odor
  falling off her person and clothes as she walks by,
The father, strong, self-sufficient, manly, mean, anger'd, unjust,
The blow, the quick loud word, the tight bargain, the crafty lure,
The family usages, the language, the company, the furniture, the yearning and
  swelling heart,
Affection that will not be gainsay'd, the sense of what is real, the thought if
  after all it should prove unreal,
The doubts of day-time and the doubts of night-time, the curious whether and
  how,
Whether that which appears so is so, or is it all flashes and specks?
Men and women crowding fast in the streets, if they are not flashes and specks
  what are they?
The streets themselves and the façades of houses, and goods in the windows,
Vehicles, teams, the heavy-plank'd wharves, the huge crossing at the ferries,

The village on the highland seen from afar at sunset, the river between,
Shadows, aureola and mist, the light falling on roofs and gables of white or
brown two miles off,
The schooner near by sleepily dropping down the tide, the little boat slack-
tow'd astern,
The hurrying tumbling waves, quick-broken crests, slapping,
The strata of color'd clouds, the long bar of maroon-tint away solitary by
itself, the spread of purity it lies motionless in,
The horizon's edge, the flying sea-crow, the fragrance of salt marsh and shore
mud,   40
These became part of that child who went forth every day, and who now goes,
and will always go forth every day.

                                                              1855, 1871

CROSSING BROOKLYN FERRY

1

Flood-tide below me! I see you face to face!
Clouds of the west—sun there half an hour high—I see you also face to face.

Crowds of men and women attired in the usual costumes, how curious you are
to me!
On the ferry-boats the hundreds and hundreds that cross, returning home, are
more curious to me than you suppose,
And you that shall cross from shore to shore years hence are more to me, and
more in my meditations, than you might suppose.

2

The impalpable sustenance of me from all things at all hours of the day,
The simple, compact, well-joined scheme, myself disintegrated, every one dis-
integrated yet part of the scheme,
The similitudes of the past and those of the future,
The glories strung like beads on my smallest sights and hearings, on the walk
in the street and the passage over the river,
The current rushing so swiftly and swimming with me far away,   10
The others that are to follow me, the ties between me and them,
The certainty of others, the life, love, sight, hearing of others.

Others will enter the gates of the ferry and cross from shore to shore,
Others will watch the run of the flood-tide,
Others will see the shipping of Manhattan north and west, and the heights of
Brooklyn to the south and east,
Others will see the islands large and small;
Fifty years hence, others will see them as they cross, the sun half an hour high,
A hundred years hence, or ever so many hundred years hence, others will see
them,
Will enjoy the sunset, the pouring-in of the flood-tide, the falling-back to the
sea of the ebb-tide.

3

It avails not, time nor place—distance avails not, [20]
I am with you, you men and women of a generation, or ever so many genera-
tions hence,
Just as you feel when you look on the river and sky, so I felt,
Just as any of you is one of a living crowd, I was one of a crowd,
Just as you are refreshed by the gladness of the river and the bright flow, I
was refreshed,
Just as you stand and lean on the rail, yet hurry with the swift current, I
stood yet was hurried,
Just as you look on the numberless masts of ships and the thick-stemmed pipes
of steamboats, I looked.

I too many and many a time crossed the river of old,
Watched the Twelfth-month sea-gulls, saw them high in the air floating with
motionless wings, oscillating their bodies,
Saw how the glistening yellow lit up parts of their bodies and left the rest
in strong shadow,
Saw the slow-wheeling circles and the gradual edging toward the south, [30]
Saw the reflection of the summer sky in the water,
Had my eyes dazzled by the shimmering track of beams,
Looked at the fine centrifugal spokes of light round the shape of my head in
the sunlit water,
Looked on the haze on the hills southward and south-westward,
Looked on the vapor as it flew in fleeces tinged with violet,
Looked toward the lower bay to notice the vessels arriving,
Saw their approach, saw aboard those that were near me,
Saw the white sails of schooners and sloops, saw the ships at anchor,
The sailors at work in the rigging or out astride the spars,
The round masts, the swinging motion of the hulls, the slender serpentine
pennants, [40]
The large and small steamers in motion, the pilots in their pilot-houses,
The white wake left by the passage, the quick tremulous whirl of the wheels,
The flags of all nations, the falling of them at sunset,
The scallop-edged waves in the twilight, the ladled cups, the frolicsome crests
and glistening,
The stretch afar growing dimmer and dimmer, the gray walls of the granite
storehouses by the docks,
On the river the shadowy group, the big steam-tug closely flanked on each
side by the barges, the hay-boat, the belated lighter,
On the neighboring shore the fires from the foundry chimneys burning high
and glaringly into the night,
Casting their flicker of black contrasted with wild red and yellow light over
the tops of houses, and down into the clefts of streets.

4

These and all else were to me the same as they are to you,
I loved well those cities, loved well the stately and rapid river, [5]
The men and women I saw were all near to me,

Others the same—others who look back on me because I looked forward to them
(The time will come, though I stop here to-day and to-night).

5

What is it then between us?
What is the count of the scores or hundreds of years between us?

Whatever it is, it avails not—distance avails not, and place avails not,
I too lived, Brooklyn of ample hills was mine,
I too walked the streets of Manhattan island, and bathed in the waters
    around it,
I too felt the curious abrupt questionings stir within me.
In the day among crowds of people sometimes they came upon me,   60
In my walks home late at night or as I lay in my bed they came upon me,
I too had been struck from the float forever held in solution,
I too had received identity by my body,
That I was I knew was of my body, and what I should be I knew I should
    be of my body.

6

It is not upon you alone the dark patches fall,
The dark threw its patches down upon me also,
The best I had done seemed to me blank and suspicious,
My great thoughts as I supposed them, were they not in reality meager?
Nor is it you alone who know what it is to be evil,
I am he who knew what it was to be evil,   70
I too knitted the old knot of contrariety,
Blabbed, blushed, resented, lied, stole, grudged,
Had guile, anger, lust, hot wishes I dared not speak,
Was wayward, vain, greedy, shallow, sly, cowardly, malignant,
The wolf, the snake, the hog, not wanting in me,
The cheating look, the frivolous word, the adulterous wish, not wanting,
Refusals, hates, postponements, meanness, laziness, none of these wanting,
Was one with the rest, the days and haps of the rest,
Was called by my nighest name by clear loud voices of young men as they saw
    me approaching or passing,
Felt their arms on my neck as I stood, or the negligent leaning of their flesh
    against me as I sat,   80
Saw many I loved in the street or ferry-boat or public assembly, yet never
    told them a word,
Lived the same life with the rest, the same old laughing, gnawing, sleeping,
Played the part that still looks back on the actor or actress,
The same old role, the role that is what we make it, as great as we like,
Or as small as we like, or both great and small.

7

Closer yet I approach you,
What thought you have of me now, I had as much of you—I laid in my stores
    in advance,

I considered long and seriously of you before you were born.

Who was to know what should come home to me?
Who knows but I am enjoying this?   9
Who knows, for all the distance, but I am as good as looking at you now, fo
    all you cannot see me?

                              8

Ah, what can ever be more stately and admirable to me than mast-hemme
    Manhattan?
River and sunset and scallop-edged waves of flood-tide?
The sea-gulls oscillating their bodies, the hay-boat in the twilight, and th
    belated lighter?
What gods can exceed these that clasp me by the hand, and with voices
    love call me promptly and loudly by my nighest name as I approach?

What is more subtle than this which ties me to the woman or man that look
    in my face?
Which fuses me into you now, and pours my meaning into you?

We understand then do we not?
What I promised without mentioning it, have you not accepted?
What the study could not teach—what the preaching could not accomplish i
    accomplished, is it not?   10

                              9

Flow on, river! flow with the flood-tide, and ebb with the ebb-tide!
Frolic on, crested and scallop-edged waves!
Gorgeous clouds of the sunset! drench with your splendor me, or the men an
    women generations after me!
Cross from shore to shore, countless crowds of passengers!
Stand up, tall masts of Mannahatta! stand up, beautiful hills of Brooklyn!
Throb, baffled and curious brain! throw out questions and answers!
Suspend here and everywhere, eternal float of solution!
Gaze, loving and thirsting eyes, in the house or street or public assembly!
Sound out, voices of young men! loudly and musically call me by my nighe
    name!
Live, old life! play the part that looks back on the actor or actress!   1
Play the old role, the role that is great or small according as one makes it!
Consider, you who peruse me, whether I may not in unknown ways be lookin
    upon you;
Be firm, rail over the river, to support those who lean idly, yet haste wi
    the hasting current;
Fly on, sea-birds! fly sideways, or wheel in large circles high in the air;
Receive the summer sky, you water, and faithfully hold it till all downca
    eyes have time to take it from you!
Diverge, fine spokes of light, from the shape of my head, or any one's hea
    in the sunlit water!

Come on, ships from the lower bay! pass up or down, white-sailed schooners,
 sloops, lighters!
Flaunt away, flags of all nations! be duly lowered at sunset!
Burn high your fires, foundry chimneys! cast black shadows at night-fall!
 cast red and yellow light over the tops of the houses!
Appearances, now or henceforth, indicate what you are,   120
You necessary film, continue to envelop the soul,
About my body for me, and your body for you, be hung our divinest aromas,
Thrive, cities—bring your freight, bring your shows, ample and sufficient rivers,
Expand, being than which none else is perhaps more spiritual,
Keep your places, objects than which none else is more lasting.

You have waited, you always wait, you dumb, beautiful ministers,
We receive you with free sense at last, and are insatiate henceforward,
Not you any more shall be able to foil us, or withhold yourselves from us,
We use you, and do not cast you aside—we plant you permanently within us,
We fathom you not—we love you—there is perfection in you also,   130
You furnish your parts toward eternity,
Great or small, you furnish your parts toward the soul.

                1856, 1881

OUT OF THE CRADLE ENDLESSLY ROCKING

Out of the cradle endlessly rocking,
Out of the mocking-bird's throat, the musical shuttle,
Out of the Ninth-month midnight,
Over the sterile sands and the fields beyond, where the child leaving his bed
 wandered alone, bareheaded, barefoot,
Down from the showered halo,
Up from the mystic play of shadows twining and twisting as if they were alive,
Out from the patches of briers and blackberries,
From the memories of the bird that chanted to me,
From your memories sad brother, from the fitful risings and fallings I heard,
From under that yellow half-moon late-risen and swollen as if with tears,   10
From those beginning notes of yearning and love there in the mist,
From the thousand responses of my heart never to cease,
From the myriad thence-aroused words,
From the word stronger and more delicious than any,
From such as now they start the scene revisiting,
As a flock, twittering, rising, or overhead passing,
Borne hither, ere all eludes me, hurriedly,
A man, yet by these tears a little boy again,
Throwing myself on the sand, confronting the waves,
I, chanter of pains and joys, uniter of here and hereafter,   20
Taking all hints to use them, but swiftly leaping beyond them,
A reminiscence sing.

Once Paumanok,
When the lilac-scent was in the air and Fifth-month grass was growing,
Up this seashore in some briers,

Two feathered guests from Alabama, two together,
And their nest, and four light-green eggs spotted with brown,
And every day the he-bird to and fro near at hand,
And every day the she-bird crouched on her nest, silent, with bright eyes,
And every day I, a curious boy, never too close, never disturbing them,   30
Cautiously peering, absorbing, translating.

Shine! shine! shine!
Pour down your warmth, great sun!
While we bask, we two together,
Two together!
Winds blow south, or winds blow north,
Day come white, or night come black,
Home, or rivers and mountains from home,
Singing all time, minding no time,
While we two keep together.   40

Till of a sudden,
May-be killed, unknown to her mate,
One forenoon the she-bird crouched not on the nest,
Nor returned that afternoon, nor the next,
Nor ever appeared again.

And thenceforward all summer in the sound of the sea,
And at night under the full of the moon in calmer weather,
Over the hoarse surging of the sea,
Or flitting from brier to brier by day,
I saw, I heard at intervals the remaining one, the he-bird,   50
The solitary guest from Alabama.

Blow! blow! blow!
Blow up sea-winds along Paumanok's shore;
I wait and I wait till you blow my mate to me.

Yes, when the stars glistened,
All night long on the prong of a moss-scalloped stake,
Down almost amid the slapping waves,
Sat the lone singer wonderful causing tears.

He called on his mate,
He poured forth the meanings which I of all men know.   60

Yes my brother I know,
The rest might not, but I have treasured every note,
For more than once dimly down to the beach gliding,
Silent, avoiding the moonbeams, blending myself with the shadows,
Recalling now the obscure shapes, the echoes, the sounds and sights after their
          sorts,
The white arms out in the breakers tirelessly tossing,
I, with bare feet, a child, the wind wafting my hair,
Listened long and long.

Listened to keep, to sing, now translating the notes,
Following you my brother.   70

Soothe! soothe! soothe!
Close on its wave soothes the wave behind,
And again another behind embracing and lapping, every one close,
But my love soothes not me, not me.

Low hangs the moon, it rose late,
It is lagging—O I think it is heavy with love, with love.

O madly the sea pushes upon the land,
With love, with love.

O night! do I not see my love fluttering out among the breakers?
What is that little black thing I see there in the white?   80

Loud! loud! loud!
Loud I call to you, my love!
High and clear I shoot my voice over the waves,
Surely you must know who is here, is here,
You must know who I am, my love.

Low-hanging moon!
What is that dusky spot in your brown yellow?
O it is the shape, the shape of my mate!
O moon do not keep her from me any longer.

Land! land! O land!   90
Whichever way I turn, O I think you could give me my mate back again if you
     only would,
For I am almost sure I see her dimly whichever way I look.

O rising stars!
Perhaps the one I want so much will rise, will rise with some of you.

O throat! O trembling throat!
Sound clearer through the atmosphere!
Pierce the woods, the earth,
Somewhere listening to catch you must be the one I want.

Shake out carols!
Solitary here, the night's carols!   100
Carols of lonesome love! death's carols!
Carols under that lagging, yellow, waning moon!
O under that moon where she droops almost down into the sea!
O reckless despairing carols.

But soft! sink low!
Soft! let me just murmur,

And do you wait a moment you husky-noised sea,
For somewhere I believe I heard my mate responding to me,
So faint, I must be still, be still to listen,
But not altogether still, for then she might not come immediately to me.   110

Hither my love!
Here I am! here!
With this just-sustained note I announce myself to you,
This gentle call is for you my love, for you.

Do not be decoyed elsewhere,
That is the whistle of the wind, it is not my voice,
That is the fluttering, the fluttering of the spray,
Those are the shadows of leaves.

O darkness! O in vain!
O I am very sick and sorrowful.   120

O brown halo in the sky near the moon, drooping upon the sea!
O troubled reflection in the sea!
O throat! O throbbing heart!
And I singing uselessly, uselessly all the night.

O past! O happy life! O songs of joy!
In the air, in the woods, over fields,
Loved! loved! loved! loved! loved!
But my mate no more, no more with me!
We two together no more.

The aria sinking,   130
All else continuing, the stars shining,
The winds blowing, the notes of the bird continuous echoing,
With angry moans the fierce old mother incessantly moaning,
On the sands of Paumanok's shore gray and rustling,
The yellow half-moon enlarged, sagging down, drooping, the face of the sea
      almost touching,
The boy ecstatic, with his bare feet the waves, with his hair the atmosphere
      dallying,
The love in the heart long pent, now loose, now at last tumultuously bursting,
The aria's meaning, the ears, the soul, swiftly depositing,
The strange tears down the cheeks coursing,
The colloquy there, the trio, each uttering,   140
The undertone, the savage old mother incessantly crying,
To the boy's soul's questions sullenly timing, some drowned secret hissing,
To the outsetting bard.

Demon or bird! (said the boy's soul)
Is it indeed toward your mate you sing? or is it really to me?
For I, that was a child, my tongue's use sleeping, now I have heard you,
Now in a moment I know what I am for, I awake,

And already a thousand singers, a thousand songs, clearer, louder and more
    sorrowful than yours,
A thousand warbling echoes have startled to life within me, never to die.

O you singer solitary, singing by yourself, projecting me,   150
O solitary me listening, never more shall I cease perpetuating you,
Never more shall I escape, never more the reverberations,
Never more the cries of unsatisfied love be absent from me,
Never again leave me to be the peaceful child I was before what there in
    the night,
By the sea under the yellow and sagging moon,
The messenger there aroused, the fire, the sweet hell within,
The unknown want, the destiny of me.

O give me the clew! (it lurks in the night here somewhere)
O if I am to have so much, let me have more!

A word then (for I will conquer it),   160
The word final, superior to all,
Subtle, sent up—what is it?—I listen;
Are you whispering it, and have been all the time, you sea waves?
Is that it from your liquid rims and wet sands?

Whereto answering, the sea,
Delaying not, hurrying not,
Whispered me through the night, and very plainly before daybreak,
Lisped to me the low and delicious word death,
And again death, death, death, death,
Hissing melodious, neither like the bird nor like my aroused child's heart, 170
But edging near as privately for me rustling at my feet,
Creeping thence steadily up to my ears and laving me softly all over,
Death, death, death, death, death.

Which I do not forget,
But fuse the song of my dusky demon and brother,
That he sang to me in the moonlight on Paumanok's gray beach,
With the thousand responsive songs at random,
My own songs awaked from that hour,
And with them the key, the word up from the waves,
The word of the sweetest song and all songs,   180
That strong and delicious word which, creeping to my feet
Or like some old crone rocking the cradle, swathed in sweet garments, bending
    aside),
The sea whispered me.

                              1859, 1881

I HEAR AMERICA SINGING

I hear America singing, the varied carols I hear,
Those of mechanics, each one singing his as it should be blithe and strong,
The carpenter singing his as he measures his plank or beam,

The mason singing his as he makes ready for work, or leaves off work,
The boatman singing what belongs to him in his boat, the deck-hand singing
    on the steamboat deck,
The shoemaker singing as he sits on his bench, the hatter singing as he stands,
The wood-cutter's song, the ploughboy's on his way in the morning, or at noon
    intermission or at sundown,
The delicious singing of the mother, or of the young wife at work, or of the
    girl sewing or washing,
Each singing what belongs to him or her and to none else,
The day what belongs to the day—at night the party of young fellows, robust,
    friendly,   10
Singing with open mouths their strong melodious songs.

                                                              1860, 1867

ME IMPERTURBE

Me imperturbe, standing at ease in Nature,
Master of all or mistress of all, aplomb in the midst of irrational things,
Imbued as they, passive, receptive, silent as they,
Finding my occupation, poverty, notoriety, foibles, crimes, less important than
    I thought,
Me toward the Mexican Sea, or in the Mannahatta or the Tennessee, or far
    north or inland,
A river man, or a man of the woods or of any farm-life of these States or of
    the coast, or the lakes or Kanada,
Me wherever my life is lived, O to be self-balanced for contingencies,
To confront night, storms, hunger, ridicule, accidents, rebuffs, as the trees and
    animals do.

                                                              1860, 1881

I SAW IN LOUISIANA A LIVE-OAK GROWING

I saw in Louisiana a live-oak growing,
All alone stood it and the moss hung down from the branches,
Without any companion it grew there uttering joyous leaves of dark green,
And its look, rude, unbending, lusty, made me think of myself,
But I wonder'd how it could utter joyous leaves standing alone there without
    its friend near, for I knew I could not,
And I broke off a twig with a certain number of leaves upon it, and twined
    around it a little moss,
And brought it away, and I have placed it in sight in my room,
It is not needed to remind me as of my own dear friends,
(For I believe lately I think of little else than of them,)
Yet it remains to me a curious token, it makes me think of manly love;   10
For all that, and though the live-oak glistens there in Louisiana solitary in a
    wide flat space,
Uttering joyous leaves all its life without a friend a lover near,
I know very well I could not.

                                                              1860, 1867

RECORDERS AGES HENCE

Recorders ages hence,
Come, I will take you down underneath this impassive exterior, I will tell you
    what to say of me,
Publish my name and hang up my picture as that of the tenderest lover,
The friend the lover's portrait, of whom his friend his lover was fondest,
Who was not proud of his songs, but of the measureless ocean of love within
    him, and freely poured it forth,
Who often walked lonesome walks thinking of his dear friends, his lovers,
Who pensive away from one he loved often lay sleepless and dissatisfied at
    night,
Who knew too well the sick, sick dread lest the one he loved might secretly
    be indifferent to him,
Whose happiest days were far away through fields, in woods, on hills, he and
    another wandering hand in hand, they twain apart from other men,
Who oft as he sauntered the streets curved with his arm the shoulder of his
    friend, while the arm of his friend rested upon him also.   10

1860, 1867

I HEAR IT WAS CHARGED AGAINST ME

I hear it was charged against me that I sought to destroy institutions,
But really I am neither for nor against institutions
(What indeed have I in common with them? or what with the destruction
    of them?),
Only I will establish in the Mannahatta and in every city of these States inland
    and seaboard,
And in the fields and woods, and above every keel little or large that dents
    the water,
Without edifices or rules or trustees or any argument,
The institution of the dear love of comrades.

1860, 1867

FACING WEST FROM CALIFORNIA'S SHORES

Facing west from California's shores,
Inquiring, tireless, seeking what is yet unfound,
I, a child, very old, over waves, towards the house of maternity, the land of
    migrations, look afar,
Look off the shores of my Western sea, the circle almost circled;
For starting westward from Hindustan, from the vales of Kashmere,
From Asia, from the north, from the God, the sage, and the hero,
From the south from the flowery peninsulas and the spice islands,
Long having wander'd since, round the earth having wander'd,
Now I face home again, very pleas'd and joyous,
(But where is what I started for so long ago?   10
And why is it yet unfound?)

1860, 1867

PIONEERS! O PIONEERS!

Come my tan-faced children,
Follow well in order, get your weapons ready,
Have you your pistols? have you your sharp-edged axes?
　　　　Pioneers! O pioneers!

For we cannot tarry here,
We must march my darlings, we must bear the brunt of danger,
We the youthful sinewy races, all the rest on us depend,
　　　　Pioneers! O pioneers!

O you youths, Western youths,
So impatient, full of action, full of manly pride and friendship,　　10
Plain I see you Western youths, see you tramping with the foremost,
　　　　Pioneers! O pioneers!

Have the elder races halted?
Do they droop and end their lesson, wearied over there beyond the seas?
We take up the task eternal, and the burden and the lesson,
　　　　Pioneers! O pioneers!

All the past we leave behind,
We debouch upon a newer mightier world, varied world,
Fresh and strong the world we seize, world of labor and the march,
　　　　Pioneers! O pioneers!　　20

We detachments steady throwing,
Down the edges, through the passes, up the mountains steep,
Conquering, holding, daring, venturing as we go the unknown ways,
　　　　Pioneers! O pioneers!

We primeval forests felling,
We the rivers stemming, vexing we and piercing deep the mines within,
We the surface broad surveying, we the virgin soil upheaving,
　　　　Pioneers! O pioneers!

Colorado men are we,
From the peaks gigantic, from the great sierras and the high plateaus,　　30
From the mine and from the gully, from the hunting trail we come,
　　　　Pioneers! O pioneers!

From Nebraska, from Arkansas,
Central inland race are we, from Missouri, with the continental blood inter-
　　　vein'd,
All the hands of comrades clasping, all the Southern, all the Northern,
　　　　Pioneers! O pioneers!

O resistless restless race!
O beloved race in all! O my breast aches with tender love for all!
O I mourn and yet exult, I am rapt with love for all,
　　　　Pioneers! O pioneers!　　40

Raise the mighty mother mistress,
Waving high the delicate mistress, over all the starry mistress, (bend your
     heads all,)
Raise the fang'd and warlike mistress, stern, impassive, weapon'd mistress,
               Pioneers! O pioneers!

See my children, resolute children,
By those swarms upon our rear we must never yield or falter,
Ages back in ghostly millions frowning there behind us urging,
               Pioneers! O pioneers!

On and on the compact ranks,
With accessions ever waiting, with the places of the dead quickly fill'd,   50
Through the battle, through defeat, moving yet and never stopping,
               Pioneers! O pioneers!

O to die advancing on!
Are there some of us to droop and die? has the hour come?
Then upon the march we fittest die, soon and sure the gap is fill'd,
               Pioneers! O pioneers!

All the pulses of the world,
Falling in they beat for us, with the Western movement beat,
Holding single or together, steady moving to the front, all for us,
               Pioneers! O pioneers!   60

Life's involv'd and varied pageants,
All the forms and shows, all the workmen at their work,
All the seamen and the landsmen, all the masters with their slaves,
               Pioneers! O pioneers!

All the hapless silent lovers,
All the prisoners in the prisons, all the righteous and the wicked,
All the joyous, all the sorrowing, all the living, all the dying,
               Pioneers! O pioneers!

I too with my soul and body,
We, a curious trio, picking, wandering on our way,   70
Through these shores amid the shadows, with the apparitions pressing,
               Pioneers! O pioneers!

Lo, the darting bowling orb!
Lo, the brother orbs around, all the clustering suns and planets,
All the dazzling days, all the mystic nights with dreams,
               Pioneers! O pioneers!

These are of us, they are with us,
All for primal needed work, while the followers there in embryo wait behind,
We to-day's procession heading, we the route for travel clearing,
               Pioneers! O pioneers!   80

O you daughters of the West!
O you young and elder daughters! O you mothers and you wives!
Never must you be divided, in our ranks you move united,
            Pioneers! O pioneers!

            Minstrels latent on the prairies!
(Shrouded bards of other lands, you may rest, you have done your work,)
Soon I hear you coming warbling, soon you rise and tramp amid us,
            Pioneers! O pioneers!

            Not for delectations sweet,
Not the cushion and the slipper, not the peaceful and the studious,   90
Not the riches safe and palling, not for us the tame enjoyment,
            Pioneers! O pioneers!

            Do the feasters gluttonous feast?
Do the corpulent sleepers sleep? have they lock'd and bolted doors?
Still be ours the diet hard, and the blanket on the ground,
            Pioneers! O pioneers!

            Has the night descended?
Was the road of late so toilsome? did we stop discouraged nodding on our way?
Yet a passing hour I yield you in your tracks to pause oblivious,
            Pioneers! O pioneers!   100

            Till with sound of trumpet,
Far, far off the daybreak call—hark! how loud and clear I hear it wind,
Swift! to the head of the army!—swift! spring to your place,
            Pioneers! O pioneers!

                                        1865, 1881

VIGIL STRANGE I KEPT ON THE FIELD ONE NIGHT

Vigil strange I kept on the field one night;
When you my son and my comrade dropt at my side that day,
One look I but gave which your dear eyes return'd with a look I shall never
            forget,
One touch of your hand to mine O boy, reach'd up as you lay on the ground,
Then onward I sped in the battle, the even-contested battle,
Till late in the night reliev'd to the place at last again I made my way,
Found you in death so cold dear comrade, found your body son of responding
            kisses, (never again on earth responding,)
Bared your face in the starlight, curious the scene, cool blew the moderate
            night-wind,
Long there and then in vigil I stood, dimly around me the battlefield
            spreading,   10
Vigil wondrous and vigil sweet there in the fragrant silent night,
But not a tear fell, not even a long-drawn sigh, long, long I gazed,

Then on the earth partially reclining sat by your side leaning my chin in my
    hands,
Passing sweet hours, immortal and mystic hours with you dearest comrade—
    not a tear, not a word,
Vigil of silence, love and death, vigil for you my son and my soldier,
As onward silently stars aloft, eastward new ones upward stole,
Vigil final for you brave boy, (I could not save you, swift was your death,
I faithfully loved you and cared for you living, I think we shall surely meet
    again,)
Till at latest lingering of the night, indeed just as the dawn appear'd,
My comrade I wrapt in his blanket, envelop'd well his form,   20
Folded the blanket well, tucking it carefully over head and carefully under feet,
And there and then and bathed by the rising sun, my son in his grave, in his
    rude-dug grave I deposited,
Ending my vigil strange with that, vigil of night and battle-field dim,
Vigil for boy of responding kisses, (never again on earth responding,)
Vigil for comrade swiftly slain, vigil I never forget, how as day brighten'd,
I rose from the chill ground and folded my soldier well in his blanket,
And buried him where he fell.

1865, 1867

COME UP FROM THE FIELDS FATHER

Come up from the fields father, here's a letter from our Pete,
And come to the front door mother, here's a letter from thy dear son.

Lo, 'tis autumn,
Lo, where the trees, deeper green, yellower and redder,
Cool and sweeten Ohio's villages with leaves fluttering in the moderate wind,
Where apples ripe in the orchards hang and grapes on the trellised vines.
(Smell you the smell of the grapes on the vines?
Smell you the buckwheat where the bees were lately buzzing?)

Above all, lo, the sky so calm, so transparent after the rain, and with wondrous
    clouds,
Below too, all calm, all vital and beautiful, and the farm prospers well.   10

Down in the fields all prospers well,
But now from the fields come father, come at the daughter's call,
And come to the entry mother, to the front door come right away.

Fast as she can she hurries, something ominous, her steps trembling,
She does not tarry to smooth her hair nor adjust her cap.

Open the envelope quickly,
O this is not our son's writing, yet his name is signed,
O a strange hand writes for our dear son, O stricken mother's soul!
All swims before her eyes, flashes with black, she catches the main words only,

Sentences broken, *gunshot wound in the breast, cavalry skirmish, taken to hospital,*   20
At present low, but will soon be better.

Ah now the single figure to me,
Amid all teeming and wealthy Ohio with all its cities and farms,
Sickly white in the face and dull in the head, very faint,
By the jamb of a door leans.

Grieve not so, dear mother (the just-grown daughter speaks through her sobs,
The little sisters huddle around speechless and dismayed),
See, dearest mother, the letter says Pete will soon be better.

Alas poor boy, he will never be better (nor may-be needs to be better, that
     brave and simple soul),
While they stand at home at the door he is dead already,   30
The only son is dead.

But the mother needs to be better,
She with thin form presently dressed in black,
By day her meals untouched, then at night fitfully sleeping, often waking,
In the midnight waking, weeping, longing with one deep longing,
O that she might withdraw unnoticed, silent from life escape and withdraw,
To follow, to seek, to be with her dear dead son.

                 1865, 1867

GIVE ME THE SPLENDID SILENT SUN

1

Give me the splendid silent sun with his beams full-dazzling,
Give me juicy autumnal fruit ripe and red from the orchard,
Give me a field where the unmow'd grass grows,
Give me an arbor, give me the trellis'd grape,
Give me fresh corn and wheat, give me the serene-moving animals teaching content,
Give me nights perfectly quiet as on high plateaus west of the Mississippi, and
     I looking up at the stars,
Give me odorous at sunrise a garden of beautiful flowers where I can walk
     undisturb'd,
Give me for marriage a sweet-breath'd woman of whom I should never tire,
Give me a perfect child, give me away aside from the noise of the world a
     rural domestic life,
Give me to warble spontaneous songs recluse by myself, for my own ears
     only,   10
Give me solitude, give me Nature, give me again O Nature your primal sanities!

These demanding to have them, (tired with ceaseless excitement, and rack'd by
     the war-strife,)
These to procure incessantly asking, rising in cries from my heart,
While yet incessantly asking still I adhere to my city.

Day upon day and year upon year O city, walking your streets,
Where you hold me enchain'd a certain time refusing to give me up,
Yet giving to make me glutted, enrich'd of soul, you give me forever faces;
(O I see what I sought to escape, confronting, reversing my cries,
I see my own soul trampling down what it ask'd for.)

2
20

Keep your splendid silent sun,
Keep your woods O Nature, and the quiet places by the woods,
Keep your fields of clover and timothy, and your corn-fields and orchards,
Keep the blossoming buckwheat fields where the Ninth-month bees hum;
Give me faces and streets—give me these phantoms incessant and endless along
   the trottoirs!
Give me interminable eyes—give me women—give me comrades and lovers by
   the thousand!
Let me see new ones every day—let me hold new ones by the hand every day!
Give me such shows—give me the streets of Manhattan!
Give me Broadway, with the soldiers marching—give me the sound of the
   trumpets and drums!
(The soldiers in companies or regiments—some starting away, flush'd and
   reckless,
Some, their time up, returning with thinn'd ranks, young, yet very old, worn,
   marching, noticing nothing;)   30
Give me the shores and wharves heavy-fringed with black ships!
O such for me! O an intense life, full to repletion and varied!
The life of the theater, bar-room, huge hotel, for me!
The saloon of the steamer! the crowded excursion for me! the torchlight pro-
   cession!
The dense brigade bound for the war, with high piled military wagons following;
People, endless, streaming, with strong voices, passions, pageants,
Manhattan streets with their powerful throbs, with beating drums as now,
The endless and noisy chorus, the rustle and clank of muskets, (even the sight
   of the wounded,)
Manhattan crowds, with their turbulent musical chorus!
Manhattan faces and eyes forever for me.   40
                                                            1865, 1867

WHEN I HEARD THE LEARN'D ASTRONOMER

When I heard the learn'd astronomer,
When the proofs, the figures, were ranged in columns before me,
When I was shown the charts and diagrams, to add, divide, and measure them,
When I sitting heard the astronomer where he lectured with much applause
   in the lecture-room,
How soon unaccountable I became tired and sick,
Till rising and gliding out I wander'd off by myself,
In the mystical moist night-air, and from time to time,
Look'd up in perfect silence at the stars.

                                                            1865, 1867

SHUT NOT YOUR DOORS

Shut not your doors to me proud libraries,
For that which was lacking on all your well-filled shelves, yet needed most,
    I bring,
Forth from the war emerging, a book I have made,
The words of my book nothing, the drift of it every thing,
A book separate, not linked with the rest nor felt by the intellect,
But you ye untold latencies will thrill to every page.

                                                    1865, 1881

WHEN LILACS LAST IN THE DOORYARD BLOOMED

1

When lilacs last in the dooryard bloomed,
And the great star early drooped in the western sky in the night,
I mourned, and yet shall mourn with ever-returning spring.

Ever-returning spring, trinity sure to me you bring,
Lilac blooming perennial and drooping star in the west,
And thought of him I love.

2

O powerful western fallen star!
O shades of night—O moody, tearful night!
O great star disappeared—O the black murk that hides the star!
O cruel hands that hold me powerless—O helpless soul of me!   10
O harsh surrounding cloud that will not free my soul.

3

In the dooryard fronting an old farm-house near the whitewashed palings,
Stands the lilac-bush tall-growing with heart-shaped leaves of rich green,
With many a pointed blossom rising delicate, with the perfume strong I love,
With every leaf a miracle—and from this bush in the dooryard,
With delicate-colored blossoms and heart-shaped leaves of rich green,
A sprig with its flower I break.

4

In the swamp in secluded recesses,
A shy and hidden bird is warbling a song.

Solitary the thrush,   20
The hermit withdrawn to himself, avoiding the settlements,
Sings by himself a song.

Song of the bleeding throat,
Death's outlet song of life (for well dear brother I know,
If thou wast not granted to sing thou would'st surely die).

5

Over the breast of the spring, the land, amid cities,
Amid lanes and through old woods, where lately the violets peeped from the
    ground, spotting the gray debris,
Amid the grass in the fields each side of the lanes, passing the endless grass,
Passing the yellow-speared wheat, every grain from its shroud in the dark-
    brown fields uprisen,
Passing the apple-tree blows of white and pink in the orchards,   30
Carrying a corpse to where it shall rest in the grave,
Night and day journeys a coffin.

6

Coffin that passes through lanes and streets,
Through day and night with the great cloud darkening the land,
With the pomp of the inlooped flags with the cities draped in black,
With the show of the States themselves as of crape-veiled women standing,
With processions long and winding and the flambeaus of the night,
With the countless torches lit, with the silent sea of faces and the unbared
    heads,
With the waiting depot, the arriving coffin, and the somber faces,
With dirges through the night, with the thousand voices rising strong and
    solemn,   40
With all the mournful voices of the dirges poured around the coffin,
The dim-lit churches and the shuddering organs—where amid these you journey,
With the tolling tolling bells' perpetual clang,
Here, coffin that slowly passes,
I give you my sprig of lilac.

7

Nor for you, for one alone,
Blossoms and branches green to coffins all I bring,
For fresh as the morning, thus would I chant a song for you O sane and
    sacred death.

All over bouquets of roses,
O death, I cover you over with roses and early lilies,   50
But mostly and now the lilac that blooms the first,
Copious I break, I break the sprigs from the bushes,
With loaded arms I come, pouring for you,
For you and the coffins all of you O death.)

8

O western orb sailing the heaven,
Now I know what you must have meant as a month since I walked,
As I walked in silence the transparent shadowy night,
As I saw you had something to tell as you bent to me night after night,
As you drooped from the sky low down as if to my side (while the other stars
    all looked on),

As we wandered together the solemn night (for something I know not what
    kept me from sleep),   60
As the night advanced, and I saw on the rim of the west how full you were
    of woe,
As I stood on the rising ground in the breeze in the cool transparent night,
As I watched where you passed and was lost in the netherward black of the
    night,
As my soul in its trouble dissatisfied sank, as where you sad orb,
Concluded, dropped in the night, and was gone.

9

Sing on there in the swamp,
O singer bashful and tender. I hear your notes, I hear your call,
I hear, I come presently, I understand you,
But a moment I linger, for the lustrous star has detained me,
The star my departing comrade holds and detains me.   70

10

O how shall I warble myself for the dead one there I loved?
And how shall I deck my song for the large sweet soul that has gone?
And what shall my perfume be for the grave of him I love?

Sea-winds blown from east and west,
Blown from the Eastern sea and blown from the Western sea, till there on
    the prairies meeting,
These and with these and the breath of my chant,
I'll perfume the grave of him I love.

11

O what shall I hang on the chamber walls?
And what shall the pictures be that I hang on the walls,
To adorn the burial-house of him I love?   80

Pictures of growing spring and farms and homes,
With the Fourth-month eve at sundown, and the gray smoke lucid and bright
With floods of the yellow gold of the gorgeous, indolent, sinking sun, burning
    expanding the air,
With the fresh sweet herbage under foot, and the pale green leaves of the
    trees prolific,
In the distance the flowing glaze, the breast of the river, with a wind-dapple
    here and there,
With ranging hills on the banks, with many a line against the sky, and shadows
And the city at hand with dwellings so dense, and stacks of chimneys,
And all the scenes of life and the workshops, and the workmen homeward
    returning.

12

Lo, body and soul—this land,
My own Manhattan with spires, and the sparkling and hurrying tides, and
    the ships,   9

The varied and ample land, the South and the North in the light, Ohio's shores
    and flashing Missouri,
And ever the far-spreading prairies covered with grass and corn.

Lo, the most excellent sun so calm and haughty,
The violet and purple morn with just-felt breezes,
The gentle soft-born measureless light,
The miracle spreading bathing all, the fulfilled noon,
The coming eve delicious, the welcome night and the stars,
Over my cities shining all, enveloping man and land.

13

Sing on, sing on you gray-brown bird,
Sing from the swamps, the recesses, pour your chant from the bushes,   100
Limitless out of the dusk, out of the cedars and pines.

Sing on dearest brother, warble your reedy song,
Loud human song, with voice of uttermost woe.

O liquid and free and tender!
O wild and loose to my soul—O wondrous singer!
You only I hear—yet the star holds me (but will soon depart),
Yet the lilac with mastering odor holds me.

14

Now while I sat in the day and looked forth,
In the close of the day with its light and the fields of spring, and the farmers
    preparing their crops,
In the large unconscious scenery of my land with its lakes and forests,   110
In the heavenly aerial beauty (after the perturbed winds and the storms),
Under the arching heavens of the afternoon swift passing, and the voices of
    children and women,
The many-moving sea-tides, and I saw the ships how they sailed,
And the summer approaching with richness, and the fields all busy with labor,
And the infinite separate houses, how they all went on, each with its meals
    and minutia of daily usages,
And the streets how their throbbings throbbed, and the cities pent—lo, then
    and there,
Falling upon them all and among them all, enveloping me with the rest,
Appeared the cloud, appeared the long black trail,
And I knew death, its thought, and the sacred knowledge of death.

Then with the knowledge of death as walking one side of me,   120
And the thought of death close-walking the other side of me,
And I in the middle as with companions, and as holding the hands of com-
    panions,
I fled forth to the hiding receiving night that talks not,
Down to the shores of the water, the path by the swamp in the dimness,
To the solemn shadowy cedars and ghostly pines so still.

And the singer so shy to the rest received me,
The gray-brown bird I know received us comrades three,
And he sang the carol of death, and a verse for him I love.

From deep secluded recesses,
From the fragrant cedars and the ghostly pines so still,
Came the carol of the bird.

And the charm of the carol rapt me,
As I held as if by their hands my comrades in the night,
And the voice of my spirit tallied the song of the bird.

Come lovely and soothing death,
Undulate round the world, serenely arriving, arriving,
In the day, in the night, to all, to each,
Sooner or later delicate death.

Praised be the fathomless universe,
For life and joy, and for objects and knowledge curious,
And for love, sweet love—but praise! praise! praise!
For the sure-enwinding arms of cool-enfolding death.

Dark mother always gliding near with soft feet,
Have none chanted for thee a chant of fullest welcome?
Then I chant it for thee, I glorify thee above all,
I bring thee a song that when thou must indeed come, come unfalteringl

Approach strong deliveress,
When it is so, when thou hast taken them I joyously sing the dead,
Lost in the loving floating ocean of thee,
Laved in the flood of thy bliss O death.

From me to thee glad serenades,
Dances for thee I propose saluting thee, adornments and feastings for the
And the sights of the open landscape and the high-spread sky are fitting,
And life and the fields, and the huge and thoughtful night.

The night in silence under many a star,
The ocean shore and the husky whispering wave whose voice I know,
And the soul turning to thee O vast and well-veiled death,
And the body gratefully nestling close to thee.

Over the tree-tops I float thee a song,
Over the rising and sinking waves, over the myriad fields and the prairie
*   wide,*
Over the dense-packed cities all and the teeming wharves and ways,
I float this carol with joy, with joy to thee O death.

15

To the tally of my soul,
Loud and strong kept up the gray-brown bird,
With pure deliberate notes spreading filling the night.

oud in the pines and cedars dim,
lear in the freshness moist and the swamp-perfume,
nd I with my comrades there in the night.

hile my sight that was bound in my eyes unclosed,
s to long panoramas of visions.   170

nd I saw askant the armies,
 saw as in noiseless dreams hundreds of battle-flags,
orne through the smoke of the battles and pierced with missiles I saw them,
nd carried hither and yon through the smoke, and torn and bloody,
nd at last but a few shreds left on the staffs (and all in silence),
nd the staffs all splintered and broken.

 saw battle-corpses, myriads of them,
nd the white skeletons of young men, I saw them,
 saw the debris and debris of all the slain soldiers of the war,
ut I saw they were not as was thought,   180
ley themselves were fully at rest, they suffered not,
ne living remained and suffered, the mother suffered,
nd the wife and the child and the musing comrade suffered,
nd the armies that remained suffered.

16

ssing the visions, passing the night,
ssing, unloosing the hold of my comrades' hands,
ssing the song of the hermit bird and the tallying song of my soul,
ctorious song, death's outlet song, yet varying ever-altering song,
 low and wailing, yet clear the notes, rising and falling, flooding the night,
dly sinking and fainting, as warning and warning, and yet again bursting
    with joy,   190
vering the earth and filling the spread of the heaven,
   that powerful psalm in the night I heard from recesses,
ssing, I leave thee lilac with heart-shaped leaves,
leave thee there in the dooryard, blooming, returning with spring.

ease from my song for thee,
om my gaze on thee in the west, fronting the west, communing with thee,
 comrade lustrous with silver face in the night.

t each to keep and all, retrievements out of the night,
e song, the wondrous chant of the gray-brown bird,
d the tallying chant, the echo aroused in my soul,   200
th the lustrous and drooping star with the countenance full of woe,
th the holders holding my hand nearing the call of the bird,
mrades mine and I in the midst, and their memory ever to keep, for the
    dead I loved so well,
r the sweetest, wisest soul of all my days and lands—and this for his dear
    sake,

Lilac and star and bird twined with the chant of my soul,
There in the fragrant pines and the cedars dusk and dim.

1865–66, 188

O CAPTAIN! MY CAPTAIN!

O Captain! my Captain! our fearful trip is done,
The ship has weathered every rack, the prize we sought is won,
The port is near, the bells I hear, the people all exulting,
While follow eyes the steady keel, the vessel grim and daring;
　　　　　But O heart! heart! heart!
　　　　　　O the bleeding drops of red,
　　　　　　　Where on the deck my Captain lies,
　　　　　　　Fallen cold and dead.

O Captain! my Captain! rise up and hear the bells;
Rise up—for you the flag is flung—for you the bugle trills,
For you bouquets and ribboned wreaths—for you the shores a-crowding,
For you they call, the swaying mass, their eager faces turning;
　　　　　Here Captain! dear father!
　　　　　　The arm beneath your head!
　　　　　　It is some dream that on the deck,
　　　　　　　You've fallen cold and dead.

My Captain does not answer, his lips are pale and still,
My father does not feel my arm, he has no pulse nor will,
The ship is anchored safe and sound, its voyage closed and done,
From fearful trip the victor ship comes in with object won:
　　　　　Exult O shores, and ring O bells!
　　　　　　But I with mournful tread,
　　　　　　Walk the deck my Captain lies,
　　　　　　Fallen cold and dead.

1865, 18?

BEAT! BEAT! DRUMS!

Beat! beat! drums!—blow! bugles! blow!
Through the windows—through doors—burst like a ruthless force,
Into the solemn church, and scatter the congregation,
Into the school where the scholar is studying;
Leave not the bridegroom quiet—no happiness must he have now with his
　　bride,
Nor the peaceful farmer any peace, ploughing his field or gathering his grain,
So fierce you whirr and pound you drums—so shrill you bugles blow.

Beat! beat! drums!—blow! bugles! blow!
Over the traffic of cities—over the rumble of wheels in the streets;
Are beds prepared for sleepers at night in the houses? no sleepers must sleep
　　in those beds,

No bargainers' bargains by day—no brokers or speculators—would they con-
        tinue?
Would the talkers be talking? would the singer attempt to sing?
Would the lawyer rise in the court to state his case before the judge?
Then rattle quicker, heavier drums—you bugles wilder blow.

Beat! beat! drums!—blow! bugles! blow!
Make no parley—stop for no expostulation,
Mind not the timid—mind not the weeper or prayer,
Mind not the old man beseeching the young man,
Let not the child's voice be heard, nor the mother's entreaties,
Make even the trestles to shake the dead where they lie awaiting the hearses, [20]
So strong you thump O terrible drums—so loud you bugles blow.

                                                      1867, 1867

RECONCILIATION

Word over all, beautiful as the sky,
Beautiful that war and all its deeds of carnage must in time be utterly lost,
That the hands of the sisters Death and Night incessantly softly wash again,
        and ever again, this soil'd world;
For my enemy is dead, a man divine as myself is dead,
I look where he lies white-faced and still in the coffin—I draw near,
Bend down and touch lightly with my lips the white face in the coffin.

                                                      1865-66, 1881

ONE'S-SELF I SING

One's-self I sing, a simple separate person,
Yet utter the word Democratic, the word En-Masse.

Of physiology from top to toe I sing,
Not physiognomy alone nor brain alone is worthy for the Muse, I say the
        Form complete is worthier far,
The Female equally with the Male I sing.

Of Life immense in passion, pulse, and power,
Cheerful, for freest action form'd under the laws divine,
The Modern Man I sing.

                                                      1867, 1871

WHISPERS OF HEAVENLY DEATH

Whispers of heavenly death murmured I hear,
Labial gossip of night, sibilant chorals,
Footsteps gently ascending, mystical breezes wafted soft and low,
Ripples of unseen rivers, tides of a current flowing, forever flowing
(Or is it the plashing of tears? the measureless waters of human tears?).

I see, just see skyward, great cloud-masses,
Mournfully slowly they roll, silently swelling and mixing,
With at times a half-dimmed saddened far-off star,
Appearing and disappearing.

(Some parturition rather, some solemn immortal birth;   1(
On the frontiers to eyes impenetrable,
Some soul is passing over.)

                                                                    1868, 188

DAREST THOU NOW O SOUL

Darest thou now O soul,
Walk out with me toward the unknown region,
Where neither ground is for the feet nor any path to follow?

No map there, nor guide,
Nor voice sounding, nor touch of human hand,
Nor face with blooming flesh, nor lips, nor eyes, are in that land.

I know it not O soul,
Nor dost thou, all is a blank before us,
All waits undream'd of in that region, that inaccessible land.

Till when the ties loosen,   1(
All but the ties eternal, Time and Space,
Nor darkness, gravitation, sense, nor any bounds bounding us.

Then we burst forth, we float,
In Time and Space O soul, prepared for them,
Equal, equipt at last, (O joy! O fruit of all!) them to fulfil O soul.

                                                                    1868, 188

A NOISELESS PATIENT SPIDER

A noiseless patient spider,
I mark'd where on a little promontory it stood isolated,
Mark'd how to explore the vacant vast surrounding,
It launch'd forth filament, filament, filament, out of itself,
Ever unreeling them, ever tirelessly speeding them.

And you O my soul where you stand,
Surrounded, detached, in measureless oceans of space,
Ceaselessly musing, venturing, throwing, seeking the spheres to connect them
Till the bridge you will need be form'd, till the ductile anchor hold,
Till the gossamer thread you fling catch somewhere, O my soul.   1
(1862-63)   1871, 188

ETHIOPIA SALUTING THE COLORS

Who are you dusky woman, so ancient hardly human,
With your woolly-white and turban'd head, and bare bony feet?
Why rising by the roadside here, do you the colors greet?

('Tis while our army lines Carolina's sands and pines,
Forth from thy hovel door thou Ethiopia com'st to me,
As under doughty Sherman I march toward the sea.)

Me master years a hundred since from my parents sunder'd
A little child, they caught me as the savage beast is caught,
Then hither me across the sea the cruel slaver brought.

No further does she say, but lingering all the day,   1 ʳ
Her high-borne turban'd head she wags, and rolls her darkling eye,
And courtesies to the regiments, the guidons moving by.

What is it fateful woman, so blear, hardly human?
Why wag your head with turban bound, yellow, red and green?
Are the things so strange and marvelous you see or have seen?
                                                        1871, 1871

THE BASE OF ALL METAPHYSICS

And now gentlemen,
A word I give to remain in your memories and minds,
As base and finalè too for all metaphysics.

(So to the students the old professor,
At the close of his crowded course.)

Having studied the new and antique, the Greek and Germanic systems,
Kant having studied and stated, Fichte and Schelling and Hegel,
Stated the lore of Plato, and Socrates greater than Plato,
And greater than Socrates sought and stated, Christ divine having studied long,
I see reminiscent to-day those Greek and Germanic systems,   10
See the philosophies all, Christian churches and tenets see,
Yet underneath Socrates clearly see, and underneath Christ the divine I see,
The dear love of man for his comrade, the attraction of friend to friend,
Of the well-married husband and wife, of children and parents,
Of city for city and land for land.
                                                        1871, 1871

TO A LOCOMOTIVE IN WINTER

Thee for my recitative,
Thee in the driving storm even as now, the snow, the winter-day declining,
Thee in thy panoply, thy measur'd dual throbbing and thy beat convulsive,
Thy black cylindric body, golden brass and silvery steel,

Thy ponderous side-bars, parallel and connecting rods, gyrating, shuttling at
    thy sides,
Thy metrical, now swelling pant and roar, now tapering in the distance,
Thy great protruding head-light fix'd in front,
Thy long, pale, floating vapor-pennants, tinged with delicate purple,
The dense and murky clouds out-belching from thy smokestack,
Thy knitted frame, thy springs and valves, the tremulous twinkle of thy
    wheels,   10
Thy train of cars behind, obedient, merrily following,
Through gale or calm, now swift, now slack, yet steadily careering;
Type of the modern—emblem of motion and power—pulse of the continent,
For once come serve the Muse and merge in verse, even as here I see thee,
With storm and buffeting gusts of wind and falling snow,
By day thy warning ringing bell to sound its notes,
By night thy silent signal lamps to swing.

Fierce-throated beauty!
Roll through my chant with all thy lawless music, thy swinging lamps at night,
Thy madly-whistled laughter, echoing, rumbling like an earthquake, rousing
    all,   20
Law of thyself complete, thine own track firmly holding,
(No sweetness debonair of tearful harp or glib piano thine,)
Thy trills of shrieks by rocks and hills return'd,
Launch'd o'er the prairies wide, across the lakes,
To the free skies unpent and glad and strong.

1876, 1881

SPIRIT THAT FORM'D THIS SCENE

WRITTEN IN PLATTE CANYON, COLORADO

Spirit that form'd this scene,
These tumbled rock-piles grim and red,
These reckless heaven-ambitious peaks,
These gorges, turbulent-clear streams, this naked freshness,
These formless wild arrays, for reasons of their own.
I know thee, savage spirit—we have communed together,
Mine too such wild arrays, for reasons of their own;
Was't charged against my chants they had forgotten art?
To fuse within themselves its rules precise and delicatesse?
The lyrist's measur'd beat, the wrought-out temple's grace—column
    and polish'd arch forgot?   10
But thou that revelest here—spirit that form'd this scene,
They have remember'd thee.

1881, 1881

GOOD-BYE MY FANCY!

Good-bye my Fancy!
Farewell dear mate, dear love!

'm going away, I know not where,
)r to what fortune, or whether I may ever see you again,
o Good-bye my Fancy.

Jow for my last—let me look back a moment;
:he slower fainter ticking of the clock is in me,
:xit, nightfall, and soon the heart-thud stopping.
,ong have we lived, joy'd, caress'd together;
)elightful!—now separation—Good-bye my Fancy.   10

Vet let me not be too hasty,
,ong indeed have we lived, slept, filter'd, become really blended into one;
:hen if we die we die together, (yes, we'll remain one,)
f we go anywhere we'll go together to meet what happens,
Jay-be we'll be better off and blither, and learn something,
Jay-be it is yourself now really ushering me to the true songs (who knows?)
Jay-be it is you the mortal knob really undoing, turning—so now finally,
;ood-bye—and hail! my Fancy.

                                        1891, 1891–92

From *DEMOCRATIC VISTAS*

[THE MASS AND THE INDIVIDUAL]

* * * Sole among nationalities, these
tates have assumed the task to put
1 forms of lasting power and prac-
icality, on areas of amplitude rival-
ing the operations of the physical
osmos, the moral political specula-
ions of ages, long, long deferred, the
lemocratic republican principle, and
he theory of development and per-
ection by voluntary standards, and
elf-reliance. Who else, indeed, ex-
ept the United States, in history, so
ar, have accepted in unwitting faith,
nd, as we now see, stand, act upon,
nd go security for, these things? * * *
For my part, I would alarm and
:aution even the political and business reader, and to the utmost ex-
ent, against the prevailing delusion
hat the establishment of free political

institutions, and plentiful intellectual
smartness, with general good order,
physical plenty, industry, etc. (desirable and precious advantages as they
all are), do, of themselves, determine
and yield to our experiment of democracy the fruitage of success. With
such advantages at present fully, or
almost fully, possessed—the Union
just issued, victorious, from the struggle with the only foes it need ever
fear (namely, those within itself, the
interior ones), and with unprecedented
materialistic advancement—society, in
these States, is cankered, crude, superstitious and rotten. Political, or law-
made society is, and private, or voluntary society, is also. In any vigor,
the element of the moral conscience,
the most important, the verteber to
State or man, seems to me either entirely lacking, or seriously enfeebled
or ungrown.

I say we had best look our times
and lands searchingly in the face, like

a physician diagnosing some deep disease. Never was there, perhaps, more hollowness at heart than at present, and here in the United States. Genuine belief seems to have left us. The underlying principles of the States are not honestly believed in (for all this hectic glow, and these melodramatic screamings). nor is humanity itself believed in. What penetrating eye does not everywhere see through the mask? The spectacle is appalling. We live in an atmosphere of hypocrisy throughout. The men believe not in the women, nor the women in the men. A scornful superciliousness rules in literature. The aim of all the *littérateurs* is to find something to make fun of. A lot of churches, sects, etc., the most dismal phantasms I know, usurp the name of religion. Conversation is a mass of badinage. From deceit in the spirit, the mother of all false deeds, the offspring is already incalculable. An acute and candid person, in the revenue department in Washington, who is led by the course of his employment to regularly visit the cities, north, south, and west, to investigate frauds, has talked much with me about his discoveries. The depravity of the business classes of our country is not less than has been supposed, but infinitely greater. The official services of America, national, state, and municipal, in all their branches and departments, except the judiciary, are saturated in corruption, bribery, falsehood, mal-administration; and the judiciary is tainted. The great cities reek with respectable as much as non-respectable robbery and scoundrelism. In fashionable life, flippancy, tepid amours, weak infidelism, small aims, or no aims at all,

only to kill time. In business (th all-devouring modern word, business the one sole object is, by any mean pecuniary gain. The magician's se pent in the fable ate up all the oth serpents; and money-making is o magician's serpent, remaining to-d sole master of the field. The be class we show, is but a mob of fas ionably dressed speculators and v garians. True, indeed, behind th fantastic farce, enacted on the visib stage of society, solid things and st pendous labors are to be discovere existing crudely and going on in th background, to advance and tell then selves in time. Yet the truths a none the less terrible. I say that ou New World democracy, however gre a success in uplifting the masses ou of their sloughs, in materialistic deve opment, products, and in a certa highly-deceptive superficial popular in tellectuality, is, so far, an almo complete failure in its social aspect and in really grand religious, mora literary, and esthetic results. In va do we march with unprecedente strides to empire so colossal, outvyin the antique, beyond Alexander's, b yond the proudest sway of Rome. I vain have we annexed Texas, Cal fornia, Alaska, and reach north fo Canada and south for Cuba. It is a if we were somehow being endowe with a vast and more and more thor oughly-appointed body, and then le with little or no soul. * * *

And now, in the full conception o these facts and points, and all tha they infer, pro and con—with yet un shaken faith in the elements of th American masses, the composites, o both sexes, and even considered a individuals—and ever recognizing i

em the broadest bases of the best
terary and esthetic appreciation—I
roceed with my speculations, Vistas.

First, let us see what we can make
ut of a brief, general, sentimental
onsideration of political democracy,
nd whence it has arisen, with re-
ard to some of its current features,
s an aggregate, and as the basic
ructure of our future literature and
uthorship. We shall, it is true,
uickly and continually find the origin-
lea of the singleness of man, individ-
alism, asserting itself, and cropping
orth, even from the opposite ideas.
ut the mass, or lump character, for
nperative reasons, is to be ever care-
ılly weighed, borne in mind, and pro-
ided for. Only from it, and from
s proper regulation and potency,
omes the other, comes the chance of
dividualism. The two are contradic-
ry, but our task is to reconcile
em.*

The political history of the past
ay be summed up as having grown
ıt of what underlies the words, or-
er, safety, caste, and especially out
˙ the need of some prompt deciding
ıthority, and of cohesion at all cost.
eaping time, we come to the period
ithin the memory of people now liv-
 g, when, as from some lair where
ey had slumbered long, accumulat-

* The question hinted here is one which
ne only can answer. Must not the virtue
modern Individualism, continually en-
rging, usurping all, seriously affect, per-
ps keep down entirely, in America, the like
the ancient virtue of Patriotism, the fervid
d absorbing love of general country? I
ve no doubt myself that the two will merge,
d will mutually profit and brace each other,
d that from them a greater product, a
ird, will arise. But I feel that at present
ey and their oppositions form a serious
oblem and paradox in the United States.
Author's note.]

ing wrath, sprang up and are yet
active (1790, and on even to the present, 1870), those noisy eructations, de-
structive iconoclasms, a fierce sense of
wrongs, amid which moves the form,
well known in modern history, in the
old world, stained with much blood,
and marked by savage reactionary
clamors and demands. These bear,
mostly, as on one inclosing point of
need.

For after the rest is said—after the
many time-honored and really true
things for subordination, experience,
rights of property, etc., have been listened to and acquiesced in—after the
valuable and well-settled statement of
our duties and relations in society is
thoroughly conned over and exhausted
—it remains to bring forward and
modify everything else with the idea
of that Something a man is (last
precious consolation of the drudging
poor), standing apart from all else,
divine in his own right, and a woman
in hers, sole and untouchable by any
canons of authority, or any rule derived from precedent, state-safety, the
acts of legislatures, or even from
what is called religion, modesty, or
art. The radiation of this truth is
the key of the most significant doings
of our immediately preceding three
centuries, and has been the political
genesis and life of America. Advancing visibly, it still more advances invisibly. Underneath the fluctuations
of the expressions of society, as well
as the movements of the politics of
the leading nations of the world, we
see steadily pressing ahead and
strengthening itself, even in the midst
of immense tendencies toward aggregation, this image of completeness in
separation, of individual personal dig-

nity, of a single person, either male or female, characterized in the main, not from extrinsic acquirements or position, but in the pride of himself or herself alone; and, as an eventual conclusion and summing up (or else the entire scheme of things is aimless, a cheat, a crash), the simple idea that the last, best dependence is to be upon humanity itself, and its own inherent, normal, full-grown qualities without any superstitious support whatever. This idea of perfect individualism it is indeed that deepest tinges and gives character to the idea of the aggregate. For it is mainly or altogether to serve independent separatism that we favor a strong generalization, consolidation. As it is to give the best vitality and freedom to the rights of the States (every bit as important as the right of nationality, the union), that we insist on the identity of the Union at all hazards.

The purpose of democracy—supplanting old belief in the necessary absoluteness of established dynastic rulership, temporal, ecclesiastical, and scholastic, as furnishing the only security against chaos, crime, and ignorance—is, through many transmigrations and amid endless ridicules, arguments, and ostensible failures, to illustrate, at all hazards, this doctrine or theory that man, properly trained in sanest, highest freedom, may and must become a law, and series of laws, unto himself, surrounding and providing for, not only his own personal control, but all his relations to other individuals, and to the State; and that, while other theories, as in the past histories of nations, have proved wise enough, and indispensable perhaps for their conditions, *this*, as matters now

stand in our civilized world, is th only scheme worth working from, a warranting results like those of Na ture's laws, reliable, when once estab lished, to carry on themselves.

The argument of the matter is ex tensive, and, we admit, by no mean all on one side. What we shall offe will be far, far from sufficient. Bu while leaving unsaid much that shoul properly even prepare the way fo the treatment of this many-sided ques tion of political liberty, equality, o republicanism—leaving the whole his tory and consideration of the feuda plan and its products, embodying hu manity, its politics and civilizatior through the retrospect of past tim (which plan and products, indeec make up all of the past, and a larg part of the present)—leaving unan swered, at least by any specific an local answer, many a well-wrough argument and instance, and many conscientious declamatory cry an warning—as, very lately, from an emi nent and venerable person abroad *— things, problems, full of doubt, dreac suspense (not new to me, but old oc cupiers of many an anxious hour i city's din, or night's silence), we sti may give a page or so, whose drif

* *Shooting Niagara.*—I was at first rouse to much anger and abuse by this essay fro Mr. Carlyle, so insulting to the theory c America—but happening to think afterwarc how I had more than once been in the lik mood, during which his essay was evidentl cast, and seen persons and things in the san light (indeed, some might say there are sigr of the same feeling in these Vistas)—I hav since read it again, not only as a study, e: pressing as it does certain judgments fro the highest feudal point of view, but hav read it with respect as coming from an ea nest soul, and as contributing certain shar cutting metallic grains, which, if not gold c silver, may be good, hard, honest iro [Author's note]

is opportune. Time alone can finally answer these things. But as a substitute in passing, let us, even if fragmentarily, throw forth a short direct or indirect suggestion of the premises of that other plan, in the new spirit, under the new forms, started here in our America.

As to the political section of Democracy, which introduces and breaks ground for further and vaster sections, few probably are the minds, even in these republican States, that fully comprehend the aptness of that phrase, "THE GOVERNMENT OF THE PEOPLE, BY THE PEOPLE, FOR THE PEOPLE," which we inherit from the lips of Abraham Lincoln; a formula whose verbal shape is homely wit, but whose scope includes both the totality and all minutiæ of the lesson.

The People! Like our huge earth itself, which, to ordinary scansion, is full of vulgar contradictions and offence, man, viewed in the lump, displeases, and is a constant puzzle and affront to the merely educated classes. The rare, cosmical, artist-mind, lit with the Infinite, alone confronts his manifold and oceanic qualities—but taste, intelligence and culture (so-called), have been against the masses, and remain so. There is plenty of glamour about the most damnable crimes and hoggish meannesses, special and general, of the feudal and dynastic world over there, with its *personnel* of lords and queens and courts, so well-dressed and so handsome. But the People are ungrammatical, untidy, and their sins gaunt and ill-bred.

Literature, strictly considered, has never recognized the People, and, whatever may be said, does not to-day. Speaking generally, the tendencies of literature, as hitherto pursued, have been to make mostly critical and querulous men. It seems as if, so far, there were some natural repugnance between a literary and professional life, and the rude rank spirit of the democracies. There is, in later literature, a treatment of benevolence, a charity business, rife enough it is true; but I know nothing more rare, even in this country, than a fit scientific estimate and reverent appreciation of the People—of their measureless wealth of latent power and capacity, their vast, artistic contrasts of lights and shades—with, in America, their entire reliability in emergencies, and a certain breadth of historic grandeur, of peace or war, far surpassing all the vaunted samples of book-heroes, or any *haut ton* coteries, in all the records of the world.

The movements of the late secession war, and their results, to any sense that studies well and comprehends them, show that popular democracy, whatever its faults and dangers, practically justifies itself beyond the proudest claims and wildest hopes of its enthusiasts. Probably no future age can know, but I well know, how the gist of this fiercest and most resolute of the world's war-like contentions resided exclusively in the unnamed, unknown rank and file; and how the brunt of its labor of death was, to all essential purposes, volunteered. The People, of their own choice, fighting, dying for their own idea, insolently attacked by the secession-slave-power, and its very existence imperilled. Descending to detail, entering any of the armies, and mixing with the private soldiers, we see

and have seen august spectacles. We
have seen the alacrity with which the
American-born populace, the peace-
ablest and most good-natured race in
the world, and the most personally
independent and intelligent, and the
least fitted to submit to the irksome-
ness and exasperation of regimental
discipline, sprang, at the first tap of
the drum, to arms—not for gain, nor
even glory, nor to repel invasion—but
for an emblem, a mere abstraction—
for the life, *the safety of the flag*.
We have seen the unequalled docility
and obedience of these soldiers. We
have seen them tried long and long
by hopelessness, mismanagement, and
by defeat; have seen the incredible
slaughter toward or through which the
armies (as at first Fredericksburg, and
afterward at the Wilderness), still unhesitatingly obey'd orders to advance.
We have seen them in trench, or
crouching behind breastwork, or
tramping in deep mud, or amid pouring rain or thick-falling snow, or under forced marches in hottest summer
(as on the road to get to Gettysburg)
—vast suffocating swarms, divisions,
corps, with every single man so grimed
and black with sweat and dust, his
own mother would not have known
him—his clothes all dirty, stained and
torn, with sour, accumulated sweat for
perfume—many a comrade, perhaps a
brother, sun-struck, staggering out,
dying, by the roadside, of exhaustion
—yet the great bulk bearing steadily
on, cheery enough, hollow bellied from
hunger, but sinewy with unconquerable resolution.

We have seen this race proved by
wholesale, by drearier, yet more fearful tests—the wound, the amputation,
the shattered face or limb, the slow

hot fever, long impatient anchorag
in bed, and all the forms of maiming
operation, and disease. Alas! America
have we seen, though only in he
early youth, already to hospita
brought. There have we watche
these soldiers, many of them onl
boys in years—marked their decorum
their religious nature and fortitude
and their sweet affection. Wholesale
truly. For at the front, and throug
the camps, in countless tents, stoo
the regimental, brigade, and divisio
hospitals; while everywhere amid th
land, in or near cities, rose cluster
of huge, white-washed, crowded, one
story wooden barracks; and ther
ruled agony with bitter scourge, ye
seldom brought a cry; and ther
stalked death by day and night alon
the narrow aisles between the row
of cots, or by the blankets on th
ground, and touched lightly many
poor sufferer, often with blessed, wel
come touch.

I know not whether I shall be un
derstood, but I realize that it is finall
from what I learned personally mi
ing in such scenes that I am no
penning these pages. One night i
the gloomiest period of the war, i
the Patent office hospital in Wash
ington city, as I stood by the be
side of a Pennsylvania soldier, wh
lay, conscious of quick approachin
death, yet perfectly calm, and wit
noble, spiritual manner, the vetera
surgeon, turning aside, said to m
that though he had witnessed man
many deaths of soldiers, and had bee
a worker at Bull Run, Antietan
Fredericksburg, etc., he had not see
yet the first case of man or boy tha
met the approach of dissolution wit
cowardly qualms or terror. My ow

observation fully bears out the remark.

What have we here, if not, towering above all talk and argument, the plentifully-supplied, last-needed proof of democracy, in its personalities? Curiously enough, too, the proof on his point comes, I should say, every bit as much from the south, as from the north. Although I have spoken only of the latter, yet I deliberately include all. Grand, common stock! To me the accomplished and convincing growth, prophetic of the future; proof undeniable to sharpest sense, of perfect beauty, tenderness and pluck, that never feudal lord, nor Greek, nor Roman breed, yet rivalled. Let no tongue ever speak in disparagement of the American races, north or south, to one who has been through the war in the great army hospitals.

Meantime, general humanity (for to that we return, as, for our purposes, what it really is, to bear in mind), has always, in every department, been full of perverse maleficence, and is so yet. In downcast hours the soul thinks it always will be—but soon recovers from such sickly moods. I myself see clearly enough the crude, defective streaks in all the strata of the common people; the specimens and vast collections of the ignorant, the credulous, the unfit and uncouth, the incapable, and the very low and poor. The eminent person just mentioned sneeringly asks whether we expect to elevate and improve a nation's politics by absorbing such morbid collections and qualities therein. The point is a formidable one, and there will doubtless always be numbers of solid and reflective citizens who will never get over it. Our answer is general, and is involved in the scope and letter of this essay. We believe the ulterior object of political and all other government (having, of course, provided for the police, the safety of life, property, and for the basic statute and common law, and their administration, always first in order), to be among the rest, not merely to rule, to repress disorder, etc., but to develop, to open up to cultivation, to encourage the possibilities of all beneficent and manly outcroppage, and of that aspiration for independence, and the pride and self-respect latent in all characters. (Or, if there be exceptions, we cannot, fixing our eyes on them alone, make theirs the rule for all.)

I say the mission of government, henceforth, in civilized lands, is not repression alone, and not authority alone, not even of law, nor by that favorite standard of the eminent writer, the rule of the best men, the born heroes and captains of the race (as if such ever, or one time out of a hundred, get into the big places, elective or dynastic)—but higher than the highest arbitrary rule, to train communities through all their grades, beginning with individuals and ending there again, to rule themselves. What Christ appeared for in the moral-spiritual field for human-kind, namely, that in respect to the absolute soul, there is in the possession of such by each single individual, something so transcendent, so incapable of gradations (like life), that, to that extent, it places all beings on a common level, utterly regardless of the distinctions of intellect, virtue, station, or any height or lowliness whatever—is tallied in like manner, in this other field, by democracy's rule that men, the nation, as a common aggregate of living identities, affording in each a separate and complete subject for freedom, worldly thrift and happiness, and for a fair chance for growth, and for protection in citizenship, etc., must, to the political extent of the suffrage or vote, if no further, be placed, in each and in the whole, on one broad, primary, universal, common platform.

The purpose is not altogether direct; perhaps it is more indirect. For it is not that democracy is of exhaustive account in itself. Perhaps, indeed, it is (like Nature), of no account in itself. It is that, as we see, it is the best, perhaps only, fit and full means, formulater, general caller-forth, trainer, for the million, not for grand material personalities only, but for immortal souls. To be a voter with the rest is not so much; and this, like every institute, will have its imperfections. But to become an enfranchised man, and now, impediments removed, to stand and start without humiliation, and equal with the rest; to commence, or have the road cleared to commence, the grand experiment of development, whose end (perhaps requiring several generations), may be the forming of a full-grown man or woman —that *is* something. To ballast the State is also secured, and in our times is to be secured, in no other way. * * *

1871

CIVIL CONFLICT

I. ABRAHAM LINCOLN
(1809–1865)

FAREWELL REMARKS AT SPRINGFIELD

[FEBRUARY 11, 1861]

MY FRIENDS: No one, not in my situation, can appreciate my feeling of sadness at this parting. To this place, and the kindness of these people, I owe everything. Here I have lived a quarter of a century, and have passed from a young to an old man. Here my children have been born, and one is buried. I now leave, not knowing when or whether ever I may return, with a task before me greater than that which rested upon Washington. Without the assistance of that Divine Being who ever attended him, I cannot succeed. With that assistance, I cannot fail. Trusting in Him, who can go with me, and remain with you, and be everywhere for good, let us confidently hope that all will yet be well. To His care commending you, as I hope in your prayers you will commend me, I bid you an affectionate farewell.

REPLY TO GREELEY

Executive Mansion, Washington,
August 22, 1862.

HON. HORACE GREELEY.

DEAR SIR: I have just read yours of the 19th, addressed to myself through the New York *Tribune*. If there be in it any statements or assumptions of fact which I may know to be erroneous, I do not, now and here, controvert them. If there be in it any inferences which I may believe to be falsely drawn, I do not, now and here, argue against them. If there be perceptible in it an impatient and dictatorial tone, I waive it in deference to an old friend, whose heart I have always supposed to be right.

As to the policy I "seem to be pursuing," as you say, I have not meant to leave anyone in doubt.

I would save the Union. I would save it the shortest way under the Constitution. The sooner the national authority can be restored, the nearer the Union will be "the Union as it was." If there be those who would not save the Union unless they could at the same time save slavery, I do not agree with them. If there be those who would not save the Union unless they could at the same time destroy slavery, I do not agree with them. My paramount object in this struggle is to save the Union, and is not either to save or to destroy slavery. If I could save the Union without freeing any slave, I would do it; and if I could save it by freeing all the slaves, I would do it; and if I could save it by freeing some and leaving others alone, I would also do that. What I do about slavery and the colored race, I do because I believe it helps to save the Union; and what I

113

forbear, I forbear because I do not believe it would help to save the Union. I shall do less whenever I shall believe what I am doing hurts the cause, and I shall do more whenever I shall believe doing more will help the cause. I shall try to correct errors when shown to be errors, and I shall adopt new views so fast as they shall appear to be true views.

I have here stated my purpose according to my view of official duty, and I intend no modification of my oft-expressed personal wish that all men, everywhere, could be free.

Yours,

A. LINCOLN.

MEDITATION ON THE DIVINE WILL

[SEPTEMBER 30, 1862]

The will of God prevails. In great contests each party claims to act in accordance with the will of God. Both may be, and one must be wrong. God cannot be for and against the same thing at the same time. In the present civil war it is quite possible that God's purpose is something different from the purpose of either party; and yet the human instrumentalities, working just as they do, are of the best adaptation to effect His purpose. I am almost ready to say that this is probably true; that God wills this contest, and wills that it shall not end yet. By His mere great power on the minds of the now contestants, he could have either saved or destroyed the Union without a human contest. Yet the contest began. And, having begun, He could give the final victory to either side any day. Yet the contest proceeds.

ADDRESS AT GETTYSBURG

[NOVEMBER 19, 1863]

Four score and seven years ago our fathers brought forth on this continent a new nation, conceived in liberty, and dedicated to the proposition that all men are created equal.

Now we are engaged in a great civil war; testing whether that nation, or any nation so conceived and so dedicated, can long endure. We are met on a great battlefield of that war. We have come to dedicate a portion of that field as a final resting-place for those who here gave their lives that that nation might live. It is altogether fitting and proper that we should do this.

But, in a larger sense, we cannot dedicate—we cannot consecrate—we cannot hallow—this ground. The brave men, living and dead, who struggled here have consecrated it, far above our poor power to add or detract. The world will little note, nor long remember, what we say here, but it can never forget what they did here. It is for us the living, rather, to be dedicated here to the unfinished work which they who fought here have thus far so nobly advanced. It is rather for us to be here dedicated to the great task remaining before us—that from these honored dead we take increased devotion to that cause for which they gave the last full measure of devotion; that we here highly resolve that these dead shall not have died in vain; that this nation, under God, shall have a new birth of freedom; and that government of the people, by the people, for the people, shall not perish from the earth.

SECOND INAUGURAL ADDRESS

[MARCH 4, 1865]

FELLOW COUNTRYMEN: At this second appearing to take the oath of the presidential office, there is less occasion for an extended address than there was at the first. Then a statement, somewhat in detail of a course to be pursued, seemed fitting and proper. Now, at the expiration of four years, during which public declarations have been constantly called forth on every point and phase of the great contest which still absorbs the attention and engrosses the energies of the nation, little that is new could be presented. The progress of our arms, upon which all else chiefly depends, is as well known to the public as to myself; and it is, I trust, reasonably satisfactory and encouraging to all. With high hope for the future, no prediction in regard to it is ventured.

On the occasion corresponding to this four years ago, all thoughts were anxiously directed to an impending civil war. All dreaded it—all sought to avert it. While the inaugural address was being delivered from this place, devoted altogether to saving the Union without war, insurgent agents were in the city seeking to destroy it without war—seeking to dissolve the Union, and divide effects, by negotiation. Both parties deprecated war; but one of them would make war rather than let the nation survive; and the other would accept war rather than let it perish. And the war came.

One-eighth of the whole population were colored slaves, not distributed generally over the Union, but localized in the southern part of it. These slaves constituted a peculiar and powerful interest. All knew that this interest was, somehow, the cause of the war. To strengthen, perpetuate, and extend this interest was the object for which the insurgents would rend the Union, even by war; while the government claimed no right to do more than to restrict the territorial enlargement of it.

Neither party expected for the war the magnitude or the duration which it has already attained. Neither anticipated that the cause of the conflict might cease with, or even before, the conflict itself should cease. Each looked for an easier triumph, and a result less fundamental and astounding. Both read the same Bible, and pray to the same God; and each invokes His aid against the other. It may seem strange that any men should dare to ask a just God's assistance in wringing their bread from the sweat of other men's faces; but let us judge not, that we be not judged. The prayers of both could not be answered—that of neither has been answered fully.

The Almighty has his own purposes. "Woe unto the world because of offenses! for it must needs be that offenses come; but woe to that man by whom the offense cometh." If we shall suppose that American slavery is one of those offenses which, in the providence of God, must needs come, but which, having continued through His appointed time, He now wills to remove, and that He gives to both North and South this terrible war, as the woe due to those by whom the offense came, shall we discern therein any departure from those divine attributes which the believers in a living God always ascribe to Him? Fondly do we hope—fervently do we pray—that this mighty scourge of war may speedily pass away. Yet, if God wills that it continue until all the wealth piled by the bondman's two hundred and fifty years of unrequited toil shall be sunk, and until every drop of blood drawn with the lash shall be paid by another drawn with the sword, as was said three thousand years ago, so still it must be said, "The judgments of the Lord are true and righteous altogether."

With malice toward none; with charity for all; with firmness in the right, as God gives us to see the right, let us strive on to finish the work we are in; to bind up the nation's wounds; to care for him who shall have borne the battle, and for his widow, and his orphan—to do all which may achieve and cherish a just and lasting peace among ourselves, and with all nations.

LETTERS

To John D. Johnston

[JANUARY 2, 1851]

DEAR JOHNSTON: Your request for eighty dollars I do not think it best to comply with now. At the various times when I have helped you a little you have said to me, "We can get along very well now"; but in a very short time I find you in the same difficulty again. Now this can only happen by some defect in your conduct. What that defect is, I think I know. You are not lazy, and still you are an idler. I doubt whether, since I saw you, you have done a good whole day's work in any one day.

You do not very much dislike to work, and still you do not work much, merely because it does not seem to you that you could get much for it. This habit of uselessly wasting time is the whole difficulty; it is vastly important to you, and still more so to your children, that you should break the habit. It is more important to them, because they have longer to live, and can keep out of an idle habit before they are in it, easier than they can get out after they are in.

You are now in need of some money; and what I propose is, that you shall go to work, "tooth and nail," for somebody who will give you money for it. Let father and your boys take charge of your things at home, prepare for a crop, and make the crop, and you go to work for the best money wages, or in discharge of any debt you owe, that you can get; and to secure you a fair reward for your labor, I now promise you, that for every dollar that you will, between this and the first of May, get for your own labor, either in money or as your own indebtedness, I will then give you one other dollar. By this, if you hire yourself at ten dollars a month, from me you will get ten more, making twenty dollars a month for your work. In this I do not mean you shall go off to St. Louis, or the lead mines, or the gold mines in California, but I mean for you to go at it for the best wages you can get close to home in Coles County. Now, if you will do this, you will be soon out of debt, and, what is better, you will have a habit that will keep you from getting into debt again. But if I should now clear you out of debt, next year you would be just as deep in as ever. You say you would almost give your place in heaven for seventy or eighty dollars. Then you value your place in heaven very cheap, for I am sure you can, with the offer I make, get the seventy or eighty dollars for four or five months' work. You say if I will furnish you the money you will deed me the land, and, if you don't pay the money back, you will deliver possession. Nonsense! If you can't now live with the land, how will you then live without it? You have always been kind to me, and I do not mean to be unkind to you. On the contrary, if you will but follow my advice, you will find it worth more than eighty times eighty dollars to you.

Affectionately your brother,

To General Joseph Hooker

[January 26, 1863]

General: I have placed you at the head of the Army of the Potomac. Of course I have done this upon what appear to me to be sufficient reasons, and yet I think it best for you to know that there are some things in regard to which I am not quite satisfied with you. I believe you to be a brave and skillful soldier, which of course I like. I also believe you do not mix politics with your profession, in which you are right. You have confidence in yourself, which is a valuable if not an indispensable quality. You are ambitious, which, within reasonable bounds, does good rather than harm; but I think that during General Burnside's command of the army you have taken counsel of your ambition and thwarted him as much as you could, in which you did a great wrong to the country and to a most meritorious and honorable brother officer. I have heard, in such a way as to believe it, of your recently saying that both the army and the government needed a dictator. Of course it was not for this, but in spite of it, that I have given you the command. Only those generals who gain successes can set up dictators. What I now ask of you is military success, and I will risk the dictatorship. The government will support you to the utmost of its ability, which is neither more nor less than it has done and will do for all commanders. I much fear that the spirit which you have aided to infuse into the army, of criticizing their commander and withholding confidence from him, will now turn upon you. I shall assist you as far as I can to put it down. Neither you nor Napoleon, if he were alive again, could get any good out of an army while such a spirit prevails in it; and now beware of rashness. Beware of rashness, but with energy and sleepless vigilance go forward and give us victories.

To General U. S. Grant

[July 13, 1863]

My dear General: I do not remember that you and I ever met personally. I write this now as a grateful acknowledgment for the almost inestimable service you have done the country. I wish to say a word further. When you first reached the vicinity of Vicksburg, I thought you should do what you finally did— march the troops across the neck, run the batteries with the transports, and thus go below; and I never had any faith, except a general hope that you knew better than I, that the Yazoo Pass expedition and the like could succeed. When you got below and took

Port Gibson, Grand Gulf and vicinity, I thought you should go down the river and join General Banks, and when you turned northward, east of the Big Black, I feared it was a mistake. I now wish to make the personal acknowledgment that you were right and I was wrong.

TO MRS. BIXBY

[NOVEMBER 21, 1864]

DEAR MADAM: I have been shown in the files of the War Department a statement of the Adjutant-General of Massachusetts that you are the mother of five sons who have died gloriously on the field of battle. I feel how weak and fruitless must be any words of mine which should attempt to beguile you from the grief of a loss so overwhelming. But I cannot refrain from tendering to you the consolation that may be found in the thanks of the Republic they died to save. I pray that our heavenly Father may assuage the anguish of your bereavement, and leave you only the cherished memory of the loved and lost, and the solemn pride that must be yours to have laid so costly a sacrifice upon the altar of freedom.

II. EDWARD EVERETT HALE
(1822–1909)

THE MAN WITHOUT A COUNTRY

I suppose that very few casual readers of the *New York Herald* of August 13th observed, in an obscure corner, among the "Deaths," the announcement,

NOLAN. Died on board U. S. Corvette *Levant,* Lat. 2° 11′ S., Long. 131° W., on the 11th of May, PHILIP NOLAN.

I happened to observe it, because I was stranded at the old Mission-House in Mackinac, waiting for a Lake Superior steamer which did not choose to come; and I was devouring to the very stubble all the current literature I could get hold of, even down to the deaths and marriages in the *Herald.* My memory for names and people is good, and the reader will see, as he goes on, that I had reason enough to remember Philip Nolan. There are hundreds of readers who would have paused at that announcement, if the officer of the *Levant* who reported it had chosen to make it thus: "Died, May 11th, The Man without a Country." For it was as "The Man without a Country" that poor Philip Nolan had generally been known by the officers who had him in charge during some fifty years, as, indeed, by all the men who sailed under them. I dare say there is many a man who has taken wine with him once a fortnight, in a three years' cruise, who never knew that his name was "Nolan," or whether the poor wretch had any name at all.

There can now be no possible harm in telling this poor creature's story. Reason enough there has been till now, ever since Madison's administration went out in 1817, for very strict secrecy, the secrecy of honor itself, among the gentlemen of the navy who have had Nolan in successive charge. And certainly it speaks well for the *esprit de corps* of the profession, and

e personal honor of its members,
at to the press this man's story has
en wholly unknown,—and, I think,
the country at large also. I have
ason to think, from some investiga-
ons I made in the Naval Archives
en I was attached to the Bureau
Construction, that every official re-
rt relating to him was burned when
oss burned the public buildings at 10
ashington. One of the Tuckers, or
ssibly one of the Watsons, had No-
n in charge at the end of the war;
d when, on returning from his
uise, he reported at Washington to
e of the Crowninshields,—who was
the Navy Department when he
me home,—he found that the De-
rtment ignored the whole business.
hether they really knew nothing 20
out it, or whether it was a *"Non mi
cordo,"* determined on as a piece of
licy, I do not know. But this I
know, that since 1817, and possibly
fore, no naval officer has mentioned
olan in his report of a cruise.

But, as I say, there is no need for
crecy any longer. And now the
or creature is dead, it seems to me
rth while to tell a little of his story, 30
way of showing young Americans
to-day what it is to be A Man
thout a Country.

Philip Nolan was as fine a young
ficer as there was in the "Legion
the West," as the Western divi-
on of our army was then called.
hen Aaron Burr made his first dash-
g expedition down to New Orleans
1805, at Fort Massac, or somewhere 40
ove on the river, he met, as the
evil would have it, this gay, dash-
g, bright young fellow; at some
nner-party, I think. Burr marked
m, talked to him, walked with him,

took him a day or two's voyage in his
flat-boat, and, in short, fascinated
him. For the next year, barrack-life
was very tame to poor Nolan. He
occasionally availed himself of the
permission the great man had given
him to write to him. Long, high-
worded, stilted letters the poor boy
wrote and rewrote and copied. But
never a line did he have in reply from
the gay deceiver. The other boys in
the garrison sneered at him, because
he sacrificed in this unrequited affection for a politician the time which
they devoted to Monongahela, sledge,
and high-low-jack. Bourbon, euchre,
and poker were still unknown. But
one day Nolan had his revenge. This
time Burr came down the river, not
as an attorney seeking a place for his
office, but as a disguised conqueror.
He had defeated I know not how
many district-attorneys; he had dined
at I know not how many public dinners; he had been heralded in I know
not how many *Weekly Arguses;* and it
was rumored that he had an army behind him and an empire before him.
It was a great day—his arrival—to
poor Nolan. Burr had not been at
the fort an hour before he sent for
him. That evening he asked Nolan
to take him out in his skiff to show
him a cane-brake or a cotton-wood
tree, as he said,—really to seduce him;
and by the time the sail was over,
Nolan was enlisted body and soul.
From that time, though he did not
yet know it, he lived as a man without a country.

What Burr meant to do I know no
more than you, dear reader. It is
none of our business just now. Only,
when the grand catastrophe came, and
Jefferson and the House of Virginia

of that day undertook to break on the wheel all the possible Clarences of the then House of York, by the great treason trial at Richmond, some of the lesser fry in that distant Mississippi Valley, which was farther from us than Puget's Sound is to-day, introduced the like novelty on their provincial stage; and, to while away the monotony of the summer at Fort Adams, got up, for *spectacles*, a string of court-martials on the officers there. One and another of the colonels and majors were tried, and, to fill out the list, little Nolan, against whom, Heaven knows, there was evidence enough,—that he was sick of the service, had been willing to be false to it, and would have obeyed any order to march any-whither with any one who would follow him, had the order only been signed, "By command of His Exc. A. Burr." The courts dragged on. The big flies escaped,—rightly for all I know. Nolan was proved guilty enough, as I say; yet you and I would never have heard of him, reader, but that, when the president of the court asked him at the close whether he wished to say anything to show that he had always been faithful to the United States, he cried out, in a fit of frenzy:

"D—n the United States! I wish I may never hear of the United States again!"

I suppose he did not know how the words shocked old Colonel Morgan who was holding the court. Half the officers who sat in it had served through the Revolution; and their lives, not to say their necks, had been risked for the very idea which he so cavalierly cursed in his madness. He, on his part, had grown up in the West

of those days, in the midst of "Spanish plot," "Orleans plot," and all the rest. He had been educated on plantation, where the finest company was a Spanish officer or a French merchant from Orleans. His education such as it was, had been perfected in commercial expeditions to Vera Cruz and I think he told me his father once hired an Englishman to be a private tutor for a winter on the plantation He had spent half his youth with an older brother, hunting horses in Texas and, in a word, to him "United States" was scarcely a reality. Yet he had been fed by "United States" for all the years since he had been in the army. He had sworn on his faith as a Christian to be true to "United States." It was "United States" which gave him the uniform he wore, and the sword by his side Nay, my poor Nolan, it was only because "United States" had picked you out first as one of her own confidential men of honor that "A. Burr" cared for you a straw more than for the flat-boat men who sailed his ark for him. I do not excuse Nolan; I only explain to the reader why he damned his country, and wished he might never hear her name again.

He never did hear her name but once again. From that moment, September 23, 1807, till the day he died May 11, 1863, he never heard her name again. For that half century and more he was a man without a country.

Old Morgan, as I said, was terribly shocked. If Nolan had compared George Washington to Benedict Arnold, or had cried, "God save King George," Morgan would not have felt worse. He called the court into his ivate room, and returned in fifteen inutes, with a face like a sheet, to y,—

"Prisoner, hear the sentence of the ourt! The Court decides, subject to ie approval of the President, that you ever hear the name of the United ates again."

Nolan laughed. But nobody else ughed. Old Morgan was too solemn, id the whole room was hushed dead night for a minute. Even Nolan st his swagger in a moment. Then Iorgan added,—

"Mr. Marshal, take the prisoner to)rleans in an armed boat, and de- ver him to the naval commander iere."

The marshal gave his orders, and ie prisoner was taken out of court.

"Mr. Marshal," continued old Mor- an, "see that no one mentions the 'nited States to the prisoner. Mr. Iarshal, make my respects to Lieu- enant Mitchell at Orleans, and re- uest him to order that no one shall iention the United States to the pris- ier while he is on board ship. You ill receive your written orders from ie officer on duty here this evening. he Court is adjourned without day."

I have always supposed that Colo- el Morgan himself took the pro- eedings of the court to Washington ity, and explained them to Mr. Jef- erson. Certain it is that the Presi- ent approved them,—certain, that is,

I may believe the men who say ley have seen his signature. Before ie Nautilus got round from New Or- ans to the northern Atlantic coast ith the prisoner on board, the sen- ence had been approved, and he was man without a country.

The plan then adopted was substan-

tially the same which was necessarily followed ever after. Perhaps it was suggested by the necessity of sending him by water from Fort Adams and Orleans. The Secretary of the Navy —it must have been the first Crownin- shield, though he is a man I do not remember—was requested to put No- lan on board a government vessel bound on a long cruise, and to direct that he should be only so far confined there as to make it certain that he never saw or heard of the country. We had few long cruises then, and the navy was very much out of favor; and as almost all of this story is tra- ditional, as I have explained, I do not know certainly what his first cruise was. But the commander to whom he was entrusted,—perhaps it was Tingey or Shaw, though I think it was one of the younger men,—we are all old enough now—regulated the eti- quette and the precautions of the af- fair, and according to his scheme they were carried out, I suppose, till Nolan died.

When I was second officer of the *Intrepid,* some thirty years after, ? saw the original paper of instructions I have been sorry ever since that] did not copy the whole of it. It ran, however, much in this way:—

Washington (with a date, which must have been late in 1807).

Sir,—You will receive from Lt. Neale the person of Philip Nolan, late a lieu- tenant in the United States Army.

This person on his trial by court- martial expressed, with an oath, the wish that he might "never hear of the United States again."

The Court sentenced him to have his wish fulfilled.

For the present, the execution of the

order is entrusted by the President to this Department.

You will take the prisoner on board your ship, and keep him there with such precautions as shall prevent his escape.

You will provide him with such quarters, rations, and clothing as would be proper for an officer of his late rank, if he were a passenger on your vessel on the business of his Government.

The gentlemen on board will make any arrangements agreeable to themselves regarding his society. He is to be exposed to no indignity of any kind, nor is he ever unnecessarily to be reminded that he is a prisoner.

But under no circumstances is he ever to hear of his country or to see any information regarding it; and you will specially caution all the officers under your command to take care, that, in the various indulgences which may be granted, this rule, in which his punishment is involved, shall not be broken.

It is the intention of the Government that he shall never again see the country which he has disowned. Before the end of your cruise you will receive orders which will give effect to this intention.

Resp'y yours,

W. Southard, for the
Sec'y of the Navy.

If I had only preserved the whole of this paper, there would be no break in the beginning of my sketch of this story. For Captain Shaw, if it was he, handed it to his successor in the charge, and he to his; and I suppose the commander of the *Levant* has it today as his authority for keeping this man in this mild custody.

The rule adopted on board the ships on which I have met "the man without a country" was, I think, transmitted from the beginning. No mess liked to have him permanently, because his presence cut off all talk of

home or of the prospect of return of politics or letters, of peace or o war,—cut off more than half the tal men like to have at sea. But it wa always thought too hard that he shoul never meet the rest of us, except t touch hats; and we finally sank int one system. He was not permitte to talk with the men, unless an o ficer was by. With officers he ha unrestrained intercourse, as far as the and he chose. But he grew shy, thoug he had favorites: I was one. The the captain always asked him to din ner on Monday. Every mess in suc cession took up the invitation in it turn. According to the size of th ship, you had him at your mess mor or less often at dinner. His break fast he ate in his own state-room,— he always had a state-room,—whic was where a sentinel or somebody o the watch could see the door. An whatever else he ate or drank, he at or drank alone. Sometimes, when th marines or sailors had any special jo lification, they were permitted to in vite "Plain-Buttons," as they calle him. Then Nolan was sent with som officer, and the men were forbidden t speak of home while he was there. believe the theory was that the sigh of his punishment did them gooc They called him "Plain-Buttons," be cause, while he always chose to wea a regulation army uniform, he wa not permitted to wear the army but ton, for the reason that it bore eithe the initials or the insignia of th country he had disowned.

I remember, soon after I joined th navy, I was on shore with some o the older officers from our ship an from the *Brandywine,* which we ha met at Alexandria. We had leav make a party and go up to Cairo and the Pyramids. As we jogged along (you went on donkeys then), some of the gentlemen (we boys called them "Dons," but the phrase has long since changed) fell to talking about Nolan, and some one told the system which was adopted from the first about his books and other reading. As he was almost never permitted to go on shore, even though the vessel lay in port for months, his time at the best hung heavy; and everybody was permitted to lend him books, if they were not published in America and made no allusion to it. These were common enough in the old days, when people in the other hemisphere talked of the United States as little as we do of Paraguay. He had almost all the foreign papers that came into the ship, sooner or later, only somebody must go over them first, and cut out any advertisement or stray paragraph that alluded to America. This was a little cruel sometimes, when the back of what was cut out might be as innocent as Hesiod. Right in the midst of one of Napoleon's battles, or one of Canning's speeches, poor Nolan would find a great hole, because on the back of the page of that paper there had been an advertisement of a packet for New York, or a scrap from the President's message. I say this was the first time I ever heard of this plan, which afterwards I had enough and more than enough to do with. I remember it because poor Phillips, who was of the party, as soon as the allusion to reading was made, told a story of something which happened at the Cape of Good Hope on Nolan's first voyage; and it is the only thing I ever knew

of that voyage. They had touched at the Cape, and had done the civil thing with the English Admiral and the fleet; and then, leaving for a long cruise up the Indian Ocean, Phillips had borrowed a lot of English books from an officer, which, in those days, as indeed in these, was quite a windfall. Among them, as the Devil would order, was the *Lay of the Last Minstrel*, which they had all of them heard of, but which most of them had never seen. I think it could not have been published long. Well, nobody thought there could be any risk of anything national in that, though Phillips swore old Shaw had cut out *The Tempest* from Shakespeare before he let Nolan have it, because he said "the Bermudas ought to be ours, and, by Jove, should be one day." So Nolan was permitted to join the circle one afternoon when a lot of them sat on deck smoking and reading aloud. People do not do such things so often now; but when I was young we got rid of a great deal of time so. Well, so it happened that in his turn Nolan took the book and read to the others; and he read very well, as I know. Nobody in the circle knew a line of the poem, only it was all magic and Border chivalry, and was ten thousand years ago. Poor Nolan read steadily through the fifth canto, stopped a minute and drank something, and then began, without a thought of what was coming,—

Breathes there the man, with soul so dead,
Who never to himself hath said,—

It seems impossible to us that anybody ever heard this for the first time; but all these fellows did then, and

poor Nolan himself went on, still unconsciously or mechanically,—

This is my own, my native land!

Then they all saw something was to
pay; but he expected to get through,
I suppose, turned a little pale, but
plunged on,—

Whose heart hath ne'er within him
  burned,
As home his footsteps he hath turned
  From wandering on a foreign strand?—
If such there breathe, go, mark him
  well,—

By this time the men were all beside
themselves, wishing there was any way
to make him turn over two pages; but
he had not quite presence of mind for
that; he gagged a little, colored crimson, and staggered on,—

For him no minstrel raptures swell;
High though his titles, proud his name,
Boundless his wealth as wish can claim,
Despite these titles, power, and pelf,
The wretch, concentered all in self,—

and here the poor fellow choked, could
not go on, but started up, swung the
book into the sea, vanished into his
state-room, "and by Jove," said Phillips, "we did not see him for two
months again. And I had to make up
some beggarly story to that English
surgeon why I did not return his
Walter Scott to him."

That story shows about the time
when Nolan's braggadocio must have
broken down. At first, they said, he
took a very high tone, considered his
imprisonment a mere farce, affected to
enjoy the voyage, and all that; but
Phillips said that after he came out
of his state-room he never was the
same man again. He never read aloud
again, unless it was the Bible or

Shakespeare, or something else he wa
sure of. But it was not that merely
He never entered in with the othe
young men exactly as a companio:
again. He was always shy afterwards
when I knew him,—very seldon
spoke, unless he was spoken to, ex
cept to a very few friends. H
lighted up occasionally,—I remembe
late in his life hearing him fairly elo
quent on something which had bee
suggested to him by one of Fléchier'
sermons,—but generally he had th
nervous, tired look of a heart-wounde
man.

When Captain Shaw was comin
home,—if, as I say, it was Shaw,—
rather to the surprise of everybod
they made one of the Windward Is
lands, and lay off and on for nearl
a week. The boys said the officer
were sick of salt-junk, and meant t
have turtle-soup before they cam
home. But after several days th
Warren came to the same rendezvous
they exchanged signals; she sent t
Philips and these homewardbounc
men letters and papers, and told then
she was outwardbound, perhaps to th
Mediterranean, and took poor Nolar
and his traps on the boat back to tr
his second cruise. He looked ver
blank when he was told to get read
to join her. He had known enougl
of the signs of the sky to know tha
till that moment he was going "home.'
But this was a distinct evidence o
something he had not thought of
perhaps,—that there was no goin
home for him, even to a prison. And
this was the first of some twenty suc
transfers, which brought him soone
or later into half our best vessels, bu
which kept him all his life at leas
some hundred miles from the country

e had hoped he might never hear
f again.

It may have been on that second
ruise,—it was once when he was up
he Mediterranean,—that Mrs. Graff,
he celebrated Southern beauty of
hose days, danced with him. They
ad been lying a long time in the Bay
f Naples, and the officers were very
ntimate in the English fleet, and there
ad been great festivities, and our
nen thought they must give a great
all on board the ship. How they
ver did it on board the *Warren* I am
ure I do not know. Perhaps it was
ot the *Warren*, or perhaps ladies did
ot take up so much room as they do
ow. They wanted to use Nolan's
tate-room for something, and they
ated to do it without asking him to
he ball; so the captain said they
night ask him, if they would be re-
ponsible that he did not talk with
he wrong people, "who would give
im intelligence." So the dance went
n, the finest party that had ever
een known, I dare say; for I never
eard of a man-of-war ball that was
ot. For ladies they had the family
f the American consul, one or two
ravelers who had adventured so far,
nd a nice bevy of English girls and
natrons, perhaps Lady Hamilton her-
elf.

Well, different officers relieved each
ther in standing and talking with
Nolan in a friendly way, so as to be
ure that nobody else spoke to him.
The dancing went on with spirit, and
fter a while even the fellows who
ook this honorary guard of Nolan
eased to fear any *contretemps*. Only
vhen some English lady—Lady Ham-
lton, as I said, perhaps—called for
set of "American dances," an odd

thing happened. Everybody then
danced contra-dances. The black
band, nothing loath, conferred as to
what "American dances" were, and
started off with "Virginia Reel,"
which they followed with "Money-
Musk," which, in its turn in those
days, should have been followed by
"The Old Thirteen." But just as
Dick, the leader, tapped for his fiddles
to begin, and bent forward, about to
say, in true negro state, "'The Old
Thirteen,' gentlemen and ladies!" as
he had said "'Virginny Reel,' if you
please!" and "'Money-Musk,' if you
please!" the captain's boy tapped
him on the shoulder, whispered to
him, and he did not announce the
name of the dance; he merely bowed,
began on the air, and they all fell to,
—the officers teaching the English
girls the figure, but not telling them
why it had no name.

But that is not the story I started
to tell. As the dancing went on,
Nolan and our fellows all got at ease,
as I said,—so much so, that it
seemed quite natural for him to bow
to that splendid Mrs. Graff, and
say,—

"I hope you have not forgotten me,
Miss Rutledge. Shall I have the
honor of dancing?"

He did it so quickly, that Shubrick,
who was with him, could not hinder
him. She laughed and said,—

"I am not Miss Rutledge any
longer, Mr. Nolan; but I will dance
all the same," just nodded to Shubrick, as if to say he must leave
Mr. Nolan to her, and led him off
to the place where the dance was
forming.

Nolan thought he had got his
chance. He had known her at Phila-

delphia, and at other places had met her, and this was a godsend. You could not talk in contra-dances, as you do in cotillions, or even in the pauses of waltzing; but there were chances for tongues and sounds, as well as for eyes and blushes. He began with her travels, and Europe, and Vesuvius, and the French; and then, when they had worked down, and had that long talking time at the bottom of the set, he said boldly, —a little pale, she said, as she told me the story years after,—

"And what do you hear from home, Mrs. Graff?"

And that splendid creature looked through him. Jove! how she must have looked through him!

"Home!! Mr. Nolan!!! I thought you were the man who never wanted to hear of home again!"—and she walked directly up the deck to her husband, and left poor Nolan alone, as he always was.—He did not dance again.

I cannot give any history of him in order; nobody can now: and, indeed, I am not trying to. These are the traditions, which I sort out, as I believe them, from the myths which have been told about this man for forty years. The lies that have been told about him are legion. The fellows used to say he was the "Iron Mask"; and poor George Pons went to his grave in the belief that this was the author of "Junius," who was being punished for his celebrated libel on Thomas Jefferson. Pons was not very strong in the historical line. A happier story than either of these I have told is of the war. That came along soon after. I have heard this affair told in three or four ways,—

and, indeed, it may have happened more than once. But which ship was on I cannot tell. However, in one, at least, of the great frigate duels with the English, in which the navy was really baptized, it happened that a round shot from the enemy entered one of our ports square, and took right down the officer of the gun himself, and almost every man of the gun's crew. Now you may say what you choose about courage, but that is not a nice thing to see. But, as the men who were not killed picked themselves up, and as they and the surgeon's people were carrying off the bodies, there appeared Nolan, in his shirt-sleeves, with the rammer in his hand, and, just as if he had been the officer, told them off with authority,—who should go to the cockpit with the wounded men, who should stay with him,—perfectly cheery, and with that way which makes men feel sure all is right and is going to be right. And he finished loading the gun with his own hands, aimed it, and bade the men fire. And there he stayed, captain of that gun, keeping those fellows in spirits, till the enemy struck,—sitting on the carriage while the gun was cooling, though he was exposed all the time,—showing them easier ways to handle heavy shot,—making the raw hands laugh at their own blunders,—and when the gun cooled again, getting it loaded and fired twice as often as any other gun on the ship. The captain walked forward by way of encouraging the men, and Nolan touched his hat and said,—

"I am showing them how we do this in the artillery, Sir."

And this is the part of the story

where all the legends agree: that the Commodore said,—

"I see you do, and I thank you, Sir; and I shall never forget this day, Sir, and you never shall, Sir."

And after the whole thing was over, and he had the Englishman's sword, in the midst of the state and ceremony of the quarterdeck, he said,—

"Where is Mr. Nolan? Ask Mr. Nolan to come here."

And when Nolan came, the captain said,—

"Mr. Nolan, we are all very grateful to you to-day; you are one of us to-day; you will be named in the despatches."

And then the old man took off his own sword of ceremony, and gave it to Nolan, and made him put it on. The man told me this who saw it. Nolan cried like a baby, and well he might. He had not worn a sword since that infernal day at Fort Adams. But always afterwards, on occasions of ceremony, he wore that quaint old French sword of the Commodore's.

The captain did mention him in the despatches. It was always said he asked that he might be pardoned. He wrote a special letter to the 'Secretary of War. But nothing ever came of it. As I said, that was about the time when they began to ignore the whole transaction at Washington, and when Nolan's imprisonment began to carry itself on because there was nobody to stop it without any new orders from home.

I have heard it said that he was with Porter when he took possession of the Nukahiwa Islands. Not this Porter, you know, but old Porter, his father, *Essex* Porter,—that is, the old

Essex Porter, not this *Essex*. As an artillery officer, who had seen service in the West, Nolan knew more about fortifications, embrasures, ravelins, stockades, and all that, than any of them did; and he worked with a right good-will in fixing that battery all right. I have always thought it was a pity Porter did not leave him in command there with Gamble. That would have settled all the question about his punishment. We should have kept the islands, and at this moment we should have one station in the Pacific Ocean. Our French friends, too, when they wanted this little watering-place, would have found it was preoccupied. But Madison and the Virginians, of course, flung all that away.

All that was near fifty years ago. If Nolan was thirty then, he must have been near eighty when he died. He looked sixty when he was forty. But he never seemed to me to change a hair afterwards. As I imagine his life, from what I have seen and heard of it, he must have been in every sea and yet almost never on land. He must have known, in a formal way, more officers in our service than any man living knows. He told me once, with a grave smile, that no man in the world lived so methodical a life as he. "You know the boys say I am the Iron Mask, and you know how busy he was." He said it did not do for any one to try to read all the time, more than to do anything else all the time; and that he read just five hours a day. "Then," he said, "I keep up my notebooks, writing in them at such and such hours from what I have been reading; and I include in these my scrap-books." These were very curious indeed. He had six or eight, of different subjects. There was one of History, one of Natural Science, one which he called "Odds and Ends." But they were not merely books of extracts from newspapers. They had bits of plants and ribbons, shells tied on, and carved scraps of bone and wood, which he had taught the men to cut for him, and they were beautifully illustrated. He drew admirably. He had some of the funniest drawings there, and some of the most pathetic, that I have ever seen in my life. I wonder who will have Nolan's scrap-books.

Well, he said his reading and his notes were his profession, and that they took five hours and two hours respectively of each day. "Then," said he, "every man should have a diversion as well as a profession. My Natural History is my diversion." That took two hours a day more. The men used to bring him birds and fish, but on a long cruise he had to satisfy himself with centipedes and cockroaches and such small game. He was the only naturalist I ever met who knew anything about the habits of the house-fly and the mosquito. All those people can tell you whether they are *Lepidoptera* or *Steptopotera;* but as for telling how you can get rid of them, or how they get away from you when you strike them,—why Linnæus knew as little of that as John Foy the idiot did. These nine hours made Nolan's regular daily "occupation." The rest of the time he talked or walked. Till he grew very old, he went aloft a great deal. He always kept up his exercise; and I never

heard that he was ill. If any other man was ill, he was the kindest nurse in the world; and he knew more than half the surgeons do. Then if anybody was sick or died, or if the captain wanted him to, on any other occasion, he was always ready to read prayers. I have remarked that he read beautifully.

My own acquaintance with Philip Nolan began six or eight years after the war, on my first voyage after I was appointed a midshipman. It was in the first days after our Slave-Trade treaty, while the Reigning House, which was still the House of Virginia, had still a sort of sentimentalism about the suppression of the horrors of the Middle Passage, and something was sometimes done that way. We were in the South Atlantic on that business. From the time I joined, I believe I thought Nolan was a sort of lay chaplain,—a chaplain with a blue coat. I never asked about him. Everything in the ship was strange to me. I knew it was green to ask questions, and I suppose I thought there was a "Plain-Buttons" on every ship. We had him to dine in our mess once a week, and the caution was given that on that day nothing was to be said about home. But if they had told us not to say anything about the planet Mars or the Book of Deuteronomy, I should not have asked why; there were a great many things which seemed to me to have as little reason. I first came to understand anything about "the man without a country" one day when we overhauled a dirty little schooner which had slaves on board. An officer was sent to take charge of her, and, after a few minutes, he sent back his boat to ask that some one might be sent him who could speak Portuguese. We were all looking over the rail when the message came, and we all wished we could interpret, when the captain asked who spoke Portuguese. But none of the officers did; and just as the captain was sending forward to ask if any of the people could, Nolan stepped out and said he should be glad to interpret, if the captain wished, as he understood the language. The captain thanked him, fitted out another boat with him, and in this boat it was my luck to go.

When we got there, it was such a scene as you seldom see, and never want to. Nastiness beyond account, and chaos run loose in the midst of the nastiness. There were not a great many of the negroes; but by way of making what there were understand that they were free, Vaughan had had their handcuffs and ankle-cuffs knocked off, and, for convenience' sake, was putting them upon the rascals of the schooner's crew. The negroes were, most of them, out of the hold, and swarming all round the dirty deck, with a central throng surrounding Vaughan and addressing him in every dialect, and *patois* of a dialect, from the Zulu "click" up to the Parisian of Beledeljereed.

As we came on deck, Vaughan looked down from a hogshead, on which he had mounted in desperation, and said:

"For God's love, is there anybody who can make these wretches understand something? The men gave them rum, and that did not quiet them. I knocked that big fellow down twice, and that did not soothe him. And then I talked Choctaw to all of them together; and I'll be hanged if they understand that as well as they understood the English."

Nolan said he could speak Portuguese, and one or two fine-looking Kroomen were dragged out, who, as it had been found already, had worked for the Portuguese on the coast at Fernando Po.

"Tell them they are free," said Vaughan; "and tell them that these rascals are to be hanged as soon as we can get rope enough."

Nolan "put that into Spanish,"— that is, he explained it in such Portuguese as the Kroomen could understand, and they in turn to such of the negroes as could understand them. Then there was such a yell of delight, clinching of fists, leaping and dancing, kissing of Nolan's feet, and a general rush made to the hogshead by way of spontaneous worship of Vaughan, as the *deus ex machina* of the occasion.

"Tell them," said Vaughan, well pleased, "that I will take them all to Cape Palmas."

This did not answer so well. Cape Palmas was practically as far from the homes of most of them as New Orleans or Rio Janeiro was; that is, they would be eternally separated from home there. And their interpreters, as we could understand, instantly said, *"Ah, non Palmas,"* and began to propose infinite other expedients in most voluble language. Vaughan was rather disappointed at this result of his liberality, and asked Nolan eagerly what they said. The drops stood on poor Nolan's white forehead, as he hushed the men down, and said:—

"He says, 'Not Palmas.' He says,

'Take us home, take us to our own country, take us to our own house, take us to our own pickaninnies and our own women.' He says he has an old father and mother who will die if they do not see him. And this one says he left his people all sick, and paddled down to Fernando to beg the white doctor to come and help them, and that these devils caught him in the bay just in sight of home, and that he has never seen anybody from home since then. And this one says," choked out Nolan, "that he has not heard a word from his home in six months, while he has been locked up in an infernal barracoon."

Vaughan always said he grew gray himself while Nolan struggled through this interpretation. I, who did not understand anything of the passion involved in it, saw that the very elements were melting with fervent heat, and that something was to pay somewhere. Even the negroes themselves stopped howling, as they saw Nolan's agony, and Vaughan's almost equal agony of sympathy. As quick as he could get words, he said:—

"Tell them yes, yes, yes; tell them they shall go to the Mountains of the Moon, if they will. If I sail the schooner through the Great White Desert, they shall go home!"

And after some fashion Nolan said so. And then they all fell to kissing him again, and wanted to rub his nose with theirs.

But he could not stand it long; and getting Vaughan to say he might go back, he beckoned me down into our boat. As we lay back in the stern-sheets and the men gave way, he said to me: "Youngster, let that show you what it is to be without a family, without a home, and without a country. And if you are ever tempted to say a word or to do a thing that shall put a bar between you and your family, your home, and your country, pray God in His mercy to take you that instant home to His own heaven. Stick by your family, boy; forget you have a self, while you do everything for them. Think of your home, boy; write, and send, and talk about it. Let it be nearer and nearer to your thought, the farther you have to travel from it; and rush back to it when you are free, as that poor black slave is doing now. And for your country, boy," and the words rattled in his throat, "and for that flag," and he pointed to the ship, "never dream a dream but of serving her as she bids you, though the service carry you through a thousand hells. No matter what happens to you, no matter who flatters you or who abuses you, never look at another flag, never let a night pass but you pray God to bless that flag. Remember, boy, that behind all these men you have to do with, behind officers, and government, and people even, there is the Country Herself, your Country, and that you belong to Her as you belong to your own mother. Stand by Her, boy, as you would stand by your mother, if those devils there had got hold of her to-day!"

I was frightened to death by his calm, hard passion; but I blundered out that I would, by all that was holy, and that I had never thought of doing anything else. He hardly seemed to hear me; but he did, almost in a whisper, say,—"Oh, if anybody had said so to me when I was of your age!"

I think it was this half-confidence of

his, which I never abused, for I never told this story till now, which afterward made us great friends. He was very kind to me. Often he sat up, or even got up, at night, to walk the deck with me, when it was my watch. He explained to me a great deal of my mathematics, and I owe to him my taste for mathematics. He lent me books, and helped me about my reading. He never alluded so directly to his story again; but from one and another officer I have learned, in thirty years, what I am telling. When we parted from him in St. Thomas harbor, at the end of our cruise, I was more sorry than I can tell. I was very glad to meet him again in 1830; and later in life, when I thought I had some influence in Washington, I moved heaven and earth to have him discharged. But it was like getting a ghost out of prison. They pretended there was no such man, and never was such a man. They will say so at the Department now! Perhaps they do not know. It will not be the first thing in the service of which the Department appears to know nothing!

There is a story that Nolan met Burr once on one of our vessels, when a party of Americans came on board in the Mediterranean. But this I believe to be a lie; or rather, it is a myth, *ben trovato,* involving a tremendous blowing-up with which he sunk Burr,—asking him how he liked to be "without a country." But it is clear, from Burr's life, that nothing of the sort could have happened; and I mention this only as an illustration of the stories which get a-going where there is the least mystery at bottom. . . .

For him, poor fellow, he repented of his folly; and then, like a man, submitted to the fate he had asked for. He never intentionally added to the difficulty or delicacy of the charge of those who had him in hold. Accidents would happen; but they never happened from his fault. Lieutenant Truxton told me that, when Texas was annexed, there was a careful discussion among the officers, whether they should get hold of Nolan's handsome set of maps and cut Texas out of it,—from the map of the world and the map of Mexico. The United States had been cut out when the atlas was bought for him. But it was voted rightly enough, that to do this would be virtually to reveal to him what had happened, or, as Harry Cole said, to make him think Old Burr had succeeded. So it was from no fault of Nolan's that a great botch happened at my own table, when, for a short time, I was in command of the *George Washington,* corvette, on the South American station. We were lying in the La Plata; and some of the officers, who had been on shore and had just joined again, were entertaining us with accounts of their misadventures in riding the half-wild horses of Buenos Ayres. Nolan was at table, and was in an unusually bright and talkative mood. Some story of a tumble reminded him of an adventure of his own when he was catching wild horses in Texas with his brother Stephen, at a time when he must have been quite a boy. He told the story with a good deal of spirit,—so much so that the silence which often follows a good story hung over the table for an instant, to be broken by Nolan himself. For

he asked perfectly unconsciously,—
"Pray, what has become of Texas?
After the Mexicans got their independence, I thought that province of
Texas would come forward very fast.
It is really one of the finest regions
on earth; it is the Italy of this continent. But I have not seen or heard
a word of Texas for near twenty
years."

There were two Texan officers at
the table. The reason he had never
heard of Texas was that Texas and
her affairs had been painfully cut out
of his newspapers since Austin began
his settlements; so that, while he read
of Honduras and Tamaulipas, and till
quite lately, of California, this virgin
province, in which his brother had
traveled so far, and, I believe, had
died, had ceased to be to him. Waters and Williams, the two Texas men,
looked grimly at each other and tried
not to laugh. Edward Morris had
his attention attracted by the third
link in the chain of the captain's
chandelier. Watrous was seized with
a convulsion of sneezing. Nolan himself saw that something was to pay,
he did not know what. And I, as
master of the feast, had to say,—

"Texas is out of the map, Mr. Nolan. Have you seen Captain Back's
curious account of Sir Thomas Roe's
Welcome?"

After that cruise I never saw Nolan
again. I wrote to him at least twice
a year, for in that voyage we became
even confidentially intimate; but he
never wrote to me. The other men
tell me that in those fifteen years he
aged very fast, as well he might indeed; but that he was still the same
gentle, uncomplaining, silent sufferer
that he ever was, bearing as best he
could his self-appointed punishment,—
rather less social, perhaps, with new
men whom he did not know, but more
anxious, apparently, than ever to serve
and befriend and teach the boys,
some of whom fairly seemed to worship him. And now it seems the
dear old fellow is dead. He has
found a home at last, and a country.
Since writing this, and while considering whether or no I would print
it, as a warning to the young Nolans
and Vallandighams and Tatnalls of
today of what it is to throw away
a country, I have received from Danforth, who is on board the *Levant*,
a letter which gives an account of
Nolan's last hours. It removes all
my doubts about telling this story.

To understand the first word of
the letter, the non-professional reader
should remember that after 1817, the
position of every officer who had
Nolan in charge was one of the
greatest delicacy. The government
had failed to renew the order of 1807
regarding him. What was a man to
do? Should he let him go? What,
then, if he were called to account
by the Department for violating the
order of 1807? Should he keep him?
What, then, if Nolan should be lib-
erated some day, and should bring
an action for false imprisonment or
kidnapping against every man who
had had him in charge? I urged and
pressed this upon Southard, and I
have reason to think that other officers did the same thing. But the
Secretary always said, as they often
do at Washington, that there were
no special orders to give, and that
we must act on our own judgment.
That means, "if you succeed, you will
be sustained; if you fail, you will be

disavowed." Well, as Danforth says, all that is over now; though I do not know but I expose myself to a criminal prosecution on the evidence of the very revelation I am making. Here is the letter:—

Levant, 2° 2′ S. @ 131° W.

"Dear Fred:—I try to find heart and life to tell you that it is all over with dear old Nolan. I have been with him on this voyage more than I ever was, and I can understand wholly now the way in which you used to speak of the dear old fellow. I could see that he was not strong, but I had no idea the end was so near. The doctor had been watching him very carefully, and yesterday morning came to me and told me that Nolan was not so well, and had not left his state-room,—a thing I never remember before. He had let the doctor come and see him as he lay there,— the first time the doctor had been in the state-room,—and he said he should like to see me. Oh, dear! do you remember the mysteries we boys used to invent about his room in the old *Intrepid* days? Well, I went in, and there, to be sure, the poor fellow lay in his berth, smiling pleasantly as he gave me his hand, but looking very frail. I could not help a glance round, which showed me what a little shrine he had made of the box he was lying in. The stars and stripes were triced up above and around a picture of Washington, and he had painted a majestic eagle, with lightings blazing from his beak and his foot just clasping the whole globe, which his wings overshadowed. The dear old boy saw my glance, and said, with a sad smile, 'Here, you see, I

have a country!' And then he pointed to the foot of his bed, where I had not seen before a great map of the United States, as he had drawn it from memory, and which he had there to look upon as he lay. Quaint, queer old names were on it, in large letters: 'Indiana Territory,' 'Mississippi Territory,' and 'Louisiana Territory,' as I suppose our fathers learned such things: but the old fellow had patched in Texas, too; he had carried his western boundary all the way to the Pacific, but on that shore he had defined nothing.

" 'Oh, Danforth,' he said, 'I know I am dying. I cannot get home. Surely you will tell me something now?—Stop! stop! Do not speak till I say what I am sure you know, that there is not in this ship, that there is not in America,—God bless her!— a more loyal man than I. There cannot be a man who loves the old flag as I do, or prays for it as I do, or hopes for it as I do. There are thirty-four stars in it now, Danforth. I thank God for that, though I do not know what their names are. There has never been one taken away: I thank God for that. I know by that that there has never been any successful Burr. O Danforth, Danforth,' he sighed out, 'how like a wretched night's dream a boy's idea of personal fame or of separate sovereignty seems, when one looks back on it after such a life as mine! But tell me,—tell me something,—tell me everything, Danforth, before I die!'

"Ingham, I swear to you that I felt like a monster that I had not told him everything before. Danger or no danger, delicacy or no delicacy, who was I, that I should have been acting the tyrant all this time over this dear, sainted old man, who had years ago expiated, in his whole manhood's life, the madness of a boy's treason? 'Mr. Nolan,' said I, 'I will tell you everything you ask about. Only, where shall I begin?'

"Oh, the blessed smile that crept over his white face! and he pressed my hand and said, 'God bless you! Tell me their names,' he said, and he pointed to the stars on the flag. 'The last I know is Ohio. My father lived in Kentucky. But I have guessed Michigan and Indiana and Mississippi,—that was where Fort Adams is,—they make twenty. But where are your other fourteen? You have not cut up any of the old ones, I hope?'

"Well, that was not a bad text, and I told him the names in as good order as I could, and he bade me take down his beautiful map and draw them in as I best could with my pencil. He was wild with delight about Texas, told me how his brother died there; he had marked a gold cross where he supposed his brother's grave was; and he had guessed at Texas. Then he was delighted as he saw California and Oregon;—that, he said, he had suspected partly, because he had never been permitted to land on that shore, though the ships were there so much. 'And the men,' said he, laughing, 'brought off a good deal besides furs.' Then he went back— heavens, how far!—to ask about the *Chesapeake*, and what was done to Barron for surrendering her to the *Leopard*, and whether Burr ever tried again,—and he ground his teeth with the only passion he showed. But in a moment that was over, and he said,

'God forgive me, for I am sure I forgive him.' Then he asked about the old war,—told me the true story of his serving the gun the day we took the *Java*,—asked about dear old David Porter, as he called him. Then he settled down more quietly, and very happily, to hear me tell in an hour the history of fifty years.

"How I wished it had been somebody who knew something! But I did as well as I could. I told him of the English war. I told him about Fulton and the steamboat beginning. I told him about old Scott, and Jackson; told him all I could think about the Mississippi, and New Orleans, and Texas, and his own old Kentucky. And do you think, he asked me who was in command of the 'Legion of the West.' I told him it was a very gallant officer named Grant, and that, by our last news, he was about to establish his headquarters at Vicksburg. Then, 'Where was Vicksburg?' I worked that out on the map; it was about a hundred miles, more or less, above his old Fort Adams; and I thought Fort Adams must be a ruin now. 'It must be at old Vick's plantation,' said he: 'well, that is a change!'

"I tell you, Ingham, it was a hard thing to condense the history of half a century into that talk with a sick man. And I do not now know what I told him,—of emigration, and the means of it,—of steamboats, and railroads, and telegraphs,—of inventions, and books, and literature—of the colleges, and West Point, and the Naval School,—but with the queerest interruptions that ever you heard. You see it was Robinson Crusoe asking all the accumulated questions of fifty-six years!

"I remember he asked, all of a sudden, who was President now; and when I told him, he asked if Old Abe was General Benjamin Lincoln's son. He said he met old General Lincoln, when he was quite a boy himself, at some Indian treaty. I said no, that Old Abe was a Kentuckian like himself, but I could not tell him of what family; he had worked up from the ranks. 'Good for him!' cried Nolan; I am glad of that. As I have brooded and wondered, I have thought our danger was in keeping up those regular successions in the first families.' Then I got talking about my visit to Washington. I told him of meeting the Oregon Congressman, Harding; I told him about the Smithsonian, and the Exploring Expedition; I told him about the Capitol, and the statues for the pediment, and Crawford's Liberty, and Greenough's Washington. Ingham, I told him everything I could think of that would show the grandeur of his country and its prosperity; but I could not make up my mouth to tell him a word about this infernal rebellion!

"And he drank it in and enjoyed it as I cannot tell you. He grew more and more silent, yet I never thought he was tired or faint. I gave him a glass of water, but he just wet his lips, and told me not to go away. Then he asked me to bring the Presbyterian 'Book of Public Prayer' which lay there, and said, with a smile, that it would open at the right place,—and so it did. There was his double red mark down the page; and I knelt down and read, and he repeated with me, 'For ourselves and our country, O gracious God, we thank Thee, that, notwithstanding our manifold transgressions of Thy holy laws, Thou hast continued to us Thy marvelous kindness,'—and so to the end of that thanksgiving. Then he turned to the end of the same book, and I read the words more familiar to me: 'Most heartily we beseech Thee with Thy favor to behold and bless Thy servant, the President of the United States, and all others in authority,'—and the rest of the Episcopal collect. 'Danforth,' said he, 'I have repeated those prayers night and morning, it is now fifty-five years.' And then he said he would go to sleep. He bent me down over him and kissed me; and he said, 'Look in my Bible, Danforth, when I am gone.' And I went away.

"But I had no thought it was the end. I thought he was tired and would sleep. I knew he was happy, and I wanted him to be alone.

"But in an hour, when the doctor went in gently, he found Nolan had breathed his life away with a smile. He had something pressed close to his lips. It was his father's badge of the Order of Cincinnati.

"We looked in his Bible, and there was a slip of paper at the place where he had marked the text:—

" 'They desire a country, even a heavenly: wherefore God is not ashamed to be called their God: for He hath prepared for them a city.'

"On this slip of paper he had written:

" 'Bury me in the sea; it has been my home, and I love it. But will not some one set up a stone for my memory at Fort Adams or at Orleans, that my disgrace may not be more than I ought to bear? Say on it:—

'In Memory of

'PHILIP NOLAN,

'Lieutenant in the Army of the
United States.

'He loved his country as no other man
has loved her; but no man de-
served less at her hands.' "

1863

III. SONGS AND BALLADS OF THE CIVIL WAR

GLORY HALLELUJAH! OR JOHN BROWN'S BODY

CHARLES SPRAGUE HALL

John Brown's body lies a-mold'ring
in the grave,
John Brown's body lies a-mold'ring
in the grave,
John Brown's body lies a-mold'ring
in the grave,
His soul is marching on!

Chorus

Glory! Glory Hallelujah!
Glory! Glory Hallelujah!
Glory! Glory Hallelujah!
His soul is marching on.

He's gone to be a soldier in the army
of the Lord!
His soul is marching on.   10

John Brown's knapsack is strapped
upon his back.
His soul is marching on.

His pet lambs will meet him on the
way,
And they'll go marching on.

They'll hang Jeff Davis on a sour
apple tree,
As they go marching on.

Now for the Union let's give thre
rousing cheers,
As we go marching on.
Hip, hip, hip, hip, Hurrah!
1861

MARYLAND! MY MARYLAND!

JAMES R. RANDALL

The despot's heel is on thy shore,
Maryland!
His torch is at thy temple door,
Maryland!
Avenge the patriotic gore
That flecked the streets of Baltimor
And be the battle queen of yore,
Maryland! My Maryland!

Hark to an exiled son's appeal,
Maryland!
My mother State! to thee I kneel,
Maryland!
For life and death, for woe and wea
Thy peerless chivalry reveal,
And gird thy beauteous limbs wi
steel,
Maryland! My Maryland!

Thou wilt not cower in the dust,
Maryland!
Thy beaming sword shall never rus
Maryland!
Remember Carroll's sacred trust,
Remember Howard's warlike thrust,
And all thy slumberers with the ju
Maryland! My Maryland!

Come! 'tis the red dawn of the da
Maryland!
Come with thy panoplied array,
Maryland!
With Ringgold's spirit for the fray,
With Watson's blood at Monterey,
With fearless Lowe and dashing Ma
Maryland! My Maryland!

Come! for thy shield is bright a
strong,
Maryland!

Come! for thy dalliance does thee
        wrong,
    Maryland!
Come to thine own heroic throng,
Stalking with Liberty along,
And chaunt thy dauntless slogan song,
    Maryland! My Maryland!   40

Dear Mother! burst the tyrant's
        chain,
    Maryland!
Virginia should not call in vain,
    Maryland!
She meets her sisters on the plain—
Sic semper!" 'tis the proud refrain
That baffles minions back again,
    Maryland! My Maryland!

I see the blush upon thy cheek,
    Maryland!   50
For thou wast ever bravely meek,
    Maryland!
But lo! there surges forth a shriek
From hill to hill, from creek to
        creek—
Potomac calls to Chesapeake,
    Maryland! My Maryland!

Thou wilt not yield the Vandal toll,
    Maryland!
Thy wilt not crook to his control,
    Maryland!   60
Better the fire upon thee roll,
Better the blade, the shot, the bowl,
Than crucifixion of the soul,
    Maryland! My Maryland!

I hear the distant thunder-hum,
    Maryland!
The Old Line's bugle, fife, and drum,
    Maryland!
She is not dead, nor deaf, nor
        dumb—
Huzza! she spurns the Northern
        scum!   70
She breathes! she burns! she'll come!
        she'll come!
    Maryland! My Maryland!
                                    1861

DIXIE

GENERAL ALBERT PIKE

Southrons, hear your Country call
        you!
Up, lest worse than death befall you!
    To arms! To arms! To arms, in
        Dixie!
Lo! all the beacon fires are lighted—
Let all hearts be now united!
    To arms! To arms! To arms, in
        Dixie!
    Advance the flag of Dixie!
        Hurrah! Hurrah!
    For Dixie's land we take our
        stand,
    And live or die for Dixie!   10
        To arms! To arms!
    And conquer peace for Dixie!
        To arms! To arms!
    And conquer peace for Dixie!

Hear the Northern thunders mutter!
Northern flags in South winds flutter!
        To arms!
Send them back your fierce defiance!
Stamp upon the accursed alliance!
        To arms!   20
    Advance the flag of Dixie!

Fear no danger! Shun no labor!
Lift up rifle, pike, and saber!
        To arms!
Shoulder pressing close to shoulder,
Let the odds make each heart bolder!
        To arms!
    Advance the flag of Dixie!

How the South's great heart rejoices,
At your cannons' ringing voices!   30
        To arms!
For faith betrayed, and pledges
        broken,
Wrongs inflicted, insults spoken,
        To arms!
    Advance the flag of Dixie!

Strong as lions, swift as eagles,
Back to their kennels hunt these
        beagles!
        To arms!

Cut the unequal bonds asunder!
Let them hence each other plunder!
    To arms!   41
     Advance the flag of Dixie!

Swear upon your country's altar
Never to submit or falter!
    To arms!
Till the spoilers are defeated,
Till the Lord's work is completed.
    To arms!
     Advance the flag of Dixie!
                1861

THE PICKET-GUARD

ETHEL LYNN BEERS(?)

"All quiet along the Potomac," they
   say,
  "Except now and then a stray picket
Is shot, as he walks on his beat to
   and fro,
  By a rifleman hid in the thicket.
'Tis nothing: a private or two, now
   and then,
  Will not count in the news of the
   battle;
Not an officer lost—only one of the
   men
  Moaning out, all alone, the death
   rattle."

All quiet along the Potomac to-night,
  Where the soldiers lie peacefully
   dreaming;   10
Their tents in the rays of the clear
   autumn moon,
  Or the light of the watch-fire, are
   gleaming.
A tremulous sigh of the gentle night-
   wind
  Through the forest leaves softly is
   creeping;
While the stars up above, with their
   glittering eyes,
  Keep guard, for the army is sleeping.

There's only the sound of the lone
   sentry's tread

As he tramps from the rock to the
   fountain,
And thinks of the two in the low
   trundle-bed
  Far away in the cot on the mountain.   2
His musket falls slack; his face, dark
   and grim,
  Grows gentle with memories tender
As he mutters a prayer for the children asleep—
  For their mother—may Heaven defend her!

The moon seems to shine just as
   brightly as then
  That night, when the love yet un-
   spoken
Leaped up to his lips—when low
   murmured vows
  Were pledged to be ever unbroken
Then drawing his sleeve roughly over
   his eyes,
  He dashes off tears that are well-
   ing,   8
And gathers his gun closer up to its
   place
  As if to keep down the heart-swell-
   ing.

He passes the fountain, the blasted
   pine-tree;
  The footstep is lagging and weary;
Yet onward he goes, through the
   broad belt of light,
  Towards the shade of the forest so
   dreary.
Hark! was it the night-wind that
   rustled the leaves?
  Was it moonlight so wondrously
   flashing?
It looked like a rifle. . . . "Ha!
   Mary, goodby!"
  The red life-blood is ebbing and
   plashing.

All quiet along the Potomac to-night,
  No sound save the rush of the
   river,

While soft falls the dew on the face
    of the dead—
The picket's off duty forever!

1861

BATTLE-HYMN OF THE REPUBLIC

JULIA WARD HOWE

Mine eyes have seen the glory of the
    coming of the Lord:
He is trampling out the vintage where
    the grapes of wrath are
    stored;
He hath loosed the fateful lightning of
    his terrible swift sword;
    His truth is marching on.

I have seen Him in the watch-fires of
    a hundred circling camps;
They have builded Him an altar in
    the evening dews and damps;
I can read His righteous sentence by
    the dim and flaring lamps;
    His day is marching on.

I have read a fiery gospel, writ in
    burnished rows of steel:
"As ye deal with my contemners, so
    with you my grace shall
    deal;   10
Let the Hero, born of woman, crush
    the serpent with his heel,
    Since God is marching on."

He has sounded forth the trumpet
    that shall never call retreat;
He is sifting out the hearts of men be-
    fore his judgment-seat:
Oh! be swift, my soul, to answer
    Him! be jubilant, my feet!
    Our God is marching on.

In the beauty of the lilies Christ was
    born across the sea,
With a glory in his bosom that trans-
    figures you and me:
As he died to make men holy, let us
    die to make men free,
    While God is marching on.   20

1862

THREE HUNDRED THOUSAND MORE

JOHN SLOAN GIBBONS

We are coming, Father Abraham,
    three hundred thousand more,
From Mississippi's winding stream
    and from New England's shore;
We leave our ploughs and workshops,
    our wives and children dear,
With hearts too full for utterance,
    with but a silent tear;
We dare not look behind us, but
    steadfastly before:
We are coming, Father Abraham,
    three hundred thousand more!

If you look across the hill-tops that
    meet the northern sky,
Long moving lines of rising dust
    your vision may descry;
And now the wind, an instant, tears
    the cloudy veil aside,
And floats aloft our spangled flag in
    glory and in pride;   10
And bayonets in the sunlight gleam,
    and bands brave music pour:
We are coming, Father Abraham,
    three hundred thousand more!

If you look all up our valleys where
    the growing harvests shine,
You may see our sturdy farmer boys
    fast forming into line;
And children from their mother's
    knees are pulling at the weeds,
And learning how to reap and sow
    against their country's needs;
And a farewell group stands weeping
    at every cottage door:
We are coming, Father Abraham,
    three hundred thousand more!

You have called us, and we're coming,
    by Richmond's bloody tide
To lay us down, for Freedom's sake,
    our brothers' bones beside;   20
Or from foul treason's savage grasp
    to wrench the murderous blade.

And in the face of foreign foes its
    fragments to parade.
Six hundred thousand loyal men and
    true have gone before:
We are coming, Father Abraham,
    three hundred thousand more!
                    1862

STONEWALL JACKSON'S WAY

John W. Palmer

Come, stack arms, men: pile on the
    rails;
    Stir up the camp fire bright!
No growling if the canteen fails:
    We'll make a roaring night.
Here Shenandoah brawls along,
There burly Blue Ridge echoes strong
To swell the Brigade's rousing song,
    Of Stonewall Jackson's Way.

We see him now—the queer slouched
    hat,
    Cocked over his eye askew: 10
The shrewd, dry smile; the speech so
    pat,
    So calm, so blunt, so true.
The "Blue-light Elder" knows 'em
    well:
Says he, "That's Banks: he's fond of
    shell.
Lord save his soul: we'll give him—":
    well,
    That's Stonewall Jackson's Way.

Silence! Ground arms! Kneel all!
    Caps off!
    Old Massa's going to pray.
Strangle the fool that dares to scoff:
    Attention!—it's his way.   20
Appealing from his native sod,
In forma pauperis to God,
"Lay bare Thine arm! Stretch forth
    Thy rod:
    Amen!" That's Stonewall's Way.

He's in the saddle now. Fall in!
    Steady! the whole brigade.

Hill's at the ford, cut off; we'll wi
    His way out, ball and blade.
What matter if our shoes are worn?
What matter if our feet are torn?
Quick step! we're with him befor
    morn:
    That's Stonewall Jackson's Way.

The sun's bright lances rout the mist
    Of morning; and, by George!
Here's Longstreet, struggling in th
    lists,
    Hemmed in an ugly gorge.
Pope and his Dutchmen! whippe
    before.
"Bay'nets and grape!" hear Stonewa
    roar.
Charge, Stuart! Pay off Ashby
    score,
    In Stonewall Jackson's Way.

Ah, Maiden! wait, and watch, ar
    yearn,
    For news of Stonewall's band.
Ah, Widow! read, with eyes that bur
    That ring upon thy hand.
Ah, Wife! sew on, pray on, hope o
Thy life shall not be all forlorn.
The foe had better ne'er been born,
    That gets in Stonewall's Way.
                    186

TENTING ON THE OLD CAMP GROUND

Walter Kittredge

We're tenting to-night on the o
    camp ground;
    Give us a song to cheer
Our weary hearts, a song of home,
    And friends we love so dear.

    Many are the hearts that a
        weary to-night,
        Wishing for the war to cease
    Many are the hearts, looking f
        the right,
        To see the dawn of peace.

Tenting to-night, tenting to-night,
　Tenting on the old camp
　　ground.　　　　　　　10

We've been tenting to-night on the
　　old camp ground,
Thinking of days gone by,
Of the loved ones at home, that gave
　　us the hand,
And the tear that said "Good-by!"

We are tired of war on the old camp
　　ground,
Many are dead and gone,
Of the brave and true who've left
　　their homes
Others been wounded long.

We've been fighting to-day on the old
　　camp ground,
Many are lying near;　　　　　20
Some are dead, and some are dying,
Many are in tears.

　　　　　　　　　　　1863

LITTLE GIFFEN

Francis Orrery Ticknor

Out of the focal and foremost fire,
Out of the hospital walls as dire;
Smitten of grape-shot and gangrene,
(Eighteenth battle and *he* sixteen!)
Spectre such as you seldom see—
Little Giffen, of Tennessee!

"Take him and welcome!" the sur-
　geons said;
"Little the doctor can help the dead!"
So we took him; and brought him
　where
The balm was sweet in the summer
　air;　　　　　　　　　10
And we laid him down on a whole-
　some bed—
Utter Lazarus, heel to head!

And we watched the war with bated
　breath—
Skeleton Boy against skeleton Death.

Months of torture, how many such?
Weary weeks of the stick and the
　crutch;
And still a glint of the steel-blue eye
Told of a spirit that wouldn't die,

And didn't. Nay more, in Death's
　despite
The crippled skeleton learned to
　write.　　　　　　　　20
"Dear Mother," at first, of course;
　and then
"Dear Captain," inquiring about the
　men.
Captain's answer: "Of eighty and
　five
Giffen and I are left alive."

Word of gloom from the war one day:
Johnston pressed at the front, they
　say.
Little Giffen was up and away;
A tear—his first—as he bade good-bye
Dimmed the glint of his steel-blue eye.
"I'll write, if spared." There was
　news of the fight,　　　　30
But none of Giffen; he did not write.

I sometimes fancy, that, were I king
Of the princely Knights of the Golden
　Ring,
With the song of the minstrel in mine
　ear,
And the tender legend that trembles
　here,
I'd give the best on his bended knee,
The whitest soul of my chivalry,
For "Little Giffen," of Tennessee.

　　　　　　　　　　　1863?

MARCHING THROUGH GEORGIA

Henry Clay Work

Bring the good old bugle, boys, we'll
　sing another song—
Sing it with the spirit that will start
　the world along—
Sing it as we used to sing it fifty thou-
　sand strong,

While we were marching through
Georgia.

Chorus

"Hurrah! Hurrah! we bring the
  jubilee!
Hurrah! Hurrah! the flag that
  makes you free!"
So we sang the chorus from At-
  lanta to the sea,
While we were marching through
  Georgia.

How the darkies shouted when they
  heard the joyful sound!
How the turkeys gobbled which our
  commissary found!   10
How the sweet potatoes even started
  from the ground,
  While we were marching through
  Georgia.

Yes, and there were Union men who
  wept with joyful tears,
When they saw the honored flag they
  had not seen for years;
Hardly could they be restrained from
  breaking forth in cheers,
  While we were marching through
  Georgia.

"Sherman's dashing Yankee boys will
  never reach the coast!"
So the saucy rebels said—and 'twas a
  handsome boast,
Had they not forgot, alas! to reckon
  on a host,
  While we were marching through
  Georgia.   20

So we made a thoroughfare for Free-
  dom and her train,
Sixty miles in latitude—three hundred
  to the main;
Treason fled before us, for resistance
  was in vain,
  While we were marching through
  Georgia.

          1864?

SHERIDAN'S RIDE

October 19, 1864

THOMAS BUCHANAN READ

Up from the South, at break of day
Bringing to Winchester fresh dismay
The affrighted air with a shudder bore
Like a herald in haste to the chief-
  tain's door,
The terrible grumble, and rumble, and
  roar,
Telling the battle was on once more
  And Sheridan twenty miles away.

And wider still those billows of war
Thundered along the horizon's bar;
And louder yet into Winchester
  rolled   1
The roar of that red sea uncontrolled
Making the blood of the listener cold
As he thought of the stake in that
  fiery fray,
  With Sheridan twenty miles away.

But there is a road from Winchester
  town,
A good, broad highway leading down
And there, through the flush of the
  morning light,
A steed as black as the steeds of night
Was seen to pass, as with eagle flight
As if he knew the terrible need,   2
He stretched away with his utmost
  speed.
Hills rose and fell, but his heart was
  gay,
  With Sheridan fifteen miles away.

Still sprang from those swift hoofs
  thundering south
The dust like smoke from the cannon's mouth,
Or the trail of a comet, sweeping
  faster and faster,
Foreboding to traitors the doom of
  disaster.
The heart of the steed and the heart
  of the master

Vere beating like prisoners assaulting
    their walls,
mpatient to be where the battle-field
    calls;   30
very nerve of the charger was
    strained to full play,
  With Sheridan only ten miles away.

Jnder his spurning feet, the road
like an arrowy Alpine river flowed,
.nd the landscape sped away behind
like an ocean flying before the wind;
.nd the steed like a bark fed with fur-
    nace ire,
wept on, with his wild eye full of
    fire;
ut, lo! he is nearing his heart's de-
    sire;
Ie is snuffing the smoke of the roar-
    ing fray,   40
  With Sheridan only five miles away.

he first that the general saw were
    the groups
f stragglers, and then the retreating
    troops;
Vhat was done? what to do? a glance
    told him both.
hen striking his spurs with a terrible
    oath,
Ie dashed down the line, 'mid a storm
    of huzzas,
nd the wave of retreat checked its
    course there, because
he sight of the master compelled it
    to pause.
Vith foam and dust the black charger
    was gray;
y the flash of his eye, and the red
    nostril's play,   50
Ie seemed to the whole great army
    to say:
I have brought you Sheridan all the
    way
  From Winchester down to save the
    day."

urrah! hurrah for Sheridan!
urrah! hurrah for horse and man

And when their statues are placed on
    high
Under the dome of the Union sky,
The American soldier's Temple of
    Fame,
There, with the glorious general's
    name,
Be it said, in letters both bold and
    bright: 60
"Here is the steed that saved the day
By carrying Sheridan into the fight,
  From Winchester—twenty miles
    away!"

                   1864?

THE BLUE AND THE GRAY

FRANCIS MILES FINCH

By the flow of the inland river,
  Whence the fleets of iron have fled,
Where the blades of the grave grass
    quiver,
  Asleep are the ranks of the dead:
    Under the sod and the dew,
      Waiting the judgment day;
    Under the one, the Blue,
      Under the other, the Gray.

These in the robings of glory,
  Those in the gloom of defeat,   10
All with the battle-blood gory,
  In the dusk of eternity meet:
    Under the sod and the dew,
      Waiting the judgment day;
    Under the laurel, the Blue,
      Under the willow, the Gray.

From the silence of sorrowful hours
  The desolate mourners go,
Lovingly laden with flowers
  Alike for the friend and the foe: 20
    Under the sod and the dew,
      Waiting the judgment day;
    Under the roses, the Blue,
      Under the lilies, the Gray.

So with an equal splendor,
  The morning sun rays fall,

With a touch impartially tender,
  On the blossoms blooming for all:
    Under the sod and the dew,
      Waiting the judgment day;   30
    Broidered with gold, the Blue,
      Mellowed with gold, the Gray.

So, when the summer calleth,
  On forest and field of grain,
With an equal murmur falleth
  The cooling drip of the rain:
    Under the sod and the dew,
      Waiting the judgment day;
    Wet with the rain, the Blue,
      Wet with the rain, the Gray. 40

Sadly, but not with upbraiding,
  The generous deed was done,
In the storm of the years that are
      fading
  No braver battle was won:
    Under the sod and the dew,
      Waiting the judgment day;
    Under the blossoms, the Blue,
      Under the garlands, the Gray.

No more shall the war cry sever,
  Or the winding rivers be red;   50
They banish our anger forever
  When they laurel the graves of our
      dead!
    Under the sod and the dew,
      Waiting the judgment day:
    Love and tears for the Blue,
      Tears and love for the Gray.
                              1867

IV. HENRY TIMROD
(1829–1867)

SONNET: I SCARCELY
GRIEVE

I scarcely grieve, O Nature! at the lot
That pent my life within a city's
      bounds,
And shut me from thy sweetest sights
  and sounds.

Perhaps I had not learned, if som
  lone cot
Had nursed a dreamy childhood, wha
  the mart
Taught me amid its turmoil; so m
  youth
Had missed full many a stern bu
  wholesome truth.
Here, too, O Nature! in this haunt o
  Art,
Thy power is on me, and I own th
  thrall.
There is no unimpressive spot o
  earth!   1
The beauty of the stars is over all,
And Day and Darkness visit ever
  hearth.
Clouds do not scorn us: yonder fac
  tory's smoke
Looked like a golden mist when morn
  ing broke.
                              1860

SONNET: I KNOW NOT WHY

I know not why, but all this wear
  day,
Suggested by no definite grief or pair
Sad fancies have been flitting throug
  my brain;
Now it has been a vessel losing way
Rounding a stormy headland; now
  gray
Dull waste of clouds above a wintr
  main;
And then, a banner, drooping in th
  rain,
And meadows beaten into bloody clay
Strolling at random with this shadow
  woe
At heart, I chanced to wander hither
  Lo!   1
A league of desolate marsh-land, wit
  its lush,
Hot grasses in a noisome, tide-left bec
And faint, warm airs, that rustle i
  the hush,
Like whispers round the body of th
  dead.
                              1860

ETHNOGENESIS

WRITTEN DURING THE MEETING OF THE
FIRST   SOUTHERN   CONGRESS,   AT
MONTGOMERY, FEBRUARY, 1861

I

Hath not the morning dawned with
    added light?
And shall not evening call another star
Out of the infinite regions of the night,
To mark this day in Heaven?   At
    last, we are
A nation among nations; and the
    world
Shall soon behold in many a distant
    port
    Another flag unfurled!
Now, come what may, whose favor
    need we court?
And, under God, whose thunder need
    we fear?
    Thank him who placed us here   10
Beneath so kind a sky—the very sun
Takes part with us; and on our er-
    rands run
All breezes of the ocean; dew and rain
Do noiseless battle for us; and the
    Year,
And all the gentle daughters in her
    train,
March in our ranks, and in our serv-
    ice wield
    Long spears of golden grain!
A yellow blossom as her fairy shield,
June flings her azure banner to the
    wind,
    While in the order of their birth   20
Her sisters pass, and many an ample
    field
Grows white beneath their steps, till
    now, behold,
    Its endless sheets unfold
The Snow of Southern Summers!
    Let the earth
Rejoice! beneath those fleeces soft and
    warm
    Our happy land shall sleep
    In a repose as deep

As if we lay intrenched behind
Whole leagues of Russian ice and
    Arctic storm!

II

And what if, mad with wrongs them-
    selves have wrought,   30
    In their own treachery caught,
    By their own fears made bold,
    And leagued with him of old,
Who long since in the limits of the
    North
Set up his evil throne, and warred with
    God—
What if, both mad and blinded in their
    rage,
Our foes should fling us down their
    mortal gage,
And with a hostile step profane our
    sod!
We shall not shrink, my brothers, but
    go forth
To meet them, marshaled by the Lord
    of Hosts,   40
And overshadowed by the mighty
    ghosts
Of Moultrie and of Eutaw—who shall
    foil
Auxiliars such as these?   Nor these
    alone,
    But every stock and stone
    Shall help us; but the very soil,
And all the generous wealth it gives
    to toil,
And all for which we love our noble
    land,
Shall fight beside, and through us; sea
    and strand,
    The heart of woman, and her hand,
Tree, fruit, and flower, and every in-
    fluence,   50
    Gentle, or grave, or grand;
    The winds in our defence
Shall seem to blow; to us the hills
    shall lend
    Their firmness and their calm;
And in our stiffened sinews we shall
    blend
    The strength of pine and palm!

III

Nor would we shun the battle-ground,
   Though weak as we are strong;
Call up the clashing elements around,
   And test the right and wrong! 60
On one side, creeds that dare to teach
What Christ and Paul refrained to
      preach;
Codes built upon a broken pledge,
And Charity that whets a poniard's
      edge;
Fair schemes that leave the neighbor-
      ing poor
To starve and shiver at the schemer's
      door,
While in the world's most liberal ranks
      enrolled,
He turns some vast philanthropy to
      gold;
Religion, taking every mortal form
But that a pure and Christian faith
      makes warm,   70
Where not to vile fanatic passion
      urged,
Or not in vague philosophies sub-
      merged,
Repulsive with all Pharisaic leaven,
And making laws to stay the laws of
      Heaven!
And on the other, scorn of sordid gain,
Unblemished honor, truth, without a
      stain,
Faith, justice, reverence, charitable
      wealth,
And, for the poor and humble, laws
      which give,
Not the mean right to buy the right
      to live,
   But life, and home, and health! 80
To doubt the end were want of trust
      in God,
      Who, if he has decreed
   That we must pass a redder sea
Than that which rang to Miriam's holy
      glee,
      Will surely raise at need
   A Moses with his rod!

IV

But let our fears—if fears we have—
      be still,
And turn us to the future! Could we
      climb
Some mighty Alp, and view the com-
      ing time,
The rapturous sight would fill   90
   Our eyes with happy tears!
Not only for the glories which the
      years
Shall bring us; not for lands from
      sea to sea,
And wealth, and power, and peace
      though these shall be;
But for the distant peoples we shall
      bless,
And the hushed murmurs of a world's
      distress:
For, to give labor to the poor,
   The whole sad planet o'er,
And save from want and crime the
      humblest door,
Is one among the many ends for which
   God makes us great and rich!   100
The hour perchance is not yet wholly
      ripe
When all shall own it, but the type
Whereby we shall be known in every
      land
Is that vast gulf which lips our South-
      ern strand,
And through the cold, untempered
      ocean pours
Its genial streams, that far off Arctic
      shores
May sometimes catch upon the sof-
      tened breeze
Strange tropic warmth and hints of
      summer seas.

                                  1861

CHARLESTON

Calm as that second summer which
      precedes
   The first fall of the snow,
In the broad sunlight of heroic deeds
   The City bides the foe.

As yet, behind their ramparts stern
    and proud,
  Her bolted thunders sleep—
Dark Sumter, like a battlemented
    cloud,
  Looms o'er the solemn deep.

No Calpe frowns from lofty cliff or
    scar
  To guard the holy strand;   10
But Moultrie holds in leash her dogs
    of war
  Above the level sand.

And down the dunes a thousand guns
    lie couched,
  Unseen, beside the flood—
Like tigers in some Orient jungle
    crouched
  That wait and watch for blood.

Meanwhile, through streets still echo-
    ing with trade,
  Walk grave and thoughtful men,
Whose hands may one day wield the
    patriot's blade
  As lightly as the pen.   20

And maidens, with such eyes as would
    grow dim
  Over a bleeding hound,
Seem each one to have caught the
    strength of him
  Whose sword she sadly bound.

Thus girt without and garrisoned at
    home,
  Day patient following day,
Old Charleston looks from roof, and
    spire, and dome,
  Across her tranquil bay.

Ships, through a hundred foes, from
    Saxon lands
  And spicy Indian ports,   30
Bring Saxon steel and iron to her
    hands,
  And summer to her courts.

But still, along yon dim Atlantic line,
  The only hostile smoke

Creeps like a harmless mist above the
    brine,
  From some frail, floating oak.

Shall the Spring dawn, and she still
    clad in smiles,
  And with an unscathed brow,
Rest in the strong arms of her palm-
    crowned isles,
  As fair and free as now?   40

We know not; in the temple of the
    Fates
  God has inscribed her doom;
And, all untroubled in her faith, she
    waits
  The triumph or the tomb.

                                    1862?

THE COTTON BOLL

While I recline
At ease beneath
This immemorial pine,
Small sphere!
(By dusky fingers brought this morn-
    ing here
And shown with boastful smiles),
I turn thy cloven sheath,
Through which the soft white fibers
    peer,
That, with their gossamer bands,
Unite, like love, the sea-divided
    lands,   10
And slowly, thread by thread,
Draw forth the folded strands,
Than which the trembling line,
By whose frail help yon startled
    spider fled
Down the tall spear-grass from his
    swinging bed,
Is scarce more fine;
And as the tangled skein
Unravels in my hands,
Betwixt me and the noonday light,
A veil seems lifted, and for miles and
    miles   20
The landscape broadens on my sight,
As, in the little boll, there lurked a
    spell

Like that which, in the ocean shell,
With mystic sound,
Breaks down the narrow walls that
    hem us round,
And turns some city lane
Into the restless main,
With all his capes and isles!

Yonder bird,
Which floats, as if at rest,   30
In those blue tracts above the thunder,
    where
No vapors cloud the stainless air,
And never sound is heard,
Unless at such rare time
When, from the City of the Blest,
Rings down some golden chime,
Sees not from his high place
So vast a cirque of summer space
As widens round me in one mighty
    field,
Which, rimmed by seas and sands, 40
Doth hail its earliest daylight in the
    beams
Of gray Atlantic dawns;
And, broad as realms made up of
    many lands,
Is lost afar
Behind the crimson hills and purple
    lawns
Of sunset, among plains which roll
    their streams
Against the Evening Star!

And lo!
To the remotest point of sight,
Although I gaze upon no waste of
    snow,   50
The endless field is white;
And the whole landscape glows,
For many a shining league away,
With such accumulated light
As Polar lands would flash beneath a
    tropic day!
Nor lack there (for the vision grows,
And the small charm within my
    hands—
More potent even than the fabled one,
Which oped whatever golden mystery

Lay hid in fairy wood or magic
    vale,   60
The curious ointment of the Arabian
    tale—
Beyond all mortal sense
Doth stretch my sight's horizon, and
    I see,
Beneath its simple influence,
As if with Uriel's crown,
I stood in some great temple of the
    Sun,
And looked, as Uriel, down!)
Nor lack there pastures rich and fields
    all green
With all the common gifts of God,
For temperate airs and torrid sheen 70
Weave Edens of the sod;
Through lands which look one sea
    of billowy gold
Broad rivers wind their devious ways;
A hundred isles in their embraces fold
A hundred luminous bays;
And through yon purple haze
Vast mountains lift their plumèd
    peaks cloud-crowned;
And, save where up their sides the
    plowman creeps,
An unhewn forest girds them grandly
    round,
In whose dark shades a future navy
    sleeps!   80
Ye Stars, which, though unseen, yet
    with me gaze
Upon this loveliest fragment of the
    earth!
Thou Sun, that kindlest all thy gen-
    tlest rays
Above it, as to light a favorite hearth!
Ye Clouds, that in your temples in the
    West
See nothing brighter than its humblest
    flowers!
And you, ye Winds, that on the
    ocean's breast
Are kissed to coolness ere ye reach
    its bowers!
Bear witness with me in my song of
    praise,
And tell the world that, since the
    world began,   90

No fairer land hath fired a poet's lays,
Or given a home to man!

But these are charms already widely
    blown!
His be the meed whose pencil's trace
Hath touched our very swamps with
    grace,
And round whose tuneful way
All Southern laurels bloom;
The Poet of "The Woodlands," unto
    whom
Alike are known
The flute's low breathing and the
    trumpet's tone,   100
And the soft west wind's sighs;
But who shall utter all the debt,
O land wherein all powers are met
That bind a people's heart,
The world doth owe thee at this day,
And which it never can repay,
Yet scarcely deigns to own!
Where sleeps the poet who shall fitly
    sing
The source wherefrom doth spring
That mighty commerce which, con-
    fined   110
To the mean channels of no selfish
    mart,
Goes out to every shore
Of this broad earth, and throngs the
    sea with ships
That bear no thunders; hushes hun-
    gry lips
In alien lands;
Joins with a delicate web remotest
    strands;
And gladdening rich and poor,
Doth gild Parisian domes,
Or feed the cottage-smoke of English
    homes,
And only bounds its blessings by man-
    kind!   120
In offices like these, thy mission lies,
My Country! and it shall not end
As long as rain shall fall and Heaven
    bend
In blue above thee; though thy foes
    be hard

And cruel as their weapons, it shall
    guard
Thy hearth-stones as a bulwark; make
    thee great
In white and bloodless state;
And haply, as the years increase—
Still working through its humbler
    reach
With that large wisdom which the
    ages teach—   130
Revive the half-dead dream of uni-
    versal peace!
As men who labor in that mine
Of Cornwall, hollowed out beneath
    the bed
Of ocean, when a storm rolls over-
    head,
Hear the dull booming of the world
    of brine
Above them, and a mighty muffled roar
Of winds and waters, yet toil calmly
    on,
And split the rock, and pile the mas-
    sive ore,
Or carve a niche, or shape the archèd
    roof;
So I, as calmly, weave my woof   140
Of song, chanting the days to come,
Unsilenced, though the quiet sum-
    mer air
Stirs with the bruit of battles, and
    each dawn
Wakes from its starry silence to the
    hum
Of many gathering armies.   Still,
In that we sometimes hear,
Upon the Northern winds, the voice
    of woe
Not wholly drowned in triumph,
    though I know
The end must crown us, and a few
    brief years
Dry all our tears,   150
I may not sing too gladly.   To Thy
    will
Resigned, O Lord! we cannot all for-
    get
That there is much even Victory must
    regret.
And, therefore, not too long

From the great burthen of our coun-
　　try's wrong
Delay our just release!
And, if it may be, save
These sacred fields of peace
From stain of patriot or of hostile
　　blood!
Oh, help us, Lord! to roll the crimson
　　flood   160
Back on its course, and while our
　　banners wing
Northward, strike with us! till the
　　Goth shall cling
To his own blasted altar-stones, and
　　crave
Mercy; and we shall grant it, and
　　dictate
The lenient future of his fate
There, where some rotting ships and
　　crumbling quays
Shall one day mark the Port which
　　ruled the Western seas.
(1862?)   1873

ODE

SUNG AT THE OCCASION OF DECORAT-
ING THE GRAVES OF THE CONFEDER-
ATE DEAD, AT MAGNOLIA CEMETERY,
CHARLESTON, S. C., JUNE 16, 1866

Sleep sweetly in your humble graves,
　　Sleep, martyrs of a fallen cause;
Though yet no marble column craves
　　The pilgrim here to pause.

In seeds of laurel in the earth
　　The blossom of your fame is blown,
And somewhere, waiting for its birth,
　　The shaft is in the stone!

Meanwhile, behalf the tardy years
　　Which keep in trust your storied
　　　tombs,   10
Behold! your sisters bring their tears.
　　And these memorial blooms.

Small tributes! but your shades will
　　smile

More proudly on these wreaths to
　　day,
Than when some cannon-molded pile
　　Shall overlook this bay.

Stoop, angels, hither from the skies!
　　There is no holier spot of ground
Than where defeated valor lies,
　　By mourning beauty crowned!   20
                                     1866

V. PAUL HAMILTON HAYNE *
(1830–1886)

VICKSBURG—A BALLAD

For sixty days and upwards,
　　A storm of shell and shot
Rained round us in a flaming shower
　　But still we faltered not.
"If the noble city perish,"
　　Our grand young leader said,
"Let the only walls our foe shall scale
　　Be ramparts of the dead!"

For sixty days and upwards,
　　The eye of heaven waxed dim;   10
And e'en throughout God's holy morn
　　O'er Christian prayer and hymn,
Arose a hissing tumult,
　　As if the fiends in air
Strove to engulf the voice of faith
　　In the shrieks of their despair.

There was wailing in the houses,
　　There was trembling in the marts,
While the tempest raged and thun
　　dered,
　　'Mid the silent thrill of hearts; 20
But the Lord, our Shield, was with us
　　And ere a month had sped,
Our very women walked the streets
　　With scarce one throb of dread.

* All selections from Hayne are from
Poems of Paul Hamilton Hayne, 1882. Re
printed by permission of Dr Henry Middle
ton Michel.

And the little children gamboled,
  Their faces purely raised,
Just for a wondering moment,
  As the huge bombs whirled and
    blazed,
Then turned with silvery laughter
  To the sports which children love, 30
Thrice-mailed in the sweet, instinctive
    thought
  That the good God watched above.

Yet the hailing bolts fell faster,
  From scores of flame-clad ships,
And about us, denser, darker,
  Grew the conflict's wild eclipse,
Till a solid cloud closed o'er us,
  Like a type of doom and ire,
Whence shot a thousand quivering
    tongues
  Of forked and vengeful fire.   40

But the unseen hands of angels
  Those death-shafts warned aside,
And the dove of heavenly mercy
  Ruled o'er the battle tide;
In the houses ceased the wailing,
  And through the war-scarred marts
The people strode, with step of hope,
  To the music in their hearts.
                              1863

UNDER THE PINE

TO THE MEMORY OF HENRY TIMROD

The same majestic pine is lifted high
  Against the twilight sky,
The same low, melancholy music
    grieves
  Amid the topmost leaves,
As when I watched, and mused, and
    dreamed with him,
  Beneath these shadows dim.

O Tree! hast thou no memory at thy
    core
  Of one who comes no more?
No yearning memory of those scenes
    that were

So richly calm and fair,   10
When the last rays of sunset, shim-
    mering down,
  Flashed like a royal crown?

And he, with hand outstretched and
    eyes ablaze,
  Looked forth with burning gaze,
And seemed to drink the sunset like
    strong wine,
  Or, hushed in trance divine,
Hailed the first shy and timorous
    glance from far
  Of evening's virgin star?

O Tree! against thy mighty trunk he
    laid
  His weary head; thy shade   20
Stole o'er him like the first cool spell
    of sleep:
  It brought a peace *so* deep
The unquiet passion died from out his
    eyes,
  As lightning from stilled skies.

And in that calm he loved to rest,
    and hear
  The soft wind-angels, clear
And sweet, among the uppermost
    branches sighing:
  Voices he heard replying
(Or so he dreamed) far up the mystic
    height,
  And pinions rustling light.   30

O Tree! have not his poet-touch, his
    dreams
  So full of heavenly gleams,
Wrought through the folded dullness
    of thy bark,
  And all thy nature dark
Stirred to slow throbbings, and the
    fluttering fire
  Of faint, unknown desire?

At least to me there sweeps no rugged
    ring
  That girds the forest-king,
No immemorial stain, or awful rent
  (The mark of tempest spent),   40

No delicate leaf, no lithe bough, vine-
o'ergrown,
No distant, flickering cone,

But speaks of him, and seems to bring
once more
The joy, the love of yore;
But most when breathed from out the
sunset-land
The sunset airs are bland,
That blow between the twilight and
the night,
Ere yet the stars are bright.

For then that quiet eve comes back
to me,
When, deeply, thrillingly,   50
He spake of lofty hopes which van-
quish Death;
And on his mortal breath
A language of immortal meanings
hung,
That fired his heart and tongue.

For then unearthly breezes stir and
sigh,
Murmuring, "Look up! 'tis I:
Thy friend is near thee! Ah, thou
canst not see!"
And through the sacred tree
Passes what seems a wild and sentient
thrill—
Passes, and all is still!—   60

Still as the grave which holds his
tranquil form,
Hushed after many a storm,—
Still as the calm that crowns his
marble brow,
No pain can wrinkle now,—
Still as the peace,—pathetic peace of
God—
That wraps the holy sod,

Where every flower from our dead
minstrel's dust
Should bloom, a type of trust,—
That faith which waxed to wings of
heavenward light
To bear his soul from night,—   70

That faith, dear Christ! whereby we
pray to meet
His spirit at God's feet!

1882

ASPECTS OF THE PINES

Tall, sombre, grim, against the morning sky
They rise, scarce touched by melancholy airs,
Which stir the fadeless foliage dream-
fully,
As if from realms of mystical despairs.

Tall, sombre, grim, they stand with
dusky gleams
Brightening to gold within the
woodland's core,
Beneath the gracious noontide's tranquil beams—
But the weird winds of morning
sigh no more.

A stillness, strange, divine, ineffable,
Broods round and o'er them in the
wind's surcease,   10
And on each tinted copse and shimmering dell
Rests the mute rapture of deep-
hearted peace.

Last, sunset comes—the solemn joy
and might
Borne from the West when cloudless day declines—
Low, flutelike breezes sweep the waves
of light,
And lifting dark green tresses of
the pines,

Till every lock is luminous—gently
float,
Fraught with hale odors up the
heavens afar
To faint when twilight on her virginal throat

Wears for a gem the tremulous
  vesper star.   20
                                         1872

A LITTLE WHILE I FAIN WOULD LINGER YET

A little while (my life is almost set!)
  I fain would pause along the down-
      ward way,
  Musing an hour in this sad sunset-
      ray,
While, Sweet! our eyes with tender
      tears are wet;
A little hour I fain would linger yet.

A little while I fain would linger yet,
  All for love's sake, for love that
      cannot tire;
  Though fervid youth be dead, with
      youth's desire,
And hope has faded to a vague regret,
A little while I fain would linger
      yet.   10

A little while I fain would linger
      here:
  Behold! who knows what strange,
      mysterious bars
  'Twixt souls that love, may rise in
      other stars?
Nor can love deem the face of death
      is fair;
A little while I still would linger here.

A little while I yearn to hold thee fast,
  Hand locked in hand, and loyal
      heart to heart;
    (O pitying Christ! those woeful
      words, "We part!")
So ere the darkness fall, the light be
      passed,
A little while I fain would hold thee
      fast.   20

A little while, when night and twi-
      light meet;
  Behind, our broken years; before,
      the deep

Weird wonder of the last unfath-
      omed sleep.
A little while I still would clasp thee,
      Sweet;
A little while, when night and twi-
      light meet.

A little while I fain would linger
      here;
  Behold! who knows what soul-
      dividing bars
  Earth's faithful loves may part in
      other stars?
Nor can love deem the face of death
      is fair:
A little while I still would linger
      here.   30
                                         1882

IN HARBOR

I think it is over, over,
  I think it is over at last,
Voices of foeman and lover,
  The sweet and the bitter have
      passed:
Life, like a tempest of ocean
  Hath outblown its ultimate blast;
There's but a faint sobbing sea-ward
While the calm of the tide deepens
      leeward,
And behold! like the welcoming
      quiver
Of heart-pulses throbbed thro' the
      river,   10
  Those lights in the harbor at last,
  The heavenly harbor at last!

I feel it is over, over!
  For the winds and the waters sur-
      cease;
Ah!—few were the days of the rover
  That smiled in the beauty of
      peace!
And distant and dim was the omen
  That hinted redress or release:
From the ravage of life, and its riot
What marvel I yearn for the quiet   20
  Which bides in the harbor at last?

For the lights with their welcoming
    quiver
That throbbed through the sanctified
    river
    Which girdles the harbor at last,
    This heavenly harbor at last?

I *know* it is over, over,
    I know it is over at last!
Down sail! the sheathed anchor un-
    cover,
    For the stress of the voyage has
    passed:
Life, like a tempest of ocean,   30
Hath outbreathed its ultimate blast;
There's but a faint sobbing sea-ward;
While the calm of the tide deepens
    lee-ward;
And behold! like the welcoming
    quiver
Of heart-pulses throbbed thro' the
    river,
    Those lights in the harbor at last,
    The heavenly harbor at last!
                    1882

VI. ABRAM JOSEPH RYAN*
(1839–1886)

THE CONQUERED BANNER

Furl that Banner, for 'tis weary;
Round its staff 'tis drooping dreary;
    Furl it, fold it,—it is best;
For there's not a man to wave it,
And there's not a sword to save it,
And there's not one left to lave it
In the blood which heroes gave it;
    And its foes now scorn and brave it;
    Furl it, hide it,—let it rest!

Take that Banner down! 'tis tat-
    tered;   10
Broken is its staff and shattered;

* All selections from Ryan are from *Poems*,
by Abram J. Ryan, 1880. Reprinted by
permission of P. J. Kenedy & Sons, owners
of the copyright.

And the valiant hosts are scattered
    Over whom it floated high.
Oh, 'tis hard for us to fold it;
Hard to think there's none to hold it;
Hard that those who once unrolled it
    Now must furl it with a sigh.

Furl that Banner!—furl it sadly!
Once ten thousands hailed it gladly,
And ten thousands wildly, madly,   20
    Swore it should forever wave;
Swore that foeman's sword should
    never
Hearts like theirs entwined dissever,
Till that flag should float forever
    O'er their freedom or their grave!

Furl it! for the hands that grasped it,
And the hearts that fondly clasped it,
    Cold and dead are lying low;
And that Banner—it is trailing!
While around it sounds the wailing   30
    Of its people in their woe.

For, though conquered, they adore it!
Love the cold, dead hands that bore
    it!
    Weep for those who fell before it!
Pardon those who trailed and tore it!
But, oh! wildly they deplore it,
    Now who furl and fold it so!

Furl that Banner! True, 'tis gory,
Yet 'tis wreathed around with glory,
And 'twill live in song and story,   40
    Though its folds are in the dust:
For its fame on brightest pages,
Penned by poets and by sages,
Shall go sounding down the ages—
    Furl its folds though now we
    must.

Furl that Banner, softly, slowly!
Treat it gently—it is holy—
    For it droops above the dead.
Touch it not—unfold it never,
Let it droop there, furled forever,   50
    For its people's hopes are dead!
                    1868

THE SWORD OF ROBERT LEE

Forth from its scabbard, pure and
    bright,
    Flashed the sword of Lee!
Far in the front of the deadly fight,
High o'er the brave in the cause of
    Right,
Its stainless sheen, like a beacon light,
    Led us to Victory.

Out of its scabbard, where, full long,
    It slumbered peacefully,
Roused from its rest by the battle's
    song,
Shielding the feeble, smiting the
    strong,   10
Guarding the right, avenging the
    wrong,
    Gleamed the sword of Lee.

Forth from its scabbard, high in air
    Beneath Virginia's sky—
And they who saw it gleaming there,
And knew who bore it, knelt to swear

That where that sword led they would
    dare
    To follow—and to die.

Out of its scabbard! Never hand
    Waved sword from stain as free, 20
Nor purer sword led braver band,
Nor braver bled for a brighter land,
Nor brighter land had a cause so
    grand,
    Nor cause a chief like Lee!

Forth from its scabbard! How we
    prayed
    That sword might victor be;
And when our triumph was delayed,
And many a heart grew sore afraid,
We still hoped on while gleamed the
    blade
    Of noble Robert Lee.   30

Forth from its scabbard all in vain
    Bright flashed the sword of Lee;
'Tis shrouded now in its sheath again,
It sleeps the sleep of our noble slain,
Defeated, yet without a stain,
    Proudly and peacefully.

                1865?

VII. ALBION W. TOURGÉE
(1838–1905)

From *A FOOL'S ERRAND*

CHAPTER XXVII

A NEW INSTITUTION

There had been rumors in the air, for some months, of a strangely mysterious organization, said to be spreading over the Southern States, which added to the usual intangibility of the secret society an element of grotesque superstition unmatched in the history of any other.

It was at first regarded as farcical, and the newspapers of the North unwittingly accustomed their readers to regard it as a piece of the broadest and most ridiculous fun. Here and there throughout the South, by a sort of sporadic instinct, bands of ghostly horsemen, in quaint and horrible guise, appeared, and admonished the lazy and trifling of the African race, and threatened the vicious. They claimed to the affrighted negroes, it was said, to be the ghosts of departed Confederates who had come straight from the confines of hell to regulate affairs about their former homes.

All this was a matter of infinite jest and amusement to the good and wise people of the North. What could be funnier, or a more appropriate subject of mirth, than that the chivalric but humorous and jocose Southrons should organize a ghostly police to play upon the superstitious fears of the colored people, who were no doubt very trifling, and needed a good deal of regulation and restraint? So the Northern patriot sat back in his safe and quiet home, and laughed himself into tears and spasms at the grotesque delineations of ghostly K. K. K.'s and terrified darkies, for months before any idea of there being any impropriety therein dawned on his mind or on the minds of the wise men who controlled the affairs of the nation. That a few hundreds, a few thousands, or even millions, of the colored race, should be controlled and dominated by their superstitious fears, deprived of their volition, and compelled to follow the behests of others, was not regarded as at all dangerous in a republic, and as worthy of remark only from its irresistibly amusing character.

It was in the winter of 1868–69, therefore, when the wise men were jubilant over the success of the Great Experiment; when it was said that already Reconstruction had been an approved success, the traces of the war been blotted out, and the era of the millennium anticipated,—that a little company of colored men came to the Fool one day; and one of them, who acted as spokesman, said,—

"What's dis we hear, Mars Kunnel, bout de Klux?"

"The what?" he asked.

"De Klux—de Ku-Kluckers dey calls demselves."

"Oh! the Ku-Klux, Ku-Klux-Klan, K. K. K's, you mean."

"Yes: dem folks what rides about at night a-pesterin' pore colored people, an' a-pertendin' tu be jes from hell, or some of de battle-fields ob ole Virginny."

"Oh, that's all gammon! There is nothing in the world in it,—nothing at all. Probably a parcel of boys now and then take it into their heads to scare a few colored people; but that's all. It is mean and cowardly, but nothing more. You needn't have any trouble about it, boys."

"An' you tink dat's all, Kunnel?"

"All? Of course it is! What else should there be?"

"I dunno, Mars Kunnel," said one.

"You don't think dey's ghostses, nor nothin' of dat sort?" asked another.

"Think! I know they are not."

"So do I," growled one of their number who had not spoken before, in a tone of such meaning that it drew the eyes of the Fool upon him at once.

"So your mind's made up on that point too, is it, Bob?" he asked laughingly.

"I know dey's not ghosts, Kunnel. I wish ter God dey was!" was the reply.

"Why, what do you mean, Bob?" asked the colonel in surprise.

"Will you jes help me take off my shirt, Jim?" said Bob meaningly, as he turned to one of those with him.

The speaker was taller than the average of his race, of a peculiarly jetty complexion, broad-shouldered, straight, of compact and powerful build. His countenance, despite its blackness, was sharply cut; his head well shaped; and his whole appearance and demeanor marked him as a superior specimen of his race. Servosse had seen him before, and knew him well as an industrious and thrifty blacksmith, living in a distant part of the county, who was noted as being one of the most independent and self-reliant of his people in all political as well as pecuniary matters, —Bob Martin by name.

When his clothing had been removed, he turned his back towards the Fool, and, glancing over his shoulder, said coolly,—

"What d'ye tink of dat, Kunnel?"

"My God!" exclaimed the Fool, starting back in surprise and horror. "What does this mean, Bob?"

"Seen de Kluckers, sah," was the grimly-laconic answer.

The sight which presented itself to the Fool's eyes was truly terrible. The broad muscular back, from the nape down to and below the waist, was gashed and marked by repeated blows. Great furrows were plowed in the black integument, whose greenly-livid lips were drawn back, while the coagulated fibrine stretched across, and mercifully protected the lacerated flesh. The whole back was livid and swollen, bruised as if it had been brayed in a mortar. Apparently, after having cut the flesh with closely-laid welts and furrows, sloping downward from the left side towards the right, with that peculiar skill in castigation which could only be obtained through the abundant opportunity for severe and deliberate flagellation which prevailed under the benign auspices of slavery, the operator had changed his position, and scientifically cross-checked the whole. That he was an expert whose skill justified Bob's remark—"Nobody but an ole oberseer ebber dun dat, Kunnel"—was evident even on a casual inspection. The injury which the man had sustained, though extensive and severe, was not dangerous to one of his constitution and hardened physique. To the eye of the Northern man who gazed at it, however, unused as are all his compeers to witness the effects of severe whipping, it seemed horrible beyond the power of words to express. He did not reflect that the African could have had none of that sense of indignity and degradation with which the Caucasian instinctively regards the application of the emblem of servility, and that he was but fulfilling the end of his dusky being in submitting to such castigation. He was filled with anger, surprise, and horror.

"What?—Who?—How? My God! Tell me all about it. Can't I do something for you, my man?"

"Thank ye, Kunnel, nothing," said Bob seriously. "It's been washed in salt an' water. Dat's de bes' ting dere is to take out de soreness; an' it's doin' as well as can be expected, I s'pose. I don't know much 'bout sech matters, Boss. I'se bin a slave goin' on forty-three years, but never hed a lash on my back sence I was a waitin'-boy till las' night."

His face was working with passion, and his eyes had a wicked fire in them, which clearly showed that he did not take this visitation in such a subdued and grateful spirit as his position properly demanded that he should. When his clothing had been resumed, he sat down and poured into the wondering ears of the Fool this story:—

BOB'S EXPERIENCE

"Yer see, I'se a blacksmith at Burke's Cross-Roads. I've been thar ever sence a few days arter I heerd ob de surrender. I rented an ole house dar, an' put up a sort of shop, an' got togedder a few tools, an' went to work. It's a right good stan'. Never used ter be ob any count, coz all de big plantations roun' dar hed der own smifs. But now de smifs hez scattered off, an' dey hev ter pay fer der work, dey finds it cheaper ter come ter my shop dan ter hire a black-smif when dey's only half work fer him to do. So I'se been doin' right well, an' hev bought de house an' lot, an' got it all paid fer, tu. I've allers tended to my own business. 'Arly an' late Bob's bin at his shop, an' allers at work. I 'llowed to get me a snug home fer myself an' de ole 'ooman afore we got tu old ter work; an' I wanted to give de boys an' gals a little eddication, an' let em hev a fa'r start in life wid de rest ob de worl', if I could. Dat's what Bob's bin wuk-kin' fer; an' der ain't no man ner woman, black ner white, can say he hain't wukked honestly an fa'rly,— honestly an' fa'rly, ebbery day sence he's bin his own master.

"Long a while back—p'raps five er six months—I refused ter du some work fer Michael Anson or his boy, 'cause they'd run up quite a score at de shop, an' allers put me off when I wanted pay. I couldn't work jes fer de fun ob scorin' it down: so I quit. It made smart ob talk. Folks said I waz gettin' too smart fer a nigger, an' sech like; but I kep right on; tole em I waz a free man,—not born free, but made free by a miracle,—an' I didn't propose ter do any man's work fer noffin'. Most everybody hed somefin' to say about it; but it didn't seem ter hurt my trade very much. I jes went on gittin' all I could do, an' sometimes moah. I s'pose I acted

pretty independent: I felt so, any-how. I staid at home, an' axed no-body any favors. I know'd der wa'n't a better blacksmif in de country, an' thought I hed things jes' ez good ez I wanted 'em. When ther come an elec-tion, I sed my say, did my own votin', an' tole de other colored peo-ple dey waz free, an' hed a right ter du de same. Thet's bad doctrine up in our country. De white folks don't like ter hear it, and 'specially don't like ter hear a nigger say it. Dey don't mind 'bout our gittin' on ef dey hev a mortgage, so't de 'arnin's goes into ther pockets; nor 'bout our votin', so long ez we votes ez dey tells us. Dat's dare idea uv liberty fer a nigger.

"Well, here a few weeks ago, I foun' a board stuck up on my shop one mornin', wid dese words on to it:—

BOB MARTIN,—You're gettin' too dam smart! The white folks round Burke's Cross-Roads don't want any sech smart niggers round thar. You'd better git, er you'll hev a call from the

K. K. K.

"I'd heerd 'bout the Klux, an' 'llowed jes' ez you did, Kunnel,—dat dey waz some triflin' boys dat fixed up an' went round jes' ter scare pore ignorant niggers, an' it made me all the madder ter think dey should try dat ar game on me. So I sed boldly, an' afore everybody, thet ef the Kluckers wanted enny thin' uv Bob Martin, they'd better come an' git it; thet I didn't 'bleve any nonsense about ther comin' straight from hell, an' drinkin' the rivers dry, an' all that: but, ef they'd come ter meddle with me, I 'llowed some on 'em mout go to hell afore it was over.

"I worked mighty hard an' late yesterday, an' when I went into de house, I was so tired thet I jes' fell down on de trundle-bed dat hed bin pulled out in front ob de souf do'. When my ole 'ooman got supper ready, an' called me, I jes' turned over, an' was thet beat out an' sleepy, that I tole her to let me alone. So I lay thar, an' slep'. She put away de supperings, an' tuk part ob de chillen into bed wid her; an' de rest crawled in wid me, I s'pose. I donno nothin' about it, fer I nebber woke up till some time in de night. I kinder remember hearin' de dog bark, but I didn't mind it; an', de fust ting I knew, de do' was bust in, an' fell off de hinges ober on de trundle-bed whar I was lyin'. It's a mercy I was thar. I don't s'pose I've lain down on it er a year afore, an', ef de chillen hed all been thar alone, it's mor'n likely they'd all been killed. They hed taken a house-log I hed got (tinkin' ter put up a kitchen arter Christmas), an' free or four of 'em hed run wid it endwise agin de do'. So, when I woke from de crash, I hed o' an' house-log bofe on me, an' de ole 'ooman an' chillen screamin', so't I couldn't make out fer a minnit what was, er whar I was. De moon was a-shinin' bright, an' I 'spect de rascals thought I'd run, an' dey would shoot me as I come out. But, as soon as dey saw me heavin' an' strugglin' under de do', two on 'em run in, an' sot on top of it. It was no use fer me to struggle any more under dat load. Besides dat, I was feared dey'd kill de chillen. So I tole 'em ef dey'd get off, an' spar' de chillen, I'd surrender. Dey wouldn't bleve me, though, till they'd tied my han's. Den

dey got off de do', an' I riz up, an' kind o' pushed it an' de house-log off de trundle-bed. Den dey pulled me out o' do's. Dar was 'bout tirty of 'em standin' dar in de moonlight, all dressed in black gowns thet come down to ther boots, an' some sort of high hat on, dat come down ober der faces, jes' leavin' little holes ter see fru, an' all trimmed wid different colored cloth, but mos'ly white.

"I axed 'em what dey wanted o' me. Dey sed I was gittin tu dam smart, an' dey'd jes' come roun' ter teach me some little manners. Den dey tied me tu a tree, an' done what you've seen. Dey tuk my wife an' oldes' gal out ob de house, tore de close nigh about off 'em, an' abused 'em shockin' afore my eyes. Arter tarin' tings up a heap in de house, dey rode off, tellin' me dey reckoned I'd larn to be 'spectful to white folks herearter, an' not refuse to work unless I hed pay in advance, an' not be so anxious 'bout radical votes. Den my ole woman cut me loose, an' we went into de house ter see what devilment dey'd done dar. We called de chillen. Dar's five on 'em,—de oldes' a gal 'bout fifteen, an' de younges' only little better'n a year ole. We foun' 'em all but de baby. I don' tink he ebber breaved arter de do' fell on us."

The tears stood in the eyes of the poor man as he finished. The Fool looked at him in a glamour of amazement, pity, and shame. He could not help feeling humiliated, that, in his own Christian land, one should be so treated by such a cowardly-seeming combination, simply for having used the liberty which the law had given him to acquire competence and independence by his own labor.

"Why have you not complained of this outrage to the authorities?" he asked after a moment.

"I tole Squire Haskins an' Judge Thompson what I hev tole you," answered Bob.

"And what did they say?"

"Dat dey couldn't do noffin' unless I could sw'ar to de parties."

"Did you not recognize any of them?"

"Not to say recognize; dat is, not so dat I could tell you so dat you could know de persons as de ones I named. I'm nigh 'bout sartin, from a lot of little tings, who dey was; but I couldn't sw'ar."

"Did you not know the voices of any of them?"

"Yes, I did. But de judge says I would jes' be makin' trouble fer myself to no 'count; fer he says no jury would convict on sech evidence when unsupported."

"I suppose he is right," mused the Colonel. "And there does not seem to be any way for you to get redress for what has been done to you, unless you can identify those who did the injury so clearly that no jury can resist a conviction. I suppose the vast majority of jurymen will be disinclined even to do justice. Perhaps some of the very men who were engaged in the act may be on the jury, or their brothers, fathers, or friends. So it would be useless for you to attempt a prosecution unless you had the very strongest and clearest testimony. I doubt not the judge was right in the advice he gave you."

"And do you tink der is any chance o' my gittin' sech testimony?" asked Bob.

"I confess," answered the Fool, "that I see very little. Time and care might possibly enable you to get it."

"Der's no hope o' dat,—no hope at all," answered the freedman sadly.

There was a moment's silence. Then the colored man asked,—

"Isn't dere no one else, Kunnel, dat could do any ting? Can't de President or Congress do somefin'? De gov'ment sot us free, an' it 'pears like it oughtn't to let our old masters impose on us in no sech way now. I ain't no coward, Kunnel, an' I don't want to brag; but I ain't 'feared o' no man. I don't min' sufferin' nor dyin' ef I could see any good to come from it. I'd be willin' ter fight fe my liberty, er fer de country dat giv me liberty. But I don't tink liberty was any favor ef we are to be cut up an' murdered jes' de same as in slav times, an' wuss too. Bob'll take kee of himself, an' his wife an' chillen too ef dey'll only give him a white man' chance. But ef men can come to hi house in de middle ob de night, ki his baby, an' beat an' abuse him an his family ez much ez dey please, je by puttin' a little black cloth ober de faces, I may ez well give up, an' be slave agin."

"If it keeps on, and grows general responded the Caucasian, "the gov ernment will have to interfere. Th necessity will be such that they ca not resist it. I don't quite see ho it can be done, now that these Stat are restored; but the government mu protect the lives of its citizens, a it ought to protect their liberties. don't know how it may be done. may declare such acts treasonable, a outlaw the offenders, authorizing a nan to kill them when engaged in uch unlawful acts."

"If dey would only do dat, Kunnel, we'd soon put an end to de Ku-Kluckers. We'd watch de roads, an', bery time dey rode frue de bushes, ere'd be some less murderin' Kluck-rs dan when dey started out. Hav' em du dat, Kunnel, an' we's all right. es' gib us a fa'r chance, an' de culled nen'll tak' keer o' dersel's. We ain't owards. We showed dat in de wah. 'se seen darkeys go whar de white roops wa'n't anxious to foller 'em nor'n once."

"Where was that, Bob?"

"Wal, at Fo't Wagner, for one."

"How did you know about that?"

"How did I know 'bout dat? Bress er soul, Kunnel, I was dar!"

"How did that happen? I thought ou were raised in the up country ere?"

"So I was, Kunnel; but, when I eerd dat Abram Linkum had gib us ur freedom, I made up my mine I'd o an' git my sheer, an', ef dar was ny ting I could do to help de rest f my folks to git dars, I was gwine r du it. So I managed to slip away, ne wayer 'nother, an' got fru de lines own 'bout Charleston, an' jined de ifty-fo' Massachusetts Culled, Kun-el. Dat's how I come to be at Wagner."

"That explains, in part, the feeling gainst you, I suppose," said Servosse.

"It s'plains annudder ting tu, Kun-el," said the colored man doggedly.

"What is that?" asked the white ex-soldier.

"It s'plains why, ef dere's any mo' luckers raidin' roun' Burke's Cor-rs, dar'll be some funerals tu," was e grim reply.

"I can't blame you, Bob," said the white man, looking frankly into his face as it worked with agony and rage. "A man has a right to protect himself and his family; and, if our government is too blind or too weak to put down this new rebellion, there are only three courses before us,—you and me, and those who stood with us: the one is to fight the devil with fire,—to kill those who kill,—guard the fords, and, whenever we see a man in disguise, shoot him down; another is to give up everything else for the privilege of living here; and the third is to get away."

"It will come to dat, Kunnel. Ef de gubment won't take keer o' de darkeys y'her, an' gib 'em a white man's chance, dey'll run away, jes' ez dey did in slave times. Dat's my notion," said the freedman, who had fought to save the life of the nation, which would not lift a finger to save his in return.

"God only knows," answered the soldier, who had been branded as a "Carpet-bagger" throughout the land, because he was born at the North, had fought for the country, and thought he had a right to live where he chose.

A hearty dinner and a glass of liquor were the only substantial benefits which he could confer on the suffering fellow, who went away with his companions to consult with friends in the village which had grown up as the colored suburb of Verdenton, and was now known as Huntsville, being named from the owner of the plantation out of which it was principally carved. It had been sold at public sale, and bought up by the Fool, who had divided it up into lots, and sold it out in this manner, together with a part of Warrington.

It was a new and terrible revelation to the Fool. He saw at once how this potent instrumentality might be used so as to effectually destroy the liberty of the newly enfranchised citizen, and establish a serfdom more barbarous and horrible than any on earth, because it would be the creature of lawless insolence. He saw, too, that this might easily be effected without any tangible and punishable violation of the law. His heart was wrung in agony for his poor neighbors. For himself, it did not yet occur to him to fear.

There was much excitement in the little village of Huntsville that day. Betwixt fear and rage, the heart of every one was in a ferment at the outrage committed upon Bob Martin. For once, Uncle Jerry forgot his accustomed prudence, and moved by a very unreasonable anger at the impotency of the law, which could not punish those who could not be clearly identified, he openly and boldly declared the monstrous doctrine that the colored people ought to defend themselves and each other. That he should entertain such ideas was in itself a misfortune; that he should give expression to such incendiary notions was a fatal error.

1879

VIII. HENRY WOODFIN GRADY
(1851–1889)

THE NEW SOUTH

"There was a South of slavery and secession—that South is dead. There is a South of union and freedom—that South, thank God, is living, breathing, growing every hour." These words, delivered from the immortal lips of Benjamin H. Hill, at Tammany Hall, in 1866, true then and truer now, I shall make my text tonight.

Mr. President and Gentlemen: Let me express to you my appreciation of the kindness by which I am permitted to address you. I make this abrupt acknowledgment advisedly, for I feel that if, when I raise my provincial voice in this ancient and august presence, it could find courage for no more than the opening sentence, it would be well if in that sentence I had met in a rough sense my obligation as a guest, and had perished, so to speak, with courtesy on my lips and grace in my heart.

Permitted, through your kindness, to catch my second wind, let me say that I appreciate the significance of being the first Southerner to speak at this board; which bears the substance, if it surpasses the semblance, of original New England hospitality—and honors the sentiment that in turn honors you, but in which my personality is lost, and the compliment to my people made plain.

I bespeak the utmost stretch of your courtesy to-night. I am not troubled about those from whom I come. You remember the man whose wife sent him to a neighbor with a pitcher of milk, and who, tripping on the top step, fell with such casual interruptions as the landings afforded into the basement; and, while picking himself up, had the pleasure of hearing his wife call out: "John, did you break the pitcher?"

"No, I didn't," said John, "but I'll be dinged if I don't."

So, while those who call me from behind may inspire me with energy, if not with courage, I ask an indulgent hearing from you. I beg that you will bring your full faith in American fairness and frankness to judgment upon what I shall say. There was an old preacher once who told some boys of the Bible lesson he was going to read in the morning. The boys, finding the place, glued together the connecting pages. The next morning he read on the bottom of one page, "When Noah was one hundred and twenty years old he took unto himself a wife, who was" —then turning the page—"140 cubits long—40 cubits wide, built of gopher wood—and covered with pitch inside and out." He was naturally puzzled at this. He read it again, verified it, and then said: "My friends, this is the first time I ever met this in the Bible, but I accept this as an evidence of the assertion that we are fearfully and wonderfully made." If I could get you to hold such faith to-night I could proceed cheerfully to the task I otherwise approach with a sense of consecration.

Pardon me one word, Mr. President, spoken for the sole purpose of putting into the volumes that go out annually freighted with the rich eloquence of your speakers—the fact that the Cavalier as well as the Puritan, was on the continent in his early days, and that he was "up and able to be out." I have read your books carefully and I find no mention of the fact, which seems to me an important one for preserving a sort of historical equilibrium, if for nothing else.

Let me remind you that the Virginia Cavalier first challenged France on the continent; that a Cavalier, John Smith, gave New England its very name, and was so pleased with the job that he has been handing his own name around ever since; and that while Myles Standish was cutting off men's ears for courting a girl without her parents' consent, and forbidding men to kiss their wives on Sunday, the Cavalier was courting everything in sight; and that the Almighty had vouchsafed great increase to the Cavalier colonies, the huts in the wilderness being as full as the nests in the woods.

But having incorporated the Cavalier as a fact in your charming little books, I shall let him work out his own salvation, as he has always done, with engaging gallantry, and we will hold no controversy as to his merits. Why should we? Neither Puritan nor Cavalier long survived as such. The virtues and good traditions of both happily still live for the inspiration of their sons and the saving of the old fashion. But both Puritan and Cavalier were lost in the storm of the first Revolution; and the American citizen, supplanting both and stronger than either, took possession of the republic bought by their common blood and fashioned to wisdom, and charged himself with teaching men government and establishing the voice of the people as the voice of God.

My friends, Dr. Talmage has told you that the typical American has yet to come. Let me tell you that he has already come. Great types, like valuable plants, are slow to flower and fruit. But from the union of these colonists, Puritans and Cavaliers, from the straightening of their purposes and the crossing of their blood, slow perfecting through a century, càme he who stands as the first typical American, the first who comprehended within himself all the strength and gentleness, all the majesty and grace of this republic—Abraham Lincoln. He was the sum of Puritan and Cavalier, for in his ardent nature were fused the virtues of both; and in the depths of his great soul the faults of both were lost. He was greater than Puritan, greater than Cavalier, in that he was American, and that in his honest form were first gathered the vast and thrilling forces of his ideal government—charging it with such tremendous meaning and elevating it above human suffering that martyrdom, though infamously aimed, came as a fitting crown to a life consecrated from the cradle to human liberty. Let us, each cherishing the traditions and honoring his fathers, build with reverent hands to the type of this simple but sublime life, in which all types are honored, and in our common glory as Americans there will be plenty and to spare for your forefathers and for mine.

Dr. Talmage has drawn for you, with a master's hand, the picture of your returning armies. He has told you how, in the pomp and circumstance of war, they came back to you, marching with proud and victorious tread, reading their glory in a nation's eyes! Will you bear with me while I tell you of another army that sought its home at the close of the late war —an army that marched home in defeat and not in victory—in pathos and not in splendor; but in glory that equaled yours, and to hearts as loving as ever welcomed heroes home!

Let me picture to you the footsore Confederate soldier, as, buttoning up in his faded gray jacket the parole which was to bear testimony to hi children of his fidelity and faith, he turned his face southward from Appomattox in April, 1865. Think of him as, ragged, half-starved, heavy hearted, enfeebled by want an wounds, having fought to exhaustion he surrenders his gun, wrings the hands of his comrades in silence, and lifting his tear-stained and pallid fac for the last time to the graves that dot the old Virginia hills, pulls hi gray cap over his brow and begin the slow and painful journey.

What does he find—let me ask yo who went to your homes eager t find, in the welcome you had just earned, full payment for four year sacrifice—what does he find when having followed the battle-staine cross against overwhelming odd dreading death not half so much a surrender, he reaches the home he le so prosperous and beautiful? He find his house in ruins, his farm devastate his slaves free, his stock killed, h barns empty, his trade destroyed, h money worthless; his social syste feudal in its magnificence, swept away his people without law or legal statu his comrades slain, and the burde of others heavy on his shoulde Crushed by defeat, his very traditio are gone. Without money, credit, e ployment, material, or training; a besides all this, confronted with t gravest problems that ever met hum intelligence—the establishment of status for the vast body of his l erated slaves.

What does he do—this hero in gr with a heart of gold? Does he own in sullenness and despair? Not or a day. Surely God, who had stripped him of his prosperity, inspired him in his adversity. As ruin was never before so overwhelming, never was restoration swifter.

The soldier stepped from the trenches into the furrow; horses that had charged Federal guns marched before the plow, and fields that ran red with human blood in April were green with the harvest in June; women reared in luxury cut up their dresses and made breeches for their husbands, and, with a patience and heroism that fit women always as a garment, gave their hands to work. There was little bitterness in all this. Cheerfulness and frankness prevailed. "Bill Arp" struck the keynote when he said: "Well, I killed as many of them as they did of me; and now I'm going to work." So did the soldier returning home after defeat and roasting some corn on the roadside, who made the remark to his comrades: "You may leave the South if you want to; but I'm going to Sandersville, kiss my wife, and raise a crop; and if the Yankees fool with me any more, I'll whip 'em again."

I want to say to General Sherman, who is considered an able man in our parts, though some people think he was a kind of careless man about fire, that from the ashes he left us in 1864 we have raised a brave and beautiful city; that somehow or other we have caught the sunshine in the bricks and mortar of our homes, and have builded therein not one ignoble prejudice or memory.

But what is the sum of our work? We have found out that in the summing up the free negro counts for more than he did as a slave. We have planted the schoolhouse on the hilltop, and made it free to white and black. We have sowed towns and cities in the place of theories, and put business above politics. We have challenged your spinners in Massachusetts and your ironmakers in Pennsylvania. We have learned that the $400,000,000 annually received from our cotton crop will make us rich when the supplies that make it are homeraised. We have reduced the commercial rate of interest from 24 to 6 per cent., and are floating 4 per cent. bonds. We have learned that one Northern immigrant is worth fifty foreigners, and have smoothed the path to the Southward, wiped out the place where Mason and Dixon's line used to be, and hung out the latchstring to you and yours.

We have reached the point that marks perfect harmony in every household, when the husband confesses that the pies which his wife cooks are as good as those his mother used to bake; and we admit that the sun shines as brightly and the moon as softly as it did "before the war." We have established thrift in city and country. We have fallen in love with work. We have restored comfort to homes from which culture and elegance never departed. We have let economy take root and spread among us as rank as the crab-grass which sprung from Sherman's cavalry camps, until we are ready to lay odds on the Georgia Yankee, as he manufactures relics of the battlefield in a one-story shanty and squeezes pure olive-oil out of his cottonseed, against any down-easter that ever swapped wooden nutmegs for flannel sausage in the valleys of

Vermont. Above all, we know that we have achieved in these "piping times of peace" a fuller independence for the South than that which our fathers sought to win in the forum by their eloquence or compel in the field by their swords.

It is a rare privilege, sir, to have had a part, however humble, in this work. Never was nobler duty confided to human hands than the uplifting and upbuilding of the prostrate and bleeding South—misguided, perhaps, but beautiful in her suffering, and honest, brave, and generous always. In the record of her social, industrial, and political institutions we await with confidence the verdict of the world.

But what of the negro? Have we solved the problem he presents, or progressed in honor and equity toward solution? Let the record speak to the point. No section shows a more prosperous laboring population than the negroes of the South, none in fuller sympathy with the employing and land-owning class. He shares our school fund, has the fullest protection of our laws and the friendship of our people. Self-interest, as well as honor, demand that he should have this. Our future, our very existence depend upon our working out this problem in full and exact justice. We understand that when Lincoln signed the emancipation proclamation, your victory was assured; for he then committed you to the cause of human liberty, against which the arms of man cannot prevail—while those of our statesmen who trusted to make slavery the cornerstone of the Confederacy doomed us to defeat as far as they could, committing us to a cause that reason could not defend or the sword maintain in sight of advancing civilization.

Had Mr. Toombs said, which he did not say, that "he would call the roll of his slaves at the foot of Bunker Hill," he would have been foolish; for he might have known that whenever slavery became entangled in war it must perish, and that the chattel in human flesh ended forever in New England when your fathers—not to be blamed for parting with what didn't pay—sold their slaves to our fathers —not to be praised for knowing a paying thing when they saw it. The relations of the Southern people with the negro are close and cordial. We remember with what fidelity for four years he guarded our defenseless women and children, whose husbands and fathers were fighting against his freedom. To his eternal credit be it said that whenever he struck a blow for his own liberty he fought in open battle; and when at last he raised his black and humble hands that the shackles might be struck off, those hands were innocent of wrong against his helpless charges, and worthy to be taken in loving grasp by every man who honors loyalty and devotion. Ruffians have maltreated him, rascals have misled him, philanthropists established a bank for him; but the South, with the North, protests against injustice to this simple and sincere people.

To liberty and enfranchisement is as far as law can carry the negro. The rest must be left to conscience and common sense. It must be left to those among whom his lot is cast, with whom he is indissolubly connected, and whose prosperity depends upon their possessing his intelligent sympathy and confidence. Faith has been kept with him, in spite of calumnious assertions to the contrary by those who assume to speak for us, or by frank opponents. Faith will be kept with him in the future, if the South holds her reason and integrity.

But have we kept faith with you? In the fullest sense, yes. When Lee surrendered—I don't say when Johnston surrendered, because I understand he still alludes to the time when he met General Sherman last, as the time when he determined to abandon any further prosecution of the struggle—when Lee surrendered, I say, and Johnston quit, the South became, and has since been, loyal to this Union. We fought hard enough to know that we were whipped, and in perfect frankness accept as final the arbitrament of the sword to which we had appealed. The South found her jewel in the toad's head of defeat. The shackles that had held her in narrow limitations fell forever when the shackles of the negro slave were broken. Under the old régime the negroes were slaves to the South; the South was a slave to the system. The old plantation, with its simple police regulations and feudal habit, was the only type possible under slavery. Thus was gathered in the hands of a splendid and chivalric oligarchy the substance that should have been diffused among the people; as the rich blood, under certain artificial conditions is gathered at the heart, filling that with affluent rapture, but leaving the body chill and colorless.

The old South rested everything on slavery and agriculture, unconscious that these could neither give nor maintain healthy growth. The new South presents a perfect democracy, the oligarchs leading in the popular movement—a social system, compact and closely knitted, less splendid on the surface, but stronger at the core—a hundred farms for every plantation, fifty homes for every palace—and a diversified industry that meets the complex needs of this complex age.

The new South is enamored of her new work. Her soul is stirred with the breath of a new life. The light of a grander day is falling fair on her face. She is thrilling with the consciousness of growing power and prosperity. As she stands upright, full-statured and equal among the people of the earth, breathing the keen air and looking out upon the expanded horizon, she understands that her emancipation came because through the inscrutable wisdom of God her honest purpose was crossed, and her brave armies were beaten.

This is said in no spirit of time-serving or apology. The South has nothing for which to apologize. She believes that the late struggle between the States was war and not rebellion; revolution and not conspiracy, and that her convictions were as honest as yours. I should be unjust to the dauntless spirit of the South and to my own convictions if I did not make this plain in this presence. The South has nothing to take back.

In my native town of Athens is a monument that crowns its central hill —a plain, white shaft. Deep cut into its shining side is a name dear to me above the names of men—that of a brave and simple man who died in brave and simple faith. Not for all the glories of New England, from Plymouth Rock all the way, would I exchange the heritage he left me in his soldier's death. To the foot of that I shall send my children's children to reverence him who ennobled their name with his heroic blood. But, sir, speaking from the shadow of that memory which I honor as I do nothing else on earth, I say that the cause in which he suffered and for which he gave his life was adjudged by higher and fuller wisdom than his or mine; and I am glad that the omniscient God held the balance of battle in His Almighty hand, and that human slavery was swept forever from American soil—that the American Union was saved from the wreck of war.

This message, Mr. President, comes to you from consecrated ground. Every foot of soil about the city in which I live is sacred as a battleground of the republic. Every hill that invests it is hallowed to you by the blood of your brothers who died for your victory, and doubly hallowed to us by the blood of those who died hopeless, but undaunted, in defeat— sacred soil to all of us—rich with memories that make us purer and stronger and better—silent but staunch witnesses in its red desolation of the matchless valor of American hearts and the deathless glory of American arms—speaking an eloquent witness in its white peace and prosperity to the indissoluble union of American States, and the imperishable brotherhood of the American people.

Now, what answer has New England to this message? Will she permit the prejudice of war to remain in the hearts of the conquerors, when it has died in the hearts of the conquered? Will she transmit this prejudice to the next generation, that in their hearts which never felt the generous ardor of conflict it may perpetuate itself? Will she withhold, save in strained courtesy, the hand which straight from his soldier's heart Grant offered to Lee at Appomattox? Will she make the vision of a restored and happy people, which gathered above the couch of your dying captain, filling his heart with grace, touching his lips with praise, and glorifying his path to the grave—will she make this vision on which the last sigh of his expiring soul breathed a benediction, a cheat and delusion?

If she does, the South, never abject in asking for comradeship, must accept with dignity its refusal; but if she does not refuse to accept in frankness and sincerity this message of good will and friendship, then will the prophecy of Webster, delivered in this very society forty years ago amid tremendous applause, become true, be verified in its fullest sense, when he said: "Standing hand to hand and clasping hands, we should remain united as we have been for sixty years, citizens of the same country, members of the same government, united, all united now and united forever." There have been difficulties, contentions, and controversies, but I tell you that in my judgment,

Those opposed eyes,
Which like the meteors of a troubled heaven,
All of one nature, of one substance bred,
Did lately meet in th' intestine shock,
Shall now, in mutual well-beseeming ranks,
March all one way.

SIDNEY LANIER*
(1842–1881)

NIGHT AND DAY

The innocent, sweet Day is dead.
Dark Night hath slain her in her bed.
O, Moors are as fierce to kill as to
    wed!
    —Put out the light, said he.

A sweeter light than ever rayed
From star of heaven or eye of maid
Has vanished in the unknown Shade.
    —She's dead, she's dead, said he.

Now, in a wild, sad after-mood
The tawny Night sits still to brood 10
Upon the dawn-time when he wooed.
    —I would she lived, said he.

Star-memories of happier times,
Of loving deeds and lovers' rhymes,
Throng forth in silvery pantomimes.
    —Come back, O Day! said he.
(1866)   1884

SONG FOR "THE JACQUERIE"

The hound was cuffed, the hound
    was kicked,
O' the ears was cropped, o' the
    tail was nicked;
(All) "Oo-hoo-o!" howled the hound.
The hound into his kennel
    crept;
He rarely wept, he never slept;
His mouth he always open kept
    Licking his bitter wound,
      The hound.
(All) "U-lu-lo!" howled the hound.

A star upon his kennel shone 10
That showed the hound a meat-
    bare bone:
(All) O hungry was the hound!
The hound had but a churlish
    wit:
He seized the bone, he crunched,
    he bit.
"An thou wert Master, I had
    slit
    Thy throat with a huge
      wound,"
      Quo' hound;
(All) O, angry was the hound.

The star in castle-window shone;
The Master lay abed, alone: 20
(All) "Oh ho, why not?" quo'
    hound.
He leapt, he seized the throat,
    he tore
The Master, head from neck, to
    floor,
And rolled the head i' the ken-
    nel door,
    And fled and salved his
      wound,
      Good hound!
(All) "U-lu-lo!" howled the hound.
(1868)   1884

CORN

To-day the woods are trembling
    through and through
With shimmering forms, that flash
    before my view,
Then melt in green as dawn-stars
    melt in blue.
The leaves that wave against my
    cheek caress

* All poems of Lanier are reprinted from
The Poems of Sidney Lanier (1884) by permission of Charles Scribner's Sons, the
publishers.

Like women's hands; the embracing
  boughs express
A subtlety of mighty tenderness;
The copse-depths into little noises
  start,
That sound anon like beatings of a
  heart,
Anon like talk 'twixt lips not far
  apart.
The beech dreams balm, as a dreamer
  hums a song;   10
Through that vague wafture, expira-
  tions strong
Throb from young hickories breathing
  deep and long
With stress and urgence bold of pris-
  oned spring
And ecstasy of burgeoning.
Now, since the dew-plashed road of
  morn is dry,
Forth venture odors of more quality
And heavenlier giving. Like Jove's
  locks awry,
Long muscadines
Rich-wreathe the spacious foreheads
  of great pines,
And breathe ambrosial passion from
  their vines.   20
I pray with mosses, ferns and flowers
  shy
That hide like gentle nuns from hu-
  man eye
To lift adoring perfumes to the sky.
I hear faint bridal-sighs of brown and
  green
Dying to silent hints of kisses keen
As far lights fringe into a pleasant
  sheen.
I start at fragmentary whispers,
  blown
From undertalks of leafy souls un-
  known,
Vague purports sweet, of inarticulate
  tone.
Dreaming of gods, men, nuns and
  brides, between   30
Old companies of oaks that inward
  lean
To join their radiant amplitudes of
  green

I slowly move, with ranging look
  that pass
Up from the matted miracles of grass
Into yon veined complex of space
Where sky and leafage interlace
So close, the heaven of blue is seen
Interwoven with a heaven of green.

I wander to the zigzag-cornered fence
Where sassafras, intrenched in bram-
  bles dense,   4
Contests with stolid vehemence
The march of culture, setting limb
  and thorn
As pikes against the army of the corn

There, while I pause, my fieldward
  faring eyes
Take harvests, where the stately corn-
  ranks rise,
      Of inward dignities
And large benignities and insight
  wise,
      Graces and modest majesties.
Thus, without theft, I reap another's
  field;
Thus, without tilth, I house a wondrous yield,   5
And heap my heart with quintuple
  crops concealed.

Look, out of line one tall corn-captain
  stands
Advanced beyond the foremost of his
  bands,
And waves his blades upon the very
  edge
And hottest thicket of the battling
  hedge.
Thou lustrous stalk, that ne'er mayst
  walk nor talk,
Still shalt thou type the poet-soul
  sublime
That leads the vanward of his timid
  time
And sings up cowards with commanding rhyme—
Soul calm, like thee, yet fain, like
  thee, to grow   6
By double increment, above, below

Soul homely, as thou art, yet rich in
    grace like thee,
Teaching the yeomen selfless chivalry
That moves in gentle curves of
    courtesy;
Soul filled like thy long veins with
    sweetness tense,
    By every godlike sense
Transmuted from the four wild ele-
    ments.
    Drawn to high plans,
Thou lift'st more stature than a mor-
    tal man's,
Yet ever piercest downward in the
    mould   70
    And keepest hold
Upon the reverend and steadfast earth
    That gave thee birth;
Yea, standest smiling in thy future
    grave,
    Serene and brave,
With unremitting breath
Inhaling life from death,
Thine epitaph writ fair in fruitage
    eloquent,
    Thyself thy monument.

    As poets should,   80
Thou hast built up thy hardihood
With universal food,
Drawn in select proportion fair
From honest mold and vagabond air;
From darkness of the dreadful night,
    And joyful light;
From antique ashes, whose departed
    flame
In thee has finer life and longer fame;
From wounds and balms,
From storms and calms,   90
From potsherds and dry bones
    And ruin-stones.
Into thy vigorous substance thou hast
    wrought
Whate'er the hand of Circumstance
    hath brought;
Yea, into cool solacing green hast
    spun
White radiance hot from out the sun.
So thou dost mutually leaven

Strength of earth with grace of
    heaven;
So thou dost marry new and old
Into a one of higher mold;   100
So thou dost reconcile the hot and
    cold,
    The dark and bright,
And many a heart-perplexing oppo-
    site,
    And so,
Akin by blood to high and low,
Fitly thou playest out thy poet's part,
Richly expending thy much-bruisèd
    heart
In equal care to nourish lord in hall
    Or beast in stall:
Thou took'st from all that thou
    might'st give to all.   110

O steadfast dweller on the selfsame
    spot
Where thou wast born, that still re-
    pinest not—
Type of the home-fond heart, the
    happy lot!—
Deeply thy mild content rebukes the
    land
Whose flimsy homes, built on the
    shifting sand
Of trade, for ever rise and fall
With alternation whimsical,
    Enduring scarce a day,
    Then swept away
By swift engulfments of incalculable
    tides   120
Whereon capricious Commerce rides.
Look, thou substantial spirit of con-
    tent!
Across this little vale, thy continent,
To where, beyond the moldering mill,
Yon old deserted Georgian hill
Bares to the sun his piteous aged
    crest
    And seamy breast,
By restless-hearted children left to lie
Untended there beneath the heedless
    sky,
As barbarous folk expose their old to
    die.   130

Upon that generous-rounding side,
    With gullies scarified
Where keen Neglect his lash hath
    plied,
Dwelt one I knew of old, who played
    at toil,
And gave to coquette Cotton soul
    and soil.
Scorning the slow reward of patient
    grain,
He sowed his heart with hopes of
    swifter gain,
Then sat him down and waited for the
    rain.
He sailed in borrowed ships of
    usury—
A foolish Jason on a treacherous
    sea,   140
Seeking the Fleece and finding misery.
Lulled by smooth-rippling loans, in
    idle trance
He lay, content that unthrift Circum-
    stance
Should plough for him the stony field
    of Chance,
Yea, gathering crops whose worth no
    man might tell,
He staked his life on games of Buy-
    and-Sell,
And turned each field into a gam-
    bler's hell.
Aye, as each year began,
My farmer to the neighboring city
    ran;
Passed with a mournful anxious
    face   150
Into the banker's inner place;
Parleyed, excused, pleaded for longer
    grace;
Railed at the drought, the worm, the
    rust, the grass;
Protested ne'er again 'twould come to
    pass;
With many an *oh* and *if* and *but alas!*
Parried or swallowed searching ques-
    tions rude,
And kissed the dust to soften Dives's
    mood.
At last, small loans by pledges great
    renewed,

He issues smiling from the fatal door
And buys with lavish hand his yearly
    store   160
Till his small borrowings will yield no
    more.
Aye, as each year declined,
With bitter heart and ever-brooding
    mind
He mourned his fate unkind.
In dust, in rain, with might and main
He nursed his cotton, cursed his grain
Fretted for news that made him fre
    again,
Snatched at each telegram of Futur
    Sale,
And thrilled with Bulls' or Bears' al
    ternate wail—
In hope or fear alike for ever pale.   17
And thus from year to year, throug
    hope and fear,
With many a curse and many a secre
    tear,
Striving in vain his cloud of debt t
    clear,
        At last
He woke to find his foolish dreamin
    past,
And all his best-of-life the easy pre
Of squandering scamps and quack
    that lined his way
        With vile array,
From rascal statesman down to pett
    knave;
Himself, at best, for all his braggin
    brave,   18
A gamester's catspaw and a banker
    slave.
Then, worn and gray, and sick wit
    deep unrest,
He fled into the oblivious West,
        Unmourned, unblest.

Old hill! old hill! thou gashed an
    hairy Lear
Whom the divine Cordelia of th
    year,
E'en pitying Spring, will vainly striv
    to cheer—
King, that no subject man nor bea
    may own,

Discrowned, undaughtered and alone—
Yet shall the great God turn thy
    fate,   190
And bring thee back into thy monarch
    state
      And majesty immaculate.

Lo, through hot waverings of the
    August morn,
Thou givest from thy vasty sides
    forlorn
Visions of golden treasuries of corn—
Ripe largesse lingering for some
    bolder heart
That manfully shall take thy part,
      And lend thee,
      And defend thee,
With antique sinew and with modern
    art.   200
(1874–75)   1875

THE POWER OF PRAYER; OR,
THE FIRST STEAMBOAT UP
THE ALABAMA

By Sidney and Clifford Lanier

You, Dinah! Come and set me whar
    de ribber-roads does meet.
De Lord, *He* made dese black-jack
    roots to twis' into a seat.
Umph, dar! De Lord have mussy
    on dis blin' ole nigger's feet.

It 'pear to me dis mornin' I kin smell
    de fust o' June.
'clar, I b'lieve dat mockin'-bird
    could play de fiddle soon!
Dem yonder town-bells sounds like
    dey was ringin' in de moon.

Well, ef dis nigger *is* been blind for
    fo'ty year or mo',
Dese ears, *dey* sees the world, like,
    th'u' de cracks dat's in de do'.
For de Lord has built dis body wid
    de windows 'hind and 'fo'.

I know my front ones *is* stopped up,
    and things is sort o' dim,   10

But den, th'u' *dem,* temptation's rain
    won't leak in on ole Jim!
De back ones show me earth enough,
    aldo' dey's mons'ous slim.

And as for Hebben,—bless de Lord,
    and praise His holy name—
Dat shines in all de co'ners of dis
    cabin jes' de same
As ef dat cabin hadn't nar' a plank
    upon de frame!

Who *call* me? Listen down de ribber,
    Dinah! Don't you hyar
Somebody holl'in *"Hoo, Jim, hoo"?*
    My Sarah died las' y'ar;
Is dat black angel done come back
    to call ole Jim f'om hyar?

My stars, dat cain't be Sarah, shuh!
    Jes, listen, Dinah, *now!*
What *kin* be comin' up dat bend,
    a-makin' sich a row?   20
Fus' bellerin' like a pawin' bull, den
    squealin' like a sow?

De Lord 'a' mussy sakes alive, jes'
    hear,—ker-woof, ker-woof—
De Debble's comin' round dat bend
    he's comin' shuh enuff,
A-splashin' up de water wid his tail
    and wid his hoof!

I'se pow'ful skeered; but neversome-
    less I ain't gwine run away:
I'm gwine to stand stiff-legged for de
    Lord dis blessèd day.
You screech, and swish de water,
    Satan! I'se a gwine to pray.

O hebbenly Marster, what thou will-
    est, dat mus' be jes' so,
And ef Thou hast bespoke de word,
    some nigger's bound to go.
Den, Lord, please take ole Jim, and
    lef young Dinah hyar below!   30

'Scuse Dinah, 'scuse her, Marster; for
    she's sich a little chile,
She hardly jes' begin to scramble up
    de homeyard stile,

But dis ole traveller's feet been tired
    dis many a many a mile.

I'se wufless as de rotten pole of las'
    year's fodderstack.
De rheumatiz done bit my bones; you
    hear 'em crack and crack?
I cain't sit down 'dout gruntin' like
    'twas breakin' o' my back.

What use de wheel, when hub and
    spokes is warped and split, and
    rotten?
What use dis dried-up cotton-stalk,
    when Life done picked my
    cotton?
I'se like a word dat somebody said,
    and den done been forgotten.

But, Dinah! Shuh dat gal jes' like
    dis little hick'ry tree,   40
De sap 's jes' risin in her; she do
    grow owdaciouslee—
Lord, ef you 's clarin' de underbrush,
    don't cut her down, cut me!

I would not proud persume—but I'll
    boldly make reques';
Sence Jacob had dat wrastlin'-match,
    I, too, gwine do my bes';
When Jacob got all underholt, de
    Lord he answered Yes!

And what for waste de vittles, now,
    and th'ow away de bread,
Jes' for to strength dese idle hands
    to scratch dis ole bald head?
T'ink of de 'conomy, Marster, ef dis
    ole Jim was dead!

Stop;—ef I don't believe de Debble's
    gone on up stream!
Jes' now he squealed down dar;—
    hush; dat's a mighty weakly
    scream!   50
Yas, sir, he's gone, he's gone;—he
    snort way off, like in a dream!

O glory hallelujah to de Lord dat
    reigns on high!

De Debble's fai'ly skeered to def, he
    done gone flyin' by;
I know'd he couldn' stand dat pra'r,
    I felt my Marster nigh!

You, Dinah; ain't you 'shamed, now,
    dat you didn' trust to grace?
I heerd you thrashin' th'u' de bushes
    when he showed his face!
You fool, you think de Debble
    couldn't beat *you* in a race?

I tell you, Dinah, jes' as shuh as you
    is standin' dar,
When folks starts prayin', answer-
    angels drop down th'u' de a'r.
Yas, Dinah, whar 'ould you be now
    jes' 'ceptin' fur dat pra'r?   60
                      1875

THE SYMPHONY

"O Trade! O Trade! would thou
    wert dead!
The Time needs heart—'tis tired of
    head:
We're all for love," the violins said.
"Of what avail the rigorous tale
Of bill for coin and box for bale?
Grant thee, O Trade! thine uttermost
    hope:
Level red gold with blue sky-slope,
And base it deep as devils grope:
When all's done, what hast thou won
Of the only sweet that's under the
    sun?   10
Ay, canst thou buy a single sigh
Of true love's least, least ecstasy?"
Then, with a bridegroom's heart-beat
    trembling,
All the mightier strings assembling
Ranged them on the violin's side
As when the bridegroom leads the
    bride,
And, heart in voice, together cried:
"Yea, what avail the endless tale
Of gain by cunning and plus by sale
Look up the land, look down the
    land,   2

The poor, the poor, the poor, they
    stand
Wedged by the pressing of Trade's
    hand
Against an inward-opening door
That pressure tightens evermore:
They sigh a monstrous foul-air sigh
For the outside leagues of liberty,
Where Art, sweet lark, translates the
    sky
Into a heavenly melody.
'Each day, all day' (these poor folks
    say),
'In the same old year-long, drear-long
    way,   30
We weave in the mills and heave in
    the kilns,
We sieve mine-meshes under the hills,
And thieve much gold from the Devil's
    bank tills,
To relieve, O God, what manner of
    ills?—
The beasts, they hunger, and eat, and
    die;
And so do we, and the world's a sty;
Hush, fellow-swine: why nuzzle and
    cry?
Swinehood hath no remedy
Say many men, and hasten by,
Clamping the nose and blinking the
    eye.   40
But who said once, in the lordly tone,
Man shall not live by bread alone
But all that cometh from the Throne?
    Hath God said so?
    But Trade saith *No:*
And the kilns and the curt-tongued
    mills say *Go!*
There's plenty that can, if you can't:
    we know.
Move out, if you think you're under-
    paid.
The poor are prolific; we're not
    afraid;
Trade is trade.'"   50
Thereat this passionate protesting
Meekly changed, and softened till
It sank to sad requesting
And suggesting sadder still:
'And oh, if men might sometime see

How piteous-false the poor decree
That trade no more than trade must
    be!
Does business mean, *Die, you—live, I?*
Then 'Trade is trade' but sings a lie:
'Tis only war grown miserly.   60
If business is battle, name it so:
War-crimes less will shame it so,
And widows less will blame it so.
Alas, for the poor to have some part
In yon sweet living lands of Art,
Makes problem not for head, but
    heart.
Vainly might Plato's brain revolve it:
Plainly the heart of a child could
    solve it."
And then, as when from words that
    seem but rude
We pass to silent pain that sits
    abrood   70
Back in our heart's great dark and
    solitude,
So sank the strings to gentle throb-
    bing
Of long chords change-marked with
    sobbing—
Motherly sobbing, not distinctlier
    heard
Than half wing-openings of the sleep-
    ing bird,
Some dream of danger to her young
    hath stirred.
Then stirring and demurring ceased,
    and lo!
Every least ripple of the strings'
    song-flow
Died to a level with each level bow
And made a great chord tranquil-
    surfaced so,   80
As a brook beneath his curving bank
    doth go
To linger in the sacred dark and green
Where many boughs the still pool
    overlean
And many leaves make shadow with
    their sheen.
    But presently
A velvet flute-note fell down pleas-
    antly
Upon the bosom of that harmony,

And sailed and sailed incessantly,
As if a petal from a wild-rose blown
Had fluttered down upon that pool of
tone   90
And boatwise dropped o' the convex
side
And floated down the glassy tide
And clarified and glorified
The solemn spaces where the shadows
bide.
From the warm concave of that fluted
note
Somewhat, half song, half odor, forth
did float,
As if a rose might somehow be a
throat:
"When Nature from her far-off glen
Flutes her soft messages to men,
     The flute can say them o'er
     again;   100
     Yea, Nature, singing sweet and
     lone,
Breathes through life's strident poly-
phone
The flute-voice in the world of tone.
     Sweet friends,
     Man's love ascends
To finer and diviner ends
Than man's mere thought e'er com-
prehends:
For I, e'en I,
As here I lie,
A petal on a harmony,   110
Demand of Science whence and why
Man's tender pain, man's inward cry,
When he doth gaze on earth and sky?
I am not overbold:
     I hold
Full powers from Nature manifold.
I speak for each no-tonguèd tree
That, spring by spring, doth nobler be,
And dumbly and most wistfully
His mighty prayerful arms out-
spreads   120
Above men's oft-unheeding heads,
And his big blessing downward sheds.
I speak for all-shaped blooms and
leaves,
Lichens on stones and moss on eaves,

Grasses and grains in ranks and
sheaves;
Broad-fronded ferns and keen-leaved
canes,
And briery mazes bounding lanes,
And marsh-plants, thirsty-cupped for
rains,
And milky stems and sugary veins;
For every long-armed woman-vine   130
That round a piteous tree doth twine;
For passionate odors, and divine
Pistils, and petals crystalline;
All purities of shady springs,
All shynesses of film-winged things
That fly from tree-trunks and bark-
rings;
All modesties of mountain-fawns
That leap to covert from wild lawns,
And tremble if the day but dawns;
All sparklings of small beady eyes   140
Of birds, and sidelong glances wise
Wherewith the jay hints tragedies;
All piquancies of prickly burs,
And smoothnesses of downs and furs,
Of eiders and of minevers;
All limpid honeys that do lie
At stamen-bases, nor deny
The humming-birds' fine roguery,
Bee-thighs, nor any butterfly;
All gracious curves of slender wings,   150
Bark-mottlings, fibre-spiralings,
Fern-wavings and leaf-flickerings;
Each dial-marked leaf and flower-bell
Wherewith in every lonesome dell
Time to himself his hours doth tell;
All tree sounds, rustlings of pine-cones,
Wind-sighings, doves' melodious moans,
And night's unearthly under-tones;
All placid lakes and waveless deeps,
All cool reposing mountain-steeps,   160
Vale-calms and tranquil lotos-sleeps;—
Yea, all fair forms, and sounds, and
lights,
And warmths, and mysteries, and
mights,
Of Nature's utmost depths and
heights,
—These doth my timid tongue pre-
sent,

Their mouthpiece and leal instru-
    ment
And servant, all love-eloquent.
I heard, when *'All for love'* the violins
    cried:
So, Nature calls through all her sys-
    tem wide,
Give me thy love, O man, so long
    denied.   170
Much time is run, and man hath
    changed his ways,
Since Nature, in the antique fable-
    days,
Was hid from man's true love by
    proxy fays,
False fauns and rascal gods that stole
    her praise.
The nymphs, cold creatures of man's
    colder brain,
Chilled Nature's streams till man's
    warm heart was fain
Never to lave its love in them again.
Later, a sweet Voice *Love thy neigh-*
    bor said,
Then first the bounds of neighbor-
    hood outspread
Beyond all confines of old ethnic
    dread.   180
Vainly the Jew might wag his cove-
    nant head:
'All men are neighbors,' so the sweet
    Voice said.
So, when man's arms had circled all
    man's race,
The liberal compass of his warm em-
    brace
Stretched bigger yet in the dark
    bounds of space;
With hands a-grope he felt smooth
    Nature's grace,
Drew her to breast and kissed her
    sweetheart face:
Yea, man found neighbors in great
    hills and trees
And streams and clouds and suns and
    birds and bees,
And throbbed with neighbor-loves in
    loving these.   190
But oh, the poor! the poor! the poor!

That stand by the inward-opening
    door
Trade's hand doth tighten ever more,
And sigh their monstrous foul-air sigh
For the outside hills of liberty,
Where Nature spreads her wild blue
    sky
For Art to make into melody!
Thou Trade! thou king of the modern
    days!
    Change thy ways,
    Change thy ways;   200
Let the sweaty laborers file
    A little while,
    A little while,
Where Art and Nature sing and smile.
Trade! is thy heart all dead, all
    dead?
And hast thou nothing but a head?
I'm all for heart," the flute-voice said,
And into sudden silence fled,
Like as a blush that while 'tis red
Dies to a still, still white instead. 210

    Thereto a thrilling calm succeeds,
Till presently the silence breeds
A little breeze among the reeds
That seems to blow by sea-marsh
    weeds:
Then from the gentle stir and fret
Sings out the melting clarionet,
Like as a lady sings while yet
Her eyes with salty tears are wet.
"O Trade! O Trade!" the Lady said,
"I too will wish thee utterly dead 220
If all thy heart is in thy head.
For O my God! and O my God!
What shameful ways have women
    trod
At beckoning of Trade's golden rod!
Alas when sighs are traders' lies,
And heart's-ease eyes and violet eyes
    Are merchandise!
O purchased lips that kiss with pain!
O cheeks coin-spotted with smirch and
    stain!
O trafficked hearts that break in
    twain!   230
—And yet what wonder at my sisters'
    crime?

So hath Trade withered up Love's
   sinewy prime,
Men love not women as in olden time.
Ah, not in these cold merchantable
   days
Deem men their life an opal gray,
   where plays
The one red Sweet of gracious ladies'-
   praise.
Now, comes a suitor with sharp pry-
   ing eye—
Says, *Here, you Lady, if you'll sell,
   I'll buy:*
*Come, heart for heart—a trade?
   What! weeping? why?*
Shame on such wooers' dapper mer-
   cery!   240
I would my lover kneeling at my feet
In humble manliness should cry, *O
   sweet!*
*I know not if thy heart my heart will
   greet:*
*I ask not if thy love my love can
   meet:*
*Whate'er thy worshipful soft tongue
   shall say,*
*I'll kiss thine answer, be it yea or
   nay:*
I do but know I love thee, and I pray
To be thy knight until my dying day.
Woe him that cunning trades in
   hearts contrives!
Base love good women to base loving
   drives   250
If men loved larger, larger were our
   lives;
And wooed they nobler, won they
   nobler wives."

There thrust the bold straightfor-
   ward horn
To battle for that lady lorn,
With heartsome voice of mellow
   scorn,
Like any knight in knighthood's
   morn.
   "Now comfort thee," said he,
         "Fair Lady.
For God shall right thy grievous
   wrong,

And man shall sing thee a true-love
   song,   260
Voiced in act his whole life long,
   Yea, all thy sweet life long,
         Fair Lady.
Where's he that craftily hath said,
The day of chivalry is dead?
I'll prove that lie upon his head,
   Or I will die instead,
         Fair Lady.
Is Honor gone into his grave?
Hath Faith become a caitiff knave, 270
And Selfhood turned into a slave
   To work in Mammon's cave,
         Fair Lady?
Will Truth's long blade ne'er gleam
   again?
Hath Giant Trade in dungeons slain
All great contempts of mean-got gain
   And hates of inward stain,
         Fair Lady?
For aye shall name and fame be sold,
And place be hugged for the sake of
   gold,   280
And smirch-robed Justice feebly scold
   At Crime all money-bold,
         Fair Lady?
Shall self-wrapt husbands aye forget
Kiss-pardons for the daily fret
Wherewith sweet wifely eyes are
   wet—
   Blind to lips kiss-wise set—
         Fair Lady?
Shall lovers higgle, heart for heart,
Till wooing grows a trading mart 290
Where much for little, and all for
   part,
   Make love a cheapening art,
         Fair Lady?
Shall woman scorch for a single sin
That her betrayer may revel in,
And she be burnt, and he but grin
   When that the flames begin,
         Fair Lady?
Shall ne'er prevail the woman's plea,
We maids would far, far whiter be 300
If that our eyes might sometimes see
   Men maids in purity,
         Fair Lady?

Shall Trade aye salve his conscience-
aches
With jibes at Chivalry's old mis-
takes—
The wars that o'erhot knighthood
makes
For Christ's and ladies' sakes,
Fair Lady?
Now by each knight that e'er hath
prayed
To fight like a man and love like a
maid,   310
Since Pembroke's life, as Pembroke's
blade,
I' the scabbard, death, was laid,
Fair Lady,
I dare avouch my faith is bright
That God doth right and God hath
might.
Nor time hath changed His hair to
white,
Nor His dear love to spite,
Fair Lady.
I doubt no doubts: I strive, and
shrive my clay,
And fight my fight in the patient mod-
ern way   320
For true love and for thee—ah me!
and pray
To be thy knight until my dying
day,
Fair Lady."
Made end that knightly horn, and
spurred away
Into the thick of the melodious fray.
And then the hautboy played and
smiled,
And sang like any large-eyed child,
Cool-hearted and all undefiled.
"Huge Trade!" he said,
"Would thou wouldst lift me on thy
head   330
And run where'er my finger led!
Once said a Man—and wise was He—
Never shalt thou the heavens see,
Save as a little child thou be."
Then o'er sea-lashings of commingling
tunes

The ancient wise bassoons,
Like weird
Gray-beard
Old harpers sitting on the high sea-
dunes,
Chanted runes: 340
"Bright-waved gain, gray-waved loss,
The sea of all doth lash and toss,
One wave forward and one across:
But now 'twas trough, now 'tis crest,
And worst doth foam and flash to
best,
And curst to blest.

"Life! Life! thou sea-fugue, writ
from east to west,
Love, Love alone can pore
On thy dissolving score
Of harsh half-phrasings,   350
Blotted ere writ,
And double erasings
Of chords most fit.
Yea, Love, sole music-master blest,
May read thy weltering palimpsest.
To follow Time's dying melodies
through,
And never to lose the old in the new,
And ever to solve the discords true—
Love alone can do.
And ever Love hears the poor-folks'
crying,   360
And ever Love hears the women's
sighing,
And ever sweet knighthood's death-
defying,
And ever wise childhood's deep im-
plying,
But never a trader's glozing and lying.

"And yet shall Love himself be heard,
Though long deferred, though long
deferred:
O'er the modern waste a dove hath
whirred:
Music is Love in search of a word."
(1875)   1875

THE CENTENNIAL MEDITATION OF COLUMBIA
(1776–1876)

A CANTATA

I

From this hundred-terraced height
Sight more large with nobler light
Ranges down yon towering years:
Humbler smiles and lordlier tears
 Shine and fall, shine and fall,
While old voices rise and call
Yonder where the to-and-fro
Weltering of my Long-Ago
Moves about the moveless base
Far below my resting-place.　　　　　10

Musical Annotations. Full chorus: sober, measured and yet majestic progressions of chords.

II

Mayflower, Mayflower, slowly hither flying,
Trembling Westward o'er yon balking sea,
Hearts within *Farewell dear England* sighing,
Winds without *But dear in vain* replying,
Gray-lipp'd waves about thee shouted, crying
 "*No! It shall not be!*"

Chorus: the sea and the winds mingling their voices with human sighs.

III

Jamestown, out of thee—
Plymouth, thee—thee, Albany—
Winter cries, *Ye freeze: away!*　　　20
Fever cries, *Ye burn: away!*
Hunger cries, *Ye starve: away!*
Vengeance cries, *Your graves shall stay!*

Quartette: a meagre and despairing minor.

IV

Then old Shapes and Masks of Things,
Framed like Faiths or clothed like Kings—
Ghosts of Goods once fleshed and fair,
Grown foul Bads in alien air—
War, and his most noisy lords,
Tongued with lithe and poisoned swords—
Error, Terror, Rage, and Crime,
All in a windy night of time　　　　30
Cried to me from land and sea,
 No! Thou shalt not be!

Full chorus: return of the motive of the second movement, but worked up with greater fury, to the climax of the shout at the last line.

V

Hark!
Huguenots whispering *yea* in the dark,
Puritans answering *yea* in the dark!
Yea, like an arrow shot true to his mark,

A rapid and intense whisper-chorus.

Darts through the tyrannous heart of Denial.
Patience and Labor and solemn-souled Trial,
    Foiled, still beginning,
  Soiled, but not sinning,   40
Toil through the stertorous death of the Night,
Toil when wild brother-wars new-dark the Light,
Toil, and forgive, and kiss o'er, and replight.

VI

Now Praise to God's oft-granted grace,

Chorus of
jubilation, until
the appeal of
the last two
lines introduces
a tone of doubt:
it then sinks to
pianissimo.

Now Praise to Man's undaunted face,
Despite the land, despite the sea,
I was: I am: and I shall be—
How long, Good Angel, O how long?
Sing me from Heaven a man's own song!

VII

"Long as thine Art shall love true love,   50

Basso solo:
the good Angel
replies.

Long as thy Science truth shall know,
Long as thine Eagle harms no Dove,
Long as thy Law by law shall grow,
Long as thy God is God above,
Thy brother every man below,
So long, dear Land of all my love,
Thy name shall shine, thy fame shall glow!"

VIII

O Music, from this height of time my Word unfold:

Full chorus:
jubilation and
welcome.

In thy large signals all men's hearts Man's Heart behold:
Mid-heaven unroll thy chords as friendly flags unfurled, 60
And wave the world's best lover's welcome to the world.
                   1876, 1884

THE REVENGE OF HAMISH

It was three slim does and a ten-tined buck in the bracken lay;
  And all of a sudden the sinister smell of a man,
  Awaft on a wind-shift, wavered and ran
Down the hill-side and sifted along through the bracken and passed that way.

Then Nan got a-tremble at nostril; she was the daintiest doe;
  In the print of her velvet flank on the velvet fern
  She reared, and rounded her ears in turn.
Then the buck leapt up, and his head as a king's to a crown did go

Full high in the breeze, and he stood as if Death had the form of a deer;
  And the two slim does long lazily stretching arose,   10
  For their day-dream slowlier came to a close,
Till they woke and were still, breath-bound with waiting and wonder and fear.

Then Alan the huntsman sprang over the hillock, the hounds shot by,
  The does and the ten-tined buck made a marvellous bound,
  The hounds swept after with never a sound,
But Alan loud winded his horn in sign that the quarry was nigh.

For at dawn of that day proud Maclean of Lochbuy to the hunt had waxed
    wild,
  And he cursed at old Alan till Alan fared off with the hounds
  For to drive him the deer to the lower glen-grounds:
"I will kill a red deer," quoth Maclean, "in the sight of the wife and the
  . child."   20

So gayly he paced with the wife and the child to his chosen stand;
  But he hurried tall Hamish the henchman ahead: "Go turn,"—
  Cried Maclean,—"if the deer seek to cross to the burn,
Do thou turn them to me: nor fail, lest thy back be red as thy hand."

Now hard-fortuned Hamish, half blown of his breath with the height of the
    hill,
  Was white in the face when the ten-tined buck and the does
  Drew leaping to burn-ward; huskily rose
His shouts, and his nether lip twitched and his legs were o'er-weak for his will.

So the deer darted lightly by Hamish and bounded away to the burn.
  But Maclean never bating his watch tarried waiting below;   30
  Still Hamish hung heavy with fear for to go
All the space of an hour; then he went, and his face was greenish and stern,

And his eye sat back in the socket, and shrunken the eye-balls shone,
  As withdrawn from a vision of deeds it were shame to see.
  "Now, now, grim henchman, what is't with thee?"
Brake Maclean, and his wrath rose red as a beacon the wind hath upblown.

"Three does and a ten-tined buck made out," spoke Hamish, full mild,
  "And I ran for to turn, but my breath it was blown, and they passed;
  I was weak, for ye called ere I broke me my fast."
Cried Maclean: "Now a ten-tined buck in the sight of the wife and the
  child   40

I had killed if the gluttonous kern had not wrought me a snail's own wrong!"
  Then he sounded, and down came kinsmen and clansmen all:
  "Ten blows, for ten tine, on his back let fall,
And reckon no stroke if the blood follow not at the bite of thong!"

So Hamish made bare, and took him his strokes; at the last he smiled.
  "Now I'll to the burn," quoth Maclean, "for it still may be,
  If a slimmer-paunched henchman will hurry with me,
I shall kill me the ten-tined buck for a gift to the wife and the child!"

Then the clansmen departed, by this path and that; and over the hill
  Sped Maclean with an outward wrath for an inward shame;   50

And that place of the lashing full quiet became;
And the wife and the child stood sad; and bloody-backed Hamish sat still.

But look! red Hamish has risen; quick about and about turns he.
"There is none betwixt me and the crag-top!" he screams under breath.
Then, livid as Lazarus lately from death,
He snatches the child from the mother, and clambers the crag toward the sea.

Now the mother drops breath; she is dumb, and her heart goes dead for a space,
Till the motherhood, mistress of death, shrieks, shrieks through the glen,
And that place of the lashing is live with men,
And Maclean, and the gillie that told him, dash up in a desperate race.   60

Not a breath's time for asking; an eye-glance reveals all the tale untold.
They follow mad Hamish afar up the crag toward the sea,
And the lady cries: "Clansmen, run for a fee!—
Yon castle and lands to the two first hands that shall hook him and hold

"Fast Hamish back from the brink!"—and ever she flies up the steep,
And the clansmen pant, and they sweat, and they jostle and strain.
But, mother, 'tis vain; but, father, 'tis vain;
Stern Hamish stands bold on the brink, and dangles the child o'er the deep.

Now a faintness falls on the men that run, and they all stand still.
And the wife prays Hamish as if he were God, on her knees,   70
Crying: "Hamish! O Hamish! but please, but please
For to spare him!" and Hamish still dangles the child, with a wavering will.

On a sudden he turns; with a sea-hawk scream, and a gibe, and a song,
Cries: "So; I will spare ye the child if, in sight of ye all,
Ten blows on Maclean's bare back shall fall,
And ye reckon no stroke if the blood follow not at the bite of the thong!"

Then Maclean he set hardly his tooth to his lip that his tooth was red,
Breathed short for a space, said: "Nay, but it never shall be!
Let me hurl off the damnable hound in the sea!"
But the wife: "Can Hamish go fish us the child from the sea, if dead?   80

"Say yea!—Let them lash *me*, Hamish?"—"Nay!"—"Husband, the lashing
will heal;
But, oh, who will heal me the bonny sweet bairn in his grave?
Could ye cure me my heart with the death of a knave?
Quick! Love! I will bare thee—so—kneel!" Then Maclean 'gan slowly to
kneel.

With never a word, till presently downward he jerked to the earth.
Then the henchman—he that smote Hamish—would tremble and lag;
"Strike, hard!" quoth Hamish, full stern, from the crag;
Then he struck him, and "One" sang Hamish, and danced with the child in
his mirth.

And no man spake beside Hamish; he counted each stroke with a song.
  When the last stroke fell, then he moved him a pace down the height,   9
  And he held forth the child in the heartaching sight
Of the mother, and looked all pitiful grave, as repenting a wrong.

And there as the motherly arms stretched out with the thanksgiving prayer—
  And there as the mother crept up with a fearful swift pace,
  Till her finger nigh felt of the bairnie's face—
In a flash fierce Hamish turned round and lifted the child in the air,

And sprang with the child in his arms from the horrible height in the sea,
  Shrill screeching, "Revenge!" in the wind-rush; and pallid Maclean,
  Age-feeble with anger and impotent pain,
Crawled up on the crag, and lay flat, and locked hold of dead roots of a tree. 10

And gazed hungrily o'er, and the blood from his back drip-dripped in the brine
  And a sea-hawk flung down a skeleton fish as he flew,
  And the mother stared white on the waste of blue,
And the wind drove a cloud to seaward, and the sun began to shine.

                                                       1878

THE MARSHES OF GLYNN

Glooms of the live-oaks, beautiful-braided and woven
With intricate shades of the vines that myriad-cloven
  Clamber the forks of the multiform boughs,—
      Emerald twilights,—
      Virginal shy lights,
Wrought of the leaves to allure to the whisper of vows,
When lovers pace timidly down through the green colonnades
Of the dim sweet woods, of the dear dark woods,
  Of the heavenly woods and glades,
That run to the radiant marginal sand-beach within   10
    The wide sea-marshes of Glynn;—

Beautiful glooms, soft dusks in the noon-day fire,—
Wildwood privacies, closets of lone desire,
Chamber from chamber parted with wavering arras of leaves,—
Cells for the passionate pleasure of prayer to the soul that grieves,
Pure with a sense of the passing of saints through the wood,
Cool for the dutiful weighing of ill with good;—

O braided dusks of the oak and woven shades of the vine,
While the riotous noon-day sun of the June-day long did shine
Ye held me fast in your heart and I held you fast in mine;   20
But now when the noon is no more, and riot is rest,
And the sun is a-wait at the ponderous gate of the West,
And the slant yellow beam down the wood-aisle doth seem
Like a lane into heaven that leads from a dream,—
Ay, now, when my soul all day hath drunken the soul of the oak,

And my heart is at ease from men, and the wearisome sound of the stroke
    Of the scythe of time and the trowel of trade is low,
     And belief overmasters doubt, and I know that I know,
    And my spirit is grown to a lordly great compass within,
That the length and the breadth and the sweep of the marshes of Glynn   30
Will work me no fear like the fear they have wrought me of yore
When length was fatigue, and when breadth was but bitterness sore,
And when terror and shrinking and dreary unnamable pain
Drew over me out of the merciless miles of the plain,—

Oh, now, unafraid, I am fain to face
    The vast sweet visage of space.
To the edge of the wood I am drawn, I am drawn,
Where the gray beach glimmering runs, as a belt of the dawn,
     For a mete and a mark
      To the forest-dark:—   40
        So:
Affable live-oak, leaning low,—
Thus—with your favor—soft, with a reverent hand,
(Not lightly touching your person, Lord of the land!)
Bending your beauty aside, with a step I stand
On the firm-packed sand,
      Free
By a world of marsh that borders a world of sea.
    Sinuous southward and sinuous northward the shimmering band
     Of the sand-beach fastens the fringe of the marsh to the folds of the
      land.   50
Inward and outward to northward and southward the beach-lines linger and curl
As a silver-wrought garment that clings to and follows the firm sweet limbs
    of a girl.
Vanishing, swerving, evermore curving again into sight,
Softly the sand-beach wavers away to a dim gray looping of light.
And what if behind me to westward the wall of the woods stands high?
The world lies east: how ample, the marsh and the sea and the sky!
A league and a league of marsh-grass, waist-high broad in the blade,
Green, and all of a height, and unflecked with a light or a shade,
Stretch leisurely off, in a pleasant plain,
To the terminal blue of the main.   60

Oh, what is abroad in the marsh and the terminal sea?
    Somehow my soul seems suddenly free
From the weighing of fate and the sad discussion of sin,
By the length and the breadth and the sweep of the marshes of Glynn.

Ye marshes, how candid and simple and nothing-withholding and free
Ye publish yourselves to the sky and offer yourselves to the sea!
Tolerant plains, that suffer the sea and the rains and the sun,
Ye spread and span like the catholic man who hath mightily won
God out of knowledge and good out of infinite pain
And sight out of blindness and purity out of a stain.   70

As the marsh-hen secretly builds on the watery sod,
Behold I will build me a nest on the greatness of God:
I will fly in the greatness of God as the marsh-hen flies
In the freedom that fills all the space 'twixt the marsh and the skies:
By so many roots as the marsh-grass sends in the sod
I will heartily lay me a-hold on the greatness of God:
Oh, like to the greatness of God is the greatness within
The range of the marshes, the liberal marshes of Glynn.

And the sea lends large, as the marsh: lo, out of his plenty the sea
Pours fast: full soon the time of the flood-tide must be: 80
Look how the grace of the sea doth go
About and about through the intricate channels that flow
       Here and there,
          Everywhere,
Till his waters have flooded the uttermost creeks and the low-lying lanes,
And the marsh is meshed with a million veins,
That like as with rosy and silvery essences flow
In the rose-and-silver evening glow.
       Farewell, my lord Sun!
The creeks overflow: a thousand rivulets run   90
'Twixt the roots of the sod; the blades of the marsh-grass stir;
Passeth a hurrying sound of wings that westward whirr;
Passeth, and all is still; and the currents cease to run;
And the sea and the marsh are one.

How still the plains of the waters be!
The tide is in his ecstasy.
The tide is at his highest height:
       And it is night.

And now from the Vast of the Lord will the waters of sleep
Roll in on the souls of men,   100
But who will reveal to our waking ken
The forms that swim and the shapes that creep
       Under the waters of sleep?
And I would I could know what swimmeth below when the tide comes in
On the length and the breadth of the marvelous marshes of Glynn.
(1878)   1879

SUNRISE

In my sleep I was fain of their fellowship, fain
   Of the live-oak, the marsh, and the main.
The little green leaves would not let me alone in my sleep;
Up-breathed from the marshes, a message of range and of sweep,
Interwoven with waftures of wild sea-liberties, drifting,
     Came through the lapped leaves sifting, sifting,
       Came to the gates of sleep.
Then my thoughts, in the dark of the dungeon-keep

Of the Castle of Captives hid in the City of Sleep,   10
Upstarted, by twos and by threes assembling:
    The gates of sleep fell a-trembling
Like as the lips of a lady that forth falter *yes,*
      Shaken with happiness:
    The gates of sleep stood wide.

I have waked, I have come, my beloved! I might not abide:
I have come ere the dawn, O beloved, my live-oaks, to hide
    In your gospelling glooms,—to be
As a lover in heaven, the marsh my marsh and the sea my sea.

Tell me, sweet burly-bark'd, man-bodied Tree   20
That mine arms in the dark are embracing, dost know
From what fount are these tears at thy feet which flow?
They rise not from reason, but deeper inconsequent deeps.
    Reason's not one that weeps.
    What logic of greeting lies
Betwixt dear over-beautiful trees and the rain of the eyes?

O cunning green leaves, little masters! like as ye gloss
All the dull-tissued dark with your luminous darks that emboss
The vague blackness of night into pattern and plan,
    So,
    (But would I could know, but would I could know,)   30
With your question embroidering the dark of the question of man,—
So, with your silences purfling this silence of man
While his cry to the dead for some knowledge is under the ban,
      Under the ban,—
    So, ye have wrought me
Designs on the night of our knowledge,—yea, ye have taught me,
    So,
    That haply we know somewhat more than we know.

    Ye lispers, whisperers, singers in storms,
      Ye consciences murmuring faiths under forms,   40
      Ye ministers meet for each passion that grieves,
      Friendly, sisterly, sweetheart leaves,
Oh, rain me down from your darks that contain me
Wisdoms ye winnow from winds that pain me,—
Sift down tremors of sweet-within-sweet
That advise me of more than they bring,—repeat
Me the woods-smell that swiftly but now brought breath
From the heaven-side bank of the river of death,—
    Teach me the terms of silence,—preach me
    The passion of patience,—sift me,—impeach me,—   50
      And there, oh there
As ye hang with your myriad palms upturned in the air,
    Pray me a myriad prayer.
    My gossip, the owl,—is it thou

That out of the leaves of the low-hanging bough,
    As I pass to the beach, art stirred?
    Dumb woods, have ye uttered a bird?

. . . .

Reverend Marsh, low-couched along the sea,
    Old chemist, rapt in alchemy,
        Distilling silence,—lo,
That which our father-age had died to know—
    The menstruum that dissolves all matter—thou
Hast found it: for this silence, filling now
The globéd clarity of receiving space
This solves us all: man, matter, doubt, disgrace,
Death, love, sin, sanity,
Must in yon silence clear solution lie.
Too clear! That crystal nothing who'll peruse?
The blackest night could bring us brighter news.
Yet precious qualities of silence haunt
Round these vast margins, ministrant.
Oh, if thy soul's at latter gasp for space,
With trying to breathe no bigger than thy race
Just to be fellow'd, when that thou hast found
No man with room, or grace enough of bound
To entertain that New thou tell'st, thou art,—
'Tis here, 'tis here thou canst unhand thy heart
And breathe it free, and breathe it free,
By rangy marsh, in lone sea-liberty.

The tide's at full; the marsh with flooded streams
Glimmers, a limpid labyrinth of dreams.
Each winding creek in grave entrancement lies
A rhapsody of morning-stars. The skies
Shine scant with one forked galaxy,—
The marsh brags ten: looped on his breast they lie.

Oh, what if a sound should be made!
Oh, what if a bound should be laid
To this bow-and-string tension of beauty and silence aspiring,—
To the bend of beauty the bow, or the hold of silence the string!
I fear me, I fear me yon dome of diaphanous gleam
Will break as a bubble o'er-blown in a dream,—
Yon dome of too-tenuous tissues of space and of night,
Over-weighted with stars, over-freighted with light,
Over-sated with beauty and silence, will seem
    But a bubble that broke in a dream,
If a bound of degree to this grace be laid,
    Or a sound or a motion made.

But no: it is made: list! somewhere,—mystery, where?
    In the leaves? in the air?

In my heart? is a motion made: 100
'Tis a motion of dawn, like a flicker of shade on shade.
In the leaves 'tis palpable: low multitudinous stirring
Upwards through the woods; the little ones, softly conferring,
Have settled my lord's to be looked for; so; they are still;
But the air and my heart and the earth are a-thrill,—
And look where the wild duck sails round the bend of the river,—
        And look where a passionate shiver
        Expectant is bending the blades
Of the marsh-grass in serial shimmers and shades,—
And invisible wings, fast fleeting, fast fleeting,   110
            Are beating
The dark overhead as my heart beats,—and steady and free
Is the ebb-tide flowing from marsh to sea—
        (Run home, little streams,
        With your lapfulls of stars and of dreams),—
And a sailor unseen is hoisting a-peak,
For list, down the inshore curve of the creek
        How merrily flutters the sail,—
And lo, in the East! Will the East unveil?
The East is unveiled, the East hath confessed   120
A flush: 'tis dead; 'tis alive; 'tis dead, ere the West
Was aware of it: nay, 'tis abiding, 'tis unwithdrawn:
        Have a care, sweet Heaven! 'Tis Dawn.

Now a dream of a flame through that dream of a flush is uprolled:
        To the zenith ascending, a dome of undazzling gold
Is builded, in shape as a bee-hive, from out of the sea:
The hive is of gold undazzling, but oh, the Bee,
        The star-fed Bee, the build-fire Bee,
        Of dazzling gold is the great Sun-Bee   130
That shall flash from the hive-hole over the sea.

        Yet now the dew-drop, now the morning gray,
        Shall live their little lucid sober day
        Ere with the sun their souls exhale away.
Now in each prettiest personal sphere of dew
The summ'd morn shines complete as in the blue
Big dew-drop of all heaven: with these lit shrines
O'er-silvered to the farthest sea-confines,
The sacramental marsh one pious plain
Of worship lies. Peace to the ante-reign   140
Of Mary Morning, blissful mother mild,
Minded of nought but peace, and of a child.
Not slower than Majesty moves, for a mean and a measure
Of motion,—not faster than dateless Olympian leisure
Might pace with unblown ample garments from pleasure to pleasure,—
The wave-serrate sea-rim sinks unjarring, unreeling,
        Forever revealing, revealing, revealing,

Edgewise, bladewise, halfwise, wholewise,—'tis done!
      Good-morrow, lord Sun!
With several voice, with ascription one,
The woods and the marsh and the sea and my soul   150
Unto thee, whence the glittering stream of all morrows doth roll,
Cry good and past-good and most heavenly morrow, lord Sun!

O Artisan born in the purple,—Workman Heat,—
Parter of passionate atoms that travail to meet
And be mixed in the death-cold oneness,—innermost Guest
At the marriage of elements,—fellow of publicans,—blest
Kind in the blouse of flame, that loiterest o'er
The idle skies laborest fast evermore,—
Thou, in the fine forge-thunder, thou, in the beat
Of the heart of a man, thou Motive,—Laborer Heat: 160
Yea, Artist, thou, of whose art yon sea's all news,
With his inshore greens and manifold mid-sea blues,
Pearl-glint, shell-tint, ancientest perfectest hues,
Ever shaming the maidens,—lily and rose
Confess thee, and each mild flame that glows
In the clarified virginal bosoms of stones that shine,
      It is thine, it is thine:

Thou chemist of storms, whether driving the winds a-swirl
Or a-flicker the subtler essences polar that whirl
In the magnet earth,—yea, thou with a storm for a heart,   170
Rent with debate, many-spotted with question, part
From part oft sundered, yet ever a globéd light,
Yet ever the artist, ever more large and bright
Than the eye of a man may avail of:—manifold One,
I must pass from thy face, I must pass from the face of the Sun:
Old Want is awake and agog, every wrinkle a-frown;
The worker must pass to his work in the terrible town:
But I fear not, nay, I fear not the thing to be done;
    I am strong with the strength of my lord the Sun:
How dark, how dark soever the race that needs be run,   180
    I am lit with the Sun.

Oh, never the mast-high run of the seas
    Of traffic shall hide thee,
Never the hell-colored smoke of the factories
      Hide thee,
Never the reek of the time's fen-politics
      Hide thee,
And ever my heart through the night shall with knowledge abide thee,
And ever by day shall my spirit, as one that hath tried thee,
    Labor, at leisure, in art,—till yonder beside thee,   190
      My soul shall float, friend Sun,
        The day being done.
1880   1882

From *TIGER LILIES*

[THE WAR-FLOWER]

Thou shalt not kill.

Love your enemies.

Father, forgive them: they know not what they do.

—CHRIST.

The early spring of 1861 brought to bloom, besides innumerable violets and jessamines, a strange, enormous, and terrible flower.

This was the blood-red flower of war, which grows amid thunders; a flower whose freshening dews are blood and hot tears, whose shadow chills a land, whose odors strangle a people, whose giant petals droop downward, and whose roots are in hell.

It is a species of the great genus, sin-flower, which is so conspicuous in the flora of all ages and all countries, and whose multifarious leafage and fruitage so far overgrow a land that the violet, or love-genus, has often small chance to show its quiet hue.

The cultivation of this plant is an expensive business, and it is a wonder, from this fact alone, that there should be so many fanciers of it. A most profuse and perpetual manuring with human bones is absolutely necessary to keep it alive, and it is well to have these powdered, which can be easily done by hoofs of cavalry-horses and artillery-wheels, not to speak of the usual method of mashing with cannon-balls. It will not grow, either, except in some wet place near a stream of human blood; and you must be active in collecting your widows' tears and orphans' tears and mothers' tears to freshen the petals with in the mornings.

It requires assiduous working; and your labor-hire will be a large item in the expense, not to speak of the amount disbursed in preserving the human bones alive until such time as they may be needed, for, I forgot to mention, they must be fresh, and young, and newly-killed.

It is, however, a hardy plant, and may be grown in any climate, from snowy Moscow to hot India.

It blooms usually in the spring, continuing to flower all summer until the winter rains set in: yet in some instances it has been known to remain in full bloom during a whole inclement winter, as was shown in a fine specimen which I saw the other day, grown in North America by two wealthy landed proprietors, who combined all their resources of money, of blood, of bones, of tears, of sulphur and what not, to make this the grandest specimen of modern horticulture, and whose success was evidenced by the pertinacious blossoms which the plant sent forth even amid the hostile rigors of snow and ice and furious storms. It is supposed by some that seed of this American specimen (now dead) yet remain in the land; but as for this author (who, with many friends, suffered from the unhealthy odors of the plant), he could find it in his heart to wish fervently that these seed, if there be verily any, might perish in the germ, utterly out of sight and life and memory and out of the remote hope of resurrection, forever and ever, no matter in whose granary they are cherished!

But, to return.

It is a spreading plant, like the banyan, and continues to insert new branch-roots into the ground, so as

sometimes to overspread a whole continent. Its black-shadowed jungles
afford fine cover for such wild beasts
as frauds and corruptions and thefts
to make their lair in; from which,
often, these issue with ravening teeth
and prey upon the very folk that
have planted and tended and raised
their flowery homes!

Now, from time to time, there have
appeared certain individuals (wishing,
it may be, to disseminate and make
profit upon other descriptions of
plants) who have protested against
the use of this war-flower.

Its users, many of whom are surely
excellent men, contend that they grow
it to protect themselves from oppressive hailstorms, which destroy
their houses and crops.

But some say the plant itself is
worse than any hailstorm; that its
shades are damp and its odors unhealthy, and that it spreads so rapidly as to kill out and uproot all
corn and wheat and cotton crops.
Which the plant-users admit; but rejoin that it is cowardly to allow hailstorms to fall with impunity, and that
manhood demands a struggle against
them of some sort.

But the others reply, fortitude is
more manly than bravery, for noble
and long endurance wins the shining
love of God; whereas brilliant bravery is momentary, is easy to the enthusiastic, and only dazzles the admiration of the weak-eyed since it
is as often shown on one side as the
other.

But then, lastly, the good war-
flower cultivators say, our preachers
recommend the use of this plant, and
help us mightily to raise it in resistance to the hailstorms.

And reply, lastly, the intereste[d]
other-flower men, that the preache[r]
should preach Christ; that Christ w[as]
worse hailed upon than anybody, b[e]
fore or since; that he always refuse[d]
to protect himself, though fully ab[le]
to do it, by any war-banyan; an[d]
that he did upon all occasions, n[ot]
only discourage the resort to th[at]
measure, but did inveigh against [it]
more earnestly than any thing els[e]
as the highest and heaviest crim[e]
against Love—the Father of Ada[m]
Christ, and all of us.

Friends and horticulturists, c[...]
these men, stickling for the last wor[d]
if war was ever right, then Christ w[as]
always wrong; and war-flowers a[nd]
the vine of Christ grow differe[nt]
ways, insomuch that no man ma[y]
grow with both!

KING HENRY.—How now, good Blun[t]
  Thy looks are full of speed.
BLUNT.—So hath the business that
  come to speak of.
Lord Mortimer of Scotland hath se[nt]
  word
That Douglas and the English reb[els]
  met,
The eleventh of this month, at Shrew[s]
  bury:
A mighty and a fearful head they are,
If promises are kept on every hand,
As ever offered foul play in a state.
                    —King Henry IV.

But these sentiments, even if an[y]
body could have been found patie[nt]
enough to listen to them, would ha[ve]
been called sentimentalities, or wors[e]
in the spring of 1861, by the inhab[i]
tants of any of those States lying b[e]
tween Maryland and Mexico. An a[f]
flatus of war was breathed upon [us]
Like a great wind, it drew on a[nd]
blew upon men, women, and childre[n]
Its sound mingled with the solemni[ty]
of the church-organs and arose wi[th]

e earnest words of preachers pray-
g for guidance in the matter. It
ghed in the half-breathed words of
veethearts conditioning impatient
vers with war-services. It thun-
red splendidly in the impassioned
ppeals of orators to the people. It
iistled through the streets, it stole
to the firesides, it clinked glasses
bar-rooms, it lifted the gray hairs
our wise men in conventions, it
rilled through the lectures in col-
ge halls, it rustled the thumbed
ok-leaves of the school-rooms.

This wind blew upon all the vanes
all the churches of the country,
d turned them one way—toward
r. It blew, and shook out, as if
' magic, a flag whose device was
known to soldier or sailor before,
t whose every flap and flutter made
e blood bound in our veins.

Who could have resisted the fair
ticipations which the new war-idea
ought? It arrayed the sanctity of
righteous cause in the brilliant trap-
igs of military display; pleasing, so,
e devout and the flippant which in
rious proportions are mixed ele-
nts in all men. It challenged the
triotism of the sober citizen, while
inflamed the dream of the states-
in, ambitious for his country or for
nself. It offered test to all al-
iances and loyalties; of church, of
te; of private loves, of public de-
tion; of personal consanguinity; of
cial ties. To obscurity it held out
inence; to poverty, wealth; to
eed, a gorged maw; to speculation,
alized gambling; to patriotism, a
intry; to statesmanship, a govern-
nt; to virtue, purity; and to love,
aat all love most desires—a field
erein to assert itself by action.

The author devoutly wishes that
some one else had said what is here
to be spoken—and said it better. That
is: if there was guilt in any, there
was guilt in nigh all of us, between
Maryland and Mexico; that Mr.
Davis, if he be termed the ring-leader
of the rebellion, was so not by virtue
of any instigating act of his, but
purely by the unanimous will and appointment of the Southern people;
and that the hearts of the Southern
people bleed to see how their own
act has resulted in the chaining of
Mr. Davis, who was as innocent as
they, and in the pardon of those who
were as guilty as he!

All of us, if any of us, either for
pardon or for punishment: this is fair,
and we are willing. * * *

1867

LETTERS *

To Paul Hamilton Hayne

Macon, Ga., April 13, 1870.

My dear Mr. Hayne: Watching,
night and day, for two weeks past,
by the bedside of a sick friend, I
have had no spiritual energy to escape out of certain gloomy ideas
which always possess me when I am
in the immediate presence of physical
ailment; and I did not care to write
you that sort of letter which one is
apt to send under such circumstances,
since I gather from your letters that
you have enough and to spare of these
dismal down-weighings of the flesh's
ponderous cancer upon suffering and
thoughtful souls.

I am glad, therefore, that I waited until this divine day. If the year were an Orchestra, to-day would be the Flute-tone in it. A serene Hope, just on the very verge of realizing itself: a tender loneliness,—what some German calls *Waldeinsamkeit*, wood-loneliness,—the ineffable withdrawal-feeling that comes over one when he hides himself in among the trees, and knows himself shut in by their purity, as by a fragile yet impregnable wall, from the suspicions and trade regulations of men; and an inward thrill, in the air, or in the sunshine, one knows not which, half like the thrill of the passion of love, and half like the thrill of the passion of friendship:—these, which make up the office of the flute-voice in those poems which the old masters wrote for the Orchestra, also prevail throughout to-day.

Do you like—as I do—on such a day to go out into the sunlight and *stop thinking*,—lie fallow, like a field, and absorb those certain liberal *potentialities* which will in after days reappear, duly formulated, duly grown, du'y perfected, as poems? I have a curiosity to know if to you, as to me, there comes such as this day: —a day exquisitely satisfying with all the fulnesses of the Spring, and filling you as full of nameless tremors as a girl on a wedding-morn; and yet, withal, a day which utterly denies you the gift of speech, which puts its finger on the lip of your inspiration, which inexorably enforces upon your soul a silence that you infinitely long to break, a day, in short, which takes absolute possession of you and says to you, in tones which command obedience, *to-day you*

must forego expression and all ou come, you must remain a fallow fiel for the sun and wind to fertilize, no shall any corn or flowers sprout int visible green and red until to-morro —mandates, further, that you hav learned after a little experience n only not to fight against, but to lov and revere as the wise communica tion of the Unseen Powers.

Have you seen Browning's "Th Ring and the Book"? I am con dent that, at the birth of this ma among all the good fairies who show ered him with magnificent endov ments, one bad one—as in the o tale—crept in by stealth and gav him a constitutional twist i' the nec whereby his windpipe became, and ha ever since remained, a marvellou tortuous passage. Out of this glotti labyrinth his words won't, and can come straight. A hitch and a shar crook in every sentence bring y up with a shock. But what a shoc it is? Did you ever see a picture o a lasso, in the act of being flung In a thousand coils and turns, ine: tricably crooked and involved ar whirled, yet, if you mark the noo at the end, you see that it is direct in front of the bison's head, ther and is bound to catch him! That the way Robert Browning catch you. The first sixty or seventy pag of "The Ring and the Book" are a together the most doleful reading, i point either of idea or of music, the English language; and yet th monologue of Giuseppe Caponsacch that of Pompilia Comparini, and th two of Guido Franceschini, are u approachable, in their kind, by living or dead poet, *me judice.* Her Browning's jerkiness comes in with i vitable effect. You get lightning-glimpses—and, as one naturally expects from lightning, zig-zag glimpses into the intense night of the passion of these souls. It is entirely wonderful and without precedent. The ful play of Guido's lust, and scorn, and hate, and cowardice, closes with a master-stroke:

. . Christ! Maria! God! . . .
ompilia, will you let them murder me?
Pompilia, mark you, is dead, by Guido's own hand; deliberately stabbed, because he hated her purity, which all along he has reviled and mocked with the Devil's own malignant ingenuity of sarcasm.

You spoke of a project you wished to tell me. Let me hear it. Your plans are always of interest to me. Can I help you? I've not put pen to paper, in the literary way, in a long time. How I thirst to do so, how I long to sing a thousand various songs that oppress me, unsung,—inexpressible. Yet, the mere work that brings bread gives me no time. I know not, after all, if this is a sorrowful thing. Nobody likes my poems except two or three friends,—who are themselves poets, and can supply themselves!

Strictly upon Scriptural principle, I've written you (as you see) almost entirely about myself. This is doing to you as I would you should do to me. Go, and do likewise. Write me about yourself.

Your Friend,
SIDNEY LANIER.

TO MRS. LANIER
Baltimore, December 2, 1873.
Well, Flauto Primo hath been to first rehearsal.

Fancy thy poor lover, weary, worn, and stuffed with a cold, arriving after a brisk walk—he was *so* afraid he might be behind time—at the hall of Peabody Institute. He passeth down betwixt the empty benches, turneth through the green-room, emergeth on the stage, greeteth the Maestro, is introduced by the same to Flauto Secondo, and then, with as much carelessness as he can assume, he sauntereth in among the rows of music-stools, to see if peradventure he can find the place where he is to sit—for he knoweth not, and liketh not to ask. He remembereth where the flutes sit in Thomas' Orchestra; but on going to the corresponding spot he findeth the part of Contra-Basso on the music-stand, and fleeth therefrom in terror. In despair, he is about to endeavor to get some information on the sly, when he seeth the good Flauto Secondo sitting down far in front, and straightway marcheth to his place on the left of the same, with an air of one that had played there since babyhood. This Hamerik of ours hath French ideas about his orchestral arrangements and places his pieces very differently from Thomas. Well, I sit down, some late-comers arrive, stamping and blowing—for it is snowing outside—and pull the green-baize covers off their big horns and bass-fiddles. Presently the Maestro, who is rushing about, hither and thither, in some excitement, falleth to striking a great tuning fork with a mallet, and straightway we all begin to toot A to puff it, to groan it, to squeak it, to scrape it, until I sympathize with the poor letter, and glide off in some delicate little runs; and presently the others begin to flourish also, and here we have it, up chromatics, down diatonics, unearthly buzzings from the big fiddles, diabolical four-string chords from the 'cellos, passionate shrieks from the clarionets and oboes, manly remonstrances from the horns, querulous complaints from the bassoons, and so on. Now the Maestro mounteth to his perch. I am seated immediately next the audience, facing the first violins, who are separated from me by the conductor's stand. I place my part (of the Fifth Symphony of Beethoven, which I had procured two days before, in order to look over it, being told that on the first rehearsal we would try nothing but the Fifth Symphony) on my stand, and try to stop my heart from beating so fast—with unavailing arguments. Maestro rappeth with his *bâton,* and magically stilleth all the shrieks and agonies of the instruments. "Fierst" (he saith, with the Frenchiest of French accents—tho' a Dane, he was educated in Paris) "I wish to present to ze gentlemen of ze orchestra our fierst flutist, Mr. Sidney Lanier, also our fierst oboe, Mr. (I didn't catch his name)." Whereupon, not knowing what else to do— and the pause being somewhat awkward—I rise and make a profound bow to the Reeds, who sit behind me, another to the 'Celli, the Bassi, and the Tympani, in the middle, and a third to the Violins opposite. This appeareth to be the right thing, for Oboe jumpeth up also, and boweth, and the gentlemen of the orchestra all rise and bow, some of them with great *empressement.* Then there is a little idiotic hum and simper, such as newly introduced people usually affect. Then cometh a man—whom I should always hate, if I *could* hate anybo[d] always—and, to my horror, putteth [on] my music-stand the flauto primo pa[rt] of Niels Gade's Ossian Overture, an[d] thereupon the Maestro saith, "We w[ill] try *that* fierst." Horrors! They to[ld] me they would play nothing but t[he] Fifth Symphony, and this Ossi[an] Overture I have never seen or hear[d]. This does not help my heart-beats n[or] steady my lips—thou canst believ[e]. However, there is no time to tar[ry], the *bâton* rappeth, the horns blo[w], my five bars' rest is out—I plunge.

—Oh! If thou couldst but be [by] me in this sublime glory of mus[ic]! All through it I yearned for thee wi[th] heart-breaking eagerness. The beau[ty] of it maketh me catch my breath— write of it. I will not attempt [to] describe it. It is the spirit of t[he] poems of Ossian done in music [by] the wonderful Niels Gade.

I got through it without causi[ng] any disturbance. Maestro had to st[op] twice on account of some other pla[y]ers. I failed to come in on ti[me] twice in the Symphony. I am t[oo] tired now to give thee any furth[er] account. I go again to rehearsal [to-] morrow.

To Bayard Taylor

180 St. Paul St., Baltimore, M[d.]
October 20, 18[72]

MY DEAREST MINISTER,—always [a] minister of grace to me,—I have lo[ng] forborne to write you because I kn[ew] your whole mind would be occupi[ed] with a thousand new cares, and [I] could not bear to add the bur[den] of a letter thereto. But you m[ay] be getting easy in the new saddle [by] this; and somehow I feel that I ca[n]

ait longer before sending you a little
ve-letter that shall at least carry my
nging over the big seas to you.
ot long ago I was in New York
r some days; but you were in Ger-
any;—and the city seemed depopu-
ted. There were multitudes of what
alt Whitman calls

ttle plentiful manikins
ipping about in collars and tailed
    coats,

it my Man, my haeleð a leofost (as
is in Beówulf) was wanting, and I
andered disconsolately towards 142
 18th St.—where I used so often
d so ruthlessly to break in upon
ur labors—as if I could *wish* you
ck into your chair rolling out the
ophecy of Deucalion. Even the
estminister Hotel had new pro-
ietors and I felt a sense of inten-
onal irony in its having changed
om the European to the American
an,—as if for pure spite because
ou had left America and gone to
urope. My dear, when *are* you
ming back?

A short time ago I found in a
cond-hand bookstall a copy of Sir
enry Wotton's works and letters
inted in 1685, and bought it—with
out all the money I had: for a joke
old Sir Henry's on a minister car-
d my mind to you. Having been
ced (he narrates the story himself,
ing then on a ministerial journey
ough Germany) to write in an al-
m, he chose to define a Minister,
l said: *A Minister is a man sent
lie abroad for the good of his
ntry.*

have seen your "Deucalion" an-
unced, but nothing more. Indeed
have been so buried in study for
 past six months that I know not

news nor gossip of any kind. Such
days and nights of glory as I have
had! I have been studying Early
English, Middle English and Eliza-
bethan poetry, from Beówulf to Ben
Jonson: and the world seems twice
as large. I enclose a programme of
lectures I am going to give before a
class of subscribers at the Peabody
Institute this winter, from which you
will see the drift of my work.

You will also care to know that
Scribner's has accepted three papers
of mine on "The Physics of Poetry,"
in which I have succeeded in develop-
ing a complete system of prosody for
all languages from the physical constitution of sound. It has given me
indescribable pleasure to be able,
through the principles therein announced, to put formal poetry on a
scientific basis which renders all its
processes perfectly secure.

If you should see an Appleton's
Journal for the current month—November—you may be interested in an
experiment of mine therein with
logaœdic dactyls called "The Revenge
of Hamish." Another freer treatment
of the same rhythm by me will appear in a book to be issued by Roberts Brothers in the "No Name Series" (called the "Masque of Poets")
under the heading "The Marshes of
Glynn":—though all this last is as yet
a secret and not to be spoken of till
the book shall have been out and
been cast to the critics for a while.
I hope to find a publisher for my
book on English Prosody * next
spring; also for my historical and
critical account, in two volumes, of
"The English Sonnet-Makers from
Surrey to Shakespeare"; and I am in

    * *The Science of English Verse.*

treaty with Scribner's Sons for a "Boy's Froissart" which I have proposed to them and which they like the idea of so far. By next autumn I trust I will have a volume of poetry ("The Songs of Aldhelm") in print, which is now in a pigeon-hole of my desk half-jotted down. During the coming week I go to Washington and Philadelphia to arrange, if possible, for delivering my course of lectures before classes in those cities.

There! I have reported progress up to date. Who better than you—who looked so kindly upon my poo[r] little beginning—has the right t[o] know how far I've gone?

Give me some little account o[f] yourself, if you are not too busy. M[y] wife and I send grateful and affe[c]tionate messages to you: adding co[r]dial postscripts for Mrs. Taylor an[d] Miss Lilian.

God bless you and keep you eve[r] in such fair ways as follow the fa[ir] wishes of

*Your faithful
SIDNEY L.

THE GENTEEL TRADITION

I. GEORGE WILLIAM CURTIS
(1824–1892)

[JOSEPH JEFFERSON AS RIP VAN WINKLE]

As delight in a work of art is perennial, criticism upon it is always renewed. Raphael's Madonnas are the texts of the latest travelers, and a fresh eye sometimes sees a fresh beauty in the most familiar work. There are, of course, traditions of admiration which are universal, and even tyrannical, so that difference from the general opinion appears often to be willfulness and affectation. So we come to the contemplation of some works of art as to shrines at which worship is imperative, and regard them as reverentially and uncritically as the Roman peasant from the Campagna looks at the Pieta in St. Peter's. Yet this is, perhaps, the best of all tributes to human genius, that when one of its works in any lofty kind has become long renowned, it acquires something of the character of a noble, natural object, and it is as idle and impertinent not to like it as to profess indifference to a beautiful landscape, or to Niagara, or to a sunset.

But of all arts, none is so difficult to comprehend as acting; and it is doubtful whether the "playing" of any actor could ever command that universal and unfading admiration, irrespective of times and fashions and feelings, which is given to certain buildings and pictures and statues and music. If Garrick should play at Booth's Theater, should we enjoy the evening with the same naturalness of emotion with which we enjoy Goldsmith's "Deserted Village"? Would Mrs. Oldfield craze the golden youth of New York? Would Mrs. Siddons, even, seem to us the superb Muse of Tragedy which Sir Joshua painted? It may be fairly replied that the question answers itself. For only his own time can see the great actor, or hear the great orator and singer. There is something contemporary in the very nature of such art. It is suggested by every detail. We can not conceive of Lord Chatham without his wig. But how much would a bewigged Lord Chatham move an American assembly with his eloquence to-day? If Mr. Booth or Mr. Fletcher should enter as Hamlet, wearing the Shakespearean costume which Garrick wore, the theater would ring with merriment at the melancholy Dane. But nothing can touch the noble grace of the Parthenon, nor make Raphael's Virgins quaint or old, nor harm the proud beauty of the Venus of Milo, as it was so long called. They borrow nothing from accidents. Like the line of the horizon, they are always beautiful to every beholder.

There may possibly be something

of this unchangeableness even upon the stage when the play is the telling of a familiar story, in which the costume itself is defined. If "Rip Van Winkle" is played a hundred years hence in New York, or elsewhere, it must be substantially as it is now. There may be actual houses instead of painted scenes; there may be turf and sand upon the stage instead of boards; but the changes will not be essential nor comical. There will be a sleepy colonial village upon the river; a tavern, with the sign of King George; the landlord and the usurer and the shrewish wife and the good-for-nothing Rip; and they will be dressed as we see them, because the costume of the time is perfectly well known, and any innovation would be resisted by that severe censor, the public. The grotesque Dutch ghost would always, doubtless, wear the high-pointed hats, and old Rip would awaken white-bearded and tattered, and all the rest would follow as we see it. But would the conception of Rip two or three hundred years hence be our conception? In this case, while the costume would be the same, would the character remain?

Such questions ask themselves as the curtain comes down upon what is the most familiar and famous rôle in the American theater to-day—the Rip Van Winkle of Mr. Jefferson. He lately played it for one hundred and fifty times in succession. The Easy Chair saw him in the evening, when he had played it in the afternoon, but it seemed as fresh as it could ever have been. There seemed to be no reason why he should not play it every day and every night without end so unwearied was he, and so large

and delighted the audience. The who wonder whether he does not ti to death of it forget that a man nev tires of telling a good story to a fre audience. We all know excellent ge tlemen who still dine out, and st tell to a new and delighted gener tion the same old stories that the fathers enjoyed. A public speak who repeats the same discourse i cessantly knows that each new au ence is a new interest, and there a speakers who do not feel the d course is in proper form unless has been spoken for at least a doz times. And it is unquestionable th the Lyceum audience which hears lecture on the fiftieth evening of i delivery is very likely to hear a ve much better lecture than those w heard it upon the first evening. T first repetitions are like varnishi days to the painters before the e hibition opens. Their pictures a hung, but they must be touched in proper effect. A picture studied up the easel in the studio is a very di ferent work from the same pictu seen upon the walls of the galle

It is probably so with the act and doubtless it is only gradually a by constant repetition that he satisfi himself with his rendering of a cha acter. Like an orator, he feels audience at every moment, and constantly studying it, and adapti himself to the method of produci the impression he seeks. And t character itself develops and reve itself to him by greater familiari It is no more likely that Mr. Jeffe son is tired of his part, and of success, than a beautiful belle is tir of her conquests, forever renewed, of the dance in which she glides, e

anting, every evening. The Easy
hair, indeed, was surprised to find a
end near it who had also not seen
e play. It had supposed that in
gard to Jefferson's Rip Van Winkle
was like the friend of Dickens, to
nom he wrote at the time of the
ystal Palace Fair: "I see; you are
ibitious of notoriety—You wish to
 the only man in the world who
dn't come to the Great Exhibition."
 did not occur to the Easy Chair
at the rest of the audience had
me, like itself, for the first time,
cause it had been constantly told
at the pleasure was greater at the
ird or fourth seeing. But what a
easant feeling it is, as you sit in
e parquet waiting for the curtain
 rise, and glancing around at the
iet, expectant audience, to know that
ey are all there to enjoy them-
lves; and how instinctively you
onder whether the enjoyment will
 like the sweet vapor that breathes
om soda-water, or like the sparkling
am that leaves a clear, sweet wine
low!

If any body has in his mind an
age of Rip Van Winkle before he
ent up into the mountains and slept
s long sleep, it is, doubtless, just
e good-humored, careless, affection-
e, shrewd, loitering fellow who
mes in with the children hanging
l about him; and those children,
th the little lovers afterward at his
ees, give us the key to the man.
ey are his good angels always. Un-
nsciously, in the midst of his idle-
ss, and the maudlin folly that ex-
perates his wife, the children plead
r him in our hearts. He is not
d whom children love. Shiftless,
ckless, even drunken, he may be,

but not bad. The wife orders him
out into the black night and storm,
but the little daughter clings to him.
He, after all, is a child, and they
mutually love with the fondness of
children. The pathos of the play
culminates in Rip's fearful consciousness that his child does not know
him. Perhaps the author was wiser
than he knew. But Rip would not
be so perpetually absolved by us, as
we look, if we did not know that the
children love him.

It is wholly a study of character.
There is no proper action in the play.
The plot is slight: a good-natured,
drunken idler squanders his property,
and leaves his wife to scrub and toil
hopelessly. She loves and frets and
despairs, and he, drunk or sober, only
smiles good-naturedly, until, stung by
the fatal discovery that his pretended
affectionate sympathy for her passionate sorrow is only a trick to steal
the bottle from her pocket, she de-
livers in one terrible sentence the
accumulated heart-break of a life by
bidding him begone from the house,
which is hers, and never to return.
He obeys, although, as the door opens
into the awful tempest, she prays him
to turn back. He disappears in the
storm; reappears upon the mountain,
and among the ghostly crew of Hen-
drick Hudson; drinks, and sleeps for
twenty years; then awakens, an old
man, and descends to the village to
find himself forgotten, his wife married to the usurer, who beats her, his
house itself destroyed, and even his
daughter repelling him. Then comes
the proof that it is he—that his property was never rightfully lost; and
with his restored wife and daughter
pressing upon him the cup which has

caused all the sorrow, the curtain falls.

Rip is a racy original, one of the men who are everywhere, and always delightful, from what is fondly called their profuse human nature, by which we really mean entire simplicity and kindliness—a heart overflowing with love and sympathy, but brave as a lion under all. This character is portrayed by Mr. Jefferson with such subtile felicity that if we only fancy him sometimes writing poetry, we can imagine that we see Robert Burns. There are always those in the audience who feel toward Rip as many good people in Dumfries felt toward Burns. They were impatient with him. They were ashamed of human nature when they thought of him. He was an idle, dissolute, reprobate. If Death hadn't wanted him, says Robert Collyer in his noble lecture upon Burns, the sheriff was waiting for him. "So he died, and the good people hurried to bury him and all his nastiness out of sight; but they might as well have tried to bury the sunshine!" Mr. Jefferson shows us this kind of character perfectly—the man who is beloved by children and the unprosperous, by hostlers and fishermen and plow-boys, who brings no dinner to his wife unless he has had good luck in shooting or trapping, but who, despite all, is a kindly human soul.

"Yes, but look at it," says Conscience, in the sixth row from the stage, "here is a good-for-nothing rascal, who wastes his substance in riotous living; who breaks his wife's heart, and enslaves her to the hardest labor; and when the catastrophe comes, what happens? He goes quietly to sleep for twenty years, an she, for her daughter's sake, marri a man who abuses her, and she wretched beyond words, as if she ha been guilty; and at last my lazy lo opens his eyes, and rubs them, an descends after his sound nap to ha his wife fall upon her knees befo him, as if she were the sinner, an to beg him to drink at his pleasure *seculâ seculorum*. What do you thin of this for a moral lesson?" asks Co science; "what do you think the Re Dr. Sabine would think of it?"

But, if we come to morals, wh do we think of the prodigal son? not its best significance this, th while eating the husks and living ri ously, he was still a human being be loved and not despaired of? A if Conscience insists upon this ki of morality, is it not the excellen of the representation of Rip that, u der all the shiftlessness and idlene we love the human sunshine that w not be buried? Besides, Dan Co science, if you will be so stringen did not his wife banish him from h hearth? and was it no atonement no penalty for the folly of his you that he slept all his manhood aw unconscious? Your debit and cre morality, and your trial balances virtue and vice, are not very sat factory. In the moral estimate of li temperament and circumstances a often the most powerful elemen The virtue of an untempted doctor not very seraphic. It is Anthony w is truly saintly. You may take yo most material text, and tell us wheth you think that young Ferdinand, w sits entranced beside you, is likely choose idleness and drinking for profession in life because he is

elighted with the play, or the curly-
aired Miranda approve her future
usband's dissipation because she sees
Irs. Van Winkle, so broken-hearted
ith Rip, so abused with her second
ouse, at last proffer the cup to Rip's
assionless and unthirsting lips. If
e are on the look-out for a moral,
all we not find it in the perception
at, however good-for-nothing a man
ay be who means no ill, and how-
ver wretched he may make his fam-
y, he is still a man, and to be
nderly entreated?

How delicately and with what ex-
uisite tone, as the painters would
y, Mr. Jefferson plays the part,
erybody knows. People return again
d again to see him, as to see a
vely landscape or a favorite picture.
deed, it is the test of high art that
does not pall in its impression.
here is no acting, perhaps, so ex-
gerated as this of Rip Van Winkle,
t there is none so effective. It is
holly free from declamation, and
om every kind of fustian. It is ab-
lutely nature, but it is the nature
art. There is something touching
the intentness of the audience,
ich is seldom broken by ordinary
plause, but which responds sensi-
ely to every emotion of the actor.
d the curious felicity of his natural-
ss is observable in the slightest de-
l. No wholly imaginary object was
er more palpably real than the dog
hneider. And he is made so merely
a word or two from Rip. There
no more doubt that there *is* a dog
hneider than that there is a William
ye who went for a heathen Chinee.
But the most remarkable illustra-
n of the power of illusion is in the
ysical difference between the young

and the old Rip—Rip of the village
and Rip of the mountains. The
younger man is hearty, solid, large-
framed. The guest of the ghosts
awakens withered and shrunken, an
old man, but still the old Rip. With
what subtility this change is expressed
in the acting can not be described.
The simple bewilderment; the gleam
of the old humor in a mind too steady
to be disturbed by any event, and instinctively but vaguely conscious of
some inconceivable jest; the patient
effort to comprehend, but without the
least tendency to suspect the truth,
which would not occur to a man so
totally unreflective; the intolerable
sense of desolation when his daughter,
even, recoils from him—all this is,
indeed, no more skillfully indicated
than the rest of the rôle, but it deals
with a higher and more novel experience. So, in the mountain, the tranquil steadiness of self-reliance mingled
with simple awe in the presence of the
ghost; the wish that he were somewhere else, but with a constant wary
mastery of the situation; the incessant talking, yet never loudly nor hurriedly, as if the sound of his own
human voice were necessary to reas-
sure him—all this, with its varying
tones and looks, eludes description. It
is a fine picture of heroic human nature, and if Conscience insists upon
a moral which may be measured
and specified, it could easily find it
here.

The peculiar charm of the old
legend is only deepened by seeing this
play. In nothing that he wrote was
the genius of Irving happier than in
his version of the tale. It casts a
drowsy, dreamy spell upon the scenery of the Hudson, which it is not

:asy to throw off, and which will
cling to it for many and many a year.
And when the story has taken form
in the memory from the acting of
Mr. Jefferson, it will be impossible
ever to glide under the Catskills upon
the river, or to see their distant,

rounded outline mingling with t
summer clouds, without believing th
somewhere among them the low voi
that we have heard will be heard fo
ever—"You know'd I didn'n want
come up here, didn'n you?"

18

II. RICHARD HENRY
STODDARD *
(1825–1903)

THE WITCH'S WHELP

Along the shore the slimy brine-pits
     yawn,
Covered with thick green scum; the
     billows rise,
And fill them to the brim with clouded
     foam,
And then subside, and leave the
     scum again.
The ribbèd sand is full of hollow gulfs,
Where monsters from the waters come
     and lie.
Great serpents bask at noon along the
     rocks,
To me no terror; coil on coil they roll
Back to their holes before my flying
     feet.
The Dragon of the Sea, my mother's
     god,   10
Enormous Setebos, comes here to
     sleep;
Him I molest not; when he flaps his
     wing
A whirlwind rises, when he swims the
     deep
It threatens to engulf the trembling
     isle.
Sometimes when winds do blow, and
     clouds are dark,
I seek the blasted wood whose bark-
     less trunks

* All poems of Stoddard reprinted by permission of Charles Scribner's Sons.

Are bleached with summer suns; t
     creaking trees
Stoop down to me, and swing
     right and left
Through crashing limbs, but not a
     care I,
The thunder breaks above, and in th
     lairs
The panthers roar; from out t
     stormy clouds
Whose hearts are fire sharp lightnin
     rain around
And split the oaks; not faster lizar
     run
Before the snake up the slant trun
     than I,
Not faster down, sliding with han
     and feet.
I stamp upon the ground, and adde
     rouse,
Sharp-eyed, with poisonous fangs;
     neath the leaves
They couch, or under rocks, and ro
     of trees
Felled by the winds; through brie
     undergrowth
They slide with hissing tongues,
     neath my feet
To writhe, or in my fingers squee
     to death.
There is a wild and solitary pi
Deep in the meadows; all the isla
     birds
From far and near fly there, a
     learn new songs.
Something imprisoned in its wrink
     bark
Wails for its freedom; when the b
     ger light

urns in mid-heaven, and dew else-
　　where is dried,
here it still falls; the quivering
　　leaves are tongues
nd load the air with syllables of woe.
ne day I thrust my spear within a
　　cleft   40
o wider than its point, and some-
　　thing shrieked,
nd falling cones did pelt me sharp
　　as hail:
picked the seeds that grew between
　　their plates,
nd strung them round my neck with
　　sea-mew eggs.
Hard by are swamps and marshes,
　　reedy fens
nee deep in water; monsters wade
　　therein
hick-set with plated scale; sometimes
　　in troops
ney crawl on slippery banks; some-
　　times they lash
ne sluggish waves among themselves
　　at war.
ften I heave great rocks from off
　　the crags,   50
eep in their drowsy eyes, at which
　　they howl
nd chase me inland; then I mount
　　their humps
nd prick them back again, unwieldly,
　　slow.
: night the wolves are howling round
　　the place,
nd bats sail there athwart the silver
　　light,
apping their wings; by day in hol-
　　low trees
ney hide, and slink into the gloom of
　　dens.
We live, my mother Sycorax and I,
　caves with bloated toads and
　　crested snakes.
e can make charms, and philters,
　　and brew storms,   60
nd call the great Sea Dragon from
　　his deeps.
othing of this know I, nor care to
　　know.

Give me the milk of goats in gourds
　　or shells,
The flesh of birds and fish, berries and
　　fruit,
Nor want I more, save all day long
　　to lie,
And hear, as now, the voices of the
　　sea.

1852

"POEMS OF THE ORIENT"

We read your little book of Orient
　　lays,
And half believe old superstitions true;
No Saxon like ourselves, an Arab, you,
Stolen in your babyhood by Saxon
　　fays.
That you in fervid songs recall the
　　blaze
Of eastern suns, behold the deep-blue
　　skies,
Lie under rustling palms, breathe
　　winds of spice,
And dream of veiled sultanas, is no
　　praise.
All this is native to you as the air;
You but regain the birthright lost of
　　yore: 10
The marvel is it now becomes your
　　own.
We wind the turban round our Frank-
　　ish hair,
Spring on our steeds that paw the
　　desert's floor,
And take the sandy solitude alone.

1857

THERE ARE GAINS FOR ALL
OUR LOSSES

There are gains for all our losses,
　　There are balms for all our pain:
But when youth, the dream, departs,
It takes something from our hearts,
　　And it never comes again.

We are stronger, and are better,
　　Under manhood's sterner reign:

Still we feel that something sweet
Followed youth, with flying feet,
    And will never come again.   10

Something beautiful is vanished,
    And we sigh for it in vain:
We behold it everywhere,
    On the earth, and in the air,
    But it never comes again!

                                1857

IMOGEN

Unknown to her the maids supplied
    Her wants, and gliding noiseless
        round
    Passed out again, while Leon's
        hound
Stole in and slumbered at her side:
Then Cloten came, a silly ape,
    And wooed her in his boorish way,
Barring the door against escape;
    But the hound woke, and stood at
        bay,
Defiant at the lady's feet,
And made the ruffian retreat.   10
        Then for a little moment's space
        A smile did flit across the face
        Of Lady Imogen.

Without the morning dried the dews
    From shaven lawns and pastures
        green:
    Meantime the court dames and the
        queen
Did pace the shaded avenues:
And Cymbeline amid his train
    Rode down the winding palace
        walks,
Behind the hounds that snuffed the
        plain,   20
    And in the track of wheeling
        hawks;
And soon in greenwood shaws anear
They blew their horns, and chased
        the deer.
        But she nor saw nor heard it
            there,
        But sat, a statue of despair,
        The mournful Imogen.

She shook her ringlets round her hea
    And clasped her hands, and thoug
        and thought,
    As every faithful lady ought,
Whose lord is far away—or dead.
She pressed in books his faded flowe
    That never seemed so sweet befor
Upon his picture gazed for hours,
    And read his letters o'er and o'
Dreaming about the loving Past,
Until her tears were flowing fast.
        With aches of heart, and aches
            brain,
        Bewildered in the realms of pa
        The wretched Imogen!

She tried to rouse herself again,
    Began a broider quaint and rich,
    But pricked her fingers every stitc
And left in every bud a stain.
She took her distaff, tried to spin,
    But tangled up the golden threa
She touched her lute, but could n
        win
    A happy sound, her skill had fl
The letters in her books were blurr
She could not understand a word.
        Bewildered still, and still
            tears,
        The dupe of hopes, the prey
            fears,
        The weeping Imogen!

Her curtains opened in the bree
    And showed the slowly-setting s
    Through vines that up the sash
        run,
And hovering butterflies and bees
A silver fountain gushed below,
    Where swans superbly swam
        spray:
And pages hurried to and fro,
    And trim gallants with ladies gay,
And many a hooded monk and friar
Went barefoot by in coarse attire.
        But like a picture, or a dream,
        The outward world did only see
        To thoughtful Imogen.

When curfews rang, and day was d
    She glided to her chapel desk,

Unclasped her missal arabesque,
And sang the solemn vesper hymn:
Before the crucifix knelt down,   70
    And told her beads, and strove to
        pray;
But Heaven was deaf, and seemed to
        frown,
    And push her idle words away:
And when she touched the holy urn
The icy water seemed to burn!
    No faith had she in saints above,
    She only wanted human love,
        The pining Imogen.

The pale moon walked the waste
        o'erhead,
    And filled the room with sickly
        light;   80
Then she arose in piteous plight,
Disrobed herself, and crept to bed.
The wind without was loud and deep,
    The rattling casements made her
        start:
At last she slept, but in her sleep
    She pressed her fingers o'er her
        heart,
And moaned, and once she gave a
        scream,
To break the clutches of a dream.
    Even in her sleep she could not
        sleep,
    For   ugly   visions   made   her
        weep,   90
        The troubled Imogen.
                                     1857

WE PARTED IN THE STREETS
        OF ISPAHAN

We parted in the streets of Ispahan.
I stopped my camel at the city gate;
Why did I stop? I left my heart
        behind.

I heard the sighing of thy garden
        palms,
I saw the roses burning up with love,
I saw thee not: thou wert no longer
        there.

We parted in the streets of Ispahan.

A moon has passed since that unhappy
        day;
It seems an age: the days are long as
        years.

I send thee gifts by every caravan, 10
I send thee flasks of attar, spices,
        pearls,
I write thee loving songs on golden
        scrolls.

I meet the caravans when they return.
"What news?" I ask. The drivers
        shake their heads.
We parted in the streets of Ispahan.
                                     1857

III. BAYARD TAYLOR *
        (1825–1878)

SONG

Daughter of Egypt, veil thine eyes!
    I cannot bear their fire;
Nor will I touch with sacrifice
    Those altars of Desire.
For they are flames that shun the day,
    And their unholy light
Is fed from natures gone astray
    In passion and in night.

The stars of Beauty and of Sin,
    They burn amid the dark,   10
Like beacons that to ruin win
    The fascinated bark.
Then veil their glow, lest I forswear
    The hopes thou canst not crown,
And in the black waves of thy hair
    My struggling manhood drown!
(1853)   1854

BEDOUIN SONG

From the Desert I come to thee
    On a stallion shod with fire;
And the winds are left behind
    In the speed of my desire.

* All poems of Taylor are used by permission of, and by arrangement with, Houghton
Mifflin Company.

Under thy window I stand,
  And the midnight hears my cry:
I love thee! I love but thee!
  With a love that shall not die
    Till the sun grows old,
    And the stars are old,   10
  And the leaves of the Judgment
    Book unfold!

Look from thy window and see
  My passion and my pain!
I lie on the sands below,
  And I faint in thy disdain.
Let the night-winds touch thy brow
  With the heat of my burning sigh,
And melt thee to hear the vow
  Of a love that shall not die
    Till the sun grows cold,   20
    And the stars are old,
  And the leaves of the Judgment
    Book unfold!

My steps are nightly driven,
  By the fever in my breast,
To hear from thy lattice breathed
  The word that shall give me rest.
Open the door of thy heart,
  And open thy chamber door,
And my kisses shall teach thy lips
  The love that shall fade no more 30
    Till the sun grows cold,
    And the stars are old,
  And the leaves of the Judgment
    Book unfold!

(1853)   1854

THE QUAKER WIDOW

Thee finds me in the garden, Hannah
  —come in! 'Tis kind of thee
To wait until the Friends were gone,
  who came to comfort me:
The still and quiet company a peace
  may give, indeed,
But blessed is the single heart that
  comes to us at need.

Come, sit thee down! Here is the
  bench where Benjamin would sit
On First-day afternoons in spring, and
  watch the swallows flit:

He loved to smell the sprouting box,
  and hear the pleasant bees
Go humming round the lilacs and
  through the apple-trees.

I think he loved the spring: not that
  he cared for flowers—most men
Think such things foolishness—but we
  were first acquainted then,   10
One spring; the next he spoke his
  mind; the third I was his wife;
And in the spring (it happened so)
  our children entered life.

He was but seventy-five: I did not
  think to lay him yet
In Kennett graveyard, where at
  Monthly Meeting first we met.
The Father's mercy shows in this: 'tis
  better I should be
Picked out to bear the heavy cross—
  alone in age—than he.

We've lived together fifty years: it
  seems but one long day,
One quiet Sabbath of the heart, till
  he was called away;
And as we bring from Meeting-time
  a sweet contentment home,
So, Hannah, I have store of peace for
  all the days to come.   20

I mind (for I can tell thee now) how
  hard it was to know
If I had heard the spirit right, that
  told me I should go;
For father had a deep concern upon
  his mind that day,
But mother spoke for Benjamin—she
  knew what best to say.

Then she was still. They sat awhile
  at last she spoke again:
"The Lord incline thee to the right!"
  And "Thou shalt have him,
  Jane!"
My father said. I cried. Indeed
  'twas not the least of shocks,
For Benjamin was Hicksite, and father
  Orthodox.

I thought of this ten years ago, when
    daughter Ruth we lost:
Her husband's of the world, and yet
    I could not see her crossed.   30
She wears, thee knows, the gayest
    gowns, she hears a hireling
    priest—
Ah, dear! the cross was ours: her life's
    a happy one, at least.

Perhaps she'll wear a plainer dress
    when she's as old as I—
Would thee believe it, Hannah? once
    I felt temptation nigh!
My wedding-gown was ashen silk, too
    simple for my taste:
I wanted lace around the neck, and a
    ribbon at the waist.

How strange it seemed to sit with him
    upon the women's side!
I did not dare to lift my eyes: I felt
    more fear than pride,
Till "In the presence of the Lord,"
    he said, and then there came
A holy strength upon my heart and I
    could say the same.   40

I used to blush when he came near,
    but then I showed no sign;
With all the meeting looking on, I held
    his hand in mine.
It seemed my bashfulness was gone,
    now I was his for life:
Thee knows the feeling, Hannah—thee
    too, hast been a wife.

As home we rode, I saw no fields look
    half so green as ours;
The woods were coming into leaf, the
    meadows full of flowers;
The neighbors met us in the lane, and
    every face was kind—
'Tis strange how lively everything
    comes back upon my mind.

I see, as plain as thee sits there, the
    wedding-dinner spread:
At our own table we were guests, with
    father at the head: 50

And Dinah Passmore helped us both—
    'twas she stood up with me,
And Abner Jones with Benjamin,—
    and now they're gone, all three!

It is not right to wish for death; the
    Lord disposes best.
His Spirit comes to quiet hearts, and
    fits them for His rest;
And that He halved our little flock
    was merciful, I see:
For Benjamin has two in heaven, and
    two are left with me.

Eusebius never cared to farm—'twas
    not his call, in truth:
And I must rent the dear old place,
    and go to daughter Ruth.
Thee'll say her ways are not like mine
    —young people now-a-days
Have fallen sadly off, I think, from
    all the good old ways.   60

But Ruth is still a Friend at heart;
    she keeps the simple tongue,
The cheerful, kindly nature we loved
    when she was young;
And it was brought upon my mind, re-
    membering her, of late,
That we on dress and outward things
    perhaps lay too much weight.

I once heard Jesse Kersey say, a spirit
    clothed with grace,
And pure, almost as angels are, may
    have a homely face.
And dress may be of less account: the
    Lord will look within:
The soul it is that testifies of right-
    eousness or sin.

Thee mustn't be too hard on Ruth,
    she's anxious I should go,
And she will do her duty as a daugh-
    ter should, I know.   70
'Tis hard to change so late in life, but
    we must be resigned:
The Lord looks down contentedly
    upon a willing mind.

(1860)   1860

WALT WHITMAN

Who was it sang of the procreant urge, recounted sextillions of subjects?
Who but myself, the Kosmos, yawping abroad, concerned not at all abou
    either the effect or the answer;
Straddling the Continent, gathering into my hairy bosom the growths, whateve
    they were, and nothing slighted, nothing forgotten?
Allez! I am the One, the only One, and this is my Chant Democratique.
Where is he that heard not, and she that heard not, and they that heard no
    before and during and after?
All is wholesome and clean, and all is the effluent strain, impeccable, sweet, o
    the clasper of comrades.
If there were anything else, I would sing it;
But there is nothing, no jot or tittle, or least little scraping of subject o
    matter:
No, there is nothing at all, and all of you know it.

187

From *EL DORADO*

CHAPTER XII

SAN FRANCISCO BY DAY AND NIGHT

A better idea of San Francisco, in the beginning of September, 1849, cannot be given than by the description of a single day. Supposing the visitor to have been long enough in the place to sleep on a hard plank and in spite of the attacks of innumerable fleas, he will be awakened at daylight by the noises of building, with which the hills are all alive. The air is temperate, and the invariable morning fog is just beginning to gather. By sunrise, which gleams hazily over the Coast Mountains across the Bay, the whole populace is up and at work. The wooden buildings unlock their doors, the canvas houses and tents throw back their front curtains; the lighters on the water are warped out from ship to ship; carts and porters are busy along the beach; and only the gaming-table thronged all night by the votaries o chance, are idle and deserted. Th temperature is so fresh as to inspir an active habit of body, and eve without the stimulus of trade an speculation there would be few slug gards at this season.

As early as half-past six the bel begin to sound to breakfast, and fo an hour thenceforth, their incessan clang and the braying of immens gongs drown all the hammers th are busy on a hundred roofs. Th hotels, restaurants, and refectories o all kinds are already as numerous a gaming-tables, and equally various i kind. The tables d'hôte of the fir class (which charge $2 and upware the meal), are abundantly supplie There are others, with more simp and solid fare, frequented by the lar class who have their fortunes yet make. At the United States and Cal fornia restaurants, on the plaza, yo may get an excellent beefsteak, scan ily garnished with potatoes, and a c of good coffee or chocolate, for $1. Fresh beef, bread, potatoes, and all provisions which will bear importation, are plenty; but milk, fruit and vegetables are classed as luxuries, and fresh butter is rarely heard of. On Montgomery street, and the vacant space fronting the water, venders of coffee, cakes and sweetmeats have erected their stands, in order to tempt the appetite of sailors just arrived in port, or miners coming down from the mountains.

By nine o'clock the town is in the full flow of business. The streets running down to the water, and Montgomery street which fronts the Bay, are crowded with people, all in hurried motion. The variety of characters and costumes is remarkable. Our own countrymen seem to lose their local peculiarities in such a crowd, and it is by chance epithets rather than by manner, that the New-Yorker is distinguished from the Kentuckian, the Carolinian from the Down-Easter, the Virginian from the Texan. The German and Frenchman are more easily recognized. Peruvians and Chilians go by in their brown ponchos, and the sober Chinese, cool and impassive in the midst of excitement, look out of the oblique corners of their long eyes at the bustle, but are never tempted to venture from their own line of business. The eastern side of the Plaza, in front of the Parker House and a canvas hell called the Eldorado, are the general rendezvous of business and amusement—combining change, park, club-room and promenade all in one. There, everybody not constantly employed in one spot, may be seen at some time of the day. The character of the groups scattered along the plaza is oftentimes very interesting. In one place are three or four speculators bargaining for lots, buying and selling "fifty varas square" in towns, some of which are canvas and some only paper; in another, a company of miners, brown as leather, and rugged in features as in dress; in a third, perhaps, three or four naval officers speculating on the next cruise, or a knot of genteel gamblers, talking over the last night's operations.

The day advances. The mist which after sunrise hung low and heavy for an hour or two, has risen above the hills, and there will be two hours of pleasant sunshine before the wind sets in from the sea. The crowd in the streets is now wholly alive. Men dart hither and thither, as if possessed with a never-resting spirit. You speak to an acquaintance—a merchant, perhaps. He utters a few hurried words of greeting, while his eyes send keen glances on all sides of you; suddenly he catches sight of somebody in the crowd; he is off, and in the next five minutes has bought up half a cargo, sold a town lot at treble the sum he gave, and taken a share in some new and imposing speculation. It is impossible to witness this excess and dissipation of business, without feeling something of its influence. The very air is pregnant with the magnetism of bold, spirited, unwearied action, and he who but ventures into the outer circle of the whirlpool, is spinning, ere he has time for thought, in its dizzy vortex.

But see! the groups in the plaza suddenly scatter; the city surveyor jerks his pole out of the ground and leaps on a pile of boards; the venders of cakes and sweetmeats follow his example, and the place is cleared, just as a wild bull which has been racing down Kearney street makes his appearance. Two vaqueros, shouting and swinging their lariats, follow at a hot gallop; the dust flies as they dash across the plaza. One of them, in mid-career, hurls his lariat in the air. Mark how deftly the coil unwinds in its flying curve, and with what precision the noose falls over the bull's horns! The horse wheels as if on a pivot, and shoots off in an opposite line. He knows the length of the lariat to a hair, and the instant it is drawn taut, plants his feet firmly for the shock and throws his body forward. The bull is "brought up" with such force as to throw him off his legs. He lies stunned a moment, and then, rising heavily, makes another charge. But by this time the second vaquero has thrown a lariat around one of his hind legs, and thus checked on both sides, he is dragged off to slaughter.

The plaza is refilled as quickly as it was emptied, and the course of business is resumed. About twelve o'clock, a wind begins to blow from the northwest, sweeping with most violence through a gap between the hills, opening towards the Golden Gate. The bells and gongs begin to sound for dinner, and these two causes tend to lessen the crowd in the streets for an hour or two. Two o'clock is the usual dinner-time for business men, but some of the old and successful merchants have adopted the fashionable hour of five. Where shall we dine to-day? the restaurants display their signs invitingly on all sides; we have choice of the United States, Tortoni's,

the Alhambra, and many other equally classic resorts, but Delmonico's, like its distinguished original in New York has the highest prices and the greatest variety of dishes. We go down Kearney street to a two-story wooden house on the corner of Jackson. The lower story is a market; the walls are garnished with quarters of beef and mutton; a huge pile of Sandwich Island squashes fills one corner, and several cabbage-heads, valued at $. each, show themselves in the window. We enter a little door at the end of the building, ascend a dark, narrow flight of steps and find ourselves in a long, low room, with ceiling and wall of white muslin and a floor covered with oil-cloth.

There are about twenty tables disposed in two rows, all of them so well filled that we have some difficulty in finding places. Taking up the written bill of fare, we find such items as the following:

SOUPS

Mock Turtle $0 7
St. Julien 1 0

FISH

Boiled Salmon Trout, anchovy
    sauce 1 7

BOILED

Leg Mutton, caper sauce 1 0
Corned Beef, Cabbage 1.0
Ham and Tongues 0 7

ENTREES

Fillet of Beef, mushroom sauce...$1 7
Veal Cutlets, breaded 1 0
Mutton Chop 1 0
Lobster Salad 2 0
Sirloin of Venison 1 5
Baked Maccaroni 0 7
Beef Tongue, sauce piquante 1 0

So that, with but a moderate appetite the dinner will cost us $5, if we are at all epicurean in our tastes. There are cries of "steward!" from all parts of the room—the word "waiter" is not considered sufficiently respectful, seeing that the waiter may have been a lawyer or merchant's clerk a few months before. The dishes look very small as they are placed on the table, but they are skilfully cooked and very palatable to men that have ridden in from the diggings. The appetite one acquires in California is something remarkable. For two months after my arrival, my sensations were like those of a famished wolf.

In the matter of dining, the tastes of all nations can be gratified here. There are French restaurants on the Plaza and on Dupont street; an extensive German establishment on Pacific street; the *Fonda Peruana;* the Italian Confectionary; and three Chinese houses, denoted by their long three-cornered flags of yellow silk. The latter are much frequented by Americans, on account of their excellent cookery, and the fact that meals are $1 each, without regard to quantity. Kong-Sung's house is near the water; Whang-Tong's in Sacramento street, and Tong-Ling's in Jackson street. There the grave Celestials serve up their chow-chow and curry, besides many genuine English dishes; their tea and coffee cannot be surpassed.

The afternoon is less noisy and active than the forenoon. Merchants keep within-doors, and the gambling-rooms are crowded with persons who step in to escape the wind and dust. The sky takes a cold gray cast, and the hills over the bay are barely visible in the dense, dusty air. Now and then a watcher, who has been stationed on the hill above Fort Montgomery, comes down and reports an inward-bound vessel, which occasions a little excitement among the boatmen and the merchants who are awaiting consignments. Towards sunset, the plaza is nearly deserted; the wind is merciless in its force, and a heavy overcoat is not found unpleasantly warm. As it grows dark, there is a lull, though occasional gusts blow down the hill and carry the dust of the city out among the shipping.

The appearance of San Francisco at night, from the water, is unlike anything I ever beheld. The houses are mostly of canvas, which is made transparent by the lamps within, and transforms them, in the darkness, to dwellings of solid light. Seated on the slopes of its three hills, the tents pitched among the chapparal to the very summits, it gleams like an amphitheatre of fire. Here and there shine out brilliant points, from the decoy-lamps of the gaming-houses; and through the indistinct murmur of the streets comes by fits the sound of music from their hot and crowded precincts. The picture has in it something unreal and fantastic; it impresses one like the cities of the magic lantern, which a motion of the hand can build or annihilate.

The only objects left for us to visit are the gaming-tables, whose day has just fairly dawned. We need not wander far in search of one. Denison's Exchange, the Parker House and Eldorado stand side by side; across the way are the Verandah and Aguila de Oro; higher up the plaza the St. Charles and Bella Union; while dozens of second-rate establishments are scattered through the less frequented streets. The greatest crowd is about the Eldorado; we find it difficult to effect an entrance. There are about eight tables in the room, all of which are thronged; copper-hued Kanakas, Mexicans rolled in their sarapes and Peruvians thrust through their ponchos, stand shoulder to shoulder with the brown and bearded American miners. The stakes are generally small, though when the bettor gets into "a streak of luck," as it is called, they are allowed to double until all is lost or the bank breaks. Along the end of the room is a spacious bar, supplied with all kinds of bad liquors, and in a sort of gallery, suspended under the ceiling, a female violinist tasks her talent and strength of muscle to minister to the excitement of play.

The Verandah, opposite, is smaller, but boasts an equal attraction in a musician who has a set of Pandean pipes fastened at his chin, a drum on his back, which he beats with sticks at his elbows, and cymbals in his hands. The piles of coin on the monte tables clink merrily to his playing, and the throng of spectators, jammed together in a sweltering mass, walk up to the bar between the tunes and drink out of sympathy with his dry and breathless throat. At the Aguila de Oro there is a full band of Ethiopian serenaders, and at the other hells, violins, guitars or wheezy accordions, as the case may be. The atmosphere of these places is rank with tobacco-smoke, and filled with a feverish, stifling heat, which communicates an unhealthy glow to the faces of the players.

We shall not be deterred from entering by the heat and smoke, or the motley characters into whose company we shall be thrown. There are rare chances here for seeing human nature in one of its most dark and exciting phases. Note the variety of expression in the faces gathered around this table! They are playing monte, the favorite game in California, since the chances are considered more equal and the opportunity of false play very slight. The dealer throws out his cards with a cool, nonchalant air; indeed, the gradual increase of the hollow square of dollars at his left hand is not calculated to disturb his equanimity. The two Mexicans in front, muffled in their dirty sarapes, put down their half-dollars and dollars and see them lost, without changing a muscle. Gambling is born habit with them, and they would lose thousands with the same indifference. Very different is the demeanor of the Americans who are playing; their good or ill luck is betrayed at once by involuntary exclamations and changes of countenance, unless the stake should be very large and absorbing, when their anxiety, though silent, may be read with no less certainty. They have no power to resist the fascination of the game. Now counting their winnings by thousands, now dependent on the kindness of a friend for a few dollars to commence anew, they pass hour after hour in those hot, unwholesome dens. There is no appearance of arms, but let one of the players, impatient with his losses and maddened by the poisonous fluids he has drunk, threaten one of the profession, and there will be no scarcity of knives and revolvers.

There are other places, where gaming is carried on privately and to more ruinous extent—rooms in the rear of the Parker House, in the City Hotel and other places, frequented only by the initiated. Here the stakes are almost unlimited, the players being men of wealth and apparent respectability. Frequently, in the absorbing interest of some desperate game the night goes by unheeded and morning breaks upon haggard faces and reckless hearts. Here are lost, in a few turns of a card or rolls of a ball, the product of fortunate ventures

by sea or months of racking labor on land. How many men, maddened by continual losses, might exclaim in their blind vehemence of passion, on leaving these hells:

Out, out, thou strumpet, Fortune! All
    you gods
In general synod, take away her power;
Break all the spokes and fellies from her
    wheel,
And bowl the round nave down the hill
    of heaven,
A low as to the fiends!

                                1850

IV. EDMUND CLARENCE
STEDMAN *
(1833–1908)

HOW OLD BROWN TOOK
HARPER'S FERRY

John Brown in Kansas settled, like a
    steadfast Yankee farmer,
  Brave and godly, with four sons, all
    stalwart men of might.
There he spoke aloud for freedom, and
    the Border-strife grew warmer,
  Till the Rangers fired his dwelling,
    in his absence, in the night;
        And Old Brown,
        Osawatomie Brown,
Came homeward in the morning—to
    find his house burned down.

Then he grasped his trusty rifle and
    boldly fought for freedom;
  Smote from border unto border the
    fierce, invading band;
And he and his brave boys vowed—so
    might Heaven help and speed
    'em—   10

* All selections from Stedman are used by permission of, and by arrangement with, Houghton Mifflin Company.

They would save those grand old
    prairies from the curse that
    blights the land;
        And Old Brown,
        Osawatomie Brown,
Said, "Boys, the Lord will aid us!"
    and he shoved his ramrod down.

And the Lord *did* aid these men, and
    they labored day and even,
  Saving Kansas from its peril; and
    their very lives seemed
    charmed,
Till the ruffians killed one son, in the
    blessed light of Heaven,—
  In cold blood the fellows slew him,
    as he journeyed all unarmed;
        Then Old Brown,
        Osawatomie Brown,   20
Shed not a tear, but shut his teeth, and
    frowned a terrible frown!

Then they seized another brave boy,
    —not amid the heat of battle,
  But in peace, behind his plough-
    share,—and they loaded him
    with chains,
And with pikes, before their horses,
    even as they goad their cattle,
  Drove him cruelly, for their sport,
    and at last blew out his brains;
        Then Old Brown,
        Osawatomie Brown,

Raised his right hand up to Heaven,
  calling Heaven's vengeance
  down.

And he swore a fearful oath, by the
  name of the Almighty,
  He would hunt this ravening evil
  that had scathed and torn him
  so;   30
He would seize it by the vitals; he
  would crush it day and night;
  he
  Would so pursue its footsteps, so
  return it blow for blow,
    That Old Brown,
    Osawatomie Brown,
Should be a name to swear by, in
  backwoods or in town!

Then his beard became more grizzled,
  and his wild blue eye grew
  wilder,
  And more sharply curved his hawk's-
  nose, snuffing battle from afar;
And he and the two boys left, though
  the Kansas strife waxed milder,
  Grew more sullen, till was over the
  bloody Border War;
    And Old Brown,   40
    Osawatomie Brown,
Had gone crazy, as they reckoned by
  his fearful glare and frown.

So he left the plains of Kansas and
  their bitter woes behind him,
  Slipt off into Virginia, where the
  statesmen all are born;
Hired a farm by Harper's Ferry, and
  no one knew where to find him,
  Or whether he'd turned parson, or
  was jacketed and shorn;
    For Old Brown,
    Osawatomie Brown,
Mad as he was, knew texts enough to
  wear a parson's gown.

He bought no ploughs and harrows,
  spades and shovels, and such
  trifles;   50
  But quietly to his rancho there
  came, by every train,

Boxes full of pikes and pistols, and
  his well-beloved Sharp's rifles;
  And eighteen other madmen joined
  their leader there again.
    Says Old Brown,
    Osawatomie Brown,
"Boys, we've got an army large enough
  to march and take the town!

"Take the town, and seize the muskets,
  free the negroes and then arm
  them;
  Carry the County and the State, ay,
  and all the potent South.
On their own heads be the slaughter,
  if their victims rise to harm
  them—
  These Virginians who believed not,
  nor would heed the warning
  mouth."   60
    Says Old Brown,
    Osawatomie Brown,
"The world shall see a Republic, or
  my name is not John Brown."

'Twas the sixteenth of October, on the
  evening of a Sunday.
  "This good work," declared the captain, "shall be on a holy night!"
It was on a Sunday evening, and before the noon of Monday,
  With two sons, and Captain Ste-
  phens, fifteen privates—black
  and white,
    Captain Brown,
    Osawatomie Brown,
Marched across the bridged Potomac,
  and knocked the sentry
  down;   70

Took the guarded armory-building,
  and the muskets and the cannon;
  Captured all the county majors and
  the colonels, one by one;
Scared to death each gallant scion of
  Virginia they ran on
  And before the noon of Monday, I
  say, the deed was done.
    Mad Old Brown,
    Osawatomie Brown,

With his eighteen other crazy men,
    went in and took the town.

Very little noise and bluster, little
    , smell of powder made he;
It was all done in the midnight, like
    the Emperor's *coup d'état*.
'Cut the wires! Stop the rail-cars!
Hold the streets and bridges!" said
    he,   80
Then declared the new Republic, with
    himself for guiding star,—
        This Old Brown
        Osawatomie Brown,
And the bold two thousand citizens
    ran off and left the town.

Then was riding and railroading and
    expressing here and thither;
And Martinsburg Sharpshooters
    and the Charlestown Volun-
    teers,
And the Shepherdstown and Winches-
    ter Militia hastened whither
Old Brown was said to muster his
    ten thousand grenadiers.
        General Brown!
        Osawatomie Brown!!   90
Behind whose rampant banner all the
    North was pouring down.

But at last, 'tis said, some prisoners
    escaped from Old Brown's dur-
    ance,
And the effervescent valor of the
    Chivalry broke out,
When they learned that nineteen mad-
    men had the marvellous assur-
    ance—
Only nineteen—thus to seize the
    place and drive them straight
    about;
        And Old Brown,
        Osawatomie Brown,
'ound an army come to take him, en-
    camped around the town.

But to storm, with all the forces I
    have mentioned, was too risky;
So they hurried off to Richmond for
    the Government Marines,   100

Tore them from their weeping ma-
    trons, fired their souls with
    Bourbon whiskey,
Till they battered down Brown's
    castle with their ladders and
    machines;
        And Old Brown,
        Osawatomie Brown,
Received three bayonet stabs, and a
    cut on his brave old crown.

Tallyho! the old Virginia gentry gather
    to the baying!
In they rushed and killed the game,
    shooting lustily away;
And whene'er they slew a rebel, those
    who came too late for slaying,
Not to lose a share of glory, fired
    their bullets in his clay;
        And Old Brown,   110
        Osawatomie Brown,
Saw his sons fall dead beside him, and
    between them laid him down.

How the conquerors wore their laurels;
    how they hastened on the trial;
How Old Brown was placed half
    dying, on the Charlestown
    courthouse floor;
How he spoke his grand oration, in the
    scorn of all denial;
What the brave old madman told
    them,—these are known the
    country o'er.
        "Hang Old Brown,
        Osawatomie Brown."
Said the judge, "and all such rebels!"
    with his most judicial frown.

But, Virginians, don't do it! for I tell
    you that the flagon   120
Filled with blood of Old Brown's
    offspring, was first poured by
    Southern hands;
And each drop from Old Brown's life-
    veins, like the red gore of the
    dragon,
May spring up a vengeful Fury,
    hissing through your slave-
    worn lands!

And Old Brown,
    Osawatomie Brown,
May trouble you more than ever,
    when you've nailed his coffin
    down!
(1859)   1859

WANTED—A MAN

Back from the trebly crimsoned field
    Terrible words are thunder-tost;
Full of the wrath that will not yield,
    Full of revenge for battles lost!
Hark to their echo, as it crost
The Capital, making faces wan:
    "End this murderous holocaust;
Abraham Lincoln, give us a MAN!

"Give us a man of Gold's own mould,
    Born to marshal his fellow men; [10]
One whose fame is not bought and
    sold
    At the stroke of a politician's pen;
    Give us the man of thousands ten,
Fit to do as well as to plan;
    Give us a rallying-cry, and then,
Abraham Lincoln, give us a MAN!

"No leader to shirk the boasting foe,
    And to march and countermarch our
    brave,
Till they fall like ghosts in the
    marshes low,
    And swamp-grass covers each name-
    less grave;   [20]
    Nor another, whose fatal banners
    wave
Aye in Disaster's shameful van;
    Nor another, to bluster, and lie, and
    rave;—
Abraham Lincoln, give us a MAN!

"Hearts are mourning in the North,
    While the sister rivers seek the main,
Red with our life-blood flowing
    forth,—
    Who shall gather it up again?
    Though we march to the battle-plain

Firmly as when the strife began, [3]
    Shall all our offering be in vain?—
Abraham Lincoln, give us a MAN!

"Is there never one in all the land,
    One on whose might the Cause may
    lean?
Are all the common ones so grand,
    And all the titled ones so mean?
    What if your failure may have been
In trying to make good bread from
    bran
    From worthless metal a weapon
    keen?—
Abraham Lincoln, find us a MAN! [4]

"O, we will follow him to the death,
    Where the foeman's fiercest column
    are!
O, we will use our latest breath,
    Cheering for every sacred star!
    His to marshall us high and far;
Ours to battle, as patriots can
    When a Hero leads the Holy
    War!—
Abraham Lincoln, give us a MAN!"
(1862)   186[2]

PAN IN WALL STREET

(A.D. 1867)

Just where the Treasury's marble front
    Looks over Wall Street's mingled
    nations;
Where Jews and Gentiles most are
    wont
    To throng for trade and last quota-
    tions;
Where, hour by hour, the rates of gold
    Outrival, in the ears of the people
The quarter-chimes, serenely tolled
    From Trinity's undaunted steeple,—

Even there I heard a strange, wild
    strain
    Sound high above the modern
    clamor,   [10]
Above the cries of greed and gain,

The curbstone war, the auction's
  hammer;
And swift, on Music's misty ways,
  It led, from all this strife for mil-
    lions,
To ancient, sweet-do-nothing days
  Among the kirtle-robed Sicilians.

And as it stilled the multitude,
  And yet more joyous rose, and
    shriller,
I saw the minstrel, where he stood
  At ease against a Doric pillar;   20
One hand a droning organ played,
  The other held a Pan's-pipe (fash-
    ioned
Like those of old) to lips that made
  The reeds give out that strain im-
    passioned.

'Twas Pan himself had wandered here,
  A-strolling through this sordid city,
And piping to the civic ear
  The prelude of some pastoral ditty!
The demigod had crossed the seas,—
  From haunts of shepherd, nymph,
    and satyr,   30
And Syracusian times, to these
  Far shores and twenty centuries
    later.

A ragged cap was on his head:
  But—hidden thus—there was no
    doubting
That, all with crispy locks o'erspread,
  His gnarled horns were somewhere
    sprouting;
His club-feet, cased in rusty shoes,
  Were crossed, as on some frieze you
    see them,
And trousers, patched of divers hues,
  Concealed his crooked shanks be-
    neath them.   40

He filled the quivering reeds with
    sound,
  And o'er his mouth their changes
    shifted,
And with his goat's-eyes looked
  around

Where'er the passing current
  drifted;
And soon, as on Trinacrian hills
  The nymphs and herdsmen ran to
    hear him,
Even now the tradesmen from their
  tills,
  With clerks and porters, crowded
    near him.

The bulls and bears together drew
  From Jauncey Court and New-
    Street Alley,   50
As erst, if pastorals be true,
  Came beasts from every wooded
    valley;
The random passers stayed to list:
  A boxer Ægon, rough and merry;
A Broadway Daphnis on his tryst
  With Naïs at the Brooklyn Ferry;

A one-eyed Cyclops halted long
  In tattered cloak of army pattern;
And Galatea joined the throng—
  A blowsy, apple-vending slattern;   60
While old Silenus staggered out
  From some new-fangled lunch-house
    handy,
And bade the piper, with a shout,
  To strike up Yankee Doodle Dandy!

A newsboy and a peanut-girl
  Like little Fauns began to caper—
His hair was all in tangled curl,
  Her tawny legs were bare and taper;
And still the gathering larger grew,
  And gave its pence and crowded
    nigher,   70
While aye the shepherd-minstrel blew
  His pipe and struck the gamut
    higher.

O heart of Nature, beating still
  With throbs her vernal passion
    taught her,—
Even here, as on the vine-clad hill
  Or by the Arethusan water!
New forms may fold the speech, new
  lands

Arise within these ocean-portals,
But Music waves eternal wands,—
  Enchantress of the souls of mor-
      tals;   80

So thought I—but among us trod
  A man in blue, with legal baton,
And scoffed the vagrant demigod,
    And pushed him from the step I
      sat on.
Doubting, I mused upon the cry,
  "Great Pan is dead!"—and all the
    people
Went on their ways; and clear and
  high
  The quarter sounded from the
    steeple.
                  1867

FALSTAFF'S SONG

Where's he that died o' Wednesday?
  What place on earth hath he?
A tailor's yard beneath, I wot,
  Where worms approaching be;
For the wight that died o' Wednesday,
  Just laid the light below,
Is dead as the varlet turned to clay
  A score of years ago.

Where's he that died o' Sabba' day?
  Good Lord, I'd not be he!   10
The best of days is foul enough
  From this world's fare to flee;
And the saint that died o' Sabba' day,

With his grave turf yet to grow
Is dead as the sinner brought to pray
  A hundred years ago.

Where's he that died o' yesterday?
  What better chance hath he
To clink the can and toss the pot
  When this night's junkets be?   2
For the lad that died o' yesterday
  Is just as dead—ho! ho!—
As the whoreson knave men laid away
  A thousand years ago.
                  189

W. W.

LINES SENT TO HIS FUNERAL WITH AN
IVY WREATH, MARCH 30, 1892

GOOD-BYE, Walt!
Good-bye, from all you loved o:
  earth—
Rock, tree, dumb creature, man and
  woman—
  To you, their comrade human.
    The last assault
Ends now; and now in some grea
  world has birth
A minstrel, whose strong soul finds
  broader wings,
  More brave imaginings.
Stars crown the hilltop where you:
  dust shall lie,
  Even as we say good-bye,
    Good-bye, Old Walt!
                  189:

From *POETS OF AMERICA*

EDGAR ALLAN POE

* * * "Poetry," said Poe, "has been
with me a passion, not a purpose,"—
a remarkable sentence to be found
in a boyish preface, and I believe that
he wrote the truth. But here, again,
he displays an opposite failing. If

poetry had been with him no less a
passion, and equally a purpose, we
now should have had something more
to represent his rhythmical genius than
the few brief, occasional lyrics which
are all that his thirty years of life as
a poet—the life of his early choice
—have left us.

In estimating him as a poet, the
dates of these lyrics are of minor con-

sequence. They make but a thin volume, smaller than one which might hold the verse of Collins or Gray. Their range is narrower still. It is a curious fact that Poe struck, in youth, the key-notes of a few themes, and that some of his best pieces, as we now have them, are but variations upon their earlier treatment.

His first collection, as we have seen, was made in his twentieth year, and reprinted with changes and omissions, just after he left West Point. The form of the longer poems is copied from Byron and Moore, while the spirit of the whole series vaguely reminds us of Shelley in his obscurer lyrical mood. Poe's originality can be found in them, but they would be valueless except for his after career. They have unusual significance as the shapeless germs of much that was to grow into form and beauty. Crude and wandering pieces, entitled "Fairy Land" and "Irene," "To ——," "A Pæan," etc., were the originals of "The Sleeper," "A Dream within a Dream," and "Lenore"; while "The Doomed City" and "The Valley of Nis" reappear as "The City in the Sea" and the "Valley of Unrest." Others were less thoroughly rewritten. Possibly he thus remodeled his juvenile verse to show that, however inchoate, it contained something worth a master's handling. Mr. Stoddard thinks, and not without reason, that he found it an easy way of making saleable "copy." The poet himself intimates that circumstances beyond his control restricted his lyrical product. I scarcely remember another instance where a writer has so hoarded his early songs, and am in doubt whether to commend or deprecate their repro-duction. It does not betoken affluence, but it was honest in Poe that he would not write in cold blood for the mere sake of composing. This he undoubtedly had the skill to do, and would have done, if his sole object had been creation of the beautiful, or art for art's sake. He used his lyrical gift mostly to express veritable feelings and moods—I might almost say a single feeling or mood —to which he could not otherwise give utterance, resorting to melody when prose was insufficient. Herein he was true to the cardinal, antique conception of poesy, and in keeping it distinct from his main literary work he confirmed his own avowal that it was to him a passion, and neither a purpose nor a pursuit.

A few poems, just as they stood in his early volume, are admirable in thought or finish. One is the sonnet, "To Science," which is striking, not as a sonnet, but for its premonition of attitudes which poetry and science have now more clearly assumed. Another is the exquisite lyric, "To Helen," which every critic longs to cite. Its confusion of imagery is wholly forgotten in the delight afforded by melody, lyrical perfection, sweet and classic grace. I do not understand why he omitted this charming trifle from the juvenile poems which he added to the collection of 1845. It is said that he wrote it when fourteen, and nothing more fresh and delicate came from his pen in maturer years.

The instant success of "The Raven" —and this was within a few years of his death—first made him popular as a poet, and resulted in a new collection of his verses. The lyrics which it contained, and a few written afterward,—"Ulalume," "The Bells," "For Annie," etc.,—now comprise the whole of his poetry as retained in the standard editions. The most glaring faults of "Al Aaraaf" and "Tamerlane," phrases such as "the eternal condor years," have been selected by eulogists for special praise. Turning from this practice-work to the . poems which made his reputation, we come at once to the most widely known of all.

Poe could not have written "The Raven" in youth. It exhibits a method so positive as almost to compel us to accept, against the denial of his associates, his own account of its building. The maker *does* keep a firm hand on it throughout, and for once seems to set his purpose above his passion. This appears in the gravely quaint diction, and in the contrast between the reality of everyday manners and the profounder reality of a spiritual shadow upon the human heart. The grimness of fate is suggested by phrases which it requires a masterly hand to subdue to the meaning of the poem. "Sir," said I, "or madam," "this ungainly fowl," and the like, sustain the air of grotesqueness, and become a foil to the pathos, an approach to the tragical climax, of this unique production. Only genius can deal so closely with the grotesque and make it add to the solemn beauty of structure an effect like that of the gargoyles seen by moonlight on the façade of Notre Dame.

In no other lyric is Poe so self-possessed. No other is so determinate in its repetends and alliterations. Hence I am far from deeming it his most poetical poem. Its artificial

qualities are those which catch the fancy of the general reader; and it is of all his ballads, if not the most imaginative, the most peculiar. His more ethereal productions seem to me those in which there is the appearance, at least, of spontaneity,—in which he yields to his feelings, while dying falls and cadences most musical, most melancholy, come from him unawares. Literal criticisms of "The Raven" are of small account. If the shadow of the bird could not fall upon the mourner, the shadows of its evil presence could brood upon his soul; the seraphim whose foot-falls tinkle upon the tufted floor may be regarded as seraphim of the Orient, their anklets hung with celestial bells. At all events, Poe's raven is the very genius of the Night's Plutonian shore, different from other ravens, entirely his own, and none other can take its place. It is an emblem of the Irreparable, the guardian of pitiless memories, whose burden ever recalls to us the days that are no more.

As a new creation, then, "The Raven" is entitled to a place in literature, and keeps it. But how much more imaginative is such a poem as "The City in the Sea"! As a picture, this reminds us of Turner, and, again, of that sublime madman, John Martin. Here is a strange city where Death has raised a throne. Its

> shrines and palaces and towers
> (Time-eaten towers that tremble not!)
> Resemble nothing that is ours.
> Around, by lifting winds forgot,
> Resignedly beneath the sky
> The melancholy waters lie.

This mystical town is aglow with light, not from heaven, but from out

the lurid sea,—light which streams up
the turrets and pinnacles and domes,—

Up many and many a marvelous shrine,
Whose wreathed friezes intertwine
The viol, the violet, and the vine.

.   .   .   .   .   .

While, from a proud tower in the town,
Death looks gigantically down.

The sea about is hideously serene, but
at last there is a movement; the towers seem slightly to sink; the dull tide
has a redder glow:

And when, amid no earthly moans,
    Down, down that town shall settle
        hence,
Hell, rising from a thousand thrones,
    Shall do it reverence.

This poem, notwithstanding its som-
berness and terror, depends upon effects which made Poe the forerunner
of our chief experts in form and
sound, and both the language and the
conception are suggestive in a high
degree.

"The Sleeper" is even more poetic.
It distills, like drops from the opiate
vapor of the swooning moonlight night,
all the melody, the fantasy, the exaltation, that befit the vision of a beautiful woman lying in her shroud, silent
in her length of tress, waiting to exchange her death chamber

        for one more holy,
This bed for one more melancholy.

Poe's ideality cannot be gainsaid,
but it aided him with few, very few,
images, and those seemed to haunt
his brain perpetually. Such an image
is that of the beings who lend their
menace to the tone of the funeral
bells:

And the people,—ah, the people,—
They that dwell up in the steeple
    All alone,

And who, tolling, tolling, tolling,
    In that muffled monotone,
Feel a glory in so rolling
    On the human heart a stone,—
They are neither man nor woman,
They are neither brute nor human,
    They are Ghouls.

In the same remarkable fantasia the
bells themselves become human, and
it is a master-stroke that makes us
hear them shriek out of tune,

In a clamorous appealing to the mercy
    of the fire,

and forces us to the very madness
with which they are

    Leaping higher, higher, higher,
    With a desperate desire
    And a resolute endeavor
    Now—now to sit, or never,
    By the side of the pale-faced moon.

Clearly this extravagance was suggested by the picture and the rime.
But it so carries us with it that we
think not of its meaning; we share
in the delirium of the bells, and nothing can be too extreme for the abandon to which we yield ourselves, led
by the faith and frenzy of the poet.

The hinting, intermittent qualities
of a few lyrics remind us of Shelley
and Coleridge, with whom Poe always
was in sympathy. The conception of
"The Raven" was new, but in method
it bears a likeness to "Lady Ger-
aldine's Courtship," so closely, in fact,
that the rhythm of the one probably
was suggested by that of the other.
In motive they are so different that
neither Poe nor Mrs. Browning could
feel aggrieved. After an examination
of dates, and of other matters relating
to the genesis of each poem, I have
satisfied myself, against much reasoning to the contrary, that Poe derived
his use of the refrain and repetend,

here and elsewhere, from the English sibyl, by whom they were employed to the verge of mannerism in her earliest lyrics.

"The Conqueror Worm" expresses in a single moan the hopelessness of the poet's vigils among the tombs, where he demanded of silence and the night some tidings of the dead. All he knew was that

No voice from that sublimer world hath ever
To sage or poet these responses given.

The most he dared to ask for "The Sleeper" was oblivion; that her sleep might be as deep as it was lasting. We lay the dead "in the cold ground" or in the warm, flower-springing bosom of dear Earth, as best may fit the hearts of those who mourn them. But the tomb, the end of mortality, is voiceless still. If you would find the beginning of immortality, seek some other oracle. "The Conqueror Worm" is the most despairing of lyrics, yet quite essential to the mystical purpose of the tale "Ligeia." But to brood upon men as mimes, ironically cast "in the form of God on high,"—mere puppets, where

the play is the tragedy, "Man,"
And its hero the Conqueror Worm,

—that way madness lies, indeed. In the lyric, "For Annie," death is a trance; the soul lingers, calm and at rest, for the fever, called living, is conquered. Human love remains, and its last kiss is still a balm. Something may be hereafter,—but what, who knows? For repose, and for delicate and unstudied melody, it is one of Poe's truest poems, and his tenderest. During the brief period in

which he survived his wife, he seemed to have a vision of rest in death, and not of horror. Two lyrics, widely different, and one of them of a most singular nature, are thought to be requiems for his lost companion. It is from no baseness, but from a divine instinct, that genuine artists are compelled to go on with their work and to make their own misery, no less than their joy, promote its uses. Their most sacred experiences become, not of their volition, its themes and illustrations. Every man as an individual is secondary to what he is as a worker for the progress of his kind and the glory of the gift allotted to him.

Therefore, whether Poe adored his wife or not, her image became the ideal of these poems. I shall add little here to all that has been written of "Ulalume." It is so strange, so unlike anything that preceded it, so vague and yet so full of meaning, that of itself it might establish a new method. To me it seems an improvisation, such as a violinist might play upon the instrument which had become his one thing of worth after the death of a companion had left him alone with his own soul. Poe remodeled and made the most of his first broken draft, and had the grace not to analyze the process. I have accepted his analysis of "The Raven" as more than half true. Poets know that an entire poem often is suggested by one of its lines, even by a refrain or a bit of rhythm. From this it builds itself. The last or any other stanza may be written first; and what at first is without form is not void,— for ultimately it will be perfected into shape and meaning. If "Ulalume" may be termed a requiem, "Annabel

Lee" is a tuneful dirge,—the simplest of Poe's melodies, and the most likely to please the common ear. It is said to have been his last lyric, and was written, I think, with more spontaneity than others. The theme is carried along skilfully, the movement hastened and heightened to the end and there dwelt upon, as often in a piece of music. Before considering the poet's method of song, I will mention the two poems which seem to me to represent his highest range, and sufficient in themselves to preserve the memory of a lyrist.

We overlook the allegory of "The Haunted Palace," until it has been read more than once; we think of the sound, the phantasmagoric picture, the beauty, the lurid close. The magic muse of Coleridge, in "Kubla Khan," or elsewhere, hardly went beyond such lines as these:

Banners yellow, glorious, golden,
  On its roof did float and flow,
(This—all this—was in the olden
  Time long ago;)
And every gentle air that dallied,
  In that sweet day,
Along the ramparts, plumed and pallid,
  A wingèd odor went away.

The conception of a "Lost Mind" never has been so imaginatively created, whether by poet or by painter. Questioning Poe's own mental state, look at this poem and see how sane, as an artist, he was that made it. "Do you act best when you forget yourself in the part?" "No, for then I forget to perfect the part." Even more striking is the song of "Israfel," whose heart-strings are a lute. Of all these lyrics is not this the most lyrical, —not only charged with music, but with light? For once, and in his

freest hour of youth, Poe got above the sepulchers and mists, even beyond the pale-faced moon, and visited the empyrean. There is joy in this carol, and the radiance of the skies, and ecstatic possession of the gift of song:

If I could dwell
Where Israfel
  Hath dwelt, and he where I,
He might not sing so wildly well
  A mortal melody,
While a bolder note than this might
    swell
  From my lyre within the sky!

All this, with the rapturous harmony of the first and third stanza, is awakened in the poet's soul by a line from the Koran, and the result is even finer than the theme. If I had any claim to make up a "Parnassus," not perhaps of the most famous English lyrics, but of those which appeal strongly to my own poetic sense, and could select but one of Poe's, I confess that I should choose "Israfel," for pure music, for exaltation, and for its original, satisfying quality of rhythmic art.

Few and brief are these *reliquiæ* which determine his fame as a poet. What do they tell us of his lyrical genius and method? Clearly enough, that he possessed an exquisite faculty which he exercised within definite bounds. It may be that within those bounds he would have done more if events had not hindered him, as he declared, "from making any serious effort" in the field of his choice. In boyhood he had decided views as to the province of song, and he never afterwards changed them. The preface to his West Point edition, rambling and conceited as it is—affording such a contrast to the proud humility of Keats's preface to "Endymion"— gives us the gist of his creed, and shows that the instinct of the young poet was scarcely less delicate than that of his nobler kinsman. Poe thought the object of poetry was pleasure, not truth; the pleasure must not be definite, but subtle, and therefore poetry is opposed to romance; music is an *essential*, "since the comprehension of sweet sound is our most indefinite conception." Metaphysics in verse he hated, pronouncing the Lake theory a new form of didacticism that had injured even the tuneful Coleridge. For a neophyte this was not bad, and after certain reservations few will disagree with him. Eighteen years later, in his charming lecture, "The Poetic Principle," he offered simply an extension of these ideas, with reasons why a long poem "cannot exist." One is tempted to rejoin that the standard of length in a poem, as in a piece of music, is relative, depending upon the power of the maker and the recipient to prolong their exalted moods. We might, also, quote Landor's "Pentameron," concerning the greatness of a poet, or even Beecher's saying that "pint measures are soon filled." The lecture justly denounces the "heresy of the didactic," and then declares poetry to be the child of Taste,—devoted solely to the Rhythmical Creation of Beauty, as it is in music that the soul most nearly attains the supernal end for which it struggles. In fine, Poe, with "the mad pride of intellectuality," refused to look beyond the scope of his own gift, and would restrict the poet to one method and even to a single theme. In his *post facto* analysis of "The Raven" he conceives the highest tone of beauty to be sadness, caused by the pathos of existence and our inability to grasp the unknown. Of all beauty that of a beautiful woman is the supremest, her death is the saddest loss—and therefore "the most poetical topic in the world." He would treat this musically by application of the refrain, increasing the sorrowful loveliness of his poem by contrast of something homely, fantastic or quaint.

Poe's own range was quite within his theory. His juvenile versions of what afterward became poems were so very "indefinite" as to express almost nothing; they resembled those marvelous stanzas of Dr. Chivers, that sound magnificently—I have heard Bayard Taylor and Mr. Swinburne rehearse them with shouts of delight—and that have no meaning at all. Poe could not remain a Chivers, but sound always was his *forte*. We rarely find his highest imagination in his verse, or the creation of poetic phrases such as came to the lips of Keats without a summons. He lacked the dramatic power of combination and produced no symphony in rhythm; was strictly a melodist, who achieved wonders in a single strain. Neither Mrs. Browning nor any other poet has "applied" the refrain in Poe's fashion, nor so effectively. In "The Bells" its use is limited almost to one word, the only English word, perhaps, that could be repeated incessantly as the burden of such a poem. In "The Raven," "Lenore," and elsewhere, he employed the repetend also, and with still more novel and poetical results:

An anthem for the queenliest dead that
    ever died so young,

A dirge for her, the doubly dead, in that
    she died so young.

Our talk had been serious and sober,
But our thoughts they were palsied and
    sere,
Our memories were treacherous and sere.

One thing profitably may be noted
by latter day poets. Poe used none
but elementary English measures, re-
lying upon his music and atmosphere
for their effect. This is true of those
which seem most intricate, as in "The
Bells" and "Ulalume." "Lenore" and
"For Annie" are the simplest of ballad forms. I have a fancy that our
Southern poet's ear caught the music
of "Annabel Lee" and "Eulalie," if
not their special quality, from the
plaintive, melodious negro songs utilized by those early writers of "min-
strelsy" who have been denominated
the only composers of a genuine
American school. This suggestion
may be scouted, but an expert might
suspect the one to be a patrician refinement upon the melody, feeling, and
humble charm of the other.

Poe was not a single-poem poet,
but the poet of a single mood. His
materials were seemingly a small stock
in trade, chiefly of Angels and Demons,
with an attendance of Dreams, Echoes,
Ghouls, Gnomes and Mimes, ready
at hand. He selected or coined, for
use and re-use, a number of what Mr.
Miller would call "beautiful words,"
—"albatros," "halcyon," "scintillant,"
"Ligeia," "Weir," "Yaanek," "Auber,"
"D'Elormie," and the like. Everything was subordinate to sound. But
his poetry, as it places us under the
spell of the senses, enables us to enter, through their reaction upon the
spirit, his indefinable mood; nor
should we forget that Coleridge owes
his specific rank as a poet, not to his
philosophic verse, but to melodious
fragments, and greatly to the rhythm
of "The Ancient Mariner" and of
"Christabel." Poe's melodies lure us
to the point where we seem to hear
angelic lutes and citherns, or elfin instruments that make music in "the
land east of the sun and west of the
moon." The enchantment may not be
that of Israfèl, nor of the harper who
exorcised the evil genius of Saul, but
it is at least that of some plumed being
of the middle air, of a charmer charming so sweetly that his numbers are
the burden of mystic dreams. * * *
                  1880

V. THOMAS BAILEY ALDRICH *
(1836–1907)

PALABRAS CARIÑOSAS

Good-night! I have to say good-
    night
To such a host of peerless things!

* All poems of Aldrich are used by permission of, and by arrangement with, Houghton Mifflin Company.

Good-night unto the slender hand
All queenly with its weight of rings;
Good-night to fond, uplifted eyes,
Good-night to chestnut braids of hair,
Good-night unto the perfect mouth,
And all the sweetness nestled there—
    The snowy hand detains me, then
    I'll have to say Good-night again! 10

But there will come a time, my love,
When, if I read our stars aright,
I shall not linger by this porch

With my farewells. Till then, good-
   night!
You wish the time were now? And I.
You do not blush to wish it so?
You would have blushed yourself to
   death
To own so much a year ago—
   What, both these snowy hands! ah,
   then
   I'll have to say Good-night again! 20
                  1859

IDENTITY

Somewhere—in desolate wind-swept
   space—
   In Twilight-land—in No-man's-land
Two hurrying Shapes met face to face,
   And bade each other stand.

"And who are you?" cried one a-gape,
   Shuddering in the gloaming light.
"I know not," said the second Shape,
   "I only died last night!"
                  1875

ENAMORED ARCHITECT OF AIRY RHYME

Enamored architect of airy rhyme,
Build as thou wilt, heed not what each
   man says:
Good souls, but innocent of dreamers'
   ways,
Will come, and marvel why thou wast-
   est time;
Others, beholding how thy turrets
   climb
'Twixt theirs and heaven, will hate
   thee all thy days;
But most beware of those who come
   to praise.
O Wondersmith, O worker in sublime
And heaven-sent dreams, let art be all
   in all;
Build as thou wilt, unspoiled by praise
   or blame,   10
Build as thou wilt, and as thy light
   is given;

Then, if at last the airy structure fall
Dissolve, and vanish—take thyself no
   shame.
They fail, and they alone, who have
   not striven.
                1876

PAULINE PAVLOVNA

Scene: St. Petersburg.
Period: The present time. A ball-
   room in the winter palace of the
   Prince ——. The ladies in character
   costumes and masks. The gentlemen in official dress and unmasked
   with the exception of six tall figures
   in scarlet kaftans, who are treated
   with marked distinction as they
   move here and there among the
   promenaders.   Quadrille   music
   throughout the dialogue.
Count Sergius Pavlovich Panshine
   who has just arrived, is standing
   anxiously in the doorway of an
   antechamber with his eyes fixed
   upon a lady in the costume of
   a maid of honor in the time of
   Catharine II. The lady presently
   disengages herself from the crowd
   and passes near Count Panshine
   who impulsively takes her by the
   hand and leads her across the
   threshold of the inner apartment
   which is unoccupied.

He.   Pauline!
She.   You knew me?
He.   How could I have failed?
A mask may hide your features, but
   not your soul.
There is an air about you like the air
That holds a star. A blind man knows
   the night,
And feels the constellations. No
   coarse sense
Of eye or ear had made you plain
   to me.
Through these I had not found you;
   for your eyes,
As blue as violets of our Novgorod,

ook black behind your mask there,
    and your voice—
  had not known that either. My
    heart said,
Pauline Pavlovna."   10
  SHE.   Ah! Your heart
    said that?
ou trust your heart, then! 'Tis a
    serious risk!—
Iow is it you and others wear no
    mask?
  HE. The Emperor's orders.
  SHE.   Is the Emperor here?
have not seen him.
  HE.   He is one of
    the six
n scarlet kaftans and all masked
    alike.
Vatch—you will note how every one
    bows down
efore those figures, thinking each by
    chance
Iay be the Tsar; yet none knows
    which is he.
ven his counterparts are left in
    doubt.   20
nhappy Russia! No serf ever wore
uch chains as gall our Emperor
    these sad days.
Ie dare trust no man.
  SHE.   All men are so false.
  HE. Save one, Pauline Pavlovna.
  SHE.   No; all, all!
think there is no truth left in the
    world,
 man or woman. Once were noble
    souls.—
ount Sergius, is Nastasia here to-
    night?
  HE. Ah! then you know! I
    thought to tell you first.
ot here, beneath these hundred curi-
    ous eyes,
 all this glare of light; but in some
    place   30
here I could throw me at your feet
    and weep.
 what shape came the story to
    your ear?

Decked in the teller's colors, I'll be
    sworn;
The truth, but in the livery of a lie,
And so must wrong me. Only this is
    true:
The Tsar, because I risked my
    wretched life
To shield a life as wretched as my
    own,
Bestows upon me, as supreme re-
    ward—
O irony!—the hand of this poor girl.
He stayed me at the bottom of a
    stair,   40
And said, *We have the pearl of pearls
    for you,*
*Such as from out the sea was never
    plucked*
By Indian diver, for a Sultan's crown.
Your joy's decreed, and stabbed me
    with a smile.
  SHE. And she—she loves you?
  HE.   I much question that.
Likes me, perhaps. What matters it?
    —her love!
The guardian, Sidor Yurievich, con-
    sents,
And she consents. Love weighs not
    in such scales—
A mere caprice, a young girl's spring-
    tide dream.
Sick of her ear-rings, weary of her
    mare,   50
She'll have a lover, something ready-
    made,
Or improvised between two cups of
    tea—
A lover by imperial ukase!
Fate said her word—I chanced to be
    the man!
If that grenade the crazy student
    threw
Had not spared me, as well as spared
    the Tsar,
All this would not have happened.
    I'd have been
A hero, but quite safe from her
    romance.
She takes me for a hero—think of
    that!

Now by our holy Lady of Kazan,   60
When I have finished pitying myself,
I'll pity her.
    SHE.   Oh no; begin with her;
She needs it most.
    HE.   At her door lies the blame,
Whatever falls. She, with a single
    word,
With half a tear, had stopped it at
    the first,
This cruel juggling with poor human
    hearts.
    SHE.   The Tsar commanded it—
    you said the Tsar.
    HE.   The Tsar does what she
    wishes—God knows why.
Were she his mistress, now! but
    there's no snow
Whiter within the bosom of a
    cloud,   70
No colder either. She is very
    haughty,
For all her fragile air of gentleness;
With something vital in her, like
    those flowers
That on our desolate steppes outlast
    the year.
Resembles you in some things. It
    was that
First made us friends. I do her jus-
    tice, mark.
For we were friends in that smooth
    surface way
We Russians have imported out of
    France—
Forgetting Alma and Sevastopol.
Alas! from what a blue and tranquil
    heaven   80
This bolt fell on me! After these
    two years,
My suit with Alexandrovitch at end,
The old wrong righted, the estates re-
    stored,
And my promotion, with the ink not
    dry!
Those fairies which neglected me at
    birth
Seemed now to lavish all good gifts
    on me—

Gold roubles, office, sudden deares
    friends.
The whole world smiled; then, as
    stooped to taste
The sweetest cup, freak dashed i
    from my lip.
This very night—just think, this ver
    night—   .   9
I planned to come and beg of you th
    alms
I dared not ask for in my poverty.
I thought me poor then. Hov
    stripped am I now!
There's not a ragged mendicant on
    meets
Along the Nevski Prospekt but ha
    leave
To tell his love, and I have not tha
    right!
Pauline Pavlovna, why do you stan
    there
Stark as a statue, with no word t
    say?
    SHE.   Because this thing ha
    frozen up my heart.
I think that there is something kille
    in me,   10
A dream that would have mocked a
    other bliss.
What shall I say? What would yo
    have me say?
    HE. If it be possible, the word c
    words!
    SHE [*very slowly*]. Well, then—
    I love you. I may tell you s
This once, . . . and then for eve
    hold my peace.
We cannot longer stay here unol
    served.
No—do not touch me! but stan
    farther off,
And seem to laugh, as if we talke
    in jest,
Should we be watched. Now tur
    your face away.
I love you.
    HE.   With such music in m
    ears   11
I would death found me. It wer
    sweet to die

listening! You love me—prove it.
SHE.   Prove it—how?
prove it saying it. How else?
HE.   Pauline,
have three things to choose from;
    you shall choose:
This marriage, or Siberia, or France.
The first means hell; the second,
    purgatory;
The third—with you—were nothing
    less than heaven!
SHE [*starting*]. How dared you
    even dream it!
HE. I was mad.
This business has touched me in the
    brain.
Have patience! the calamity is new.
    [*Pauses.*]   120
There is a fourth way; but that gate
    is shut
To brave men who hold life a thing
    of God.
SHE. Yourself spoke there; the
    rest was not of you.
HE. Oh, lift me to your level!
    Where you move
The air is temperate, and no pulses
    beat.
What's to be done?
SHE.   I lack invention—stay,
Perhaps the Emperor—
HE.   Not a shred of hope!
His mind is set on this with that in-
    sistence
Which seems to seize on all match-
    making folk.
The fancy bites them, and they
    straight go mad.   130
SHE. Your father's friend, the
    Metropolitan—
A word from him. . . .
HE.   Alas, he too is bitten!
Gray-haired, gray-hearted, worldly
    wise, he sees
This marriage makes me the Tsar's
    protégé,
And opens every door to preference.
SHE. Then let him be. There
    surely is some way

Out of the labyrinth, could we but
    find it.
Nastasia!
HE.   What! beg life of her?
    Not I.
SHE. Beg love. She is a woman,
    young, perhaps
Untouched as yet of this too poison-
    ous air.   140
Were she told all, would she not pity
    us?
For if she love you, as I think she
    must,
Would not some generous impulse
    stir in her,
Some latent, unsuspected spark il-
    lume?
How love thrills even commonest
    girl-clay,
Ennobling it an instant, if no more!
You said that she is proud; then
    touch her pride,
And turn her into marble with the
    touch.
But yet the gentler passion is the
    stronger.
Go to her, tell her, in some tenderest
    phrase   150
That will not hurt too much—ah, but
    'twill hurt!—
Just how your happiness lies in her
    hand
To make or mar for all time; hint,
    not say,
Your heart is gone from you, and
    you may find—
HE. A casemate in St. Peter and
    St. Paul
For, say, a month; then some Siberian
    town.
Not this way lies escape. At my first
    word
That sluggish Tartar blood would
    turn to fire
In every vein.
SHE.   How blindly you
    read her,
Or any woman! Yes, I know. I
    grant   160

How small we often seem in our
    small world
Of trivial cares and narrow prece-
    dents—
Lacking that wide horizon stretched
    for men—
Capricious, spiteful, frightened at a
    mouse;
But when it comes to suffering mortal
    pangs,
The weakest of us measures pulse with
    you.
    HE.   Yes, you, not she. If she
        were at your height!
But there's no martyr wrapped in *her*
    rose flesh.
There should have been; for Nature
    gave you both
The self-same purple for your eyes
    and hair,   170
The self-same Southern music to your
    lips,
Fashioned you both, as 'twere, in the
    same mold,
Yet failed to put the soul in one of
    you!
I know her wilful—her light head
    quite turned
In this court atmosphere of flatteries;
A Moscow beauty, petted and spoiled
    there,
And since spoiled here; as soft as
    swan's-down now,
With words like honey melting from
    the comb,
But being crossed, vindictive, cruel,
    cold.
I fancy her, between two languid
    smiles,   180
Saying, "Poor fellow, in the Nert-
    chinsk mines!"
I know her pitiless.
    SHE.   You know her not.
Count Sergius Pavlovich, you said no
    mask
Could hide the soul, yet how you
    have mistaken
The soul these two months—and the
    face to-night!
    [*Removes her mask.*]

    HE. You!—it was *you!*
    SHE.   Count Sergius Pavlovich
Go find Pauline Pavlovna—she i
    here—
And tell her that the Tsar has se
    you free.
[*She goes out hurriedly, replacing he
    mask.*]
                    188

UNGUARDED GATES

Wide open and unguarded stand ou
    gates,
Named of the four winds, North
    South, East, and West;
Portals that lead to an enchanted lan
Of cities, forests, fields of living gold
Vast prairies, lordly summits touche
    with snow,
Majestic rivers sweeping proudly pas
The Arab's date-palm and the Norse
    man's pine—
A realm wherein are fruits of ever
    zone,
Airs of all climes, for, lo! through
    out the year
The red rose blossoms somewhere—
    rich land,   1
A later Eden planted in the wilds,
With not an inch of earth within it
    bound
But if a slave's foot press it sets hin
    free,
Here, it is written, Toil shall have it
    wage,
And Honor honor, and the humbles
    man
Stand level with the highest in the law
Of such a land have men in dungeon
    dreamed,
And with the vision brightening i
    their eyes
Gone smiling to the fagot and th
    sword.

Wide open and unguarded stan
    our gates,   2
And through them presses a wild mot
    ley throng—

Men from the Volga and the Tartar
        steppes,
Featureless figures of the Hoang-Ho,
Malayan, Scythian, Teuton, Kelt, and
        Slav,
Flying the Old World's poverty and
        scorn;
These bringing with them unknown
        gods and rites,
Those, tiger passions, here to stretch
        their claws.
In street and alley what strange
        tongues are loud,
Accents of menace alien to our air,
Voices that once the Tower of Babel
        knew!   30

O Liberty, white Goddess! is it well
To leave the gates unguarded? On
        thy breast
Fold Sorrow's children, soothe the
        hurts of fate,
Lift the down-trodden, but with hand
        of steel
Stay those who to thy sacred portals
        come
To waste the gifts of freedom. Have
        a care
Lest from thy brow the clustered stars
        be torn
And trampled in the dust. For so
        of old
The thronging Goth and Vandal
        trampled Rome,

And where the temples of the Cæsars
        stood   40
The lean wolf unmolested made her
        lair.
(1892)   1892

REALISM

Romance beside his unstrung lute
    Lies stricken mute.
The old-time fire, the antique grace,
You will not find them anywhere.
To-day we breathe a commonplace,
Polemic, scientific air:
We strip Illusion of her veil;
We vivisect the nightingale
To probe the secret of his note.
The Muse in alien ways remote   10
    Goes wandering.
                                1896

MEMORY

My mind lets go a thousand things,
Like dates of wars and deaths of kings,
And yet recalls the very hour—
'Twas noon by yonder village tower,
And on the last blue noon in May—
The wind came briskly up this way,
Crisping the brook beside the road;
Then, pausing here, set down its load
Of pine-scents, and shook listlessly
Two petals from that wild-rose tree. 10
                                1896

MARJORIE DAW

I

Dr. Dillon to Edward Delaney,
    Esq., at The Pines, near
    Rye, N. H.

                    August 8, 187—.
My dear Sir: I am happy to as-   10
sure you that your anxiety is without reason. Flemming will be confined to the sofa for three or four
weeks, and will have to be careful
at first how he uses his leg. A fracture of this kind is always a tedious
affair.   Fortunately, the bone was
very skilfully set by the surgeon who
chanced to be in the drug-store where
Flemming was brought after his fall,
and I apprehend no permanent inconvenience from the accident. *Flemming is doing perfectly well physically;* but I must confess that the
irritable and morbid state of mind

into which he has fallen causes me a great deal of uneasiness. He is the last man in the world who ought to break his leg. You know how impetuous our friend is ordinarily, what a soul of restlessness and energy, never content unless he is rushing at some object, like a sportive bull at a red shawl; but amiable withal. He is no longer amiable. His temper has become something frightful. Miss Fanny Flemming came up from Newport, where the family are staying for the summer, to nurse him; but he packed her off the next morning in tears. He has a complete set of Balzac's works, twenty-seven volumes, piled up near his sofa, to throw at Watkins whenever that exemplary serving-man appears with his meals. Yesterday I very innocently brought Flemming a small basket of lemons. You know it was a strip of lemon-peel on the curbstone that caused our friend's mischance. Well, he no sooner set his eyes upon these lemons than he fell into such a rage as I cannot adequately describe. This is only one of his moods, and the least distressing. At other times he sits with bowed head regarding his splintered limb, silent, sullen, despairing. When this fit is on him—and it sometimes lasts all day—nothing can distract his melancholy. He refuses to eat, does not even read the newspapers; books, except as projectiles for Watkins, have no charms for him. His state is truly pitiable.

Now, if he were a poor man, with a family depending on his daily labor, this irritability and despondency would be natural enough. But in a young fellow of twenty-four, with plenty of money and seemingly not a care in the world, the thing is monstrous If he continues to give way to his vagaries in this manner, he will end by bringing on an inflammation of the fibula. It was the fibula he broke I am at my wits' end to know what to prescribe for him. I have an æsthetics and lotions, to make people sleep and to soothe pain; but I've no medicine that will make a man have a little common-sense. That is beyond my skill, but maybe it is not beyond yours. You are Flemming's intimate friend, his *fidus Achates* Write to him, write to him frequently, distract his mind, cheer him up, and prevent him from becoming a confirmed case of melancholia. Perhaps he has some important plans disarranged by his present confinement. If he has you will know, and will know how to advise him judiciously. I trust your father finds the change beneficial? I am, my dear sir, with great respect, etc.

II

EDWARD DELANEY TO JOHN FLEMMING, WEST 38TH STREET, NEW YORK

Aug 9,—.

MY DEAR JACK: I had a line from Dillon this morning, and was rejoiced to learn that your hurt is not so bad as reported. Like a certain personage, you are not so black and blue as you are painted. Dillon will put you on your pins again in two or three weeks, if you will only have patience and follow his counsels. Did you get my note of last Wednesday? I was greatly troubled when I heard of the accident.

I can imagine how tranquil and

saintly you are with your leg in a trough! It is deuced awkward, to be sure, just as we had promised ourselves a glorious month together at the seaside; but we must make the best of it. It is unfortunate, too, that my father's health renders it impossible for me to leave him. I think he has much improved; the sea air is his native element; but he still needs my arm to lean upon in his walks, and requires some one more careful than a servant to look after him. I cannot come to you, dear Jack, but I have hours of unemployed time on hand, and I will write you a whole post-office full of letters if that will divert you. Heaven knows, I haven't anything to write about. It isn't as if we were living at one of the beach houses; then I could do you some character studies, and fill your imagination with groups of sea-goddesses, with their (or somebody else's) raven and blond manes hanging down their shoulders. You should have Aphrodite in morning wrapper, in evening costume, and in her prettiest bathing suit. But we are far from all that here. We have rooms in a farm-house, on a cross-road, two miles from the hotels, and lead the quietest of lives.

I wish I were a novelist. This old house, with its sanded floors and high wainscots, and its narrow windows looking out upon a cluster of pines that turn themselves into æolian-harps every time the wind blows, would be the place in which to write a summer romance. It should be a story with the odors of the forest and the breath of the sea in it. It should be a novel like one of that Russian fellow's, — what's his name? — Tour-guénieff, Turguenef, Toorguniff, Turgénjew,—nobody knows how to spell him. I think his own mother must be in some doubt about him. Yet I wonder if even a Liza or an Alexandra Paulovna could stir the heart of a man who has constant twinges in his leg. I wonder if one of our own Yankee girls of the best type, haughty and *spirituelle*, would be of any comfort to you in your present deplorable condition. If I thought so, I would hasten down to the Surf House and catch one for you; or, better still, I would find you one over the way.

Picture to yourself a large white house just across the road, nearly opposite our cottage. It is not a house, but a mansion, built, perhaps, in the colonial period, with rambling extensions, and gambrel roof, and a wide piazza on three sides,—a self-possessed, high-bred piece of architecture, with its nose in the air. It stands back from the road, and has an obsequious retinue of fringed elms and oaks and weeping willows. Sometimes in the morning, and oftener in the afternoon, when the sun has withdrawn from that part of the mansion, a young woman appears on the piazza with some mysterious Penelope web of embroidery in her hand, or a book. There is a hammock over there,—of pineapple fiber, it looks from here. A hammock is very becoming when one is eighteen, and has golden hair, and dark eyes, and an emerald-colored illusion dress looped up after the fashion of a Dresden china shepherdess, and is *chaussée* like a belle of the time of Louis Quatorze. All this splendor goes into that hammock, and sways there like a pond-lily in the golden afternoon. The window of my bedroom looks down on that piazza,—and so do I.

But enough of this nonsense, which ill becomes a sedate young attorney taking his vacation with an invalid father. Drop me a line, dear Jack, and tell me how you really are. State your case. Write me a long, quiet letter. If you are violent or abusive, I'll take the law to you.

III

JOHN FLEMMING TO EDWARD DELANEY

August 11,—.

Your letter, dear Ned, was a godsend. Fancy what a fix I am in,—I, who never had a day's sickness since I was born. My left leg weighs three tons. It is embalmed in spices and smothered in layers of fine linen, like a mummy. I can't move. I haven't moved for five thousand years. I'm of the time of Pharaoh.

I lie from morning till night on a lounge, staring into the hot street. Everybody is out of town enjoying himself. The brown-stone-front houses across the street resemble a' row of particularly ugly coffins set up on end. A green mould is settling on the names of the deceased, carved on the silver door-plates. Sardonic spiders have sewed up the key-holes. All is silence and dust and desolation.—I interrupt this a moment, to take a shy at Watkins with the second volume of César Birotteau. Missed him! I think I could bring him down with a copy of Sainte-Beuve or the Dictionnaire Universel, if I had it. These small Balzac books somehow don't quite fit my hand; but I shall fetch him yet.

I've an idea Watkins is tapping the old gentleman's Château Yquem Duplicate key of the wine-cellar Hibernian swarries in the front basement. Young Cheops upstairs, snug in his cerements. Watkins glides into my chamber, with that colorless, hypocritical face of his drawn out long like an accordion; but I know he grins all the way down stairs, and is glad I have broken my leg. Was not my evil star in the very zenith when I ran up to town to attend that dinner at Delmonico's? I didn't come up altogether for that. It was partly to buy Frank Livingstone's roan mare Margot. And now I shall not be able to sit in the saddle these two months. I'll send the mare down to you at The Pines,—is that the name of the place?

Old Dillon fancies that I have something on my mind. He drives me wild with lemons. Lemons for a mind diseased! Nonsense, I am only as restless as the devil under this confinement,—a thing I'm not used to. Take a man who has never had so much as a headache or a toothache in his life, strap one of his legs in a section of water-spout, keep him in a room in the city for weeks, with the hot weather turned on, and then expect him to smile and purr and be happy! It is preposterous. I can't be cheerful or calm.

Your letter is the first consoling thing I have had since my disaster, a week ago. It really cheered me up for half an hour. Send me a screed, Ned, as often as you can, if you love me. Anything will do. Write me more about that little girl in the hammock. That was very pretty, all that about the Dresden china shepherdess and the pond-lily; the imagery a little

nixed, perhaps, but very pretty. I
iidn't suppose you had so much sen-
imental furniture in your upper story.
t shows how one may be familiar
or years with the reception-room of
.is neighbor, and never suspect what
s directly under his mansard. I sup-
osed your loft stuffed with dry legal
archments, mortgages and affidavits;
ou take down a package of manu-
cript, and lo! there are lyrics and
onnets and canzonettas. You really
ave a graphic descriptive touch, Ed-
vard Delaney, and I suspect you of
nonymous love-tales in the maga-
ines.

I shall be a bear until I hear from
ou again. Tell me all about your
retty *inconnue* across the road.
Vhat is her name? Who is she?
Vho's her father? Where's her
nother? Who's her lover? You
annot imagine how this will oc-
upy me. The more trifling the bet-
r. My imprisonment has weakened
ne intellectually to such a degree that
find your epistolary gifts quite con-
derable. I am passing into my sec-
nd childhood. In a week or two I
nall take to India-rubber rings and
rongs of coral. A silver cup, with
n appropriate inscription, would be
delicate attention on your part. In
ne meantime, write!

IV

EDWARD DELANEY TO JOHN FLEM-
MING

August 12,—.

The sick pasha shall be amused.
ismillah! he wills it so. If the story-
-ller becomes prolix and tedious,—
e bow-string and the sack, and two
ubians to drop him into the Pis-

cataqua! But, truly, Jack, I have a
hard task. There is literally nothing
here,—except the little girl over the
way. She is swinging in the hammock at this moment. It is to me
compensation for many of the ills
of life to see her now and then put
out a small kid boot, which fits like
a glove, and set herself going. Who
is she, and what is her name? Her
name is Daw. Only daughter of Mr.
Richard W. Daw, ex-colonel and
banker. Mother dead. One brother
at Harvard, elder brother killed at
the battle of Fair Oaks, nine years
ago. Old, rich family, the Daws.
This is the homestead, and where
father and daughter pass eight months
of the twelve; the rest of the year
in Baltimore and Washington. The
New England winter too many for
the old gentleman. The daughter is
called Marjorie, — Marjorie Daw.
Sounds odd at first, doesn't it? But
after you say it over to yourself half
a dozen times, you like it. There's
a pleasing quaintness to it, something
prim and violet-like. Must be a nice
sort of girl to be called Marjorie
Daw.

I had mine host of The Pines in
the witness-box last night, and drew
the foregoing testimony from him. He
has charge of Mr. Daw's vegetable-
garden, and has known the family
these thirty years. Of course I shall
make the acquaintance of my neighbors before many days. It will be
next to impossible for me not to meet
Mr. Daw or Miss Daw in some of
my walks. The young lady has a favorite path to the sea-beach. I shall
intercept her some morning, and touch
my hat to her. Then the princess will
bend her fair head to me with courte-

ous surprise not unmixed with haughtiness. Will snub me, in fact. All this for thy sake, O Pasha of the Snapt Axle-tree! . . . How oddly things fall out! Ten minutes ago I was called down to the parlor,—you know the kind of parlors in farmhouses on the coast, a sort of amphibious parlor, with sea-shells on the mantel-piece and spruce branches in the chimney-place,—where I found my father and Mr. Daw doing the antique polite to each other. He had come to pay his respects to his new neighbors. Mr. Daw is a tall, slim gentleman of fifty-five, with a florid face and snow-white mustache and side-whiskers. Looks like Mr. Dombey, or as Mr. Dombey would have looked if he had served a few years in the British Army. Mr. Daw was a colonel in the late war, commanding the regiment in which his son was a lieutenant. Plucky old boy, backbone of New Hampshire granite. Before taking his leave, the colonel delivered himself of an invitation as if he were issuing a general order. Miss Daw has a few friends coming, at 4 P.M., to play croquet on the lawn (parade-ground) and have tea (cold rations) on the piazza. Will we honor them with our company? (or be sent to the guard-house). My father declines on the plea of ill-health. My father's son bows with as much suavity as he knows, and accepts.

In my next I shall have something to tell you. I shall have seen the little beauty face to face. I have a presentiment, Jack, that this Daw is a *rara avis!* Keep up your spirits, my boy, until I write you another letter,—and send me along word how's your leg.

V

EDWARD DELANEY TO JOHN FLEMMING

August 13,—

The party, my dear Jack, was as dreary as possible. A lieutenant of the navy, the rector of the Episcopal church at Stillwater, and a society swell from Nahant. The lieutenant looked as if he had swallowed a couple of his buttons, and found the bullion rather indigestible; the rector was a pensive youth, of the daffy-downdilly sort; and the swell from Nahant was a very weak tidal wave indeed. The women were much better, as they always are; the two Miss Kingsburys of Philadelphia, staying at the Sea-shell House, two bright and engaging girls. But Marjorie Daw!

The company broke up soon after tea, and I remained to smoke a cigar with the colonel on the piazza. It was like seeing a picture to see Miss Marjorie hovering around the old soldier and doing a hundred gracious little things for him. She brought the cigars and lighted the tapers with her own delicate fingers, in the most enchanting fashion. As we sat there she came and went in the summer twilight, and seemed, with her white dress and pale gold hair, like some lovely phantom that had sprung into existence out of the smoke-wreaths. If she had melted into air, like the statue of Galatea in the play, I should have been more sorry than surprised.

It was easy to perceive that the old colonel worshipped her, and she him. I think the relation between an elderly father and a daughter just blooming into womanhood the most beautiful possible. There is in it a su

le sentiment that cannot exist in
he case of mother and daughter, or
hat of son and mother. But this is
etting into deep water.

I sat with the Daws until half past
en, and saw the moon rise on the
ea. The ocean, that had stretched
motionless and black against the hori-
on, was changed by magic into a
roken field of glittering ice, inter-
persed with marvellous silvery fjords.
n the far distance the Isles of Shoals
oomed up like a group of huge bergs
rifting down on us. The Polar Re-
ions in a June thaw! It was ex-
eedingly fine. What did we talk
bout? We talked about the weather
—and *you!* The weather has been
isagreeable for several days past,—
nd so have you. I glided from one
opic to the other very naturally. I
old my friends of your accident; how
had frustrated all our summer plans,
nd what our plans were. I played
quite a spirited solo on the fibula.
Then I described you; or, rather, I
idn't. I spoke of your amiability,
f your patience under this severe af-
iction; of your touching gratitude
when Dillon brings you little presents
f fruit; of your tenderness to your
ister Fanny, whom you would not
llow to stay in town to nurse you,
nd how you heroically sent her back
o Newport, preferring to remain
lone with Mary, the cook, and your
nan Watkins, to whom, by the way,
ou were devotedly attached. If you
had been there, Jack, you wouldn't
ave known yourself. I should have
xcelled as a criminal lawyer, if I had
ot turned my attention to a different
ranch of jurisprudence.

Miss Marjorie asked all manner of
eading questions concerning you. It
did not occur to me then, but it struck
me forcibly afterwards, that she
evinced a singular interest in the conversation. When I got back to my
room, I recalled how eagerly she
leaned forward, with her full, snowy
throat in strong moonlight, listening
to what I said. Positively, I think
I made her like you!

Miss Daw is a girl whom you would
like immensely, I can tell you that.
A beauty without affectation, a high
and tender nature,—if one can read
the soul in the face. And the old
colonel is a noble character, too.

I am glad the Daws are such pleasant people. The Pines is an isolated
spot, and my resources are few. I
fear I should have found life here
somewhat monotonous before long,
with no other society than that of
my excellent sire. It is true, I might
have made a target of the defence-
less invalid; but I haven't a taste for
artillery, *moi.*

VI

JOHN FLEMMING TO EDWARD DELANEY

August 17,—.

For a man who hasn't a taste for
artillery, it occurs to me, my friend,
you are keeping up a pretty lively
fire on my inner works. But go on.
Cynicism is a small brass field-piece
that eventually bursts and kills the
artilleryman.

You may abuse me as much as you
like, and I'll not complain; for I
don't know what I should do without your letters. They are curing me.
I haven't hurled anything at Watkins
since last Sunday, partly because I
have grown more amiable under your

teaching, and partly because Watkins captured my ammunition one night, and carried it off to the library. He is rapidly losing the habit he had acquired of dodging whenever I rub my ear, or make any slight motion with my right arm. He is still suggestive of the wine-cellar, however. You may break, you may shatter Watkins, if you will, but the scent of the Roederer will hang round him still.

Ned, that Miss Daw must be a charming person. I should certainly like her. I like her already. When you spoke in your first letter of seeing a young girl swinging in a hammock under your chamber window, I was somehow strangely drawn to her. I cannot account for it in the least. What you have subsequently written of Miss Daw has strengthened the impression. You seem to be describing a woman I have known in some previous state of existence, or dreamed of in this. Upon my word, if you were to send me her photograph, I believe I should recognize her at a glance. Her manner, that listening attitude, her traits of character, as you indicate them, the light hair and the dark eyes,—they are all familiar things to me. Asked a lot of questions, did she? Curious about me? That is strange.

You would laugh in your sleeve, you wretched old cynic, if you knew how I lie awake nights, with my gas turned down to a star, thinking of The Pines and the house across the road. How cool it must be down there! I long for the salt smell of the air. I picture the colonel smoking his cheroot on the piazza. I send you and Miss Daw off on afternoon rambles along the beach. Sometimes I let you stroll

with her under the elms in the moonlight, for you are great friends by this time, I take it, and see each other every day. I know your ways and your manners! Then I fall into a truculent mood, and would like to destroy somebody. Have you noticed anything in the shape of a lover hanging around the colonial Lares and Penates? Does that lieutenant of the horse-marines or that young Stillwater parson visit the house much? Not that I am pining for news of them, but any gossip of the kind would be in order. I wonder, Ned, you don't fall in love with Miss Daw. I am ripe to do it myself. Speaking of photographs, couldn't you manage to slip one of her *cartes-de-visite* from her album,—she must have an album, you know,—and send it to me? I will return it before it could be missed. That's a good fellow. Did the mare arrive safe and sound? It will be a capital animal this autumn for Central Park.

O—my leg? I forgot about my leg. It's better.

VII

EDWARD DELANEY TO JOHN FLEMMING

August 20,—

You are correct in your surmises. I am on the most friendly terms with our neighbors. The colonel and my father smoke their afternoon cigar together in our sitting-room or on the piazza opposite, and I pass an hour or two of the day or the evening with the daughter. I am more and more struck by the beauty, modesty, and intelligence of Miss Daw.

You ask me why I did not fall

n love with her. I will be frank,
ack: I have thought of that. She
s young, rich, accomplished, uniting
n herself more attractions, mental
nd personal, than I can recall in any
irl of my acquaintance; but she lacks
he something that would be necessary
o inspire in me that kind of interest.
Possessing this unknown quantity, a
woman neither beautiful nor wealthy
or very young could bring me to her
eet. But not Miss Daw. If we were
hipwrecked together on an uninhab-
ed island,—let me suggest a tropical
sland, for it costs no more to be
picturesque,—I would build her a
amboo hut, I would fetch her bread-
ruit and cocoanuts, I would fry
ams for her, I would lure the in-
enuous turtle and make her nourish-
ng soups, but I wouldn't make love
o her,—not under eighteen months.
would like to have her for a sister,
hat I might shield her and counsel
er, and spend half my income on
hread-laces and camel's-hair shawls.
We are off the island now.) If such
vere not my feeling, there would
ill be an obstacle to my loving Miss
Daw. A greater misfortune could
carcely befall me than to love her.
Flemming, I am about to make a
evelation that will astonish you. I
nay be all wrong in my premises and
onsequently in my conclusions; but
ou shall judge.

That night when I returned to my
oom after the croquet party at the
Daw's, and was thinking over the
rivial events of the evening, I was
uddenly impressed by the air of
ager attention with which Miss Daw
nad followed my account of your
ccident. I think I mentioned this to
ou. Well, the next morning, as I

went to mail my letter, I overtook
Miss Daw on the road to Rye, where
the post-office is, and accompanied
her thither and back, an hour's walk.
The conversation again turned on
you, and again I remarked that inexplicable look of interest which had
lighted up her face the previous evening. Since then, I have seen Miss
Daw perhaps ten times, perhaps
oftener, and on each occasion I found
that when I was not speaking of you,
or your sister, or some person or place
associated with you, I was not holding her attention. She would be
absent-minded, her eyes would wander away from me to the sea, or to
some distant object in the landscape;
her fingers would play with the leaves
of a book in a way that convinced
me she was not listening. At these
moments if I abruptly changed the
theme,—I did it several times as an
experiment,—and dropped some remark about my friend Flemming, then
the sombre blue eyes would come
back to me instantly.

Now, is not this the oddest thing
in the world? No, not the oddest.
The effect which you tell me was produced on you by my casual mention
of an unknown girl swinging in a
hammock is certainly as strange.
You can conjecture how that passage
in your letter of Friday startled me.
Is it possible, then, that two people
who have never met, and who are
hundreds of miles apart, can exert
a magnetic influence on each other?
I have read of such psychological phenomena, but never credited them. I
leave the solution of the problem to
you. As for myself, all other things
being favorable, it would be impossible for me to fall in love with a

woman who listens to me only when I am talking of my friend!

I am not aware that any one is paying marked attention to my fair neighbor. The lieutenant of the navy —he is stationed at Rivermouth— sometimes drops in of an evening, and sometimes the rector from Stillwater; the lieutenant the oftener. He was there last night. I would not be surprised if he had an eye to the heiress; but he is not formidable. Mistress Daw carries a neat little spear of irony, and the honest lieutenant seems to have a particular facility for impaling himself on the point of it. He is not dangerous, I should say; though I have known a woman to satirize a man for years, and marry him after all. Decidedly, the lowly rector is not dangerous; yet, again, who has not seen Cloth of Frieze victorious in the lists where Cloth of Gold went down?

As to the photograph. There is an exquisite ivorytype of Marjorie, in passe-partout, on the drawing-room mantel-piece. It would be missed at once, if taken. I would do anything reasonable for you, Jack; but I've no burning desire to be hauled up before the local justice of the peace, on a charge of petty larceny.

P. S.—Enclosed is a spray of mignonette, which I advise you to treat tenderly. Yes, we talked of you again last night, as usual. It is becoming a little dreary for me.

VIII

EDWARD DELANEY TO JOHN FLEMMING

August 22,—.

Your letter in reply to my last has occupied my thoughts all the morning. I do not know what to think Do you mean to say that you ar seriously half in love with a woman whom you have never seen,—with shadow, a chimera? for what else can Miss Daw be to you? I do not un derstand it at all. I understand neither you nor her. You are a cou ple of ethereal beings moving in fine air than I can breathe with my com monplace lungs. Such delicacy o sentiment is something I admire with out comprehending. I am bewildered I am of the earth earthy, and I fine myself in the incongruous position o having to do with mere souls, with natures so finely tempered that I ru some risk of shattering them in my awkwardness. I am as Caliban among the spirits!

Reflecting on your letter, I am no sure it is wise in me to continue thi correspondence. But no, Jack; I d wrong to doubt the good sense tha forms the basis of your character You are deeply interested in Mis Daw; you feel that she is a person whom you may perhaps greatly ad mire when you know her: at the sam time you bear in mind that th chances are ten to five that, when yo do come to know her, she will fal far short of your ideal, and you wil not care for her in the least. Loo at it in this sensible light, and I wil hold back nothing from you.

Yesterday afternoon my father and myself rode over to Rivermouth with the Daws. A heavy rain in the morn ing had cooled the atmosphere an laid the dust. To Rivermouth is drive of eight miles, along a windin road lined all the way with wild bar berry-bushes. I never saw anythin more brilliant than these bushes, th

reen of the foliage and the pink of
he coral berries intensified by the
ain. The colonel drove, with my
ather in front, Miss Daw and I on
he back seat. I resolved that for
he first five miles your name should
not pass my lips. I was amused by
he artful attempts she made, at the
start, to break through my reticence.
Then a silence fell upon her; and
then she became suddenly gay. That
keenness which I enjoyed so much
when it was exercised on the lieutenant was not so satisfactory directed
against myself. Miss Daw has great
sweetness of disposition, but she can
be disagreeable. She is like the young
lady in the rhyme, with the curl on
her forehead,

> When she is good,
> She is very, very good,
> And when she is bad, she is horrid!

I kept to my resolution, however; but
on the return home I relented, and
talked of your mare! Miss Daw is
going to try a side-saddle on Margot
some morning. The animal is a trifle
too light for my weight. By the by,
I nearly forgot to say Miss Daw sat
for a picture yesterday to a Rivermouth artist. If the negative turns
out well, I am to have a copy. So
our ends will be accomplished without crime. I wish, though, I could
send you the ivorytype in the drawing-room; it is cleverly colored, and
would give you an idea of her hair and
eyes, which of course the other will not.
No, Jack, the spray of mignonette
did not come from me. A man of
twenty-eight doesn't enclose flowers in
his letters—to another man. But
don't attach too much significance to
the circumstance. She gives sprays
of mignonette to the rector, sprays

to the lieutenant. She has even given
a rose from her bosom to your slave.
It is her jocund nature to scatter
flowers, like Spring.

If my letters sometimes read dis-
jointedly, you must understand that
I never finish one at a sitting, but
write at intervals, when the mood is
on me.

The mood is not on me now.

IX

EDWARD DELANEY TO JOHN
FLEMMING

August 23,—.

I have just returned from the
strangest interview with Marjorie.
She has all but confessed to me her
interest in you. But with what modesty and dignity! Her words elude
my pen as I attempt to put them
on paper; and, indeed, it was not
so much what she said as her manner;
and that I cannot reproduce. Perhaps it was of a piece with the
strangeness of this whole business,
that she should tacitly acknowledge to
a third party the love she feels for
a man she has never beheld! But I
have lost, through your aid, the faculty of being surprised. I accept
things as people do in dreams. Now
that I am again in my room, it all
appears like an illusion,—the black
masses of Rembrandtish shadow under the trees, the fire-flies whirling in
Pyrrhic dances among the shrubbery,
the sea over there, Marjorie sitting
on the hammock!

It is past midnight, and I am too
sleepy to write more.

Tuesday Morning.—My father has
suddenly taken it into his head to

spend a few days at the Shoals. In the mean while you will not hear from me. I see Marjorie walking in the garden with the colonel. I wish I could speak to her alone, but shall probably not have an opportunity before we leave.

x

EDWARD DELANEY TO JOHN FLEMMING

August 28,—.

You were passing into your second childhood, were you? Your intellect was so reduced that my epistolary gifts seemed quite considerable to you, did they? I rise superior to the sarcasm in your favor of the 11th instant, when I notice that five days' si-20 ence on my part is sufficient to throw you into the depths of despondency.

We returned only this morning from Appledore, that enchanted island,—at four dollars per day. I find on my desk three letters from you! Evidently there is no lingering doubt in your mind as to the pleasure I derive from your correspondence. These letters are undated, but in what I 30 take to be the latest are two passages that require my consideration. You will pardon my candor, dear Flemming, but the conviction forces itself upon me that as your leg grows stronger your head becomes weaker. You ask my advice on a certain point. I will give it. In my opinion you could do nothing more unwise than to address a note to Miss Daw, thank-40 ing her for the flower. It would, I am sure, offend her delicacy beyond pardon. She knows you only through me; you are to her an abstraction, a figure in a dream,—a dream from which the faintest shock would

awaken her. Of course, if you e close a note to me and insist on i delivery, I shall deliver it; but I a vise you not to do so.

You say you are able, with the a of a cane, to walk about your chan ber, and that you purpose to con to The Pines the instant Dillon thinl you strong enough to stand the jou
10 ney. Again I advise you not to. D you not see that, every hour you re main away, Marjorie's glamour dee ens, and your influence over her in creases? You will ruin everything b precipitancy. Wait until you are e tirely recovered; in any case, do n come without giving me warning. fear the effect of your abrupt adver here—under the circumstances.
20 Miss Daw was evidently glad see us back again, and gave me bot hands in the frankest way. Sh stopped at the door a moment, th afternoon, in the carriage; she ha been over to Rivermouth for her pi tures. Unluckily the photographe had spilt some acid on the plate, an she was obliged to give him anothe sitting. I have an intuition that som
30 thing is troubling Marjorie. She ha an abstracted air not usual with he However, it may be only my fancy . . . I end this, leaving several thing unsaid, to accompany my father o one of those long walks which a now his chief medicine,—and mine!

XI

EDWARD DELANEY TO JOHN FLEMMING

August 29,—

I write in great haste to tell yo what has taken place here since m letter of last night. I am in th utmost perplexity. Only one thin

s plain,—*you* must not dream of
.oming to The Pines. Marjorie has
:old her father everything! I saw
.er for a few minutes, an hour ago,
n the garden; and, as near as I could
;ather from her confused statement,
he facts are these: Lieutenant Bradly
—that's the naval officer stationed at
Rivermouth—has been paying court to
Miss Daw for some time past, but
not so much to her liking as to that
of the colonel, who it seems is an old
friend of the young gentleman's
father. Yesterday (I knew she was
n some trouble when she drove up
:o our gate) the colonel spoke to
Marjorie of Bradly,—urged his suit,
I infer. Marjorie expressed her dis-
ike for the lieutenant with character-
stic frankness, and finally confessed
o her father—well, I really do not
:now what she confessed. It must
.ave been the vaguest of confessions,
.nd must have sufficiently puzzled the
:olonel. At any rate, it exasperated
.im. I suppose I am implicated in
he matter, and that the colonel feels
.itterly towards me. I do not see
vhy: I have carried no messages be-
ween you and Miss Daw; I have be-
.aved with the greatest discretion. I
:an find no flaw anywhere in my pro-
.eeding. I do not see that anybody
.as done anything,—except the colo-
.el himself.

It is probable, nevertheless, that the
friendly relations between the two
.ouses will be broken off. "A plague
)' both your houses," say you. I
vill keep you informed, as well as I
:an, of what occurs over the way.
.Ve shall remain here until the second
.eek in September. Stay where you
.re, or, at all events, do not dream
.f joining me. . . . Colonel Daw is
.itting on the piazza looking rather

ferocious. I have not seen Marjorie
since I parted with her in the garden.

XII

EDWARD DELANEY TO THOMAS DIL-
LON, M.D., MADISON SQUARE,
NEW YORK

August 30,—.

MY DEAR DOCTOR: If you have any
influence over Flemming, I beg of
you to exert it to prevent his coming to this place at present. There
are circumstances, which I will explain to you before long, that make
it of the first importance that he
should not come into this neighborhood. His appearance here, I speak
advisedly, would be disastrous to him.
In urging him to remain in New York,
or to go to some inland resort, you
will be doing him and me a real
service. Of course you will not mention my name in this connection.
You know me well enough, my dear
doctor, to be assured that, in begging
your secret co-operation, I have reasons that will meet your entire approval when they are made plain to
you. My father, I am glad to state,
has so greatly improved that he can
no longer be regarded as an invalid.
With great esteem, I am, etc., etc.

XIII

EDWARD DELANEY TO JOHN
FLEMMING

August 31,—.

Your letter, announcing your mad
determination to come here, has just
reached me. I beg of you to reflect
a moment. The step would be fatal
to your interests and hers. You
would furnish just cause for irritation to R. W. D.; and, though he

loves Marjorie tenderly, he is capable
of going to any lengths if opposed.
You would not like, I am convinced,
to be the means of causing him to
treat *her* with severity. That would
be the result of your presence at The
Pines at this juncture. Wait and see
what happens. Moreover, I understand from Dillon that you are in no
condition to take so long a journey.
He thinks the air of the coast would
be the worst thing possible for you;
that you ought to go inland, if anywhere. Be advised by me. Be advised by Dillon.

XIV

TELEGRAMS

September 1,—.

1.—TO EDWARD DELANEY

*Letter received. Dillon be hanged.
I think I ought to be on the ground.*
            J. F.

2.—TO JOHN FLEMMING

*Stay where you are. You would
only complicate matters. Do not
move until you hear from me.*
            E. D.

3.—TO EDWARD DELANEY

*My being at The Pines could be
kept secret. I must see her.   J. F.*

4.—TO JOHN FLEMMING

*Do not think of it. It would be
useless. R. W. D. has locked M. in
her room. You would not be able to
effect an interview.   E. D.*

5.—TO EDWARD DELANEY

*Locked her in her room. Good God.
That settles the question. I shall
leave by the twelve-fifteen express.*
            J. F.

XV

THE ARRIVAL

On the 2d of September, 187–, a
the down express due at 3.40 left the
station at Hampton, a young man
leaning on the shoulder of a servant
whom he addressed as Watkins
stepped from the platform into a
hack, and requested to be driven to
"The Pines." On arriving at the gate
of a modest farmhouse, a few mile
from the station, the young man descended with difficulty from the car
riage, and, casting a hasty glance
across the road, seemed much im
pressed by some peculiarity in th
landscape. Again leaning on th
shoulder of the person Watkins, h
walked to the door of the farm-house
and inquired for Mr. Edward De
laney. He was informed by the aged
man who answered his knock, tha
Mr. Edward Delaney had gone to
Boston the day before, but that Mr
Jonas Delaney was within. This information did not appear satisfactory
to the stranger, who inquired if Mr
Edward Delaney had left any mes
sage for Mr. John Flemming. There
was a letter for Mr. Flemming, if he
were that person. After a brief ab
sence the aged man reappeared with
a letter.

XVI

EDWARD DELANEY TO JOHN
FLEMMING

September 1,—

I am horror-stricken at what I have
done! When I began this correspondence I had no other purpose
than to relieve the tedium of your
sick-chamber. Dillon told me to cheer
you up. I tried to. I thought you

entered into the spirit of the thing.
I had no idea, until within a few days,
that you were taking matters *au
serieux*.

What can I say? I am in sack-
cloth and ashes. I am a pariah, a
dog of an outcast. I tried to make
a little romance to interest you, something soothing and idyllic, and, by
Jove! I have done it only too well! 10

My father doesn't know a word of
this, so don't jar the old gentleman
any more than you can help. I fly
from the wrath to come—when you
arrive! For O, dear Jack, there isn't
any colonial mansion on the other
side of the road, there isn't any piazza,
there isn't any hammock,—there isn't
any Marjorie Daw!!

1873

VI. EDWARD ROWLAND · SILL *
(1841–1887)

MORNING

I entered once, at break of day,
A chapel, lichen-stained and gray,
Where a congregation dozed and
    heard
An old monk read from a written
    Word.
No light through the window-panes
    could pass,
For shutters were closed on the rich
    stained glass;
And in a gloom like the nether night
The monk read on by a taper's light.
Ghostly with shadows, that shrank
    and grew
As the dim light flared, were aisle and
    pew;   10
And the congregation that dozed
    around
Listened without a stir or sound—
Save one, who rose with wistful face,
And shifted a shutter from its place.
Then light flashed in like a flashing
    gem—
For dawn had come unknown to
    them—
And a slender beam, like a lance of
    gold,

*All selections from Sill are used by per-
mission of, and by arrangement with,
Houghton Mifflin Company.

Shot to the crimson curtain-fold,
Over the bended head of him
Who pored and pored by the taper
    dim;   20
And it kindled over his wrinkled
    brow
Such words: "The law which was till
    now";
And I wondered that, under that
    morning ray,
When night and shadow were scat-
    tered away,
The monk should bow his locks of
    white
By a taper's feebly flickering light—
Should pore, and pore, and never
    seem
To notice the golden morning-beam.
                                    1868

THE FOOL'S PRAYER

The royal feast was done; the King
    Sought some new sport to banish
        care,
And to his jester cried: "Sir Fool,
    Kneel now, and make for us a
        prayer!"

The jester doffed his cap and bells,
    And stood the mocking court be-
        fore;
They could not see the bitter smile
    Behind the painted grin he wore.

He bowed his head, and bent his knee
    Upon the monarch's silken stool; 10

His pleading voice arose: "O Lord,
  Be merciful to me, a fool!

"No pity, Lord, could change the
  heart
  From red with wrong to white as
    wool:
The rod must heal the sin; but,
  Lord,
  Be merciful to me, a fool!

" 'Tis not by guilt the onward sweep
  Of truth and right, O Lord, we
    stay;
'Tis by our follies that so long
  We hold the earth from heaven
    away.   20

"These clumsy feet, still in the mire,
  Go crushing blossoms without end;
These hard, well-meaning hands we
    thrust
  Among the heart-strings of a friend.

"The ill-timed truth we might have
    kept—
  Who knows how sharp it pierced
    and stung!
The word we had not sense to say—
  Who knows how grandly it had
    rung!

"Our faults no tenderness should ask,
  The chastening stripes must cleanse
    them all;   30
But for our blunders—oh, in shame
  Before the eyes of heaven we fall.

"Earth bears no balsam for mis-
    takes;
  Men crown the knave; and scourge
    the tool
That did his will; but Thou, O Lord,
  Be merciful to me, a fool!"

The room was hushed; in silence rose
  The King, and sought his gardens
    cool,
And walked apart, and murmured low,
  "Be merciful to me, a fool!"   40
             1879

AMONG THE REDWOODS

Farewell to such a world! Too long
  I press
  The crowded pavement with un-
    willing feet.
Pity makes pride, and hate breeds
  hatefulness,
  And both are poisons. In the for-
    est, sweet
The shade, the peace! Immensity
  that seems
To drown the human life of doubts
  and dreams.

Far off the massive portals of the
  wood,
  Buttressed with shadow, misty-
    blue, serene,
Waited my coming. Speedily I stood
  Where the dun wall rose roofed in
    plumy green.   10
Dare one go in?—Glance backward!
  Dusk as night
Each column, fringed with sprays of
  amber light.

Let me, along this fallen bole, at
  rest,
  Turn to the cool, dim roof my glow-
    ing face.
Delicious dark on weary eyelids prest!
  Enormous solitude of silent space,
But for a low and thunderous ocean
  sound,
Too far to hear, felt thrilling through
  the ground!

No stir nor call the sacred hush pro-
  fanes;
  Save when from some bare treetop,
    far on high,   20
Fierce disputations of the clamorous
  cranes
  Fall muffled, as from out the upper
    sky.
So still, one dreads to wake the
  dreaming air,
Breaks a twig softly, moves the foot
  with care.

The hollow dome is green with empty
  shade,
  Struck through with slanted shafts
    of afternoon;
Aloft, a little rift of blue is made,
  Where slips a ghost that last night
    was the moon;
Beside its pearl a sea-cloud stays its
    wing,
Beneath a tilted hawk is balanc-
    ing.   30

The heart feels not in every time and
    mood
  What is around it. Dull as any
    stone
  lay; then, like a darkening dream,
    the wood
  Grew Karnak's temple, where I
    breathed alone
n the awed air strange incense, and
    uprose
Dim, monstrous columns in their
    dread repose.

The mind not always sees; but if
    there shine
  A bit of fern-lace bending over
    moss,
A silky glint that rides a spider-line,
  On a trefoil two shadow-spears that
    cross,   40
Three grasses that toss up their
    nodding heads,
With spring and curve like clustered
    fountain-threads,—

Suddenly, through side windows of the
    eye,
  Deep solitudes, where never souls
    have met;
Vast spaces, forest corridors that lie
  In a mysterious world, unpeopled
    yet.
Because the outward eye elsewhere
    was caught,
The awfulness and wonder come un-
    sought.

f death be but resolving back again
  Into the world's deep soul, this is
    a kind   50

Of quiet, happy death, untouched by
    pain
  Or sharp reluctance. For I feel my
    mind
Is interfused with all I hear and see;
As much a part of All as cloud or
    tree.

Listen! A deep and solemn wind on
    high;
  The shafts of shining dust shift to
    and fro;
The columned trees sway impercep-
    tibly,
  And creak as mighty masts when
    trade-winds blow.
The cloudy sails are set; the earth-
    ship swings
Along the sea of space to grander
    things.   60
                              1883

BEFORE SUNRISE IN WINTER

A purple cloud hangs half-way down;
  Sky, yellow gold below;
The naked trees, beyond the town,
  Like masts against it show,—

Bare masts and spars of our earth-
    ship,
  With shining snow-sails furled;
And through the sea of space we slip,
  That flows all round the world.
                              1900?

ON SECOND THOUGHT

  The end's so near,
    It is all one
  What track I steer,
    What work's begun.
    It is all one
    If *nothing's* done,
  The end's so near!

  The end's so near,
    It is all one
  What track thou steer,   10
    What work's begun—

Some deed, *some* plan,
As thou 'rt a man!
The end 's so near!

1899

VII. RICHARD WATSON GILDER *
(1844–1909)

THE SONNET

What is a sonnet? 'Tis the pearly
  shell
  That murmurs of the far-off mur-
  muring sea;
  A precious jewel carved most curi-
  ously;
  It is a little picture painted well.
What is a sonnet? 'Tis the tear that
  fell
  From a great poet's hidden ecstasy;
  A two-edged sword, a star, a song—
  ah me!
  Sometimes a heavy-tolling funeral
  bell.
This was the flame that shook with
  Dante's breath;
  The solemn organ whereon Milton
  played,   10
  And the clear glass where Shake-
  speare's shadow falls:
A sea this is—beware who ventureth!
  For like a fiord the narrow floor is
  laid
  Mid-ocean deep sheer to the moun-
  tain walls.

1885?

THE NIGHT PASTURE

I

In a starry night in June, before the
moon had come over into our valley
from the high valley beyond,
  Up the winding mountain-lane I

---

* All selections from Gilder are used by
permission of, and by arrangement with,
Houghton Mifflin Company.

---

wandered, and, stopping, leaned on the
bars, and listened:
  And I heard the little brook sliding
from stone to stone; and I heard the
sound of the bells as the cows moved
—heavily, slowly,
  In various keys, deep, or like sleigh
bells tinkling, sounded the chiming
cow-bells—
  Starting and stilling, irregular; near
or far away in the dusk—
  And the nearer cows I heard chew
ing the cud, and breathing warm on
the cool air of the mountain slope
  In the night pasture.

II

Terrace on terrace rises the farm
from meadow and winding river to
forest of chestnut and pine;
  There by the high-road, among the
embowering maples, nestles the ancient homestead;
  From each new point of vantage
lovelier seems the valley, and the hill
framed sunset ever more and more
moving and glorious;   10
  But when in the thunderous city I
think of the mountain farm, nothing
so sweet of remembrance,—holding
me as in a dream,—
  As the silver note of the unseen
brook, and the clanging of the cow
bells fitfully in the dark, and the deep
breathing of the cows
  In the night pasture.

III

Then I think, not of myself—but
an image comes to me of one who
has passed,
  Of an old man bent with labor;
  He, like his father before him, for
many and many a year,
  When the cows down the mountain

ave trudged in the summer evening,
nd after the evening milking,
Night after night, and year after
ear, back up the lane he has driven
hem, while the shepherd-dog leaped
nd barked—
Back up the lane, and past the
rchard, and through the bars
Into the night pasture.   20

IV

There in the twilight I see him
tand:
He listens to the sounds of the field
nd the forest,
On his brow strikes the cool moun-
ain air;
Hard is the old man's life and full
ndeed of sorrow—
But now, for a moment, respite
rom labor, in the pause 'twixt day
nd night!
Perhaps to his heart comes a sense
f the beauty that fills all this exqui-
ite valley—
A sense of peace and of rest; a
hought of the long and toilless night
hat comes to all,
As he leans on the bars and listens,
nd hears the deep-breathed cows,
nd the scattered sound of the bells
In the night pasture.
                          1901?

VIII. EMMA LAZARUS *
(1849–1887)

VENUS OF THE LOUVRE

)own the long hall she glistens like a
    star,
he foam-born mother of Love, trans-
    fixed to stone,

* From *The Poems of Emma Lazarus*. In
wo Volumes. 1889 Copyright 1888 by
ary and Annie Lazarus.

Yet none the less immortal, breath-
    ing on.
Time's brutal hand hath maimed but
    could not mar.
When first the enthralled enchantress
    from afar
Dazzled mine eyes, I saw not her
    alone,
Serenely poised on her world-wor-
    shipped throne,
As when she guided once her dove-
    drawn car,—
But at her feet a pale, death-stricken
    Jew,
Her life adorer, sobbed farewell to
    love.   10
Here *Heine* wept! Here still he
    weeps anew,
Nor ever shall his shadow lift or
    move,
While mourns one ardent heart, one
    poet-brain,
For vanished Hellas and Hebraic pain.
                          1889

HOW LONG?

How long, and yet how long,
Our leaders will we hail from over
    seas,
Masters and kings from feudal mon-
    archies,
And mock their ancient song
With echoes weak of foreign melo-
    dies?

That distant isle mist-wreathed,
Mantled in unimaginable green,
Too long hath been our mistress and
    our queen.
Our fathers have bequeathed
Too deep a love for her, our hearts
    within.   10

She made the whole world ring
With the brave exploits of her chil-
    dren strong,
And with the matchless music of her
    song.

Too late, too late we cling
To alien legends, and their strains
    prolong.

This fresh young world I see,
With heroes, cities, legends of her
    own;
With a new race of men, and over-
    blown
By winds from sea to sea,
Decked with the majesty of every
    zone.   20

I see the glittering tops
Of snow-peaked mounts, the wid'ning
    vale's expanse,
Large prairies where free herds of
    horses prance,
Exhaustless wealth of crops,
In vast, magnificent extravagance.

These grand, exuberant plains,
These stately rivers, each with many
    a mouth,
The exquisite beauty of the soft-
    aired south,
The boundless seas of grains,
Luxuriant forests' lush and splendid
    growth.   30

The distant siren-song
Of the green island in the eastern sea,
Is not the lay for this new chivalry,
    It is not free and strong
To chant on prairies 'neath this bril-
    liant sky.

The echo faints and fails;
It suiteth not, upon this western
    plain,
Our voice or spirit; we should stir
    again
The wilderness, and make the vales
Resound unto a yet unheard-of
    strain.   40
                                    1871

THE BANNER OF THE JEW

Wake, Israel, wake! Recall to-day
The glorious Maccabean rage,

The sire heroic, hoary-gray,
    His five-fold lion-lineage:
The Wise, the Elect, the Help-of-God
The Burst-of-Spring, the Avenging
    rod.*

From Mizpeh's mountain-ridge they
    saw
Jerusalem's empty streets, he
    shrine
Laid waste where Greeks profaned
    the Law,
    With idol and with pagan sign. 1
Mourners in tattered black were
    there,
With ashes sprinkled on their hair.

Then from the stony peak there ran
    A blast to ope the graves: down
    poured
The Maccabean clan, who sang
    Their battle-anthem to the Lord.
Five heroes lead, and, following, see
Ten thousand rush to victory!

Oh for Jerusalem's trumpet now,
    To blow a blast of shattering
    power,   2
To wake the sleepers high and low,
    And rouse them to the urgent hour
No hand for vengeance—but to save
A million naked swords should wave

Oh deem not dead that martial fire,
    Say not the mystic flame is spent
With Moses' law and David's lyre,
    Your ancient strength remains un-
    bent.
Let but an Ezra rise anew,
To lift the *Banner of the Jew!*   3

A rag, a mock at first—erelong,
    When men have bled and women
    wept,
To guard its precious folds from
    wrong,
    Even they who shrunk, even they
    who slept,

---

* The sons of Mattathias—Jonathan, John
Eleazar, Simon (also called the Jewel), an
Judas, the Prince. [Author's note.]

Shall leap to bless it, and to save.
Strike! for the brave revere the
    brave!

1882

THE NEW COLOSSUS *

Not like the brazen giant of Greek
    fame,
With conquering limbs astride from
    land to land;
Here at our sea-washed, sunset gates
    shall stand
A mighty woman with a torch, whose
    flame
Is the imprisoned lightning, and her
    name

* Written in aid of Bartholdi Pedestal
Fund, 1883. [Author's note.]

Mother of Exiles. From her beacon-
    hand
Glows world-wide welcome; her mild
    eyes command
The air-bridged harbor that twin
    cities frame.
"Keep, ancient lands, your storied
    pomp!" cries she
With silent lips. "Give me your
    tired, your poor,   10
Your huddled masses yearning to
    breathe free,
The wretched refuse of your teeming
    shore.
Send these, the homeless, tempest-
    tost to me,
I lift my lamp beside the golden
    door!"

1883

THE WESTERN HUMORISTS

I. JOHN PHOENIX (GEORGE HORATIO DERBY)
(1823–1861)

From *PHOENIXIANA; OR, SKETCHES AND BURLESQUES*

MUSICAL REVIEW EXTRAORDINARY

San Diego, July 10th, 1854.

DEAR EWER:

As your valuable magazine is not supposed to be so entirely identified with San Francisco interests, as to be careless what takes place in other portions of this great *kedntry,* and as it is received and read in San Diego with great interest (I have loaned my copy to over four different literary gentlemen, most of whom have read some of it), I have thought it not improbable that a few critical notices of the musical performances and the drama of this place might be acceptable to you, and interest your readers. I have been, moreover, encouraged to this task by the perusal of your interesting musical and theatrical critiques on San Francisco performers and performances; as I feel convinced that, if you devote so much space to them, you will not allow any little feeling of rivalry between the two great cities to prevent your noticing ours, which, without the slightest feeling of prejudice, I must consider as infinitely superior. I propose this month to call your attention to the two great events in our theatrical and musical world—the appearance of the talented Miss PELICAN, and the production of Tarboxes' celebrated "Ode Symphonie" of "The Plains."

The critiques on the former are from the columns of *The Vallecetos Sentinel,* to which they were originally contributed by me, appearing on the respective dates of June 1st and June 31st.

FROM THE VALLECETOS SENTINEL, JUNE 1ST

MISS PELICAN.—Never during our dramatic experience, has a more exciting event occurred than the sudden bursting upon our theatrical firmament, full, blazing, unparalleled, of the bright, resplendent and particular star, whose honored name shines refulgent at the head of this article. Coming among us unheralded, almost unknown, without claptrap, in a wagon drawn by oxen across the plains, with no agent to get up a counterfeit enthusiasm in her favor, she appeared before us for the first time at the San Diego Lyceum, last evening, in the trying and difficult character of Ingomar, or the Tame Savage. We are at a loss to describe our sensations, our admiration, at her magnificent, her superhuman efforts. We do not hesitate to say that she is by far the superior of any living actress; and, as we believe hers to be the perfection of acting, we cannot be wrong in the belief that no one hereafter will ever be found to ap-

254

roach her. Her conception of the character of Ingomar was perfection itself; er playful and ingenuous manner, her ght girlish laughter, in the scene with ir Peter, showed an appreciation of the avage character, which nothing but the ost arduous study, the most elaborate aining could produce; while her awful hange to the stern, unyielding, uncompromising father in the tragic scene of uncan's murder, was indeed nature itlf. Miss Pelican is about seventeen ears of age, of miraculous beauty, and ost thrilling voice. It is needless to ay she dresses admirably, as in fact we ave said all we can say when we called er most truthfully, perfection. Mr. ohn Boots took the part of Parthenia ery creditably, etc., etc.

FROM THE VALLECETOS SENTINEL,
JUNE 31ST

MISS PELICAN.—As this lady is about o leave us to commence an engagement n the San Francisco stage, we should egret exceedingly if any thing we have aid about her, should send with her a *restige* which might be found undeerved on trial. The fact is, Miss Pelian is a very ordinary actress; indeed, ne of the most indifferent ones we ever appened to see. She came here from he Museum at Fort Laramie, and we raised her so injudiciously that she beame completely spoiled. She has performed a round of characters during the st week, very miserably, though we re bound to confess that her perormance of King Lear last evening, was uperior to any thing of the kind we ver saw. Miss Pelican is about fortyhree years of age, singularly plain in er personal appearance, awkward and mbarrassed, with a cracked and squeakng voice, and really dresses quite outageously. *She has much to learn—poor hing!*

I take it the above notices are ather ingenious. The fact is, I'm no judge of acting, and don't know how Miss Pelican will turn out. If well, why there's my notice of June the 1st; if ill, then June 31st comes in play, and, as there is but one copy of the *Sentinel* printed, it's an easy matter to destroy the incorrect one; *both can't be wrong;* so I've made a sure thing of it in any event. Here follows my musical critique, which I flatter myself is of rather superior order:

THE PLAINS. ODE SYMPHONIE PAR JABEZ TARBOX.—This glorious composition was produced at the San Diego Odeon, on the 31st of June, ult., for the first time in this or any other country, by a very full orchestra (the performance taking place immediately after supper), and a chorus composed of the entire "Sauer Kraut-Verein," the "Wee Gates Association," and choice selections from the "Gyascutus" and "Pikeharmonic" societies. The solos were rendered by Herr Tuden Links, the recitations by Herr Von Hyden Schnapps, both performers being assisted by Messrs. John Smith and Joseph Brown, who held their coats, fanned them, and furnished water during the more overpowering passages.

The Plains we consider the greatest musical achievement that has been presented to an enraptured public. Like Waterloo among battles; Napoleon among warriors; Niagara among falls, and Peck among senators, this magnificent composition stands among Oratorios, Operas, Musical Melodramas and performances of Ethiopian Serenaders, peerless and unrivaled. *Il frappe toute chose parfaitment froid.*

"It does not depend for its success"

upon its plot, its theme, its school or its master, for it has very little if any of them, but upon its soul-subduing, all-absorbing, high-faluting effect upon the audience, every member of which it causes to experience the most singular and exquisite sensations. Its strains at times remind us of those of the old master of the steamer McKim, who never went to sea without being unpleasantly affected;—a straining after effect he used to term it. Blair in his lecture on beauty, and Mills in his treatise on logic, (p. 31,) have alluded to the feeling which might be produced in the human mind, by something of this transcendentally sublime description, but it has remained for M. Tarbox, in the production of *The Plains,* to call this feeling forth.

The symphonie opens upon the wide and boundless plains, in longitude 115° W., latitude 35° 21′ 03″ N., and about sixty miles from the west bank of Pitt River. These data are beautifully and clearly expressed by a long (topographically) drawn note from an E flat clarionet. The sandy nature of the soil, sparsely dotted with bunches of cactus and artemisia, the extended view, flat and unbroken to the horizon, save by the rising smoke in the extreme verge, denoting the vicinity of a Pi Utah village, are represented by the bass drum. A few notes on the piccolo, calls the attention to a solitary antelope, picking up mescal beans in the foreground. The sun having an altitude of 36° 27′, blazes down upon the scene in indescribable majesty. "Gradually the sounds roll forth in a song" of rejoicing to the God of Day.

Of thy intensity
And great immensity
  Now then we sing;
Beholding in gratitude
Thee in this latitude,
  Curious thing.

Which swells out into "Hey Jim along, Jim along Josey," then *decrescendo, mas o menos, poco pocita,* die away and dries up.

Suddenly we hear approaching train from Pike County, consisting o seven families, with forty-six wagons each drawn by thirteen oxen; eac family consists of a man in butternut colored clothing driving the oxen; wife in butternut-colored clothing rid ing in the wagon, holding a butternu baby, and seventeen butternut chil dren running promiscuously about th establishment; all are barefootec dusty, and smell unpleasantly. (A these circumstances are expressed b pretty rapid fiddling for some min utes, winding up with a puff from th orpheclide, played by an intoxicate Teuton with an atrocious breath—i is impossible to misunderstand the de scription.) Now rises o'er the plain in mellifluous accents, the grand Pik County Chorus.

Oh we'll soon be thar
In the land of gold,
Through the forest old,
O'er the mounting cold,
With spirits bold—
Oh, we come, we come,
And we'll soon be thar.
  Gee up Bolly! whoo, up, whoo haw

The train now encamp. The un packing of the kettles and mess-pans the unyoking of the oxen, the gather ing about the various camp-fires, th frizzling of the pork, are so clearly expressed by the music, that the mos untutored savage could readily com prehend it. Indeed, so vivid and life ike was the representation, that a lady sitting near us, involuntarily exclaimed aloud, at a certain passage, *"Thar, that pork's burning!"* and it was truly interesting to watch the gratified expression of her face, when by a few notes of the guitar, the pan was removed from the fire, and the blazing pork extinguished.

This is followed by the beautiful *aria:*—

> O! marm, I want a pancake!

Followed by that touching *recitative:*—

> Shet up, or I will spank you!

To which succeeds a grand *crescendo* movement, representing the flight of the child with the pancake, the pursuit of the mother, and the final arrest and summary punishment of the former, represented by the rapid and successive strokes of the castanet.

The turning in for the night follows: and the deep and stertorous breathing of the encampment, is well given by the bassoon, while the sufferings and trials of an unhappy father with an unpleasant infant, are touchingly set forth by the *cornet à piston.*

Part Second—The night attack of the Pi Utahs; the fearful cries of the demoniac Indians; the shrieks of the females and children; the rapid and effective fire of the rifles; the stampede of the oxen; their recovery and the final repulse; the Pi Utahs being routed after a loss of thirty-six killed and wounded, while the Pikes lose but one scalp (from an old fellow who wore a wig, and lost it in the scuffle,) are faithfully given and excite the most intense interest in the minds of the hearers; the emotions of fear, admiration and delight, succeeding each other in their minds, with almost painful rapidity. Then follows the grand chorus:

> Oh! we gin them fits,
> The Ingen Utahs,
> With our six-shooters—
> We gin 'em pertickuler fits.

After which, we have the charming recitative of Herr Tuden Links, to the infant, which is really one of the most charming gems in the performance:

> Now, dern your skin, *can't* you be easy?

Morning succeeds. The sun rises magnificently (octavo flute)—breakfast is eaten,—in a rapid movement on three sharps; the oxen are caught and yoked up—with a small drum and triangle; the watches, purses, and other valuables of the conquered Pi Utahs, are stored away in a campkettle, to a small movement on the piccolo, and the train moves on, with the grand chorus:—

> We'll soon be thar,
> Gee up Bolly! Whoo hup! whoo haw!

The whole concludes with the grand hymn and chorus:—

> When we die we'll go to Benton,
> Whup! Whoo, haw!
> The greatest man that e'er land saw,
> Gee!
> Who this little airth was sent on
> Whup! Whoo, haw!
> To tell a "hawk from a hand-saw!"
> Gee!

The immense expense attending the production of this magnificent work; the length of time required to prepare the chorus; the incredible number of instruments destroyed at each rehearsal; have hitherto prevented M.

Tarbox from placing it before the American public, and it has remained for San Diego to show herself superior to her sister cities of the Union, in musical taste and appreciation, and in high souled liberality, by patronizing this immortal prodigy, and enabling its author to bring it forth in accordance with his wishes and its capabilities. We trust every citizen of San Diego and Vallecetos will listen to it ere it is withdrawn; and if there yet lingers in San Francisco, one spark of musical fervor, or a remnant of taste for pure harmony, we can only say that the Southerner sails from that place once a fortnight, and that the passage-money is but forty-five dollars.

JOHN PHOENIX.

1855

II. ARTEMUS WARD (CHARLES FARRAR BROWNE) (1834–1867)

From THE LONDON PUNCH LETTERS

VI. THE TOWER OF LONDON

MR. PUNCH, MY DEAR SIR,—I skurcely need inform you that your excellent Tower is very pop'lar with peple from the agricultooral districks, and it was chiefly them class which I found waitin at the gates the other mornin.

I saw at once that the Tower was established on a firm basis. In the entire history of firm basisis I don't find a basis more firmer than this one.

"You have no Tower in America?" said a man in the crowd, who had somehow detected my denomination.

"Alars! no," I ansered; "we boste of our enterprise and improovements and yit we are devoid of a Tower America, oh my onhappy country thou hast not got no Tower! It's a sweet Boon."

The gates was opened after awhile and we all purchist tickets and went into a waitin-room.

"My frens," said a pale-faced little man, in black close, "this is a sad day."

"Inasmuch as to how?" I said.

"I mean it is sad to think that so many peple have been killed within these gloomy walls. My frens, let us drop a tear!"

"No," I said, "you must excuse me. Others may drop one if they feel like it; but as for me, I decline The early managers of this institootion were a bad lot, and their crimes were trooly orful; but I can't sob for those who died four or five hundred years ago. If they was my own relations I couldn't. It's absurd to shed sobs over things which occurd durin the rain of Henry the Three. Let us be cheerful," I continnerd. "Look at the festiv Warders, in their red flannil jackets. They are cheerful and why should it not be thusly with us?"

A Warder now took us in charge and showed us the Trater's Gate, the armers, and things. The Trater's Gate is wide enuff to admit about twenty trater's abrest, I should jedge; but beyond this, I couldn't see that it was superior to gates in gen'ral.

Traters, I will here remark, are a onfortnit class of peple. If they wasn't, they wouldn't be traters. They conspire to bust up a country —they fail, and they're traters. They bust her, and they become statesmen and heroes.

Take the case of Gloster, afterwards Old·Dick the Three, who may be seen at the Tower, on horseback, in a heavy tin overcoat—take Mr. Gloster's case. Mr. G. was a conspirater of the basist dye, and if he'd failed, he would have been hung on a sour apple tree. But Mr. G. suceeded, and became great. He was lewd by Col. Richmond, but he lives in histry, and his equestrian figger may be seen daily for a sixpence, in conjuction with other em'nent persons, and no extra charge for the Varder's able and bootiful lectur.

There's one king in the room who is mounted onto a foamin steed, his right hand graspin a barber's pole. I didn't learn his name.

The room where the daggers and pistils and other weppins is kept is interestin. Among this collection of choice cutlery I notist the bow and arrer which those hot-heded old chaps used to conduct battles with. It is quite like the bow and arrer used at this day by certin tribes of American Injuns, and they shoot 'em off with such a excellent precision that I almost sigh'd to be a Injun, when I was in the Rocky Mountin regin. They are a pleasant lot them Injuns. Mr. Cooper and Dr. Catlin have told us of the red man's wonerful eloquence, and I found it so. Our party was stopt on the plains of Utah by a band of Shoshones, whose chief said, "Brothers! the pale-face is welcome. Brothers! the sun is sinkin in the West, and Warra-bucky-she will

soon cease speakin. - Brothers! the poor red man belongs to a race which is fast becomin extink." He then whooped in a shrill manner, stole all our blankets and whisky, and fled to the primeval forest to conceal his emotions.

I will remark here, while on the subjeck of Injuns, that they are in the main a very shaky set, with even less sense than the Fenians, and when I hear philanthropists bewailin the fack that every year "carries the noble red man nearer the settin sun," I simply have to say I'm glad of it, tho' it is rough on the settin sun. They call you by the sweet name of Brother one minit, and the next they scalp you with their Tomashawks. But I wander. Let us return to the Tower.

At one end of the room where the weppins is kept, is a wax figger of Queen Elizabeth, mounted on a fiery stuffed hoss, whose glass eye flashes with pride, and whose red morocker nostril dilates hawtily, as if conscious of the royal burden he bears. I have associated Elizabeth with the Spanish Armady. She's mixed up with it at the Surry Theater, where *Troo to the Core* is bein acted, and in which a full bally core is introjooced on board the Spanish Admiral's ship, givin the audiens the idee that he intends openin a moosic-hall in Plymouth the moment he conkers that town. But a very interesting drammer is *Troo to the Core,* notwitstandin the eccentric conduck of the Spanish Admiral; and very nice it is in Queen Elizabeth to make Martin Truegold a baronet.

The Warder shows us some instrooments of tortur, such as thumbscrews, throat-collars, etc., statin that these was conkerd from the Spanish Armady, and addin what a crooil peple the Spaniards was in them days—which elissited from a bright eyed little girl of about twelve summers the remark that she tho't it *was* rich to talk about the crooilty of the Spaniards usin thumbscrews, when we was in a Tower where so many poor peple's heads had been cut off. This made the Warder stammer and turn red.

I was so blessed with the little girl's brightness that I could have kissed the dear child, and I would if she'd been six years older.

I think my companions intended makin a day of it, for they all had sandwiches, sassiges, etc. The sad-lookin man, who had wanted us to drop a tear afore we started to go round, fling'd such quantities of sassige into his mouth, that I expected to see him choke hisself to death. He said to me, in the Beauchamp Tower, where the poor prisoners writ their onhappy names on the cold wall, "This is a sad sight."

"It is, indeed," I ansered. "You're black in the face. You shouldn't eat sassige in public without some rehearsals beforehand. You manage it orkwardly."

"No," he said, "I mean this sad room."

Indeed, he was quite right. Tho' so long ago all these drefful things happened, I was very glad to git away from this gloomy room, and go where the rich and sparklin Crown Jewils is kept. I was so pleased with the Queen's Crown, that it occurd to me what a agree'ble surprise it would be to send a sim'lar one home to my wife; and I asked the Warder what

was the vally of a good, well constructed Crown like that. He told me, but on cypherin up with a penci the amount of funs I have in the Jin' Stock Bank, I conclooded I'd send he a genteel silver watch instid.

And so I left the Tower. It is a solid and commandin edifis, but I deny that it is cheerful. I bid it adod without a pang.

I was droven to my hotel by the most melancholy driver of a four wheeler that I ever saw. He heaved a deep sigh as I gave him two shillings. "I'll give you six *d.*'s more," I said, "if it hurts you so."

"It isn't that," he said, with a hart-rendin groan, "it's only a way I have My mind's upset to-day. I at one time tho't I'd drive you into the Thames. I've been readin all the daily papers to try and understand about Governor Ayre, and my mind is totterin. It's really wonderful I didn't drive you into the Thames."

I asked the onhappy man what his number was, so I could redily find him in case I should want him agin, and bad him good-bye. And then I tho't what a frollicksome day I'd made of it.

Respectably, &c.
ARTEMUS WARD.
1866

III. JOSH BILLINGS
(HENRY WHEELER SHAW)
(1818–1885)

GLASS DIMONDS

If we could see the sekret motives that prompt even the good ackshuns

v men, we should see more tew re-
rove than admire.

The best specimens ov calm resig-
ashun tew their fate that I hav met
vith thus far, hav been amung thoze
vho had an inkum ov 40 thousand
ollars a year, less government tax.

Diogenes and Seneca were two az
rate philosophers az the world haz
ver produced; one lived in a tub, [10]
nd the other in a palace.

Most ov the happiness in this world
onsists in possessing what others
ant git.

Take all the phools and the good
ak out of this world, and it would
other menny ov us tew git a living.

Thare iz a grate menny ghosts trav-
lling around loose, but no one ever
aw one yet.

Honesty iz like money, yu hav got
ew work hard tew git it, and then
vork harder to keep it.

I alwus git my boots made bi the
humaker that other shumakers praze.

Philosophy iz born in the head, and
ies in the heart.

I hav noticed one thing, that just
bout in proporshun that the pashuns
re weak, men are seemingly virtew- [30]
us.

Here iz just what's the matter—if
u shut yureself up folks will run
fter yu, and if yu run after folks
ey will shut themselfs up.

Thare iz az mutch difference be-
ween wit and humor, az thare iz
etween the ile and the essence of
eppermint.

It iz a safe kalkulashun that the [40]
ore praze a man iz willing to take,
e less he deserves.

Thare iz but phew people in this
orld underrated.

Honesty iz the only aristokrasy that

i acknoweledge; an honest man iz
alwus a well-bred man and a gentleman.

Politeness iz not only the most
powerful, but the cheapest argument
I kno ov. The more wrinkles i kan
see in a man's face the better i like
it, provided a smile lays in each one
ov the gutters.

The philosophers tell us that "natur
abhors a vacum." This ackounts for
the sawdust in sum mens heds.

Thare iz now and then a person
to whom sosiety owes menny obli-
gashuns, but most people owe all
thare iz ov them tew sosiety.

If yu pull the sting out ov a hor-
net hiz moral power iz gone in a
minnit.

We are all ov us willing tew divide [20]
our sorrows amung our nabors, but
our plezzures we are more stingy
with.

Sages and phools are the only two
kinds ov people that the world kan
afford tew hav liv in solitude.

If a man waz kompletely virtewous,
i doubt whether he would be happy
here, he would be so lonesum.

It dont require mutch tallent tew [30]
giv good advice, but tew follow it
duz.

Altho the mule iz looked upon az a
stupid kritter, he makes sum most
brilliant hits.

Every man haz a weak side, and
sum hav two or three.

He who demands respekt almost
allways deserves it.

Ridikule that ain't true haz no partikular power.

I wouldn't giv 250 dollars cash, or
good dicker, for all the fame thare iz
in the world at this partikular junktur.

Mi opinyun ov mankind, az a brilliant suckcess, needs a good deal ov nussing.

No church kan expekt tew be very suckcessful now days, unless it haz got a good orkestra in it.

Hope iz a thoughtless jade—she often cheats us, but she haz no malace.

When i waz yung i thought all money spent waz well invested, but as i get older i cypher different.

God makes opportunitys, but man must hunt for them.

Invenshun and judgement are seldom found together.

Ambishun tew shine in everything iz a sure way tew put a man's kandell all out.

Man's make up iz ov natur and custom, and i don't kno which ov the two iz the most powerfullest.

A grate brag iz either a phool or a coward, and probably he iz both.

Az long az we are lucky we attribit it tew our smartness; our bad luck we giv the gods credit for.

Thare iz one person in this world that every boddy kan tell yu all about, and that iz the next door nabor.

Thare are people who love too well to ever be jealous.

I know lots ov people who always think at least 3 times before they speak once, and then never say enny thing worth listening to.

It takes a certain amount ov back ground in a man's karakter tew sho hiz virtews to good advantage.

It iz better tew overshute the mark than tew fall short; this shows that the fault ain't in the amunishun.

Thare iz plenty ov individuals who, if they kan go up like a baloon, are willing tew cum down like a chunk.

1876

IV. PETROLEUM V. NASBY
(DAVID ROSS LOCKE)
(1833–1888)

From "SWINGIN' ROUND THE CIRKLE"

A FEW LAST WORDS

XLI

A Few Last Words.—The Write hereof bids his Readers Farewell and hurls a Trifle of Exhortatio after them.

Confedrit X Road
(which is in the Stait uv Kentucky)
November 19, 1866

Poets hev remarked a great many times, too tejus to enoomerate, tha "farewell" is the saddistist word t pronounce wich hez to be pronounst It may be so among poets, wich ar spozd to be continyooally carryi about with em a load uv sadnis, an sensibilities, and sich; but I hev neve found it so. The fact is, it depend very much on how yoo say it, unde wat circumstances, and to whom Wen, in my infancy, I wuz inkar seratid in the common jail uv m native village, in Noo Gersey, a vic tim to the prejudisis uv twelve men who believed, on the unsupportid tes timony uv three men, and the mer accident uv the missin property bei found in my possession (notwith standin the fact that I solemnly as shoored em that I didn't know nothi about it, and if I did it, it must he bin in a somnamboolic state), that hed bin guilty uv bustin open a gro sery store, and takin twelve boxes u cheroot cigars, I asshoor yoo that, a

he end uv the sentence,—hevin bin
ed on bread and water,—the sayin
arewell to the inhuman jailer wuzn't
t all onpleasant. Likewise, when, in
he State uv Pennsylvany, in the eggs-
itin campane uv 1856, I votid twict
or four times for that eminent and
'ilelis patriot, Jeems Bookannon, and
vuz hauled up therefor, and sen-
enced by a Ablishn Judge to a year
n the Western Penitentiary, after an
lokent speech, in wich I reviewed
he whole question at issue between
he parties, and ashoored him that my
riflin irregularity in the matter uv
otin grew out uv an overweenin de-
ire for the salvashen uv my beloved
ountry,—that, feelin that rooin wuz
head uv us, onless that leveler Fre-
mont was defeated, I felt that my
onshence wood not be easy onless I
id all in my power to avert the evil,
—when I emerged from them gloomy
valls, with one soot uv close, and a
olable knowledge uv the shoemakin
iznis, wuz it a sad thing for me to
ay "Farewell" to the grim jailer,
'hose key turned one way wuz lib-
rty, and tother way captivity?
Jary.

These two instances, I beleeve, is
he only ones in wich I hev ever hed
o say farewell. In the course uv
ny long and checkered career (I do
ot here allood to the style uv clothin
n the Penitentiary), I am, when I
hink uv it, surprised at the com-
aratively few times wich I ever left
place at wich I hed bin stayin, in
aylite! I ginerally went in the
ite,—

Foldin my tent like the Arab,
And ez silently steelin away,

evin too much sensibility to be an

onwillin witnis uv the agony uv landladies, when they diskivered that I
cood not pay. Knowin the softnis
uv my heart, I hev alluz hed a great
regard for my feelins.

Still, I feel some disinclinashen to
commence sayin Farewell at this time.
I wood like to continyoo this work.
Methinks I wood like to go on pilin
up pages ontil the Dimocrisy uv the
Yoonited States wuz thoroughly in-
doctrinatid with *my* Dimocrisy. But
it is impossible.

I bid my readers farewell in a
period uv gloom rarely ekalled, and
never surpast, for the Dimocrisy.
Never in my recollekshun wuz the
party in sich a state uv abject cus-
sitood. The Northern States hev
slipt from our grasp one by one, ontil
none remains wich we kin fondly call
ourn. The Border States are losin
their Dimocrisy, and rallyin under the
black banner uv Ablishinism; and the
ten States which we kin control on-
fortinitly ain't got no voice in the
Guvment. From the mountin tops uv
Maine, and the level praries uv Illinoy,
the remnants uv the Dimocrisy holler
to us uv the South, "Be firm! we'll
stand by yoo!" and from the rich
cotton fields uv the South the Dimocrisy holler to them uv the North,
"Keep up yoor sperits! we are troo
to yoo!" all uv wich is very cheerin,
when them uv the North is in sich
a hopelis minority ez to be unable
to elect a township constable, and
them in the South hain't got no vote
at all!

I appeal, however, with the rest
of the leaders, to the Dimocrisy to
remain firm. Suthin will come in
time,—what, I can't, with any degree
uv certainty, now state; but suthin

will come. The Ablishnists cannot alluz rool. The cuss uv the old Whig party wuz, that the respective individooal members thereof cood read and write, and hed a knack uv doin their own thinkin, and therefore it cood not be brot into that state uv dissipline so necessary to success ez a party. That same cuss is a hangin onto the Ablishnists. They hung together from 1856 to 1860 coz there wuz wat they called a prinsipple at stake; and on that prinsipple they elected Linkin. They wood hev fallen to peeces then, but our Southern brethren decided to commence operashens for the new government it hed so long desired; and the overwhelmin pressur uv the war smothered all miner ishoos and all individooal feelin, and they hung together long enough to see that throo. Now, still for the principle wich welded em doorin the war, they are holdin together yit, and probably will ontil they think this question wich they are disposin of is disposed of. Then they will split up, and our openin is made. We hev a solid phalanx, wich they can't win over or detach from us. We hev them old veterans who voted for Jaxon, and who are still votin for him. We hev them sturdy old yeomanry who still swear that Bloo Lite Fedralism ought to be put down, and can't be tolerated in a Republikin Government, and who, bless their old souls! don't know no more what Bloo Lite Fedralism wuz than an unborn baby does uv Guy Fawkes. We hev that solid army uv voters whose knees yawn hidjusly, and whose coats is out at elbows, and whose children go barefoot in winter, while their dads is a drinkin cheap whiskey, and damin the Goverment for imposin a income tax. We hev the patriotic citizins whose noses blossom like the lobster, and who liv in mortal fear uv nigger ekality; and we hev John Morrissey's constitooents

These classes argyment won't move and reasonin' won't faze. They like to abooze the Goverment for levyin taxes, hopin to deseeve somebody into the idea that they pay taxes, and that it bears hard onto em; and they oppose nigger ekality becoz it soothe em, like laudnum, to think that ther is somebody in the country lowe down than themselves. The Dimocrisy alluz hed these, and alluz will

Ez I remarked, the Ablishnists when releeved uv the pressure now bearin onto em, will grow fractious and split, and these classes will he no trouble to git into a majority, an then our time comes.

The discouraged Dimokrat may sa that preechers, and noosepapers, an Sundy skools, and sich, are under minin their party. In time they will but not yet. There is still whiske in the land, and the nigger is not ye extinct. Uv wat danger is preecher to these men, when yoo coodent gi one uv em within gun-shot uv one and wat harm is noospapers to em when they can't read? Besides, w are not at the end uv our resource yet. When the wust comes to th wust, there is the nigger left us When he is no longer uv use to u ez he is now,—when the prejoodis i so far removed ez to invest him wit the suffrage,—then we'll give him th ballot,—we'll lead him out uv Egypt and we'll make him vote with us. Th Dimocrisy never yet failed to contro all uv the lower orders uv sosiet They hev the lowest grade uv fu iners; they hev Delaware and Maryland; they hev Noo York city and Suthern Illinoy; and ef the nigger gets the ballot afore he does the spellinbook, he's ourn beyond peradvencher.

Again: Ef our politikel stumiks isn't yet toned up to swallerin the nigger, we kin compermise on the Mexican. That country Johnson hez his eagle eye on now, and ef we demand it, he'll take it. Wat a glorious prospeck opens to us! Mexico wood cut up into at least twenty States, wich, added to the ten we hev, wood make a clean majority wich we cood hold for years. Massahoosets cood do nuthin in Mexico. The Greasers ain't adapted to Massahoosets. Ef they sent their longhaired teachers there with their spellin books, they'd end their labors by lettin a knife into their intestines for the clothes they wore, wich would put a check on the mishnary biznis. They re, it is troo, several degrees lower in the skale uv humanity than the niggers, but then they ain't niggers, and we cood marry em without feelin that we'd degraded ourselves. Ther s undoubtedly cusses on em, but the only cuss we hev Constooshnel objecions to is the cuss uv Ham, and that they ain't labrin under. Mexico afords us room for hope; we never hel run out uv material for Dimocratic votes until she is convertid, and ut few mishnaries wood hev the nerve to tackle her.

Therefore I say to the Dimocrisy, e uv good cheer! Ther's a brite day dawnin. We hev now the Post Offisis, and nothin short uv impeachment kin take em from us for two years. We may be beaten in 1868; it may be that our managin men promised the nominashen to our present Head—A. Johnson; but I hope not. Ef we are laid out agin, we kin console ourselves with the reflection that we're yoost to it, and we kin go on hopin for the good time that must come.

Let us hold onto our faith, and continyoo to run, hopin eventooally to be glorified. Let us remember that all the majorities agin us don't change the fact that Noah cust Ham, and that Hager wuz sent back to her mistress. Let us remember that Paul, or some one uv them possels, remarked, "Servance, obey yoor masters," and that, under Ablishn rool, we are exposed to the danger uv marryin niggers. Let us still cherish the faith that evenchooally, when reason returns, the Amerikin people will not throw away the boon we offer em uv filling the cuss uv labor imposed by the Almity for disobedience in the garden, ez the Dimocrisy served in the army, by substitoot, and persevere even unto the perfeck end. When this good time is come, then will the anshent Dimocrisy, uv wich I hev bin to-wunst a piller and a ornament for thirty years, triumph, and the position wich I now hold, wich is rather too temporary to be agreeable, be continyood unto me for keeps, and layin off the armor uv actooal warfare, I shel rest in that haven uv worn-out patriots,—a perpetooal Post Offis. May the day be hastened! Farewell!

PETROLEUM V. NASBY, P. M.
(wich is Postmaster).
1866

FOLK LITERATURE

I. THE COWBOY AND FRONTIERSMAN *

THE COWBOY'S DREAM

[JOHN A. LOMAX]

Last night as I lay on the prairie,
And looked at the stars in the sky,
I wondered if ever a cowboy
Would drift to that sweet by and by.

    Roll on, roll on;
    Roll on, little dogies, roll on,
      roll on,
    Roll on, roll on;
    Roll on, little dogies, roll on.

The road to that bright, happy region
Is a dim, narrow trail, so they say;   10
But the broad one that leads to perdition
Is posted and blazed all the way.

They say there will be a great round-up,
And cowboys, like dogies, will stand,
To be marked by the Riders of Judgment,
Who are posted and know every brand.

I know there's many a stray cowboy
Who'll be lost at the great, final sale,
When he might have gone in the green pastures
Had he known of the dim, narrow trail.   20

* All of the songs and ballads in this group are from *Cowboy Songs and Other Frontier Ballads* (1925), by John A. Lomax, by whose permission as owner of the copyright they are here reprinted.

I wonder if ever a cowboy
Stood ready for that Judgment Day
And could say to the Boss of the Riders,
"I'm ready, come drive me away."

For they, like the cows that are locoed,
Stampede at the sight of a hand,
Are dragged with a rope to the round up,
Or get marked with some crooked man's brand.

And I'm scared that I'll be a stray yearling,—
A maverick, unbranded on high,—   30
And get cut in the bunch with the "rusties"
When the Boss of the Riders goes by.

For they tell of another big owner
Who's ne'er overstocked, so they say,
But who always makes room for the sinner
Who drifts from the straight, narrow way.

They say he will never forget you,
That he knows every action and look
So, for safety, you'd better get branded,
Have your name in the great Tall Book.   40

THE OLD CHISHOLM TRAIL

[JOHN A. LOMAX]

Come along, boys, and listen to my tale,
I'll tell you of my troubles on the old Chisholm trail.

Coma ti yi youpy, youpy ya,
    youpy ya,
Coma ti yi youpy, youpy ya.

I started up the trail October twenty-
    third,
I started up the trail with the 2-U
    herd.

Oh, a ten dollar hoss and a forty dol-
    lar saddle,
And I'm goin' to punchin' Texas
    cattle.

I woke up one morning on the old
    Chisholm trail,
Rope in my hand and a cow by the
    tail.   10

I'm up in the mornin' afore daylight,
And afore I sleep the moon shines
    bright.

Old Ben Bolt was a blamed good boss,
But he'd go to see the girls on a
    sore-backed hoss.

Old Ben Bolt was a fine old man
And you'd know there was whiskey
    wherever he'd land.

My hoss throwed me off at the creek
    called Mud,
My hoss throwed me off round the
    2-U herd.

Last time I saw him he was going
    cross the level
A-kicking up his heels and a-running
    like the devil.   20

It's cloudy in the West, a-looking like
    rain,
And my damned old slicker's in the
    wagon again.

I crippled my hoss, I don't know how,
Ropin' at the horn of a 2-U cow.

We hit Caldwell and we hit her on
    the fly,
We bedded down the cattle on the hill
    close by.

No chaps, no slicker, and it's pouring
    down rain,
And I swear by god, I'll never night-
    herd again.

Feet in the stirrups and seat in the
    saddle,
I hung and rattled with them long-
    horn cattle.   30

Last night I was on guard and the
    leader broke the ranks,
I hit my horse down the shoulders
    and I spurred him in the flanks.

The wind commenced to blow, and
    the rain began to fall,
Hit looked, by grab, like we was
    goin' to lose 'em all.

I jumped in the saddle and grabbed
    holt the horn,
Best blamed cow-puncher ever was
    born.

I popped my foot in the stirrup and
    gave a little yell,
The tail cattle broke and the leaders
    went to hell.

I don't give a damn if they never do
    stop,
I'll ride as long as an eight-day
    clock.   40

Foot in the stirrup and hand on the
    horn,
Best damned cowboy ever was born.

I herded and I hollered and I done
    very well,
Till the boss said, "Boys, just let 'em
    go to hell."

Stray in the herd and the boss said
    kill it,
So I shot him in the rump with the
    handle of the skillet.

We rounded 'em up and put 'em on
    the cars,
And that was the last of the old Two
    Bars.

Oh it's bacon and beans 'most every
    day,—
I'd as soon be a-eatin' prairie hay. 50

I'm on my best horse and I'm goin'
    at a run,
I'm the quickest shootin' cowboy that
    ever pulled a gun.

I went to the wagon to get my roll,
To come back to Texas, dad-burn my
    soul.

I went to the boss to draw my roll,
He had it figgered out I was nine dol-
    lars in the hole.

I'll sell my outfit just as soon as I
    can,
I won't punch cattle for no damned
    man.

Goin' back to town to draw my
    money,
Goin back home to see my honey. 60

With my knees in the saddle and my
    seat in the sky,
I'll quit punchin' cows in the sweet
    by and by.

    Coma ti yi youpy, youpy ya,
      youpy ya,
    Coma ti yi youpy, youpy ya.

WHOOPEE TI YI YO, GIT ALONG LITTLE DOGIES *

[John A. Lomax]

As I walked out one morning for
    pleasure,
I spied a cow-puncher all riding
    alone;
His hat was throwed back and his
    spurs was a-jingling,
As he approached me a-singin' this
    song.

* Yearling steers.

Whoopee ti yi yo, git along
    little dogies,
It's your misfortune, and none
    of my own,
Whoopee ti yi yo, git along
    little dogies,
For you know Wyoming will
    be your new home.

Early in the spring we round up the
    dogies,
Mark and brand and bob off their
    tails; 1
Round up our horses, load up the
    chuck-wagon,
Then throw the dogies upon the trail

It's whooping and yelling and driving
    the dogies;
Oh, how I wish you would go on;
It's whooping and punching and go on
    little dogies,
For you know Wyoming will be your
    new home.

Some boys goes up the trail for
    pleasure,
But that's where you get it most
    awfully wrong;
For you haven't any idea the trouble
    they give us
While we go driving them all along. 2

When the night comes on and we hold
    them on the bedground,
These little dogies that roll on so
    slow;
Roll up the herd and cut out the
    strays,
And roll the little dogies that never
    rolled before.

Your mother she was raised way down
    in Texas,
Where the jimson weed and sand
    burrs grow;
Now we'll fill you up on prickly pear
    and cholla
Till you are ready for the trail to
    Idaho.

Oh you'll be soup for Uncle Sam's
  Injuns;
'It's beef, heap beef," I hear them
  cry.   30
Git along, git along, git along little
  dogies,
You're going to be beef steers by and
  by.

JESSE JAMES

[John A. Lomax]

Jesse James was a lad that killed
  a-many a man;
He robbed the Danville train.
But that dirty little coward that shot
  Mr. Howard
Has laid poor Jesse in his grave.

Poor Jesse had a wife to mourn for
  his life,
Three children, they were brave,
But that dirty little coward that
  shot Mr. Howard
Has laid poor Jesse in his grave.

It was Robert Ford, that dirty little
  coward,
I wonder how he does feel,   10
For he ate of Jesse's bread and he
  slept in Jesse's bed,
Then laid poor Jesse in his grave.

Jesse was a man, a friend to the poor,
He never would see a man suffer pain;
And with his brother Frank he
  robbed the Chicago bank,
And stopped the Glendale train.

It was his brother Frank that robbed
  the Gallatin bank,
And carried the money from the
  town;
It was in this very place that they
  had a little race,

For they shot Captain Sheets to the
  ground.   20

They went to the crossing not very
  far from there,
And there they did the same;
With the agent on his knees, he de-
  livered up the keys
To the outlaws, Frank and Jesse
  James.

It was on Wednesday night, the
  moon was shining bright,
They robbed the Glendale train;
The people they did say, for many
  miles away,
It was robbed by Frank and Jesse
  James.

It was on Saturday night, Jesse was
  at home
Talking with his family brave,   30
Robert Ford came along like a thief
  in the night
And laid poor Jesse in his grave.

The people held their breath when
  they heard of Jesse's death,
And wondered how he ever came to
  die.
It was one of the gang called little
  Robert Ford,
He shot poor Jesse on the sly.

Jesse went to his rest with his hand
  on his breast;
The devil will be upon his knee.
He was born one day in the county
  of Clay
And came from a solitary race.   40

This song was made by Billy Gashade,
As soon as the news did arrive;
He said there was no man with the
  law in his hand
Who could take Jesse James when
  alive.

II. THE LUMBERJACK

PAUL BUNYAN PROVIDES FOR HIS CREW *

Homer A. Watt

"The year I logged for Paul Bunyan on the pyramid forty," began the old lumberjack, deftly shifting his cud of Battleaxe to his other cheek, "he sure had a monstrous crew. *Three* crews there was, one always goin' to work, one always comin' back, and one always on the job. Of course you all know Paul."

It was more of an assertion than a question, simply a narrative formula, and the men in the ring around the glowing sugarloaf stove did not think it necessary to answer. They gazed at the tale-teller with straight faces and solemn eyes, and only the tenderfoot who had arrived at camp the day before displayed his interest by leaning forward, chin cupped in his hands, eager-eyed. Some eighteen or twenty bronzed men lounged on rude chairs and benches around a stove that glowed red with blazing pine-knots, and perhaps a dozen more stretched their hulks within the shadows of the bunks that lined the long room. Above, on ropes looped from rafter to rafter, hung many soggy pairs of thick socks and heavy wool packs, steaming from the heat and throwing off the pungent smell of sweat to mingle with the other elemental odors of the bunk-house. Without, the wind drove the snow smartly against the panes, but it was warm enough within, and cozy in a

* Printed by permission of the author. Further publication rights reserved.

crude, man's way. The story-teller ejected a mahogany parabola of tobacco juice against the red-hot fluting of the stove and watched it hiss and bubble. Then he shifted his cud, turned his head in the general direction of the tenderfoot, and went on with his yarn.

"Paul needed a big crew to log the pyramid forty. Straight up she went on four sides, and we logged a million foot o' pine off her that winter. The men got short legs on the up-hill side. Look here."

He stretched his two legs before him, and verily the right one *was* an inch or two shorter than the left.

"Rockin'-horse the boys called me after I got away from that camp, and Rockin'-horse I'll always be for loggin' on that mountain. This here bunk-house"—and he stretched his arms generously to right and left—"is nothin' to the one Paul had. An hour it took to walk aroun' it, and the stove in the cook-shanty was so big it et up a whole cord o' wood with one stokin'."

"Really?" asked the tenderfoot, hitching his chair nearer the speaker.

"Really," responded Rocking-horse solemnly. "An' the top o' the stove was so big that when Joe Mufferon the bull-cook, made flap-jacks for the crew, he had the cookees grease it by skatin' on the lid with hams strapped to their feet. Eat? Golly, how those beggars did eat. Flapjacks and pea-soup and loggin' berries. It took two men to wheel away the prune-pits after every meal, and the chipmunks aroun' camp that et the pits got as big as dogs and scrapped with the side-hill dodgers up on the pyramid forty. A nuisance

was at night to have them chipmunks come barkin' aroun' the camp
nd keepin' us all awake.

"I guess only Paul could 'a fed
hat crew, and they had him stumped
sometimes. One time I remember
him standin' outside the bunk-house,
smokin' away and a swamper with a
scoop-shovel keepin' his pipe filled
for him. He was thinkin' up a way 10
to get fresh meat for the men. 'I
have it,' says Paul, an' he slaps his
leg and shakes down two acres o'
pine off the hill. We had been loggin' high up on one side, and the
logs was all piled behind a key-log,
ready to be rolled down to the river.
Them woods was full o' deer, and
they kept runnin' down to the water
to drink, like a flock o' chickens 20
when you throw the corn out. When
Paul sees five hundred or more o'
them deer all lined up nice an' even
on the bank with their muzzles
stuck into the water up to their eyes,
he trips the key-log and down comes
the logs and knocks the deer right
into the river. It was easy enough
to haul 'em out with peavies. Venison? We had enough for a week or 30
more. An' out o' the skins old Ole
Olson, the blacksmith, makes a buckskin harness for Babe."

The tenderfoot hitched his chair
forward another notch.

"Babe?" he asked in puzzled tones.

"What," exclaimed Rocking-horse
reproachfully, "you never heard o'
Babe, Paul's blue ox? He was a
calf when Paul found him the winter 40
o' the blue snow. Blue he was from
his snoot to his tail from sleepin' out
in the snow, and Paul, who always
liked animals, brought him home
and nursed him on a bottle. When

I saw him he was a whale for size
and a glutton for fodder. Between
the tips o' his horns he measured exactly twelve axe-handles and a plug
o' Star tobacco. I've heard say that
a crow got lost flyin' from one horn
to the other, but I don't believe such
stories myself. And strong! It was
Babe that pulled the bunk-houses to
the new camp whenever Paul moved.
Only Ole the blacksmith could shoe
him, and Babe's shoes was so heavy
that whenever Ole carried one, he
sank in the ground up to his knees
with every step. Babe et hay, mostly,
et it so fast that the men couldn't
take the wire off but had to pick it
out o' Babe's teeth afterwards. These
pieces Paul used for shingle-nails on
the bunk-houses, for he never would
waste anything."

"But what about the buckskin
harness?" asked the tenderfoot.

"The harness that Ole made out o'
the deer-skins?" repeated Rocking-
horse. "Oh, yes. It was gettin' toward spring when Paul killed all
them deer, and the river was open.
It rained, too, sometimes, and the
tote-roads was gettin' spongy. The
logs was runnin' low in the cook-
shanty, and Joe Mufferon, the bull-
cook, puts the new buckskin harness
on Babe and starts down the tote-
road to get a fire log, aimin' to get
back afore noon. But long before
he gets back it begins to drizzle, and
pretty soon it's rainin' steady. You
know how buckskin stretches when
it gets wet? Well, when Joe drives
Babe into camp and turns around to
see how wet his log got, he doesn't
see any log but just the buckskin tugs
stretchin' no end of a way down the
tote-road and into the pines. Too

late to go back for the log then, so
Joe ties Babe up and goes in to his
grub. And while he's in the cook-
shanty, the sun comes out real
strong, and dries the buckskin, and
hauls that there log right into camp.

"A third o' the crew, as I was
sayin', was always on the job, and
Paul had his own way o' gettin'
their grub to 'em. Pea-soup was 10
what he gave 'em while they was
swampin' and cuttin' and haulin', but
he couldn't send it out in kettles so
he sends it on ropes."

"Ropes?" asked the tenderfoot,
opening his eyes inquiringly.

"Ropes," responded Rocking-horse.
"Maybe y've seen wimmin make
these here candles by dippin' wicks
into hot wax and lettin' it harden? 20
There's where Paul gets his idea for
his soup strings. He takes lengths o'
tow-rope, dips 'em into the pea-soup,
an' freezes 'em stiff. Just like sticks
they are when he's done with 'em,
and he can tie 'em up in bundles and
send 'em down to the men. Once
after Babe had broke his halter and
et up a thousand feet o' tow-rope,
Paul had to freeze the pea-soup on 30
pine splinters, but what he used
mostly was rope.

"Paul always did take care o' his
men fine. The spring after we'd
logged off the pyramid forty, Joe
Mufferon told Paul that he was runnin' out o' peas and would he please
to send to town for a load. Paul
always made out his own orders. He
couldn't write a line and used to say 40
that he went through school by
climbin' through one window and out
o' the other, but he could draw good.
Only one mistake I remember him
makin'. The men used to sharpen

their axes by rollin' round ston
down the side o' the pyramid for
and grindin' the edges by runni
alongside. That was before Paul i
vented the double-bitted axe ar
showed the men how to let the wi
sharpen the up-blade on the bac
stroke. Well, anyway, when the m
gets tired o' runnin' after the rolli
stones, Paul sends to town for a hu
dred grind-stones by drawin' pitche
on a piece o' bark. The teamst
brings back a hundred round chees
'O,' says Paul, 'I forgot to put t
holes in my grind-stones.' "

"But you were going to tell abo
Paul's order of peas," protested t
tenderfoot.

"So I was," replied Rocking-hors
"so I was. A whole load o' peas t
teamster was bringin' back to can
with a wagon and two span o' oxe
and Paul and Joe Mufferon w
standin' in front o' the bunk-hou
awaitin' for 'em. A piece or two b
yond the bottom o' the pyram
forty was a lake which outletted in
a bit o' a stream that run down
where the crew was gettin' the lo
ready for the drive, for it was ne
spring and the snow was meltin' a
runny. The lake had been froz
solid enough in the winter, but it w
gettin' rotten and spongy, and Pa
and Joe was wonderin' if it was sa
when all o' a sudden they hears
cracklin' and a yellin' and sees t
pea wagon and the four oxen breaki
through the ice and bein' swallow
up in the lake. The driver had be
watchin' a pinnacle grouse wheeli
on his one wing 'round and 'round t
top o' the pyramid forty and had
been payin' no sort o' attention
where he was goin' until he fin

himself breakin' through. He gets out all right by steppin' on the horns o' the oxen and off them onto a log or two, but the beasts was drowned and the peas was gone. A dead loss, you'd think, but you don't know Paul. He was the most inventive man that ever swung an axe. 'Get busy, boys,' he sings out to those aroun' camp. Then he takes us down to the outlet o' the lake, and tells us to make a log dam across the stream. We done it. Then Paul fires the slashin's aroun' the lake and *cooks* the peas right in the water. When the whole mess

gets to sizzlin' and bubblin' good, Paul gives the word, and we opens up the dam with a shot o' dynamite, and down to the men who was workin' a mile below Paul sluices all that hot pea-soup—with ox-tail flavor."

The tenderfoot gave a start and an exclamation. From one of the bunks came a stentorian snore. Rocking-horse took a final salivary shot at the glowing flutes of the sugarloaf, rose slowly, and stretched himself.

"It is about time," said Rocking-horse to nobody in particular, "to turn in."

III. THE MOUNTAINEER

THE WRECK ON THE C. & O.*

[JOHN HARRINGTON COX]

Along came the old F.F.V., the fast-
    est on the line,
Running over the C. & O. Road,
    twenty minutes behind time;
Running into Sewell, she was quar-
    tered on the line,
And there received strict orders:
    Hinton, away behind time.

Chorus

Many a man's been murdered by the
    railroad,
By the railroad, by the railroad;
Many a man's been murdered by the
    railroad,
And sleeping in his lonesome grave.

When she got to Hinton, that engi-
    neer was there,
George Allen was his name, with
    bright and golden hair;   10

His fireman, Jack Dickinson, was
    standing by his side,
Waiting for strict orders, and in his
    cab did ride.

George's mother came to the train,
    with a bucket on her arm.
Says she to him, "My darling son, be
    careful how you run;
For many a man has lost his life in
    trying to make lost time,
And if you run your engine right,
    you'll get there yet on time."

"Mother, I know your advice is good;
    to the letter I'll take heed,
I know my engine is all right, and
    sure that she will steam;
But over this road I mean to fly with
    a speed unknown to all,
And when I blow for the Stock Yard
    Gates, they'll surely hear my
    call."   20

Then he said to his fireman, "Jack, a
    rock ahead I see;
I know that death is waiting there to
    grab both you and me;
And from the cab you must fly, your
    darling life to save,

* Reprinted from *Folk-Songs of the South* (1925), edited by John Harrington Cox, and ere used by permission of the editor and the Harvard University Press, the publishers.

For I want you to be an engineer
   when I'm sleeping in my grave."

"No, no!" said Jack, "I will not go,
   I want to die with you!"
"No, no!" said George, "I'll die, I'll
   die for you and me."
And from the cab poor Jack did fly,
   the river it was high,
And as he kissed his hand to George,
   old No. 4 flew by.

Down the road she darted; against
   the rock she crashed;
Upside down his engine turned, upon
   his breast she smashed;   30
His head upon the firebox door, the
   rolling scenes rolled o'er:
"I'm glad I was born an engineer and
   died on No. 4."

George's mother came to him: "My
   son, what have you done?"
"Too late, too late! the dome is almost done.
But if I had a local train, the truth
   to you I'll tell,
I'd pull her into Clifton Forge, or bid
   you all farewell."

The doctor said to George, "My
   darling son, lie still;
Your life may yet be saved, if it's
   God's own blessed will."
"No, no!" said George, "I want to
   die so free;
I want to die with my engine, 143."   40

THE ROWAN COUNTY CREW *

[JOHN HARRINGTON COX]

Come all of you young people,
   fathers, mothers, too,
I'll relate to you the history of the
   Rowan County crew,

* Printed by permission of the collector,
Professor John Harrington Cox. Further publication rights reserved.

Concerning bloody Rowan and many
   a dreadful deed,
I pray you pay attention, come, listen how it reads.

It was a day in August, all on election
   day,
John Martin was shot and wounded
   some say by John Day;
But Martin wouldn't believe it, he
   wouldn't have it so,
He said it was Floyd Tolliver that
   struck the fatal blow.

Martin he recovered, some months
   had come and passed,
It was in the town of Morehead
   these two men met at last;   10
Martin and a friend or two about the
   streets did walk,
They seemed to be uneasy, and no
   one wished to talk.

He walked into Judge Carer's grocery, he walked up to the bar,
But little did he think, dear friends
   it was his fatal hour.
Martin saw the situation, he rushed
   in at the door,
A few words passed between them
   concerning the row before.

The people all got excited, they began
   to leave the room,
When a ball from Martin's pistol laid
   Tolliver in his tomb.
His friends all gathered round him,
   his wife to weep and wail,
And Martin was soon arrested and
   lodged in Rowan jail.   2

In the jail in Rowan County, there to
   remain a while,
In the hands of law and justice, to
   bravely stand his trial;
Some people talked of lynching him,
   at present it did fail,
And Martin's friends removed him to
   the Winchester jail.

Some persons forged an order, their
names I do not know,
The terms were soon agreed upon,
for Martin they did go.
Martin seemed to be uneasy, he
seemed to be in dread,
"They've set up a plan to kill me,"
to the jailer Martin said.

They put the handcuffs on him, his
heart was in distress,
They took him to the station, aboard
the night express,   30
The night express she rambled on, all
at her usual speed,
They were only two in number to
commit the dreadful deed.

When the train arrived at Farmers,
they had no time to lose,
They stepped up to the engineer and
told him not to move;
They stepped up to the prisoner, with
pistols in their hands,
To death he soon was sinking, he died
in iron bands.

Martin was in the smoking car, accompanied by his wife,
They did not wish her present, when
they took her husband's life;
When the dreadful deed was committed, she was in another car,
She said, "O Lord, they've killed
him"! when she heard the pistol
fire.   40

The death of these two men caused
great trouble in our land,
Caused men to leave their wives and
families and take the parting
hand;
Relations still at war, oh, will it never
cease,
I pray to God that I may see our
land once more in peace.

They shot and killed Sol Bradley, a
poor and innocent man,
They leave his wife and children to
do the best they can;

They wounded young Ed Sizemore,
although his life was saved,
He seems to shun the grog-shop, since
he stood so near the grave.

They killed the deputy sheriff, Bum-
gardner was his name,
They shot him from the bushes, they
took deliberate aim;   50
The death of this man was dreadful,
oh, may it ne'er be forgot,
His body was pierced and torn by
thirty-three buckshot.

Come all of you young gentlemen,
take warning from a friend,
Your pistols will get you into trouble,
on this you may depend,
At the bottom of the whiskey glass a
lurking devil dwells,
It ruins the minds of those that drink
it and sends their souls to hell.

IV. THE NEGRO

ROOM IN THERE

[T. W. HIGGINSON]

"O, my mudder is gone! my mudder
is gone!
My mudder is gone into heaven, my
Lord!
  I can't stay behind!
Dere's room in dar, room in dar,
Room in dar, in de heaven, my Lord!
  I can't stay behind,
Can't stay behind, my dear,
  I can't stay behind!

"O, my fader is gone!" etc.

"O, de angels are gone!" etc.   10

"O, I'se been on de road! I'se been
on de road!
I'se been on de road into heaven, my
Lord!
  I can't stay behind!

O, room in dar, room in dar,
Room in dar, in de heaven, my Lord!
I can't stay behind!"

JOHN HENRY *

[JOHN HARRINGTON COX]

When John Henry was a little babe,
  A-holding to his mama's hand,
Says, "If I live till I'm twenty-one,
  I'm going to make a steel-driving
    man, my babe,
  I'm going to make a steel-driving
    man."

When John Henry was a little boy,
  A-sitting on his father's knee,
Says, "The Big Bend Tunnel on the
    C. & O. Road
  Is going to be the death of me, my
    babe," etc.

John he made a steel-driving man, 10
  They took him to the tunnel to
    drive;
He drove so hard he broke his heart,
  He laid down his hammer and he
    died, my babe, etc.

O now John Hardy is a steel-driving
    man,
  He belongs to the steel-driving
    crew,
And every time the hammer comes
    down,
  You can see that steel walking
    through, etc.

The steam drill standing on the right-
    hand side,
  John Henry standing on the left;
He says, "I'll beat that steam drill
    down, 20

* Reprinted from *Folk-Songs of the South*
(1925), edited by John Harrington Cox, and
here used by permission of the editor and
the Harvard University Press, the publishers.

Or I'll die with my hammer in m[y]
    breast," etc.

He placed his drill on the top of th[e]
    rock,
  The steam drill standing close [a]
    hand;
He beat it down one inch and a ha[lf]
  And laid down his hammer like [a]
    man, etc.

Johnny looked up to his boss-man an[d]
    said,
  "O boss-man, how can it be?
For the rock is so hard and the ste[el]
    is so tough
  I can feel my muscles giving way.

Johnny looked down to his turne[r]
    and said,
  "O turner, who can it be?
The rock is so hard and the steel
    so tough
  That everybody's turning after me

They took poor Johnny to the ste[el]
    hillside,
  He looked to his heavens above;
He says, "Take my hammer and wra[p]
    it in gold
  And give it to the girl I love."

They took his hammer and wrapped [it]
    in gold
  And gave it to Julia Ann;
And the last word John Hardy sa[id]
    to her
  Was, "Julia, do the best you can[."]

"If I die a railroad man,
  Go bury me under the tie,
So I can hear old Number Four,
  As she goes rolling by.

"If I die a railroad man,
  Go bury me under the sand,
With a pick and shovel at my he[ad]
    and feet,
  And a nine-pound hammer in m[y]
    hand."

PROMISES OF FREEDOM *

[Thomas W. Talley]

My ole Mistiss promise me,
W'en she died, she'd set me free.
She lived so long dat 'er head got bal',
An' she give out'n de notion a dyin'
    at all.

My ole Mistiss say to me:
"Sambo, I'se gwine ter set you free."
But w'en dat head git slick an' bal',
De Lawd couldn' a' killed 'er wid a
    big green maul.

My ole Mistiss never die,
Wid 'er nose all hooked an' skin all
    dry.   10
But my ole Miss, she's somehow gone,
An' she lef' "Uncle Sambo" a-hillin'
    up co'n.

Ole Mosser lakwise promise me,
W'en he died, he'd set me free.
But ole Mosser go an' make his Will
Fer to leave me a-plowin' ole Beck
    still.

Yes, my ole Mosser promise me;
But "his papers" didn' leave me free.
A dose of pizen he'ped 'im along.
May de Devil preach 'is fūner'l
    song.   20

HALF WAY DOINGS *

[Thomas W. Talley]

My dear Brudders an' Sisters,
As I comes here to-day,
I hain't gwineter take no scripture
    verse
Fer what I'se gwineter say.

My words I'se gwineter cut off short
An' I 'spects to use dis tex':
"Dis half way doin's hain't no 'count
Fer dis worl' nor de nex'."

Dis half way doin's, Brudderin,
Won't never do, I say.   10
Go to yō' wuk, an' git it done,
An' den's de time to play.

Fer w'en a Nigger gits lazy,
An' stops to take short naps,
De weeds an' grass is shore to grow
An' smudder out his craps.

Dis worl' dat we's a livin' in
Is sumpen lak a cotton row:
Whar each an' ev'ry one o' us
Is got his row to hoe.   20

SHE HUGGED ME AND KISSED ME *

[Thomas W. Talley]

I see'd her in de Springtime,
I see'd her in de Fall,
I see'd her in de Cotton patch,
A cameing from de Ball.

She hug me, an' she kiss me,
She wrung my han' an' cried.
She said I wus de sweetes' thing
Dat ever lived or died.

She hug me an' she kiss me.
Oh Heaben! De touch o' her han'!   10
She said I wus de puttiest thing
In de shape o' mortal man.

I told her dat I love her,
Dat my love wus bed-cord strong;
Den I axed her w'en she'd have me,
An' she jes say "Go long!"

* Reprinted from *Negro Folk Rhymes*
(1922), by Thomas W. Talley, and here used
by permission of the Macmillan Company,
publishers.

* Reprinted from *Negro Folk Rhymes*
(1922), by Thomas W. Talley, and here used
by permission of the Macmillan Company,
publishers.

LOCAL COLOR AND REALISM: THE FAR WEST

I. BRET HARTE
(1836–1902)

THE WORK ON RED MOUNTAIN *

By Bret

In Four Parts

PART I.—THE POCKET

Just where the Sierra Nevada begins to subside in gentler undulations, and the rivers grow more rapid and yellow, on the side of a great red Mountain stands "Smith's Pocket." Seen from the red road at sunset—in the red light and the red dust, its white houses look like the outcroppings of quartz on the mountain side. There are two ways to get to Smith's Pocket. One is by the stage road which loses itself half a dozen times in the tortuous descent, turns up unexpectedly in out of the way places and vanishes altogether within a hundred yards of the town. The other is that odd fancy which springs up in the mind of the impatient traveler, and causes him to wish for a balloon to waft him across from mountain to mountain. Near the end of the awful declivity, a long flume stretches across the chasm. Viewed from above, its narrow body and disproportionate legs

give it the appearance of a gigant[ic] centipede. The advent of a strang[er] at Smith's Pocket is usually attend[ed] with a peculiar circumstance. It [is] probably owing to the sudden twist [of] the road before entering town. D[is]mounting from the vehicle at t[he] stage office, the imbecile traveler i[n]variably walks straight out of tow[n] under the impression that it lies [in] quite another direction. It is relate[d] that one of the tunnel men, two mil[es] from town, met a self-reliant passe[n]ger with a carpet-bag, umbrella, Ha[r]per's Magazine and other evidences [of] "civilization and refinement," ploddi[ng] along over the road he had just ri[d]den, vainly endeavoring to find t[he] settlement of Smith's Pocket.

The settlement of Smith's Pock[et] owed its origin to the finding of [a] pocket on its site, by a veritab[le] Smith. Five thousand dollars we[re] taken out of it in one half hour b[y] Smith. Three thousand dollàrs we[re] expended by Smith and others in erec[t]ing a flume, and in tunneling. A[nd] then Smith's Pocket was found to b[e] only a pocket, and subject like oth[er] pockets to depletion. Although Smit[h] pierced the bowels of the earth, th[is] five thousand dollars was the first a[nd] last return of his labor. Then Smit[h] went into quartz mining. Then in[to] quartz milling. Then into hydrauli[cs] and ditching; and then by easy d[e]grees into saloon keeping. Presentl[y] it was whispered that Smith drank

---

* The *Golden Era* copy has here been reproduced verbatim; thus even gross inconsistencies in spelling and punctuation are retained.

good deal more liquor than he sold; then it was known that he was an habitual drunkard, and then people began to think, as they always do, that he had never been anything else. But the settlement of Smith's Pocket was, happily, not dependent on Smith, for other parties projected tunnels and found pockets. So Smith's Pocket became a settlement with its two fancy stores, its two hotels, its one express office, its two fine cottages, and its two first families. Occasionally its one long straggling street was humiliated and crushed of a sunny Sabbath morning, by the sudden assumption of the latest San Francisco fashions, imported per express, exclusively to the first families; making outraged nature in the ragged outlines of her torn gulches and furrowed surface look still more homely and unlovely, and putting personal insult on the rest of the inhabitants. Then there was a Methodist church, and a little beyond the town on the mountain side, a grave-yard; and then, a little school-house.

"The Master,"—as he was known to his little flock—sat alone one night in the school-house with some open copy-books before him, carefully making those bold and full characters inculcating such moral sentiments as, "Knowledge is Power" or "Riches are Deceitful;" and had got as far as "Love your Par—," and was elegantly recurving the tail of the P when he heard a gentle tapping. The woodpeckers had been busy about the roof during the day and the noise did not disturb his work. But the opening of the door, and the tapping continuing from the inside, made him turn around. He was startled slightly at the figure of a young girl—dirty, and shabbily clad. Still, the great blackeyes, the coarse uncombed, lusterless black hair falling over a sunburned face; the red arms and feet streaked with the redder soil, were all familiar to him. It was Melissa Smith—Smith's motherless child.

What can she want here, thought the master. Everybody knew "M'liss," as she was called, throughout the length and height of Red Mountain. Everybody knew her to be an incorrigible girl. Her coarse and rude manners; her mad freaks and hoyden pranks; her fierce ungovernable and untameable disposition are all proverbial. She wrangled and fought the school-boys with wickeder speech and more spiteful arm. She wandered away miles from town, and had often been met, shoeless, stockingless and bareheaded on the mountain road. She followed the trails with woodman's craft. She was known to all the miner's camps along the stream and subsisted during her voluntary pilgrimages by their freely offered alms. M'liss was not a beggar nor gipsy. She was ready to dance Juba, climb trees, or jump ditches for their amusement. She had climbed the liberty pole, and had walked the dizzy height of the flume on a dark night at a foolish banter from some drunken brute. She was untameable as she was fearless. She had been taken by the Rev. McSnagley, the Methodist parson, and placed in the hotel as servant, and introduced to the reverend gentleman's scholars at Sunday school. But she threw plates at the landlord, and shocked the reverend gentleman's piety to such an extent that with a decent regard for the two pink and white faced children of the first families she was ignominiously expelled. Such were the antecedents, and such the character of M'liss as she stood before the Master. They spake in her poor dress and dirty and bleeding feet, and asked his pity. They looked out of her big black and fearless eyes, and flung that pity in his face.

"I came here to-night"—she said rapidly and boldly, keeping her hard glance on his, "because I knew you was alone. I couldn't come here when them gals was here. I hate 'em and they hate me. You keep school,— don't you? I want to go to school!"

If with her ragged dress, uncombed hair and dirty face, she had cried and whined, the master would have pitied her but could hardly have stifled his disgust. But in her strangely contrasted imperiousness, there was something that awakened the respect which all original natures pay unconsciously to one another in any grade. She went on still more rapidly, her hand on the door latch and her eyes still fixed on the master's.

"Do you know me? My name's M'liss. M'liss Smith's my name. That's what it is. My father's old drunken Smith. There now! That's what I am. M'liss Smith, and I'm coming to school."

"Well?" said the master.

Accustomed to be thwarted and opposed, often wantonly and cruelly for no other purpose than to excite her painfully impulsive nature, the Master's phlegm evidently took her by surprise. She commenced to twist her hair between her fingers and the rigid white line of upper lip drawn tightly over the little wicked white teeth, relaxed and quivered slightly.—Then her eyes dropped, and something like a blush struggled up to her cheek and tried to assert itself through the splashes of redder soil and the sunburn of years. Suddenly she threw herself forward, calling on God to strike her dead, and fell quite weak and helpless, with her face on the Master's desk, crying and sobbing as if her heart would break.

The Master lifted her quietly and waited for the paroxysm to pass. When with face still averted, she was saying, between her sobs, that she wished to do better and be like other girls, it came to him to ask her why she had left the Sabbath school?

Why had she left the Sunday school? Why? Oh! What did he (McSnagly) want to tell her she was wicked for. What did he tell her that God hated her for. If God hated her what did she want to go to Sabbath school for. *She* didn't want to be "beholden" to anybody who hated her

Had she told McSnagly this?

Yes, she had!

The Master turned away for a moment with an expression very probably the reverse of the dignified McSnagly's on hearing the same announcement.

But her father?

Her father? What father? Whose father?—What had he ever done for her? Why did the girls hate her? Come now! What made the folks say "Old Bummer Smith's M'liss," when she passed. Yes; oh, yes! She wished he was dead—she was dead—everybody was dead!—And her sobs broke forth anew.

The Master then leaning over her, told her as well as he could, what you or I might have said, after hearing

such unnatural sentiments from childish lips—only bearing in mind, better than you or I, the soiled and
ragged dress, the poor bleeding feet,
the flashing but truthful eye, and the
darkening shadow of the drunken
father.—Then, raising her to her feet
once more, he wrapped his shawl about
her, and bidding her come early in
the morning, he walked a few steps
down the road. There he bade her
"good-night." The moon shone
brightly on the narrow path before
them. He stood still and watched the
bent little figure as it staggered down
the road—not, oh, not, with the buoy-
ant feet of childhood; and waited
until it had passed the little graveyard
and the Red Mountain hid it from
view. Then he went back to his
work. But the lines of the copy books
only faded into long parallels of weary,
never-ending road, down which bending childish figures seemed to pass,
crying and sobbing passionately to the
night. Then the little school-house
seeming lonelier than before, he shut
the door and went home.

The next morning M'liss came to
school. Her face had been washed,
and her coarse, black hair bore evidence of recent struggles with a comb,
in which the latter had evidently
been sacrificed. The old defiant look
shone occasionally in her eyes, but her
manner was tamer and more subdued.
Then commenced a series of little
trials and self-sacrifices, both on the
part of Master and pupil, which perhaps strengthened the bond of sympathy between them. Although obedient under the Master's eye, at times
during recess, if thwarted or stung
by a fancied slight, M'liss would rage
in ungovernable fury, and many a

palpitating lubberly boy would seek
the Master with torn jacket and
scratched face, and complaints of the
awful M'liss. There was a serious
division among the townspeople on the
subject; some threatening to withdraw their children from such evil
companionship, and others as warmly
upholding the course of the Master
in his work of reclamation. Still with
a steady persistence, that even astonished him, the Master drew M'liss
gradually out of the shadow of her
past life, and set her feet again upon
the narrow path, as on the moonlit
night of their first meeting. Remembering the dreadful experience of the
evangelical McSnagly, he carefully
avoided that rock of ages on which
her young faith had been shipwrecked.
Sometimes when the old light was in
her eyes, he spoke to her soothingly,
and tried to tell her of that faith
which is symbolized by suffering—
haply made clearer to his own pur-
blind vision by occasional chastening
—of those few words which had lifted
such as she above the level of the
older, and wise and more prudent—and
so, holding her hand in his, he groped
his way, himself a child, toward that
mysterious world of Light and Life
which is so near and yet so distant.
—Strangely enough, some few of the
plainer people had made up a little
sum by which the ragged M'liss was
enabled to assume the garments of
respect and civilization, and many a
rough shake of the hand, and words of
homely commendation, from a red
shirted and burly figure, sent a glow to
the cheek of the young Master.

Three months had passed from the
time of their first meeting, and the
Master was sitting late one evening

over the moral and sententious copies, when there came a tap at the door, and again M'liss stood before him. She was neatly clad and clean faced; and there was nothing, perhaps, but the twisting long black hair, and the big, bright, black eyes to remind him of his former apparition. "Are you busy?" she asked—"can you come with me?"—and on his signifying his readiness, she held out her hand, and in her old willful way said—"come then quick."

They passed out of the door together and into the dark road. As they entered the town, the Master asked her whither she was going. She replied "to see father."

It was the first time he had heard her call him by that filial title, or indeed anything more than "Old Smith" or the "Old Man." It was the first time in three months that she had spoken of him at all, and the Master knew she had kept resolutely aloof from him since her great change. Satisfied from her manner that it was fruitless to question her purpose, he passively followed. In out of the way places, low groggeries, restaurants and saloons; in gambling hells and dance houses, the Master preceded by M'liss came and went. In the reeking smoke and blasphemous outcries of low dens, the child, holding the Master's hand, stood and anxiously gazed, seemingly unconscious of all in the one absorbing nature of her pursuit. Some of the revelers recognizing M'liss called to the child, to sing and dance for them, and would have forced liquor upon her but for the interference of the Master. Others recognizing him mutely made way for them to pass. So an hour slipped by. Then the child

whispered in his ear that there was a cabin on the other side of the creek crossed by the long flume, where she thought he still might be. Thither they crossed—a toilsome half-hours' walk—but in vain. They were returning by the ditch at the abutment of the flume gazing at the lights of the town on the opposite bank, when, suddenly, sharply, a quick report rang out on the clear night air. The echoes caught it, and carried it round and round Red Mountain and set the dogs to barking all along the streams. Lights seemed to dance and move quickly on the outskirts of the town for a few moments, the stream rippled quite audibly beside them, a few stones loosened themselves from the hill-side and splashed into the stream, a heavy wind seemed to surge the branches of the funereal pines, and then the silence seemed to fall thicker, heavier and deadlier. The Master turned towards M'liss with an unconscious gesture of protection, but the child had gone. Oppressed by a strange fear, he ran quickly down the trail to the river's bed and jumping from boulder to boulder, reached the base of Red Mountain, and the outskirts of the village. Midway of the crossing he looked up and held his breath in awe. For high above him on the narrow flume, he saw the fluttering little figure of his late companion, crossing swiftly in the darkness.

He climbed the bank and guided by a few lights moving about a central point on the mountain, soon found himself breathless, among a crowd of awe-stricken and sorrowful men. Out from among them the child appeared and taking the Master's hand, led him silently before what seemed a ragged hole in the mountain. Her face was quite white, but her excited manner gone and her look that of one to whom some long expected event had at last happened,—an expression that to the Master in his bewilderment, seemed almost like relief. The walls of the cavern were partly propped by decaying timbers. The child pointed to what appeared to be some ragged, cast-off clothes left in the hole by the late occupant. The Master approached nearer with his flaming dip and bent over them. It was Smith, already cold, with a pistol in his hand and a bullet in his heart, lying beside his empty pocket.

PART II.—THE LEAD

The opinion which McSnagly expressed in reference to a "change of heart" supposed to be experienced by M'liss, was more forcibly described in the gulches and tunnels. It was thought there that M'liss had "struck a good lead." So when there was a new grave added to the little enclosure, and, at the expense of the Master, a little board and inscription put above it, the *Red Mountain Banner* came out quite handsomely, and did the fair thing to the memory of one of "our oldest Pioneers" alluding gracefully to that "bane of noble intellects" and otherwise genteely shelving our dear brother with the past. "He leaves an only child to mourn his loss," says the *Banner*, "who is now an exemplary scholar, thanks to the efforts of the Rev. McSnagly." The Rev. McSnagly, in fact made a strong point of M'liss's conversion, and indirectly attributing to the unfortunate child the suicide of her father, made affecting allusions in Sunday school to the beneficial effects of the "silent tomb" and in this cheerful contemplation—drove most of the children into speechless horror, and caused the pink and white scions of the first families to howl dismally and refuse to be comforted.

The long dry summer came. As each fierce day burned itself out in little whiffs of pearl-grey smoke on the mountain summits, and the upspringing breeze scattered its red embers over the landscape, the green wave which in early spring upheaved above Smith's grave grew sere and dry and hard. In those days the Master strolling in the little church-yard of a Sabbath afternoon was sometimes surprised to find a few wild flowers plucked from the damp pine forests scattered there, and oftener rude wreaths hung upon the little pine cross. Most of these wreaths were formed of a sweet-scented grass—which the children loved to keep in their desks —entwined with the pompions plumes of the buck-eye and syringa, the wood anemone, and here and there the Master noticed the dark blue cowl of the Monk's hood—or deadly aconite. There was something in the odd association of this noxious plant with these memorials which occasioned a painful sensation to the Master deeper than his aesthetic sense. One day, during a long walk, in crossing a wooded ridge he came upon M'liss in the heart of the forest, perched upon a prostrate pine, on a fantastic throne formed by the hanging plumes of lifeless branches, her lap full of grasses and pine burrs, and crooning to herself one of the negro melodies of her younger life. Recognizing him at a distance, she made room for him on her elevated throne, and with a grave assumption of hospitality and patronage, that would have been ridiculous had it not been so terribly earnest, she fed him with pine nuts and crab-apples. The master took that opportunity to point out to her the noxious and deadly qualities of the Monk's-hood, whose dark blossoms he saw in her lap, and extorted from her a promise not to meddle with it as long as she remained his pupil. This done —as the Master had tested her integrity before—he rested satisfied and the strange feeling which had overcome him on seeing them, died away.

Of the homes that were offered M'liss when her conversion became known, the Master preferred that of Mrs. Morpher, a womanly and kind-hearted specimen of South-western efflorescence, known in her maidenhood as the "Per-rairie Rose." Being one of those who contend resolutely against their own natures, Mrs. M. by a long series of self sacrifices and struggles, had at last subjugated her naturally careless disposition to principles of "order" which she considered in common with Mr. Pope, as "Heaven's first law." But she could not entirely govern the orbits of her satellites, however regular her own movements, and even her own "Jeemes" sometimes collided with her. Again her old nature asserted itself in her children. Lycurgus dipped in the cupboard "between meals," and Aristides came home from school without shoes, leaving those important articles on the threshold, for the delight of a barefooted walk down the ditches. Octavia and Cassandra were "keerless" of their clothes. So

with but one exception, however much the "Prairie Rose" might have trimmed and pruned and trained her own matured luxuriance, the little shoots came up defiantly wild and straggling. That one exception was Clytemnestra Morpher aged 15. She was the realization of her mother's immaculate conception—neat, orderly and dull.

It was an amiable weakness of Mrs. Morpher to imagine that "Clytie" was a consolation, and model for M'liss. Following this fallacy, Mrs. M. threw Clytie at the head of M'liss when she was "bad" and set her up before the child for adoration in her penitential moments. It was not surprising to the Master to hear therefore that "Clytie" was coming to school, obviously as a favor to the Master and an example for M'liss and others. For "Clytie" was quite a young lady. Inheriting her mother's physical peculiarities, and in obedience to the climatic laws of the Red Mountain region she was an early bloomer. The youth of Smith's Pocket to whom this kind of flower was rare, sighed for her in April and languished in May. Enamored swains haunted the schoolhouse at the hour of dismissal. A few were jealous of the Master.

Perhaps it was this circumstance which opened the Master's eyes to another. He could not help noticing that "Clytie" was romantic. That in school she required a great deal of attention. That her pens were uniformly bad and wanted "fixing." That she usually accompanied the request with a look out of her large blue eyes—which the Master knew conveyed more expression than her whole life time was capable of. That she sometimes allowed the curves of a round plump white arm to rest on his, when he was writing her copies; that she always blushed and flung back her blonde curls when she did so. Had not the Master, who was a young man, been severely educated in the school in which "Clytie" was only taking her first lesson, he might have succumbed to the flexible curves and the factitious glance. But with that modicum of self-satisfaction and conceit which enters into most young men's composition, one evening, when Clytie returned to the school-house after something she had forgotten, and found suddenly that it was quite dark, the Master walked home with the plump little thing hanging on his arm, endeavoring to make himself particularly agreeable, partly from the fact, I imagine, that his conduct was adding gall and bitterness to the already overcharged hearts of Clytemnestra's admirers.

The morning after this affecting episode M'liss did not come to school. Noon came, but not M'liss. Questioning Clytie on the subject it appeared that they had left the school together but the willful M'liss had taken another road. The afternoon brought no M'liss. In the evening he called on Mrs. Morpher, whose motherly heart was really alarmed. John had been all day in search of her but without discovering a trace that might lead to her discovery. Mrs. Morpher entertained a vivid impression that the child would yet be found drowned in a ditch—or what was almost as terrible—muddied and soiled beyond the redemption of soap and water. Sick at heart the Master returned to the little school-house. Resolving on pursuing the search the next morning, he lit his lamp and seating himself by his desk was pleasantly surprised at finding a three-cornered note lying on his table addressed to himself in M'liss's well known, strong and nervous hand. To prevent sacrilegious trifling, it had been sealed with six large wafers, placed like brass rivets on its lips. Opening it almost tenderly the Master read as follows:

HONORED SIR:—When you read this I am run away. Never to come back. *Never,* NEVER, NEVER. Tell Mrs. Morpher not to look for me; say I am dead and buried in the graveyard with father. Give my beads to Mary Jennings, and my America's Pride, (a highly colored lithograph from a tobacco case) to Sally Flanders. Give all my pine nuts, for I don't want them, to the rest of the little girls but DON'T give anything to Clytie Morpher. Don't you dare to. Fairwell. She is not mad who kneels to thee. Good by. Farewell.
                          Yours Respectfully,
                              MELISSA SMITH.

The Master sat pondering on this strange epistle till the moon lifted its bright face above the distant hills, and illuminated the trail that led to the school-house, beaten quite hard with the coming and going of little feet. Then more satisfied in mind, he tore the missive into fragments and scattered it along the road.

The Master was up in the chill of the morning and long before the sun had risen he had reached the wooded ridge spoken of. Making his way through the palm-like fern and the thick underbrush, starting the hare from its form and awakening the chattering jay, he proceeded directly toward the prostrate pine and its tasselated drooping branches. As he neared it, what might have been some frightened animal started through the crackling branches. It ran up the tossed roots of the fallen monarch and sheltered itself in some friendly foliage. The Master reaching the old seat, found the nest still warm; looking up in the intertwining branches he met the black eyes of the errant M'liss. They stood gazing at each other. She was the first to speak.

"What do you want?" she asked curtly.

"I want some pine nuts," said the Master humbly.

"Shan't have them. Go away. Why don't you get 'em of Clytemneresterer? (In her excessive dignity she thought it necessary to give the classical young woman's title in full.) Oh! you wicked thing!"

"I am hungry, Lissy. Have had no breakfast. I am famishing," and the young man in a state of excessive exhaustion lapsed against the tree.

Melissa's heart was touched. In the bitter days of her gipsy life she had known the sensation he so artfully simulated. Overcome by his heartbroken tone, but not entirely divested of suspicion, she said.

"Dig under the tree near the roots, and you'll find lots, but mind you don't tell," for M'liss had *her* hoards as well as the rats and squirrels.

But the Master of course could not find it: the effects of hunger blinding his senses. M'liss grew uneasy. At length she peered at him through the leaves and said.

"If I come down and give you some, you'll promise you won't touch me?"

The Master promised.

"Hope you'll die if you do?"

The Master accepted instant dissolution as a forfeit. M'liss slid down the tree. For a few moments nothing transpired but the munching of the pine nuts. "Do you feel better?" she asked with some solicitude. The Master confessed to a recuperated feeling. and then gravely thanking her, proceeded to retrace his steps. As he expected, he had not gone far before she called him. He turned. She was standing there quite white, with tears in her widely opened orbs. The Master felt that the right moment had come. Going up to her he took both her hands and looking in her tearful eyes, said gravely: "Lissy, do you remember the first evening you came to see me?"

Lissy remembered.

"You asked me if you might come to school, for you wanted to learn something and be better, and I said"—

"Come," responded the child promptly.

"What would *you* say if the Master now came to you and said that he was lonely without his little scholar, and that he wanted her to come and teach him to be better?"

The child hung her head for a few moments in silence. The Master waited patiently. Tempted by the quiet, a hare ran close to the couple, and raising her bright eyes and velvet forepaws, sat and gazed at them. A squirrel ran half-way down the furrowed bark of the fallen tree, and there stopped.

"We are waiting, Lissy," said the Master in a whisper, and the child smiled. Stirred by a passing breeze, the tree tops rocked, and a long pencil of light stole through their interlaced boughs, full on the doubting face and irresolute little figure. Suddenly she took the Master's hand in her quick way. What she said was scarcely audible, but the Master, putting the black hair back from her forehead, kissed her, and so, hand in hand, they passed out of the damp aisles and forest odors into the open sunlit road.

PART III.—THE BED ROCK

Somewhat less spiteful in her intercourse with other scholars, M'liss still retained an offensive attitude in regard to Clytemnestra. Perhaps the jealous element was not entirely lulled in her passionate little breast. Perhaps it was only, that the round curves and plump outline offered more extended pinching surface. But while such ebullitions were under the Master's control, her enmity occasionally took a new and irrepressible form.

The Master in his first estimate of the child's character could not conceive that she had ever possessed a doll. But the Master, like many other professed readers of character, was safer in *a posteriori* than *a priori* reasoning. M'liss had a doll, but then it was emphatically M'liss's doll—a smaller copy of herself. It's unhappy existence had been a secret discovered accidentally by Mrs. Morpher. It had been the old time companion of M'liss's wanderings and bore evident marks of suffering. Its original complexion was long since washed away by the weather and anointed by the lime of ditches. It looked very much as M'liss had in days past. It's one gown of faded stuff was dirty and ragged as hers had been. M'liss had never been known to apply to it any childish term of endearment. She never exhibited it in the presence of other children. It was put severely to bed in a hollow tree near the school-house, and only allowed exercise during M'liss's rambles. Fulfilling a stern duty to her doll—as she would to herself—it knew no luxuries.

Now Mrs. M. obeying a commendable impulse, bought another doll and gave it to M'liss. The child received it gratefully, but doubtingly. The Master, in looking at it one day, discovered as he thought a slight resemblance in its round red cheeks and mild blue eyes to Clytemnestra. It became evident before long that M'liss had noticed the same resemblance. Accordingly she hammered its waxen head on the rocks when she was alone, and sometimes dragged it with a string around its neck to and from school. At other times, setting it up in her desk, she made a pin cushion of its inoffensive body. Whether this was done in revenge for what she considered a second figurative obtrusion of Clytie's excellencies upon her; or whether she had an intuitive appreciation of the superstition of certain other heathens, and indulging in a Fetish rite, imagined that the original of her wax model would pine away and finally die, the Master was puzzled to determine.

In her different tasks the Master could not help noticing the workings of a quick, restless and vigorous perception. Truth came to her active little brain in electric flashes and telegraphed its record in short, sharp, sententious symbols. She knew not the hesitancy nor the doubts of childhood. Her answers in class were always slightly dashed with audacity. Of course she was not infallible. But her

courage and daring in venturing beyond her own depth and that of the
floundering little swimmers around
her, in their minds outweighed all errors of judgment. Children are no
better than grown people in this respect; and whenever the little red
hand flashed above her desk, there was
a wondering silence, and even the
Master was sometimes oppressed with
a doubt of his own experience and
judgment.

In common with most childless
young men, the interest which the
Master first possessed for this wayward child was of a fleeting and
superficial character, unembarrassed
with the weight of responsibility. Certain attributes which at first amused
and entertained his fancy began to
afflict him at last with grave doubts.
He could not but notice that she was
wilful, that she was revengeful, that
she was irreverent. There was but
one virtue which pertained to her
semi-savage disposition, that the Master when summing up her character
always placed to her credit in large
letters. It was the basis of M'liss's
peculiar nature—the bed rock of her
faith—TRUTH.

The Master had been doing some
hard thinking on this subject and had
arrived at the conclusion which is
common to all who think sincerely,
that he was generally the slave of his
own prejudices and idiosyncrasy, when
he thought he would make a call on
the Rev. Mr. McSnagley, and get his
advice and opinion. The decision was
humiliating to his pride as he and
McSnagley were not friends. But he
thought of M'liss, and the evening of
their first meeting; and perhaps with a
pardonable superstition that it was not

chance alone that had guided her wilful feet to the little school-house, he
choked back his dislike and went to
McSnagly.

The Reverend gentleman was glad
to see him. He found him looking
"peartish," and hoped he had got over
the "Neuralagy" and "Rheumatiz."
He himself had been troubled with a
dumb "ager" since last "Conference."
But he had learned to "rastle and
pray." Pausing a moment to enable
the Master to write this certain
method of curing the dumb "ager"
upon the book and volume of his
brain, Mr. McSnagley proceeded to
enquire after "Sister Morpher." "She
is an adornment to Christ*ew*anity and
has a likely growin' young family,"
said Mr. McS., "and then there's that
mannerly young gal—so well be
haved—Miss Clytie." In fact Clytie's
perfections seemed to affect Mr. Mc-
Snagley to such an extent, that he
dwelt for several minutes upon them
The Master was doubly embarrassed
In the first place, there was an en
forced contrast of poor M'liss in al
this praise of Clytie. Secondly: there
was something unpleasantly confiden
tial in his tone in speaking of Mor
pher's earliest born. After vainly en
deavoring to get him out of the old
worn ruts of common-places the Mas
ter effectually "chocked" his wheels by
a single interruption. He commenced
"Melissa"—McSnagley bumped
against the name with something like
an interjection and a very disagreeabl
expression on his face and stopped
Then the Master commenced.

He told the story of Melissa, as it
had grown upon him since the first
night of their meeting. Putting for
ward her best qualities with conscien

ious truthfulness, he dwelt upon them s praiseworthy trophies brought out f the battle of her past life. Speaking of her astonishing quickness and alent he hinted that such faculties night have greater scope than it was is power to give. Speaking modestly, s became the younger man, he asked or guidance for himself—for advice rom the graver and more experienced pastor. Without mentioning the hild's unconquerable aversion to the unday school and its worthy preeptor, he believed that he alone had btained influence over her disposition. Therefore, whatever knowledge of a igher and graver character she acuired must come from him. It was e who must ask the teachings of McSnagley—the Master who must beome the pupil. "As to her irreverence," said the young man, warmng with the subject "only consider her past life. From whom was she to earn reverence? From a drunken ather? From the fickle fancies of her ld companions? From a hard discipline whose only teachings have been listrust of all things, and selfeliance? Could she see the hand that ed her to my school? God help her!" aid the young man, suddenly bursting the bonds of logic and reason. 'Why 'sir, I should have been worse han she, had I suffered as she has. should sir, indeed I would," and with his natural but illogical anti-climax —feeling that he had not expressed alf that he might—the young man at down.

His fatal supposition supplied McSnagley with the longest kind of a ever. He felt that he could not "conent" without admitting the principle f "Works without Faith." If Melissy Smith wanted to come to the "founting," he could only say the "founting" was "theer." He was quite certain that the child could not drink by proxy. He had a number of lambs in his fold and there was always room for more. Then (using the lever) he could not think of entrusting the salvation of a mortal soul to a young man of the World and of the Flesh, but hinting that his eyes might be opened to his folly, he cleverly shifted the errors of M'liss's present life upon the Master's shoulders. Growing more careless and singular in his speech as he went on, and using a sacred name occasionally with a coarse familiarity which made the young man shrink, he gave, as he afterwards expressed it, "a right smart lettin' down" to the young Master. Then with a heavy heart the young man took his leave, and left the Rev. Mr. McSnagley to incorporate the subject of their remarks at next Sunday's class meeting, in the form of "Conversations with a gifted Infidel"—which gifted Infidel of course everybody knew.

Perhaps this rebuff placed the Master and pupil once more in the close communion of old. The child seemed to notice the change in the Master's manner which had of late been constrained, and in one of their long postprandial walks, she stopped suddenly and mounting a stump looked full in his face with big searching eyes. "You ain't mad?" said she with an interrogative shake of the black braids. "No!" "Nor bothered?" "No!" "Nor hungry?" (Hunger was to M'liss a kind of sickness which might attack a person at any moment.) "No!" "Nor thinking of her?" "Of whom, Lissy?" "The white girl!" (This was the latest epithet invented by M'liss who was a very dark brunette, to express Clytemnestra.) "No!" "Upon your word?" (a substitute for "Hope you'll die," proposed by the Master). "Yes!" "And sacred honor?" "Yes!" Then M'liss gave him a fierce little kiss, and hopping down, fluttered off. For two or three days after that she condescended to appear more like other children and be, as she expressed it, "good."

Two years had passed since the Master's advent at Smith's Pocket, and as his salary was not large, and the prospects of Smith's Pocket eventually becoming the capital of the State not entirely definite, he contemplated a change. He had informed the school trustees privately of his intentions, but educated young men of unblemished moral character being scarce at that time, he consented to continue his school term through the winter to early spring. None else knew of his intention except his one friend, a Dr. Duchesne, a young Creole physician known to the people of 'Wingdam,' as 'Duchesny.' He never mentioned it to Mrs. Morpher, Clytie, or any of his scholars. His reticence was partly the result of a constitutional indisposition to fuss, partly a desire to be spared the questions and surmises of vulgar curiosity, and partly that he never really believed he was going to do anything, before it was done.

He did not like to think of M'liss. It was a selfish instinct perhaps, which made him try to fancy his feeling for the child was foolish, romantic and impractical. He even tried to imagine that she would do better under the control of an older, and sterne teacher. Then she was nearly eleven and in a few years, by the rules of Red Mountain would be a woman. He had done his duty. After Smith death he addressed letters to Smith relatives, and received one answer from a sister of Melissa's mother Thanking the Master, she stated her intention of leaving the Atlantic State for California with her husband in few months. This was a slight super structure for the airy castle which the Master pictured for M'liss's home, but it was easy to fancy that some loving sympathetic woman with the claim of kindred, might better guide her wayward nature. Yet when the Master had read the letter, M'liss listened to it carelessly, received it submissively, and afterwards cut figures out of it with her scissors, supposed to represent Clytemnestra, labeled "the white girl" to [prevent] mistakes, and impaled them upon the outer walls of the schoolhouse.

When the Summer was almost spent and the last harvest had been gathered in the valleys, the Master bethought him of gathering in a few of the ripened shoots of the young idea, and of having his Harvest Home, or Examination. So the savans and professionals of Smith's Pocket were gathered, according to that memorable custom, which consists in placing timid children in a constrained position, and bullying them as in a witness box. As usual in such cases, the most audacious and most self possessed were the lucky recipients of the honors. The reader will imagine that in the present instance, M'liss and Clytie were pre-eminent. They divided public attention; M'liss with her learness of material perception and self-reliance, Clytie with her placid self-esteem and saint-like correctness and deportment. The other little ones were timid and blundering. M'liss' readiness and brilliancy of course captivated the greatest number and provoked the greatest applause.—M'liss' antecedents had unconsciously awakened the strongest sympathies of a class whose athletic forms were ranged against the walls, or whose handsome bearded faces looked in at the windows. But M'liss's popularity was overthrown by an unexpected circumstance.

McSnagley had invited himself, and had been going through the pleasing entertainment of frightening the more timid pupils by the vaguest and most ambiguous questions delivered in an impressive funereal tone; and M'liss had soared into Astronomy, and was tracking the course of our spotted ball through space, and keeping time with the music of the spheres, and defining the tethered orbits of the planets— when McSnagley impressively arose. "Meelissy! ye were speaking of the revolutions of this yere yearth and the move-*ments* of the sun, and I think ye said it had been a doing of it 'nce the creashun, eh?" M'liss nodded a scornful affirmative. "Well, ar that the truth!" said McSnagley folding his arms. "Yes," said M'liss, shutting up her little red lips tightly. The handsome outlines at the windows peered further in the school-room, and a saintly Raphael-face with blonde beard and soft blue eyes belonging to the biggest scamp in the diggings, turned toward the child, and whispered, "stick to it, M'liss!" The Reverend gentleman heaved a deep sigh, and cast a compassionate glance at the Master, then at the children, and then rested his look on Clytie. That young woman softly elevated her round, white arm. Its seductive curves were enhanced by a gorgeous and massive specimen bracelet, the gift of one of her humblest worshippers, worn in honor of the occasion. There was a momentary silence.—Clytie's round cheeks were very pink and soft. Clytie's big eyes were very bright and blue.—Clytie's low-necked white book-muslin rested softly on Clytie's white, plump shoulders. Clytie looked at the Master, and the Master nodded. Then Clytie spoke softly:

"Joshua commanded the sun to stand still and it obeyed him!" There was a low hum of applause in the school-room, a triumphant expression on McSnagley's face, a grave shadow on the Master's, and a comical look of disappointment reflected from the windows. M'liss skimmed rapidly over her Astronomy, and then shut the book with a loud snap. A groan burst from McSnagley, an expression of astonishment from the school-room, a yell from the windows as M'liss brought her tiny fist down on the desk with the emphatic declaration:

"It's a *lie!* *I* don't believe it!"

PART IV.—"CLEANING UP"

The long wet season drew near its close.—Signs of Spring were visible in the swelling buds and rushing torrents. The pine forests exhaled a fresher spicery. The azalias were already budding; the Ceanothus getting ready its lilac livery for Spring. On the green upland which climbed Red Mountain at its southern aspect, the long spike of the Monkshood shot up from its broad leaved stool, and once more shook its dark blue-bells. Again the billow above Smith's grave was soft and green, its crest just tossed with the foam of daisies and buttercups. The little graveyard had gathered a few new dwellers in the past year, and the mounds were placed two by two by the little paling, until they reached Smith's grave, and there there was but the one. General superstition had apparently shunned the enforced companionship. So the plot beside Smith was still vacant.

There had been several placards posted about the town, intimating that at a certain period, a celebrated dramatic company would perform for a few days, a series of "side-splitting" and "screaming farces." That, alternating pleasantly with this, there would be some Melo-drama and a Grand Divertisement, which would include singing, dancing, etc. These announcements occasioned a great fluttering among the little folk, and were the theme of much excitement and great speculation among the Master's scholars. The Master had promised M'liss, to whom this sort of thing, was sacred and rare—that she should go, and on that momentous evening the Master and M'liss "assisted."

The performance was the prevalent style of heavy mediocrity; the melodrama was not bad enough to laugh at, nor good enough to excite. But the Master turning wearily to the child was astonished and felt something like self-accusation in noticing the peculiar effect upon her excitable nature. The red blood flushed in her cheeks at each stroke of her panting little heart. Her small passionate lips were slightly parted to give vent to her hurried breath. Her widely opened lids threw up and arched her black eyebrows. She did not laugh at the dismal comicalities of the funny man—for M'liss seldom laughed. Nor was she discreetly affected to the delicate extremes of the corner of a white handkerchief, as was the tender hearted "Clytie," who was talking with her "feller," and ogling the Master at the same moment. But when the performance was over and the green curtain fell on the little stage, M'liss drew a long, deep breath, and turned to the Master's grave face with half apologetic smile, and wearied gesture. Then she said "now take me home!" and dropped the lids of her black eyes, as if to dwell once more in fancy on the mimic stage.

On their way to Mrs. Morpher's the Master thought proper to ridicule the whole performance. Now he shouldn't wonder if M'liss thought that the young lady who acted so beautifully was really in earnest, and in love with the gentleman who wore such fine clothes. Well if she were in love with him it was a very unfortunate thing. "Why?" said M'liss with an upward sweep of the drooping lid. "Oh! well he couldn't support his wife at his present salary, and pay so much week for his fine clothes, and then they wouldn't receive as much wages if they were married as if they were merely lovers,—that is" added the Master "if they are not already married to somebody else, but I think the husband of the pretty young countess takes the tickets at the door, or pulls up the curtain or snuffs the candles or does something equally refined and elegant. As to the young man with the nice clothes which are really ninow—and must cost at least two and a half or three dollars—not to speak of that mantle of red drugget which I happen to know the price of, as I bought some of it for my room once. As to this young man 'Lissy, he is a pretty good fellow, and if he does drink occasionally I don't think people ought to take advantage of it and give him black eyes and throw him in the mud. Do you? I am sure he might owe me two dollars and a half a long time, before I would throw it up in his face as the fellow did the other night at Wingdam."

M'liss had taken his hand in both of her's and was trying to look in his eyes, which the young man kept as resolutely averted. M'liss had a faint idea of irony, indulging herself sometimes in a species of sardonic humor, which was as much visible in her actions as her speech. But the young man continued on this strain until they had reached Mrs. Morpher's, and he had deposited M'liss in her maternal charge. Waiving the invitation of Mrs. M. to refreshment and rest, and shading his eyes with his hand to keep out the blue-eyed Clytemnestra's syren glances, he excused himself, and went home.

For two or three days after the advent of the Dramatic Company, M'liss was late at school and the Master's usual Friday afternoon ramble was for once pretermitted owing to the absence of his trustworthy guide. As he was putting away his books and preparing to leave the school-house a small voice piped at his side, "please sir?" the Master turned and there stood Aristides Morpher.

"Well, my little man," said the Master impatiently, "what is it; quick?" "Please sir, me and 'Kerg' thinks that M'liss is a going to run away again."

"What's that, sir," said the Master, with that unjust testiness with which we always receive disagreeable news.

"Why sir, she don't stay home any more, and 'Kerg' and me see her talking with one of those actor fellers, and she's with him now—and 'please sir,' yesterday she told 'Kerg' and me she could make a speech as well as Miss Cellerstina Montmoressy, and she spouted right off by heart," and the little fellow paused in a collapsed condition.

"What actor?" asked the Master.

"Him as wears the shiny hat. And hair. And gold pin. And gold chain," said the just Aristides putting periods for commas to eke out his breath.

The Master put on his gloves and hat, feeling an unpleasant tightness in his chest and thorax, and walked out in the road. Aristides trotted along by his side endeavoring to keep pace with his short legs to the Master's strides, when the Master stopped suddenly, and Aristides bumped up against him. "Where were they talking," said the Master as if continuing the conversation. "At the Arcade" said Aristides.

When they reached the main street the Master paused. "Run down home" said he to the boy. "If M'liss is there come to the Arcade and tell me. If she isn't there—stay home, run!" And off trotted the short-legged Aristides.

The Arcade was just across the way —a long rambling building containing a bar-room, billiard room, and restaurant. As the young man crossed the plaza, he noticed that two or three of the passers-by turned and looked after him. He looked at his clothes, took out his handkerchief and wiped his face before he entered the bar-room. It contained the usual number of loungers who stared at him as he entered. One of them looked at him so fixedly and with such a strange expression that the Master stopped and looked again, and then saw it was only his own reflection in a large mir-ror. This made the Master think that perhaps he was a little excited, and so he took up a copy of the Red Mountain Banner from one of the tables and tried to recover his composure by reading the column of advertisements.

He then walked through the bar-room, through the restaurant and into the billiard room. The child was not there. In the latter apartment a person was standing by one of the tables with a broad-brimmed glazed hat on his head. The Master recognized him as the agent of the Dramatic Company; he had taken a dislike to him at their first meeting from the peculiar fashion of wearing his beard and hair. Perhaps there was more of intuition in the belligerent instincts of Benvolio than the witty Mercutio imagined—for the Master was naturally a peaceful man. Satisfied that the object of his search was not there, he turned to the man with a glazed hat. He had noticed the Master, but tried that common trick of unconsciousness, in which vulgar natures always fail. Balancing a billiard cue in his hand, he pretended to play with a ball in the center of the table. The Master stood opposite to him until he raised his eyes; when their glances met the Master walked up to him.

He had intended to avoid a scene or quarrel—but when he began to speak something kept rising in his throat and retarded his utterance, and his own voice frightened him, it sounded so distant, low and resonant. "I understand," he began, "that Melissa Smith an orphan and one of my scholars ha talked with you about adopting you profession. Is that so?"

The man with the glazed hat leaned over the table, and made an imaginary shot, that sent the ball spinning round the cushions. Then walking round the table he recovered the ball and placed it upon the spot. This duty discharged—getting ready for another shot, he said:

" 'Spose she has?"

The Master choked up again, but squeezing the cushion of the table in his gloved hand, he went on:

"If you are a gentleman I have only to tell you that I am her guardian and responsible for her career. You know as well as I do, the kind of life you offer her. As you may learn of any one here, I have already brought her out of an existence worse than death —out of the streets and the contamination of vice. I am trying to do so again. Let us talk like men. She has neither father, mother, sister or brother. Are you seeking to give her an equivalent for these?"

The man with the glazed hat examined the point of his cue and then looked around for somebody to enjoy the joke with him.

"I know that she is a strange wilful girl," continued the Master, "but she is better than she was. I believe that I have some influence over her still. I beg and hope therefore that you will take no further steps in this matter—but as a man—as a gentleman—

leave her to me. I am willing"—, but here something rose again in the Master's throat, and the sentence remained unfinished.

The man with the glazed hat mistaking the Master's silence, raised his head with a coarse brutal laugh, and said in a loud voice:

"Want her yourself, do you? That cock won't fight here, young man!"

The insult, was more in the tone than words,—more in the glance than tone, and more in the man's instinctive nature than all these.—The only appreciable rhetoric to this kind of animal is a blow. The Master felt this, and with his pent up nervous energy finding expression in the one act, he struck the brute full in his grinning face.—The blow sent the glazed hat one way and the cue another, and tore the glove and skin from the Master's hand from knuckle to joint. It opened up the corners of the fellow's mouth, and spoilt the peculiar shape of his beard for sometime to come.

There was a shout, an imprecation, a scuffle, and the trampling of many feet. Then the crowd parted right and left, and two sharp quick reports followed each other in rapid succession. Then they closed again about his opponent, and the Master was standing alone. He remembered of picking bits of burning wadding from his coat sleeve with his left hand. Some one was holding his other hand. Looking at it, he saw it was still bleeding from the blow, but his fingers were clenched around the handle of a glittering knife. He could not remember when, or how he got it.

The man who [was] holding his hand was Mr. Morpher. He hurried the Master to the door, but the Mas-ter held back, and tried to tell him as well as he could with his parched throat, about "M'liss." "It's all right my boy," said Mr. M. "She's home!" And they passed out into the street together. As they walked along, Mr. Morpher said that M'liss had come running in to the house, a few moments before, and had dragged him out, saying that somebody was trying to kill the Master at the Arcade. Wishing to be alone, in his present unpleasant state of feeling, the Master, promised Mr. Morpher that he would not seek the agent again that night, and parted from him, taking the road toward the school-house. He was surprised in nearing it to find the door open—still more surprised to see M'liss sitting at his desk.

The Master's nature, as I have hinted before, had, like most sensitive organizations, a selfish basis. The brutal taunt thrown out by his late adversary still rankled in his heart. It was possible, he thought, that such a construction might be put upon his affection for the child—which at best was foolish, Quixotic and impractical. Besides, had she not voluntarily abnegated his authority and affection. And what had everybody else said about her? Why should he alone combat the opinion of all, and be at last obliged to tacitly confess the truth of all they had predicted. And he had been a participant in a low bar-room fight with a common boor, and risked his life, to prove what? What had he proved? Nothing? What would the people say? What would his friends say? What would McSnagley say?

In his self-accusation the last person he should have wished to meet was

M'liss. He entered the door, and going up to his desk, told the child in a few cold words, that he was busy and wished to be alone. As she rose, he took her vacant seat and sitting down buried his head in his hands. When he looked up again she was still standing there. She was looking at his face with an anxious expression. "Did you kill him," she asked. "No!" said the Master. "That's what I gave you the knife for," said the child quickly. "Gave me the knife?" repeated the Master in bewilderment. "Yes, gave you the knife—I was there under the bar. Saw you hit him. Saw you both fall. He dropped his old knife. I gave it to you. Why didn't you stick him?" said M'liss rapidly, with an expressive twinkle of the black eyes, and a gesture of the little red hand.

The Master could only look his astonishment.

"Yes," said M'liss. "If you'd asked me, I'd told you I was off with the play-actors. Why was I off with the play-actors? Because you wouldn't tell me you was going away. I knew it. I heard you tell the Doctor so. I wasn't a'goin' to stay here alone with those Morphers. I'd rather die first."

With a theatric gesture which was perfectly consonant with her character, she drew from her bosom a few limp green leaves, and holding them out at arms length said in her quick vivid way, and in the queer pronunciation of her old life, which she fell into when unduly excited:

"That's the poison plant you said would kill me. I ain't your scholar any longer, but I'll do what you say to-night. I'll go with the play actors, or I'll eat this and die here. I don't care which. I won't stay here, where they hate and despise me! Nor would you let me, if you didn't hate and despise me, too!"

The passionate little breast heaved and two big tears peeped over the edge of M'liss's eye-lids, but she whisked them away with the corner of her apron as if they had been wasps.

"If you lock me up in jail," said M'liss fiercely, "to keep me from the play-actors, I'll poison myself. Father killed himself—why shouldn't I? You said a mouthful of that root would kill me, and I always carry it here"—and she struck her breast passionately with her clenched fist.

The Master thought of the vacant plot beside Smith's grave, and of the passionate little figure before him. Then a wild thought sprang up in his heart, which, when fully grown, seemed to have been the resolve of his lifetime. Seizing her hands in his and looking full into her truthful eyes, he said:

"Lissy, will you go with *me?*"

The child put her arms around his neck, and said joyfully, "Yes."

"But now—to-night?"

"To-night."

.   .   .   .   .   .

There were two passengers by the Wingdam Mail stage from Smith's Pocket at two o'clock that night. A young man and a girl of twelve. Although it made some trouble and annoyance to the school trustees to get another teacher, they could not blame him for he had given them three months' warning. And the Master's WORK ON RED MOUNTAIN was done!

1860

From *CONDENSED NOVELS*

MUCK-A-MUCK *

A MODERN INDIAN NOVEL AFTER
COOPER

CHAPTER I

It was toward the close of a bright
October day. The last rays of the setting sun were reflected from one of
those sylvan lakes peculiar to the
Sierras of California. On the right the
curling smoke of an Indian village
rose between the columns of the lofty
pines, while to the left the log cottage
of Judge Tompkins, embowered in
buckeyes, completed the enchanting
picture.

Although the exterior of the cottage
was humble and unpretentious, and in
keeping with the wildness of the
landscape, its interior gave evidence
of the cultivation and refinement of
its inmates. An aquarium, containing
goldfishes, stood on a marble center-
table at one end of the apartment,
while a magnificent grand piano occupied the other. The floor was covered with a yielding tapestry carpet,
and the walls were adorned with paintings from the pencils of Van Dyke,
Rubens, Tintoretto, Michael Angelo,
and the productions of the more modern Turner, Kensett, Church, and
Bierstadt. Although Judge Tompkins
had chosen the frontiers of civilization as his home, it was impossible
for him to entirely forego the habits
and tastes of his former life. He was
seated in a luxurious armchair, writing
at a mahogany escritoire, while his
daughter, a lovely young girl of seven-

teen summers, plied her crochet-needle
on an ottoman beside him. A bright
fire of pine logs flickered and flamed
on the ample hearth.

Genevra Octavia Tompkins was
Judge Tompkins's only child. Her
mother had long since died on the
Plains. Reared in affluence, no pains
had been spared with the daughter's
education. She was a graduate of one
of the principal seminaries, and spoke
French with a perfect Benicia accent.
Peerlessly beautiful, she was dressed
in a white Moiré antique robe trimmed
with tulle. That simple rosebud, with
which most heroines exclusively decorate their hair, was all she wore in her
raven locks.

The Judge was the first to break
the silence.

"Genevra, the logs which compose
yonder fire seem to have been incau-
tiously chosen. The sibilation produced by the sap, which exudes copi-
ously therefrom, is not conductive to
composition."

"True, father, but I thought it
would be preferable to the constant
crepitation which is apt to attend the
combustion of more seasoned ligneous
fragments."

The Judge looked admiringly at the
intellectual features of the graceful
girl, and half forgot the slight an-
noyances of the green wood in the
musical accents of his daughter. He
was smoothing her hair tenderly, when
the shadow of a tall figure, which suddenly darkened the doorway, caused
him to look up.

CHAPTER II

It needed but a glance at the new-
comer to detect at once the form and
features of the haughty aborigine,—

* Used by permission of, and by arrangement with, Houghton Mifflin Company.

the untaught and untrammeled son of the forest. Over one shoulder a blanket, negligently but gracefully thrown, disclosed a bare and powerful breast, decorated with a quantity of three-cent postage-stamps which he had despoiled from an Overland Mail stage a few weeks previous. A cast-off beaver of Judge Tompkins's, adorned by a simple feather, covered his erect head, from beneath which his straight locks descended. His right hand hung lightly by his side, while his left was engaged in holding on a pair of pantaloons, which the lawless grace and freedom of his lower limbs evidently could not brook.

"Why," said the Indian, in a low sweet tone,—"why does the Pale Face still follow the track of the Red Man? Why does he pursue him, even as O-kee chow, the wild cat, chases Ka-ka, the skunk? Why are the feet of Sorrel-top, the white chief, among the acorns of Muck-a-Muck, the mountain forest? Why," he repeated, quietly but firmly abstracting a silver spoon from the table,—"why do you seek to drive him from the wigwams of his fathers? His brothers are already gone to the happy hunting-grounds. Will the Pale Face seek him there?" And, averting his face from the Judge, he hastily slipped a silver cake-basket beneath his blanket, to conceal his emotion.

"Muck-a-Muck has spoken," said Genevra softly. "Let him now listen. Are the acorns of the mountain sweeter than the esculent and nutritious bean of the Pale Face miner? Does my brother prize the edible qualities of the snail above that of the crisp and oleaginous bacon? Delicious are the grasshoppers that sport on the hillside,—are they better than the dried apples of the Pale Faces? Pleasant is the gurgle of the torrent, Kish-Kish, but is it better than the cluck-cluck of old Bourbon from the old stone bottle?"

"Ugh!" said the Indian,—"ugh! good. The White Rabbit is wise. Her words fall as the snow on Tootoonolo, and the rocky heart of Muck-a-Muck is hidden. What says my brother the Gray Gopher of Dutch Flat?"

"She has spoken, Muck-a-Muck," said the Judge, gazing fondly on his daughter. "It is well. Our treaty is concluded. No, thank you,—you need *not* dance the Dance of Snow-shoes, or the Moccasin Dance, the Dance of Green Corn, or the Treaty Dance. I would be alone. A strange sadness overpowers me."

"I go," said the Indian. "Tell your great chief in Washington, the Sachem Andy, that the Red Man is retiring before the footsteps of the adventurous pioneer. Inform him, if you please, that westward the star of empire takes its way, that the chiefs of the Pi-Ute nation are for Reconstruction to a man, and that Klamath will poll a heavy Republican vote in the fall."

And folding his blanket more tightly around him, Muck-a-Muck withdrew.

CHAPTER III

Genevra Tompkins stood at the door of the log-cabin, looking after the retreating Overland Mail stage which conveyed her father to Virginia City. "He may never return again," sighed the young girl, as she glanced at the frightfully rolling vehicle and wildly careering horses,—"at least, with unbroken bones. Should he meet with an accident! I mind me now a fearful legend, familiar to my childhood. Can it be that the drivers on this line are privately instructed to dispatch all passengers maimed by accident, to prevent tedious litigation? No, no. But why this weight upon my heart?"

She seated herself at the piano and lightly passed her hand over the keys. Then, in a clear mezzo-soprano voice, she sang the first verse of one of the most popular Irish ballads:—

) *Arrah ma dheelish,* the distant *dudheen*
Lies soft in the moonlight, *ma bouchal vourneen:*
The springing *gossoons* on the heather are still,
And the *caudeens* and *colleens* are heard on the hill.

But as the ravishing notes of her sweet voice died upon the air, her hands sank listlessly to her side. Music could not chase away the mysterious shadow from her heart. Again she rose. Putting on a white crape bonnet, and carefully drawing a pair of lemon-colored gloves over her taper fingers, she seized her parasol and plunged into the depths of the pine forest.

CHAPTER IV

Genevra had not proceeded many miles before a weariness seized upon her fragile limbs, and she would fain seat herself upon the trunk of a prostrate pine, which she previously dusted with her handkerchief. The sun was just sinking below the horizon, and the scene was one of gorgeous and sylvan beauty. "How beautiful is nature!" murmured the innocent girl, as, reclining gracefully against the root of the tree, she gathered up her skirts and tied a handkerchief around her throat. But a low growl interrupted her meditation. Starting to her feet, her eyes met a sight which froze her blood with terror.

The only outlet to the forest was the narrow path, barely wide enough for a single person, hemmed in by trees and rocks, which she had just traversed. Down this path, in Indian file, came a monstrous grizzly, closely followed by a California lion, a wild cat, and a buffalo, the rear being brought up by a wild Spanish bull. The mouths of the three first animals were distended with frightful significance, the horns of the last were lowered as ominously. As Genevra was preparing to faint, she heard a low voice behind her.

"Eternally dog-gone my skin ef this ain't the puttiest chance yet!"

At the same moment, a long, shining barrel dropped lightly from behind her, and rested over her shoulder.

Genevra shuddered.

"Dern ye—don't move!"

Genevra became motionless.

The crack of a rifle rang through the woods. Three frightful yells were heard, and two sullen roars. Five animals bounded into the air and five lifeless bodies lay upon the plain. The well-aimed bullet had done its work. Entering the open throat of the grizzly it had traversed his body only to enter the throat of the California lion, and in like manner the catamount, until it passed through into the respective foreheads of the bull and the buffalo, and finally fell flattened from the rocky hillside.

Genevra turned quickly. "My preserver!" she shrieked, and fell into the arms of Natty Bumpo, the celebrated Pike Ranger of Donner Lake.

CHAPTER V

The moon rose cheerfully above Donner Lake. On its placid bosom a dug-out canoe glided rapidly, containing Natty Bumpo and Genevra Tompkins.

Both were silent. The same thought possessed each, and perhaps there was sweet companionship even in the unbroken quiet. Genevra bit the handle of her parasol, and blushed. Natty Bumpo took a fresh chew of tobacco. At length Genevra said, as if in half-spoken reverie:—

"The soft shining of the moon and the peaceful ripple of the waves seem to say to us various things of an instructive and moral tendency."

"You may bet yer pile on that, miss," said her companion gravely. "It's all the preachin' and psalm-singin' I've heern since I was a boy."

"Noble being!" said Miss Tompkins to herself, glancing at the stately Pike as he bent over his paddle to conceal his emotion. "Reared in this wild seclusion, yes he has become penetrated with visible consciousness of a Great First Cause." Then, collecting herself, she said aloud: "Methinks 't were pleasant to glide ever thus down the stream of life, hand in hand with the one being whom the soul claims as its affinity. But what am I saying?"—and the delicate-minded girl hid her face in her hands.

A long silence ensued, which was at length broken by her companion.

"Ef you mean you're on the marry," he said thoughtfully, "I ain't in no wise partikler."

"My husband!" faltered the blushing girl; and she fell into his arms.

In ten minutes more the loving couple had landed at Judge Tompkins's.

CHAPTER VI

A year had passed away. Natty Bumpo was returning from Gold Hill where he had been to purchase provisions. On his way to Donner Lake rumors of an Indian uprising met his ears. "Dern their pesky skins, ef they dare to touch my Jenny," he muttered between his clinched teeth.

It was dark when he reached the borders of the lake. Around a glittering fire he dimly discerned dusky figures dancing. They were in war paint. Conspicuous among them was the renowned Muck-a-Muck. But why did the fingers of Natty Bumpo tighten convulsively around his rifle?

The chief held in his hand long tufts of raven hair. The heart of the pioneer sickened as he recognized the clustering curls of Genevra. In a moment his rifle was at his shoulder and with a sharp "ping" Muck-a-Muck leaped into the air a corpse. To knock out the brains of the remaining savages, tear the tresses from the stiffening hand of Muck-a-Muck and dash rapidly forward to the cottage of Judge Tompkins was the work of a moment.

He burst open the door. Why did he stand transfixed with open mouth and distended eyeballs? Was the sight too horrible to be borne? On the contrary, before him, in her peerless beauty, stood Genevra Tompkins leaning on her father's arm.

"Ye'r not scalped, then!" gasped her lover.

"No. I have no hesitation in saying that I am not; but why this abruptness?" responded Genevra.

Bumpo could not speak, but frantically produced the silken tresses. Genevra turned her face aside.

"Why, that's her waterfall!" said the Judge.

Bumpo sank fainting to the floor.

The famous Pike chieftain never recovered from the deceit and refused to marry Genevra, who died, twenty years afterwards, of a broken heart. Judge Tompkins lost his fortune in Wild Cat. The stage passes twice a week the deserted cottage at Donner Lake. Thus was the death of Muck-a-Muck avenged.

1867

THE LUCK OF ROARING CAMP *

There was commotion in Roaring Camp. It could not have been a fight, for in 1850 that was not novel enough to have called together the entire settlement. The ditches and claims were not only deserted, but "Tuttle's grocery" had contributed its gamblers, who, it will be remembered, calmly continued their game the day that French Pete and Kanaka Joe shot each other to death over the bar in the front room. The whole camp was collected before a rude cabin on the outer edge of the clearing. Conversation was carried on in a low tone, but the name of a woman was frequently repeated. It was a name familiar enough in the camp,—"Cherokee Sal."

Perhaps the less said of her the better. She was a coarse and, it is to be feared, a very sinful woman. But at

* Used by permission of, and by arrangement with, Houghton Mifflin Company.

that time she was the only woman in Roaring Camp, and was just then lying in sore extremity, when she most needed the ministration of her own sex. Dissolute, abandoned, and irreclaimable, she was yet suffering a martyrdom hard enough to bear even when veiled by sympathizing womanhood, but now terrible in her loneliness. The primal curse had come to her in that original isolation which must have made the punishment of the first transgression so dreadful. It was, perhaps, part of the expiation of her sin that, at a moment when she most lacked her sex's intuitive tenderness and care, she met only the half-contemptuous faces of her masculine associates. Yet a few of the spectators were, I think, touched by her sufferings. Sandy Tipton thought it was "rough on Sal," and, in the contemplation of her condition, for a moment rose superior to the fact that he had an ace and two bowers in his sleeve.

It will be seen also that the situation was novel. Deaths were by no means uncommon in Roaring Camp, but a birth was a new thing. People had been dismissed the camp effectively, finally, and with no possibility of return; but this was the first time that anybody had been introduced *ab initio*. Hence the excitement.

"You go in there, Stumpy," said a prominent citizen known as "Kentuck," addressing one of the loungers. "Go in there, and see what you kin do. You've had experience in them things."

Perhaps there was a fitness in the selection. Stumpy, in other climes, had been the putative head of two families; in fact, it was owing to some legal informality in these proceedings that Roaring Camp—a city of refuge —was indebted to his company. The crowd approved the choice, and Stumpy was wise enough to bow to the majority. The door closed on the extempore surgeon and midwife, and Roaring Camp sat down outside, smoked its pipe, and awaited the issue.

The assemblage numbered about a hundred men. One or two of these were actual fugitives from justice, some were criminal, and all were reckless. Physically they exhibited no indication of their past lives and character. The greatest scamp had a Raphael face, with a profusion of blonde hair; Oakhurst, a gambler, had the melancholy air and intellectual abstraction of a Hamlet; the coolest and most courageous man was scarcely over five feet in height, with a soft voice and an embarrassed, timid manner. The term "roughs" applied to them was a distinction rather than a definition. Perhaps in the minor details of fingers, toes, ears, etc., the camp may have been deficient, but these slight omissions did not detract from their aggregate force. The strongest man had but three fingers on his right hand; the best shot had but one eye.

Such was the physical aspect of the men that were dispersed around the cabin. The camp lay in a triangular valley between two hills and a river. The only outlet was a steep trail over the summit of a hill that faced the cabin, now illuminated by the rising moon. The suffering woman might have seen it from the rude bunk whereon she lay,—seen it winding like a silver thread until it was lost in the stars above.

A fire of withered pine boughs added sociability to the gathering. By degrees the natural levity of Roaring Camp returned. Bets were freely offered and taken regarding the result. Three to five that "Sal would get through with it"; even that the child would survive; side bets as to the sex and complexion of the coming stranger. In the midst of an excited discussion an exclamation came from those nearest the door, and the camp stopped to listen. Above the swaying and moaning of the pines, the swift rush of the river, and the crackling of the fire rose a sharp, querulous cry,— a cry unlike anything heard before in the camp. The pines stopped moaning, the river ceased to rush, and the fire to crackle. It seemed as if Nature had stopped to listen too.

The camp rose to its feet as one man! It was proposed to explode a barrel of gun-powder; but in consideration of the situation of the mother better counsels prevailed, and only a few revolvers were discharged; for whether owing to the rude surgery of the camp, or some other reason Cherokee Sal was sinking fast. Within an hour she had climbed, as it were that rugged road that led to the stars, and so passed out of Roaring Camp its sin and shame, forever. I do not think that the announcement disturbed them much, except in speculation as to the fate of the child. "Can he live now?" was asked of Stumpy. The answer was doubtful. The only other being of Cherokee Sal's sex and maternal condition in the settlement was an ass. There was some conjecture as to fitness, but the experiment was tried. It was less problematical than the ancient treat-ıent of Romulus and Remus, and pparently as successful.

When these details were completed, hich exhausted another hour, the ɔor was opened, and the anxious rowd of men, who had already ɔrmed themselves into a queue, en‐ ‐red in single file. Beside the low ınk or shelf, on which the figurᵉ of ιe mother was starkly outlined below ιe blankets, stood a pine table. On ιis a candle-box was placed, and ithin it, swathed in staring red flan‐ ᵉl, lay the last arrival at Roaring amp. Beside the candle-box was aced a hat. Its use was soon indi‐ ιted. "Gentlemen," said Stumpy, ith a singular mixture of authority ιd *ex officio* complacency,—"gentle‐ ᵉn will please pass in at the front ɔor, round the table, and out at the ιck door. Them as wishes to con‐ ibute anything toward the orphan 'll find a hat handy." The first man ιtereᵈ with his hat on; he uncovered, ɔwever, as he looked about him, and unconsciously set an example to ᵉ next. In such communities good d bad actions are catching. As the ɔcession filed in comments were dible,—criticisms addressed perhaps ther to Stumpy in the character of ɔwman: "Is that him?" "Mighty ιall specimen"; "Hasn't more'n got ᵉ color"; "Ain't bigger nor a der‐ ιger." The contributions were as ιaracteristic: A silver tobacco box; doubloon; a navy revolver, silver ɔunted; a gold specimen; a very ιutifully embroidered lady's hand‐ ιchief (from Oakhurst the gam‐ ɔr); a diamond breastpin; a diamond g (suggested by the pin, with the ιark from the giver that he "saw ιt pin and went two diamonds bet‐

ter"); a slung-shot; a Bible (con‐ tributor not detected); a golden spur; a silver teaspoon (the initials, I re‐ gret to say, were not the giver's); a pair of surgeon's shears; a lancet; a Bank of England note for £5; and about $200 in loose gold and silver coin. During these proceedings Stumpy maintained a silence as im‐ passive as the dead on his left, a grav‐ ity as inscrutable as that of the newly born on his right. Only one incident occurred to break the monotony of the curious procession. As Kentuck bent over the candle-box half curiously, the child turned, and, in a spasm of pain, caught at his groping finger, and held it fast for a moment. Kentuck looked foolish and embarrassed. Something like a blush tried to assert itself in his weather-beaten cheek. "The d—d lit‐ tle cuss!" he said, as he extricated his finger, with perhaps more tenderness and care than he might have been deemed capable of showing. He held that finger a little apart from its fel‐ lows as he went out, and examined it curiously. The examination provoked the same original remark in regard to the child. In fact, he seemed to en‐ joy repeating it. "He rastled with my finger," he remarked to Tipton, hold‐ ing up the member, "the d—d little cuss!"

It was four o'clock before the camp sought repose. A light burnt in the cabin where the watchers sat, for Stumpy did not go to bed that night. Nor did Kentuck. He drank quite freely, and related with great gusto his experience, invariably ending with his characteristic condemnation of the newcomer. It seemed to relieve him of any unjust implication of sentiment, and Kentuck had the weaknesses of the nobler sex. When everybody else had gone to bed, he walked down to the river and whistled reflectingly. Then he walked up the gulch past the cabin, still whistling with demonstrative un-concern. At a large redwood-tree he paused and retraced his steps, and again passed the cabin. Halfway down to the river's bank he again paused, and then returned and knocked at the door. It was opened by Stumpy. "How goes it?" said Kentuck, looking past Stumpy toward the candle-box. "All serene!" replied Stumpy. "Anything up?" "Nothing." There was a pause—an embarrassing one—Stumpy still holding the door. Then Kentuck had recourse to his finger, which he held up to Stumpy. "Rastled with it,—the d—d little cuss," he said, and retired.

The next day Cherokee Sal had such rude sepulture as Roaring Camp afforded. After her body had been committed to the hillside, there was a formal meeting of the camp to discuss what should be done with her infant. A resolution to adopt it was unanimous and enthusiastic. But an animated discussion in regard to the manner and feasibility of providing for its wants at once sprang up. It was remarkable that the argument partook of none of those fierce personalities with which discussions were usually conducted at Roaring Camp. Tipton proposed that they should send the child to Red Dog,—a distance of forty miles,—where female attention could be procured. But the unlucky suggestion met with fierce and unanimous opposition. It was evident that no plan which entailed parting from their new acquisition would for a moment be entertained. "Besides," said Tom Ryder, "them fellows at Red Dog would swap it, and ring in somebody else on us." A disbelief in the honesty of other camps prevailed at Roaring Camp, as in other places.

The introduction of a female nurse in the camp also met with objection. It was argued that no decent woman could be prevailed to accept Roaring Camp as her home, and the speaker urged that "they didn't want any more of the other kind." This unkind allusion to the defunct mother, harsh as it may seem, was the first spasm of propriety,—the first symptom of the camp's regeneration. Stumpy advanced nothing. Perhaps he felt a certain delicacy in interfering with the selection of a possible successor in office. But when questioned, he averred stoutly that he and "Jinny"—the mammal before alluded to—could manage to rear the child. There was something original, independent, and heroic about the plan that pleased the camp. Stumpy was retained. Certain articles were sent for to Sacramento. "Mind," said the treasurer, as he pressed a bag of gold-dust into the expressman's hand, "the best that can be got,—lace, you know, and filigree-work and frills,—d—n the cost!"

Strange to say, the child thrived. Perhaps the invigorating climate of the mountain camp was compensation for material deficiencies. Nature took the foundling to her broader breast. In that rare atmosphere of the Sierra foothills,—that air pungent with balsamic odor, that ethereal cordial at once bracing and exhilarating—he may have found food and nourishment, or a subtle chemistry that transmuted ass's milk to lime and phosphorus. Stumpy inclined to the belief that it was the latter and good nursing. "Me and that ass," he would say, "has been father and mother to him! Don't you," he would add, apostrophizing the helpless bundle before him, "never go back on us."

By the time he was a month old the necessity of giving him a name became apparent. He had generally been known as "The Kid," "Stumpy's Boy," "The Coyote" (an allusion to his vocal powers), and even by Kentuck's endearing diminutive of "The d—d little cuss." But these were felt to be vague and unsatisfactory, and were at last dismissed under another influence. Gamblers and adventurers are generally superstitious, and Oakhurst one day declared that the baby had brought "the luck" to Roaring Camp. It was certain that of late they had been successful. "Luck" was the name agreed upon, with the prefix of Tommy for greater convenience. No allusion was made to the mother, and the father was unknown. "It's better," said the philosophical Oakhurst, "to take a fresh deal all round. Call him Luck, and start him fair." A day was accordingly set apart for the christening. What was meant by this ceremony the reader may imagine who has already gathered some idea of the reckless irreverence of Roaring Camp. The master of ceremonies was one "Boston," a noted wag, and the occasion seemed to promise the greatest facetiousness. This ingenious satirist had spent two days in preparing a burlesque of the Church service, with pointed local allusions. The choir was properly trained, and Sandy Tipton was to stand godfather. But after the procession had marched to the grove with music and banners, and the child had been deposited before a mock altar, Stumpy stepped before the expectant crowd. "It ain't my style to spoil fun, boys," said the little man, stoutly eying the faces around him, "but it strikes me that this thing ain't exactly on the squar. It's playing it pretty low down on this yer baby to ring in fun on him that he ain't goin' to understand. And ef there's goin' to be any godfathers round, I'd like to see who's got any better rights than me." A silence followed Stumpy's speech. To the credit of all humorists be it said that the first man to acknowledge its justice was the satirist thus stopped of his fun. "But," said Stumpy, quickly following up his advantage, "we're here for a christening, and we'll have it. I proclaim you Thomas Luck, according to the laws of the United States and the State of California, so help me God." It was the first time that the name of the Deity had been otherwise uttered than profanely in the camp. The form of christening was perhaps even more ludicrous than the satirist had conceived; but strangely enough, nobody saw it and nobody laughed. "Tommy" was christened as seriously as he would have been under a Christian roof, and cried and was comforted in as orthodox fashion.

And so the work of regeneration began in Roaring Camp. Almost imperceptibly a change came over the settlement. The cabin assigned to "Tommy Luck"—or "The Luck," as he was more frequently called—first showed signs of improvement. It was kept scrupulously clean and whitewashed. Then it was boarded, clothed and papered. The rosewood cradle, packed eighty miles by mule, had, in

Stumpy's way of putting it, "sorter killed the rest of the furniture." So the rehabilitation of the cabin became a necessity. The men who were in the habit of lounging in at Stumpy's to see "how 'The Luck' got on" seemed to appreciate the change, and in self-defense the rival establishment of "Tuttle's grocery" bestirred itself and imported a carpet and mirrors. The reflections of the latter on the appearance of Roaring Camp tended to produce stricter habits of personal cleanliness. Again Stumpy imposed a kind of quarantine upon those who aspired to the honor and privilege of holding The Luck. It was a cruel mortification to Kentuck—who, in the carelessness of a large nature and the habits of frontier life, had begun to regard all garments as a second cuticle, which, like a snake's, only sloughed off through decay—to be debarred this privilege from certain prudential reasons. Yet such was the subtle influence of innovation that he thereafter appeared regularly every afternoon in a clean shirt and face still shining from his ablutions. Nor were moral and social sanitary laws neglected. "Tommy," who was supposed to spend his whole existence in a persistent attempt to repose, must not be disturbed by noise. The shouting and yelling, which had gained the camp its infelicitous title, were not permitted within hearing distance of Stumpy's. The men conversed in whispers or smoked with Indian gravity. Profanity was tacitly given up in these sacred precincts, and throughout the camp a popular form of expletive, known as "D—n the luck!" and "Curse the luck!" was abandoned, as having a new personal bearing. Vocal music was not interdicted, being supposed to have a soothing, tranquilizing quality; and one song, sung by "Man-o'-War Jack," an English sailor from her Majesty's Australian colonies, was quite popular as a lullaby. It was a lugubrious recital of the exploits of "the Arethusa, Seventy-four," in a muffled minor, ending with a prolonged dying fall at the burden of each verse, "On b-oo-o-ard of the Arethusa." It was a fine sight to see Jack holding The Luck, rocking from side to side as if with the motion of a ship, and crooning forth this naval ditty. Either through the peculiar rocking of Jack or the length of his song,—it contained ninety stanzas, and was continued with conscientious deliberation to the bitter end,—the lullaby generally had the desired effect. At such times the men would lie at full length under the trees in the soft summer twilight, smoking their pipes and drinking in the melodious utterances. An indistinct idea that this was pastoral happiness pervaded the camp. "This 'ere kin o' think," said the Cockney Simmons, meditatively reclining on his elbow, "is 'evingly." It reminded him of Greenwich.

On the long summer days The Luck was usually carried to the gulch from whence the golden store of Roaring Camp was taken. There, on a blanket spread over pine boughs, he would lie while the men were working in the ditches below. Latterly there was a rude attempt to decorate this bower with flowers and sweet-smelling shrubs, and generally some one would bring him a cluster of wild honeysuckle, azaleas, or the painted blossoms of Las Mariposas. The men had suddenly awakened to the fact that there were beauty and significance in these trifles, which they had so long trodden carelessly beneath their feet. A flake of glittering mica, a fragment of variegated quartz, a bright pebble from the bed of the creek, became beautiful to eyes thus cleared and strengthened, and were invariably put aside for The Luck. It was wonderful how many treasures the woods and hillsides yielded that "would do for Tommy." Surrounded by playthings such as never child out of fairyland had before, it is to be hoped that Tommy was content. He appeared to be serenely happy, albeit there was an infantine gravity about him, a contemplative light in his round gray eyes, that sometimes worried Stumpy. He was always tractable and quiet, and it is recorded that once, having crept beyond his "corral,"—a hedge of tessellated pine boughs, which surrounded his bed,—he dropped over the bank on his head in the soft earth, and remained with his mottled legs in the air in that position for at least five minutes with unflinching gravity. He was extricated without a murmur. I hesitate to record the many other instances of his sagacity, which rest, unfortunately, upon the statements of prejudiced friends. Some of them were not without a tinge of superstition. "I crep' up the bank just now," said Kentuck one day, in a breathless state of excitement, "and dern my skin if he wasn't a-talking to a jaybird as was a-sittin' on his lap. There they was, just as free and sociable as anything you please, a-jawin' at each other just like two cherrybums." Howbeit, whether creeping over the pine boughs or lying lazily on his back blinking at the leaves above him, to him the birds sang, the squirrels chattered, and the flowers bloomed. Nature was his nurse and playfellow. For him she would let slip between the leaves golden shafts of sunlight that fell just within his grasp; she would send wandering breezes to visit him with the balm of bay and resinous gum; to him the tall redwoods nodded familiarly and sleepily, the bumblebees buzzed, and the rooks cawed a slumbrous accompaniment.

Such was the golden summer of Roaring Camp. They were "flush times," and the luck was with them. The claims had yielded enormously. The camp was jealous of its privileges and looked suspiciously on strangers. No encouragement was given to immigration, and, to make their seclusion more perfect, the land on either side of the mountain wall that surrounded the camp they duly preëmpted. This, and a reputation for singular proficiency with the revolver, kept the reserve of Roaring Camp inviolate. The expressman—their only connecting link with the surrounding world —sometimes told wonderful stories of the camp. He would say, "They've a street up there in 'Roaring' that would lay over any street in Red Dog. They've got vines and flowers round their houses, and they wash themselves twice a day. But they're mighty rough on strangers, and they worship an Ingin baby."

With the prosperity of the camp came a desire for further improvement. It was proposed to build a hotel in the following spring, and to invite one or two decent families to reside there for the sake of The Luck, who might perhaps profit by female companionship. The sacrifice that this concession to the sex cost these men who were fiercely skeptical in regard to its general virtue and usefulness, can only be accounted for by their affection for Tommy. A few still held out. But the resolve could not be carried into effect for three months, and the minority meekly yielded in the hope that something might turn up to prevent it. And it did.

The winter of 1851 will long be remembered in the foothills. The snow lay deep on the Sierras, and every mountain creek became a river, and every river a lake. Each gorge and gulch was transformed into a tumultuous water-course that descended the hillsides, tearing down giant trees and scattering its drift and débris along the plain. Red Dog had been twice under water, and Roaring Camp had been forewarned. "Water put the gold into them gulches," said Stumpy. "It's been here once and will be here again!" And that night the North Fork suddenly leaped over its banks and swept up the triangular valley of Roaring Camp.

In the confusion of rushing water, crashing trees, and crackling timber, and the darkness which seemed to flow with the water and blot out the fair valley, but little could be done to collect the scattered camp. When the morning broke, the cabin of Stumpy, nearest the river-bank, was gone. Higher up the gulch they found the body of its unlucky owner; but the pride, the hope, the joy, The Luck, of Roaring Camp had disappeared. They were returning with sad hearts when a shout from the bank recalled them.

It was a relief-boat from down the river. They had picked up, they said, a man and an infant, nearly exhausted, about two miles below. Did anybody know them, and did they belong here?

It needed but a glance to show them Kentuck lying there, cruelly crushed and bruised, but still holding The Luck of Roaring Camp in his arms. As they bent over the strangely assorted pair, they saw that the child was cold and pulseless. "He is dead," said one. Kentuck opened his eyes. "Dead?" he repeated feebly. "Yes, my man, and you are dying too." A smile lit the eyes of the expiring Kentuck. "Dying!" he repeated; "he's a-taking me with him. Tell the boys I've got The Luck with me now"; and the strong man, clinging to the frail babe as a drowning man is said to cling to a straw, drifted away into the shadowy river that flows forever to the unknown sea.

1868

THE ANGELUS *

(HEARD AT THE MISSION DOLORES, 1868)

Bells of the Past, whose long-forgotten music
  Still fills the wide expanse,

* All poems by Harte are used by permission of, and by arrangement with, Houghton Mifflin Company.

Tingeing the sober twilight of the Present
  With color of romance!

I hear your call, and see the sun descending,
  On rock and wave and sand,
As down the coast the Mission voices blending,
  Girdle the heathen land

Within the circle of your incantation
  No blight nor mildew falls;   10
Nor fierce unrest, nor lust, nor low
    ambition
  Passes those airy walls.

Borne on the swell of your long waves
    receding,
  I touch the farther Past;
I see the dying glow of Spanish glory,
  The sunset dream and last!

Before me rise the dome-shaped Mis-
    sion towers,
  The white Presidio;
The swart commander in his leathern
    jerkin,
  The priest in stole of snow.   20

Once more I see Portolá's cross up-
    lifting
  Above the setting sun;
And past the headland, northward,
    slowly drifting,
  The freighted galleon.

O solemn bells! Whose consecrated
    masses
  Recall the faith of old;
O tinkling bells! that lulled with twi-
    light music
  The spiritual fold!

Your voices break and falter in the
    darkness,—
  Break, falter, and are still;   30
And veiled and mystic, like the Host
    descending,
  The sun sinks from the hill!

                    1868

IN THE TUNNEL

  Didn't know Flynn,—
  Flynn of Virginia,—
  Long as he's been 'yar?
  Look 'ee here, stranger,
  Whar *hev* you been?

  Here in this tunnel
    He was my pardner,

That same Tom Flynn,—
  Working together,
  In wind and weather,   10
Day out and in.

Didn't know Flynn!
  Well, that *is* queer;
Why, it's a sin
To think of Tom Flynn,—
  Tom, with his cheer,
  Tom without fear,—
Stranger, look 'yar!

Thar in the drift,
  Back to the wall,   20
He held the timbers
  Ready to fall;
Then in the darkness
I heard him call:
  "Run for your life, Jake!
  Run for your wife's sake!
  Don't wait for me."

And that was all
  Heard in the din,
  Heard of Tom Flynn,—   30
    Flynn of Virginia.

That's all about
  Flynn of Virginia.
That lets me out.
  Here in the damp,—
Out of the sun,—
  That 'ar derned lamp
Makes my eyes run.
Well, there,—I'm done!

But, sir, when you'll   40
Hear the next fool
  Asking of Flynn,—
Flynn of Virginia,—
  Just you chip in,
  Say you knew Flynn;
Say that you've been 'yar.

                    1869

HER LETTER

I'm sitting alone by the fire,
  Dressed just as I came from the
    dance,

In a robe even *you* would admire,—
  It cost a cool thousand in France;
I'm be-diamonded out of all reason,
  My hair is done up in a cue:
In short, sir, "the belle of the season"
  Is wasting an hour upon you.

A dozen engagements I've broken;
  I left in the midst of a set;   10
Likewise a proposal, half spoken,
  That waits—on the stairs—for me
    yet.
They say he'll be rich,—when he
    grows up,—
  And then he adores me indeed;
And you, sir, are turning your nose up,
  Three thousand miles off, as you
    read.

"And how do I like my position?"
  "And what do I think of New
    York?"
"And now, in my higher ambition,
  With whom do I waltz, flirt, or
    talk?"   20
"And isn't it nice to have riches,
  And diamonds and silks, and all
    that?"
"And aren't they a change to the
    ditches
  And tunnels of Poverty Flat?"

Well, yes,—if you saw us out driving
  Each day in the Park, four-in-hand,
If you saw poor dear mamma con-
    triving
  To look supernaturally grand,—
If you saw papa's picture, as taken
  By Brady, and tinted at that,— 30
You'd never suspect he sold bacon
  And flour at Poverty Flat.

And yet, just this moment, when sit-
    ting
  In the glare of the grand chande-
    lier,—
In the bustle and glitter befitting
  The "finest *soirée* of the year,"—
In the mists of a *gaze de Chambéry*,
  And the hum of the smallest of
    talk,—

Somehow, Joe, I thought of the
    "Ferry,"
  And the dance that we had on "The
    Fork;"   40

Of Harrison's barn, with its muster
  Of flags festooned over the wall;
Of the candles that shed their soft
    luster
  And tallow on head-dress and shawl;
Of the steps that we took to one fiddle;
  Of the dress of my queer *vis-à-vis*;
And how I once went down the middle
  With the man that shot Sandy
    McGee;

Of the moon that was quietly sleeping
  On the hill, when the time came
    to go;   50
Of the few baby peaks that were peep-
    ing
  From under their bedclothes of
    snow;
Of that ride,—that to me was the
    rarest;
  Of—the something you said at the
    gate.
Ah! Joe, then I wasn't an heiress
  To "the best-paying lead in the
    State."

Well, well, it's all past; yet it's funny
  To think, as I stood in the glare
Of fashion and beauty and money,
  That I should be thinking, right
    there,   60
Of some one who breasted high water,
  And swam the North Fork, and all
    that,
Just to dance with old Folinsbee's
    daughter,
  The Lily of Poverty Flat.

But goodness! what nonsense I'm
    writing!
  (Mamma says my taste still is low)
Instead of my triumphs reciting,
  I'm spooning on Joseph,—heigh-ho!
And I'm to be "finished" by travel,—
  Whatever's the meaning of that. 70

Oh, why did papa strike pay gravel
  In drifting on Poverty Flat?

Good-night!—here's the end of my
  paper;
  Good-night! — if the longitude
    please,—
For maybe, while wasting my taper,
  Your sun's climbing over the trees.
But know, if you haven't got riches,
  And are poor, dearest Joe, and all
    that,
That my heart's somewhere there in
  the ditches,
  And you've struck it,—on Poverty
  Flat.   80

                   1869

PLAIN LANGUAGE FROM TRUTHFUL JAMES

(TABLE MOUNTAIN, 1870)

Which I wish to remark,
  And my language is plain,
That for ways that are dark
  And for tricks that are vain,
The heathen Chinee is peculiar,
  Which the same I would rise to
  explain.

Ah Sin was his name;
  And I shall not deny,
In regard to the same,
  What that name might imply; 10
But his smile, it was pensive and child-
  like,
  As I frequent remarked to Bill
  Nye.

It was August the third,
  And quite soft was the skies;
Which it might be inferred
  That Ah Sin was likewise;
Yet he played it that day upon Wil-
  liam
  And me in a way I despise.

Which we had a small game,
  And Ah Sin took a hand: 20
It was Euchre. The same
  He did not understand;
But he smiled as he sat by the table,
  With a smile that was childlike and
  bland.

Yet the cards they were stocked
  In a way that I grieve,
And my feelings were shocked
  At the state of Nye's sleeve,
Which was stuffed full of aces and
  bowers,
  And the same with intent to de-
  ceive.   30

But the hands that were played
  By that heathen Chinee,
And the points that he made,
  Were quite frightful to see,—
Till at last he put down a right bower
  Which the same Nye had dealt
  unto me.

Then I looked up at Nye,
  And he gazed upon me;
And he rose with a sigh,
  And said, "Can this be?   40
We are ruined by Chinese cheap
  labor,"
  And he went for that heathen
  Chinee.

In the scene that ensued
  I did not take a hand,
But the floor it was strewed
  Like the leaves on the strand
With the cards that Ah Sin had been
  hiding,
  In the game "he did not under-
  stand."

In his sleeves, which were long,
  He had twenty-four jacks,—   50
Which was coming it strong,
  Yet I state but the facts;
And we found on his nails, which
  were taper,
  What is frequent in tapers,—that's
  wax.

Which is why I remark,
    And my language is plain,
That for ways that are dark
    And for tricks that are vain,
The heathen Chinee is peculiar,—
    Which the same I am free to main-
        tain.   60
                                    1870

THE SOCIETY UPON THE STANISLAUS

I reside at Table Mountain, and my
    name is Truthful James;
I am not up to small deceit or any
    sinful games;
And I'll tell in simple language what
    I know about the row
That broke up our Society upon the
    Stanislow.

But first I would remark, that it is not
    a proper plan
For any scientific gent to whale his
    fellow-man,
And, if a member don't agree with
    his peculiar whim,
To lay for that same member for to
    "put a head" on him.

Now nothing could be finer or more
    beautiful to see
Than the first six months' proceedings
    of that same Society,   10
Till Brown of Calaveras brought a
    lot of fossil bones
That he found within a tunnel near
    the tenement of Jones.

Then Brown he read a paper, and he
    reconstructed there,
From those same bones, an animal
    that was extremely rare;
And Jones then asked the Chair for
    a suspension of the rules,
Till he could prove that those same
    bones was one of his lost mules.

Then Brown he smiled a bitter smile,
    and said he was at fault.

It seemed he had been trespassing on
    Jones's family vault;
He was a most sarcastic man, this
    quiet Mr. Brown,
And on several occasions he had
    cleaned out the town.   20

Now I hold it is not decent for a
    scientific gent
To say another is an ass,—at least, to
    all intent;
Nor should the individual who hap-
    pens to be meant
Reply by heaving rocks at him, to
    any great extent.

Then Abner Dean of Angel's raised a
    point of order, when
A chunk of old red sandstone took
    him in the abdomen,
And he smiled a kind of sickly smile
    and curled up on the floor,
And the subsequent proceedings in-
    terested him no more.

For, in less time than I write it,
    every member did engage
In a warfare with the remnants of a
    palæozoic age;   30
And the way they heaved those fos-
    sils in their anger was a sin,
Till the skull of an old mammoth
    caved the head of Thompson in.

And this is all I have to say of these
    improper games,
For I live at Table Mountain, and my
    name is Truthful James;
And I've told in simple language what
    I know about the row
That broke up our Society upon the
    Stanislow.
                                    1871

"CROTALUS"

(RATTLESNAKE BAR, SIERRAS)

No life in earth, or air, or sky;
The sunbeams, broken silently,
On the bared rocks around me lie,—

Cold rocks with half-warmed lichens
    scarred,
And scales of moss; and scarce a yard
Away, one long strip, yellow-barred.

Lost in a cleft! 'Tis but a stride
To reach it, thrust its roots aside,
And lift it on thy stick astride!

Yet stay! That moment is thy
    grace!   10
For round thee, thrilling air and
    space,
A chattering terror fills the place!

A sound as of dry bones that stir
In the Dead Valley! By yon fir
The locust stops its noonday whir!

The wild bird hears; smote with the
    sound,
As if by bullet brought to ground,
On broken wing, dips, wheeling
    round!

The hare, transfixed, with trembling
    lip,
Halts, breathless, on pulsating hip,   20
And palsied tread, and heels that slip.
. . . .

Enough, old friend! 'tis thou. Forget
My heedless foot, nor longer fret
The peace with thy grim castanet!

I know thee! Yes! Thou mayst
    forego
That lifted crest; the measured blow
Beyond which thy pride scorns to go,

Or yet retract! For me no spell
Lights those slit orbs, where, some
    think, swell
Machicolated fires of hell!   30

I only know thee humble, bold,
Haughty, with miseries untold,
And the old Curse that left thee cold,

And drove thee ever to the sun,
On blistering rocks; nor made thee
    shun

Our cabin's hearth, when day was
    done,

And the spent ashes warmed thee
    best;
We knew thee,—silent, joyless guest
Of our rude ingle. E'en thy quest

Of the rare milk-bowl seemed to be   40
Naught but a brother's poverty,
And Spartan taste that kept thee free

From lust and rapine. Thou! whose
    fame
Searchest the grass with tongue of
    flame,
Making all creatures seem thy game;

When the whole woods before thee
    run,
Asked but—when all was said and
    done—
To lie, untrodden, in the sun!
                      1882?

RELIEVING GUARD

THOMAS STARR KING. OBIIT MAR. 4,
1864

Came the relief. "What, sentry, ho!
How passed the night through thy
    long waking?"
"Cold, cheerless, dark,—as may befit
The hour before the dawn is break-
    ing."

"No sight? no sound?" "No; nothing
    save
The plover from the marshes calling,
And in yon western sky, about
An hour ago, a star was falling."

"A star? There's nothing strange in
    that."
"No, nothing; but, above the
    thicket,   10
Somehow it seemed to me that God
Somewhere had just relieved a picket."
                      1873

THE AGED STRANGER

AN INCIDENT OF THE WAR

"I was with Grant"—the stranger
    said;
  Said the farmer, "Say no more,
But rest thee here at my cottage
    porch,
  For thy feet are weary and sore."

"I was with Grant"—the stranger
    said;
  Said the farmer, "Nay, no more,—
I prithee sit at my frugal board,
  And eat of my humble store.

"How fares my boy,—my soldier boy,
  Of the old Ninth Army Corps? 10
I warrant he bore him gallantly
  In the smoke and the battle's roar!"

"I know him not," said the aged man,
  "And, as I remarked before,
I was with Grant"—"Nay, nay, I
    know,"
Said the farmer, "say no more:

"He fell in battle,—I see, alas!
  Thou'dst smooth these tidings
    o'er,—
Nay, speak the truth, whatever it be,
  Though it rend my bosom's core. 20

"How fell he? With his face to the
    foe,
  Upholding the flag he bore?
Oh, say not that my boy disgraced
  The uniform that he wore!"

"I cannot tell," said the aged man,
  "And should have remarked before,
That I was with Grant,—in Illinois,—
  Some three years before the war."

Then the farmer spake him never a
    word,
  But beat with his fist full sore 30
That aged man who had worked for
    Grant
  Some three years before the war.
                 1873

II. JOAQUIN MILLER (CINCINNATUS HINER MILLER) (1841–1913)

KIT CARSON'S RIDE *

*Room! room to turn round in, to
  breathe and be free,*
To grow to be giant, to sail as at sea
*With the speed of the wind on a steed
  with his mane*
*To the wind, without pathway or
  route or a rein.*
*Room! room to be free where the
  white border'd sea*
*Blows a kiss to a brother as boundless
  as he;*
*Where the buffalo come like a cloud
  on the plain,*
*Pouring on like the tide of a storm-
  driven main,*
*And the lodge of the hunter to friend
  or to foe*
*Offers rest; and unquestion'd you
  come or you go. 10*
*My plains of America! Seas of wild
  lands!*
*From a land in the seas in a raiment
  of foam,*
*That has reached to a stranger the
  welcome of home,*
*I turn to you, lean to you, lift you my
  hands.*

  Run? Run? See this flank, sir, and
    I do love him so!
But he's blind, badger blind. Whoa,
    Pache, boy, whoa,
No, you wouldn't believe it to look at
    his eyes,
But he's blind, badger blind, and it
    happen'd this wise:

* All poems by Miller are reprinted from
the Bear Edition (1909) and are here used
by permission of Abbie Leland Miller and
the publishers, the Harr Wagner Publishing
Company.

"We lay in the grass and the sun-
  burnt clover
That spread on the ground like a great
  brown cover   20
Northward and southward, and west
  and away
To the Brazos, where our lodges lay,
One broad and unbroken level of
  brown.
We were waiting the curtains of night
  to come down
To cover us trio and conceal our flight
With my brown bride, won from an
  Indian town
That lay in the rear the full ride of a
  night.

"We lounged in the grass—her eyes
  were in mine,
And her hands on my knee, and her
  hair was as wine
In its wealth and its flood, pouring on
  and all over   30
Her bosom wine red, and press'd
  never by one.
Her touch was as warm as the tinge
  of the clover
Burnt brown as it reach'd to the kiss
  of the sun.
Her words they were low as the lute-
  throated dove,
And as laden with love as the heart
  when it beats
In its hot, eager answer to earliest
  love,
Or the bee hurried home by its
  burthen of sweets.

"We lay low in the grass on the
  broad plain levels,
Old Revels and I, and my stolen
  brown bride;
Forty full miles if a foot, and the
  devils   40
Of red Comanches are hot on the
  track
When once they strike it. Let the
  sun go down
Soon, very soon,' muttered bearded
  old Revels

As he peer'd at the sun, lying low on
  his back,
Holding fast to his lasso. Then he
  jerk'd at his steed
And he sprang to his feet, and
  glanced swiftly around,
And then dropp'd, as if shot, with an
  ear to the ground;
Then again to his feet, and to me, to
  my bride,
While his eyes were like flame, his
  face like a shroud,
His form like a king, and his beard
  like a cloud,   50
And his voice loud and shrill, as both
  trumpet and reed,—
'Pull, pull in your lassoes, and bridle
  to steed,
And speed you if ever for life you
  would speed.
Aye, ride for your lives, for your
  lives you must ride!
For the plain is aflame, the prairie on
  fire,
And the feet of wild horses hard flying before
I heard like a sea breaking high on
  the shore,
While the buffalo come like a surge
  of the sea,
Driven far by the flame, driving fast
  on the three
As a hurricane comes, crushing palms
  in his ire.'   60

"We drew in the lassoes, seized the
  saddle and rein,
Threw them on, cinched them on,
  cinched them over again,
And again drew the girth; and spring
  we to horse,
With head to Brazos, with a sound in
  the air
Like the surge of a sea, with a flash
  in the eye,
From that red wall of flame reaching
  up to the sky;
A red wall of flame and a black rolling sea

Rushing fast upon us, as the wind
　　sweeping free
And afar from the desert blown hol-
　　low and hoarse.

"Not a word, not a wail from a lip
　　was let fall,　　　　　　70
We broke not a whisper, we breathed
　　not a prayer,
There was work to be done, there was
　　death in the air,
And the chance was as one to a
　　thousand for all.
"Twenty miles! . . . thirty miles!
　　. . . a dim distant speck . . .
Then a long reaching line, and the
　　Brazos in sight!
And I rose in my seat with a shout
　　of delight.
I stood in my stirrup, and look'd to
　　my right—
But Revels was gone; I glanced by
　　my shoulder
And saw his horse stagger; I saw his
　　head drooping
Hard down on his breast, and his
　　naked breast stooping　　80
Low down to the mane, as so swifter
　　and bolder
Ran reaching out for us the red-
　　footed fire.
He rode neck to neck with a buffalo
　　bull,
That made the earth shake where he
　　came in his course,
The monarch of millions, with shaggy
　　mane full
Of smoke and of dust, and it shook
　　with desire
Of battle, with rage and with bellow-
　　ings hoarse.
His keen, crooked horns, through the
　　storm of his mane,
Like black lances lifted and lifted
　　again;
And I looked but this once, for the
　　fire licked through,　　90
And Revels was gone, as we rode two
　　and two.

"I look'd to my left then—and
　　nose, neck, and shoulder
Sank slowly, sank surely, till back to
　　my thighs,
And up through the black blowing
　　veil of her hair
Did beam full in mine her two mar-
　　velous eyes,
With a longing and love yet a look
　　of despair
And of pity for me, as she felt the
　　smoke fold her,
And flames leaping far for her glori-
　　ous hair.
Her sinking horse falter'd, plunged
　　fell and was gone
As I reach'd through the flame and I
　　bore her still on.　　100
On! into the Brazos, she, Pache and
　　I—
Poor, burnt, blinded Pache.　I love
　　him . . .
That's why."

　　　　　　　　　　　1871, 1909

From THE LAST TASCHASTAS

III

. . . .

From cold east shore to warm west
　　sea
The red men followed the red sun,
And faint and failing fast as he,
They knew too well their race was
　　run.
This ancient tribe, press'd to the wave
There fain had slept a patient slave,
And died out as red embers die
From flames that once leapt hot and
　　high;
But, roused to anger, half arose
Around that chief, a sudden flood,　210
A hot and hungry cry for blood;
Half drowsy shook a feeble hand,
Then sank back in a tame repose,
And left him to his fate and foes,
A stately wreck upon the strand.

. . . .

His eye was like the lightning's wing,
His voice was like a rushing flood;
And when a captive bound he stood
His presence look'd the perfect king.

'Twas held at first that he should
          die: 220
I never knew the reason why
A milder council did prevail,
Save that we shrank from blood, and
          save
That brave men do respect the brave.
Down sea sometimes there was a sail,
And far at sea, they said, an isle,
And he was sentenced to exile;
In open boat upon the sea
To go the instant on the main,
And never under penalty   230
Of death to touch the shore again.
A troop of bearded buckskinn'd men
Bore him hard-hurried to the wave,
Placed him swift in the boat; and then
Swift pushing to the gristling sea,
His daughter rush'd down suddenly,
Threw him his bow, leapt from the
          shore
Into the boat beside the brave,
And sat her down and seized the oar,
And never questioned, made re-
          plies,   240
Or moved her lips, or raised her eyes.

His breast was like a gate of brass,
His brow was like a gather'd storm;
There is no chisell'd stone that has
So stately and complete a form
In sinew, arm, and every part,
In all the galleries of art.

Gray, bronzed, and naked to the
          waist,
He stood half halting in the prow,
With quiver bare and idle bow.   250
The warm sea fondled with the shore,
And laid his white face to the sands.
His daughter sat with her sad face
Bent on the wave, with her two hands
Held tightly to the dripping oar;
And as she sat, her dimpled knee
Bent lithe as wand or willow tree,

So round and full, so rich and free,
That no one would have ever known
That it had either joint or bone.   260

Her eyes were black, her face was
          brown,
Her breasts were bare, and there fell
          down
Such wealth of hair, it almost hid
The two, in its rich jetty fold—
Which I had sometime fain forbid,
They were so richer, fuller far
Than any polished bronzes are,
And richer hued than any gold.
On her brown arms and her brown
          hands
Were bars of gold and golden
          bands,   270
Rough hammer'd from the virgin ore,
So heavy, they could hold no more.

I wonder now, I wonder'd then,
That men who fear'd not gods nor
          men
Laid no rude hands at all on her,—
I think she had a dagger slid
Down in her silver'd wampum belt;
It might have been, instead of hilt,
A flashing diamond hurry-hid
That I beheld—I could not know   280
For certain, we did hasten so;
And I know now less sure than then:
Deeds strangle memories of deeds,
Red blossoms wither, choked with
          weeds,
And years drown memories of men.
Some things have happened since—
          and then
This happen'd years and years ago.

"Go, go!" the captain cried, and
          smote
With sword and boot the swaying
          boat,
Until it quiver'd as at sea
And brought the old chief to his knee.
He turn'd his face, and turning rose   290
With hand raised fiercely to his foes:
"Yes, I will go, last of my race,
Push'd by you robbers ruthlessly

Into the hollows of the sea,
From this my last, last resting-place.
Traditions of my fathers say
A feeble few reach'd for this land,
And we reach'd them a welcome hand
Of old, upon another shore;
Now they are strong, we weak as
　　　they,　　　　　　　　　　300
And they have driven us before
Their faces, from that sea to this:
Then marvel not if we have sped
Sometime an arrow as we fled,
So keener than a serpent's kiss."

He turn'd a time unto the sun
That lay half hidden in the sea,
As in his hollows rock'd asleep,
All trembled and breathed heavily;
Then arch'd his arm, as you have
　　　done,　　　　　　　　　　310
For sharp masts piercing through the
　　　deep.
No shore or kind ship met his eye,
Or isle, or sail, or anything,
Save white sea gulls on dipping wing,
And mobile sea and molten sky.

"Farewell!—push seaward, child!"
　　　he cried,
And quick the paddle-strokes replied.
Like lightning from the panther-skin,
That bound his loins round about,
He snatched a poison'd arrow out,　320
That like a snake lay hid within,
And twang'd his bow.　The captain
　　　fell
Prone on his face, and such a yell
Of triumph from that savage rose
As man may never hear again.
He stood as standing on the main,
The topmast main, in proud repose,
And shook his clench'd fist at his foes,
And call'd and cursed them every one.
He heeded not the shouts and shot　330
That follow'd him, but grand and
　　　grim
Stood up against the level sun;
And, standing so, seem'd in his ire
So grander than some ship on fire.

And when the sun had left the se[a]
That laves Abrup, and Blanco laves,
And left the land to death and me,
The only thing that I could see
Was, ever as the light boat lay
High lifted on the white-back[']
　　　waves,　　　　　　　　　　34[0]
A head as gray and toss'd as they.

　　We raised the dead, and from hi[s]
　　　hands
Pick'd out some shells, clutched as h[e]
　　　lay
And two by two bore him away,
And wiped his lips of blood and sands[.]

We bent and scooped a shallo[w]
　　　home,
And laid him warm-wet in his blood[,]
Just as the lifted tide a-flood
Came charging in with mouth a-foam
And as we turn'd, the sensate thing　35[0]
Reached up, lick'd out its foam[y]
　　　tongue,
Lick'd out its tongue and taste[d]
　　　blood:
The white lips to the red earth clung
An instant, and then loosening
All hold just like a living thing,
Drew back sad-voiced and shuddering[,]
All stained with blood, a stripéd flood[.]
　　　　　　　　　　　　　　187[1]

EXODUS FOR OREGON

A tale half told and hardly under-
　　　stood;
The talk of bearded men that chance[d]
　　　to meet,
That lean'd on long quaint rifles i[n]
　　　the wood,
That look'd in fellow faces, spoke
　　　discreet
And low, as half in doubt and i[n]
　　　defeat
Of hope; a tale it was of lands of gold
That lay below the sun.　Wild-wing'[d]
　　　and fleet

It spread among the swift Missouri's
    bold
Unbridled men, and reach'd to where
    Ohio roll'd.

Then long chain'd lines of yoked
    and patient steers;   10
Then long white trains that pointed
    to the west,
Beyond the savage west; the hopes
    and fears
Of blunt, untutor'd men, who hardly
    guess'd
Their course; the brave and silent
    women, dress'd
In homely spun attire, the boys in
    bands,
The cheery babes that laugh'd at all,
    and bless'd
The doubting hearts, with laughing
    lifted hands! . . .
What exodus for far untraversed
    lands!

The Plains! The shouting drivers
    at the wheel;
The crash of leather whips; the crush
    and roll   20
Of wheels; the groan of yokes and
    grinding steel
And iron chain, and lo! at last the
    whole
Vast line, that reach'd as if to touch
    the goal,
Began to stretch and stream away
    and wind
Toward the west as if with one con-
    trol;
Then hope loom'd fair, and home lay
    far behind;
Before, the boundless plain, and fierc-
    est of their kind.

At first the way lay green and fresh
    as seas,
And far away as any reach of wave;
The sunny streams went by in belt
    of trees;   30
And here and there the tassell'd
    tawny brave

Swept by on horse, look'd back,
    stretch'd forth and gave
A yell of warn, and then did wheel
    and rein
Awhile, and point away, dark-brow'd
    and grave,
Into the far and dim and distant plain
With signs and prophecies, and then
    plunged on again.

Some hills at last began to lift and
    break;
Some streams began to fail of wood
    and tide,
The somber plain began betime to
    take
A hue of weary brown, and wild and
    wide   40
It stretch'd its naked breast on every
    side.
A babe was heard at last to cry for
    bread
Amid the deserts; cattle low'd and
    died,
And dying men went by with broken
    tread,
And left a long black serpent line of
    wreck and dead.

Strange hunger'd birds, black-
    wing'd and still as death,
And crown'd of red with hooked
    beaks, blew low
And close about, till we could touch
    their breath—
Strange unnamed birds, that seem'd
    to come and go
In circles now, and now direct and
    slow,   50
Continual, yet never touch the earth;
Slim foxes slid and shuttled to and
    fro
At times across the dusty weary
    dearth
Of life, look'd back, then sank like
    crickets in a hearth.

Then dust arose, a long dim line
    like smoke

From out of riven earth. The wheels
    went groaning by,
Ten thousand feet in harness and in
    yoke,
They tore the ways of ashen alkali,
And desert winds blew sudden, swift
    and dry.
The dust! it sat upon and fill'd the
    train!   60
It seem'd to fret and fill the very sky.
Lo! dust upon the beasts, the tent,
    the plain,
And dust, alas! on breasts that rose
    not up again.

    They sat in desolation and in dust
By dried-up desert streams; the
    mother's hands
Hid all her bended face; the cattle
    thrust
Their tongues and faintly call'd across
    the lands.
The babes, that knew not what this
    way through sands
Could mean, did ask if it would end
    today . . .
The panting wolves slid by, red-
    eyed, in bands   70
To pools beyond. The men look'd
    far away,
And, silent, saw that all a boundless
    desert lay.

    They rose by night; they struggled
    on and on
As thin and still as ghosts; then here
    and there
Beside the dusty way before the
    dawn,
Men silent laid them down in their
    despair,
And died. But woman! Woman,
    frail as fair,
May man have strength to give to
    you your due;
You falter'd not, nor murmured any-
    where,
You held your babes, held to your
    course, and you   80

Bore on through burning hell you
    double burdens through.

    Men stood at last, the decimate
    few,
Above a land of running streams, and
    they?
They push'd aside the boughs, and
    peering through
Beheld afar the cool, refreshing bay
Then some did curse, and some bend
    hands to pray;
But some look'd back upon the desert
    wide
And desolate with death, then all the
    day
They mourned. But one, with noth-
    ing left beside
His dog to love, crept down among
    the ferns and died.   9
                    187

DEAD IN THE SIERRAS

    His footprints have failed us,
  Where berries are red,
  And madroños are rankest,—
    The hunter is dead!

    The grizzly may pass
  By his half-open door;
  May pass and repass
  On his path, as of yore;

    The panther may crouch
  In the leaves on his limb;   1
  May scream and may scream,—
  It is nothing to him.

    Prone, bearded, and breasted
  Like columns of stone;
  And tall as a pine—
  As a pine overthrown!

    His camp-fires gone,
  What else can be done
  Than let him sleep on
  Till the light of the sun?   2

Ay, tombless! what of it?
Marble is dust,
Cold and repellent;
And iron is rust.

1873

ALASKA

Ice built, ice bound and ice bounded,
uch cold seas of silence! such room!
uch snow-light, such sea light con-
    founded
Vith thunders that smite like a
    doom!
uch grandeur! such glory! such
    gloom!
[ear that boom! hear that deep dis-
    tant boom
»f an avalanche hurled
»own this unfinished world!

Ice seas! and ice summits! ice
    spaces
ɪ splendor of white, as God's
    throne!   10
·e worlds to the pole! and ice places
ntracked, and unnamed, and un-
    known!
[ear that boom! Hear the grinding,
    the groan
f the ice-gods in pain! Hear the
    moan
f yon ice mountain hurled
own this unfinished world.

1909

COLUMBUS

ehind him lay the gray Azores,
  Behind the Gates of Hercules;
efore him not the ghost of shores,
  Before him only shoreless seas.
he good mate said: "Now must we
    pray,
  For lo! the very stars are gone,
rave Adm'r'l speak; what shall I
    say?"
  "Why, say: 'Sail on! sail on! and
    on!' "

"My men grow mutinous day by day;
  My men grow ghastly wan and
    weak."   10
The stout mate thought of home; a
    spray
  Of salt wave washed his swarthy
    cheek.
"What shall I say, brave Adm'r'l, say,
  If we sight naught but seas at
    dawn?"
"Why, you shall say at break of day:
  'Sail on! sail on! and on!' "

They sailed and sailed, as winds might
    blow,
  Until at last the blanched mate
    said:
"Why, now not even God would
    know
  Should I and all my men fall
    dead.   20
These very winds forget their way,
  For God from these dread seas is
    gone.
Now speak, brave Adm'r'l, speak and
    say"—
  He said: "Sail on! sail on! and
    on!"

They sailed. They sailed. Then
    spake the mate:
  "This mad sea shows his teeth to-
    night.
He curls his lip, he lies in wait,
  He lifts his teeth, as if to bite!
Brave Adm'r'l, say but one good
    word:
  What shall we do when hope is
    gone?"   30
The words leapt like a leaping sword:
  "Sail on! sail on! sail on! and on!"

Then pale and worn, he paced his
    deck,
  And peered through darkness. Ah,
    that night
Of all dark nights! And then a
    speck—
  A light! A light! At last a light!
It grew, a starlit flag unfurled!

It grew to be Time's burst of dawn.
He gained a world; he gave that world
    Its grandest lesson: "On! sail
        on!"   40

                                1896

TWILIGHT AT THE HEIGHTS

The brave young city by the Balboa
    seas
Lies compassed about by the hosts
    of night—
Lies humming, low, like a hive of
    bees;
And the day lies dead. And its
    spirit's flight

Is far to the west; while the golden
    bars
That bound it are broken to a dust
    of stars.

Come under my oaks, oh, drowsy
    dusk!
The wolf and the dog; dear incense
    hour
When Mother Earth hath a smell of
    musk,
And things of the spirit assert their
    power—   10
When candles are set to burn in the
    west—
Set head and foot to the day at rest.
                                1909

From *LIFE AMONGST THE MO-
DOCS: UNWRITTEN HISTORY*

CHAPTER I

SHADOWS OF SHASTA

Lonely as God, and white as a
winter moon, Mount Shasta starts up
sudden and solitary from the heart
of the great black forests of North- 10
ern California.

You would hardly call Mount
Shasta a part of the Sierras; you
would say rather that it is the great
white tower of some ancient and
eternal wall, with here and there the
white walls overthrown.

It has no rival! There is not even
a snow-crowned subject in sight of
its dominion. A shining pyramid in 20
mail of everlasting frosts and ice, the
sailor sometimes, in a day of singular
clearness, catches glimpses of it from
the sea a hundred miles away to the
west; and it may be seen from the
dome of the capital 300 miles distant. The immigrant coming from

the east beholds the snowy, solitary
pillar from afar out on the arid sage-
brush plains, and lifts his hands in
silence as in answer to a sign.

Column upon column of storm-
stained tamarack, strong-tossing pines,
and warlike-looking firs have rallied
here. They stand with their backs
against this mountain, frowning down
dark-browed, and confronting the face
of the Saxon. They defy the advance
of civilization into their ranks. What
if these dark and splendid columns,
a hundred miles in depth, should be
the last to go down in America!
What if this should be the old guard
gathered here, marshalled around their
emperor in plumes and armor, that
may die but not surrender!

Ascend this mountain, stand against
the snow above the upper belt of
pines, and take a glance below. Toward the sea nothing but the black
and unbroken forest. Mountains, it
is true, dip and divide and break the
monotony as the waves break up the
sea; yet it is still the sea, still the un-

broken forest, black and magnificent. To the south the landscape sinks and declines gradually, but still maintains its column of dark-plumed grenadiers, till the Sacramento Valley is reached, nearly a hundred miles away. Silver rivers run here, the sweetest in the world. They wind and wind among the rocks and mossy roots, with California lilies, and the yew with scarlet berries dipping in the water, and trout idling in the eddies and cool places by the basketful. On the east, the forest still keeps up unbroken rank till the Pit River valley is reached; and even there it surrounds the valley, and locks it up tight in its black embrace. To the north, it is true, Shasta valley makes quite a dimple in the sable sea, and men plough there, and Mexicans drive mules or herd their mustang ponies on the open plain. But the valley is limited, surrounded by the forest, confined and imprisoned.

Look intently down among the black and rolling hills, forty miles away to the west, and here and there you will see a haze of cloud or smoke hung up above the trees; or, driven by the wind that is coming from the sea, it may drag and creep along as tangled in the tops.

These are mining camps. Men are here, down in these dreadful cañons, out of sight of the sun, swallowed up, buried in the impenetrable gloom of the forest, toiling for gold. Each one of these camps is a world in itself. History, romance, tragedy, poetry in every one of them. They are connected together, and reach the outer world only by a narrow little pack trail, stretching through the timber, swinging round the mountains, barely wide enough to admit of footmen and little Mexican mules with their *apparajos,* to pass in single file. We will descend into one of these camps by-and-by. I dwelt there a year, many and many a year ago. I shall picture that camp as it was, and describe events as they happened. Giants were there, great men were there.

They were very strong, energetic and resolute, and hence were neither gentle or sympathetic. They were honorable, noble, brave and generous, and yet they would have dragged a Trojan around the wall by the heels and thought nothing of it. Coming suddenly into the country with prejudices against and apprehensions of the Indians, of whom they knew nothing save through novels, they of course were in no mood to study their nature. Besides, they knew that they were in a way, trespassers if not invaders, that the Government had never treated for the land or offered any terms whatever to the Indians. and like most men who feel that they are somehow in the wrong, did not care to get on terms with their antagonists. They would have named the Indian a Trojan, and dragged him around, not only by the heels but by the scalp, rather than have taken time or trouble, as a rule, to get in the right of the matter.

I say that the greatest, the grandest body of men that have ever been gathered together since the siege of Troy, was once here on the Pacific. I grant that they were rough enough sometimes. I admit that they took a peculiar delight in periodical six-shooter war dances, these wild-bearded, hairy-breasted men, and that they did a great deal of promiscuous killing among each other, but then they did it in such a manly sort of way!

There is another race in these forests. I lived with them nearly five years. A great sin it was thought then, indeed. You do not see the smoke of their wigwams through the trees. They do not smite the mountain rocks for gold, nor fell the pines, nor roil up the waters and ruin them for the fishermen. All this magnificent forest is their estate. The Great Spirit made this mountain first of all, and gave it to them, they say, and they have possessed it ever since. They preserve the forest, keep out the fires, for it is the park for their deer.

I shall endeavor to make this sketch of my life with the Indians—a subject about which so much has been written and so little is known—true in every particular. In so far as I succeed in doing that I think the work will be novel and original. No man with a strict regard for truth should attempt to write his autobiography with a view to publication during his life; the temptations are too great.

A man standing on the gallows, without hope of descending and mixing again with his fellow men, might trust himself to utter "the truth, the whole truth, and nothing but the truth," as the law hath it; and a Crusoe on his island, without sail in sight or hope of sail, might be equally sincere, but I know of few other conditions in which I could follow a man through his account of himself with perfect confidence.

This narrative, however, while the

thread of it is necessarily spun aroun[d] a few years of my early life, is no[t] particularly of myself, but of a rac[e] of people that has lived centuries o[f] history and never yet had a historian[,] that has suffered nearly four hundre[d] years of wrong, and never yet ha[d] an advocate.

I must write of myself, because [I] was among these people of whom [I] write, though often in the backgroun[d] giving place to the inner and actu[al] lives of a silent and mysterious pe[o]ple, a race of prophets; poets wit[h]out the gift of expression—a race tha[t] has been often, almost always, mi[s]treated, and never understood—a rac[e] that is moving noiselessly from t[he] face of the earth; dreamers that som[e]times waken from their mysteriou[s]ness and simplicity, and then, bloo[d] brutality, and all the ferocity tha[t] marks a man of maddened passion[,] women without mercy and witho[ut] reason, brand them with the appr[o]priate name of savages.

But beyond this, I have a word [to] say for the Indian. I saw him as [he] was, not as he is. In one litt[le] spot of our land, I saw him [as] he was centuries ago in every pa[rt] of it perhaps, a Druid and a dream[er] —the mildest and the tamest of b[e]ings. I saw him as no man can s[ee] him now. I saw him as no ma[n] ever saw him who had not the des[ire] and patience to observe, the sympat[hy] to understand, and the intelligence [to] communicate his observations to tho[se] who would really like to understa[nd] him. He is truly "the gentle sa[v]age"; the worst and the best of me[n,] the tamest and the fiercest of bein[g.] The world cannot understand t[he] combination of these two qualiti[es]

or want of a truer comparison let
s liken him to a jealous woman—
whole-souled uncultured woman,
trong in her passions and her love.
sort of Parisian woman, now made
esperate by a long siege and an end-
ss war.

A singular combination of circum-
tances laid his life bare to me. I
as a child and he was a child. He
ermitted me to enter his heart.

As I write these opening lines here
-day in the Old World, a war of
xtermination is declared against the
Iodoc Indians in the New. I know
iese people. I know every foot of
ieir once vast possessions, stretch-
ig away to the north and east of
Iount Shasta. I know their rights
d their wrongs. I have known them
r nearly twenty years.

Peace commissioners have been
lled by the Modocs, and the civi-
zed world condemns them. I am not
repared to defend their conduct.
his narrative is not for their defence,
for the defence of the Indian, or
y one; but I could, by a ten-line
ragraph, throw a bombshell into the
mp of the civilized world at this
oment, and change the whole drift
public opinion. But it would be
o late to be of any particular use
this one doomed tribe.

Years and years ago, when Cap-
in Jack was but a boy, the Modocs
ere at war with the whites, who
ere then scouring the country in
arch of gold. A company took the
ld under the command of a brave
d reckless ruffian named Ben
right.

The Indians were not so well armed
d equipped as their enemies. The
cessities of the case, to say nothing of their nature, compelled them
to fight from behind the cover of
the rocks and trees. They were hard
to reach, and generally came out best
in the few little battles that were
fought.

In this emergency Captain Wright
proposed to meet the chiefs in council, for the purpose of making a lasting and permanent treaty. The Indians consented, and the leaders
came in. "Go back," said Wright,
"and bring in all your people; we
will have council, and celebrate our
peace with a feast."

The Indians came in in great numbers, laid down their arms, and then
at a sign Wright and his men fell
upon them, and murdered them without mercy. Captain Wright boasted
on his return that he had made a
permanent treaty with at least a thousand Indians.

Captain Jack was but a boy then,
but he was a true Indian. He was
not a chief then. I believe he was
not even of the blood which entitles
him to that place by inheritance, but
he was a bold, shrewd Indian, and
won the confidence of the tribe. He
united himself to a band of the Modocs, worked his way to their head,
and bided his time for revenge. For
nearly half a lifetime he and his warriors waited their chance, and when
it came they were not unequal to the
occasion.

They have murdered, perhaps, one
white man to one hundred Indians
that were butchered in the same way,
and not so very far from the same
spot. I deplore the conduct of the
Modocs. It will contribute to the
misfortune of nearly every Indian in
America, however well some of the

rulers of the land may feel towards the race.

With these facts before you, considering our superiority in understanding right and wrong, and all that, you may not be so much surprised at the faithful following in this case of the example we set the Modoc Indians, which resulted in the massacre, and the universal condemnation of Captain Jack and his clan.

To return to my reason for publishing this sketch at this time. You will see that treating chiefly of the Indians, as it does, it may render them a service, that by-and-by would be of but little use, by instructing good men who have to deal with this peculiar people.

I know full well how many men there are on the border who are ready to rise up and contradict everything that looks like clemency or an apology for the Indian, and have therefore given only a brief account of the Ben Wright treachery and tragedy, and only such an account as I believe the fiercest enemy of the Indians living in that region admits to be true, or, at least, such an account as Ben Wright gave and was accustomed to boast of.

The Indian account of the affair, however, which I have heard a hundred times around their camp fires, and over which they seemed to never tire of brooding and mourning, is quite another story. It is dark and dreadful. The day is even yet with them, a sort of St. Bartholomew's Eve, and their mournful narration of all the bloody and brutal events would fill a volume.

They waited for revenge, a very bad thing for Indians to do, I find; though a Christian king can wait a lifetime, and a Christian nation wait a century. They saw their tribe wasting away every year; every year the hordes of white settlers were eating into the heart of their hunting grounds, still they lay in their lava beds or moved like shadows through the stormy forests and silently waited, and then when the whites came into their camp to talk for peace, as they had gone into the camp of the whites, they showed themselves but too apt scholars in the bloody lesson of long ago. * * *

1874

LOCAL COLOR AND REALISM: THE EAST AND MIDDLE WEST

I. REBECCA HARDING DAVIS
(1831–1910)

LIFE IN THE IRON MILLS

Is this the end?
O Life, as futile, then, as frail!
What hope of answer or redress?

A cloudy day: do you know what that is in a town of iron-works? The sky sank down before dawn, muddy, flat, immovable. The air is thick, clammy with the breath of crowded human beings. It stifles me. I open the window, and, looking out, can scarcely see through the rain the grocer's shop opposite, where a crowd of drunken Irishmen are puffing Lynchburg tobacco in their pipes. I can detect the scent through all the foul smells ranging loose in the air.

The idiosyncrasy of this town is smoke. It rolls sullenly in slow folds from the great chimneys of the iron-foundries, and settles down in black, slimy pools on the muddy streets. Smoke on the wharves, smoke on the dingy boats, on the yellow river,—clinging in a coating of greasy soot to the house-front, the two faded poplars, the faces of the passers-by. The long train of mules, dragging masses of pig iron through the narrow street, have a foul vapor hanging to their reeking sides. Here, inside, is a little broken figure of an angel pointing upward from the mantel-shelf; but even its wings are covered with smoke, clotted and black. Smoke everywhere! A dirty canary chirps desolately in a cage beside me. Its dream of green fields and sunshine is a very old dream,—almost worn out, I think.

From the back-window I can see a narrow brick-yard sloping down to the riverside, strewed with rain-butts and tubs. The river, dull and tawny-colored, (*la belle rivière!*) drags itself sluggishly along, tired of the heavy weight of boats and coal-barges. What wonder? When I was a child, I used to fancy a look of weary, dumb appeal upon the face of the negro-like river slavishly bearing its burden day after day. Something of the same idle notion comes to me to-day, when from the street-window I look on the slow stream of human life creeping past, night and morning, to the great mills. Masses of men, with dull, besotted faces bent to the ground, sharpened here and there by pain or cunning; skin and muscle and flesh begrimed with smoke and ashes; stooping all night over boiling caldrons of metal, laired by day in dens of drunkenness and infamy; breathing from infancy to death an air saturated with fog and grease and soot, vileness for soul and body. What do you make of a case like that, amateur psychologist? You call it an altogether serious thing to be alive: to these men it is a drunken jest, a joke,—horrible to angels perhaps, to them commonplace enough. My fancy about the river was an idle one: it is no type of such a life. What if it be stagnant and slimy here? It knows that beyond there waits for it odorous sunlight,—quaint old gardens, dusky with soft, green foliage of apple-trees, and flushing crimson with roses,—air, and fields, and mountains. The future of the Welsh puddler passing just now is not so pleasant. To be stowed away, after his grimy work is done, in a hole in the muddy graveyard, and after that,—*not* air, nor green fields, nor curious roses.

Can you see how foggy the day is? As I stand here, idly tapping the windowpane, and looking out through the rain at the dirty back-yard and the coal-boats below, fragments of an old story float up before me,—a story of this old house into which I happened to come to-day. You may think it a tiresome story enough, as foggy as the day, sharpened by no sudden flashes of pain or pleasure.—I know: only the outline of a dull life, that long since, with thousands of dull lives like its own, was vainly lived and lost: thousands of them,—massed, vile, slimy lives, like those of the torpid lizards in yonder stagnant water-butt.—Lost? There is a curious point for you to settle, my friend, who study psychology in a lazy, *dilettante* way. Stop a moment. I am going to be honest. This is what I want you to do. I want you to hide your disgust, take no heed to your clean clothes, and come right down with me,—here, into the thickest of the fog and mud an foul effluvia. I want you to he this story. There is a secret dow here, in this nightmare fog, that h lain dumb for centuries: I want make it a real thing to you. Yo Egoist, or Pantheist, or Arminian, bu in making straight paths for your fe on the hills, do not see it clearly,— this terrible question which men he have gone mad and died trying answer. I dare not put this secr into words. I told you it was dum These men, going by with drunke faces and brains full of unawakene power, do not ask it of Society or God. Their lives ask it; their death ask it. There is no reply. I w tell you plainly that I have a grea hope; and I bring it you to be teste It is this: that this terrible dum question is its own reply; that it not the sentence of death we thir it, but, from the very extremity its darkness, the most solemn prop ecy which the world has known the Hope to come. I dare make m meaning no clearer, but will only te my story. It will, perhaps, seem you as foul and dark as this thic vapor about us, and as pregnant wit death; but if your eyes are free mine are to look deeper, no perfum tinted dawn will be so fair with prom ise of the day that shall surely com

My story is very simple,—onl what I remember of the life of on of these men,—a furnace-tender one of Kirby & John's rolling-mill —Hugh Wolfe. You know the mills They took the great order for th Lower Virginia railroads there la winter; run usually with about a thou sand men. I cannot tell why I choos the half-forgotten story of this Wol more than that of myriads of these furnace-hands. Perhaps because there is a secret underlying sympathy between that story and this day with its impure fog and thwarted sunshine, —or perhaps simply for the reason that this house is the one where the Wolfes lived. There were the father and son,—both hands, as I said, in one of Kirby & John's mills for making railroad-iron,—and Deborah, their cousin, a picker in some of the cotton-mills. The house was rented then to half a dozen families. The Wolfes had two of the cellar-rooms. The old man, like many of the puddlers and feeders of the mills, was Welsh,—had spent half of his life in the Cornish tin-mines. You may pick the Welsh emigrants, Cornish miners, out of the throng passing the windows, any day. They are a trifle more lthy; their muscles are not so brawny; they stoop more. When they are drunk, they neither yell, nor shout, nor stagger, but skulk along like beaten hounds. A pure, unmixed blood, I fancy: shows itself in the light angular bodies and sharply-cut facial lines. It is nearly thirty years since the Wolfes lived here. Their lives were like those of their class: incessant labor, sleeping in kennel-like rooms, eating rank pork and molasses, drinking—God and the distillers only knew what; with an occasional night in jail, to atone for some drunken excess. Is that all of their lives?—of the portion given to them and these their duplicates swarming the streets to-day?—nothing beneath? —all? So many a political reformer will tell you,—and many a private reformer, too, who has gone among them with a heart tender with Christ's charity, and come out outraged, hardened.

One rainy night, about eleven o'clock, a crowd of half-clothed women stopped outside of the cellar-door. They were going home from the cotton-mill.

"Good-night, Deb," said one, a mulatto, steadying herself against the gas-post. She needed the post to steady her. So did more than one of them.

"Dah's a ball to Miss Potts' to-night. Ye'd best come."

"Inteet, Deb, if hur'll come, hur'll hef fun," said a shrill Welsh voice in the crowd.

Two or three dirty hands were thrust out to catch the gown of the woman, who was groping for the latch of the door.

"No."

"No? Where's Kit Small, then?"

"Begorra! on the spools. Alleys behint, though we helped her, we dud. An wid ye! Let Deb alone! It's ondacent frettin' a quiet body. Be the powers, an' we'll have a night of it! there'll be lashin's o' drink,—the Vargent be blessed and praised for 't!"

They went on, the mulatto inclining for a moment to show fight, and drag the woman Wolfe off with them; but, being pacified, she staggered away.

Deborah groped her way into the cellar, and, after considerable stumbling, kindled a match, and lighted a tallow dip, that sent a yellow glimmer over the room. It was low, damp, —the earthen floor covered with a green, slimy moss,—a fetid air smothering the breath. Old Wolfe lay asleep on a heap of straw, wrapped in a torn horse-blanket. He was a pale, meek little man, with a white face and red rabbit-eyes. The woman Deborah was like him; only her face was even more ghastly, her lips bluer, her eyes more watery. She wore a faded cotton gown and a slouching bonnet. When she walked, one could see that she was deformed, almost a hunchback. She trod softly, so as not to waken him, and went through into the room beyond. There she found by the half-extinguished fire an iron saucepan filled with cold boiled potatoes, which she put upon a broken chair with a pint-cup of ale. Placing the old candlestick beside this dainty repast, she untied her bonnet, which hung limp and wet over her face, and prepared to eat her supper. It was the first food that had touched her lips since morning. There was enough of it, however: there is not always. She was hungry,—one could see that easily enough,—and not drunk, as most of her companions would have been found at this hour. She did not drink, this woman,—her face told that, too,—nothing stronger than ale. Perhaps the weak, flaccid wretch had some stimulant in her pale life to keep her up,—some love or hope, it might be, or urgent need. When that stimulant was gone, she would take to whisky. Man cannot live by work alone. While she was skinning the potatoes, and munching them, a noise behind her made her stop.

"Janey!" she called, lifting the candle and peering into the darkness. "Janey, are you there?"

A heap of ragged coats was heaved up, and the face of a young girl emerged, staring sleepily at the woman.

"Deborah," she said, at last, "I'm here the night."

"Yes, child. Hur's welcome," sh[e] said, quietly eating on.

The girl's face was haggard an[d] sickly; her eyes were heavy wit[h] sleep and hunger: real Milesian eye[s] they were, dark, delicate blue, gloom[-] ing out from black shadows with [a] pitiful fright.

"I was alone," she said, timidly.

"Where's the father?" asked Deb[-] orah, holding out a potato, which th[e] girl greedily seized.

"He's beyant,—wid Haley,—in th[e] stone house." (Did you ever hea[r] the word *jail* from an Irish mouth?[)] "I came here. Hugh told me neve[r] to stay me-lone."

"Hugh?"

"Yes."

A vexed frown crossed her fac[e.] The girl saw it, and added quickly,—

"I have not seen Hugh the day[,] Deb. The old man says his watc[h] lasts till the mornin'."

The woman sprang up, and hastil[y] began to arrange some bread an[d] flitch in a tin pail, and to pour he[r] own measure of ale into a bottle[.] Tying on her bonnet, she blew ou[t] the candle.

"Lay ye down, Janey dear," sh[e] said, gently, covering her with the ol[d] rags. "Hur can eat the potatoes, i[f] hur's hungry."

"Where are ye goin', Deb? Th[e] rain's sharp."

"To the mill, with Hugh's supper.["]

"Let him bide till th' morn. Si[t] ye down."

"No, no,"—sharply pushing her off[.] "The boy'll starve."

She hurried from the cellar, whil[e] the child wearily coiled herself up fo[r] sleep. The rain was falling heavily, as the woman, pail in hand, emerged from the mouth of the alley, and turned down the narrow street, that stretched out, long and black, miles before her. Here and there a flicker of gas lighted an uncertain space of muddy footwalk and gutter; the long rows of house, except an occasional lager-bier shop, were closed; now and then she met a band of mill-hands skulking to or from their work.

Not many even of the inhabitants of a manufacturing town know the vast machinery of system by which the bodies of workmen are governed, that goes on unceasingly from year to year. The hands of each mill are divided into watches that relieve each other as regularly as the sentinels of an army. By night and day the work goes on, the unsleeping engines groan and shriek, the fiery pools of metal boil and surge. Only for a day in the week, in half-courtesy to public censure, the fires are partially veiled; but as soon as the clock strikes midnight, the great furnaces break forth with renewed fury, the clamor begins with fresh, breathless vigor, the engines sob and shriek like "gods in pain."

As Deborah hurried down through the heavy rain, the noise of these thousand engines sounded through the deep and shadow of the city like far-off thunder. The mill to which she was going lay on the river, a mile below the city-limits. It was far, and she was weak, aching from standing twelve hours at the spools. Yet it was her almost nightly walk to take this man his supper, though at every square she sat down to rest, and she knew she should receive small word of thanks.

Perhaps, if she had possessed an artist's eye, the picturesque oddity of the scene might have made her step stagger less, and the path seem shorter; but to her the mills were only "summat deilish to look at by night."

The road leading to the mills had been quarried from the solid rock, which rose abrupt and bare on one side of the cinder-covered road, while the river, sluggish and black, crept past on the other. The mills for rolling iron are simply immense tent-like roofs, covering acres of ground, open on every side. Beneath these roofs Deborah looked in on a city of fires, that burned hot and fiercely in the night. Fire in every horrible form: pits of flame waving in the wind; liquid metal-flames writhing in tortuous streams through the sand; wide caldrons filled with boiling fire, over which bent ghastly wretches stirring the strange brewing; and through all, crowds of half-clad men, looking like revengeful ghosts in the red light, hurried, throwing masses of glittering fire. It was like a street in Hell. Even Deborah muttered, as she crept through, " 'T looks like t' Devil's place!" It did,—in more ways than one.

She found the man she was looking for, at last, heaping coal on a furnace. He had not time to eat his supper; so she went behind the furnace, and waited. Only a few men were with him, and they noticed her only by a "Hyur comes t' hunchback, Wolfe."

Deborah was stupid with sleep; her back pained her sharply; and her

teeth chattered with cold, with the
rain that soaked her clothes and
dripped from her at every step. She
stood, however, patiently holding the
pail, and waiting.

"Hout, woman! ye look like a
drowned cat. Come near to the fire,"
—said one of the men, approaching to
scrape away the ashes.

She shook her head. Wolfe had
forgotten her. He turned, hearing the
man, and came closer.

"I did no' think; gi' me my supper, woman."

She watched him eat with a painful eagerness. With a woman's quick
instinct, she saw that he was not
hungry,—was eating to please her.
Her pale, watery eyes began to gather
a strange light.

"Is 't good, Hugh? T' ale was a
bit sour, I feared."

"No, good enough." He hesitated a
moment. "Ye're tired, poor lass!
Bide here till I go. Lay down there
on that heap of ash, and go to sleep."

He threw her an old coat for a
pillow, and turned to his work. The
heap was the refuse of the burnt
iron, and was not a hard bed; the
half-smothered warmth, too, penetrated her limbs, dulling their pain
and cold shiver.

Miserable enough she looked, lying
there on the ashes like a limp, dirty
rag,—yet not an unfitting figure to
crown the scene of hopeless discom-
fort and veiled crime: more fitting,
if one looked deeper into the heart
of things,—at her thwarted woman's
form, her colorless life, her waking
stupor that smothered pain and hunger,—even more fit to be a type of
her class. Deeper yet if one could
look, was there nothing worth read-

ing in this wet, faded thing, half-co
ered with ashes? no story of a so
filled with groping passionate lov
heroic unselfishness, fierce jealousy
of years of weary trying to please th
one human being whom she loved,
gain one look of real heart-kindne
from him? If anything like this wer
hidden beneath the pale, bleared eye
and dull, washed-out-looking face, r
one had ever taken the trouble to rea
its faint signs: not the half-clothe
furnace-tender, Wolfe, certainly. Y
he was kind to her: it was his natur
to be kind, even to the very rats th
swarmed in the cellar: kind to her
just the same way. She knew tha
And it might be that very knowled
had given to her face its apathy an
vacancy more than her low, torp
life. One sees that dead, vacant loo
steal sometimes over the rarest, fine
of women's faces,—in the very mids
it may be, of their warmest summer
day; and then one can guess at th
secret of intolerable solitude that li
hid beneath the delicate laces an
brilliant smile. There was no warmt
no brilliancy, no summer for th
woman; so the stupor and vacanc
had time to gnaw into her face pe
petually. She was young, too, thoug
no one guessed it; so the gnawi
was the fiercer.

She lay quiet in the dark corne
listening, through the monotonous di
and uncertain glare of the works,
the dull plash of the rain in the fa
distance,—shrinking back wheneve
the man Wolfe happened to look t
wards her. She knew, in spite of a
his kindness, that there was that i
her face and form which made hi
loathe the sight of her. She felt b
instinct, although she could not con

rehend it, the finer nature of the
an, which made him among his
llow-workmen something unique, set
art. She knew, that, down under
l the vileness and coarseness of his
e, there was a groping passion for
hatever was beautiful and pure,—
at his soul sickened with disgust at
r deformity, even when his words
ere kindest. Through this dull con-
iousness, which never left her, came,
ke a sting, the recollection of the
rk blue eyes and lithe figure of the
tle Irish girl she had left in the cel-
r. The recollection struck through
en her stupid intellect with a vivid
ow of beauty and of grace. Little
ney, timid, helpless, clinging to
ugh as her only friend: that was
e sharp thought, the bitter thought,
at drove into the glazed eyes a
rce light of pain. You laugh at
? Are pain and jealousy less savage
alities down here in this place I am
king you to than in your own house
your own heart,—your heart, which
ey clutch at sometimes? The note
the same, I fancy, be the octave
gh or low.

If you could go into this mill where
eborah lay, and drag out from the
arts of these men the terrible
agedy of their lives, taking it as
symptom of the disease of their
ass, no ghost Horror would terrify
u more. A reality of soul-starva-
n, of living death, that meets you
ery day under the besotted faces
the street,—I can paint nothing of
is, only give you the outside out-
es of a night, a crisis in the life of
e man: whatever muddy depth of
ul-history lies beneath you can read
cording to the eyes God has given
u.

Wolfe, while Deborah watched him
as a spaniel its master, bent over the
furnace with his iron pole, unconscious
of her scrutiny, only stopping to receive orders. Physically, Nature had
promised the man but little. He had
already lost the strength and instinct
vigor of a man, his muscles were thin,
his nerves weak, his face (a meek,
woman's face) haggard, yellow with
consumption. In the mill he was
known as one of the girl-men: "Molly
Wolfe" was his *sobriquet*. He was
never seen in the cockpit, did not
own a terrier, drank but seldom;
when he did, desperately. He fought
sometimes, but was always thrashed,
pommelled to a jelly. The man was
game enough, when his blood was up:
but he was no favorite in the mill;
he had the taint of school-learning
on him,—not to a dangerous extent,
only a quarter or so in the free-school
in fact, but enough to ruin him as a
good hand in a fight.

For other reasons, too, he was not
popular. Not one of themselves, they
felt that, though outwardly as filthy
and ash-covered; silent, with foreign
thoughts and longings breaking out
through his quietness in innumerable
curious ways: this one, for instance.
In the neighboring furnace-buildings
lay great heaps of the refuse from the
ore after the pig-metal is run. *Korl*
we call it here: a light, porous substance, of a delicate, waxen, flesh-
colored tinge. Out of the blocks of
this korl, Wolfe, in his off-hours from
the furnace, had a habit of chipping
and molding figures,—hideous, fantastic enough, but sometimes strangely
beautiful: even the mill-men saw that,
while they jeered at him. It was a
curious fancy in the man, almost a

passion. The few hours for rest he spent hewing and hacking with his blunt knife, never speaking, until his watch came again,—working at one figure for months, and, when it was finished, breaking it to pieces, perhaps, in a fit of disappointment. A morbid, gloomy man, untaught, unled, left to feed his soul in grossness and crime, and hard, grinding labor.

I want you to come down and look at this Wolfe, standing there among the lowest of his kind, and see him just as he is, that you may judge him justly when you hear the story of this night. I want you to look back, as he does every day, at his birth in vice, his starved infancy; to remember the heavy years he has groped through as boy and man,—the slow, heavy years of constant, hot work. So long ago he began, that he thinks sometimes he has worked there for ages. There is no hope that it will ever end. Think that God put into this man's soul a fierce thirst for beauty,—to know it, to create it; to *be*—something, he knows not what,— other than he is. There are moments when a passing cloud, the sun glinting on the purple thistles, a kindly smile, a child's face, will rouse him to a passion of pain,—when his nature starts up with a mad cry of rage against God, man, whoever it is that has forced this vile, slimy life upon him. With all this groping, this mad desire, a great blind intellect stumbling through wrong, a loving poet's heart, the man was by habit only a coarse, vulgar laborer, familiar with sights and words you would blush to name. Be just: when I tell you about this night, see him as he is. Be just,— not like man's law, which seizes on one isolated fact, but like God's judging angel, whose clear, sad eye saw all the countless cankering days of this man's life, all the countless nights when, sick with starving, his soul fainted in him, before it judged him for this night, the saddest of all.

I called this night the crisis of his life. If it was, it stole on him unawares. These great turning-days of life cast no shadow before, slip by us unconsciously. Only a trifle, a little turn of the rudder, and the ship goes to heaven or hell.

Wolfe, while Deborah watched him, dug into the furnace of melting iron with his pole, dully thinking only how many rails the lump would yield. It was late,—nearly Sunday morning; another hour, and the heavy work would be done,—only the furnaces to replenish and cover for the next day. The workmen were growing more noisy, shouting, as they had to do to be heard over the deep clamor of the mills. Suddenly they grew less boisterous,—at the far end, entirely silent. Something unusual had happened. After a moment, the silence came nearer; the men stopped their jeers and drunken choruses. Deborah, stupidly lifting up her head, saw the cause of the quiet. A group of five or six men were slowly approaching, stopping to examine each furnace as they came. Visitors often came to see the mills after night: except by growing less noisy, the men took no notice of them. The furnace where Wolfe worked was near the bounds of the works; they halted there hot and tired: a walk over one of these great foundries is no trifling task. The woman, drawing out of sight, turned over to sleep. Wolfe, seeing them stop, suddenly roused from his indifferent stupor, and watched them keenly. He knew some of them: the overseer, Clarke,—a son of Kirby, one of the mill-owners,—and a Doctor May, one of the town-physicians. The other two were strangers. Wolfe came closer. He seized eagerly every chance that brought him into contact with this mysterious class that shone down on him perpetually with the clamor of another order of being. What made the difference between them? That was the mystery of his life. He had a vague notion that perhaps to-night he could find it out. One of the strangers sat down on a pile of bricks, and beckoned young Kirby to his side.

"This *is* hot, with a vengeance. A match, please?"—lighting his cigar. "But the walk is worth the trouble. If it were not that you must have heard it so often, Kirby, I would tell you that your works look like Dante's Inferno."

Kirby laughed.

"Yes. Yonder is Farinata himself in the burning tomb,"—pointing to some figure in the shimmering shadows.

"Judging from some of the faces of your men," said the other, "they bid fair to try the reality of Dante's vision, some day."

Young Kirby looked curiously round, as if seeing the faces of his hands for the first time.

"They're bad enough, that's true. A desperate set, I fancy. Eh, Clarke?"

The overseer did not hear him. He was talking of net profits just then,—giving, in fact, a schedule of the annual business of the firm to a sharp peering little Yankee, who jotted down notes on a paper laid on the crown of his hat: a reporter for one of the city-papers, getting up a series of reviews of the leading manufactories. The other gentlemen had accompanied them merely for amusement. They were silent until the notes were finished, drying their feet at the furnaces, and sheltering their faces from the intolerable heat. At last the overseer concluded with—

"I believe that is a pretty fair estimate, Captain."

"Here, some of you men!" said Kirby, "bring up those boards. We may as well sit down, gentlemen, until the rain is over. It cannot last much longer at this rate."

"Pig-metal,"— mumbled the reporter,—"um! — coal facilities,— um! —hands employed, twelve hundred,— bitumen,—um!—all right, I believe, Mr. Clarke;—sinking-fund,—what did you say was your sinking-fund?"

"Twelve hundred hands?" said the stranger, the young man who had first spoken. "Do you control their votes, Kirby?"

"Control? No." The young man smiled complacently. "But my father brought seven hundred votes to the polls for his candidate last November. No force-work, you understand, —only a speech or two, a hint to form themselves into a society, and a bit of red and blue bunting to make them a flag. The Invincible Roughs,—I believe that is their name. I forget the motto: 'Our country's hope,' I think."

There was a laugh. The young man talking to Kirby sat with an amused light in his cool gray eye, surveying critically the half-clothed figures of the puddlers, and the slow swing of their brawny muscles. He was a stranger in the city,—spending a couple of months in the borders of a Slave State, to study the institutions of the South,—a brother-in-law of Kirby's,—Mitchell. He was an amateur gymnast,—hence his anatomical eye; a patron, in a *blasé* way, of the prize-ring; a man who sucked the essence out of a science or philosophy in an indifferent, gentlemanly way; who took Kant, Novalis, Humboldt, for what they were worth in his own scales; accepting all, despising nothing, in heaven, earth, or hell, but one-idead men; with a temper yielding and brilliant as summer water, until his Self was touched, when it was ice, though brilliant still. Such men are not rare in the States.

As he knocked the ashes from his cigar, Wolfe caught with a quick pleasure the contour of the white hand, the blood-glow of a red ring he wore. His voice, too, and that of Kirby's, touched him like music,—low, even, with chording cadences. About this man Mitchell hung the impalpable atmosphere belonging to the thorough-bred gentleman. Wolfe, scraping away the ashes beside him, was conscious of it, did obeisance to it with his artist sense, unconscious that he did so.

The rain did not cease. Clarke and the reporter left the mills; the others, comfortably seated near the furnace, lingered, smoking and talking in a desultory way. Greek would not have been more unintelligible to the furnace-tenders, whose presence they soon forgot entirely. Kirby drew out a newspaper from his pocket and read aloud some article, which they discussed eagerly. At every sentence,

Wolfe listened more and more like a dumb, hopeless animal, with a duller more stolid look creeping over his face, glancing now and then at Mitchell, marking acutely every smallest sign of refinement, then back to himself, seeing as in a mirror his filthy body, his more stained soul.

Never! He had no words for such a thought, but he knew now, in all the sharpness of the bitter certainty that between them there was a great gulf never to be passed. Never!

The bell of the mills rang for midnight. Sunday morning had dawned. Whatever hidden message lay in the tolling bells floated past these men unknown. Yet it was there. Veiled in the solemn music ushering the risen Saviour was a key-note to solve the darkest secrets of a world gone wrong,—even this social riddle which the brain of the grimy puddler grappled with madly to-night.

The men began to withdraw the metal from the caldrons. The mills were deserted on Sundays, except by the hands who fed the fires, and those who had no lodgings and slept usually on the ash-heaps. The three strangers sat still during the next hour watching the men cover the furnaces, laughing now and then at some jest of Kirby's.

"Do you know," said Mitchell, "I like this view of the works better than when the glare was fiercest. These heavy shadows and the amphitheater of smothered fires are ghostly, unreal. One could fancy these red smoldering lights to be the half-shut eyes of wild beasts, and the spectral figures their victims in the den."

Kirby laughed. "You are fanciful

Come, let us get out of the den. The spectral figures, as you call them, are a little too real for me to fancy a close proximity in the darkness,—unarmed, too."

The others rose, buttoning their overcoats, and lighting cigars.

"Raining, still," said Doctor May, "and hard. Where did we leave the coach, Mitchell?"

"At the other side of the works.— Kirby, what's that?"

Mitchell started back, half-frightened, as, suddenly turning a corner, he white figure of a woman faced him in the darkness,—a woman, white, of giant proportions, crouching on the ground, her arms flung out in some wild gesture of warning.

"Stop! Make that fire burn there!" cried Kirby, stopping short.

The flame burst out, flashing the gaunt figure into bold relief.

Mitchell drew a long breath.

"I thought it was alive," he said, going up curiously.

The others followed.

"Not marble, eh?" asked Kirby, touching it.

One of the lower overseers stopped.

"Korl, Sir."

"Who did it?"

"Can't say. Some of the hands; chipped it out in off-hours."

"Chipped to some purpose, I should say. What a flesh-tint the stuff has! Do you see, Mitchell?"

"I see."

He had stepped aside where the light fell boldest on the figure, looking at it in silence. There was not one line of beauty or grace in it: a nude woman's form, muscular, grown coarse with labor, the powerful limbs instinct with some one poignant longing. One idea: there it was in the tense, rigid muscles, the clutching hands, the wild, eager face, like that of a starving wolf's. Kirby and Doctor May walked around it, critical, curious. Mitchell stood aloof, silent. The figure touched him strangely.

"Not badly done," said Doctor May. "Where did the fellow learn that sweep of the muscles in the arm and hand? Look at them! They are groping,—do you see?—clutching: the peculiar action of a man dying of thirst."

"They have ample facilities for studying anatomy," sneered Kirby, glancing at the half-naked figures.

"Look," continued the Doctor, "at this bony wrist, and the strained sinews of the instep! A working-woman, —the very type of her class."

"God forbid!" muttered Mitchell.

"Why?" demanded May. "What does the fellow intend by the figure? I cannot catch the meaning."

"Ask him," said the other, dryly. "There he stands,"—pointing to Wolfe, who stood with a group of men, leaning on his ash-rake.

The Doctor beckoned him with the affable smile which kind-hearted men put on, when talking to these people.

"Mr. Mitchell has picked you out as the man who did this,—I'm sure I don't know why. But what did you mean by it?"

"She be hungry."

Wolfe's eyes answered Mitchell, not the Doctor.

"Oh-h! But what a mistake you have made, my fine fellow! You have given no sign of starvation to the body. It is strong,—terribly strong. It has the mad, half-despairing gesture of drowning."

Wolfe stammered, glanced appealingly at Mitchell, who saw the soul of the thing, he knew. But the cool, probing eyes were turned on himself now,—mocking, cruel, relentless.

"Not hungry for meat," the furnace-tender said at last.

"What then? Whisky?" jeered Kirby, with a coarse laugh.

Wolfe was silent a moment, thinking.

"I dunno," he said, with a bewildered look. "It mebbe. Summat to make her live, I think,—like you. Whisky ull do it, in a way."

The young man laughed again. Mitchell flashed a look of disgust somewhere,—not at Wolfe.

"May," he broke out impatiently, "are you blind? Look at that woman's face! It asks questions of God, and says, 'I have a right to know.' Good God, how hungry it is!"

They looked a moment; then May turned to the mill-owner:—

"Have you many such hands as this? What are you going to do with them? Keep them at puddling iron?"

Kirby shrugged his shoulders. Mitchell's look had irritated him.

"*Ce n'est pas mon affaire.* I have no fancy for nursing infant geniuses. I suppose there are some stray gleams of mind and soul among these wretches. The Lord will take care of his own; or else they can work out their own salvation. I have heard you call our American system a ladder which any man can scale. Do you doubt it? Or perhaps you want to banish all social ladders, and put us all on a flat table-land,—eh, May?"

The Doctor looked vexed, puzzled. Some terrible problem lay hid in this woman's face, and troubled these men.

Kirby waited for an answer, and, receiving none, went on, warming with his subject.

"I tell you, there's something wrong that no talk of '*Liberté*' or '*Egalité*' will do away. If I had the making of men, these men who do the lowest part of the world's work should be machines,—nothing more,—hands. It would be kindness. God help them! What are taste, reason, to creatures who must live such lives as that?" He pointed to Deborah, sleeping on the ash-heap. "So many nerves to sting them to pain. What if God had put your brain, with all its agony of touch into your fingers, and bid you work and strike with that?"

"You think you could govern the world better?" laughed the Doctor.

"I do not think at all."

"That is true philosophy. Drift with the stream, because you cannot dive deep enough to find bottom, eh?"

"Exactly," rejoined Kirby. "I do not think. I wash my hands of all social problems,—slavery, caste, white or black. My duty to my operatives has a narrow limit, the pay-hour on Saturday night. Outside of that, if they cut korl, or cut each other' throats, (the more popular amusement of the two,) I am not responsible."

The Doctor sighed,—a good honest sigh, from the depths of his stomach.

"God help us! Who is responsible?"

"Not I, I tell you," said Kirby testily. "What has the man who pays them money to do with their souls' concerns, more than the grocer or butcher who takes it?"

"And yet," said Mitchell's cynical

voice, "look at her! How hungry she is!"

Kirby tapped his boot with his cane. No one spoke. Only the dumb face of the rough image looking into their faces with the awful question, "What shall we do to be saved?" Only Wolfe's face, with its heavy weight of brain, its weak, uncertain mouth, its desperate eyes, out of which looked the soul of his class,—only Wolfe's face turned towards Kirby's. Mitchell laughed,—a cool, musical laugh.

"Money has spoken!" he said, seating himself lightly on a stone with the air of an amused spectator at a play. "Are you answered?"—turning to Wolfe his clear, magnetic face.

Bright and deep and cold as Arctic air, the soul of the man lay tranquil beneath. He looked at the furnace-tender as he had looked at a rare mosaic in the morning; only the man was the more amusing study of the two.

"Are you answered? Why, May, look at him! 'De profundis clamavi.' Or, to quote in English, 'Hungry and thirsty, his soul faints in him.' And so Money sends back its answer into the depths through you, Kirby! Very clear the answer, too!—I think I remember reading the same words somewhere:—washing your hands in Eau de Cologne, and saying, 'I am innocent of the blood of this man. See yet to it!'"

Kirby flushed angrily.

"You quote Scripture freely."

"Do I not quote correctly? I think I remember another line, which may mend my meaning: 'Inasmuch as ye did it unto one of the least of these, ye did it unto me.' Deist? Bless you, man, I was raised on the milk of the Word. Now, Doctor, the pocket of the world having uttered its voice, what has the heart to say? You are a philanthropist, in a small way,—n'est ce pas? Here, boy, this gentleman can show you how to cut korl better,—or your destiny. Go on, May!"

"I think a mocking devil possesses you to-night," rejoined the Doctor, seriously.

He went to Wolfe and put his hand kindly on his arm. Something of a vague idea possessed the Doctor's brain that much good was to be done here by a friendly word or two: a latent genius to be warmed into life by a waited-for sunbeam. Here it was: he had brought it. So he went on complacently:—

"Do you know, boy, you have it in you to be a great sculptor, a great man?—do you understand?" (talking down to the capacity of his hearer: it is a way people have with children, and men like Wolfe,) —"to live a better, stronger life than I, or Mr. Kirby here? A man may make himself anything he chooses. God has given you stronger powers than many men,—me, for instance."

May stopped, heated, glowing with his own magnanimity. And it was magnanimous. The puddler had drunk in every word, looking through the Doctor's flurry, and generous heat, and self-approval, into his will, with those slow, absorbing eyes of his.

"Make yourself what you will. It is your right."

"I know," quietly. "Will you help me?"

Mitchell laughed again. The Doctor turned now, in a passion,—

"You know, Mitchell, I have not

the means. You know, if I had, it is in my heart to take this boy and educate him for"—

"The glory of God, and the glory of John May."

May did not speak for a moment; then, controlled, he said,—

"Why should one be raised, when myriads are left?—I have not the money, boy," to Wolfe, shortly.

"Money?" He said it over slowly, as one repeats the guessed answer to a riddle, doubtfully. "That is it? Money?"

"Yes, money,—that is it," said Mitchell, rising and drawing his furred coat about him. "You've found the cure for all the world's diseases.— Come, May, find your good-humor, and come home. This damp wind chills my very bones. Come and preach your Saint-Simonian doctrines to-morrow to Kirby's hands. Let them have a clear idea of the rights of the soul, and I'll venture next week they'll strike for higher wages. That will be the end of it."

"Will you send the coach-driver to this side of the mills?" asked Kirby, turning to Wolfe.

He spoke kindly: it was his habit to do so. Deborah, seeing the puddler go, crept after him. The three men waited outside. Doctor May walked up and down, chafed. Suddenly he stopped.

"Go back, Mitchell! You say the pocket and the heart of the world speak without meaning to these people. What has its head to say? Taste, culture, refinement? Go!"

Mitchell was leaning against a brick wall. He turned his head indolently, and looked into the mills. There hung about the place a thick, unclean

odor. The slightest motion of his hand marked that he perceived it and his insufferable disgust. That was all. May said nothing, only quickened his angry tramp.

"Besides," added Mitchell, giving a corollary to this answer, "it would be of no use. I am not one of them."

"You do not mean"—said May facing him.

"Yes, I mean just that. Reform is born of need, not pity. No vital movement of the people's has worked down, for good or evil; fermented instead, carried up the heaving, cloggy mass. Think back through history and you will know it. What will thi lowest deep,—thieves, Magdalens, ne groes—do with the light filtered through ponderous Church creeds, Ba conian theories, Goethe schemes Some day, out of their bitter nee will be thrown up their own light bringer,—their Jean Paul, their Crom well, their Messiah."

"Bah!" was the Doctor's inward criticism. However, in practice, he adopted the theory; for, when, nigh and morning, afterwards, he praye that power might be given these de graded souls to rise, he glowed a heart, recognizing an accomplished duty.

Wolfe and the woman had stood in the shadow of the works as th coach drove off. The Doctor ha held out his hand in a frank, generou way, telling him to "take care of himself, and to remember it was h right to rise." Mitchell had simpl touched his hat, as to an equal, with quiet look of thorough recognitio Kirby had thrown Deborah som money, which she found, and clutche eagerly enough. They were gone now, all of them. The man sat down on the cinder-road, looking up into the murky sky.

" 'T be late, Hugh. Wunnot hur come?"

He shook his head doggedly, and the woman crouched out of his sight against the wall. Do you remember rare moments when a sudden light flashed over yourself, your world, God? when you stood on a mountain-peak, seeing your life as it might have been, as it is? one quick instant, when custom lost its force and every-day usage? when your friend, wife, brother, stood in a new light? your soul was bared, and the grave,— a foretaste of the nakedness of the Judgment-Day? So it came before him, his life, that night. The slow tides of pain he had borne gathered themselves up and surged against his soul. His squalid daily life, the brutal coarseness eating into his brain, as the ashes into his skin: before, these things had been a dull aching into his consciousness; to-night, they were reality. He gripped the filthy red shirt that clung, stiff with soot, about him, and tore it savagely from his arm. The flesh beneath was muddy with grease and ashes,—and the heart beneath that! And the soul? God knows.

Then flashed before his vivid poetic sense the man who had left him,— the pure face, the delicate, sinewy limbs, in harmony with all he knew of beauty or truth. In his cloudy fancy he had pictured a Something like this. He had found it in this Mitchell, even when he idly scoffed at his pain: a Man all-knowing, all-seeing, crowned by Nature, reigning,—the keen glance of his eye falling like a scepter on other men. And yet his instinct taught him that he too— He! He looked at himself with sudden loathing, sick, wrung his hands with a cry, and then was silent. With all the phantoms of his heated, ignorant fancy, Wolfe had not been vague in his ambitions. They were practical, slowly built up before him out of his knowledge of what he could do. Through years he had day by day made this hope a real thing to himself,—a clear, projected figure of himself, as he might become.

Able to speak, to know what was best, to raise these men and women working at his side up with him: sometimes he forgot this defined hope in the frantic anguish to escape,— only to escape,—out of the wet, the pain, the ashes, somewhere, anywhere, —only for one moment of free air on a hill-side, to lie down and let his sick soul throb itself out in the sunshine. But to-night he panted for life. The savage strength of his nature was aroused; his cry was fierce to God for justice.

"Look at me!" he said to Deborah, with a low, bitter laugh, striking his puny chest savagely. "What am I worth, Deb? Is it my fault that I am no better? My fault? My fault?"

He stopped, stung with a sudden remorse, seeing her hunchback shape writhing with sobs. For Deborah was crying thankless tears, according to the fashion of women.

"God forgi' me, woman! Things go harder wi' you nor me. It's a worse share."

He got up and helped her to rise;

and they went doggedly down the muddy street, side by side.

"It's all wrong," he muttered, slowly,—"all wrong! I dunnot understan'. But it'll end some day."

"Come home, Hugh!" she said, coaxingly; for he had stopped, looking around bewildered.

"Home,—and back to the mill!" He went on saying this over to himself, as if he would mutter down every pain in this dull despair.

She followed him through the fog, her blue lips chattering with cold. They reached the cellar at last. Old Wolfe had been drinking since she went out, and had crept nearer the door. The girl Janey slept heavily in the corner. He went up to her, touching softly the worn white arm with his fingers. Some bitterer thought stung him, as he stood there. He wiped the drops from his forehead, and went into the room beyond, livid, trembling. A hope, trifling, perhaps, but very dear, had died just then out of the poor puddler's life, as he looked at the sleeping, innocent girl,—some plan for the future, in which she had borne a part. He gave it up that moment, then and forever. Only a trifle, perhaps, to us: his face grew a shade paler,—that was all. But, somehow, the man's soul, as God and the angels looked down on it, never was the same afterwards.

Deborah followed him into the inner room. She carried a candle, which she placed on the floor, closing the door after her. She had seen the look on his face, as he turned away: her own grew deadly. Yet, as she came up to him, her eyes glowed. He was seated on an old chest, quiet, holding his face in his hands.

"Hugh!" she said, softly.

He did not speak.

"Hugh, did hur hear what the man said,—him with the clear voice? Did hur hear? Money, money,—that it wud do all?"

He pushed her away,—gently, but he was worn out; her rasping tone fretted him.

"Hugh!"

The candle flared a pale yellow light over the cobwebbed brick walls, and the woman standing there. He looked at her. She was young, in deadly earnest; her faded eyes, and wet ragged figure caught from their frantic eagerness a power akin to beauty.

"Hugh, it is true! Money ull do it! Oh, Hugh, boy, listen till me! He said it true! It is money!"

"I know. Go back! I do not want you here."

"Hugh, it is t' last time. I'll never worrit hur again."

There were tears in her voice now, but she choked them back.

"Hear till me only to-night! If one of t' witch people wud come, then we heard of t' home, and gif hur all hur wants, what then? Say, Hugh!"

"What do you mean?"

"I mean money."

Her whisper shrilled through his brain.

"If one of t' witch dwarfs wud come from t' lane moors to-night, and gif hur money, to go out,—*out*, I say,—out, lad, where t' sun shines, and t' heath grows, and t' ladies walk in silken gownds, and God stays all t' time,—where t' man lives that talked to us to-night,—Hugh knows, —Hugh could walk there like a king!"

He thought the woman mad, tried

to check her, but she went on, fierce in her eager haste.

"If *I* were t' witch dwarf, if I had t' money, wud hur thank me? Wud hur take me out o' this place wid hur and Janey? I wud not come into the gran' house hur wud build, to vex hur wid t' hunch,—only at night, when t' shadows were dark, stand far off to see hur."

Mad? Yes! Are many of us mad in this way?

"Poor Deb! poor Deb!" he said, soothingly.

"It is here," she said, suddenly jerking into his hand a small roll. "I took it! I did it! Me, me!—not hur! I shall be hanged, I shall be burnt in hell, if anybody knows I took it! Out of his pocket, as he leaned against t' bricks. Hur knows?"

She thrust it into his hand, and then, her errand done, began to gather chips together to make a fire, choking down hysteric sobs.

"Has it come to this?"

That was all he said. The Welsh Wolfe blood was honest. The roll was a small green pocket-book containing one or two gold pieces, and a check for an incredible amount, as it seemed to the poor puddler. He laid it down, hiding his face again in his hands.

"Hugh, don't be angry wud me! It's only poor Deb,—hur knows?"

He took the long skinny fingers kindly in his.

"Angry? God help me, no! Let me sleep. I am tired."

He threw himself heavily down on the wooden bench, stunned with pain and weariness. She brought some old rags to cover him.

It was late on Sunday evening before he awoke. I tell God's truth, when I say he had then no thought of keeping this money. Deborah had hid it in his pocket. He found it there. She watched him eagerly, as he took it out.

"I must gif it to him," he said, reading her face.

"Hur knows," she said with a bitter sigh of disappointment. "But it is hur right to keep it."

His right! The word struck him. Doctor May had used the same. He washed himself, and went out to find this man Mitchell. His right! Why did this chance word cling to him so obstinately? Do you hear the fierce devils whisper in his ear, as he went slowly down the darkening street?

The evening came on, slow and calm. He seated himself at the end of an alley leading into one of the larger streets. His brain was clear to-night, keen, intent, mastering. It would not start back, cowardly, from any hellish temptation, but meet it face to face. Therefore the great temptation of his life came to him veiled by no sophistry, but bold, defiant, owning its own vile name, trusting to one bold blow for victory.

He did not deceive himself. Theft! That was it. At first the word sickened him; then he grappled with it. Sitting there on a broken cart-wheel, the fading day, the noisy groups, the church-bells' tolling, passed before him like a panorama, while the sharp struggle went on within. This money! He took it out, and looked at it. If he gave it back, what then? He was going to be cool about it.

People going by to church saw only a sickly mill-boy watching them quietly at the alley's mouth. They did not know that he was mad, or they would not have gone by so quietly: mad with hunger; stretching out his hands to the world, that had given so much to them, for leave to live the life God meant him to live. His soul within him was smothering to death; he wanted so much, thought so much, and *knew*—nothing. There was nothing of which he was certain, except the mill and things here. Of God and heaven he had heard so little, that they were to him what fairyland is to a child: something real, but not here; very far off. His brain, greedy, dwarfed, full of thwarted energy and unused powers, questioned these men and women going by, coldly, bitterly, that night. Was it not his right to live as they,—a pure life, a good, true-hearted life, full of beauty and kind words? He only wanted to know how to use the strength within him. His heart warmed, as he thought of it. He suffered himself to think of it longer. If he took the money?

Then he saw himself as he might be, strong, helpful, kindly. The night crept on, as this one image slowly evolved itself from the crowd of other thoughts and stood triumphant. He looked at it. As he might be! What wonder, if it blinded him to delirium, —the madness that underlies all revolution, all progress, and all fall?

You laugh at the shallow temptation? You see the error underlying its argument so clearly,—that to him a true life was one of full development rather than self-restraint? that he was deaf to the higher tone in a cry of voluntary suffering for truth's sake than in the fullest flow of spontaneous harmony? I do not plead his

cause. I only want to show you the mote in my brother's eye: then you can see clearly to take it out.

The money,—there it lay on his knee, a little blotted slip of paper, nothing in itself; used to raise him out of the pit; something straight from God's hand. A thief! Well what was it to be a thief? He met the question at last, face to face, wiping the clammy drops of sweat from his forehead. God made this money —the fresh air, too—for his children's use. He never made the difference between poor and rich. The Something who looked down on him that moment through the cool gray sky had a kindly face, he knew,—loved his children alike. Oh, he knew that!

There were times when the soft floods of color in the crimson and purple flames, or the clear depth of amber in the water below the bridge, had somehow given him a glimpse of another world than this,—of an infinite depth of beauty and of quiet somewhere,—somewhere,—a depth of quiet and rest and love. Looking up now, it became strangely real. The sun had sunk quite below the hills, but his last rays struck upward, touching the zenith. The fog had risen, and the town and river were steeped in its thick, gray damp; but overhead, the sun-touched smoke-clouds opened like a cleft ocean,—shifting, rolling seas of crimson mist, waves of billowy silver veined with blood-scarlet, inner depths unfathomable of glancing light. Wolfe's artist-eye grew drunk with color. The gates of that other world! Fading, flashing before him now! What, in that world of Beauty, Content, and Right, were the petty laws, the mine and thine, of mill-owners and mill-hands?

A consciousness of power stirred within him. He stood up. A man, —he thought, stretching out his hands,—free to work, to live, to love! Free! His right! He folded the scrap of paper in his hand. As his nervous fingers took it in, limp and blotted, so his soul took in the mean temptation, lapped it in fancied rights, in dreams of improved existences, drifting and endless as the cloud-seas of color. Clutching it, as if the tightness of his hold would strengthen his sense of possession, he went aimlessly down the street. It was his watch at the mill. He need'not go, need never go again, thank God!—shaking off the thought with unspeakable loathing.

Shall I go over the history of the hours of that night? how the man wandered from one to another of his old haunts, with a half-consciousness of bidding them farewell,—lanes and alleys and back-yards where the mill-hands lodged,—noting, with a new eagerness, the filth and drunkenness, the pig-pens, the ash-heaps covered with potato-skins, the bloated, pimpled women at the doors,—with a new disgust, a new sense of sudden triumph, and, under all, a new, vague dread, unknown before, smothered down, kept under, but still there? It left him but once during the night, when, for the second time in his life, he entered a church. It was a somber Gothic pile, where the stained light lost itself in far-retreating arches; built to meet the requirements and sympathies of a far other class than Wolfe's. Yet it touched, moved him uncontrollably. The distances, the shadows, the still,

marble figures, the mass of silent kneeling worshippers, the mysterious music, thrilled, lifted his soul with a wonderful pain. Wolfe forgot himself, forgot the new life he was going to live, the mean terror gnawing underneath. The voice of the speaker strengthened the charm; it was clear, feeling, full, strong. An old man, who had lived much, suffered much; whose brain was keenly alive, dominant; whose heart was summer-warm with charity. He taught it to-night. He held up Humanity in its grand total; showed the great world-cancer to his people. Who could show it better? He was a Christian reformer; he had studied the age thoroughly; his outlook at man had been free, world-wide, over all time. His faith stood sublime upon the Rock of Ages; his fiery zeal guided vast schemes by which the gospel was to be preached to all nations. How did he preach it to-night? In burning, light-laden words he painted the incarnate Life, Love, the universal Man: words that became reality in the lives of these people,—that lived again in beautiful words and actions, trifling, but heroic. Sin, as he defied it, was a real foe to them; their trials, temptations, were his. His words passed far over the furnace-tender's grasp, toned to suit another class of culture; they sounded in his ears a very pleasant song in an unknown tongue. He meant to cure this world-cancer with a steady eye that had never glared with hunger, and a hand that neither poverty nor strychnine-whisky had taught to shake. In this morbid, distorted heart of the Welsh puddler he had failed.

Wolfe rose at last, and turned from the church down the street. He looked up; the night had come on foggy, damp; the golden mists had vanished, and the sky lay dull and ash-colored. He wandered again aimlessly down the street, idly wondering what had become of the cloud-sea of crimson and scarlet. The trial-day of this man's life was over, and he had lost the victory. What followed was mere drifting circumstance,—a quicker walking over the path,—that was all. Do you want to hear the end of it? You wish me to make a tragic story out of it? Why, in the police-reports of the morning paper you can find a dozen such tragedies: hints of shipwrecks unlike any that ever befell on the high seas; hints that here a power was lost to heaven,—that there a soul went down where no tide can ebb or flow. Commonplace enough the hints are,—jocose sometimes, done up in rime.

Doctor May, a month after the night I have told you of, was reading to his wife at breakfast from this fourth column of the morning-paper: an unusual thing,—these police-reports not being, in general, choice reading for ladies; but it was only one item he read.

"Oh, my dear! You remember that man I told you of, that we saw at Kirby's mill?—that was arrested for robbing Mitchell? Here he is; just listen:—'Circuit Court. Judge Day. Hugh Wolfe, operative in Kirby & John's Loudon Mills. Charge, grand larceny. Sentence, nineteen years hard labor in penitentiary.—Scoundrel! Serves him right! After all our kindness that night! Picking Mitchell's pocket at the very time!"

His wife said something about the ingratitude of that kind of people, and then they began to talk of something else.

Nineteen years! How easy that was to read! What a simple word for Judge Day to utter! Nineteen years! Half a lifetime!

Hugh Wolfe sat on a window-ledge of his cell, looking out. His ankles were ironed. Not usual in such cases; but he had made two desperate efforts to escape. "Well," as Haley, the jailer, said, "small blame to him! Nineteen years' imprisonment was not a pleasant thing to look forward to." Haley was very good-natured about it, though Wolfe had fought him savagely.

"When he was first caught," the jailer said afterwards, in telling the story, "before the trial, the fellow was cut down at once,—laid there on that pallet like a dead man, with his hands over his eyes. Never saw a man so cut down in my life. Time of the trial, too, came the queerest dodge of any customer I ever had. Would choose no lawyer. Judge gave him one, of course. Gibson it was. He tried to prove the fellow crazy; but it wouldn't go. Thing was plain as daylight: money found on him. 'Twas a hard sentence,—all the law allows; but it was for 'xample's sake. These mill-hands are gettin' onbearable. When the sentence was read, he just looked up, and said the money was his by rights, and that all the world had gone wrong. That night, after the trial, a gentleman came to see him here, name of Mitchell,—him as he stole from. Talked to him for an hour. Thought he came for curiosity, like. After he was gone, thought Wolfe was remarkable quiet, and went into his cell. Found him very low; bed all bloody. Doctor said he had been bleeding at the lungs. He was as weak as a cat; yet, if ye'll b'lieve me, he tried to get a-past me and get out. I just carried him like a baby, and threw him on the pallet. Three days after, he tried it again: that time reached the wall. Lord help you! he fought like a tiger,—giv' some terrible blows. Fightin' for life, you see; for he can't live long, shut up in the stone crib down yonder. Got a death-cough now. 'T took two of us to bring him down that day; so I just put the irons on his feet. There he sits, in there. Goin' to-morrow, with a batch more of 'em. That woman, hunchback, tried with him, —you remember?—she's only got three years. 'Complice. But *she's* a woman, you know. He's been quiet ever since I put on irons: giv' up, I suppose. Looks white, sick-lookin'. It acts different on 'em, bein' sentenced. Most of 'em gets reckless, devilish-like. Some prays awful, and sings them vile songs of the mills, all in a breath. That woman, now, she's desper't. Been begging to see Hugh, as she calls him, for three days. I'm a-goin' to let her in. She don't go with him. Here she is in this next cell. I'm a-goin' now to let her in."

He let her in. Wolfe did not see her. She crept into a corner of the cell, and stood watching him. He was scratching the iron bars of the window with a piece of tin which he had picked up, with an idle, uncertain, vacant stare, just as a child or idiot would do.

"Tryin' to get out, old boy?" laughed Haley. "Them irons will need a crowbar beside your tin, before you can open 'em."

Wolfe laughed, too, in a senseless way.

"I think I'll get out," he said.

"I believe his brain's touched," said Haley, when he came out.

The puddler scraped away with the tin for half an hour. Still Deborah did not speak. At last she ventured nearer, and touched his arm.

"Blood?" she said, looking at some spots on his coat with a shudder.

He looked up at her. "Why, Deb!" he said, smiling,—such a bright, boyish smile, that it went to poor Deborah's heart directly, and she sobbed and cried out loud.

"Oh, Hugh, lad! Hugh! dunnot look at me, when it wur my fault! To think I brought hur to it! And I loved hur so! Oh, lad, I dud!"

The confession, even in this wretch, came with the woman's blush through the sharp cry.

He did not seem to hear her,— scraping away diligently at the bars with the bit of tin.

Was he going mad? She peered closely into his face. Something she saw there made her draw suddenly back,—something which Haley had not seen, that lay beneath the pinched, vacant look it had caught since the trial, or the curious gray shadow that rested on it. That gray shadow,— yes, she knew what that meant. She had often seen it creeping over women's faces for months, who died at last of slow hunger or consumption. That meant death, distant, lingering: but this— Whatever it was the woman saw, or thought she saw, used as she was to crime and misery, seemed to make her sick with a new horror. Forgetting her fear of him, she caught his shoulders, and looked keenly, steadily, into his eyes.

"Hugh!" she cried, in a desperate whisper,—"oh, boy, not that! for God's sake not *that!*"

The vacant laugh went off his face, and he answered her in a muttered word or two that drove her away. Yet the words were kindly enough. Sitting there on his pallet, she cried silently a hopeless sort of tears, but did not speak again. The man looked up furtively at her now and then. Whatever his own trouble was, her distress vexed him with a momentary sting.

It was market-day. The narrow window of the jail looked down directly on the carts and wagons drawn up in a long line, where they had unloaded. He could see, too, and hear distinctly the clink of money as it changed hands, the busy crowd of whites and blacks shoving, pushing one another, and the chaffering and swearing at the stalls. Somehow, the sound, more than anything else had done, wakened him up,—made the whole real to him. He was done with the world and the business of it. He let the tin fall, and looked out, pressing his face close to the rusty bars. How they crowded and pushed! And he,—he should never walk that pavement again! There came Neff Sanders, one of the feeders at the mill, with a basket on his arm. Sure enough, Neff was married the other week. He whistled, hoping he would look up; but he did not. He wondered if Neff remembered he was there,—if any of the boys thought of him up there, and thought that he never was to go down that old cinder-road again. Never again! He had not quite understood it before; but now he did. Not for days or years, but never!—that was i[t]

How clear the light fell on that sta[tion] in front of the market! and how lik[e] a picture it was, the dark-green heap[s] of corn, and the crimson beets, an[d] golden melons! There was anothe[r] with game: how the light flickered o[n] that pheasant's breast, with the pu[r]plish blood dripping over the brow[n] feathers! He could see the red shin[n]ing of the drops, it was so near. I[n] one minute he could be down there[.] It was just a step. So easy, as i[t] seemed, so natural to go! Yet i[t] could never be—not in all the thou[s]ands of years to come—that h[e] should put his foot on that stree[t] again! He thought of himself wit[h] a sorrowful pity, as of some one els[e.] There was a dog down in the market[,] walking after his master with such [a] stately, grave look!—only a dog, ye[t] he could go backwards and forward just as he pleased: he had good luck[.] Why, the very vilest cur, yelping ther[e] in the gutter, had not lived his life[,] had been free to act out whateve[r] thought God had put into his brain while he— No, he would not thin[k] of that! He tried to put the though[t] away, and to listen to a dispute be[-] tween a countryman and a woma[n] about some meat; but it would com[e] back. He, what had he done to bea[r] this?

Then came the sudden picture o[f] what might have been, and now. H[e] knew what it was to be in the peni[-] tentiary,—how it went with men there[.] He knew how in these long years h[e] should slowly die, but not until sou[l] and body had become corrupt an[d] rotten,—how, when he came out, if h[e] lived to come, even the lowest of the[e] mill-hands would jeer him,—how hi[s] hands would be weak, and his brain senseless and stupid. He believed he was almost that now. He put his hand to his head, with a puzzled, weary look. It ached, his head, with thinking. He tried to quiet himself. It was only right, perhaps; he had done wrong. But was there right or wrong for such as he? What was right? And who had ever taught him? He thrust the whole matter away. A dark, cold quiet crept through his brain. It was all wrong; but let it be! It was nothing to him more than the others. Let it be!

The door grated, as Haley opened it.

"Come, my woman! Must lock up for t' night. Come, stir yerself!"

She went up and took Hugh's hand.

"Good-night, Deb," he said, carelessly.

She had not hoped he would say more; but the tired pain on her mouth just then was bitterer than death. She took his passive hand and kissed it.

"Hur'll never see Deb again!" she ventured, her lips growing colder and more bloodless.

What did she say that for? Did he not know it? Yet he would not be impatient with poor old Deb. She had trouble of her own, as well as he.

"No, never again," he said, trying to be cheerful.

She stood just a moment, looking at him. Do you laugh at her, standing there, with her hunchback, her rags, her bleared, withered face, and the great despised love tugging at her heart?

"Come, you!" called Haley, impatiently.

She did not move.

"Hugh!" she whispered.

It was to be her last word. What was it?

"Hugh, boy, not THAT!"

He did not answer. She wrung her hands, trying to be silent, looking in his face in an agony of entreaty. He smiled again, kindly.

"It is best, Deb. I cannot bear to be hurted any more."

"Hur knows," she said, humbly.

"Tell my father good-by; and—and kiss little Janey."

She nodded, saying nothing, looked in his face again, and went out of the door. As she went, she staggered.

"Drinkin' to-day?" broke out Haley, pushing her before him. "Where the Devil did you get it? Here, in with ye!" and he shoved her into her cell, next to Wolfe's, and shut the door.

Along the wall of her cell there was a crack low down by the floor, through which she could see the light from Wolfe's. She had discovered it days before. She hurried in now, and, kneeling down by it, listened, hoping to hear some sound. Nothing but the rasping of the tin on the bars. He was at his old amusement again. Something in the noise jarred on her ear, for she shivered as she heard it. Hugh rasped away at the bars. A dull old bit of tin, not fit to cut korl with.

He looked out of the window again. People were leaving the market now. A tall mulatto girl, following her mistress, her basket on her head, crossed the street just below, and looked up. She was laughing; but, when she caught sight of the haggard face peering out through the bars, suddenly grew grave, and hurried by. A free, firm step, a clear-cut olive face, with a scarlet turban tied on one side, dark, shining eyes, and on the head the basket poised, filled with fruit and flowers, under which the scarlet turban and bright eyes looked out half-shadowed. The picture caught his eye. It was good to see a face like that. He would try to-morrow, and cut one like it. *To-morrow!* He threw down the tin, trembling, and covered his face with his hands. When he looked up again, the daylight was gone.

Deborah, crouching near by on the other side of the wall, heard no noise. He sat on the side of the low pallet, thinking. Whatever was the mystery which the woman had seen on his face, it came out now slowly, in the dark here, and became fixed,—a something never seen on his face before. The evening was darkening fast. The market had been over for an hour; the rumbling of the carts over the pavement grew more infrequent: he listened to each as it passed, because he thought it was to be for the last time. For the same reason, it was, I suppose, that he strained his eyes to catch a glimpse of each passer-by, wondering who they were, what kind of homes they were going to, if they had children,—listening eagerly to every chance word in the street, as if—(God be merciful to the man! what strange fancy was this?)—as if he never should hear human voices again.

It was quite dark at last. The street was a lonely one. The last passenger, he thought, was gone. No, —there was a quick step: Joe Hill, lighting the lamps. Joe was a good old chap; never passed a fellow without some joke or other. He remembered once seeing the place where he lived with his wife. "Granny Hill," the boys called her. Bedridden she

was; but so kind as Joe was to her! kept the room so clean!—and the old woman, when he was there, was laughing at "some of t' lad's foolishness." The step was far down the street; but he could see him place the ladder, run up, and light the gas. A longing seized him to be spoken to once more.

"Joe!" he called, out of the grating. "Good-bye, Joe!"

The old man stopped a moment, listening uncertainly; then hurried on. The prisoner thrust his hand out of the window, and called again, louder; but Joe was too far down the street. It was a little thing; but it hurt him, —this disappointment.

"Good-bye, Joe!" he called, sorrowfully enough.

"Be quiet!" said one of the jailers, passing the door, striking on it with his club.

Oh, that was the last, was it?

There was an inexpressible bitterness on his face, as he lay down on the bed, taking the bit of tin, which he had rasped to a tolerable degree of sharpness, in his hand,—to play with, it may be. He bared his arms, looking intently at their corded veins and sinews. Deborah, listening in the next cell, heard a slight clicking sound, often repeated. She shut her lips tightly, that she might not scream; the cold drops of sweat broke over her, in her dumb agony.

"Hur knows best," she muttered at last, fiercely clutching the boards where she lay.

If she could have seen Wolfe, there was nothing about him to frighten her. He lay quite still, his arms outstretched, looking at the pearly stream of moonlight coming into the window. I think in that one hour that came then

e lived back over all the years that
had gone before. I think that all
he low, vile life, all his wrongs, all
is starved hopes, came then, and
tung him with a farewell poison that
made him sick unto death. He made
either moan nor cry, only turned his
worn face now and then to the pure
ght, that seemed so far off, as one
hat said, "How long, O Lord? how
ong?"

The hour was over at last. The
moon, passing over her nightly path,
lowly came nearer, and threw the
ght across his bed on his feet. He
watched it steadily, as it crept up,
nch by inch, slowly. It seemed to
im to carry with it a great silence.
He had been so hot and tired there
ways in the mills! The years had
een so fierce and cruel! There was
oming now quiet and coolness and
eep. His tense limbs relaxed, and
ttled in a calm languor. The blood
an fainter and slow from his heart.
e did not think now with a savage
nger of what might be and was not;
e was conscious only of deep still-
ess creeping over him. At first he
w a sea of faces: the mill-men,—
omen he had known, drunken and
loated,—Janeys timid and pitiful,—
oor old Debs: then they floated to-
ether like a mist, and faded away,
aving only the clear, pearly moon-
ght.

Whether, as the pure light crept up
he stretched-out figure, it brought
ith it calm and peace, who shall say?
is dumb soul was alone with God
judgment. A Voice may have spoken
or it from far-off Calvary, "Father,
rgive them, for they know not what
ey do!" Who dare say? Fainter
d fainter the heart rose and fell,

slower and slower the moon floated
from behind a cloud, until, when at
last its full tide of white splendor
swept over the cell, it seemed to wrap
and fold into a deeper stillness the
dead figure that never should move
again. Silence deeper than the Night!
Nothing that moved, save the black,
nauseous stream of blood dripping
slowly from the pallet to the floor!

There was outcry and crowd enough
in the cell the next day. The coroner
and his jury, the local editors, Kirby
himself, and boys with their hands
thrust knowingly into their pockets
and heads on one side, jammed into
the corners. Coming and going all
day. Only one woman. She came
late, and outstayed them all. A
Quaker, or Friend, as they call themselves. I think this woman was known
by that name in heaven. A homely
body, coarsely dressed in gray and
white. Deborah (for Haley had let
her in) took notice of her. She
watched them all—sitting on the end
of the pallet, holding his head in her
arms—with the ferocity of a watch-
dog, if any of them touched the body.
There was no meekness, or sorrow, in
her face; the stuff out of which mur-
derers are made, instead. All the time
Haley and the woman were laying
straight the limbs and cleaning the
cell, Deborah sat still, keenly watching
the Quaker's face. Of all the crowd
there that day, this woman alone had
not spoken to her,—only once or twice
had put some cordial to her lips.
After they all were gone, the woman,
in the same still, gentle way, brought
a vase of wood-leaves and berries, and
placed it by the pallet, then opened
the narrow window. The fresh air
blew in, and swept the woody fra-

grance over the dead face. Deborah looked up with a quick wonder.

"Did hur know my boy would like it? Did hur know Hugh?"

"I know Hugh now."

The white fingers passed in a slow, pitiful way over the dead, worn face. There was a heavy shadow in the quiet eyes.

"Did hur know where they'll bury Hugh?" said Deborah in a shrill tone, catching her arm.

This had been the question hanging on her lips all day.

"In t' town-yard? Under t' mud and ash? T' lad'll smother, woman! He wur born on t' lane moor, where t' air is frick and strong. Take hur out, for God's sake, take hur out where t' air blows!"

The Quaker hesitated, but only for a moment. She put her strong arm around Deborah and led her to the window.

"Thee sees the hills, friend, over the river? Thee sees how the light lies warm there, and the winds of God blow all the day? I live there,— where the blue smoke is, by the trees. Look at me." She turned Deborah's face to her own, clear and earnest. "Thee will believe me? I will take Hugh and bury him there to-morrow."

Deborah did not doubt her. As the evening wore on, she leaned against the iron bars, looking at the hills that rose far off, through the thick sodden clouds, like a bright, unattainable calm. As she looked, a shadow of their solemn repose fell on her face: its fierce discontent faded into a pitiful, humble quiet. Slow, solemn tears gathered in her eyes: the poor weak eyes turned so hopelessly to the place where Hugh was to rest, the grave heights looking higher and brighter and more solemn than ever before. The Quaker watched her keenly. She came to her at last, and touched her arm.

"When thee comes back," she said in a low, sorrowful tone, like one who speaks from a strong heart deeply moved with remorse or pity, "the shall begin thy life again,—there on the hills. I came too late; but not for thee,—by God's help, it may be."

Not too late. Three years after, the Quaker began her work. I end my story here. At evening-time it was light. There is no need to tire you with the long years of sunshine, and fresh air, and slow, patient Christ-love, needed to make healthy and hopeful this impure body and soul. There is a homely pine house, on one of these hills, whose windows overlook broad, wooded slopes and clover crimsoned meadows,—niched into the very place where the light is warmest, the air freest. It is the Friends' meeting-house. Once a week they sit there, in their grave, earnest way, waiting for the Spirit of Love to speak, opening their simple hearts to receive His words. There is a woman, old, deformed, who takes a humble place among them: waiting like them in her gray dress, her worn face, pure and meek, turned now and then to the sky. A woman much loved by these silent, restful people; more silent than they, more humble, more loving. Waiting: with her eyes turned to hills higher and purer than these on which she lives,—dim and far off now, but to be reached some day. There may be in her heart some latent hope to meet there the love denied her here —that she shall find him whom she ost, and that then she will not be all-unworthy. Who blames her? Something is lost in the passage of every soul from one eternity to the other, —something pure and beautiful, which might have been and was not: a hope, talent, a love, over which the soul mourns, like Esau deprived of his birthright. What blame to the meek Quaker, if she took her lost hope to make the hills of heaven more fair?

Nothing remains to tell that the poor Welsh puddler once lived, but his figure of the mill-woman cut in corl. I have it here in a corner of my library. I keep it hid behind a curtain,—it is such a rough, ungainly thing. Yet there are about it touches, grand sweeps of outline, that show a master's hand. Sometimes,—to-night, for instance,—the curtain is accidentally drawn back, and I see a bare arm stretched out imploringly in the darkness, and an eager, wolfish face watching mine: a wan, woful face, through which the spirit of the dead korl-cutter looks out, with its thwarted life, its mighty hunger, its unfinished work. Its pale, vague lips seem to tremble with a terrible question. "Is this the end?" they say,—"nothing beyond? —no more?" Why, you tell me you have seen that look in the eyes of dumb brutes,—horses dying under the lash. I know.

The deep of the night is passing while I write. The gas-light wakens from the shadows here and there the objects which lie scattered through the room: only faintly, though: for they belong to the open sunlight. As I glance at them, they each recall some task or pleasure of the coming day. A half-molded child's head; Aphrodite; a bough of forest-leaves;

music; work; homely fragments, in which lie the secrets of all eternal truth and beauty. Prophetic all! Only this dumb, woful face seems to belong to and end with the night. I turn to look at it. Has the power of its desperate need commanded the darkness away? While the room is yet steeped in heavy shadow, a cool, gray light suddenly touches its head like a blessing hand, and its groping arm points through the broken cloud to the far East, where, in the flickering, nebulous crimson, God has set the promise of the Dawn.

1861

II. HARRIET BEECHER STOWE
(1811–1896)

THE GHOST IN THE MILL

"Come, Sam, tell us a story," said I, as Harry and I crept to his knees, in the glow of the bright evening firelight, while Aunt Lois was busily rattling the tea-things, and grand-mamma was quietly setting the heel of a blue-mixed yarn stocking at the other end of the fireplace.

In those days we had no magazines and daily papers, each reeling off a serial story. Once a week, the *Columbian Sentinel* came from Boston with its slender stock of news and editorial; but all the multiform devices, pictorial, narrative, and poetical, which keep the mind of the present generation ablaze with excitement, had not then even an existence. There was no theater, no opera; there were in Oldtown no parties or balls, except, perhaps, the annual election or Thanksgiving festival; and when winter came, and the sun went down at half past four o'clock and left the long dark hours of evening to be provided for, the necessity of amusement became urgent. Hence in those days chimney-corner story-telling became an art and an accomplishment. Society then was full of traditions and narratives which had all the uncertain glow and shifting mystery of the firelit hearth upon them. They were told to sympathetic audiences, by the rising and falling light of the solemn embers, with the hearth crickets filling up every pause. Then the aged told their stories to the young,—tales of early life, tales of war and adventure, of forest-days, of Indian captivities and escapes, of bears and wild-cats and panthers, of rattlesnakes, of witches and wizards, and strange and wonderful dreams and appearances and providences.

In those days of early Massachusetts, faith and credence were in the very air. Two-thirds of New England was then dark, unbroken forest, through whose tangled paths the mysterious winter wind groaned and shrieked and howled with weird noises and unaccountable clamors. Along the iron-bound shore the stormful Atlantic raved and thundered, and dashed its moaning waters, as if to deaden and deafen any voice that might tell of the settled life of the old civilized world, and shut us forever into the wilderness. A good story-teller, in those days, was always sure of a warm seat at the hearth-stone, and the delighted homage of children; and in all Oldtown

there was no better story-teller than Sam Lawson.

"Do, do, tell us a story," said Harry, pressing upon him and opening very wide blue eyes, in which undoubting faith shone as in a mirror, "and let it be something strange, and different from common."

"Wal, I know lots o' strange things," said Sam, looking mysteriously into the fire. "Why, I know things, that ef I should tell, why people might say they wa'n't so; but then they is so, for all that."

"Oh, do, do, tell us."

"Why, I should scare ye to death, mebbe," said Sam, doubtingly.

"Oh, pooh! no, you wouldn't," we both burst out at once.

But Sam was possessed by a reticent spirit, and loved dearly to be wooed and importuned; and so he only took up the great kitchen tongs, and smote on the hickory forestick, when it flew apart in the middle and scattered a shower of clear, bright coals all over the hearth.

"Mercy on us, Sam Lawson!" said Aunt Lois, in an indignant voice, spinning round from her dish-washing.

"Don't you worry a grain, Miss Lois," said Sam, composedly. "I see that are stick was e'en a'most in two, and I thought I'd jest settle it. I sweep up the coals now," he added, vigorously applying a turkey-wing to the purpose, as he knelt on the hearth, his spare, lean figure glowing in the blaze of the firelight, and getting quite flushed with exertion.

"There, now," he said, when he had brushed over and under and between the fire-irons, and pursued the retreating ashes so far into the re-ery citadel, that his finger-ends were urning and tingling, "that are's done ow as well as Hepsy herself could ,' done it. I allers sweeps up the aarth: I think it's part o' the man's isness when he makes the fire. But Iepsy's so used to seein' me a-doin' n't that she don't see no kind o' uerit in't. It's just as Parson Lothrop uid in his sermon,—folks allers over- ok their common marcies—"

"But come, Sam, that story," said Iarry and I, coaxingly, pressing upon im, and pulling him down into his at in the corner.

"Lordy massy, these 'ere young ns!" said Sam, "there's never no ontentin' on 'em; ye tell 'em one ory, and they jest swallows it as a og does a gob o' meat, and they're l ready for another. What do ye ant to hear now?"

Now the fact was that Sam's ories had been told us so often that ey were all arranged and ticketed our minds. We knew every word them, and could set him right if varied a hair from the usual track, id still the interest in them was un- ated. Still we shivered, and clung his knee at the mysterious parts, id felt gentle, cold chills run down ir spines at appropriate places. We re always in the most receptive and mpathetic condition. To-night, in rticular, was one of those thunder- g stormy ones when the winds ap- ared to be holding a perfect mad rnival over my grandfather's house. hey yelled and squealed round the rners. They collected in troops and me tumbling and roaring down the imney. They shook and rattled the ttery door and the sink-room door d the cellar door and the chamber

door, with a constant undertone of squeak and clatter, as if at every door were a cold, discontented spirit, tired of the chill outside, and longing for the warmth and comfort within.

"Wal, boys," said Sam, confiden- tially, "what'll ye have?"

"Tell us 'Come down, come down,'" we both shouted with one voice. This was in our mind an A No. 1 among Sam's stories.

"Ye mus'n't be frightened, now," said Sam, paternally.

"Oh, no! we ar'n't frightened *ever*," said we both in one breath.

"Not when ye go down the cellar arter cider?" said Sam, with severe scrutiny. "Ef ye should be down cellar, and the candle should go out, now?"

"I ain't," said I: "I ain't afraid of any thing. I never knew what it was to be afraid in my life."

"Wal, then," said Sam, "I'll tell ye. This 'ere's what Cap'n Eb Sawin told me when I was a boy about your big- ness, I reckon.

"Cap'n Eb Sawin was a most re- spectable man; your gran'ther knew him very well, and he was a deacon in the church in Dedham afore he died. He was at Lexington when the fust gun was fired agin the British. He was a dreffle smart man, Cap'n Eb was, and driv team a good many years atween here and Boston. He married Lois Peabody, that was cousin to your gran'ther then. Lois was a rael sensible woman, and I've heard her tell the story as he told her, and it was jest as he told it to me, jest exactly; and I shall never forget it if I live to be nine hundred years old, like Mathusaleh.

"Ye see, along back in them times,

there used to be a fellow come round these 'ere parts, spring and fall, a peddlin' goods, with his pack on his back; and his name was Jehiel Lommedieu. Nobody rightly knew where he come from. He wasn't much of a talker, but the women rather liked him, and kind o' liked to have him round; women will like some fellows, when men can't see no sort o' reason why they should, and they liked this 'ere Lommedieu, though he was kind o' mournful and thin and shad-bellied, and hadn't nothin' to say for himself. But it got to be so that the women would count and calculate, so many weeks afore 'twas time for Lommedieu to be along, and they'd make up ginger-snaps and preserves and pies, and make him stay to tea at their houses, and feed him up on the best there was: and the story went round that he was acourtin' Phebe Ann Parker, or Phebe Ann was acourtin' him,—folks didn't rightly know which. Wal, all of a sudden Lommedieu stopped comin' round, and nobody knew why, only jest he didn't come. It turned out that Phebe Ann Parker had got a letter from him, sayin' he'd be along afore Thanksgiving, but he didn't come, neither afore nor at Thanksgiving time, nor arter, nor next spring; and finally the women they gin up lookin' for him. Some said he was dead, some said he was gone to Canada, and some said he hed gone over to the old country. As to Phebe Ann, she acted like a gal o' sense, and married 'Bijah Moss and thought no more 'bout it. She said she was sartin that all things was ordered out for the best; and it was jest as well folks couldn't always have their own way; and so in time

Lommedieu was gone out o' folks minds, much as a last year's apple blossom. It's relly affectin' to thin how little these 'ere folks is misse that's so much sot by! There ain nobody, ef they's ever so importan but what the world gets to goin' o without 'em pretty much as it di with 'em, though there's some litt flurry at fust. Wal, the last thin that was in anybody's mind was tha they ever should hear from Lom medieu ag'in. But there ain't nothir but what has its time o' turnin' up and it seems his turn was to come.

"Wal, ye see, 'twas the nineteent o' March, when Cap'n Eb Sawi started with a team for Boston. Tha day there come on about the bigges snow-storm that there'd been in the parts sence the oldest man could re member. 'Twas this 'ere fine, siftin snow, that drives in your face lik needles, with a wind to cut your nos off: it made teamin' pretty tedio work. Cap'n Eb was about th toughest man in them parts. He' spent days in the woods aloggin', an he'd been up to the deestrict Maine a lumberin', and was about u to any sort o' thing a man gen'all could be up to; but these 'ere Marc winds sometimes does set on a fello so that neither natur' nor grace ca stan' 'em. The Cap'n used to say could stan' any wind that blew on way't time for five minutes, but com to winds that blew all four p'ints the same minit, why, they flustere him.

"Wal, that was the sort o' weath it was all day, and by sundow Cap'n Eb he got clean bewildered, s that he lost his road; and when nigl came on he didn't know nothi where he was. Ye see the country was all under drift, and the air so thick with snow that he couldn't see a foot afore him, and the fact was he got off the Boston road without knowin' it and come out at a pair o' bars nigh upon Sherburn, where old Cack Sparrock's mill is. Your gran'- her used to know old Cack, boys. He was a dreful drinkin' old crittur that lived there all alone in the woods by himself, a tendin' saw and grist mill. He wa'n't all jest what he was then. Time was that Cack was a pretty consid'ably likely young man, and his wife was a very respectable woman,—Deacon Amos Petengalls's darter, from Sherburn.

"But ye see, the year arter his wife died, Cack he gin up goin' to meetin' Sundays, and all the tithing- men and selectmen could do they couldn't get him out to meetin'; and when a man neglects means o' grace and sanctuary privileges there ain't no sayin' *what* he'll do next. Why, boys, jist think on't! an immortal crittur lyin' round loose all day Sun- day, and not puttin' on so much as a clean shirt, when all 'spectable folks has on their best close, and is to meetin' worshippin the Lord! What can you spect to come of it, when he es idlin' round in his old week-day close, fishing or some sich, but what the Devil should be arter him at last, as he was arter old Cack?"

Here Sam winked impressively to my grandfather in the opposite cor- ner, to call his attention to the moral which he was interweaving with his narrative.

"Wal, ye see, Cap'n Eb he told me that when he come to them bars and looked up and saw the dark a comin' down and the storm a thickenin' up, he felt that things was gettin' pretty consid'able serious. There was a dark piece o' woods on ahead of him inside the bars, and he knew come to get in there the light would give out clean. So he jest thought he'd take the hoss out o' the team, and go ahead a little, and see where he was. So he driv his oxen up ag'in the fence, and took out the hoss, and got on him, and pushed along through the woods, not rightly knowin' where he was goin'.

"Wal, afore long he see a light through the trees, and sure enough he come out to Cack Sparrock's old mill.

"It was a pretty consid'able gloomy sort of a place, that are old mill was. There was a great fall of water that come rushin' down the rocks and fell in a deep pool, and it sounded sort o' wild and lonesome, but Cap'n Eb he knocked on the door with his whip- handle and got in.

"There, to be sure, sot old Cack beside a great blazin' fire, with his rum-jug at his elbow; he was a dreful fellow to drink, Cack was; for all that, there was some good in him, for he was pleasant spoken and 'bliging, and he made the Cap'n welcome.

"'Y see, Cack,' said Cap'n Eb, 'I'm off my road, and got snowed up down by your bars,' says he.

"'Want ter know!' says Cack; 'calculate you'll jest have to camp down here till mornin',' says he.

"Wal, so old Cack he got out his tin lantern, and went with Cap'n Eb back to the bars to help him fetch along his critturs; he told him he could put 'em under the mill-shed. So they got the critturs up to the shed and got the cart under; and by that time the storm was awful.

"But Cack he made a great roarin' fire, 'cause ye see Cack allers had slab-wood a plenty from his mill, and a roarin' fire is jest so much company. It sort o' keeps a fellow's spirits up, a good fire does. So Cack he sot on his old teakettle and made a swingeing lot o' toddy, and he and Cap'n Eb were havin' a tol'able comfortable time there. Cack was a pretty good hand to tell stories, and Cap'n Eb warn't no ways backward in that line, and kep' up his end pretty well, and pretty soon they was a roarin' and haw-hawin' inside about as loud as the storm outside; when all of a sudden, 'bout midnight, there come a loud rap on the door.

" 'Lordy massy! what's that?' says Cack. Folks is rather startled allers to be checked up sudden when they are a carryin' on and laughin', and it was such an awful blowy night, it was a little scary to have a rap on the door.

"Wal, they waited a minit, and didn't hear nothin' but the wind a screechin' round the chimbley; and old Cack was jest goin' on with his story, when the rap come ag'in, harder'n ever, as if it'd shook the door open.

" 'Wal,' says old Cack, 'if 'tis the Devil, we'd jest as good's open, and have it out with him to onst,' says he; and so he got up and opened the door, and, sure enough, there was old Ketury there. Expect you've heard your grandma tell about old Ketury. She used to come to meetin's sometimes, and her husband was one o' the prayin' Indians; but Ketury was one of the rael wild sort, and you couldn't no more convert *her* tha you could convert a wild-cat or painter (panther). Lordy massy Ketury used to come to meetin', an sit there on them Indian benches, an when the second bell was a-tollin and when Parson Lothrop and hi wife was comin' up the broad aisle and everybody in the house ris' u and stood, Ketury would sit there an look at 'em out o' the corner o' he eyes, and folks used to say she rattled them necklaces o' rattlesnake tails and wild-cat teeth and sich like heathen trumpery, and looked for a the world as if the spirit of the ol Sarpent himself was in her. I've see her sit and look at Lady Lothrop ou of the corner o' her eyes, and he old brown baggy neck would kind o twist and work; and her eyes the looked so, that 'twas enough to scar a body. For all the world she looke jest as if she was aworkin' up t spring at her. Lady Lothrop wa jest as kind to Ketury as she alway was to every poor crittur. She'd bo and smile as gracious to her whe meetin' was over, and she come dow the aisle, passin' out o' meetin'; b Ketury never took no notice. Ye se Ketury's father was one o' those grea powwows of Martha's Vineyard, an people used to say she was set apa when she was a child to the servic o' the Devil; any way, she never coul be made nothin' of in a Christia way. She come down to Parso Lothrop's study once or twice to b catechised, but he couldn't get word out o' her, and she kind seemed to sit scornful while he wa atalkin'. Folks said, if it was in o times, Ketury wouldn't have been a lowed to go on so, but Parson Lot op's so sort o' mild, he let her take pretty much her own way. Everybody thought that Ketury was a witch; at least she knew consid'able more'n she ought to know, and so they was kind o' 'fraid on her. Cap'n Eb says he never see a fellow seem scareder than Cack did when he see Ketury astandin' there.

"Why, ye see, boys, she was as withered and wrinkled and brown as an old frosted punkin-vine, and her little snaky eyes sparkled and snapped, and it made yer head kind o' dizzy to look at 'em, and folks used to say that anybody that Ketury got mad at was sure to get the worst of it, just or last; and so, no matter what day or hour Ketury had a mind to rap at anybody's door, folks gen'lly thought it was best to let her in; but then, they never thought her coming was for any good, for she was just like the wind,—she came when the fit was on her, she staid jest so long as it pleased her, and went when she got ready, and not before. Ketury understood English, and could talk it well enough, but always seemed to scorn it, and was allers mowin' and mutterin' to herself in Indian, and winkin' and blinkin' as if she saw more folks round than you did, so that she wa'n't no ways pleasant company; and yet everybody took good care to be polite to her.

"So old Cack asked her to come in, and didn't make no question where she come from, or what she come on; but he knew it was twelve good miles from where she lived to his hut, and the snow was drifted 'bove her middle, and Cap'n Eb declared that there wa'n't no track nor sign o' a track, of anybody's coming

through that snow next morning."

" 'How did she get there, then?' said I.

" 'Didn't ye never see brown leaves a ridin' on the wind? Well,' Cap'n Eb, he says, 'she came on the wind,' and I'm sure it was strong enough to fetch her. But Cack he got her down into the warm corner, and he poured her out a mug o' hot toddy, and give her; but ye see her bein' there sort o' stopped the conversation, for she sot there a rockin' back'ards and for'ards, a sippin' her toddy, and a mutterin' and lookin' up chimbley.

"Cap'n Eb says in all his born days he never hearn such screeches and yells as the wind give over that chimbley; and old Cack got so frightened you could fairly hear his teeth chatter.

"But Cap'n Eb he was a putty brave man, and he wa'n't goin' to have conversation stopped by no woman, witch or no witch; and so, when he see her mutterin', and lookin' up chimbley, he spoke up, and says he, 'Well, Ketury, what do you see?' says he. 'Come, out with it; don't keep it to yourself.' Ye see Cap'n Eb was a hearty fellow, and then he was a leetle warmed up with the toddy.

"Then he said he see an evil kind o' smile on Ketury's face, and she rattled her necklace o' bones and snakes' tails; and her eyes seemed to snap, and she looked up the chimbley and called out, 'Come down, come down. Let's see who ye be.'

"Then there was a scratchin' and a rumblin' and a groan; and a pair of feet come down the chimbley, and stood right in the middle of the haarth, the toes pi'ntin' out'rds, with shoes and silver buckles a-shinin' in the firelight. Cap'n Eb says he never come so near bein' scared in his life, and as to old Cack he jest wilted right down in his chair.

"Then old Ketury got up, and reached her stick up chimbley, and called out louder, 'Come down, come down! let's see who ye be'; and sure enough down came a pair o' legs, and j'ined right on to the feet; good fair legs they was, with ribbed stockings and leather breeches.

" 'Wal, we're in for it now,' says Cap'n Eb; 'go it, Ketury, and let's have the rest on him.'

"Ketury didn't seem to mind him; she stood there as stiff as a stake and kep' callin' out, 'Come down, come down! let's see who ye be,' and then come down the body of a man with a brown coat and yellow vest, and j'ined right on to the legs; but there wa'n't no arms to it. Then Ketury shook her stick up chimbley, and called, 'Come down, come down!' And there came down a pair o' arms, and went on each side o' the body; and there stood a man all finished, only there wa'n't no head on him.

" 'Wal, Ketury,' says Cap'n Eb, 'this 'ere's getting serious. I 'spec you must finish him up, and let's see what he wants of us.'

"Then Ketury called out once more, louder'n ever, 'Come down, come down! let's see who ye be'; and sure enough, down comes a man's head and settled on the shoulders straight enough, and Cap'n Eb, the minit he sot eyes on him knew he was Jehiel Lommedieu.

"Old Cack knew him too, and he fell flat on his face, and prayed the Lord to have mercy on his soul; bu Cap'n Eb he was for gettin' to th bottom of matters, and not have hi scare for nothin', so he says to him 'What do you want, now you hav come?'

"The man he didn't speak, he onl sort o' moaned and p'inted to th chimbley; he seemed to try to spea but couldn't, for ye see it isn't ofte that his sort o' folks is permitted t speak; but just then there came screechin' blast o' wind, and blowe the door open, and blowed the smok and fire all out into the room, an there seemed to be a whirlwind an darkness and moans and screeches and when it all cleared up, Ketur and the man was both gone, and onl old Cack lay on the ground rollin and moaning as if he'd die.

"Wal, Cap'n Eb he picked him up and built up the fire, and sort o' com forted him up, 'cause the crittur wa in distress o' mind that was dreffu The awful Providence ye see ha awakened him, and his sin had bee set home to his soul, and he was unde such conviction that it all had t come out,—how old Cack's fathe had murdered poor Lommedieu fo his money, and Cack had been priv to it, and helped his father build th body up in that very chimbley; an he said that he hadn't had neithe peace nor rest since then, and tha was what had driv' him away fror ordinances, for ye know sinnin' wi always make a man leave prayin Wal, Cack didn't live but a day o two. Cap'n Eb he got the ministe o' Sherburn and one o' the selectme down to see him; and they took hi deposition. He seemed railly quit penitent; and Parson Carryl h

rayed with him, and was faithful in
ettin' home the providence to his
oul, and so at the eleventh hour poor
ld Cack might have got in,—at least
. looks a leetle like it. He was dis-
ressed to think he couldn't live to
e hung. He sort o' seemed to think,
hat if he was fairly tried, and hung,
would make it all square. He made
'arson Carryl promise to have the old
ill pulled down and bury the body,
nd after he was dead they did it.

"Cap'n Eb he was one of a party
' eight that pulled down the chim-
ley, and there sure enough was the
keleton of poor Lommedieu.

"So there you see, boys, there
an't be no iniquity so hid but what
t'll come out. The wild Indians of
he forest and the stormy winds and
empests j'ined together to bring out
his 'ere."

"For my part," said Aunt Lois
harply, "I never believed that story."

"Why, Lois," said my grandmother,
Cap'n Eb Sawin was a regular
hurch-member, and a most respecta-
ole man."

"Law, mother, I don't doubt he
thought so. I suppose he and Cack
got drinking toddy together, till he
got asleep, and dreamed it. I
wouldn't believe such a thing if it did
happen right before my face and
eyes. I should only think I was
crazy, that's all."

"Come, Lois, if I was you I
wouldn't talk so like a Sadducee,"
said my grandmother. "What would
become of all the accounts in Dr.
Cotton Mather's 'Magnilly' if folks
were like you?"

"Wal," said Sam Lawson, drooping
contemplatively over the coals, and
gazing into the fire, "there's a putty
consid'able sight o' things in this
world that's true; and then ag'in
there's a sight o' things that ain't
true. Now, my old gran'ther used to
say, 'Boys, says he, 'if ye want to
lead a pleasant and prosperous life,
ye must contrive allers to keep jest
the *happy medum* between truth and
falsehood.' Now, that are's my doctrine."

1870

III. JOHN JAMES PIATT
(1835–1917)

RIDING TO VOTE

THE OLD DEMOCRAT IN THE WEST

Yonder the bleak old Tavern stands
  —the faded sign before,
That years ago a setting sun and
  banded harvest bore;
The Tavern stands the same to-day—
  the sign you look upon
Has glintings of the dazzled sheaves,
  but nothing of the sun.

In Jackson's days a gay young man,
  with spirit hale and blithe,
And form like the young hickory, so
  tough and tall and lithe,
I first remember coming up—we came
  a wagon-load,
A dozen for Old Hickory—this rough
  November road.

Ah! forty years—they help a man,
  you see, in getting gray;
They can not take the manly soul,
  that makes a man, away!
It's forty years, or near: to-day I go
  to vote once more;

Here, half a mile away, we see the
crowd about the door.

My boys, in Eighteen Sixty—what!
my boys? my men, I mean!
(No better men nor braver souls in
flesh-and-blood are seen!)
One twenty-six, one twenty-three,
rode with their father then:
The ballot-box remembers theirs—my
vote I'll try again!

The ballot-box remembers theirs, the
country well might know—
Though in a million only two for
little seem to go;
But, somehow, when my ticket
slipp'd I dream'd of Jackson's
day:
The land, I thought, has need of One
whose will will find a way!   20

"*He* did not waver when the need had
call'd for steadfast thought—
The word he spoke made plain the
deed that lay behind it wrought;"
And while I mused the Present fell,
and breathing back the Past,
Again it seem'd the hale young man
his vote for Jackson cast!

Thank God it was not lost!—my vote
I did not cast in vain!
I go alone to drop my vote—the
glorious vote again;
Alone—where three together fell but
one to-day shall fall;
But though I go alone to-day, one
voice shall speak for all!

For, when our men, awaking quick,
from hearth and threshold came,
Mine did not say, "Another day!" but
started like a flame;   30
I'll vote for them as well as me; they
died as soldiers can,
But in my vote their voices each
shall claim the right of man.

The elder left his wife and child—my
vote for these shall tell;

The younger's sweet-heart has a claim
—I'll vote for her as well!
Yes! for the myriad speechless
tongues, the myriad offer'd lives,
The desolation at the heart of orphans
and of wives!

I go to give my vote alone—I curse
your shameless shame
Who fight for traitors here at home
in Peace's holy name!
I go to give my vote alone, but even
while I do,
I vote for dead and living, all—the
living dead and you!   40

See yonder tree beside the field
caught in the sudden sough,
How conscious of its strength it
leans, how straight and steadfast
now!
If Lincoln bends (for all, through
him, my vote I mean to cast)—
What winds have blown! what storms
he's known! the hickory's straight
at last!

                                186

[TORCH-LIGHT IN AUTUMN]

I pluck this sumach bough of crim
son flare,
    And, touched with subtle pangs of
    dreamy pain,
Through the dark woods a torch I
    seem to bear,
    In Autumn's funeral train.
(Before 1881?)   193

FARTHER

Far-off a young State rises, full of
might:
I paint its brave escutcheon. Near
at hand
See the log-cabin in the rough clear
ing stand;

woman by its door, with steadfast
sight,
rustful, looks Westward, where, uplifted bright,
me city's Apparition, weird and
grand,
dazzling quiet fronts the lonely
land,
ith vast and marvellous structures
wrought of light,

Motionless on the burning cloud
afar:—
The haunting vision of a time to
be,   10
After the heroic age is ended here,
Built on the boundless, still horizon's
bar
By the low sun, his gorgeous prophecy
Lighting the doorway of the pioneer!
                                        1871

---

7. EDWARD EGGLESTON
(1837–1902)

From *THE HOOSIER SCHOOL-MASTER*

CHAPTER I

A PRIVATE LESSON FROM A BULLDOG

"Want to be a school-master, do
u? You? Well, what would *you*
in Flat Crick deestrick, *I'd* like to
ow? Why, the boys have driv off
e last two, and licked the one afore
em like blazes. You might teach a
mmer school, when nothin' but chil-
en come. But I 'low it takes a
ght smart *man* to be school-master
Flat Crick in the winter. They'd 20
ch you out of doors, sonny, neck
d heels, afore Christmas."

The young man, who had walked
n miles to get the school in this dis-
ict, and who had been mentally re-
ewing his learning at every step he
ok, trembling lest the committee
ould find that he did not know
ough, was not a little taken aback
this greeting from "Old Jack 30
eans," who was the first trustee that
lighted on. The impression made
these ominous remarks was em-
asized by the glances which he re-

ceived from Jack Means' two sons.
The older one eyed him from the top
of his brawny shoulders with that
amiable look which a big dog turns
on a little one before shaking him.
Ralph Hartsook had never thought of
being measured by the standard of
muscle. This notion of beating education into young savages in spite of
themselves dashed his ardor.

He had walked right to where Jack
Means was at work shaving shingles
in his own front yard. While Mr.
Means was making the speech which
we have set down above, and punc-
tuating it with expectorations, a large
brindle bulldog had been sniffing at
Ralph's heels, and a girl in a new
linsey-woolsey dress, standing by the
door, had nearly giggled her head off
at the delightful prospect of seeing a
new school-teacher eaten up by the
ferocious brute.

Between the disheartening words of
the old man, the immense muscles of
the young man who was to be his rebellious pupil, the jaws of the ugly
bulldog, and the heartless giggle of
the girl, Ralph had a delightful sense
of having precipitated himself into a
den of wild beasts. Faint with weariness and discouragement, and shiver-
ing with fear, he sat down on a
wheelbarrow.

"You, Bull!" said the old man to the dog, which was showing more and more a disposition to make a meal of the incipient pedagogue, "you, Bull! git aout, you pup!" The dog walked sullenly off, but not until he had given Ralph a look full of promise of what he meant to do when he got a good chance. Ralph wished himself back in the village of Lewisburg, whence he had come.

"You see," continued Mr. Means, spitting in a meditative sort of a way, "you see, we a'n't none of your saft sort in these diggin's. It takes a *man* to boss this deestrick. Howsumdever, ef you think you kin trust your hide in Flat Crick school-house, I ha'n't got no 'bjection. But ef you git licked, don't come on us. Flat Crick don't pay no 'nsurance, you bet! Any other trustees? Wal, yes. But as I pay the most taxes, t'others jist let me run the thing. You can begin right off a Monday. They a'n't been no other applications. You see, it takes grit to apply for this school. The last master had a black eye for a month. But, as I wuz sayin', you can jist roll up and wade in. I 'low you've got pluck, maybe, and that goes for a heap sight more'n sinnoo with boys. Walk in, and stay over Sunday with me. You'll hev' to board roun', and I guess you better begin here."

Ralph did not go in, but sat out on the wheelbarrow, watching the old man shave shingles, while the boys split the blocks and chopped wood. Bull smelled of the new-comer again in an ugly way, and got a good kick from the older son for his pains. But out of one of his red eyes the dog warned the young school-master that *he* should yet suffer for all kicks re ceived on his account.

"Ef Bull once takes a holt, heav and yarth can't make him let go said the older son to Ralph, by wa of comfort.

It was well for Ralph that he b gan to "board roun'" by stopping Mr. Means's. Ralph felt that Fl Creek was what he needed. He ha lived a bookish life; but here was h lesson in the art of managing peopl for he who can manage the untam and strapping youths of a wint school in Hoopole County has go far toward learning one of the har est of lessons. And twenty-five yea ago, in Ralph's time, things we worse than they are now.

The older son of Mr. Means w called Bud Means. What his re name was, Ralph could not find ou for in many of these families t nickname of "Bud" given to the ol est boy, and that of "Sis," which the birthright of the oldest girl, co pletely bury the proper Christi name. Ralph was a general. He sa his first strategic point, which was capture Bud Means.

After supper, the boys began to g ready for something. Bull stuck his ears in a dignified way, and t three or four yellow curs who we Bull's satellites yelped delighted and discordantly.

"Bill," said Bud Means to h brother, "ax the master ef he'd li to hunt coons. I'd like to take t starch out uv the stuck-up fellow

" 'Nough said," was Bill's reply.

"You durn't do it," said Bud.

"I don't take no sech a dare," r turned Bill, and walked down to t gate, by which Ralph stood watchi he stars come out, and half wishing he had never seen Flat Creek.

"I say, mister," began Bill, "mister, hey's a coon what's been a eatin' our hickens lately, and we're goin' to try o ketch the varmint. You wouldn't like to take a coon hunt nor nothin', would you?"

"Why, yes," said Ralph, "there's nothing I should like better, if I could only be sure Bull wouldn't mistake me for the coon."

And so, as a matter of policy, Ralph dragged his tired legs eight or ten miles, on hill and in hollow, after Bud, and Bill, and Bull, and the coon. But the raccoon climbed a tree. The boys got into a quarrel about whose business it was to have brought the ax, and who was to blame that the tree could not be felled. Now, if there was anything Ralph's muscles were good for, it was climbing. So, asking Bud to give him a start, he soon reached the limb above the one on which the raccoon was. Ralph did not know how ugly a customer a raccoon can be, and so got credit for more courage than he had. With much peril to his legs from the raccoon's teeth, he succeeded in shaking the poor creature off among the yelping brutes and yelling boys. Ralph could not help sympathizing with the hunted animal, which sold its life as dearly as possible, giving the dogs many a scratch and bite. It seemed to him that he was like the raccoon, precipitated into the midst of a party of dogs who would rejoice in worrying his life out, as Bull and his crowd were destroying the poor raccoon. When Bull at last seized the raccoon and put an end to it, Ralph could not but admire the decided way in which he did it, calling to mind Bud's comment, "Ef Bull once takes a holt, heaven and yarth can't make him let go."

But as they walked home, Bud carrying the raccoon by the tail, Ralph felt that his hunt had not been in vain. He fancied that even red-eyed Bull, walking uncomfortably close to his heels, respected him more since he had climbed that tree.

"Purty peart kind of a master," remarked the old man to Bud, after Ralph had gone to bed. "Guess you better be a little easy on *him*. Hey?"

But Bud deigned no reply. Perhaps because he knew that Ralph heard the conversation through the thin partition.

Ralph woke delighted to find it raining. He did not want to hunt or fish on Sunday, and this steady rain would enable him to make friends with Bud. I do not know how he got started, but after breakfast he began to tell stories. Out of all the books he had ever read he told story after story. And "old man Means," and "old *Miss* Means," and Bud Means, and Bill Means, and Sis Means listened with great eyes while he told of Sinbad's adventures, of the Old Man of the Sea, of Robinson Crusoe, of Captain Gulliver's experiences in Liliput, and of Baron Munchausen's exploits.

Ralph had caught his fish. The hungry minds of these backwoods people, were refreshed with the new life that came to their imaginations in these stories. For there was but one book in the Means library, and that, a well-thumbed copy of "Captain Riley's Narrative," had long since lost all freshness.

"I'll be dog-on'd," said Bill, emphatically, "ef I hadn't 'ruther hear the master tell them whoppin' yarns than to go to a circus the best day I ever seed!" Bill could pay no higher compliment.

What Ralph wanted was to make a friend of Bud. It's a nice thing to have the seventy-four-gun ship on your own side, and the more Hartsook admired the knotted muscles of Bud Means the more he desired to attach him to himself. So, whenever he struck out a peculiarly brilliant passage, he anxiously watched Bud's eye. But the young Philistine kept his own counsel. He listened, but said nothing, and the eyes under his shaggy brow gave no sign. Ralph could not tell whether those eyes were deep and inscrutable or only stolid. Perhaps a little of both. When Monday morning came, Ralph was nervous. He walked to school with Bud.

"I guess you're a little skeered by what the old man said, a'n't you?"

Ralph was about to deny it, but on reflection concluded that it was the best to speak the truth. He said that Mr. Means's description of the school had made him feel a little down-hearted.

"What will you do with the tough boys? You a'n't no match for 'em." And Ralph felt Bud's eyes not only measuring his muscles, but scrutinizing his countenance. He only answered:

"I don't know."

"What would you do with me, for instance?" and Bud stretched himself up as if to shake out the reserve power coiled up in his great muscles.

"I sha'n't have any trouble with you."

"Why, I'm the wust chap of all. thrashed the last master, myself."

And again the eyes of Bud Mear looked out sharply from his shadow ing brows to see the effect of th speech on the slender young man.

"You won't thrash me, though, said Ralph.

"Pshaw! I 'low I should whip yo in an inch of your life with my le hand, and never half try," said youn Means, with a threatening sneer.

"I know that as well as you do."

"Well, a'n't you afraid of m then?" and again he looked sidewis at Ralph.

"Not a bit," said Ralph, wonderin at his own courage.

They walked on in silence a mi ute. Bud was turning the matter ove

"Why a'n't you afraid of me?" h said presently.

"Because you and I are going to b friends."

"And what about t'others?"

"I am not afraid of all the othe boys put together."

"You a'n't! The mischief! How that?"

"Well, I'm not afraid of them be cause you and I are going to b friends, and you can whip all of the together. You'll do the fighting an I'll do the teaching."

The diplomatic Bud only chuckle a little at this; whether he assente to the alliance or not Ralph cou not tell.

When Ralph looked round on t faces of the scholars—the little face full of mischief and curiosity, the b faces full of an expression which wa not further removed than secon cousin from contempt—when your Hartsook looked into these faces, h

art palpitated with stage-fright.
here is no audience so hard to face
one of school-children, as many a
an has found to his cost. Perhaps
is that no conventional restraint can
eep down their laughter when you
or say anything ridiculous.

Hartsook's first day was hurried and
nsatisfactory. He was not master
himself, and consequently not mas-
r of anybody else. When evening
me, there were symptoms of insub-
rdination through the whole school.
oor Ralph was sick at heart. He
lt that if there had ever been the
adow of an alliance between himself
nd Bud, it was all "off" now. It
emed to Hartsook that even Bull had
st his respect for the teacher. Half
at night the young man lay awake.
t last comfort came to him. A
eminiscence of the death of the rac-
oon flashed on him like a vision. He
emembered that quiet and annihilat-
g bite which Bull gave. He remem-
ered Bud's certificate, that "Ef Bull
nce takes a holt, heaven and yarth
an't make him let go." He thought
at what Flat Creek needed was a
ulldog. He would be a bulldog,
uiet, but invincible. He would take
old in such a way that nothing
ould make him let go. And then
e went to sleep.

In the morning Ralph got out of bed
owly. He put his clothes on slowly.
e pulled on his boots in a bulldog
ood. He tried to move as he thought
ull would move if he were a man.
e ate with deliberation, and looked
verybody in the eyes with a manner
at made Bud watch him curiously.
e found himself, continually com-
aring himself with Bull. He found
ull possessing a strange fascination

for him. He walked to school alone,
the rest having gone on before. He
entered the school-room preserving a
cool and dogged manner. He saw
in the eyes of the boys that there was
mischief brewing. He did not dare
sit down in his chair for fear of a
pin.

Everybody looked solemn. Ralph
lifted the lid of his desk. "Bow-wow!
wow-wow!" It was the voice of an
imprisoned puppy, and the school giggled and then roared. Then everything was quiet.

The scholars expected an outburst
of wrath from the teacher. For they
had come to regard the whole world
as divided into two classes, the teacher
on the one side representing lawful
authority, and the pupils on the other
in a state of chronic rebellion. To
play a trick on the master was an
evidence of spirit; to "lick" the master
was to be the crowned hero of Flat
Creek district. Such a hero was Bud
Means; and Bill, who had less muscle,
saw a chance to distinguish himself
on a teacher of slender frame. Hence
the puppy in the desk.

Ralph Hartsook grew red in the
face when he saw the puppy. But
the cool, repressed, bulldog mood in
which he had kept himself saved him.
He lifted the dog into his arms and
stroked him until the laughter subsided. Then, in a solemn and set way,
he began:

"I am sorry," and he looked round
the room with a steady, hard eye—
everybody felt that there was a conflict coming—"I am sorry that any
scholar in this school could be so
mean"—the word was uttered with a
sharp emphasis, and all the big boys
felt sure that there would be a fight

with Bill Means, and perhaps with Bud—"could be so *mean*—as to—shut up his *brother* in such a place as that!"

There was a long, derisive laugh. The wit was indifferent, but by one stroke Ralph had carried the whole school to his side. By the significant glances of the boys, Hartsook detected the perpetrator of the joke, and with the hard and dogged look in his eyes, with just such a look as Bull would give a puppy, but with the utmost suavity in his voice, he said:

"William Means, will you be so good as to put this dog out of doors?" *

There was a moment of utter stillness; but the magnetism of Ralph's eye was too much for Bill Means. The request was so polite, the master's look was so innocent and yet so

* Marks the end of Chapter I.

determined. Bill often wondere afterward that he had not "fit" rathe than obeyed the request. But som how he put the dog out. He wa partly surprised, partly inveigle partly awed into doing just what h had not intended to do. In the wee that followed, Bill had to fight half dozen boys for calling him "Pupp Means." Bill said he wished he' licked the master on the spo 'Twould 'a' saved five fights out c the six.

And all that day and the next, th bulldog in the master's eye was a ter ror to evil-doers. At the close c school on the second day Bud wa heard to give it as his opinion tha "the master wouldn't be much in a tus sle, but he had a heap of thunder an lightning in him." * * *

187

V. JOHN HAY
(1838–1905)

From *PIKE COUNTY BALLADS* *

LITTLE BREECHES

I don't go much on religion,
   I never ain't had no show;
But I've got a middlin' tight grip, sir,
   On the handful o' things I know.
I don't pan out on the prophets
   And free-will and that sort of
      thing,—
But I b'lieve in God and the angels,
   Ever sence one night last spring.

I come into town with some turnips,
   And my little Gabe come along,— 10

* All selections from Hay are used by permission of, and by arrangement with, Houghton Mifflin Company.

No four-year-old in the county
   Could beat him for pretty an
     strong,—
Peart and chipper and sassy,
   Always ready to swear and fight,—
And I'd larnt him to chaw terbacke
   Jest to keep his milk-teeth white.

The snow come down like a blanke
   As I passed by Taggart's store;
I went in for a jug of molasses
   And left the team at the door.   2
They scared at something an
    started,—
   I heard one little squall,
And hell-to-split over the prairie
   Went team, Little Breeches, and al

Hell-to-split over the prairie!
   I was almost froze with skeer;
But we rousted up some torches,
   And sarched for 'em far and near

At last we struck hosses and wagon,
   Snowed under a soft white
      mound,   30
Upsot, dead beat,—but of little Gabe
   No hide nor hair was found.

And here all hope soured on me
   Of my fellow-critter's aid;—
I jest flopped down on my marrow-
      bones,
   Crotch-deep in the snow, and
      prayed.

.   .   .   .

By this, the torches was played out,
   And me and Isrul Parr
Went off for some wood to a sheep-
      fold
   That he said was somewhar thar. 40

We found it at last, and a little shed
   Where they shut up the lambs at
      night.
We looked in and seen them huddled
      thar,
   So warm and sleepy and white;
And thar sot Little Breeches and
      chirped,
   As peart as ever you see,
"I want a chaw of terbacker,
   And that's what's the matter of me."

How did he git thar? Angels.
   He could never have walked in that
      storm: 50
They jest scooped down and toted him
   To whar it was safe and warm.
And I think that saving a little child,
   And fotching him to his own,
Is a derned sight better business
   Than loafing around The Throne.
            1870

JIM BLUDSO

(OF THE PRAIRIE BELLE)

Wall, no! I can't tell whar he lives,
   Because he don't live, you see;
Leastways, he's got out of the habit
   Of livin' like you and me.

Whar have you been for the last three
      year
   That you haven't heard folks tell
How Jimmy Bludso passed in his
      checks,
   The night of the Prairie Belle?

He weren't no saint—them engineers
   Is all pretty much alike—   10
One wife in Natchez-under-the-Hill
   And another here, in Pike.
A keerless man in his talk was Jim,
   And an awkward man in a row—
But he never flunked, and he never
      lied,
   I reckon he never knowed how.

And this was all the religion he had—
   To treat his engine well;
Never be passed on the river;
   To mind the Pilot's bell;   20
And if ever the Prairie Belle took
      fire—
A thousand times he swore,
He'd hold her nozzle agin the bank
   Till the last soul got ashore.

All boats has their day on the Missis-
      sipp,
   And her day come at last—
The Movastar was a better boat,
   But the Belle she *wouldn't* be
      passed.
And so she come tarin' along that
      night—
   The oldest craft on the line,   30
With a nigger squat on her safety
      valve
   And her furnace crammed, rosin and
      pine.

The fire bust out as she clared the
      bar,
   And burnt a hole in the night,
And quick as flash she turned, and
      made
   For that willer-bank on the right.
There was running and cursing, but
      Jim yelled out,
   Over all the infernal roar,

"I'll hold her nozzle agin the bank
  Till the last galoot's ashore."   40

Through the hot, black breath of the
    burnin' boat
Jim Bludso's voice was heard,
And they all had trust in his cussed-
    ness,
  And knowed he would keep his
    word.
And sure's you're born, they all got off
Afore the smokestacks fell—

And Bludso's ghost went up alone
  In the smoke of the Prairie Belle.

He weren't no saint—but at jedgment
  I'd run my chance with Jim,   50
'Longside of some pious gentlemen
  That wouldn't shook hands with
    him.
He seen his duty, a dead sure thing—
  And went for it thar and then:
And Christ ain't a goin' to be too hard
  On a man that died for men.
                     1871

VI. ROSE TERRY COOKE
(1827–1892)

TOO LATE
'Tis true 'tis pity! pity 'tis, 'tis true!

In one of those scanty New England
towns that fill a stranger with the
acutest sense of desolation, more desolate than the desert itself, because 10
there are human inhabitants to suffer
from its solitude and listlessness, there
stood, and still stands, a large red
farm-house, with sloping roof, and
great chimney in the middle, where
David Blair lived. Perhaps Wingfield
was not so forlorn to him as to another, for he had Scotch blood in his
veins, and his shrewd thrift found full
exercise in redeeming the earth from 20
thorns and briars, and eating his bread
under the full force of the primeval
curse. He was a "dour" man, with a
long, grim visage that would have become any Covenanter's conventicle in
his native land; and his prayers were
as long and grim as his face. Of
life's graces and amenities he had no
idea; they would have been scouted
as profane vanities had they blossomed 30
inside his threshold. Existence to him

was a heavy and dreadful responsibility; a drear and doubtful working out
of his own salvation; a perpetual flee-
ing from the wrath to come, that
seemed to dog his heels and rear
threatening heads at every turn. A
cowardly man, with these ever-present
terrors, would have taken refuge in
some sweet and lulling sin or creed,
some belief of a universal salvation,
some epicurean "let us eat and drink,
for to-morrow we die," or some idea
of nothing beyond the grave.

But David Blair was full of courage. Like some knotty, twisted oak,
that offers scant solace to the eye, he
endured, oak-like, all storms, and bent
not an atom to any fierce blast of nature or Providence; for he made a
distinction between them. His wife
was a neat, quiet, subdued woman,
who held her house and her husband
in as much reverence as a Feejee holds
his idols. Like most women, she had
an instinctive love for grace and
beauty, but from long repression it
was only a blind and groping instinct.
Her house was kept in a state of spotless purity, but was bald as any vine-
less rock within. Flies never intruded
there; spiders still less. The windows

f the "best room" were veiled and double veiled with green paper shades and snow-white cotton curtains, and the ghastly light that strayed in through these obstructions revealed a speckless but hideous home-spun carpet, four straight-backed chairs, with horse-hair seats, an equally black and shining sofa, and a round mahogany table with a great Bible in the midst. No vases, no shells, no ornament of useless fashion stood on the white wooden mantelpiece over the open fireplace; no stencil border broke the monotonous whitewash of the walls. You could see your face in a state of distortion and jaundice anywhere in the andirons, so brilliant were their brassy columns; and the very bricks of the chimney were scraped and washed from the soot of the rare fire. You could hardly imagine that even the leaping, wood fire could impart any cheer to the funereal order of that chill and musty apartment. Bedroom, kitchen, shed, woodhouse—all shared his scrupulous array. The processes that in other households are wont to give tokens of cheery life, and bounty, and natural appetites and passions, seemed here to be carried on under protest. No flour was spilled when Thankful Blair made bread! no milk ever slopped from an overfull pail; no shoe ever brought in mud or sand across the mats that lay inside and outside of every door. The very garret preserved an aspect of serenity, since all its bundles of herbs hung evenly side by side, and the stores of nuts had each their separate boundaries, lest some jarring door or intrusive mouse should scatter them.

In the midst of all this order there was yet a child, if little Hannah Blair ever was a child in more than name. From her babyhood she was the model of all Wingfield babies; a child that never fretted, that slept nights through all the pangs and perils of teething, that had every childish disease with perfect decency and patience, was a child to be held up to every mother's admiration. Poor little soul! the mother love that crushed those other babies with kisses, that romped and laughed with them, when she was left straight and solemn in her cradle, that petted, and slapped, and spoiled, and scolded all those common children, Thankful Blair kept under lock and key in her inmost heart.

"Beware of idols!" was the stern warning that had fallen on her first outburst of joy at the birth of one living child at last, and from that time the whole tenor of her husband's speech and prayer had been that they both might be saved from the awful sin of idolatry, and be enabled to bring up their child in the fear of the Lord, a hater of sin and a follower of the Law: the gospel that a baby brought to light was not yet theirs! So Hannah grew to girlhood, a feminine reproduction of her father. Keen, practical insight is not the most softening trait for a woman to possess. It is iron and steel in the soul that does not burn with love mighty and overflowing enough to fuse all other elements in its own glow, and as Hannah grew older and read her mother's repressed nature through and through, the tender heart, the timid conscience, the longing after better and brighter things than life offered to her only moved her child to an unavowed contempt for a soul so weak and so childish. In a certain way Hannah Blair loved her mother, but it was more as if she had been her child than her parent. Toward her father her feelings were far different. She respected him; he was her model. She alone knew, from a like experience, what reserved depth of feeling lay unawakened under his rigid exterior—she knew, for there were times when her own granite nature shuddered through and through with volcanic forces, when her only refuge against generous indignation or mighty anger was in solitary prayer or grievous wrestlings of the flesh against the spirit as well as the spirit against the flesh. So Hannah grew up to womanhood. Tall and slight as any woodland sapling, but without the native grace of a free growth, her erect and alert figure pleased only by its alacrity and spotless clothing. She was "dredful spry," as old Moll Thunder, the half-breed Indian woman used to say—"dredful spry; most like squaw —so still, so straight; blue eyes, most like ice. Ho! Moll better walk a chalk 'fore Miss Hanner!"

And Moll spoke from bitter experience, for old Deacon Campbell himself never gave her severer lectures on her ungodly life and conversation than dropped with cutting distinctness from those prim, thin, red lips. Yet Hannah Blair was not without charms for the youth of Wingfield. Spare as she was, her face had the fresh bloom of youth upon its high, straight features; her eyes were blue and bright, her hair, smoothed about her small head, glittered like fresh flax, and made a heavy coil, that her slender white throat seemed over small to sustain. She was cool, serene, rather unapproachable to lovers or love makers,

but she was David Blair's only child and his farm lay fair and wide on the high plains of Wingfield. She was well-to-do and pious—charms which hold to this day potent sway over the youth of her native soil—and after she was eighteen no Saturday night passed in solitude in the Blair keeping room, for young men of all sorts and sizes ranged themselves against the wall, sometimes four at once, tilted their chairs, twirled their thumbs, crossed one foot and then the other over their alternate knees, dropped sparse remarks about the corn, or the weather, or the sermon, sometimes even the village politics, but one and all stared at Hannah as she sat upright and prim by the fireplace or the window, arrayed in a blue stuff gown or a flowered chintz, as the season might be, and sitting as serene, as cool, as uninteresting as any cherub on a tombstone, until the old Dutch clock struck nine, the meeting-house bell tolled and the young men, one and all, made their awkward farewells and went home, uttering, no doubt, a sigh of relief when the painful pleasure was over.

By and by the Wingfield store, long kept by Uncle Gid Mayhew, began to have a look of new life, for the old man's only son, Charley Mayhew, had come home from Boston, where he had been ten years in a dry-goods shop to take the business off his father's hands. Just in time, too, for the store was scarce set to rights in symmetrical fashion when Uncle Gid was struck with paralysis and put to bed for all the rest of his life—a brief one at that. Wingfield gossips shook their heads and muttered that the new order of things was enough to kill him

After so many years of dust and confusion, to see the pepper corns, candy, and beeswax sorted into fresh, clean jars; the shoes and ribbons, cut nails and bar soap neatly disentangled and arranged; the plows, harrows, cheeses, hoes, and bales of cotton and calico divorced and placed at different ends of the store; the grimy windows washed, and the dirty floor cleaned and swept, was perhaps a shock to the old man, but not enough to kill him. His eighty years of vegetation sufficed for that; but he left behind him this son, so full of life, and spirit, and fun, so earnest at work, so abounding in energy, but withal so given over to frolic in its time, that it seemed as if even Wingfield stagnation never could give him a proper dullness or paralyze his handsome face and manly figure. Of course Charley Mayhew fell in love with Hannah Blair. A mischievous desire at first to wake up those cold blue eyes and flush that clear set face with blushes soon deepened into a very devoted affection. The ranks of Saturday night lovers began to look at him with evil eyes, for not even the formality of the best parlor restrained his fun, or the impassive visage of David Blair awed him into silence. Even Hannah began to glow and vivify in his presence; a warmer color flushed her cheeks, her thin lips relaxed into real smiles, her eyes shone with deeper and keener gleams than the firelight lent them, and, worst of all, the sheepish suitors themselves could not help an occasional giggle, a broad grin, or even a decided horse laugh, at his sallies; and when at last David Blair himself relaxed into an audible laugh, and declared to Charley he was "a master hand at telling stories," the vexed ranks gave it up, allowed that the conquering hero had come, and left Charley Mayhew a free field thereafter, which of course he improved. But even after Hannah Blair had promised in good set terms to be his wife, and David had given his slow consent, it was doubtful to Charley if this treasure was his merely out of his own determined persistence or with any genuine feeling of her own, any real response of heart, for the maiden was so inaccessible, so chill, so proper, that his warm, impulsive nature dashed against hers and recoiled as the wild sea from a rocky coast. Yet after many days the rock does show signs of yielding; there are traces on its surface, though it needs years to soften and disintegrate its nature. They were a handsome couple, these two, and admiring eyes followed them in their walks. Never had Hannah's face mantled with so rich a color, or her eyes shone with so deep and soft a blue; the stern, red lips relaxed into a serene content, and here and there a tint of gaiety about her prim dress—a fresh ribbon, a flower at her throat, a new frill—told of her shy blossom time. She was like one of those prim, old-fashioned pinks, whose cold color, formal shape, stiff growth, and dagger-shaped gray-green leaves, stamp them the quaint old-maid sisterhood of flowers, yet which hold in their hearts a breath of passionate spice, and odor of the glowing Orient or the sweet and ardent South, that seems fitter for the open-breasted roses, looking frankly and fervently up to the sun. No, not even her lover knew the madness of Hannah Blair's hungry heart, now for the first time fed—a madness that filled her with sweet delirium, that she regarded as nothing less than a direct Satanic impulse, against which she fought and prayed, all in vain; for God was greater than her heart, and He had filled it with that love which every wife and mother needs, strong enough to endure all things, to be forever faithful and forever fresh. But no vine-planted and grass-strewn volcano ever showed more placidly than Hannah Blair. Her daily duties were done with such exactness and patience, her lover's demands so coolly set aside till those duties were attended to, her face kept so calm even when the blood thrilled to her finger tips at the sound of his voice, that, long as her mother had known her, she looked on with wonder, and admired afar off the self-control she never could have exhibited. For Hannah's wooing was carried on in no such style as her mother's had been. Thankful Parsons had accepted David Blair from a simple sense of duty, and he had asked her because she was meek and pious, had a good farm and understood cows; no troublesome sentiment, no turbulent passion disturbed their rather dull courtship. A very different wooer was this handsome, merry young fellow, with his dark curls and keen, pleasant eyes, who came into the house like a fresh dancing breeze, and stirred its dusty stagnation into absolute sparkle. Mrs. Blair loved him dearly already; her repressed heart opened to him all its motherly instincts. She cooked for him whatever she observed he liked, with simple zeal and pleasure. She unconsciously smiled to hear his voice. Deeply she wondered at Hannah, who, day by day, stitched on her quilts,

her sheets, her pillow-cases, and her napery, with as diligent sternness as ever she applied to more irksome tasks, and never once blushed or smiled over the buying or shaping of her personal bridal gear, only showing, if possible a keener eye for business a more infallible judgment of good and prices, wear and tear, use and fitness, than ever before. So the long winter wore away. Hannah's goods lay piled in the "spare chamber"—heaps of immaculate linen, home-spun flannel, patchwork of gayest hues, and towels woven and hemmed by her own hand; and in the clothes-press, whose deep drawers were filled with her own garments in neat array, hung the very wedding dress of dove-colored padu asoy, the great Leghorn bonnet, with white satin ribbons, and the black silk cardinal. Hannah had foregone all the amusements of the past months at no time consonant to her taste, in order to construct these treasures for her new life. In vain had Charley coaxed her to share in the sleighing frolics, the huskings, the quilting bees of the neighborhood. It did not once enter into his mind that Hannah had rather be alone with the fullness of her great joy than to have its sacred rapture intermeddled with by the kindly or unkindly jokes and jeers of other people. He never knew that her delight was full even to oppression when she sat by herself and sewed like an automaton, setting with every stitch a hope or a thought of her love and life.

It was spring now. The long, cold winter had passed at last; the woods began to bud, the pastures grew green even in Wingfield, and brave little blossoms sprung up in the very mois-

ure of the just melted snow-drifts.
May had brought the robins and the
wallows back; here and there an
oriole darted like a flake of fire from
one drooping elm to another; the stiff
arches put out little crimson cones;
he gracious elm boughs grew dusk and
dense with swelling buds, and the
maple hung out its dancing yellow tas-
els high in the air. The swamps were
ransfigured with vivid verdure and lit
with rank yellow blossoms.

The wild marsh marigold shone like
fire, and the quaint, sad-colored tril-
ium made its protest in fence corners
and by the low buttresses of granite
on the hills far and near, and the
rough-leaved arbutus nestled its baby
faces of sweetest bloom deep in the
gray grass and stiff moss beds. The
day drew near for the wedding. It
was to be the last Wednesday in May.

"Darned unlucky," muttered Moll
Thunder, drying her ragged shoes before Mrs. Blair's kitchen fire, having
just brought a fagot of herbs and roots
for the brewing of root-beer—even
then a favorite beverage in New England, as it is to-day. "Darned un-
ucky! Married in May, repent alway. Guess Hanner pretty good like
her set up 'ginst ole debbil heself. No
good, no good; debbil pretty good
trong. Moll knows! He! he! he!'"

Mrs. Blair shivered. She was super-
titious like all women, and old Moll
was a born witch, everybody knew.
But then her daughter's pure, fair,
and resolute face rose up before
her, and the superstitious fear flickered and went out. She thought Hannah altogether beyond the power of
ole debbil." At last the last Wednesday came—a day as serene and lovely
as if new created: flying masses of

white cloud chased each other through
the azure sky, and cast quick shadows
on the long, green range of hills that
shut in Wingfield on the west. Shine
and shadow added an exquisite grace
of expression to the shades of tender
green veiling those cruel granite rocks;
a like flitting grace at last transfigured
Hannah Blair's cold-featured face.
The apple trees blossomed everywhere
with festive garlands of faint pink
bloom, and filled the air with their
bitter-sweet, subtle odor, clean and
delicate, yet the parent of that luscious, vinous, oppressive perfume that
autumn should bring from the heaps
of gold and crimsoned fruit as yet un-
formed below those waxen petals. To-
day at last Hannah had resolved to
give her beating heart one day of freedom—one long day of unrestrained
joy—if she could bear the freedom of
that ardent rapture so long so conscientiously repressed. For once in
her life she sung about her work;
psalm tunes, indeed, but one can put
a deal of vitality into Mear and
Bethesda, and Cambridge, with its
glad exultant repeat, has all the capacity of a love song. Mrs. Blair
heard it from the kitchen where she
was watching the last pan of cake
come to crisp perfection in the brick
oven. The old words had a curious
adaptation to the sweet, intense triumph of the air, and Hannah carried the three parts of the tune as they
came in with a flexibility of voice new
to her as to her sole hearer.

" 'Twas in the watches of the night
    I thought upon thy power;
    I kept thy lovely face in sight
    Amid the darkest hour!"

What a subdued ecstasy rose and fell
in her voice as she swept and gar-

nished the old house. "Amid the darkest hour!" Oh, there never could be a dark hour for her again, she thought—never a doubt, or fear, or trouble. "My beloved is mine, and I am his" rose to her lips from the oldest of all love songs. Half profane she seemed to herself, but to-day her deeper nature got the better of her deep prejudices; she was at heart for once a simple love-smitten girl.

The quiet wedding was to be after tea. Nobody was asked, for the few relatives David Blair possessed were almost strangers to him, and lived far away. His wife had been an only child, and Hannah had made no girl friends in the village. The minister was to come at eight o'clock, and the orthodox cake and wine handed round after the ceremony. The young couple were to go to their own house, and settle down at once to the duties and cares of life. Charley had been ordered not to appear till tea-time, and after the dinner was eaten and everything put to rights, Mrs. Blair went to her room to plait a cap ruffle, and Hannah sat down in the spare room by herself, to rest, she said— really to dream, to hope, to bury her face in her trembling hand, and let a mighty wave of rapture overflow her whole entranced soul. The cap ruffle troubled Mrs. Blair much. Twice it had to be taken from the prim plaits and relaid, then to be sprinkled and ironed out. This involved making a fresh fire to heat the flat-iron, and it got to be well on in the afternoon, and Mrs. Blair was tired. There was nobody to reflect on her waste of time, so she lay down a moment on the bed. David had gone to plow a lot on the furthest part of the farm. He

neglected work for no emergency. A a godless neighbor once said, "Dav Blair would sow rye on the edge o hell if he thought he could get the cat tle there to plow it up!" A daugh ter's wedding day was no excuse fo idleness in him. So Mrs. Blair wa safe in her nap. Meanwhile, as Han nah sat a little withdrawn from th open window, where for once th afternoon sun streamed in unguard edly, and the passionate warble of th song-sparrows, and the indescribabl odor of spring followed too, she wa suddenly half aware of an outsid shadow, and a letter skimmed throug the window, and fell at her feet Scarce roused from her dream, sh looked at it fixedly a moment befor she stooped to pick it up. Its coming was so sudden, so startling, it did no once occur to her to look out to se who brought it. She hesitated befor she broke the broad, red seal, an swept her hands across her eyes as i to brush away the dreams that ha filled and clouded them. But the first few words brought back to those eyes their native steely glint, and as sh read on life, light, love withdrew thei tender glories from her face. I settled into stone, into flint. He mouth set in lines of dreadful im placable portent, her cheek paled t the whiteness of a marble monument and the red lips faded to pale, col purple. What she read in that lette neither man or woman save the write and the reader ever knew, for whe it was read Hannah Blair walked, lik an unrepentant conspirator to th stake, fearless, careless, hopeless, ou into the small, silent kitchen, and lay ing that missive of evil on the smol dering coals, stood by stark and stif ill every ash was burned or floated up the chimney. Then she turned, and said in the voice of one who calls from his grave,

"Mother!"

Mrs. Blair sprung from her doze at the sound. Her mother instinct was keen as the hen's who hears the hawk scream in the sky, and knows her brood in danger. She was on the threshold of the kitchen door almost as soon as Hannah spoke, but her heart sunk to its furthest depth when she saw the face before her. Death would have left no such traces—given her no such shock. This was death in life, and it spoke, slowly, deliberately, with an awful distinctness.

"Mother, when Charles Mayhew comes here to-night, you must tell him I will not marry him."

"What?" half screamed the terrified woman, doubtful of her own hearing. Again the cold, relentless tones, in accents as clear and certain as the voice of fate itself—

"When Charles Mayhew comes here to-night, you must see him, and tell him I will not marry him."

"Hanner, I can't! I can't! What for? What do you mean? What is it?"

The words syllabled themselves again out of the thin, rigid lips.

"I will not marry him."

"Oh, I can't tell him! he will die! I cannot, Hanner. You must tell him yourself—you must! you must!"

Still the same answer, only the words lessening each time:

"I will not!"

"But, Hanner, child, stop and think —do. All your things made; you're published; the minister's spoke to. Why do you act so? You can't, Han-

ner. Oh, I never can tell him! What shall I say? What will he do? Oh dear! You must tell him yourself; I can't—I won't! I ain't goin' to; you must!"

A shade of mortal weariness stole across the gray, still face, most like the relaxation of the features after death; but that was all the shrill tirade produced, except the dull, cold repetition—

"I will not!"

And then Hannah Blair turned and crept up the narrow stairway to her bedroom; her mother, stunned with terror and amazement, still with a mother's alert ear, heard the key grate in the lock, the window shut quietly down, and heard no more. The house was silent even to breathlessness. In her desperation Mrs. Blair began to wish that David would come; and then the unconscious spur of life-long habit stung her into action. It was five o'clock, and she must get tea; for tea must be prepared though the crack of doom were impending. So she built the fire, filled the kettle, hung it on the crane, laid the table, all with the accuracy of habit, her ear strained to its utmost to hear some voice, some sigh, some movement from that bolted chamber above. All in vain. There might have been a corpse there for any sound of life, and Mrs. Blair felt the awe of death creep over her as she listened. For once it was glad relief to hear David coming with the oxen; to see them driven to their shed; to watch his gaunt, erect figure come up the path to the back door; but how hard it was to tell him. He asked no question, he made no comment, but the cold, gray eye quickened into fire like the sudden glitter of lightning, and without a word he strode up the stairs to Hannah's room.

"Hannah!"

There was no answer. David Blair was ill-used to disobedience. His voice was sterner than ever as he repeated the call:

"Hannah, open your door!"

Slowly the key turned, slowly the door opened, and the two faced each other. The strong man recoiled. Was this his child—this gray, rigid masque, this old woman? But he had a duty to do.

"Hannah, why is this?"

"I cannot tell you, father."

"But you must see Charles Mayhew."

"I will not."

Still calm, but inexpressibly bitter and determined, like one repeating a dreadful lesson after some tyrant's torture. David Blair could not speak. He stood still on that threshold without speech or motion, and softly as it had opened, the door closed in his face, the key turned, he was shut out —not merely from the chamber, but forever from the deepest recess of Hannah's heart and life, if indeed he had ever, even in imagination, entered there. He stood a moment in silent amazement, and then went down into the kitchen utterly speechless. He swallowed his supper mechanically, reached down his hat, but on the doorstep turned and said:

"Thankful, you must tell Charles Mayhew: Hannah will not; I cannot. It's women's work—yea, it was a woman that first time in Paradise!"

And with this Scriptural sneer he left his frightened wife to do the thing he dared not. Not the first man who has done so, nor the last. An hour later the joyful bridegroom came in his dark eyes full of happy light, his handsome figure set off by a new suit of clothes, the like of which Wingfield never had seen, much less originated; his face fairly radiant; but it clouded quickly as a storm-reflecting lake when he saw the cold wet face of Mrs. Blair, the reddened eyes, the quivering lips, and felt the close yet trembling pressure of the kind old arms for the first time clasped round his neck as he stooped toward her. How Thankful Blair contrived to tell him what she had to tell she never knew. It was forced from her lips in incoherent snatches; it was received at first with total incredulity, and she needed to repeat it again and again—to recall Hannah's words, to describe, as she best might, her ghastly aspect, her hollow, hoarse voice, her reply to her father. At last Charles Mayhew began to believe—to rave, to give way to such passionate, angry grief that Thankful Blair trembled, and longed for Parson Day to come, or for David to return. But neither thing happened, for David had warned the parson, and then hidden his own distress and dismay as far as he could get from the house in his own woodland, sitting on a log for hours lest in coming back to the house he should face the man he could not but pity and fear both; for what reason or shadow of excuse could he offer to him for his daughter's cruel and mysterious conduct? So Mrs. Blair had to bear the scene alone. At last the maddened man insisted on going up stairs to Hannah's door, but that her mother withstood. He should not harass Hannah; she would keep her from one more anguish, if she stood in the doorway and resisted physically.

"But I will see her! I will speak to her! I will know myself what this means! I am not a fool or a dog, to be thrown aside for nothing!"

And with this he rushed out of the kitchen door, round the end of the house, to the grass-plot below Hannah's window. Well he knew that little window, with its prim white curtain, where he had so often watched the light go out from the hillside, where he always lingered in his homeward walks. The curtain was down now, and no ray of light quivered from behind it.

"Hannah! Hannah! *my* Hannah!" he called with anguish in every tone. "Hannah, look at me! only just look at me! tell me one word!" And then came the fondest pleadings, the most passionate remonstrances—all in vain. He might as well have agonized by her coffin side—by her grass-grown grave. Now a different mood inspired him, and he poured out threats and commands till the cool moonlight air seemed quivering with passion and rage. Still there was no voice nor answer, nor any that replied. The calmness of immortal repose lay upon this quiet dwelling, though the torment and tumult without stormed like a tempest. Was there then neither tumult nor torment within? At last, when hours—ages it seemed to the desperate man—had passed by, nature could endure no more. The apathy of exhaustion stole over him; he felt a despair that was partly bodily weariness take entire possession of him; he ceased to adjure, to remonstrate, to cry out.

"Good-by, Hannah, good-by!" he called at length. The weak, sad accents beat like storm-weary birds vainly against that blank, deaf window. Nothing spoke to him, not even the worn-out and helpless woman who sat on the kitchen door-step with her apron over her head, veiling her hopeless distress, nor lifting that homely screen to see a ruined man creep away from his own grave—the grave of all his better nature, to be seen there no more, for from that hour no creature in Wingfield ever saw or heard of him again.

There was a mighty stir among the gossips of the village at once. Not often did so piquant and mysterious a bit of scandal regale them at sewing societies, at tea-fights, even at prayer-meetings, for it became a matter of certain religious interest, since all the parties therein were church members. But in vain did all the gossips lay their heads together. Nothing was known beyond the bare facts that at the last minute Hannah Blair had "gin the mitten" to Charley Mayhew, and he had then and there disappeared. His store was sold to a new-comer from Grenville Center, who was not communicative—perhaps because he had nothing to tell—and Charley dropped out of daily talk before long, as one who is dead and buried far away, as we all do, after how brief a time, how vanishing a grief. As for the Blairs, they endured in stoical silence, and made no sign. Sunday saw both the old people in their places early; nobody looked for Hannah, but before the bell ceased its melancholy toll, just before Parson Day ambled up the broad aisle, her slender figure, straight and still as ever, came up to her seat in the square pew. True her face was colorless; the shadow of death lingered there yet; and though her eyes shone with keener glitter than ever, and her lips burned like a scarlet streak, an acute observer would have seen upon her face traces of a dreadful conflict, lines around the mouth that years of suffering might have grown; a relaxation of the muscles about the eye and temple; a look as of one who sees only something afar off, who is absent from the body as far as consciousness goes. There she sat, through short prayer and long prayer, hymn, psalm, and sermon, and the battery of looks both direct and furtive that assailed her, all unmoved. And at home it was the same—utterly listless, cold, silent, she took up her life again; day by day did her weary round of household duties with the same punctilious neatness and dispatch—spun and knit and turned cheeses, for her mother had been broken down visibly for a time by this strange and sad catastrophe, and was more incapable than ever in her life before of earnest work, so Hannah had her place to supply in part as well as her own. We hear of martyrs of the stake, the fagot, the arena, the hunger-maddened beasts, the rising tide, the rack, and our souls shudder, our flesh creeps; we wonder and adore. I think the gladdest look of her life would have illuminated Hannah Blair's face had it been possible now to exchange her endurance for any of these deaths; but it is woman who must endure; for them are those secret agonies no enthusiasm gilds, no hope assuages, no sympathy consoles. God alone stoops to this anguish, and He not always, for there is a stubborn pride that will not lift its eyes to heaven lest it should be a tacit acknowledgment that they were fixed once upon poor earth. For these remains only the outlook daily lessening to all of us—the outlook whose vista ends in a grave.

But the unrelenting days stole on; their dead-march with monotonous tramp, left traces on even Hannah's wretched, haughty soul. They trampled down the past in thick dust; it became ashes under their feet. Her life from torture subsided into pain; then into bitterness, stoicism, contempt —at last into a certain tread-mill of indifference; only not indifference from the strong cruel grasp she still found it needful to keep upon thought and memory: once let that iron hand relax its pressure, and chaos threatened her again; she dared not. Lovers came no more to Hannah; a certain instinct of their sure fate kept them away; the store of linen and cotton she had gathered, her mother's careful hands had packed away directly in the great garret. The lavender silk, the cardinal, the big bonnet, had been worn to church year after year in the same spirit in which a Hindoo woman puts on her gorgeous garments and her golden ornaments for suttee. Mrs. Blair looked on in solemn wonder, but said not a word. Nor were these bridal robes worn threadbare ten years after, when another change came to Hannah's life; when Josiah Maxwell, a well-to-do bachelor from Newfield, the next village, was recommended to her, and came over to try his chance. Josiah was a personable, hale, florid man of forty; generous, warm-hearted; a little blustering perhaps, but thoroughly good, and a rich man for those days. He had a tannery, a foundry, and a flourishing farm. Newfield was a place of great water-privileges, sure to grow; it was pretty, bright, and successful; the sleepy, mullein-growing farms of Wingfield had in them no such cheer or life. Hannah was thirty years old; the matter was set before her purely as a matter of business. Josiah wanted a pious, capable wife. He had been too busy to fall in love all his life; now he was too sensible (he thought), so he looked about him calmly, after royal fashion, and hearing good report of Hannah Blair, proceeded to make her acquaintance and visit her. She too was a rational woman; feeling she had long set aside as a weak indulgence of the flesh; all these long and lonely years had taught her a lesson—more than one. She had learned too that a nature as strong, as dominant, as full of power and pride as hers must have some outlet or burn itself out, and here was a prospect offered that appealed to her native instincts, save and except that one so long trodden under foot. She accepted Mr. Maxwell; listened to his desire for a short engagement favorably; took down the stores prepared for a past occasion from the chests in the garret, washed and bleached them with her own hands; and purchased once more her bridal attire, somewhat graver, much more costly than before—a plum-colored satin dress, a white merino shawl, a hat of chip with rich white ribbons. Moll Thunder, who served as chorus to this homely tragedy, was at hand with her quaint shrewd comment, as she brought Mrs. Blair her yearly tribute of hickory nuts the week before the wedding.

"He! He! She look pretty much fine; same as cedar tree out dere, all red vine all ober; nobody tink him ole cedar been lightnin'-struck las' year. He! he! Hain't got no heart in him——pretty much holler."

One bright October day Hannah was married. Parson Day's successor performed the ceremony in the afternoon, and the "happy couple" went home to Newfield in a gig directly. Never was a calmer bride, a more matter-of-fact wedding. Sentiment was at a discount in the Blair family; if David felt anything at parting with his only child, he repressed its expression; and since that day her mother never could forget, Hannah had wrought in poor Mrs. Blair's mind a sort of terror toward her that actually made her absence a relief, and the company of the little "bound girl" she had taken to bring up a pleasant substitute for Hannah's stern, quiet activity. Everybody was suited; it was almost a pleasure to Mrs. Maxwell to rule over her sunny farmhouse and become a model to all backsliding housekeepers about her. Her butter always "came," her bread never soured, her hens laid and set, her chickens hatched, in the most exemplary manner; nobody had such a garden, such a loom and wheel, such spotless linen, such shiny mahogany; there was never a hole in her husband's garments or a button off his shirt; the one thing that troubled her was that her husband, good, honest, tender man, had during their first year of married life fallen thoroughly in love with her; it was not in his genial nature to live in the house a year with even a cat and not love it. Hannah was a handsome woman and his wife: what could one expect? But she did not expect it; she was bored and put out by his demonstrations; almost felt a cold contempt for the love he lavished on her, icy and irresponsive as she was, though all the time ostentatiously submissive. Josiah felt after a time that he had made a mistake; but he had the sense to adapt himself to it, and to be content, like many another idolator, with worship instead of response. Not even the little daughter born in the second year of their marriage thawed the heart so long frost-sealed in Hannah's breast; she had once worshiped a false god, and endured the penalty; henceforward she would be warned. Baby was baptized Dorothy, after her father's dead mother, and by every one but Hannah that quaint style was softened into Dolly. Never was a child better brought up, everybody said——a rosy, sturdy, saucy little creature, doing credit to fresh air and plain food; a very romp in the barn and fields with her father, whom she loved with all her warm, wayward heart; but alas! a child whose strong impulses, ardent feeling, violent temper, and stormy will were never to know the softening, tempering sweetness of real mother love. She knew none of those tender hours of caressing and confidence that even a very little child enjoys in the warmth of any mother heart, if not its own mother's; no loving arms clasped her to a mother's bosom to soothe her baby-griefs, to rest her childish weariness. There were even times when Hannah Maxwell seemed to resent her existence; to repel her affection, though her duty kept her inexorably just to the child. Dolly was never punished for what she had

not done, but always for nearly every thing she did do, and services were exacted from her that made her childhood a painful memory to all her later life. Was there butter or eggs wanted from Wingfield on any emergency? at five years old Dolly would be mounted on the steady old horse that Josiah had owned fifteen years and with saddle-bags swinging on either side, sent over to her grandfather's at Wingfield to bring home the supplies—a long and lonely road of five full-measured miles for the tiny creature to traverse; and one could scare believe the story did it not come direct to these pages from her own lips. In vain was Josiah's remonstrance; for by this time Hannah was fully the head of the house and the first principle of her rule was silent obedience. All her husband could do was to indulge and spoil Dolly in private, persistently and bravely. Alas for her, there was one day in the week, when even father could not interfere to help his darling Sunday was a sound of terror in her ears: first the grim and silent breakfast, where nobody dared smile, and where even a fixed routine of food, not in itself enticing, became at last tasteless by mere habit: codfish-cakes and tea; of these, "as of all carnal pleasure, cometh satiety at the last," according to the monk in *Hypatia;* then, fixed in a high stiff-backed chair, the pretty little vagrant must be still and read her Bible till it was time to ride to church—till she was taken down and arrayed in spotlessness and starch, and set bodkinwise into the gig between her silent mother and subdued father. Once at meeting, began the weariest routine of all.

hrough all the long services, her lit-
e fat legs swinging from the high
at, Dolly was expected to sit per-
ctly quiet; not a motion was al-
wed, not a whisper permitted; she
ared not turn her head to watch a
rofane butterfly or a jolly bumble-
ee wandering about that great roof
r tall window. Of course she did
p it instinctively, recovering herself
ith a start of terror, and a glance
t her mother's cold blue eyes, al-
ays fixed on Parson Buck, but al-
ays aware of all going on beside
er, as Dolly knew too well. At noon,
ter a hurried lunch of gingerbread
ad cheese, the child was taken to the
earest house, there to sit through
e noon prayer-meeting, her weary
gs swinging this time off the edge
f the high bed and her wearier ears
nned with long prayers. Then, as
on as the bell tolled, off to the
eeting-house to undergo another long
rmon, till, worn out mentally and
ysically, the last hour of the service
came a struggle with sleep painful
the extreme, as well in present
sistance as in certainty of results;
r as soon as poor Dolly reached
me, after another silent drive, she
as invariably taken into the spare
droom and soundly whipped for be-
g restless in meeting. And, adding
sult to injury, after dinner, enjoyed
th the eager appetite of a healthy
ild used to three meals on a week-
y, she was required to repeat that
eological torture, the Assembly's
atechism, from end to end. But
spite of all this, partly because
nday came only once a week, partly
cause of her father's genial nature
d devoted affection for his girl,
hich grew deeper and stronger con-

stantly, Dolly did not miss of her
life as many a morbid character might
have in her place. She grew up a
rosy, sunny, practical young woman,
with a dominant temper toward everybody but her mother. Plump, healthy,
and pretty, her cheeriness and usefulness would have made her popular
had she been a poor man's daughter;
and by this time Josiah Maxwell was
the richest man in town, so Dolly
had plenty of lovers, and in due time
married a fine young fellow and settled down at home with her parents,
who were almost as much pleased
with Mr. Henderson as was their
daughter. But all this time Mrs. Maxwell preserved the calm austerity of
her manner, even to her child. She
did her duty by Dolly. She prepared
for her marriage with liberal hand
and unerring judgment, but no caress,
no sympathetic word, no slightest expression of affection soothed the girl's
agitated heart or offered her support
in this tender yet exciting crisis of
her life.

Hannah Maxwell made her life a
matter of business—it had been nothing else to her for years; it was an
old habit at sixty; and she was well
over that age when one day Dolly,
rocking her first baby to sleep, was
startled to see her mother, who sat
in her upright chair reading the county
paper, fall quietly to the floor and
lie there. Baby was left to fret while
her mother ran to the old lady and
lifted her spare thin shape to the
sofa; but she did not need to do
more, for Mrs. Maxwell's eyes opened
and her hand clasped tight on Dolly's.

"Do not call any one," she whispered faintly, and leaning on her
daughter's shoulder, her whole body

shook with agonized sobs. At last that heart of granite had broken in her breast; lightning-struck so long ago, now it crumbled. With her head still on Dolly's kind arm, she told her then and there the whole story of her one love, her solitary passion, and its fatal ending. She still kept to herself the contents of that anonymous letter, only declaring that she knew, and the writer must have been aware she would know, from the handwriting as well as the circumstances detailed, who wrote it, and that the information it conveyed of certain lapses from virtue on the part of Charles Mayhew must be genuine.

"Oh, Dolly," groaned the smitten woman, "when he stood under my window and called me, I was wrung to my heart's core. The pains of hell got hold upon me. I was upon the floor, with my arms wound about the bed rail and my teeth shut like a vice, lest I should listen to the voice of nature, and going to the window to answer him, behold his face. Had I seen him I must have gone down and done what I thought a sin; so I steeled myself to resist, although I thought flesh would fail in the end; but it did not. I conquered then and after. Oh, how long it has been! I meant to do right, Dolly, but to-day, when I saw in the paper that he died last week in a barn over Goshen way, a lonely drunken pauper—Dolly, my heart came out of its grave and smote me. Had I been a meeker woman, having mercy instead of judgment, I might have helped him to right ways. I might have saved him—I loved him so."

The last words struck upon her hearer with the force of a blow, so burning, so eager, so intense was the emphasis: "I loved him *so!*"

Ah, who could ever know the depth out of which that regretful utterance sprang!

"Dear mother, dear mother," sobbed Dolly, altogether overcome by this sudden revelation of gulfs she had never dreamed of—a heart which, long repressed, convulsively burst at last, and revealed its bleeding arteries.

"Dear, good mother, don't feel so —don't! You meant right. Try to forgive yourself. If you made a mistake then, try to forget it now. Try to believe it was all for the best— do dear."

187

VII. SARAH ORNE JEWETT
(1849–1909)

DEEPHAVEN CRONIES

During the summer which Kate Lancaster and I spent at Deephaven we made many desirable friends and acquaintances, besides those of whom I spoke in The Shore House. It was curious to notice, in this quaint little fishing village by the sea, how clearly the gradations of society were defined. The place prided itself most upon having been long ago the residence of one Governor Chantrey, who was a rich ship-owner and East India merchant, and whose fame and magnificence were almost fabulous. It was a never-ceasing regret that his house should have burned down after he died, and there is no doubt that if it were still standing it would rival any ruin of the Old World.

The elderly people, though laying claim to no slight degree of present consequence, modestly ignored it, and spoke with pride of the grand way in which life was carried on by their ancestors, the Deephaven families of old times. I think Kate and I were assured at least a hundred times that Governor Chantrey kept a valet, and his wife, Lady Chantrey, kept a maid, and that the governor had an uncle in England who was a baronet; and I believe this must have been why our friends felt so deep an interest in the affairs of the English nobility: they no doubt felt themselves entitled to seats near the throne itself. There were formerly five families who kept their coaches, in Deephaven; there were balls at the governor's, and regal entertainments at other of the grand mansions; there is not a really distinguished person in the country who will not prove to have been directly or indirectly connected with Deephaven. We were shown the cellar of the Chantrey house, and the terraces, and a few clumps of lilacs, and the grand rows of elms. There are still two of the governor's warehouses left, but his ruined wharves are fast disappearing, and are almost deserted, except by small, barefooted boys, who sit on the edges to fish for sea-perch when the tide comes in. There is an imposing monument in the burying-ground to the great man and his amiable consort. I am sure that if there were any surviving relatives of the governor, they would receive in Deephaven far more deference than is consistent with the principles of a republican government; but the family became extinct long since, and I have heard, though it is not a subject that one may speak of lightly, that the sons were unworthy their noble descent and came to inglorious ends.

There were still remaining a few representatives of the old families, who were treated with much reverence by the rest of the towns-people, although they were like the conies of Scripture, a feeble folk.

Deephaven is utterly out of fashion. It never recovered from the effects of the embargo of 1807, and a sand-bar has been steadily filling in the mouth of the harbor. Though the fishing gives what occupation there is for the inhabitants of the place, it is by no means sufficient to draw recruits from abroad. But nobody in Deephaven cares for excitement, and if some one once in a while has the low taste to prefer a more active life, he is obliged to go elsewhere in search of it, and is spoken of afterward with kind pity. I well remember the Widow Moses said to me, in speaking of a certain misguided nephew of hers, "I never could see what could 'a' sot him out to leave so many privileges and go way off to Lynn, with all them children too. Why, they lived here no more than a cable's length from the meetin'-house!"

There were two schooners owned in town, and 'Bijah Manley and Jo Sands owned a trawl. There were two schooners and a small brig slowly going to pieces by the wharves, and indeed all Deephaven looked more or less out of repair. All along shore one might see dories and wherries and whale-boats, which had been left to die a lingering death. There is something piteous to me in the sight of an old boat. If one I had used much and cared for were past its useful-

ness, I should say good-by to it, and
have it towed out to sea and sunk;
it never should be left to fall to
pieces above high-water mark.

Even the commonest fishermen felt
a satisfaction, and seemed to realize
their privilege, in being residents of
Deephaven; but among the nobility
and gentry there lingered a fierce pride
in their family and town records, and
a hardly concealed contempt and pity
for people who were obliged to live
in other parts of the world. There
were acknowledged to be a few disadvantages,—such as living nearly a
dozen miles from the railway,—but,
as Miss Honora Carew said, the tone
of Deephaven society had always been
very high, and it was very nice that
there had never been any manufacturing elements introduced. She could
not feel too grateful herself that there
was no disagreeable foreign population.

"But," said Kate one day, "would
n't you like to have some pleasant
new people brought into town?"

"Certainly, my dear," said Miss
Honora, rather doubtfully; "I have
always been public-spirited; but then,
we always have guests in summer,
and I am growing old. I should not
care to enlarge my acquaintance to
any great extent." Miss Honora and
Mrs. Dent had lived gay lives in their
younger days, and were interested and
connected with the outside world more
than any of our Deephaven friends;
but they were quite contented to stay
in their own house, with their books
and letters and knitting, and they carefully read Littell and "the new magazine," as they called The Atlantic.

The Carews were very intimate
with the minister and his sister, and

there were one or two others wh
belonged to this set. There was M:
Joshua Dorsey, who wore his hair i
a queue, was very deaf, and carrie
a ponderous cane which had belonge
to his venerated father,—a much talle
man than he. He was polite to Ka
and me, but we never knew him mucl
He went to play whist with th
Carews every Monday evening, an
commonly went out fishing once
week. He had begun the practic
of law, but he had lost his hearin
and at the same time his lady-lov
had inconsiderately fallen in love wit
somebody else; after which he retire
from active business life. He had
fine library, which he invited us t
examine. He had many new book
but they looked shockingly ove
dressed in their fresher bindings, b
side the old brown volumes of essay
and sermons, and lighter works i
many-volume editions.

A prominent link in society wa
Widow Tully, who had been the muc
respected housekeeper of old Captai
Manning for forty years. When h
died, he left her the use of his hous
and family pew, besides an annuit
The existence of Mr. Tully seeme
to be a myth. During the first of h
widow's residence in town, she ha
been much affected when obliged t
speak of him, and always represente
herself as having seen better day
and as being highly connected. Bu
she was apt to be ungrammatical whe
excited, and there was a whispere
tradition that she used to keep a bake
shop in a town in Connecticut; thoug
the mystery of her previous state o
existence will probably never b
solved. She wore mourning for th
captain which would have befitted h

dow, and patronized the towns-
ople conspicuously, while she her-
lf was treated with much conde-
nsion by the Carews and Lorimers.
e occupied, on the whole, much the
me position that "Mrs. Betty
arker" did in Cranford. And ined Kate and I were often reminded
that estimable town. We heard
at Kate's aunt, Katherine Brandon,
d never been appreciative of Mrs.
lly's merits, and that since her
ath the others had received Mrs.
lly into their society rather more.
It seemed as if all the clocks in
eephaven, and all the people with
em, had stopped years ago, and the
ople had been doing over and over
at they had been busy about during
e last week of their unambitious
ogress. Their clothes had lasted
nderfully well, and they had no
ed to earn money when there was
little chance to spend it; indeed
ere were several families who
emed to have no more visible means
support than a balloon. There
re no young people whom we knew,
ough a number used to come to
urch on Sunday from the inland
rms, or "the country," as we learned
say. There were children among
e fishermen's families at the shore,
t a few years will see Deephaven
ssessed by two classes instead of
e time-honored three.
We always went to church, and we
joyed our first Sunday morning
ost heartily. We felt that we were
nsidered as Miss Brandon's repre-
ntatives, and we had already found
at it was no slight responsibility,
she had received much honor and
spect from her neighbors. We really
ed, that summer, to do nothing to

lessen the family reputation, and to
give pleasure as well as take it,
though we were singularly persistent
in our pursuit of "a good time." It
was very pleasant having Kate for
one's companion, for she has an unusual power of winning people's confidence, and knows with surest instinct how to meet them on their own
ground. It is the girl's being so genuinely sympathetic and interested
which makes every one ready to talk
to her and be friends with her; just
as the sunshine makes it easy for
flowers to grow up out of the ground,
which the chilly winds have hindered.
She is not polite for the sake of being
polite, but polite for the sake of being kind; and there is not a particle
of what Hugh Miller justly calls "the
insolence of condescension" about
her.

But to go back to our first Sunday
at church: it must be in vain to ask
you to imagine our delight when we
heard the tuning of a bass-viol in the
gallery just before service. We
pressed each other's hands most tenderly, looked up at the singers' seats,
and then trusted ourselves to look at
each other. It was more than we
had hoped for. There were also a
violin and sometimes a flute, and a
choir of men and women singers,
though the congregation were expected
to join in the psalm-singing. It was
all so delightfully old-fashioned; our
pew was a square pew, and was by
an open window looking seaward. We
also had a view of the entire congregation, and as we were somewhat
early, we watched the people come
in, with great interest. The Deephaven aristocracy came with stately
step up the aisle; this was all the

chance there was for displaying their unquestioned dignity in public.

Many of the people drove to church in wagons that were low and old and creaky, with worn buffalo-robes over the seat, and some hay tucked underneath for the sleepy, undecided old horse. Some of the younger farmers and their wives had high, shiny wagons, with tall horsewhips,—which they sometimes brought into church,—and they drove up to the steps with a consciousness of being conspicuous and enviable. They had a bashful look when they came in, and for a few minutes after they took their seats they evidently felt that all eyes were fixed upon them, but after a little while they were quite at their ease, and looked critically at the new arrivals.

The old folks interested us most. "Do you notice how many more old women there are than old men?" whispered Kate to me; and we wondered if the husbands and brothers had been drowned, and if it must not be sad to look at the blue, sunshiny sea beyond the marshes, if the faraway white sails reminded them of some ships that had never sailed home into Deephaven harbor, or of fishing-boats that had never come back to land.

The girls and young women adorned themselves in what they believed to be the latest fashion, but the elderly women were usually relics of old times in manner and dress. They wore to church thin, soft silk gowns that must have been brought from over the seas years upon years before, and wide collars fastened with mourning-pins holding a lock of hair. They had big black bonnets, some of them with

stiff capes, such as Kate and I h[ad] not seen before, since our childhoo[d] They treasured large, rusty lace ve[ils] of scraggly pattern, and wore som[e] times, on pleasant Sundays, whi[te] China-crape shawls with attenuat[ed] fringes; and there were two or thr[ee] of these shawls in the congregati[on] which had been dyed black, and ga[ve] an aspect of meekness and gene[ral] unworthiness to the aged wearer, th[ey] clung and drooped about the figure [in] such a hopeless way. We used [to] notice often the most interesti[ng] scarfs, without which no Deephav[en] woman considered herself in f[ull] dress. Sometimes there were red I[n] dia scarfs in spite of its being h[ot] weather; but our favorite ones we[re] long strips of silk, embroidered alo[ng] the edges and at the ends with dism[al] colored floss in odd patterns. I thi[nk] there must have been a fashion on[ce] in Deephaven, of working these scar[fs] and I should not be surprised to fi[nd] that it was many years before t[he] fashion of working samplers ca[me] about. Our friends always wore bla[ck] mitts on warm Sundays, and ma[ny] of them carried neat little bags [of] various designs on their arms, co[n] taining a precisely folded pock[et] handkerchief, and a frugal lunch [of] caraway seeds or red and white pe[p]permints. I should like you to s[ee] with your own eyes, Widow Wa[r]e a[nd] Miss Exper'ence Hull, two old sist[ers] whose personal appearance we [de] lighted in, and whom we saw fee[bly] approaching down the street this fi[rst] Sunday morning under the shadow [of] the two last members of an otherw[ise] extinct race of parasols.

There were two or three old m[en] who sat near us. They were sailo[rs]

—there is something unmistakable bout a sailor,—and they had a curiusly ancient, uncanny look, as if ney might have belonged to the crew f the Mayflower, or even have ruised about with the Northmen in ne times of Harold Harfager and his omrades. They had been blown bout by so many winter winds, so rowned by summer suns, and wet by alt spray, that their hands and faces joked like leather with a few deep olds instead of wrinkles. They had ale blue eyes, very keen and quick; heir hair looked like the fine seaveed which clings to the kelp roots nd mussel shells in little locks. hese friends of ours sat solemnly t the heads of their pews and looked nflinchingly at the minister, when ney were not dozing, and they sang ith voices like the howl of the wind, ith an occasional deep note or vo.

Have you never seen faces that eemed old-fashioned? Many of the eople in Deephaven church looked as they must be—if not supernaturally ld—exact copies of their remote anestors. I wonder if it is not possible aat the features and expression may e almost perfectly reproduced. These ces were not modern American faces, ut belonged rather to the days of ae early settlement of the country, ne old colonial times. We often eard quaint words and expressions hich we never had known anywhere se but in old books. There was a eat deal of sea-lingo in use; indeed, e learned a great deal ourselves, unonsciously, and used it afterward to e great amusement of our friends; ut there were also many peculiar ovincialisms, and among the people who lived on the lonely farms inland, we often noticed words we had seen in Chaucer, and studied out at school in our English literature class. Everything in Deephaven was more or less influenced by the sea; the minister spoke oftenest of Peter and his fishermen-companions, and prayed most earnestly every Sunday morning for those who go down to the sea in ships. He made frequent allusions and drew numberless illustrations of a similar kind for his sermons, and indeed I am in doubt whether, if the Bible had been written wholly in inland countries, it would have been much valued in Deephaven.

The singing was very droll, for there was a majority of old voices. which had seen their best days long before, and the bass-viol was excessively noticeable and apt to be a little ahead of the time the singers kept, while the violin lingered after. Somewhere on the other side of the church we heard an acute voice which rose high above all the rest of the congregation, sharp as a needle, and slightly cracked, with a limitless supply of breath. It rose and fell gallantly, and clung long to the high notes of Dundee. It was like the wail of the banshee, which sounds clear to the fated hearer above all other noises. We afterward became acquainted with the owner of this voice, and were surprised to find her a meek widow, who was like a thin black beetle in her pathetic cypress veil and big black bonnet. She looked as if she had forgotten who she was, and spoke with an apologetic whine; but we heard she had a temper as high as her voice, and as much to be dreaded as the equinoctial gale.

I should consider my sketch of Deephaven society incomplete if I did not tell you something of the ancient mariners who may be found every pleasant morning, sunning themselves like turtles, on one of the wharves. There were always three of them, and sometimes several others, but the less constant members of the club were older than the rest, and the epidemics of rheumatism in town were sadly frequent. They sat close together, because most of them were deaf, and when we heard the conversation, it seemed to concern their adventures at sea, or the freight carried out by the Sea-Duck, the Ocean Rover, or some other Deephaven ship, the particulars of the voyage and its disasters and successes being as familiar as the wanderings of the children of Israel to an old parson. There were sometimes violent altercations when "the cap'ns" differed as to the tonnage of some ship that had been a prey to the winds and waves, dry-rot, or barnacles, fifty years before. The old fellows puffed away at little black pipes with short stems, and otherwise consumed tobacco in fabulous quantities. We used to wish we could join this agreeable company, but we found that the appearance of an outsider caused a disapproving silence, and that the club was evidently not to be interfered with. Once we were impertinent enough to hide ourselves for a while, just round the corner of the warehouse, but we were afraid or ashamed to try it again, though the conversation was inconceivably edifying. Captain Isaac Bean, the oldest and wisest of all, was discoursing upon some cloth he had purchased once in Bristol, which the shopkeeper delayed sending until just as they were read to weigh anchor.

"I happened to take a look at tha cloth," said the captain in a lou droning voice, "and as quick as I gc sight of it, I spoke onpleasant of tha swindling English fellow, and the crew they stood back. I was dreadful high tempered in them days, mind ye; an I had the gig manned. We was ou in the stream, just ready to sail, nic wind a-coming in from the no'east. went ashore, and when I walks int his shop, ye never see a creatur' s wilted. Ye see the miser'ble sculpi thought I'd never stop to open th goods, an' it was a chance I di mind ye! 'Lor,' says he, grinning an turning the color of a b'iled lobster 'I s'posed ye were a-standing out t sea by this time.' 'No,' says I, 'an I've got some men out here on th quay a-landing that cloth o' yourn and if you don't send just what bought and paid for, down there t go back in the gig within fifteer minutes, I'll take ye by the colla and drop ye into the dock.' I wa twice the size of him, mind yè, an master strong. 'Don't ye like it says he, edging round. 'I'll change i for ye, then.' Ter'ble perlite he wa 'Like it?' says I, 'it looks as if i were built of dog's hair and divil wool, kicked together by spiders; an it's coarser than Irish frieze; thre threads to an *armful*,' says I."

This was evidently one of the cap tain's favorite stories, for we hear an approving grumble from the audi ence.

In the course of a long walk in land we made a new acquaintance Captain Lant, whom we had notice at church, and who sometimes joine

he company on the wharf. We had
been walking through the woods, and,
coming out to his fields, we went on
to the house for some water. There
was no one at home but the captain,
who announced cheerfully that he
should be pleased to serve us, though
his women-folks had gone off to a
funeral, the other side of the P'int.
He brought out a pitcher full of milk,
and after we had drunk some, we all
sat down together in the shade. The
captain brought an old flag-bottomed
chair from the wood-house and sat
down facing Kate and me, with an
air of certainty that he was going
to hear something new and make some
desirable new acquaintances, and also
as if he knew something it would be
worth our while to hear. He looked
more and more like a well-to-do old
English sparrow, and chippered faster
and faster.

"Queer ye should know I'm a sailor
so quick; why, I've been a-farming it
his twenty years; have to go down
to the shore and take a day's fishing
every hand's turn, though, to keep the
old hulk clear of barnacles. There!
I do wish I lived nigher the shore,
where I could see the folks I know,
and talk about what's been a-goin' on.
You don't know anything about it,
you don't; but it's tryin' to a man
to be called 'old Cap'n Lant,' and so
to speak be forgot when there's anything stirring, and be called gran'ther
by clumsy creatur's goin' on fifty and
sixty, who can't do no more work
to-day than I can; an' then the
women-folks keep a-tellin' me to be
ceerful and not fall, and as how I'm
too old to go out fishing; and when
they want to be soft-spoken, they say
is how they don't see as I fail, and

how wonderful I keep my hearin'. I
never did want to farm it, but 'she'
always took it to heart when I was
off on a v'y'ge, and this farm and some
consider'ble means beside come to her
from her brother, and they all sot to
and give me no peace of mind till I
sold out my share of the Ann Eliza
and come ashore for good. I did
keep an eighth of the Pactolus, and
I was ship's husband for a long spell,
but she never was heard from on her
last voyage to Singapore. I was the
lonesomest man, when I first come
ashore, that ever you see. Well, you
are master hands to walk, if you come
way up from the Brandon House. I
wish the women was at home. Know
Miss Brandon? Why, yes; and I remember all her brothers and sisters,
and her father and mother. I can see
'em now, coming into meeting, proud
as Lucifer and straight as a mast,
every one of 'em. Miss Catherine, she
always had her butter from this very
farm. Some of the folks used to go
down every Saturday, and my wife,
she's been in the house a hundred
times, I s'pose. So you are Hath-
away Brandon's granddaughter?" (to
Kate); "why, he and I have been out
fishing together many's the time,—he
and Chantrey, his next younger
brother. Henry, he was a disapp'intment; he went to furrin parts and
turned out a Catholic priest, I s'pose
ye've heard? I never was so set agin
Mr. Henry as some folks was. He
was the pleasantest spoken of the
whole on 'em. You do look like the
Brandons; you really favor 'em consider'ble. Well, I'm pleased to see ye,
I'm sure."

We asked him many questions
about the old people, and found he

knew all the family histories and told them with great satisfaction. We found he had his pet stories, and it must have been gratifying to have an entirely new and fresh audience. He was adroit in leading the conversation around to a point where the stories would come in appropriately, and we helped him as much as possible. In a small neighborhood all the people know each other's stories and experiences by heart, and I have no doubt the old captain had been snubbed many times on beginning a favorite anecdote. There was a story which he told us that first day, which he assured us was strictly true, and it is certainly a remarkable instance of the influence of one mind upon another at a distance. It seems to me worth preserving, at any rate; and as we heard it from the old man, with his solemn voice and serious expression and quaint gestures, it was singularly impressive.

"When I was a youngster," said Captain Lant, "I was an orphan, and I was bound out to old Mr. Peletiah Daw's folks, over on the Ridge Road. It was in the time of the last war, and he had a nephew, Ben Dighton, a dreadful high-strung, wild fellow, who had gone off on a privateer The old man, he set everything by Ben; he would disoblige his own boys any day to please him. This was in his latter days, and he used to have spells of wandering and being out of his head; and he used to call for Ben and talk sort of foolish about him, till they would tell him to stop. Ben never did a stroke of work for him, either, but he was a handsome fellow and had a way with him when he was good-natured. One night old Peletiah

had been very bad all day and was getting quieted down, and it was after supper; we sat round in the kitchen and he lay in the bedroom opening out. There were some pitch-knots blazing and the light shone in on the bed, and all of a sudden something made me look up and look in; and there was the old man setting up straight, with his eyes shining at me like a cat's. 'Stop 'em!' says he *'Stop 'em!'* and his two sons run in then to catch hold of him, for they thought he was beginning with one of his wild spells, but he fell back on the bed and began to cry like a baby 'Oh dear me,' says he, 'they've hung him—hung him right up to the yard arm! Oh, they oughtn't to have done it; cut him down quick! he didn' think; he means well, Ben does; he was hasty. Oh my God, I can't bear to see him swing round by the neck It's poor Ben hung up to the yard arm. Let me alone, I say!' Andrew and Moses, they were holding him with all their might, and they were both hearty men, but he most got away from them once or twice, and he screeched and howled like a mad creatur', and then he would cry again like a grieving child. He was worn out after a while and lay back quiet and said over and over, 'Poor Ben! and 'hung at the yard-arm'; and he told the neighbors next day, but nobody noticed him much, and h seemed to forget it as his mind come back. All that summer he was mis er'ble, and towards cold weather h failed right along, though he had bee a master strong man in his day, an his timbers held together well. Alon late in the fall he had taken to hi bed, and one day there came to th

ouse a fellow named Sim Decker, a
eckless fellow he was, too, who had
one out in the same ship with Ben.
Ie pulled a long face when he came
i, and said he had brought bad
ews. They had been taken prisoner
nd carried into port and put in
iil, and Ben Dighton had got a fever
iere and died.

"'You lie!' says the old man from
ie bedroom, speaking as loud and
erce as ever you heard. 'They hung
im to the yard-arm!'

"'Don't mind him,' says Andrew;
ie's wandering-like, and he had a
ad dream along back in the spring;
s'posed he'd forgotten it.' But the
ecker fellow he turned pale, and kept
ilking crooked while he listened to
d Peletiah a-scolding to himself. He
iswered the questions the women
ilks asked him,—they took on a good
eal,—but pretty soon he got up and
inked to me and Andrew, and we
ent out in the yard. He began to
vear, and then says he, 'When did
ie old man have his dream?' An-
rew couldn't remember, but I knew
was the night before he sold the
ray colt, and that was the twenty-
urth of April.

"'Well,' says Sim Decker, 'on the
venty-third day of April Ben Dighton
as hung to the yard-arm, and I see
m do it, Lord help him! I didn't
ean to tell the women, and I s'posed
iu'd never know, for I'm all the one
: the ship's company you're ever
kely to see. We were taken prisoner,
id Ben was mad as fire, and they
ere scared of him and chained him
i the deck; and while he was raving
iere, a little parrot of a midshipman
ime up and grinned at him, and
iapped his fingers in his face; and

Ben lifted his hands with the heavy
irons and sprung at him like a tiger,
and the boy dropped dead as a stone;
and they put the bight of a rope round
Ben's neck and slung him right up
to the yard-arm, and there he swung
back and forth until as soon as we
dared one of us clim' up and cut
the rope and let him go over the
ship's side; and they put us in irons
for that, curse 'em. How did that
old man in there know, and he bedridden here, nigh upon three thousand
miles off?' says he; but I guess there
wasn't any of us could tell him," said
Captain Lant in conclusion. "It's
something I never could account for,
but it's true as truth. I've known
more such cases; some folks laughs at
me for believing 'em,—'the cap'n's
yarns' they calls 'em,—but if you'll
notice, everybody's got some yarn of
that kind they do believe, if they
won't believe yours. And there's a
good deal happens in the world that's
mysterious. Now there was Widder
Oliver Pinkham, over to the P'int,
told me with her own lips that she"—
But just here we saw the captain's
expression alter suddenly, and looked
around, to see a wagon coming up
the lane. We immediately said we
must go home, for it was growing late,
but asked permission to come again
and hear the Widow Oliver Pinkham
story. We stopped however to see
"the women folks," and afterward became so intimate with them that we
were invited to spend the afternoon
and take tea, which invitation we accepted with great pride. We went
out fishing, also, with the captain and
"Danny," of whom I will tell you
presently. I often think of Captain
Lant in the winter, for he told Kate

once that he "felt master old in winter to what he did in summer." He likes reading, fortunately, and we had a letter from him, not long ago, acknowledging the receipt of some books of travel by land and water which we had luckily thought to send him. He gave the latitude and longitude of Deephaven at the beginning of his letter, and signed himself "respectfully yours with esteem, Jacob Lant (condemned as unseaworthy)."

Kate and I went to a show that summer, the memory of which will never fade. It is somewhat impertinent to call it a show, and "public entertainment" is equally inappropriate, though we certainly were entertained. It had been raining for two or three days; the Deephavenites spoke of it as "a spell of weather." Just after tea, one Thursday evening, Kate and I went down to the post-office. When we opened the great hall door the salt air was delicious, but we found the town apparently wet through and discouraged; though it had almost stopped raining just then, there was a Scotch mist, like a snowstorm with the chill taken off, and the Chantrey elms dripped hurriedly and creaked occasionally in the east wind.

"There will not be a cap'n on the wharf for a week after this," said I to Kate; "only think of the cases of rheumatism!"

We stopped for a few minutes at the Carews', who were as surprised to see us as if we had been mermaids out of the sea, and begged us to give ourselves something warm to drink and to change our boots, the moment we got home. Then we went on to the post-office. Kate went in, but

stopped, as she came out with our letters, to read a written notice securely fastened to the grocery door by four large carpet-tacks with wide leathers round their necks.

"Dear," said she, exultantly, "there going to be a lecture to-night in th church, a free lecture on The Elements of True Manhood. Wouldn you like to go?" And we went.

We were fifteen minutes later tha the time appointed, and were sorr to find that the audience was almo imperceptible. The dampness had a fected the old-fashioned lamps that those on the walls and on th front of the gallery were the dim mest lights I ever saw, and sen their feeble rays through a sma space, the edges of which were clearl defined. There were two rather mor energetic lights on the table near th pulpit, where the lecturer sat, an as we were in the rear of the churc we could see the yellow fog betwee ourselves and him. There were fou teen persons in the audience, and w were all huddled together in a cow ardly way in the pews nearest th door: three old men, four wome and four children, besides ourselv and the sexton, a deaf little old ma with a wooden leg.

The children whispered noisily, an soon, to our surprise, the lectur rose and began. He bowed, an treated us with beautiful deferenc and read the dreary lecture with e thusiasm. I wish I could say for h sake that it was interesting, but cannot tell a lie, and it was so lon He went on and on, until I felt a if I had been there ever since I wa a little girl. Kate and I did not da to look at each other, and in my de

eration at feeling her quiver with
aughter, I moved to the other end
f the pew, knocking over a big hymn-
ook on the way, which attracted so
much attention that I have seldom
elt more embarrassed in my life.
ate's great dog rose several times
o shake himself and yawn loudly,
nd then lay down again despair-
gly.

You would have thought the man
was addressing an enthusiastic Young
Men's Christian Association. He ex-
orted us with fervor upon our duties
s citizens and as voters, and told us
 great deal about George Washing-
on and Benjamin Franklin, whom he
rged us to choose as our examples.
He waited for applause after each of
is outbursts of eloquence, and pres-
tly went on again, in no wise dis-
ncerted at the silence, and with re-
oubled energy, as if he were sure
e would fetch us next time. The
rain had begun to fall again heavily,
nd the wind wailed around the
meeting-house. If the lecture had
een upon any other subject it would
ot have been so hard for Kate and
me to keep sober faces, but it was
rected entirely toward young men,
nd there was not a single young man
here.

The children in front of us mildly
uffled with each other at one time,
til the one at the end of the pew
opped a marble, which struck the
oor and rolled with a frightful noise
wn the edge of the aisle, where
ere was no carpet. The congrega-
on instinctively started up to look
er it, but we recollected ourselves
d leaned back again in our places,
ile the awed children, after keeping
naturally quiet, fell asleep and

tumbled against each other helplessly.
After a time the man sat down and
wiped his forehead, looking well satisfied; and when we were wondering
whether we might with propriety come
away, he rose again, and said it was
a free lecture, and he thanked us for
our kind patronage on that inclement
night, but in other places which he
had visited there had been a contribution taken up for the cause. It would
perhaps do no harm—would the sexton—

But the sexton could not have heard
a cannon at that distance, and slumbered on. Neither Kate nor I had
any money except a twenty-dollar
bill in my purse, and some coppers
in the pocket of her water-proof
cloak, which she assured me she was
prepared to give; but we saw no signs
of the sexton's waking, and, as one
of the women kindly went forward
to wake the children, we all rose and
came away.

After we had made fun of the affair
and laughed as long as we pleased
that night, we became suddenly conscious of the pitiful side of it all; and
being anxious that every one should
have the highest opinion of Deephaven, we sent Tom Dockum out
early in the morning with an
anonymous note for the lecturer,
whom he found without much trouble;
but afterward we were disturbed at
hearing that he was going to repeat
his lecture that evening,—the wind
having gone round to the northwest,
—and I have no doubt there were a
good many women able to be out, and
that he harvested enough ten-cent
pieces to pay his expenses without
our help, though he had particularly told us it was "for the cause"

the evening before, and that ought
to have been a consolation.

None of our cronies were more interesting than the fishermen. The
fish-houses, which might be called the
business center of the town, were at a
little distance from the old warehouses, and were ready to fall down
in despair. There were some fishermen who lived near by, but most of
them were also farmers in a small
way, and lived inland. From our
eastern windows we could see the
moorings, and we always liked to
watch the boats go out and come
straying in, one after the other, tip-
ping and skimming under the square
little sails, and we sometimes went
down to the fish-houses to see what
kind of a catch there had been.

I said we liked to see the boats go
out, but I must not give you the
impression that we saw them often,
for they weighed anchor at an early
hour in the morning. I remember
once there was a light fog over the
sea, lifting fast, as the sun was coming up, and the brownish sails soon
disappeared, while voices could be
heard occasionally for some minutes
after the men were hidden from sight.
But afterward, when the sun had
risen, we found everything looked
much the same as usual; the fog had
gone, and the dories and even the
larger boats were distant specks on
the sparkling sea.

One afternoon we made a new acquaintance in this wise. We went
down to the shore to see if we could
hire a conveyance to the light-house
the next morning. We often went out
in one of the fishing-boats, and after
we stayed as long as we pleased, Mr.
Kew—do you remember him?—would

bring us home. It was quiet enoug
that day, for not a single boat ha
come in, and there were no men t
be seen along shore. There was
solemn company of lobster-coops
"cages" which had been brought i
to be mended. They always amuse
Kate. She said they seemed lik
droll old women telling each oth
secrets. These were scattered abo
in different attitudes, and looked mo
confidential than usual.

Just as we were going away w
happened to see a man at work
one of the sheds. He was the fishe
man whom we knew least of all; a
odd-looking, silent sort of man, mo
sunburnt and weather-beaten than an
of the others. We had learned
know him by the bright red flann
shirt he always wore, and besides, l
was lame; some one told us he ha
had a bad fall once, on board shi
Kate and I had always wished
could find a chance to talk with hir
He looked up at us pleasantly, ar
when we nodded and smiled, he sa
"Good day" in a gruff, hearty voic
and went on with his work, cleani
mackerel.

"Do you mind our watching you
asked Kate.

"No, *ma'am!*" said the fisherm
emphatically, so there we stood.

Those fish-houses were curio
places, so different from any oth
kind of work-shop. In this there w
a seine, or part of one, festoon
among the cross-beams overhead, a
there were snarled fishing-lines, a
barrows to carry fish in, like whe
barrows without wheels; there we
the queer round lobster-nets, a
"kits" of salt mackerel, tubs of ba
and piles of clams: and some que

ones, and parts of remarkable fish, and lobster-claws of surprising size fastened on the walls for ornament. There was a pile of rubbish down at the end; I dare say it was all useful, however,—there is such mystery about the business.

Kate and I were never tired of hearing of the fish that come at different times of the year, and go away again, like the birds; or of the actions of the dog-fish, which the 'longshore-men hate so bitterly; and then there are such curious legends and traditions, of which almost all fishermen have a store.

"I think mackerel are the prettiest fish that swim," said I presently, in an interested way.

"So do I, miss," said the man, "not to say but I've seen more fancy-looking fish down in southern waters, bright as any flower you ever see; but a mackerel," holding one up admiringly, "why, they're so clean-built and trig-looking! Put a cod alongside, and he looks as lumbering as an old-fashioned Dutch brig aside a yacht.

"Those are good-looking fish, but they an't made much account of," continued our friend, as he pushed aside the mackerel and took another tub; "they're hake, I s'pose you know. But I forgot—I can't stop to bother with them now"; and he pulled forward a barrow full of small fish, flat and hard, with pointed, bony heads.

"Those are porgies, aren't they?" asked Kate.

"Yes," said the man, "an' I'm going to sliver them for the trawls."

We knew what the trawls were, and supposed that the porgies were to be used for bait; and we soon found out what "slivering" meant, by seeing him take them by the head and cut a slice from first one side and then the other in such a way that the pieces looked not unlike smaller fish.

"It seems to me," said I, "that fishermen always have sharper knives than other people."

"Yes, we do like a sharp knife in our trade, and then we are mostly strong-handed."

He was throwing the porgies' heads and back-bones—all that was left of them after slivering—in a heap, and now several cats walked in as if they felt at home, and began a hearty lunch. "What a troop of pussies there is round here," said I; "I wonder what will become of them in the winter, though to be sure the fishing goes on just the same."

"The better part of them don't get through the cold weather," said Danny. "Two or three of the old ones have been here for years, and are as much belonging to Deephaven as the meetin'-house; but the rest of them aren't to be depended on. You'll miss the young ones by the dozen, come spring. I don't know myself but they move inland in the fall of the year; they're knowing enough, if that's all!"

Kate and I stood in the wide door-way, arm in arm, looking sometimes at the queer fisherman and the porgies, and sometimes out to sea. It was low tide; the wind had risen a little, and the heavy salt air blew toward us from the wet brown ledges in the rocky harbor. The sea was bright blue, and the sun was shining. Two gulls were swinging lazily to and fro; there was a flock of sandpipers down by the water's edge, in a great hurry, as usual.

Presently the fisherman spoke again, beginning with an odd laugh:—

"I *was* scared last winter! Jim Toggerson and me, we were up in the Cap'n Manning storehouse hunting for a half-bar'l of salt the skipper said was there. It was an awful blustering kind of day, with a thin, icy rain blowing from all points at once; sea roaring as if it wished it could come ashore and put a stop to everything. Bad days at sea, them are; rigging all froze up. As I was saying, we were hunting for a half-bar'l of salt, and I laid hold of a bar'l that had something heavy in the bottom, and tilted it up, and my eye! there was a stir and a scratch and a squeal, and out went some kind of a creatur', and I jumped back, not looking for anything live, but I see in a minute it was a cat; and perhaps you think it is a big story, but there were eight more in there, hived in together to keep warm. I car'd 'em up some new fish that night; they seemed short of provisions. We hadn't been out fishing as much as common, and they hadn't dared to be round the fish-houses much, for a fellow who came in on a coaster had a dog, and he used to chase 'em. Hard chance they had, and lots of 'em died, I guess; but there seems to be some survivin' relatives, an' al'ays just so hungry! I used to feed them some when I was ashore. I think likely you've heard that a cat will fetch you bad luck; but I don't know's that made much difference to me. I kind of like to keep on the right side of 'em, too; if ever I have a bad dream there's sure to be a cat in it; but I was brought up to be clever to dumb beasts, an' I guess it's my natur'. Except fish," said Danny after a minute's thought; "but then, it never seem like they had feelin's like creatur' that live ashore"; and we all laughed heartily and felt well acquainted.

"I s'pose you misses will laugh if I tell ye I kept a kitty once myself." This was said rather shyly, and there was evidently a story, so we were much interested, and Kate said "Please tell us about it; was it at sea?"

"Yes, it was at sea; leastways, on a coaster. I got her in a sing'lar kind of way: it was one afternoon we were lying alongside Charlestown bridge and I heard a young cat screeching real pitiful; and after I looked around, I see her in the water clutching on to the pier of the bridge, and some little divils of boys were heaving rocks down at her. I got into the schooner's tag-boat, quick, I tell ye and pushed off for her, 'n she let go just as I got there, 'n I guess you never saw a more miser'ble-looking creatur' than I fished out of the water Cold weather it was. Her leg was hurt, and her eye, and I thought first I'd drop her overboard again, and then I didn't, and I took her aboard the schooner and put her by the stove I thought she might as well die where it was warm. She eat a little mite of chowder before night, but she was very slim; but next morning, when I went to see if she was dead, she fell to licking my finger, and she did purr away like a dolphin. One of her eyes was out, where a stone had took her, and she never got any use of it but she used to look at you so clever with the other, and she got well of her

me foot after a while. I got to be
er'ble fond of her. She was just
he knowingest thing you ever saw,
nd she used to sleep alongside of me
n my bunk, and like as not she would
o on deck with me when it was my
atch. I was coasting then for a year
nd eight months, and I kept her all
he time. We used to be in harbor
onsider'ble, and about eight o'clock
n the forenoon I used to drop a line
nd catch her a couple of cunners.
Now, it is cur'us that she used to
now when I was fishing for her. She
ould pounce on them fish and carry
hem off and growl, and she knew
hen I got a bite,—she'd watch the
ne; but when we were mackereling
he never give us any trouble. She
ould never lift a paw to touch any
f our fish. She didn't have the
ieving ways common to most cats.
he used to set round on deck in fair
eather, and when the wind blew she
ays kept herself below. Sometimes
hen we were in port she would go
hore a while, and fetch back a bird
 a mouse, but she wouldn't eat it
ll she come and showed it to me.
he never wanted to stop long ashore,
ough I never shut her up; I always
ve her her liberty. I got a good
al of joking about her from the fel-
ws, but she was a sight of company.
 don' know as I ever had anything
ke me as much as she did. Not to
y as I ever had much of any trouble
th anybody, ashore or afloat. I'm
 still kind of fellow for all I look
 rough.

"But then, I han't had a home, what
 call a home, since I was going on
ne year old."

"How has that happened?" inquired
ate.

"Well, mother, she died, and I was
bound out to a man in the tanning
trade, and I hated him, and I hated
the trade; and when I was a little bigger I ran away, and I've followed the
sea ever since. I wasn't much use
to him, I guess; leastways, he never
took the trouble to hunt me up.

"About the best place I ever was
in was a hospital. It was in foreign
parts. Ye see I'm crippled some?
I fell from way up the mainmast rig-
gin', and I struck my shoulder and
broke my leg and banged myself all
up. It was to a nuns' hospital where
they took me. All of the nuns were
Catholics, and they wore big white
things on their heads. I don't suppose
you ever saw any. Have you? Well,
now, that's queer! When I was first
there I was scared of them; they were
real ladies, and I wasn't used to being
in a house, any way. One of them,
that took care of me most of the time,
why, she would even set up half the
night with me, and I couldn't begin
to tell you how good-natured she was,
an' she'd look real sorry too. I used
to be ugly, I ached so, along in the
first of my being there, but I spoke
of it when I was coming away, and
she said it was all right. She used
to feed me, that lady did; and there
were some days I couldn't lift my
head, and she would rise it on her
arm. She give me a little mite of a
book, when I come away. I'm not
much of a hand at reading, but I always kept it on account of her. She
was so pleased when I got so's to set
up in a chair and look out of the
window. She wasn't much of a hand
to talk English. I did feel bad to
come away from there. I 'most wished
I could be sick a while longer. I

never said much of anything either, and I don't know but she thought it was queer, but I am a dreadful clumsy man to say anything, and I got flustered. I don't know's I mind telling you; I was most a-crying. I used to think I'd lay by some money and ship for there and carry her something real pretty. But I don't rank able-bodied seaman like I used, and it's as much as I can do to get a berth on a coaster: I suppose I might go as cook. I liked to have died with my hurt at that hospital, but when I was getting well it made me think of when I was a mite of a chap to home before mother died, to be laying there in a clean bed with somebody to do for me. Guess you think I'm a master hand to spin long yarns; somehow it comes easy to talk to-day."

"What became of your cat?" asked Kate, after a pause, during which our friend sliced away at the porgies.

"I never rightfully knew; it was in Salem harbor, and a windy night. I was on deck consider'ble, for the schooner pitched lively, and once or twice she dragged her anchor. I never saw the kitty after she eat her supper. I remember I gave her some milk—I used to buy her a pint once in a while for a treat; I don't know but she might have gone off on a cake of ice, but it did seem as if she had too much sense for that. Most likely she missed her footing, and fell overboard in the dark. She was marked real pretty, black and white, and kep' herself just as clean! She knew as well as could be when foul weather was coming; she would bother round and act queer; but when the sun was out she would sit round on deck as pleased as a queen. There!

I feel bad sometimes when I think o her, and I never went into Sale since without kind of hoping I shoul see her. I don't know but if I wa a-going to begin my life over agai I'd settle down ashore and have snug little house and farm it. Bu I guess I shall do better at fishin Give me a trig-built fore-and-a schooner painted up nice, with stripe on her, and clean sails, and fresh wind with the sun a-shining, an I feel first-rate."

"Do you believe that codfish swal low stones before a storm?" aske Kate. I had been thinking about th lonely fisherman in a sentimental wa and so irrelevant a question shocke me. "I saw he felt slightly emba rassed at having talked about his a fairs so much," Kate told me afte ward, "and I thought we should lea him feeling more at his ease if w talked about fish for a while." An sure enough he did seem relieved, an gave us his opinion about the codfis at once, adding that he never care much for cod any way; folks up cou try bought 'em a good deal, he hear Give him a haddock right out of th water for his dinner!

"I never can remember," said Kat "whether it is cod or haddock tha have a black stripe along the sides"—

"Oh, those are haddock," said "they say that the devil caught a ha dock once, and it slipped through fingers and got scorched; so all t haddock had the same mark afte ward."

"Well, now, how did you know th old story?" said Danny, laughi heartily; "ye mustn't believe all t old stories ye hear, mind ye!"

"Oh, no," said we.

"Hullo! There's Jim Toggerson's boat close in shore. She sets low in the water, so he's done well. He's been out deep-sea fishing since yesterday." Our friend pushed the porgies back into a corner, stuck his knife into a beam, and we hastened down to the shore. Kate and I sat on the pebbles, and he went out to the moorings in a dirty dory to help unload the fish.

We afterward saw a great deal of Danny, as all the men called him. But though Kate and I tried our best and used our utmost skill and tact to make him tell us more about himself, he never did. But perhaps there was nothing more to be told,

The day we left Deephaven we went down to the shore to say good-by to him, and to some other friends, and he said, "Goin', are ye? Well, I'm sorry; ye've treated me first-rate; the Lord bless ye!" and then was so much mortified at his speech that he turned and fled round the corner of the fish-house.

It is bewildering to try to write one's impressions of Deephaven, there is so much to be said. Beside the quaintness and unworldliness of the people, there was the delight we had in our housekeeping, in that fascinating old Shore House. I think it did Kate and me much good in more ways than one. I have the good fortune and the misfortune to belong to the navy,—that is, my father does,—and I have lived the consequent unsettled life. The thought of Deephaven brings up long, quiet summer days, and reading aloud on the rocks by the sea, the fresh salt air, and gorgeous sunsets; the wail of the Sunday psalm-singing; the yellow lichen that grew over the trees, the houses, and the stone wall; our importance as members of society, and how kind every one was to us both. By and by the Deephaven warehouses will fall and be used for firewood by the fisherpeople, and the wharves will be worn away by the tides. The few old gentlefolks who still linger will be dead; and I wonder if some day Kate Lancaster and I shall not go down to Deephaven for the sake of old times, and read the epitaphs in the burying-ground, look out to sea, and talk quietly about the girls who were so happy there one summer long before. I should like to walk along the beach at sunset, and watch the color of the marshes and the sea change as the light of the sky goes out. It would make the old days come back vividly. We should see the roofs and chimneys of the village, and the great Chantrey elms look black against the sky. A little later the marsh fog would show faintly white, and we should feel it deliciously cold and wet against our hands and faces; when we looked up, there would be a star, the crickets would chirp loudly, perhaps some late sea-birds would fly inland. Turning, we could see the light-house lamp shine out over the water, and the great sea would move and speak to us lazily in its idle high-tide sleep.

1875

MARK TWAIN
(SAMUEL LANGHORNE CLEMENS)
(1835–1910)

THE CELEBRATED JUMPING FROG OF CALAVERAS COUNTY *

In compliance with the request of a friend of mine, who wrote me from the East, I called on good-natured, garrulous old Simon Wheeler, and inquired after my friend's friend, *Leonidas W.* Smiley, as requested to do, and I hereunto append the result. I have a lurking suspicion that *Leonidas W.* Smiley is a myth; that my friend never knew such a personage; and that he only conjectured that, if I asked old Wheeler about him, that it would remind him of his infamous *Jim Smiley,* and he would go to work and bore me nearly to death with some infernal reminiscence of him as long and tedious as it would be useless to me. If that was the design, it certainly succeeded.

I found Simon Wheeler dozing comfortably by the bar-room stove of the old dilapidated tavern in the ancient mining camp of Angel's, and I noticed that he was fat and bald-headed, and had an expression of winning gentleness and simplicity upon his tranquil countenance. He roused up and gave me good-day. I told him

a friend of mine had commissioned me to make some inquiries about a cherished companion of his boyhood named *Leonidas W.* Smiley—*Rev Leonidas W.* Smiley—a young minister of the Gospel, who he had heard was at one time a resident of Angel's Camp. I added that, if Mr. Wheeler could tell me anything about this Rev Leonidas W. Smiley, I would feel under many obligations to him.

Simon Wheeler backed me into a corner and blockaded me there with his chair, and then sat me down and reeled off the monotonous narrative which follows this paragraph. He never smiled, he never frowned, he never changed his voice from the gentle-flowing key to which he tuned the initial sentence, he never betrayed the slightest suspicions of enthusiasm; but all through the interminable narrative there ran a vein of impressive earnestness and sincerity, which showed me plainly that, so far from his imagining that there was anything ridiculous or funny about his story, he regarded it as a really important matter, and admitted its two heroes as men of transcendent genius in *finesse.* To me, the spectacle of a man drifting serenely along through such a queer yarn without ever smiling, was exquisitely absurd. As I said before, I asked him to tell me what he knew of Rev. Leonidas W.

* Reprinted from *The Celebrated Jumping Frog of Calaveras County, and other Sketches,* by Mark Twain, 1867, and here used by permission of Harper and Brothers, the authorized publishers.

Smiley, and he replied as follows. I let him go on in his own way, and never interrupted him once:

There was a feller here once by the name of *Jim* Smiley, in the winter of '49—or maybe it was the spring of '50—I don't recollect exactly, somehow, though what makes me think it was one or the other is because I remember the big flume wasn't finished when he first came to the camp; but anyway, he was the curiousest man about always betting on anything that turned up you ever see, if he could get anybody to bet on the other side; and if he couldn't, he'd change sides. Any way, that suited the other man would suit him—any way just so's he got a bet, *he* was satisfied. But still he was lucky, uncommon lucky—he most always come out winner. He was always ready and laying for a chance; there couldn't be no solit'ry thing mentioned but that feller'd offer to bet on it, and take any side you please, as I was just telling you. If there was a horse-race, you'd find him flush, or you'd find him busted at the end of it; if there was a dog-fight, he'd bet on it; if there was a cat-fight, he'd bet on it; if there was a chicken-fight, he'd bet on it; why, if there was two birds setting on a fence, he would bet you which one would fly first; or if there was a camp-meeting, he would be there reg'lar, to bet on Parson Walker, which he judged to be the best exhorter about here, and so he was, too, and a good man. If he even see a straddle-bug start to go anywheres, he would bet you how long it would take him to get wherever he was going to, and if you took him up, he would foller that straddle-bug to Mexico but what he

would find out where he was bound for and how long he was on the road. Lots of the boys here has seen that Smiley, and can tell you about him. Why, it never made no difference to *him*—he would bet on *any*thing—the dangdest feller. Parson Walker's wife laid very sick once, for a good while, and it seemed as if they warn't going to save her; but one morning he came in, and Smiley asked how she was, and he said she was considerable better— thank the Lord for his inf'nit mercy —and coming on so smart that, with the blessing of Prov'dence, she'd get well yet; and Smiley, before he thought, says, "Well, I'll risk two-and-a-half that she don't anyway."

Thish-yer Smiley had a mare—the boys called her the fifteen-minute nag, but that was only in fun, you know, because, of course, she was faster than that—and he used to win money on that horse, for all she was so slow and always had the asthma, or the distemper, or the consumption, or something of that kind. They used to give her two or three hundred yards start, and then pass her under way; but always at the fag-end of the race she'd get excited and desperate-like, and come cavorting and straddling up, and scattering her legs around limber, sometimes in the air, and sometimes out to one side amongst the fences, and kicking up m-o-r-e dust, and raising m-o-r-e racket with her coughing and sneezing and blowing her nose—and always fetch up at the stand just about a neck ahead, as near as you could cipher it down.

And he had a little small bull pup, that to look at him you'd think he wan't worth a cent but to set around and look ornery and lay for a chance to steal something. But as soon as money was up on him, he was a different dog; his under-jaw'd begin to stick out like the fo'castle of a steamboat, and his teeth would uncover, and shine savage like the furnaces. And a dog might tackle him, and bully-rag him, and bite him, and throw him over his shoulder two or three times, and Andrew Jackson—which was the name of the pup—Andrew Jackson would never let on but what *he* was satisfied, and hadn't expected nothing else—and the bets being doubled and doubled on the other side all the time, till the money was all up; and then all of a sudden he would grab that other dog jest by the j'int of his hind leg and freeze to it—not claw, you understand, but only jest grip and hang on till they throwed up the sponge, if it was a year. Smiley always come out winner on that pup, till he harnessed a dog once that didn't have no hind legs, because they'd been sawed off by a circular saw, and when the thing had gone along far enough, and the money was all up, and he come to make a snatch for his pet holt, he saw in a minute how he'd been imposed on, and how the other dog had him in the door, so to speak, and he 'peared surprised, and then he looked sorter discouraged-like, and didn't try no more to win the fight, and so he got shucked out bad. He give Smiley a look, as much to say his heart was broke and it was *his* fault for putting up a dog that hadn't no hind legs for him to take holt of, which was his main dependence in a fight, and then he limped off a piece and laid down and died. It was a good pup, was that Andrew Jackson, and would have made a name for hisself if

he'd lived, for the stuff was in him and he had genius—I know it, because he hadn't no opportunities to speak of, and it don't stand to reason that a dog could make such a fight as he could under them circumstances, if he hadn't no talent. It always makes me feel sorry when I think of that last fight of his'n, and the way it turned out.

Well, this-yer Smiley had rat tarriers, and chicken-cocks, and tom cats, and all them kind of things, till you couldn't rest, and you couldn't fetch nothing for him to bet on but he'd match you. He ketched a frog one day, and took him home, and said he cal'klated to edercate him; and so he never done nothing for thes three months but set in his back yard and learn that frog to jump. And you bet you he *did* learn him, too. He'd give him a little punch behind, and the next minute you'd see that frog whirling in the air like a doughnut—see him turn one summerset, or maybe a couple, if he got a good start, and come down flat-footed and all right, like a cat. He got him up so in the matter of catching flies, and kept him in practice so constant, that he'd nail a fly every time as far as he could see him. Smiley said all a frog wanted was education, and he could do most anything—and I believe him. Why, I've seen him set Dan'l Webster down here on this floor—Dan'l Webster was the name of the frog—and sing out, "Flies, Dan'l, flies!" an quicker'n you could wink, he'd spring straight up, and snake a fly off'n the counter there, and flop down on the floor again as solid as a gob of mud, and fall to scratching the side of his head with his hind foot as indifferent as if he hadn't no idea he's been doin

ny more'n any frog might do. You
ever see a frog so modest and
traight-for'ard as he was, for all he
vas so gifted. And when it come to
air and square jumping on the dead
evel, he could get over more ground
t one straddle than any animal of his
reed you ever see. Jumping on a
ead level was his strong suit, you
nderstand; and when it come to that,
miley would ante up money on him
s long as he had a red. Smiley was
onstrous proud of his frog, and well
e might be, for fellers that had trav-
led and been everywhere all said he
id over any frog that ever *they* see.

Well, Smiley kept the beast in a
ttle lattice box, and he used to fetch
im downtown sometimes and lay for
bet. One day a feller—a stranger
a the camp, he was—come across
im with his box, and says:

"What might it be that you've got
a the box?"

And Smiley says, sorter indifferent
ke, "It might be a parrot, or it might
e a canary, maybe, but it ain't—it's
nly just a frog."

An' the feller took it, and looked
t it careful, and turned it round this
ay and that, and says, "H'm—so 'tis.
Vell, what's *he* good for?"

"Well," Smiley says, easy and caress, "he's good enough for *one* thing,
should judge—he can outjump ary
og in Calaveras county."

The feller took the box again, and
ok another long, particular look,
ad give it back to Smiley, and says,
ery deliberate, "Well, I don't see no
ints about that frog that's any bet-
r'n any other frog."

"Maybe you don't," Smiley says.
Maybe you understand frogs,
d maybe you don't understand

'em; maybe you've had experience,
and maybe you ain't only a amature,
as it were. Anyways, I've got *my*
opinion, and I'll risk forty dollars
that he can outjump any frog in
Calaveras county."

And the feller studied a minute, and
then says, kinder sad like, "Well, I'm
only a stranger here, and I ain't got
no frog; but if I had a frog, I'd bet
you."

And then Smiley says, "That's all
right—that's all right—if you'll hold
my box a minute, I'll go and get you
a frog." And so the feller took the
box, and put up his forty dollars along
with Smiley's, and set down to wait.

So he set there a good while thinking and thinking to hisself, and then
he got the frog out and prized his
mouth open and took a teaspoon and
filled him full of quail shot—filled
him pretty near up to his chin—and
set him on the floor. Smiley he went
to the swamp and slopped around in
the mud for a long time, and finally
he ketched a frog and fetched him in,
and give him to this feller, and says:

"Now, if you're ready, set him
alongside of Dan'l, with his fore-paws
just even with Dan'l, and I'll give
the word." Then he says, "One—two
—three—jump!" and him and the
feller touched up the frogs from behind, and the new frog hopped off,
but Dan'l gave a heave, and hysted
up his shoulders—so—like a Frenchman, but it wasn't no use—he couldn't
budge; he was planted as solid as an
anvil, and he couldn't no more stir
than if he was anchored out. Smiley
was a good deal surprised, and he was
disgusted, too, but he didn't have no
idea what the matter was, of course.

The feller took the money and

started away; and when he was going out at the door, he sorter jerked his thumb over his shoulder—this way—at Dan'l, and says again, very deliberate, "Well, *I* don't see no p'ints about that frog that's any better'n any other frog."

Smiley he stood scratching his head and looking down at Dan'l a long time, and at last he says, "I do wonder what in the nation that frog throw'd off for—I wonder if there ain't something the matter with him—he 'pears to look mighty baggy, somehow." And he ketched Dan'l by the nap of the neck, and lifted him up and says, "Why, blame my cats, if he don't weight five pounds!" and turned him upside down, and he belched out a double handful of shot. And then he see how it was, and he was the maddest man—he set the frog down and took out after that feller, but he never ketched him. And—

(Here Simon Wheeler heard his name called from the front yard, and got up to see what was wanted.) And turning to me as he moved away, he said: "Jest set where you are, stranger, and rest easy—I ain't going to be gone a second."

But, by your leave, I did not think that a continuation of the history of the enterprising vagabond *Jim* Smiley would be likely to afford me much information concerning the Rev. *Leonidas W.* Smiley, and so I started away.

At the door I met the sociable Wheeler returning, and he buttonholed me and recommenced:

"Well, thish-yer Smiley had a yeller one-eyed cow that didn't have no tail, only jest a short stump like a bannanner, and—"

"Oh, hang Smiley and his afflicted cow!" I muttered good-naturedly, and bidding the old gentleman good-day, departed.

186

From *THE INNOCENTS ABROAD* *

BOOK I

CHAPTER XXIII

[VENICE]

The Venetian gondola is as free and graceful, in its gliding movement, as a serpent. It is twenty or thirty feet long, and is narrow and deep, like a canoe; its sharp bow and stern sweep upward from the water like the horns of a crescent with the abruptness of the curve slightly modified.

The bow is ornamented with a steel comb with a battle-ax attachment which threatens to cut passing boats in two occasionally, but never does. The gondola is painted black because in the zenith of Venetian magnificence the gondolas became too gorgeous altogether, and the Senate decreed that all such display must cease, and a solemn, unembellished black be substituted. If the truth were known, it would doubtless appear that rich plebeians grew too prominent in their affectation of patrician show on the Grand Canal, and required a wholesome snubbing. Reverence for the hallowed Past and its traditions keep the dismal fashion in force now that the compulsion exists no longer. So let it remain. It is the color of mourning. Venice mourns. The stern of

* Reprinted from *The Innocents Abroad*, by Mark Twain, 1869, and here used by permission of Harper and Brothers, the authorized publishers.

the boat is decked over and the gondolier stands there. He uses a single oar—a long blade, of course, for he stands nearly erect. A wooden peg, a foot and a half high, with two slight crooks or curves in one side of it and one in the other, projects above the starboard gunwale. Against that peg the gondolier takes a purchase with his oar, changing it at intervals to the other side of the peg or dropping it into another of the crooks, as the steering of the craft may demand— and how in the world he can back and fill, shoot straight ahead, or flirt suddenly around a corner, and make the oar stay in those insignificant notches, is a problem to me and a never-diminishing matter of interest. I am afraid I study the gondolier's marvelous skill more than I do the sculptured palaces we glide among. He cuts a corner so closely, now and then, or misses another gondola by such an imperceptible hair-breadth, that I feel myself "scrootching," as the children say, just as one does when a buggy-wheel grazes his elbow. But he makes all his calculations with the nicest precision, and goes darting in and out among a Broadway confusion of busy craft with the easy confidence of the educated hackman. He never makes a mistake.

Sometimes we go flying down the great canals at such a gait that we can get only the merest glimpses into front doors, and again, in obscure alleys in the suburbs, we put on a solemnity suited to the silence, the mildew, the stagnant waters, the clinging weeds, the deserted houses, and the general lifelessness of the place, and move to the spirit of grave meditation.

The gondolier *is* a picturesque rascal for all he wears no satin harness, no plumed bonnet, no silken tights. His attitude is stately; he is lithe and supple; all his movements are full of grace. When his long canoe, and his fine figure, towering from its high perch on the stern, are cut against the evening sky, they make a picture that is very novel and striking to a foreign eye.

We sit in the cushioned carriage-body of a cabin, with the curtains drawn, and smoke, or read, or look out upon the passing boats, the houses, the bridges, the people, and enjoy ourselves much more than we could in a buggy jolting over our cobblestone pavements at home. This is the gentlest, pleasantest locomotion we have ever known.

But it seems queer—ever so queer—to see a boat doing duty as a private carriage. We see business men come to the front door, step into a gondola, instead of a street-car, and go off down-town to the counting-room.

We see visiting young ladies stand on the stoop, and laugh, and kiss good-by, and flirt their fans and say "Come soon—now *do*—you've been just as mean as ever you can be—mother's dying to see you—and we've moved into the new house, oh, such a love of a place!—so convenient to the post-office and the church, and the Young Men's Christian Association; and we do have such fishing, and such carrying on, and *such* swimming-matches in the back yard—Oh, you *must* come —no distance at all, and if you go down through by St. Mark's and the Bridge of Sighs, and cut through the alley and come up by the church of Santa Maria dei Frari, and into the

Grand Canal, there isn't a *bit* of current—now *do* come, Sally Maria—by-by!" and then the little humbug trips down the steps, jumps into the gondola, says, under her breath, "Disagreeable old thing, I hope she *won't!*" goes skimming away, round the corner; and the other girl slams the street door and says, "Well, *that* infliction's over, anyway,—but I suppose I've got to go and see her—tiresome, stuck-up thing!" Human nature appears to be just the same, all over the world. We see the diffident young man, mild of mustache, affluent of hair, indigent of brain, elegant of costume, drive up to *her* father's mansion, tell his hackman to bail out and wait, start fearfully up the steps and meet "the old gentleman" right on the threshold!—hear him ask what street the new British Bank is in—as if *that* were what he came for—and then bounce into his boat and scurry away with his coward heart in his boots!—see him come sneaking around the corner again, directly, with a crack of the curtain open toward the old gentleman's disappearing gondola, and out scampers his Susan with a flock of little Italian endearments fluttering from her lips, and goes to drive with him in the watery avenues down toward the Rialto.

We see the ladies go out shopping, in the most natural way, and flit from street to street and from store to store, just in the good old fashion, except that they leave the gondola, instead of a private carriage, waiting at the curbstone a couple of hours for them,—waiting while they make the nice young clerks pull down tons and tons of silks and velvets and moire antiques and those things; and then they buy a paper of pins and go paddling away to confer the rest of their disastrous patronage on some other firm. And they always have their purchases sent home just in the good old way. Human nature is *very* much the same all over the world; and it is *so* like my dear native home to see a Venetian lady go into a store and buy ten cents' worth of blue ribbon and have it sent home in a scow. Ah, it is these little touches of nature that move one to tears in these far-off foreign lands.

We see little girls and boys go out in gondolas with their nurses, for an airing. We see staid families, with prayer-book and beads, enter the gondola dressed in their Sunday best, and float away to church. And at midnight we see the theater break up and discharge its swarm of hilarious youth and beauty; we hear the cries of the hackmen-gondoliers, and behold the struggling crowd jump aboard, and the black multitude of boats go skimming down the moonlit avenues; we see them separate here and there; and disappear up divergent streets; we hear the faint sounds of laughter and of shouted farewells floating up out of the distance; and then, the strange pageant being gone, we have lonely stretches of glittering water—of stately buildings—of blotting shadows—of weird stone faces creeping into the moonlight—of deserted bridges—of motionless boats at anchor. And over all broods that mysterious stillness, that stealthy quiet, that befits so well this old dreaming Venice.

We have been pretty much everywhere in our gondola. We have bought beads and photographs in the stores, and wax matches in the Great Square of St. Mark. The last remark suggests a digression. Everybody goes to this vast square in the evening. The military bands play in the center of it and countless couples of ladies and gentlemen promenade up and down on either side, and platoons of them are constantly drifting away toward the old cathedral, and by the venerable column with the Winged Lion of St. Mark on its top, and out to where the boats lie moored; and other platoons are as constantly arriving from the gondolas and joining the great throng. Between the promenaders and the sidewalks are seated hundreds and hundreds of people at small tables, smoking and taking *granita* (a first cousin to ice-cream); on the sidewalks are more employing themselves in the same way. The shops in the first floor of the tall rows of buildings that wall in three sides of the square are brilliantly lighted, the air is filled with music and merry voices, and altogether the scene is as bright and spirited and full of cheerfulness as any man could desire. We enjoy it thoroughly. Very many of the young women are exceedingly pretty and dress with rare good taste. We are gradually and laboriously learning the ill manners of staring them unflinchingly in the face—not because such conduct is agreeable to us, but because it is the custom of the country and they say the girls like it. We wish to learn all the curious, outlandish ways of all the different countries, so that we can "show off" and astonish people when we get home. We wish to excite the envy of our untraveled friends with our strange foreign fashions which we can't shake off. All our passengers are paying strict attention to this thing, with the end in view which I have mentioned. The gentle reader will never, never know what a consummate ass he can become until he goes abroad. I speak now, of course, in the supposition that the gentle reader has not been abroad, and therefore is not already a consummate ass. If the case be otherwise, I beg his pardon and extend to him the cordial hand of fellowship and call him brother. I shall always delight to meet an ass after my own heart when I shall have finished my travels.

On this subject let me remark that there are Americans abroad in Italy who have actually forgotten their mother-tongue in three months—forgot it in France. They cannot even write their address in English in a hotel-register. I append these evidences, which I copied *verbatim* from the register of a hotel in a certain Italian city:

John P. Whitcomb, *États Unis.*
William L. Ainsworth, *travailleur* (he meant traveler, I suppose), *États Unis.*
George P. Morton, *et fils, d'Amérique.*
Lloyd B. Williams, *et trois amis, ville de* Boston, *Amérique.*

J. Ellsworth Baker, *tout de suite de France, place de naissance Amérique, destination la Grande Bretagne.*

I love this sort of people. A lady passenger of ours tells of a fellow-citizen of hers who spent eight weeks in Paris and then returned home and addressed his dearest old bosom friend Herbert as Mr. "Er-bare!" He apologized, though, and said, " 'Pon my soul it is aggravating, but I cahn't help it—I have got so used to speak-

ing nothing but French, my dear Er-
bare—damme there it goes again!—
got so used to French pronunciation
that I cahn't get rid of it—it is positively annoying, I assure you." This
enterprising idiot, whose name was
Gordon, allowed himself to be hailed
three times in the street before he
paid any attention, and then begged a
thousand pardons and said he had
grown so accustomed to hearing himself addressed as "M'sieu Gor-r-*dong,*"
with a roll to the *r,* that he had forgotten the legitimate sound of his
name! He wore a rose in his buttonhole; he gave the French salutation
—two flips of the hand in front of the
face; he called Paris *Pairree* in ordinary English conversation; he carried
envelopes bearing foreign postmarks
protruding from his breast pocket;
he cultivated a mustache and imperial,
and did what else he could do to suggest to the beholder his pet fancy that
he resembled Louis Napoleon—and in
a spirit of thankfulness which is entirely unaccountable, considering the
slim foundation there was for it, he
praised his Maker that he was *as* he
was, and went on enjoying his little
life just the same as if he really *had*
been deliberately designed and erected
by the great Architect of the Universe.

Think of our Whitcombs and our
Ainsworths and our Williamses writing
themselves down in dilapidated French
in a foreign hotel-register! We laugh
at Englishmen, when we are at home,
for sticking so sturdily to their national ways and customs, but we look
back upon it from abroad very forgivingly. It is not pleasant to see an
American thrusting his nationality forward *obtrusively* in a foreign land, but
oh, it is pitiable to see him making

of himself a thing that is neither male
nor female, neither fish, flesh, nor
fowl—a poor, miserable, hermaphro-
dite Frenchman!

Among a long list of churches, art-
galleries, and such things, visited by
us in Venice, I shall mention only one
—the Church of Santa Maria dei
Frari. It is about five hundred years
old, I believe, and stands on twelve
hundred thousand piles. In it lie the
body of Canova and the heart of
Titian, under magnificent monuments.
Titian died at the age of almost one
hundred years. A plague which swept
away fifty thousand lives was raging
at the time, and there is notable evidence of the reverence in which the
great painter was held, in the fact
that to him alone the state permitted
a public funeral in all that season of
terror and death.

In this church, also, is a monument
to the doge Foscari, whose name a
once resident of Venice, Lord Byron,
has made permanently famous.

The monument to the doge Giovanni
Pesaro, in this church, is a curiosity in
the way of mortuary adornment. It
is eighty feet high and is fronted like
some fantastic pagan temple. Against
it stand four colossal Nubians, as
black as night, dressed in white marble
garments. The black legs are bare,
and through rents in sleeves and
breeches, the skin, of shiny black
marble, shows. The artist was as ingenious as his funeral designs were
absurd. There are two bronze skeletons bearing scrolls, and two great
dragons uphold the sarcophagus. On
high, amid all this grotesqueness, sits
the departed doge.

In the conventual buildings attached
to this church are the state archives

of Venice. We did not see them, but they are said to number millions of documents. "They are the records of centuries of the most watchful, observant, and suspicious government that ever existed—in which everything was written down and nothing spoken out." They fill nearly three hundred rooms. Among them are manuscripts from the archives of nearly two thousand families, monasteries, and convents. The secret history of Venice for a thousand years is here—its plots, its hidden trials, its assassinations, its commissions of hireling spies and masked bravoes—food, ready to hand, for a world of dark and mysterious romances.

Yes, I think we have seen all of Venice. We have seen, in these old churches, a profusion of costly and elaborate sepulcher ornamentation such as we never dreamt of before. We have stood in the dim religious light of these hoary sanctuaries, in the midst of long ranks of dusty monuments and effigies of the great dead of Venice, until we seemed drifting back, back, back, into the solemn past, and looking upon the scenes and mingling with the peoples of a remote antiquity. We have been in a half-waking sort of dream all the time. I do not know how else to describe the feeling. A part of our being has remained still in the nineteenth century, while another part of it has seemed in some unaccountable way walking among the phantoms of the tenth.

We have seen famous pictures until our eyes are weary with looking at them and refuse to find interest in them any longer. And what wonder, when there are twelve hundred pic-

tures by Palma the Younger in Venice and fifteen hundred by Tintoretto? And behold, there are Titians and the works of other artists in proportion. We have seen Titian's celebrated "Cain and Abel," his "David and Goliath," his "Abraham's Sacrifice." We have seen Tintoretto's monster picture, which is seventy-four feet long and I do not know how many feet high, and thought it a very commodious picture. We have seen pictures of martyrs enough, and saints enough, to regenerate the world. I ought not to confess it, but still, since one has no opportunity in America to acquire a critical judgment in art, and since I could not hope to become educated in it in Europe in a few short weeks, I may therefore as well acknowledge with such apologies as may be due, that to me it seemed that when I had seen one of these martyrs I had seen them all. They all have a marked family resemblance to each other, they dress alike, in coarse monkish robes and sandals, they are all bald-headed, they all stand in about the same attitude, and without exception they are gazing heavenward with countenances which the Ainsworths, the Mortons, and the Williamses, et fils, inform me are full of "expression." To me there is nothing tangible about these imaginary portraits, nothing that I can grasp and take a living interest in. If great Titian had only been gifted with prophecy, and had skipped a martyr, and gone over to England and painted a portrait of Shakespeare, even as a youth, which we could all have confidence in now, the world down to the latest generations would have forgiven the lost martyr in the rescued seer. I think posterity could have spared one more martyr for the sake of a great historical picture of Titian's time and painted by his brush—such as Columbus returning in chains from the discovery of a world, for instance. The old masters did paint some Venetian historical pictures, and these we did not tire of looking at, notwithstanding representations of the formal introduction of defunct doges to the Virgin Mary in regions beyond the clouds clashed rather harshly with the proprieties, it seemed to us.

But, humble as we are, and unpretending, in the matter of art, our researches among the painted monks and martyrs have not been wholly in vain. We have striven hard to learn. We have had some success. We have mastered some things, possibly of trifling import in the eyes of the learned, but to us they give pleasure, and we take as much pride in our little acquirements as do others who have learned far more, and we love to display them full as well. When we see a monk going about with a lion and looking tranquilly up to heaven, we know that that is St. Mark. When we see a monk with a book and pen, looking tranquilly up to heaven, trying to think of a word, we know that that is St. Matthew. When we see a monk sitting on a rock, looking tranquilly up to heaven, with a human skull beside him, and without other baggage, we know that that is St. Jerome. Because we know that he always went flying light in the matter of baggage. When we see a party looking tranquilly up to heaven, unconscious that his body is shot through and through with arrows, we know that that is St. Sebastian. When we see other monks looking tranquilly up to heaven, but having no trade-mark, we always ask who those parties are. We do this because we humbly wish to learn. We have seen thirteen thousand St. Jeromes, and twenty-two thousand St. Marks, and sixteen thousand St. Matthews, and sixty thousand St. Sebastians, and four millions of assorted monks, undesignated, and we feel encouraged to believe that when we have seen some more of these various pictures, and had a larger experience, we shall begin to take an absorbing interest in them like our cultivated countrymen from *Amérique*.

Now it does give me real pain to speak in this almost unappreciative way of the old masters and their martyrs, because good friends of mine in the ship—friends who do thoroughly and conscientiously appreciate them and are in every way competent to discriminate between good pictures and inferior ones—have urged me for my own sake not to make public the fact that I lack this appreciation and this critical discrimination myself. I believe that what I have written and may still write about pictures will give them pain, and I am honestly sorry for it. I even promised that I would hide my uncouth sentiments in my own breast. But alas! I never could keep a promise. I do not blame myself for this weakness, because the fault must lie in my physical organization. It is likely that such a very liberal amount of space was given to the organ which enables me to *make* promises, that the organ which should enable me to keep them was crowded out. But I grieve not. I like no half-way things. I had rather have one faculty nobly developed than two faculties of mere ordinary capacity. I certainly meant to keep that promise, but I find I cannot do it. It is impossible to travel through Italy without speaking of pictures, and can I see them through other's eyes?

If I did not so delight in the grand pictures that are spread before me every day of my life by that monarch of all the old masters, Nature, I should come to believe, sometimes, that I had in me no appreciation of the beautiful, whatsoever.

It seems to me that whenever I glory to think that for once I have discovered an ancient painting that is beautiful and worthy of all praise, the pleasure it gives me is an infallible proof that it is *not* a beautiful picture and not in any wise worthy of commendation. This very thing has occurred more times than I can mention, in Venice. In every single instance the guide has crushed out my swelling enthusiasm with the remark:

"It is nothing—it is of the *Renaissance.*"

I did not know what in the mischief the Renaissance was, and so always I had to simply say:

"Ah! so it is—I had not observed it before."

I could not bear to be ignorant before a cultivated negro, the offspring of a South Carolina slave. But it occurred too often for even my self-complacency, did that exasperating "It is nothing—it is of the *Renaissance.*" I said at last:

"*Who* is this Renaissance? Where did he come from? Who gave him permission to cram the Republic with his execrable daubs?"

We learned, then, that Renaissance was not a man; that *renaissance* was a term used to signify what was at best but an imperfect rejuvenation of art. The guide said that after Titian's time and the time of the other great names we had grown so familiar with, high art declined; then it partially rose again—an inferior sort of painters sprang up, and these shabby pictures were the work of their hands. Then I said, in my heat, that I "wished to goodness high art had declined five hundred years sooner." The Renaissance pictures suit me very well, though sooth to say its school were too much given to painting real men and did not indulge enough in martyrs.

The guide I have spoken of is the only one we have had yet who knew anything. He was born in South Carolina, of slave parents. They came to Venice while he was an infant. He has grown up here. He is well educated. He reads, writes, and speaks English, Italian, Spanish, and French, with perfect facility; is a worshiper of art and thoroughly conversant with it; knows the history of Venice by heart and never tires of talking of her illustrious career. He dressed better than any of us, I think, and is daintily polite. Negroes are deemed as good as white people in Venice, and so this man feels no desire to go back to his native land. His judgment is correct.

I have had another shave. I was writing in our front room this afternoon and trying hard to keep my attention on my work and refrain from looking out upon the canal. I was resisting the soft influences of the climate as well as I could, and endeavoring to overcome the desire to be indolent and happy. The boys sent for a barber. They asked me if I would be shaved. I reminded them of my tortures in Genoa, Milan, Como;

of my declaration that I would suffer
no more on Italian soil. I said: "Not
any for me, if you please."

I wrote on. The barber began on
the doctor. I heard him say:

"Dan, this is the easiest shave I
have had since we left the ship."

He said again, presently:

"Why, Dan, a man could go to sleep
with this man shaving him."

Dan took the chair. Then he said:
"Why, this is Titian. This is one
of the old masters."

I wrote on. Directly Dan said:
"Doctor, it is a perfect luxury. The
ship's barber isn't anything to him."

My rough beard was distressing me
beyond measure. The barber was
rolling up his apparatus. The temptation was too strong. I said:

"Hold on, please. Shave me also."

I sat down in the chair and closed
my eyes. The barber soaped my face,
and then took his razor and gave me
a rake that well-nigh threw me into
convulsions. I jumped out of the chair:
Dan and the doctor were both wiping
blood off their faces and laughing.

I said it was a mean, disgraceful
fraud.

They said that the misery of this
shave had gone so far beyond anything they had ever experienced before, that they could not bear the idea
of losing such a chance of hearing a
cordial opinion from me on the
subject.

It was shameful. But there was no
help for it. The skinning was begun
and had to be finished. The tears
flowed with every rake, and so did the
fervent execrations. The barber grew
confused, and brought blood every
time. I think the boys enjoyed it
better than anything they have

seen or heard since they left home.

We have seen the Campanile, and
Byron's house, and Balbi's the geog-
rapher, and the palaces of all the
ancient dukes and doges of Venice, and
we have seen their effeminate descendants airing their nobility in fashionable
French attire in the Grand Square of
St. Mark, and eating ices and drinking cheap wines, instead of wearing
gallant coats of mail and destroying
fleets and armies as their great ancestors did in the days of Venetian
glory. We have seen no bravoes with
poisoned stilettoes, no masks, no wild
carnival; but we have seen the ancient pride of Venice, the grim Bronze
Horses that figure in a thousand
legends. Venice may well cherish
them, for they are the only horses she
ever had. It is said there are hundreds of people in this curious city
who never have seen a living horse in
their lives. It is entirely true, no
doubt.

And so, having satisfied ourselves,
we depart to-morrow, and leave the
venerable Queen of the Republics to
summon her vanished ships, and marshal her shadowy armies, and know
again in dreams the pride of her old
renown.

1869

From *ROUGHING IT* *

VOLUME II

CHAPTER VI

[BUCK FANSHAW'S FUNERAL]

Somebody has said that in order
to know a community, one must ob-

* Reprinted from *Roughing It,* by Mark
Twain, 1872, and here used by permission
of Harper and Brothers, the authorized publishers.

erve the style of its funerals and
know what manner of men they bury
with most ceremony. I cannot say
which class we buried with most éclat
in our "flush times," the distinguished
public benefactor or the distinguished
rough—possibly the two chief grades
or grand divisions of society honored
their illustrious dead about equally;
and hence, no doubt, the philosopher
I have quoted from would have
needed to see two representative
funerals in Virginia before forming his
estimate of the people.

There was a grand time over Buck
Fanshaw when he died. He was a
representative citizen. He had "killed
his man"—not in his own quarrel,
it is true, but in defence of a stranger
unfairly beset by numbers. He had
kept a sumptuous saloon. He had
been the proprietor of a dashing help-
meet whom he could have discarded
without the formality of a divorce.
He held a high position in the fire
department and been a very Warwick
in politics. When he died there was
great lamentation throughout the
town, but especially in the vast
bottom-stratum of society.

On the inquest it was shown that
Buck Fanshaw, in the delirium of a
wasting typhoid fever, had taken
arsenic, shot himself through the body,
cut his throat, and jumped out of a
four-storey window and broken his
neck—and after due deliberation, the
jury, sad and tearful, but with intelligence unblinded by its sorrow,
brought a verdict of death "by the
visitation of God." What could the
world do without juries?

Prodigious preparations were made
for the funeral. All the vehicles in
town were hired, all the saloons put

in mourning, all the municipal and
fire-company flags hung at half-mast,
and all the firemen ordered to muster
in uniform and bring their machines
duly draped in black. Now—let us
remark in parenthesis—as all the peoples of the earth had representative
adventurers in Silverland, and as each
adventurer had brought the slang of
his nation or his locality with him, the
combination made the slang of Nevada the richest and the most infinitely varied and copious that had
ever existed anywhere in the world,
perhaps, except in the mines of California in the "early days." Slang was
the language of Nevada. It was hard
to preach a sermon without it, and to
be understood. Such phrases as "You
bet!" "Oh, no, I reckon not!" "No
Irish need apply," and a hundred
others, became so common as to fall
from the lips of a speaker unconsciously—and very often when they
did not touch the subject under discussion and consequently failed to
mean anything.

After Buck Fanshaw's inquest, a
meeting of the short-haired brotherhood was held, for nothing can be
done on the Pacific coast without a
public meeting and an expression of
sentiment. Regretful resolutions were
passed and various committees appointed; among others, a committee
of one was deputed to call on the minister, a fragile, gentle, spirituel new
fledgling from an Eastern theological
seminary, and as yet unacquainted
with the ways of the mines. The
committeeman, "Scotty" Briggs, made
his visit; and in after days it was
worth something to hear the minister
tell about it. Scotty was a stalwart
rough, whose customary suit, when

on weighty official business, like committee work, was a fire helmet, flaming red flannel shirt, patent leather belt with spanner and revolver attached, coat hung over his arm, and pants stuffed into boot tops. He formed something of a contrast to the pale theological student. It is fair to say of Scotty, however, in passing, that he had a warm heart, and a strong love for his friends, and never entered into a quarrel when he could reasonably keep out of it. Indeed, it was commonly said that whenever one of Scotty's fights were investigated, it always turned out that it had originally been no affair of his, but that out of native goodheartedness he had dropped in of his own accord to help the man who was getting the worst of it. He and Buck Fanshaw were bosom friends, for years, and had often taken adventurous "potluck" together. On one occasion, they had thrown off their coats and taken the weaker side in a fight among strangers, and after gaining a hard-earned victory, turned and found that the men they were helping had deserted early, and not only that, but had stolen their coats and made off with them! But to return to Scotty's visit to the minister. He was on a sorrowful mission, now, and his face was the picture of woe. Being admitted to the presence he sat down before the clergyman, placed his fire-hat on an unfinished manuscript sermon under the minister's nose, took from it a red silk handkerchief, wiped his brow and heaved a sigh of dismal impressiveness, explanatory of his business. He choked, and even shed tears; but with an effort he mastered

his voice and said in lugubrious tones:

"Are you the duck that runs the gospel-mill next door?"

"Am I the—pardon me, I believe I do not understand?"

With another sigh, and half-sob, Scotty rejoined:

"Why you see we are in a bit of trouble, and the boys thought maybe you would give us a lift, if we'd tackle you—that is, if I've got the rights of it and you are the head clerk of the doxology-works next door."

"I am the shepherd in charge of the flock whose fold is next door."

"The which?"

"The spiritual adviser of the little company of believers whose sanctuary adjoins these premises."

Scotty scratched his head, reflected a moment, and then said:

"You ruther hold over me, pard. I reckon I can't call that hand. Ante and pass the buck."

"How? I beg pardon. What did I understand you to say?"

"Well, you've ruther got the bulge on me. Or maybe we've both got the bulge somehow. You don't smoke me and I don't smoke you. You see, one of the boys has passed in his checks and we want to give him a good send-off, and so the thing I'm on now is to roust out somebody to jerk a little chin-music for us and waltz him through handsome."

"My friend, I seem to grow more and more bewildered. Your observations are wholly incomprehensible to me. Cannot you simplify them in some way? At first I thought perhaps I understood you, but I grope now. Would it not expedite matters if you restricted yourself to categorical state

nents of fact unencumbered with ob-
structing accumulations of metaphor
and allegory?"

Another pause, and more reflection.
Then, said Scotty:

"I'll have to pass, I judge."

"How?"

"You've raised me out, pard."

"I still fail to catch your meaning."

"Why, that last lead of yourn is too
many for me—that's the idea. I can't
neither trump nor follow suit."

The clergyman sank back in his
chair perplexed. Scotty leaned his
head on his hand and gave himself
up to thought. Presently his face
came up, sorrowful but confident.

"I've got it now, so's you can
savvy," he said. "What we want is
gospel-sharp. See?"

"A what?"

"Gospel-sharp. Parson."

"Oh! Why did you not say so before? I am a clergyman—a parson."

"Now you talk! You see my blind
and straddle it like a man. Put it
there!"—extending a brawny paw,
which closed over the minister's small
hand and gave it a shake indicative
of fraternal sympathy and fervent
ratification.

"Now we're all right, pard. Let's
start fresh. Don't you mind my snuf-
ing a little—becuz we're in a power
f trouble. You see one of the boys
has gone up the flume—"

"Gone where?"

"Up the flume—throwed up the
sponge, you understand."

"Thrown up the sponge?"

"Yes—kicked the bucket—"

"Ah—has departed to that mysterious country from whose bourne no
traveler returns."

"Return! I reckon not. Why pard,
he's *dead!*"

"Yes, I understand."

"Oh, you do? Well I thought
maybe you might be getting tangled
some more. Yes, you see he's dead
again—"

"*Again?* Why, has he ever been
dead before?"

"Dead before? No! Do you
reckon a man has got as many lives
as a cat? But you bet you he's awful
dead now, poor old boy, and I wish I'd
never seen this day. I don't want no
better friend than Buck Fanshaw. I
knowed him by the back; and when
I know a man and like him, I freeze
to him—you hear *me.* Take him all
round, pard, there never was a bullier
man in the mines. No man ever
knowed Buck Fanshaw to go back on
a friend. But it's all up, you know,
it's all up. It ain't no use. They've
scooped him."

"Scooped him?"

"Yes—death has. Well, well, well,
we've got to give him up. Yes indeed.
It's a kind of a hard world, after all,
ain't it? But pard, he was a rustler!
You ought to see him get started once.
He was a bully boy with a glass eye!
Just spit in his face and give him
room according to his strength, and
it was just beautiful to see him peel
and go in. He was the worst son of a
thief that ever drawed breath. Pard,
he was *on* it! He was on it bigger
than an Injun!"

"On it? On what?"

"On the shoot. On the shoulder. On
the fight, you understand. *He* didn't
give a continental for *any*body. *Beg*
your pardon, friend, for coming so
near saying a cuss-word—but you see

I'm on an awful strain, in this palaver, on account of having to camp down and draw everything so mild. But we've got to give him up. There ain't any getting around that, I don't reckon. Now if we can get you to help plant him—"

"Preach the funeral discourse? Assist at the obsequies?"

"Obs'quies is good. Yes. That's it—that's our little game. We are going to get the thing up regardless, you know. He was always nifty himself, and so you bet you his funeral ain't going to be no slouch—solid silver door-plate on his coffin, six plumes on the hearse, and a nigger on the box in a biled shirt and a plug hat—how's that for high? And we'll take care of *you*, pard. We'll fix you all right. There'll be a kerridge for you; and whatever you want, you just 'scape out and we'll tend to it. We've got a shebang fixed up for you to stand behind, in No. 1's house, and don't you be afraid. Just go in and toot your horn, if you don't sell a clam. Put Buck through as bully as you can, pard, for anybody that knowed him will tell you that he was one of the whitest men that was ever in the mines. You can't draw it too strong. He never could stand it to see things going wrong. He's done more to make this town quiet and peaceable than any man in it. I've seen him lick four Greasers in eleven minutes, myself. If a thing wanted regulating, *he* warn't a man to go browsing around after somebody to do it, but he would prance in and regulate it himself. He warn't a Catholic. Scasely. He was down on 'em. His word was, 'No Irish need apply!' But it didn't make no

difference about that when it cam down to what a man's rights was— and so, when some roughs jumped th Catholic bone-yard and started in t stake out town-lots in it he *went* f 'em! And he *cleaned* 'em, too! was there, pard, and I seen it myself.

"That was very well indeed—least the impulse was—whether th act was strictly defensible or no Had deceased any religious convi tions? That is to say, did he fe a dependance upon, or acknowledg allegiance to a higher power?"

More reflection.

"I reckon you've stumped me agai pard. Could you say it over onc more, and say it slow?"

"Well, to simplify it somewhat, wa he, or rather had he ever been co nected with any organization seque tered from secular concerns and d voted to self-sacrifice in the interes of morality?"

"All down but nine—set 'em up o the other alley, pard."

"What did I understand you t say?"

"Why, you're most too many f me, you know. When you get in wit your left I hunt grass every tim Every time you draw, you fill; b I don't seem to have any luck. Let have a new deal."

"How? Begin again?"

"That's it."

"Very well. Was he a good ma and—"

"There—I see that; don't put u another chip till I look at my han A good man, says you? Pard, it ain no name for it. He was the best ma that ever—pard, you would have dote on that man. He could lam an galoot of his inches in America. It was him that put down the riot last election before it got a start; and everybody said he was the only man that could have done it. He waltzed in with a spanner in one hand and a trumpet in the other, and sent four-teen men home on a shutter in less than three minutes. He had that riot all broke up and prevented nice before anybody ever got a chance to strike a blow. He was always for peace, and he would *have* peace—he could not stand disturbances. Pard, he was a great loss to this town. It would please the boys if you could chip in something like that and do him justice. Here once when the Micks got to throwing stones through the Methodis' Sunday-school windows, Buck Fan-shaw, all of his own notion, shut up his saloon and took a couple of six-shooters and mounted guard over the Sunday school. Says he, 'No Irish need apply!' And they didn't. He was the bulliest man in the mountains, pard! He could run faster, jump higher, hit harder, and hold more tangle-foot whisky without spilling it than any man in seventeen counties. Put that in, pard—it'll please the boys more than anything you could say. And you can say, pard, that he never shook his mother."

"Never shook his mother?"

"That's it—any of the boys will tell you so."

"Well, but why *should* he shake her?"

"That's what *I* say—but some peo-ple does."

"Not people of any repute?"

"Well, some that averages pretty so-so."

"In my opinion the man that would offer personal violence to his own mother, ought to—"

"Cheese it, pard; you've banked your ball clean outside the string. What I was drivin' at, was, that he never *throwed off* on his mother—don't you see? No indeedy. He gave her a house to live in, and town lots, and plenty of money; and he looked after her and took care of her all the time; and when she was down with the small-pox I'm d—d if he didn't set up nights and nuss her himself! *Beg* your pardon for saying it, but it hopped out too quick for yours truly. You've treated me like a gentleman, pard, and I ain't the man to hurt your feelings intentional. I think you're white. I think you're a square man, pard. I like you, and I'll lick any man that don't. I'll lick him till he can't tell himself from a last year's corpse! Put it *there!*" [Another fra-ternal hand-shake—and exit.]

The obsequies were all that "the boys" could desire. Such a marvel of funeral pomp had never been seen in Virginia. The plumed hearse, the dirge-breathing brass bands, the closed marts of business, the flags drooping at half mast, the long, plodding pro-cession of uniformed secret societies, military battalions and fire companies, draped engines, carriages of officials; and citizens in vehicles and on foot, attracted multitudes of spectators to the sidewalks, roofs and windows; and for years afterward, the degree of grandeur attained by any civic dis-play in Virginia was determined by comparison with Buck Fanshaw's funeral.

Scotty Briggs, as a pall-bearer and a

mourner, occupied a prominent place at the funeral, and when the sermon was finished and the last sentence of the prayer for the dead man's soul ascended, he responded, in a low voice, but with feeling:

"AMEN. No Irish need apply."

As the bulk of the response was without apparent relevancy, it was probably nothing more than a humble tribute to the memory of the friend that was gone; for, as Scotty had once said, it was "his word."

Scotty Briggs, in after days, achieved the distinction of becoming the only convert to religion that was ever gathered from the Virginia roughs; and it transpired that the man who had it in him to espouse the quarrel of the weak out of inborn nobility of spirit was no mean timber whereof to construct a Christian. The making him one did not warp his generosity or diminish his courage; on the contrary it gave intelligent direction to the one and a broader field to the other. If his Sunday-school class progressed faster than the other classes, was it matter for wonder? I think not. He talked to his pioneer small-fry in a language they understood! It was my large privilege, a month before he died, to hear him tell the beautiful story of Joseph and his brethren to his class "without looking at the book." I leave it to the reader to fancy what it was like, as it fell, riddled with slang, from the lips of that grave, earnest teacher, and was listened to by his little learners with a consuming interest that showed that they were as unconscious as he was that any violence was being done to the sacred proprieties!

1872

From *THE GILDED AGE* *

CHAPTER VIII

COL. SELLERS ENTERTAINS WASHINGTON HAWKINS

—Whan þe borde is thynne, as of seruys
   Nought replenesshed with grete diuersi
Of mete & drinke, good chere may the
   suffise
With honest talkyng——
       —*The Book of Curtesy*

MAMMON. Come on, sir. Now, you se
   your foot on shore
In *Novo Orbe;* here's the rich Peru:
And there, within, sir, are the golden mine
Great Solomon's Ophir!——
    —BEN JONSON, *The Alchemis*

The supper at Col. Sellers's was no sumptuous, in the beginning, but improved on acquaintance. That to say, that what Washington regarde at first sight as mere lowly potatoe presently became awe-inspiring agr cultural productions that had bee reared in some ducal garden beyon the sea, under the sacred eye of th duke himself, who had sent them t Sellers; the bread was from cor which could be grown in only on favored locality in the earth and onl a favored few could get it; the R coffee, which at first seemed execrab to the taste, took to itself an improve flavor when Washington was told drink it slowly and not hurry wh should be a lingering luxury in ord to be fully appreciated—it was fro the private stores of a Brazilian nob man with an unrememberable nam The Colonel's tongue was a magiciar wand that turned dried apples in figs and water into wine as easily it could change a hovel into a pala

* Reprinted from *The Gilded Age*, by M Twain and Charles Dudley Warner, 18 and here used by permission of Harper a Brothers, the authorized publishers.

and present poverty into imminent future riches.

Washington slept in a cold bed in a carpetless room and woke up in a palace in the morning; at least the palace lingered during the moment that he was rubbing his eyes and getting his bearings—and then it disappeared and he recognized that the Colonel's inspiring talk had been influencing his dreams. Fatigue had made him sleep late; when he entered the sitting-room he noticed that the old haircloth sofa was absent; when he sat down to breakfast the Colonel tossed six or seven dollars in bills on the table, counted them over, said he was a little short and must call upon his banker; then returned the bills to his wallet with the indifferent air of a man who is used to money. The breakfast was not an improvement upon the supper, but the Colonel talked it up and transformed it into an oriental feast. By and by, he said: "I intend to look out for you, Washington, my boy. I hunted up a place for you yesterday, but I am not referring to that, now—that is a mere livelihood—mere bread and butter; but when I say I mean to look out for you I mean something very different. I mean to put things in our way that will make a mere livelihood a trifling thing. I'll put you in a way to make more money than you'll ever know what to do with. You'll be right here where I can put my hand on you when anything turns up. I've got some prodigious operations on foot; but I'm keeping quiet; mum's the word; your old hand don't go around pow-wowing and letting everybody see his k'yards and find out his little game. But all in good time,

Washington, all in good time. You'll see. Now, there's an operation in corn that looks well. Some New York men are trying to get me to go into it—buy up all the growing crops and just boss the market when they mature—ah, I tell you it's a great thing. And it only costs a trifle; two millions or two and a half will do it. I haven't exactly promised yet—there's no hurry—the more indifferent I seem, you know, the more anxious those fellows will get. And then there is the hog speculation— that's bigger still. We've got quiet men at work" [he was very impressive here] "mousing around, to get propositions out of all the farmers in the whole West and Northwest for the hog crop, and other agents quietly getting propositions and terms out of all the manufacturies—and don't you see, if we can get all the hogs and all the slaughter-houses into our hands on the dead quiet—whew! it would take three ships to carry the money. I've looked into the thing —calculated all the chances for and all the chances against, and though I shake my head and hesitate and keep on thinking, apparently, I've got my mind made up that if the thing can be done on a capital of six millions, that's the horse to put up money on! Why, Washington—but what's the use of talking about it—any man can see that there's whole Atlantic oceans of cash in it, gulfs and bays thrown in. But there's a bigger thing than that, yet—a bigger—"

"Why, Colonel, you can't want anything bigger!" said Washington, his eyes blazing. "Oh, I wish I could go into either of those speculations—I only wish I had money—I wish

I wasn't cramped and kept down and fettered with poverty, and such prodigious chances lying right here in sight! Oh, it is a fearful thing to be poor. But don't throw away those things—they are so splendid and I can see how sure they are. Don't throw them away for something still better and maybe fail in it! I wouldn't, Colonel. I would stick to these. I wish father were here and were his old self again. Oh, he never in his life had such chances as these are. Colonel, you *can't* improve on these—no man can improve on them!"

A sweet, compassionate smile played about the Colonel's features, and he leaned over the table with the air of a man who is "going to show you" and do it without the least trouble:

"Why Washington, my boy, these things are nothing. They *look* large —of course they look large to a novice, but to a man who has been all his life accustomed to large operations—shaw! They're well enough to while away an idle hour with, or furnish a bit of employment that will give a trifle of idle capital a chance to earn its bread while it is waiting for something to *do,* but—now just listen a moment—just let me give you an idea of what we old veterans of commerce call 'business.' Here's the Rothschilds' proposition—this is between you and me, you understand—"

Washington nodded three or four times impatiently, and his glowing eyes said, "Yes, yes—hurry—I understand—"

"—for I wouldn't have it get out for a fortune. They want me to go in with them on the sly—agent was here two weeks ago about it—go in on

the sly" [voice down to an impressiv whisper, now] "and buy up a hun dred and thirteen wildcat banks i Ohio, Indiana, Kentucky, Illinois, an Missouri—notes of these banks are a all sorts of discount now—average dis count of the hundred and thirteen i forty-four per cent.—buy them all u you see, and then all of a sudden le the cat out of the bag! Whiz! th stock of every one of those wildcat would spin up to a tremendou premium before you could turn handspring—profit on the speculatio not a dollar less than forty millions! [An eloquent pause, while the ma velous vision settled into W.'s focus. "Where's your hogs now! Why, m dear innocent boy, we would just si down on the front doorsteps and pec dle banks like lucifer matches!"

Washington finally got his breat and said:

"Oh, it is perfectly wonderful! Wh couldn't these things have happene in father's day? And I—it's of n use—they simply lie before my fac and mock me. There is nothing fc me but to stand helpless and see othe people reap the astonishing harvest.

"Never mind, Washington, don you worry. I'll fix you. There plenty of chances. How much mone have you got?"

In the presence of so many mi lions, Washington could not keep fror blushing when he had to confess th: he had but eighteen dollars in tł world.

"Well, all right—don't despai Other people have been obliged to be gin with less. I have a small id: that may develop into something fc us both, all in good time. Keep yo money close and add to it. I'll mal it breed. I've been experimenting (to pass away the time) on a little preparation for curing sore eyes—a kind of decoction nine-tenths water and the other tenth drugs that don't cost more than a dollar a barrel; I'm still experimenting; there's one ingredient wanted yet to perfect the thing, and somehow I can't just manage to hit upon the thing that's necessary, and I don't dare talk with a chemist, of course. But I'm progressing, and before many weeks I wager the country will ring with the fame of Beriah Sellers's Inafllible Imperial Oriental Optic Liniment and Salvation for Sore Eyes—the Medical Wonder of the Age! Small bottles fifty cents, large ones a dollar. Average cost, five and seven cents for the two sizes. The first year sell, say ten thousand bottles in Missouri, seven thousand in Iowa, three thousand in Arkansas, four thousand in Kentucky, six thousand in Illinois, and say twenty-five thousand in the rest of the country. Total, fifty-five thousand bottles; profit clear of all expenses, twenty thousand dollars at the very lowest calculation. All the capital needed is to manufacture the first two thousand bottles—say a hundred and fifty dollars—then the money would begin to flow in. The second year, sales would reach 200,000 bottles—clear profit, say, $75,000—and in the meantime the great factory would be building in St. Louis, to cost, say, $100,000. The third year we could easily sell 1,000,000 bottles in the United States and—"

"O, splendid!" said Washington. "Let's commence right away—let's—"

"—1,000,000 bottles in the United States—profit at least $350,000—and

then it would begin to be time to turn our attention toward the *real* idea of the business."

"The *real* idea of it! Ain't $350,000 year a pretty real"—

"Stuff! Why, what an infant you are, Washington—what a guileless, short-sighted, easily-contented innocent you are, my poor little country-bred know-nothing! Would I go to all that trouble and bother for the poor crumbs a body might pick up in *this* country? Now do I look like a man who—does my history suggest that I am a man who deals in trifles, contents himself with the narrow horizon that hems in the common herd, sees no further than the end of his nose? Now, *you* know that that is not me—couldn't *be* me. *You* ought to know that if I throw my time and abilities into a patent medicine, it's a patent medicine whose field of operations is the solid earth! its clients the swarming nations that inhabit it! Why what is the republic of America for an eye-water country? Lord bless you, it is nothing but a barren highway that you've got to cross to get *to* the true eye-water market! Why, Washington, in the Oriental countries people swarm like the sands of the desert; every square mile of ground upholds its thousands upon thousands of struggling human creatures—and every separate and individual devil of them's got the ophthalmia! It's as natural to them as noses are—and sin. It's born with them, it stays with them, it's all that some of them have left when they die. Three years of introductory trade in the Orient and what will be the result? Why, our headquarters would be in Constantinople and our hindquarters in Further

India! Factories and warehouses in Cairo, Ispahan, Bagdad, Damascus, Jerusalem, Yedo, Peking, Bangkok, Delhi, Bombay, and Calcutta! Annual income—well, God only knows how many millions and millions apiece!"

Washington was so dazed, so bewildered—his heart and his eyes had wandered so far away among the strange lands beyond the seas, and such avalanches of coin and currency had fluttered and jingled confusedly down before him, that he was now as one who has been whirling round and round for a time, and, stopping all at once, finds his surroundings still whirling and all objects a dancing chaos. However, little by little the Sellers family cooled down and crystallized into shape, and the poor room lost its glitter and resumed its poverty. Then the youth found his voice and begged Sellers to drop everything and hurry up the eye-water; and he got his eighteen dollars and tried to force it upon the Colonel—pleaded with him to take it—implored him to do it. But the Colonel would not; said he would not need the capital (in his native magnificent way he called that eighteen dollars capital) till the eye-water was an accomplished fact. He made Washington easy in his mind, though, by promising that he would call for it just as soon as the invention was finished, and he added the glad tidings that nobody but just they two should be admitted to a share in the speculation.

When Washington left the breakfast table he could have worshiped that man. Washington was one of that kind of people whose hopes are in the very clouds one day, and in the gutter the next. He walked on air now. The Colonel was ready to take him around and introduce him to the employment he had found for him, but Washington begged for a few moments in which to write home; with his kind of people, to ride to-day's new interest to death and put off yesterday's till another time, is nature itself. He ran upstairs and wrote glowingly, enthusiastically, to his mother about the hogs and the corn, the banks and the eye-water—and added a few inconsequential millions to each project. And he said that people little dreamed what a man Col. Sellers was, and that the world would open its eyes when it found out. And he closed his letter thus:

So make yourself perfectly easy mother—in a little while you shall have everything you want, and more. I am not likely to stint you in anything, I fancy. This money will not be for me alone, but for all of us. I want all to share alike; and there is going to be far more for each than one person can spend. Break it to father cautiously—you understand the need of that—break it to him cautiously, for he has had such cruel hard fortune, and is so stricken by it that great good news might prostrate him more surely than even bad, for he is used to the bad but is grown sadly unaccustomed to the other. Tell Laura—tell all the children And write to Clay about it if he is not with you yet. You may tell Clay that whatever I get he can freely share in—freely. He knows that that is true—there will be no need that I should swear to that to make him believe it. Good-bye—and mind what I say: Rest perfectly easy, one and all of you, for our troubles are nearly at an end.

Poor lad, he could not know that his mother would cry some loving,

ompassionate tears over his letter and
out off the family with a synopsis of
ts contents which conveyed a deal
of love to them but not much idea of
his prospects or projects. And he
never dreamed that such a joyful let-
er could sadden her and fill her night
with sighs, and troubled thoughts, and
oodings of the future, instead of filling
t with peace and blessing it with rest-
ul sleep.

When the letter was done, Washing-
on and the Colonel sallied forth, and
as they walked along Washington
earned what he was to be. He was
o be a clerk in a real estate office.
Instantly the fickle youth's dreams
orsook the magic eye-water and flew
oack to the Tennessee Land. And the
gorgeous possibilities of that great
lomain straightway began to occupy
his imagination to such a degree that
he could scarcely manage to keep even
enough of his attention upon the
Colonel's talk to retain the general
un of what he was saying. He was
glad it was a real estate office—he was
a made man now, sure.

The Colonel said that General Boswell was a rich man and had a good
and growing business; and that Wash-
ngton's work would be light and he
would get forty dollars a month and
oe boarded and lodged in the General's
family—which was as good as ten dol-
ars more; and even better, for he
could not live as well even at the
"City Hotel" as he would there, and
yet the hotel charged fifteen dollars
a month where a man had a good
room.

General Boswell was in his office; a
comfortable looking place, with plenty
of outline maps hanging about the
walls and in the windows, and a spec-

tacled man was marking out another
one on a long table. The office was in
the principal street. The General received Washington with a kindly but
reserved politeness. Washington
rather liked his looks. He was about
fifty years old, dignified, well preserved, and well dressed. After the
Colonel took his leave, the General
talked a while with Washington—his
talk consisting chiefly of instructions
about the clerical duties of the place.
He seemed satisfied as to Washington's
ability to take care of the books, he
was evidently a pretty fair theoretical
bookkeeper, and experience would
soon harden theory into practice. By
and by dinner-time came, and the two
walked to the General's house; and
now Washington noticed an instinct
in himself that moved him to keep
not in the General's rear, exactly, but
yet not at his side—somehow the old
gentleman's dignity and reserve did
not inspire familiarity.

1873

From OLD TIMES ON THE
MISSISSIPPI

II

A "CUB" PILOT'S EXPERIENCE, OR, LEARNING THE RIVER

What with lying on the rocks four
days at Louisville, and some other
delays, the poor old *Paul Jones* fooled
away about two weeks in making the
voyage from Cincinnati to New
Orleans. This gave me a chance to
get acquainted with one of the pilots,
and he taught me how to steer the
boat, and thus made the fascination
of river life more potent than ever
for me.

It also gave me a chance to get acquainted with a youth who had taken deck passage—more's the pity; for he easily borrowed six dollars of me on a promise to return to the boat and pay it back to me the day after we should arrive. But he probably died or forgot, for he never came. It was doubtless the former, since he had said his parents were wealthy, and he only traveled deck passage because it was cooler.*

I soon discovered two things. One was that a vessel would not be likely to sail for the mouth of the Amazon under ten or twelve years; and the other was that the nine or ten dollars still left in my pocket would not suffice for so impossible an exploration as I had planned, even if I could afford to wait for a ship. Therefore it followed that I must contrive a new career. The *Paul Jones* was now bound for St. Louis. I planned a siege against my pilot, and at the end of three hard days he surrendered. He agreed to teach me the Mississippi River from New Orleans to St. Louis for five hundred dollars, payable out of the first wages I should receive after graduating. I entered upon the small enterprise of "learning" twelve or thirteen hundred miles of the great Mississippi River with the easy confidence of my time of life. If I had really known what I was about to require of my faculties, I should not have had the courage to begin. I supposed that all a pilot had to do was to keep his boat in the river, and I did not consider that that could be much of a trick, since it was so wide. The boat backed out from New

Orleans at four in the afternoon, and it was "our watch" until eight. Mr. B——, my chief, "straightened her up," plowed her along past the sterns of the other boats that lay at the Levee and then said, "Here, take her; shave those steamships as close as you'd peel an apple." I took the wheel and my heart went down into my boots; for it seemed to me that we were about to scrape the side off every ship in the line, we were so close. I held my breath and began to claw the boat away from the danger; and I had my own opinion of the pilot who had known no better than to get us into such peril, but I was too wise to express it. In half a minute I had a wide margin of safety intervening between the *Paul Jones* and the ships, and within ten seconds more I was set aside in disgrace, and Mr. B—— was going into danger again and flaying me alive with abuse of my cowardice. I was stung, but I was obliged to admire the easy confidence with which my chief loafed from side to side of his wheel, and trimmed the ships so closely that disaster seemed ceaselessly imminent. When he had cooled a little he told me that the easy water was close ashore and the current outside, and therefore we must hug the bank, up-stream, to get the benefit of the former, and stay well out, down-stream, to take advantage of the latter. In my own mind I resolved to be a down-stream pilot and leave the up-streaming to people dead to prudence.

Now and then Mr. B—— called my attention to certain things. Said he, "This is Six-Mile Point." I assented It was pleasant enough information but I could not see the bearing of it

* "Deck" passage—*i. e.*, steerage passage. [Author's note.]

was not conscious that it was a matter of any interest to me. Another time he said, "This is Nine-Mile Point." Later he said, "This is Twelve-Mile Point." They were all about level with the water's edge; they all looked about alike to me; they were monotonously unpicturesque. I hoped Mr. B—— would change the subject. But no; he would crowd up around a point, hugging the shore with affection, and then say: "The slack water ends here, abreast this bunch of Chinarees; now we cross over." So he crossed over. He gave me the wheel once or twice, but I had no luck. I either came near chipping off the edge of a sugar-plantation, or I yawed too far from shore, and so dropped back into disgrace again and got bused.

The watch was ended at last, and we took supper and went to bed. At midnight the glare of a lantern shone in my eyes, and the night watchman said:

"Come, turn out!"

And then he left. I could not understand this extraordinary procedure; so I presently gave up trying to, and dozed off to sleep. Pretty soon the watchman was back again, and this time he was gruff. I was annoyed. I said:

"What do you want to come bothering around here in the middle of the night for? Now, as like as not, I'll not get to sleep again to-night."

The watchman said:

"Well, if this ain't good, I'm blessed."

The "off-watch" was just turning in, and I heard some brutal laughter from them, and such remarks as

"Hello, watchman! an't the new cub turned out yet? He's delicate, likely. Give him some sugar in a rag, and send for the chambermaid to sing rock-a-by baby, to him."

About this time Mr. B—— appeared on the scene. Something like a minute later I was climbing the pilot-house steps with some of my clothes on and the rest in my arms. Mr. B—— was close behind, commenting. Here was something fresh—this thing of getting up in the middle of the night to go to work. It was a detail in piloting that had never occurred to me at all. I knew that boats ran all night, but somehow I had never happened to reflect that somebody had to get up out of a warm bed to run them. I began to fear that piloting was not quite so romantic as I had imagined it was; there was something very real and work-like about this new phase of it.

It was a rather dingy night, although a fair number of stars were out. The big mate was at the wheel, and he had the old tub pointed at a star and was holding her straight up the middle of the river. The shores on either hand were not much more than half a mile apart, but they seemed wonderfully far away and ever so vague and indistinct. The mate said:—

"We've got to land at Jones's plantation, sir."

The vengeful spirit in me exulted. I said to myself, "I wish you joy of your job, Mr. B——; you'll have a good time finding Mr. Jones's plantation such a night as this; and I hope you never *will* find it as long as you live."

Mr. B—— said to the mate:

"Upper end of the plantation, or the lower?"

"Upper."

"I can't do it. The stumps there are out of water at this stage. It's no great distance to the lower, and you'll have to get along with that."

"All right, sir. If Jones don't like it, he'll have to lump it, I reckon."

And then the mate left. My exultation began to cool and my wonder to come up. Here was a man who not only proposed to find this plantation on such a night, but to find either end of it you preferred. I dreadfully wanted to ask a question, but I was carrying about as many short answers as my cargo-room would admit of, so I held my peace. All I desired to ask Mr. B—— was the simple question whether he was ass enough to really imagine he was going to find that plantation on a night when all plantations were exactly alike and all of the same color. But I held in. I used to have fine inspirations of prudence in those days.

Mr. B—— made for the shore and soon was scraping it, just the same as if it had been daylight. And not only that, but singing:

"Father in heaven, the day is declining," etc.

It seemed to me that I had put my life in the keeping of a peculiarly reckless outcast. Presently he turned on me and said:

"What's the name of the first point above New Orleans?"

I was gratified to be able to answer promptly, and I did. I said I didn't know.

"Don't *know?*"

This manner jolted me. I was

down at the foot again, in a moment But I had to say just what I had said before.

"Well, you're a smart one!" said Mr. B——. "What's the name of the *next* point?"

Once more I didn't know.

"Well, this beats anything. Tell me the name of *any* point or place I told you."

I studied awhile and decided that I couldn't.

"Look-a-here! What do you start out from, above Twelve-Mile Point to cross over?"

"I—I—don't know."

"You—you—don't know?" mimicking my drawling manner of speech "What *do* you know?"

"I—I—nothing, for certain."

"By the great Cæsar's ghost, I believe you! You're the stupidest dunderhead I ever saw or ever heard of, so help me Moses! The idea of *you* being a pilot—*you!* Why, you don't know enough to pilot a cow down a lane."

Oh, but his wrath was up! He was a nervous man, and he shuffled from one side of his wheel to the other as if the floor was hot. He would boil awhile to himself, and then overflow and scald me again.

"Look-a-here! What do you suppose I told you the names of those points for?"

I tremblingly considered a moment and then the devil of temptation provoked me to say:

"Well to—to—be entertaining, I thought."

This was a red rag to the bull. He raged and stormed so (he was crossing the river at the time) that I judged it made him blind, because he ran over the steering-oar of a trading-scow. Of course the traders sent up a volley of red-hot profanity. Never was a man so grateful as Mr. B—— was; because he was brim full, and here were subjects who could *talk back*. He threw open a window, thrust his head out, and such an iruption followed as I never had heard before. The fainter and farther away the scowmen's curses drifted, the higher Mr. B—— lifted his voice and he weightier his adjectives grew. When he closed the window he was empty. You could have drawn a seine through his system and not caught curses enough to disturb your mother with. Presently he said to me in the gentlest way:

"My boy, you must get a little memorandum-book; and every time I tell you a thing, put it down right away. There's only one way to be a pilot, and that is to get this entire river by heart. You have to know it just like A B C."

That was a dismal revelation to me; for my memory was never loaded with anything but blank cartridges. However, I did not feel discouraged long. I judged that it was best to make some allowances, for doubtless Mr. B—— was "stretching." Presently he pulled a rope and struck a few strokes on the big bell. The stars were all gone now, and the night was as black as ink. I could hear the wheels churn along the bank, but I was not entirely certain that I could see the shore. The voice of the invisible watchman called up from the hurricane-deck:

"What's this, sir?"

"Jones's plantation."

I said to myself, "I wish I might venture to offer a small bet that it isn't." But I did not chirp. I only waited to see. Mr. B—— handled the engine-bells, and in due time the boat's nose came to the land, a torch glowed from the forecastle, a man skipped ashore, a darky's voice on the bank said: "Gimme de carpet-bag, Mars' Jones," and the next moment we were standing up the river again, all serene. I reflected deeply awhile, and then said,—but not aloud,—Well, the finding of that plantation was the luckiest accident that ever happened; but it couldn't happen again in a hundred years. And I fully believed it *was* an accident, too.

By the time we had gone seven or eight hundred miles up the river, I had learned to be a tolerably plucky up-stream steersman, in daylight; and before we reached St. Louis I had made a trifle of progress in night work, but only a trifle. I had a note-book that fairly bristled with the names of towns, "points," bars, islands, bends, reaches, etc.; but the information was to be found only in the note-book—none of it was in my head. It made my heart ache to think I had only got half of the river set down; for as our watch was four hours off and four hours on, day and night, there was a long four-hour gap in my book for every time I had slept since the voyage began.

My chief was presently hired to go on a big New Orleans boat, and I packed my satchel and went with him. She was a grand affair. When I stood in her pilot-house I was so far above the water that I seemed perched on a mountain; and her decks stretched so far away, fore and aft, below me, that I wondered how I could ever have

considered the little *Paul Jones* a large
craft. There were other differences,
too. The *Paul Jones's* pilot-house was
a cheap, dingy, battered rattle-trap,
cramped for room: but here was a
sumptuous glass temple; room enough
to have a dance in; showy red and
gold window-curtains; an imposing
sofa; leather cushions and a back to
the high bench where visiting pilots sit, 10
to spin yarns and "look at the river;"
bright, fanciful "cuspadores," instead
of a broad wooden box filled with sawdust; nice new oil-cloth on the floor;
a hospitable big stove for winter; a
wheel as high as my head, costly with
inlaid work; a wire tiller-rope; bright
brass knobs for the bells; and a tidy,
white-aproned, black "texas-tender,"
to bring up tarts and ices and coffee 20
during the mid-watch, day and night.
Now this was "something like;" and
so I began to take heart once more to
believe that piloting was a romantic
sort of occupation after all. The moment we were under way I began to
prowl about the great steamer and fill
myself with joy. She was as clean
and as dainty as a drawing-room;
when I looked down her long, gilded 30
saloon, it was like gazing through a
splendid tunnel; she had an oil-picture,
by some gifted sign-painter, on every
state-room door; she glittered with
no end of prism-fringed chandeliers;
the clerk's office was elegant, the bar
was marvelous, and the bar-keeper had
been barbered and upholstered at incredible cost. The boiler-deck (*i.e.*,
the second story of the boat, so to 40
speak) was as spacious as a church, it
seemed to me; so with the forecastle;
and there was no pitiful handful of
deck-hands, firemen, and roustabouts
down there, but a whole battalion of

men. The fires were fiercely glarin
from a long row of furnaces, and ove
them were eight huge boilers! Thi
was unutterable pomp. The might
engines—but enough of this. I ha
never felt so fine before. And whe
I found that the regiment of natt
servants respectfully "sir'd" me, m
satisfaction was complete.

When I returned to the pilot-hous
St. Louis was gone and I was los
Here was a piece of river which wa
all down in my book, but I coul
make neither head nor tail of it: yo
understand, it was turned around.
had seen it when coming up-stream
but I had never faced about to se
how it looked when it was behind me
My heart broke again, for it was plai
that I had got to learn this trouble
some river *both ways*.

The pilot-house was full of pilots
going down to "look at the river.
What is called the "upper river" (th
two hundred miles between St. Loui
and Cairo, where the Ohio comes in
was low; and the Mississippi change
its channel so constantly that the pilot
used to always find it necessary t
run down to Cairo to take a fres
look, when their boats were to lie i
port a week, that is, when th
water was at a low stage. A deal o
this "looking at the river" was don
by poor fellows who seldom had
berth, and whose only hope of gettin
one lay in their being always freshl
posted and therefore ready to dro
into the shoes of some reputable pilot
for a single trip, on account of suc
pilot's sudden illness, or some othe
necessity. And a good many of then
constantly ran up and down inspectin
the river, not because they ever reall
hoped to get a berth, but becaus

(they being guests of the boat) it was cheaper to "look at the river" than stay ashore and pay board. In time these fellows grew dainty in their tastes, and only infested boats that had an established reputation for setting good tables. All visiting pilots were useful, for they were always ready and willing, winter or summer, night or day, to go out in the yawl and help buoy the channel or assist the boat's pilots in any way they could. They were likewise welcomed because all pilots are tireless talkers, when gathered together, and as they talk only about the river they are always understood and are always interesting. Your true pilot cares nothing about anything on earth but the river, and his pride in his occupation surpasses the pride of kings.

We had a fine company of these river inspectors along this trip. There were eight or ten; and there was abundance of room for them in our great pilot-house. Two or three of them wore polished silk hats, elaborate shirt-fronts, diamond breastpins, kid gloves, and patent-leather boots. They were choice in their English, and bore themselves with a dignity proper to men of solid means and prodigious reputation as pilots. The others were more or less loosely clad, and wore upon their heads tall felt cones that were suggestive of the days of the Commonwealth.

I was a cipher in this august company, and felt subdued, not to say torpid. I was not even of sufficient consequence to assist at the wheel when it was necessary to put the tiller hard down in a hurry; the guest that stood nearest did that when oc-

casion required—and this was pretty much all the time, because of the crookedness of the channel and the scant water. I stood in a corner; and the talk I listened to took the hope all out of me. One visitor said to another:

"Jim, how did you run Plum Point, coming up?"

"It was in the night, there, and I ran it the way one of the boys on the *Diana* told me; started out about fifty yards above the wood-pile on the false point, and held on the cabin under Plum Point till I raised the reef—quarter less twain—then straightened up for the middle bar till I got well abreast the old one-limbed cotton-wood in the bend, then got my stern on the cotton-wood, and head on the low place above the point, and came through a-booming—nine and a half."

"Pretty square crossing, an't it?"

"Yes, but the upper bar's working down fast."

Another pilot spoke up and said:

"I had better water than that, and ran it lower down; started out from the false point—mark twain—raised the second reef abreast the big snag in the bend, and had quarter less twain."

One of the gorgeous ones remarked:

"I don't want to find fault with your leadsmen, but that's a good deal of water for Plum Point, it seems to me."

There was an approving nod all around as this quiet snub dropped on the boaster and "settled" him. And so they went on talk-talk-talking. Meantime, the thing that was running in my mind was, "Now if my ears hear aright, I have not only to get the names of all the towns and islands and bends, and so on, by heart, but I must even get up a warm personal acquaintanceship with every old snag and one-limbed cotton-wood and obscure wood-pile that ornaments the banks of this river for twelve hundred miles; and more than that, I must actually know where these things are in the dark, unless these guests are gifted with eyes that can pierce through two miles of solid blackness. I wish the piloting business was in Jericho and I had never thought of it."

At dusk Mr. B—— tapped the big bell three times (the signal to land), and the captain emerged from his drawing-room in the forward end of the "texas," and looked up inquiringly. Mr. B—— said:

"We will lay up here all night, captain."

"Very well, sir."

That was all. The boat came to shore and was tied up for the night. It seemed to me a fine thing that the pilot could do as he pleased, without asking so grand a captain's permission. I took my supper and went immediately to bed, discouraged by my day's observations and experiences. My late voyage's note-booking was but a confusion of meaningless names. It had tangled me all up in a knot every time I had looked at it in the daytime. I now hoped for respite in sleep; but no, it reveled all through my head till sunrise again, a frantic and tireless nightmare.

Next morning I felt pretty rusty and low-spirited. We went booming along, taking a good many chances, for we were anxious to "get out of the river" (as getting out to Cairo was called) before night should overtake us. But Mr. B——'s partner, the other pilot, presently grounded the boat, and we lost so much time getting her off that it was plain the darkness would overtake us a good long way above the mouth. This was a great misfortune, especially to certain of our visiting pilots, whose boats would have to wait for their return, no matter how long that might be. It sobered the pilot-house talk a good deal. Coming up-stream pilots did not mind low water or any kind of darkness; nothing stopped them but fog. But down-stream work was different; a boat was too nearly helpless, with a stiff current pushing behind her; so it was not customary to run down-stream at night in low water.

There seemed to be one small hope, however: if we could get through the intricate and dangerous Hat Island crossing before night, we could venture the rest, for we would have plainer sailing and better water. But it would be insanity to attempt Hat Island at night. So there was a deal of looking at watches all the rest of the day, and a constant ciphering upon the speed we were making; Hat Island was the eternal subject; sometimes hope was high and sometimes we were delayed in a bad crossing, and down it went again. For hours all hands lay under the burden of this suppressed excitement; it was even communicated to me, and I got to feeling so solicitous about Hat Island, and under such an awful pressure of responsibility, that I wished I might have five minutes on shore to draw a good, full, relieving breath, and start over again. We were standing no regular watches. Each of our pilots ran such portions of the river as he had run when coming up-stream, because of his greater familiarity with it; but both remained in the pilot-house constantly.

An hour before sunset Mr. B—— took the wheel, and Mr. W—— stepped aside. For the next thirty minutes every man held his watch in his hand and was restless, silent, and uneasy. At last somebody said, with a doomful sigh.

"Well, yonder's Hat Island—and we can't make it."

All the watches closed with a snap, everybody sighed and muttered something about its being "too bad, too bad—ah, if we could *only* have got here half an hour sooner!" and the place was thick with the atmosphere of disappointment. Some started to go out, but loitered, hearing no bell-tap to land. The sun dipped behind the horizon, the boat went on. Inquiring looks passed from one guest to another; and one who had his hand on the door-knob, and had turned it, waited, then presently took away his hand, then let the knob turn back again. We bore steadily down the bend. More looks were exchanged, and nods of surprised admiration—but no words. Insensibly the men drew together behind Mr. B——, as the sky darkened and one or two dim stars came out. The dead silence and sense of waiting became oppressive. Mr. B—— pulled the cord, and two deep, mellow notes from the big bell floated off on the night. Then a pause, and one more note was struck. The watchman's voice followed, from the hurricane-deck:

"Labboard lead, there! Stabboard lead!"

The cries of the leadsmen began to rise out of the distance, and were gruffly repeated by the word-passers on the hurricane-deck.

"M-a-r-k three! M-a-r-k three! Quarter-less-three! Half twain! Quarter twain! M-a-r-k twain! Quarter-less—"

Mr. B—— pulled two bell-ropes, and was answered by faint jinglings far below in the engine-room, and our speed slackened. The steam began to whistle through the gauge-cocks. The cries of the leadsmen went on—and it is a weird sound, always, in the night. Every pilot in the lot was watching, now, with fixed eyes, and talking under his breath. Nobody was calm and easy but Mr. B——. He would put his wheel down and stand on a spoke, and as the steamer swung into her (to me) utterly invisible marks —for we seemed to be in the midst of a wide and gloomy sea—he would meet and fasten her there. Talk was going on, now, in low voices:—

"There; she's over the first reef all right!"

After a pause, another subdued voice:—

"Her stern's coming down just *exactly* right, by *George!*"

"Now she's in the marks; over she goes!"

Somebody else muttered:—

"Oh, it was done beautiful—*beautiful!*"

Now the engines were stopped altogether, and we drifted with the current. Not that I could see the boat drift, for I could not, the stars being all gone by this time. This drifting was the dismalest work; it held one's heart still. Presently I discovered a blacker gloom than that which surrounded us. It was the head of the island. We were closing right down upon it. We entered its deeper shadow, and so imminent seemed the peril that I was likely to suffocate; and I had the strongest impulse to do *something*, anything, to save the vessel. But still Mr. B—— stood by his wheel, silent, intent as a cat, and all the pilots stood shoulder to shoulder at his back.

"She'll not make it!" somebody whispered.

The water grew shoaler and shoaler by the leadsman's cries, till it was down to:

"Eight-and-a-half! E-i-g-h-t feet! E-i-g-h-t feet! Seven-and—"

Mr. B—— said warningly through his speaking-tube to the engineer:

"Stand by, now!"

"Aye, aye, sir!"

"Seven-and-a-half! Seven feet! *Six*-and—"

We touched bottom! Instantly Mr. B—— set a lot of bells ringing, shouted through the tube, *"Now,* let her have it—every ounce you've got!" then to his partner, "Put her hard down! snatch her! snatch her!" The boat rasped and ground her way through the sand, hung upon the apex of disaster a single tremendous instant, and then over she went! And such a shout as went up at Mr. B——'s back never loosened the roof of a pilot-house before!

There was no more trouble after that. Mr. B—— was a hero that night; and it was some little time, too, before his exploit ceased to be talked about by river-men.

Fully to realize the marvelous precision required in laying the great steamer in her marks in that murky waste of water, one should know that not only must she pick her intricate way through snags and blind reefs, and then shave the head of the island so closely as to brush the overhanging foliage with her stern, but at one place she must pass almost within arm's reach of a sunken and invisible wreck that would snatch the hull timbers from under her if she should strike it, and destroy a quarter of a million dollars' worth of steamboat and cargo in five minutes, and maybe a hundred and fifty human lives into the bargain.

The last remark I heard that night was a compliment to Mr. B——, uttered in soliloquy and with unction by one of our guests. He said:—

"By the Shadow of Death, but he's a lightning pilot!"

1875

From *THE ADVENTURES OF HUCKLEBERRY FINN* *

CHAPTER XVI

[WE MISS CAIRO]

We slept most all day, and started out at night, a little ways behind a monstrous long raft that was as long going by as a procession. She had four long sweeps at each end, so we judged she carried as many as thirty men, likely. She had five big wigwams aboard, wide apart, and an open camp-fire in the middle, and a tall flag-pole at each end. There was a

* From *The Adventures of Huckleberry Finn,* by Mark Twain, 1884, and here used by permission of Harper and Brothers, the authorized publishers.

power of style about her. It *amounted* to something being a raftsman on such a craft as that.

We went drifting down into a big bend, and the night clouded up and got hot. The river was very wide, and was walled with solid timber on both sides; you couldn't see a break in it hardly ever, or a light. We talked about Cairo, and wondered whether we would know it when we got to it. I said likely we wouldn't, because I had heard say there warn't but about a dozen houses there, and if they didn't happen to have them lit up, how was we going to know we was passing a town? Jim said if the two big rivers joined together there, that would show. But I said maybe we might think we was passing the foot of an island and coming into the same old river again. That disturbed Jim—and me too. So the question was, what to do? I said, paddle ashore the first time a light showed, and tell them pap was behind, coming along with a trading-scow, and was a green hand at the business, and wanted to know how far it was to Cairo. Jim thought it was a good idea, so we took a smoke on it and waited.

There warn't nothing to do now but to look out sharp for the town, and not pass it without seeing it. He said he'd be mighty sure to see it, because he'd be a free man the minute he seen it, but if he missed it he'd be in a slave country again and no more show for freedom. Every little while he jumps up and says:

"Dah she is?"

But it warn't. It was Jack-o'-lanterns, or lightning-bugs; so he set down again, and went to watching, same as before. Jim said it made him all over trembly and feverish to be so close to freedom. Well, I can tell you it made me all over trembly and feverish, too, to hear him, because I begun to get it through my head that he *was* most free—and who was to blame for it? Why, *me*. I couldn't get that out of my conscience, no how nor no way. It got to troubling me so I couldn't rest; I couldn't stay still in one place. It hadn't ever come home to me before, what this thing was that I was doing. But now it did; and it stayed with me, and scorched me more and more. I tried to make out to myself that *I* warn't to blame, because *I* didn't run Jim off from his rightful owner; but it warn't no use, conscience up and says, every time, "But you knowed he was running for his freedom, and you could 'a' paddled ashore and told somebody." That was so—I couldn't get around that no way. That was where it pinched. Conscience says to me, "What had poor Miss Watson done to you that you could see her nigger go off right under your eyes and never say one single word? What did that poor old woman do to you that you could treat her so mean? Why, she tried to learn you your book, she tried to learn you your manners, she tried to be good to you every way she knowed how. *That's* what she done."

I got to feeling so mean and so miserable I most wished I was dead. I fidgeted up and down the raft, abusing myself to myself, and Jim was fidgeting up and down past me. We neither of us could keep still. Every time he danced around and says, "Dah's Cairo!" it went through me like a shot, and I thought if it *was* Cairo I reckoned I would die of miserableness.

Jim talked out loud all the time while I was talking to myself. He was saying how the first thing he would do when he got to a free state he would go to saving up money and never spend a single cent, and when he got enough he would buy his wife, which was owned on a farm close to where Miss Watson lived; and then they would both work to buy the two children, and if their master wouldn't sell them, they'd get an Ab'litionist to go and steal them.

It most froze me to hear such talk. He wouldn't ever dared to talk such talk in his life before. Just see what a difference it made in him the minute he judged he was about free. It was according to the old saying, "Give a nigger an inch and he'll take an ell." Thinks I, this is what comes of my not thinking. Here was this nigger, which I had as good as helped to run away, coming right out flat-footed and saying he would steal his children— children that belonged to a man I didn't even know; a man that hadn't ever done me no harm.

I was sorry to hear Jim say that, it was such a lowering of him. My conscience got to stirring me up hotter than ever, until at last I says to it, "Let up on me—it ain't too late yet —I'll paddle ashore at the first light and tell." I felt easy and happy and light as a feather right off. All my troubles was gone. I went to looking out sharp for a light, and sort of singing to myself. By and by one showed. Jim sings out:

"We's safe, Huck, we's safe! Jump up and crack yo' heels! Dat's de good ole Cairo at las', I jis knows it!"

I says:

"I'll take the canoe and go and see, Jim. It mightn't be, you know."

He jumped and got the canoe ready, and put his old coat in the bottom for me to set on, and give me the paddle; and as I shoved off, he says:

"Pooty soon I'll be a-shout'n' for joy, en I'll say, it's all on accounts o' Huck; I's a free man, en I couldn't ever ben free ef it hadn' ben for Huck; Huck done it. Jim won't ever forgit you, Huck; you's de bes' fren' Jim's ever had; en you's de *only* fren' ole Jim's got now."

I was paddling off, all in a sweat to tell on him; but when he says this, it seemed to kind of take the tuck all out of me. I went along slow then, and I warn't right down certain whether I was glad I started or whether I warn't. When I was fifty yards off, Jim says:

"Dah you goes, de ole true Huck; de on'y white genlman dat ever kep' his promise to ole Jim."

Well, I just felt sick. But I says, I *got* to do it—I can't get *out* of it. Right then along comes a skiff with two men in it with guns, and they stopped and I stopped. One of them says:

"What's that yonder?"

"A piece of a raft," I says.

"Do you belong on it?"

"Yes, sir."

"Any men on it?"

"Only one, sir."

"Well, there's five niggers run off to-night up yonder, above the head of the bend. Is your man white or black?"

I didn't answer up prompt. I tried

to, but the words wouldn't come. I tried for a second or two to brace up and out with it, but I warn't man enough—hadn't the spunk of a rabbit. I see I was weakening; so I just give up trying, and up and says:

"He's white."

"I reckon we'll go and see for ourselves."

"I wish you would," says I, "because it's pap that's there, and maybe you'd help me tow the raft ashore where the light is. He's sick—and so is mam and Mary Ann."

"Oh, the devil! we're in a hurry, boy. But I s'pose we've got to. Come, buckle to your paddle, and let's get along."

I buckled to my paddle and they laid to their oars. When we had made a stroke or two, I says:

"Pap'll be mighty much obleeged to you, I can tell you. Everybody goes away when I want them to help me tow the raft ashore, and I can't do it by myself."

"Well, that's infernal mean. Odd, too. Say, boy, what's the matter with your father?"

"It's the—a—the—well, it ain't anything much."

They stopped pulling. It warn't but a mighty little ways to the raft now. One says:

"Boy, that's a lie. What *is* the matter with your pap? Answer up square now, and it'll be the better for you."

"I will, sir, I will, honest—but don't leave us, please. It's the—the— Gentlemen, if you'll only pull ahead, and let me heave you the headline, you won't have to come a-near the raft—please do."

"Set her back, John, set her back!"

says one. They backed water. "Keep away, boy—keep to looard. Confound it, I just expect the wind has blowed it to us. Your pap's got the small-pox, and you know it precious well. Why didn't you come out and say so? Do you want to spread it all over?"

"Well," says I, a-blubbering, "I've told everybody before, and they just went away and left us."

"Poor devil, there's something in that. We are right down sorry for you, but we—well, hang it, we don't want the smallpox, you see. Look here, I'll tell you what to do. Don't you try to land by yourself, or you'll smash everything to pieces. You float along down about twenty miles, and you'll come to a town on the left-hand side of the river. It will be long after sun-up then, and when you ask for help you tell them your folks are all down with chills and fever. Don't be a fool again, and let people guess what is the matter. Now we're trying to do you a kindness; so you just put twenty miles between us, that's a good boy. It wouldn't do any good to land yonder where the light is—it's only a wood-yard. Say, I reckon your father's poor, and I'm bound to say he's in pretty hard luck. Here, I'll put a twenty-dollar gold piece on this board, and you get it when it floats by. I feel mighty mean to leave you; but my kingdom! it won't do to fool with smallpox, don't you see?"

"Hold on, Parker," says the man, "here's a twenty to put on the board for me. Good-by, boy; you do as Mr. Parker told you, and you'll be all right."

"That's so, my boy—good-by, good-by. If you see any runaway niggers you get help and nab them, and you can make some money by it."

"Good-by, sir," says I; "I won't let no runaway niggers get by me if I can help it."

They went off and I got aboard the raft, feeling bad and low, because I knowed very well I had done wrong, and I see it warn't no use for me to try to learn to do right; a body that don't get *started* right when he's little ain't got no show—when the pinch comes there ain't nothing to back him up and keep him to his work, and so he gets beat. Then I thought a minute, and says to myself, hold on; s'pose you'd 'a' done right and give Jim up, would you felt better than what you do now? No, says I, I'd feel bad—I'd feel just the same way I do now. Well, then, says I, what's the use you learning to do right when it's troublesome to do right and ain't no trouble to do wrong, and the wages is just the same? I was stuck. I couldn't answer that. So I reckoned I wouldn't bother no more about it, but after this always do whichever come handiest at the time.

I went into the wigwam; Jim warn't there. I looked all around; he warn't anywhere. I says:

"Jim!"

"Here I is, Huck. Is dey out o' sight yit? Don't talk loud."

He was in the river under the stern oar, with just his nose out. I told him they were out of sight, so he come aboard. He says:

"I was a-listenin' to all de talk, en I slips into de river en was gwyne to shove for sho' if dey come aboard. Den I was gwyne to swim to de raf'

agin when dey was gone. But lawsy, how you did fool 'em, Huck! Dat *wuz* de smartes' dodge! I tell you, chile, I 'spec it save' ole Jim—ole Jim ain't going to forgit you for dat, honey."

Then we talked about the money. It was a pretty good raise—twenty dollars apiece. Jim said we could take deck passage on a steamboat now, and the money would last us as far as we wanted to go in the free states. He said twenty mile more warn't far for the raft to go, but he wished we was already there.

Towards daybreak we tied up, and Jim was mighty particular about hiding the raft good. Then he worked all day fixing things in bundles, and getting all ready to quit rafting.

That night about ten we hove in sight of the lights of a town away down in a left-hand bend.

I went off in the canoe to ask about it. Pretty soon I found a man out in the river with a skiff, setting a trotline. I ranged up and says:

"Mister, is that town Cairo?"

"Cairo? no. You must be a blame' fool."

"What town is it, mister?"

"If you want to know, go and find out. If you stay here botherin' around me for about a half a minute longer you'll get something you won't want."

I paddled to the raft. Jim was awful disappointed, but I said never mind, Cairo would be the next place, I reckoned.

We passed another town before daylight, and I was going out again; but it was high ground, so I didn't go. No high ground about Cairo, Jim said. I had forgot it. We laid up for the day on a towhead tolerable close to the left-hand bank. I begun to suspicion something. So did Jim. I says:

"Maybe we went by Cairo in the fog that night."

He says:

"Doan' le's talk about it, Huck. Po' niggers can't have no luck. I awluz 'spected dat rattlesnake-skin warn't done wid its work."

"I wish I'd never seen that snake-kin, Jim—I do wish I'd never laid eyes on it."

"It ain't yo' fault, Huck; you didn't know. Don't you blame yo'self bout it."

When it was daylight, here was the clear Ohio water inshore, sure enough, and outside was the old regular Muddy! So it was all up with Cairo.

We talked it all over. It wouldn't do to take to the shore; we couldn't take the raft up the stream, of course. There warn't no way but to wait for dark, and start back in the canoe and take the chances. So we slept all day amongst the cotton-wood thicket, so as to be fresh for the work, and when we went back to the raft about dark the canoe was gone!

We didn't say a word for a good while. There warn't anything to say. We both knowed well enough it was some more work of the rattlesnake-skin; so what was the use to talk bout it? It would only look like we was finding fault, and that would be bound to fetch more bad luck—and keep on fetching it, too, till we knowed enough to keep still.

By and by we talked about what we better do, and found there warn't no way but just to go along down with the raft till we got a chance to buy a canoe to go back in. We warn't going to borrow it when there warn't anybody around, the way pap would do, for that might set people after us.

So we shoved out after dark on the raft.

Anybody that don't believe yet that it's foolishness to handle a snake-skin, after all that that snake-skin done for us, will believe it now if they read of and see what more it done for us.

The place to buy canoes is off of rafts laying up at shore. But we didn't see no rafts laying up; so we went along during three hours and more. Well, the night got gray and ruther thick, which is the next meanest thing to fog. You can't tell the shape of the river, and you can't see no distance. It got to be very late and still, and then along comes a steamboat up the river. We lit the lantern, and judged she would see it. Up-stream boats didn't generly come close to us; they go out and follow the bars and hunt for easy water under the reefs; but nights like this they bull right up the channel against the whole river.

We could hear her pounding along, but we didn't see her good till she was close. She aimed right for us. Often they do that and try to see how close they can come without touching; sometimes the wheel bites off a sweep, and then the pilot sticks his head out and laughs, and thinks he's mighty smart. Well, here she comes, and we said she was going to try and shave us; but she didn't seem to be sheering off a bit. She was a big one, and she was coming in a hurry, too, looking like a black cloud with rows of glow-worms around it; but all of a sudden she bulged out, big and scary, with a long row of wide-open furnace doors shining like red-hot teeth, and her monstrous bows and guards hanging right over us. There was a yell at us, and a jingling of bells to stop the engines, a powwow of cussing, and whistling of steam—and as Jim went overboard on one side and I on the other, she come smashing straight through the raft.

I dived—and I aimed to find the bottom, too, for a thirty-foot wheel had got to go over me, and I wanted it to have plenty of room. I could always stay under water a minute; this time I reckon I stayed under a minute and a half. Then I bounced for the top in a hurry, for I was nearly busting. I popped out to my armpits and blowed the water out of my nose, and puffed a bit. Of course there was a booming current; and of course that boat started her engines again ten seconds after she stopped them, for they never cared much for raftsmen; so now she was churning along up the river, out of sight in the thick weather, though I could hear her.

I sung out for Jim about a dozen times, but I didn't get any answer; so I grabbed a plank that touched me while I was "treading water," and struck out for shore, shoving it ahead of me. But I made out to see that the drift of the current was towards the left-hand shore, which meant that I was in a crossing; so I changed off and went that way.

It was one of these long, slanting, two-mile crossings; so I was a good long time in getting over. I made a safe landing, and clumb up the bank.

I couldn't see but a little ways, bu I went poking along over roug ground for a quarter of a mile c more, and then I run across a bi old-fashioned double log house befor I noticed it. I was going to rush b and get away, but a lot of dog jumped out and went to howling an barking at me, and I knowed bette than to move another peg.

CHAPTER XIX

[HIS LORDSHIP AND HIS GRACE]

Two or three days and nights wer by; I reckon I might say they swu by, they slid along so quiet an smooth and lovely. Here is the wa we put in the time. It was a mon strous big river down there—som times a mile and a half wide; we ru nights, and laid up and hid daytimes soon as night was most gone w stopped navigating and tied up nearly always in the dead water un der a towhead; and then cut your cotton-woods and willows, and hid th raft with them. Then we set ov the lines. Next we slid into the riv and had a swim, so as to freshen u and cool off; then we set down o the sandy bottom where the wat was about knee-deep, and watched th daylight come. Not a sound an wheres—perfectly still—just like th whole world was asleep, only som times the bullfrogs a-cluttering, mayb The first thing to see, looking awa over the water, was a kind of du line—that was the woods on t'oth side; you couldn't make nothing el out; then a pale place in the sk then more paleness spreading aroun then the river softened up away o nd warn't black any more, but gray; ou could see little dark spots drifting along ever so far away—trading-cows, and such things; and long black streaks—rafts; sometimes you could hear a sweep screaking; or jumbled-up voices, it was so still, and sounds come so far; and by and by you could see a streak on the water which you know by the look of the streak that there's a snag there in a swift current which breaks on it and makes that streak look that way; and you see the mist curl up off of the water, and the east reddens up, and the river, and you make out a log cabin in the edge of the woods, away on the bank on t'other side of the river, being a wood-yard, likely, and piled by them cheats so you can throw a dog through it anywheres; then the nice breeze springs up, and comes fanning you from over there, so cool and fresh and sweet to smell on account of the woods and the flowers; but sometimes not that way, because they've left dead fish laying around, gars and such, and they do get pretty rank; and next you've got the full day, and everything smiling in the sun, and the song-birds just going it!

A little smoke couldn't be noticed now, so we would take some fish off of the lines and cook up a hot breakfast. And afterwards we would watch the lonesomeness of the river, and kind of lazy along, and by and by lazy off to sleep. Wake up by and by, and look to see what done it, and maybe see a steamboat coughing along up-stream, so far off towards the other side you couldn't tell nothing about her only whether she was a stern-wheel or side-wheel; then

for about an hour there wouldn't be nothing to hear nor nothing to see— just solid lonesomeness. Next you'd see a raft sliding by, away off yonder, and maybe a galoot on it chopping, because they're most always doing it on a raft; you'd see the ax flash and come down—you don't hear nothing; you see that ax go up again, and by the time it's above the man's head then you hear the *k'chunk!*—it had took all that time to come over the water. So we would put in the day, lazying around, listening to the stillness. Once there was a thick fog, and the rafts and things that went by was beating tin pans so the steamboats wouldn't run over them. A scow or a raft went by so close we could hear them talking and cussing and laughing—heard them plain; but we couldn't see no sign of them; it made you feel crawly; it was like spirits carrying on that way in the air. Jim said he believed it was spirits; but I says:

"No, spirits wouldn't say, 'Dern the dern fog.'"

Soon as it was night out we shoved; when we got her out to about the middle we let her alone, and let her float wherever the current wanted her to; then we lit the pipes, and dangled our legs in the water, and talked about all kinds of things—we was always naked, day and night, whenever the mosquitoes would let us—the new clothes Buck's folks made for me was too good to be comfortable, and besides I didn't go much on clothes, nohow.

Sometimes we'd have that whole river all to ourselves for the longest time. Yonder was the banks and the islands, across the water; and maybe a spark—which was a candle in a cabin window; and sometimes on the water you could see a spark or two —on a raft or a scow, you know; and maybe you could hear a fiddle or a song coming over from one of them crafts: It's lovely to live on a raft. We had the sky up there, all speckled with stars, and we used to lay on our backs and look up at them, and discuss about whether they was made or only just happened. Jim he allowed they was made, but I allowed they happened; I judged it would have took too long to *make* so many. Jim said the moon could 'a' *laid* them; well, that looked kind of reasonable, so I didn't say nothing against it, because I've seen a frog lay most as many, so of course it could be done. We used to watch the stars that fell, too, and see them streak down. Jim allowed they'd got spoiled and was hove out of the nest.

Once or twice of a night we would see a steamboat slipping along in the dark, and now and then she would belch a whole world of sparks up out of her chimbleys, and they would rain down in the river and look awful pretty; then she would turn a corner and her lights would wink out and her powwow shut off and leave the river still again; and by and by her waves would get to us, a long time after she was gone, and joggle the raft a bit, and after that you wouldn't hear nothing for you couldn't tell how long, except maybe frogs or something.

After midnight the people on shore went to bed, and then for two or three hours the shores was black— no more sparks in the cabin windows.

These sparks was our clock—the first one that showed again meant morning was coming, so we hunted a place to hide and tie up right away.

One morning about daybreak found a canoe and crossed over a chute to the main shore—it was only two hundred yards—and paddled about a mile up a crick amongst the cypress woods, to see if I couldn't get some berries. Just as I was passing a place where a kind of a cow path crossed the crick, here comes a couple of men tearing up the path as tight as they could foot it. I thought I was a goner, for whenever anybody was after anybody I judged it was *me* —or maybe Jim. I was about to dig out from there in a hurry, but they was pretty close to me then, and sung out and begged me to save their lives—said they hadn't been doing nothing, and was being chased for it— said there was men and dogs a-coming. They wanted to jump right in but I says:

"Don't you do it. I don't hear the dogs and horses yet; you've got time to crowd through the brush and get up the crick a little ways; then you take to the water and wade down to me and get in—that'll throw the dogs off the scent."

They done it, and soon as they was aboard I lit out for our tow head, and in about five or ten minutes we heard the dogs and the men away off, shouting. We heard them come along towards the crick, but couldn't see them; they seemed to stop and fool around awhile; then as we got further and further away all the time, we couldn't hardly hear them at all; by the time we had left a mile of woods behind us and struck he river, everything was quiet, and we paddled over to the towhead and hid in the cottonwoods and was safe.

One of these fellows was about seventy or upwards, and had a bald head and very gray whiskers. He had an old battered-up slouch hat on, and a greasy blue woolen shirt, and ragged old blue jeans britches stuffed into his boot-tops, and home-knit gal-luses—no, he only had one. He had an old long-tailed blue jeans coat with slick brass buttons flung over his arm, and both of them had big, fat, ratty-looking carpet-bags.

The other fellow was about thirty, and dressed about as ornery. After breakfast we all laid off and talked, and the first thing that come out was that these chaps didn't know one another.

"What got you into trouble?" says the baldhead to t'other chap.

"Well, I'd been selling an article to take the tartar off the teeth—and it does take it off, too, and generly the enamel along with it—but I stayed about one night longer than I ought to, and was just in the act of sliding out when I ran across you on the trail this side of town, and you told me they were coming, and begged me to help you to get off. So I told you I was expecting trouble myself, and would scatter out *with* you. That's the whole yarn—what's yourn?"

"Well, I'd ben a-runnin' a little temperance revival thar 'bout a week, and was the pet of the women folks, big and little, for I was makin' it mighty warm for the rummies, I *tell* you, and takin' as much as five or six dollars a night—ten cents a head, children and niggers free—and business a-growin' all the time, when somehow or another a little report got around last night that I had a way of puttin' in my time with a private jug on the sly. A nigger rousted me out this mornin', and told me the people was getherin' on the quiet with their dogs and horses, and they'd be along pretty soon and give me 'bout half an hour's start, and then run me down if they could; and if they got me they'd tar and feather me and ride me on a rail, sure. I didn't wait for no breakfast—I warn't hungry."

"Old man," said the young one, "I reckon we might double-team it to-gether; what do you think?"

"I ain't undisposed. What's your line—mainly?"

"Jour printer by trade; do a little in patent medicines; theater-actor—tragedy, you know; take a turn to mesmerism and phrenology when there's a chance; teach singing-geography school for a change; sling a lecture sometimes—oh, I do lots of things—most anything that comes handy, so it ain't work. What's your lay?"

"I've done considerble in the doctoring way in my time. Layin' on o' hands is my best holt—for cancer and paralysis, and sich things; and I k'n tell a fortune pretty good when I've got somebody along to find out the facts for me. Preachin's my line, too, and workin' camp-meetin's, and missionaryin' around."

Nobody never said anything for a while; then the young man hove a sigh and says:

"Alas!"

"What're you alassin' about?" says the baldhead.

"To think I should have lived to

be leading such a life, and be degraded down into such company." And he begun to wipe the corner of his eye with a rag.

"Dern your skin, ain't the company good enough for you?" says the bald-head, pretty pert and uppish.

"Yes, it *is* good enough for me; it's as good as I deserve; for who fetched me so low when I was so high? *I* did myself. I don't blame *you,* gentlemen—far from it; I don't blame anybody. I deserve it all. Let the cold world do its worst; one thing I know—there's a grave somewhere for me. The world may go on just as it's always done, and take everything from me—loved ones, property, everything; but it can't take that. Some day I'll lie down in it and forget it all, and my poor broken heart will be at rest." He went on a-wiping.

"Drot your pore broken heart," says the bald-head; "what are you heaving your pore broken heart at *us* f'r? *We* hain't done nothing."

"No, I know you haven't. I ain't blaming you, gentlemen. I brought myself down—yes, I did it myself. It's right I should suffer—perfectly right—I don't make any moan."

"Brought you down from whar? Whar was you brought down from?"

"Ah, you would not believe me; the world never believes—let it pass —'tis no matter. The secret of my birth—"

"The secret of your birth! Do you mean to say—"

"Gentlemen," says the young man, very solemn, "I will reveal it to you, for I feel I may have confidence in you. By rights I am a duke!"

Jim's eyes bugged out when he heard that; and I reckon mine did,

too. Then the baldhead says: "No you can't mean it?"

"Yes. My great-grandfather, eldest son of the Duke of Bridgewater fled to this country about the end of the last century, to breathe the pure air of freedom; married here and died, leaving a son, his own father dying about the same time. The second son of the late duke seize the titles and estates—the infant real duke was ignored. I am the lineal descendant of that infant—I am the rightful Duke of Bridgewater; and here am I, forlorn, torn from my high estate, hunted of men, despised by the cold world, ragged, worn, heartbroken and degraded to the companionship of felons on a raft!"

Jim pitied him ever so much, and so did I. We tried to comfort him but he said it warn't much use, h couldn't be much comforted; said if we was a mind to acknowledge him that would do him more good tha most anything else; so we said w would, if he would tell us how. H said we ought to bow when we spok to him, and say "Your Grace," o "My Lord," or "Your Lordship"— and he wouldn't mind it if we calle him plain "Bridgewater," which, h said, was a title anyway, and not name; and one of us ought to wai on him at dinner, and do any littl thing for him he wanted done.

Well, that was all easy, so we don it. All through dinner Jim stoo around and waited on him, and says "Will yo' Grace have some o' dis o some o' dat?" and so on, and a bod could see it was mighty pleasing t him.

But the old man got pretty silen by and by—didn't have much to say nd didn't look comfortable over all aat petting that was going on around aat duke. He seemed to have something on his mind. So, along in the fternoon, he says:

"Looky here, Bilgewater," he says, I'm nation sorry for you, but you in't the only person that's had trou- les like that."

"No?"

"No, you ain't. You ain't the only erson that's ben snaked down wrong- ılly out'n a high place."

"Alas!"

"No, you ain't the only person aat's had a secret of his birth." And, y jings, *he* begins to cry.

"Hold! What do you mean?"

"Bilgewater, kin I trust you?" says ıe old man, still sort of sobbing.

"To the bitter death!" He took ıe old man by the hand and squeezed , and says, "That secret of your eing: speak!"

"Bilgewater, I am the late Dau- hin!"

You bet you, Jim and me stared ıis time. Then the duke says:

"You are what?"

"Yes, my friend, it is too true— our eyes is lookin' at this very mo- ıent on the pore disappeared ›auphin, Looy the Seventeen, son of ₀ooy the Sixteen and Marry An- ›nette."

"You! At your age! No! You ıean you're the late Charlemagne; ou must be six or seven hundred ears old, at the very least."

"Trouble has done it, Bilgewater, rouble has done it; trouble has brung hese gray hairs and this premature ›alditude. Yes, gentlemen, you see efore you, in blue jeans and misery, he wanderin', exiled, trampled-on,

and sufferin' rightful King of France."

Well, he cried and took on so that me and Jim didn't know hardly what to do, we was so sorry—and so glad and proud we'd got him with us, too. So we set in, like we done be- fore with the duke, and tried to comfort *him*. But he said it warn't no use, nothing but to be dead and done with it all could do him any good; though he said it often made him feel easier and better for a while if people treated him according to his rights, and got down on one knee to speak to him, and always called him "Your Majesty," and waited on him first at meals, and didn't set down in his presence till he asked them. So Jim and me set to majesty- ing him, and doing this and that and t'other for him, and standing up till he told us we might set down. This done him heaps of good, and so he got cheerful and comfortable. But the duke kind of soured on him, and didn't look a bit satisfied with the way things was going; still, the king acted real friendly towards him, and said the duke's great grandfather and all the other Dukes of Bilgewater was a good deal thought of by *his* father, and was allowed to come to the pal- ace considerable; but the duke stayed huffy a good while, till by and by the king says:

"Like as not we got to be together a blamed long time on this h-yer raft, Bilgewater, and so what's the use o' your bein' sour? It'll only make things oncomfortable. It ain't my fault I warn't born a duke, it ain't your fault you warn't born a king— so what's the use to worry? Make the best o' things the way you find 'em, says I—that's my motto. This ain't no bad thing that we've struck here—plenty grub and an easy life—come, give us your hand, duke, and le's all be friends."

The duke done it, and Jim and me was pretty glad to see it. It took away all the uncomfortableness and we felt mighty good over it, because it would 'a' been a miserable business to have any unfriendliness on the raft; for what you want, above all things, on a raft, is for everybody to be satisfied, and feel right and kind towards the others.

It didn't take me long to make up my mind that these liars warn't no kings nor dukes at all, but just low-down humbugs and frauds. But I never said nothing, never let on; kept it to myself; it's the best way; then you don't have no quarrels, and don't get into no trouble. It they wanted us to call them kings and dukes, I hadn't no objections, 'long as it would keep peace in the family; and it warn't no use to tell Jim, so I didn't tell him. If I never learnt nothing else out of pap, I learnt that the best way to get along with his kind of people is to let them have their own way.

1884

From *THE MYSTERIOUS STRANGER: A ROMANCE* *

CHAPTER IX

[HUMAN SHEEP]

It was wonderful, the mastery Satan had over time and distance. For him they did not exist. He

* Reprinted from *The Mysterious Stranger: A Romance*, by Mark Twain, 1916, and here used by permission of Harper and Brothers, the authorized publishers.

called them human inventions, an said they were artificialities. W often went to the most distant part of the globe with him, and staye weeks and months, and yet were gon only a fraction of a second, as a rule You could prove it by the clock. On day when our people were in suc awful distress because the witch com mission were afraid to proceed agains the astrologer and Father Peter' household, or against any, indeed, bu the poor and the friendless, they los patience and took to witch-huntin on their own score, and began to chas a born lady who was known to hav the habit of curing people by devilis arts, such as bathing them, washin them, and nourishing them instead o bleeding them and purging then through the ministrations of a barber surgeon in the proper way. She cam flying down, with the howling an cursing mob after her, and tried t take refuge in houses, but the door were shut in her face. They chase her more than half an hour, we fol lowing to see it, and at last she wa exhausted and fell, and they caugh her. They dragged her to a tree an threw a rope over the limb, and be gan to make a noose in it, some hold ing her, meantime, and she crying an begging, and her young daughte looking on and weeping, but afraid t say or do anything.

They hanged the lady, and I threv a stone at her, although in my hear I was sorry for her; but all wer throwing stones and each was watch ing his neighbor, and if I had no done as the others did it would hav been noticed and spoken of. Sata burst out laughing.

All that were nearby turned upo

im, astonished and not pleased. It was an ill time to laugh, for his free and scoffing ways and his supernatural music had brought him under suspicion all over the town and turned many privately against him. The big blacksmith called attention to him now, raising his voice so that all should hear, and said:

"What are you laughing at? Answer! Moreover, please explain to the company why you threw no stone."

"Are you sure I did not throw a stone?"

"Yes. You needn't try to get out of it; I had my eye on you."

"And I—I noticed you!" shouted two others.

"Three witnesses," said Satan: "Mueller, the blacksmith; Klein, the butcher's man; Pfeiffer, the weaver's journeyman. Three very ordinary liars. Are there any more?"

"Never mind whether there are others or not, and never mind about what you consider us—three's enough to settle your matter for you. You'll prove that you threw a stone, or it shall go hard with you."

"That's so!" shouted the crowd, and surged up as closely as they could to the center of interest.

"And first you will answer that other question," cried the blacksmith, pleased with himself for being mouthpiece to the public and hero of the occasion. "What are you laughing at?"

Satan smiled and answered, pleasantly: "To see three cowards stoning a dying lady when they were so near death themselves."

You could see the superstitious crowd shrink and catch their breath, under the sudden shock. The blacksmith, with a show of bravado, said:

"Pooh! What do you know about it?"

"I? Everything. By profession I am a fortune-teller, and I read the hands of you three—and some others—when you lifted them to stone the woman. One of you will die to-morrow week; another of you will die to-night; the third has but five minutes to live—and yonder is the clock!"

It made a sensation. The faces of the crowd blanched, and turned mechanically toward the clock. The butcher and the weaver seemed smitten with an illness, but the blacksmith braced up and said, with spirit:

"It is not long to wait for prediction number one. If it fails, young master, you will not live a whole minute after, I promise you that."

No one said anything; all watched the clock in a deep stillness which was impressive. When four and a half minutes were gone the blacksmith gave a sudden gasp and clapped his hand upon his heart, saying, "Give me breath! Give me room!" and began to sink down. The crowd surged back, no one offering to support him, and he fell lumbering to the ground and was dead. The people stared at him, then at Satan, then at one another; and their lips moved, but no words came. Then Satan said:

"Three saw that I threw no stone. Perhaps there are others; let them speak."

It struck a kind of panic into them, and although no one answered him, many began to violently accuse one another, saying, "You said he didn't throw," and getting for reply, "It is a lie, and I will make you eat it!"

And so in a moment they were in a raging and noisy turmoil, and beating and banging one another; and in the midst was the only indifferent one —the dead lady hanging from her rope, her troubles forgotten, her spirit at peace.

So we walked away, and I was not at ease, but was saying to myself, "He told them he was laughing at them, but it was a lie—he was laughing at me."

That made him laugh again, and he said, "Yes, I was laughing at you, because, in fear of what others might report about you, you stoned the woman when your heart revolted at the act—but I was laughing at the others, too."

"Why?"

"Because their case was yours."

"How is that?"

"Well, there were sixty-eight people there, and sixty-two of them had no more desire to throw a stone than you had."

"Satan!"

"Oh, it's true. I know your race. It is made up of sheep. It is governed by minorities, seldom or never by majorities. It suppresses its feelings and its beliefs and follows the handful that makes the most noise. Sometimes the noisy handful is right, sometimes wrong; but no matter, the crowd follows it. The vast majority of the race, whether savage or civilized, are secretly kind-hearted and shrink from inflicting pain, but in the presence of the aggressive and pitiless minority they don't dare to assert themselves. Think of it! One kind-hearted creature spies upon another, and sees to it that he loyally helps in iniquities which revolt both of them.

Speaking as an expert, I know that ninety-nine out of a hundred of your race were strongly against the killing of witches when that foolishness was first agitated by a handful of pious lunatics in the long ago. And I know that even to-day, after ages of transmitted prejudice and silly teaching, only one person in twenty puts any real heart into the harrying of a witch. And yet apparently everybody hates witches and wants them killed. Some day a handful will rise up on the other side and make the most noise—perhaps even a single daring man with a big voice and a determined front will do it—and in a week all the sheep will wheel and follow him, and witch-hunting will come to a sudden end.

"Monarchies, aristocracies, and religions are all based upon that large defect in your race—the individual's distrust of his neighbor, and his desire, for safety's or comfort's sake, to stand well in his neighbor's eye. These institutions will always remain, and always flourish, and always oppress you, affront you, and degrade you, because you will always be and remain slaves of minorities. There was never a country where the majority of the people were in their secret hearts loyal to any of these institutions."

I did not like to hear our race called sheep, and said I did not think they were.

"Still, it is true, lamb," said Satan. "Look at you in war—what mutton you are, and how ridiculous!"

"In war? How?"

"There has never been a just one, never an honorable one—on the part of the instigator of the war. I can see a million years ahead, and this rule will never change in so many as half a dozen instances. The loud little handful—as usual—will shout for the war. The pulpit will—warily and cautiously—object—at first; the great, big, dull bulk of the nation will rub its sleepy eyes and try to make out why there should be a war, and will say, earnestly and indignantly, "It is unjust and dishonorable, and there is no necessity for it." Then the handful will shout louder. A few fair men on the other side will argue and reason against the war with speech and pen, and at first will have a hearing and be applauded; but it will not last long; those others will outshout them, and presently the anti-war audiences will thin out and lose popularity. Before long you will see this curious thing: the speakers stoned from the platform, and free speech strangled by hordes of furious men who in their secret hearts are still at one with those stoned speakers—as earlier—but do not dare to say so. And now the whole nation—pulpit and all—will take up the war-cry, and shout itself hoarse, and mob any honest man who ventures to open his mouth; and presently such mouths will cease to open. Next the statesmen will invent cheap lies, putting the blame upon the nation that is attacked, and every man will be glad of those conscience-soothing falsities, and will diligently study them, and refuse to examine any refutations of them; and thus he will by and by convince himself that the war is just, and will thank God for the better sleep he enjoys after this process of grotesque self-deception."

(1898)   1916

From *MARK TWAIN'S AUTO-BIOGRAPHY* *

[ON BIOGRAPHY AND CRITICISM]

Susy Clemens's biography of her father.—Mr. Clemens's opinion of critics, etc.

[*Wednesday, February 7, 1906.*]

When Susy was thirteen, and was a slender little maid with plaited tails of copper-tinged brown hair down her back, and was perhaps the busiest bee in the household hive, by reason of the manifold studies, health exercises, and recreations she had to attend to, she secretly, and of her own motion, and out of love, added another task to her labors—the writing of a biography of me. She did this work in her bedroom at night, and kept her record hidden. After a little, the mother discovered it and filched it, and let me see it; then told Susy what she had done, and how pleased I was and how proud. I remember that time with a deep pleasure. I had had compliments before, but none that touched me like this; none that could approach it for value in my eyes. It has kept that place always since. I have had no compliment, no praise, no tribute from any source, that was so precious to me as this one was and still is. As I read it *now*, after all these many years, it is still a king's message to me, and brings me the same dear surprise it brought me then—with the pathos added of the thought that the eager and hasty hand that sketched it and scrawled it will

* Reprinted from *Mark Twain's Autobiography*, 1924, and here used by permission of Harper and Brothers, the authorized publishers.

not touch mine again—and I feel as the humble and unexpectant must feel when their eyes fall upon the edict that raises them to the ranks of the noble.

Yesterday while I was rummaging in a pile of ancient note-books of mine which I had not seen for years, I came across a reference to that biography. It is quite evident that several times, at breakfast and dinner, in those long-past days, I was posing for the biography. In fact, I clearly remember that I *was* doing that—and I also remember that Susy detected it. I remember saying a very smart thing, with a good deal of an air, at the breakfast table one morning, and that Susy observed to her mother privately, a little later, that papa was doing that for the biography.

I cannot bring myself to change any line or word in Susy's sketch of me, but will introduce passages from it now and then just as they came in —their quaint simplicity out of her honest heart, which was the beautiful heart of a child. What comes from that source has a charm and grace of its own which may transgress all the recognized laws of literature, if it choose, and yet be literature still, and worthy of hospitality.

The spelling is frequently desperate, but it was Susy's, and it shall stand. I love it, and cannot profane it. To me, it is gold. To correct it would alloy it, not refine it. It would spoil it. It would take from it its freedom and flexibility and make it stiff and formal. Even when it is most extravagant I am not shocked. It is Susy's spelling, and she was doing the best she could—and nothing could better it for me.

She learned languages easily; she learned history easily; she learned music easily; she learned all things easily, quickly, and thoroughly—except spelling. She even learned that, after a while. But it would have grieved me but little if she had failed in it—for, although good spelling was my one accomplishment, I was never able to greatly respect it. When I was a schoolboy, sixty years ago, we had two prizes in our school. One was for good spelling, the other for amiability. These things were thin, smooth, silver disks, about the size of a dollar. Upon the one was engraved in flowing Italian script the words "Good Spelling," on the other was engraved the word "Amiability." The holders of these prizes hung them about the neck with a string—and those holders were the envy of the whole school. There wasn't a pupil that wouldn't have given a leg for the privilege of wearing one of them a week, but no pupil ever got a chance except John RoBards and me. John RoBards was eternally and indestructibly amiable. I may even say devilishly amiable; fiendishly amiable; exasperatingly amiable. That was the sort of feeling that we had about that quality of his. So he always wore the amiability medal. I always wore the other medal. That word "always" is a trifle too strong. We lost the medals several times. It was because they became so monotonous. We needed a change—therefore several times we traded medals. It was a satisfaction to John RoBards to *seem* to be a good speller—which he wasn't. And it was a satisfaction to me to seem to be amiable, for a change. But of course these changes could not long endure—for some schoolmate or other would presently notice what had been happening, and that schoolmate would not have been human if he had lost any time in reporting this treason. The teacher took the medals away from us at once, of course—and we always had them back again before Friday night. If we lost the medals Monday morning, John's amiability was at the top of the list Friday afternoon when the teacher came to square up the week's account. The Friday-afternoon session always closed with "spelling down." Being in disgrace, I necessarily started at the foot of my division of spellers, but I always slaughtered both divisions and stood alone with the medal around my neck when the campaign was finished. I *did* miss on a word once, just at the end of one of these conflicts, and so lost the medal. I left the first *r* out of February— but that was to accommodate a sweetheart. My passion was so strong just at that time that I would have left out the whole alphabet if the word had contained it.

As I have said before, I never had any large respect for good spelling. That is my feeling yet. Before the spelling-book came with its arbitrary forms, men unconsciously revealed shades of their characters, and also added enlightening shades of expression to what they wrote by their spelling, and so it is possible that the spelling-book has been a doubtful benevolence to us.

Susy began the biography in 1885, when I was in the fiftieth year of my age, and she in the fourteenth of hers. She begins in this way:

We are a very happy family. We consist of Papa, Mamma, Jean, Clara and me. It is papa I am writing about, and I shall have no trouble in not knowing what to say about him, as he is a *very* striking character.

But wait a minute—I will return to Susy presently. In the matter of slavish imitation, man is the monkey's superior all the time. The average man is destitute of independence of opinion. He is not interested in contriving an opinion of his own, by study and reflection, but is only anxious to find out what his neighbor's opinion is and slavishly adopt it. A generation ago, I found out that the latest review of a book was pretty sure to be just a reflection of the *earliest* review of it. That whatever the first reviewer found to praise or censure in the book would be repeated in the latest reviewer's report, with nothing fresh added.* Therefore more than once I took the precaution of sending my book, in manuscript, to Mr. Howells, when he was editor of the *Atlantic Monthly,* so that he could prepare a review of it at leisure. I knew he would say the truth about the book—I also knew that he would find more merit than demerit in it, because I already knew that that was the condition of the book. I allowed no copy of that book to go out to the press until after Mr. Howells's notice of it had appeared. That book was always safe. There wasn't a man behind a pen in all America that had the courage to find anything in the book which Mr. Howells had not found—there wasn't a man behind a pen in America that

* Hardly true to-day.—A. B. P. [Albert Bigelow Paine.]

had spirit enough to say a brave and original thing about the book on his own responsibility.

I believe that the trade of critic, in literature, music, and the drama, is the most degraded of all trades, and that it has no real value—certainly no large value. When Charles Dudley Warner and I were about to bring out *The Gilded Age,* the editor of the *Daily Graphic* persuaded me to let him have an advance copy, he giving me his word of honor that no notice of it should appear in his paper until after the *Atlantic Monthly* notice should have appeared. This reptile published a review of the book within three days afterward. I could not really complain, because he had only given me his word of honor as security. I ought to have required of him something substantial. I believe his notice did not deal mainly with the merit of the book, or the lack of it, but with my moral attitude toward the public. It was charged that I had used my reputation to play a swindle upon the public—that Mr. Warner had written as much as half of the book, and that I had used my name to float it and give it currency—a currency which it could not have acquired without my name—and that this conduct of mine was a grave fraud upon the people. The *Graphic* was not an authority upon any subject whatever. It had a sort of distinction in that it was the first and only illustrated daily newspaper that the world had seen; but it was without character, it was poorly and cheaply edited, its opinion of a book or of any other work of art was of no consequence. Everybody knew this, yet all the critics in America, one after the other,

copied the *Graphic's* criticism, merely changing the phraseology, and left me under that charge of dishonest conduct. Even the great Chicago *Tribune* the most important journal in the Middle West, was not able to invent anything fresh, but adopted the view of the humble *Daily Graphic,* dishonesty charge and all. However, let it go. It is the will of God that we must have critics, and missionaries and congressmen, and humorists, and we must bear the burden.

What I have been traveling toward all this time is this: The first critic that ever had occasion to describe my personal appearance littered his description with foolish and inexcusable errors whose aggregate furnished the result that I was distinctly and distressingly unhandsome. That description floated around the country in the papers, and was in constant use and wear for a quarter of a century. It seems strange to me that apparently no critic in the country could be found who could look at me and have the courage to take up his pen and destroy that lie. That lie began its course on the Pacific coast in 1864, and it likened me in personal appearance to Petroleum V. Nasby who had been out there lecturing. For twenty-five years afterward, no critic could furnish a description of me without fetching in Nasby to help out my portrait. I knew Nasby well, and he was a good fellow, but in my life I have not felt malignantly enough about any more than three persons to charge those persons with resembling Nasby. It hurts me to the heart, these things. To this day, it hurts me to the heart, and it had long been a distress to my family—in

luding Susy—that the critics should
o on making this wearisome mistake,
ear after year, when there was no
oundation for it. Even when a
ritic wanted to be particularly
riendly and complimentary to me, he
lidn't dare to go beyond my clothes.
Ie did not venture beyond that fron-
ier. When he had finished with my
lothes he had said all the kind [10]
hings, the pleasant things, the com-
limentary things he could risk. Then
ie dropped back on Nasby.

Yesterday I found this clipping in
he pocket of one of those ancient
nemorandum-books of mine. It is of
he date of thirty-nine years ago, and
ooth the paper and the ink are
ellow with the bitterness that I
elt in that old day when I clipped [20]
t out to preserve it and brood over
t and grieve about it. I will copy it
iere, to wit:

A correspondent of the Philadelphia
Press, writing of one of Schuyler Col-
ax's receptions, says of our Washington
orrespondent: "Mark Twain, the deli-
ate humorist, was present; quite a lion,
is he deserves to be. Mark is a bache-
or, faultless in taste, whose snowy vest [30]
s suggestive of endless quarrels with
Washington washerwomen; but the hero-
sm of Mark is settled for all time, for
uch purity and smoothness were never
een before. His lavender gloves might
iave been stolen from some Turkish
iarem, so delicate were they in size; but

more likely—anything else were more
likely than that. In form and feature he
bears some resemblance to the immortal
Nasby; but whilst Petroleum is brunette
to the core, Twain is golden, amber-
hued, melting, blonde."

Let us return to Susy's biography
now, and get the opinion of one who
is unbiased.

Papa's appearance has been described
many times, but very incorrectly. He
has beautiful gray hair, not any too
thick or any too long, but just right; a
Roman nose, which greatly improves the
beauty of his features; kind blue eyes
and a small mustache. He has a wonderfully shaped head and profile. He
has a very good figure—in short, he is
an extrodinarily fine looking man. All
his features are perfect, except that he
hasn't extrodinary teeth. His complexion is very fair, and he doesn't
ware a beard. He is a very good man
and a very funny one. He *has* got a
temper, but we all of us have in this
family. He is the loveliest man I ever
saw or ever hope to see—and oh, so
absent-minded. He does tell perfectly
delightful stories. Clara and I used to
sit on each arm of his chair and listen
while he told us stories about the pictures on the wall.

I remember the story-telling days
vividly. They were a difficult and
exacting audience—those little creatures.

1924

WILLIAM DEAN HOWELLS
(1837–1920)

From *THE RISE OF SILAS
LAPHAM* *

I

[AN INTERVIEW]

When Bartley Hubbard went to interview Silas Lapham for the "Solid Men of Boston" series, which he undertook to finish up in *The Events,* after he replaced their original projector on that newspaper, Lapham received him in his private office by previous appointment.

"Walk right in!" he called out to the journalist, whom he caught sight of through the door of the counting-room.

He did not rise from the desk at which he was writing, but he gave Bartley his left hand for welcome, and he rolled his large head in the direction of a vacant chair. "Sit down! I'll be with you in just half a minute."

"Take your time," said Bartley, with the ease he instantly felt. "I'm in no hurry." He took a notebook from his pocket, laid it on his knee, and began to sharpen a pencil.

"There!" Lapham pounded with his great hairy fist on the envelope he had been addressing. "William!" he called out, and he handed the letter to a boy who came to get it. "I

* Copyright 1884 by Houghton Mifflin Co. Copyright 1912 by Mildred Howells and John Mead Howells.

want that to go right away. Well sir," he continued, wheeling round in his leather-cushioned swivel-chair, and facing Bartley, seated so near that their knees almost touched, "so you want my life, death, and Christian sufferings, do you, young man?"

"That's what I'm after," said Bartley. "Your money or your life."

"I guess you wouldn't want my life without the money," said Lapham, as if he were willing to prolong these moments of preparation.

"Take 'em both," Bartley suggested "Don't want your money without your life, if you come to that. But you're just one million times more interesting to the public than if you hadn't a dollar; and you know that as well as I do, Mr. Lapham. There's no use beating about the bush."

"No," said Lapham, somewhat absently. He put out his huge foot and pushed the ground-glass door shut between his little den and the book-keepers, in their larger den outside.

"In personal appearance," wrote Bartley in the sketch for which he now studied his subject, while he waited patiently for him to continue, "Silas Lapham is a fine type of the successful American. He has a square, bold chin, only partially concealed by the short reddish-grey beard, growing to the edges of his firmly closing lips. His nose is short and straight; his forehead good, but broad rather than high; his eyes blue, and with a light them that is kindly or sharp according to his mood. He is of medium height, and fills an average armchair with a solid bulk, which on the day of our interview was unpretentiously clad in a business suit of blue serge. His head droops somewhat from a short neck, which does not trouble itself to rise far from a pair of massive shoulders."

"I don't know as I know just where you want me to begin," said Lapham.

"Might begin with your birth; that's where most of us begin," replied Bartley.

A gleam of humorous appreciation shot into Lapham's blue eyes.

"I didn't know whether you wanted me to go quite so far back as that," he said. "But there's no disgrace in having been born, and I was born in the State of Vermont, pretty well up under the Canada line—so well up, in fact, that I came very near being an adoptive citizen; for I was bound to be an American of *some* sort, from the word Go! That was about—well, let me see!—pretty near sixty years ago: this is '75, and that was '20. Well, say I'm fifty-five years old; and I've *lived* 'em, too; not an hour of waste time about *me,* anywheres! I was born on a farm, and—"

"Worked in the fields summers and went to school winters: regulation thing?" Bartley cut in.

"Regulation thing," said Lapham, accepting this irreverent version of his story somewhat dryly.

"Parents poor, of course," suggested the journalist. "Any barefoot business? Early deprivations of any kind, that would encourage the youthful reader to go and do likewise? Orphan yourself, you know," said Bartley, with a smile of cynical good-comradery.

Lapham looked at him silently, and then said with quiet self-respect, "I guess if you see these things as a joke, my life won't inter*est* you."

"Oh, yes, it will," returned Bartley, unabashed. "You'll see; it'll come out all right." And in fact it did so, in the interview which Bartley printed.

"Mr. Lapham," he wrote, "passed rapidly over the story of his early life, its poverty and its hardships, sweetened, however, by the recollections of a devoted mother, and a father who, if somewhat her inferior in education, was no less ambitious for the advancement of his children. They were quiet, unpretentious people, religious, after the fashion of that time, and of sterling morality, and they taught their children the simple virtues of the Old Testament and Poor Richard's Almanac."

Bartley could not deny himself this gibe; but he trusted to Lapham's unliterary habit of mind for his security in making it, and most other people would consider it sincere reporter's rhetoric.

"You know," he explained to Lapham, "that we have to look at all these facts as material, and we get the habit of classifying them. Sometimes a leading question will draw out a whole line of facts that a man himself would never think of." He went on to put several queries, and it was from Lapham's answers that he generalised the history of his childhood. "Mr. Lapham, although he did not dwell on his boyish trials and struggles, spoke of them with deep feeling and an abiding sense of their reality." This was what he added in the interview, and by the time he had got

Lapham past the period where risen Americans are all pathetically alike in their narrow circumstances, their sufferings, and their aspirations, he had beguiled him into forgetfulness of the check he had received, and had him talking again in perfect enjoyment of his autobiography.

"Yes, sir," said Lapham, in a strain which Bartley was careful not to interrupt again, "a man never sees all that his mother has been to him till it's too late to let her know that he sees it. Why, *my* mother—" he stopped. "It gives me a lump in the throat," he said apologetically, with an attempt at a laugh. Then he went on: "She was a little, frail thing, not bigger than a good-sized intermediate school-girl; but she did the whole work of a family of boys, and boarded the hired men besides. She cooked, swept, washed, ironed, made and mended from daylight till dark—and from dark till daylight, I was going to say; for I don't know how she got any time for sleep. But I suppose she did. She got time to go to church, and to teach us to read the Bible, and to misunderstand it in the old way. She was *good*. But it ain't her on her knees in church that comes back to me so much like the sight of an angel as her on her knees before me at night, washing my poor, dirty little feet, that I'd run bare in all day, and making me decent for bed. There were six of us boys; it seems to me we were all of a size; and she was just so careful with all of us. I can feel her hands on my feet yet!" Bartley looked at Lapham's No. 10 boots, and softly whistled through his teeth. "We were patched all over; but we wa'n't ragged. *I* don't know how she got

through it. She didn't seem to thin it was anything; and I guess it wa no more than my father expected c her. *He* worked like a horse in doo and out—up at daylight, feeding th stock, and groaning round all day wit his rheumatism, but not stopping."

Bartley hid a yawn over his not book, and probably, if he could hav spoken his mind, he would have su; gested to Lapham that he was n there for the purpose of interviewir his ancestry. But Bartley had learne to practice a patience with his victin which he did not always feel, and feign an interest in their digressio till he could bring them up with round turn.

"I tell you," said Lapham, jabbi the point of his penknife into t writing-pad on the desk before hir "when I hear women complaini nowadays that their lives are stunt and empty, I want to tell 'em abo my *mother's* life. *I* could paint out for 'em."

Bartley saw his opportunity at t word paint, and cut in. "And you sa Mr. Lapham, that you discovered t mineral paint on the old farm you self?"

Lapham acquiesced in the return business. "*I* didn't discover it," said scrupulously. "My father fou it one day, in a hole made by a tr blowing down. There it was, ly loose in the pit, and sticking to t roots that had pulled up a big cake dirt with 'em. *I* don't know what gi him the idea that there was mon in it, but he did think so from t start. I guess, if they'd had the wo in those days, they'd considered h pretty much of a crank about it. was trying as long as he lived to at paint introduced; but he couldn't ake it go. The country was so poor ey couldn't paint their houses with ything; and father hadn't any cilities. It got to be a kind of joke th us; and I guess that paint-mine d as much as any one thing to make boys clear out as soon as we got d enough. All my brothers went est, and took up land; but I hung to New England, and I hung on to e old farm, not because the paint-ine was on it, but because the old use was—and the graves. Well," id Lapham, as if unwilling to give mself too much credit, "there uldn't been any market for it, any-y. You can go through that part the State and buy more farms than u can shake a stick at for less oney than it cost to build the barns 'em. Of course, it's turned out a od thing. I keep the old house up good shape, and we spend a month so there every summer. M' wife nd of likes it, and the girls. Pretty ace; sightly all round it. I've got orce of men at work there the whole ne, and I've got a man and his wife the house. Had a family meeting ere last year; the whole connection om out West. There!" Lapham se from his seat and took down a ge warped, unframed photograph om the top of his desk, passing his nd over it, and then blowing vigor-sly upon it, to clear it of the dust. here we are, *all* of us."

"I don't need to look twice at *you*," id Bartley, putting his finger on one the heads.

"Well, that's Bill," said Lapham, th a gratified laugh. "He's about brainy as any of us, I guess. He's e of their leading lawyers. out Du-

buque way; been judge of the Common Pleas once or twice. That's his son—just graduated at Yale—alongside of my youngest girl. Good-looking chap, ain't he?"

"She's a good-looking chap," said Bartley, with prompt irreverence. He hastened to add, at the frown which gathered between Lapham's eyes, "What a beautiful creature she is! What a lovely, refined, sensitive face! And she looks *good,* too."

"She *is* good," said the father, re-lenting.

"And, after all, that's about the best thing in a woman," said the potential reprobate. "If my wife wasn't good enough to keep both of us straight, I don't know what would become of me."

"My other daughter," said Lapham, indicating a girl with eyes that showed large, and a face of singular gravity. "Mis' Lapham," he continued, touching his wife's effigy with his little finger. "My brother Willard and his family—farm at Kankakee. Hazard Lapham and his wife—Baptist preacher in Kansas. Jim and his three girls—milling business at Minneapolis. Ben and his family—practicing medicine in Fort Wayne."

The figures were clustered in an irregular group in front of an old farm-house, whose original ugliness had been smartened up with a coat of Lapham's own paint, and heightened with an incongruous piazza. The photographer had not been able to conceal the fact that they were all decent, honest-looking, sensible people, with a very fair share of beauty among the young girls; some of these were extremely pretty, in fact. He had put them into awkward and constrained attitudes, of course; and they all looked as if they had the instrument of torture which photographers call a head-rest under their occiputs. Here and there an elderly lady's face was a mere blur; and some of the younger children had twitched themselves into wavering shadows, and might have passed for spirit-photographs of their own little ghosts. It was the standard family-group photograph, in which most Americans have figured at some time or other; and Lapham exhibited a just satisfaction in it. "I presume," he mused aloud, as he put it back on top of his desk, "that we sha'n't soon get together again, all of us."

"And you say," suggested Bartley, "that you stayed right along on the old place, when the rest cleared out West?"

"No-o-o-o," said Lapham, with a long, loud drawl; "I cleared out West too, first off. Went to Texas. Texas was all the cry in those days. But I got enough of the Lone Star in about three months, and I come back with the idea that Vermont was good enough for me."

"Fatted calf business?" queried Bartley, with his pencil poised above his note-book.

"I presume they were glad to see me," said Lapham, with dignity. "Mother," he added gently, "died that winter, and I stayed on with father. I buried him in the spring; and then I came down to a little place called Lumberville, and picked up what jobs I could get. I worked round at the saw-mills, and I was ostler a while at the hotel—I always *did* like a good horse. Well, I *wa'n't* exactly a college graduate, and I went to school odd

times. I got to driving the sta[ge] after while, and by and by I *boug[ht]* the stage and run the business m[y]self. Then I hired the tavern-stan[d] and—well to make a long story sho[rt] then I got married. Yes," sa[id] Lapham, with pride, "I married t[he] school-teacher. We did pretty w[ell] with the hotel, and my wife she w[as] always at me to paint up. Well, [I] put it off, and *put* it off, as a man wi[ll] till one day I give in, and says I, 'We[ll] *let's* paint up. Why, Pert,'—m' wif[e's] name's Persis,—'I've got a whole pai[nt] mine out on the farm. Let's go o[ut] and look at it.' So we drove out. [I] let the place for seventy-five dolla[rs] a year to a shif'less kind of a Kanu[ck] that had come down that way; a[nd] I'd hated to see the house with h[im] in it; but we drove out one Saturd[ay] afternoon, and we brought back abo[ut] a bushel of the stuff in the bugg[y] seat, and I tried it crude, and I tri[ed] it burnt; and I liked it. M' wife s[he] liked it too. There wa'n't any pain[ter] by trade in the village, and I mix[ed] it myself. Well, sir, that tavern's g[ot] that coat of paint on it yet, and [it] hain't ever had any other, and I do[n't] know's it ever will. Well, you kno[w] I felt as if it was a kind of haru[m]scarum experiment, all the while; a[nd] I presume I shouldn't have tried [it] but I kind of liked to do it becau[se] father'd always set so much store [by] his paint-mine. And when I'd [got] the first coat on,"—Lapham called [it] *cut*,—"I presume I must have set [as] much as half an hour, looking at [it] and thinking how he would have e[n]joyed it. I've had my share of l[uck] in this world, and I ain't a-going [to] complain on my *own* account, [but] I've noticed that most things get al[ong]

o late for most people. It made me
el bad, and it took all the pride out
y success with the paint, thinking of
ther. Seemed to me I might 'a'
ken more interest in it when he
as by to see; but we've got to live
d learn. Well, I called my wife out,
-I'd tried it on the back of the house,
u know,—and she left her dishes,—
can remember she came out with
r sleeves rolled up and set down
ongside of me on the trestle,—and
ys I, 'What do you think, Persis?'
d says she, 'Well, you hain't got a
int-mine, Silas Lapham; you've got
gold-mine.' She always was just so
thusiastic about things. Well, it
is just after two or three boats had
irnt up out West, and a lot of lives
st, and there was a great cry about
n-inflammable paint, and I guess
at was what was in her mind. 'Well,
guess it ain't any gold-mine, Persis,'
ys I; 'but I guess it is a paint-mine.
n going to have it analysed, and if
turns out what I think it is, I'm
ing to work it. And if father hadn't
d such a long name, I should call
the Nehemiah Lapham Mineral
int. But, any rate, every barrel
it, and every keg, and every bottle,
d every package, big or little, has
t to have the initials and figures
L. f. 1835, S. L. t. 1855, on it.
ther found it in 1835, and I tried it
1855.'"

" 'S. T.—1860—X.' business," said
rtley.

"Yes," said Lapham, "but I hadn't
ard of Plantation Bitters then, and
adn't seen any of the fellow's labels.
et to work and I got a man down
m Boston; and I carried him out
the farm, and he analysed it—made
egular job of it. Well, sir, we built

a kiln, and we kept a lot of that
paint-ore red-hot for forty-eight
hours; kept the Kanuck and his family
up, firing. The presence of iron in
the ore showed with the magnet from
the start; and when he came to test
it, he found out that it contained
about seventy-five per cent. of the
peroxide of iron."

Lapham pronounced the scientific
phrases with a sort of reverent satisfaction, as if awed through his pride
by a little lingering uncertainty as to
what peroxide was. He accented it
as if it were purr-ox-*eyed;* and Bartley had to get him to spell it.

"Well, and what then?" he asked,
when he had made a note of the per-
centage.

"What then?" echoed Lapham.
"Well, then, the fellow set down and
told me, 'You've got a paint here,'
says he, 'that's going to drive every
other mineral paint out of the market.
Why,' says he, 'it'll drive 'em right
into the Back Bay!' Of course, *I*
didn't know what the Back Bay was
then; but I begun to open my eyes;
thought I'd had 'em open before, but
I guess I hadn't. Says he, 'That paint
has got hydraulic cement in it, and it
can stand fire and water and acids;'
he named over a lot of things. Says
he, 'It'll mix easily with linseed oil,
whether you want to use it boiled or
raw; and it ain't a-going to crack nor
fade any; and it ain't a-going to scale.
When you've got your arrangements
for burning it properly, you're going
to have a paint that will stand like
the everlasting hills, in every climate
under the sun.' Then he went into a
lot of particulars, and I begun to
think he was drawing a long-bow, and
meant to make his bill accordingly

So I kept pretty cool; but the fellow's bill didn't amount to anything hardly—said I might pay him after I got going; young chap, and pretty easy; but every word he said was gospel. Well, I ain't a-going to brag up my paint; I don't suppose you came here to hear me blow—"

"Oh, yes, I did," said Bartley. "That's what I want. Tell all there is to tell, and I can boil it down afterward. A man can't make a greater mistake with a reporter than to hold back anything out of modesty. It may be the very thing we want to know. What we want is the whole truth; and more; we've got so much modesty of our own that we can temper almost any statement."

Lapham looked as if he did not quite like this tone, and he resumed a little more quietly. "Oh, there isn't really very much more to say about the paint itself. But you can use it for almost anything where a paint is wanted, inside or out. It'll prevent decay, and it'll stop it, after it's begun, in tin or iron. You can paint the inside of a cistern or a bath-tub with it, and water won't hurt it; and you can paint a steam-boiler with it, and heat won't. You can cover a brick wall with it, or a railroad car, or the deck of a steamboat, and you can't do a better thing for either."

"Never tried it on the human conscience, I suppose," suggested Bartley.

"No, sir," replied Lapham gravely. "I guess you want to keep that as free from paint as you can, if you want much use of it. I never cared to try any of it on mine." Lapham suddenly lifted his bulk up out of his swivel-chair, and led the way out into the wareroom beyond the office par-

titions, where rows and ranks of cask[s] barrels, and kegs stretched dimly ba[ck] to the rear of the building, and di[f-] fused an honest, clean, wholeso[me] smell of oil and paint. They we[re] labelled and branded as containi[ng] each so many pounds of Laphan[m] Mineral Paint, and each bore t[he] mystic devices, N. L. f. 1835—S. t. 1855. "There!" said Lapham, kic[k-] ing one of the largest casks with t[he] toe of his boot, "that's about our bi[g-] gest package; and here," he adde[d] laying his hand affectionately on t[he] head of a very small keg, as if it we[re] the head of a child, which it resembl[ed] in size, "this is the smallest. We us[ed] to put the paint on the market d[ry] but now we grind every ounce of [it] in oil—very best quality of linse[ed] oil—and warrant it. We find [it] gives more satisfaction. Now, co[me] back to the office, and I'll show y[ou] our fancy brands."

It was very cool and pleasant [in] that dim wareroom, with the rafte[rs] showing overhead in a cloudy perspe[c-] tive, and darkening away into the p[er-] petual twilight at the rear of t[he] building; and Bartley had found [an] agreeable seat on the head of a ha[lf] barrel of the paint, which he was [re-] luctant to leave. But he rose and f[ol-] lowed the vigorous lead of Lapha[m] back to the office, where the sun [of] a long summer afternoon was j[ust] beginning to glare in at the wind[ow] On the shelves opposite Lapha[m's] desk were tin cans of various si[ze] arranged in tapering cylinders, a[nd] showing, in a pattern diminish[ing] toward the top, the same label bo[rne] by the casks and barrels in the wa[re] room. Lapham merely waved his ha[nd] toward these; but when Bartley, af[ter] comprehensive glance at them, gave s whole attention to a row of clean, nooth jars, where different tints of e paint showed through flawless ass, Lapham smiled, and waited in eased expectation.

"Hello!" said Bartley. "That's etty!"

"Yes," assented Lapham, "it is ther nice. It's our latest thing, and e find it takes with customers first-te. Look here!" he said, taking wn one of the jars, and pointing the first line of the label.

Bartley read, "THE PERSIS RAND," and then he looked at pham and smiled.

"After *her*, of course," said Lapham. Got it up and put the first of it on e market her last birthday. She as pleased."

"I should think she might have en," said Bartley, while he made a te of the appearance of the jars.

"I don't know about your mention-g it in your interview," said Lapham biously.

"That's going into the interview, r. Lapham, if nothing else does. ot a wife myself, and I know just w you feel." It was in the dawn of rtley's prosperity on the *Boston ents,* before his troubles with arcia had seriously begun.

"Is that so?" said Lapham, recog-zing with a smile another of the vast jority of married Americans; a few derrate their wives, but the rest nk them supernal in intelligence and pability. "Well," he added, "we ust see about that. Where'd you y you lived?"

"We don't live; we board. Mrs. sh, 13 Canary Place."

"Well, we've all got to commence that way," suggested Lapham con-solingly.

"Yes; but we've about got to the end of our string. I expect to be under a roof of my own on Clover Street before long. I suppose," said Bartley, returning to business, "that you didn't let the grass grow under your feet much after you found out what was in your paint-mine?"

"No, sir," answered Lapham, with-drawing his eyes from a long stare at Bartley, in which he had been seeing himself a young man again, in the first days of his married life. "I went right back to Lumberville and sold out everything, and put all I could rake and scrape together into paint. And Mis' Lapham was with me every time. No hang back about *her*. I tell you she was a *woman!*"

Bartley laughed. "That's the sort most of us marry."

"No, we don't," said Lapham. "Most of us marry silly little girls grown up to *look* like women."

"Well, I guess that's about so," as-sented Bartley, as if upon second thought.

"If it hadn't been for her," resumed Lapham, "the paint wouldn't have come to anything. I used to tell her it wa'n't the seventy-five per cent. of purr-ox-eyed of iron in the *ore* that made that paint go; it was the seventy-five per cent. of purr-ox-eyed of iron in *her*."

"Good!" cried Bartley. "I'll tell Marcia that."

"In less 'n six months there wa'n't a board-fence, nor a bridge-girder, nor a dead wall, nor a barn, nor a face of rock in that whole region that didn't have 'Lapham's Mineral Paint—Specimen' on it in the three colors we begun by making." Bartley had taken his seat on the window-sill, and Lapham, standing before him, now put up his huge foot close to Bartley's thigh; neither of them minded that.

"I've heard a good deal of talk about that S. T.—1860—X. man, and the stove-blacking man, and the kidney-cure man, because they advertised in that way; and I've read articles about it in the papers; but I don't see where the joke comes in, exactly. So long as the people that own the barns and fences don't object, I don't see what the public has got to do with it. And I never saw anything so very sacred about a big rock, along a river or in a pasture, that it wouldn't do to put mineral paint on it in three colors. I wish some of the people that talk about the landscape, and *write* about it, had to bu'st one of them rocks *out* of the landscape with powder, or dig a hole to bury it in, as we used to have to do up on the farm; I guess they'd sing a little different tune about the profanation of scenery. There ain't any man enjoys a sightly bit of nature—a smooth piece of interval with half a dozen good-sized wine-glass elms in it—more than *I* do. But I ain't a-going to stand up for every big ugly rock I come across, as if we were all a set of dumn Druids. I say the landscape was made for man, and not man for the landscape."

"Yes," said Bartley carelessly; "it was made for the stove-polish man and the kidney-cure man."

"It was made for any man that knows how to use it," Lapham returned, insensible to Bartley's irony. "Let 'em go and live with nature in the *winter*, up there along the Canada line, and I guess they'll get enough her for one while. Well—wher was I?"

"Decorating the landscape," sa Bartley.

"Yes, sir; I started right there Lumberville, and it give the place start too. You won't find it on t map now; and you won't find it the gazetteer. I give a pretty go lump of money to build a town-ha about five years back, and the fir meeting they held in it they voted change the name,—Lumberville *wa'n* a name,—and it's Lapham now."

"Isn't it somewhere up in that r gion that they get the old Brand red?" asked Bartley.

"We're about ninety miles fro Brandon. The Brandon's a go paint," said Lapham conscientiousl "Like to show you round up at o place some odd time, if you get off

"Thanks. I should like it first-ra Works there?"

"Yes; works there. Well, sir, ju about the time I got started, the w brok▪ ▪ut; and it knocked my pai high ▪r t ▪an a kite. The thing dropp perf▪ctl y dead. I presume that if ▪ had a▪ y sort of influence, I mig have got it into Government han for gu▪-carriages and army wago and may be on board Government v sels. But I hadn't, and we had face the music. I was about broke hearted, but m' wife she looked at another way. '*I* guess it's a pro dence,' says she. 'Silas, I guess you got a cou ntry that's worth fighti for. Any rate, you better go ▪ and give it a chance.' Well, sir, went. I knew she meant business. might kill her to have me go, but would kill her sure if I stayed. S was one of that kind. I went. Her last words was, 'I'll look after the paint, Si.' We hadn't but just one little girl then,—boy'd died,—and Mis' Lapham's mother was livin' with us; and I knew if times *did* anyways come up again, m' wife'd know just what to do. So I went. I got through; and you can call me Colonel, if you want to. Feel there!" Lapham took Bartley's thumb and forefinger and put them on a bunch in his leg, just above the knee. "Anything hard?"

"Ball?"

Lapham nodded. "Gettysburg. That's my thermometer. If it wa'n't for that, I shouldn't know enough to come in when it rains."

Bartley laughed at a joke which betrayed some evidences of wear. "And when you came back, you took hold of the paint and rushed it."

"I took hold of the paint and rushed it—all I could," said Lapham, with less satisfaction than he had hitherto shown in his autobiography. "But I found that I had got back to another world. The day of small things was past, and I don't suppose it will ever come again in this country. My wife was at me all the time to take a partner—somebody with capital; but I couldn't seem to bear the idea. That paint was like my own blood to me. To have anybody else concerned in it was like—well, I don't know what. I saw it was the thing to do; but I tried to fight it off, and I tried to joke it off. I used to say, 'Why didn't you take partner yourself, Persis, while I was away?' And she'd say, 'Well, if you hadn't come back, I should, Si.' Always *did* like a joke about as well as any woman *I* ever saw. Well, I had to come to it. I took a partner."

Lapham dropped the bold blue eyes with which he had been till now staring into Bartley's face, and the reporter knew that here was a place for asterisks in his interview, if interviews were faithful. "He had money enough," continued Lapham, with a suppressed sigh; "but he didn't know anything about paint. We hung on together for a year or two. And then we quit."

"And he had the experience," suggested Bartley, with companionable ease.

"I had some of the experience, too," said Lapham, with a scowl; and Bartley divined, through the freemasonry of all who have some sore places in their memories, that this was a point which he must not touch again.

"And since that, I suppose, you've played it alone."

"I've played it alone."

"You must ship some of this paint of yours to foreign countries, Colonel?" suggested Bartley, putting on a professional air.

"We ship it to all parts of the world It goes to South America, lots of it. It goes to Australia, and it goes to India, and it goes to China, and it goes to the Cape of Good Hope. It'll stand any climate. Of course, we don't export these fancy brands much. They're for home use. But we're introducing them elsewhere. Here." Lapham pulled open a drawer, and showed Bartley a lot of labels in different languages—Spanish, French, German, and Italian. "We expect to do a good business in all those countries. We've got our agencies in Cadiz now, and in Paris, and in Hamburg, and in Leghorn. It's a thing that's bound to make its way. Yes, sir.

Wherever a man has got a ship, or a bridge, or a dock, or a house, or a car, or a fence, or a pig-pen anywhere in God's universe to paint, that's the paint for him, and he's bound to find it out sooner or later. You pass a ton of that paint dry through a blast-furnace, and you'll get a quarter of a ton of pig-iron. I believe in my paint. I believe it's a blessing to the world. When folks come in, and kind of smell round, and ask me what I mix it with, I always say, 'Well, in the first place, I mix it with *Faith*, and after that I grind it up with the best quality of boiled linseed oil that money will buy.'"

Lapham took out his watch and looked at it, and Bartley perceived that his audience was drawing to a close. " 'F you ever want to run down and take a look at our works, pass you over the road,"—he called it *rud*,—"and it sha'n't cost you a cent."

"Well, may be I shall, sometime," said Bartley. "Good afternoon, Colonel."

"Good afternoon. Or—hold on! My horse down there yet, William?" he called to the young man in the counting-room who had taken his letter at the beginning of the interview. "Oh! All right!" he added, in response to something the young man said. "Can't I set you down somewhere, Mr. Hubbard? I've got my horse at the door, and I can drop you on my way home. I'm going to take Mis' Lapham to look at a house I'm driving piles for, down on the New Land."

"Don't care if I do," said Bartley.

Lapham put on a straw hat, gathered up some papers lying on his desk, pulled down its rolling cover, turned the key in it, and gave the papers to an extremely handsome young woman at one of the desks in the outer office. She was stylishly dressed, as Bartley saw, and her smooth, yellow hair was sculpturesquely waved over a low white forehead. "Here," said Lapham with the same prompt gruff kindness that he had used in addressing the young man, "I want you should put these in shape, and give me a type-writer copy to-morrow."

"What an uncommonly pretty girl!" said Bartley, as they descended the rough stairway and found their way out to the street, past the dangling rope of a block and tackle wandering up into the cavernous darkness overhead.

"She does her work," said Lapham shortly.

Bartley mounted to the left side of the open buggy standing at the curbstone, and Lapham, gathering up the hitching-weight, slid it under the buggy-seat and mounted beside him. "No chance to speed a horse here of course," said Lapham, while the horse with a spirited gentleness picked her way, with a high, long action, over the pavement of the street. The streets were all narrow, and most of them crooked, in that quarter of the town; but at the end of one the spar of a vessel pencilled themselves delicately against the cool blue of the afternoon sky. The air was full of a smell pleasantly compounded of oakum, of leather, and of oil. It was not the busy season, and they met only two or three trucks heavily straggling toward the wharf with their long string teams; but the cobblestones of the pavement were worn with the din of ponderous wheels, and discolored with iron-rust from them; here and there, in wandering streaks over its surface, was the grey stain of the salt water with which the street had been sprinkled.

After an interval of some minutes, which both men spent in looking round the dash-board from opposite sides to watch the stride of the horse, Bartley said, with a light sigh, "I had a colt once down in Maine that stepped just like that mare."

"Well!" said Lapham, sympathetically recognising the bond that this fact created between them. "Well, now, I tell you what you do. You let me come for you 'most any afternoon, now, and take you out over the Milldam, and speed this mare a little. I'd like to show you what this mare can do. Yes, I would."

"All right," answered Bartley; "I'll let you know my first day off."

"Good," cried Lapham.

"Kentucky?" queried Bartley.

"No, sir. I don't ride behind anything but Vermont; never did. Touch of Morgan, of course; but you can't have much Morgan in a horse if you want speed. Hambletonian mostly. Where'd you say you wanted to get out?"

"I guess you may put me down at the *Events* Office, just round the corner here. I've got to write up this interview while it's fresh."

"All right," said Lapham, impersonally assenting to Bartley's use of him as material.

He had not much to complain of in Bartley's treatment, unless it was the strain of extravagant compliment which it involved. But the flattery was mainly for the paint, whose virtues Lapham did not believe could be overstated, and himself and his history had been treated with as much respect as Bartley was capable of showing any one. He made a very picturesque thing of the discovery of the paintmine. "Deep in the heart of the virgin forests of Vermont, far up toward the line of the Canadian snows, on a desolate mountain-side, where an autumnal storm had done its wild work, and the great trees, strewn hither and thither, bore witness to its violence, Nehemiah Lapham discovered, just forty years ago, the mineral which the alchemy of his son's enterprise and energy has transmuted into solid ingots of the most precious of metals. The colossal fortune of Colonel Silas Lapham lay at the bottom of a hole which an uprooted tree had dug for him, and which for many years remained a paint-mine of no more appreciable value than a soap-mine."

Here Bartley had not been able to forego another grin; but he compensated for it by the high reverence with which he spoke of Colonel Lapham's record during the war of the rebellion, and of the motives which impelled him to turn aside from an enterprise in which his whole heart was engaged, and take part in the struggle. "The Colonel bears embedded in the muscle of his right leg a little memento of the period in the shape of a minie-ball, which he jocularly referred to as his thermometer, and which relieves him from the necessity of reading 'The Probabilities' in his morning paper. This saves him just so much time; and for a man who, as he said, has not a moment of waste time on him anywhere, five minutes a day are something in the course of a year. Simple, clear, bold, and straightforward in mind and action, Colonel Silas

Lapham, with a prompt comprehensiveness and a never-failing business sagacity, is, in the best sense of that much-abused term, one of nature's noblemen, to the last inch of his five eleven and a half. His life affords an example of single-minded application and unwavering perseverance which our young business men would do well to emulate. There is nothing showy or meretricious about the man. He believes in mineral paint, and he puts his heart and soul into it. He makes it a religion; though we would not imply that it *is* his religion. Colonel Lapham is a regular attendant at the Rev. Dr. Langworthy's church. He subscribes liberally to the Associated Charities, and no good object or worthy public enterprise fails to receive his support. He is not now actively in politics, and his paint is not partisan; but it is an open secret that he is, and always has been, a staunch Republican. Without violating the sanctities of private life, we cannot speak fully of various details which came out in the free and unembarrassed interview which Colonel Lapham accorded our representative. But we may say that the success of which he is justly proud he is also proud to attribute in great measure to the sympathy and energy of his wife—one of those women who, in whatever walk of life, seem born to honor the name of American Woman, and to redeem it from the national reproach of Daisy Millerism. Of Colonel Lapham's family, we will simply add that it consists of two young lady daughters.

"The subject of this very inadequate sketch is building a house on the water side of Beacon Street, after designs by one of our leading architectural firms, which, when complete, will be one of the finest ornaments of that exclusive avenue. It will, we believe, be ready for the occupancy of the family sometime in the spring."

When Bartley had finished his article, which he did with a good deal of inward derision, he went home to Marcia, still smiling over the thought of Lapham, whose burly simplicity had peculiarly amused him.

"He regularly turned himself inside out to me," he said, as he sat describing his interview to Marcia.

"Then I know you could make something nice out of it," said his wife; "and that will please Mr. Witherby."

"Oh, yes, I've done pretty well; but I couldn't let myself loose on him the way I wanted to. Confound the limitations of decency, anyway! I should like to have told just what Colonel Lapham thought of landscape advertising in Colonel Lapham's own words. I'll tell you one thing, Marsh: he had a girl there at one of the desks that you wouldn't let *me* have within gunshot of *my* office. Pretty? It ain't any name for it!" Marcia's eyes began to blaze, and Bartley broke out into a laugh, in which he arrested himself at sight of a formidable parcel in the corner of the room.

"Hello! What's that?"

"Why, I don't know what it is," replied Marcia tremulously. "A man brought it just before you came in, and I didn't like to open it."

"Think it was some kind of infernal machine?" asked Bartley, getting down on his knees to examine the package. "*Mrs.* B. Hubbard, heigh?" He cut the heavy hemp string with his penknife. "We must look into this thing. I should like to know who's sending packages to Mrs. Hubbard in my absence." He unfolded the wrappings of paper, growing softer and finer inward, and presently pulled out a handsome square glass jar, through which a crimson mass showed richly. "The Persis Brand!" he yelled. "I knew it!"

"Oh, what is it, Bartley?" quavered Marcia. Then, courageously drawing a little nearer: "Is it some kind of jam?" she implored.

"Jam? No!" roared Bartley. "It's *paint!* It's mineral paint—Lapham's paint!"

"Paint?" echoed Marcia, as she stood over him while he stripped their wrappings from the jars which showed the dark blue, dark green, light brown, dark brown, and black, with the dark crimson, forming the gamut of color of the Lapham paint. "Don't *tell* me it's paint that *I* can use, Bartley!"

"Well, I shouldn't advise you to use much of it—all at once," replied her husband. "But it's paint that you can use in moderation."

Marcia cast her arms round his neck and kissed him. "Oh, Bartley, I think I'm the happiest girl in the world! I was just wondering what I should do. There are places in that Clover Street house that need touching up so dreadfully. I shall be very careful. You needn't be afraid I shall overdo. But, this just saves my life. Did you *buy* it, Bartley? You know we couldn't afford it, and you oughtn't to have done it! And what does the Persis Brand mean?"

"Buy it?" cried Bartley. "No! The old fool's sent it to you as a present. You'd better wait for the facts before you pitch into me for extravagance, Marcia. Persis is the name of his wife; and he named it after her because it's his finest brand. You'll see it in my interview. Put it on the market her last birthday for a surprise to her."

"What old fool?" faltered Marcia.

"Why, Lapham—the mineral paint man."

"Oh, what a good man!" sighed Marcia from the bottom of her soul. "Bartley! you *won't* make fun of him as you do of some of those people? *Will* you?"

"Nothing that *he*'ll ever find out," said Bartley, getting up and brushing off the carpet-lint from his knees.

1885

From *A HAZARD OF NEW FORTUNES* *

PART THIRD: CHAPTER IX

[A MUSICALE]

The Dryfooses went late to Mrs. Horn's *musicale,* in spite of Mrs. Mandel's advice. Christine made the delay, both because she wished to show Miss Vance that she was anxious, and because she had some vague notion of the distinction of arriving late at any sort of entertainment. Mrs. Mandel insisted upon the difference between this *musicale* and an ordinary reception; but Christine rather fancied disturbing a company that had got seated, and perhaps making people rise and stand, while she found her way to her place, as she had seen them do for a tardy comer at the theater.

Mela, whom she did not admit to her reasons or feelings always, followed her with the servile admiration she had for all that Christine did; and she took on trust as somehow successful the result of Christine's obstinacy, when they were allowed to stand against the wall at the back of the room through the whole of the long piece begun just before they came in. There had been no one to receive them; a few people, in the rear rows of chairs near them, turned their heads to glance at them, and then looked away again. Mela had her misgivings; but at the end of the piece Miss Vance came up to them at once, and then Mela knew that she had her eyes on them all the time, and that Christine must have been right. Christine said nothing about their coming late, and so Mela did not make any excuse, and Miss Vance seemed to expect none. She glanced with a sort of surprise at Conrad, when Christine introduced him; Mela did not know whether she liked their bringing him, till she shook hands with him, and said: "Oh, I am very glad indeed! Mr. Dryfoos and I have met before." Without explaining where or when, she led them to her aunt and presented them, and then said, "I'm going to put you with some friends of yours," and quickly seated them next the Marches. Mela liked that well enough; she thought she might have some joking with Mr. March, for all his wife was so stiff; but the look which Christine wore seemed to forbid, provisionally at least, any such recreation. On her part, Christine was cool with the Marches. It went through her mind

that they must have told Miss Vance they knew her; and perhaps they had boasted of her intimacy. She relaxed a little toward them when she saw Beaton leaning against the wall at the end of the row next Mrs. March. Then she conjectured that he might have told Miss Vance of her acquaintance with the Marches, and she bent forward and nodded to Mrs. March across Conrad, Mela, and Mr. March. She conceived of him as a sort of hand of her father's, but she was willing to take them at their apparent social valuation for the time. She leaned back in her chair, and did not look up at Beaton after the first furtive glance, though she felt his eyes on her.

The music began again almost at once, before Mela had time to make Conrad tell her where Miss Vance had met him before. She would not have minded interrupting the music; but everyone else seemed so attentive, even Christine, that she had not the courage.

The concert went on to an end without realizing for her the ideal of pleasure which one ought to find in society. She was not exacting, but it seemed to her there were very few young men, and when the music was over, and their opportunity came to be sociable, they were not very sociable. They were not introduced, for one thing, but it appeared to Mela that they might have got introduced, if they had any sense; she saw them looking at her, and she was glad she had dressed so much; she was dressed more than any other lady there, and either because she was the most dressed of any person there, or because it had got around who her father was, she felt that she had made an impression on the young men. In her satisfaction with this, and from her good nature, she was contented to be served with her refreshments after the concert by Mr. March, and to remain joking with him. She was at her ease; she let her hoarse voice out in her largest laugh; she accused him, to the admiration of those near, of getting her into a perfect gale. It appeared to her, in her own pleasure, her mission to illustrate to the rather subdued people about her what a good time really was, so that they could have it if they wanted it. Her joy was crowned when March modestly professed himself unworthy to monopolize her, and explained how selfish he felt in talking to a young lady when there were so many young men dying to do so.

"Oh, pshaw, dyun', yes!" cried Mela, tasting the irony. "I guess I see them!"

He asked if he might really introduce a friend of his to her, and she said, Well, yes, if he thought he could live to get to her; and March brought up a man whom he thought very young and Mela thought very old. He was a contributor to *Every Other Week,* and so March knew him; he believed himself a student of human nature in behalf of literature, and he now set about studying Mela. He tempted her to express her opinion on all points, and he laughed so amiably at the boldness and humorous vigor of her ideas that she was delighted with him. She asked him if he was a New-Yorker by birth; and she told him she pitied him, when he said he had never been West. She professed herself perfectly sick of New York, and urged him to go to

Moffitt if he wanted to see a real live town. He wondered if it would do to put her into literature just as she was, with all her slang and brag, but he decided that he would have to subdue her a great deal: he did not see how he could reconcile the facts of her conversation with the facts of her appearance: her beauty, her splendor of dress, her apparent right to be where she was. These things perplexed him; he was afraid the great American novel, if true, must be incredible. Mela said he ought to hear her sister go on about New York when they first came; but she reckoned that Christine was getting so she could put up with it a little better, now. She looked significantly across the room to the place where Christine was now talking with Beaton; and the student of human nature asked, Was she here? and, Would she introduce him? Mela said she would, the first chance she got; and she added, They would be much pleased to have him call. She felt herself to be having a beautiful time, and she got directly upon such intimate terms with the student of human nature that she laughed with him about some peculiarities of his, such as his going so far about to ask things he wanted to know from her; she said she never did believe in beating about the bush much. She had noticed the same thing in Miss Vance when she came to call that day; and when the young man owned that he came rather a good deal to Mrs. Horn's house, she asked him, Well, what sort of a girl was Miss Vance, anyway, and where did he suppose she had met her brother? The student of human nature could not say as to this, and as to Miss Vance he judged it safest to treat of the non-society side of her character, her activity in charity, her special devotion to the work among the poor on the East Side, which she personally engaged in.

"Oh, that's where Conrad goes, too!" Mela interrupted. "I'll bet anything that's where she met him. I *wisht* I could tell Christine! But I suppose she would want to kill me, if I was to speak to her *now*."

The student of human nature said, politely, "Oh, shall I take you to her?"

Mela answered, "I guess you better *not!*" with a laugh so significant that he could not help his inferences concerning both Christine's absorption in the person she was talking with and the habitual violence of her temper. He made note of how Mela helplessly spoke of all her family by their names, as if he were already intimate with them; he fancied that if he could get that in skilfully, it would be a valuable color in his study; the English lord whom she should astonish with it began to form himself out of the dramatic nebulosity in his mind, and to whirl on a definite orbit in American society. But he was puzzled to decide whether Mela's willingness to take him into her confidence on short notice was typical or personal: the trait of a daughter of the natural-gas millionaire, or a foible of her own.

Beaton talked with Christine the greater part of the evening that was left after the concert. He was very grave, and took the tone of a fatherly friend; he spoke guardedly of the people present, and moderated the severity of some of Christine's judgments of their looks and costumes. He did this out of a sort of unrea-soned allegiance to Margaret, whom he was in the mood of wishing to please by being very kind and good, as she always was. He had the sense also of atoning by this behavior for some reckless things he had said before that to Christine; he put on a sad, reproving air with her, and gave her the feeling of being held in check. She chafed at it, and said, glancing at Margaret in talk with her brother, "I don't think Miss Vance is so very pretty, do you?"

"I never think whether she's pretty or not," said Beaton, with dreamy affectation. "She is merely perfect. Does she know your brother?"

"So *she* says. I didn't suppose Conrad ever went anywhere, except to tenement-houses."

"It might have been there," Beaton suggested. "She goes among friendless people everywhere."

"Maybe that's the reason she came to see *us!*" said Christine.

Beaton looked at her with his smoldering eyes, and felt the wish to say, "Yes, it was exactly that," but he only allowed himself to deny the possibility of any such motive in that case. He added: "I am so glad you know her, Miss Dryfoos. I never met Miss Vance without feeling myself better and truer, somehow; or the wish to be so."

"And you think *we* might be improved, too?" Christine retorted. "Well, I must say you're not very flattering, Mr. Beaton, anyway."

Beaton would have liked to answer her according to her cattishness, with a good clawing sarcasm that would leaves its smart in her pride; but he was being good, and he could no change all at once. Besides, the girl' attitude under the social honor done her interested him. He was sure she had never been in such good company before, but he could see that she was not in the least affected by the experience. He had told her who this person and that was; and he saw she had understood that the names were of consequence; but she seemed to feel her equality with them all. Her serenity was not obviously akin to the savage stoicism in which Beaton hid his own consciousness of social inferiority; but having won his way in the world so far by his talent, his personal quality, he did not conceive the simple fact in her case. Christine was self-possessed because she felt that a knowledge of her father's fortune had got around, and she had the peace which money gives to ignorance; but Beaton attributed her poise to indifference to social values. This, while he inwardly sneered at it, avenged him upon his own too keen sense of them, and, together with his temporary allegiance to Margaret's goodness, kept him from retaliating Christine's vulgarity. He said, "I don't see how that could be," and left the question of flattery to settle itself.

The people began to go away, following each other up to take leave of Mrs. Horn. Christine watched them with unconcern, and either because she would not be governed by the general movement, or because she liked being with Beaton, gave no sign of going. Mela was still talking to the student of human nature, sending out her laugh in deep gurgles amid the unimaginable confidences she was making him about herself, her family, the staff of *Every Other Week*, Mrs. Mandel, and the kind of life they had

all led before she came to them. He was not a blind devotee of art for art's sake, and though he felt that if one could portray Mela just as she was she would be the richest possible material, he was rather ashamed to know some of the things she told him; and he kept looking anxiously about for a chance of escape. The company had reduced itself to the Dryfoos groups and some friends of Mrs. Horn's who had the right to linger, when Margaret crossed the room with Conrad to Christine and Beaton.

"I'm so glad, Miss Dryfoos, to find that I was not quite a stranger to you all when I ventured to call, the other day. Your brother and I are old acquaintances, though I never knew who he was before. I don't know just how to say we met where he is valued so much. I suppose I mustn't try to say how much," she added, with a look of deep regard at him.

Conrad blushed and stood folding his arms tight over his breast, while his sister received Margaret's confession with the suspicion which was her first feeling in regard to any new thing. What she concluded was that this girl was trying to get in with them, for reasons of her own. She said: "Yes; it's the first I ever heard of his knowing you. He's so much taken up with his meetings, he didn't want to come to-night."

Margaret drew in her lip before she answered, without apparent resentment of the awkwardness or ungraciousness, whichever she found it: "I don't wonder! You become so absorbed in such work that you think nothing else is worth while. But I'm glad Mr. Dryfoos could come with you; I'm *so* glad you could all come;

I knew you would enjoy the music. Do sit down—"

"No," said Christine, bluntly; "we must be going. Mela!" she called out, "come!"

The last group about Mrs. Horn looked around, but Christine advanced upon them undismayed, and took the hand Mrs. Horn promptly gave her. "Well, I must bid you good-night."

"Oh, good-night," murmured the elder lady. "So very kind of you to come."

"I've had the best kind of a time," said Mela, cordially. "I hain't laughed so much, I don't know when."

"Oh, I'm glad you enjoyed it," said Mrs. Horn, in the same polite murmur she had used with Christine; but she said nothing to either sister about any future meeting.

They were apparently not troubled. Mela said over her shoulder to the student of human nature, "The next time I see you I'll *give* it to you for what you said about Moffitt."

Margaret made some entreating paces after them, but she did not succeed in covering the retreat of the sisters against critical conjecture. She could only say to Conrad, as if recurring to the subject, "I *hope* we can get our friends to play for us some night. I know it isn't any real help, but such things take the poor creatures out of themselves for the time being, don't you think?"

"Oh yes," he answered. "They're good in that way." He turned back hesitatingly to Mrs. Horn, and said, with a blush, "I thank you for a happy evening."

"Oh, I am very glad," she replied, in her murmur.

One of the old friends of the house

arched her eyebrows in saying good-night, and offered the two young men remaining seats home in her carriage. Beaton gloomily refused, and she kept herself from asking the student of human nature, till she had got him into her carriage, "What *is* Moffit, and what did you say about it?"

"Now you see, Margaret," said Mrs. Horn, with bated triumph, when the people were all gone.

"Yes, I see," the girl consented. "From one point of view, of course it's been a failure. I don't think we've given Miss Dryfoos a pleasure, but perhaps nobody could. And at least we've given her the opportunity of enjoying herself."

"Such people," said Mrs. Horn, philosophically, "people with their money, must of course be received sooner or later. You can't keep them out. Only, I believe I would rather let some one else begin with them. The Leightons didn't come?"

"I sent them cards. I *couldn't* call again."

Mrs. Horn sighed a little. "I suppose Mr. Dryfoos is one of your fellow-philanthropists?"

"He's one of the workers," said Margaret. "I met him several times at the Hall, but I only knew his first name. I think he's a great friend of Father Benedict; he seems devoted to the work. Don't you think he looks *good?*"

"Very," said Mrs. Horn, with a color of censure in her assent. "The younger girl seemed more amiable than her sister. But what manners!"

"Dreadful!" said Margaret, with knit brows, and a pursed mouth of humorous suffering. "But she appeared to feel very much at home."

"Oh, as to that, neither of them was much abashed. Do you suppose Mr. Beaton gave the other one some hints for that quaint dress of hers? I don't imagine that black and lace is her own invention. She seems to have some sort of strange fascination for him."

"She's very picturesque," Margaret explained. "And artists see points in people that the rest of us don't."

"Could it be her money?" Mrs. Horn insinuated. "He must be very poor."

"But he isn't base," retorted the girl, with a generous indignation that made her aunt smile.

"Oh no; but if he fancies her so picturesque, it doesn't follow that he would object to her being rich."

"It would with a man like Mr. Beaton!"

"You are an idealist, Margaret. I suppose your Mr. March has some disinterested motive in paying court to Miss Mela—Pamela, I suppose, is her name. He talked to her longer than her literature would have lasted."

"He seems a very kind person," said Margaret.

"And Mr. Dryfoos pays his salary?"

"I don't know anything about that. But that wouldn't make any difference with him."

Mrs. Horn laughed out at this security; but she was not displeased by the nobleness which it came from. She liked Margaret to be high-minded, and was really not distressed by any good that was in her.

The Marches walked home, both because it was not far, and because they must spare in carriage hire at any rate. As soon as they were out

of the house, she applied a point of conscience to him.

"I don't see how you could talk to that girl so long, Basil, and make her laugh so."

"Why, there seemed no one else to do it, till I thought of Kendricks."

"Yes, but I kept thinking, now he's pleasant to her because he thinks it's to his interest. If she had no relation to *Every Other Week,* he wouldn't waste his time on her."

"Isabel," March complained, "I wish you wouldn't think of me in *he, him,* and *his;* I never personalize you in my thoughts: you remain always a vague unindividualized essence, not quite without form and void, but nounless and pronounless. I call that a much more beautiful mental attitude toward the object of one's affections. But if you must *he* and *him* and *his* me in your thoughts, I wish you'd have more kindly thoughts of me."

"Do you deny that it's true, Basil?"

"Do you believe that it's true, Isabel?"

"No matter. But could you excuse it if it were?"

"Ah, I see you'd have been capable of it in my place, and you're ashamed."

"Yes," sighed the wife, "I'm afraid that I should. But tell me that *you* wouldn't, Basil!"

"I can tell you that I wasn't. But I suppose that in a real exigency, I could truckle to the proprietary Dryfooses as well as you."

"Oh no; you mustn't, dear! I'm woman, and I'm dreadfully afraid. But you must always be a man, especially with that horrid old Mr. Dryfoos. Promise me that you'll never yield the least point to him in a matter of right and wrong!"

"Not if he's right and I'm wrong?"

"Don't trifle, dear! You know what I mean. Will you promise?"

"I'll promise to submit the point to you, and let you do the yielding. As for me, I shall be adamant. Nothing I like better."

"They're dreadful, even that poor, good young fellow, who's so different from all the rest; he's awful, too, because you feel that he's a martyr to them."

"And I never did like martyrs a great deal," March interposed.

"I wonder how they came to be there," Mrs. March pursued, unmindful of his joke.

"That is exactly what seemed to be puzzling Miss Mela about us. She asked, and I explained as well as I could; and then she told me that Miss Vance had come to call on them and invited them; and first they didn't know how they could come till they thought of making Conrad bring them. But she didn't say why Miss Vance called on them. Mr. Dryfoos doesn't employ *her* on *Every Other Week*. But I suppose she has her own vile little motive."

"It can't be their *money;* it *can't* be!" sighed Mrs. March.

"Well, I don't know. We all respect money."

"Yes, but Miss Vance's position is so secure. She needn't pay court to those stupid, vulgar people."

"Well, let's console ourselves with the belief that she would, if she needed. Such people as the Dryfooses are the raw material of good society. It isn't made up of refined or meritorious people—professors and littéra-teurs, ministers and musicians, and their families. All the fashionable people there to-night were like the Dryfooses a generation or two ago. I dare say the material works up faster now, and in a season or two you won't know the Dryfooses from the other plutocrats. *They* will—a little better than they do now; they'll see a difference, but nothing radical, nothing painful. People who get up in the world by service to others—through letters, or art, or science—may have their modest little misgivings as to their social value, but people that rise by money—especially if their gains are sudden—never have. And that's the kind of people that form our nobility; there's no use pretending that we haven't a nobility; we might as well pretend we haven't first-class cars in the presence of a vestibuled Pullman. Those girls had no more doubt of their right to be there than if they had been duchesses: *we* thought it was very nice of Miss Vance to come and ask us, but *they* didn't; they weren't afraid, or the least embarrassed; they were perfectly natural—like born aristocrats. And you may be sure that if the plutocracy that now owns this country ever sees fit to take on the outward signs of an aristocracy —titles, and arms, and ancestors—it won't falter from any inherent question of its worth. Money prizes and honors itself, and if there is anything it hasn't got, it believes it can buy it."

"Well, Basil," said his wife, "I hope you won't get infected with Lindau's ideas of rich people. Some of them are very good and kind."

"Who denies that? Not even Lindau himself. It's all right. And the great thing is that the evening's enjoyment is over. I've got my society smile off, and I'm radiantly happy. Go on with your little pessimistic diatribes, Isabel; you can't spoil *my* pleasure."

"I could see," said Mela, as she and Christine drove home together, "that she was as jealous as she could be, all the time you was talkun' to Mr. Beaton. She pretended to be talkun' to Conrad, but she kep' her eye on you pretty close, I can tell you. I bet she just got us there to see how him and you would act together. And I reckon she was satisfied. He's dead gone on you, Chris."

Christine listened with a dreamy pleasure to the flatteries with which Mela plied her in the hope of some return in kind, and not at all because she felt spiteful toward Miss Vance, or in anywise wished her ill. "Who was that fellow with you so long?" asked Christine. "I suppose you turned yourself inside out to him, like you always do."

Mela was transported by the cruel ingratitude. "It's a lie! I didn't tell him a single thing."

Conrad walked home, choosing to do so because he did not wish to hear his sisters' talk of the evening, and because there was a tumult in his spirit which he wished to let have its way. In his life with its single purpose, defeated by stronger wills than his own, and now struggling partially to fulfill itself in acts of devotion to others, the thought of women had entered scarcely more than in that of a child. His ideals were of a virginal vagueness; faces, voices, gestures had filled his fancy at times, but almost passionately; and the sensation that he now indulged was a kind of worship, ardent, but reverent and exalted. The brutal experiences of the world make us forget that there are such natures in it, and that they seem to come up out of the lowly earth as well as down from the high heaven. In the heart of this man well on toward thirty there had never been left the stain of a base thought; not that suggestion and conjecture had not visited him, but that he had not entertained them, or in anywise made them his. In a Catholic age and country, he would have been one of those monks who are sainted after death for the angelic purity of their lives, and whose names are invoked by believers in moments of trial, like San Luigi Gonzaga. As he now walked along thinking, with a lover's beatified smile on his face, of how Margaret Vance had spoken and looked, he dramatized scenes in which he approved himself to her by acts of goodness and unselfishness, and died to please her for the sake of others. He made her praise him for them, to his face, when he disclaimed their merit, and after his death, when he could not. All the time he was poignantly sensible of her grace, her elegance, her style; they seemed to intoxicate him; some tones of her voice thrilled through his nerves, and some looks turned his brain with a delicious, swooning sense of her beauty; her refinement bewildered him. But all this did not admit the idea of possession, even of aspiration. At the most his worship only set her beyond the love of other men as far as beyond his own.

1890

THE UNEXPECTED GUESTS *

CAST

WILLIS CAMPBELL
DR. LAWTON
EDWARD ROBERTS
MR. BEMIS
MR. CURWEN
YOUNG MR. BEMIS
MR. BELFORT
MRS. CAMPBELL
MRS. CRASHAW
MRS. CURWEN
YOUNG MRS. BEMIS
MISS REYNOLDS
MRS. BELFORT

Scene: A drawing-room.
Time: The present.

MRS. WILLIS CAMPBELL'S *drawing-room.*

I

[MRS. CAMPBELL, CAMPBELL, DR. LAWTON.]

DR. LAWTON. Then truth, as I understand you, Mrs. Campbell, is a female virtue.

MRS. CAMPBELL. It is one of them.

DR. LAWTON. Oh! You have several?

MRS. CAMPBELL. Legions, Dr. Lawton.

DR. LAWTON. What do you do with them all?

MRS. CAMPBELL. Oh, we just keep them. You may be sure we don't waste them on *men*. What would be the use, for instance, of always telling Willis the truth? He wouldn't believe it, to begin with.

CAMPBELL. You had better try me once, Amy. My impression is that

it's the other thing I can't get away with. And yet I'm a great deal more accustomed to it!

MRS. CAMPBELL. That is neither here nor there. But what I say, and what I insist, is that the conventional lies that people tell are just as much lies as any—just as wicked, and altogether unnecessary. Why should I send word to the door that I'm not at home, or that I'm engaged, when I'm not, merely to get out of seeing a person?

CAMPBELL. Because you are such a liar, my love.

DR. LAWTON. No! Excuse me, Campbell! I don't wish to intercept any little endearments, but really I think that in this case Mrs. Campbell's sacrifice of the truth is a piece of altruism. She knows how it is herself; she wouldn't like to be in the place of the person she wants to get out of seeing. So she sends word that she is not at home, or that she's engaged.

MRS. CAMPBELL. Of course I do. Willis's idea of *truth* would be to send word that he didn't want to see them.

DR. LAWTON [*laughing*]. I haven't the least doubt of it.

CAMPBELL. Well, you hoary-headed imposter, what would yours be?

DR. LAWTON. Mine? I have none! I have been a general practitioner for forty years. But what time did you ask me for, Mrs. Campbell?

MRS. CAMPBELL. Seven. I don't see what's keeping them all.

CAMPBELL. The women are not coming.

MRS. CAMPBELL. Why?

CAMPBELL. Because they said they were. Truth is a female virtue.

MRS. CAMPBELL. I must say, I

don't see why they're so late. I can't understand, when every woman knows the anxiety of a hostess, how any one can be late. It's very heartless, I think.

[MRS. CAMPBELL *is in dinner dress; she remains tranquilly seated on the sofa while she speaks, but the movement of her alternately folded and expanded fan betrays the agitation of her spirits.* DR. LAWTON, *lounging at large ease in a low chair, regards her with a mixture of admiration and scientific interest. Her husband walks up and down with a surcharge of nervous energy which the husband of a dinner-giver naturally expends when the guests are a little late.*]

CAMPBELL. They will probably come in a lump—if they come at all. Don't be discouraged, Amy. If they don't come, I shall be hungry enough, by-and-by, to eat the whole dinner myself.

MRS. CAMPBELL. That is a man's idea; you think that the great thing about a dinner is to get it eaten.

DR. LAWTON. Oh, not *all* of us, Mrs. Campbell!

MRS. CAMPBELL. Well, I will except you, Dr. Lawton.

CAMPBELL. And what is a woman's idea of a dinner, I should like to know?

MRS. CAMPBELL. To get it over.

CAMPBELL. In this instance, then, I think you're going to fail. I see no prospect of your getting it over. The people are not coming. I guess you wrote Thursday when you meant Tuesday; didn't you, Amy? Your Tuesdays always look like Thursdays, anyway.

MRS. CAMPBELL. Now, Willis, if you begin your teasing!

CAMPBELL. Well, what I want you to do is to tell them what you really think of them when they do come. I don't want any hollow-hearted pretense that it isn't at all late, and that you did not expect them before, and all that kind of thing. You just say, *Yes, you are rather behind time;* and, *No, I didn't write half-past seven; I wrote seven.* With all your devotion to truth, I'll bet you wouldn't dare to speak it once.

MRS. CAMPBELL. What will you bet? Come, now! Dr. Lawton will hold the stakes.

CAMPBELL. Ah, *I* should have to pay, whichever lost, and Lawton would pocket the stakes.

DR. LAWTON. Try me!

CAMPBELL. I'd rather not. It would be too expensive. [*A ring is heard; and then voices below and on the stairs.*] The spell is broken! I hear the stentorian tones of my sister Agnes.

MRS. CAMPBELL. Yes, it *is* Agnes; and now they'll all come. [*She runs out to the space at the top of the stairs which forms a sort of passageway between the drawing-room and library.*] Oh, Agnes! I'm *so* glad to see you! And Mr. Roberts! [*She says this without, and the shock of kisses penetrates to the drawing-room, where* CAMPBELL *and* DR. LAWTON *remain.*]

MRS. ROBERTS [*without*]. Amy, I'm quite ashamed of myself! I'm afraid we're late. I think Edward's watch must be slow.

MRS. CAMPBELL [*without*]. Not at all! I don't believe it's seven yet. I've only just got into my gown.

CAMPBELL. It *is* a female virtue, Doctor!

DR. LAWTON. Oh, there's no doubt of its sex.

MRS. CAMPBELL [without]. You'll find Willis in the drawing-room with Dr. Lawton, Mr. Roberts.

II

[ROBERTS, CAMPBELL, DR. LAWTON.]

CAMPBELL [as ROBERTS meekly appears]. Hello, Roberts! You're late, old fellow. You ought to start Agnes dressing just after lunch.

ROBERTS. No, I'm afraid it's my fault. How do you do, Dr. Lawton? I think my watch is losing time.

CAMPBELL. You didn't come your old dodge of stealing a garroter's watch on your way through the Common? That was a tremendous exploit of yours, Roberts.

DR. LAWTON. And you were at your best that night, Campbell. For a little while I wasn't sure but truth was a boy.

CAMPBELL. I don't believe old Bemis has quite forgiven Roberts to this day. By-the-way, Bemis is late, too. Wouldn't have helped much to grab his watch to-night, Roberts. Hold on! That's his voice, now. [As MR. BEMIS enters] Good evening, Mr. Bemis. Roberts and I were just talking of that night when you tried to garrote him in the Common, and he got away with your watch.

III

[MR. BEMIS and the OTHERS.]

MR. BEMIS [reluctantly]. Oh! very good. Ha, ha, ha!

ROBERTS [cringingly]. Ha, ha, ha! Capital!

MR. BEMIS. Talking of watches, I hope I'm not late.

CAMPBELL. About half an hour.

MRS. CAMPBELL [reëntering and giving her hand]. Don't believe a word of it, Mr. Bemis. You're just in time. Why, even Aunt Mary is not here yet!

AUNT MARY CRASHAW [without]. Yes, I am, my dear—half-way up your ridiculous stairs.

MRS. CAMPBELL. Oh, Aunt Mary! [She runs out to meet her.]

CAMPBELL [to DR. LAWTON]. You see! she can't tell the truth even by accident.

ROBERTS. What in the world do you mean, Willis?

CAMPBELL. 'Sh! It's a bet. [To MRS. CRASHAW, coming in with his wife.] You are pretty well blown, Aunt Mary.

IV

[MRS. CRASHAW, MRS. CAMPBELL, and the OTHERS.]

MRS. CRASHAW. Blown? I wonder I'm alive to reproach Amy for these stairs. Why don't you live in a flat?

CAMPBELL. I am going to put in an elevator here, and you can get stuck in it.

MRS. CRASHAW. I dare say I shall, if you put it in. What a frightful experience! I shall never forget that night. How d'ye do, Edward? [She shakes hands with ROBERTS and MR. BEMIS.] How do you do, Mr. Bemis? I know how Dr. Lawton does, without asking.

DR. LAWTON [gallantly]. All the better for—

MRS. CRASHAW. Don't say, for

seeing me! We may *be* chestnuts, doctor, but we needn't speak them. [*To* MRS. CAMPBELL] Are you going to have the whole elevator company, as usual?

MRS. CAMPBELL. Yes—all but Mr. and Mrs. Miller. I asked them, but they had an engagement.

MRS. CRASHAW. So much the worse for them. Mrs. Curwen will be 10 very much disappointed not to see— Mrs. Miller. [*The men laugh. She shakes her fan at them.*] You ought to be ashamed to provoke me to say such things. Well, now, since I'm here, I wish the others would come. I'm rather hungry, and it's late, isn't it?

MRS. CAMPBELL. Not at all! I don't see why you all think it's late. 20 I'm sure it's very early. Ah, Mrs. Curwen! [*She advances upon this lady, who enters with her husband behind her.*] So glad you could come. And Mr. Curwen! I didn't hear you coming!

V

[MR. *and* MRS. CURWEN *and the* OTHERS.]

MRS. CURWEN. That proves you didn't eavesdrop at the head of the stairs, my dear. We were quarrelling all the way up to this threshold. After I'd answered it, I mislaid your invitation, and Mr. Curwen was sure we were asked for Wednesday. But I knew better. As it is, I'm afraid we're rather late.

MRS. CAMPBELL [*forcing a laugh*]. We rarely sit down before eight. Oh, 40 Mrs. Bemis! How do you do, Mr. Bemis? [*She greets young* MR. *and* MRS. BEMIS *with effusion, as they come in with an air of haste.*]

VI

[YOUNG MR. *and* MRS. BEMIS *and the* OTHERS.]

MRS. BEMIS. Oh, I *know* we're frightfully late!

BEMIS. Yes, it's quite shocking—

MRS. CAMPBELL. Not at all! Really, I think it must be a conspiracy. Everybody says they are late, and I don't know why.

CAMPBELL. I do; but I don't like to tell.

DR. LAWTON. Much safer, my dear boy! Much!

MRS. CAMPBELL [*ignoring this passage*]. If I should make you wait, just to *show* you that it was early, I don't think it would be more than you deserve.

CAMPBELL. Probably, if you did that, Miss Reynolds would get here too soon.

MRS. CAMPBELL. Yes; and she's usually so prompt.

MRS. CURWEN. I'm beginning to have the courage of my convictions, Mrs. Campbell. Are you *sure* you didn't say half-past?

MRS. CAMPBELL. I'm sure I can't say. Very likely I may have done so in your note. But I don't see why we are so inflexible about dinner engagements. I think we ought to give people at least three-quarters of an hour's grace, instead of that wretched fifteen minutes that keeps everybody's heart in their mouth. [*The door-bell sounds.*] Ah! That's Miss Reynolds' ring, and—

CAMPBELL. We are saved! I was afraid we were going to be thirteen at table.

MRS. ROBERTS. Thirteen! What do you mean, Willis?

CAMPBELL. Why, one from twelve, you know.

MRS. ROBERTS. Oh, yes. [*The* OTHERS *laugh.*]

MRS. CAMPBELL. Don't notice him, Agnes. He's in one of his very worst ways to-night.

MRS. ROBERTS. But I don't see what the joke is!

MRS. CAMPBELL. Neither do I, Agnes. I—

A GHOSTLY VOICE [*as of an asthmatic specter speaking through an imperfectly attached set of artificial teeth, makes itself heard from the library*]. Truth crushed to earth will rise again. For God's eternal years are hers—er—r—r—ck—ck—cr—cr —cr—ee—ck—

MRS. CRASHAW. Good heavens, Willis, what in the world is that?

THE VOICE. This is the North America Company's perfected phonograph, invented by Thomas A.—cr— cr—cr—ee—ee—ck—ck—ck— New Jersey. This cylinder was cr— cr—elocutionist—ee—ee—ck—Cullen Bryant— Truth crushed to—cr—cr —ck—ck—

CAMPBELL. Don't be alarmed, Aunt Mary. It's just a phonograph that I had got in to amuse you after dinner. It don't seem to be exactly in order. Perhaps the cylinder's got dry, or Jim hasn't got quite the right pressure on—

MRS. CRASHAW. Is Jim in there?

MRS. CAMPBELL. Yes; Agnes has lent him to us to-day. I adore boys, and Jim has been angelic the whole afternoon.

MRS. ROBERTS. Oh, you're *too* good, Amy!

MRS. CRASHAW. I don't wonder he's been angelic, with a thing like that to play with. I should be an gelic myself. Why can't we go an be amused with it a little before din ner, Willis?

THE OTHERS [*respectively*]. O yes. Do. By all means. I neve heard one before. We really can wait. Let us hear it now, Mr. Camp bell! Do make him, Mrs. Campbel

CAMPBELL. Well, all right. I'll g with you— [*He stops, feeling him self significantly clutched by th wrist, and arrested in mid-career, b* MRS. CAMPBELL.] Or, Jim can sho it off. It'll do him so much goo I'll let Jim. [*The guests follow on another out with cries of real an simulated interest, and* CAMPBEL *turns to his wife.*] What in the worl is it, Amy?

VII

[MR. *and* MRS. CAMPBELL.]

MRS. CAMPBELL. What is it? shall die, Willis!

CAMPBELL. Well, speak first.

MRS. CAMPBELL. Something's hap pened to the dinner, I know. An I'm afraid to go and see. The cook so cross!

CAMPBELL. Well, shall *I* go?

MRS. CAMPBELL. And if you kee up this teasing of yours, you'll simpl kill me.

CAMPBELL. Well, I won't, ther But it's very lucky your guests ar belated, too, Amy. Now, if yo *could* get the dinner on in about te minutes, we should be just right. Bu you've told them all they were s early that they'll believe the delay all yours.

MRS. CAMPBELL. They won't be lieve anything of the kind! The know better. But I don't dare—

JANE [*the waitress, appearing through the portière of the drawing-room*]. Dinner is ready, Mrs. Campbell.

MRS. CAMPBELL. Oh, well, then, to get them started, Willis! Don't forget, it's young Mrs. Bemis you're to take down—*not* Mrs. Curwen.

CAMPBELL. Oh, no! I sha'n't forget that. I hope Mrs. Curwen won't. Hello! There's another ring. Who in the world is that?

MRS. CAMPBELL. 'Sh! If that horrid, squeaking phonograph—

THE PHONOGRAPH [*from the library*]. Truth crushed to earth will—

MRS. CAMPBELL. Good gracious! I can't hear a word. Hark! It's Miss Reynolds talking with some one in the reception-room, and it sounds like—but it can't be—no, it can't—it—it—*is*—yes! And that's *his* voice, too, Willis! What does it mean? Am I losing my five senses? Or am I simply going stark, staring mad?

CAMPBELL. You don't say the Millers have come?

MRS. CAMPBELL. The Millers? No! Who cares anything about the Millers? 'Sh!   [*She listens.*]

CAMPBELL [*listening*]. Why, it's the Belforts!

MRS. CAMPBELL. How can you are to say it, Willis? Of course it's the Belforts. Hark!   [*She listens.*]

CAMPBELL [*listening*]. But I thought you said they declined, too.

MRS. CAMPBELL. They did. It's some frightful mystery. Be still, do, Willis!

CAMPBELL. Why, I'm not making any noise. It's the froufrou of that dress of yours.

MRS. CAMPBELL. It's your shirt bosom. You always *will* have them so stiff; and you keep breathing so.

CAMPBELL. Oh, well, if you don't want me to breathe!

MRS. CAMPBELL [*desperately*]. It doesn't matter. It wouldn't help now if you *never* breathed again. Don't joke, Willis! I can't bear it. If you do, I shall scream.

CAMPBELL. I wasn't going to joke. It's too serious. What are you going to do?

MRS. CAMPBELL. I don't know. We must do anything to keep them from finding out that they weren't expected.

CAMPBELL. But how do you suppose it's happened, Amy?

MRS. CAMPBELL. I don't know. They meant to decline somewhere else and accept here, and they mixed the letters. It's always happening. But be still now! They're coming up, and all we can do is to keep them in the dark as well as we can. You must help me, Willis.

CAMPBELL. Oh, there's nothing I like better than throwing dust in people's eyes. It's my native element.

MRS. CAMPBELL. Of course it puts the table all out, and we've got to rearrange the places, and think who is going to take out who again as soon as we can get rid of them. Be making up some pretext, Willis. We've got to consult together, or else we are completely lost. You'll have to stay and keep talking, while I run down and make them put another leaf into the table. I don't believe there's room enough now, and I'm not certain about the quails. The cook said she didn't believe they were all nice. How can people be so careless about notes? I think it's really criminal.

There ought to be something done about it. If people won't read their notes over they ought to be told about it, and I've the greatest mind to say at once that they sent a refusal, and I wasn't expecting them. It would serve them right.

CAMPBELL. Yes, and it would be such a relief to your feelings. I wish you *would* do it, Amy. Just for once.

MRS. CAMPBELL. I shall have to take the tablecloth off if I put another leaf in, and the whole thing has got to be rearranged, decorations and everything; and I'd got the violets scattered so carelessly. Now I shall just *fling* them on. I don't care how they look. I'm completely discouraged, and I shall just go through it all like a stone.

CAMPBELL. Like a precious stone. You *are* such a perfect little brick, Amy.

MRS. CAMPBELL. I guess you wouldn't like it yourself, Willis. And the Belforts are just the people I should have liked to do my best before, and now their being here spoils everything.

CAMPBELL [*smiling*]. It *is* a complication!

MRS. CAMPBELL. Oh, yes, giggle, do! I suppose you'd expect me to be logical, as you call it, with my dying breath.

CAMPBELL. No, I shouldn't, Amy; out I know you'd be delightful under any circumstances. You always get there just the same, whether you take the steps or not. But brace up now, dear, and you'll come out all right. Tell them the truth and I'll stand by you. I don't want any better fun. [*He slips behind his wife,*

who gives him a ghastly glance ove her shoulder as the BELFORTS ente the room with MISS REYNOLDS.]

VIII

[*The* BELFORTS, MISS REYNOLDS, an *the* CAMPBELLS.]

MRS. CAMPBELL. Oh, how do yo do, Maria? [*She kisses* MISS REYN OLDS, *and then, with gay cordialit; gives her hand to* MRS. BELFORT. I'm *so* glad to see you! [*She shake hands with* BELFORT.] So kind o you to come.

MISS REYNOLDS. I'm sorry to b a little late, Amy; but better lat than never, I suppose.

MRS. BELFORT. I'm not so sur of that. Dear Mrs. Campbell! wish you would be quite frank wit me!

MRS. CAMPBELL. Late? Frank What do you mean, both of you You know you're never late, Maria and why should I be frank with yo Mrs. Belfort?

CAMPBELL. What do you take u for?

MRS. BELFORT [*holding* MR CAMPBELL'S *hand clasped betwee both of hers*]. For the very nices and kindest people in the world, wh wouldn't let me have the mortificatio of deranging them on any accoun Did you expect us this evening?

MRS. CAMPBELL. Expect you What a strange question! Why i the world shouldn't we expect yo

CAMPBELL. What an extraordinar idea!

MRS. BELFORT. Because I had t hurry away from Mrs. Miller's te when I went home to dress, and whe I told her we were coming here t dinner, she said, "Oh, you are *goin*

hen?" in such a way that, though
he covered it up afterwards, and said
he didn't mean anything, and she
idn't know why she had spoken, I
elt sure there must be some misun-
erstanding, and I've come quite
eady to be sent away again if there
. Didn't you get my note?

MRS. CAMPBELL. Your note? Why,
f course I did!

MRS. BELFORT. Then it's all right.
uch a relief! Now I feel that I can
reathe freely again.

MR. BELFORT. I assure you, Mrs.
ampbell, it's a relief to me, too.
ve never seen my wife of quite so
any minds as she's been for the last
our and a half. She was quite en-
clopedic.

CAMPBELL. Oh, I know how that
, my dear boy. I've known Mrs.
ampbell to change hers as often as
a unabridged dictionary in great
nergencies.

MRS. BELFORT. But really, the
aly thing for us to do was to come,
I felt from the beginning, in spite
my doubts what to do. I thought
could depend upon you to send us
vay if we weren't wanted; but if
were, and didn't come, you
uldn't very well have sent for us.

MRS. CAMPBELL [gayly]. Indeed
should!

CAMPBELL [gallantly]. The din-
r would have been nothing without
u.

MRS. BELFORT. I don't know
out that, but I'm sure we should
ve been nothing without the din-
r. We were so glad to come. I
ited a little while about answering
I I could see whether we could be
ee of a sort of provisional engage-
ent we had hanging over us. Even

after we got here, though, I'd half
a mind to run away, and we've been
catechising poor Miss Reynolds down
in the reception-room till she
wouldn't stand it any longer, and so
here we are.

MRS. CAMPBELL. And I'm perfectly delighted. If you had yielded
to any such ridiculous misgiving, I
should never have forgiven you. I'm
sure I don't know what Mrs. Miller
could have—

THE PHONOGRAPH [in the library.]
Truth crushed to earth will cr—cr-r-
r-r—ck—ck—cr—

MRS. BELFORT. A phonograph!
Oh, have you got one? I must hear
it!

CAMPBELL. Well, won't you come
into the library? My nephew is in
there, driving everybody mad with it.
He'll be perfectly delighted with a
fresh victim.

MRS. BELFORT. And I shall be
charmed to offer myself up. Come,
Miss Reynolds. Come, Roger.

CAMPBELL. Yes, come along, Belfort. [He leads the way to the door,
and then adroitly slips back to his
wife, who has abandoned herself
wildly upon the sofa.]

IX

[CAMPBELL and MRS. CAMPBELL.]

MRS. CAMPBELL. Well, now, what
are you going to do, Willis?

CAMPBELL. I'm not going to do
anything. I haven't been flying in
the face of Providence. If ever there
was a woman offered a clean and safe
way out! But since you preferred to
remain in this labyrinth—this Black
Forest of improbabilities—

MRS. CAMPBELL. Oh, don't torment me, Willis! Don't you see that

her taking it that way made it all the more impossible for me to tell her of the blunder she had committed? I simply couldn't do it, then.

CAMPBELL. I don't see how you could help doing it then.

MRS. CAMPBELL. When she behaved so magnanimously about it, and put herself in my power? I would sooner have died, and she knew it perfectly well. That's the reason she *was* so magnanimous. You wouldn't have done it yourself after that. But it's no use talking about that now. We've got to do something, and you've got to think what we shall do. Now think!

CAMPBELL. What about?

MRS. CAMPBELL. Oh, don't tease, dearest! About the trouble—and who shall take out who—and the quails. You know what!

CAMPBELL. Well, I think if we leave those people alone much longer, they'll all come out here and ask if they weren't mistaken in supposing they were expected.

MRS. CAMPBELL [whimpering]. Oh, there you go! How perfectly heartless!

X

[MRS. ROBERTS *and the* CAMPBELLS.]

MRS. ROBERTS [showing herself at the door]. Amy, dear, what *is* the matter? Didn't you tell me the Belforts were not coming? Is that what's keeping you out here? I just knew it was!

MRS. CAMPBELL. Yes, Agnes; but do go back to them, and keep them amused. Willis and I are trying to think what to do. I've got to rearrange the whole table, you know, and

I'm not sure whether there'll be quail enough to go round.

MRS. ROBERTS. Don't worry about that, Amy. I won't take any, and I'll give Edward a hint about them.

CAMPBELL. And Roberts is capable of asking you before the whole company why you don't want him to take quail. There's nothing like Roberts for presence of mind and any little bit of *finesse* like that. No, it won't do for the entire connection to fight shy of quail. Mrs. Belfort has got her suspicions roused, and she'd be on to a thing of that kind like lightning. She's got the notion that she wasn't expected, somehow, and she's been making it hot for Amy—trying to get her to own up, and all that. If it hadn't been for me, Amy *would* have owned up, too. But I kept my eye on her, and she lied out of it like a little man.

MRS. CAMPBELL. It isn't so, Agnes. He *wanted* me to tell the truth about it, as he calls it—

MRS. ROBERTS. What an idea! You might as well have died at once. I don't see what you could have been thinking of, Willis!

MRS. CAMPBELL. Yes, he can't understand yet why I shouldn't, when Mrs. Belfort asked me if there wasn't some mistake, and literally threw herself on my mercy. She had no business to do it, and I shall always think it was taking a mean advantage; but I wasn't going to let myself be outdone in magnanimity. I shouldn't have thought she would be capable of it.

MRS. ROBERTS. It wasn't very nice, but I suppose she was excited. We mustn't blame her, and you did the only thing that any human creature ould do. I'm surprised at Willis; or, rather, I'm *not* surprised.

CAMPBELL. Well, don't let it keep you away from our other guests, Agnes.

MRS. CAMPBELL. Oh, yes; *do* go back to them, Agnes, dear! I have got to arrange all over again now, about who's to go out with who, you know. I shall want you to let Edward take Mrs. Curwen, and—

MRS. ROBERTS. Oh, Amy, you know I'd do anything for you, especially in a case like this; but I *can't* let Edward take Mrs. Curwen out. I don't mind her flirting; she does that with everyone; but she always gets Edward to laughing so that it attracts the attention of the whole table, and—

CAMPBELL. That's a very insignificant matter. I'll take out Mrs. Curwen, myself—

MRS. CAMPBELL. No, indeed you won't! You always get *her* laughing, and that's a great deal worse.

CAMPBELL. Well, well, I won't, then. But we can arrange that afterwards.

MRS. CAMPBELL. No, we'll settle it now, if you please; and I don't want you to go *near* Mrs. Curwen. She'll be sure to see that there's something wrong from the delay, and she'll try to find it out, and if she should I shall simply perish on the spot. She'll try to get round you and make you tell, and I want you to promise me, Willis, on your bended knees, that you won't let it out. She's insufferable enough as it is, but if she got to sympathizing with me, or patronizing me about such a thing, as she'd be sure to do, I don't know what I *should* do. Will you promise?

CAMPBELL. Oh, I promise. Look out you don't tell her yourself, Amy! But now I've got to see that there's enough to eat, under this new deal, and the great question is about the quail, and I've thought how to manage that. I'll just run down to the telephone, and send to the club for them. We can have them here inside of a half-hour, and never turn a feather.

MRS. CAMPBELL. Oh, Willis, you *are* inspired. Well, I shall always say that when there is any real thinking to be done— But hurry back, do, dear, and Agnes and I will be trying to settle who shall take out— Oh, I'm afraid you won't get back in time to help us! It takes so long to telephone the simplest thing.

CAMPBELL. I'll be back in one-quarter of a second. [*He rushes out, brushing by* MR. CRASHAW, *who enters at the same moment from the library.*]

XI

[MRS. CRASHAW *and the* OTHER LADIES; *then* CAMPBELL.]

MRS. CRASHAW. Amy, child, what in the world has happened? What are you staying out here away from your company for? Where's Willis going? What's Agnes doing here? It's perfectly scandalous to leave all those people alone!

MRS. CAMPBELL. Oh, Aunt Mary, if you only knew, you wouldn't scold us! Don't you see the Belforts have come?

MRS. CRASHAW. Yes, of course, they've come, and after they declined; I understand that. But it's only a matter of two plates more at the table—

MRS. CAMPBELL. Oh, is it? And am I to let *him* go down with *her?*

The whole affair has got to be planned over, and another leaf put in, and the table rearranged, and I don't know what all.

MRS. ROBERTS. And Willis has gone down to telephone to the club for more quails.

MRS. CRASHAW [to MRS. CAMPBELL]. You don't mean that you only got just quails enough?

MRS. CAMPBELL [indignantly]. A dinner for ten is not a dinner for twelve. I may not have kept house so long as you, Aunt Mary, but I'm not quite a child! [At this critical moment CAMPBELL returns.] Well, will they send them?

CAMPBELL. Yes, yes. It's all right. I couldn't get the club, just now; Central was busy; but I've primed Green's man, down below, and he'll call them up in a minute. He understands it. I thought I'd hurry back and see if I could be of use. Well, have you got things all straight?

MRS. CRASHAW. No; we've spent the time in getting them crookeder, if possible. I've insinuated that Amy didn't know how to order her dinner, and she's told me I'm an old woman. I am an old woman, Amy, and you mustn't regard me. I think my mind's going. [She kisses MRS. CAMPBELL, who clasps her in a forgiving embrace.]

MRS. CAMPBELL. Mine's gone, Aunt Mary, or I could have taken anything amiss from you! I don't see how I shall live through it. I don't know what to do; it seems to get worse every moment.

MRS. CRASHAW. Why, you don't suppose the Belforts suspect anything, do you?

MRS. CAMPBELL. That's the worst of it. I thought I ought to let th Millers know who had failed when asked them so late; and the Belfort were there at tea this afternoon, an Mrs. Miller let out her surprise tha they were coming. So, of course, had a double duty.

CAMPBELL. But, thank goodnes she was equal to it, Aunt Mary. I'v had to do some tall lying in my tim but I never soared to the heights tha Amy reached with the Belforts, in m palmiest days.

MRS. CRASHAW. Well, then, if sh convinced them that their suspicior were wrong, it's all right; and if th quails are coming from the club, don't see what there is to worry abou We must be thankful that you coul get out of it so easily.

MRS. CAMPBELL. But we're not ov of it. The table has to be rearrange but I can have that done now som how, while we're waiting for th quails. The great thing is to manag about the going out. It happens ver fortunately that if I tell all the othe men whom they're to take out, M Belfort can't suppose that he was a after-thought. But I can't seem t make a start with a new arrangemen in my own mind.

CAMPBELL. You've used up a your invention in convincing the Be forts that they were expected. Goo gracious, here's Dr. Lawton! Wha do you want here, you venerable op probrium of science?

XII

[DR. LAWTON and the OTHERS.]

DR. LAWTON [standing at ease o the threshold of the drawing-room Nothing. I merely got tired of hear ing the praises of truth chanted i here, and came out here for—a little change.

CAMPBELL. Well, you can't stay. You've got to go back, and help keep the Belforts from supposing they weren't expected, if it takes all your hoarded wisdom as a general practitioner for forty years.

MRS. CAMPBELL. Oh, yes; do go back, doctor!

DR. LAWTON. What has been the treatment up to the present time?

CAMPBELL. The most heroic kind. Amy has spared neither age nor sex, in the use of whoppers. You know what she is, doctor, when she has a duty to perform.

DR. LAWTON. But whoppers, as I understand, are always of one sex. They may be old; they often are, I believe; but they are invariably masculine.

CAMPBELL. Oh, that doesn't prevent women's using them. They use all of us.

DR. LAWTON. Well, then, there's no need of my going back on that account. In fact, I may congratulate Mrs. Campbell on the most complete success. The Belforts are thoroughly deceived.

MRS. CAMPBELL [with tremulous eagerness]. Oh, do you think so, doctor? If I could only believe that, how happy I should be!

DR. LAWTON. You may be sure of it, Mrs. Campbell. Belfort doesn't count, of course?

MRS. CRASHAW. Of course not; men will believe anything that's told them.

DR. LAWTON. And I don't allude to him. But Mrs. Belfort got me to one side as soon as she saw me, and told me she had been afraid there

was something wrong, but Mrs. Campbell had assured her that she had got her note of acceptance, and now she was going to give her whole mind to the phonograph's beautiful rendering of Bryant's poem on truth.

MRS. ROBERTS. There, Amy, you see there's no reason to worry about that!

MRS. CRASHAW. No; the only thing now is to get your dinner on the table, child, and let us eat it as soon as possible.

CAMPBELL. Yes, if Lawton's telling the truth.

THE LADIES. Willis!

DR. LAWTON. Don't mind him, ladies! The experiences of his early life in California, you know, must have been very unfavorable to a habit of confidence in his fellow-men. I pity him.

XIII

[MRS. CURWEN and the OTHERS.]

MRS. CURWEN [appearing with young MR. BEMIS]. Dr. Lawton, I wish you would go and bring your daughter here. She's flirting outrageously with my husband. [In making this accusation, MRS. CURWEN casts the eye of experienced coquetry at young MR. BEMIS, who laughs foolishly.]

DR. LAWTON. Oh, I dare say he won't mind; he must be so used to it.

MRS. CURWEN. What do you mean, Dr. Lawton? What does he mean, Mr. Campbell?

CAMPBELL. I couldn't imagine, for the life of me.

MRS. CURWEN. Can you tell me, Mrs. Campbell?

MRS. CAMPBELL. Oh, I never tell —such things.

MRS. CURWEN. What mysteries! Well, can you tell me what makes Mrs. Belfort so uncommonly gay, this evening? She seems to be in the greatest spirits, laughing with everybody—Mr. Bemis *père,* and Mr. Roberts.

MRS. CAMPBELL. Mrs. Belfort?

MRS. CURWEN. Yes. She seems a little hysterical. I wonder if anything's happened?

MRS. CAMPBELL [*sweeping the circle of her confidants with a look of misery*]. What could have happened?

DR. LAWTON. It's merely the pleasure of finding herself in your company, Mrs. Curwen.

MRS. CURWEN. Oh, thank you, Dr. Lawton. I know that I scatter sunshine in my path, but not to that extent, I think. [*With winning appeal.*] Oh, what *is* the cat in the meal, doctor? [*To young* MR. BEMIS, *archly*] Do make them tell me, Mr. Bemis!

YOUNG MR. BEMIS [*with the air of epigram*]. I'm sure *I* don't know. [*He chokes with flattered laughter.*]

MRS. CURWEN. How cruel of you not even to try! [*She makes eyes at young* MR. BEMIS, *and then transfers them rapidly to* CAMPBELL.] Won't you just whisper it in my ear, Mr. Campbell? Mrs. Roberts, you can't imagine what nice things your husband's been saying to me! I didn't know he paid compliments. And now I suppose he's devoting himself to Mrs. Belfort. Perhaps it was that made her so lively. He began at once. He's *so* amusing. I envy you having such a husband always about.

YOUNG MR. BEMIS [*in the belief that he is saying something gallant*].

I'm sure we're none of us so hard hearted as to envy *you,* Mrs. Curwen.

MRS. CURWEN. Oh, *thank* you, Mr Bemis! I shall really be afraid to tell Mr. Curwen *all* you say. [*She laughs and* CAMPBELL *joins her, even under the reproachful gaze of his wife and sister.* MRS. CURWEN *turns coaxingly to him.*] *Do* tell!

CAMPBELL. Tell what?

MRS. CURWEN. Well— [*She pause thoughtfully, and then suddenly adds.*] Who's going to take me out to dinner?

MRS. CAMPBELL [*surprised into saying it*]. Why, it's all disarranged now by the Belforts— [*She stops, and a thrill of dismay at her self-betrayal makes itself apparent to the spectators.*]

MRS. CURWEN [*with claspe hands*]. *Don't* say by the Belforts coming unexpectedly! Oh, *dear* Mrs Campbell, I know how to pity you That very thing happened to me last winter. Only, it was Mrs. Miller who came after she'd declined; she said Mr. Miller wouldn't come without her But why do you mind it? *We* all went out pell-mell. Such fun! But it must have taken all Mr. Campbell's ingenuity to keep them from suspecting

CAMPBELL. More, too. I was no where.

MRS. CURWEN [*with caressing def erence to* MRS. CAMPBELL]. O course you were not needed. But isn' it shocking how one has to manage in such an emergency? I really believe it would be better to tell the truth sometimes. Don't you?

MRS. CAMPBELL. It's all very well telling the truth if they don't suspect anything. But when people tax you with their mistakes, and try to make you own up that they've blundered hen of course you *have* to deny it.

MRS. ROBERTS. You simply *have* to.

MRS. CRASHAW. There's no other way, in that case, even if you'd prefer to tell the truth.

MRS. CURWEN. Oh, in that case, yes, indeed. *Poor* Mrs. Campbell! I can imagine how annoying it must have been; but I *should* have liked to hear you getting out of it! What did you say? *I'm* so transparent, people see through me at once.

CAMPBELL. Are you?

DR. LAWTON. Don't you think you're a little hard on yourself, Mrs. Curwen?

MRS. CURWEN [*with burlesque meekness and sincerity*]. No, not the least. It's simple justice. [MR. CURWEN *enters with* ROBERTS.] You can ask my husband if you don't believe me. Or no, I'll put the case to him myself. Fred, dear, if people whom I didn't expect to dinner came, *could* I keep them from discovering that they weren't expected? You know how awkward I am about such things —little fibs, and all that?

XIV

ROBERTS, CURWEN, *and the* OTHERS; *then the* BELFORTS.]

CURWEN. Well, I don't know—

MRS. CURWEN [*shaking her fan at him during the general laughing*]. Oh, what a wicked husband! *You* don't believe I could fib out of such a thing, do you, Mr. Roberts?

ROBERTS [*gallantly*]. If I knew what the thing was?

MRS. CURWEN. Why, like the Belforts— Oh, *poor* Mrs. Campbell! I *didn't* mean to let it out!

MRS. CAMPBELL. Oh, it doesn't matter. Would you like to go and tell the Belforts themselves? Or, you needn't go; they're coming here.

MRS. BELFORT [*returning from the library, followed by her husband and the elder* MR. BEMIS]. How perfectly the phonograph renders that piece, Mr. Campbell! I've never heard anything like it.

CAMPBELL. It's all in practice. You wouldn't hear anything else here, Mrs. Belfort. It's my favorite poem. And I'm happy to find that Mrs. Curwen likes it as much as I do.

MRS. CURWEN. I adore it!

THE PHONOGRAPH [*within*]. Truth crushed to earth will rise again.

CAMPBELL. Every time! But I wish Jim would change the cylinder. I like a little vari—

A SOUND [*from the regions below, something like this*]. Woor, roor, roor; woor, roor, roor! [*And then a voice.*] Hello! Is that you, Central? Well, give me two hundred and forty-one, please! Yes, two, four, one: Iroquois Club. Yes! What? Yes, Iroquois Club—two forty-one. Well, hurry up! Is that you, Iroquois? Yes? Busy? Well, that won't work. I don't care if you *are* busy. You've got to take my message, and take it right away. Hear that?

CAMPBELL. Hear it? I should think they could! That confounded fool has left the closet-door open! [*He rushes out and down the stairs, while the* OTHERS *assume various attitudes of sympathy and dismay, and* MRS. CURWEN *bows herself into her fan, and the voice below continues.*]

THE VOICE. Well, why don't you send them quails you promised half an hour ago? What? Who is it? It's Mr. Campbell. C, a, m, Cam, m, e, l, mel, Campbell. One hump!

What? Oh, hump yourself! It's Mr.
Cam—

CAMPBELL'S VOICE [*from below*].
Why the deuce don't you shut that
closet-door? Shut it! Shut it! We
can hear you all over the house, the
way you yell. Don't you know how
to use a telephone? Shut that door,
anyway!

THE VOICE. Oh, I beg your pardon,
sir, I didn't think about the door. I
didn't know it was open. All right,
sir. [*There is the sound of a closing
door, and then, as* CAMPBELL *rejoins
his guests with a flushed face, the
woor-roor-rooring of the electric bell
begins again.*] Iroquois! Is this
Iroquois? No, I don't want you; I
want Iroquois. Well, is that Iroquois
now? [*The words are at first muf-*
*fled; then they grow more and more
distinct, in spite of the intervening
door.*] Yes, quails! A dozen roast
quails. You got the order half an
hour ago. There's a lot of folks come
that they didn't expect, and they got
to have some more birds. Well, hurry
up, then! Good-by! Woor-roor!

CAMPBELL [*amid the consternation
of the company, while* MR. BELFORT
*fixes his wife with an eye of mute
reproach*]. Now, my dear, this is so
awful that nothing can be done about
it on the old lines.

MRS. CAMPBELL. Yes; I give it
up. Mrs. Belfort, I tried my very best
to keep you from suspecting, and even
when you did suspect, I'm sure you
must say that I did all I could. But
fate was against me.

MRS. CURWEN. Oh, *poor* Mrs.
Campbell! *Must* you own up?

MRS. BELFORT. But I don't understand. You got my note of acceptance, didn't you?

MRS. CAMPBELL. But it *wasn't*
note of acceptance: it was a note o
regret!

MRS. BELFORT. Indeed it was not

MRS. CAMPBELL. I knew just ho
it happened as soon as I saw you th
evening, and I determined that wil
horses should not get the truth out o
me. [CAMPBELL *and* DR. LAWTO
exchange signals of admiration.] Yo
must have been writing two notes, de
clining somewhere else, and then go
them mixed. It's always happenin

CAMPBELL. It's one of the com
monest things in the world—on th
stage; and ever since a case of th
kind happened to Mrs. Campbell dow
at the Shore, one summer, she's know
how to deal with it.

MRS. BELFORT. But I *didn't* writ
two notes and get them mixed.
wrote but one, to tell Mrs. Campbel
how very glad I was to come. D
you happen to have kept my note?

MRS. CAMPBELL. They are all her
in this desk, and—[*running to it, an*
pulling it open.]—here is yours. [*Sh*
reads.] "Dear Mrs. Campbell, I a
very sorry to be so late in answering
An out-of-town engagement for th
tenth, which has been hanging over u
in a threatening way for the past fort
night—" [MRS. CAMPBELL *turns th
leaf, and continues reading in a mur
mur that finally fades into the silenc
of utter dismay.*]

CAMPBELL. Well, my dear?

MRS. CRASHAW. What in the worl
is it, child?

MRS. ROBERTS. Amy!

MRS. CURWEN. Oh, not *anothe
mystery*, I hope!

CAMPBELL. Go on, Amy, or shal
I—

MRS. CAMPBELL [*reading desper*

ely on]. "—for the past fortnight,
happily off at last, and I am very
ad indeed to accept your kind invi-
tion for dinner at seven on that day,
r Mr. Belfort and myself—" [She
ts her hands, with the letter stretched
tween them, fall dramatically be-
re her.]

CAMPBELL. Well, my dear, there
ems to be a pretty clear case against
u, and unless you can plead mind-
ansference, or something like that—

MRS. ROBERTS. I'm sure it's mind-
ansference, Amy! I've often been
rough the same experience myself.
st take the opposite of what's
id.

MRS. CAMPBELL [in a daze]. But
don't see— Yes, now I begin to re-
ember how it must have been—how
was. I know now, but I don't know
w I can ever forgive myself for
ch carelessness, when I'm always so
rticular about notes—

CAMPBELL. Yes, I've even heard
u say it was criminal to read them
relessly. I can bear witness for
u there.

MRS. ROBERTS. I'm sure I could,
o, Amy, in a court of justice.

MRS. CAMPBELL. Yes, I was just
ing out when your note came, Mrs.
lfort, and I read the first page—
wn to "for the past fortnight"—and
ook it for granted that the opening
ret meant a refusal, and just
opped it into my desk and gave you
. It's inexcusable, perfectly in-
cusable! I'm quite at your feet,
rs. Belfort, and I shall not blame
u at all if you can't forgive me.
at shall I say to you?

MRS. BELFORT [amiably]. Nothing,
dear, except that you will let me
y, now I'm here!

MRS. CAMPBELL. How sweet you
are! You shall live with us!

CAMPBELL. Truth crushed to earth!
It's perfectly wonderful! Mrs. Campbell can't get away from it when she
tries her best. She tells it in spite
of herself. She supposed she wasn't
telling it when she said there was no
mistake on your part; but she was.
Well, it is a feminine virtue, doctor.

DR. LAWTON. Unquestionably, I
think that it came into the world with
woman.

MRS. CAMPBELL [with mounting
courage]. Yes, a pretty predicament
I should have been in, Willis, if I had
taken your advice, and told the truth,
as you call it, in the beginning. But
now we won't wait any longer. The
quails will come in their own good
time. My dear, will you give Mrs.
Belfort your arm? And, Mr. Belfort,
will you give me yours?

MRS. CURWEN. And all the rest
of us?

MRS. CAMPBELL. Oh, you can come
out pell-mell.

MRS. CURWEN. Oh, dear Mrs.
Campbell!

1893

From *CRITICISM AND FICTION* *

XXIII

[ON DECENCY]

One of the great newspapers the
other day invited the prominent
American authors to speak their minds
upon a point in the theory and practice of fiction which had already vexed
some of them. *It was the question of*

how much or how little the American novel ought to deal with certain facts of life which are not usually talked of before young people, and especially young ladies. Of course the question was not decided, and I forget just how far the balance inclined in favor of a larger freedom in the matter. But it certainly inclined that way; one or two writers of the sex which is somehow supposed to have purity in its keeping (as if purity were a thing that did not practically concern the other sex, preoccupied with serious affairs) gave it a rather vigorous tilt to that side. In view of this fact it would not be the part of prudence to make an effort to dress the balance; and indeed I do not know that I was going to make any such effort. But there are some things to say, around and about the subject, which I should like to have some one else say, and which I may myself possibly be safe in suggesting.

One of the first of these is the fact, generally lost sight of by those who censure the Anglo-Saxon novel for its prudishness, that it is really not such a prude after all; and that if it is sometimes apparently anxious to avoid those experiences of life not spoken of before young people, this may be an appearance only. Sometimes a novel which has this shuffling air, this effect of truckling to propriety, might defend itself, if it could speak for itself, by saying that such experiences happened not to come within its scheme, and that, so far from maiming or mutilating itself in ignoring them, it was all the more faithfully representative of the tone of modern life in dealing with love that was chaste, and with passion so honest that it could be openly spoken of before the tenderest society bud at dinner. It might say that the guilty intrigue, the betrayal, the extreme flirtation even, was the exceptional thing in life, and unless the scheme of the story necessarily involved it that it would be bad art to lug it in and as bad taste as to introduce such topics in a mixed company. It could say very justly that the novel in our civilization now always addresses mixed company, and that the vast majority of the company are ladies, and that very many, if not most, of these ladies are young girls. If the novel were written for men and for married women alone, as in continental Europe, it might be altogether different. But the simple fact is that is not written for them alone among us, and it is a question of writing, under cover of our universal acceptance, things for young girls to read which you would be put out-of-doors for saying to them, or of frankly giving notice of your intention, and so cutting yourself off from the pleasure—and it is a very high and sweet one—of appealing to these vivid, responsive intelligences, which are none the less brilliant and admirable because they are innocent.

One day a novelist who liked, after the manner of other men, to repine his hard fate, complained to his friend a critic, that he was tired of the restriction he had put upon himself this regard; for it is a mistake, can be readily shown, to suppose that others impose it. "See how free those French fellows are!" he rebelled. "Shall we always be shut up to our tradition of decency?"

"Do you think it's much worse than

being shut up to their tradition of indecency?" said his friend.

Then that novelist began to reflect, and he remembered how sick the invariable motive of the French novel made him. He perceived finally that, convention for convention, ours was not only more tolerable, but on the whole was truer to life, not only to its complexion, but also to its texture. No one will pretend that there is not vicious love beneath the surface of our society; if he did, the fetid explosions of the divorce trials would refute him; but if he pretended that it was in any just sense characteristic of our society, he could be still more easily refuted. Yet it exists, and it is unquestionably the material of tragedy, the stuff from which intense effects are wrought. The question, after owning this fact, is whether these intense effects are not rather cheap effects. I incline to think they are, and I will try to say why I think so, if I may do so without offence. The material itself, the mere mention of it, has an instant fascination; it arrests, it detains, till the last word is said, and while there is anything to be hinted. This is what makes a love intrigue of some sort all but essential to the popularity of any fiction. Without such an intrigue the intellectual equipment of the author must be of the highest, and then he will succeed only with the highest class of readers. But any author who will deal with a guilty love intrigue holds all readers in his hand, the highest with the lowest, as long as he hints the slightest hope of the smallest potential naughtiness. He needs not at all be a great author; he may be a very shabby wretch, if he has but the courage or the trick of

that sort of thing. The critics will call him "virile" and "passionate"; decent people will be ashamed to have been limned by him; but the low average will only ask another chance of flocking into his net. If he happens to be an able writer, his really fine and costly work will be unheeded, and the lure to the appetite will be chiefly remembered. There may be other qualities which make reputations for other men, but in his case they will count for nothing. He pays this penalty for his success in that kind; and every one pays some such penalty who deals with some such material.

But I do not mean to imply that his case covers the whole ground. So far as it goes, though, it ought to stop the mouths of those who complain that fiction is enslaved to propriety among us. It appears that of a certain kind of impropriety it is free to give us all it will, and more. But this is not what serious men and women writing fiction mean when they rebel against the limitations of their art in our civilization. They have no desire to deal with nakedness, as painters and sculptors freely do in the worship of beauty; or with certain facts of life, as the stage does, in the service of sensation. But they ask why, when the conventions of the plastic and histrionic arts liberate their followers to the portrayal of almost any phase of the physical or of the emotional nature, an American novelist may not write a story on the lines of *Anna Karenina* or *Madame Bovary*. They wish to touch one of the most serious and sorrowful problems of life in the spirit of Tolstoy and Flaubert, and they ask why they may not. At one time, they remind us, the Anglo-Saxon novelist did deal with such problems—De Foe in his spirit, Richardson in his, Goldsmith in his. At what moment did our fiction lose this privilege? In what fatal hour did the Young Girl arise and seal the lips of Fiction, with a touch of her finger, to some of the most vital interests of life?

Whether I wished to oppose them in their aspirations for greater freedom, or whether I wished to encourage them, I should begin to answer them by saying that the Young Girl has never done anything of the kind. The manners of the novel have been improving with those of its readers; that is all. Gentlemen no longer swear or fall drunk under the table, or abduct young ladies and shut them up in lonely country-houses, or so habitually set about the ruin of their neighbors' wives, as they once did. Generally, people now call a spade an agricultural implement; they have not grown decent without having also grown a little squeamish, but they have grown comparatively decent; there is no doubt about that. They require of a novelist whom they respect unquestionable proof of his seriousness, if he proposes to deal with certain phases of life; they require a sort of scientific decorum. He can no longer expect to be received on the ground of entertainment only; he assumes a higher function, something like that of a physician or a priest, and they expect him to be bound by laws as sacred as those of such professions; they hold him solemnly pledged not to betray them or abuse their confidence. If he will accept the conditions, they give him their confidence, and he may then treat to his

greater honor, and not at all to his disadvantage, of such experiences such relations of men and women a George Eliot treats in *Adam Bede*, in *Daniel Deronda*, in *Romola*, in almost all her books; such as Hawthorne treats in *The Scarlet Letter;* such as Dickens treats in *David Copperfield* such as Thackeray treats in *Pendennis* and glances at in every one of his fictions; such as most of the masters of English fiction have at some time treated more or less openly. It is quite false or quite mistaken to suppose that our novels have left untouched these most important realities of life. They have only not made them their stock in trade; they have kept a true perspective in regard to them; they have relegated them in their pictures of life to the space an place they occupy in life itself, as we know it in England and America. They have kept a correct proportion knowing perfectly well that unless the novel is to be a map, with everything scrupulously laid down in it, a faithful record of life in far the greater extent could be made to the exclusion of guilty love and all its circumstance and consequences.

I justify them in this view not only because I hate what is cheap and meretricious, and hold in peculiar loathing the cant of the critics who require "passion" as something in itself admirable and desirable in a novel but because I prize fidelity in the historian of feeling and character. Most of these critics who demand "passion" would seem to have no conception of any passion but one. Yet there are several other passions: the passion of grief, the passion of avarice, the passion of pity, the passion of ambition

e passion of hate, the passion of
vy, the passion of devotion, the pas-
on of friendship; and all these have
greater part in the drama of life than
e passion of love, and infinitely
eater than the passion of guilty love.
ittingly or unwittingly, English fic-
on and American fiction have recog-
ized this truth, not fully, not in the
easure it merits, but in greater de-
ree than most other fiction.

1891

rom *MY LITERARY PASSIONS* *

XXXII

TOURGUENIEF, AUERBACH

In those years at Cambridge my
ost notable literary experience with-
ut doubt was the knowledge of Tour-
uenief's novels, which began to be
ecognized in all their greatness about
e middle seventies. I think they
ade their way with such of our pub-
c as were able to appreciate them
efore they were accepted in Eng-
nd; but that does not matter. It
enough for the present purpose that
moke, and *Lisa,* and *On the Eve,*
d *Dimitri Roudine,* and *Spring
loods,* passed one after another
rough my hands, and that I formed
r their author one of the pro-
undest literary passions of my
fe.

I now think that there is a finer
nd truer method than his, but in its
ay, Tourguenief's method is as far
s art can go. That is to say, his
ction is to the last degree dramatic.
he persons are sparely described,

and briefly accounted for, and then
they are left to transact their affair,
whatever it is, with the least possible
comment or explanation from the
author. The effect flows naturally
from their characters, and when they
have done or said a thing you conjecture why as unerringly as you
would if they were people whom you
knew outside of a book. I had already conceived of the possibility of
this from Björnson, who practises
the same method, but I was still too
sunken in the gross darkness of English fiction to rise to a full consciousness of its excellence. When I
remembered the deliberate and impertinent moralizing of Thackeray, the
clumsy exegesis of George Eliot, the
knowing nods and winks of Charles
Reade, the stage-carpentering and
lime-lighting of Dickens, even the fine
and important analysis of Hawthorne,
it was with a joyful astonishment that
I realized the great art of Tourguenief.

Here was a master who was apparently not trying to work out a plot,
who was not even trying to work out
a character, but was standing aside
from the whole affair, and letting the
characters work the plot out. The
method was revealed perfectly in
Smoke, but each successive book of
his that I read was a fresh proof of
its truth, a revelation of its transcendent superiority. I think now that
I exaggerated its value somewhat;
but this was inevitable in the first
surprise. The sane aesthetics of the
first Russian author I read, however,
have seemed more and more an essential part of the sane ethics of all
the Russians I have read. It was
not only that Tourguenief had painted

life truly, but that he had painted it conscientiously.

Tourguenief was of that great race which has more than any other fully and freely uttered human nature, without either false pride or false shame in its nakedness. His themes were oftenest those of the French novelist, but how far he was from handling them in the French manner and with the French spirit! In his hands sin suffered no dramatic punishment; it did not always show itself as unhappiness, in the personal sense, but it was always unrest, and without the hope of peace. If the end did not appear, the fact that it must be miserable always appeared. Life showed itself to me in different colors after I had once read Tourguenief; it became more serious, more awful, and with mystical responsibilities I had not known before. My gay American horizons were bathed in the vast melancholy of the Slav, patient, agnostic, trustful. At the same time nature revealed herself to me through him with an intimacy she had not hitherto shown me. There are passages in this wonderful writer alive with a truth that seems drawn from the reader's own knowledge; who else but Tourguenief and one's own most secret self ever felt all the rich, sad meaning of the night air drawing in at the open window, of the fires burning in the darkness on the distant fields? I try in vain to give some notion of the subtle sympathy with nature which scarcely puts itself into words with him. As for the people of his fiction, though they were of orders and civilizations so remote from my experience, they were of the eternal human types whose origin and potentialities ever one may find in his own heart, and felt their verity in every touch.

I cannot describe the satisfaction his work gave me; I can only impart some sense of it, perhaps, by saying that it was like a happiness I had been waiting for all my life, and now that it had come, I was richly content forever. I do not mean to say that the art of Tourguenief surpasses the art of Björnson; I think Björnson quite as fine and true. But the Norwegian deals with simple and primitive circumstances for the most part, and always with a small world; and the Russian has to do with human nature inside of its conventional shells, and his scene is often as large as Europe. Even when it is as remote as Norway, it is still related to the great capitals by the history if not the actuality of the characters. Most of Tourguenief's books I have read many times over, all of them have read more than twice. For a number of years I read them again and again without much caring for other fiction. It was only the other day that I read *Smoke* through once more, with no diminished sense of its truth, but with somewhat less than my first satisfaction in its art. Perhaps this was because I had reached the point through my acquaintance with Tolstoy where I was impatient even of the artifice that hid itself. In *Smoke* I was now aware of an artifice that kept out of sight, but was still always present somewhere, invisibly operating the story.

I must not fail to own the great pleasure that I have had in some of the stories of Auerbach. It is true that I have never cared greatly for

On the Heights, which in its dealing with royalties seems too far aloof from the ordinary human life, and which on the moral side finally fades out into a German mistiness. But I speak of it with the imperfect knowledge of one who was never able to read it quite through, and I have really no right to speak of it. The book of his that pleased me most was *Edelweiss*, which, though the story was somewhat too catastrophical, seemed to me admirably good and true. I still think it very delicately done, and with a deep insight; but there is something in all Auerbach's work which in the retrospect affects me as if it dealt with pigmies.

XXXV

TOLSTOY

I come now, though not quite in the order of time, to the noblest of all these enthusiasms—namely, my devotion for the writings of Lyof Tolstoy. I should wish to speak of him with his own incomparable truth, yet I do not know how to give a notion of his influence without the effect of exaggeration. As much as one merely human being can help another I believe that he has helped me; he has not influenced me in aesthetics only, but in ethics, too, so that I can never again see life in the way I saw it before I knew him. Tolstoy awakens in his reader the will to be a man; not effectively, not spectacularly, but simply, really. He leads you back to the only true ideal, away from that false standard of the gentleman, to the Man who sought not to be distinguished from other men, but identified with them, to that Presence in which the finest gentleman shows his alloy of vanity, and the greatest genius shrinks to the measure of his miserable egotism. I learned from Tolstoy to try character and motive by no other test, and though I am perpetually false to that sublime ideal myself, still the ideal remains with me, to make me ashamed that I am not true to it. Tolstoy gave me heart to hope that the world may yet be made over in the image of Him who died for it, when all Caesar's things shall be finally rendered unto Caesar, and men shall come into their own, into the right to labor and the right to enjoy the fruits of their labor, each one master of himself and servant to every other. He taught me to see life not as a chase of a forever impossible personal happiness, but as a field for endeavor towards the happiness of the whole human family; and I can never lose this vision, however I close my eyes, and strive to see my own interest as the highest good. He gave me new criterions, new principles, which, after all, were those that are taught us in our earliest childhood, before we have come to the evil wisdom of the world. As I read his different ethical books, *What to Do, My Confession,* and *My Religion,* I recognized their truth with a rapture such as I have known in no other reading, and I rendered them my allegiance, heart and soul, with whatever sickness of the one and despair of the other. They have it yet, and I believe they will have it while I live. It is with inexpressible astonishment that I hear them attainted of pessimism, as if the teaching of a man whose ideal was simple goodness must mean the prevalence of evil. The way he showed me seemed indeed impossible to my will, but to my conscience it was and is the only possible way. If there is any point on which he has not convinced my reason it is that of our ability to walk this narrow way alone. Even there he is logical, but as Zola subtly distinguishes in speaking of Tolstoy's essay on "Money," he is not reasonable. Solitude enfeebles and palsies, and it is as comrades and brothers that men must save the world from itself, rather than themselves from the world. It was so the earliest Christians, who had all things common, understood the life of Christ, and I believe that the latest will understand it so.

I have spoken first of the ethical works of Tolstoy, because they are of the first importance to me, but I think that his aesthetical works are as perfect. To my thinking they transcend in truth, which is the highest beauty, all other works of fiction that have been written, and I believe that they do this because they obey the law of the author's own life. His conscience is one ethically and one aesthetically; with his will to be true to himself he cannot be false to his knowledge of others. I thought the last word in literary art had been said to me by the novels of Tourguenief, but it seemed like the first, merely, when I began to acquaint myself with the simpler method of Tolstoy. I came to it by accident, and without any manner of preoccupation in *The Cossacks,* one of his early books, which had been on my shelves unread for five or six years. I did not know even Tolstoy's name when

I opened it, and it was with a kind o amaze that I read it, and felt wor by word, and line by line, the trut of a new art in it.

I do not know how it is that th great Russians have the secret of sim plicity. Some say it is because the have not a long literary past and ar not conventionalized by the usage o many generations of other writers but this will hardly account for th brotherly directness of their dealin with human nature; the absence o experience elsewhere characterizes th artist with crudeness, and simplicity is the last effect of knowledge. Tol stoy is, of course, the first of them in this supreme grace. He has no only Tourguenief's transparency o style, unclouded by any mist of th personality which we mistakenly valu in style, and which ought no more t be there than the artist's personality should be in a portrait; but he has a method which not only seems without artifice, but is so. I can get at the manner of most writers, and tell what it is, but I should be baffled to tel what Tolstoy's manner is; perhaps he has no manner. This appears to me true of his novels, which, with their vast variety of character and incident are alike in their single endeavor to get the persons living before you both in their action and in the peculiarly dramatic interpretation of their emotion and cogitation. There are plenty of novelists to tell you that their characters felt and thought so and so, but you have to take it on trust; Tolstoy alone makes you know how and why it was so with them and not otherwise. If there is anything in him which can be copied or burlesqued it is this ability of his to now men inwardly as well as outwardly; it is the only trait of his which I can put my hand on.

After *The Cossacks* I read *Anna Karenina* with a deepening sense of the author's unrivalled greatness. I thought that I saw through his eyes human affair of that most sorrowful sort as it must appear to the Infinite Compassion; the book is a sort of revelation of human nature in circumstances that have been so perpetually lied about that we have almost lost the faculty of perceiving the truth concerning an illicit love. When you have once read *Anna Karenina* you know how fatally miserable and essentially unhappy such a love must be. But the character of Karenin himself is quite as important as the intrigue of Anna and Vronsky. It is wonderful how such a man, cold, Philistine and even mean in certain ways, towers into a sublimity unknown (to me, at least), in fiction when he forgives, and yet knows that he cannot forgive with dignity. There is something crucial, and something triumphant, not beyond the power, but hitherto beyond the imagination of men in this effect, which is not solicited, not forced, not in the least romantic, but comes naturally, almost inevitably, from the make of man.

The vast prospects, the far-reaching perspectives of *War and Peace* made it as great a surprise for me in the historical novel as *Anna Karenina* had been in the study of contemporary life; and its people and interests did not seem more remote, since they are of a civilization always as strange and of a humanity always as known.

I read some shorter stories of Tolstoy's before I came to this greatest work of his: I read *Scenes of the Siege of Sebastopol,* which is so much of the same quality as *War and Peace;* and I read *Policoushka* and most of his short stories with a sense of my unity with their people such as I had never felt with the people of other fiction.

His didactic stories, like all stories of the sort, dwindle into allegories; perhaps they do their work the better for this, with the simple intelligences they address; but I think that where Tolstoy becomes impatient of his office of artist, and prefers to be directly a teacher, he robs himself of more than half his strength with those he can move only through the realization of themselves in others. The simple pathos, and the apparent indirectness of such a tale as that of *Policoushka,* the peasant conscript, is of vastly more value to the world at large than all his parables; and *The Death of Ivan Ilyitch,* the Philistine worldling, will turn the hearts of many more from the love of the world than such pale fables of the early Christian life as "Work while ye have the Light." A man's gifts are not given him for nothing, and the man who has the great gift of dramatic fiction has no right to cast it away or to let it rust out in disuse.

Terrible as the *Kreutzer Sonata* was, it had a moral effect dramatically which it lost altogether when the author descended to exegesis, and applied to marriage the lesson of one evil marriage. In fine, Tolstoy is certainly not to be held up as infallible. He is very distinctly fallible, but I think his life is not less instructive because in certain things it seems a failure. There was but one life ever lived upon the earth which was without failure, and that was Christ's, whose erring and stumbling follower Tolstoy is. There is no other example, no other ideal, and the chief use of Tolstoy is to enforce this fact in our age, after nineteen centuries of hopeless endeavor to substitute ceremony for character, and the creed for the life. I recognize the truth of this without pretending to have been changed in anything but my point of view of it. What I feel sure is that I can never look at life in the mean and sordid way that I did before I read Tolstoy.

Artistically, he has shown me a greatness that he can never teach me. I am long past the age when I could wish to form myself upon another writer, and I do not think I could now insensibly take on the likeness of another; but his work has been a revelation and a delight to me, such as I am sure I can never know again. I do not believe that in the whole course of my reading, and not even in the early moment of my literary enthusiasms, I have known such utter satisfaction in any writer, and this supreme joy has come to me at a time of life when new friendships, not to say new passions, are rare and reluctant. It is as if the best wine at this high feast where I have sat so long had been kept for the last, and I need not deny a miracle in it in order to attest my skill in judging vintages. In fact, I prefer to believe that my life has been full of miracles, and that the good has always come to me at the right time, so that I could profit most by it. I believe if I had not turned the corner of my fiftieth year, when I first knew Tolstoy, I should not have been able to know him as fully as I did. He has been to me that final consciousness, which he speaks of so wisely in his essay on "Life." I came into to the knowledge of myself in ways I had not dreamt of before, and began at least to discern my relation to the race, without which we are each nothing. The supreme art in literature had its highest effect in making me set art forever below humanity, and it is with the wish to offer the greatest homage to his heart and mind, which any man can pay another, that I close this record with the name of Lyof Tolstoy.

1898

From *LITERARY FRIENDS AND ACQUAINTANCE* *

PART FIRST

MY FIRST VISIT TO NEW ENGLAND

* * * I had stopped in Boston at the Tremont House, which was still one of the first hostelries of the country, and I must have inquired my way to Cambridge there; but I was sceptical of the direction the Cambridge horse-car took when I found it, and I hinted to the driver my anxieties as to why he should be starting east when I had been told that Cambridge was west of Boston. He reassured me in the laconic and sarcastic manner of his kind, and we really reached Cambridge by the route he had taken.

* Copyright 1900 by Harper & Brothers Copyright 1928 by Mildred Howells and John Mead Howells.

The beautiful elms that shaded a great part of the way massed themselves in the "groves of academe" the Square, and showed pleasant glimpses of "Old Harvard's scholar factories red," then far fewer than now. It must have been in vacation, for I met no one as I wandered through the college yard, trying to make up my mind as to how I should learn where Lowell lived; for it was he whom I had come to find. He had not only taken the poems I sent him, but he had printed two of them in a single number of the *Atlantic*, and had even written me a little note about them, which I wore next my heart in my breast pocket till I almost wore it out; and so I thought I might fitly report myself to him. But I have always been helpless in finding my way, and I was still depressed by my failure to convince the horse-car driver that he had taken the wrong road. I let several people go by without questioning them, and those I did ask abashed me farther by not knowing what I wanted to know. When I had remitted my search for the moment, an ancient man, with an open mouth and an inquiring eye, whom I never afterwards made out in Cambridge, addressed me with a hospitable offer to show me the Washington Elm. I thought this would give me time to embolden myself for the meeting with the editor of the *Atlantic* if I should ever find him, and I went with that kind old man, who, when he had shown me the tree, and the spot where Washington stood when he took command of the Continental forces, said that he had a branch of it, and that if I would come to his house

with him he would give me a piece. In the end, I meant merely to flatter him into telling me where I could find Lowell, but I dissembled my purpose and pretended a passion for a piece of the historic elm, and the old man led me not only to his house but his wood-house, where he sawed me off a block so generous that I could not get it into my pocket. I feigned the gratitude which I could see that he expected, and then I took courage to put my question to him. Perhaps that patriarch lived only in the past, and cared for history and not literature. He confessed that he could not tell me where to find Lowell; but he did not forsake me; he set forth with me upon the street again, and let no man pass without asking him. In the end we met one who was able to say where Mr. Lowell was, and I found him at last in a little study at the rear of a pleasant, old-fashioned house near the Delta.

Lowell was not then at the height of his fame; he had just reached this thirty years after, when he died; but I doubt if he was ever after a greater power in his own country or more completely embodied the literary aspiration which would not and could not part itself from the love of freedom and the hope of justice. For the sake of these he had been willing to suffer the reproach which followed their friends in the earlier days of the anti-slavery struggle. He had outlived the reproach long before; but the fear of his strength remained with those who had felt it, and he had not made himself more generally loved by the *Fable for Critics* than by the *Biglow Papers*, probably. But in the *Vision of Sir Launfal* and the *Leg-*

end of Brittany he had won a liking if not a listening far wider than his humor and his wit had got him; and in his lectures on the English poets, given not many years before he came to the charge of the *Atlantic*, he had proved himself easily the wisest and finest critic in our language. He was already, more than any American poet,

> Dowered with the hate of hate, the scorn of scorn,
> The love of love,

and he held a place in the public sense which no other author among us has held. I had myself never been a great reader of his poetry, when I met him, though when I was a boy of ten years I had heard my father repeat passages from the *Biglow Papers* against war and slavery and the war for slavery upon Mexico, and later I had read those criticisms of English poetry, and I knew Sir Launfal must be Lowell in some sort; but my love for him as a poet was chiefly centered in my love for his tender rhyme, *Auf Wiedersehen,* which I cannot yet read without something of the young pathos it first stirred in me. I knew and felt his greatness somehow apart from the literary proofs of it; he ruled my fancy and held my allegiance as a character, as a man; and I am neither sorry nor ashamed that I was abashed when I first came into his presence; and that in spite of his words of welcome I sat inwardly quaking before him. He was then forty-one years old, and nineteen my senior, and if there had been nothing else to awe me, I might well have been quelled by the disparity of our ages. But I have always been willing and even eager to do homage to men who have do something, and notably to men wh have done something in the sort wished to do something in, myse I could never recognize any oth sort of superiority; but that I a proud to recognize; and I had befo Lowell some such feeling as an o scure subaltern might have before h general. He was by nature a bit a disciplinarian, and the effect wa from him as well as in me; I da say he let me feel whatever differen there was as helplessly as I felt i At the first encounter with people always was apt to have a certai frosty shyness, a smiling cold, as fro the long, high-sunned winters of h Puritan race; he was not quite him self till he had made you aware his quality: then no one could sweeter, tenderer, warmer than h then he made you free of his whol heart; but you must be his captiv before he could do that. His whol personality had now an instant char for me; I could not keep my eye from those beautiful eyes of hi which had a certain starry serenit and looked out so purely from unde his white forehead, shadowed wit auburn hair untouched by age; from the smile that shaped the au burn beard, and gave the face in it form and color the Christ-look whic Page's portrait has flattered in it.

His voice had as great a fascina tion for me as his face. The vibran tenderness and the crisp clearness o the tones, the perfect modulation, th clear enunciation, the exquisite ac cent, the elect diction—I did no know enough then to know that thes were the gifts, these were the graces of one from whose tongue our rough

English became music such as I should never hear from any other. In this speech there was nothing of our slip-hod American slovenliness, but a truly Italian conscience and an artistic sense of beauty in the instrument.

I saw, before he sat down across his writing-table from me, that he was not far from the medium height; but his erect carriage made the most of his five feet and odd inches. He had been smoking the pipe he loved, and he put it back in his mouth, presently, as if he found himself at greater ease with it, when he began to chat, or rather to let me show what manner of young man I was by giving me the first word. I told him of the trouble I had in finding him, and I could not help dragging in something about Heine's search for Börne, when he went to see him in Frankfort; but I felt at once this was a false start, for Lowell was such an impassioned lover of Cambridge, which was truly his patria, in the Italian sense, that it must have hurt him to be unknown to anyone in it; he said, a little dryly, that he should not have thought I would have so much difficulty; but he added, forgivingly, that this was not his own house, which he was out of for the time. Then he spoke to me of Heine, and when I showed my ardor for him, he sought to temper it with some judicious criticisms, and told me that he had kept the first poem I sent him, for the long time it had been unacknowledged, to make sure that it was not a translation. He asked me about myself, and my name, and its Welsh origin, and seemed to find the vanity I had in this harmless enough. When I said I had tried

hard to believe that I was at least the literary descendant of Sir James Howels, he corrected me gently with "James Howel," and took down a volume of the *Familiar Letters* from the shelves behind him to prove me wrong. This was always his habit, as I found afterward: when he quoted anything from a book he liked to get it and read the passage over, as if he tasted a kind of hoarded sweetness in the words. It visibly vexed him if they showed him in the least mistaken; but

The love he bore to learning was at fault

for this foible, and that other of setting people right if he thought them wrong. I could not assert myself against his version of Howel's name, for my edition of his letters was far away in Ohio, and I was obliged to own that the name was spelt in several different ways in it. He perceived, no doubt, why I had chosen the form likest my own, with the title which the pleasant old turncoat ought to have had from the many masters he served according to their many minds, but never had except from that erring edition. He did not afflict me for it, though; probably it amused him too much; he asked me about the West, and when he found that I was as proud of the West as I was of Wales, he seemed even better pleased, and said he had always fancied that human nature was laid out on rather a larger scale there than in the East, but he had seen very little of the West. In my heart I did not think this then, and I do not think it now; human nature has had more ground to spread over in the West; that is all; but "it was not for me to bandy words with my sovereign." He said he liked to hear of the differences between the different sections, for what we had most to fear in our country was a wearisome sameness of type.

He did not say now, or at any other time during the many years I knew him, any of those slighting things of the West which I had so often to suffer from Eastern people, but suffered me to praise it all I would. He asked me what way I had taken in coming to New England, and when I told him, and began to rave of the beauties and quaintness of French Canada, and to pour out my joy in Quebec, he said, with a smile that had now lost all its frost, Yes, Quebec was a bit of the seventeenth century; it was in many ways more French than France, and its people spoke the language of Voltaire, with the accent of Voltaire's time.

I do not remember what else he talked of, though once I remembered it with what I believed an ineffaceable distinctness. I set nothing of it down at the time; I was too busy with the letters I was writing for a Cincinnati paper; and I was severely bent upon keeping all personalities out of them. This was very well, but I could wish now that I had trans-

gressed at least so far as to repor some of the things that Lowell said for the paper did not print my le ters, and it would have been perfectl safe, and very useful for the preser purpose. But perhaps he did not sa anything very memorable; to do tha you must have something positive i your listener; and I was the mer response, the hollow echo, that yout must be in like circumstances. I wa all the time afraid of wearing m welcome out, and I hurried to g when I would so gladly have staid. do not remember where I meant t go, or why he should have undertake to show me the way across-lots, bu this was what he did; and when w came to a fence, which I clambere gracelessly over, he put his hands o the top, and tried to take it at bound. He tried twice, and the laughed at his failure, but not wit any great pleasure, and he was nc content till a third trial carried hi across. Then he said, "I commonl do that the first time," as if it wer a frequent habit with him, while remained discreetly silent, and fo that moment at least felt myself th elder of the man who had so muc of the boy in him. He had, indeec much of the boy in him to the las and he parted with each hour of hi youth reluctantly, pathetically. * *

190

HENRY JAMES, JR.
(1843–1916)

From *THE AMERICAN* *

I

[THE LITTLE COPYIST]

On a brilliant day in May, of the year 1868, a gentleman was reclining at his ease on the great circular divan which at that period occupied the center of the Salon Carré, in the Museum of the Louvre. This commodious ottoman has since been removed, to the extreme regret of all weak-kneed lovers of the fine arts; but the gentleman in question had taken serene possession of its softest spots, and, with his head thrown back and his legs outstretched, he was staring at Murillo's beautiful moon-borne Madonna in profound enjoyment of his posture. He had removed his hat, and flung down beside him a little red guide-book and an opera-glass. The day was warm, he was heated with walking, and he repeatedly passed his handkerchief over his forehead, with a somewhat wearied gesture. And yet he was evidently not a man to whom fatigue was familiar; long, lean, and muscular, he suggested the sort of vigor that is commonly known as toughness. But his exertions on this particular day had been of an unwonted sort, and he had often performed great physical feats which left him .

* Used by permission of, and arrangement with, Houghton Mifflin Company.

less jaded than his tranquil stroll through the Louvre. He had looked out all the pictures to which an asterisk was affixed in those formidable pages of fine print in his Bädeker; his attention had been strained and his eyes dazzled, and he had sat down with an aesthetic headache. He had looked, moreover, not only at all the pictures, but at all the copies that were going forward around them, in the hands of those innumerable young women in irreproachable toilets who devote themselves, in France, to the propagation of masterpieces; and if the truth must be told, he had often admired the copy much more than the original. His physiognomy would have sufficiently indicated that he was a shrewd and capable fellow, and in truth he had often sat up all night over a bristling bundle of accounts and heard the cock crow without a yawn. But Raphael and Titian and Rubens were a new kind of arithmetic, and they inspired our friend for the first time in his life, with a vague self-mistrust.

An observer with anything of an eye for national types would have had no difficulty in determining the local origin of this undeveloped connoisseur, and indeed such an observer might have felt a certain humorous relish of the almost ideal completeness with which he filled out the national mold. The gentleman on the divan was a powerful specimen of an American. But he was not only a fine American; he was in the first place, physically, a fine man. He appeared to possess that kind of health and strength which, when found in perfection, are the most impressive—the physical capital which the owner does nothing to "keep up." If he was a muscular Christian, it was quite without knowing it. If it was necessary to walk to a remote spot, he walked, but he had never known himself to "exercise." He had no theory with regard to cold bathing or the use of Indian clubs; he was neither an oarsman, a rifleman nor a fencer—he had never had time for these amusements,—and he was quite unaware that the saddle is recommended for certain forms of indigestion. He was by inclination a temperate man; but he had supped the night before his visit to the Louvre at the Café Anglais,—some one had told him it was an experience not to be omitted,—and he had slept none the less the sleep of the just. His usual attitude and carriage were of a rather relaxed and lounging kind, but when, under a special inspiration, he straightened himself, he looked a grenadier on parade. He never smoked. He had been assured—such things are said—that cigars were excellent for the health, and he was quite capable of believing it; but he knew as little about tobacco as about homoeopathy. He had a very well-formed head, with a shapely, symmetrical balance of the frontal and the occipital development, and a good deal of straight, rather dry brown hair. His complexion was brown, and his nose had a bold, well-marked arch. His eye was of a clear, cold grey, and save for a rather abundant moustache he was clean-shaved. He had the flat jaw and the sinewy neck which are frequent in the American type; but the traces of national origin are a matter of expression even more than of feature, and it was in this respect that our friend's countenance was supremely eloquent. The discriminating observer we have been supposing might, however, perfectly have measured its expressiveness, and yet have been at a loss to describe it. It had that typical vagueness which is not vacuity, that blankness which is not simplicity, that look of being committed to nothing in particular, of standing in an attitude of general hospitality to the chances of life, of being very much at one's own disposal, so characteristic of many American faces. It was our friend's eye that chiefly told his story; an eye in which innocence and experience were singularly blended. It was full of contradictory suggestions, and though it was by no means the glowing orb of a hero of romance, you could find in it almost anything you looked for. Frigid and yet friendly, frank yet cautious, shrewd yet credulous, positive yet sceptical, confident yet shy, extremely intelligent and extremely good-humored, there was something vaguely defiant in its concessions and something profoundly reassuring in its reserve. The cut of this gentleman's moustache, with the two premature wrinkles in the cheek above it, and the fashion of his garments, in which an exposed shirt-front and a cerulean cravat played perhaps an obtrusive part, completed the conditions of his identity. We have approached him, perhaps, at a not especially favourable moment; he is by no means sitting for his portrait. But listless as he lounges there, rather baffled on the aesthetic question, and guilty of the damning fault (as we have lately discovered it to be) of confounding the merit of the artist with that of his work (for he admires the squinting Madonna of the young lady with the boyish coiffure, because he thinks the young lady herself uncommonly taking), he is a sufficiently promising acquaintance. Decision, salubrity, jocosity, prosperity, seem to hover within his call; he is evidently a practical man, but the idea, in his case, has undefined and mysterious boundaries, which invite the imagination to bestir itself on his behalf.

As the little copyist proceeded with her work, she sent every now and then a responsive glance toward her admirer. The cultivation of the fine arts appeared to necessitate, to her mind, a great deal of by-play, a great standing off with folded arms and head dropping from side to side, stroking of a dimpled chin with a dimpled hand, sighing and frowning and patting of the foot, fumbling in disordered tresses for wandering hairpins. These performances were accompanied by a restless glance, which lingered longer than elsewhere upon the gentleman we have described. At last he rose abruptly, put on his hat, and approached the young lady. He placed himself before her picture and looked at it for some moments, during which she pretended to be quite unconscious of his inspection. Then, addressing her with the single word which constituted the strength of his French vocabulary, and holding up one finger in a manner that appeared to him to illuminate his meaning, "Combien?" he abruptly demanded.

The artist stared a moment, gave a little pout, shrugged her shoulders, put down her palette and brushes, and stood rubbing her hands.

"How much?" said our friend, in English. "Combien?"

"Monsieur wishes to buy it?" asked the young lady in French.

"Very pretty, splendide. Combien?" repeated the American.

"It pleases monsieur, my little picture? It's a very beautiful subject," said the young lady.

"The Madonna, yes; I'm not a real Catholic, but I want to buy it. Combien? Write it here." And he took a pencil from his pocket and showed her the fly-leaf of his guide-book. She stood looking at him and scratching her chin with the pencil. "Isn't it for sale?" he asked. And as she still stood reflecting, and looking at him with an eye which, in spite of her desire to treat this avidity of patronage as a very old story, betrayed an almost touching incredulity, he was afraid he had offended her. She was simply trying to look indifferent, and wondering how far she might go. "I haven't made a mistake—pas insulté, no?" her interlocutor continued. "Don't you understand a little English?"

The young lady's aptitude for playing a part at short notice was remarkable. She fixed him with all her conscious perceptive eye and asked him if he spoke no French. Then "Donnez!" she said briefly, and took the open guide-book. In the upper corner of the fly-leaf she traced a number, in a minute and extremely neat hand. Then she handed back the book and took up her palette again.

Our friend read the number: "2000 francs." He said nothing for a time, but stood looking at the picture while the copyist began actively to dabble with her paint. "For a copy, isn't that a good deal?" he inquired at last. *"Pas beaucoup?"*

The young lady raised her eyes from her palette, scanned him from head to foot, and alighted with admirable sagacity upon exactly the right answer. "Yes, it's a good deal. But my copy has certain qualities; it is worth nothing less."

The gentleman in whom we are interested understood no French, but I have said he was intelligent, and here is a good chance to prove it. He apprehended, by a natural instinct, the meaning of the young woman's phrase, and it gratified him to think she was so honest. Beauty, talent, virtue; she combined everything! "But you must finish it," he said. *"Finish,* you know;" and he pointed to the unpainted hand of the figure.

"Oh, it shall be finished in perfection; in the perfection of perfections!" cried mademoiselle; and, to confirm her promise she deposited a rosy blotch in the middle of the Madonna's cheek.

But the American frowned. "Ah, too red, too red!" he objected. "Her complexion," pointing to the Murillo, "is more delicate."

"Delicate? Oh it shall be delicate, monsieur; delicate as Sèvres *biscuit.* I am going to tone that down; I know all the secrets of the art. And where will you allow us to send it to you? Your address."

"My address? Oh yes!" And the gentleman drew a card from his pocket-book and wrote something on it. Then hesitating a moment he said, "If I don't like it when it is finished, you know, I shall not be obliged to pay for it."

The young lady seemed as good a guesser as himself. "Oh, I'm very sure that monsieur is not capricious," she said with a roguish smile.

"Capricious?" And at this monsieur began to laugh. "Oh no, I'm not capricious. I am very faithful. I'm very constant. *Comprenez?"*

"Monsieur is constant; I understand perfectly. It's a rare virtue. To recompense you, you shall have your picture on the first possible day; next week—as soon as it is dry. I will take the card of monsieur." And she took it and read his name: "Christopher Newman." Then she tried to repeat it aloud and laughed at her bad accent. "Your English names are so droll!"

"Droll?" said Mr. Newman, laughing too. "Did you ever hear of Christopher Columbus?"

"Bien sûr! He invented America; a very great man. And is he your patron?"

"My patron?"

"Your patron-saint, in the calendar."

"Oh, exactly; my parents named me for him."

"Monsieur is American?"

"Don't you see it?" monsieur inquired.

"And you mean to carry my little picture away over there?" and she explained her phrase with a gesture.

"Oh, I mean to buy a great many

pictures—*beaucoup, beaucoup,*" said Christopher Newman.

"The honor is not less for me," the young lady answered, "for I'm sure monsieur has a great deal of taste."

"But you must give me your card," Newman went on; "your card, you know."

The young lady looked severe an instant. "My father will wait upon you."

But this time Mr. Newman's powers of divination were at fault. "Your card, your address," he simply repeated.

"My address?" said mademoiselle. Then, with a little shrug: "Happily for you, you are an American! It is the first time I ever gave my card to a gentleman." And, taking from her pocket a rather greasy *porte-monnaire,* she extracted from it a small glazed visiting card and presented the latter to her patron. It was neatly inscribed in pencil, with a great many flourishes, "Mlle. Noémie Nioche." But Mr. Newman, unlike his companion, read the name with perfect gravity; all French names to him were equally droll.

"And precisely here is my father, he has come to escort me home," said Mademoiselle Noémie. "He speaks English. He will arrange with you." And she turned to welcome a little old gentleman who came shuffling up, peering over his spectacles at Newman.

M. Nioche wore a glossy wig, of an unnatural color, which overhung his little meek, white, vacant face, leaving it hardly more expressive than the unfeatured block upon which these articles are displayed in the barber's window. He was an exquisite image of shabby gentility. His little, ill-made coat, desperately brushed, his darned gloves, his highly polished boots, his rusty, shapely hat, told the story of a person who had "had losses," and who clung to the spirit of nice habits, though the letter had been hopelessly effaced. Among other things, M. Nioche had lost courage. Adversity had not only ruined him, it had frightened him, and he was going through his remnant of life on tiptoe, for fear of waking up the hostile fate. If this strange gentleman should be saying anything improper to his daughter M. Nioche would entreat him huskily, as a particular favor, to forbear; but he would admit at the same time that he was very presumptuous to ask for particular favors.

"Monsieur has bought my picture," said Mademoiselle Noémie. "When it is finished you will carry it to him in a cab."

"In a cab!" cried M. Nioche; and he stared, in a bewildered way, as if he had seen the sun rising at midnight.

"Are you the young lady's father?" said Newman. "I think she said you speak English."

"Speak English—yes," said the old man, slowly rubbing his hands. "I'll bring it in a cab."

"Say something, then," cried his daughter. "Thank him a little—not too much."

"A little, my daughter, a little?" said M. Nioche, perplexed. "How much?"

"Two thousand!" said Mademoiselle Noémie. "Don't make a fuss or he'll take back his word."

"Two thousand!" gasped the old man; and he began to fumble for his snuff-box. He looked at Newman, from head to foot, at his daughter, and then at the picture. "Take care you don't spoil it!" he cried, almost sublimely.

"We must go home," said Mademoiselle Noémie. "This is a good day's work. Take care how you carry it!" And she began to put up her painting materials.

"How can I thank you?" said M. Nioche. "My English does not suffice."

"I wish I spoke French half so well," said Newman good-naturedly. "Your daughter is very clever."

"Oh sir!" and M. Nioche looked over his spectacles with tearful eyes and nodded several times with a world of sadness. "She has had an education—très-supérieure! Nothing was spared. Lessons in pastel at ten francs the lesson, lessons in oil at twelve francs. I didn't look at the francs, then. She's an artiste, ah!"

"Do I understand you to say that you have had reverses?" asked Newman.

"Reverses? Oh sir, misfortunes—terrible!"

"Unsuccessful in business?"

"Very unsuccessful, sir."

"Oh, never fear, you'll get on your legs again," said Newman cheerily.

The old man dropped his head on one side and looked at him with an expression of pain, as if this were an unfeeling jest.

"What does he say?" demanded Mademoiselle Noémie.

M. Nioche took a pinch of snuff. "He says I shall make my fortunes again."

"Perhaps he'll help you. And what else?"

"He says thou art very clever."

"It is very possible. You believe it yourself, my father?"

"Believe it, my daughter? With this evidence!" And the old man turned afresh with a staring, wondering homage, to the audacious daub on the easel.

"Ask him, then, if he'd not like to learn French."

"To learn French?"

"To take lessons."

"To take lessons, my daughter? From you?"

"From you!"

"From me, my child? How should I give lessons?"

"Pas de raisons! Ask him immediately!" said Mademoiselle Noémie with soft brevity.

M. Nioche stood aghast, but under his daughter's eye he collected his wits, and, doing his best to assume an agreeable smile, executed her commands. "Would it please you to receive instruction in our beautiful language?" he inquired with an appealing quaver.

"To study French?" asked Newman, staring.

M. Nioche pressed his finger-tips together and slowly raised his shoulders. "A little conversation!"

"Conversation—that's it!" murmured Mademoiselle Noémie, who had caught the word. "The conversation of the best society."

"Our French conversation is rather famous, you know," M. Nioche ventured to continue. "It's a great talent."

"But isn't it awfully difficult?" asked Newman very simply.

"Not to a man of *esprit,* like mon-
eur, an admirer of beauty in every
orm!" and M. Nioche cast a sig-
ficant glance at his daughter's Ma-
onna.

"I can't fancy myself chattering
rench!" said Newman with a laugh.
And yet, I suppose the more a man
nows the better."

"Monsieur expresses that very haply. *Hélas, oui!*"

"I suppose it would help me a
reat deal, knocking about Paris, to
now the language."

"Ah, there are so many things mon-
eur must want to say; difficult
ings!"

"Everything I want to say is dif-
cult. But you give lessons?"

Poor M. Nioche was embarrassed;
e smiled more appealingly. "I am
ot a regular professor," he admitted.
I can't nevertheless tell him that
m a professor," he said to his daugh-
r.

"Tell him it's a very exceptional
ance," answered Mademoiselle Noé-
ie, "an *homme du monde*—one per-
ct gentleman conversing with an-
her! Remember what you are—
hat you have been!"

"A teacher of languages in neither
se! Much more in the one and
uch less in the other! And if he
ks the price of the lessons?"

"He won't ask it," said Mademoi-
lle Noémie.

"What he pleases, I may say?"

"Never! That's bad style."

"If he asks, then?"

Mademoiselle Noémie had put on
er bonnet and was tying the ribbons.
he smoothed them out, with her soft
ttle chin thrust forward. "Ten
ancs," she said quickly.

"Oh my daughter! I shall never
dare."

"Don't dare, then! He won't ask
till the end of the lessons, and then
I will make out the bill."

M. Nioche turned to the confiding
foreigner again and stood rubbing his
hands with an air of seeming to plead
guilty which was not intenser only
because it was habitually so striking.
It never occurred to Newman to ask
him for a guarantee of his skill in im-
parting instruction; he supposed of
course M. Nioche knew his own language, and his appealing forlornness
was quite the perfection of what the
American, for vague reasons, had always associated with all elderly for-
eigners of the lesson-giving class.
Newman had never reflected upon
philological processes. His chief impression with regard to ascertaining
those mysterious correlatives of his
familiar English vocables which were
current in this extraordinary city of
Paris was, that it was a good deal of
unwonted and rather ridiculous muscular effort on his own part. "How
did you learn English?" he asked of
the old man.

"When I was young, before my
miseries. Oh, I was wide awake,
then. My father was a great *com-
merçant;* he placed me for a year in
a counting-house in England. Some
of it stuck to me, but much I have
forgotten!"

"How much French can I learn in
about a month?"

"What does he say?" asked Mademoiselle Noémie.

M. Nioche explained.

"He will speak like an angel," said
his daughter.

But the native integrity which had

been vainly exerted to secure M. Nioche's commercial prosperity flickered up again. *"Dame,* monsieur!" he answered. "All I can teach you!" And then, recovering himself at a sign from his daughter, "I will wait upon you at your hotel."

"Oh yes, I should like to learn French," Newman went on, with democratic confidingness. "Hang me if I should ever have thought of it! I took for granted it, was impossible. But if you learned my language, why shouldn't I learn yours?" and his frank, friendly laugh drew the sting from the jest. "Only, if we are going to converse, you know, you must think of something cheerful to converse about."

"You are very good, sir; I'm overcome!" said M. Nioche throwing up his hands. "But you have cheerfulness and happiness for two!"

"Oh no," said Newman, more seriously. "You must be bright and lively; that's part of the bargain."

M. Nioche bowed, with his hand on his heart. "Very well, sir; you have already made me lively."

"Come and bring me my picture then; I will pay you for it, and we will talk about that. That will be a cheerful subject!"

Mademoiselle Noémie had collected her accessories, and she gave the precious Madonna in charge to her father, who retreated backwards out of sight, holding it at arm's length and reiterating his obeisances. The young lady gathered her shawl about her like a perfect Parisienne, and it was with the smile of a Parisienne that she took leave of her patron.

1876

THE LESSON OF THE MASTER

I

He had been informed that th ladies were at church, but that wa corrected by what he saw from th top of the steps (they descended fro a great height in two arms, with circular sweep of the most charmin effect) at the threshold of the doc which, from the long, bright galler overlooked the immense lawn. Thre gentlemen, on the grass, at a distanc sat under the great trees; but th fourth figure was not a gentlema the one in the crimson dress whic made so vivid a spot, told so as "bit of color" amid the fresh, ri green. The servant had come so fa with Paul Overt to show him the wa and had asked him if he wished firs to go to his room. The young ma declined this privilege, having no di order to repair after so short and eas a journey and liking to take a genera perceptive possession of the new scen immediately, as he always did. H stood there a little with his eyes o the group and on the admirable pic ture—the wide grounds of an ol country-house near London (that onl made it better,) on a splendid Sun day in June. "But that lady, wh is she?" he said to the servant be fore the man went away.

"I think it's Mrs. St. George, sir.

"Mrs. St. George, the wife of th distinguished—". Then Paul Ove checked himself, doubting whether th footman would know.

"Yes, sir—probably, sir," said th servant, who appeared to wish to int ate that a person staying at Sumersoft would naturally be, if only y alliance, distinguished. His maner, however, made poor Overt feel or the moment as if he himself were ut little so.

"And the gentlemen?" he inquired. "Well, sir, one of them is General ancourt."

"Ah yes, I know; thank you." Genal Fancourt was distinguished, there as no doubt of that, for something e had done, or perhaps even had not one (the young man could not remember which) some years before in idia. The servant went away, leaving the glass doors open into the galry, and Paul Overt remained at the ead of the wide double staircase, saysg to himself that the place was sweet nd promised a pleasant visit, while e leaned on the balustrade of fine d ironwork which, like all the other etails, was of the same period as the ouse. It all went together and spoke 1 one voice—a rich English voice of ne early part of the eighteenth century. It might have been churchme on a summer's day in the reign f Queen Anne; the stillness was too erfect to be modern, the nearness ounted so as distance and there was omething so fresh and sound in the riginality of the large smooth house, he expanse of whose beautiful brickork, which had been kept clear of nessy creepers (as a woman with a are complexion disdains a veil,) was ink rather than red. When Paul Overt perceived that the people under he trees were noticing him he turned ack through the open doors into the reat gallery which was the pride of he place. It traversed the mansion rom end to end and seemed—with its bright colors, its high panelled windows, its faded, flowered chintzes, its quickly-recognized portraits and pictures, the blue and white china of its cabinets and the attenuated festoons and rosettes of its ceiling—a cheerful upholstered avenue into the other century.

The young man was slightly nervous; that belonged in general to his disposition as a student of fine prose, with his dose of the artist's restlessness; and there was a particular excitement in the idea that Henry St. George might be a member of the party. For the younger writer he had remained a high literary figure, in spite of the lower range of production to which he had fallen after his three first great successes, the comparative absence of quality in his later work. There had been moments when Paul Overt almost shed tears upon this; but now that he was near him (he had never met him,) he was conscious only of the fine original source and of his own immense debt. After he had taken a turn or two up and down the gallery he came out again and descended the steps. He was but slenderly supplied with a certain social boldness (it was really a weakness in him,) so that, conscious of a want of acquaintance with the four persons in the distance, he indulged in a movement as to which he had a certain safety in feeling that it did not necessarily appear to commit him to an attempt to join them. There was a fine English awkwardness in it—he felt this too as he sauntered vaguely and obliquely across the lawn, as if to take an independent line. Fortunately there was an equally fine English directness in the way one of the gentlemen presently rose and made as if to approach him, with an air of conciliation and reassurance. To this demonstration Paul Overt instantly responded, though he knew the gentleman was not his host. He was tall, straight and elderly, and had a pink, smiling face and a white moustache. Our young man met him half way while he laughed and said: "A—Lady Watermouth told us you were coming; she asked me just to look after you." Paul Overt thanked him (he liked him without delay,) and turned round with him, walking toward the others. "They've all gone to church—all except us," the stranger continued as they went; "we're just sitting here —it's so jolly." Overt rejoined that it was jolly indeed—it was such a lovely place; he mentioned that he had not seen it before—it was a charming impression.

"Ah, you've not been here before?" said his companion. "It's a nice little place—not much to *do*, you know." Overt wondered what he wanted to "do"—he felt as if he himself were doing a good deal. By the time they came to where the others sat he had guessed his initiator was a military man, and (such was the turn of Overt's imagination), this made him still more sympathetic. He would naturally have a passion for activity—for deeds at variance with the pacific, pastoral scene. He was evidently so good-natured, however, that he accepted the inglorious hour for what it was worth. Paul Overt shared it with him and with his companions for the next twenty minutes; the latter looked at him and he looked at them without knowing much who they were, while the talk went on without

enlightening him much as to what it was about. It was indeed about nothing in particular, and wandered with casual, pointless pauses and short terrestrial flights, amid the names of persons and places—names which, for him, had no great power of evocation. It was all sociable and slow, as was right and natural on a warm Sunday morning.

Overt's first attention was given to the question, privately considered, of whether one of the two younger men would be Henry St. George. He knew many of his distinguished contemporaries by their photographs, but he had never, as it happened, seen a portrait of the great misguided novelist. One of the gentlemen was out of the question—he was too young; and the other scarcely looked clever enough, with such mild, undiscriminating eyes. If those eyes were St. George's the problem presented by the ill-matched parts of his genius was still more difficult of solution. Besides, the deportment of the personage possessing them was not, as regards the lady in the red dress, such as could be natural towards his wife, even to a writer accused by several critics of sacrificing too much to manner. Lastly, Paul Overt had an indefinite feeling that if the gentleman with the sightless eyes bore the name that had set his heart beating faster (he also had contradictory, conventional whiskers—the young admirer of the celebrity had never in a mental vision seen *his* face in so vulgar a frame), he would have given him a sign of recognition or of friendliness—would have heard of him a little, would know something about *Ginistrella*, would have gathered at least that that recent work of fiction ad made an impression on the discerning. Paul Overt had a dread of being grossly proud, but it seemed to him that his self-consciousness took no undue license in thinking that the authorship of *Ginistrella* constituted a degree of identity. His soldierly friend became clear enough; he was "Fancourt," but he was also the General; and he mentioned to our young man in the course of a few moments that he had but lately returned from twenty years' service abroad.

"And do you mean to remain in England?" Overt asked.

"Oh yes, I have bought a little house in London."

"And I hope you like it," said Overt, looking at Mrs. St. George.

"Well, a little house in Manchester Square—there's a limit to the enthusiasm that that inspires."

"Oh, I meant being at home again—being in London."

"My daughter likes it—that's the main thing. She's very fond of art and music and literature and all that kind of thing. She missed it in India and she finds it in London, or she hopes she will find it. Mr. St. George has promised to help her—he has been awfully kind to her. She has gone to church—she's fond of that too—but they'll all be back in a quarter an hour. You must let me introduce you to her—she will be so glad to know you. I dare say she has had every word you have written."

"I shall be delighted—I haven't written very many," said Overt, who felt without resentment that the General at least was very vague about that. But he wondered a little why, once he expressed this friendly disposition, it did not occur to him to pronounce the word which would put him in relation with Mrs. St. George. If it was a question of introductions Miss Fancourt (apparently she was unmarried,) was far away and the wife of his illustrious *confrère* was almost between them. This lady struck Paul Overt as a very pretty woman, with a surprising air of youth and a high smartness of aspect which seemed to him (he could scarcely have said why,) a sort of mystification. St. George certainly had every right to a charming wife, but he himself would never have taken the important little woman in the aggressively Parisian dress for the domestic partner of a man of letters. That partner in general, he knew, was far from presenting herself in a single type: his observation had instructed him that she was not inveterately, not necessarily dreary. But he had never before seen her look so much as if her prosperity had deeper foundations than an ink-spotted study-table littered with proof-sheets. Mrs. St. George might have been the wife of a gentleman who "kept" books rather than wrote them, who carried on great affairs in the City and made better bargains than those that poets make with publishers. With this she hinted at a success more personal, as if she had been the most characteristic product of an age in which society, the world of conversation, is a great drawing-room with the City for its antechamber. Overt judged her at first to be about thirty years of age; then, after a while, he perceived that she was much nearer fifty. But she juggled away the twenty years somehow—you only saw them in a rare glimpse, like the rabbit in the conjurer's sleeve. She was extraordinarily white, and everything about her was pretty—her eyes, her ears, her hair, her voice, her hands, her feet (to which her relaxed attitude in her wicker chair gave a great publicity,) and the numerous ribbons and trinkets with which she was bedecked. She looked as if she had put on her best clothes to go to church, and then had decided that they were too good for that and had stayed at home. She told a story of some length about the shabby way Lady Jane had treated the Duchess, as well as an anecdote in relation to a purchase she had made in Paris (on her way back from Cannes,) for Lady Egbert, who had never refunded the money. Paul Overt suspected her of a tendency to figure great people as larger than life, until he noticed the manner in which she handled Lady Egbert, which was so subversive that it reassured him. He felt that he should have understood her better if he might have met her eye; but she scarcely looked at him. "Ah, here they come—all the good ones!" she said at last; and Paul Overt saw in the distance the return of the churchgoers—several persons, in couples and threes, advancing in a flicker of sun and shade at the end of a large green vista formed by the level grass and the overarching boughs.

"If you mean to imply that we are bad, I protest," said one of the gentlemen—"after making oneself agreeable all the morning!"

"Ah, if they've found you agreeable!" Mrs. St. George exclaimed, smiling. "But if we are good the others are better."

"They must be angels then," observed the General.

"Your husband was an angel, t[he] way he went off at your bidding," t[he] gentleman who had first spoken sa[id] to Mrs. St. George.

"At my bidding?"

"Didn't you make him go [to] church?"

"I never made him do anything [in] my life but once, when I made hi[m] burn up a bad book. That's all[!]" At her "That's all!" Paul broke in[to] an irrepressible laugh; it lasted on[ly] a second, but it drew her eyes to hi[m.] His own met them, but not lo[ng] enough to help him to understand he[r,] unless it were a step towards this th[at] he felt sure on the instant that t[he] burnt book (the way she alluded [to] it!) was one of her husband's fine[st] things.

"A bad book?" her interlocutor r[e]peated.

"I didn't like it. He went to chur[ch] because your daughter went," she co[n]tinued, to General Fancourt. "I thi[nk] it my duty to call your attention [to] his demeanor to your daughter."

"Well, if you don't mind it, [I] don't," the General laughed.

"Il s'attache à ses pas. But I do[n't] wonder—she's so charming."

"I hope she won't make him bu[rn] any books!" Paul Overt ventured [to] exclaim.

"If she would make him write [a] few it would be more to the purpose[,]" said Mrs. St. George. "He has be[en] of an indolence this year!"

Our young man stared—he was struck with the lady's phraseolog[y.] Her "write a few" seemed to him a[l]most as good as her "That's all[.]" Didn't she, as the wife of a rare arti[st,] know what it was to produce one pe[r]fect work of art? How in the wor[ld]

id she think they were turned off?
His private conviction was that admirably as Henry St. George wrote,
e had written for the last ten years,
nd especially for the last five, only
oo much, and there was an instant
uring which he felt the temptation
o make this public. But before he
ad spoken a diversion was effected
y the return of the absent guests.
hey strolled up dispersedly—there
ere eight or ten of them—and the
ircle under the trees rearranged itself
s they took their place in it. They
made it much larger; so that Paul
vert could feel (he was always feel-
ng that sort of thing, as he said to
imself,) that if the company had
lready been interesting to watch it
ould now become a great deal more
o. He shook hands with his hostess,
ho welcomed him without many
ords, in the manner of a woman able
o trust him to understand—conscious
nat, in every way, so pleasant an oc-
asion would speak for itself. She
fered him no particular facility for
tting by her, and when they had all
bsided again he found himself still
ext to General Fancourt, with an un-
nown lady on his other flank.

"That's my daughter—that one op-
osite," the General said to him with-
nt loss of time. Overt saw a tall girl,
ith magnificent red hair, in a dress
f a pretty grey-green tint and of a
mp silken texture, in which every
odern effect had been avoided. It
ad therefore somehow the stamp of
ne latest thing, so that Overt quickly
erceived she was eminently a con-
mporary young lady.

"She's very handsome—very hand-
me," he repeated, looking at her.
here was something noble in her

head, and she appeared fresh and
strong.

Her father surveyed her with complacency; then he said: "She looks
too hot—that's her walk. But she'll
be all right presently. Then I'll make
her come over and speak to you."

"I should be sorry to give you that
trouble; if you were to take me over
there—" the young man murmured.

"My dear sir, do you suppose I put
myself out that way? I don't mean
for you, but for Marian," the General added.

"*I* would put myself out for her,
soon enough," Overt replied; after
which he went on: "Will you be so
good as to tell me which of those
gentlemen is Henry St. George?"

"The fellow talking to my girl. By
Jove, he *is* making up to her—they're
going off for another walk."

"Ah, is that he, really?" The young
man felt a certain surprise, for the
personage before him contradicted a
preconception which had been vague
only till it was confronted with the
reality. As soon as this happened the
mental image, retiring with a sigh, became substantial enough to suffer a
slight wrong. Overt, who had spent
a considerable part of his short life
in foreign lands, made now, but not
for the first time, the reflection that
whereas in those countries he had almost always recognised the artist and
the man of letters by his personal
"type," the mould of his face, the
character of his head, the expression
of his figure and even the indications
of his dress, in England this identification was as little as possible a matter of course, thanks to the greater
conformity, the habit of sinking the
profession instead of advertising it,

the general diffusion of the air of the gentleman—the gentleman committed to no particular set of ideas. More than once, on returning to his own country, he had said to himself in regard to the people whom he met in society: "One sees them about and one even talks with them; but to find out what they *do* one would really have to be a detective." In respect to several individuals whose work he was unable to like (perhaps he was wrong) he found himself adding, "No wonder they conceal it—it's so bad!" He observed that oftener than in France and in Germany his artist looked like a gentleman (that is, like an English one,) while he perceived that outside of a few exceptions his gentleman didn't look like an artist. St. George was not one of the exceptions; that circumstance he definitely apprehended before the great man had turned his back to walk off with Miss Fancourt. He certainly looked better behind than any foreign man of letters, and beautifully correct in his tall black hat and his superior frock coat. Somehow, all the same, these very garments (he wouldn't have minded them so much on a weekday,) were disconcerting to Paul Overt, who forgot for the moment that the head of the profession was not a bit better dressed than himself. He had caught a glimpse of a regular face, with a fresh colour, a brown moustache and a pair of eyes surely never visited by a fine frenzy, and he promised himself to study it on the first occasion. His temporary opinion was that St. George looked like a lucky stockbroker—a gentleman driving eastward every morning from a sanitary suburb in a smart dog-cart. That carried out

the impression already derived from his wife. Paul Overt's glance, after a moment, traveled back to this lady and he saw that her own had followed her husband as he moved off with Miss Fancourt. Overt permitted himself to wonder a little whether she were jealous when another woman took him away. Then he seemed to perceive that Mrs. St. George was not glaring at the indifferent maiden—her eye rested only on her husband, and with unmistakable serenity. That was the way she wanted him to be—she liked his conventional uniform. Overt had a great desire to hear more about the book she had induced him to destroy.

II

As they all came out from luncheon General Fancourt took hold of Paul Overt and exclaimed, "I say, I want you to know my girl!" as if the idea had just occurred to him and he had not spoken of it before. With the other hand he possessed himself of the young lady and said: "You know all about him. I've seen you with his books. She reads everything—everything!" he added to the young man. The girl smiled at him and then laughed at her father. The General turned away and his daughter said:

"Isn't papa delightful?"

"He is indeed, Miss Fancourt."

"As if I read you because I read 'everything'!"

"Oh, I don't mean for saying that," said Paul Overt. "I liked him from the moment he spoke to me. Then he promised me this privilege."

"It isn't for you he means it, it's for me. If you flatter yourself that he thinks of anything in life but me you'll find you are mistaken. He introduces every one to me. He thinks me insatiable."

"You speak like him," said Paul Overt, laughing.

"Ah, but sometimes I want to," the girl replied, colouring. "I don't read everything—I read very little. But I *have* read you."

"Suppose we go into the gallery," said Paul Overt. She pleased him greatly, not so much because of this last remark (though that of course was not disagreeable to him,) as because, seated opposite to him at luncheon, she had given him for half an hour the impression of her beautiful face. Something else had come with it—a sense of generosity, of an enthusiasm which, unlike many enthusiasms, was not all manner. That was not spoiled for him by the circumstance that the repast had placed her again in familiar contact with Henry St. George. Sitting next to her he was also opposite to our young man, who had been able to observe that he multiplied the attentions which his wife had brought to the General's notice. Paul Overt had been able to observe further that this lady was not in the least discomposed by these demonstrations and that she gave very sign of an unclouded spirit. She had Lord Masham on one side of her and on the other the accomplished Mr. Mulliner, editor of the new high-class, lively evening paper which was expected to meet a want felt in circles increasingly conscious that Conservatism must be made amusing, and unconvinced when assured by those of another political colour that it was already amusing enough. At the end of an hour spent in her company Paul

Overt thought her still prettier than she had appeared to him at first, and if her profane allusions to her husband's work had not still rung in his ears he should have liked her—so far as it could be a question of that in connection with a woman to whom he had not yet spoken and to whom probably he should never speak if it were left to her. Pretty women evidently were necessary to Henry St. George, and for the moment it was Miss Fancourt who was most indispensable. If Overt had promised himself to take a better look at him the opportunity now was of the best, and it brought consequences which the young man felt to be important. He saw more in his face, and he liked it the better for its not telling its whole story in the first three minutes. That story came out as one read, in little instalments (it was excusable that Overt's mental comparisons should be somewhat professional,) and the text was a style considerably involved—a language not easy to translate at sight. There were shades of meaning in it and a vague perspective of history which receded as you advanced. Of two facts Paul Overt had taken especial notice. The first of these was that he liked the countenance of the illustrious novelist much better when it was in repose than when it smiled; the smile displeased him (as much as anything from that source could,) whereas the quiet face had a charm which increased in proportion as it became completely quiet. The change to the expression of gaiety excited on Overt's part a private protest which resembled that of a person sitting in the twilight and enjoying it, when the lamp is brought in too soon. His second reflection was that, though generally he disliked the sight of a man of that age using arts to make himself agreeable to a pretty girl, he was not struck in this case by the ugliness of the thing, which seemed to prove that St. George had a light hand or the air of being younger than he was, or else that Miss Fancourt showed that *she* was not conscious of an anomaly.

Overt walked with her into the gallery, and they strolled to the end of it, looking at the pictures, the cabinets, the charming vista, which harmonised with the prospect of the summer afternoon, resembling it in its long brightness, with great divans and old chairs like hours of rest. Such a place as that had the added merit of giving persons who came into it plenty to talk about. Miss Fancourt sat down with Paul Overt on a flowered sofa, the cushions of which, very numerous, were tight, ancient cubes, of many sizes, and presently she said: "I'm so glad to have a chance to thank you."

"To thank me?"

"I liked your book so much. I think it's splendid."

She sat there smiling at him, and he never asked himself which book she meant; for after all he had written three or four. That seemed a vulgar detail, and he was not even gratified by the idea of the pleasure she told him—her bright, handsome face told him—he had given her. The feeling she appealed to, or at any rate the feeling she excited, was something larger—something that had little to do with any quickened pulsation of his own vanity. It was responsive admiration of the life she embodied, the young purity and richness of which

appeared to imply that real success was to resemble *that*, to live, to bloom, to present the perfection of a fine type, not to have hammered out headachy fancies with a bent back at an ink-stained table. While her grey eyes rested on him (there was a wideish space between them, and the division of her rich-colored hair, which was so thick that it ventured to be smooth, made a free arch above them,) he was almost ashamed of that exercise of the pen which it was her present inclination to eulogise. He was conscious that he should have liked better to please her in some other way. The lines of her face were those of a woman grown, but there was something childish in her complexion and the sweetness of her mouth. Above all she was natural—that was indubitable now—more natural than he had supposed at first, perhaps on account of her æsthetic drapery, which was conventionally unconventional, suggesting a tortuous spontaneity. He had feared that sort of thing in other cases, and his fears had been justified, though he was an artist to the essence, the modern reactionary nymph, with the brambles of the woodland caught in her folds and a look as if the satyrs had toyed with her hair, was apt to make him uncomfortable. Miss Fancourt was really more candid than her costume, and the best proof of it was her supposing that such garment suited her liberal character. She was robed like a pessimist, but Overt was sure she liked the taste of life. He thanked her for her appreciation—aware at the same time that he didn't appear to thank her enough and that she might think him ungracious. He was afraid she would ask him to ex-lain something that he had written, nd he always shrank from that (peraps too timidly,) for to his own ear he explanation of a work of art ounded fatuous. But he liked her so much as to feel a confidence that in he long run he should be able to show er that he was not rudely evasive. Moreover it was very certain that she was not quick to take offence; she was not irritable, she could be trusted to wait. So when he said to her, "Ah! on't talk of anything I have done, ere; there is another man in the ouse who is the actuality!" when he ttered this short, sincere protest, it was with the sense that she would see in the words neither mock humility or the ungraciousness of a successful man bored with praise.

"You mean Mr. St. George—isn't e delightful?"

Paul Overt looked at her a moment; ere was a species of morning-light in her eyes.

"Alas, I don't know him. I only admire him at a distance."

"Oh, you must know him—he wants to talk to you," rejoined Miss Fancourt, who evidently had the habit of .ying the things that, by her quick alculation, would give people pleasre. Overt divined that she would ways calculate on everything's being mple between others.

"I shouldn't have supposed he knew ything about me," Paul said, oiling.

"He does then—everything. And he didn't, I should be able to tell m."

"To tell him everything?"

"You talk just like the people in ur book!" the girl exclaimed.

"Then they must all talk alike."

"Well, it must be so difficult. Mr. St. George tells me it is, terribly. I've tried too and I find it so. I've tried to write a novel."

"Mr. St. George oughtn't to discourage you," said Paul Overt.

"You do much more—when you wear that expression."

"Well, after all, why try to be an artist?" the young man went on. "It's so poor—so poor!"

"I don't know what you mean," said Marian Fancourt, looking grave.

"I mean as compared with being a person of action—as living your works."

"But what is art but a life—if it be real?" asked the girl. "I think it's the only one—everything else is so clumsy!" Paul Overt laughed, and she continued: "It's so interesting, meeting so many celebrated people."

"So I should think; but surely it isn't new to you."

"Why, I have never seen any one —any one: living always in Asia."

"But doesn't Asia swarm with personages? Haven't you administered provinces in India and had captive rajahs and tributary princes chained to your car?"

"I was with my father, after I left school to go out there. It was delightful being with him—we are alone together in the world, he and I—but there was none of the society I like best. One never heard of a picture —never of a book, except bad ones."

"Never of a picture? Why, wasn't all life a picture?"

Miss Fancourt looked over the delightful place where they sat. "Nothing to compare with this. I adore England!" she exclaimed.

"Ah, of course I don't deny that

we must do something with it yet."

"It hasn't been touched, really," said the girl.

"Did Henry St. George say that?"

There was a small and, as he felt it, venial intention of irony in his question; which, however, the girl took very simply, not noticing the insinuation. "Yes, he says it has not been touched—not touched comparatively," she answered, eagerly. "He's so interesting about it. To listen to him makes one want so to do something."

"It would make me want to," said Paul Overt, feeling strongly, on the instant, the suggestion of what she said and of the emotion with which she said it, and what an incentive, on St. George's lips, such a speech might be.

"Oh, you—as if you hadn't! I should like so to hear you talk together," the girl added, ardently.

"That's very genial of you; but he would have it all his own way. I'm prostrate before him."

Marian Fancourt looked earnest for a moment. "Do you think then he's so perfect?"

"Far from it. Some of his later books seem to me awfully queer."

"Yes, yes—he knows that."

Paul Overt stared. "That they seem to me awfully queer?"

"Well, yes, or at any rate that they are not what they should be. He told me he didn't esteem them. He has told me such wonderful things— he's so interesting."

There was a certain shock for Paul Overt in the knowledge that the fine genius they were talking of had been reduced to so explicit a confession and had made it, in his misery, to the first comer; for though Miss Fancourt was charming, what was she after all but an immature girl encountered at a country-house? Yet precisely this was a part of the sentiment that he himself had just expressed; he would make way completely for the poor peccable great man, not because he didn't read him clear, but altogether because he did. His consideration was half composed of tenderness for superficialities which he was sure St. George judged privately with supreme sternness and which denoted some tragic intellectual secret. He would have his reasons for his psychology à fleur de peau, and these reasons could only be cruel ones, such as would make him dearer to those who already were fond of him. "You excite my envy. I judge him, I discriminate—but I love him," Overt said in a moment. "And seeing him for the first time this way is a great event for me."

"How momentous—how magnificent!" cried the girl. "How delicious to bring you together!"

"*Your* doing it—that makes it perfect," Overt responded.

"He's as eager as you," Miss Fancourt went on. "But it's so odd you shouldn't have met."

"It's not so odd as it seems. I've been out of England so much—repeated absences during all these last years."

"And yet you write of it as well as if you were always here."

"It's just the being away perhaps. At any rate the best bits, I suspect, are those that were done in dreary places abroad."

"And why were they dreary?"

"Because they were health-resorts —where my poor mother was dying."

"Your poor mother?" the girl murmured, kindly.

"We went from place to place to help her to get better. But she never did. To the deadly Riviera (I hate it!) to the high Alps, to Algiers, and far away—a hideous journey—to Colorado."

"And she isn't better?" Miss Fancourt went on.

"She died a year ago."

"Really?—like mine! Only that is far away. Some day you must tell me about your mother," she added.

Overt looked at her a moment. "What right things you say! If you say them to St. George I don't wonder he's in bondage."

"I don't know what you mean. He doesn't make speeches and professions at all—he isn't ridiculous."

"I'm afraid you consider that I am."

"No, I don't," the girl replied, rather shortly. "He understands everything."

Overt was on the point of saying jocosely: "And I don't—is that it?" but these words, before he had spoken, changed themselves into others slightly less trivial: "Do you suppose he understands his wife?"

Miss Fancourt made no direct answer to his question; but after a moment's hesitation she exclaimed: "Isn't she charming?"

"Not in the least!"

"Here he comes. Now you must know him," the girl went on. A small group of visitors had gathered at the other end of the gallery and they had been joined for a moment by Henry St. George, who strolled in from a neighbouring room. He stood near them a moment, not, apparently, falling into the conversation, but taking up an old miniature from a table and vaguely examining it. At the end of a minute he seemed to perceive Miss Fancourt and her companion in the distance; whereupon, laying down his miniature, he approached them with the same procrastinating air, with his hands in his pockets, looking to right and left at the pictures. The gallery was so long that this transit took some little time, especially as there was a moment when he stopped to admire the fine Gainsborough. "He says she has been the making of him," Miss Fancourt continued, in a voice slightly lowered.

"Ah, he's often obscure!" laughed Paul Overt.

"Obscure?" she repeated, interrogatively. Her eyes rested upon her other friend, and it was not lost upon Paul that they appeared to send out great shafts of softness. "He is going to speak to us!" she exclaimed, almost breathlessly. There was a sort of rapture in her voice; Paul Overt was startled. "Bless my soul, is she so fond of him as that—is she in love with him?" he mentally inquired. "Didn't I tell you he was eager?" she added, to her companion.

"It's eagerness dissimulated," the young man rejoined, as the subject of their observation lingered before his Gainsborough. "He edges toward us shyly. Does he mean that she saved him by burning that book?"

"That book? what book did she burn?" The girl turned her face quickly upon him.

"Hasn't he told you, then?"

"Not a word."

"Then he doesn't tell you everything!" Paul Overt had guessed that Miss Fancourt pretty much supposed he did. The great man had now resumed his course and come nearer; nevertheless Overt risked the profane observation: "St. George and the dragon, the anecdote suggests!"

Miss Fancourt, however, did not hear it; she was smiling at her approaching friend. "He *is* eager—he is!" she repeated.

"Eager for you—yes."

The girl called out frankly, joyously: "I know you want to know Mr. Overt. You'll be great friends, and it will always be delightful to me to think that I was here when you first met and that I had something to do with it."

There was a freshness of intention in this speech which carried it off; nevertheless our young man was sorry for Henry St. George, as he was sorry at any time for any one who was publicly invited to be responsive and delightful. He would have been so contented to believe that a man he deeply admired attached an importance to him that he was determined not to play with such a presumption if it possibly were vain. In a single glance of the eye of the pardonable master he discovered (having the sort of divination that belonged to his talent,) that this personage was full of general good-will, but had not read a word he had written. There was even a relief, a simplification, in that: liking him so much already for what he had done, how could he like him more for having been struck with a certain promise? He got up, trying to show his compassion, but at the same instant he found himself encompassed by St. George's happy personal art—a manner of which it was the essence to. conjure away false positions. It all

took place in a moment. He was con scious that he knew him now, con scious of his handshake and of the ver quality of his hand; of his face, see nearer and consequently seen bette of a general fraternising assurance, an in particular of the circumstance tha St. George didn't dislike him (as yet a least,) for being imposed by a charm ing but too gushing girl, valuabl enough without such danglers. At an rate no irritation was reflected in th voice with which he questioned Mis Fancourt in respect to some projec of a walk—a general walk of the com pany round the park. He had sai something to Overt about a talk—"W must have a tremendous lot of talk there are so many things, aren there?"—but Paul perceived that th idea would not in the present case tak very immediate effect. All the sam he was extremely happy, even after th matter of the walk had been settle (the three presently passed back the other part of the gallery, whe it was discussed with several membe of the party,) even when, after the had all gone out together, he four himself for half an hour in conta with Mrs. St. George. Her husba had taken the advance with Miss Fa court, and this pair were quite o of sight. It was the prettiest rambles for a summer afternoon— grassy circuit, of immense exte skirting the limit of the park with The park was completely surround by its old mottled but perfect r wall, which, all the way on their le made a picturesque accompanime Mrs. St. George mentioned to him t surprising number of acres that we thus enclosed, together with numero other facts relating to the proper

nd the family, and its other prop-
rties; she could not too strongly urge
pon him the importance of seeing
heir other houses. She ran over the
ames of these and rang the changes
n them with the facility of practice,
naking them appear an almost end-
ess list. She had received Paul Overt
ery amiably when he broke ground
vith her by telling her that he had
ust had the joy of making her hus-
and's acquaintance, and struck him as
 alert and so accommodating a little
oman that he was rather ashamed of
is *mot* about her to Miss Fancourt;
hough he reflected that a hundred
ther people, on a hundred occasions,
ould have been sure to make it. He
ot on with Mrs. St. George, in short,
etter than he expected; but this did
ot prevent her from suddenly becom-
g aware that she was faint with fa-
gue and must take her way back
 the house by the shortest cut. She
adn't the strength of a kitten, she
id—she was awfully seedy; a state
f things that Overt had been too pre-
ccupied to perceive—preoccupied
ith a private effort to ascertain in
hat sense she could be held to have
een the making of her husband. He
ad arrived at a glimmering of the
nswer when she announced that she
ust leave him, though this percep-
on was of course provisional. While
e was in the very act of placing him-
elf at her disposal for the return the
tuation underwent a change; Lord
Iasham suddenly turned up, coming
ack to them, overtaking them, emerg-
g from the shrubbery—Overt could
carcely have said how he appeared,
nd Mrs. St. George had protested
at she wanted to be left alone and
ot to break up the party. A moment

later she was walking off with Lord
Masham. Paul Overt fell back and
joined Lady Watermouth, to whom he
presently mentioned that Mrs. St.
George had been obliged to renounce
the attempt to go further.

"She oughtn't to have come out at
all," her ladyship remarked, rather
grumpily.

"Is she so very much of an invalid?"

"Very bad indeed." And his hostess
added, with still greater austerity:
"She oughtn't to come to stay with
one!" He wondered what was implied
by this, and presently gathered that
it was not a reflection on the lady's
conduct or her moral nature: it only
represented that her strength was not
equal to her aspirations.

III

The smoking-room at Summersoft
was on the scale of the rest of the
place; that is it was high and light and
commodious, and decorated with such
refined old carvings and mouldings
that it seemed rather a bower for
ladies who should sit at work at fading crewels than a parliament of
gentlemen smoking strong cigars. The
gentlemen mustered there in considerable force on the Sunday evening, collecting mainly at one end, in front
of one of the cool fair fireplaces of
white marble, the entablature of which
was adorned with a delicate little
Italian "subject." There was another
in the wall that faced it, and, thanks
to the mild summer night, there was
no fire in either; but a nucleus for
aggregation was furnished on one side
by a table in the chimney-corner
laden with bottles, decanters and tall
tumblers. Paul Overt was an insin-

cere smoker; he puffed cigarettes occasionally for reasons with which tobacco had nothing to do. This was particularly the case on the occasion of which I speak; his motive was the vision of a little direct talk with Henry St. George. The "tremendous" communion of which the great man had held out hopes to him earlier in the day had not yet come off, and this saddened him considerably, for the party was to go its several ways immediately after breakfast on the morrow. He had, however, the disappointment of finding that apparently the author of *Shadowmere* was not disposed to prolong his vigil. He was not among the gentlemen assembled in the smoking-room when Overt entered it, nor was he one of those who turned up, in bright habiliments, during the next ten minutes. The young man waited a little, wondering whether he had only gone to put on something extraordinary; this would account for his delay as well as contribute further to Overt's observation of his tendency to do the approved superficial thing. But he didn't arrive —he must have been putting on something more extraordinary than was probable. Paul gave him up, feeling a little injured, a little wounded at his not having managed to say twenty words to him. He was not angry, but he puffed his cigarette sighingly, with the sense of having lost a precious chance. He wandered away with his regret, moved slowly round the room, looking at the old prints on the walls. In this attitude he presently felt a hand laid on his shoulder and a friendly voice in his ear. "This is good. I hoped I should find you. I came down on purpose." St. George

was there, without a change of dres and with a kind face—his graver on —to which Overt eagerly responded He explained that it was only for th Master—the idea of a little talk—tha he had sat up and that, not findin, him, he had been on the point o going to bed.

"Well, you know, I don't smoke— my wife doesn't let me," said S George, looking for a place to si down. "It's very good for me—ver good for me. Let us take that sofa.

"Do you mean smoking is good fo you?"

"No, no, her not letting me. It a great thing to have a wife wh proves to one all the things one ca do without. One might never fin them out for oneself. She doesn allow me to touch a cigarette."

They took possession of the sofa which was at a distance from th group of smokers, and St George wen on: "Have you got one yourself?"

"Do you mean a cigarette?"

"Dear no! a wife."

"No; and yet I would give up m cigarette for one."

"You would give up a good de more than that," said St. Georg "However, you would get a great de in return. There is a great deal to b said for wives," he added, folding h arms and crossing his outstretche legs. He declined tobacco altogethe and sat there without returning fir Paul Overt stopped smoking, touche by his courtesy; and after all th were out of the fumes, their sofa wa in a far-away corner. It would hav been a mistake, St. George went on, great mistake for them to have sep rated without a little chat; "for know all about you," he said, "I kno

ou're very remarkable. You've writ-
en a very distinguished book."

"And how do you know it?" Overt
sked.

"Why, my dear fellow, it's in the
ir, it's in the papers, it's everywhere,"
t. George replied, with the immediate
amiliarity of a *confrère*—a tone that
eemed to his companion the very
ustle of the laurel. "You're on all
nen's lips and, what's better, you're
n all women's. And I've just been
eading your book."

"Just? You hadn't read it this
fternoon," said Overt.

"How do you know that?"

"You know how I know it," the
oung man answered, laughing.

"I suppose Miss Fancourt told you."

"No, indeed; she led me rather to
uppose that you had."

"Yes; that's much more what she
vould do. Doesn't she shed a rosy
low over life? But you didn't be-
ieve her?" asked St. George.

"No, not when you came to us
here."

"Did I pretend? did I pretend
adly?" But without waiting for an
nswer to this St. George went on:
You ought always to believe such
girl as that—always, always. Some
omen are meant to be taken with al-
owances and reserves; but you must
ake *her* just as she is."

"I like her very much," said Paul
)vert.

Something in his tone appeared to
xcite on his companion's part a mo-
nentary sense of the absurd; perhaps
was the air of deliberation attend-
g this judgment. St. George broke
nto a laugh and returned: "It's the
est thing you can do with her. She's
rare young lady!. In point of fact,

however, I confess I hadn't read you
this afternoon."

"Then you see how right I was in
this particular case not to believe Miss
Fancourt."

"How right? how can I agree to
that, when I lost credit by it?"

"Do you wish to pass for exactly
what she represents you? Certainly
you needn't be afraid," Paul said.

"Ah, my dear young man, don't
talk about passing—for the likes of
me! I'm passing away—nothing else
than that. She has a better use for
her young imagination (isn't it fine?)
than in 'representing' in any way
such a weary, wasted, used-up animal!" St. George spoke with a sudden sadness which produced a protest
on Paul's part; but before the protest could be uttered he went on, re-
verting to the latter's successful novel:
"I had no idea you were so good—one
hears of so many things. But you're
surprisingly good."

"I'm going to be surprisingly better," said Overt.

"I see that and it's what fetches me.
I don't see so much else—as one looks
about—that's going to be surprisingly
better. They're going to be consist-
ently worse—most of the things. It's
so much easier to be worse—heaven
knows I've found it so. I'm not in a
great glow, you know, about what's
being attempted, what's being done.
But you *must* be better—you must
keep it up. I haven't, of course. It's
very difficult—that's the devil of the
whole thing; but I see you can. It
will be a great disgrace if you don't."

"It's very interesting to hear you
speak of yourself; but I don't know
what you mean by your allusions to
your having fallen off," Paul Overt re-

marked, with pardonable hypocrisy. He liked his companion so much now that it had ceased for the moment to be vivid to him that there had been any decline.

"Don't say that—don't say that," St. George replied gravely, with his head resting on the top of the back of the sofa and his eyes on the ceiling. "You know perfectly what I mean. I haven't read twenty pages of your book without seeing that you can't help it."

"You make me very miserable," Paul murmured.

"I'm glad of that, for it may serve as a kind of warning. Shocking enough it must be, especially to a young, fresh mind, full of faith,—the spectacle of a man meant for better things sunk at my age in such dishonor." St. George, in the same contemplative attitude, spoke softly but deliberately, and without perceptible emotion. His tone indeed suggested an impersonal lucidity which was cruel —cruel to himself—and which made Paul lay an argumentative hand on his arm. But he went on, while his eyes seemed to follow the ingenuities of the beautiful Adams ceiling: "Look at me well and take my lesson to heart, for it *is* a lesson. Let that good come of it at least that you shudder with your pitiful impression and that this may help to keep you straight in the future. Don't become in your old age what I am in mine—the depressing, the deplorable illustration of the worship of false gods!"

"What do you mean by your old age?" Paul Overt asked.

"It has made me old. But I like your youth."

Overt answered nothing—they sat for a minute in silence. They hear the others talking about the gover mental majority. Then, "What d you mean by false gods?" Paul in quired.

"The idols of the market—mone and luxury and 'the world,' placir one's children and dressing one's wi —everything that drives one to th short and easy way. Ah, the vi things they make one do!"

"But surely one is right to want t place one's children."

"One has no business to have an children," St. George declared, pla idly. "I mean of course if one wan to do something good."

"But aren't they an inspiration—a incentive?"

"An incentive to damnation, artist cally speaking."

"You touch on very deep things— things I should like to discuss wi you," Paul Overt said. "I shou like you to tell me volumes abo yourself. This is a festival for *me* !"

"Of course it is, cruel youth. B to show you that I'm still not i capable, degraded as I am, of an a of faith, I'll tie my vanity to the stak for you and burn it to ashes. Yc must come and see me—you mu come and see us. Mrs. St. George charming; I don't know whether yc have had any opportunity to talk wit her. She will be delighted to see you she likes great celebrities, whether i cipient or predominant. You mu come and dine—my wife will wri to you. Where are you to be found?

"This is my little address"—an Overt drew out his pocketbook an extracted a visiting-card. On secor thoughts, however, he kept it bac remarking that he would not troub his friend to take charge of it but would come and see him straightway in London and leave it at his door if he should fail to obtain admittance.

"Ah! you probably will fail; my wife's always out, or when she isn't out she's knocked up from having been out. You must come and dine —though that won't do much good either, for my wife insists on big dinners. You must come down and see us in the country, that's the best way; we have plenty of room, and it isn't bad."

"You have a house in the country?" Paul asked, enviously.

"Ah, not like this! But we have sort of place we go to—an hour from Euston. That's one of the reasons."

"One of the reasons?"

"Why my books are so bad."

"You must tell me all the others!" Paul exclaimed, laughing.

St. George made no direct rejoinder to this; he only inquired rather abruptly: "Why have I never seen you before?"

The tone of the question was singularly flattering to his new comrade; it seemed to imply that he perceived now that for years he had missed something. "Partly, I suppose, because there has been no particular reason why you should see me. I haven't lived in the world—in your world. I have spent many years out of England, in different places abroad."

"Well, please don't do it any more. You must do England—there's such a lot of it."

"Do you mean I must write about ?" Paul asked, in a voice which had the note of the listening candor of a child.

"Of course you must. And tremendously well, do you mind? That takes off a little of my esteem for this thing of yours—that it goes on abroad. Hang abroad! Stay at home and do things here—do subjects we can measure."

"I'll do whatever you tell me," said Paul Overt, deeply attentive. "But excuse me if I say I don't understand how you have been reading my book," he subjoined. "I've had you before me all the afternoon, first in that long walk, then at tea on the lawn, till we went to dress for dinner, and all the evening at dinner and in this place."

St. George turned his face round with a smile. "I only read for a quarter of an hour."

"A quarter of an hour is liberal, but I don't understand where you put it in. In the drawing-room, after dinner, you were not reading, you were talking to Miss Fancourt."

"It comes to the same thing, because we talked about *Ginistrella*. She described it to me—she lent it to me."

"Lent it to you?"

"She travels with it."

"It's incredible," Paul Overt murmured, blushing.

"It's glorious for you; but it also turned out very well for me. When the ladies went off to bed she kindly offered to send the book down to me. Her maid brought it to me in the hall and I went to my room with it. I hadn't thought of coming here, I do that so little. But I don't sleep early, I always have to read for an hour or two. I sat down to your novel on the spot, without undressing, without taking off anything but my coat. I think that's a sign that my curiosity had been strongly aroused about it. I read a quarter of an hour, as I tell you, and even in a quarter of an hour I was greatly struck."

"Ah, the beginning isn't very good —it's the whole thing!" said Overt, who had listened to this recital with extreme interest. "And you laid down the book and came after me?" he asked.

"That's the way it moved me. I said to myself, 'I see it's off his own bat, and he's there, by the way, and the day's over and I haven't said twenty words to him.' It occurred to me that you would probably be in the smoking-room and that it wouldn't be too late to repair my omission. I wanted to do something civil to you, so I put on my coat and came down. I shall read your book again when I go up."

Paul Overt turned round in his place —he was exceedingly touched by the picture of such a demonstration in his favor. "You're really the kindest of men. *Cela s'est passé comme ça?* and I have been sitting here with you all this time and never apprehended it and never thanked you!"

"Thank Miss Fancourt—it was she who wound me up. She has made me feel as if I had read your novel."

"She's an angel from heaven!" Paul Overt exclaimed.

"She is indeed. I have never seen anyone like her. Her interest in literature is touching—something quite peculiar to herself; she takes it all so seriously. She feels the arts and she wants to feel them more. To those who practise them it's almost humiliating—her curiosity, her sympathy, her good faith. How can anything be as fine as she supposes it?"

"She's a rare organisation," Paul Overt sighed.

"The richest I have ever seen—an artistic intelligence really of the first order. And lodged in such a form! St. George exclaimed.

"One would like to paint such girl as that," Overt continued.

"Ah, there it is—there's nothing like life! When you're finished squeezed dry and used up and you think the sack's empty, you're still spoken to, you still get touches and thrills, the idea springs up—out of the lap of the actual—and shows you there's always something to be done. But I shan't do it—she's not for me!"

"How do you mean, not for you?

"Oh, it's all over—she's for you, if you like."

"Ah, much less!" said Paul Overt. "She's not for a dingy little man of letters; she's for the world, the bright rich world of bribes and rewards. And the world will take hold of her—it will carry her away."

"It will try; but it's just a case in which there may be a fight. It would be worth fighting, for a man who has it in him, with youth and talent on his side."

These words rang not a little in Paul Overt's consciousness—they held him silent a moment. "It's a wonder she has remained as she is—giving herself away so, with so much to give away."

"Do you mean so ingenuous—so natural? Oh, she doesn't care a straw —she gives away because she overflows. She has her own feelings, her own standards; she doesn't keep remembering that she must be proud. And then she hasn't been here long enough to be spoiled; she has picked up a fashion or two, but only the musing ones. She's a provincial—a provincial of genius; her very blunders are charming, her mistakes are interesting. She has come back from Asia with all sorts of excited curiosities and unappeased appetites. She's first-rate herself and she expends herself on the second-rate. She's life herself and she makes a rare interest in imitations. She mixes all things up, but there are none in regard to which she hasn't perceptions. She sees things in a perspective—as if from the top of the Himalayas—and she enlarges everything she touches. Above all she exaggerates—to herself, I mean. She exaggerates you and me!"

There was nothing in this description to allay the excitement produced in the mind of our younger friend by such a sketch of a fine subject. It seemed to him to show the art of St. George's admired hand, and he lost himself in it, gazing at the vision (it hovered there before him,) of a woman's figure which should be part of the perfection of a novel. At the end of a moment he became aware that it had turned into smoke, and out of the smoke—the last puff of a big cigar—proceeded the voice of General Fancourt, who had left the others and come and planted himself before the gentlemen on the sofa. "I suppose that when you fellows get talking you sit up half the night."

"Half the night?—*jamais de la vie!* I follow a hygiene," St. George replied, rising to his feet.

"I see, you're hothouse plants," laughed the General. "That's the way you produce your flowers."

"I produce mine between ten and one every morning; I bloom with a regularity!" St. George went on.

"And with a splendour!" added the polite General, while Paul Overt noted how little the author of *Shadow-mere* minded, as he phrased it to himself, when he was addressed as a celebrated story-teller. The young man had an idea that *he* should never get used to that—it would always make him uncomfortable (from the suspicion that people would think they had to,) and he would want to prevent it. Evidently his more illustrious congener had toughened and hardened —had made himself a surface. The group of men had finished their cigars and taken up their bedroom candlesticks; but before they all passed out Lord Watermouth invited St. George and Paul Overt to drink something. It happened that they both declined, upon which General Fancourt said: "Is that the hygiene? You don't sprinkle the flowers?"

"Oh, I should drown them!" St. George replied; but leaving the room beside Overt he added whimsically, for the latter's benefit, in a lower tone: "My wife doesn't let me."

"Well, I'm glad I'm not one of you fellows!" the General exclaimed.

The nearness of Summersoft to London had this consequence, chilling to a person who had had a vision of sociability in a railway-carriage, that most of the company, after breakfast, drove back to town, entering their own vehicles, which had come out to fetch them, while their servants returned by train with their luggage. Three or four young men, among whom was Paul Overt, also availed themselves of the common convenience; but they stood in the portico of the house and saw the others roll away. Miss Fan-

court got into a victoria with her
father, after she had shaken hands
with Paul Overt and said, smiling in
the frankest way in the world—"I
must see you more. Mrs. St. George
is so nice: she has promised to ask
us both to dinner together." This
lady and her husband took their places
in a perfectly-appointed brougham
(she required a closed carriage,) and
as our young man waved his hat to
them in response to their nods and
flourishes he reflected that, taken together, they were an honourable image
of success, of the material rewards and
the social credit of literature. Such
things were not the full measure, but
all the same he felt a little proud for
literature.

IV

Before a week had elapsed Paul
Overt met Miss Fancourt in Bond
Street, at a private view of the works
of a young artist in "black and white"
who had been so good as to invite him
to the stuffy scene. The drawings
were admirable, but the crowd in the
one little room was so dense that he
felt as if he were up to his neck in a
big sack of wool. A fringe of people
at the outer edge endeavoured by
curving forward their backs and presenting, below them, a still more convex surface of resistance to the
pressure of the mass, to preserve an
interval between their noses and the
glazed mounts of the pictures; while
the central body, in the comparative
gloom projected by a wide horizontal
screen, hung under the skylight and allowing only a margin for the day, remained upright, dense and vague, lost
in the contemplation of its own in-
gredients. This contemplation sat

especially in the sad eyes of certai
female heads, surmounted with ha
of strange convolution and plumag
which rose on long necks above th
others. One of the heads, Paul Ove
perceived, was much the most beau
tiful of the collection, and his next dis
covery was that it belonged to Mis
Fancourt. Its beauty was enhanced b
the glad smile that she sent him acros
surrounding obstructions, a smi
which drew him to her as fast as h
could make his way. He had divine
at Summersoft that the last thin
her nature contained was an affecta
tion of indifference; yet even with thi
circumspection he had a freshness o
pleasure in seeing that she did nc
pretend to await his arrival with com
posure. She smiled as radiantly a
if she wished to make him hurry, an
as soon as he came within earshot sh
said to him, in her voice of joy: "He
here—he's here—he's coming back i
a moment!"

"Ah, your father?" Paul responde
as she offered him her hand.

"Oh, dear no, this isn't in my poo
father's line. I mean Mr. St. Georg
He has just left me to speak to som
one—he's coming back. It's he wh
brought me—wasn't it charming?"

"Ah, that gives him a pull over m
—I couldn't have 'brought' yo
could I?"

"If you had been so kind as to prc
pose it—why not you as well as he?
the girl asked, with a face which ex
pressed no cheap coquetry, but simpl
affirmed a happy fact.

"Why, he's a *père de famille*. The
have privileges," Paul Overt explaine
And then, quickly: "Will you go t
see places with *me?*" he broke out.

"Anything you like!" she smile

I know what you mean, that girls have to have a lot of people—" She interrupted herself to say: "I don't know; I'm free. I have always been like that," she went on; "I can go anywhere with any one. I'm so glad to meet you," she added, with a sweet distinctness that made the people near her turn round.

"Let me at least repay that speech by taking you out of this squash," said Paul Overt. "Surely people are not happy here!"

"No, they are *mornes*, aren't they? But I am very happy indeed, and I promised Mr. St. George to remain in this spot till he comes back. He's going to take me away. They send him invitations for things of this sort —more than he wants. It was so kind of him to think of me."

"They also send me invitations of his kind—more than I want. And thinking of *you* will do it—!" Paul went on.

"Oh, I delight in them—everything that's life—everything that's London!"

"They don't have private views in Asia, I suppose. But what a pity that for this year, in this fertile city, they re pretty well over."

"Well, next year will do, for I hope you believe we are going to be friends always. Here he comes!" Miss Fancourt continued, before Paul had time to respond.

He made out St. George in the laps of the crowd, and this perhaps led to his hurrying a little to say: "I hope that doesn't mean that I'm to wait till next year to see you."

"No, no; are we not to meet at dinner on the 25th?" she answered, with an eagerness greater even than his own.

"That's almost next year. Is there no means of seeing you before?"

She stared, with all her brightness. "Do you mean that you would *come?*"

"Like a shot, if you'll be so good as to ask me!"

"On Sunday, then—this next Sunday?"

"What have I done that you should doubt it?" the young man demanded, smiling.

Miss Fancourt turned instantly to St. George, who had now joined them, and announced triumphantly: "He's coming on Sunday—this next Sunday!"

"Ah, my day—my day too!" said the famous novelist, laughing at Paul Overt.

"Yes, but not yours only. You shall meet in Manchester Square; you shall talk—you shall be wonderful!"

"We don't meet often enough," St. George remarked, shaking hands with his disciple. "Too many things—ah, too many things! But we must make it up in the country in September. You won't forget that you've promised me that?"

"Why, he's coming on the 25th; you'll see him then," said Marian Fancourt.

"On the 25th?" St. George asked, vaguely.

"We dine with you; I hope you haven't forgotten. He's dining out," she added gaily to Paul Overt.

"Oh, bless me, yes; that's charming! And you're coming? My wife didn't tell me," St. George said to Paul. "Too many things—too many things!" he repeated.

"Too many people—too many people!" Paul exclaimed, giving ground before the penetration of an elbow.

"You oughtn't to say that; they all read you."

"Me? I should like to see them! Only two or three at most," the young man rejoined.

"Did you ever hear anything like that? He knows how good he is!" St. George exclaimed, laughing, to Miss Fancourt. "They read *me*, but that doesn't make me like them any better. Come away from them, come away!" And he led the way out of the exhibition.

"He's going to take me to the Park," the girl said, with elation, to Paul Overt, as they passed along the corridor which led to the street.

"Ah, does he go there?" Paul asked, wondering at the idea as a somewhat unexpected illustration of St. George's *moeurs*.

"It's a beautiful day; there will be a great crowd. We're going to look at the people, to look at types," the girl went on. "We shall sit under the trees; we shall walk by the Row."

"I go once a year, on business," said St. George, who had overheard Paul's question.

"Or with a country cousin, didn't you tell me? I'm the country cousin!" she went on, over her shoulder, to Paul, as her companion drew her toward a hansom to which he had signalled. The young man watched them get in; he returned, as he stood there, the friendly wave of the hand with which, ensconced in the vehicle beside Miss Fancourt, St. George took leave of him. He even lingered to see the vehicle start away and lose itself in the confusion of Bond Street. He followed it with his eyes; it was embarrassingly suggestive. "She's not for me!" the great novelist had said

emphatically at Summersoft; but his manner of conducting himself toward her appeared not exactly in harmony with such a conviction. How could he have behaved differently if she had been for him? An indefinite envy rose in Paul Overt's heart as he took his way on foot alone, and the singular part of it was that it was directed to each of the occupants of the hansom. How much he should like to rattle about London with such a girl! How much he should like to go and look at "types" with St. George!

The next Sunday, at four o'clock, he called in Manchester Square, where his secret wish was gratified by his finding Miss Fancourt alone. She was in a large, bright, friendly, occupied room, which was painted red all over, draped with the quaint, cheap, flori stuffs that are represented as coming from southern and eastern countries, where they are fabled to serve as the counterpanes of the peasantry, and bedecked with pottery of vivid hue, ranged on casual shelves, and with many water-colour drawings from the hand (as the visitor learned,) of the young lady, commemorating, with courage and skill, the sunsets, the mountains, the temples and palaces of India. Overt sat there an hour—more than an hour, two hours—and all the while no one came in. Miss Fancourt was so good as to remark, with her liberal humanity, that it was delightful they were not interrupted; it was so rare in London, especially at that season, that people got good talk. But fortunately now, on a fine Sunday, half the world went out of town, and that made it better for those who didn't go, when they were in sympathy. It was the defect of London (one of two or three, the very short list of those she recognised in the teeming world-city that she adored,) that there were too few good chances for talk; one never had time to carry anything far.

"Too many things—too many things!" Paul Overt said, quoting St. George's exclamation of a few days before.

"Ah yes, for him there are too many; his life is too complicated."

"Have you seen it *near?* That's what I should like to do; it might explain some mysteries," Paul Overt went on. The girl asked him what mysteries he meant, and he said: "Oh, peculiarities of his work, inequalities, superficialities. For one who looks at it from the artistic point of view it contains a bottomless ambiguity."

"Oh, do describe that more—it's so interesting. There are no such suggestive questions. I'm so fond of them. He thinks he's a failure—fancy!" Miss Fancourt added.

"That depends upon what his ideal may have been. Ah, with his gifts it ought to have been high. But till one knows what he really proposed to himself— Do *you* know, by chance?" the young man asked, breaking off.

"Oh, he doesn't talk to me about himself. I can't make him. It's too provoking."

Paul Overt was on the point of asking what then he did talk about; but discretion checked this inquiry, and he said instead: "Do you think he's unhappy at home?"

"At home?"

"I mean in his relations with his wife. He has a mystifying little way of alluding to her."

"Not to me," said Marian Fancourt, with her clear eyes. "That wouldn't be right, would it?" she asked, seriously.

"Not particularly; so I am glad he doesn't mention her to you. To praise her might bore you, and he has no business to do anything else. Yet he knows you better than me."

"Ah, but he respects *you!*" the girl exclaimed, enviously.

Her visitor stared a moment; then he broke into a laugh. "Doesn't he respect you?"

"Of course, but not in the same way. He respects what you've done —he told me so, the other day."

"When you went to look at types?"

"Ah, we found so many—he has such an observation of them! He talked a great deal about your book. He says it's really important."

"Important! Ah! the grand creature," Paul murmured, hilarious.

"He was wonderfully amusing, he was inexpressibly droll, while we walked about. He sees everything; he has so many comparisons, and they are always exactly right. *C'est d'un trouvé!* as they say."

"Yes, with his gifts, such things as he ought to have done!" Paul Overt remarked.

"And don't you think he *has* done them?"

He hesitated a moment. "A part of them—and of course even that part is immense. But he might have been one of the greatest! However, let us not make this an hour of qualifications. Even as they stand, his writings are a mine of gold."

To this proposition Marian Fancourt ardently responded, and for half an hour the pair talked over the master's principal productions. She knew them well—she knew them even better than her visitor, who was struck with her critical intelligence and with something large and bold in the movement in her mind. She said things that startled him and that evidently had come to her directly; they were not picked-up phrases, she placed them too well. St. George had been right about her being first-rate, about her not being afraid to gush, not remembering that she must be proud. Suddenly something reminded her, and she said: "I recollect that he did speak of Mrs. St. George to me once. He said, *à propos* of something or other, that she didn't care for perfection."

"That's a great crime, for an artist's wife," said Paul Overt.

"Yes, poor thing!" and the young lady sighed, with a suggestion of many reflections, some of them mitigating. But she added in a moment, "Ah, perfection, perfection—how one ought to go in for it! I wish I could."

"Every one can, in his way," said Paul Overt.

"In *his* way, yes; but not in hers. Women are so hampered—so condemned! But it's a kind of dishonour if you don't, when you want to *do* something, isn't it?" Miss Fancourt pursued, dropping one train in her quickness to take up another, an accident that was common with her. So these two young persons sat discussing high themes in their electric drawing-room, in their London season—discussing, with extreme seriousness, the high theme of perfection. And it must be said, in extenuation of this eccentricity, that they were interested in the business; their tone was genuine, their emotion real; they were not posturing for each other or for some one else.

The subject was so wide that they found it necessary to contract it; the perfection to which for the moment they agreed to confine their speculations was that of which the valid work of art is susceptible. Miss Fancourt's imagination, it appeared, had wandered far in that direction, and her visitor had the rare delight of feeling that their conversation was a full interchange. This episode will have lived for years in his memory and even in his wonder; it had the quality that fortune distils in a single drop at a time—the quality that lubricates ensuing weeks and months. He has still a vision of the room whenever he likes—the bright, red sociable, talkative room, with the curtains that, by a stroke of successful audacity, had the note of vivid blue. He remembers where certain things stood, the book that was open on the table and the particular odour of the flowers that were placed on the left somewhere behind him. These facts were the fringe, as it were, of a particular consciousness which had its birth in those two hours and of which perhaps the most general description would be to mention that it led him to say over and over again to himself: "I had no idea there was any one like this—I had no idea there was any one like this!" Her freedom amazed him and charmed him—it seemed so to simplify the practical question. She was on the footing of an independent personage—a motherless girl who had passed out of her teens and had a position, responsibilities, and was not held down to the limitations of a little miss. She came and went without the clumsiness of a chaperon; she received people alone and, though she was totally without hardness, the question of protection or patronage had no relevancy in regard to her. She gave such an impression of purity combined with naturalness that, in spite of her eminently modern situation, she suggested no sort of sisterhood with the "fast" girl. Modern she was, indeed, and made Paul Overt, who loved old colour, the golden glaze of time, think with some alarm of the muddled palette of the future. He couldn't get used to her interest in the arts he cared for; it seemed too good to be real—it was so unlikely an adventure to tumble into such a well of sympathy. One might stray into the desert easily—that was on the cards and that was the law of life; but it was too rare an accident to stumble on a crystal well. Yet if her aspirations seemed at one moment too extravagant to be real, they struck him at the next as too intelligent to be false. They were both noble and crude, and whims for whims, he liked them better than any he had met. It was probable enough she would leave them behind—exchange them for politics, or "smartness," or mere prolific maternity, as was the custom of scribbling, daubing, educated, flattered girls, in an age of luxury and a society of leisure. He noted that the water-colours on the walls of the room she sat in had mainly the quality of being *naïves*, and reflected that *naïveté* in art is like a cipher in a number: its importance depends upon the figure it

is united with. But meanwhile he had fallen in love with her.

Before he went away he said to Miss Fancourt: "I thought St. George was coming to see you to-day —but he doesn't turn up."

For a moment he supposed she was going to reply, "*Comment donc?* Did you come here only to meet him?" But the next he became aware of how little such a speech would have fallen in with any flirtatious element he had as yet perceived in her. She only replied: "Ah yes, but I don't think he'll come. He recommended me not to expect him." Then she added, laughing: "He said it wasn't fair to you. But I think I could manage two."

"So could I," Paul Overt rejoined, stretching the point a little to be humorous. In reality his appreciation of the occasion was so completely an appreciation of the woman before him that another figure in the scene, even so esteemed a one as St. George, might for the hour have appealed to him vainly. As he went away he wondered what the great man had meant by its not being fair to him; and, still more than that, whether he had actually stayed away out of the delicacy of such an idea. As he took his course, swinging his stick, through the Sunday solitude of Manchester Square, with a good deal of emotion fermenting in his soul, it appeared to him that he was living in a world really magnanimous. Miss Fancourt had told him that there was an uncertainty about her being, and her father's being, in town on the following Sunday, but that she had the hope of a visit from him if they should not go away. She promised to let him know if they stayed at home, then he could act accordingly. After he had passed into one of the streets that lead out of the square, he stopped, without definite intentions, looking sceptically for a cab. In a moment he saw a hansom roll through the square from the other side and come a part of the way toward him. He was on the point of hailing the driver when he perceived that he carried a fare; then he waited, seeing him prepare to deposit his passenger by pulling up at one of the houses. The house was apparently the one he himself had just quitted; at least he drew that inference as he saw that the person who stepped out of the hansom was Henry St. George. Paul Overt turned away quickly, as if he had been caught in the act of spying. He gave up his cab—he preferred to walk; he would go nowhere else. He was glad St. George had not given up his visit altogether—that would have been too absurd. Yes, the world was magnanimous, and Overt felt so too as, on looking at his watch, he found it was only six o'clock, so that he could mentally congratulate his successor on having an hour still to sit in Miss Fancourt's drawing-room. He himself might use that hour for another visit, but by the time he reached the Marble Arch the idea of another visit had become incongruous to him. He passed beneath that architectural effort and walked into the Park till he got upon the grass. Here he continued to walk; he took his way across the elastic turf and came out by the Serpentine. He watched with a friendly eye the diversions of the London people, and bent a glance almost encouraging upon the young ladies paddling their sweethearts on the lake, and the guardsmen tickling tenderly with their bearskins the artificial flowers in the Sunday hats of their partners. He prolonged his meditative walk; he went into Kensington Gardens—he sat upon the penny chairs—he looked at the little sail-boats launched upon the round pond —he was glad he had no engagement to dine. He repaired for this purpose, very late, to his club, where he found himself unable to order a repast and told the waiter to bring whatever he would. He did not even observe what he was served with, and he spent the evening in the library of the establishment, pretending to read an article in an American magazine. He failed to discover what it was about; it appeared in a dim way to be about Marian Fancourt.

Quite late in the week she wrote to him that she was not to go into the country—it had only just been settled. Her father, she added, would never settle anything—he put it all on her. She felt her responsibility—she had to—and since she was forced that was the way she had decided. She mentioned no reasons, which gave Paul Overt all the clearer field for bold conjecture about them. In Manchester Square, on this second Sunday, he esteemed his fortune less good for she had three or four other visitors. But there were three or four compensations; the greatest, perhaps, of which was that, learning from her that her father had, after all, at the last hour, gone out of town alone, the bold conjecture I just now spoke of found itself becoming a shade more bold. And then her presence was her presence, and the personal red room was there and was full of it, whatever phantoms passed and vanished, emitting incomprehensible sounds. Lastly, he had the resource of staying till every one had come and gone and of supposing that this pleased her, though she gave no particular sign. When they were alone together he said to her: "But St. George did come—last Sunday. I saw him as I looked back."

"Yes; but it was the last time."

"The last time?"

"He said he would never come again."

Paul Overt stared. "Does he mean that he wishes to cease to see you?"

"I don't know what he means," the girl replied, smiling. "He won't, at any rate, see me here."

"And, pray, why not?"

"I don't know," said Marian Fancourt; and her visitor thought he had not yet seen her more beautiful than in uttering these unsatisfactory words.

v

"Oh, I say, I want you to remain," Henry St. George said to him at eleven o'clock, the night he dined with the head of the profession. The company had been numerous and they were taking their leave; our young man, after bidding good-night to his hostess, had put out his hand in farewell to the master of the house. Besides eliciting from St. George the protest I have quoted this movement provoked a further observation about such a chance to have a talk, their going into his room, his having still everything to say. Paul Overt was delighted to be asked to stay; nevertheless he mentioned jocularly the literal fact that he had promised to go to another place, at a distance.

"Well then, you'll break your promise, that's all. You humbug!" St. George exclaimed, in a tone that added to Overt's contentment.

"Certainly, I'll break it; but it was a real promise."

"Do you mean to Miss Fancourt? You're following her?" St. George asked.

Paul Overt answered by a question. "Oh, is *she* going?"

"Base impostor!" his ironic host went on; "I've treated you handsomely on the article of that young lady: I won't make another concession. Wait three minutes—I'll be with you." He gave himself to his departing guests, went with the long-trained ladies to the door. It was a hot night, the windows were open, the sound of the quick carriages and of the linkmen's call came into the house. The company had been brilliant; a sense of festal things was in the heavy air: not only the influence of that particular entertainment, but the suggestion of the wide hurry of pleasure which, in London, on summer nights, fills so many of the happier quarters of the complicated town. Gradually Mrs. St. George's drawing-room emptied itself; Paul Overt was left alone with his hostess, to whom he explained the motive of his waiting. "Ah yes, some intellectual, some *professional,* talk," she smiled; "at this season doesn't one miss it? Poor dear Henry, I'm so glad!" The young man looked out of the window a moment, at the called hansoms that lurched up, at the smooth broughams that rolled away. When he turned round Mrs. St. George had disappeared; her husband's voice came up to him from below—he was laughing and talking, in the portico, with some lady who awaited her carriage. Paul had solitary possession, for some minutes, of the warm, deserted rooms, where the covered, tinted lamplight was soft, the seats had been pushed about and the odour of flowers lingered. They were large, they were pretty, they contained objects of value; everything in the picture told of a "good house." At the end of five minutes a servant came in with a request from Mr. St. George that he would join him downstairs; upon which, descending, he followed his conductor through a long passage to an apartment thrown out, in the rear of the habitation, for the special requirements, as he guessed, of a busy man of letters.

St. George was in his shirt-sleeves in the middle of a large, high room—a room without windows, but with a wide sky-light at the top, like a place of exhibition. It was furnished as a library, and the serried bookshelves rose to the ceiling, a surface of incomparable tone, produced by dimly-gilt "backs," which was interrupted here and there by the suspension of old prints and drawings. At the end furthest from the door of admission was a tall desk, of great extent, at which the person using it could only write standing, like a clerk in a counting-house; and stretching from the door to this structure was a large plain band of crimson cloth, as straight as a garden-path and almost as long, where, in his mind's eye, Paul Overt immediately saw his host pace to and fro during his hours of composition. The servant gave him a coat, an old jacket with an air of experience, from a cupboard in the wall, retiring afterwards with the garment he had taken off. Paul Overt welcomed the coat; it was a coat for talk and promised confidences—it must have received so many—and had pathetic literary elbows. "Ah, we're practical—we're practical!" St. George said, as he saw his visitor looking the place over. "Isn't it a good big cage, to go round and round? My wife invented it and she locks me up here every morning."

"You don't miss a window—a place to look out?"

"I did at first, awfully; but her calculation was just. It saves time, it has saved me many months in these ten years. Here I stand, under the eye of day—in London of course, very often, it's rather a bleared old eye—walled in to my trade. I can't get away, and the room is a fine lesson in concentration. I've learned the lesson, I think; look at that big bundle of proof and admit that I have." He pointed to a fat roll of papers, on one of the tables, which had not been undone.

"Are you bringing out another—?" Paul Overt asked, in a tone of whose deficiencies he was not conscious till his companion burst out laughing, and indeed not even then.

"You humbug—you humbug! Don't I know what you think of them?" St. George inquired, standing before him with his hands in his pockets and with a new kind of smile. It was as if he were going to let his young votary know him well now.

"Upon my word, in that case you know more than I do!" Paul ventured to respond, revealing a part of the torment of being able neither clearly to esteem him nor distinctly to renounce him.

"My dear fellow," said his companion, "don't imagine I talk about my books, specifically; it isn't a decent subject—*il ne manquerait plus que ça*—I'm not so bad as you may apprehend! About myself, a little, if you like; though it wasn't for that I brought you down here. I want to ask you something—very much indeed—I value this chance. Therefore sit down. We are practical, but there *is* a sofa, you see, for she does humour me a little, after all. Like all really great administrators she knows when to." Paul Overt sank into the corner of a deep leathern couch, but his interlocutor remained standing and said: "If you don't mind, in this room this is my habit. From the door to the desk and from the desk to the door. That shakes up my imagination, gently; and don't you see what a good thing it is that there's no window for her to fly out of? The eternal standing as I write (I stop at that bureau and put it down, when anything comes, and so we go on,) was rather wearisome at first, but we adopted it with an eye to the long run; you're in better order (if your legs don't break down!) and you can keep it up for more years. Oh, we're practical—we're practical!" St. George repeated, going to the table and taking up, mechanically, the bundle of proofs. He pulled off the wrapper, he turned the papers over with a sudden change of attention which only made him more interesting to Paul Overt. He lost himself a moment, examining the sheets of his new book, while the younger man's eyes wandered over the room again.

"Lord, what good things I should do if I had such a charming place as this to do them in!" Paul reflected. The outer world, the world of accident and ugliness was so successfully excluded, and within the rich, protecting square, beneath the patronising sky, the figures projected for an artistic purpose could hold their particular revel. It was a prevision of Paul Overt's rather than an observation on actual data, for which the occasions had been too few, that his new friend would have the quality, the charming quality, of surprising him by flashing out in personal intercourse, at moments of suspended, or perhaps even of diminished expectation. A happy relation with him would be a thing proceeding by jumps, not by traceable stages.

"Do you read them—really?" he asked, laying down the proofs on Paul's inquiring of him how soon the work would be published. And when the young man answered, "Oh yes, always," he was moved to mirth again by something he caught in his manner of saying that. "You go to see your grandmother on her birthday—and very proper it is, especially as she won't last for ever. She has lost every faculty and every sense; she neither sees, nor hears, nor speaks; but all customary pieties and kindly habits are respectable. But you're strong if you *do* read 'em! *I* couldn't, my dear fellow. You *are* strong, I know; and that's just a part of what I wanted to say to you. You're very strong indeed. I've been going into your other things—they've interested me exceedingly. Some one ought to have told me about them before—some one I could believe. But whom can one believe? You're wonderfully in the good direction—it's extremely curious work. Now do you mean to keep it up?—that's what I want to ask you."

"Do I mean to do others?" Paul Overt asked, looking up from his sofa at his erect inquisitor and feeling partly like a happy little boy when the schoolmaster is gay and partly like some pilgrim of old who might have consulted the oracle. St. George's own performance had been infirm, but as an adviser he would be infallible.

"Others—others? Ah, the number won't matter; one other would do, if it were really a further step—a throb of the same effort. What I mean is, have you it in your mind to go in for some sort of little perfection?"

"Ah, perfection!" Overt sighed, "I talked of that the other Sunday with Miss Fancourt."

"Oh yes, they'll talk of it, as much as you like! But they do mighty little to help one to it. There's no obligation, of course; only you strike me as capable," St. George went on. "You must have thought it all over. I can't believe you're without a plan. That's the sensation you give me, and it's so rare that it really stirs up one; it makes you remarkable. If you haven't a plan and you don't mean to keep it up, of course it's all right, it's no one's business, no one can force you, and not more than two or three people will notice that you don't go straight. The others—*all* the rest, every blessed soul in England, will think you do—will think you *are* keeping it up: upon my honour they will! I shall be one of the two or three who know better. Now the question is whether you can do it for two or three. Is that the stuff you're made of?"

"I could do it for one, if you were the one."

"Don't say that—I don't deserve it; it scorches me," St. George exclaimed, with eyes suddenly grave and glowing. "The 'one' is of course oneself—one's conscience, one's idea, the singleness of one's aim. I think of that pure spirit as a man thinks of a woman whom, in some detested hour of his youth, he has loved and forsaken. She haunts him with reproachful eyes, she lives for ever before him. As an artist, you know, I've married for money." Paul stared and even blushed a little, confounded by this avowal; whereupon his host, observing the expression of his face, dropped a quick laugh and went on: "You don't follow my figure. I'm not speaking of my dear wife, who had a small fortune, which, however, was not my bribe. I fell in love with her, as many other people have done. I refer to the mercenary muse whom I led to the altar of literature. Don't do that, my boy. She'll lead you a life!"

"Haven't you been happy!"

"Happy? It's a kind of hell."

"There are things I should like to ask you," Paul Overt said, hesitating.

"Ask me anything in all the world. I'd turn myself inside out to save you."

"To save me?" Paul repeated.

"To make you stick to it—to make you see it through. As I said to you the other night at Summersoft, let my example be vivid to you."

"Why, your books are not so bad as that," said Paul, laughing and feeling that he breathed the air of art.

"So bad as what?"

"Your talent is so great that it is n everything you do, in what's less ood as well as in what's best. You've ome forty volumes to show for it— orty volumes of life, of observation, f magnificent ability."

"I'm very clever, of course I know hat," St. George replied, quietly. "Lord, what rot they'd all be if I adn't been! I'm a successful harlatan—I've been able to pass off ly system. But do you know what is? It's *carton-pierre*."

"*Carton-pierre?*"

"Lincrusta-Walton!"

"Ah, don't say such things—you lake me bleed!" the younger man rotested. "I see you in a beautiful, ortunate home, living in comfort id honour."

"Do you call it honour?" St. George iterrupted, with an intonation that ften comes back to his companion. That's what I want *you* to go in for. mean the real thing. This is brum-lagaem."

"Brummagaem?" Paul ejaculated, hile his eyes wandered, by a move-lent natural at the moment, over the xurious room.

"Ah, they make it so well to-day; s wonderfully deceptive!"

"Is it deceptive that I find you liv-lg with every appearance of domestic licity—blessed with a devoted, ac-implished wife, with children whose :cquaintance I haven't yet had the leasure of making, but who *must* be lelightful young people, from what know of their parents?"

"It's all excellent, my dear fellow -heaven forbid I should deny it. I've ade a great deal of money; my wife is known how to take care of it,

to use it without wasting it, to put a good bit of it by, to make it fructify. I've got a loaf on the shelf; I've got everything, in fact, but the great thing—"

"The great thing?"

"The sense of having done the best —the sense, which is the real life of the artist and the absence of which is his death, of having drawn from his intellectual instrument the finest music that nature had hidden in it, of having played it as it should be played. He either does that or he doesn't—and if he doesn't he isn't worth speaking of. And precisely those who really know don't speak of him. He may still hear a great chatter, but what he hears most is the incorruptible silence of Fame. I have squared her, you may say, for my little hour—but what is my little hour? Don't imagine for a moment I'm such a cad as to have brought you down here to abuse or to com-plain of my wife to you. She is a woman of very distinguished quali-ties, to whom my obligations are im-mense; so that, if you please, we will say nothing about her. My boys —my children are all boys—are straight and strong, thank God; and have no poverty of growth about them, no penury of needs. I receive, periodically, the most satisfactory at-testation from Harrow, from Oxford, from Sandhurst (oh, we have done the best for them!) of their being living, thriving, consuming organisms."

"It must be delightful to feel that the son of one's loins is at Sandhurst," Paul remarked enthusiastically.

"It is—it's charming. Oh, I'm a patriot!"

"Then what did you mean—the

other night at Summersoft—by saying that children are a curse?"

"My dear fellow, on what basis are we talking?" St. George asked, dropping upon the sofa, at a short distance from his visitor. Sitting a little sideways he leaned back against the opposite arm with his hands raised and interlocked behind his head. "On the supposition that a certain perfection is possible and even desirable—isn't it so? Well, all I say is that one's children interfere with perfection. One's wife interferes. Marriage interferes."

"You think then the artist shouldn't marry?"

"He does so at his peril—he does so at his cost."

"Not even when his wife is in sympathy with his work?"

"She never is—she can't be! Women don't know what work is."

"Surely, they work themselves," Paul Overt objected.

"Yes, very badly. Oh, of course, often, they think they understand, they think they sympathise. Then it is that they are most dangerous. Their idea is that you shall do a great lot and get a great lot of money. Their great nobleness and virtue, their exemplary conscientiousness as British females, is in keeping you up to that. My wife makes all my bargains with my publishers for me, and she has done so for twenty years. She does it consummately well; that's why I'm really pretty well off. Are you not the father of their innocent babes, and will you withhold from them their natural sustenance? You asked me the other night if they were not an immense incentive. Of course they are—there's no doubt of that!"

"For myself, I have an idea I nee incentives," Paul Overt dropped.

"Ah well, then, *n'en parlons plus!* said his companion, smiling.

"You are an incentive, I maintain, the young man went on. "You don' affect me in the way you apparentl would like to. Your great success what I see—the pomp of Ennismor Gardens!"

"Success?—do you call it success t be spoken of as you would speak c me if you were sitting here with an other artist—a young man intelliger and sincere like yourself? Do you ca it success to make you blush—as yo would blush—if some foreign crit (some fellow, of course, I mean, wh should know what he was talkir about and should have shown yc he did, as foreign critics like to sho it!) were to say to you: 'He's th one, in this country, whom they co: sider the most perfect, isn't he?' it success to be the occasion of young Englishman's having to star mer as you would have to stamm at such a moment for old Englanc No, no; success is to have made pe ple tremble after another fashio Do try it!"

"Try it?"

"Try to do some really good work

"Oh, I want to, heaven knows!"

"Well, you can't do it without sacr fices; don't believe that for a m ment," said Henry St. George. "I' made none. I've had everything. other words, I've missed ever thing."

"You've had the full, rich, masc line, human, general life, with all tl responsibilities and duties and burde and sorrows and joys—all the dome tic and social initiations and comp ations. They must be immensely suggestive, immensely amusing."

"Amusing?"

"For a strong man—yes."

"They've given me subjects without number, if that's what you mean; but they've taken away at the same time the power to use them. I've touched a thousand things, but which one of them have I turned into gold? The artist has to do only with that —he knows nothing of any baser metal. I've led the life of the world, with my wife and my progeny; the clumsy, expensive, materialised, brutalised, Philistine, snobbish life of London. We've got everything handsome, even a carriage—we are prosperous, hospitable, eminent people. But, my dear fellow, don't try to nullify yourself and pretend you don't know what we *haven't* got. It's bigger than all the rest. Between artists —come! You know as well as you sit there that you would put a pistol-ball into your brain if you had written my books!"

It appeared to Paul Overt that the tremendous talk promised by the master at Summersoft had indeed come off, and with a promptitude, a fulness, with which his young imagination had scarcely reckoned. His companion made an immense impression on him and he throbbed with the excitement of such deep soundings and such strange confidences. He throbbed indeed with the conflict of his feelings —bewilderment and recognition and alarm, enjoyment and protest and assent, all commingled with tenderness and a kind of shame in the participation,) for the sores and bruises exhibited by so fine a creature, and with sense of the tragic secret that he nursed under his trappings. The idea of *his* being made the occasion of such an act of humility made him flush and pant, at the same time that his perception, in certain directions, had been too much awakened to conceal from him anything that St. George really meant. It had been his odd fortune to blow upon the deep waters, to make them surge and break in waves of strange eloquence. He launched himself into a passionate contradiction of his host's last declaration; tried to enumerate to him the parts of his work he loved, the splendid things he had found in it, beyond the compass of any other writer of the day. St. George listened awhile, courteously; then he said, laying his hand on Paul Overt's:

"That's all very well; and if your idea is to do nothing better there is no reason why you shouldn't have as many good things as I—as many human and material appendages, as many sons or daughters, a wife with as many gowns, a house with as many servants, a stable with as many horses, a heart with as many aches." He got up when he had spoken thus, and then stood a moment near the sofa, looking down on his agitated pupil. "Are you possessed of any money?" it occurred to him to ask.

"None to speak of."

"Oh, well, there's no reason why you shouldn't make a goodish income —if you set about it the right way. Study *me* for that—study me well. You may really have a carriage."

Paul Overt sat there for some moments without speaking. He looked straight before him—he turned over many things. His friend had wandered away from him, taking up a parcel of letters that were on the table where the roll of proofs had lain. "What was the book Mrs. St. George made you burn—the one she didn't like?" he abruptly inquired.

"The book she made me burn— how did you know that?" St. George looked up from his letters.

"I heard her speak of it at Summersoft."

"Ah, yes; she's proud of it. I don't know—it was rather good."

"What was it about?"

"Let me see." And St. George appeared to make an effort to remember. "Oh, yes, it was about myself." Paul Overt gave an irrepressible groan for the disappearance of such a production, and the elder man went on: "Oh, but *you* should write it—*you* should do me. There's a subject, my boy: no end of stuff in it!"

Again Paul was silent, but after a little he spoke. "Are there no women that really understand—that can take part in a sacrifice?"

"How can they take part? They themselves are the sacrifice. They're the idol and the altar and the flame."

"Isn't there even *one* who sees further?" Paul continued.

For a moment St. George made no answer to this; then, having torn up his letters, he stood before his disciple again, ironic. "Of course I know the one you mean. But not even Miss Fancourt."

"I thought you admired her so much."

"It's impossible to admire her more. Are you in love with her?" St. George asked.

"Yes," said Paul Overt.

"Well, then, give it up."

Paul stared. "Give up my love?"

"Bless me, no; your idea."

"My idea?"

"The one you talked with her abou The idea of perfection."

"She would help it—she would he it!" cried the young man.

"For about a year—the first yea yes. After that she would be as millstone round its neck."

"Why, she has a passion for con pleteness, for good work—for ever thing you and I care for most."

"'You and I' is charming, my de fellow! She has it indeed, but sl would have a still greater passion fo her children; and very proper to She would insist upon everything being made comfortable, advantageou propitious for them. That isn't tl artist's business."

"The artist—the artist! Isn't a man all the same?"

St. George hesitated. "Sometim I really think not. You know as w as I what he has to do: the conce tration, the finish, the independen that he must strive for, from the m ment that he begins to respect l work. Ah, my young friend, his re tion to women, especially in mat mony, is at the mercy of this damni fact—that whereas he can in the n ture of things have but one standar they have about fifty. That's wh makes them so superior," St. Geor added, laughing. "Fancy an artist wi a plurality of standards," he went ("To *do* it—to do it and make it (vine is the only thing he has to thi about. 'Is it done or not?' is his on question. Not 'Is it done as well a proper solicitude for my dear lit family will allow?' He has nothi to do with the relative, nothing do with a dear little family!"

"Then you don't allow him the common passions and affections of men?"

"Hasn't he a passion, an affection, which includes all the rest? Besides, let him have all the passions he likes —if he only keeps his independence. He must afford to be poor."

Paul Overt slowly got up. "Why did you advise me to make up to her, then?"

St. George laid his hand on his shoulder. "Because she would make an adorable wife! And I hadn't read you then."

"I wish you had left me alone!" murmured the young man.

"I didn't know that that wasn't good enough for you," St. George continued.

"What a false position, what a condemnation of the artist, that he's a mere disfranchised monk and can produce his effect only by giving up personal happiness. What an arraignment of art!" Paul Overt pursued, with a trembling voice.

"Ah, you don't imagine, by chance, that I'm defending art? Arraignment, I should think so! Happy the societies in which it hasn't made its appearance; for from the moment it comes they have a consuming ache, they have an incurable corruption in their bosom. Assuredly, the artist is in a false position. But I thought we were taking him for granted. Pardon me," St. George continued; *"Ginistrella* made me!"

Paul Overt stood looking at the floor —one o'clock struck, in the stillness, from a neighbouring church-tower. "Do you think she would ever look at me?" he asked at last.

"Miss Fancourt—as a suitor? Why shouldn't I think it? That's why

I've tried to favour you—I have had a little chance or two of bettering your opportunity."

"Excuse my asking you, but do you mean by keeping away yourself?" Paul said, blushing.

"I'm an old idiot—my place isn't there," St. George replied, gravely.

"I'm nothing, yet; I've no fortune; and there must be so many others."

"You're a gentleman and a man of genius. I think you might do something."

"But if I must give that up—the genius?"

"Lots of people, you know, think I've kept mine."

"You have a genius for torment!" Paul Overt exclaimed; but taking his companion's hand in farewell as a mitigation of this judgment.

"Poor child, I do bother you. Try, try, then! I think your chances are good, and you'll win a great prize."

Paul held the other's hand a minute; he looked into his face. "No, I *am* an artist—I can't help it!"

"Ah, show it then!" St. George broke out—"let me see before I die the thing I most want, the thing I yearn for—a life in which the passion is really intense. If you can be rare, don't fail of it! Think what it is —how it counts—how it lives!" They had moved to the door and St. George had closed both his own hands over that of his companion. Here they paused again and Paul Overt ejaculated—"I want to live!"

"In what sense?"

"In the greatest sense."

"Well then, stick to it—see it through."

"With your sympathy—your help?"

"Count on that—you'll be a great

figure to me. Count on my highest appreciation, my devotion. You'll give me satisfaction!—if that has any weight with you." And as Paul appeared still to waver, St. George added: "Do you remember what you said to me at Summersoft?"

"Something infatuated, no doubt!"

" 'I'll do anything in the world you tell me.' You said that."

"And you hold me to it?"

"Ah, what am I?" sighed the master, shaking his head.

"Lord, what things I shall have to do!" Paul almost moaned as he turned away.

VI

"It goes on too much abroad—hang abroad!" These, or something 20 like them, had been St. George's remarkable words in relation to the action of *Ginistrella;* and yet, though they had made a sharp impression on Paul Overt, like almost all the master's spoken words, the young man, a week after the conversation I have narrated, left England for a long absence and full of projects of work. It is not a perversion of the truth 30 to say that that conversation was the direct cause of his departure. If, the oral utterance of the eminent writer had the privilege of moving him deeply it was especially on his turning it over at leisure, hours and days afterward, that it appeared to yield its full meaning and exhibit its extreme importance. He spent the summer in Switzerland, and having, in September, begun a new 40 task, he determined not to cross the Alps till he should have made a good start. To this end he returned to a quiet corner that he knew well, on the edge of the Lake of Geneva,

within sight of the towers of Chillon a region and a view for which he ha an affection springing from old asso ciations, capable of mysterious littl revivals and refreshments. Here h lingered late, till the snow was o the nearer hills, almost down to th limit to which he could climb whe his stint was done, on the shortenin 10 afternoons. The autumn was fine, th lake was blue, and his book took for and direction. These circumstance for the time, embroidered his life, an he suffered it to cover him with i mantle. At the end of six weeks h appeared to himself to have learne St. George's lesson by heart—to hav tested and proved its doctrin Nevertheless he did a very inconsisten 20 thing: before crossing the Alps h wrote to Marian Fancourt. He wa aware of the perversity of this ac and it was only as a luxury, an amus ment, the reward of a strenuo autumn, that he justified it. She ha not asked any such favour of hi when he went to see her three da before he left London—three da after their dinner in Ennismore Ga 30 dens. It is true that she had no re son to, for he had not mentioned th he was on the eve of such an excu sion. He hadn't mentioned it becau he didn't know it; it was that partic lar visit that made the matter clea He had paid the visit to see how mu he really cared for her, and quick d parture, without so much as a far well, was the sequel to this inquiry, t 40 answer to which had been a distin superlative. When he wrote to h from Clarens he noted that he ow her an explanation (more than thr months after!) for the omission such a form.

She answered him briefly but very promptly, and gave him a striking piece of news: the death, a week before, of Mrs. St. George. This exemplary woman had succumbed, in the country, to a violent attack of inflammation of the lungs—he would remember that for a long time she had been delicate. Miss Fancourt added that she heard her husband was overwhelmed with the blow; he would miss her unspeakably—she had been everything to him. Paul Overt immediately wrote to St. George. He had wished to remain in communication with him, but had hitherto lacked the right excuse for troubling so busy a man. Their long nocturnal talk came back to him in every detail, but this did not prevent his expressing a cordial sympathy with the head of the profession, for had not that very talk made it clear that the accomplished lady was the influence that ruled his life? What catastrophe could be more cruel than the extinction of such an influence? This was exactly the tone that St. George took in answering his young friend, upwards of a month later. He made no allusion, of course, to their important discussion. He spoke of his wife as frankly and generously as if he had quite forgotten that occasion, and the feeling of deep bereavement was visible in his words. She took everything off my hands—off my mind. She carried on our life with the greatest art, the rarest devotion, and I was free, as few men can have been, to drive my pen, to shut myself up with my trade. This was a rare service—the highest she could have rendered me. Would I could have acknowledged it more fitly!"

A certain bewilderment, for Paul Overt, disengaged itself from these remarks: they struck him as a contradiction, a retraction. He had certainly not expected his correspondent to rejoice in the death of his wife, and it was perfectly in order that the rupture of a tie of more than twenty years should have left him sore. But if she was such a benefactress as that, what in the name of consistency had St. George meant by turning *him* upside down that night—by dosing him to that degree, at the most sensitive hour of his life, with the doctrine of renunciation? If Mrs. St. George was an irreparable loss, then her husband's inspired advice had been a bad joke and renunciation was a mistake. Overt was on the point of rushing back to London to show that, for his part, he was perfectly willing to consider it so, and he went so far as to take the manuscript of the first chapters of his new book out of his table-drawer, to insert it into a pocket of his portmanteau. This led to his catching a glimpse of some pages he had not looked at for months, and that accident, in turn, to his being struck with the high promise they contained —a rare result of such retrospections, which it was his habit to avoid as much as possible. They usually made him feel that the glow of composition might be a purely subjective and a very barren emotion. On this occasion a certain belief in himself disengaged itself whimsically from the serried erasures of his first draft, making him think it best after all to carry out his present experiment to the end. If he could write as well as that under the influence of renunciation, it would be a pity to change the conditions before the termination of the work. He would go back to London of course, but he would go back only when he should have finished his book. This was the vow he privately made, restoring his manuscript to the table-drawer. It may be added that it took him a long time to finish his book, for the subject was as difficult as it was fine and he was literally embarrassed by the fulness of his notes. Something within him told him that he must make it supremely good—otherwise he should lack, as regards his private behaviour, a handsome excuse. He had a horror of this deficiency and found himself as firm as need be on the question of the lamp and the file. He crossed the Alps at last and spent the winter, the spring, the ensuing summer, in Italy, where still, at the end of a twelvemonth, his task was unachieved. "Stick to it—see it through:" this general injunction of St. George's was good also for the particular case. He applied it to the utmost, with the result that when in its slow order, the summer had come round again he felt that he had given all that was in him. This time he put his papers into his portmanteau, with the address of his publisher attached, and took his way northward.

He had been absent from London for two years—two years which were a long period and had made such a difference in his own life (through the production of a novel far stronger, he believed, than *Ginistrella*) that he turned out into Piccadilly, the morning after his arrival, with an indefinite expectation of changes, of finding that things had happened. But there were few transformations in Piccadilly (only three or four big red houses where there had been low black ones),

and the brightness of the end of Jun peeped through the rusty railings the Green Park and glittered in th varnish of the rolling carriages as h had seen it in other, more curso Junes. It was a greeting that he a preciated; it seemed friendly an pointed, added to the exhilaration his finished book, of his having h own country and the huge, oppressiv amusing city that suggested ever thing, that contained everything, u der his hand again. "Stay at hom and do things here—do subjects can measure," St. George had sai and now it appeared to him that should ask nothing better than to sta at home for ever. Late in the afte noon he took his way to Manchest Square, looking out for a number had not forgotten. Miss Fancou however, was not within, so that turned, rather dejectedly, from t door. This movement brought h face to face with a gentleman who w approaching it and whom he prompt perceived to be Miss Fancourt's fath Paul saluted this personage, and t General returned his greeting with customary good manner—a manner good, however, that you could nev tell whether it meant that he plac you. Paul Overt felt the impulse speak to him; then, hesitating, becar conscious both that he had noth particular to say and that though t old soldier remembered him he reme bered him wrong. He therefo passed on, without calculating on t irresistible effect that his own evide recognition would have upon the Ge eral, who never neglected a cha to gossip. Our young man's face w expressive, and observation seldom it pass. He had not taken ten ste before he heard himself called after with a friendly, semi-articulate "A—I beg your pardon!" He turned round and the General, smiling at him from the steps, said: "Won't you come in? I won't leave you the advantage of me!" Paul declined to come in, and then was sorry he had done so, for Miss Fancourt, so late in the afternoon, might return at any moment. But her father gave him no second chance; he appeared mainly to wish not to have struck him as inhospitable. A further look at the visitor told him more about him, enough at least to enable him to say—"You've come back, you've come back?" Paul was on the point of replying that he had come back the night before, but he bethought himself to suppress this strong light on the immediacy of his visit, and, giving merely a general assent, remarked that he was extremely sorry not to have found Miss Fancourt. He had come late, in the hope that she would be in. "I'll tell her—I'll tell her," said the old man; and then he added quickly, gallantly, "You'll be giving us something new? It's a long time, isn't it?" Now he remembered him right.

"Rather long. I'm very slow," said Paul. "I met you at Summersoft a long time ago."

"Oh, yes, with Henry St. George. I remember very well. Before his poor wife—" General Fancourt paused a moment, smiling a little less. "I daresay you know."

"About Mrs. St. George's death? Oh, yes, I heard at the time."

"Oh, no; I mean—I mean he's to be married."

"Ah! I've not heard that." Just as Paul was about to add, "To

whom?" the General crossed his intention with a question.

"When did you come back? I know you've been away—from my daughter. She was very sorry. You ought to give her something new."

"I came back last night," said our young man, to whom something had occurred which made his speech, for the moment, a little thick.

"Ah, most kind of you to come so soon. Couldn't you turn up at dinner?"

"At dinner?" Paul Overt repeated, not liking to ask whom St. George was going to marry, but thinking only of that.

"There are several people, I believe. Certainly St. George. Or afterwards, if you like better. I believe my daughter expects—" He appeared to notice something in Overt's upward face (on his steps he stood higher) which led him to interrupt himself, and the interruption gave him a momentary sense of awkwardness, from which he sought a quick issue. "Perhaps then you haven't heard she's to be married."

"To be married?" Paul stared.

"To Mr. St. George—it has just been settled. Odd marriage, isn't it?" Paul uttered no opinion on this point: he only continued to stare. "But I daresay it will do—she's so awfully literary!" said the General.

Paul had turned very red. "Oh, it's a surprise—very interesting, very charming! I'm afraid I can't dine—so many thanks!"

"Well, you must come to the wedding!" cried the General. "Oh, I remember that day at Summersoft. He's a very good fellow."

"Charming—charming!" Paul stammered, retreating. He shook hands with the General and got off. His face was red and he had the sense of its growing more and more crimson. All the evening at home—he went straight to his rooms and remained there dinnerless—his cheek burned at intervals as if it had been smitten. He didn't understand what had happened to him, what trick had been played him, what treachery practised. "None, none," he said to himself. "I've nothing to do with it. I'm out of it—it's none of my business." But that bewildered murmur was followed again and again by the incongruous ejaculation—"Was it a plan—was it a plan?" Sometimes he cried to himself, breathless, "Am I a dupe—am I a dupe?" If he was, he was an absurd, and abject one. It seemed to him he had never lost her till now. He had renounced her, yes; but that was another affair—that was a closed but not a locked door. Now he felt as if the door had been slammed in his face. Did he expect her to wait—was she to give him his time like that: two years at a stretch? He didn't know what he had expected—he only knew what he hadn't. It wasn't this—it wasn't this. Mystification, bitterness and wrath rose and boiled in him when he thought of the deference, the devotion, the credulity with which he had listened to St. George. The evening wore on and the light was long; but even when it had darkened he remained without a lamp. He had flung himself on the sofa, and he lay there through the hours with his eyes either closed or gazing into the gloom, in the attitude of a man teaching himself to bear something, to bear having been made a fool of. He had

made it too easy—that idea passed over him like a hot wave. Suddenly, as he heard eleven o'clock strike, he jumped up, remembering what General Fancourt had said about his coming after dinner. He would go—he would see her at least; perhaps he should see what it meant. He felt as if some of the elements of a hard sum had been given him and the others were wanting: he couldn't do his sum till he was in possession of them all.

He dressed quickly, so that by half-past eleven he was at Manchester Square. There were a good many carriages at the door—a party was going on; a circumstance which at the last gave him a slight relief, for now he would rather see her in a crowd People passed him on the staircase; they were going away, going "on," with the hunted, herdlike movement of London society at night. But sundry groups remained in the drawing-room, and it was some minutes, as she didn't hear him announced, before he discovered her and spoke to her In this short interval he had perceived that St. George was there, talking to a lady before the fireplace; but he looked away from him, for the moment, and therefore failed to see whether the author of *Shadowmere* noticed him. At all events he didn't come to him. Miss Fancourt did, as soon as she saw him; she almost rushed at him, smiling, rustling, radiant, beautiful. He had forgotten what her head, what her face offered to the sight; she was in white, there were gold figures on her dress, and her hair was like a casque of gold In a single moment he saw she was happy, happy with a kind of ag gressiveness of splendour. But she would not speak to him of that, she would speak only of himself.

"I'm so delighted; my father told me. How kind of you to come!" She struck him as so fresh and brave, while his eyes moved over her, that he said to himself, irresistibly: "Why to *him*, why not to youth, to strength, to ambition, to a future? Why, in her rich young capacity, to failure, to abdication, to superannuation?" In his thought, at that sharp moment, he blasphemed even against all that had been left of his faith in the peccable master. "I'm so sorry I missed you," she went on. "My father told me. How charming of you to have come so soon!"

"Does that surprise you?" Paul Overt asked.

"The first day? No, from you—nothing that's nice." She was interrupted by a lady who bade her good-night, and he seemed to read that it cost her nothing to speak to one in that tone; it was her old bounteous, demonstrative way, with a certain added amplitude that time had brought; and if it began to operate on the spot, at such a juncture in her history, perhaps in the other days too it had meant just as little or as much—a sort of mechanical charity, with the difference now that she was satisfied, ready to give but asking nothing. Oh, she was satisfied—and why shouldn't she be? Why shouldn't she have been surprised at his coming the first day —for all the good she had ever got from him? As the lady continued to hold her attention Paul Overt turned from her with a strange irritation in his complicated artistic soul and a kind of disinterested disappointment. She was so happy that it was almost stupid—it seemed to deny the extraordinary intelligence he had formerly found in her. Didn't she know how bad St. George could be, hadn't she perceived the deplorable thinness—? If she didn't she was nothing, and if she did why such an insolence of serenity? This question expired as our young man's eyes settled at last upon the genius who had advised him in a great crisis. St. George was still before the chimney-piece, but now he was alone (fixed, waiting, as if he meant to remain after every one), and he met the clouded gaze of the young friend who was tormented with uncertainty as to whether he had the right (which his resentment would have enjoyed,) to regard himself as his victim. Somehow, the fantastic inquiry I have just noted was answered by St. George's aspect. It was as fine in its way as Marian Fancourt's—it denoted the happy human being; but somehow it represented to Paul Overt that the author of *Shadowmere* had now definitely ceased to count—ceased to count as a writer. As he smiled a welcome across the room he was almost *banal*, he was almost smug. Paul had the impression that for a moment he hesitated to make a movement forward, as if he had a bad conscience; but the next they had met in the middle of the room and had shaken hands, expressively, cordially on St. George's part. Then they had passed together to where the elder man had been standing, while St. George said: "I hope you are never going away again. I have been dining here; the General told me." He was handsome, he was young, he looked as if he had still a great fund of life. He bent the friendliest, most unconfessing eyes upon Paul Overt; asked him about everything, his health, his plans, his late occupations, the new book. "When will it be out—soon, soon, I hope? Splendid, eh? That's right; you're a comfort! I've read you all over again, the last six months." Paul waited to see if he would tell him what the General had told him in the afternoon, and what Miss Fancourt, verbally at least, of course had not. But as it didn't come out he asked at last: "Is it true, the great news I hear, that you're to be married?"

"Ah, you *have* heard it then?"

"Didn't the General tell you?" Paul Overt went on.

"Tell me what?"

"That he mentioned it to me this afternoon?"

"My dear fellow, I don't remember. We've been in the midst of people. I'm sorry, in that case, that I lose the pleasure, myself, of announcing to you a fact that touches me so nearly. It *is* a fact, strange as it may appear. It has only just become one. Isn't it ridiculous?" St. George made this speech without confusion, but on the other hand, so far as Paul could see, without latent impudence. It appeared to his interlocutor that, to talk so comfortably and coolly, he must simply have forgotten what had passed between them. His next words, however, showed that he had not, and they had, as an appeal to Paul's own memory, an effect which would have been ludicrous if it had not been cruel. "Do you recollect the talk we had at my house that night, into which Miss Fancourt's name entered? I've often thought of it since."

"Yes—no wonder you said what you did," said Paul, looking at him

"In the light of the present occasion? Ah! but there was no light then. How could I have foreseen this hour?"

"Didn't you think it probable?"

"Upon my honour, no," said Henry St. George. "Certainly, I owe you that assurance. Think how my situation has changed."

"I see—I see," Paul murmured.

His companion went on, as if, now that the subject had been broached, he was, as a man of imagination and tact, perfectly ready to give every satisfaction—being able to enter fully into everything another might feel. "But it's not only that—for honestly at my age, I never dreamed—a widower, with big boys and with so little else! It has turned out differently from any possible calculation and I am fortunate beyond all measure. She has been so free, and yet she consents. Better than any one else perhaps—for I remember how you liked her, before you went away, and how she liked you—you can intelligently congratulate me."

"She has been so free!" Those words made a great impression on Paul Overt, and he almost writhed under that irony in them as to which it little mattered whether it was intentional or casual. Of course she had been free and, appreciably perhaps by his own act; for was not St. George's allusion to her having liked him a part of the irony too? "I thought that by your theory you disapproved of a writer's marrying."

"Surely—surely. But you don't call me a writer?"

"You ought to be ashamed," said Paul

"Ashamed of marrying again?"

"I won't say that—but ashamed of our reasons."

"You must let me judge of them, my friend."

"Yes; why not? For you judged wonderfully of mine."

The tone of these words appeared suddenly, for Henry St. George, to suggest the unsuspected. He stared as if he read a bitterness in them. Don't you think I have acted fair?"

"You might have told me at the time, perhaps."

"My dear fellow, when I say I couldn't pierce futurity!"

"I mean afterwards."

St. George hesitated. "After my wife's death?"

"When this idea came to you."

"Ah, never, never! I wanted to save you, rare and precious as you are."

"Are you marrying Miss Fancourt to save me?"

"Not absolutely, but it adds to the pleasure. I shall be the making of you," said St. George, smiling. "I was greatly struck, after our talk, with the resolute way you quitted the country and still more, perhaps, with your force of character in remaining abroad. You're very strong—you're wonderfully strong."

Paul Overt tried to sound his pleasant eyes; the strange thing was that he appeared sincere—not a mocking fiend. He turned away, and as he did he heard St. George say something about his giving them the proof, being the joy of his old age. He faced him again, taking another look. "Do you mean to say you've stopped writing?"

"My dear fellow, of course I have. It's too late. Didn't I tell you?"

"I can't believe it!"

"Of course you can't—with your own talent! No, no; for the rest of my life I shall only read you."

"Does she know that—Miss Fancourt?"

"She will—she will." Our young man wondered whether St. George meant this as a covert intimation that the assistance he should derive from that young lady's fortune, moderate as it was, would make the difference of putting it in his power to cease to work, ungratefully, an exhausted vein. Somehow, standing there in the ripeness of his successful manhood, he did not suggest that any of his veins were exhausted. "Don't you remember the moral I offered myself to you—that night—as pointing?" St. George continued. "Consider, at any rate, the warning I am at present."

This was too much—he *was* the mocking fiend. Paul separated from him with a mere nod for good-night; the sense that he might come back to him some time in the far future but could not fraternise with him now. It was necessary to his sore spirit to believe for the hour that he had a grievance—all the more cruel for not being a legal one. It was doubtless in the attitude of hugging this wrong that he descended the stairs without taking leave of Miss Fancourt, who had not been in view at the moment he quitted the room. He was glad to get out into the honest, dusky, unsophisticating night, to move fast, to take his way home on foot. He walked a long time, missing his way, not thinking of it. He was thinking of too many other things. His steps recovered their direction, however, and at the end of an hour he found himself before his door, in the small, inexpensive, empty street. He lingered, questioning himself still, before going in, with nothing around and above him but moonless blackness, a bad lamp or two and a few far-away dim stars. To these last faint features he raised his eyes; he had been saying to himself that there would have been mockery indeed if now, on his new foundation, at the end of a year, St. George should put forth something with his early quality—something of the type of *Shadowmere* and finer than his finest. Greatly as he admired his talent Paul literally hoped such an incident would not occur; it seemed to him just then that he scarcely should be able to endure it. St. George's words were still in his ears, "You're very strong—wonderfully strong." Was he really? Certainly, he would have to be; and it would be a sort of revenge. *Is* he? the reader may ask in turn, if his interest has followed the perplexed young man so far. The best answer to that perhaps is that he is doing his best but that it is too soon to say. When the new book came out in the autumn Mr. and Mrs. St. George found it really magnificent. The former still has published nothing, but Paul Overt does not even yet feel safe. I may say for him, however, that if this event were to befall he would really be the very first to appreciate it: which is perhaps a proof that St. George was essentially right and that Nature dedicated him to intellectual, not to personal passion.

1888

From *PARTIAL PORTRAITS**

THE ART OF FICTION

I should not have affixed so comprehensive a title to these few remarks, necessarily wanting in any completeness upon a subject the full consideration of which would carry us far, did I not seem to discover a pretext for my temerity in the interesting pamphlet lately published under his name by Mr. Walter Besant. Mr. Besant's lecture at the Royal Institution—the original form of his pamphlet—appears to indicate that many persons are interested in the art of fiction, and are not indifferent to such remarks, as those who practise it may attempt to make about it. I am therefore anxious not to lose the benefit of this favourable association, and to edge in a few words under cover of the attention which Mr. Besant is sure to have excited. There is something very encouraging in his having put into form certain of his ideas on the mystery of story telling.

It is a proof of life and curiosity—curiosity on the part of the brotherhood of novelists as well as on the part of their readers. Only a short time ago it might have been supposed that the English novel was not what the French call *discutable*. It had no air of having a theory, a conviction, a consciousness of itself behind it—of being the expression of an artistic faith, the result of choice and comparison. I do not say it was necessarily the worse for that: it would

* Reprinted from *Partial Portraits* (1888 by permission of the Macmillan Company.

take much more courage than I possess to intimate that the form of the novel as Dickens and Thackeray (for instance) saw it had any taint of incompleteness. It was, however, *naïf* (if I may help myself out with another French word); and evidently if it be destined to suffer in any way for having lost its *naïveté* it has now an idea of making sure of the corresponding advantages. During the period I have alluded to there was a comfortable, good-humoured feeling abroad that a novel is a novel, as a pudding is a pudding, and that our only business with it could be to swallow it. But within a year or two, for some reason or other, there have been signs of returning animation—the era of discussion would appear to have been to a certain extent opened. Art lives upon discussion, upon experiment, upon curiosity, upon variety of attempt, upon the exchange of views and the comparison of standpoints; and there is a presumption that those times when no one has anything particular to say about it, and has no reason to give for practice or preference, though they may be times of honour, are not times of development—are times, possibly even, a little of dulness. The successful application of any art is a delightful spectacle, but the theory too is interesting; and though there is a great deal of the latter without the former I suspect there has never been a genuine success that has not had a latent core of conviction. Discussion, suggestion, formulation, these things are fertilising when they are frank and sincere. Mr. Besant has set an excellent example in saying what he thinks, for his part, about the way in which fiction should

be written, as well as about the way in which it should be published; for his view of the "art," carried on into an appendix, covers that too. Other labourers in the same field will doubtless take up the argument, they will give it the light of their experience, and the effect will surely be to make our interest in the novel a little more what it had for some time threatened to fail to be—a serious, active, inquiring interest, under protection of which this delightful study may, in moments of confidence, venture to say a little more what it thinks of itself.

It must take itself seriously for the public to take it so. The old superstition about fiction being "wicked" has doubtless died out in England; but the spirit of it lingers in a certain oblique regard directed toward any story which does not more or less admit that it is only a joke. Even the most jocular novel feels in some degree the weight of the proscription that was formerly directed against literary levity: the jocularity does not always succeed in passing for orthodoxy. It is still expected, though perhaps people are ashamed to say it, that a production which is after all only a "make-believe" (for what else is a "story"?) shall be in some degree apologetic—shall renounce the pretension of attempting really to represent life. This, of course, any sensible, wide-awake story declines to do, for it quickly perceives that the tolerance granted to it on such a condition is only an attempt to stifle it disguised in the form of generosity. The old evangelical hostility to the novel, which was as explicit as it was narrow, and which regarded it as little less favourable to our immortal part than a stage-play, was in reality far less insulting. The only reason for the existence of a novel is that it does attempt to represent life. When it relinquishes this attempt, the same attempt that we see on the canvas of the painter, it will have arrived at a very strange pass. It is not expected of the picture that it will make itself humble in order to be forgiven; and the analogy between the art of the painter and the art of the novelist is, so far as I am able to see, complete. Their inspiration is the same, their process (allowing for the different quality of the vehicle) is the same, their success is the same. They may learn from each other, they may explain and sustain each other. Their cause is the same, and the honour of one is the honour of another. The Mahometans think a picture an unholy thing, but it is a long time since any Christian did, and it is therefore the more odd that in the Christian mind the traces (dissimulated though they may be) of a suspicion of the sister art should linger to this day. The only effectual way to lay it to rest is to emphasise the analogy to which I just alluded— to insist on the fact that as the picture is reality, so the novel is history. That is the only general description (which does it justice) that we may give of the novel. But history also is allowed to represent life; it is not, any more than painting, expected to apologise. The subject-matter of fiction is stored up likewise in documents and records, and if it will not give itself away, as they say in California, it must speak with assurance, with the tone of the historian. Certain accomplished novelists have a habit of giving themselves away which must often bring tears to the eyes of people who take their fiction seriously. I was lately struck, in reading over many pages of Anthony Trollope, with his want of discretion in this particular. In a digression, a parenthesis or an aside, he concede to the reader that he and this trusting friend are only "making believe." He admits that the events he narrate have not really happened, and that he can give his narrative any turn the reader may like best. Such a betrayal of a sacred office seems to me, I confess, a terrible crime; it is what mean by the attitude of apology, and it shocks me every whit as much in Trollope as it would have shocked me in Gibbon or Macaulay. It implie that the novelist is less occupied in looking for the truth (the truth, of course I mean, that he assumes, the premises that we must grant him whatever they may be), than the historian, and in doing so it deprives him at a stroke of all his standing-room. To represent and illustrate the past the actions of men, is the task of either writer, and the only difference that I can see is, in proportion as he succeeds, to the honour of the novelist, consisting as it does in his having more difficulty in collecting his evidence, which is so far from being purely literary. It seems to me to give him a great character, the fact that he has at once so much in common with the philosopher and the painter; this double analogy is a magnificent heritage.

It is of all this evidently that M. Besant is full when he insists upon the fact that fiction is one of th ne arts, deserving in its turn of all the honours and emoluments that have hitherto been reserved for the successful profession of music, poetry, painting, architecture. It is impossible to insist too much on so important a truth, and the place that Mr. Besant demands for the work of the novelist may be represented, a trifle less abstractly, by saying that he demands not only that it shall be reputed artistic, but that it shall be reputed very artistic indeed. It is excellent that he should have struck his note, for his doing so indicates that there was need of it, that his proposition may be to many people a novelty. One rubs one's eyes at the thought; but the rest of Mr. Besant's essay confirms the revelation. I suspect in truth that it would be possible to confirm it still further, and that he would not be far wrong in saying that in addition to the people to whom it has never occurred that a novel ought to be artistic, there are great many others who, if this principle were urged upon them, would be filled with an indefinable mistrust. They would find it difficult to explain their repugnance, but it would operate strongly to put them on their guard. "Art," in our Protestant communities, where so many things have got so strangely twisted about, is supposed in certain circles to have some vaguely injurious effect upon those who make it an important consideration, who let it weigh in the balance. It is assumed to be opposed in some mysterious manner to morality, to amusement, to instruction. When it is embodied in the work of the painter (the sculptor is another affair!) you know what it is: it stands there before you, in the honesty of pink and green and a gilt frame; you can see the worst of it at a glance, and you can be on your guard. But when it is introduced into literature it becomes more insidious—there is danger of its hurting you before you know it. Literature should be either instructive or amusing, and there is in many minds an impression that these artistic preoccupations, the search for form, contribute to neither end, interfere indeed with both. They are too frivolous to be edifying, and too serious to be diverting; and they are moreover priggish and paradoxical and superfluous. That, I think, represents the manner in which the latent thought of many people who read novels as an exercise in skipping would explain itself if it were to become articulate. They would argue, of course, that a novel ought to be "good," but they would interpret this term in a fashion of their own, which indeed would vary considerably from one critic to another. One would say that being good means representing virtuous and aspiring characters, placed in prominent positions; another would say that it depends on a "happy ending," on a distribution at the last of prizes, pensions, husbands, wives, babies, millions, appended paragraphs, and cheerful remarks. Another still would say that it means being full of incident and movement, so that we shall wish to jump ahead, to see who was the mysterious stranger, and if the stolen will was ever found, and shall not be distracted from this pleasure by any tiresome analysis or "description." But they would all agree that the "artistic" idea would spoil some of their fun.

One would hold it accountable for all
the description, another would see it
revealed in the absence of sympathy.
Its hostility to a happy ending would
be evident, and it might even in some
cases render any ending at all impossible. The "ending" of a novel is,
for many persons, like that of a good
dinner, a course of dessert and ices,
and the artist in fiction is regarded
as a sort of meddlesome doctor who
forbids agreeable aftertastes. It is
therefore true that this conception of
Mr. Besant's of the novel as a superior form encounters not only a
negative but a positive indifference.
It matters little that as a work of art
it should really be as little or as much
of its essence to supply happy end-
ings, sympathetic characters, and an
objective tone, as if it were a work
of mechanics: the association of
ideas, however incongruous, might
easily be too much for it if an eloquent voice were not sometimes
raised to call attention to the fact
that it is at once as free and as serious a branch of literature as any
other.

Certainly this might sometimes be
doubted in presence of the enormous
number of works of fiction that appeal to the credulity of our generation, for it might easily seem that
there could be no great character in
a commodity so quickly and easily
produced. It must be admitted that
good novels are much compromised
by bad ones, and that the field at
large suffers discredit from over-
crowding. I think, however, that this
injury is only superficial, and that the
superabundance of written fiction
proves nothing against the principle
itself. It has been vulgarised, like

all other kinds of literature, li[ke]
everything else to-day, and it h[as]
proved more than some kinds acce[s-]
sible to vulgarisation. But there [is]
as much difference as there ever w[as]
between a good novel and a bad on[e;]
the bad is swept with all the daub[ed]
canvases and spoiled marble in[to]
some unvisited limbo, or infinite ru[b-]
bish-yard beneath the back-windo[ws]
of the world, and the good subsis[ts]
and emits its light and stimulates o[ur]
desire for perfection. As I sha[ll]
take the liberty of making but [a]
single criticism of Mr. Besant, who[se]
tone is so full of the love of his ar[t]
I may as well have done with it [at]
once. He seems to me to mistake [in]
attempting to say so definitely befor[e-]
hand what sort of an affair the goo[d]
novel will be. To indicate the dan[ger]
ger of such an error as that has bee[n]
the purpose of these few pages; [to]
suggest that certain traditions on th[e]
subject, applied a priori, have a[l-]
ready had much to answer for, an[d]
that the good health of an art whic[h]
undertakes so immediately to repro[o-]
duce life must demand that it be pe[r-]
fectly free. It lives upon exercis[e]
and the very meaning of exercise [is]
freedom. The only obligation [to]
which in advance we may hold a nove[l]
without incurring the accusation [of]
being arbitrary, is that it be interes[t-]
ing. That general responsibility res[ts]
upon it, but it is the only one I ca[n]
think of. The ways in which it is [at]
liberty to accomplish this result ([of]
interesting us) strike me as innume[r-]
able, and such as can only suffer fro[m]
being marked out or fenced in b[y]
prescription. They are as various [as]
the temperament of man, and the[y]
are successful in proportion as the[y]

eveal a particular mind, different rom others. A novel is in its broadst definition a personal, a direct impression of life: that, to begin with, onstitutes its value, which is greater r less according to the intensity of he impression. But there will be no ntensity at all, and therefore no alue, unless there is freedom to feel nd say. The tracing of a line to be ollowed, of a tone to be taken, of a orm to be filled out, is a limitation f that freedom and a suppression of he very thing that we are most urious about. The form, it seems to 1e, is to be appreciated after the fact: hen the author's choice has been nade, his standard has been indiated; then we can follow lines and lirections and compare tones and reemblances. Then in a word we can njoy one of the most charming of leasures, we can estimate quality, we an apply the test of execution. The xecution belongs to the author alone; t is what is most personal to him, nd we measure him by that. The dvantage, the luxury, as well as the orment and responsibility of the novlist, is that there is no limit to what 1e may attempt as an executant—no mit to his possible experiments, eforts, discoveries, successes. Here it s especially that he works, step by tep, like his brother of the brush, f whom we may always say that he 1as painted his picture in a manner 1est known to himself. His manner s his secret, not necessarily a jealous ne. He cannot disclose it as a genral thing if he would; he would be it a loss to teach it to others. I say his with a due recollection of having nsisted on the community of method f the artist who paints a picture and the artist who writes a novel. The painter *is* able to teach the rudiments of his practice, and it is possible, from the study of good work (granted the aptitude), both to learn how to paint and to learn how to write. Yet it remains true, without injury to the *rapprochement*, that the literary artist would be obliged to say to his pupil much more than the other, "Ah, well, you must do it as you can!" It is a question of degree, a matter of delicacy. If there are exact sciences, there are also exact arts, and the grammar of painting is so much more definite that it makes the difference.

I ought to add, however, that if Mr. Besant says at the beginning of his essay that the "laws of fiction may be laid down and taught with as much precision and exactness as the laws of harmony, perspective, and proportion," he mitigates what might appear to be an extravagance by applying his remark to "general" laws, and by expressing most of these rules in a manner with which it would certainly be unaccommodating to disagree. That the novelist must write from his experience, that his "characters must be real and such as might be met with in actual life;" that "a young lady brought up in a quiet country village should avoid descriptions of garrison life," and "a writer whose friends and personal experiences belong to the lower middleclass should carefully avoid introducing his characters into society;" that one should enter one's notes in a common-place book; that one's figures should be clear in outline; that making them clear by some trick of speech or of carriage is a bad method, and "describing them at length" is a worse one; that English Fiction should have a "conscious moral purpose;" that "it is almost impossible to estimate too highly the value of careful workmanship—that is, of style;" that "the most important point of all is the story," that "the story is everything": these are principles with most of which it is surely impossible not to sympathise. That remark about the lower middle-class writer and his knowing his place is perhaps rather chilling; but for the rest I should find it difficult to dissent from any one of these recommendations. At the same time, I should find it difficult positively to assent to them, with the exception, perhaps, of the injunction as to entering one's notes in a common-place book. They scarcely seem to me to have the quality that Mr. Besant attributes to the rules of the novelist—the "precision and exactness" of "the laws of harmony, perspective, and proportion." They are suggestive, they are even inspiring, but they are not exact, though they are doubtless as much so as the case admits of: which is a proof of that liberty of interpretation for which I just contended. For the value of these different injunctions—so beautiful and so vague—is wholly in the meaning one attaches to them. The characters, the situation, which strike one as real will be those that touch and interest one most, but the measure of reality is very difficult to fix. The reality of Don Quixote or of Mr. Micawber is a very delicate shade; it is a reality so coloured by the author's vision that, vivid as it may be, one would hesitate to propose it as a model: one would expose one's self to some very embarrassing ques tions on the part of a pupil. It goe without saying that you will not writ a good novel unless you possess th sense of reality; but it will be dif ficult to give you a recipe for callin that sense into being. Humanity i immense, and reality has a myria forms; the most one can affirm i that some of the flowers of fictio have the odour of it, and others hav not; as for telling you in advanc how your nosegay should be com posed, that is another affair. It i equally excellent and inconclusive t say that one must write from experi ence; to our supposititious aspiran such a declaration might savour o mockery. What kind of experienc is intended, and where does it begi and end? Experience is never lim ited, and it is never complete; it i an immense sensibility, a kind o huge spiderweb of the finest silke threads suspended in the chamber o consciousness, and catching every air borne particle in its tissue. It is th very atmosphere of the mind; an when the mind is imaginative—much more when it happens to be that o a man of genius—it takes to itself the faintest hints of life, it converts the very pulses of the air into revelations The young lady living in a village has only to be a damsel upon whom nothing is lost to make it quite un fair (as it seems to me) to declare to her that she shall have nothing to say about the military. Greater miracles have been seen than that, imagination assisting, she should speak the truth about some of these gentlemen. I re member an English novelist, a woman of genius, telling me that she was much commended for the impression

he had managed to give in one of her
ales of the nature and way of life of
ne French Protestant youth. She had
een asked where she learned so much
bout this recondite being, she had
een congratulated on her peculiar op-
ortunities. These opportunities con-
isted in her having once, in Paris,
s she ascended a staircase, passed an
pen door where, in the household of
pasteur, some of the young Prot-
stants were seated at table round a
nished meal. The glimpse made a
icture; it lasted only a moment, but
hat moment was experience. She
ad got her direct personal impres-
on, and she turned out her type.
he knew what youth was, and what
rotestantism; she also had the ad-
antage of having seen what it was
> be French, so that she converted
nese ideas into a concrete image and
roduced a reality. Above all, how-
ver, she was blessed with the faculty
hich when you give it an inch takes
n ell, and which for the artist is a
nuch greater source of strength than
ny accident of residence or of place
n the social scale. The power to
uess the unseen from the seen,
> trace the implication of things, to
udge the whole piece by the pattern,
ne condition of feeling life in general
> completely that you are well on
our way to knowing any particular
orner of it—this cluster of gifts may
lmost be said to constitute experi-
nce, and they occur in country and
n town, and in the most differing
tages of education. If experience
onsists of impressions, it may be
aid that impressions *are* experience,
ist as (have we not seen it?) they
re the very air we breathe. There-
ore, if I should certainly say to a
novice, "Write from experience and
experience only," I should feel that
this was rather a tantalising moni-
tion if I were not careful immediately
to add, "Try to be one of the people
on whom nothing is lost!"

I am far from intending by this to
minimise the importance of exactness
—of truth of detail. One can speak
best from one's own taste, and I may
therefore venture to say that the air
of reality (solidity of specification)
seems to me to be the supreme virtue
of a novel—the merit on which all
its other merits (including that conscious moral purpose of which Mr.
Besant speaks) helplessly and submissively depend. If it be not there
they are all as nothing, and if these
be there, they owe their effect to the
success with which the author has
produced the illusion of life. The
cultivation of this success, the study
of this exquisite process, form, to my
taste, the beginning and the end of
the art of the novelist. They are his
inspiration, his despair, his reward,
his torment, his delight. It is here
in very truth that he competes with
life; it is here that he competes with
his brother the painter in *his* attempt
to render the look of things, the look
that conveys their meaning, to catch
the colour, the relief, the expression,
the surface, the substance of the
human spectacle. It is in regard to
this that Mr. Besant is well inspired
when he bids him take notes. He
cannot possibly take too many, he
cannot possibly take enough. All life
solicits him, and to "render" the simplest surface, to produce the most
momentary illusion, is a very complicated business. His case would be
easier and the rule would be more

exact, if Mr. Besant had been able to tell him what notes to take. But this, I fear, he can never learn in any manual; it is the business of his life. He has to take a great many in order to select a few, he has to work them up as he can, and even the guides and philosophers who might have most to say to him must leave him alone when it comes to the application of precepts, as we leave the painter in communion with his palette. That his characters "must be clear in outline," as Mr. Besant says—he feels that down to his boots; but how he shall make them so is a secret between his good angel and himself. It would be absurdly simple if he could be taught that a great deal of "description" would make them so, or that on the contrary the absence of description and the cultivation of dialogue, or the absence of dialogue and the multiplication of "incident," would rescue him from his difficulties. Nothing, for instance, is more possible than that he be of a turn of mind for which this odd, literal opposition of description and dialogue, incident and description, has little meaning and light. People often talk of these things as if they had a kind of internecine distinctness, instead of melting into each other at every breath, and being intimately associated parts of one general effort of expression. I cannot imagine composition existing in a series of blocks, nor conceive, in any novel worth discussing at all, of a passage of description that is not in its intention narrative, a passage of dialogue that is not in its intention descriptive, a touch of truth of any sort that does not partake of the nature of incident, or an incident that

derives its interest from any other source than the general and only source of the success of a work of art—that of being illustrative. novel is a living thing, all one and continuous, like any other organism and in proportion as it lives will be found, I think, that in each of the parts there is something of each of the other parts. The critic who over the close texture of a finished work shall pretend to trace a geography of items will mark some frontier as artificial, I fear, as any that have been known to history. There is a old-fashioned distinction between the novel of character and the novel of incident which must have cost many a smile to the intending fabulist who was keen about his work. It appears to me as little to the point as the equally celebrated distinction between the novel and the romance—to answer as little to any reality. There are bad novels and good novels, as there are bad pictures and good pictures; but that is the only distinction in which I see any meaning, and I can as little imagine speaking of novel of character as I can imagine speaking of a picture of character. When one says picture one says of character, when one says novel one says of incident, and the terms may be transposed at will. What is character but the determination of incident? What is incident but the illustration of character? What is either a picture or a novel that is not of character? What else do we seek in it and find in it? It is an incident for a woman to stand up with her hand resting on a table and look out at you in a certain way; or if it be not an incident I think it will be hard say what it is. At the same time is an expression of character. If you say you don't see it (character that—allons donc!), this is exactly that the artist who has reasons of his own for thinking he *does* see it undertakes to show you. When a young man makes up his mind that he has not faith enough after all to enter the church as he intended, that an incident, though you may not hurry to the end of the chapter to see whether perhaps he doesn't change once more. I do not say that these are extraordinary or startling incidents. I do not pretend to estimate the degree of interest proceeding from them, for this will depend upon the skill of the painter. It sounds almost puerile to say that some incidents are intrinsically much more important than others, and I need not take this precaution after having professed my sympathy for the major ones in remarking that the only classification of the novel that I can understand is into that which has life and that which has it not.

The novel and the romance, the novel of incident and that of character—these clumsy separations appear to me to have been made by critics and readers for their own convenience, and to help them out of some of their occasional queer predicaments, but to have little reality or interest for the producer, from whose point of view it is of course that we are attempting to consider the art of fiction. The case is the same with another shadowy category which Mr. Besant apparently is disposed to set up—that of the "modern English novel"; unless indeed it be that in this matter he has fallen into an accidental confusion of standpoints. It is not quite clear whether he intends the remarks in which he alludes to it to be didactic or historical. It is as difficult to suppose a person intending to write a modern English as to suppose him writing an ancient English novel: that is a label which begs the question. One writes the novel, one paints the picture, of one's language and of one's time, and calling it modern English will not, alas! make the difficult task any easier. No more, unfortunately, will calling this or that work of one's fellow-artist a romance—unless it be, of course, simply for the pleasantness of the thing, as for instance when Hawthorne gave this heading to his story of *Blithedale*. The French, who have brought the theory of fiction to remarkable completeness, have but one name for the novel, and have not attempted smaller things in it, that I can see, for that. I can think of no obligation to which the "romancer" would not be held equally with the novelist; the standard of execution is equally high for each. Of course it is of execution that we are talking —that being the only point of a novel that is open to contention. This is perhaps too often lost sight of, only to produce interminable confusions and cross-purposes. We must grant the artist his subject, his idea, his *donnée:* our criticism is applied only to what he makes of it. Naturally I do not mean that we are bound to like it or find it interesting: in case we do not our course is perfectly simple—to let it alone. We may believe that of a certain idea even the most sincere novelist can make nothing at all, and the event may perfectly justify our belief; but the failure will have been a failure to execute, and it is in the execution that the fatal weakness is recorded. If we pretend to respect the artist at all, we must allow him his freedom of choice, in the face, in particular cases, of innumerable presumptions that the choice will not fructify. Art derives a considerable part of its beneficial exercise from flying in the face of presumptions, and some of the most interesting experiments of which it is capable are hidden in the bosom of common things. Gustave Flaubert has written a story about the devotion of a servant-girl to a parrot, and the production, highly finished as it is, cannot on the whole be called a success. We are perfectly free to find it flat, but I think it might have been interesting; and I, for my part, am extremely glad he should have written it; it is a contribution to our knowledge of what can be done—or what cannot. Ivan Turgénieff has written a tale about a deaf and dumb serf and a lap-dog, and the thing is touching, loving, a little masterpiece. He struck the note of life where Gustave Flaubert missed it—he flew in the face of a presumption and achieved a victory.

Nothing, of course, will ever take the place of the good old fashion of "liking" a work of art or not liking it: the most improved criticism will not abolish that primitive, that ultimate test. I mention this to guard myself from the accusation of intimating that the idea, the subject, of a novel or a picture, does not matter. It matters, to my sense, in the highest degree, and if I might put up a prayer it would be that artists should select none but the richest. Some, as have already hastened to admit, a much more remunerative than other and it would be a world happily a ranged in which persons intending t treat them should be exempt fro confusions and mistakes. This fo tunate condition will arrive only, fear, on the same day that critics be come purged from error. Meanwhil I repeat, we do not judge the artis with fairness unless we say to hin "Oh, I grant you your starting-poin because if I did not I should seer to prescribe to you, and heaven fo bid I should take that responsibilit If I pretend to tell you what yo must not take, you will call upon m to tell you then what you must take in which case I shall be prettil caught. Moreover, it isn't till I hav accepted your data that I can begi to measure you. I have the stanc ard, the pitch; I have no right t tamper with your flute and then crit icise your music. Of course I ma not care for your idea at all; I ma think it silly, or stale, or unclean; i which case I wash my hands of yo al together. I may content mysel with believing that you will not hav succeeded in being interesting, but shall, of course, not attempt t demonstrate it, and you will be a indifferent to me as I am to you. needn't remind you that there ar all sorts of tastes: who can know i better? Some people, for excellen reasons, don't like to read about car penters; others, for reasons even bet ter, don't like to read about courte sans. Many object to Americans Others (I believe they are mainl editors and publishers) won't look a Italians. Some readers don't lik quiet subjects; others don't like bustling ones. Some enjoy a complete illusion, others the consciousness of large concessions. They choose their novels accordingly, and if they don't care about your idea they won't, *a fortiori*, care about your treatment."

So that it comes back very quickly, as I have said, to the liking: in spite of M. Zola, who reasons less powerfully than he represents, and who will not reconcile himself to this absoluteness of taste, thinking that there are certain things that people ought to like, and that they can be made to like. I am quite at a loss to imagine anything (at any rate in this matter of fiction) that people *ought* to like or dislike. Selection will be sure to take care of itself, for it has a constant motive behind it. That motive is simply experience. As people feel life, so they will feel the art that is most closely related to it. This closeness of relation is what we should never forget in talking of the effort of the novel. Many people speak of it as a factitious, artificial form, a product of ingenuity, the business of which is to alter and arrange the things that surround us, to translate them into conventional, traditional moulds. This, however, is a view of the matter which carries us but a very short way, condemns the art to an eternal repetition of a few familiar *clichés,* cuts short its development, and leads us straight up to a dead wall. Catching the very note and trick, the strange irregular rhythm of life, that is the attempt whose strenuous force keeps Fiction upon her feet. In proportion as in what she offers us we see life *without*

rearrangement do we feel that we are touching the truth; in proportion as we see it *with* rearrangement do we feel that we are being put off with a substitute, a compromise and convention. It is not uncommon to hear an extraordinary assurance of remark in regard to this matter of rearranging, which is often spoken of as if it were the last word of art. Mr. Besant seems to me in danger of falling into the great error with his rather unguarded talk about "selection." Art is essentially selection, but it is a selection whose main care is to be typical, to be inclusive. For many people art means rose-coloured window-panes, and selection means picking a bouquet for Mrs. Grundy. They will tell you glibly that artistic considerations have nothing to do with the disagreeable, with the ugly; they will rattle off shallow commonplaces about the province of art and the limits of art till you are moved to some wonder in return as to the province and the limits of ignorance. It appears to me that no one can ever have made a seriously artistic attempt without becoming conscious of an immense increase—a kind of revelation—of freedom. One perceives in that case—by the light of a heavenly ray—that the province of art is all life, all feeling, all observation, all vision. As Mr. Besant so justly intimates, it is all experience. That is a sufficient answer to those who maintain that it must not touch the sad things of life, who stick into its divine unconscious bosom little prohibitory inscriptions on the end of sticks, such as we see in public gardens—"It is forbidden to walk on the grass; it is forbidden to touch the flowers; it is not allowed to introduce dogs or to remain after dark; it is requested to keep to the right." The young aspirant in the line of fiction whom we continue to imagine will do nothing without taste, for in that case his freedom would be of little use to him; but the first advantage of his taste will be to reveal to him the absurdity of the little sticks and tickets. If he have taste, I must add, of course he will have ingenuity, and my disrespectful reference to that quality just now was not meant to imply that it is useless in fiction. But it is only a secondary aid; the first is a capacity for receiving straight impressions.

Mr. Besant has some remarks on the question of "the story" which I shall not attempt to criticise, though they seem to me to contain a singular ambiguity, because I do not think I understand them. I cannot see what is meant by talking as if there were a part of a novel which is the story and part of it which for mystical reasons is not—unless indeed the distinction be made in a sense in which it is difficult to suppose that any one should attempt to convey anything. "The story," if it represents anything, represents the subject, the idea, the *donnée* of the novel; and there is surely no "school" —Mr. Besant speaks of a school— which urges that a novel should be all treatment and no subject. There must assuredly be something to treat; every school is intimately conscious of that. This sense of the story being the idea, the starting-point, of the novel, is the only one that I see in which it can be spoken of as something different from its organic whole;

and since in proportion as the work is successful the idea permeates and penetrates it, informs and animates it, so that every word and every punctuation-point contribute directly to the expression, in that proportion do we lose our sense of the story being a blade which may be drawn more or less out of its sheath. The story and the novel, the idea and the form, are the needle and thread, and I never heard of a guild of tailors who recommended the use of the thread without the needle, or the needle without the thread. Mr. Besant is not the only critic who may be observed to have spoken as if there were certain things in life which constitute stories, and certain others which do not. I find the same odd implication in an entertaining article in the *Pall Mall Gazette*, devoted, as it happens, to Mr. Besant's lecture. "The story is the thing!" says this graceful writer, as if with a tone of opposition to some other idea. I should think it was, as every painter who, as the time for "sending in" his picture looms in the distance, finds himself still in quest of a subject—as every belated artist not fixed about his theme will heartily agree. There are some subjects which speak to us and others which do not, but he would be a clever man who should undertake to give a rule—an index expurgatorius— by which the story and the no-story should be known apart. It is impossible (to me at least) to imagine any such rule which shall not be altogether arbitrary. The writer in the *Pall Mall* opposes the delightful (as I suppose) novel of *Margot la Balafrée* to certain tales in which "Bostonian nymphs" appear to have "rejected English dukes for psychological reasons." I am not acquainted with the romance just designated, and can scarcely forgive the *Pall Mall* critic for not mentioning the name of the author, but the title appears to refer to a lady who may have received a scar in some heroic adventure. I am inconsolable at not being acquainted with this episode, but am utterly at a loss to see why it is a story when the rejection (or acceptance) of a duke is not, and why a reason, psychological or other, is not a subject when a cicatrix is. They are all particles of the multitudinous life with which the novel deals, and surely no dogma which pretends to make it lawful to touch the one and unlawful to touch the other will stand for a moment on its feet. It is the special picture that must stand or fall, according as it seem to possess truth or to lack it. Mr. Besant does not, to my sense, light up the subject by intimating that a story must, under penalty of not being a story, consist of "adventures." Why adventures more than of green spectacles? He mentions a category of impossible things, and among them he places "fiction without adventure." Why without adventure, more than without matrimony, or celibacy, or parturition, or cholera, or hydropathy, or Jansenism? This seems to me to bring the novel back to the hapless little *rôle* of being an artificial, ingenious thing—bring it down from its large, free character of an immense and exquisite correspondence with life. And what *is* adventure, when it comes to that, and by what sign is the listening pupil to recognise it? It is an adventure—an immense one

—for me to write this little article; and for a Bostonian nymph to reject an English duke is an adventure only less stirring, I should say, than for an English duke to be rejected by a Bostonian nymph. I see dramas within dramas in that, and innumerable points of view. A psychological reason is, to my imagination, an object adorably pictorial; to catch the tint of its complexion—I feel as if that idea might inspire one to Titianesque efforts. There are few things more exciting to me, in short, than a psychological reason, and yet, I protest, the novel seems to me the most magnificent form of art. I have just been reading, at the same time, the delightful story of *Treasure Island,* by Mr. Robert Louis Stevenson and, in a manner less consecutive, the last tale from M. Edmond de Goncourt, which is entitled *Chérie.* One of these works treats of murders, mysteries, islands of dreadful renown, hairbreadth escapes, miraculous coincidences and buried doubloons. The other treats of a little French girl who lived in a fine house in Paris, and died of wounded sensibility because no one would marry her. I call *Treasure Island* delightful, because it appears to me to have succeeded wonderfully in what it attempts; and I venture to bestow no epithet upon *Chérie,* which strikes me as having failed deplorably in what it attempts—that is in tracing the development of the moral consciousness of a child. But one of these productions strikes me as exactly as much of a novel as the other, and as having a "story" quite as much. The moral consciousness of a child is as much a part of life as the islands of the Spanish Main, and the one sort of geography seems to me to have those "surprises" of which Mr. Besant speaks quite as much as the other. For myself (since it comes back in the last resort, as I say, to the preference of the individual), the picture of the child's experience has the advantage that I can at successive steps (an immense luxury, near to the "sensual pleasure" of which Mr. Besant's critic in the *Pall Mall* speaks) say Yes or No, as it may be, to what the artist puts before me. I have been a child in fact, but I have been on a quest for a buried treasure only in supposition, and it is a simple accident that with M. de Goncourt I should have for the most part to say No. With George Eliot, when she painted that country with a far other intelligence, I always said Yes.

The most interesting part of Mr. Besant's lecture is unfortunately the briefest passage—his very cursory allusion to the "conscious moral purpose" of the novel. Here again it is not very clear whether he be recording a fact or laying down a principle; it is a great pity that in the latter case he should not have developed his idea. This branch of the subject is of immense importance, and Mr. Besant's few words point to considerations of the widest reach, not to be lightly disposed of. He will have treated the art of fiction but superficially who is not prepared to go every inch of the way that these considerations will carry him. It is for this reason that at the beginning of these remarks I was careful to notify the reader that my reflections on so large a theme have no pretension to be exhaustive. Like Mr. Besant, I

have left the question of the morality of the novel till the last, and at the last I find I have used up my space. It is a question surrounded with difficulties, as witness the very first that meets us, in the form of a definite question, on the threshold. Vagueness, in such a discussion, is fatal, and what is the meaning of your morality and your conscious moral purpose? Will you not define your terms and explain how (a novel being a picture) a picture can be either moral or immoral? You wish to paint a moral picture or carve a moral statue: will you not tell us how you would set about it? We are discussing the Art of Fiction; questions of art are questions (in the widest sense) of execution; questions of morality are quite another affair, and will you not let us see how it is that you find it so easy to mix them up? These things are so clear to Mr. Besant that he has deduced from them a law which he sees embodied in English Fiction, and which is "a truly admirable thing and a great cause for congratulation." It is a great cause for congratulation indeed when such thorny problems become as smooth as silk. I may add that in so far as Mr. Besant perceives that in point of fact English Fiction has addressed itself preponderantly to these delicate questions he will appear to many people to have made a vain discovery. They will have been positively struck, on the contrary, with the moral timidity of the usual English novelist; with his (or with her) aversion to face the difficulties with which on every side the treatment of reality bristles. He is apt to be extremely shy (whereas the picture that Mr.

Besant draws is a picture of boldness), and the sign of his work, for the most part, is a cautious silence on certain subjects. In the English novel (by which of course I mean the American as well), more than in any other, there is a traditional difference between that which people know and that which they agree to admit that they know, that which they see and that which they speak of, that which they feel to be a part of life and that which they allow to enter into literature. There is the great difference, in short, between what they talk of in conversation and what they talk of in print. The essence of moral energy is to survey the whole field, and I should directly reverse Mr. Besant's remark and say not that the English novel has a purpose, but that it has a diffidence. To what degree a purpose in a work of art is a source of corruption I shall not attempt to inquire; the one that seems to me least dangerous is the purpose of making a perfect work. As for our novel, I may say lastly on this score that as we find it in England to-day it strikes me as addressed in a large degree to "young people," and that this in itself constitutes a presumption that it will be rather shy. There are certain things which it is generally agreed not to discuss, not èven to mention, before young people. That is very well, but the absence of discussion is not a symptom of the moral passion. The purpose of the English novel—"a truly admirable thing, and a great cause for congratulation"—strikes me therefore as rather negative.

There is one point at which the moral sense and the artistic sense lie very near together; that is in the light of the very obvious truth that the deepest quality of a work of art will always be the quality of the mind of the producer. In proportion as that intelligence is fine will the novel, the picture, the statue partake of the substance of beauty and truth. To be constituted of such elements is, to my vision, to have purpose enough. No good novel will ever proceed from a superficial mind; that seems to me an axiom which, for the artist in fiction, will cover all needful moral ground: if the youthful aspirant take it to heart it will illuminate for him many of the mysteries of "purpose." There are many other useful things that might be said to him, but I have come to the end of my article, and can only touch them as I pass. The critic in the *Pall Mall Gazette,* whom I have already quoted, draws attention to the danger, in speaking of the art of fiction, of generalising. The danger that he has in mind is rather, I imagine, that of particularising, for there are some comprehensive remarks which, in addition to those embodied in Mr. Besant's suggestive lecture, might without fear of misleading him be addressed to the ingenuous student. I should remind him first of the magnificence of the form that is open to him, which offers to sight so few restrictions and such innumerable opportunities. The other arts, in comparison, appear confined and hampered; the various conditions under which they are exercised are so rigid and definite. But the only condition that I can think of attaching to the composition of the novel is, as I have already said, that it be sincere. This freedom is a splendid privilege, and the first lesson of the young novelist is to learn to be worthy of it. "Enjoy it as it deserves," I should say to him; "take possession of it, explore it to its utmost extent, publish it, rejoice in it. All life belongs to you, and do not listen either to those who would shut you up into corners of it and tell you that it is only here and there that art inhabits, or to those who would persuade you that this heavenly messenger wings her way outside of life altogether, breathing a superfine air, and turning away her head from the truth of things. There is no impression of life, no manner of seeing it and feeling it, to which the plan of the novelist may not offer a place; you have only to remember that talents so dissimilar as those of Alexandre Dumas and Jane Austen, Charles Dickens and Gustave Flaubert, have worked in this field with equal glory. Do not think too much about optimism and pessimism; try and catch the colour of life itself. In France to-day we see a prodigious effort (that of Émile Zola, to whose solid and serious work no explorer of the capacity of the novel can allude without respect), we see an extraordinary effort, vitiated by a spirit of pessimism on a narrow basis. M. Zola is magnificent, but he strikes an English reader as ignorant; he has an air of working in the dark; if he had as much light as energy, his results would be of the highest value. As for the aberrations of a shallow optimism, the ground (of English fiction especially) is strewn with their brittle particles as with broken glass. If you must indulge in conclusions, let them have the taste of a wide knowledge. Remember that your first duty is to be as complete as possible—to make as perfect a work. Be generous and delicate and pursue the prize."

1884

I. JOHN LOTHROP MOTLEY
(1814–1877)

From *THE HISTORY OF THE UNITED NETHERLANDS*

[THE SPANISH ARMADA]

* * * On the 22nd of July (N.S.) the Armada set sail. Six days later, the Spaniards took soundings, thirty leagues from the Scilly Islands, and on Friday, the 29th of July, off the Lizard, they had the first glimpse of the land of promise presented them by Sixtus V, of which they had at last come to take possession.

On the same day and night the blaze and smoke of ten thousand beacon-fires from the Land's End to Margate, and from the Isle of Wight to Cumberland, gave warning to every Englishman that the enemy was at last upon them. Almost at that very instant intelligence had been brought from the court to the Lord-Admiral at Plymouth, that the Armada, dispersed and shattered by the gales of June, was not likely to make its appearance that year; and orders had consequently been given to disarm the four largest ships, and send them into dock. Even Walsingham, as already stated, had participated in this strange delusion.

Before Howard had time to act upon this ill-timed suggestion—even had he been disposed to do so—he received authentic intelligence that the great fleet was off the Lizard. Neither he nor Francis Drake were the men to lose time in such an emergency, and before that Friday night was spent, sixty of the best English ships had been warped out of Plymouth harbor.

On Saturday, 30th July, the wind was very light at southwest, with a mist and drizzling rain, but by three in the afternoon the two fleets could descry and count each other through the haze.

By nine o'clock, 31st July, about two miles from Looe, on the Cornish coast, the fleets had their first meeting. There were 136 sail of the Spaniards, of which ninety were large ships, and sixty-seven of the English. It was a solemn moment. The long-expected Armada presented a pompous, almost a theatrical appearance. The ships seemed arranged for a pageant, in honor of a victory already won. Disposed in form of a crescent, the horns of which were seven miles asunder, those gilded, towered, floating castles, with their gaudy standards and their martial music, moved slowly along the channel, with an air of indolent pomp. Their captain-general, the golden Duke, stood in his private shot-proof fortress, on the deck of his great galleon the *Saint Martin,* surrounded by generals of infantry, and colonels of cavalry, who knew as little as he did himself of naval matters. The English vessels, on the other hand—with a few exceptions, light, swift, and easily handled—could sail round and round those unwieldy galleons, hulks, and galleys rowed by fettered slave-gangs. The superior seamanship of free Englishmen, commanded by such experienced captains as Drake, Frobisher, and Hawkins—from infancy at home on blue water—was manifest in the very first encounter. They obtained the weather-gage at once, and cannonaded the enemy at intervals with considerable effect, easily escaping at will out of range of the sluggish Armada, which was incapable of bearing sail in pursuit, although provided with an armament which could sink all its enemies at close quarters. "We had some small fight with them that Sunday afternoon," said Hawkins. . . .

By five o'clock on Tuesday morning, 2nd of August, the Armada lay between Portland Bill and St. Albans' Head, when the wind shifted to the north-east, and gave the Spaniards the weather-gage. The English did their best to get to windward, but the Duke, standing close into the land with the whole Armada, maintained his advantage. The English then went about, making a tack seaward, and were soon afterwards assaulted by the Spaniards. A long and spirited action ensued. Howard in his little *Ark-Royal*—"the odd ship of the world for all conditions"—was engaged at different times with Bertendona, of the Italian squadron, with Alonzo de Leyva in the *Ratta,* and with other large vessels. He was hard pressed for a time, but was gallantly supported by the *Nonpareil,* Captain Tanner; and after a long and confused combat, in which the *St. Mark,* the *St. Luke,* the *St. Mat-*

thew, the *St. Philip,* the *St. John,* the *St. James,* the *St. John Baptist,* the *St. Martin,* and many other great galleons, with saintly and apostolic names, fought pell-mell with the *Lion,* the *Bear,* the *Bull,* the *Tiger,* the *Dreadnought,* the *Revenge,* the *Victory,* the *Triumph,* and other of the more profanely-baptized English ships, the Spaniards were again baffled in all their attempts to close with, and to board, their ever-attacking, ever-flying adversaries. The cannonading was incessant. "We had a sharp and long fight," said Hawkins. Boat-loads of men and munitions were perpetually arriving to the English, and many high-born volunteers—like Cumberland, Oxford, Northumberland, Raleigh, Brooke, Dudley, Willoughby, Noel, William Hatton, Thomas Cecil, and others—could no longer restrain their impatience, as the roar of battle sounded along the coasts of Dorset, but flocked merrily on board the ships of Drake, Hawkins, Howard, and Frobisher, or came in small vessels which they had chartered for themselves, in order to have their share in the delights of the long-expected struggle. . . .

All night the Spaniards, holding their course toward Calais, after the long but indecisive conflict had terminated, were closely pursued by their wary antagonists. On Wednesday, 3rd of August, there was some slight cannonading, with but slender results; and on Thursday, the 4th, both fleets were off Dunnose, on the Isle of Wight. The great hulk *Santana* and a galleon of Portugal having been somewhat damaged the previous day, were lagging behind the rest of the Armada, and were vigorously atcked by the *Triumph* and a few her vessels. Don Antonio de eyva, with some of the galeasses ld large galleons, came to the res- ie, and Frobisher, although in much eril, maintained an unequal conflict, ithin close range, with great spirit. Seeing his danger, the Lord Ad- iral in the *Ark-Royal,* accompanied ʸ the *Golden Lion,* the *White Bear,* e *Elizabeth,* the *Victory,* and the *eicester,* bore boldly down into the ery midst of the Spanish fleet, and id himself within three or four hun- ed yards of Medina's flag-ship, the *t. Martin,* while his comrades were equally close quarters with Vice- dmiral Recalde and the galleons of quendo, Mexia, and Almanza. It is the hottest conflict which had yet ken place. Here at last was thor- igh English work. The two great ets, which were there to subjugate d to defend the realm of Elizabeth, ere nearly yard-arm and yard-arm gether—all England on the lee. roadside after broadside of great ins, volley after volley of arque- isry from maintop and rigging, were irmly exchanged, and much damage is inflicted on the Spaniards, whose gantic ships were so easy a mark aim at, while from their turreted ights they themselves fired for the ost part harmlessly over the heads their adversaries. The leaders of e Armada, however, were encour- ʳed, for they expected at last to come even closer quarters, and there were me among the English who were ad enough to wish to board.

But so soon as Frobisher, who was e hero of the day, had extricated mself from his difficulty, the Lord- dmiral—having no intention of risk-

ing the existence of his fleet, and with it perhaps of the English crown, upon the hazard of a single battle, and hav- ing been himself somewhat damaged in the fight—gave the signal for re- treat, and caused the *Ark-Royal* to be towed out of action. Thus the Spaniards were frustrated of their hopes, and the English, having in- flicted much punishment at compara- tively small loss to themselves, again stood off to windward, and the Armada continued its indolent course along the cliffs of Freshwater and Blackgang.

On Friday, 5th August, the English, having received men and munitions from shore, pursued their antagonists at a moderate distance; and the Lord- Admiral, profiting by the pause—for it was almost a flat calm—sent for Martin Frobisher, John Hawkins, Roger Townsend, Lord Thomas Howard, son of the Duke of Norfolk, and Lord Edmund Sheffield, and on the deck of the *Royal Ark* conferred the honor of knighthood on each for his gallantry in the action of the previous day. Medina Sidonia, on his part, was again despatching messenger after messenger to the Duke of Parma, asking for small shot, pilots, and forty fly-boats, with which to pursue the teasing English clippers. The Catholic Armada, he said, being so large and heavy, was quite in the power of its adversaries, who could assault, re- treat, fight, or leave off fighting, while he had nothing for it but to proceed, as expeditiously as might be, to his rendezvous in Calais roads.

And in Calais roads the great fleet —sailing slowly all next day in com- pany with the English, without a shot being fired on either side—at last

dropped anchor on Saturday afternoon, August 6th.

Here then the Invincible Armada
had arrived at its appointed resting-
place. Here the great junction of
Medina Sidonia with the Duke of
Parma · was to be effected, and now
at last the curtain was to rise upon
the last act of the great drama so
slowly and elaborately prepared. . . . 10
Never, since England was England,
had such a sight been seen as now
revealed itself in those narrow straits
between Dover and Calais. Along
that long, low, sandy shore, and quite
within the range of the Calais fortifications, one hundred and thirty Spanish
ships—the greater number of them the
largest and most heavily armed in the
world—lay face to face, and scarcely 20
out of cannon-shot, with one hundred
and fifty English sloops and frigates,
the strongest and swiftest that the
island could furnish, and commanded
by men whose exploits had rung
through the world.

Farther along the coast, invisible,
but known to be performing a most
perilous and vital service, was a
squadron of Dutch vessels of all sizes, 30
lining both the inner and outer edges
of the sandbanks off the Flemish
coasts, and swarming in all the estu-
aries and inlets of that intricate and
dangerous cruising-ground between
Dunkerk and Walcheren. Those fleets
of Holland and Zeeland, numbering
some one hundred and fifty galleons,
sloops, and fly-boats, under Warmond,
Nassau, Van der Does, de Moor, and 40
Rosendael, lay patiently blockading
every possible egress from Nieuport,
or Gravelines, or Sluys, or Flushing,
or Dunkerk, and longing to grapple
with the Duke of Parma, so soon as

his fleet of gunboats and hoys, pack
with his Spanish and Italian vete
ans, should venture to set forth up
the sea for their long-prepared e
ploit.

It was a pompous spectacle, th
midsummer night, upon those narr
seas. The moon, which was at t
full, was rising calmly upon a sce
of anxious expectation. Would s
not be looking, by the morrow's nig
upon a subjugated England, a ree
slaved Holland—upon the downfall
civil and religious liberty? Tho
ships of Spain, which lay there wi
their banners waving in the moo
light, discharging salvoes of anti
pated triumph and filling the air wi
strains of insolent music, would th
not, by daybreak, be moving straig
to their purpose, bearing the co
querors of the world to the scene
their cherished hopes?

That English fleet, too, which ro
there at anchor, so anxiously on t
watch—would that swarm of nimb
lightly-handled, but slender vesse
which had held their own hitherto
hurried and desultory skirmishes—
able to cope with their great anta
onist now that the moment had a
rived for the death grapple? Wou
not Howard, Drake, Frobisher, Se
mour, Winter, and Hawkins, be swe
out of the straits at last, yielding a
open passage to Medina, Oquend
Recalde, and Farnese? Would tho
Hollanders and Zeelanders, cruisi
so vigilantly among their treachero
shallows, dare to maintain their po
now that the terrible "Holofernese
with his invincible legions, was r
solved to come forth? . . .

As the twilight deepened, the mo
became totally obscured, dark clou

asses sp.ad over the heavens, the
a grew black, distant thunder rolled,
d the sob of an approaching tempest
came distinctly audible. Such indi-
tions of a westerly gale were not
couraging to those cumbrous vessels,
ith the treacherous quicksands of
anders under their lee.

At an hour past midnight, it was
dark that it was difficult for the
ost practiced eye to pierce far into
e gloom. But a faint drip of oars
w struck the ears of the Spaniards
they watched from the decks. A
w moments afterwards the sea be-
me suddenly luminous, and six flam-
g vessels appeared at a slight dis-
nce, bearing steadily down upon
em before the wind and tide.

There were men in the Armada who
d been at the siege of Antwerp
ly three years before. They re-
embered with horror the devil-ships
Gianibelli, those floating volcanoes,
hich had seemed to rend earth and
ean, whose explosion had laid so
any thousands of soldiers dead at a
ow, and which had shattered the
idge and floating forts of Farnese,
though they had been toys of glass.
hey knew, too, that the famous
gineer was at the moment in Eng-
nd.

In a moment one of those horrible
nics, which spread with such con-
gious rapidity among large bodies
f men, seized upon the Spaniards.
here was a yell throughout the fleet
-"the fire-ships of Antwerp, the fire-
ips of Antwerp!" and in an instant
very cable was cut, and frantic at-
mpts were made by each galleon and
leasse to escape what seemed immi-
nt destruction. The confusion was
eyond description. Four or five of

the largest ships became entangled
with each other. Two others were
set on fire by the flaming vessels, and
were consumed. Medina Sidonia, who
had been warned, even before his departure from Spain, that some such
artifice would probably be attempted,
and who had even, early that morning, sent out a party of sailors in a
pinnace to search for indications of
the scheme, was not surprised or dismayed. He gave orders—as well as
might be—that every ship, after the
danger should be passed, was to return to its post, and await his further
orders. But it was useless, in that moment of unreasonable panic, to issue
commands. The despised Mantuan,
who had met with so many rebuffs
at Philip's court, and who—owing to
official incredulity—had been but partially successful in his magnificent enterprise at Antwerp, had now, by the
mere terror of his name, inflicted
more damage on Philip's Armada than
had hitherto been accomplished by
Howard and Drake, Hawkins and
Frobisher, combined. . . . The Invincible Armada, already sorely crippled, was standing N.N.E. directly
before a fresh topsail-breeze from the
S.S.W. The English came up with
them soon after nine o'clock A.M.
off Gravelines, and found them sailing in a half-moon, the admiral and
vice-admiral in the center, and the
flanks protected by the three remaining galeasses and by the great galleons of Portugal.

Seeing the enemy approaching, Medina Sidonia ordered his whole fleet
to luff to the wind, and prepare for
action. The wind shifting a few
points, was now at W.N.W., so that
the English had both the weather-

gage and the tide in their favor. A general combat began at about ten, and it was soon obvious to the Spaniards that their adversaries were intending warm work. Sir Francis Drake in the *Revenge,* followed by Frobisher in the *Triumph,* Hawkins in the *Victory,* and some smaller vessels, made the first attack upon the Spanish flagships. Lord Henry in the *Rainbow,* Sir Henry Palmer in the *Antelope,* and others engaged with three of the largest galleons of the Armada, while Sir William Winter in the *Vanguard,* supported by most of his squadron, charged the starboard wing.

The portion of the fleet thus assaulted fell back into the main body. Four of the ships ran foul of each other, and Winter, driving into their center, found himself within musketshot of many of their most formidable ships.

"I tell you, on the credit of a poor gentleman," he said, "that there were five hundred discharges of demi-cannon, culverin, and demi-culverin, from the *Vanguard;* and when I was farthest off in firing my pieces, I was not out of shot of their harquebus, and most time within speech, one of another."

The battle lasted six hours long, hot and furious; for now there was no excuse for retreat on the part of the Spaniards, but, on the contrary, it was the intention of the Captain-General to return to his station off Calais, if it were within his power. Nevertheless the English still partially maintained the tactics which had proved so successful, and resolutely refused the fierce attempts of the Spaniards to lay themselves along-

side. Keeping within musket-rang the well-disciplined English marine poured broadside after broadsi against the towering ships of t Armada, which afforded so easy mark; while the Spaniards, on the part, found it impossible, while was ing incredible quantities of powd and shot, to inflict any severe dam age on their enemies. Throughout t action, not an English ship was d stroyed, and not a hundred men we killed. On the other hand, all the be ships of the Spaniards were riddl through and through, and with mas and yards shattered, sails and riggi torn to shreds, and a north-west win still drifting them towards the fat sand-banks of Holland, they labor heavily in a chopping sea, firing wildl and receiving tremendous punishme at the hands of Howard, Drake, Se mour, Winter, and their follower Not even master-gunner Thom could complain that day of "blir exercise" on the part of the Englis with "little harm done" to the enem There was scarcely a ship in t Armada that did not suffer severel for nearly all were engaged in th memorable action off the sands Gravelines. The Captain-Gener himself, Admiral Recalde, Alonzo Leyva, Oquendo, Diego Flores Valdez, Bertendona, Don Francisc de Toledo, Don Diego de Piment Telles Enriquez, Alonzo de Luzo Garibay, with most of the great ga leons and galeasses, were in the thic est of the fight, and one after t other each of those huge ships wa disabled. Three sank before the figl was over, many others were soc drifting helpless wrecks towards hostile shore, and, before five o'cloc

the afternoon, at least sixteen of
their best ships had been sacrificed,
and from four to five thousand sol-
ers killed. . . .

Up to this period, the weather,
though occasionally threatening, had
been moderate. During the week
which succeeded the eventful night off
Calais, neither the Armada nor the
English ships had been much impeded
their manoeuvers by storms or
heavy seas. But on the following
Monday, 14th of August, there was a
change. The wind shifted again to
the south-west, and, during the whole
of that day and the Monday, blew a
tremendous gale. " 'Twas a more
violent storm," said Howard, "than
was ever seen before at this time of
the year." The retreating English fleet
was scattered, many ships were in
peril, "among the ill-favoured sands
of Norfolk," but within four or five
days all arrived safely in Margate
roads.

Far different was the fate of the
Spaniards. Over their Invincible
Armada, last seen by the departing
English midway between the coasts
of Scotland and Denmark, the blackness of night seemed suddenly to descend. A mystery hung for a long
time over their fate. Damaged, leak-
ing, without pilots, without a competent commander, the great fleet entered that furious storm, and was
whirled along the iron crags of Norway and between the savage rocks of
Faroe and the Hebrides. In those regions of tempest the insulted North
wreaked its full vengeance on the insolent Spaniards. Disaster after disaster marked their perilous track; gale
after gale swept them hither and
thither, tossing them on sandbanks or

shattering them against granite cliffs.
The coasts of Norway, Scotland, Ireland, were strewn with the wrecks of
that pompous fleet, which claimed the
dominion of the seas; with the bones
of those invincible legions which were
to have sacked London and made
England a Spanish vice-royalty.

Through the remainder of the
month of August there was a succession of storms. On the 2nd September a fierce southwester drove Admiral Oquendo in his galleon, together
with one of the great galeasses, two
large Venetian ships, the *Ratta* and the
Balauzara, and thirty-six other vessels, upon the Irish coast, where nearly
every soul on board perished, while
the few who escaped to the shore—
notwithstanding their religious affinity with the inhabitants—were
either butchered in cold blood, or sent
coupled in halters from village to
village, in order to be shipped to
England. A few ships were driven on
the English coast; others went ashore
near Rochelle.

Of the four galeasses and four galleys, one of each returned to Spain.
Of the ninety-one great galleons and
hulks, fifty-eight were lost and thirty-
three returned. Of the tenders and
zabras, seventeen were lost and eighteen returned. Of one hundred and
thirty-four vessels, which sailed from
Coruña in July, but fifty-three, great
and small, made their escape to Spain,
and these were so damaged as to be
utterly worthless. The Invincible
Armada had not only been vanquished
but annihilated.

Of the 30,000 men who sailed in
the fleet, it is probable that not more
than 10,000 ever saw their native land
again. Most of the leaders of the ex-

580   JOHN FISKE

pedition lost their lives. Medina
Sidonia reached Santander in October, and, as Philip for a moment believed, "with the greater part of the
Armada," although the King soon discovered his mistake. Recalde, Diego
Flores de Valdez, Oquendo, Maldo-
nado, Bobadilla, Manriquez, either
perished at sea, or died of exhaustion
immediately after their return. Pedro
de Valdez, Vasco de Silva, Alonzo de
Sayas, Piemontel, Toledo, with many
other nobles, were prisoners in England and Holland. There was hardly
a distinguished family in Spain not
placed in mourning, so that, to relieve
the universal gloom, an edict was
published, forbidding the wearing of
mourning at all. On the other hand, a
merchant of Lisbon, not yet recon-
ciled to the Spanish conquest of his
country, permitted himself some
tokens of hilarity at the defeat of the
Armada, and was immediately hanged
by express command of Philip. Thus
—as men said—one could neither cry
nor laugh within the Spanish do-
minions.

This was the result of the invasion,
so many years preparing, and at an
expense almost incalculable. In the
year 1588 alone, the cost of Philip's
armaments for the subjugation of
England could not have been less than
six millions of ducats, and there was
at least as large a sum on board the
Armada itself, although the Pope refused to pay his promised million.
And with all this outlay, and with the
sacrifice of so many thousand lives,
nothing had been accomplished, and
Spain, in a moment, instead of seeming terrible to all the world, had become ridiculous. . . .

1860

II. JOHN FISKE
(1842–1901)

From *OUTLINES OF COSMIC PHILOSOPHY* *

NATURAL SELECTION

In that most delightful of printed
books, the *Conversations of Goethe
with Eckermann and Soret,* there is
an amusing anecdote which shows how
distinctly the great master realized the
importance of the question of the
origin of species. The news of the
French Revolution of July, 1830, had
just reached Weimar and set the whole
town in commotion. In the course
of the afternoon, says Soret, "I went
around to Goethe's. 'Now,' exclaimed
he to me, as I entered, 'what do you
think of this great event? The volcano has come to an eruption; everything is in flames, and we have no
longer a transaction with closed
doors!' 'Terrible affair,' said I, 'but
what could be expected under such
outrageous circumstances, and with
such a ministry, otherwise than that
the whole would end with the expul-
sion of the royal family?' 'My good
friend,' gravely returned Goethe, 'we
seem not to understand each other.
I am not speaking of those creatures
there, but of something quite different.
I am speaking of the contest, so important for science, between Cuvier
and Geoffroy Saint-Hilaire, which has
just come to an open rupture in the
French Academy!'" At this unexpected turn of the subject poor Soret
knew not what to say, and for some
minutes, he tells us, his thoughts were
quite at a standstill.

* Used by permission of, and arrangement
with, Houghton Mifflin Company.

The anecdote well illustrates the immeasurable superiority of Goethe over Comte in prophetic insight into the bearings of the chief scientific question of the immediate future. While Comte was superciliously setting aside the problem of man's origin, a problem not only insoluble but utterly devoid of philosophic value even if it could be solved, the great German poet and philosopher was welcoming the outbreak of this famous contest on questions of pure morphology, as conducive to the speedy triumph of the development theory, for which he himself had so long been waging battle. But events were hastening that triumph even more rapidly than Goethe could have anticipated. In December, 1831, only a few weeks before Goethe was laid in the grave, Mr. Darwin set out upon that voyage round the world, in the course of which he fell in with the facts which suggested his theory of the origin of species. The history of the investigation is a memorable one,—worth something for the illustration it gives of the habits of a truly scientific mind. On his return to England, in 1837, Mr. Darwin began patiently to collect all kinds of facts which might be of use in the solution of the problem,—"How is organic evolution caused?" It was only after seven years of unremitting labor that he went so far as to commit to manuscript a brief sketch of his general conclusions, of which the main points were communicated to his friends Sir Charles Lyell and Dr. Hooker. A less wise and sober speculator than Mr. Darwin would now at once have rushed into print. A thinker less thoroughly imbued with the true scientific spirit would probably have suffered from not publishing his views, and profiting by the adverse criticisms of contemporary observers. It is a striking illustration of Mr. Darwin's patience and self-restraint that he continued fifteen years longer to work assiduously in testing the weak and strong points of his theory, before presenting it to the public. And it is an equally interesting illustration of his thoroughly scientific temperament that, after so many years of solitary labor, he should have been so little carried away by the fascinations of his own hypothesis as to foresee clearly all the more valid objections which might be urged against it. After a careful perusal of the recent literature of the subject, and especially of the skillful work of Mr. St. George Mivart, it still seems to me that the weightiest objections which have yet been brought to bear on the Darwinian theory are to be found in chapters vi.–ix. of Mr. Darwin's own work, where they are elaborately and in most cases conclusively answered. To such a marvellous instance of candor, patience, and sobriety, united with the utmost boldness of speculation, the history of science can show but few parallels.

In 1858 a fortunate circumstance caused Mr. Darwin to break his long silence, and to give to the public an exposition of the results of his researches. Mr. Wallace, who had been for several years engaged in studying the natural history of the Malay Archipelago, had arrived at views concerning the origin of species quite similar to Mr. Darwin's, and in 1858 he sent Mr. Darwin an essay on the subject, which in August of the same year was published in the Journal of the Linnaean Society. Sir Charles Lyell and Dr. Hooker now earnestly advised Mr. Darwin to publish his own views; and in 1859 the memorable treatise on the "Origin of Species" was given to the world.

It would, however, be incorrect to rate Mr. Wallace's merits, in the discovery of the law of natural selection, so high as Mr. Darwin's. They do not stand on precisely the same level, like Adams and Leverrier with reference to the discovery of the planet Neptune. Mr. Wallace, indeed, thought out independently all the essential points of the theory, and stated it in a way which showed that he understood its wide-reaching importance; but being a much younger man than Mr. Darwin, and having begun the investigation at a much later date, he by no means worked it out so elaborately. Nor is it likely that, with an equal length of time at his command, he could have succeeded in producing a work comparable in scientific calibre to the "Origin of Species." His lately published collection of essays, while showing unusual powers of observation and rare acuteness in the application of his theory to certain special classes of phenomena, nevertheless furnishes convincing proof that in breadth and depth of scientific attainment, as well as in philosophic capacity, he is very far inferior to his great coadjutor. In his preface, indeed, Mr. Wallace hastens to acknowledge, with a modest self-appreciation as rare as it is admirable, and especially rare in such cases, that his strength would have been quite unequal to the task which Mr. Darwin has accom plished.

As Professor Haeckel somewhe observes, it was quite fortunate f the progress of science that Mr. Da win received such a stimulus to t publication of his theory; since othe wise he might perhaps have gone several years longer, observing a experimenting in seclusion. The most immediate acquiescence of t majority of naturalists in Mr. Da win's views shows that in 1859 t scientific world was fully prepar for them. The flimsiness of the sp cial creation hypothesis was more less clearly perceived by a large nu ber of biologists, who were only wit held from committing themselves the derivation theory by the circu stance that no satisfactory explan tion of the *process* of developme had been propounded. No one h assigned an adequate cause for su a phenomenon as the gradual evol tion of a new species; and sundry a tempts which had been made in th direction were so obviously futile to excite both distrust and ridicu Lamarck, for example, placing an e aggerated stress upon an establish law of biology, contended that "d sires, by leading to increased actio of motor organs, may induce furth development of such organs," a that, consequently, animals may b come directly adapted through stru tural changes to changes in the environment. We shall see, as we co tinue the discussion, that such direct adaptive changes really take plac but Lamarck ill understood the character, and indeed could not ha been expected to understand it, sin n his day dynamical biology was in ts earliest infancy.* By insisting on volition as a chief cause of adaptive change, the illustrious naturalist not only left the causes of vegetable variation unexplained, but even in the zoölogical department laid open the way for malicious misrepresentations which the uninstructed zeal of theological adversaries has gladly transferred to the account of Mr. Darwin. Some time ago a clergyman in New York, lecturing about Darwinism, sarcastically alluded to "the bear which took to swimming, and so became a whale." Had this worthy person condescended to study the subject about which he thought himself fit to enlighten the public, he would soon have discovered that his funny remark is not even a parody upon any opinion held by Mr. Darwin. In so far as it is applicable to any opinion ever held by a scientific writer, it may perhaps be accepted as a parody, though at best a very far-fetched and feeble one, of the hypothesis of Lamarck.

It is now time to explain what the Darwinian theory is. At the outset we may observe that while it is a common error to speak of Mr. Darwin as if he were the originator of the derivation theory, the opposite error not unfrequently committed of alluding to him as if he had contributed nothing to the establishment of that theory save the doctrine of natural selection. Mr. Mivart habitually thus alludes to him. In fact, however, Mr. Darwin's merits are twofold. He was

the first to marshal the arguments from classification, embryology, morphology, and distribution, and thus fairly to establish the fact that there has been a derivation of higher forms from lower; and he was also the first to point out the *modus operandi* of the change. The first of these achievements by itself would have entitled him to associate his name with the development theory; though it was only by the second that the triumph of the theory was practically assured. Just as, in astronomy, the heliocentric theory was not regarded as completely established until the forces which it postulated were explained as identical with forces already known, so the development theory possessed comparatively little value as a working hypothesis so long as it still remained doubtful whether there were any known or knowable causes sufficient to have brought about the phenomena which that theory assumed to have taken place. It was by pointing out adequate causes of organic evolution that Mr. Darwin established the development theory upon a thoroughly scientific basis.

As Lyell explained all past geologic phenomena as due to the slow action of the same forces which are still in action over the earth's surface and beneath its crust, so Mr. Darwin, in explaining the evolution of higher from lower forms of life, appeals only to agencies which are still visibly in action. Whether species, in a state of nature, are changing or not at the present time, cannot be determined by direct observation, any more than the motion of the hour-hand of a clock could be detected by gazing at it for

* Lamarck also tried to explain organic development metaphysically, as the continuous manifestation of an "inherent tendency" toward perfection. [Author's note.]

one second.* The entire period which has elapsed since men began to observe nature systematically is but an infinitesimal portion of the period requisite for any fundamental alteration in the characteristics of a species. But there are innumerable cases in which species are made to change rapidly through the deliberate intervention of man. In the course of a few thousand years, a great number of varieties of plants and animals have been produced under domestication, many of which differ so widely from their parent-forms that, if found in a state of nature, they would be unhesitatingly classified as distinct species, and sometimes as distinct genera. Modifications in the specific characters of domesticated organisms are the only ones which take place so rapidly that we can actually observe them; and it therefore becomes highly important to inquire what is the agency which produces these modifications.

That agency is neither more nor less than *selection*, taking advantage of that slight but universal variation in organisms implied by the fact that no

two individuals in any species are exactly alike. If man, for example wishes to produce a breed of flee race-horses, he has only to take a scor of horses and select from these th fleetest to pair together: from amon the offspring of these fleet pairs h must again select the fleetest; an thus, in a few generations, he will ob tain horses whose average speed fa exceeds that of the fleetest of the undomesticated ancestors. It is in th and no other way that our breeds race-horses have been produced. I this way too have been produced th fine wools of which our clothing made. By selecting, generation aft generation, the sheep with the fine and longest wool, a breed of sheep ultimately reared with wool almo generically different from that of th undomesticated race. In this and n other way have the different races dogs—the greyhound, the mastiff, th terrier, the pointer, and the whit haired Eskimo—been artificially deve oped from two or three closely allie varieties of the wolf and jackal. Th mastiff and bloodhound are more tha ten times as large as the terrier, an if found in a state of nature, the would perhaps be classed in distin genera, like the leopard and panthe whose differences are hardly mo striking. Yet the ancestral races fro which these dogs have been rear differed but slightly from each othe The different breeds of dogs vary the number of their toes, teeth, an vertebrae, in the number and dispos tion of their mammae, in the shape their zygomatic arches, and in th position of their occiputs; althou dogs have not been selected with re erence to these peculiarities, abo

* "If we imagine mankind to be contemplated by some creature as short-lived as an ephemeron, but possessing intelligence like our own—if we imagine such a being studying men and women, during his few hours of life, and speculating as to the mode in which they came into existence; it is manifest that, reasoning in the usual way, he would suppose each man and woman to have been separately created. No appreciable changes of structure occurring during the few hours over which his observations extended, this being would probably infer that no changes of structure were taking place, or had taken place; and that from the outset, each man and woman had possessed all the characters then visible—had been originally formed with them. This would naturally be the first impression." Spencer, *Principles of Biology*, Vol. I, p. 338. [Author's note.]

which uninstructed men neither know nor care, but only with reference to their speed, fleetness, strength, or sagacity. In the case of domestic pigeons, where man has been to a great extent actuated by pure fancy in his selections, the divergences are still more remarkable. All domestic pigeons are descended from a single species of wild pigeon—yet their differences, even in bony structure, in the internal organs, and in mental disposition, are such as characterize distinct genera, and to describe them comletely would require a large volume. Pigs, rabbits, cows, fowl, silk-moths, and hive-bees furnish no less instructive evidence; and the development of the peach and the almond from a common stock, and of countless varieties of apple from the sour crab, may be cited, out of a hundred examples, to show what prodigies artificial selection has accomplished in the modification of vegetal organisms.

Now Mr. Darwin's great achievement has been to show that a similar process of selection, going on throughout the organic world without the knowledge or intervention of man, tends not only to maintain but to produce adaptive alterations in plants and animals. The process is a simple one, when once we have the clew to it. All plants and animals tend to increase in a high geometrical ratio. The old problem of the nails in the horse's shoe teaches us what an astounding affair is a geometrical rate of increase; but when we consider the reproductive capacity of insects and plants, the nails in the horse's shoe are left nowhere. When Arctic travellers tell us that the minute protococcus multiplies

so fast as to color blood-red many acres of snow in a single night, such a rate of increase appears astonishing. But it is a mere trifle compared to what would happen if reproduction were to go on unchecked. Let us take the case of a plant which yields one hundred seeds yearly, and suppose each of these seeds to reach maturity so as to yield its hundred offspring in the following year: in the tenth year the product would be one hundred quintillions * of adult plants! As this is one of those figures before which the imagination stands hopelessly baffled, let us try the effect of an illustration. Supposing each of these plants to be from three to five inches in length, so that about twenty thousand would reach nearly an English mile, the total length of the number just mentioned would be equal to five million times the radius of the earth's orbit. The ray of light, which travels from the sun to the earth in eight minutes, would be seventy-six years in passing along this line of little plants! And in similar wise it might be shown of many insects, crustaceans, and fishes, that their unchecked reproduction could not long go on without requiring the assimilation of a greater quantity of matter than is contained in the whole solar system.

We may now begin dimly to realize how prodigious is the slaughter which unceasingly goes on throughout the organic world. For obviously, when a plant like the one just cited maintains year by year a tolerable uniformity in its numbers, it does so only

* According to the American system of numeration. One hundred thousand trillions, according to the English system. [Author's note.]

because on the average ninety-nine seeds perish prematurely for one that survives long enough to produce other seeds. A single codfish has been known to lay six million eggs within a year. If these eggs were all to become adult codfishes, and the multiplications were to continue at this rate for three or four years, the ocean would not afford room for the species. Yet we have no reason to suppose that the race of codfishes is actually increasing in numbers to any notable extent. With the codfish, as with animal species in general, the numbers during many successive generations oscillate about a point which is fixed, or moves but slowly forward or backward. Instead of a geometrical increase with a ratio of six millions, there is practically no marked increase at all. Now this implies that out of the six million embryo codfish a sufficient number will survive to replace their two parents, and to replace a certain small proportion of those contemporary codfishes who leave no progeny. Perhaps a dozen may suffice for this, perhaps a hundred. The rest of the six million must die. We may thus understand what is meant by the "struggle for existence." Battles far more deadly than those of Gettysburg or Gravelotte have been incessantly waged on every square mile of the earth's life-bearing surface, since life first began. It is only thus that the enormous increase of each species has been kept within bounds. Of the many offspring produced by each plant and animal, save in the case of those highest in the scale, but few attain maturity and leave offspring behind them. The most perish for want of sustenance, or are slain to furnish food for other organisms. There is thus an unceasing struggle for life—a competition for the means of subsistence —going on among all plants and animals. In this struggle by far the greater number succumb without leaving offspring—but a few favored ones in each generation survive and propagate to their offspring the qualities by virtue of which they have survived.

Thus we see what is meant by "Natural Selection." The organisms which survive and propagate their kind are those which are best adapted to the conditions in which they live so that we may, by a legitimate use of metaphor, personify Nature as a mighty breeder, selecting from each generation those individuals which are fleetest, strongest, most sagacious, lions with supplest muscles, moths with longest antennae, mollusks with hardest shells, wolves with keenest scent, bees with surest instinct, flowers with sweetest nectar; until, in the course of untold ages, the numberless varieties of organic life have been produced by the same process of which man now takes advantage in order to produce variations to suit his own caprices. * * *

187

III. JOHN BURROUGHS
(1837–1921)

From BIRDS'-NESTS *

How alert and vigilant the birds are even when absorbed in building their nests! In an open space in the wood I see a pair of cedar-birds collecting

* Used by permission of, and by arrangement with, Houghton Mifflin Company.

noss from the top of a dead tree.
ollowing the direction in which they
ly, I soon discover the nest placed
n the fork of a small soft-maple,
vhich stands amid a thick growth of
vild-cherry trees and young beeches.
Carefully concealing myself beneath
t, without any fear that the workmen
vill hit me with a chip or let fall a
ool, I await the return of the busy
air. Presently I hear the well-known
ote, and the female sweeps down and
ettles unsuspectingly into the half-
nished structure. Hardly have her
vings rested before her eye has pene-
rated my screen, and with a hurried
novement of alarm she darts away.
n a moment the male, with a tuft of
ool in his beak, (for there is a sheep-
asture near,) joins her, and the two
econnoitre the premises from the
rrounding bushes. With their beaks
ill loaded, they move around with a
rightened look, and refuse to ap-
roach the nest till I have moved off
d lain down behind a log. Then
ne of them ventures to alight upon
e nest, but, still suspecting all is not
ght, quickly darts away again. Then
ey both together come, and after
uch peeping and spying about, and
parently much anxious consultation,
utiously proceed to work. In less
an half an hour it would seem that
ool enough has been brought to sup-
y the whole family, real and pros-
ective, with socks, if needles and
gers could be found fine enough to
it it up. In less than a week the
male has begun to deposit her eggs,
-four of them, in as many days,—
hite tinged with purple, with black
ots on the larger end. After two
eeks of incubation, the young
e out.

Excepting the American goldfinch, this bird builds later in the spring than any other—its nest, in our northern climate, seldom being undertaken till July. As with the goldfinch, the reason is, probably, that suitable food for the young cannot be had at an earlier period.

Like most of our common species, as the robin, sparrow, bluebird, pewee, wren, etc., this bird sometimes seeks wild, remote localities in which to rear its young; at others, takes up its abode near that of man. I knew a pair of cedar-birds, one season, to build in an apple-tree the branches of which rubbed against the house. For a day or two before the first straw was laid, I noticed the pair carefully exploring every branch of the tree, the female taking the lead, the male following her with an anxious look and note. It was evident that the wife was to have her choice this time; and, like one who thoroughly knew her mind, she was proceeding to take it. Finally the site was chosen upon a high branch, extending over one low wing of the house. Mutual congratulations and caresses followed, when both birds flew away in quest of building material. That most freely used is a sort of cotton-bearing plant, which grows in old, worn-out fields. The nest is large for the size of the bird, and very soft. It is in every respect a first-class domicile.

On another occasion, while walking or rather loafing in the woods (for I have discovered that one cannot run and read the book of nature) my attention was arrested by a dull hammering, evidently but a few rods off. I said to myself, "Some one is building a house." From what I had previously seen, I suspected the builder to be a red-headed woodpecker in the top of a dead oak stub near by. Moving cautiously in that direction, I perceived a round hole, about the size of that made by an inch-and-a-half auger, near the top of the decayed trunk, and the white chips of the workman strewing the ground beneath. When but a few spaces from the tree, my foot pressed upon a dry twig, which gave forth a very slight snap. Instantly the hammering ceased, and a scarlet head appeared at the door. Though I remained perfectly motionless, forbearing even to wink till my eyes smarted, the bird refused to go on with his work, but flew quietly off to a neighboring tree. What surprised me was, that amid his busy occupation down in the heart of the old tree, he should have been so alert and watchful as to catch the slightest sound from without.

The woodpeckers all build in about the same manner, excavating the trunk or branch of a decayed tree and depositing the eggs on the fine fragments of wood at the bottom of the cavity. Though the nest is not especially an artistic work,—requiring strength rather than skill,—yet the eggs and the young of few other birds are so completely housed from the elements, or protected from their natural enemies—the jays, crows, hawks, and owls. A tree with a natural cavity is never selected, but one which has been dead just long enough to have become soft and brittle throughout. The bird goes in horizontally for a few inches, making a hole perfectly round and smooth and adapted to his size, then turns downward, gradually enlarging the hole, as he proceeds,

to the depth of ten, fifteen, twent inches, according to the softness of th tree and the requirements of the fe male in laying her eggs. A few day since, I climbed up to the nest of th downy woodpecker, in the decaye top of a sugar-maple. For bette protection against driving rains, th hole, which was rather more than a inch in diameter, was made immed ately beneath a branch which stretche out almost horizontally from the mai stem. It appeared merely a deepe shadow upon the dark and mottle surface of the bark with which th branches were covered, and could no be detected by the eye until one wa within a few feet of it. The youn chirped vociferously as I approache the nest, thinking it was the old on with food; but the clamor sudden ceased as I put my hand on that pa of the trunk in which they were co cealed, the unusual jarring and ru tling alarming them into silence. Th cavity, which was about fifteen inch deep, was gourd-shaped, and wa wrought out with great skill and regu larity. The walls were quite smoot and clean and new.

I shall never forget the circum stance of observing a pair of yellow bellied woodpeckers,—the most ra and secluded, and, next to the re headed, the most beautiful speci found in our woods,—breeding in a old, truncated beech in the Beaverk Mountains, an offshoot of the Ca skills. We had been travelling, thre brothers of us, all day in search of trout lake, which lay far in amor the mountains, had twice lost o course in the trackless forest, an weary and hungry, had sat down rest upon a decayed log. The cha

ering of the young, and the passing
o and fro of the parent birds, soon
rrested my attention. The entrance
o the nest was on the east side of
he tree, about twenty-five feet from
he ground. At intervals of scarcely
minute, the old birds, one after an-
ther, would alight upon the edge of
he hole with a grub or a worm in
heir beaks; then each in turn would
nake a bow or two, cast an eye
uickly around, and by a single move-
nent place itself in the neck of the
assage. Here it would pause a mo-
nent, as if to determine in which ex-
ectant mouth to place the morsel, and
nen disappear within. In about half
minute, during which time the chat-
ering of the young gradually sub-
ded, the bird would again emerge,
ut this time bearing in its beak the
rdure of one of the helpless family.
lying away very slowly with head
wered and extended, as if anxious
hold the offensive object as far
om its plumage as possible, the bird
ropped the unsavory morsel in the
urse of a few yards, and, alighting
a tree, wiped its bill on the bark
d moss. This seems to be the order
day,—carrying in and carrying out.
watched the birds for an hour, while
y companions were taking their turn
exploring the lay of the land around
, and noted no variation of the pro-
amme. It would be curious to know
the young are fed and waited upon
regular order, and how, amid the
rkness and the crowded state of the
artment, the matter is so neatly
anaged. But the ornithologists are
silent upon the subject.

This practice of the birds is not so
common as it might at first seem.
is indeed almost an invariable rule

among all the land birds. With
woodpeckers and kindred species, and
with birds that burrow in the ground,
as bank swallows, kingfishers, etc., it
is a necessity. The accumulation of
the excrement in the nest would most
likely prove fatal to the young.

But even among birds which neither
bore nor mine, but which build a
shallow nest on the branch of a tree or
upon the ground, as the robin, the
finches, the buntings, etc., the ordure
of the young is removed to a distance
by the parent bird. When the robin is
seen going away from its brood with
a slow heavy flight, entirely different
from its manner a moment before on
approaching the nest with a cherry or
worm, it is certain to be engaged in
this office. One may observe the social sparrow, when feeding its young,
pause a moment after the worm has
been given, and hop around on the
brink of the nest, observing the movements within.

The instinct of cleanliness no doubt
prompts the action in all cases, though
the disposition to secrecy or concealment may not be unmixed with it.

The swallows, form an exception to
the rule, the excrement being voided
by the young over the brink of the
nest. They form an exception, also,
to the rule of secrecy, aiming not so
much to conceal the nest as to render
it inaccessible.

Other exceptions are the pigeons,
hawks, and water-fowls.

But to return. Having a good
chance to note the color and mark-
ings of the woodpeckers as they passed
in and out at the opening of the nest,
I saw that Audubon had made a mistake in figuring or describing the female of this species with the red spot

upon the head. I have seen a number of pairs of them, and in no instance have I seen the mother bird marked with red.

The male was in full plumage, and I reluctantly shot him for a specimen. Passing by the place again next day, I paused a moment to note how matters stood. I confess it was not without some compunctions that I heard the cries of the young birds, and saw the widowed mother, her cares now doubled, hastening to and fro in the solitary woods. She would occasionally pause expectantly on the trunk of a tree, and utter a loud call.

It usually happens, when the male of any species is killed during the breeding season, that the female soon procures another mate. There are, most likely, always a few unmated birds, of both sexes, within a given range, and through these the broken links may be restored. Audubon or Wilson, I forget which, tells of a pair of fish-hawks, or ospreys, that built their nest in an ancient oak. The male was so zealous in the defence of the young that it actually attacked with beak and claw a person who attempted to climb into its nest, putting his face and eyes in great jeopardy. Arming himself with a heavy club, the climber felled the gallant bird to the ground and killed him. In the course of a few days the female had procured another mate. But naturally enough the step-father showed none of the spirit and pluck in defence of the brood that had been displayed by the original parent. When danger was nigh, he was seen afar off, sailing around in placid unconcern.

It is generally known that when either the wild turkey or domestic turkey begins to lay, and afterward to sit and rear the brood, she seclude herself from the male, who then, very suddenly herds with others of his sex and betakes himself to haunts of hi own till male and female, old an young, meet again on commo ground, late in the fall. But rob th sitting bird of her eggs, or destro her tender young, and she immed ately sets out in quest of a male who is no laggard when he hears he call. The same is true of ducks an other aquatic fowls. The propaga ing instinct is strong, and surmount all ordinary difficulties. No doul the widowhood I had caused in th case of the woodpeckers was of sho duration, and chance brought, the widow drummed up, some forlor male, who was not dismayed by th prospect of having a large family of half-grown birds on his hands at th outset.

I have seen a fine cock robin pay ing assiduous addresses to a fema bird, as late as the middle of July and I have no doubt that his inte tions were honorable. I watched th pair for half an hour. The hen, took it, was in the market for the se ond time that season, but the coc from his bright, unfaded plumag looked like a new arrival. The h resented every advance of the mal In vain he strutted around her a displayed his fine feathers; every no and then she would make at him the most spiteful manner. He f lowed her to the ground, poured in her ear a fine half-suppressed warb offered her a worm, flew back to t tree again with a great spread plumage, hopped around her on t branches, chirruped, chattered, fl

llantly at an intruder, and was back
an instant at her side. No use,—
e cut him short at every turn.

The *dénouement* I cannot relate,
the artful bird, followed by her
dent suitor, soon flew away beyond
y sight. It may not be rash to con-
ude, however, that she held out no
nger than was prudent.

On the whole, there seems to be
system of Women's Rights prevail-
g among the birds, which, contem-
ated from the standpoint of the
ale, is quite admirable. In almost
l cases of joint interest, the female
rd is the most active. She deter-
ines the site of the nest, and is
ually the most absorbed in its con-
ruction. Generally, she is more
gilant in caring for the young, and
anifests the most concern when dan-
r threatens. Hour after hour I
ve seen the mother of a brood of
ue grossbeaks pass from the nearest
eadow to the tree that held her
st, with a cricket or grasshopper
her bill, while her better-dressed
lf was singing serenely on a dis-
nt tree, or pursuing his pleasures
id the branches.

Yet the male is most conspicuous
th by his color and manners and
his song, and is to that extent a
ield to the female. It is thought
at the female is humbler clad for
r better concealment during incuba-
n. But this is not satisfactory, as
most cases she is relieved from
ne to time by the male. In the
se of the domestic dove, for in-
nce, promptly at midday the cock
found upon the nest. I should
oner say that the dull or neutral
ts of the female were a provision
nature for her greater safety at

all times, as her life is far more precious to the species than that of the
male. The indispensable office of the
male reduces itself to little more than
a moment of time, while that of his
mate extends over days and weeks,
if not months.

In migrating northward, the males
precede the females by eight or ten
days; returning in the fall, the females and young precede the males
by about the same time.

After the woodpeckers have abandoned their nests, or rather chambers, which they do after the first
season, their cousins, the nuthatches,
chickadees, and brown creepers, fall
heir to them. These birds, especially
the creepers and nuthatches, have
many of the habits of the picidæ, but
lack their powers of bill, and so are
unable to excavate a nest for themselves. Their habitation, therefore,
is always second-hand. But each species carries in some soft material of
various kinds, or, in other words, furnishes the tenement to its liking. The
chickadee arranges in the bottom of
the cavity a little mat of a light felt-
like substance, which looks as if it
came from the hatter's, but which is
probably the work of numerous
worms or caterpillars. On this soft
lining the female deposits six white
eggs.

I recently discovered one of these
nests in a most interesting situation.
The tree containing it, a variety of the
wild-cherry, stood upon the brink of
the bald summit of a high mountain.
Gray, time-worn rocks lay piled
loosely about, or overtoppled the
just visible by-ways of the red fox.
The trees had a half-scared look, and
that indescribable wildness which

lurks about the tops of all remote mountains possessed the place. Standing there, I looked down upon the back of the red-tailed hawk as he flew out over the earth beneath me. Following him, my eye also took in farms and settlements and villages and other mountain ranges that grew blue in the distance.

The parent birds attracted my attention by appearing with food in their beaks, and by seeming much put out. Yet so wary were they of revealing the locality of their brood, or even of the precise tree that held them, that I lurked around over an hour without gaining a point on them. Finally a bright and curious boy who accompanied me secreted himself under a low, projecting rock close to the tree in which we supposed the nest to be, while I moved off around the mountain-side. It was not long before the youth had their secret. The tree, which was low and wide, branching, and overrun with lichens, appeared at a cursory glance to contain not one dry or decayed limb. Yet there was one a few feet long, in which, when my eyes were piloted thither, I detected a small round orifice.

As my weight began to shake the branches, the consternation of both old and young was great. The stump of a limb that held the nest was about three inches thick, and at the bottom of the tunnel was excavated quite to the bark. With my thumb I broke in the thin wall, and the young, which were full-fledged, looked out upon the world for the first time. Presently one of them, with a significant chirp, as much as to say, "It is time we were out of this," began

to climb up toward the proper e[ntrance]. Placing himself in the ho[le] he looked around without manifes[t]ing any surprise at the grand sce[ne] that lay spread out before him. [He] was taking his bearings, and dete[r]mining how far he could trust t[he] power of his untried wings to ta[ke] him out of harm's way. After a m[o]ment's pause, with a loud chirp, [he] launched out and made tolerab[le] headway. The others rapidly f[ol]lowed. Each one, as it started u[p]ward, from a sudden impulse, co[n]temptuously saluted the abandon[ed] nest with its excrement.

Though generally regular in the[ir] habits and instincts, yet the bir[ds] sometimes seem as whimsical and c[a]pricious as superior beings. One [is] not safe, for instance, in making a[n] absolute assertion as to their place [or] mode of building. Ground builde[rs] often get up into a bush, and tr[ee] builders sometimes get upon t[he] ground or into a tussock of gra[ss]. The song sparrow, which is a grou[nd] builder, has been known to build [in] the knot-hole of a fence rail, and [a] chimney sparrow once got tired [of] soot and smoke, and fastened its ne[st] on a rafter in a barn. A friend te[lls] me of a pair of barn swallows whic[h] taking a fanciful turn, saddled the[ir] nest in the loop of a rope that w[as] pendent from a peg in the peak, a[nd] liked it so well that they repeat[ed] the experiment next year. I ha[ve] known the social sparrow, or "ha[ir] bird," to build under a shed, in a tu[ft] of hay that hung down, through t[he] loose flooring, from the mow abov[e].

It usually contents itself with ha[lf] a dozen stalks of dry grass and a f[ew] long hairs from a cow's tail, loose[ly]

ranged on the branch of an apple-
ee. The rough-winged swallow
uilds in the wall and in old stone
eaps, and I have seen the robin build
a similar localities. Others have
ound its nest in old, abandoned wells.
he house wren will build in anything
that has an accessible cavity, from an
'd boot to a bombshell. A pair of
nem once persisted in building their
est in the top of a certain pump-
ee, getting in through the opening
oove the handle. The pump being
a daily use, the nest was destroyed
nore than a score of times. This
ealous little wretch has the wise
orethought, when the box in which
e builds contains two compartments,
o fill up one of them, so as to avoid
ne risk of troublesome neighbors.

The less skilful builders sometimes
epart from their usual habit, and
ke up with the abandoned nest of
ome other species. The blue jay
ow and then lays in an old crow's-
est or cuckoo's-nest. The crow-
lackbird, seized with a fit of indo-
nce, drops its eggs in the cavity of
decayed branch. I heard of a
uckoo that dispossessed a robin of
s nest; of another, that set a blue
y adrift. Large, loose structures,
ke the nests of the osprey and cer-
in of the herons, have been found
ith half a dozen nests of the black-
ird set in the outer edges, like so
any parasites, or, as Audubon says,
ke the retainers about the rude
ourt of a feudal baron.

The same birds breeding in a south-
rn climate construct far less elabo-
te nests than when breeding in a
orthern climate. Certain species of
aterfowl that abandon their eggs to
ne sand and the sun in the warmer

zones, build a nest and sit in the usual
way in Labrador. In Georgia, the
Baltimore oriole places its nest upon
the north side of the tree; in the
Middle and Eastern States, it fixes
it upon the south or east side, and
makes it much thicker and warmer.
I have seen one from the South that
had some kind of coarse reed or sedge
woven into it, giving it an openwork
appearance, like a basket.

Very few species use the same material uniformly. I have seen the
nest of the robin quite destitute of
mud. In one instance, it was composed mainly of long black horse-
hairs, arranged in a circular manner,
with a lining of fine yellow grass; the
whole presenting quite a novel appearance. In another case, the nest
was chiefly constructed of a species
of rock moss.

The nest for the second brood during the same season is often a mere
makeshift. The haste of the female
to deposit her eggs as the season advances seems very great, and the
structure is apt to be prematurely
finished. I was recently reminded of
this fact by happening, about the last
of July, to meet with several nests
of the wood or bush sparrow in a remote blackberry field. The nests
with eggs were far less elaborate and
compact than the earlier nests, from
which the young had flown.

Day after day, as I go to a certain
piece of woods, I observe a male indigo-bird sitting on precisely the same
part of a high branch, and singing in
his most vivacious style. As I approach, he ceases to sing, and, flirting
his tail right and left with marked
emphasis, chirps sharply. In a low
bush near by, I come upon the object

of his solicitude—a thick, compact nest composed largely of dry leaves and fine grass, in which a plain brown bird is sitting upon four pale blue eggs.

The wonder is, that a bird will leave the apparent security of the tree-tops, to place its nest in the way of the many dangers that walk and crawl upon the ground. There, far up out of reach, sings the bird; here, not three feet from the ground, are its eggs or helpless young. The truth is, birds are the greatest enemies of birds, and it is with reference to this fact that many of the smaller species build.

Perhaps the greatest proportion of birds breed along highways. I have known the ruffed grouse to come out of a dense wood, and make its nest at the root of a tree within ten paces of the road, where, no doubt, hawks and crows, as well as skunks and foxes, would be less liable to find it out. Traversing remote mountain-roads through dense woods, I have repeatedly seen the veery, or Wilson's thrush, sitting upon her nest, so near me that I could almost take her from it by stretching out my hand. Birds of prey show none of this confidence in man, and, when locating their nests, avoid rather than seek his haunts.

In a certain locality in the interior of New York, I know, every season, where I am sure to find a nest or two of the slate-colored snowbird. It is under the brink of a low, mossy bank, so near the highway that it could be reached from a passing vehicle with a whip. Every horse or wagon or foot passenger disturbs the sitting bird. But she awaits the near approach of the sound of feet or wheels, and then darts quickly across the road, barely clearing the ground and disappears amid the bushes on the opposite side.

In the trees that line one of the main streets and fashionable drive leading out of Washington City, and less than half a mile from the boundary, I have counted the nests of five different species at one time, and that without any very close scrutiny of the foliage, while in many acres of woodland, half a mile off, searched in vain for a single nest. Among the five, the nest that interested me most was that of the blue grossbeak. Here, this bird which, according to Audubon's observations in Louisiana, is shy and recluse, affecting remote marshes and the borders of large ponds of stagnant water, had placed its nest in the lowest twig of the lowest branch of a large sycamore, immediately over a great thoroughfare, and so near the ground that a person standing in a cart or sitting on a horse could have reached it with his hand. The nest was composed mainly of fragments of newspaper and stalks of grass, and though so low, was remarkably well concealed by one of the peculiar clusters of twigs and leaves which characterize this tree. The nest contained young when I discovered it, and though the parent birds were much annoyed by my loitering about beneath the tree, they paid little attention to the stream of vehicles that was constantly passing. It was a wonder to me when the birds could have built it, for they are much shyer when building than at other times. No doubt they worked

nostly in the morning, having the
arly hours all to themselves.

Another pair of blue grossbeaks
uilt in a grave-yard within the city
imits. The nest was placed in a low
oush, and the male continued to sing
t intervals till the young were ready
o fly. The song of this bird is a
apid, intricate warble, like that of
he indigo-bird, though stronger and
ouder. Indeed, these two birds so
much resemble each other in color,
orm, manner, voice, and general
abits that, were it not for the dif-
erence in size,—the grossbeak being
nearly as large again as the indigo-
oird,—it would be a hard matter to
ell them apart. The females of both
pecies are clad in the same reddish-
orown suits. So are the young the
rst season.

Of course in the deep, primitive
woods also are nests; but how rarely
ve find them! The simple art of the
ird consists in choosing common,
neutral-tinted material, as moss, dry
eaves, twigs, and various odds and
nds, and placing the structure on a
onvenient branch where it blends in
olor with its surroundings; but how
onsummate is this art, and how skil-
ully is the nest concealed! We oc-
asionally light upon it, but who, un-
ided by the movements of the bird,
ould find it out? During the pres-
nt season I went to the woods nearly
very day for a fortnight, without
naking any discoveries of this kind;
ill one day, paying them a farewell
isit, I chanced to come upon several
ests. A black and white creeping
warbler suddenly became much
darmed as I approached a crumbling
ld stump in a dense part of the
orest. He alighted upon it, chirped

sharply, ran up and down its sides,
and finally left it with much reluctance. The nest, which contained
three young birds nearly fledged, was
placed upon the ground at the foot
of the stump, and in such a position
that the color of the young harmon-
ized perfectly with the bits of bark,
sticks, etc., lying about. My eye
rested upon them for the second time
before I made them out. They
hugged the nest very closely, but as I
put down my hand, they all scam-
pered off with loud cries for help,
which caused the parent birds to
place themselves almost within my
reach. The nest was merely a little
dry grass arranged in a thick bed of
dry leaves.

This was amid a thick under-
growth. Moving on into a passage
of large stately hemlocks, with only
here and there a small beech or maple
rising up into the perennial twilight,
I paused to make out a note which
was entirely new to me. It is still
in my ear. Though unmistakably a
bird note, it yet suggested the bleat-
ing of a tiny lambkin. Presently the
birds appeared,—a pair of the solitary vireo. They came flitting from
point to point, alighting only for a
moment at a time, the male silent,
but the female uttering this strange,
tender note. It was a rendering into
some new sylvan dialect of the human
sentiment of maidenly love. It was
really pathetic in its sweetness and
childlike confidence and joy. I soon
discovered that the pair were building a nest upon a low branch a few
yards away from me. The male flew
cautiously to the spot, and adjusted
something, and the twain moved on,
the female calling to her mate at in-

tervals, *love-e, love-e,* with a cadence
and tenderness in the tone that rang
in the ear long afterward. The nest
was suspended to the fork of a small
branch, as is usual with the vireos,
plentifully lined with lichens, and
bound and rebound with masses of
coarse spider-webs. There was no attempt at concealment except in the
neutral tints, which made it look like
a natural growth of the dim, gray
woods. * * *

1869

IV. JOHN MUIR
(1838–1914)

THE SIERRA NEVADA*

Go where you may within the
bounds of California, mountains are
ever in sight, charming and glorifying every landscape. Yet so simple
and massive is the topography of the
State in general views, that the main
central portion displays only one valley, and two chains of mountains
which seem almost perfectly regular
in trend and height: the Coast Range
on the west side, the Sierra Nevada
on the east. These two ranges coming together in curves on the north
and south inclose a magnificent
basin, with a level floor more than
400 miles long, and from 35 to 60
miles wide. This is the grand Central Valley of California, the waters
of which have only one outlet to the
sea through the Golden Gate. But
with this general simplicity of fea-

* From *The Mountains of California,* by
John Muir. Copyright 1894 by The Century
Co.

tures there is great complexity
hidden detail. The Coast Range, ri
ing as a grand green barrier again
the ocean, from 2000 to 8000 fe
high, is composed of innumerab
forest-crowned spurs, ridges, ar
rolling hill-waves which inclose a mu
titude of small valleys; some lookir
out through long, forest-lined vista
to the sea; others, with but fe
trees, to the Central Valley; while
thousand others yet smaller are en
bosomed and concealed in mild, roun
browed hills, each with its own cl
mate, soil, and production.

Making your way through th
mazes of the Coast Range to the sun
mit of any of the inner peaks
passes opposite San Francisco, in th
clear spring-time, the grandest ar
most telling of all California lan
scapes is outspread before you. A
your feet lies the great Central Va
ley glowing golden in the sunshin
extending north and south farth
than the eye can reach, one smoot
flowery, lake-like bed of fertile so
Along its eastern margin rises th
mighty Sierra, miles in height, repo
ing like a smooth, cumulous cloud
the sunny sky, and so gloriously co
ored, and so luminous, it seems to l
not clothed with light, but whol
composed of it, like the wall of som
celestial city. Along the top, and e
tending a good way down, you see
pale, pearl-gray belt of snow; ar
below it a belt of blue and dark pu
ple, marking the extension of th
forests; and along the base of th
range a broad belt of rose-purple ar
yellow, where lie the miner's gol
fields and the foot-hill gardens. A
these colored belts blending smooth
make a wall of light ineffably fin

nd as beautiful as a rainbow, yet
rm as adamant.

When I first enjoyed this superb
ew, one glowing April day, from
e summit of the Pacheco Pass, the
entral Valley, but little trampled or
owed as yet, was one furred, rich
eet of golden compositæ, and the
minous wall of the mountains shone
all its glory. Then it seemed to
e the Sierra should be called not
e Nevada, or Snowy Range, but the
ange of Light. And after ten years
ent in the heart of it, rejoicing and
ondering, bathing in its glorious
oods of light, seeing the sunbursts
f morning among the icy peaks, the
onday radiance on the trees and
cks and snow, the flush of the al-
englow, and a thousand dashing
aterfalls with their marvelous abun-
nce of irised spray, it still seems to
e above all others the Range of
ight, the most divinely beautiful of
l the mountain-chains I have ever
en.

The Sierra is about 500 miles long,
) miles wide, and from 7000 to
arly 15,000 feet high. In general
ews no mark of man is visible on
, nor anything to suggest the rich-
ess of the life it cherishes, or the
pth and grandeur of its sculpture.
one of its magnificent forest-
owned ridges rises much above the
eneral level to publish its wealth.
o great valley or lake is seen, or
ver, or group of well-marked fea-
res of any kind, standing out in
stinct pictures. Even the summit-
eaks, so clear and high in the sky,
em comparatively smooth and fea-
reless. Nevertheless, glaciers are
ill at work in the shadows of the
eaks, and thousands of lakes and

meadows shine and bloom beneath
them, and the whole range is furrowed with cañons to a depth of from
2000 to 5000 feet, in which once
flowed majestic glaciers, and in which
now flow and sing a band of beautiful
rivers.

Though of such stupendous depth,
these famous cañons are not raw,
gloomy, jagged-walled gorges, savage
and inaccessible. With rough passages here and there they still make
delightful pathways for the mountaineer, conducting from the fertile
lowlands to the highest icy fountains,
as a kind of mountain streets full of
charming life and light, graded and
sculptured by the ancient glaciers,
and presenting, throughout all their
courses, a rich variety of novel and
attractive scenery, the most attractive that has yet been discovered in
the mountain-ranges of the world.

In many places, especially in the
middle region of the western flank
of the range, the main cañons widen
into spacious valleys or parks, diversified like artificial landscape-gardens,
with charming groves and meadows,
and thickets of blooming bushes,
while the lofty, retiring walls, infinitely varied in form and sculpture,
are fringed with ferns, flowering-
plants of many species, oaks, and
evergreens, which find anchorage on
a thousand narrow steps and benches;
while the whole is enlivened and
made glorious with rejoicing streams
that come dancing and foaming over
the sunny brows of the cliffs to join
the shining river that flows in tranquil beauty down the middle of each
one of them.

The walls of these park valleys of
the Yosemite kind are made up of

rocks, mountains in size, partly separated from each other by narrow
gorges and side-cañons; and they are
so sheer in front, and so compactly
built together on a level floor, that,
comprehensively seen, the parks they
inclose look like immense halls or
temples lighted from above. Every
rock seems to glow with life. Some
lean back in majestic repose; others, 10
absolutely sheer, or nearly so, for
thousands of feet, advance their
brows in thoughtful attitudes beyond
their companions, giving welcome to
storms and calms alike, seemingly
conscious yet heedless of everything
going on about them, awful in stern
majesty, types of permanence, yet
associated with beauty of the frailest
and most fleeting forms; their feet set 20
in pine-groves and gay emerald meadows, their brows in the sky; bathed
in light, bathed in floods of singing
water, while snow-clouds, avalanches,
and the winds shine and surge and
wreathe about them as the years go
by, as if into these mountain mansions Nature had taken pains to
gather her choicest treasures to draw
her lovers into close and confiding 30
communion with her.

Here, too, in the middle region of
deepest cañons are the grandest
forest-trees, the Sequoia, king of
conifers, the noble Sugar and Yellow
Pines, Douglas Spruce, Libocedrus,
and the Silver Firs, each a giant of
its kind, assembled together in one
and the same forest, surpassing all
other coniferous forests in the world, 40
both in the number of its species and
in the size and beauty of its trees.
The winds flow in melody through
their colossal spires, and they are
vocal everywhere with songs of birds

and running water. Miles of fra
grant ceanothus and manzanita bush
bloom beneath them, and lily garde
and meadows, and damp, ferny gle
in endless variety of fragrance ar
color, compelling the admiration
every observer. Sweeping on ov
ridge and valley, these noble tre
extend a continuous belt from end t
end of the range, only slightly inte
rupted by sheer-walled cañons at in
tervals of about fifteen and twent
miles. Here the great burly brow
bears delight to roam, harmonizir
with the brown boles of the trees b
neath which they feed. Deer, als
dwell here, and find food and shelt
in the ceanothus tangles, with a mu
titude of smaller people. Above th
region of giants, the trees gro
smaller until the utmost limit of tl
timber line is reached on the storm
mountain-slopes at a height of fro
ten to twelve thousand feet abo
the sea, where the Dwarf Pine is s
lowly and hard beset by storms an
heavy snow, it is pressed into fl
tangles, over the tops of which v
may easily walk. Below the ma
forest belt the trees likewise dimini
in size, frost and burning drouth r
pressing and blasting alike.

The rose-purple zone along tl
base of the range comprehends near
all the famous gold region of Califo
nia. And here it was that mine
from every country under the sun a
sembled in a wild, torrent-like rus
to seek their fortunes. On the banl
of every river, ravine, and gully the
have left their marks. Every grave
and boulder-bed has been desperate
riddled over and over again. But
this region the pick and shovel, on
wielded with savage enthusiasm, ha

been laid away, and only quartz-mining is now being carried on to any considerable extent. The zone in general is made up of low, tawny, waving foot-hills, roughened here and there with brush and trees, and outcropping masses of slate, colored gray and red with lichens. The smaller masses of slate, rising abruptly from the dry, grassy sod in leaning slabs, look like ancient tombstones in a deserted burying-ground. In early spring, say from February to April, the whole of this foot-hill is a paradise of bees and flowers. Refreshing rains then fall freely, birds are busy building their nests, and the sunshine is balmy and delightful. But by the end of May the soil, plants, and sky seem to have been baked in an oven. Most of the plants crumble to dust beneath the foot, and the ground is full of cracks; while the thirsty traveler gazes with eager longing through the burning glare to the snowy summits looming like hazy clouds in the distance.

The trees, mostly *Quercus Douglasii* and *Pinus Sabiniana,* thirty to forty feet high, with thin, pale-green foliage, stand far apart and cast but little shade. Lizards glide about on the rocks enjoying a constitution that no drouth can dry, and ants in amazing numbers, whose tiny sparks of life seem to burn the brighter with the increasing heat, ramble industriously in long trains in search of food. Crows, ravens, magpies— friends in distress—gather on the ground beneath the best shade-trees, panting with drooping wings and bills wide open, scarce a note from any of them during the midday hours. Quails, too, seek the shade during the heat of the day about tepid pools in the channels of the larger mid-river streams. Rabbits scurry from thicket to thicket among the ceanothus bushes, and occasionally a long-eared hare is seen cantering gracefully across the wider openings. The nights are calm and dewless during the summer, and a thousand voices proclaim the abundance of life, notwithstanding the desolating effect of dry sunshine on the plants and larger animals. The hylas make a delightfully pure and tranquil music after sunset; and coyotes, the little, despised dogs of the wilderness, brave, hardy fellows, looking like withered wisps of hay, bark in chorus for hours. Mining-towns, most of them dead, and a few living ones with bright bits of cultivation about them, occur at long intervals along the belt, and cottages covered with climbing roses, in the midst of orange and peach orchards, and sweet-scented hay-fields in fertile flats where water for irrigation may be had. But they are mostly far apart, and make scarce any mark in general views.

Every winter the High Sierra and the middle forest region get snow in glorious abundance, and even the foot-hills are at times whitened. Then all the range looks like a vast beveled wall of purest marble. The rough places are then made smooth, the death and decay of the year is covered gently and kindly, and the ground seems as clean as the sky. And though silent in its flight from the clouds, and when it is taking its place on rock, or tree, or grassy meadow, how soon the gentle snow finds a voice! Slipping from the heights, gathering in avalanches, it booms and roars like thunder, and makes a glorious show as it sweeps down the mountain-side, arrayed in long, silken streamers and wreathing, swirling films of crystal dust.

The north half of the range is mostly covered with floods of lava, and dotted with volcanoes and craters, some of them recent and perfect in form, others in various stages of decay. The south half is composed of granite nearly from base to summit, while a considerable number of peaks, in the middle of the range, are capped with metamorphic slates, among which are Mounts Dana and Gibbs to the east of Yosemite Valley. Mount Whitney, the culminating point of the range near its southern extremity, lifts its helmet-shaped crest to a height of nearly 14,700 feet. Mount Shasta, a colossal volcanic cone, rises to a height of 14,440 feet at the northern extremity, and forms a noble landmark for all the surrounding region within a radius of a hundred miles. Residual masses of volcanic rocks occur throughout most of the granitic southern portion also, and a considerable number of old volcanoes on the flanks, especially along the eastern base of the range near Mono Lake and southward. But it is only to the northward that the entire range, from base to summit, is covered with lava.

From the summit of Mount Whitney only granite is seen. Innumerable peaks and spires but little lower than its own storm-beaten crags rise in groups like forest-trees, in full view, segregated by cañons of tremendous depth and ruggedness. On Shasta nearly every feature in the vast view speaks of the old volcanic fires. Far to the northward, in Oregon, the icy volcanoes of Mount Pitt and the Three Sisters rise above the dark evergreen woods. Southward innumerable smaller craters and cones are distributed along the axis of the range and on each flank. Of these Lassen's Butte is the highest, being nearly 11,000 feet above sea-level. Miles of its flanks are reeking and bubbling with hot springs, many of them so boisterous and sulphurous they seem ever ready to become spouting geysers like those of the Yellowstone.

The Cinder Cone near marks the most recent volcanic eruption in the Sierra. It is a symmetrical truncated cone about 700 feet high, covered with gray cinders and ashes, and has a regular unchanged crater on its summit, in which a few small Two-leaved Pines are growing. These show that the age of the cone is not less than eighty years. It stands between two lakes, which a short time ago were one. Before the cone was built, a flood of rough vesicular lava was poured into the lake, cutting it in two, and, overflowing its banks, the fiery flood advanced into the pine woods, overwhelming the trees in its way, the charred ends of some of which may still be seen projecting from beneath the snout of the lava-stream where it came to rest. Later still there was an eruption of ashes and loose obsidian cinders, probably from the same vent, which, besides forming the Cinder Cone, scattered a heavy shower over the surrounding woods for miles to a depth of from six inches to several feet.

The history of this last Sierra eruption is also preserved in the traditions of the Pitt River Indians.

They tell of a fearful time of darkness, when the sky was black with ashes and smoke that threatened every living thing with death, and that when at length the sun appeared once more it was red like blood.

Less recent craters in great numbers roughen the adjacent region; some of them with lakes in their throats, others overgrown with trees and flowers, Nature in these old hearths and firesides having literally given beauty for ashes. On the northwest side of Mount Shasta there is a subordinate cone about 3000 feet below the summit, which has been active subsequent to the breaking up of the main ice-cap that once covered the mountain, as is shown by its comparatively unwasted crater and the streams of unglaciated lava radiating from it. The main summit is about a mile and a half in diameter, bounded by small crumbling peaks and ridges, among which we seek in vain for the outlines of the ancient crater.

These ruinous masses, and the deep glacial grooves that flute the sides of the mountain, show that it has been considerably lowered and wasted by ice; how much we have no sure means of knowing. Just below the extreme summit hot sulphurous gases and vapor issue from irregular fissures, mixed with spray derived from melting snow, the last feeble expression of the mighty force that built the mountain. Not in one great convulsion was Shasta given birth. The crags of the summit and the sections exposed by the glaciers down the sides display enough of its internal framework to prove that comparatively long periods of quiescence intervened between many distinct eruptions, during which the cooling lavas ceased to flow, and became permanent additions to the bulk of the growing mountain. With alternate haste and deliberation eruption succeeded eruption till the old volcano surpassed even its present sublime height.

Standing on the icy top of this, the grandest of all the fire-mountains of the Sierra, we can hardly fail to look forward to its next eruption. Gardens, vineyards, homes have been planted confidingly on the flanks of volcanoes which, after remaining steadfast for ages, have suddenly blazed into violent action, and poured forth overwhelming floods of fire. It is known that more than a thousand years of cool calm have intervened between violent eruptions. Like gigantic geysers spouting molten rock instead of water, volcanoes work and rest, and we have no sure means of knowing whether they are dead when still, or only sleeping.

Along the western base of the range a telling series of sedimentary rocks containing the early history of the Sierra are now being studied. But leaving for the present these first chapters, we see that only a very short geological time ago, just before the coming on of that winter of winters called the glacial period, a vast deluge of molten rocks poured from many a chasm and crater on the flanks and summit of the range, filling lake basins and river channels, and obliterating nearly every existing feature on the northern portion. At length these all-destroying floods ceased to flow. But while the great volcanic cones built up along the axis still burned and smoked, the whole Sierra passed under the domain of ice and snow. Then over the bald, featureless, fire-blackened mountains, glaciers began to crawl, covering them from the summits to the sea with a mantle of ice; and then with infinite deliberation the work went on of sculpturing the range anew. These mighty agents of erosion, halting never through unnumbered centuries, crushed and ground the flinty lavas and granites beneath their crystal folds, wasting and building until in the fullness of time the Sierra was born again, brought to light nearly as we behold it to-day, with glaciers and snow-crushed pines at the top of the range, wheat-fields and orange-groves at the foot of it.

This change from icy darkness and death to life and beauty was slow, as we count time, and is still going on, north and south, over all the world wherever glaciers exist, whether in the form of distinct rivers, as in Switzerland, Norway, the mountains of Asia, and the Pacific Coast; or in continuous mantling folds, as in portions of Alaska, Greenland, Franz-Joseph-Land, Nova Zembla, Spitzbergen, and the lands about the South Pole. But in no country, as far as I know, may these majestic changes be studied to better advantage than in the plains and mountains of California.

Toward the close of the glacial period, when the snow-clouds became less fertile and the melting waste of sunshine became greater, the lower folds of the ice-sheet in California, discharging fleets of icebergs into the sea, began to shallow and recede from the lowlands, and then move slowly up the flanks of the Sierra in compliance with the changes of climate. The great white mantle on the mountains broke up into a series of glaciers more or less distinct and river-like, with many tributaries, and these again were melted and divided into still smaller glaciers, until now only a few of the smaller residual topmost branches of the grand system exist on the cool slopes of the summit peaks.

Plants and animals, biding their time, closely followed the retiring ice, bestowing quick and joyous animation on the new-born landscape. Pine-trees marched up the sun-warmed moraines in long, hopeful files, taking the ground and establishing themselves as soon as it was ready for them; brown-spiked sedges fringed the shores of the new-born lakes; young rivers roared in the abandoned channels of the glaciers; flowers bloomed around the feet of the great burnished domes,—while with quick fertility mellow beds of soil, settling and warming, offered food to multitudes of Nature's waiting children, great and small, animals as well as plants; mice, squirrels, marmots, deer, bears, elephants, etc. The ground burst into bloom with magical rapidity, and the young forests into bird-song: life in every form warming and sweetening and growing richer as the years passed away over the mighty Sierra so lately suggestive of death and consummate desolation only.

It is hard without long and loving study to realize the magnitude of the work done on these mountains during the last glacial period by glaciers, which are only streams of closely compacted snow-crystals. Careful study of the phenomena presented goes to show that the pre-glacial condition of the range was comparatively simple: one vast wave of stone in which a thousand mountains, domes, cañons, ridges, etc., lay concealed. And in the development of these Nature chose for a tool not the earthquake or lightning to rend and split asunder, not the stormy torrent or eroding rain, but the tender snow-flowers noiselessly falling through unnumbered centuries, the offspring of the sun and sea. Laboring harmoniously in united strength they crushed and ground and wore away the rocks in their march, making vast beds of soil, and at the same time developed and fashioned the landscapes into the delightful variety of hill and dale and lordly mountain that mortals call beauty. Perhaps more than a mile in average depth has the range been thus degraded during the last glacial period,—a quantity of mechanical work almost inconceivably great. And our admiration must be excited again and again as we toil and study and learn that this vast job of rockwork, so far-reaching in its influences, was done by agents so fragile and small as are these flowers of the mountain clouds. Strong only by force of numbers, they carried away entire mountains, particle by particle, block by block, and cast them into the sea; sculptured, fashioned, modeled all the range, and developed its predestined beauty. All these new Sierra landscapes were evidently predestined, for the physical structure of the rocks on which the features of the scenery depend was acquired while they lay at least a mile deep below the pre-glacial surface. And it was while these features were taking form in the depths of the range, the particles of the rocks marching to their appointed places in the dark with reference to the coming beauty, that the particles of icy vapor in the sky marching to the same music assembled to bring them to the light. Then, after their grand task was done, these bands of snow-flowers, these mighty glaciers, were melted and removed as if of no more importance than dew destined to last but an hour. Few, however, of Nature's agents have left monuments so noble and enduring as they. The great granite domes a mile high, the cañons as deep, the noble peaks, the Yosemite valleys, these, and indeed nearly all other features of the Sierra scenery, are glacier monuments.

Contemplating the works of these flowers of the sky, one may easily fancy them endowed with life: messengers sent down to work in the mountain mines on errands of divine love. Silently flying through the darkened air, swirling, glinting, to their appointed places, they seem to have taken counsel together, saying, "Come, we are feeble; let us help one another. We are many, and together we will be strong. Marching in close, deep ranks, let us roll away the stones from these mountain sepulchers, and set the landscapes free. Let us uncover these clustering domes. Here let us carve a lake basin; there, a Yosemite Valley; here, a channel for a river with fluted steps and brows for the plunge of songful cataracts. Yonder let us spread broad sheets of soil, that man and beast may be fed;

and here pile trains of boulders for pines and giant Sequoias. Here make ground for a meadow; there, for a garden and grove, making it smooth and fine for small daisies and violets and beds of heathy bryanthus, spicing it well with crystals, garnet feldspar, and zircon." Thus and so on it has oftentimes seemed to me sang and planned and labored the hearty snow-flower crusaders; and nothing that I can write can possibly exaggerate the grandeur and beauty of their work. Like morning mist they have vanished in sunshine, all save the few small companies that still linger on the coolest mountain-sides, and, as residual glaciers, are still busily at work completing the last of the lake basins, the last beds of soil, and the sculpture of some of the highest peaks.

1873

I. IRWIN RUSSELL
(1853–1879)

NEBUCHADNEZZAR *

You, Nebuchadnezzar, whoa, sah!
Whar is you tryin' to go, sah?
I'd hab you fur to know, sah,
    I's a-holdin' ob de lines.
You better stop dat prancin';
You's pow'ful fond ob dancin',
But I'll bet my yeah's advancin'
    Dat I'll cure you ob yo' shines.

Look heah, mule! Better min' out;
Fus' t'ing you know you'll fin' out   10
How quick I'll wear dis line out
    On your ugly stubbo'n back.
You needn't try to steal up
An' lif' dat precious heel up;
You's got to plow dis fiel' up,
    You has, sah, fur a fac'.

Dar, *dat's* de way to do it!
He's comin' right down to it;
Jes watch him plowin' troo it!
    Dis nigger ain't no fool.   20
Some folks dey would 'a' beat him;
Now, dat would only heat him—
I know jest how to treat him:
    You mus' *reason* wid a mule.

He minds me like a nigger.
If he wuz only bigger
He'd fotch a mighty figger,
    He would, I *tell* you! Yes, sah!
See how he keep a-clickin'!   30
He's as gentle as a chicken,

* All selections from Russell are reprinted from *Christmas-Night in the Quarters and Other Poems,* by Irwin Russell. Copyright 1917 by The Century Co.

An' nebber thinks o' kickin'—
    Whoa dar! Nebuchadnezzah!

Is dis heah me, or not me?
Or is de debbil got me?
Wuz dat a cannon shot me?
    Hab I laid heah more'n a week?
Dat mule do kick amazin'!
De beast was sp'iled in raisin'—
But now I s'pect he's grazin'
    On de oder side de creek.   40
                                    1876

MAHSR JOHN

I heahs a heap o' people talkin', ebry-
    whar I goes,
'Bout Washintum an' Franklum, an'
    sech gen'uses as dose;
I s'pose dey's mighty fine, but heah's
    de p'int I's bettin' on:
Dere wuzn't nar a one ob 'em come
    up to Mahsr John.

He shorely wuz de greates' man de
    country ebber growed.
You better had git out de way when
    he come 'long de road!
He hel' his head up dis way, like he
    'spised to see de groun';
An' niggers had to toe de mark when
    Mahsr John wuz roun'.

I only has to shet my eyes, an' den it
    seems to me
I sees him right afore me now, jes
    like he use' to be,   10
A-settin' on de gal'ry, lookin' awful
    big an' wise,
Wid little niggers fannin' him to keep
    away de flies.

He alluz wore de berry bes' ob plant-
    ers' linen suits,

An' kep' a nigger busy jes a-blackin'
  of his boots;
De buckles on his galluses wuz made
  of solid gol',
An' diamon's!—dey wuz in his shut
  as thick as it would hol'.

You heered me! 'twas a caution, when
  he went to take a ride,
To see him in de kerridge, wid ol'
  Mistis by his side—
Mulatter Bill a-dribin', an' a nigger
  on behin',
An' two Kaintucky hosses tuk 'em
  tearin' whar dey gwine.   20
Ol' Mahsr John wuz pow'ful rich—he
  owned a heap o' lan':
Fibe cotton places, 'sides a sugar place
  in Loozyan';
He had a thousan' niggers—an' he
  wuked 'em, shore's you born!
De oberseahs 'u'd start 'em at de
  breakin' ob de morn.

I reckon dere wuz forty ob de niggers,
  young an' ol',
Dat staid about de big house jes to
  do what dey wuz tol';
Dey had a' easy time, wid skacely
  any work at all—

But dey had to come a-runnin' when
  ol' Mahsr John 'u'd call!

Sometimes he'd gib a frolic—dat's de
  time you seed de fun:
De 'ristocratic fam'lies, dey 'u'd be
  dar, ebry one;   30
Dey'd hab a band from New Orleans
  to play for 'em to dance,
An' tell you what, de *supper* was a
  'tic'lar sarcumstance.

Well, times is changed. De war it
  come an' sot de niggers free,
An' now ol' Mahsr John ain't hardly
  wuf as much as me;
He had to pay his debts, an' so his
  lan' is mos'ly gone—
An' I declar' I's sorry for my pore ol'
  Mahsr John.

But when I heahs 'em talkin' 'bout
  some sullybrated man,
I listens to 'em quiet till dey done
  said all dey can,
An' den I 'lows dat in dem days 'at
  I remembers on,
Dat gemman warn't a patchin' onto
  my ol' Mahsr John.   40

1877

II. GEORGE WASHINGTON CABLE
(1844–1925)

BELLES DEMOISELLES PLANTATION

The original grantee was Count
——, assume the name to be De
Charleu; the old Creoles never forgive   10
a public mention. He was the French
king's commissary. One day, called
to France to explain the lucky accident of the commissariat having
burned down with his account-books

inside, he left his wife, a Choctaw
Comptesse, behind.

Arrived at court, his excuses were
accepted, and that tract granted him
where afterwards stood Belles Demoiselles Plantation. A man cannot remember everything! In a fit of
forgetfulness he married a French
gentlewoman, rich and beautiful, and
"brought her out." However, "All's
well that ends well"; a famine had
been in the colony, and the Choctaw
Comptesse had starved, leaving nought
but a half-caste orphan family lurking on the edge of the settlement,

earing our French gentlewoman's own new name, and being mentioned in Monsieur's will.

And the new Comptesse—she tarried but a twelve-month, left Monsieur lovely son, and departed, led out of his vain world by the swamp-fever.

From this son sprang the proud Creole family of De Charleu. It rose straight up, up, up, generation after generation, tall, branchless, slender, palm-like; and finally, in the time of which I am to tell, flowered with all the rare beauty of a century-plant, in Artemise, Innocente, Felicité, the twins Marie and Martha, Leontine and little Septima: the seven beautiful daughters for whom their home had been fitly named Belles Demoiselles.

The Count's grant had once been a long point, round which the Mississippi used to whirl, and seethe, and foam, that it was horrid to behold. Big whirlpools would open and wheel about in the savage eddies under the low bank, and close up again, and others open, and spin, and disappear. Great circles of muddy surface would boil up from hundreds of feet below, and gloss over, and seem to float away,—sink, come back again under water, and with only a soft hiss surge up again, and again drift off, and vanish. Every few minutes the loamy bank would tip down a great load of earth upon its besieger, and fall back a foot,—sometimes a yard,—and the writhing river would press after, until at last the Pointe was quite swallowed up, and the great river glided by in a majestic curve, and asked no more; the bank stood fast, the "caving" became a forgotten misfortune, and the diminished grant was a long, sweeping, willowy bend, rustling with miles of sugar-cane.

Coming up the Mississippi in the sailing craft of those early days, about the time one first could descry the white spires of the old St. Louis Cathedral, you would be pretty sure to spy, just over to your right under the levee, Belles Demoiselles Mansion, with its broad veranda and red painted cypress roof, peering over the embankment, like a bird in the nest, half hid by the avenue of willows which one of the departed De Charleus,— he that married a Marot,—had planted on the levee's crown.

The house stood unusually near the river, facing eastward, and standing four-square, with an immense veranda about its sides, and a flight of steps in front spreading broadly downward, as we open arms to a child. From the veranda nine miles of river were seen; and in their compass, near at hand, the shady garden full of rare and beautiful flowers; farther away broad fields of cane and rice, and the distant quarters of the slaves, and on the horizon everywhere a dark belt of cypress forest.

The master was old Colonel De Charleu,—Jean Albert Henri Joseph De Charleu-Marot, and "Colonel" by the grace of the first American governor. Monsieur,—he would not speak to any one who called him "Colonel," —was a hoary-headed patriarch. His step was firm, his form erect, his intellect strong and clear, his countenance classic, serene, dignified, commanding, his manners courtly, his voice musical,—fascinating. He had had his vices,—all his life; but had borne them, as his race does, with a serenity of conscience and a cleanness of mouth that left no outward blemish on the surface of the gentleman. He had gambled in Royal Street, drank hard in Orleans Street, run his adversary through in the duelling-ground at Slaughter-house Point, and danced and quarreled at the St. Philippe street-theater quadroon balls. Even now, with all his courtesy and bounty, and a hospitality which seemed to be entertaining angels, he was bitter-proud and penurious, and deep down in his hard-finished heart loved nothing but himself, his name, and his motherless children. But these!—their ravishing beauty was all but excuse enough for the unbounded idolatry of their father. Against these seven goddesses he never rebelled. Had they even required him to defraud old De Carlos—

I can hardly say.

Old De Carlos was his extremely distant relative on the Choctaw side. With this single exception, the narrow thread-like line of descent from the Indian wife, diminished to a mere strand by injudicious alliances, and deaths in the gutters of old New Orleans, was extinct. The name, by Spanish contact, had become De Carlos; but this one surviving bearer of it was known to all, and known only, as Injin Charlie.

One thing I never knew a Creole to do. He will not utterly go back on the ties of blood, no matter what sort of knots those ties may be. For one reason, he is never ashamed of his or his father's sins; and for another,—he will tell you—he is "all heart"!

So the different heirs of the De Charleu estate had always strictly regarded the rights and interests of the De Carloses, especially their ownership of a block of dilapidated buildings in a part of the city, which had once been very poor property, but was beginning to be valuable. This block had much more than maintained the last De Carlos through a long and lazy lifetime, and, as his household consisted only of himself, and an aged and crippled negress, the inference was irresistible that he "had money." Old Charlie, though by *alias* an "Injin," was plainly a dark white man, about as old as Colonel De Charleu, sunk in the bliss of deep ignorance, shrewd, deaf, and, by repute at least, unmerciful.

The Colonel and he always conversed in English. This rare accomplishment, which the former had learned from his Scotch wife,—the latter from up-river traders,—they found an admirable medium of communication, answering, better than French could, a similar purpose to that of the stick which we fasten to the bit of one horse and breast-gear of another, whereby each keeps his distance. Once in a while, too, by way of jest, English found its way among the ladies of Belles Demoiselles, always signifying that their sire was about to have business with old Charlie.

Now a long-standing wish to buy out Charlie troubled the Colonel. He had no desire to oust him unfairly; he was proud of being always fair; yet he did long to engross the whole estate under one title. Out of his luxurious idleness he had conceived this desire, and thought little of so slight an obstacle as being already somewhat in debt to old Charlie for money borrowed, and for which Belles Demoi-

elles was, of course, good, ten times
ver. Lots, buildings, rents, all, might
s well be his, he thought, to give,
eep, or destroy. "Had he but the old
1an's heritage. Ah! he might bring
hat into existence which his *belles
emoiselles* had been begging for,
since many years;' a home,—and such
home,—in the gay city. Here he
hould tear down this row of cottages, 10
nd make his garden wall; there that
ong rope-walk should give place to
ine-covered arbors; the bakery yon-
er should make way for a costly con-
ervatory; that wine warehouse
hould come down, and the mansion
o up. It should be the finest in the
tate. Men should never pass it, but
1ey should say—'the palace of the
e Charleus; a family of grand de- 20
ent, a people of elegance and bounty,
line as old as France, a fine old man,
nd seven daughters as beautiful as
1ppy; whoever dare attempt to marry
1ere must leave his own name behind
im!'

"The house should be of stones fitly
et, brought down in ships from the
nd of '*les Yankees*', and it should
1ve an airy belvedere, with a gilded
1age tiptoeing and shining on its
eak, and from it you should see, far
cross the gleaming folds of the river,
1e red roof of Belles Demoiselles,
1e country-seat. At the big stone
1te there should be a porter's lodge,
1d it should be a privilege even to
e the ground."

Truly they were a family fine
1ough, and fancy-free enough to have 40
1e wishes, yet happy enough where
ey were, to have had no wish but
 live there always.

To those, who, by whatever for-
1e, wandered into the garden of

Belles Demoiselles some summer afternoon as the sky was reddening towards
evening, it was lovely to see the family gathered out upon the tiled pavement at the foot of the broad front
steps, gayly chatting and jesting, with
that ripple of laughter that comes so
pleasingly from a bevy of girls. The
father would be found seated in their
midst, the center of attention and
compliment, witness, arbiter, umpire,
critic, by his beautiful children's
unanimous appointment, but the single
vassal, too, of seven absolute sov-
ereigns.

Now they would draw their chairs
near together in eager discussion of
some new step in the dance, or the
adjustment of some rich adornment.
Now they would start about him with
excited comments to see the eldest
fix a bunch of violets in his buttonhole. Now the twins would move
down a walk after some unusual
flower, and be greeted on their return
with the high pitched notes of delighted feminine surprise.

As evening came on they would
draw more quietly about their paternal center. Often their chairs were
forsaken, and they grouped themselves
on the lower steps, one above another,
and surrendered themselves to the tender influences of the approaching
night. At such an hour the passer on
the river, already attracted by the dark
figures of the broad-roofed mansion,
and its woody garden standing against
the glowing sunset, would hear the
voices of the hidden group rise from
the spot in the soft harmonies of an
evening song; swelling clearer and
clearer as the thrill of music warmed
them into feeling, and presently joined
by the deeper tones of the father's

voice; then, as the daylight passed quite away, all would be still, and he would know that the beautiful home had gathered its nestlings under its wings.

And yet, for mere vagary, it pleased them not to be pleased.

"Arti!" called one sister to another in the broad hall, one morning,—mock amazement in her distended eyes,—"something is goin' to took place!"

"*Comm-e-n-t?*"—long-drawn perplexity.

"Papa is goin' to town!"

The news passed up stairs.

"Inno!"—one to another meeting in a doorway,—"something is goin' to took place!"

"*Qu'est-ce-que c'est!*" vain attempt at gruffness.

"Papa is goin' to town!"

The unusual tidings were true. It was afternoon of the same day that the Colonel tossed his horse's bridle to his groom, and stepped up to old Charlie, who was sitting on his bench under a China-tree, his head, as was his fashion, bound in a Madras handkerchief. The "old man" was plainly under the effect of spirits, and smiled a deferential salutation without trusting himself to his feet.

"Eh, well Charlie!"—the Colonel raised his voice to suit his kinsman's deafness,—"how is those times with my friend Charlie?"

"Eh?" said Charlie, distractedly.

"Is that goin' well with my friend Charlie?"

"In de house,—call her,"—making a pretense of rising.

"*Non, non!* I don't want,"—the speaker paused to breathe—" 'ow is collection?"

"Oh!" said Charlie, "every day h[...] make me more poorer!"

"What do you hask for it?" aske[...] the planter indifferently, designati[...] the house by a wave of his whip.

"Ask for w'at?" said Injin Charl[...]

"De *house!* What you ask for it[...]

"I don't believe," said Charlie.

"What you would *take* for it[...] cried the planter.

"Wait for w'at?"

"What you would *take* for the who[...] block?"

"I don't want to sell him!"

"I'll give you *ten thousand doll[...]* for it."

"Ten t'ousand dollah for dis hous[...] Oh, no, dat is no price. He is blam[...] good old house,—dat old house[...] (Old Charlie and the Colonel nev[...] swore in the presence of each other[...] "Forty years dat old house didn't h[...] to be paint! I easy can get fif[...] t'ousand dollah for dat old house."

"Fifty thousand picayunes; yes[...] said the Colonel.

"She's a good house. Can ma[...] plenty money," pursued the deaf ma[...]

"That's what make you so rich, e[...] Charlie?"

"*Non,* I don't make nothing. T[...] blame clever, me, dat's de troub[...] She's a good house,—make mon[...] fast like a steamboat,—make a barr[...] full in a week! Me, I lose money [...] de days. Too blame clever."

"Charlie!"

"Eh?"

"Tell me what you'll take."

"Make? I don't make *nothin[...]* Too blame clever."

"What will you *take?*"

"Oh! I got enough already,—ha[...] drunk now."

"What will you take for the 'ouse[...]

"You want to buy her?"

"I don't know,"—(shrug),—"may-
e,—if you sell it cheap."

"She's a bully old house."

There was a long silence. By and
y old Charlie commenced—

"Old Injin Charlie is a low-down
g."

"*C'est vrai, oui!*" retorted the
olonel in an undertone.

"He's got Injin blood in him."

The Colonel nodded assent.

"But he's got some blame good
ood, too, ain't it?"

The Colonel nodded impatiently.

"*Bien!* Old Charlie's Injin blood
ys, 'sell de house, Charlie, you blame
d fool!' *Mais,* old Charlie's good
ood says, 'Charlie! if you sell dat
d house, Charlie, you low-down old
g, Charlie, what de Compte De
arleu make for you grace-gran'-
uzzer, de dev' can eat you, Charlie,
don't care.'"

"But you'll sell it anyhow, won't
u, old man?"

"No!" And the *no* rumbled off in
uttered oaths like thunder out on
e Gulf. The incensed old Colonel
eeled and started off.

"Curl!" (Colonel) said Charlie,
nding up unsteadily.

The planter turned with an inquir-
g frown.

"I'll trade with you!" said Charlie.

The Colonel was tempted. "'Ow'll
u trade?" he asked.

"My house for yours!"

The old Colonel turned pale with
ger. He walked very quickly back,
d came close up to his kinsman.

"Charlie!" he said.

"Injin Charlie,"—with a tipsy nod.
But by this time self-control was re-
ning. "Sell Belles Demoiselles to

you?" he said in a high key, and then
laughed "Ho, ho, ho!" and rode away.

A cloud, but not a dark one, overshadowed the spirits of Belles Demoiselles' plantation. The old master,
whose beaming presence had always
made him a shining Saturn, spinning
and sparkling within the bright circle
of his daughters, fell into musing fits,
started out of frowning reveries,
walked often by himself, and heard
business from his overseer fretfully.

No wonder. The daughters knew
his closeness in trade, and attributed
to it his failure to negotiate for the
Old Charlie buildings,—so to call
them. They began to depreciate
Belles Demoiselles. If a north wind
blew, it was too cold to ride. If a
shower had fallen, it was too muddy
to drive. In the morning the garden
was wet. In the evening the grasshopper was a burden. Ennui was
turned into capital; every headache
was interpreted a premonition of
ague; and when the native exuber-
ance of a flock of ladies without a
want or a care burst out in laughter
in the father's face, they spread their
French eyes, rolled up their little
hands, and with rigid wrists and mock
vehemence vowed and vowed again
that they only laughed at their misery,
and should pine to death unless they
could move to the sweet city. "Oh!
the theater! Oh! Orleans Street!
Oh! the masquerade! the Place
d'Armes! the ball!" and they would
call upon Heaven with French irreverence, and fall into each other's
arms, and whirl down the hall singing
a waltz, end with a grand collision and
fall, and, their eyes streaming merriment, lay the blame on the slippery

floor, that would some day be the death of the whole seven.

Three times more the fond father, thus goaded, managed, by accident,—business accident,—to see old Charlie and increase his offer; but in vain. He finally went to him formally.

"Eh?" said the deaf and distant relative. "For what you want him, eh? Why you don't stay where you halways be 'appy? Dis is a blame old rat-hole,—good for old Injin Charlie, —tha's all. Why you don't stay where you be halways 'appy? Why you don't buy somewheres else?"

"That's none of your business," snapped the planter. Truth was, his reasons were unsatisfactory even to himself.

A sullen silence followed. Then said Charlie spoke:

"Well, now, look here; I sell you old Charlie's house."

"*Bien!* and the whole block," said the Colonel.

"Hold on," said Charlie. "I sell you de 'ouse and de block. Den I go and git drunk, and go to sleep; de dev' comes along and says, 'Charlie! old Charlie, you blame low-down old dog, wake up! What you doin' here? Where's de 'ouse what Monsieur le Compte give your grace-gran-muzzer? Don't you see dat fine gentyman, De Charleu, done gone and tore him down and make him over new, you blame old fool, Charlie, you low-down old Injin dog!'"

"I'll give you forty thousand dollars," said the Colonel.

"For de 'ouse?"

"For all."

The deaf man shook his head.

"Forty-five!" said the Colonel.

"What a lie? For what you tell me 'What a lie?' I don't tell you n lie."

"*Non, non!* I give you *forty-five!* shouted the Colonel.

Charlie shook his head again.

"Fifty."

He shook it again.

The figures rose and rose to—

"Seventy-five!"

The answer was an invitation to g away and let the owner alone, as h was, in certain specified respects, th vilest of living creatures, and no com pany for a fine gentyman.

The "fine gentyman" longed to bla pheme,—but before old Charlie!—i the name of pride, how could he? H mounted and started away.

"Tell you what I'll make wid you said Charlie.

The other, guessing aright, turne back without dismounting, smiling.

"How much Belles Demoiselles ho me now?" asked the deaf one.

"One hundred and eighty thousan dollars," said the Colonel, firmly.

"Yass," said Charlie. "I don't war Belles Demoiselles."

The old Colonel's quiet laugh int mated it made no difference eith way.

"But me," continued Charlie, "m —I'm got le Compte De Charleu blood in me, any'ow,—a litt' bit, any 'ow, ain't it?"

The Colonel nodded that it was.

"*Bien!* If I go out of dis place an don't go to Belles Demoiselles, de pe ples will say,—day will say, 'O Charlie he been all doze time tell blame *lie!* He ain't no kin to his o grace-gran-muzzer, not a blame bi He don't got nary drop of De Charle blood to save his blame low-down o Injin soul! No, sare! What I wa

vid money, den? No, sare! My
lace for yours!"

He turned to go into the house, just
oo soon to see the Colonel make an
gly whisk at him with his riding-
whip. Then the Colonel, too, moved
ff.

Two or three times over, as he
mbled homeward, laughter broke
hrough his annoyance, as he recalled
ld Charlie's family pride and the pre-
umption of his offer. Yet each time
e could but think better of—not the
ffer to swap, but the preposterous
ncestral loyalty. It was so much
etter than he could have expected
om his "low-down" relative, and not
nlike his own whim withal—the
roposition which went with it was
rgiven.

This last defeat bore so harshly on
ie master of Belles Demoiselles, that
ie daughters, reading chagrin in his
ce, began to repent. They loved
ieir father as daughters can, and
hen they saw their pretended dejec-
on harassing him seriously they re-
rained their complaints, displayed
ore than ordinary tenderness, and
eroically and ostentatiously con-
uded there was no place like Belles
emoiselles. But the new mood
uched him more than the old, and
ily refined his discontent. Here was
man, rich without the care of riches,
ee from any real trouble, happiness
native to his house as perfume to
s garden, deliberately, as it were
ith premeditated malice, taking joy
y the shoulder and bidding her be
ne to town, whither he might easily
ive followed, only that the very same
icestral nonsense that kept Injin
harlie from selling the old place for
vice its value prevented him from

choosing any other spot for a city
home.

Heaven sometimes pities such rich
men and sends them trouble.

But by and by the charm of nature and the merry hearts around prevailed; the fit of exalted sulks passed
off, and after a while the year flared
up at Christmas, flickered, and went
out.

New Year came and passed; the
beautiful garden of Belles Demoiselles
put on its spring attire; the seven fair
sisters moved from rose to rose; the
cloud of discontent had warmed into
invisible vapor in the rich sunlight of
family affection, and on the common
memory the only scar of last year's
wound was old Charlie's sheer imper-
tinence in crossing the caprice of the
De Charleus. The cup of gladness
seemed to fill with the filling of the
river.

How high that river was! Its tremendous current rolled and tumbled
and spun along, hustling the long
funeral flotillas of drift,—and how
near shore it came! Men were out
day and night, watching the levee.
On windy nights even the old Colonel
took part, and grew light-hearted with
occupation and excitement, as every
minute the river threw a white arm
over the levee's top, as though it
would vault over. But all held fast,
and, as the summer drifted in, the
water sunk down into its banks and
looked quite incapable of harm.

On a summer afternoon of uncommon mildness, old Colonel Jean Albert Henry Joseph De Charleu-Marot,
being in a mood for reverie, slipped
the custody of his feminine rulers
and sought the crown of the levee,
where it was his wont to promenade.

Presently he sat upon a stone bench, —a favorite seat. Before him lay his broad-spread fields; near by, his lordly mansion; and being still,—perhaps by female contact,—somewhat sentimental, he fell to musing on his past. It was hardly worthy to be proud of. All its morning was reddened with mad frolic, and far toward the meridian it was marred with elegant rioting. Pride had kept him well-nigh useless, and despised the honors won by valor; gaming had dimmed prosperity; death had taken his heavenly wife; voluptuous ease had mortgaged his lands; and yet his house still stood, his sweet-smelling fields were still fruitful, his name was fame enough; and yonder and yonder, among the trees and flowers, like angels walking in Eden, were the seven goddesses of his only worship.

Just then a slight sound behind him brought him to his feet. He cast his eyes anxiously to the outer edge of the little strip of bank between the levee's base and the river. There was nothing visible. He paused, with his ear toward the water, his face full of frightened expectation. Ha! There came a single plashing sound, like some great beast slipping into the river, and little waves in a wide semi-circle came out from under the bank and spread over the water.

"My God!"

He plunged down the levee and bounded through the low weeds to the edge of the bank. It was sheer, and the water about four feet below. He did not stand quite on the edge, but fell upon his knees a couple of yards away, wringing his hands, moaning and weeping, and staring through his watery eyes at a fine, long crevice just discernible under the matte grass, and curving outward on eithe hand toward the river.

"My God!" he sobbed aloud; "m God!" and even while he called, b God answered: the tough Bermud grass stretched and snapped, the cre ice slowly became a gape, and softl gradually, with no sound but th closing of the water at last, a ton more of earth settled into the boilin eddy and disappeared.

At the same instant a pulse of th breeze brought from the garden be hind, the joyous, thoughtless laught of the fair mistresses of Belles Dem oiselles.

The old Colonel sprang up ar clambered over the levee. Then for ing himself to a more compose movement he hastened into the hous and ordered his horse.

"Tell my children to make merr while I am gone," he left word. shall be back to-night," and the horse hoofs clattered down a by-road lea ing to the city.

"Charlie," said the planter, ridin up to a window, from which the ol man's nightcap was thrust out, "wha you say, Charlie,—my house f yours, eh, Charlie—what you say

"'Ello!" said Charlie; "from whe you come from dis time of to-night

"I come from the Exchange." (small fraction of the truth.)

"What you want?" said matter-o fact Charlie.

"I come to trade."

The low-down relative drew t worsted off his ears. "Oh! yass," l said with an uncertain air.

"Well, old man Charlie, what y say; my house for yours,—like y said,—eh, Charlie?"

"I dunno," said Charlie; "it's nearly mine now. Why you don't stay dare youse'f?"

"*Because I don't want!*" said the Colonel savagely; "is dat reason enough for you? you better take me in de notion, old man, I tell you,—yes!"

Charlie never winced; but how his answer delighted the Colonel! Quoth Charlie:

"I don't care—I take him!—*mais*, possession give right off."

"Not the whole plantation, Charlie; only"—

"I don't care," said Charlie; "we easy can fix dat. *Mais,* what for you don't want to keep him? I don't want him. You better keep him."

"Don' you try to make no fool of me, old man," cried the planter.

"Oh, no!" said the other. "Oh, no! but you make a fool of yourself, in't it?"

The dumbfounded Colonel stared; Charlie went on:

"Yass! Belles Demoiselles is more vort' dan tree block like dis one. I pass by dare since two weeks. Oh, pritty Belles Demoiselles! De cane was wave in de wind, de garden smell ike a bouquet, de white-cap was jump up and down on de river; seven *elles demoiselles* was ridin' on horses. 'Pritty, pritty, pritty!' says ld Charlie; ah! *Monsieur le père,* 'ow appy, 'appy, 'appy!"

"Yass!" he continued—the Colonel till staring—"le Compte De Charleu ave two familie. One was low-down Choctaw, one was high-up *noblesse.* Ie gave the low-down Choctaw dis ld rat-hole; he give Belles Demoiselles to you gran-fozzer; and now ou don't be *satisfait.* What I'll do

wid Belles Demoiselles? She'll break me in two years, yass. And what you'll do wid old Charlie's house, eh? You'll tear her down and make you'se'f a blame old fool. I rather wouldn't trade!"

The planter caught a big breathful of anger, but Charlie went straight on:

"I rather wouldn't, *mais* I will do it for you;—just the same, like Monsieur le Compte would say, 'Charlie, you old fool, I want to shange houses wid you.'"

So long as the Colonel suspected irony he was angry, but as Charlie seemed, after all, to be certainly in earnest, he began to feel conscience-stricken. He was by no means a tender man, but his lately-discovered misfortune had unhinged him, and this strange, undeserved, disinterested family fealty on the part of Charlie touched his heart. And should he still try to lead him into the pitfall he had dug? He hesitated;—no, he would show him the place by broad daylight, and if he chose to overlook the "caving bank," it would be his own fault;—a trade's a trade.

"Come," said the planter, "come at my house to-night; to-morrow we look at the place before breakfast, and finish the trade."

"For what?" said Charlie.

"Oh, because I got to come in town in the morning."

"I don't want," said Charlie. "How I'm goin' to come dere?"

"I git you a horse at the liberty stable."

"Well—anyhow—I don't care—I'll go." And they went.

When they had ridden a long time, and were on the road darkened by hedges of Cherokee rose, the Colonel called behind him to the "low-down" scion:

"Keep the road, old man."

"Eh?"

"Keep the road."

"Oh, yes; all right; I keep my word; we don't goin' to play no tricks, eh?"

But the Colonel seemed not to hear. His ungenerous design was beginning to be hateful to him. Not only old Charlie's unprovoked goodness was prevailing; the eulogy on Belles Demoiselles had stirred the depths of an intense love for his beautiful home. True, if he held to it, the caving of the bank, at its present fearful speed, would let the house into the river within three months; but were it not better to lose it so, than sell his birthright? Again,—coming back to the first thought,—to betray his own blood! It was only Injin Charlie; but had not the De Charleu blood just spoken out in him? Unconsciously he groaned.

After a time they struck a path approaching the plantation in the rear, and a little after, passing from behind a clump of live-oaks, they came in sight of the villa. It looked so like a gem, shining through its dark grove, so like a great glow-worm in the dense foliage, so significant of luxury and gayety, that the poor master, from an overflowing heart, groaned again.

"What?" asked Charlie.

The Colonel only drew his rein, and, dismounting mechanically, contemplated the sight before him. The high, arched doors and windows were thrown wide to the summer air; from every opening the bright light of nu-merous candelabra darted out upon the sparkling foliage of magnolia and bay, and here and there in the spacious verandas a colored lantern swayed in the gentle breeze. A sound of revel fell on the ear, the music of harps; and across one window brighter than the rest, flitted, once or twice, the shadows of dancers. But oh! the shadows flitting across the heart of the fair mansion's master

"Old Charlie," said he, gazing fondly at his house, "you and me is both old, eh?"

"Yass," said the stolid Charlie.

"And we has both been bad enough in our time, eh, Charlie?"

Charlie, surprised at the tender tone, repeated "Yass."

"And you and me is mighty close?"

"Blame close, yass."

"But you never know me to cheat old man!"

"No,"—impassively.

"And do you think I would cheat you now?"

"I dunno," said Charlie. "I don't believe."

"Well, old man, old man,"—his voice began to quiver,—"I shan't cheat you now. My God!—old man I tell you—you better not make the trade!"

"Because for what?" asked Charlie in plain anger; but both looked quickly toward the house! The Colonel tossed his hands wildly in the air, rushed forward a step or two, and giving one fearful scream of agony and fright, fell forward on his face in the path. Old Charlie stood transfixed with horror. Belles Demoiselles, the realm of maiden beauty the home of merriment, the house o lancing, all in the tremor and glow of pleasure, suddenly sunk, with one short, wild wail of terror—sunk, sunk, down, down, down, into the merciless, unfathomable flood of the Mississippi.

Twelve long months were midnight to the mind of the childless father; when they were only half gone, he took his bed; and every day, and every night, old Charlie, the "low-down," the "fool," watched him tenderly, tended him lovingly, for the sake of his name, his misfortunes and his broken heart. No woman's step crossed the floor of the sick-chamber, whose western dormer-windows overpeered the dingy architecture of old Charlie's block; Charlie and a skilled physician, the one all interest, the other all gentleness, hope, and patience—these only entered by the door; but by the window came in a sweet-scented evergreen vine, transplanted from the caving bank of Belles Demoiselles. It caught the rays of sunset in its flowery net and let them softly in upon the sick man's bed; gathered the glancing beams of the moon at midnight, and often wakened the sleeper to look, with his mindless eyes, upon their pretty silver fragments strewn upon the floor.

By and by there seemed—there was—a twinkling dawn of returning reason. Slowly, peacefully, with an increase unseen from day to day, the light of reason came into the eyes, and speech became coherent; but withal there came a failing of the wrecked body, and the doctor said that monsieur was both better and worse.

One evening, as Charlie sat by the vine-clad window with his fireless pipe in his hand, the old Colonel's eyes fell full upon his own, and rested there.

"Charl—," he said with an effort, and his delighted nurse hastened to the bedside and bowed his best ear. There was an unsuccessful effort or two, and then he whispered, smiling with sweet sadness,—

"We didn't trade."

The truth, in this case, was a secondary matter to Charlie; the main point was to give a pleasing answer. So he nodded his head decidedly, as who should say—"Oh yes, we did, it was a bona-fide swap!" but when he saw the smile vanish, he tried the other expedient and shook his head with still more vigor, to signify that they had not so much as approached a bargain; and the smile returned.

Charlie wanted to see the vine recognized. He stepped backward to the window with a broad smile, shook the foliage, nodded and looked smart.

"I know," said the Colonel, with beaming eyes, "—many weeks."

The next day—

"Charl—"

The best ear went down.

"Send for a priest."

The priest came, and was alone with him a whole afternoon. When he left, the patient was very haggard and exhausted, but smiled and would not suffer the crucifix to be removed from his breast.

One more morning came. Just before dawn Charlie, lying on a pallet in the room, thought he was called, and came to the bedside.

"Old man," whispered the failing invalid, "is it caving yet?"

Charlie nodded.

"It won't pay you out."

"Oh, dat makes not'ing," said Charlie. Two big tears rolled down his brown face. "Dat makes not'in."

The Colonel whispered once more:—

"Mes belles demoiselles! in paradise;—in the garden—I shall be with them at sunrise"; and so it was.

1874

III. LAFCADIO HEARN
(1850–1904)

From *CREOLE SKETCHES* *

THE GLAMOUR OF NEW ORLEANS

The season has come at last when strangers may visit us without fear, and experience with unalloyed pleasure the first delicious impression of the most beautiful and picturesque old city in North America. For in this season is the glamour of New Orleans strongest upon those whom she attracts to her from less hospitable climates, and fascinates by her nights of magical moonlight, and her days of dreamy languors and perfumes. There are few who can visit her for the first time without delight; and few who can ever leave her without regret; and none who can forget her strange charm when they have once felt its influence. To a native of the bleaker Northern clime—if he have any poetical sense of the beautiful in nature, any love of bright verdure and luxuriance of landscape—the approach to the city by river must be in itself something indescribable pleasant. The white steamer gliding through an unfamiliar world of blue and green—blue above and blue below, with a long strip of low green land alone to break the ethereal azure; the waving cane; the evergreen fringe of groves weird with moss; the tepid breezes and golden sunlight—all deepening in their charm as the city is neared, make the voyage seem beautiful as though one were sailing to some far-off glimmering Eden, into the garden of Paradise itself. And then, the first impression of the old Creole city slumbering under the glorious sun; of its quaint houses; its shaded streets; its suggestions of a hundred years ago; its contrasts of agreeable color; its streets reëchoing the tongues of many nations; its general look of somnolent contentment; its verdant antiquity; its venerable memorials and monuments; its eccentricities of architecture; its tropical gardens; its picturesque surprises; its warm atmosphere drowsy perhaps with the perfume of orange flowers, and thrilled with the fantastic music of mocking-birds—cannot ever be wholly forgotten. For a hundred years and more has New Orleans been drawing hither wandering souls from all the ends of the earth. The natives of India and Japan have walked upon her pavements; Chinese and swarthy natives of Manila; children of the Antilles and of South America; subjects of the Sultan and sailors of the Ionian Sea have sought homes here. All civilized nations have sent wandering children hither. All cities of the

* The selections from *Creole Sketches* are used by permission of, and by arrangement with, Houghton Mifflin Company.

North, East, and West have yielded up some restless souls to the far-off southern city, whose spell is so mystic, so sweet, so universal. And to these wondering and wandering ones, this sleepy, beautiful, quaint old city murmurs: "Rest with me. I am old; but thou hast never met with a younger more beautiful than I. I well in eternal summer; I dream in perennial sunshine; I sleep in magical moonlight. My streets are flecked with strange sharp shadows; and sometimes also the Shadow of Death falleth upon them; but if thou wilt not fear, thou art safe. My charms are not the charms of much gold and great riches; but thou mayest feel with me such hope and content as thou hast never felt before. I offer thee eternal summer, and a sky divinely blue; sweet breezes and sweet perfumes, bright fruits, and flowers fairer than the rainbow. Rest with me. For if thou leavest me, thou must forever remember me with regret." And assuredly those who wander from her may never cease to behold her in their dreams—quaint, beautiful, and sunny as of old—and feel at long intervals the return of the first charm—the first delicious fascination of the fairest city of the South.

1878

A CREOLE TYPE

It is a little curious how the old Creole element preserves its ancient customs and manners in the very heart of the changes that are going on about it. At half-past nine or ten o'clock the American city is all alive —a blaze of gas and a whirl of pleasure. The old French town is asleep; the streets are deserted; and the shadow of a pedestrian makes a moving black speck against the moonlight on the pavement only at long intervals. Creoledom wakes up as slowly and cautiously as possible; and has not fairly begun to enter upon the business of the day until the sun has warmed the streets. The comparatively new generation of American citizens, when brought into contact with this older population, is utterly unable to understand the difference of character; and shuns as much as possible the transaction of business with it—which contents the Creoles perfectly well. They seem to tolerate those who understand them, and to abominate those who do not, and propose to live in the good old way as long as possible—marrying and giving in marriage, aiding one another in a good brotherly way, and keeping themselves to themselves. If there is one virtue they possess remarkably, it is the virtue of minding their own affairs—which, alas! cannot always be said of all other people who dwell in New Orleans.

Nothing, perhaps, can be funnier than the contrast of character brought out by the attempt of a stiff-mannered stranger to do business with a typical Creole, especially if the latter be of the fair sex. Let us imagine, for example, the episode of renting a house to a foreigner—somebody whom chance or curiosity has prompted to seek quarters in the old-fashioned part of the city. The stranger is a little phlegmatic; the woman is as much the opposite as any human being could well be—a little dark, tropically dark, but quite attractive, with magnetic eyes, an electric tongue, and an utter indifference to those ordinary feelings which prompt landladies to play the agreeable;—proud as a queen, and quite as determined to show her own individuality as the stranger is to conceal his own. She has a nice little house; and the stranger would like to rent it. She would also like to rent it; but only according to her own original idea of conditions, and she would never think of concealing her inmost feelings on the subject. She is determined that nobody shall impose upon her, and that fact she proposes to explain very forcibly forthwith; the stranger appears to be a good sort of man, but appearances are so deceitful in this wicked world!

SHE—"Ah, yes, monsieur, I have a nice little house. Let me beg of you to wait a moment until I open the other door, so that you can enter my parlor."

HE—"But what is the rent of the house?"

SHE [*in a voice sweeter than the sweetest honey*]—"One minute!—this way, monsieur—come in; be seated, if you please."

HE—"But what is the rent of—"

SHE [*shutting the door, and placing herself before it like a statue of animated bronze, and suddenly changing the sweet voice for a deep and extraordinarily vibrant alto*]—"Ah, now, monsieur, let us at once understand one another. I have a nice little house. Good! You want a nice little house. Good! Let us under-

stand one another. In the first place I do not rent my house to everybody, monsieur. Oh, no, no, No!! [*crescendo*].

HE—"But what is the rent of—"

SHE [*imperiously, terrifying him into silence with a flash of her black eyes*]—"Do not interrupt me, monsieur. Three things I require from a tenant. Do you know what the first is? No?—then I will tell you. Cash, CASH, CASH! [*crescendo*]—right here in my hand—in advance—ah, yes, all the time in advance."

HE [*very timidly*]—"Yes, certainly—I know—of course!—I expected;—but what is—"

SHE [*in a voice like the deepest tone of a passionately agitated harp*]—"*Attends, donc, monsieur*. The second thing which I require from a tenant is a guarantee that he will stay. Ah, yes! I am not one of those who rent houses for a week, or a month, or six months. *Mon Dieu, non!* I must have people who Stay, STAY, STAY [*pianissimo*]; and they must stay a long, long time. You must not come to me if you want a house only for—"

HE [*with a last desperate effort which happens to be partially successful*]—"O madam, I want to stay for a number of years in the house, if I take it; but I cannot take it until I have seen it."

SHE—"You shall see it, monsieur, you shall see it [*parenthetically*]. Now the third thing which I require from a tenant is absolute cleanliness, absolute, absolute! No spitting on the walls, no dirt upon the doors, no grease upon the planking, no *cochonnerie* in the yard. You understand ne, monsieur? Yes!—you shall see he house: these are the keys."

He—"But what is the rent of—"

She [*frightening him into motionessness by a sudden gypsy-like gesure*]—"Ah, monsieur, but I cannot rust you with these keys. No; my ervant shall go with you. I cannot ave all the doors of my house left pen. No; I have had too much experience. My servant shall go with ou. She shall bring me back my eys. Marie! Come here! Go, nonsieur, see the house!"

He [*resignedly*]—"Thanks, but may ask what is—"

She [*with a superb gesture of withring disgust and another of terrible etermination*]—"Do you not know, ir, that I would rather shut the house p until the last day of the world han rent it to the *canaille!* Ah, the *anaille!* Monsieur! Ah! the *canaille, he canaille!*"

[*These last words, with an inexessible look of horror upon her face,* *which would make the stranger laugh if he were not afraid to laugh.*]

He—"And the rent is—"

She [*sweetly as a rose-fed nightingale*]—"Twenty-five dollars to a responsible party, monsieur."

The stranger is by this time fairly mesmerized. He has listened to a sermon, heard an oration, received a reproof, watched a most marvelous piece of natural acting by a beautiful woman, and felt his own will and purpose completely crushed out of him by the superior vitality and willpower of this wonderful creature, whose gestures, graceful as a bayadère's, seemed to weave a spell of magnetism about him. He sees the house; pays faithfully in advance; gives proper recommendations; and never forgets the three requisites which his landlady taught him as forcibly as though she had burned the words into his brain with a red-hot iron.

1879

CHAR-COAL

lack—coalee—coaly!
  Coaly-coaly; coaly-coaly; coal-coal-coal.
  Coaly-coaly!
  Coal-ee! Nice!
  Cha'coal!
  Twenty-five! Whew!
  O charco-oh-oh-oh-oh-oh-lee!
  Oh-lee!
  Oh-lee-e!
[You get some coal in your mout', oung fellow, if you don't keep it ut.]   10

Pretty coalee-oh-ee!
Char-coal!
Cha-ah-ah-ahr-coal!
Coaly-coaly!
Charbon! due charbon, Madame!
  Bon charbon? Point! Ai-ai!
Tonnerre de Dieu!
  Char-r-r-r-r-r-rbon!
  A-a-a-a-a-w! High-ya-a-ah! High-yah!   19
  Vingt-cinq! Nice coalee! Coalee!
  Coaly-coal-coal!
  Pretty coaly!
  Charbon de Paris!
  De Paris, Madame; de Paris!

1880

From *JAPAN: AN ATTEMPT AT INTERPRETATION* *

STRANGENESS AND CHARM

The majority of the first impressions of Japan recorded by travellers are pleasurable impressions. Indeed, there must be something lacking, or something very harsh, in the nature to which Japan can make no emotional appeal. The appeal itself is the clue to a problem; and that problem is the character of a race and of its civilization.

My own first impressions of Japan, —Japan as seen in the white sunshine of a perfect spring day,—had doubtless much in common with the average of such experiences. I remember especially the wonder and the delight of the vision. The wonder and the delight have never passed away: they are often revived for me even now, by some chance happening, after fourteen years of sojourn. But the reason of these feelings was difficult to learn, —or at least to guess; for I cannot yet claim to know much about Japan. . . . Long ago the best and dearest Japanese friend I ever had said to me, a little before his death: "When you find, in four or five years more, that you cannot understand the Japanese at all, then you will begin to know something about them." After having realized the truth of my friend's prediction,—after having discovered that I cannot understand the Japanese at all,—I feel better qualified to attempt this essay.

As first perceived, the outward strangeness of things in Japan produces (in certain minds, at least) queer thrill impossible to describe,— a feeling of weirdness which comes t us only with the perception of th totally unfamiliar. You find yoursel moving through queer small street full of odd small people, wearing robe and sandals of extraordinary shapes and you can scarcely distinguish th sexes at sight. The houses are cor structed and furnished in ways alie to all your experience; and you ar astonished to find that you cannot cor ceive the use or meaning of numbe less things on display in the shop Food-stuffs of unimaginable deriv tion; utensils of enigmatic forms emblems incomprehensible of som mysterious belief; strange masks an toys that commemorate legends gods or demons; odd figures, too, the gods themselves, with monstrou ears and smiling faces,—all these yc may perceive as you wander about though you must also notice telegrap poles and typewriters, electric lam and sewing machines. Everywhere c signs and hangings, and on the back of people passing by, you will observ wonderful Chinese characters; and th wizardry of all these texts makes th dominant tone of the spectacle.

Further acquaintance with this fa tastic world will in nowise diminis the sense of strangeness evoked by th first vision of it. You will soon ol serve that even the physical actio of the people are unfamiliar,—th their work is done in ways the opp site of Western ways. Tools are surprising shapes, and are handl after surprising methods: the blac smith squats at his anvil, wieldi a hammer such as no Western smi could use without long practice; th

* Used by permission of the Macmillan Company.

carpenter pulls, instead of pushing, his extraordinary plane and saw. Always the left is the right side, and the right side the wrong; and keys must be turned, to open or close a lock, in what we are accustomed to think the wrong direction. Mr. Percival Lowell has truthfully observed that the Japanese speak backwards, read backwards, write backwards,—and that this is "only the *abc* of their contrariety." For the habit of writing backwards there are obvious evolutional reasons; and the requirements of Japanese calligraphy sufficiently explain why the artist pushes his brush or pencil instead of pulling it. But why, instead of putting the thread through the eye of the needle, should the Japanese maiden slip the eye of the needle over the point of the thread? Perhaps the most remarkable, out of a hundred possible examples of antipodal action, is furnished by the Japanese art of fencing. The swordsman, delivering his blow with both hands, does not pull the blade towards him in the moment of striking, but pushes it from him. He uses it, indeed, as other Asiatics do, not on the principle of the wedge, but of the saw; yet there is a pushing motion where we should expect a pulling motion in the stroke. . . . These and other forms of unfamiliar action are strange enough to suggest the notion of a humanity even physically as little related to us as might be the population of another planet,—the notion of some anatomical unlikeness. No such unlikeness, however, appears to exist; and all this oppositeness probably implies, not so much the outcome of a human experience entirely independent of Aryan experience, as the outcome

of an experience evolutionally younger than our own.

Yet that experience has been one of no mean order. Its manifestations do not merely startle: they also delight. The delicate perfection of workmanship, the light strength and grace of objects, the power manifest to obtain the best results with the least material, the achieving of mechanical ends by the simplest possible means, the comprehension of irregularity as æsthetic value, the shapeliness and perfect taste of everything, the sense displayed of harmony in tints or colors,—all this must convince you at once that our Occident has much to learn from this remote civilization, not only in matters of art and taste, but in matters likewise of economy and utility. It is no barbarian fancy that appeals to you in those amazing porcelains, those astonishing embroideries, those wonders of lacquer and ivory and bronze, which educate imagination in unfamiliar ways. No: these are the products of a civilization which became, within its own limits, so exquisite that none but an artist is capable of judging its manufactures,—a civilization that can be termed imperfect only by those who would also term imperfect the Greek civilization of three thousand years ago.

But the underlying strangeness of this world,—the psychological strangeness,—is much more startling than the visible and superficial. You begin to suspect the range of it after having discovered that no adult Occidental can perfectly master the language. East and West the fundamental parts of human nature—the emotional bases of it—are much the same: the mental difference between a Japanese and a European child is mainly potential. But with growth the difference rapidly develops and widens, till it becomes, in adult life, inexpressible. The whole of the Japanese mental superstructure evolves into forms having nothing in common with Western psychological development: the expression of thought becomes regulated, and the expression of emotion inhibited in ways that bewilder and astound. The ideas of this people are not our ideas; their sentiments are not our sentiments; their ethical life represents for us regions of thought and emotion yet unexplored, or perhaps long forgotten. Any one of their ordinary phrases, translated into Western speech, makes hopeless nonsense; and the literal rendering into Japanese of the simplest English sentence would scarcely be comprehended by any Japanese who had never studied a European tongue. Could you learn all the words in a Japanese dictionary, your acquisition would not help you in the least to make yourself understood in speaking, unless you had learned also to think like a Japanese,—that is to say, to think backwards, to think upside-down and inside-out, to think in directions totally foreign to Aryan habit. Experience in the acquisition of European languages can help you to learn Japanese about as much as it could help you to acquire the language spoken by the inhabitants of Mars. To be able to use the Japanese tongue as a Japanese uses it, one would need to be born again, and to have one's mind completely reconstructed, from the foundation upwards. It is possible

that a person of European parentage born in Japan, and accustomed from infancy to use the vernacular, might retain in after-life that *instinctive* knowledge which could alone enable him to adapt his mental relations to the relations of any Japanese environment. There is actually an Englishman named Black, born in Japan, whose proficiency in the language is proved by the fact that he is able to earn a fair income as a professional story-teller (*hanashika*). But this is an extraordinary case. . . . As for the literary language, I need only observe that to make acquaintance with it requires very much more than a knowledge of several thousand Chinese characters. It is safe to say that no Occidental can undertake to render at sight any literary text laid before him—indeed the number of native scholars able to do so is very small;—and although the learning displayed in this direction by various Europeans may justly compel our admiration, the work of none could have been given to the world without Japanese help.

But as the outward strangeness of Japan proves to be full of beauty, so the inward strangeness appears to have its charm,—an ethical charm reflected in the common life of the people. The attractive aspects of that life do not indeed imply, to the ordinary observer, a psychological differentiation measurable by scores of centuries: only a scientific mind, like that of Mr Percival Lowell, immediately perceives the problem presented. The less gifted stranger, if naturally sympathetic, is merely pleased and puzzled and tries to explain, by his own ex perience of happy life on the other side of the world, the social conditions that charm him. Let us suppose that one has the good fortune of being able to live for six months or a year in some old-fashioned town of the interior. From the beginning of this sojourn he can scarcely fail to be impressed by the apparent kindliness and joyousness of the existence about him. In the relations of the people to each other, as well as in all their relations to himself, he will find a constant amenity, a tact, a good-nature such as he will elsewhere have met with only in the friendship of exclusive circles. Everybody greets everybody with happy looks and pleasant words; faces are always smiling; the commonest incidents of everyday life are transfigured by a courtesy at once so artless and so faultless that it appears to spring directly from the heart, without any teaching. Under all circumstances a certain outward cheerfulness never fails: no matter what troubles may come,—storm or fire, flood or earthquake,—the laughter of greeting voices, the bright smile and graceful bow, the kindly inquiry and the wish to please, continue to make existence beautiful. Religion brings no gloom into this sunshine: before the Buddhas and the gods folk smile as they pray; the temple-courts are playgrounds for the children; and within the enclosure of the great public shrines—which are places of festivity rather than of solemnity—dancing-platforms are erected. Family existence would seem to be everywhere characterized by gentleness: there is no visible quarrelling, no loud harshness, no tears and reproaches. Cruelty, even to animals, appears to be unknown: one sees farmers, coming to town, trudging patiently beside their horses or oxen, aiding their dumb companions to bear the burden, and using no whips or goads. Drivers or pullers of carts will turn out of their way, under the most provoking circumstances, rather than overrun a lazy dog or a stupid chicken. . . . For no inconsiderable time one may live in the midst of appearances like these, and perceive nothing to spoil the pleasure of the experience.

Of course the conditions of which I speak are now passing away; but they are still to be found in the remoter districts. I have lived in districts where no case of theft had occurred for hundreds of years,—where the newly-built prisons of Meiji remained empty and useless,—where the people left their doors unfastened by night as well as by day. These facts are familiar to every Japanese. In such a district, you might recognize that the kindness shown to you, as a stranger, is the consequence of official command; but how explain the goodness of the people to each other? When you discover no harshness, no rudeness, no dishonesty, no breaking of laws, and learn that this social condition has been the same for centuries, you are tempted to believe that you have entered into the domain of a morally superior humanity. All this soft urbanity, impeccable honesty, ingenuous kindliness of speech and act, you might naturally interpret as conduct directed by perfect goodness of heart. And the simplicity that delights you is no simplicity of barbarism. Here every one has been taught; every one knows how to write and speak beautifully, how to compose poetry, how to behave politely; there is everywhere cleanliness and good taste; interiors are bright and pure; the daily use of the hot bath is universal. How refuse to be charmed by a civilization in which every relation appears to be governed by altruism, every action directed by duty, and every object shaped by art? You cannot help being delighted by such conditions, or feeling indignant at hearing them denounced as "heathen." And according to the degree of altruism within yourself, these good folk will be able, without any apparent effort, to make you happy. The mere sensation of the *milieu* is a placid happiness: it is like the sensation of a dream in which people greet us exactly as we like to be greeted, and say to us all that we like to hear, and do for us all that we wish to have done,—people moving soundlessly through spaces of perfect repose, all bathed in vapory light. Yes—for no little time these fairy-folk can give you all the soft bliss of sleep. But sooner or later, if you dwell long with them, your contentment will prove to have much in common with the happiness of dreams. You will never forget the dream,— never; but it will lift at last, like those vapors of spring which lend preternatural loveliness to a Japanese landscape in the forenoon of radiant days. Really you are happy because you have entered bodily into Fairyland,—into a world that is not, and never could be your own. You have been transported out of your own century—over spaces enormous of perished time—into an era forgotten, into a vanished age,—back to something ancient as Egypt or Nineveh. That is the secret of the strangeness and beauty of things,—the secret of the thrill they give,—the secret of the elfish charm of the people and their ways. Fortunate mortal! the tide of Time has turned for you! But remember that here all is enchantment —that you have fallen under the spell of the dead,—that the lights and the colors and the voices must fade away at last into emptiness and silence.

·   ·   ·   ·   ·

Some of us, at least, have often wished that it were possible to live for a season in the beautiful vanished world of Greek culture. Inspired by our first acquaintance with the charm of Greek art and thought this wish comes to us even before we are capable of imagining the true conditions of the antique civilization. If the wish could be realized, we should certainly find it impossible to accommodate ourselves to those conditions,—not so much because of the difficulty of learning the environment, as because of the much greater difficulty of feeling just as people used to feel some thirty centuries ago. In spite of all that has been done for Greek studies since the Renaissance, we are still unable to understand many aspects of the old Greek life: no modern mind can really feel, for example, those sentiments and emotions to which the great tragedy of Œdipus made appeal. Nevertheless we are much in advance of our forefathers of the eighteenth century, as regards the knowledge of Greek civilization. In the time of the French revolution, it was thought possible to reëstablish in France the conditions of a Greek republic, and to educate children according to the system of Sparta. To-day we are well aware that no mind developed by modern civilization could find happiness under any of those socialistic despotisms which existed in all the cities of the ancient world before the Roman conquest. We could no more mingle with the old Greek life, if it were resurrected for us,—no more become a part of it,—than we could change our mental identities. But how much would we not give for the delight of beholding it,—for the joy of attending one festival in Corinth, or of witnessing the Pan-Hellenic games? . . .

And yet, to witness the revival of some perished Greek civilization,—to walk about the very Crotona of Pythagoras,—to wander through the Syracuse of Theocritus,—were not any more of a privilege than is the opportunity actually afforded us to study Japanese life. Indeed, from the evolutional point of view, it were less of a privilege,—since Japan offers us the living spectacle of conditions older, and psychologically much farther away from us, than those of any Greek period with which art and literature have made us closely acquainted.

The reader scarcely needs to be reminded that a civilization less evolved than our own, and intellectually remote from us, is not on that account to be regarded as necessarily inferior in all respects. Hellenic civilization at its best represented an early stage of sociological evolution; yet the arts which it developed still furnish our supreme and unapproachable ideals of beauty. So, too, this much more archaic civilization of Old Japan attained an average of æsthetic and moral culture well worthy of our wonder and praise. Only a shallow mind—a very shallow mind—will pronounce the best of that culture inferior. But Japanese civilization is peculiar to a degree for which there is perhaps no Western parallel, since it offers us the spectacle of many successive layers of alien culture superimposed above the simple indigenous basis, and forming a very bewilderment of complexity. Most of this alien culture is Chinese, and bears but an indirect relation to the real subject of these studies. The peculiar and surprising fact is that, in spite of all superimposition, the original character of the people and of their society should still remain recognizable. The wonder of Japan is not to be sought in the countless borrowings with which she has clothed herself,—much as a princess of the olden time would don twelve ceremonial robes, of divers colors and qualities, folded one upon the other so as to show their many-tinted edges at throat and sleeves and skirt;—no, the real wonder is the Wearer. For the interest of the costume is much less in its beauty of form and tint than in its significance as idea,—as representing something of the mind that devised or adopted it. And the supreme interest of the old Japanese civilization lies in what it expresses of the race-character,—that character which yet remains essentially unchanged by all the changes of Meiji.

"Suggests" were perhaps a better word than "expresses," for this race-character is rather to be divined than recognized. Our comprehension of it might be helped by some definite knowledge of origins; but such knowledge we do not yet possess. Ethnologists are agreed that the Japanese race has been formed by a mingling of peoples, and that the dominant element is Mongolian; but this dominant element is represented in two very different types,—one slender and almost feminine of aspect; the other, squat and powerful. Chinese and Korean elements are known to exist in the populations of certain districts; and there appears to have been a large infusion of Aino blood. Whether there be any Malay or Polynesian element also has not been decided. Thus much only can be safely affirmed,— that the race, like all good races, is a mixed one; and that the peoples who originally united to form it have been so blended together as to develop, under long social discipline, a tolerably uniform type of character. This character, though immediately recognizable in some of its aspects, presents us with many enigmas that are very difficult to explain.

Nevertheless, to understand it better has become a matter of importance. Japan has entered into the world's competitive struggle; and the worth of any people in that struggle depends upon character quite as much as upon force. We can learn something about Japanese character if we are able to ascertain the nature of the conditions which shaped it,—the great general facts of the moral experience of the race. And these facts we should find expressed or suggested in the history of the national beliefs, and in the history of those social institutions derived from and developed by religion.

1904

IV. CHARLES EGBERT CRADDOCK (MARY NOAILLES MURFREE) (1850–1922)

THE "HARNT" THAT WALKS CHILHOWEE *

June had crossed the borders of Tennessee. Even on the summit of Chilhowee Mountain the apples in Peter Giles's orchard were beginning to redden, and his Indian corn, planted on so steep a declivity that the stalks seemed to have much ado to keep their footing, was crested with tassels and plumed with silk. Among the dense forests, seen by no man's eye, the elder was flying its creamy banners in honor of June's coming and, heard by no man's ear, the pink and white bells of the azalea rang out melodies of welcome.

"An' it air a toler'ble for'ard season. Yer wheat looks likely; an' yer gyarden truck air thrivin' powerful. Even that cold spell we-uns hed about the full o' the moon in May ain't done sot it back none, it 'pears like ter me. But, 'cording ter my way o' thinkin', ye hev got chickens enough hyar ter eat off every pea-bloom ez soon ez it opens." And Simon Burney glanced with a gardener's disapproval at the numerous fowls, lifting their red combs and tufted top-

* From *In the Tennessee Mountains*, by Charles Egbert Craddock, 1884. Used by permission of, and by arrangement with, Houghton Mifflin Company.

knots here and there among the thick clover under the apple-trees.

"Them's Clarsie's chickens,—my darter, ye know," drawled Peter Giles, a pale, listless and lank mountaineer. "An' she hev been gin ter onderstand ez they hev got ter be kep' out 'n the gyarden; 'thout," he added indulgently,—" 'thout I'm a-plowin', when I lets 'em foller in the furrow ter pick up worms. But law! Clarsie is so spry that she don't ax no better 'n ter be let ter run them chickens off'n the peas."

Then the two men tilted their chairs against the posts of the little porch in front of Peter Giles's log cabin, and puffed their pipes in silence. The panorama spread out before them showed misty and dreamy among the delicate spiral wreaths of smoke. But was that gossamer-like illusion, lying upon the far horizon, the magic of nicotian, or the vague presence of distant heights? As ridge after ridge came down from the sky in ever-graduating shades of intenser blue, Peter Giles might have told you that this parallel system of enchantment was only "the mountings:" that here was Foxy, and there was Big 'Injun, and still beyond was another, which he had "hearn tell ran spang up into Virginny." The sky that bent to clasp this kindred blue was of varying moods. Floods of sunshine submerged Chilhowee in liquid gold, and revealed that dainty outline limned upon the northern horizon; but over the Great Smoky mountains clouds had gathered, and a gigantic rainbow bridged the valley.

Peter Giles's listless eyes were fixed upon a bit of red clay road, which was visible through a gap in the foliage far below. Even a tiny object, that ant-like crawled upon it, could be seen from the summit of Chilhowee. "I reckon that's my brother's wagon an' team," he said, as he watched the moving atom pass under the gorgeous triumphal arch. "He 'lowed he war goin' ter the Cross-Roads ter-day."

Simon Burney did not speak for a moment. When he did, his words seemed widely irrelevant. "That's a likely gal o' yourn," he drawled, with an odd constraint in his voice,—"a likely gal, that Clarsie."

There was a quick flash of surprise in Peter Giles's dull eyes. He covertly surveyed his guest, with an astounded curiosity rampant in his slow brains. Simon Burney had changed color; an expression of embarrassment lurked in every line of his honest, florid, hard-featured face. An alert imagination might have detected a deprecatory self-consciousness in every gray hair that striped the black beard raggedly fringing his chin.

"Yes," Peter Giles at length replied, "Clarsie air a likely enough gal. But she air mightily sot ter hevin' her own way. An' ef 'tain't give ter her peaceable-like, she jes' takes it, whether or no."

This statement, made by one presumably fully informed on the subject, might have damped the ardor of many a suitor,—for the monstrous truth was dawning on Peter Giles's mind that suitor was the position to which this slow, elderly widower aspired. But Simon Burney, with that odd, all-pervading constraint still prominently apparent, mildly observed, "Waal, ez much ez I hev seen of her goin's-on, it 'pears ter me ez her way air a mighty good way. An' it ain't comical that she likes it."

Urgent justice compelled Peter Giles to make some amends to the absent Clarissa. "That's a fac'," he admitted. "An' Clarsie ain't no hand ter jaw. She don't hev no words. But then," he qualified, truth and consistency alike constraining him, "she air a toler'ble hard-headed gal. That air a true word. Ye mought ez well try ter hender the sun from shining ez ter make that thar Clarsie Giles do what she don't want ter do."

To be sure, Peter Giles had a right to his opinion as to the hardness of his own daughter's head. The expression of his views, however, provoked Simon Burney to wrath; there was something astir within him that in a worthier subject might have been called a chivalric thrill, and it forbade him to hold his peace. He retorted: "Of course ye kin say that, ef so minded; but ennybody ez hev got eyes kin see the change ez hev been made in this hyar place sence that thar gal hev been growed. I ain't a-purtendin' ter know that thar Clarsie ez well ez you-uns knows her hyar at home, but I hev seen enough, an' a deal more'n enough, of her goin's-on, ter know that what she does ain't done fur *herself*. An' ef she will hev her way, it air fur the good of the whole tribe of ye. It 'pears ter me ez thar ain't many gals like that thar Clarsie. An' she air a merciful critter. She air mighty savin' of the feelin's of everything, from the cow an' the mare down ter the dogs, an' pigs, an' chickens; always a-feedin' of 'em jes' ter the time, an' never draggin', an' clawin', an' beatin' of 'em. Why, that thar Clarsie can't put her foot out'n the door, that every dumb beast is on

this hyar place ain't a-runnin' ter gi nigh her. I hev seen them pigs mos climb the fence when she shows he face at the door. 'Pears ter me e that thar Clarsie could tame a b'ar ef she looked at him a time or two she's so savin' o' the critter's feelin's An' thar's that old yaller dog o yourn," pointing to an ancient cu that was blinking in the sun, "he' older 'n Clarsie, an' no 'count in th worl'. I hev hearn ye say forty time that ye would kill him, 'ceptin' tha Clarsie purtected him, an' hed sot he heart on his a-livin' along. An' al the home-folks, an' everybody tha kems hyar to sot an' talk awhile never misses a chance ter kick tha thar old dog, or poke him with a stick or cuss him. But Clarsie!—I he seen that gal take the bread an' mea off'n her plate, an' give it ter that o dog, ez 'pears ter me ter be the wors dispositionest dog I ever see, an' n thanks lef' in him. He hain't he the grace ter wag his tail fur twenty year. That thar Clarsie air surely merciful critter, an' a mighty spry likely young gal, besides."

Peter Giles sat in stunned astonish ment during this speech, which wa delivered in a slow, drawling mono tone, with frequent meditative pauses but nevertheless emphatically. H made no reply, and as they were onc more silent there rose suddenly th sound of melody upon the air. I came from beyond that tumultuou stream that raced with the wind dow the mountain's side; a great lo thrown from bank to bank served a bridge. The song grew momentarily more distinct; among the leaves ther were fugitive glimpses of blue an white, and at last Clarsie appeared walking lightly along the log, clad in her checked homespun dress, and with a pail upon her head.

She was a tall, lithe girl, with that delicately transparent complexion often seen among the women of these mountains. Her lustreless black hair lay along her forehead without a ripple or wave; there was something in the expression of her large eyes that suggested those of a deer,—something free, untamable, and yet gentle. " 'Tain't no wonder ter me ez Clarsie is all tuk up with the wild things, an' critters ginerally," her mother was wont to say. "She sorter looks like 'em, I'm a-thinkin'."

As she came in sight there was a renewal of that odd constraint in Simon Burney's face and manner, and he rose abruptly. "Waal," he said, hastily, going to his horse, a raw-boned sorrel, hitched to the fence, 'it's about time I war a-startin' home, I reckons."

He nodded to his host, who silently nodded in return, and the old horse jogged off with him down the road, as Clarsie entered the house and placed the pail upon a shelf.

"Who d'ye think hev been hyar a-speakin' of compli*mints* on ye, Clarsie?" exclaimed Mrs. Giles, who had overheard through the open door every word of the loud, drawling voice on the porch.

Clarsie's liquid eyes widened with surprise, and a faint tinge of rose sprang into her pale face, as she looked an expectant inquiry at her mother.

Mrs. Giles was a slovenly, indolent woman, anxious, at the age of forty-five, to assume the prerogatives of advanced years. She had placed all her domestic cares upon the shapely shoulders of her willing daughter, and had betaken herself to the chimney-corner and a pipe.

"Yes, thar hev been somebody hyar a-speakin' of compli*mints* on ye, Clarsie," she reiterated, with chuckling amusement. "He war a mighty peart, likely boy,—that he war!"

Clarsie's color deepened.

"Old Simon Burney!" exclaimed her mother, in great glee at the incongruity of the idea. "*Old Simon Burney!*—jes' a-sittin' out thar, a-wastin' the time, an' a-burnin' of daylight—jes' ez perlite an' smilin' ez a basket of chips—a-speakin' of compli*mints* on ye!"

There was a flash of laughter among the sylvan suggestions of Clarsie's eyes,—a flash as of sudden sunlight upon water. But despite her mirth she seemed to be unaccountably disappointed. The change in her manner was not noticed by her mother, who continued banteringly,—

"Simon Burney air a mighty pore old man. Ye oughter be sorry fur him, Clarsie. Ye mustn't think less of folks than ye does of the dumb beastis,—that ain't religion. Ye knows ye air sorry fur mos' everything; why not fur this comical old consarn? Ye oughter marry him ter take keer of him. He said ye war a merciful critter; now is yer chance ter show it! Why, air ye a-goin' ter weavin', Clarsie, jes' when I wants ter talk ter ye 'bout'n old Simon Burney? But law! I knows ye kerry him with ye in yer heart."

The girl summarily closed the conversation by seating herself before a great hand-loom; presently the persistent thump, thump, of the batten and the noisy creak of the treadle filled the room, and through all the long, hot afternoon her deft, practiced hands lightly tossed the shuttle to and fro.

The breeze freshened, after the sun went down, and the hop and gourd vines were all astir as they clung about the little porch where Clarsie was sitting now, idle at last. The rain clouds had disappeared, and there bent over the dark, heavily wooded ridges a pale blue sky, with here and there the crystalline sparkle of a star. A halo was shimmering in the east, where the mists had gathered about the great white moon, hanging high above the mountains. Noiseless wings flitted through the dusk; now and then the bats swept by so close as to wave Clarsie's hair with the wind of their flight. What an airy, glittering, magical thing was that gigantic spider-web suspended between the silver moon and her shining eyes! Ever and anon there came from the woods a strange, weird, long-drawn sigh, unlike the stir of the wind in the trees, unlike the fret of the water on the rocks. Was it the voiceless sorrow of the sad earth? There were stars in the night besides those known to astronomers: the stellular fire-flies gemmed the black shadows with a fluctuating brilliancy; they circled in and out of the porch, and touched the leaves above Clarsie's head with quivering points of light. A steadier and an intenser gleam was advancing along the road, and the sound of languid footsteps came with it; the aroma of tobacco graced the atmosphere, and a tall figure walked up to the gate.

"Come in, come in," said Peter Giles, rising, and tendering the guest a chair. "Ye air Tom Pratt, ez well ez I kin make out by this light. Waal, Tom, we hain't furgot ye sence ye done been hyar."

As Tom had been there on the previous evening, this might be considered a joke, or an equivocal compliment. The young fellow was restless and awkward under it, but Mrs. Giles chuckled with great merriment.

"An' how air ye a-comin' on, Mrs. Giles?" he asked propitiatorily.

"Jes' toler'ble, Tom. Air they all well ter yer house?"

"Yes, they're toler'ble well, too." He glanced at Clarsie, intending to address to her some polite greeting, but the expression of her shy, half-startled eyes, turned upon the far away moon, warned him. "Thar never war a gal so skittish," he thought. "She'd run a mile, skerred ter death ef I said a word ter her."

And he was prudently silent.

"Waal," said Peter Giles, "what's the news out yer way, Tom? Enny thing a-goin' on?"

"Thar war a shower yander on the Backbone; it rained toler'ble hard fur a while, an' sot up the corn wonderful. Did ye git enny hyar?"

"Not a drap."

"'Pears ter me ez I kin see the clouds a-circlin' round Chilhowee, an' a-rainin' on everybody's corn-field 'ceptin' ourn," said Mrs. Giles. "Some folks is the favored of the Lord, an' t'others hev ter work fur everything an' git nuthin'. Waal, waal; we-uns will see our reward in the nex' worl'. Thar's a better worl' than this, Tom."

"That's a fac'," said Tom, in orthodox assent.

"An' when we leaves hyar once, w

leaves all trouble an' care behind us, Tom; fur we don't come back no more." Mrs. Giles was drifting into one of her pious moods.

"I dunno," said Tom. "Thar hev been them ez hev."

"Hev what?" demanded Peter Giles, startled.

"Hev come back ter this hyar yearth. Thar's a harnt that walks Chilhowee every night o' the worl'. I know them ez hev seen him."

Clarsie's great dilated eyes were fastened on the speaker's face. There was a dead silence for a moment, more eloquent with these looks of amazement than any words could have been.

"I reckons ye remember a puny, shriveled little man, named Reuben Crabb, ez used ter live yander, eight mile along the ridge ter that thar big sulphur spring," Tom resumed, appealing to Peter Giles. "He war born with only one arm."

"I 'members him," interpolated Mrs. Giles, vivaciously. "He war a mighty porely, sickly little critter, all the days of his life. 'Twar a wonder he war ever raised ter be a man,— an' a pity, too. An' 'twar powerful comical, the way of his takin' off; a stunted, one-armed little critter a-on-dertakin' ter fight folks an' shoot pistols. He hed the use o' his one arm, sure."

"Waal," said Tom, "his house ain't thar now, 'kase Sam Grim's brothers burned it ter the ground fur his a-killin' of Sam. That warn't all that war done ter Reuben fur killin' of Sam. The sheriff run Reuben Crabb down this hyar road 'bout a mile from hyar,—mebbe less,—an' shot him dead n the road, jes' whar it forks. Waal.

Reuben war in company with another evil-doer,—*he* war from the Cross-Roads, an' I furgits what he hed done, but he war a-tryin' ter hide in the mountings, too; an' the sheriff lef' Reuben a-lying thar in the road, while he tries ter ketch up with the t'other; but his horse got a stone in his hoof. an' he los' time, an' hed ter gin it up An' when he got back ter the forks o' the road whar he had lef' Reuben a-lyin' dead, thar war nuthin' thar 'ceptin' a pool o' blood. Waal, he went right on ter Reuben's house, an' them Grim boys hed burnt it ter the ground; but he seen Reuben's brother Joel. An' Joel, he tole the sheriff that late that evenin' he hed tuk Reuben's body out'n the road an' buried it, 'kase it hed been lyin' thar in the road ever sence early in the mornin', an' he couldn't leave it thar all night, an' he hedn't no shelter fur it, sence the Grim boys hed burnt down the house. So he war obleeged ter bury it. An' Joel showed the sheriff a new-made grave, an' Reuben's coat whar the sheriff's bullet hed gone in at the back an' kem out'n the breast. The sheriff 'lowed ez they'd fine Joel fifty dollars for a-buryin' of Reuben afore the cor'ner kem; but they never done it, ez I knows on. The sheriff said that when the cor'ner kem the body would be tuk up fur a 'quest. But thar hed been a pow-erful big frishet, an' the river 'twixt the cor'ner's house an' Chilhowee couldn't be forded fur three weeks. The cor'ner never kem, an' so thar it all stayed. That war four year ago."

"Waal," said Peter Giles, dryly, "I ain't seen no harnt yit. I knowed all that afore."

Clarsie's wondering eyes upon the young man's moonlit face had elicited these facts, familiar to the elders, but strange, he knew, to her.

"I war jes' a-goin' on ter tell," said Tom, abashed. "Waal, ever sence his brother Joel died, this spring, Reuben's harnt walks Chilhowee. He war seen week afore las', 'bout daybreak, by Ephraim Blenkins, who hed been a-fishin', an' war a-goin' home. Eph happened ter stop in the laurel ter wind up his line, when all in a minit he seen the harnt go by, his face white, an' his eye-balls like fire, an' puny an' one-armed, jes' like he lived. Eph, he owed me a haffen day's work; I holped him ter plow las' month, an' so he kem ter-day an' hoed along consider'ble ter pay fur it. He say he believes the harnt never seen him, 'kase it went right by. He 'lowed ef the harnt hed so much ez cut one o' them blazin' eyes round at him he couldn't but hev drapped dead. Waal, this mornin', 'bout sunrise, my brother Bob's little gal, three year old, strayed off from home while her mother war out milkin' the cow. An' we went a-huntin' of her, mightily worked up, 'kase thar hev been a b'ar prowlin' round our cornfield twict this summer. An' I went to the right, an' Bob went to the lef'. An' he say ez he war a-pushin' 'long through the laurel, he seen the bushes ahead of him a-rustlin'. An' he jes' stood still an' watched 'em. An' fur a while the bushes war still too; an' then they moved jes' a little, fust this way an' then that, till of a suddint the leaves opened, like the mouth of hell mought hev done, an' thar he seen Reuben Crabb's face. He say he never seen sech a face! Its mouth war open,

an' its eyes war a-startin' out'n its head, an' its skin war white till it war blue; en' ef the devil hed hed it a-hangin' over the coals that minit it couldn't hev looked no more skeered. But that war all that Bob seen, 'kase he jes' shet his eyes an' screeched an' screeched like he war destracted. An' when he stopped a second ter ketch his breath he hearn su'thin' a-answerin' him back, sorter weak-like, an' thar war little Peggy a-pullin' through the laurel. Ye know she's too little ter talk good, but the folks down ter our house believes she seen the harnt, too."

"My Lord!" exclaimed Peter Giles. "I 'low I couldn't live a minit ef I war ter see that thar harnt that walks Chilhowee!"

"I know I couldn't," said his wife.

"Nor me, nuther," murmured Clarsie.

"Waal," said Tom, resuming the thread of his narrative, "we hev all been a-talkin' down yander ter our house ter make out the reason why Reuben Crabb's harnt hev sot out ter walk *jes' sence his brother Joel died,*—'kase it war never seen afore then. An' ez nigh ez we kin make it out, the reason is 'kase thar's nobody lef' in this hyar worl' what believes he warn't ter blame in that thar killin o' Sam Grim. Joel always swore ez Reuben never killed him no more'n nuthin'; that Sam's own pistol went off in his own hand, an' shot him through the heart jes' ez he war a drawin' of it ter shoot Reuben Crabb. An' I hev hearn other men ez war a-standin' by say the same thing, though them Grims tells another tale, but ez Reuben never owned no pisto in his life, nor kerried one, it don'

'pear ter me ez what them Grims say
air reasonable. Joel always swore ez
Sam Grim war a mighty mean man,
—a great big feller like him a-rockin'
of a deformed little critter, an' a-
mockin' of him, an' a-hittin' of him.
An' the day of the fight Sam jes'
knocked him down fur nuthin' at all;
an' afore ye could wink Reuben
jumped up suddint, an' flew at him 10
like an eagle, an' struck him in the
face. An' then Sam drawed his pistol,
an' it went off in his own hand, an'
shot him through the heart, an' killed
him dead. Joel said that ef he could
hev kep' that pore little critter Reuben still, an' let the sheriff arrest him
peaceable-like, he war sure the jury
would hev let him off; 'kase how war
Reuben a-goin' ter shoot ennybody 20
when Sam Grim never left a-holt of
the only pistol between 'em, in life,
or in death? They tells me they hed
ter bury Sam Grim with that thar
pistol in his hand; his grip war too
tight fur death to unloose it. But
Joel said that Reuben war sartain
they'd hang him. He hedn't never
seen no jestice from enny one man,
an' he couldn't look fur it from twelve 30
men. So he jes' sot out ter run
through the woods, like a painter or
a wolf, ter be hunted by the sheriff,
an' he war run down an' kilt in the
road. Joel said he kep' up arter the
sheriff ez well ez he could on foot,—
fur the Crabbs never hed no horse,
—ter try ter beg fur Reuben, ef he
war cotched, an' tell how little an'
how weakly he war. I never seen a 40
young man's head turn white like
Joel's done; he said he reckoned it
war his troubles. But ter the las' he
stuck ter his rifle faithful. He war
a powerful hunter; he war out rain

or shine, hot or cold, in sech weather
ez other folks would think thar warn't
no use in tryin' ter do nuthin' in.
I'm mightily afeard o' seein' Reuben,
now, that's a fac'," concluded Tom,
frankly; " 'kase I hev hearn tell, an'
I believes it, that ef a harnt speaks
ter ye, it air sartain ye're bound ter
die right then."

" 'Pears ter me," said Mrs. Giles,
"ez many mountings ez thar air round
hyar, he mought hev tuk ter walkin'
some o' them, stidder Chilhowee."

There was a sudden noise close at
hand: a great inverted splint-basket,
from which came a sound of flapping
wings, began to move slightly back
and forth. Mrs. Giles gasped out an
ejaculation of terror, the two men
sprang to their feet, and the coy
Clarsie laughed aloud in an exuber-
ance of delighted mirth, forgetful of
her shyness. "I declar' ter goodness,
you-uns air skeered fur true! Did
ye think it war the harnt that walks
Chilhowee?"

"What's under that thar basket?"
demanded Peter Giles, rather sheep-
ishly, as he sat down again.

"Nuthin' but the duck-legged Dominicky," said Clarsie, "what air bein'
broke up from settin'." The moonlight was full upon the dimpling merriment in her face, upon her shining
eyes and parted red lips, and her
gurgling laughter was pleasant to hear.
Tom Pratt edged his chair a trifle
nearer, as he, too, sat down.

"Ye oughtn't never ter break up a
duck-legged hen, nor a Dominicky,
nuther," he volunteered, " 'kase they
air sech a good kind o' hen ter kerry
chickens; but a hen that is duck-
legged an' Dominicky too oughter be
let ter set, whether or no."

Had he been warned in a dream, he could have found no more secure road to Clarsie's favor and interest than a discussion of the poultry. "I'm a-thinkin'," she said, "that it air too hot fur hens ter set now, an' 'twill be till the las' of August."

"It don't 'pear ter me ez it air hot much in June up hyar on Chilhowee,—thar's a differ, I know, down in the valley; but till July, on Chilhowee, it don't 'pear ter me ez it air too hot ter set a hen. An' a duck-legged Dominicky air mighty hard ter break up."

"That's a fac'," Clarsie admitted; "but I'll hev ter do it, somehow, 'kase I ain't got no eggs fur her. All my hens air kerryin' of chickens."

"Waal!" exclaimed Tom, seizing his opportunity, "I'll bring ye some ter-morrer night, when I come agin. We-uns hev got eggs ter our house."

"Thanky," said Clarsie, shyly smiling.

This unique method of courtship would have progressed very prosperously but for the interference of the elders, who are an element always more or less adverse to love-making. "Ye oughter turn out yer hen now, Clarsie," said Mrs. Giles, "ez Tom air a-goin' ter bring ye some eggs ter-morrer. I wonder ye don't think it's mean ter keep her up longer'n ye air obleeged ter. Ye oughter remember ye war called a merciful critter jes' ter-day."

Clarsie rose precipitately, raised the basket, and out flew the "duck-legged Dominicky," with a frantic flutter and hysterical cackling. But Mrs. Giles was not to be diverted from her purpose; her thoughts had recurred to the absurd episode of the afternoon, and with her relish of the incongruity of the joke she opened upon the subject at once.

"Waal, Tom," she said, "we'll be hevin' Clarsie married, afore long, I'm a-thinkin'." The young man sat bewildered. He, too, had entertained views concerning Clarsie's speedy marriage but with a distinctly personal application; and this frank mention of the matter by Mrs. Giles had a sinister suggestion that perhaps her ideas might be antagonistic. "An' who d'ye think hev been hyar ter-day, a-speakin' of complimints on Clarsie?" He could not answer, but he turned his head with a look of inquiry, and Mrs. Giles continued, "He is a mighty peart, likely boy,—he is.'

There was a growing anger in the dismay on Tom Pratt's face; he leaned forward to hear the name with a fiery eagerness, altogether incongruous with his usual lack-lustre manner.

"Old Simon Burney!" cried Mrs. Giles, with a burst of laughter. "Old Simon Burney! Jes' a-speakin' of complimints on Clarsie!"

The young fellow drew back with a look of disgust. "Why, he's a old man; he ain't no fit husband fur Clarsie."

"Don't ye be too sure ter count on that. I war jes' a-layin' off ter tel Clarsie that a gal oughter keep mighty clar o' widowers, 'thout she wants ter marry one. Fur I believes," said Mrs. Giles, with a wild flight of imagination, "ez them men hev got some sort'n trade with the Evil One, an' he gives 'em the power ter witch the gals, somehow, so's ter git 'em te marry; 'kase I don't think that any gal that's got good sense air a-goin ter be a man's second ch'ice, an' th mother of a whole pack of step-chil 'ren, 'thout she air under some sort'n spell. But them men carries the day with the gals ginerally, an' I'm a-thinkin' they're banded with the devil. Ef I war a gal, an' a smart, peart boy like Simon Burney kem around a-speakin' of compli*mints*, an' sayin' I war a merciful critter, I'd jes' give it up, an' marry him fur second ch'ice. Thar's one blessin'," she continued, contemplating the possibility in a cold-blooded fashion positively revolting to Tom Pratt: "he ain't got no tribe of chil'ren fur Clarsie ter look arter; nary chick nor child hev old Simon Burney got. He hed two, but they died."

The young man took leave presently, in great depression of spirit,—the idea that the widower was banded with the powers of evil was rather overwhelming to a man whose dependence was in merely mortal attractions; and after he had been gone a little while Clarsie ascended the ladder to a nook in the roof, which she called her room.

For the first time in her life her slumber was fitful and restless, long intervals of wakefulness alternating with snatches of fantastic dreams. At last she rose and sat by the rude window, looking out through the chestnut leaves at the great moon, which had begun to dip toward the dark uncertainty of the western ridges, and at the shimmering, translucent, pearly mists that filled the intermediate valleys. All the air was dew and incense; so subtle and penetrating an odor came from that fir-tree beyond the fence that it seemed as if some invigorating infusion were thrilling along her veins; there floated upward, too, the warm fragrance of the clover,

and every breath of the gentle wind brought from over the stream a thousand blended, undistinguishable perfumes of the deep forests beyond The moon's idealizing glamour had left no trace of the uncouthness of the place which the daylight revealed; the little log house, the great overhanging chestnut-oaks, the jagged precipice before the door, the vague outlines of the distant ranges, all suffused with a magic sheen, might have seemed a stupendous alto-rilievo in silver repoussé. Still, there came here and there the sweep of the bat's dusky wings; even they were a part of the night's witchery. A tiny owl perched for a moment or two amid the dew-tipped chestnut-leaves, and gazed with great round eyes at Clarsie as solemnly as she gazed at him.

"I'm thankful enough that ye hed the grace not ter screech while ye war hyar," she said, after the bird had taken his flight. "I ain't ready ter die yit, an' a screech-ow*el* air the sure sign."

She felt now and then a great impatience with her wakeful mood. Once she took herself to task: "Jes' a-sittin' up hyar all night, the same ez ef I war a fox, or that thar harnt that walks Chilhowee!"

And then her mind reverted to Tom Pratt, to old Simon Burney, and to her mother's emphatic and oracular declaration that widowers are in league with Satan, and that the girls upon whom they cast the eye of supernatural fascination have no choice in the matter. "I wish I knowed ef that thar sayin' war true," she murmured, her face still turned to the western spurs, and the moon sinking so slowly toward them.

With a sudden resolution she rose to her feet. She knew a way of telling fortunes which was, according to tradition, infallible, and she determined to try it, and ease her mind as to her future. Now was the propitious moment. "I hev always hearn that it won't come true 'thout ye try it jes' before daybreak, an' a-kneelin' down at the forks of the road." She hesitated a moment and listened intently. "They'd never git done a-laffin' at me, ef they fund it out," she thought.

There was no sound in the house, and from the dark woods arose only those monotonous voices of the night, so familiar to her ears that she accounted their murmurous iteration as silence too. She leaned far out of the low window, caught the wide-spreading branches of the tree beside it, and swung herself noiselessly to the ground. The road before her was dark with the shadowy foliage and dank with the dew; but now and then, at long intervals, there lay athwart it a bright bar of light, where the moonshine fell through a gap in the trees. Once, as she went rapidly along her way, she saw speeding across the white radiance, lying just before her feet, the ill-omened shadow of a rabbit. She paused, with a superstitious sinking of the heart, and she heard the animal's quick, leaping rush through the bushes near at hand; but she mustered her courage, and kept steadily on. " 'Tain't no use a-goin' back ter git shet o' bad luck," she argued. "Ef old Simon Burney air my fortune, he'll come whether or no, —ef all they say air true."

The serpentine road curved to the mountain's brink before it forked, and there was again that familiar picture of precipice, and far-away ridges, and shining mist, and sinking moon, which was visibly turning from silver to gold. The changing lustre gilded the feathery ferns that grew in the marshy dip. Just at the angle of the divergent paths there rose into the air a great mass of indistinct white blossoms, which she knew were the exquisite mountain azaleas, and all the dark forest was starred with the blooms of the laurel. .

She fixed her eyes upon the mystic sphere dropping down the sky, knelt among the azaleas at the forks of the road, and repeated the time-honored invocation:—

"Ef I'm a-goin' ter marry a young man, whistle, Bird, whistle. Ef I'm a-goin' ter marry an old man, low, Cow, low. Ef I ain't a-goin' ter marry nobody, knock, Death, knock."

There was a prolonged silence in the matutinal freshness and perfume of the woods. She raised her head, and listened attentively. No chirp of half-awakened bird, no tapping of woodpecker, or the mysterious deathwatch; but from far along the dewy aisles of the forest, the ungrateful Spot, that Clarsie had fed more faithfully than herself, lifted up her voice and set the echoes vibrating. Clarsie, however, had hardly time for a pang of disappointment. While she still knelt among the azaleas her large deer-like eyes were suddenly dilated with terror. From around the curve of the road came the quick beat of hastening footsteps, the sobbing sound of panting breath, and between her and the sinking moon there passed an attenuated, one-armed figure, with

pallid, sharpened face, outlined for
moment on its brilliant disk, and
eadful starting eyes, and quivering
en mouth. It disappeared in an
stant among the shadows of the
urel, and Clarsie, with a horrible
ar clutching at her heart, sprang to
r feet.

Her flight was arrested by other
unds. Before her reeling senses
uld distinguish them, a party of
orsemen plunged down the road.
hey reined in suddenly as their eyes
ll upon her, and their leader, an
ger, authoritative man, was asking
r a question. Why could she not
nderstand him? With her nerveless
nds feebly catching at the shrubs
r support, she listened vaguely to
s impatient, meaningless words, and
w with helpless deprecation the ris-
g anger in his face. But there was
o time to be lost. With a curse
oon the stupidity of the mountaineer,
ho couldn't speak when she was
oken to, the party sped on in a
weeping gallop, and the rocks and
e steeps were hilarious with the
und.

When the last faint echo was
shed, Clarsie tremblingly made her
ay out into the road; not reassured,
wever, for she had a frightful con-
ction that there was now and then
strange stir in the laurel, and that
e was stealthily watched. Her eyes
ere fixed upon the dense growth
ith a morbid fascination, as she
oved away; but she was once more
oted to the spot when the leaves
arted and in the golden moonlight
e ghost stood before her. She
uld not nerve herself to run past
m, and he was directly in her way

homeward. His face was white, and
lined, and thin; that pitiful quiver was
never still in the parted lips; he
looked at her with faltering, beseeching eyes. Clarsie's merciful heart was
stirred. "What ails ye, ter come back
hyar, an' foller me?" she cried out,
abruptly. And then a great horror
fell upon her. Was not one to whom
a ghost should speak doomed to death,
sudden and immediate?

The ghost replied in a broken, shiv-
ering voice, like a wail of pain, "I
war a-starvin',—I war a-starvin',"
with despairing iteration.

It was all over, Clarsie thought.
The ghost had spoken, and she was
a doomed creature. She wondered
that she did not fall dead in the road.
But while those beseeching eyes were
fastened in piteous appeal on hers,
she could not leave him. "I never
hearn that 'bout ye," she said, re-
flectively. "I knows ye hed awful
troubles while ye war alive, but I
never knowed ez ye war starved."

Surely that was a gleam of sharp
surprise in the ghost's prominent eyes,
succeeded by a sly intelligence.

"Day is nigh ter breakin'," Clarsie
admonished him, as the lower rim of
the moon touched the silver mists of
the west. "What air ye a-wantin'
of me?"

There was a short silence. Mind
travels far in such intervals. Clarsie's
thoughts had overtaken the scenes
when she should have died that sudden terrible death: when there would
be no one left to feed the chickens;
when no one would care if the pigs
cried with the pangs of hunger, unless, indeed, it were time for them
to be fattened before killing. The

mare,—how often would she be taken from the plow, and shut up for the night in her shanty without a drop of water, after her hard day's work! Who would churn, or spin, or weave? Clarsie could not understand how the machinery of the universe could go on without her. And Towse, poor Towse! He was a useless cumberer of the ground, and it was hardly to be supposed that after his protector was gone he would be spared a blow or a bullet, to hasten his lagging death. But Clarsie still stood in the road, and watched the face of the ghost, as he, with his eager, starting eyes, scanned her open, ingenuous countenance.

"Ye do ez ye air bid, or it'll be the worse for ye," said the "harnt," in the same quivering, shrill tone. "Thar's hunger in the nex' worl' ez well ez in this, an' ye bring me some vittles hyar this time ter-morrer, an' don't ye tell nobody ye hev seen me, nuther, or it'll be the worse for ye."

There was a threat in his eyes as he disappeared in the laurel, and left the girl standing in the last rays of moonlight.

A curious doubt was stirring in Clarsie's mind when she reached home, in the early dawn, and heard her father talking about the sheriff and his posse, who had stopped at the house in the night, and roused its inmates, to know if they had seen a man pass that way.

"Clarsie never hearn none o' the noise, I'll be bound, 'kase she always sleeps like a log," said Mrs. Giles, as her daughter came in with the pail, after milking the cow. "Tell her bout'n it."

"They kem a-bustin' along hyar while afore day-break, a-runnin' art the man," drawled Mr. Giles, di matically. "An' they knocked me u ter know ef ennybody hed passe An' one o' them men—I never se none of 'em afore; they's all vall folks, I'm a-thinkin'—an' one of 'e bruk his saddle-girt' a good pie down the road, an' he kem back t borrer mine; an' ez we war a-fixin' it, he tole me what they war all arte He said that word war tuk ter t sheriff down yander in the valley 'pears ter me them town-folks do think nobody in the mountings h got good sense—word war tuk ter t sheriff 'bout this one-armed harnt th walks Chilhowee; an' he sot it dow that Reuben Crabb warn't dead at a an' Joel jes' purtended ter hev buri him, an' it air Reuben hisself th walks Chilhowee. An' thar air tw hundred dollars blood-money rewa fur ennybody ez kin ketch hi These hyar valley folks air powerf cur'ous critters,—two hundred dolla blood-money reward fur that th harnt that walks Chilhowee! I je sot myself ter laffin' when that th cuss tole it so solemn. I jes' 'low ter him ez he couldn't shoot a har nor hang a harnt, an' Reuben Cra hed about got done with his persec tions in this worl'. An' he said th by the time they hed scoured th mounting, like they hed laid off t do, they would find that thar pu little harnt war nuthin' but a mort man, an' could be kep' in a jail handy ez enny other flesh an' bloo He said the sheriff 'lowed ez t reason Reuben hed jes' taken ter wa Chilhowee sence Joel died is 'ka

ar air nobody ter feed him, like Joel
ne, mebbe, in the nights; an' Reu-
n always war a pore, one-armed,
:akly critter, what can't even kerry
gun, an' he air driv by hunger out'n
e hole whar he stays, ter prowl
und the cornfields an' hen-coops ter
:al suthin',—an' that's how he kem
r be seen frequent. The sheriff
·wed that Reuben can't find enough
ots an' yerbs ter keep him up; but
w!—a harnt eatin'! It jes' sot me
: ter laffin'. Reuben Crabb hev been
o busy in torment fur the las' four
ar ter be a-studyin' 'bout eatin';
,' it air his harnt that walks Chil-
·wee."

The next morning, before the moon
nk, Clarsie, with a tin pail in her
.nd, went to meet the ghost at the
pointed place. She understood now
1y the terrible doom that falls upon
ose to whom a spirit may chance
speak had not descended upon her,
.d that fear was gone; but the se-
ecy of her errand weighed heavily.
ae had been scrupulously careful to
it into the pail only such things as
.d fallen to her share at the table,
ad which she had saved from the
eals of yesterday. "A gal that goes
robbin' fur a hongry harnt," was her
oral reflection, "oughter be throwed
odaciously off'n the bluff."

She found no one at the forks of
ae road. In the ·marshy dip were
.ly the myriads of mountain azaleas,
aly the masses of feathery ferns,
aly the constellated glories of the
urel blossoms. A sea of shining
hite mist was in the valley, with
inting golden rays striking athwart it
om the great cresset of the sinking
.oon; here and there the long, dark,

horizontal line of a distant mountain's summit rose above the vaporous
shimmer, like a dreary, somber island
in the midst of enchanted waters. Her
large, dreamy eyes, so wild and yet
so gentle, gazed out through the
laurel leaves upon the floating gilded
flakes of light, as in the deep coverts
of the mountain, where the fulvous-
tinted deer were lying, other eyes, as
wild and as gentle, dreamily watched
the vanishing moon. Overhead, the
filmy, lace-like clouds, fretting the
blue heavens, were tinged with a faint
rose. Through the trees she caught
a glimpse of the red sky of dawn,
and the glister of a great lucent,
tremulous star. From the ground,
misty blue exhalations were rising,
alternating with the long lines of
golden light yet drifting through the
woods. It was all very still, very
peaceful, almost holy. One could
hardly believe that these consecrated
solitudes had once reverberated with
the echoes of man's death-dealing ingenuity, and that Reuben Crabb had
fallen, shot through and through,
amid that wealth of flowers at the
forks of the road. She heard suddenly the far-away baying of a hound
Her great eyes dilated, and she lifted
her head to listen. Only the solemn
silence of the woods, the slow sinking
of the noiseless moon, the voiceless
splendor of that eloquent day-star.

Morning was close at hand, and
she was beginning to wonder that the
ghost did not appear, when the leaves
fell into abrupt commotion, and he
was standing in the road, beside her.
He did not speak, but watched her
with an eager, questioning intentness,
as she placed the contents of the pail

upon the moss at the roadside. "I'm a-comin' agin ter-morrer," she said, gently. He made no reply, quickly gathered the food from the ground, and disappeared in the deep shades of the woods.

She had not expected thanks, for she was accustomed only to the gratitude of dumb beasts; but she was vaguely conscious of something wanting, as she stood motionless for a moment, and watched the burnished rim of the moon slip down behind the western mountains. Then she slowly walked along her misty way in the dim light of the coming dawn. There was a footstep in the road behind her; she thought it was the ghost once more. She turned, and met Simon Burney, face to face. His rod was on his shoulder, and a string of fish was in his hand.

"Ye air a-doin' wrongful, Clarsie," he said, sternly. "It air agin the law fur folks ter feed an' shelter them ez is a-runnin' from jestice. An' ye'll git yerself inter trouble. Other folks will find ye out, besides me, an' then the sheriff'll be up hyar arter ye."

The tears rose to Clarsie's eyes. This prospect was infinitely more terrifying than the awful doom which follows the horror of a ghost's speech. "I can't holp it," she said, however, doggedly swinging the pail back and forth. "I can't gin my consent ter starvin' of folks, even ef they air a-hidin' an' a-runnin' from justice."

"They mought put ye in jail, too, —I dunno," suggested Simon Burney.

"I can't holp that, nuther," said Clarsie, the sobs rising, and the tears falling fast. "Ef they comes an' gits me, and puts me in the pen'tiary

away down yander, somewhars in t[...] valley, like they done Jane Simpki[...] fur a-cuttin' of her step-mothe[...] throat with a butcher-knife, while s[...] war asleep,—though some said Ja[...] war crazy,—I can't gin my conse[...] ter starvin' of folks."

A recollection came over Sim[...] Burney of the simile of "henderi[...] the sun from shining."

"She hev done sot it down in h[...] mind," he thought, as he walked [...] beside her and looked at her resolu[...] face. Still he did not relinquish h[...] effort.

"Doin' wrong, Clarsie, ter aid fo[...] what air a-doin' wrong, an' mebbe h[...] done wrong, air powerful hurtful t[...] everybody, an' henders the law a[...] jestice."

"I can't holp it," said Clarsie.

"It 'pears toler'ble comical ter me[...] said Simon Burney, with a sudden pe[...] ception of a curious fact which h[...] proved a marvel to wiser men, "th[...] no matter how good a woman is, s[...] ain't got no respect fur the laws [...] the country, an' don't sot no store [...] jestice." After a momentary silen[...] he appealed to her on another basi[...] "Somebody will ketch him arter [...] while, ez sure ez ye air born. T[...] sheriff's a-sarchin' now, an' by t[...] time that word gits around, all t[...] mounting boys'll turn out, 'kase th[...] air two hundred dollars blood-mon[...] fur him. An' then he'll think, whe[...] they ketches him,—an' everybody[...] say so, too,—ez ye war constant [...] feedin' him jes' ter 'tice him t[...] comin' ter one place, so ez ye cou[...] tell somebody whar ter go ter ket[...] him, an' make them gin ye haffen t[...] blood-money. mebbe. That's wh[...]

e mounting will say, mos' likely."

"I can't holp it," said Clarsie, once
ore.

He left her walking on toward the
ing sun, and retraced his way to
e forks of the road. The jubilant
orning was filled with the song of
rds; the sunlight flashed on the
w; all the delicate enameled bells
 the pink and white azaleas were
inging tremulously in the wind; the
oma of ferns and mint rose on the
licious fresh air. Presently he
ecked his pace, creeping stealthily
 the moss and grass beside the road
ther than in the beaten path. He
lled aside the leaves of the laurel
th no more stir than the wind
ght have made, and stole cautiously
rough its dense growth, till he came
ddenly upon the puny little ghost,
ing in the sun at the foot of a
e. The frightened creature sprang
 his feet with a wild cry of terror,
t before he could move a step he
s caught and held fast in the strong
p of the stalwart mountaineer be-
le him. "I hev kem hyar ter tell
 a word, Reuben Crabb," said
mon Burney. "I hev kem hyar ter
ll ye that the whole mounting air
goin' ter turn out ter sarch fur ye;
e sheriff air a-ridin' now, an' ef ye
n't come along with me they'll hev
 afore night, 'kase thar air two
undred dollars reward fur ye."

What a piteous wail went up to
e smiling blue sky, seen through the
ppling leaves above them! What a
rror, and despair, and prescient
ony were in the hunted creature's
ce! The ghost struggled no longer;
 slipped from his feet down upon
e roots of the tree, and turned that

woful face, with its starting eyes and
drawn muscles and quivering parted
lips, up toward the unseeing sky.

"God A'mighty, man!" exclaimed
Simon Burney, moved to pity.
"Whyn't ye quit this hyar way of
livin' in the woods like ye war a
wolf? Whyn't ye come back an'
stand yer trial? From all I've hearn
tell, it 'pears ter me ez the jury air
obleeged ter let ye off, an' I'll take
keer of ye agin them Grims."

"I hain't got no place ter live in,"
cried out the ghost, with a keen despair.

Simon Burney hesitated. Reuben
Crabb was possibly a murderer,—at
the best could but be a burden. The
burden, however, had fallen in his
way, and he lifted it.

"I tell ye now, Reuben Crabb," he
said, "I ain't a-goin' ter holp no man
ter break the law an' hender jestice;
but ef ye will go an' stand yer trial,
I'll take keer of ye agin them Grims
ez long ez I kin fire a rifle. An' arter
the jury hev done let ye off, ye air
welcome ter live along o' me at my
house till ye die. Ye air no-'count ter
work, I know, but I ain't a-goin' ter
grudge ye fur a livin' at my house."

And so it came to pass that the
reward set upon the head of the harnt
that walked Chilhowee was never
claimed.

With his powerful ally, the forlorn
little specter went to stand his trial,
and the jury acquitted him without
leaving the box. Then he came back
to the mountains to live with Simon
Burney. The cruel gibes of his burly
mockers that had beset his feeble life
from his childhood up, the depriva-
tion and loneliness and despair and

fear that had filled those days when he walked Chilhowee, had not improved the harnt's temper. He was a helpless creature, not able to carry a gun or hold a plow, and the years that he spent smoking his cob-pipe in Simon Burney's door were idle years and unhappy. But Mrs. Giles said she thought he was "a mighty lucky little critter: fust, he hed Joel ter take keer of him an' feed him, when he tuk ter the woods ter pertend he war a harnt; an' they do say now that Clarsie Pratt, afore she war married, used ter kerry him vittles, too; an' then old Simon Burney tuk him up an' fed him ez plenty ez ef he war a good workin' hand, an' gin him clothes an' house-room, an' put up with his jawin' jes' like he never hearn a word of it. But law! some folks dunno when they air well off."

There was only a sluggish current of peasant blood in Simon Burney's veins, but a prince could not have dispensed hospitality with a more royal hand. Ungrudgingly he gave of his best; valiantly he defended his thankless guest at the risk of his life; with a moral gallantry he struggled with his sloth, and worked early and late, that there might be enough to divide. There was no possibility of a recompense for him, not even in the encomiums of discriminating friends, nor the satisfaction of tutored feelings and a practiced spiritual discernment; for he was an uncouth creature, and densely ignorant.

The grace of culture is, in its way, a fine thing, but the best that art can do—the polish of a gentleman—is hardly equal to the best that Nature can do in her higher moods.

1883

V. JOEL CHANDLER HARRIS
(1848–1908)

From *UNCLE REMUS: HIS SONG AND SAYINGS* *

IV

HOW MR. RABBIT WAS TOO SHARP FOR MR. FOX

"Uncle Remus," said the little b one evening, when he had found t old man with little or nothing to « "did the fox kill and eat the rabl when he caught him with the T Baby?"

"Law, honey, ain't I tell you 'bc dat?" replied the old darkey, chuc ling slyly. "I 'clar ter grashus ought er tole you dat, but old m Nod wuz ridin' on my eyeleds 'tv a leetle mo'n I'd a dis'membei my own name, en den on to c here come yo' mammy hollerin' att you.

"W'at I tell you w'en I fus' begi I tole you Brer Rabbit wuz a monst soon creetur; leas'ways dat's w'at laid out fer ter tell you. Well, de honey, don't you go en make udder calkalashuns, kaze in dem da Brer Rabbit en his fambly wuz de head er de gang w'en enny rack wuz on han', en dar dey stayed. 'F you begins fer ter wipe yo' eyes 'bo Brer Rabbit, you wait en see wha 'bouts Brer Rabbit gwineter fetch at. But dat's needer yer ner dar.

"W'en Brer Fox fine Brer Rabl mixt up wid de Tar-Baby, he f«

* From *Uncle Remus: His Songs and S ings,* by Joel Chandler Harris, 1880. printed by permission of the publishers, Appleton & Co.

ghty good, en he roll on de groun'
laff. Bimeby he up'n say, sezee:
"'Well, I speck I got you dis time,
er Rabbit,' sezee; 'maybe I ain't,
t I speck I is. You been runnin'
un' here sassin' atter me a mighty
ig time, but I speck you done come
de een' er de row. You bin cut-
' up yo' capers en bouncin' 'roun'
dis neighberhood ontwel you come 10
' b'leeve yo'se'f de boss er de
ole gang. En den youer allers
ne'rs whar you got no bizness,' sez
er Fox, sezee. 'Who ax you fer
' come en strike up a 'quaintance
d dish yer Tar-Baby? En who
ick you up dar whar you iz? No-
dy in de roun' worril. You des
ck en jam yo'se'f on dat Tar-Baby
dout waitin' fer enny invite,' sez 20
er Fox, sezee, 'en dar you is, en
r you'll stay twel I fixes up a bresh-
e and fires her up, kaze I'm gwineter
bbycue you dis day, sho,' sez Brer
x, sezee.

"Den Brer Rabbit talk mighty 'um-
.

"'I don't keer w'at you do wid me,
er Fox,' sezee, 'so you don't fling
e in dat brier-patch. Roas' me, Brer 30
x,' sezee, 'but don't fling me in dat
er-patch,' sezee.

"'Hit's so much trouble fer ter kin-
a fier,' sez Brer Fox, sezee, 'dat I
eck I'll hatter hang you,' sezee.

"'Hang me des ez high as you
ease, Brer Fox,' sez Brer Rab-
t, sezee, 'but do fer de Lord's sake
n't fling me in dat brier-patch.'
zee.

"'I ain't got no string,' sez Brer
x, sezee, 'en now I speck I'll hatter
wn you,' sezee.

"'Drown me des ez deep ez you
ease, Brer Fox,' sez Brer Rabbit,

sezee, 'but do don't fling me in dat
brier-patch,' sezee.

"'Dey ain't no water nigh,' sez
Brer Fox, sezee, 'en now I speck I'll
hatter skin you,' sezee.

"'Skin me, Brer Fox,' sez Brer
Rabbit, sezee, 'snatch out my eyeballs,
t'ar out my years by de roots, en
cut off my legs,' sezee, 'but do please, 10
Brer Fox, don't fling me in dat brier-
patch,' sezee.

"Co'se Brer Fox wanter hurt Brer
Rabbit bad ez he kin, so he cotch 'im
by de behime legs en slung 'im right
in de middle er de brier-patch. Dar
wuz a considerbul flutter whar Brer
Rabbit struck de bushes, en Brer Fox
sorter hang 'roun' fer ter see w'at
wuz gwineter happen. Bimeby he hear 20
somebody call 'im, en way up de hill
he see Brer Rabbit settin' cross-legged
on a chinkapin log koamin' de pitch
outen his har wid a chip. Den Brer
Fox know dat he bin swop off mighty
bad. Brer Rabbit wuz bleedzed fer
ter fling back some er his sass, en
he holler out:

"'Bred en bawn in a brier-patch,
Brer Fox—bred en bawn in a brier- 30
patch!' en wid dat he skip out des ez
lively ez a cricket in de embers."

1880

AUNT FOUNTAIN'S PRISONER *

It is curious how the smallest incident, the most unimportant circumstance, will recall old friends and old
40 associations. An old gentleman, who
is noted far and near for his prodigious memory of dates and events, once

* From *Free Joe and Other Georgian
Sketches*, by Joel Chandler Harris, 1887.
Used by permission of Charles Scribner's
Sons.

told me that his memory, so astonishing to his friends and acquaintances, consisted not so much in remembering names and dates and facts, as in associating each of these with some special group of facts and events; so that he always had at command a series of associations to which he could refer instantly and confidently. This is an explanation of the system of employing facts, but not of the method by which they are accumulated and stored away.

I was reminded of this some years ago by a paragraph in one of the county newspapers that sometimes come under my observation. It was a very commonplace paragraph; indeed, it was in the nature of an advertisement,—an announcement of the fact that orders for "gilt-edged butter" from the Jersey farm on the Tomlinson Place should be left at the drug-store in Rockville, where the first that came would be the first served. This business-like notice was signed by Ferris Trunion. The name was not only peculiar, but new to me; but this was of no importance at all. The fact that struck me was the bald and bold announcement that the Tomlinson Place was the site and center of trading and other commercial transactions in butter. I can only imagine what effect this announcement would have had on my grandmother, who died years ago, and on some other old people I used to know. Certainly they would have been horrified; and no wonder, for when they were in their prime the Tomlinson Place was the seat of all that was high, and mighty, and grand, in the social world in the neighborhood of Rockville. I remember that everybody stood in

awe of the Tomlinsons. Just w this was so, I never could make o They were very rich; the Place e braced several thousand acres; but the impressions made on me when child are worth any thing, they we extremely simple in their wa Though, no doubt, they could be fe mal and conventional enough when casion required.

I have no distinct recollection Judge Addison Tomlinson, except th he was a very tall old gentlem much older than his wife, who we about the streets of Rockville carr ing a tremendous gold-headed ca carved in a curious manner. In the days I knew more of Mrs. Tomlins than I did of the judge, mainly k cause I heard a great deal more abo her. Some of the women called h Mrs. Judge Tomlinson; but my gran mother never called her any thing e but Harriet Bledsoe, which was h maiden name. It was a name, to that seemed to suit her, so that wh you once heard her called Harri Bledsoe, you never forgot it aft ward. I do not know now, any mo than I did when a child, why th particular name should fit her so e actly; but, as I have often been tol a lack of knowledge does not alt facts.

I think my grandmother used to to church to see what kind of cloth Harriet Bledsoe wore; for I ha often heard her say, after the serm was over, that Harriet's bonnet, Harriet's dress, was perfectly charr ing. Certainly Mrs. Tomlinson w always dressed in the height of fashio though it was a very simple fashi when compared with the flounces ar furbelows of her neighbors. I r ember this distinctly, that she emed to be perfectly cool the hottest unday in summer, and comfortably irm the coldest Sunday in winter; d I am convinced that this impres-on, made on the mind of a child, ust bear some definite relation to rs. Tomlinson's good taste.

Certainly my grandmother was ver tired of telling me that Har-et Bledsoe was blessed with excep-nally good taste and fine manners; d I remember that she told me ten how she wished I was a girl, that I might one day be in a po-ion to take advantage of the op-rtunities I had had of profiting by irriet Bledsoe's example. I think ere was some sort of attachment tween my grandmother and Mrs. omlinson, formed when they were school together, though my grand-other was much the older of the o. But there was no intimacy. ie gulf that money sometimes makes tween those who have it and those o lack it lay between them. Though think my grandmother was more isitive about crossing this gulf than rs. Tomlinson.

I was never in the Tomlinson house t once when a child. Whether it s because it was two or three miles ay from Rockville, or whether it s because I stood in awe of my andmother's Harriet Bledsoe, I do t know. But I have a very vivid ollection of the only time I went ere as a boy. One of my play-tes, a rough-and-tumble little fel-v, was sent by his mother, a poor k woman, to ask Mrs. Tomlinson some preserves. I think this man and her little boy were in ne way related to the Tomlinsons.

The richest and most powerful people, I have heard it said, are not so rich and powerful but they are pestered by poor kin, and the Tomlinsons were no exception to the rule.

I went with this little boy I spoke of, and I was afraid afterward that I was in some way responsible for his boldness. He walked right into the presence of Mrs. Tomlinson, and, without waiting to return the lady's salutation, he said in a loud voice,—

"Aunt Harriet, ma says send her some of your nicest preserves."

"*Aunt Harriet,* indeed!" she exclaimed, and then she gave him a look that was cold enough to freeze him, and hard enough to send him through the floor.

I think she relented a little, for she went to one of the windows, bigger than any door you see nowadays, and looked out over the blooming orchard; and then after a while she came back to us. and was very gracious. She patted me on the head; and I must have shrunk from her touch, for she laughed and said she never bit nice little boys. Then she asked me my name; and when I told her, she said my grandmother was the dearest woman in the world. Moreover, she told my companion that it would spoil preserves to carry them about in a tin bucket; and then she fetched a big basket, and had it filled with preserves, and jelly, and cake. There were some ginger-preserves among the rest, and I remember that I appreciated them very highly; the more so, since my companion had a theory of his own that ginger-preserves and fruit-cake were not good for sick people.

I remember, too, that Mrs. Tomlinson had a little daughter about my own age. She had long yellow hair and very black eyes. She rode around in the Tomlinson carriage a great deal, and everybody said she was remarkably pretty, with a style and a spirit all her own. The negroes used to say that she was as affectionate as she was wilful, which was saying a good deal. It was characteristic of Harriet Bledsoe, my grandmother said, that her little girl should be named Lady.

I heard a great many of the facts I have stated from old Aunt Fountain, one of the Tomlinson negroes, who, for some reason or other, was permitted to sell ginger-cakes and persimmon-beer under the widespreading China-trees in Rockville on public days and during court-week. There was a theory among certain envious people in Rockville,—there are envious people everywhere,—that the Tomlinsons, notwithstanding the extent of their landed estate and the number of their negroes, were sometimes short of ready cash; and it was hinted that they pocketed the proceeds of Aunt Fountain's persimmon-beer and ginger-cakes. Undoubtedly such stories as these were the outcome of pure envy. When my grandmother heard such gossip as this, she sighed, and said that people who would talk about Harriet Bledsoe in that way would talk about anybody under the sun. My own opinion is, that Aunt Fountain got the money and kept it; otherwise she would not have been so fond of her master and mistress, nor so proud of the family and its position. I spent many an hour near Aunt Fountain's cake and beer stand, for I liked to hear her talk. Besides, she had a very funny

name, and I thought there was alway a probability that she would expla how she got it. But she never did.

I had forgotten all about the Tom linsons until the advertisement I hav mentioned was accidentally brought my notice, whereupon memory su denly became wonderfully active. am keenly alive to the happier r sults of the war, and I hope I appr ciate at their full value the emancip tion of both whites and blacks fro the deadly effects of negro slaver and the wonderful development our material resources that the w has rendered possible; but I mu confess it was with a feeling of r gret that I learned that the Tomlins Place had been turned into a dair farm. Moreover, the name of Fer Trunion had a foreign and an u familiar sound. His bluntly word advertisement appeared to come fro the mind of a man who would n hesitate to sweep away both roman and tradition if they happened stand in the way of a profitable ba gain.

I was therefore much gratifie some time after reading Trunion's a vertisement, to receive a note fro a friend who deals in real esta telling me that some land near t Tomlinson Place had been placed his hands for sale, and asking me go to Rockville to see if the land a the situation were all they were scribed to be. I lost no time in u dertaking this part of the business, I was anxious to see how the place looked in the hands of strange and unsympathetic strangers at th

It is not far from Atlanta to Ro ville,—a day and a night,—and journey is not fatiguing; so that

w hours after receiving my friend's
request I was sitting in the veranda
f the Rockville Hotel, observing,
ith some degree of wonder, the vast
changes that had taken place—the
most of them for the better. There
ere new faces and new enterprises
l around me, and there was a bustle
bout the town that must have caused
queer sensations in the minds of the
w old citizens who still gathered at
e post-office for the purpose of car-
ring on ancient political controversies
ith each other.

Among the few familiar figures that
tracted my attention was that of
unt Fountain. The old China-tree
the shade of which she used to
had been blasted by lightning or
e; but she still had her stand there,
nd she was keeping the flies and
st away with the same old turkey-
il fan. I could see no change. If
er hair was grayer, it was covered
nd concealed from view by the
ow-white handkerchief tied around
er head. From my place I could
ar her humming a tune,—the tune
had heard her sing in precisely the
me way years ago. I heard her
olding a little boy. The gesture,
e voice, the words, were the same
e had employed in trying to con-
ace me that my room was much
tter than my company, especially in
e neighborhood of her cake-stand.
see and hear her thus gave me a
culiar feeling of homesickness. I
proached and saluted her. She
wed with old-fashioned politeness,
t without looking up.

"De biggest uns, dee er ten cent,"
e said, pointing to her cakes; "en
littlest, dee er fi' cent. I make
all myse'f, suh. En de beer in

dat jug—dat beer got body, suh."

"I have eaten many a one of your
cakes, Aunt Fountain," said I, "and
drank many a glass of your beer; but
you have forgotten me."

"My eye weak, suh, but dee ain'
weak nuff fer dat." She shaded her
eyes with her fan, and looked at me.
Then she rose briskly from her chair.
"De Lord he'p my soul!" she exclaimed enthusiastically. "W'y, I
know you w'en you little boy. W'at
make I ain' know you w'en you big
man? My eye weak, suh, but dee ain'
weak nuff fer dat. Well, suh, you
mus' eat some my ginger-cake. De
Lord know you has make way wid
um w'en you wuz little boy."

The invitation was accepted, but
somehow the ginger-cakes had lost
their old-time relish; in me the taste
and spirit of youth were lacking.

We talked of old times and old
friends, and I told Aunt Fountain that
I had come to Rockville for the purpose of visiting in the neighborhood
of the Tomlinson Place.

"Den I gwine wid you, suh," she
cried, shaking her head vigorously. "I
gwine wid you." And go she did.

"I been layin' off ter go see my
young mistiss dis long time," said
Aunt Fountain, the next day, after
we had started. "I glad I gwine deer
in style. De niggers won' know me
skacely, ridin' in de buggy dis away."

"Your young mistress?" I inquired.

"Yes, suh. You know Miss Lady
w'en she little gal. She grown oman
now."

"Well, who is this Trunion I have
heard of?"

"He monst'ous nice w'ite man, suh.
He married my young mistiss. He
monst'ous nice w'ite man."

"But who is he? Where did he come from?"

Aunt Fountain chuckled convulsively as I asked these questions.

"We-all des pick 'im up, suh. Yes, suh; we-all des pick 'im up. Ain' you year talk 'bout dat, suh? I dunner whar you bin at ef you ain' never is year talk 'bout dat. He de fus' w'ite man w'at I ever pick up, suh. Yes, suh; de ve'y fus' one."

"I don't understand you," said I; "tell me about it."

At this Aunt Fountain laughed long and loudly. She evidently enjoyed my ignorance keenly.

"De Lord know I oughtn' be laughin' like dis. I ain' laugh so hearty sence I wuz little gal mos', en dat wuz de time w'en Marse Rowan Tomlinson come 'long en ax me my name. I tell 'im, I did, 'I'm name Flew Ellen, suh.' Marse Rowan he deaf ez any dead hoss. He 'low, 'Hey?' I say, 'I'm name Flew Ellen, suh.' Marse Rowan say, 'Fountain! Huh! he quare name.' I holler en laugh, en w'en de folks ax me w'at I hollerin' 'bout, I tell um dat Marse Rowan say I'm name Fountain. Well, suh, fum dat day down ter dis; stedder Flew Ellen, I'm bin name Fountain. I laugh hearty den en my name got change, en I feared ef I laugh now de hoss'll run away en turn de buggy upperside down right spang on top er me."

"But about this Mr. Trunion?" said I.

"Name er de Lord!" exclaimed Aunt Fountain, "ain' you never is bin year 'bout dat? You bin mighty fur ways, suh, kaze we all bin knowin' 'bout it fum de jump."

"No doubt. Now tell me about it."

Aunt Fountain shook her head, a[n] her face assumed a serious expre[s]sion.

"I dunno 'bout dat, suh. I ye[ar] tell dat niggers ain' got no busine[ss] fer go talkin' 'bout fambly doin's. [Y]dar wuz yo' gran'mammy. My mist[is] sot lots by her, en you been bornd right yer 'long wid um. I don't spe[ct] it'll be gwine so mighty fur out'n fambly ef I tell you 'bout it."

I made no attempt to coax Au[nt] Fountain to tell me about Truni[on] for I knew it would be difficult [to] bribe her not to talk about him. S[he] waited a while, evidently to tease [my] curiosity; but as I betrayed none, a[nd] even made an effort to talk ab[out] something else, she began:—

"Well, suh, you ax me 'bout Ma[rse] Fess Trunion. I know you bleeze [to] like dat man. He ain' b'long ter w[e] all folks, no furder dan he my you[ng] mistiss ole man, but dee ain' no fin[er] w'ite man dan him. No, suh; dee ai[n't] I tell you dat p'intedly. De nigge[rs] dee say he mighty close en pinchi[n'] but deze is mighty pinchin' times [en] you know dat yo'se'f, suh. Ef a m[an] don' fa'rly fling 'way he money, d[ese] Tomlinson niggers, dee'll say [he] mighty pinchin'. I hatter be pinch[in] myse'f, suh, kaze I know time I s[ell] my ginger-cakes dat ef I don't g[it] onter de money, dee won' be n[one] lef' fer buy flour en 'lasses fer ma[ke] mo'. It de Lord's trufe, suh, k[aze] I done had trouble dat way man[y] de time. I say dis 'bout Marse F[ess] Trunion, ef he ain' got de blood, [he] got de breedin'. Ef he ain' good [ez] de Tomlinsons, he lots better d[an] some folks w'at I know."

I gathered from all this that Tru[n]ion was a foreigner of some ki[nd]

t I found out my mistake later.
"I pick dat man up myse'f, en I
ows 'im 'most good ez ef he wuz
e er we-all.'"

"What do you mean when you say
ou picked him up'?" I asked, unable
restrain my impatience.

"Well, suh, de fus' time I see Marse
ss Trunion wuz terreckerly atter de
erman army come 'long. Dem wuz
t times, suh, col' ez de wedder wuz.
ee wuz in-about er million un um
ok like ter me, en dee des ravage
face er de yeth. Dee tuck all de
sses, en all de cows, en all de
ickens. Yes, suh; dee cert'n'y did.
an come 'long, en 'low, 'Aunty, you
ee now,' en den he tuck all my
ger-cakes w'at I bin bakin' 'g'inst
ris'mus; en den I say, 'Ef I wuz
ee ez you is, suh, I'd fling you down
take dem ginger-cakes 'way fum
u.' Yes, suh. I tole 'im dat. It
ake me mad fer see de way dat
n walk off wid my ginger-cakes.

"I got so mad, suh, dat I foller
ng atter him little ways; but dat
' do no good, kaze he come ter
ar dee wuz some yuther men, en dee
de up dem cakes till dee want no
ke lef'. Den I struck 'cross de plan'-
on, en walked 'bout in de drizzlin'
n tell I cool off my madness, suh,
ze de flour dat went in dem cakes
' me mos' a hunderd dollars in
d Confederick money. Yes, suh;
did dat. En I work for dat money
ghty hard.

'Well, suh, I ain' walk fur 'fo' it
m like I year some un talkin'. I
p, I did, en lissen, en still I year
. I ain' seen nobody, suh, but still
ear um. I walk fus' dis away en
dat away, en den I walk 'roun' en
un', en den it pop in my min' 'bout

de big gully. It ain' dar now, suh, but
in dem days we call it de big gully,
kaze it wuz wide en deep. Well, suh,
'fo' I git dar I see hoss-tracks, en dee
led right up ter de brink. I look in,
I did, en down dar dee wuz a man en
a hoss. Yes, suh; dee wuz bofe down
dar. De man wuz layin' out flat on
he back, en de hoss he wuz layin'
sorter up en down de gully en right
on top er one er de man legs, en
eve'y time de hoss'd scramble en try
fer git up de man 'ud talk at 'im. I
know dat hoss mus' des nata'lly a
groun' dat man legs in de yeth, suh.
Yes, suh. It make my flesh crawl
w'en I look at um. Yit de man ain'
talk like he mad. No, suh, he ain';
en it make me feel like somebody
done gone en hit me on de funny-
bone w'en I year 'im talkin' dat away.
Eve'y time de hoss scuffle, de man he
'low, 'Hol' up, ole fel, you er mashin'
all de shape out'n me.' Dat w'at he
say, suh. En den he 'low, 'Ef you
know how you hurtin', ole fel, I des
know you'd be still.' Yes, suh. Dem
he ve'y words.

"All dis time de rain wuz a-siftin'
down. It fall mighty saft, but 'twuz
monst'ous wet, suh. Bimeby I crope
up nigher de aidge, en w'en de man
see me he holler out, 'Hol' on, aunty;
don't you fall down yer!'

"I ax 'im, I say, 'Marster, is you
hurted much?' Kaze time I look at
'im I know he ain' de villyun w'at
make off wid my ginger-cakes. Den
he 'low, 'I speck I hurt purty bad,
aunty, en de wuss un it is dat my
hoss keep hurtin' me mo'.'

"Den nex' time de hoss move it
errortate me so, suh, dat I holler at
'im loud ez I ken, 'Wo dar, you
scan'lous villyun! Wo!' Well, suh.

I speck dat hoss mus a-bin use'n ter niggers, kaze time I holler at 'im he lay right still, suh. I slid down dat bank, en I kotch holter dat bridle— I don't look like I'm mighty strong, does I, suh?" said Aunt Fountain, pausing suddenly in her narrative to ask the question.

"Well, no," said I, humoring her as much as possible. "You don't seem to be as strong as some people I've seen."

"Dat's it, suh!" she exclaimed. "Dat w'at worry me. I slid down dat bank, en I kotch dat hoss by de bridle. De man say, 'Watch out dar, aunty! don't let he foot hit you. Dee one cripple too much now.' I ain' pay no 'tention, suh. I des grab de bridle, en I slew dat hoss head roun', en I fa'rly lif' 'im on he foots. Yes, suh, I des lif' 'im on he foots. Den I led 'im down de gully en turnt 'im a-loose, en you ain' never see no hoss supjued like dat hoss wuz, suh. Den I went back whar de man layin', en ax 'im ef he feel better, en he 'low dat he feel like he got a big load lif' offen he min', en den, mos' time he say dat, suh, he faint dead away. Yes, suh. He des faint dead away. I ain' never is see no man like dat, w'at kin be jokin' one minnit en den de nex' be dead, ez you may say. But dat's Marse Fess Trunion, suh. Dat's him up en down.

"Well, suh, I stan' dar, I did, en I ain' know w'at in de name er de Lord I gwine do. I wuz des ez wringin' wet ez if I'd a-bin baptize in de water; en de man he wuz mo' wetter dan w'at I wuz, en goodness knows how long he bin layin' dar. I run back ter de big-'ouse, suh, mighty nigh a mile, en I done my

level bes' fer fin' some er de nigge en git um fer go wid me back en git de man. But I ain' fin' no un um, suh. Dem w'at ain' gone w de Sherman army, dee done hide o Den I went in de big-'ouse, suh, tell Mistiss 'bout de man down in de gully, en how he done hurt so bad he ain' kin walk. Den Mist —I speck you done fergit Mistiss, s —Mistiss, she draw herse'f up en w'at business dat man er any yut man got on her plan'ation. I s 'Yassum, dat so; but he done dar, ef he stay dar he gwine die dar.' Y suh; dat w'at I say. I des put it Mistiss right pine-blank.

"Den my young mistiss—dat's M Lady, suh—she say dat dough spize um all dez bad az she kin, man mus' be brung away from d Kaze, she say, she don't keer h yuther folks go on, de Tomlinsons bleeze to do like Christun peop Yes, suh; she say dem ve'y wor Den Mistiss, she 'low dat de man be brung up, en put in de corn-cr but Miss Lady she say no, he m be brung en put right dar in de b 'ouse in one er de up-sta'rs roo kaze maybe some er dem State Georgy boys mought be hurted up in de Norf, en want some place stay at. Yes, suh; dat des de w she talk. Den Mistiss, she ain' nothin', yit she hol' her head migl high.

"Well, suh, I went back out in yard, en den I went 'cross ter nigger-quarter, en I ain' gone fur I year my ole man prayin' in some'r's. I know 'im by he v'ice, en he wuz prayin' des like it camp-meetin' time. I hunt 'roun' 'im, suh, en bimeby I fin' 'im squ

' down behime de do'. I grab 'im, did, en I shuck 'im, en I 'low, 'Git fum yer, you nasty, stinkin' ole lyun, you!' Yes, suh; I wuz mad. say, 'W'at you doin' squattin' down de flo'? Git up fum dar en come 'long wid me!' I hatter laugh, suh, ze w'en I shuck my ole man by de oulder, en holler at 'im, he put up two han', suh, en squall out, 'Oh, ay marster! don't kill me dis time, I ain' never gwine do it no mo'!'

"Atter he 'come pacify, suh, den I ll him 'bout de man down dar in de lly, en yit we ain' know w'at ter . My ole man done hide out some de mules en hosses down in de amp, en he feard ter go atter um, h, kaze he skeerd de Sherman army uld come marchin' back en fine n, en he 'low dat he mos' know dee comin' back atter dat man down r. Yes, suh; he de skeerdest nigger at I ever see, ef I do say it myse'f. t, bimeby he put out atter one er hosses, en he brung 'im back; en hitch 'im up in de spring-waggin, atter dat man we went. Yes, suh; did dat. En w'en we git dar, dat man wuz plum ravin' deestracted. wuz laughin' en talkin' wid hese'f, gwine on, tell it make yo' blood col' fer lissen at 'im. Yes, suh. 'Me en my ole man, we pick 'im des like he wuz baby. I come ghty nigh droppin' 'im, suh, kaze e time, wiles we kyarn 'im up de k, I year de bones in he leg rasp 'g'inst one er n'er. Yes, suh. It ke me blin' sick, suh. We kyard home en put 'im up st'ars, en dar stayed fer many's de long day."

'Where was Judge Tomlinson?' I ed. At this Aunt Fountain grew re serious than ever,—a seriousness that was expressed by an increased particularity and emphasis in both speech and manner.

"You axin' 'bout Marster? Well, suh, he wuz dar. He wuz cert'n'y dar with Mistiss en Miss Lady, suh, but look like he ain' take no intruss in w'at gwine on. *Some* folks 'low, suh, dat he ain' right in he head, but dee ain' know 'im—dee ain' know 'im, suh, like we-all. Endurin' er de war, suh, he wuz strucken wid de polzy, en den w'en he git well, he ain' take no intruss in w'at gwine on. Dey'd be long days, suh, w'en he ain' take no notice er nobody ner nuttin' but Miss Lady. He des had dem spells; en den, ag'in, he'd set out on de peazzer en sing by hese'f, en it make me feel so lonesome dat I bleeze ter cry. Yes, suh; it's de Lord's trufe.

"Well, suh, dat man w'at I fin' out dar in de gully wuz Marse Fess Trunion. Yes, suh, de ve'y same man. Dee ain' no tellin' w'at dat po' creetur gone thoo wid. He had fever, he had pneumony, en he had dat broke leg. En all 'long wid dat dee want skacely no time w'en he want laughin' en jokin'. Our w'ite folks, dee des spized 'im kase he bin wid Sherman army. Dee say he wuz Yankee; but I tell um, suh, dat ef Yankee look dat away dee wuz cert'n'y mighty like we-all. Mistiss, she ain' never go 'bout 'im wiles he sick; en Miss Lady, she keep mighty shy, en she tu'n up her nose eve'y time she year 'im laugh. Oh, yes, suh; dee cert'n'y spize de Yankees endurin' er dem times. Dee hated um rank, suh. I tell um, I say, 'You-all des wait. Dee ain' no nicer man dan w'at he is, en you-all des wait tell you know 'im.' *Shoo!* I des might ez well talk ter de win' suh.—dee hate de Yankees dat rank.

"By de time dat man git so he kin creep 'bout on crutches, he look mos' good ez he do now. He wuz dat full er life, suh, dat he bleeze ter go downsta'rs, en down he went. Well, suh, he wuz mighty lucky dat day. Kase ef he'd a run up wid Mistiss en Miss Lady by hese'f, dee'd er done sumpn' ner fer ter make 'im feel bad. Dee cert'n'y would, suh. But dee wuz walkin' 'roun' in de yard, en he come out on de peazzer whar Marster wuz sunnin' hese'f and singin'. I wouldn' b'lieve it, suh, ef I ain' see it wid my two eyes; but Marster got up out'n he cheer, en straighten hese'f, en shuck han's wid Mars Fess, en look like he know all 'bout it. Dee sot dar, suh, en talk en laugh, en laugh en talk, tell bimeby I 'gun ter git skeerd on de accounts er bofe un um. Dee talk 'bout de war, en dee talk 'bout de Yankees, en dee talk politics right straight 'long des like Marster done 'fo' he bin strucken wid de polzy. En he talk sense, suh. He cert'n'y did. Bimeby Mistiss en Miss Lady come back fum dee walk, en dee look like dee gwine drap w'en dee see w'at gwine on. Dem two mens wuz so busy talkin', suh, dat dee ain' see de wimmen folks, en dee des keep right on wid dee argafyin'. Mistiss en Miss Lady, dee ain' know w'at ter make er all dis, en dee stan' dar lookin' fus' at Marster en den at one er n'er. Bimeby dee went up de steps en start to go by, but Marster he riz up en stop um. Yes, suh. He riz right up en stop um, en right den en dar, suh, he make um interjuced ter one an'er. He stan' up, en he say, 'Mr. Trunion, dis my wife; Mr. Trunion, dis my daughter.'

"Well, suh, I wuz stannin' back de big hall, en we'n I see Marst gwine on dat away my knees con mighty nigh failin' me, suh. Dis fus' time w'at he reckermember an body name, an de fus' time he like he useter, sence he bin sick w de polzy. Mistiss en Miss Lady, d come 'long in atter w'ile, en dee lo like dee skeerd. Well, suh, I d far'ly preach at um. Yes, suh; I d dat. I say, 'You see dat? You s how Marster doin'? Ef de han' er Lord ain' in dat, den he han' ain' b in nuttin' on de top side er dis yet I say, 'You see how you bin cutti up 'roun' dat sick w'ite man wid y biggity capers, en yit de Lord ret down en make Marster soun' en w time de yuther w'ite man tetch 'in Well, suh, dey wuz dat worked up d dey sot down en cried. Yes, suh; d did dat. Dey cried. En I ain' tell you no lie, suh, I stood dar en cri wid um. Let 'lone dat, I des far boohooed. Yes, suh; dat's me. W I git ter cryin' sho' nuff, I blee ter boohoo.

"Fum dat on, Marster do like hese en talk like hese'f. It look like bin sleep long time, suh, en de sle done 'im good. All he sense co back; en you know, suh, de Toml sons, w'en dey at deese'f, got mu sense ez dee want en some fer gi way. Mistiss and Miss Lady, dee w mighty proud 'bout Marster, suh, l dee ain' fergit dat de yuther man w Yankee, en dee hol' deese'f monst'c stiff. He notice dat hese'f, en he wa ter go 'way, but Marster, he 'fuse lissen at 'im right pine-plank, suh. say de dead Tomlinsons would about turn over in dee graves ef e know he sont a cripple man 'way fr

'ouse. Den he want ter pay he
ard, but Marster ain' lissen ter dat,
needer is Mistiss; en dis mighty
nny, too, kaze right dat minnit dee
ant a half er dollar er good money
de whole fambly, ceppin' some sil-
r w'at I work fer, en w'at I hide
er chink er my chimbly. No, suh.
ee want er half er dollar in de whole
mbly, suh. En yit dee won't take
greenbacks w'at dat man offer um.
"By dat time, suh, de war wuz done
ne, en dee wuz tough times. Dee
rt'n'y wuz, suh. De railroads wuz
broke up, en eve'y thing look like
gwine helter-skelter right straight
r de Ole Boy. Dey want no law,
h, en dey want no nuttin'; en ef it
dn't er bin fer me en my ole man,
speck de Tomlinsons, proud ez dee
uz, would er bin mightily pincht fer
' bread en meat. But dee ain'
ver want fer it yit, suh, kaze w'en
e en my ole man git whar we can't
ove no furder, Marse Fess Trunion,
tuck holt er de place en he fetcht
right side up terreckerly. He say
r me dat he gwine pay he board
t away, suh, but he ain' say it whar
Tomlinsons kin year 'im, kaze den
e'd a-bin a fuss, suh. But he kotch
lt, en me, en him, en my ole man,
des he't eve'y thing hot. Mo'
eshually Marse Fess Trunion, suh.
ou ain' know 'im, suh, but dat ar
ite man, he got mo' ways ter work,
mo' short cuts ter de ways, suh,
n any w'ite man w'at I ever see,
I done see lots un um. It got so,
h, dat me en my ole man ain' have
draw no mo' rashuns fum de
eedman Bureau; but dee wuz one
ell, suh, w'en wuss rashuns dan dem
uz on de Tomlinson table.
"Well, suh, dat w'ite man, he work

en he scuffle; he hire niggers, and he
turn um off; he plan, en he projick;
en 'tain' so mighty long, suh, 'fo' he
got eve'y thing gwine straight. How
he done it, I'll never tell you, suh;
but do it he did. He put he own
money in dar, suh, kaze dee wuz two
times dat I knows un w'en he git
money out'n de pos'-office, en I see 'im
pay it out ter de niggers, suh. En all
dat time he look like he de happies'
w'ite man on top er de groun', suh.
Yes, suh. En w'en he at de 'ouse
Marster stuck right by 'im, en ef he
bin he own son he couldn't pay him
mo' 'tention. Dee wuz times, suh,
w'en it seem like ter me dat Marse
Fess Trunion wuz a-cuttin' he eye at
Miss Lady, en den I 'low ter myse'f,
'Shoo, man! you mighty nice en all
dat, but you Yankee, en you nee'nter
be a-drappin' yo' wing 'roun' Miss
Lady, kaze she too high-strung
fer dat.'

"It look like he see it de same way
I do, suh, kaze atter he git eve'y
thing straight he say he gwine home.
Marster look like he feel mighty bad,
but Mistiss en Miss Lady, dee ain'
say nuttin' 'tall. Den, atter w'ile,
suh, Marse Fess Trunion fix up, en
off he put. Yes, suh. He went off
whar he come fum, en I speck he folks
wuz mighty glad ter see 'im atter so
long, kaze ef dee ever wuz a plum
nice man it wuz dat man. He want
no great big man, suh, en he ain' make
much fuss, yit he lef' a mighty big
hole at de Tomlinson Place w'en he
pulled out fum dar. Yes, suh; he did
dat. It look like it lonesome all over
de plan'ation. Marster, he 'gun ter
git droopy, but eve'y time de dinner
bell ring he go ter de foot er de
sta'rs en call out, 'Come on, Trunion!'

Yes, suh. He holler dat out eve'y
day, en den, wiles he be talkin', he'd
stop en look roun' en say, 'Whar
Trunion?' It ain' make no diffunce
who he talkin' wid, suh, he'd des stop
right still en ax, 'Whar Trunion?'
Den de niggers, dee got slack, en
eve'y thing 'gun ter go een'-ways.
One day I run up on Miss Lady settin'
down cryin', en I ax her w'at de name 10
er goodness de matter, en she say
nuff de matter. Den I say she better
go ask her pappy whar Trunion, en
den she git red in de face, en 'low I
better go 'ten' ter my business; en
den I tell her dat ef somebody ain'
tell us whar Trunion is, en dat mighty
quick, dee won't be no business on
dat place fer 'ten' ter. Yes, suh. I
tol' her dat right p'intedly, suh.

"Well, suh, one day Marse Fess
Trunion come a-drivin' up in a shiny
double buggy, en he look like he des
step right out'n a ban'-box; en ef ever
I wuz glad ter see anybody, I wuz
glad ter see dat man. Marster wuz
glad; en dis time, suh, Miss Lady
wuz glad, en she show it right plain;
but Mistiss, she still sniff de a'r en
hol' her head high. T'want long, suh, 30
'fo' we all knowd dat Marse Fess wuz
gwine marry Miss Lady. I ain' know
how dee fix it, kaze Mistiss never is
come right out en say she 'greeable
'bout it, but Miss Lady wuz a Bledsoe
too, en a Tomlinson ter boot, en I
ain' never see nobody w'at impatient
nuff fer ter stan' out 'g'inst dat gal.
It ain' all happen, suh, quick ez I tell
it, but it happen; en but fer dat, I 40
dunno w'at in de name er goodness
would er 'come er dis place."

A few hours later, as I sat with
Trunion on the veranda of his house,
he verified Aunt Fountain's story, but

not until after he was convinced th
I was familiar with the history of t
family. There was much in that h
tory he could afford to be proud
modern though he was. A man w
believes in the results of blood in ca
tle is not likely to ignore the pos
bility of similar results in human b
ings; and I think he regarded the ma
ter in some such practical light. I
was a man, it seemed, who was d
posed to look lightly on trouble, on
it was over with; and I found he w
not so much impressed with his stru
gle against the positive scorn and co
tempt of Mrs. Tomlinson,—a strugg
that was infinitely more important a
protracted than Aunt Fountain h
described it to be,—as he was wi
his conflict with Bermuda grass. I
told me laughingly of some of
troubles with his hot-headed neig
bors in the early days after the wa
but nothing of this sort seemed to
as important as his difficulties wi
Bermuda grass. Here the practi
and progressive man showed himsel
for I have a very vivid recollecti
of the desperate attempts of the far
ers of that region to uproot and d
stroy this particular variety.

As for Trunion, he conquered it
cultivating it for the benefit of hi
self and his neighbors; and I suspe
that this is the way he conquered
other opponents. It was a great v
tory over the grass, at any rate.
walked with him over the place, a
the picture of it all is still framed
my mind,—the wonderful hedges
Cherokee roses, and the fragrant a
fertile stretches of green Bermu
through which beautiful fawn-color
cattle were leisurely making their wa
He had a theory that this was the on

grass in the world fit for the dainty Jersey cow to eat.

There were comforts and conveniences on the Tomlinson Place not dreamed of in the old days, and I think there was substantial happiness here too. Trunion himself was a wholesome man, a man full of honest affection, hearty laughter, and hard work,—a breezy, companionable, energetic man. There was something boyish, unaffected, and winsome in his manners; and I can easily understand why Judge Addison Tomlinson, in his old age, insisted on astonishing his family and his guests by exclaiming, "Where's Trunion?" Certainly he was a man to think about and inquire after. I have rarely seen a lovelier woman than his wife, and I think her happiness helped to make her so. She had inherited a certain degree of cold stateliness from her ancestors; but her experience after the war, and Trunion's unaffected ways, had acted as powerful correctives, and there was nothing in the shape of indifference or haughtiness to mar her singular beauty.

As for Mrs. Tomlinson,—the habit is still strong in me to call her Harriet Bledsoe,—I think that in her secret soul she had an ineradicable contempt for Trunion's extraordinary business energy. I think his "push and vim," as the phrase goes, shocked her sense of propriety to a far greater extent than she would have been willing to admit. But she had little time to think of these matters; for she had taken possession of her grandson, Master Addison Tomlinson Trunion, and was absorbed in his wild and boisterous ways, as grandmothers will be. This boy, a brave and manly little fellow, had Trunion's temper, but he had inherited the Tomlinson air. It became him well, too, and I think Trunion was proud of it.

"I am glad," said I, in parting, "that I have seen Aunt Fountain's Prisoner."

"Ah!" said he, looking at his wife, who smiled and blushed, "that was during the war. Since then I have been a Prisoner of Peace."

I do not know what industrial theories Trunion has impressed on his neighborhood by this time; but he gave me a practical illustration of the fact that one may be a Yankee and a Southerner too, simply by being a large-hearted, whole-souled American.

1887

VI. THOMAS NELSON PAGE
(1853–1922)

"UNC' EDINBURG'S DROWNDIN'" *

A PLANTATION ECHO

"Well, suh, dat's a fac—dat's what Marse George al'ays said. 'Tis hard to spile Christmas anyways."

The speaker was "Unc' Edinburg," the driver from Werrowcoke, where I was going to spend Christmas; the time was Christmas Eve, and the place the muddiest road in eastern Virginia —a measure which, I feel sure, will to those who have any experience establish its claim to distinction.

A half-hour before, he had met me at the station, the queerest-looking, raggedest old darky conceivable,

* Used by permission of Charles Scribner's Sons.

brandishing a cedar-staffed whip of enormous proportions in one hand, and clutching a calico letter-bag with a twisted string in the other; and with the exception of a brief interval of temporary suspicion on his part, due to the unfortunate fact that my luggage consisted of only a hand-satchel instead of a trunk, we had been steadily progressing in mutual esteem.

"Dee's a boy standin' by my mules; I got de ker-idge heah for you," had been his first remark on my making myself known to him. "Mistis say as how you might bring a trunk."

I at once saw my danger, and muttered something about "a short visit," but this only made matters worse.

"Dee don' nobody nuver pay short visits dyah," he said, decisively, and I fell to other tactics.

"You couldn' spile Christmas den noways," he repeated, reflectingly, while his little mules trudged knee-deep through the mud. "Twuz Christmas den, sho' 'nough," he added, the fires of memory smoldering, and then, as they blazed into sudden flame, he asserted, positively: "Dese heah free-issue niggers don' know what Christmas is. Hog meat an' pop crackers don' meck Christmas. Hit tecks ole times to meck a sho'-'nough, tyahin'-down Christmas. Gord! I's seen 'em! But de wuss Christmas I ever seen tunned out de best in de een," he added, with sudden warmth, "an' dat wuz de Christmas me an' Marse George an' Reveller all got drownded down at Braxton's Creek. You's hearn 'bout dat?"

As he was sitting beside me in solid flesh and blood, and looked as little ethereal in his old hat and patched clothes, as an old oak stump would

have done, and as Colonel Staunto had made a world-wide reputatio when he led his regiment through th Chickahominy thickets against M Clellan's intrenchments, I was force to confess that I had never been s favored, but would like to hear abo it now; and with a hitch of the la blanket under his outside knee, and supererogatory jerk of the reins, began:

"Well, you know, Marse George wa jes eighteen when he went to colleg I went wid him, 'cause me an' hi wuz the same age; I was born lil on a Sat-day in de Christmas, an' wuz born in de new year on a Chue day, an' my mammy nussed us bofe one breast. Dat's de reason may huccome we took so to one nurr. sutney set a heap o' sto' by me; a I 'ain' nuver see nobody yit wuz go to me as Marse George."

The old fellow, after a short reveri went on:

"Well, we growed up togerr, jes to say two stalks in one hill. cotch ole hyahs togerr, an' we hunte 'possums togerr, an' 'coons. Lor he wuz a climber! I 'member a fig he had one night up in de ve'y top a big poplar-tree wid a 'coon, wh he done gone up after, an' he flu he hat over he head; an' do' de va mint leetle mo' tyah him all to piec he fotch him down dat tree 'live; a me an' him had him at Christma 'Coon meat mighty good when d fat, you know?"

As this was a direct request for m judgment, I did not have the mor courage to raise an issue, although m views on the subject of 'coon me are well known to my family, so grunted something which I doubt n took for assent, and he proceeded: "Dee warn' nuttin he didn' lead de ow in; he wuz de bes' swimmer I ver see, an' he handled a skiff same s a fish handle heself. An' I wuz id him constant; wharever you see Marse George, dyah Edinburg sho, jes ke he shadow. So twuz, when he ent to de university; 'twarn' nuttin ould do but I got to go too. Marster he didn't teck much to de otion, but Marse George wouldn' ave it no urr way, an' co'se mistis e teck he side. So I went 'long as body-servant to teck keer on him ' help meck him a gent'man. An' wuz, too. From time he got dyah ll he come 'way he wuz de head an.

"Dee warn' but one man dyah idn' compliment him, an' dat wuz Ir. Darker. But he warn' nuttin! ot dat he didn' come o' right good mbly—'cep' dee politics; but he wuz tney pitted, jes like sometimes you e a weevly runty pig in a right good ter. Well, Mr. Darker he al'ays inst Marse George; he hate me an' im bofe, an' he sutney act mischee- ous todes us; 'cause he know he arn' as we all. De Stauntons dee wuz popularitiest folks in Virginia; an' e wuz high-larnt besides. So when Iarse George run for de medal, an' uz to meck he gret speech, Mr. arker he speak 'ginst him. Dat's hat Marse George whip him 'bout. in' nobody nuver told you 'bout t?"

I again avowed my misfortune; and though it manifestly aroused new ubts, he worked it off on the mules, d once more took up his story:

"Well, you know, dee had been eakin' 'ginst one nurr ev'y Sat-dy night; an' ev'ybody knowed Marse George wuz de bes' speaker, but dee give him one mo' sho', an' dee wuz bofe gwine spread deeselves, an' dee wuz two urr gent'mens also gwine speak. An' dat night when Mr. Darker got up he meck sich a fine speech ev'y- body wuz s'prised; an' some on 'em say Mr. Darker done beat Marse George. But shuh! I know better'n dat; an' Marse George face look so curious; but, suh, when he riz I knowed der wuz somen gwine happen —I wuz leanin' in de winder. He jes step out in front an' throwed up he head like a horse wid a rank kyurb on him, an' den he begin; an' twuz jes like de river when hit gits out he bank. He swep' ev'ything. When he fust open he mouf I know twuz comin'; he face wuz pale, an' he wuds tremble like a fiddle-string, but he eyes wuz blazin', an' in a minute he wuz jes reshin'. He voice soun' like a bell; an' he jes wallered dat turr man, an' wared him out; an' when he set down dee all yelled an' hollered so you couldn' heah you' ears. Gent'- mans, twuz royal!

"Den dee tuck de vote, an' Marse George got it munanimous, an' dee all hollered agin, all 'cep' a few o' Mr. Darker friends. An' Mr. Darker he wuz de second. An' den dee broke up. An' jes den Marse George walked thoo de crowd straight up to him, an' lookin' him right in de eyes, says to him, 'You stole dat speech you made to-night.' Well, suh, you ought to 'a hearn 'em; hit soun' like a mill-dam. You couldn' heah nuttin 'cep' roarin', an' you couldn' see nuttin 'cep' shovin'; but, big as he wuz, Marse George beat him; an' when dee pull him off, do' he face wuz mighty pale, he stan' out befo' 'em all, dem whar wuz 'ginst him, an' all, an' as straight as an arrow, an' say: 'Dat speech wuz written an' printed years ago by somebody or nurr in Congress, an' this man stole it; had he beat me only, I should not have said one word; but as he hás beaten others, I shall show him up!' Gord, suh, he voice wuz clear as a game rooster. I sutney wuz proud on him.

"He did show him up, too, but Mr. Darker ain' wait to see it; he lef' dat night. An' Marse George he wuz de popularest gent'man at dat university. He could handle dem students dyah same as a man handle a hoe.

"Well, twuz de next Christmas we meet Miss Charlotte an' Nancy. Mr. Braxton invite we all to go down to spen' Christmas wid him at he home. An' sich a time as we had!

"We got dyah Christmas Eve night —dis very night—jes befo' supper, an' jes natchelly froze to death," he pursued, dealing in his wonted hyperbole, "an' we jes had time to git a apple toddy or two when supper was ready, an' wud come dat dee wuz waitin' in de hall. I had done fix Marse George up gorgeousome, I tell you; an' when he walked down dem stairs in dat swaller-tail coat, an' dem paten'-leather pumps on, dee warn nay one dyah could tetch him; he looked like he own 'em all. I jes rest my mind. I seen him when he shake hands wid 'em all roun', an' I say, 'Um-m-m! he got 'em.'

"But he ain' teck noticement o' none much tell Miss Charlotte come. She didn' live dyah, had jes come over de river dat evenin' from her home, 'bout ten miles off, to spen' Christmas like we all, an' she come down de stairs

jes as Marse George finish shaki hands. I seen he eye light on her a she come down de steps smilin', wi her dim blue dress trainin' behind he an' her little blue foots peepin' ou so pretty, an' holdin' a little hankche lookin' like a spider-web, in one han an' a gret blue fan in turr, spread ou like a peacock tail, an' jes her roun arms an' th'oat white, an' her gr dark eyes lightin' up her face. I sa 'Dyah 'tis!' an' when de ole Cun'l sta aside an' interduce 'em, an' Mar George step for'ard an' meck he gran bow, an' she sort o' swing back a gin her curtchy, wid her dress so o' dammed up 'ginst her, an' her arm so white, an' her face sort o' sunsett I say, 'Yes, Lord! Edinburg, dyah yo mistis.' Marse George look like thinks she done come down right fro de top o' de blue sky an' bring pie on it wid her. He ain' nuver took eyes from her dat night. Dee glu to her, mun! an' she—well, do' s mighty rosy, an' look mighty unco sarned, she sutney ain' hender hi Hit look like kyarn nobody else to dat fan an' pick up dat hankch skuzin o' him; an' after supper, wh dee all playin' blindman's-buff in hall—I don' know how twuz—but d she jes as nimble as a filly, an' h ankle jes as clean, an' she kin up her dress an' dodge out de way ev'ybody else, somehow or nurr s kyarn help him ketchin' her to sa her life; he always got her corndere an' when dee'd git fur apart, dat a nuttin, dee jes as sure to come toge again as water is whar you done r you hand thoo. An' do' he kiss ev' body else under de mestletow, 'cau dee be sort o' cousins, he ain' nuv kiss her, nor nobody else nurr, 'ce

ole Cun'l. I wuz standin' down at
e een de hall wid de black folks, an'
notice it 'tic'lar, 'cause I done meck
'quintance o' Nancy; she wuz
iss Charlotte's maid; a mighty likely
oung gal she wuz den, an' jes as
pident as a fly. She see it too, do'
e ain' 'low it. Fust thing I know I
en a mighty likely light-skinned gal
andin' dyah by me, wid her hyah
os' straight as white folks, an' a
ighty good frock on, an' a clean
ron, an' her hand mos' like a lady,
ly it brown, an' she keep on 'vidin'
r eyes twix me an' Miss Charlotte;
hen I watchin' Miss Charlotte she
atchin' me, an' when I steal my eye
un' on her she noticin' Miss Char-
tte; an' presney I sort o' sidle 'long-
de her, an' I say, 'Lady, you mighty
rightly to-night.' An' she say, she
leeged to be sprightly, her mistis look
good; an' I ax her which one twuz,
' she tell me, 'Dat queen one over
vah,' an' I tell her dee's a king dyah
o, she got her eye set for; an' when
say her mistis tryin' to set her cap
r Marse George, she fly up, an' say
e an' her mistis don' have to set
e cap for nobody; *dee* got to set dee
p an' all de clo'es for dem, an' den
e ain' gwine cotch 'em, 'cause dee
n' studyin' 'bout no up-country folks
har dee ain' nobody know nuttin
out.

"Well, dat oudaciousness so aggri-
te me, I lite into dat nigger right
ah. I tell her she ain' been nowhar
all ef she don' know we all; dat
e wuz de bes' of quality, de ve'y top
pot; an' den I tell her 'bout how
et we wuz; how de ker'idges wuz
'ays hitched up night an' day, an'
ggers jes thick as weeds; an' how
nc' Torm he wared he swaller-tail

ev'y day when he wait on de table;
an' Marse George he won' wyah a coat
mo'n once or twice anyways, to save
your life. Oh! I sutney 'stonish dat
nigger, 'cause I wuz teckin up for de
fambly, an' I meck out like dee use
gold up home like urr folks use wood,
an' sow silver like urr folks sow
wheat; an' when I got thoo dee wuz
all on 'em listenin', an' she 'lowed dat
Marse George he were ve'y good, sho
'nough, ef twarn for he nigger; but
I ain' tarrifyin' myself none 'bout dat,
'cause I know she jes projickin, an'
she couldn' help bein' impident ef you
wuz to whup de frock off her back.

"Jes den dee struck up de dance.
Dee had wheel de pianer out in de
hall, an' somebody say Jack Forester
had come 'cross de river, an' all on
'em say dee mus' git Jack; an' presney
he come in wid he fiddle, grinnin' an'
scrapin', 'cause he wuz a notable fiddler, do' I don' think he may equal to
we all's Tubal, an' I know he couldn'
tetch Marse George, 'cause Marse
George wuz a natchel fiddler, jes like
'coons is natchel pacers, an' mules is
natchel kickers. Howsomever, he sutney jucked a jig sweet, an' when he
shake dat bow you couldn' help you
foot switchin' a leetle—not ef you wuz
a member of de chutch. He wuz a
mighty sinful man, Jack wuz, an' dat
fiddle had done drawed many souls to
torment.

"Well, in a minute dee wuz all
flyin', an' Jack he wuz rockin' like
boat rockin' on de water, an' he face
right shiny, an' he teef look like ear
o' corn he got in he mouf, an' he big
foot set 'way out keepin' time, an'
Marse George he wuz in de lead row
dyah too; ev'y chance he git he tunned
Miss Charlotte—'petchel motion, right

hand across, an' cauliflower, an' coquette—dee coquette plenty o' urrs, but I notice dee ain' nuver fail to tun one nurr, an' ev'y tun he gin she wrappin' de chain roun' him; once when dee wuz 'prominadin-all' down we all's een o' de hall, as he tunned her somebody step on her dress an' to' it. I heah de screech o' de silk, an' Nancy say, 'O Lord!' den she say, 'Nem mine! now I'll git it!' an' dee stop for a minute for Marse George to pin it up, while turrers went on, an' Marse George wuz down on he knee, an' she look down on him mighty sweet out her eyes, an' say, 'Hit don' meck no difference,' an' he glance up an' cotch her eye, an', jest dout a wud, he tyah a gret piece right out de silk an' slipt it in he bosom, an' when he got up, he say, right low, lookin' in her eyes right deep, 'I gwine wyah dis at my weddin',' an' she jes look sweet as candy; an' ef Nancy ever wyah dat frock I ain' see it.

"Den presney dee wuz talkin' 'bout stoppin'. De ole Cun'l say hit time to have prars, an' dee wuz beggin' him to wait a leetle while; an' Jack Forester lay he fiddle down nigh Marse George, an' he picked 't up an' drawed de bow 'cross it jes to try it, an' den jes projickin' he struck dat chune 'bout 'You'll ermember me.' He hadn' mo'n tetch de string when you could heah a pin drop. Marse George he warn noticin', an' he jes lay he face on de fiddle, wid he eyes sort o' half shet, an' drawed her out like he'd do some nights at home in de moonlight on de gret porch, tell on a sudden he looked up an' cotch Miss Charlotte eye leanin' for'ards so earnest, an' all on 'em list'nin', an' he stopt, an' dee all clapt dee hands, an'

he sudney drapt into a jig. Jack Fo\[r]ester ain' had to play no mo' d\[at] night; even de ole Cun'l ketched \[de] fever, an' he stept out in de flo', \[and] he long-tail coat an' high collar, an\[d] knocked 'em off de 'Snow-bud on \[de] Ash-bank,' an' 'Chicken in de Brea\[d] tray,' right natchel. Oh, he could j\[es] plank 'em down!

"Oh, dat wuz a Christmas like yo\[u] been read 'bout! An' twuz hard \[to] tell which gittin cotch most, Mar\[se] George or me, 'cause dat nigger s\[he] jes as confusin' as Miss Charlott\[e]. An' she sutney wuz sp'ilt dem day\[s]; ev'y nigger on dat place got he ey\[es] on her, an' she jes as oudacious a\[n] aggravatin as jes womens kin b\[e]. Dees monsus 'ceivin' critters, wome\[n] is, jes as onreliable as de hind-leg of \[a] mule; a man got to watch 'em all \[de] time; you kyarn break 'em like yo\[u] kin horses. Now dat off mule dyah (indicating, by a lazy but not lig\[ht] lash of his whip the one selected f\[or] his illustration), "dee ain' no counti\[n] on her at all; she go 'long all day, \[an'] maybe a week, jes dat easy an' s\[o]ciable, an' fust thing you know y\[ou] ain' know nuttin, she done knock yo\[ur] brains out; dee ain' no 'pendence \[to] be placed in 'em 'tall, suh; she j\[es] as sweet as a kiss one minute, an' ne\[xt] time she come out de house she g\[ot] her head up in de air, an' her ea\[rs] backed, an' goin' 'long switchin' he\[r] self like I ain' good 'nough for h\[er] to walk on.

"'Fox-huntin's?' oh, yes, suh, ev\['ry] day mos'; an' when Marse Geor\[ge] didn' git de tail, twuz 'cause twuz \[a] bob-tail fox—you heah me! He pl\[ays] de fiddle for he pastime, but \[he] fotched up in de saddle—dat \[he] cradle.

"De fust day dee went out I heah Nancy quoilin 'bout de tail layin' on Miss Charlotte dressin'-table gittin' ayahs over ev'ything.

"One day de ladies went out too, Miss Charlotte 'mongst 'em, on Miss Lucy gray myah Switchity, an' Marse George he rid Mr. Braxton's chestnut Villful. Well, suh, he stick so close o dat gray myah, he leetle mo' los' dat fox; but, Lord! he know what ae 'bout—he monsus 'ceivin' 'bout dat!—he know de way de fox gwine es as well as he know heself; an' all de time he leadin' Miss Charlotte whar she kin heah de music, but he watchin' him too, jes as narrow as , ole hound. So, when de fox tun de ead o' de creek, Marse George had Miss Charlotte on de aidge o' de flat, an' he de fust man see de fox tun lown on turr side wid de hounds right rank after him. Dat sort o' set him back, 'cause by rights de fox ought to 'a double an' come back dis side; he xyarn git out dat way, an' two or hree gent'mens dee had see it too, an' wuz jes layin' de horses to de groun' o git roun' fust, 'cause de creek wuz heap too wide to jump, an' wuz 'way ver you head, an' hit cold as Christmas, sho 'nough; well, suh, when dee unned, Mr. Clarke he wuz in de lead (he wuz ridin' for Miss Charlotte too), an' hit fyah set Marse George on fire; ae ain' said but one wud, 'Wait,' an' ies set de chestnut's head straight for le creek, whar de fox comin' wid he ail up on he back, an de dogs ravlin mos' on him. De ladies screamed, an' some de gent'mens hollered for him to come back, but he ain' mind; he went 'cross dat flat like a wild-duck; an' when he retch de water he norse try to flinch, but dat hand on

de bridle, an' dem rowels in he side, an' he 'bleeged to teck it. Lord, suh, sich a screech as dee set up! But he wuz swimmin' for life, an' he wuz up de bank an' in de middle o' de dogs time dee tetched ole Gray Jacket; an' when Mr. Clarke got dyah Marse George wuz stanin' holdin' up de tail for Miss Charlotte to see, turrer side de creek, an' de hounds wuz wallerin' all over de body, an' I don' think Mr. Clarke don got up wid 'em yit.

"He cotch de fox, an' he cotch some'n' else besides, in my 'pinion, 'cause when de ladies went upstairs dat night Miss Charlotte had to wait on de steps for a glass o' water, an' couldn' nobody git it but Marse George; an' den when she tell him good-night over de banisters, he couldn' say it good enough; he got to kiss her hand; an' she ain' do nuttin but jes peep upstairs ef anybody dyah lookin'; an' when I come thoo de do' she juck her hand 'way an' ran upstairs jes as farst as she could. Marse George look at me sort o' laughin', an' say: 'Confound you! Nancy couldn' been very good to you.' An' I say, 'She le' me squench my thirst kissin' her hand'; an' he sort o' laugh an' tell me to keep my mouf shet.

"But dat ain' de on'y time I come on 'em. Dee al'ays gittin' corndered; an' de evenin' befo' we come 'way I wuz gwine in thoo de conservity, an' dyah dee wuz sort o' hide 'way. Miss Charlotte she was settin' down, an' Marse George he wuz leanin' over her, got her hand to he face, talkin' right low an' lookin' right sweet, an' she ain' say nuttin; an' presney he dropt on one knee by her, an slip he arm roun' her, an' try to look in her eyes, an' she so 'shamed to look at him she got to hide her face on he shoulder, an' I slipt out.

"We come 'way next mornin'. When marster heah 'bout it he didn' teck to de notion at all, 'cause her pa—dat is, he warn' her own pa, 'cause he had married her ma when she wuz a widder after Miss Charlotte pa died, an' he politics warn' same as ourn. 'Why, you kin never stand him, suh,' he said to Marse George. 'We won't mix any mo'n fire and water; you ought to have found that out at college; dat fellow Darker is his son.'

"Marse George he say he know dat; but he on'y de step-brurr of de young lady, an' ain' got a drap o' her blood in he veins, an' he didn' know it when he meet her, an' anyhow hit wouldn' meck any difference; an' when de mistis see how sot Marse George is on it she teck he side, an' dat fix it; 'cause when ole mistis warn marster to do a thing, hit jes good as done. I don' keer how much he rar roun' an' say he ain' gwine do it, you jes well go 'long an' put on you hat; you gwine see him presney doin' it jes peaceable as a lamb. She tun him jes like she got bridle on him, an' he ain' nuver know it.

"So she got him jes straight as a string. An' when de time come for Marse George to go, marster he mo' consarned 'bout it 'n Marse George; he ain' say nuttin 'bout it befo', but now he walkin' roun' an' roun' axin mistis mo' questions 'bout he cloes an' he horse an' all; an' dat mornin' he gi' him he two Sunday razors, an' gi' me a pyah o' boots an' a beaver hat, 'cause I wuz gwine wid him to kyar he portmanteau, an' git he shavin' water, sence marster say ef he wuz gwine marry a Locofoco, he at least

must go like a gent'man; an' me an' Marse George had done settle it 'twix us, 'cause we al'ays set bofe we trap on de same hyah parf.

"Well, we got 'em, an' when I a dat gal out on de wood-pile at night she say bein' as her mistis gwine ow me, an' we bofe got to be in de sam estate, she reckon she ain' nuver gwin to be able to git shet o' me; an' de I clamp her. Oh, she wuz a beauty!"

A gesture and guffaw completed th recital of his conquest.

"Yes, suh, we got 'em sho!" he said presently. "Dee couldn' persist us we crowd 'em into de fence an' rur 'em off dee foots.

"Den come de 'gagement an' ev'ything wuz smooth as silk. Mars George an' me wuz ridin' over dyah constant, on'y we nuver did git over bein' skeered when we wuz ridin' up dat turpentine road facin' all dem winders. Hit 'pear like ev'ybody in de wull 'mos' wuz lookin' at us.

"One evenin' Marse George say 'Edinburg, d'you ever see as many winders p'intin' one way in you' life? When I git a house,' he say, 'I gwine have all de winders lookin' turr way.' But dat evenin', when I see Miss Charlotte come walkin' out de gret parlor wid her hyah sort o' rumpled over her face, an' some yaller roses on her bres', an' her gret eyes so soft an' sweet, an' Marse George walkin' 'long hinst her, so peaceable, like she got chain roun' him, I say, 'Winders ain' nuttin.' Oh, twuz jes like holiday all de time! An' den Miss Charlotte come over to see mistis, an' of co'se she bring her maid wid her, 'cause she 'bleeged to have her maid, you know, an' dat wuz de bes' of all. Dat evenin', 'bout sunset, dee come drivin' up in de big ker'idge, wid dee gret hyah trunk stropped on de seat behind, an' Nancy she settin' by Billy, an' Marse George settin' inside by he rose-bud, 'cause he had done gone down to bring her up; an' marster he done been drest in he blue coat an' yallow westket ever sence dinner, an' walkin' roun', watchin' up de road all de time, an' tellin' de mistis he reckon dee ain' comin', an' ole mistis she try to pacify him, an' she come out presney drest, an' rustlin' in her stiff black silk an' all, an' when de ker'idge come in sight, ev'ybody wuz runnin'; an' when dee draw up to de do', Marse George he help her out an' 'duce her to marster an' ole mistis; an' marster he start to meck her a gret bow, an' she jes put up her mouf like a little gal to be kissed, an' dat got him. An' mistis teck her right in her arms an' kiss her twice, an' de servants dee wuz all peepin' an' grinnin'. Ev'ywhar you tun you see a nigger teef, 'cause dee all warn see de young mistis whar good 'nough for Marse George. Dee ain' gwine be married tell de next fall, 'count o' Miss Charlotte bein' so young; but she jes good as b'longst to we all now; an' ole marster an' mistis dee jes as much in love wid her as Marse George. Hi! dee warn pull de house down an' buil' it over for her! An' ev'y han' on de place he peepin' to try to git a look at he young mistis whar he gwine b'longst to. One evenin' dee all on 'em come roun' de porch an' send for Marse George, an' when he come out, Charley Brown (he al'ays de speaker, 'cause he got so much mouf, kin talk pretty as white folks), he say dee warn interduce to de young mistis, an' pay dee bespects to her; an' presney Marse George lead her out on de porch laughin' at her, wid her face jes rosy as a wine-sap apple, an' she meck 'em a beautiful bow, an' speak to 'em ev'y one, Marse George namin' de names; an' Charley Brown he meck her a pretty speech, an' tell her we mighty proud to own her; an' one o' dem impident gals ax her to gin her dat white frock when she git married; an' when she say, 'Well, what am I goin' weah?' Sally say, 'Lord, honey, Marse George gwine dress you in pure gol'!' an' she look up at him wid sparks flashin' out her eyes, while he look like dat ain' good 'nough for her. An' so twuz, when she went 'way, Sally Marshall got dat frock, an' proud on it I tell you.

"Oh yes; he sutney mindin' her tender. Hi! when she go to ride in evenin' wid him, de ain' no horseblock good 'nough for her! Marse George got to have her step in he hand; an' when dee out walkin' he got de umbreller holdin' 't over her all de time, he so feared de sun'll kiss her; an' dee walk so slow down dem walks in de shade you got to sight 'em by a tree to tell ef dee movin' 'tall. She use' to look like she used to it too, I tell you, 'cause she wuz quality, one de white-skinned ones; an' she'd set in dem big cheers, wid her little foots on de cricket whar Marse George al'ays set for her, he so feared dee'd tetch de groun', jes like she on her throne; an' ole marster he'd watch her 'mos' edmirin' as Marse George; an' when she went 'way hit sutney was lonesome. Hit look like daylight gone wid her. I don' know which I miss mos', Miss Charlotte or Nancy.

"Den Marse George was 'lected to de Legislature, an' ole Jedge Darker run for de Senator, an' Marse George vote gin him an' beat him. An' dat commence de fuss; an' den dat man gi' me de whuppin, an' dat breck 'tup an' breck he heart.

"You see, after Marse George wuz 'lected ('lections wuz 'lections dem days; dee warn' no bait-gode 'lections, wid ev'y sort o' worms squirmin' up 'ginst one nurr, wid piece o' paper d' ain' know what on, drappin' in a chink; didn' nuttin but gent'mens vote den, an' dee took dee dram, an' vote out loud, like gent'mens)—well, arter Marse George wuz 'lected, de parties wuz jes as even balanced as stilyuds, an' wen dee ax Marse George who wuz to be de Senator, he vote for de Whig, 'ginst de ole jedge, an' dat beat him, of co'se. An' dee ain' got sense to know he 'bleeged to vote wid he politics. Dat he sprinciple; he kyarn vote for Locofoco, I don' keer ef he is Miss Charlotte pa, much less her step-pa. Of co'se de ole jedge ain' speak to him arter dat, nur is Marse George ax him to. But who dat gwine s'pose women-folks got to put dee mouf in too? Miss Charlotte she write Marse George a letter dat pester him mightily; he set up all night answerin' dat letter, an' he mighty solemn, I tell you. An' I wuz gittin' right grewsome myself, 'cause I studyin' 'bout dat gal down dyah whar I done gi' my wud to, an' when dee ain' no letters come torectly hit hard to tell which one de anxiouser, me or Marse George. Den presney I so 'straughted 'long o' it I ax Aunt Haly 'bouten it: she know all sich things, 'cause she 'mos' a hunderd years ole, an' seed evil sperits, an' got skoripins up her chimney, an' knowed cunjure; an' she ax me what wuz de

signification, an' I tell her I ain' abl nuther to eat nor to sleep, an' dat ga come foolin' 'long me when I slee jes like as natchel as ef I see her sh 'nough. An' she say I done conjured dat de gal done tricked me. Oh, Gord dat skeered me. You white folk: marster, don' b'lieve nuttin like dat y' all got too much sense, 'cause y' al kin read; but niggers dee ain' know n better, an' I sutney wuz skeered 'cause Aunt Haly say my coffin don seasoned, de planks up de chimney Well, I got so bad Marse George a me 'bout it, an' he sort o' laugh an sort o' cuss, an' he tell Aunt Haly e she don' stop dat foolishness skeerin me he'll sell her an' teah her ole skoripin house down. Well, co'se he jes talkin', an' he ax me next day how'd I like to go an' see my sweet-heart. Gord! suh, I got well torectly. So I set off next evenin', feelin' jes big as ole marster, wid my pass in my pocket, which I warn' to show nobody 'douten I 'bleeged to, 'cause Marse George didn' warn nobody to know he le' me go. An' den dat rascallion teck de shut off my back. But et Marse George didn' pay him de wuth o' it!

"I done git 'long so good, too. When Nancy see me she sutney was 'ston-ished. She come roun' de cornder in de back yard whar I settin' in Nat's do' (he wuz de gardener) wid her hyah all done untwist, an' breshed out mighty fine, an' a clean ap'on wid fringe on it, meckin' out she so s'prised to see me (whar wuz all a lie, 'cause some on 'em done notify her I dyah), an' she say, 'Hi! what dis black nigger doin' heah?'

"An' I say, 'Who you callin' nigger, you impident kercumber-faced thing you?' Den we shake hands, an' I tell her Marse George done set me free—dat I done buy myself; dat's de ie I done lay off to tell her.

"An' when I tole her dat, she bust out laughin', an' say, well, I better go 'long 'way, den, dat she don' warn no free nigger to be comp'ny for her. Dat sort o' set me back, an' I tell her she kickin' 'fo' she spurred, dat I ain' got her in my mine; I got a nurr gal at home, whar grievin' 'bout me dat ve'y minute. An' after I tell her all sich lies as dat, presney she ax me ain' I hongry; an' ef dat nigger didn' git her mammy to gi' me de bes' supter! Umm-m! I kin 'mos' tas'e it now. Wheat bread off de table, an' zerves, an' fat bacon, tell I couldn' 'a put a nurr moufful nowhar sep'n' I'd teck my hat. Dat night I tote Nancy water for her, an' I tell her all 'bout ev'ything an' she jes sweet as honey. Next mornin', do', she done sort o' tunned some, an' ain' so sweet. You know how milk gits sort o' bonny-clabberish? An' when she see me she 'gin to 'buse me—say I jes tryin' to fool her, an' all de time got nurr wife at home, or gittin' ready to git one, for all she know, an' she ain' know wherr Marse George ain' jes 'ceivin' as I is; an' nem mine, she got plenty warn marry her; an' as to Miss Charlotte, she got de whole wull; Mr. Darker he ain' got nobody in he way now, dat he deah all de time, an' ain' gwine West no mo'. Well, dat aggrivate me so I tell her ef she say dat 'bout Marse George I gwine knock her; an' wid dat she got so oudacious I meck out I gwine 'way, an' lef' her, an' went up todes de barn; an up dyah, fust thing I know, I come across dat ar man Mr. Darker. Soon as he

see me he begin to cuss me, an' he ax me what I doin' on dat land, an' I tell him nuttin. An' he say, well, he gwine to gi' me some'n; he gwine teach me to come prowlin' round gent'men's houses. An' he meck me go in de barn an' teck off my shut, an' he beat me wid he whup tell de blood run out my back. He sutney did beat me scandalous, 'cause he done hate me an' Marse George ever since we wuz at college togurr. An' den he say: 'Now you git right off dis land. Ef either you or you marster ever put you foot on it, you'll git de same thing agin.' An' I tell you, Edinburg he come 'way, 'cause he sutney had worry me. I ain' stop to see Nancy or nobody; I jes come 'long, shakin' de dust, I tell you. An' as I come 'long de road I pass Miss Charlotte walkin' on de lawn by herself, an' she call me: 'Why, hi! ain' dat Edinburg?'

"She look so sweet, an' her voice soun' so cool, I say, 'Yes'm; how you do, missis?' An' she say, she ve'y well, an' how I been, an' whar I gwine? I tell her I ain' feelin' so well, dat I gwine home. 'Hi!' she say, 'is anybody treat you bad?' An' I tell her, 'Yes'm.' An' she say, 'Oh! Nancy don' mean nuttin by dat; dat you mus'n mine what womens say an' do, 'cause dee feel sorry for it next minute; an' sometimes dee kyarn help it, or maybe hit you fault; an', anyhow, you ought to be willin' to overlook it; an' I better go back an' wait till tomorrow—ef—ef I ain' 'bleeged to git home to-day.'

"She got mighty mixed up in de een part o' dat, an' she looked mighty anxious 'bout me an' Nancy; an' I tell her, 'Nor'm, I 'bleeged to git home.'

"Well, when I got home Marse

George he warn know all dat gwine on; but I mighty sick—dat man done beat me so; an' he ax me what de marter, an' I upped an' tell him.

"Gord! I never see a man in sich a rage. He call me in de office an' meck me teck off my shut, an' he fyah bust out cryin'. He walked up an' down dat office like a caged lion. Ef he had got he hand on Mr. Darker den, he'd 'a kilt him, sho!

"He wuz most 'stracted. I don' know what he'd been ef I'd tell him what Nancy tell me. He call for Peter to git he horse torectly, an' he tell me to go an' git some'n' from mammy to put on my back, an' to go to bed torectly, an' not to say nuttin to nobody, but to tell he pa he'd be away for two days, maybe; an' den he got on Reveller an' galloped 'way hard as he could wid he jaw set farst, an' he heaviest whip clamped in he hand. Gord! I wuz most hopin' he wouldn' meet dat man, 'cause I feared ef he did he'd kill him; an' he would, sho, ef he had meet him right den; dee say he leetle mo' did when he fine him next day, an' he had done been ridin' den all night; he cotch him at a sto' on de road, an' dee say he leetle mo' cut him all to pieces; he drawed a weepin on him, but Marse George wrench it out he hand an' flung it over de fence; an' when dee got him 'way he had weared he whup out on him; an' he got dem whelps on him now, ef he ain' dead. Yes, suh, he ain' let nobody else do dat he ain' do heself, sho!

"Dat done de business! He sont Marse George a challenge, but Marse George sont him wud he'll cowhide him agin ef he ever heah any mo' from him, an' he 'ain't. Dat perrify him, so he shet he mouf. Den come he ring an' all he pictures an' things back—a gret box on 'em, and not a wud wid 'em. Marse George, I think he know'd dee wuz comin', but da ain' keep it from huttin him, 'cause he done been 'gaged to Miss Charlotte, an' got he mine riveted to her; an' do' befo' dat dee had stop writin', an' a riff done git 'twixt 'em he ain' satisfied in he mine dat she ain't gwine 'pologizee—I know by Nancy; but now he got de confirmation dat he done for good, an' da de gret gulf fixed 'twix him an' Abraham bosom. An', Gord, suh, twuz torment, sho 'nough! He ain' say nuttin 'bout it, but I see de light done pass from him, an' de darkness done wrap him up in it. In a leetle while you wouldn' 'a knowed him. Den ole mistis died. B'lieve me, ole marster he 'most much hut by Miss Charlotte as Marse George. He meck a 'tempt to buy Nancy for me, so I find out arterward, an' write Jedge Darker he'll pay him anything he'll ax for her, but he letter wuz sont back 'dout any answer He sutney was mad 'bout it—he say he'd horsewhip him as Marse George did dat urr young puppy, but ole mistis wouldn' le' him do nuttin, and den he grieve heself to death You see he mighty ole, anyways. He nuver got over ole mistis death. She had been failin' a long time, an' he ain' tarry long 'hinst her; hit sort o' like breckin up a holler—de ole 'coon goes 'way soon arter dat; an' marster nuver could pin he own collar or buckle he own stock—mistis she al'ays do dat; an' do' Marse George do de bes' he kin, an' mighty willin', he kyarn handle a pin like a woman; he hand tremble like a p'inter dog; an' anyvays he ain' ole mistis. So old mars-er foller her dat next fall, when dee wuz gittin in de corn, an' Marse George he ain' got nobody in de wull left; he all alone in dat gret house, an' I wonder sometimes he ain' die too, 'cause he sutney wuz fond o' ole marster. When ole mistis wuz lyin' she tell him to be good to ole marster, an' patient wid him, 'cause he ain' got nobody but him now (ole marster he had jes step out de room to cry); an' Marse George he lean over her an' kiss her an' promise her faithful he would. An' he sutney wuz tender wid him as a woman; an' when ole marster die he set by him an' hol' he hand an' kiss him sorf, like he wuz ole mistis. But, Gord! twuz lonesome arter dat, an' Marse George eyes look wistful, like he al'ays lookin' far 'way; an' Aunt Haly say he see harnts whar walk 'bout in de gret house. She say dee walk dyah constant of nights sence ole marster done alternate de rooms from what dee wuz when he gran'pa buil' 'em, an' dat dee huntin' for dee ole chambers an' kyarn git no rest 'cause dee kyarn fine 'em. I don't know how dat wuz. I know Marse George he used to walk about heself mightily of nights. All night long, all night long, I'd heah him tell de chick-ens crowin' de second crow, an' some mornin's I'd go dyah an' he ain' even rumple de bed. I thought sho' he wuz gwine die, but I suppose he done 'arn he days to be long in de land, an' dat save him. But hit sutney wuz lone-some, an' he nuver went off de plan-tation, an' he got older an' older, tell we all thought he wuz gwine die. An' one day come jes befo' Christmas, 'bout night two year after marster die, Mr. Braxton ride up to de do'. He had done come to teck Marse George home to spen' Christmas wid him. Marse George warn git out it, but Mr. Braxton won' teck no disapp'intment; he say he gwine baptize he boy, an' he done name him after Marse George (he had marry Marse George cousin, Miss Peggy Carter, an' he 'vite Marse George to de weddin', but he wouldn' go, do' I sutney did want him to go, 'cause I heah Miss Charlotte was nominated to marry Mr. Darker, an' I warn know what done 'come o' dat bright-skinned nigger gal whar I used to know down dyah); an' he say Marse George got to come an' stan' for him, an' gi' him a silver cup an' a gol' rattle. So Marse George he finally promise to come an' spend Christmas Day, an' Mr. Braxton went 'way next mornin', an' den hit tun in an' rain so I feared we couldn' go, but hit cler off de day befo' Christmas Eve an' tun cold. Well, suh, we ain' been nowhar for so long I wuz skit-tish as a young filly; an' den you know twuz de same ole place. We didn' git dyah till supper-time, an' twuz a good one too, 'cause seventy miles dat cold a weather hit whet a man's honger jes like a whetstone. Dee sutney wuz glad to see we all. We rid roun' by de back yard to gi' Billy de horses, an' we see dee wuz havin' gret fixin's; an' den we went to de house, jes as some o' de folks run in an' tell 'em we wuz come. When Marse George stept in de hall dee all clustered roun' him like dee gwine hug him, dee faces fyah dimplin' wid pleasure, an' Miss Peggy she jes retched up an' teck him in her arms an' hug him.

"Dee tell me in de kitchen dat dee wuz been 'spectin' of Miss Charlotte over to spend Christmas too, but de river wuz so high dee s'pose dee couldn' git 'cross. Chile, dat sutney disapp'int me!

"Well, after supper de niggers had a dance. Hit wuz down in de laundry, an' de table wuz set in de carpenter shop jes by. Oh, hit sutney wuz beautiful! Miss Lucy an' Miss Ailsy dee had superintend' ev'ything wid dee own hands. So dee wuz down dyah wid dee ap'ons up to dee chins, an' dee had de big silver strandeliers out de house, two on each table, an' some o' ole mistiss's best damas' tableclothes, an' ole marster's gret bowl full o' eggnog; hit look big as a mill-pond settin' dyah in de cornder; an' dee had flowers out de greenhouse on de table, an' some o' de chany out de gret house, an' de dinin'-room cheers set roun' de room. Oh! oh! nuttin warn too good for niggers dem times; an' de little niggers wuz runnin' roun' right 'stracted, squealin' an' peepin' an' gittin in de way onder you foots; an' de mens dee wuz totin' in de wood —gret hickory logs, look like stock whar you gwine saw—an' de fire so big hit look like you gwine kill horgs, 'cause hit sutney wuz cold dat night. Dis nigger ain' nuver gwine forgit it! Jack Forester he had come 'cross de river to lead de fiddlers, an' he say he had to put he fiddle onder he coat an' poke he bow in he breeches leg to keep de strings from poppin', an' dat de river would freeze over sho ef twarn so high; but twuz jes snortin', an' he had hard wuck to git over in he skiff, an' Unc' Jeems say he ain' gwine come out he boat-house no mo' dat night—he done tempt Providence often 'nough dat day. Den ev'ything wuz ready, an' de fiddlers got dee dram an' chuned up, an' twuz lively, I tell you!

Twuz jes as thick in dyah as blackberries on de blackberry bush, 'cause ev'y gal on de plantation wuz dyah shakin' her foot for some young buck an' back-steppin' for to go 'long. Den ole sleepers wuz jes a-rockin', an' Jack Forester he wuz callin' de figgers for to wake 'em up. I warn' dancin' 'cause I done got 'ligion an' longst te de chutch since de trouble done tetch us up so rank; but I tell you my foots wuz pintedly eechchin for a leettle sop on it, an' I had to come out to keep from crossin' 'em onst, anyways. Den too, I had a tetch o' misery in my back, an' I lay off to git a tas'e o' dat egg nog out dat big bowl wid snowdrift on it from Miss Lucy—she al'ays mighty fond o' Marse George; so I slip into de carpenter shop, an' ax her kyarn I do nuttin for her, an' she laugh an' say, yes, I kin drink her health, an' gi' me a gret gobletful, an jes den de white folks come in to 'spec' de tables, Marse George in de lead, an' dee all fill up dee glasses an' pledge dee health, an' all de servants' an' a merry Christmas; an' den we went in de laundry to see de dancin', an' maybe to teck a hand deeself, 'cause white folks' 'ligion ain' like niggers', you know; dee got so much larnin' dee kin dance an' fool de devil too. An' I stay roun' a little while, an' den went in de kitchen to see how supper gittin on, 'cause I wuz so hongry when I got dyah I ain' able to eat 'nough at one time to 'commodate it, an' de smell o' de turkeys an de gret saddlers o' mutton in de two kitchens wuz mos' 'nough by deeself to feed a right hongry man; an' dyah wuz a whole parcel o' niggers cookin' an' tunnin 'bout for life, an' dee faces jes as shiny as ef dee done bas'e 'em vid gravy; an' dyah, settin' back in a cheer out de way, wid her clean frock up off de flo', wuz dat gal. I utney did feel curious.

"I say, 'Hi! name o' Gord, whar'd 'ou come from?' She say, 'Oh, Marser! ef heah ain' dat free nigger!' An' v'ybody laughed. Well, presney we come out, 'cause Nancy warn see de dancin', an' we stop a leetle while hind de cornder out de wind while he tell me 'bout ev'ything. An' she ay dat's all a lie she tell me dat day out Mr. Darker an' Miss Charlotte; n' he done gone 'way now for good, cause he so low-down an' wuthless ee kyarn nobody stand him; an' all e warn marry Miss Charlotte for is o git her niggers. But Nancy say Miss Charlotte nuver could abide him, e so 'sateful, spressly sence she fine ut what a lie he told 'bout Marse eorge. You know, Mr. Darker he one meck 'em think Marse George nt me dyah to fine out ef he done ome home, an' den dat he fall on im wid he weepin when he ain' nocin' him, an' sort o' out de way too, n' git two urr mens to hold him while e beat him, all 'cause he in love wid Miss Charlotte. D'you ever, ever eah sich a lie? An' Nancy say, do' Miss Charlotte ain' b'lieve it all gerr, hit look so reasonable she done ' de ole jedge an' her ma, who wuz ending on what she heah, 'duce her send back he things; an' dee ain' ow no better not tell after de ole dge die; den dee fine out 'bout de huppin me, an' all; an' den Miss harlotte know huccome I ain' gwine ay dat day; an' she say dee wuz tney outdone 'bout it, but it too late n, an' Miss Charlotte kyarn do nut- but cry 'bout it, an' dat she did,

pintedly, 'cause she done lost Marse George, an' done 'stroy he life; an' she nuver keer 'bout nobody else sep Marse George, Nancy say. Mr. Clarke he hangin' on, but Miss Charlotte she done tell him pintedly she ain' nuver gwine marry nobody. An' dee jes done come, she say, 'cause dee had to go 'way round by de rope-ferry 'long o' de river bein' so high, an' dee ain' know tell dee done git out de ker'idge an' in de house dat we all wuz heah; an' Nancy say she glad dee ain', 'cause she 'feared ef dee had, Miss Charlotte wouldn' 'a come.

"Den I tell her all 'bout Marse George, 'cause I know she 'bleeged to tell Miss Charlotte. Twuz powerful cold out dyah, but I ain' mine dat, chile. Nancy she done had to wrop her arms up in her ap'on, an' she kyarn meck no zistance 'tall, an' dis nigger ain' keerin nuttin 'bout cold den.

"An' jes den two ladies come out de carpenter shop an' went 'long to de laundry, an' Nancy say, 'Dyah Miss Charlotte now'; an' twuz Miss Lucy an' Miss Charlotte; an' we heah Miss Lucy coaxin' Miss Charlotte to go, tellin' her she kin come right out; an' jes den dee wuz a gret shout, an' we went in hinst 'em. Twuz Marse George had done teck de fiddle, an' ef he warn' natchelly layin' hit down! He wuz up at de urr een o' de room, 'way from we all, 'cause we wuz at de do', nigh Miss Charlotte to go, tellin' her she kin come on 'em, wid her eyes on him mighty timid, like she hidin' from him, an' ev'y nigger in de room wuz on dat flo'. Gord! suh, dee wuz grinnin' so dee warn' a toof in dat room you couldn' git you tweezers on; an' you couldn' heah a wud, dee so proud o' Marse George playin' for 'em.

"Well, dee danced tell you couldn'
tell which wuz de clappers an' which
de back-steppers; de whole house look
like it wuz rockin'; an' presney somebody say supper, an' dat stop 'em, an'
dee wuz a spell for a minute, an'
Marse George standin' dyah wid de
fiddle in he hand. He face wuz
tunned away, an' he wuz studyin'—
studyin' 'bout dat urr Christmas so
long ago—an' sudney he face drapt
down on de fiddle, an' he drawed he
bow 'cross de strings, an' dat chune
begin to whisper right sorf. Hit begin so low ev'ybody had to stop
talkin' an' hold dee mouf to heah it;
an' Marse George he ain' know nuttin
'bout it, he done gone back, an'
standin' dyah in de gret hall playin'
it for Miss Charlotte whar done come
down de steps wid her little blue foots
an' gret fan, an' standin' dyah in her
dim blue dress an' her fyah arms, an'
her gret eyes lookin' in he face so
earnest, whar he ain' gwine nuver
speak to no mo'. I see it by de way
he look—an' de fiddle wuz jes pleadin'.
He drawed it out jes as fine as a stran'
o' Miss Charlotte's hyah.

"Hit so sweet, Miss Charlotte, mun,
she couldn' stan' it; she made to de
do'; an' jes while she watchin' Marse
George to keep him from seein' her
he look dat way, an' he eyes fall right
into hern.

"Well, suh, de fiddle drapt down on
de flo', an' he face wuz white as a
sycamore limb. Dee say twuz a swimmin' in de head he had; an' Jack say
de whole fiddle warn' wuff de five
dollars.

"Me an' Nancy followed 'em tell dee
went in de house, an' den we come
back to de shop whar de supper wuz

gwine on, an' got we all supper an'
leetle sop o' dat yaller gravy out da
big bowl, an' den we all rejourned t
de laundry agin, an' got onder de bi
bush o' misseltow whar hangin' fro
de jice, an' ef you ever see scuffli
dat's de time.

"Well, me an' she had jes done la
off de whole Christmas, when wu
come dat Marse George want h
horses.

"I went, but it sutney breck me up
an' I wonder whar de name o' Gor
Marse George gwine sen' me dat col
night, an' jes as I got to de do' Mars
George an' Mr. Braxton come ou
an' I know torectly Marse George w
gwine home. I seen he face by
light o' de lantern, an' twuz set j
rigid as a rock. Mr. Braxton he w
beggin' him to stay; he tell him h
ruinin' he life, dat he sho dee's som
mistake, an' 'twill be all right. A
all de answer Marse George meck w
to swing heself up in de saddle, a
Reveller he look like he gwine fya
'stracted. He al'ays mighty fool an
ways when he git cold, dat horse wu

"Well, we come 'long 'way, an' M
Braxton an' two mens come down
de river wid lanterns to see us cros
'cause twuz dark as pitch, sho 'noug
An' jes 'fo' I started I got one o'
mens to hol' my horses, an' I went
de kitchen to git warm, an' dya
Nancy wuz. An' she say Miss Cha
lotte upsteirs cryin' right now, 'cau
she think Marse George gwine cro
de river 'count o' her, an' she whimp
a little herself when I tell her goo
by. But twuz too late den. We
de river wuz jes natchelly b'ilin',
hit soun' like a mill-dam roarin' b
an' when we got dyah Marster Geor
tunned to me an' tell me he reckon

etter go back. I ax him whar he
gwine, an' he say, 'Home.' 'Den I
gwine wid you,' I says. I wuz mighty
keered, but me an' Marse George wuz
boys togerr; an' he plunged right in,
an' I after him.

"Gord! twuz cold as ice; an' we
hadn' got in befo' bofe horses wuz
swimmin' for life. He holler to me to
yah de myah head up de stream; an' I
did try, but what's a nigger to dat
water! Hit jes pick me up an' dash
me down like I ain' no mo'n a chip,
an' de fust thing I know I gwine down
de stream like a piece of bark, an'
water washin' all over me. I knowed
den I gone, an' I hollered for Marse
George for help. I heah him answer
me not to git skeered, but to hold on;
but de myah wuz lungin' an' de water
wuz all over me like ice, an' den I
washed off de myah back, an' got
drownded. I 'member comin' up an'
hollerin' agin for help, but I know
den 'tain' no use, dee ain' no help den,
an' I got to pray to Gord, an' den
some'n hit me an' I went down again,
an'—de next thing I know, I wuz in
de bed, an' I heah 'em talkin' 'bout
wherr I dead or not, an' I ain' know
myself tell I taste de whisky dee
po'rin' down my jugular. An' den dee
tell me 'bout how when I hollered
Marse George tun back an' struck
ut for me for life, an' how jes as
I went down de last time he cotch me
an' helt on to me tell we wash down
to whar de bank curve, an' dyah de
current wuz so rapid hit yuck him
ff Reveller back, but he helt on to
de reins tell de horse lunge so he hit
him wid he fo'-foot an' breck he
collar-bone, an' den he had to let him
go, an' jes helt on to me; an' jes
den we wash up agin de bank an'

cotch in a tree, an' de mens got dyah
quick as dee could, an' when dee
retched us Marse George wuz holdin' on to me, an' had he arm wropped
roun' a limb, an' we wuz lodged in de
crotch, an' bofe jes as dead as a nail;
an' de myah she got out, but Reveller
he wuz drownded, wid his foot cotch
in de rein an' de saddle tunned onder
he side; an' dee ain' know wherr Marse
George ain' dead too, 'cause he not
only drownded, but he lef' arm broke
up nigh de shoulder. An' dee say
Miss Charlotte she 'most 'stracted;
dat de fust thing anybody know 'bout
it wuz when some de servants bust in
de hall an' holler, and say Marse
George an' me done bofe washed 'way
an' drownded, an' dat she drapt down
dead on de flo', an' when dee bring
her to she 'low to Miss Lucy dat she
de 'casion on he death; an' dee say dat
when de mens wuz totin' him in de
house, an' wuz shufflin' de feets not
to meck no noige, an' a little piece o'
blue silk drapt out he breast whar
somebody picked up an' gin Miss
Lucy, Miss Charlotte breck right
down agin; an' some on 'em say she
sutney did keer for him; an' now when
he layin' upsteairs dyah dead, hit too
late for him ever to know it.

"Well, suh, I couldn' teck it in dat
Marse George and Reveller wuz dead,
an' jes den somebody say Marse
George done comin' to, an' dee gi' me
so much whisky I went to sleep. An'
next mornin' I got up an' went to
Marse George's room, an' see him
layin' dyah in de bed, wid he face so
white an' he eyes so tired-lookin', an'
he ain' know me no mo' 'n ef he
nuver see me, an' I couldn' stan' it;
I jes drap down on de flo' an' bust
out cryin'. Gord! suh, I couldn' help

it, 'cause Reveller wuz drownded, an'
Marse George he wuz mos' gone. An'
he came nigher goin' yit, 'cause he
had sich a strain, an' been so long in
de water, he heart got numbed, an' he
got 'lirium, an' all de time he thought
he tryin' to git 'cross de river to see
Miss Charlotte, an' hit so high he
kyarn git dyah. Hit sutney wuz pitiful to see him layin' dyah tossin' an' 10
pitchin', not knowin' whar he wuz, tell
it took all Mr. Braxton an' me could
do to keep him in de bed, an' de doctors say he kyarn hol' out much
longer.

"An' all dis time Miss Charlotte she
wuz gwine 'bout de house wid her face
right white, an' Nancy say she don'
do nuttin all day long in her room
but cry an' say her pra'rs, prayin' for 20
Marse George, whar dyin' upstairs by
'count o' not knowin' she love him,
an' I tell Nancy how he honin' all de
time to see her, an' how he constant
callin' her name. Well, so twuz, tell
he mos' done weah heself out; an'
jes lay dyah wid his face white as de
pillow an' he gret pitiful eyes rollin'
'bout so restless, like he still lookin'
for her whar he all de time callin' her 30
name, an' kyarn git 'cross dat river
to see; an' one evenin' 'bout sunset
he 'peared to be gwine; he weaker'n
he been at all, he ain' able to scuffle
no mo', an' jes layin' dyah so quiet,
an' presney he say, lookin' mighty
wistful,

" 'Edinburg, I'm goin' to-night; ef
I don' git 'cross dis time, I'll
gin't up.'

"Mr. Braxton wuz standin' nigh de
head o' de bed, an' he say, 'Well, by
Gord! he *shall* see her!'—jes so. An'
he went out de room, an' to Miss
Charlotte do', an' call her, an' tell her

she got to come, ef she don', he'll di
dat night; an' fust thing I know, Mis
Lucy bring Miss Charlotte in, wi
her face right white, but jes as tende
as a angel's, an' she come an' star
by the side de bed, an' lean down ove
him, an' call he name, 'George!'—
jes so.

"An' Marse George he ain' answer
he jes look at her studdy for a minute
an' den he forehead got smooth, ar
he tun he eyes to me, an' say, 'Edin
burg, I'm 'cross.' "

188

VII. GRACE ELIZABETH KING

From *BALCONY STORIES* *

A DRAMA OF THREE

It was a regular dramatic pe
formance every first of the month i
the little cottage of the old Genera
and Madame B——.

It began with the waking up c
the General by his wife, standing a
the bedside with a cup of blac
coffee.

"Hé! Ah! Oh, Honorine! Yes
the first of the month, and affairs—
affairs to be transacted."

On those mornings when affai
were to be transacted there was n
much leisure for the household; ar
it was Honorine who constituted th
household. Not the old dressin
gown and slippers, the old, old trou
sers, and the antediluvian nec
foulard of other days! Far from i
It was a case of warm water (wit

* Reprinted by permission of The Ma
millan Company.

ven a fling of cologne in it), of the
rimming of beard and mustache by
Honorine, and the black broadcloth
suit, and the brown satin stock, and
that *je ne sais quoi de dégagé* which
no one could possess or assume like
the old General. Whether he possessed or assumed it is an uncertainty
which hung over the fine manners of
all the gentlemen of his day, who
ere kept through their youth in
aris to cultivate *bon ton* and an edu-
ation.

It was also something of a gala-day
or Madame la Générale too, as it
ust be a gala-day for all old wives
to see their husbands pranked in the
manners and graces that had con-
uered their maidenhood, and exhal-
g once more that ambrosial fra-
ance which once so well incensed
eir compelling presence.

Ah, to the end a woman loves to
elebrate her conquest! It is the
st touch of misfortune with her to
se in the old, the ugly, and the com-
onplace her youthful lord and mas-
r. If one could look under the gray
irs and wrinkles with which time
atches old women, one would be
rprised to see the flutterings, the
iverings, the thrills, the emotions,
e coals of the heart-fires which
ath alone extinguishes, when he
mmands the tenant to vacate.

Honorine's hands chilled with the
e of sixteen as she approached scis-
rs to the white mustache and beard.
hen her finger-tips brushed those
s, still well formed and roseate,
e felt it, strange to say, on her
s. When she asperged the warm
ter with cologne,—it was her
cret delight and greatest effort of
onomy to buy this cologne,—she

always had one little moment of what
she called faintness—that faintness
which had veiled her eyes, and chained
her hands, and stilled her throbbing
bosom, when as a bride she came
from the church with him. It was
then she noticed the faint fragrance
of the cologne bath. Her lips would
open as they did then, and she would
stand for a moment and think
thoughts to which, it must be confessed, she looked forward from
month to month. What a man he
had been! In truth he belonged to
a period that would accept nothing
less from Nature than physical
beauty; and Nature is ever subservi-
ent to the period. If it is to-day all
small men, and to-morrow gnomes
and dwarfs, we may know that the
period is demanding them from Nature.

When the General had completed—
let it be called no less than the ceremony of—his toilet, he took his
chocolate and his *pain de Paris*. Honorine could not imagine him break-
fasting on anything but *pain de Paris*.
Then he sat himself in his large
armchair before his escritoire, and
began transacting his affairs with the
usual—

"But where is that idiot, that dolt,
that sluggard, that snail, with my
mail?"

Honorine, busy in the breakfast-
room:

"In a moment, husband. In a moment."

"But he should be here now. It
is the first of the month, it is nine
o'clock, I am ready; he should be
here."

"It is not yet nine o'clock, husband."

"Not yet nine! Not yet nine! Am I not up? Am I not dressed? Have I not breakfasted before nine?"

"That is so, husband. That is so."

Honorine's voice, prompt in cheerful acquiescence, came from the next room, where she was washing his cup, saucer, and spoon.

"It is getting worse and worse every day. I tell you, Honorine, Pompey must be discharged. He is worthless. He is trifling. Discharge him! Discharge him! Do not have him about! Chase him out of the yard! Chase him as soon as he makes his appearance! Do you hear, Honorine?"

"You must have a little patience, husband."

It was perhaps the only reproach one could make to Madame Honorine, that she never learned by experience.

"Patience! Patience! Patience is the invention of dullards and sluggards. In a well-regulated world there should be no need of such a thing as patience. Patience should be punished as a crime, or at least as a breach of the peace. Wherever patience is found police investigation should be made as for smallpox. Patience! Patience! I never heard the word—I assure you, I never heard the word in Paris. What do you think would be said there to the messenger who craved patience of you? Oh, they know too well in Paris—a rataplan from the walking-stick on his back, that would be the answer; and a, 'My good fellow, we are not hiring professors of patience, but legs.'"

"But husband, you must remember we do not hire Pompey. He only

does it to oblige us, out of his kind ness."

"Oblige us! Oblige me! Kind ness! A negro oblige me! Kind t me! That is it; that is it. That the way to talk under the new re gime. It is favor, and oblige, an education, and monsieur, and ma dame, now. What child's play to ca this a country—a government! would not be surprised"—jumping his next position on this ever-recu ring first of the month theme—" would not be surprised if Pompey ha failed to find the letter in the bo How do I know that the mail has n been tampered with? From day day I expect to hear it. What is prevent? Who is to interpose? Th honesty of the officials? Honesty the officials—that is good! What farce—honesty of officials! That evidently what has happened. Th thought has not occurred to me vain. Pompey has gone. He has n found the letter, and—well; that the end."

But the General had still anoth theory to account for the delay in t appearance of his mail which he a ways posed abruptly after the exhau tion of the arraignment of the pos office.

"And why not Journel?" Journ was their landlord, a fellow of mean but no extraction, and a favori aversion of the old gentleman "Journel himself? You think he above it, hé? You think Journ would not do such a thing? H your simplicity, Honorine—your sin plicity is incredible. It is miraculo I tell you, I have known the Jou nels, from father to son, for—yes, f seventy-five years. Was not

randfather the overseer on my fath-
r's plantation? I was not five years
ld when I began to know the Jour-
els. And this fellow, I know him
etter than he knows himself. I
now him as well as God knows him.
have made up my mind. I have
ade it up carefully that the first
me that letter fails on the first of
ne month I shall have Journel ar-
ested as a thief. I shall land him
the penitentiary. What! You
ink I shall submit to have my mail
mpered with by a Journel? Their
ntents appropriated? What! You
ink there was no coincidence in
ournel's offering me his postoffice
ox just the month—just the month,
efore those letters began to arrive?
ou think he did not have some ink-
ng of them? Mark my words, Ho-
orine, he did—by some of his sub-
rranean methods. And all these
ve years he has been arranging his
lans—that is all. He was arranging
eft, which, no doubt, has been con-
mmated to-day. Oh, I have re-
etted it—I assure you I have
gretted it, that I did not promptly
ject his proposition, that, in fact,
ever had anything to do with the
llow."

It was almost invariably, so regu-
rly do events run in this world,—it
as almost invariably that the negro
essenger made his appearance at
is point. For five years the Genal had perhaps not been interrupted
many times, either above or below
e last sentence. The mail, or rather
e letter, was opened, and the usual
nount—three ten-dollar bills—was
refully extracted and counted. And
if he scented the bills, even as the
eneral said he did, within ten min-

utes after their delivery, Journel
made his appearance to collect the
rent.

It could only have been in Paris,
among that old retired nobility, who
counted their names back, as they
expressed it, *"au de çà de déluge,"*
that could have been acquired the
proper manner of treating a *"roturier"* landlord: to measure him with
the eyes from head to foot; to
hand the rent—the ten-dollar bill—
with the tips of the fingers; to scorn
a look at the humbly tendered receipt;
to say: "The cistern needs repair-
ing, the roof leaks; I must warn you
that unless such notifications meet
with more prompt attention than in
the past, you must look for another
tenant," etc., in the monotonous tone
of supremacy, and in the French, not
of Journel's dictionary, nor the dictionary of any such as he, but in the
French of Racine and Corneille; in
the French of the above suggested
circle, which inclosed the General's
memory, if it had not inclosed—as he
never tired of recounting—his star-
like personality.

A sheet of paper always infolded
the banknotes. It always bore, in
fine but sexless tracery, "From one
who owes you much."

There, that was it, that sentence,
which, like a locomotive, bore the
General and his wife far on these
firsts of the month to two opposite
points of the horizon, in fact, one
from the other—"From one who owes
you much."

The old gentleman would toss the
paper aside with the bill receipt. In
the man to whom the bright New
Orleans itself almost owed its brightness, it was a paltry act to search and

pick for a debtor. Friends had betrayed and deserted him; relatives had forgotten him; merchants had failed with his money; bank presidents had stooped to deceive him; for he was an old man, and had about run the gamut of human disappointments—a gamut that had begun with a C major of trust, hope, happiness, and money.

His political party had thrown him aside. Neither for ambassador, plenipotentiary, senator, congressman, not even for a clerkship, could he be nominated by it. Certes! "From one who owed him much." He had fitted the cap to a new head, the first of every month, for five years, and still the list was not exhausted. Indeed, it would have been hard for the General to look anywhere and not see some one whose obligations to him far exceeded this thirty dollars a month. Could he avoid being happy with such eyes?

But poor Madame Honorine! She who always gathered up the receipts, and the "From one who owes you much"; who could at an instant's warning produce the particular ones for any month of the past half-decade. She kept them filed, not only in her armoire, but the scrawled papers—skewered, as it were, somewhere else—where women from time immemorial have skewered such unsigned papers. She was not original in her thoughts—no more, for the matter of that, than the General was. Tapped at any time on the first of the month, when she would pause in her drudgery to reimpale her heart by a sight of the written characters on the scrap of paper, her thoughts would have been found flowing thus,

"One can give everything, and ye be sure of nothing."

When Madame Honorine sai "everything," she did not, as wome in such cases often do, exaggerat When she married the General, she i reality gave the youth of sixteen, th beauty (ah, do not trust the deni of those wrinkles, the thin hair, th faded eyes!) of an angel, the dot c an heiress. Alas! It was too littl at the time. Had she in her own per son united all the youth, all th beauty, all the wealth, sprinkled pa simoniously so far and wide ove all the women in this land, woul she at that time have done augh else with this than immolate it c the burning pyre of the General affection? "And yet be sure of noth ing."

It is not necessary, perhaps, to e plain that last clause. It is ver little consolation for wives that the husbands have forgotten, when som one else remembers. Some one else Ah! there could be so many some or elses in the 'General's life, for i truth he had been irresistible to e cess. But this was one particul some one else who had been faithf for five years. Which one?

When Madame Honorine solv that enigma, she has made up h mind how to act.

As for Journel, it amused him mo and more. He would go away fro the little cottage rubbing his han with pleasure (he never saw M dame Honorine, by the way, only tl General). He would have given f more than thirty dollars a month f this drama; for he was not only ric but a great *farceur*.

18

ROMANCE AND SENTIMENT

I. LEWIS WALLACE
(1827–1905)

From *THE FAIR GOD* *

BOOK VII

CHAPTER XI

BATTLE IN THE AIR

As Cortes, at the head of his column, drew near the gate of the *coatapantli,* he saw the inclosure and the terraces on that side of the temple occupied by warriors, and the edge of the azoteas above lined with *pabas,* chanting in dismal harmony with the deep music of the great drum. Ensigns and symbols of unknown meaning, and rich regalia pranked the dull gray faces of the pile with holiday splendors. Little note, however, gave he to the beautiful effect.

"God helping us," he said to his cavaliers,—and with such gravity that they knew him unusually impressed with the task before them,—"God helping us, gentlemen, we will do a deed now that hath no likeness in the wars of men. Commend we ourselves each, and all who follow us, to the holy Christ, who cometh yonder on the staff of Father Olmedo."

So saying, he reversed his sword, and carried the crossed handle softly and reverently to the bars of his helmet, and all who heard him did likewise.

In front of the gate, under a shower of arrows, he stopped to adjust the armlets of his shield, for his hand was yet sore; then, settling in his saddle again, he spurred his horse through the entrance into the enclosure.

Right into the mass waiting to receive him he broke, and whom his sword left untouched the trained steed bore down. After him charged the choicest spirits of the conquest, animated with generous rivalry and the sublime idea that this time the fight was for God and His Church. And so, with every thrust of sword and every plunge of horse, out rang their cries.

"On, on, for love of Christ! Death to the infidels! Down with the false gods!"

On the side of the infidels there was no yielding, for the ground was holy ground to them. When their frail weapons were broken, they flung themselves empty-handed upon the nearest rider, or under the horses, and, dying even, tried to hold fast locked the hoofs that beat them to death. In their aid, the pavement became heaped with bodies, and so slippery with blood that a number of the horses fell down; and, in such cases, if the rescue came not quickly they and their riders were lost. Indeed, so much did this peril increase that Cortes, when his footmen were fairly in the yard,

* Used by permission of, and arrangement with, Houghton Mifflin Company.

680 · LEWIS WALLACE

dismounted the horsemen the better to wage the fight.

At length resistance ceased: the inclosure was won. The marble floor bore awful evidences of the prowess of one party and the desperation of the other.

The Christians took up their wounded, and carried them tenderly to the shade, for the sun blazed down from the cloudless sky.

Around Cortes gathered the captains, resting themselves.

"The Tlascalans must hold the yard," he said, well pleased, and with raised visor. "That charge I commit to thee, Lugo."

Lugo bared his face, and said, sullenly,—

"Thou knowest, Señor, that I am accustomed to obey thee questionless; but this liketh me not. I—"

"By the love of Christ—"

"Even so, Señor," said Lugo, interrupting him in turn. "I feel bidden by love of Christ to go up, and help cast down the accursed idols."

The face of the crafty leader changed quickly.

"Ola, father!" he said. "Here is one malcontent, because I would have him stay and take care of us while we climb the stairways. What say'st thou?"

Olmedo answered solemnly, "What ye have in mind now, Señores,—the disgrace of the false gods who abide in this temple of abominations,—is what hath led us here. And now that the end is at hand, the least circumstance is to be noted; for the wise hear God as often in the small voice as in the thunder. Doubt not, doubt not; the prompting of the good captain is from Him. Be this lower

duty to the unassoilzied Tlascalans: go we as the love of Christ calleth. Verily, he who doeth this work well, though his sins be many as the sands of the sea, yet shall he become as purity itself, and be blessed forever. Take thy measures quickly, Señor, and let us be gone."

"Amen, amen!" said the cavaliers; and Cortes, crossing himself, hastened in person to make dispositions for the further emprise.

The Tlascalans he set to hold the coatapantli from attack without. To the arquebusiers and cross-bowmen he gave orders to cover him with their fire while he climbed the stairways and was driving the enemy around the terraces. When the azoteas was gained, they were to ascend, and take part in the crowning struggle for the sanctuaries. The cavalry, already dismounted, were to go with him in the assault. To the latter, upon rejoining them, he said,—

"In my judgment, gentlemen, the fighting we go to now is of the kind wherein the sword is better than axe or lance; therefore, put away all else."

He took place at the head, with Alvarado and Sandoval next him in the column.

"And thou, father?" he asked.

Olmedo raised his crucifix, and looking up, said,—

"Hagase tu voluntad en la tierra asi como en el cielo."* Then to Cortes, "I will follow these, my children."

"Forward, then! Christ with us and all the saints!" cried Cortes, "Adelante! Christo y Santiago!"

* Thy will be done on earth as it is in heaven. [Author's note.]

In a moment they were swiftly climbing the lower stairway of the temple.

Meantime Io', from the *azoteas,* kept watch on the combats below. Two figures charmed his gaze,—that of Cortes and that of the 'tzin,—both, in their separate ways, moving forward slowly but certainly. Before he thought of descending, the Christians were in the precinct of the *coatapantli,* and after them streamed the long line of Tlascalans.

As we have seen, the prince had been in battles, and more than once felt the joyous frenzy nowhere else to be found; but now a dread fell upon him. Did Malinche's dream of conquest reach the gods? Again and again he turned to the sanctuaries, but the divine wrath came not forth, —only the sonorous throbs of the drum. Once he went into the presence chamber, which was full of kneeling *pabas.* The *teotuctli* stood before the altar praying. Io' joined in the invocation; but miracle there was not, neither was there help; for when he came out, all the yard around the temple was Malinche's.

Then Io' comprehended that this attack, unlike Escobar's, was of method; for the ways of succor, which were also those of retreat, were all closed. The supreme trial had come early in his career. His spirit arose; he saw himself the stay of the religion of his fathers; the gods leaned upon him. On the roof and terraces were some two thousand warriors, the fighting children of the valley: Tezcucans, with countless glorious memories to sustain their native pride; Cholulans, eager to avenge the sack of their city and the massacre of their countrymen; Aztecs, full of the superiority of race, and the inspiration of ages of empire. They would fight to the last man. He could trust them, as the 'tzin had trusted him. The struggle, moreover, besides being of special interest on account of its religious character, would be in mid-air, with the strangers and all the tribes and companies as witnesses. So, with his caciques, he went down to the landing at the top of the lower stairway.

A yell saluted Cortes when, at the head of the cavaliers, he appeared on the steps, and, sword in hand and shield overhead, commenced the perilous ascent. At the same time javelins and spears began to rain upon the party from the first terrace. Up they hurried. Half the height was gained and not a man hurt, —not a foot delayed! Then, slowly at first, but with longer leaps and increasing force, a block of stone was started down the stairs. Fortunately, the steps were broad, having been built for the accommodation of processions. Down sped a warning cry; down as swiftly plunged the danger. Olmedo saw three figures of men in iron follow it headlong to the bottom; fast they fell, but not too fast for his words of absolution; before the victims touched the pavement, their sins were forgiven, and their souls at rest in Paradise.

The stones and timbers placed on the landing by the 'tzin's order were now laid hold of, and rolled and dragged to the steps and hurled down. Thus ten Christians more were slain. Even Cortes, deeming escape impossible, turned his battle-cry into a prayer, and not in vain! From below, the arquebusiers and cross-bow-men suddenly opened fire, which they kept so close that, on the landing, the dead and wounded speedily outnumbered the living.

"The saints are with us! Forward, swords of the Church!" cried Cortes.

Before the infidels recovered from their panic, he passed the last step, and stood upon the terrace. And there, first in front of him, first to meet him, was Io', whom pride and zeal would not permit to retire.

The meeting—combat it can hardly be called—was very brief. The blades of Io's *maquahuitl* broke at the first blow. Cortes replied with a thrust of the sword,—quick, but true, riving both the shield and the arm. A cacique dragged the hapless boy out of reach of the second thrust, and took his place before the conqueror.

The terrace so hardly gained was smoothly paved, and wide enough for ten men to securely walk abreast; on the outer side there was no railing or guard of any kind, nothing but a descent of such height as to make a fall certainly fatal. Four times the smooth, foot-worn pavement extended around the temple, broken in its course by six grand stairways, the last of which landed on the *azoteas,* one hundred and fifty feet above the level of the street. Such was the highway of the gods, up which the adventurous Christians essayed to march, fighting.

"To my side, Sandoval! And ye, Alvarado, Morla, Lugo, Ordas, Duero,—to my side!" said Cortes, defending himself the while. "Make with me a line of shields across the way. Let me hear your voices. No battle-cry here but Christ and St.

James! When ye are ready, shout that I may hear ye!"

One by one the brave gentlemen took their places; then rose the cry "*Christo y Santiago! Christo y Santiago!*"

And then the voice of Cortes,—

"Forward, my friends! Push the dogs! No quarter! *Christo y Santiago!*"

Behind the line of shields moved the other cavaliers, eager to help when help should be needed.

And then were shown the excellences of the sword in a master's hand. The best shields of the infidels could not bar its point; it overcame resistance so quietly that men fell wounded, or slain outright, before they thought themselves in danger it won the terrace, and so rapidly that the Christians were themselves astonished.

"*Ola, compañeros!*" said Cortes who in the fiercest *mêlée* was still the watchful captain. "*Ola!* Yonder riseth the second stairway. That the heathen may not use the vantage against us, keep we close to this pack On their heels! Closer!"

So they mounted the steps of the second stairway, fighting; and the crowd which they kept between them and the enemy on the landing was a better cover even than the fire of the bowmen and arquebusiers. And so the terraces were all taken. Of the eight other Christians who fell under the stones and logs rolled upon them from the heights above, two lived long enough to be shrived by the faithful Olmedo.

The *azoteas* of the temple has already been described as a broad paved area, unobstructed except by

he sacrificial stones and the sanc-
uaries of Huitzil' and Tezca'. A
more dreadful place for battle cannot
e imagined. The coming and going
f worshippers, singly or in proces-
ions, and of barefooted pabas, to
whom the dizzy height was all the
world, had worn its surface smooth
s furbished iron. If, as the combat
olled slowly around the terraces, ris-
ng higher, and nearer the chiefs and
warriors on the summit,—if, in faint-
ess of heart or hope, they looked for
way of escape, the sky and the remote horizon were all they saw: es-
ape was impossible.

With many others disabled by
wounds, Io' ascended to the azoteas
n advance of the fight; not in de-
pair, but as the faithful might, never
oubting that, when the human effort
ailed, Huitzil', the Omnipotent,
would defend himself. He passed
hrough the ranks, and with brave
ords encouraged the common re-
olve to conquer or die. Stopping
pon the western verge, he looked
own upon the palace, and lo! there
as a rest in the assault, except where
he 'tzin fought, with his back to
he temple; and the thousands were
anding still, their faces upturned,—
ach where the strange truce found
im,—to behold the hunted gods in
me majestic form at last assert
heir divinity. So Io' knew, by the
hisperings of his own faith.

Again he turned prayerfully to the
anctuaries. At that instant Cortes
ounted the last step of the last
airway,—after him the line of
hields, and all the cavaliers,—after
hem again, Olmedo with his crucifix!
hen was wrought an effect, simple
nough of itself, but so timely that

the good man—forgetful that the
image of Christ dead on the cross is
nothing without the story of his perfect love and sorrowful death—found
believers when he afterwards pro-
claimed it a miracle. He held the
sacred effigy up to be seen by all the
infidels; they gazed at it as at a god
unfriendly to their gods, and waited
in awe for the beginning of a struggle between the divine rivals; and
while they waited, Cortes and his cavaliers perfected their formation upon
the azoteas, and the bowmen and arquebusiers began to climb the second
stairway of the ascent. The moment
of advantage was lost to the Aztecs,
and they paid the penalty.

Io' waited with the rest; from
crucifix to sanctuary, and sanctuary
to crucifix, he turned; yet the gods
nursed their power. At last he
awoke; too late! there was no escape.
Help of man was not possible, and the
gods seemed to have abandoned him.

"Tezcuco! Cholula! Tenochtit-
lan! Up, up, Tlateloco, up!"

Over the azoteas his words rang
piercing clear, and through the ranks
towards the Christians he rushed.
The binding of the spell was broken.
Shook the banners, pealed war-cry,
conch, and atabal,—and the battle
was joined.

"Hold fast until our brethren come;
then shall our swords drink their fill!
Christo y Santiago!"

Never was the voice of Cortes
more confident.

Need, nevertheless, had the cavaliers for all their strength and skill,
even the nicest cunning of fence and
thrust. Every joint of their harness
was searched by javelin and spear,
and the clang of maquahuitls against

the faces of their shields was as the noise of a thousand *armeros* at work. The line swayed and bent before the surge, now yielding, now recovering, at times ready to break, and then— death awaited them all on the terraces below. For life they plied their swords,—no, not for life alone; behind them to and fro strode Olmedo.

"Strike, and spare not!" he cried. "Lo, the gates of hell yonder, but they shall not prevail. Strike for Holy Church, whose swords ye are! For Holy Cross, and room to worship above the Baals of heathendom! For glory here, and eternal life hereafter!"

So he cried as he strode; and the crucifix on his lance and the saintly words on his lips were better than trumpets, better than a hundred Cids in reserve.

The great drum, which had been for a while silent, at this juncture burst out again; and still more to inflame the infidels, forth from the sanctuaries the pabas poured, and dispersed themselves, leaping, dancing, singing, through the ranks. Doubtless they answered the Christian priest, promise for promise, and with even greater effect; the calm and self-possessed among their people became zealots, and the zealots became frantic madmen.

At last the bowmen and arquebusiers appeared upon the scene. When Cortes saw them,—their line formed, matches lighted, bows drawn, —he drew out of the combat to give them directions.

"*Viva compañeros!*" he said, with a vivacity peculiar to himself, "I bid ye welcome. The temple and its keepers are ours. We with swords will now go forward. Keep ye th stairway, and take care of our flanks Ply your bolts,—ply them fast,—an spare not a cur in the kennel!"

They made no answer, spake no a word. Stolidly, grimly they gaze at him under their morions; the knew their duty, and he knew them Once more he turned to the fight.

"To the sanctuaries!" he shouted to the cavaliers. "We have come fo the false gods: let us at them Charge, gentlemen, Christ with us Forward all!"

Back came their response, "For ward! *Christo y Santiago!*"

They advanced their shields sud denly; the play of their swords re doubled; the weapons in front o them splintered like reeds; war-crie half uttered turned to screams; un der foot blood ran like water, an feathered panoply and fallen me dying and dead, blotted out the pave ment. Surprised, bewildered, baffle the bravest of the infidels perished the rest gave way or were pushe helplessly back; and the dismay thu excited rose to panic when the bow men and arquebusiers joined in th combat. A horrible confusion ensue Hundreds threw away their arms, an ran wildly around the *azoteas;* som flung themselves from the height some climbed the sanctuaries; som took to piteous imploration of th doomed idols; others, in blind fur rushed empty-handed upon the dri ping swords.

Steadily, as a good craft divide the current and its eddies, Corte made way to the sanctuaries, impa tient to possess the idols, that, at on blow, he might crush the faith the represented, after which he made n

doubt of the submission of the nations in arms. A rare faculty that
which, in the heat of battle, can
weave webs of policy, and in the
mind's eye trace out lines of wise
conduct.

When, at last, the end was nigh,
such of the pabas as survived withdrew themselves from the delirious
mob, and assembled around the sacrificial stones. Some of them were
wounded; on many the black gowns
hung in shreds; all of them had one
purpose more, usually the last to linger in an enthusiast's heart. There,
where they had witnessed so many
sacrifices, and, in eager observance
of auguries, overlooked or savagely
enjoyed the agony of the victims, they
came themselves to die,—there the
word found them; and from their
brave, patient death we may learn
that Satan hath had his martyrs as
well as Christ.

About the same time another body
collected in the space before the
presence chamber of Huitzil'. They
were the surviving caciques, with Io'
in their midst. Having borne him out
of the fray, they now took up a last
position to defend him and the gods.
Upon them also the battle had laid
heavy hand; most of them were
hurt and bleeding; of their beautiful
regalia only fragments remained;
some were without arms of any kind,
some bore headless javelins or spears;
few had *maquahuitls*. Not a word
was spoken: they, too, had come to
die, and the pride of their race forbade repining.

They saw the last of the pabas fall;
then the rapacious swords, to complete the work, came to them. In
the front strode Cortes. His armor

shone brightly, and his shield, though
spotted with blood, was as a mirror
from which the sun's rays shot, like
darts, into the eyes of the infidels attracted by its brightness.

Suddenly, three warriors, unarmed,
rushed upon him; his sword passed
through one of them; the others
caught him in their arms. So quick,
so bold and desperate was the action
that, before he could resist or his
captains help him, he was lifted from
his feet and borne away.

"Help, gentlemen! Rescue!" he
cried.

Forward sprang Sandoval, forward
Alvarado, forward the whole line.
The caciques interposed themselves.
Played the swords then never so fast
and deadly,—still the wall of men
endured.

Cortes with all his armor was a
cumbrous burthen; yet the warriors
bore him swiftly toward the verge of
the *azoteas*. No doubt of their purpose: fair and stately were the halls
awaiting them in the Sun, if they but
took the leap with him! He struggled
for life, and called on the saints, and
vowed vows; at the last moment, one
of them stumbled and fell; thereupon
he broke away, regained his feet, and
slew them both.

In the door of the sanctuary of
Huitzil', meantime, Io' stood, biding
the sure result of the unequal struggle. Again and again he had striven
to get to the enemy; but the devoted
caciques closed their circle against
him as compactly as against them.
Nearer shone the resistless blades,—
nearer the inevitable death. The
rumble and roar of the drum poured
from the chamber in mighty throbs;
at times he caught glimpses of the

azoteas strewn with bloody wreck; a sense of the greatness of the calamity seized him, followed by the sullen calm which, in brave men dying, is more an accusation of fate than courage, resignation, or despair; upon his faculties came a mist; he shouted the old war-cry of the 'tzin, and scarcely heard himself; the loves and hopes that had made his young life beautiful seemed to rise up and fly away, not in the air-line of birds, but with the slow, eccentric flight of star-winged butterflies; then the light faded and the sky darkened; he reeled and staggered, but while falling, felt himself drawn into the presence chamber, and looking up saw the face of the *teotuctli*, and heard the words, "I loved your father, and he loved the god, who may yet save us. Come, come!" The loving hands took off his warlike trappings, and covering him with the frock of a paba set him on the step of the altar at the feet of the god; then the darkness became perfect, and he knew no more.

Directly there was a great shout within the chamber, blent with the clang of armor and iron-shod feet; the *teotuctli* turned, and confronted Olmedo, with Cortes and the cavaliers.

The Christian priest dropped his lance to the floor, threw back his cowl, raised his visor, and pointing to the crucifix gazed proudly into the face of the infidel pontiff, who answered with a look high and scornful, as became the first and last servant of a god so lately the ruler of the universe. And while they faced each other, the beating of the drum ceased, and the clamor stilled, until nothing

was heard but the breathing of the conquerors, tired with slaughter.

Then Cortes said,—

"Glory to Christ, whose victory this is! Thou, father, art his priest; let thy will be done. Speak!"

Olmedo turned to that quarter of the chamber where, by permission of Montezuma, a Christian shrine and cross had been erected: shrine and cross were gone! Answered he then,—

"The despoiler hath done his work. Vengeance is mine, saith the Lord. Take this man," pointing to the *teotuctli*, "and bind him, and lead him hence."

Alvarado stepped forward, and took off the massive silver chain which he habitually wore twice encircling his neck, and falling down low over his breast-plate; with it he bound the wrists of the prisoner, who once, and once only, cast an appealing glance up to the stony face of the idol. As they started to lead him off, his eye fell upon Io'; by a sign and look of pity, he directed their attention to the boy.

"He is not dead," said Sandoval, after examination.

"Take him hence, also," Olmedo ordered. "At leisure to-morrow we can learn what importance he hath."

Hardly were the captives out when the chamber became a scene of wild iconoclasm. The smoking censers were overthrown; the sculpturings of the walls were defaced; the altar was rifled of the rich accumulation of gifts; fagots snatched from the undying fires in front of the sanctuaries were applied to the carved and gilded wood-work; and amid the smoke, and with shouting and laughter and the

ʴisy abandon of school-boys at play,
ʴe zealots despoiled the gigantic
ʴnage of its ornaments and treasure,
-of the bow and golden arrows in
s hands; the feathers of humming
ʴrds on its left foot; the necklace of
ʴld and silver hearts; the serpent
ʴfolding its waist in coils glistening
ith pearls and precious stones. A
ʴundred hands then pushed the mon- 10
ʴer from its sitting-place, and rolled
out of the door, and finally off the
zoteas. Tezca' shared the same fate.
ʴhe greedy flames mounted to the
ʴwers, and soon not a trace of the
ʴges of horrible worship remained,
ʴxcept the smoking walls of the
ʴined sanctuaries.

Down from the heights marched the
ʴictors; into the palace they marched; 20
ʴnd not a hand was raised against
ʴem on the way; the streets were
ʴlmost deserted.

"Bien!" said Cortes, as he dis-
ʴounted once more in front of his
ʴuarters. *"Muy bien!* We have their
ʴing and chief-priests; we have
ʴurned their churches, disgraced their
ʴods, and slain their nobles by the
ʴousand. The war is over, gentle- 30
ʴen; let us to our couches. Welcome
ʴst! welcome peace!"

And the weary army, accepting his
ʴords as verity, went to rest, though
ʴe sun flamed in the brassy sky; but
ʴst there was not; ere dreams could
ʴllow slumber, the trumpets sounded,
ʴnd the battle was on again, fiercer
ʴan ever.

The sun set, and the night came; 40
ʴen the companies thought to rest;
ʴut Cortes, made tireless by rage,
ʴent out after them, and burned a
ast district of houses.

And the flames so filled the sky

with brilliance that the sun seemed
to have stood still just below the
horizon.

During the lurid twilight, Olmedo
laid away, in shallow graves dug for
them in the palace-garden, more than
fifty Christians, of whom six and
forty perished on the temple and its
terraces.

1873

II. FRANK R. STOCKTON (FRANCIS RICHARD STOCKTON) (1834–1902)

RUDDER GRANGE

For some months after our marriage, Euphemia and I boarded. But
we didn't like it. Indeed, there was
no reason why we should like it. Euphemia said that she never felt at
home except when she was out, which
feeling, indicating an excessively un-
philosophic state of mind, was enough
to make me desire to have a home of
my own, where, except upon rare and
exceptional occasions, my wife would
never care to go out.

If you should want to rent a house,
there are three ways to find one. One
way is to advertise, another is to read
the advertisements of other people.
This is a comparatively cheap way.
The third method is to apply to an
agent. But none of these plans are
worth anything. The proper way is
to know some one who will tell you
of a house which will exactly suit
you. Euphemia and I thoroughly investigated this matter, and I know
that what I say is a fact.

We tried all the plans. When we advertised, we had about a dozen admirable answers, but although everything else seemed to suit, the amount of rent was not named. (None of those in which the rent was named would do at all.) And when I went to see the owners, or agents of these houses, they asked much higher rents than those mentioned in the unavailable answers—and this, notwithstanding the fact that they always asserted that their terms were either very reasonable or else greatly reduced on account of the season being advanced. (It was now the fifteenth of May.)

Euphemia and I once wrote a book, —this was just before we were married,—in which we told young married people how to go to housekeeping and how much it would cost them. We knew all about it, for we had asked several people. Now the prices demanded for yearly rental for small furnished houses by the owners and agents of whom I have been speaking, were actually more than we stated a house could be bought and furnished for!

The advertisements of other people did not serve any better. There was always something wrong about the houses when we made close inquiries, and the trouble was generally in regard to the rent. With agents we had a little better fortune. Euphemia sometimes went with me on my expeditions to real estate offices, and she remarked that these offices were always in the basement, or else you had to go up to them in an elevator. There was nothing between these extremes. And it was a good deal the same way, she said, with their houses.

They were all very low indeed price and quality, or else too hig She answered me several times th if we could find any office on t second or third floor we should ce tainly be suited. But we never four such an office.

One trouble was that we wanted house in a country place, not ve far from the city, and near a railro station or steamboat landing. W also wanted the house to be nice shaded and fully furnished, and n to be in a malarious neighborhood, one infested by mosquitoes.

"If we do go to housekeeping," sa Euphemia, "we might as well get house to suit us while we are abou it. Moving is more expensive tha a fire."

There was one man who offered a house that almost suited us. It w near the water, had rooms enoug and some—but not very much ground, and was very accessible the city. The rent, too, was qui reasonable. But it was unfurnishe The agent, however, did not thi that this would present any obstac to our taking it. He was sure th the owner would furnish it if we pa him ten per cent. on the value of t furniture he put into it. We agree that if the landlord would do this ar let us furnish the house according the plans laid down in our book, th we would take the house. But unfo tunately this arrangement did not su the landlord, although he was in t habit of furnishing houses for tenan and charging them ten per cent. the cost.

I saw him myself and talked to hi about it.

"But you see," said he, when I ha

own him our list of articles neces-
ry for the furnishing of a house,
t would not pay me to buy all these
ings and rent them out to you. If
ou only wanted heavy furniture,
hich would last for years, the plan
ould answer, but you want every-
ing. I believe the small conven-
nces you have on this list cost more
oney than the furniture and car-
ets."

"Oh, yes," said I. "We are not so
ery particular about furniture and
arpets, but these little conveniences
re the things that make housekeep-
g pleasant and,—speaking from a
ommon-sense point of view,—profit-
ble."

"That may be," he answered, "but
can't afford to make matters pleas-
nt and profitable for you in that
ay. Now, then, let us look at one
r two particulars. Here, on your
st, is an ice-pick: twenty-five cents.
ow, if I buy that ice-pick and rent
to you at two and a half cents a
ear, I shall not get my money back
nless it lasts you ten years. And
ven then, as it is not probable that
can sell that ice-pick after you have
sed it for ten years, I shall have
ade nothing at all by my bargain.
nd there are other things in that
st, such as feather-dusters and lamp-
himneys, that couldn't possibly last
en years. Don't you see my posi-
ion?"

I saw it. We did not get that fur-
ished house, and Euphemia was
reatly disappointed.

"It would have been just splendid,"
he said, "to have taken our book and
o have ordered all these things at
he stores, one after another, without
eing obliged to ask the price."

I had my private doubts in regard
to this matter of price. I am afraid
that Euphemia generally set down the
lowest price and the best things. She
did not mean to mislead, and her plan
certainly made our book attractive.
But it did not work very well in practice. We have a friend who undertook to furnish her house by our
book, and she never could get the
things as cheap as we had them
quoted.

"But you see," said Euphemia to
her, "we had to put them down at
the lowest prices, because the model
house we speak of in the book is to
be entirely furnished for just so
much."

But, in spite of this explanation,
the lady was not satisfied.

We found ourselves obliged to give
up the idea of a furnished house. We
would have taken an unfurnished one
and furnished it ourselves, but we
hadn't money enough. We were very
much afraid that we should have to
continue to board.

It was now getting on toward summer, at least there was only a part
of a month of spring left, and whenever I could get away from my business Euphemia and I made little excursions into the country round about
the city. One afternoon we went up
the Harlem river, and there we saw
a sight that transfixed us, as it were.
On the bank, a mile or so above High
Bridge, stood a canal-boat. I say
stood, because it was so firmly im-
bedded in the ground by the riverside, that it would have been almost
as impossible to move it as to have
turned the Sphinx around. This boat
we soon found was inhabited by an
oyster-man and his family. They had

lived there for many years and were
really doing quite well. The boat
was divided, inside, into rooms, and
these were papered and painted and
nicely furnished. There was a
kitchen, a living-room, a parlor and
bedrooms. There were all sorts of
conveniences—carpets on the floors,
pictures, and everything—at least so
it seemed to us, to make a home
comfortable. This was not all done
at once, the oyster-man told me.
They had lived there for years, and
had gradually added this and that
until the place was as we saw it. He
had an oyster-bed out in the river,
and he made cider in the winter, but
where he got the apples I don't know.
There was really no reason why he
should not get rich in time.

We went all over that house, and
we praised everything so much that
the oyster-man's wife was delighted,
and when we ordered some stewed
oysters afterward,—eating them at a
little table under a tree near by,—I
believe that she picked out the very
largest oysters she had, to stew for
us. When we had finished our supper and paid for it, and were going
down to take our little boat again,—
for we had rowed up the river,—Euphemia stopped and looked around
her. Then she clasped her hands and
exclaimed in an ecstatic undertone:

"We must have a canal-boat!"

And she never swerved from that
determination.

After I had seriously thought over
the matter, I could see no good reason against adopting this plan. It
certainly would be a cheap method of
living, and it would really be housekeeping. I grew more and more in
favor of it. After what the oyster-

man had done, what might not we do
He had never written a book on
housekeeping, nor, in all probability
had he considered the matter philosophically, for one moment in all h
life.

But it was not an easy thing to fin
a canal-boat. There were none ad
vertised for rent—at least, not fo
housekeeping purposes.

We made many inquiries and too
many a long walk along the water
courses in the vicinity of the city
but all in vain. Of course, we talke
a great deal about our project an
our friends became greatly intereste
in it, and, of course, also, they gav
us a great deal of advice, but we di
not mind that. We were philosoph
ical enough to know that you canno
have shad without bones. They wer
good friends and, by being careful i
regard to the advice, it didn't inter
fere with our comfort.

We were beginning to be discour
aged, at least Euphemia was. He
discouragement is like water-cresses
it generally comes up in a very shor
time after she shows her wishes. Bu
then it withers away rapidly, which i
a comfort. One evening we were sit
ting, rather disconsolately, in ou
room, and I was reading out the ad
vertisements of country board in the
"Herald," when in rushed Dr. Hear
—one of our old friends. He was s
full of something that he had to say
that he did not even ask us how we
were. In fact, he did not appear to
want to know.

"I tell you what it is, Arden," said
he, "I have found the very thing you
want."

"A canal-boat?" I cried.

"Yes," said he, "a canal-boat."

"Furnished?" asked Euphemia, her eyes glistening.

"Well, no," answered the doctor, I don't think you could expect that."

"But we can't live on the bare floor," said Euphemia; "our house must be furnished."

"Well, then, I suppose this won't do," said the doctor ruefully, "for there isn't so much as a bootjack in it. It has most things that are necessary for a boat, but it hasn't anything that you could call house-furniture; but, dear me, I should think you could furnish it very cheaply and comfortably out of your book."

"Very true," said Euphemia, "if we could pick out the cheapest things and then get some folks to buy a lot of the books."

"We could begin with very little," said I, trying hard to keep calm.

"Certainly," said the doctor; "you need make no more rooms, at first, than you could furnish."

"Then there are no rooms," said Euphemia.

"No, there is nothing but one vast apartment extending from stem to stern."

"Won't it be glorious!" said Euphemia to me. "We can first make a kitchen, and then a dining-room, and a bedroom, and then a parlor—just in the order in which our book says they ought to be furnished."

"Glorious!" I cried, no longer able to contain my enthusiasm; "I should think so. Doctor, where is this canal-boat?"

The doctor then went into a detailed statement.

The boat was stranded on the shore of the Scoldsbury river not far below Ginx's. We knew where Ginx's was, because we had spent a very happy day there, during our honeymoon.

The boat was a good one, but superannuated. That, however, did not interfere with its usefulness as a dwelling. We could get it—the doctor had seen the owner—for a small sum per annum, and there was positively no end to its capabilities.

We sat up until twenty minutes past two, talking about that house. We ceased to call it a boat at about a quarter of eleven.

The next day I "took" that boat and paid a month's rent in advance. Three days afterward we moved into it.

We had not much to move, which was a comfort, looking at it from one point of view. A carpenter had put up two partitions in it, which made three rooms,—a kitchen, a dining-room, and a very long bedroom, which was to be cut up into a parlor, study, guest-chamber, etc., as soon as circumstances should allow, or my salary should be raised. Originally, all the doors and windows were in the roof, so to speak, but our landlord allowed us to make as many windows to the side of the boat as we pleased, provided we gave him the wood we cut out. It saved him trouble, he said, but I did not understand him at the time. Accordingly, the carpenter made several windows for us, and put in sashes, which opened on hinges, like the rasp of a trunk. Our furniture did not amount to much, at first. The very thought of living in this independent, romantic way was so delightful, Euphemia said, that furniture seemed a mere secondary matter.

We were obliged, indeed, to give up

the idea of following the plan detailed in our book, because we had not the sum upon which the furnishing of a small house was therein based.

"And if we haven't the money," remarked Euphemia, "it would be of no earthly use to look at the book. It would only make us doubt our own calculations. You might as well try to make brick without mortar, as the children of Israel did."

"I could do that myself, my dear," said I, "but we won't discuss that subject now. We will buy just what we absolutely need, and then work up from that."

Acting on this plan, we bought first a small stove, because Euphemia said that we could sleep on the floor, if it were necessary, but we couldn't make a fire on the floor—at least, not often. Then we got a table and two chairs. The next thing we purchased was some hanging shelves for our books, and Euphemia suddenly remembered the kitchen utensils. These, which were few, with some crockery, nearly brought us to the end of our resources, but we had enough for a big easy-chair which Euphemia was determined I should have, because I really needed it when I came home at night, tired by my long day's work at the office. I had always been used to an easy-chair, and it was one of her most delightful dreams to see me in one, comfortably smoking my cigar in my own house, after eating my own delicious little supper in company with my own dear wife. We selected the chair, and were about to order the things sent out to our future home, when I happened to think that we had no bed. I called Euphemia's attention to the fact.

She was thunderstruck.

"I never thought of that," she sai[d] "We shall have to give up the stove["]

"Not at all," said I, "we can't d[o] that. We must give up the eas[y] chair."

"Oh, that would be too bad," sai[d] she. "The house would seem li[ke] nothing to me without the chair!"

"But we must do without it, m[y] dear," said I, "at least for awhile. [We] can sit out on deck and smoke in th[e] evening, you know."

"Yes," said Euphemia. "You ca[n] sit on the bulwarks and I can sit b[y] you. That will do very well. I'[m] sure I'm glad the boat has bulwarks.["]

So we resigned the easy-chair an[d] bought a bedstead and some ver[y] plain bedding. The bedstead wa[s] what is called a "scissors-bed." W[e] could shut it up when we did n[ot] want to sleep in it, and stand [it] against the wall.

When we packed up our trunks an[d] left the boarding-house Euphem[ia] fairly skipped with joy.

We went down to Ginx's in th[e] first boat, having arranged that ou[r] furniture should be sent to us in th[e] afternoon. We wanted to be ther[e] to receive it. The trip was wild[ly] delirious. The air was charming, th[e] sun was bright, and I had a who[le] holiday. When we reached Ginx['s] we found that the best way to ge[t] our trunks and ourselves to our hous[e] was to take a carriage, and so w[e] took one. I told the driver to driv[e] along the river road and I would te[ll] him where to stop.

When we reached our boat, and ha[d] alighted, I said to the driver:

"You can just put our trunks in[-] side, anywhere."

The man looked at the trunks and then looked at the boat. Afterward he looked at me.

"That boat ain't goin' anywhere," said he.

"I should think not," said Euphemia. "We wouldn't want to live in , if it were."

"You are going to live in it?" said the man.

"Yes," said Euphemia.

"Oh!" said the man, and he took our trunks on board without another word.

It was not very easy for him to get the trunks into our new home. In fact it was not easy for us to get there ourselves. There was a gang-plank, with a rail on one side of it, which inclined from the shore to the deck of the boat at an angle of about forty-five degrees, and when the man had staggered up this plank with the trunks (Euphemia said I ought to have helped him, but I really thought that it would be better for one person to fall off the plank than for two to go over together), and we had paid him, and he had driven away in a speechless condition, we scrambled up and stood upon the threshold, or, rather, the after-deck of our home.

It was a proud moment. Euphemia glanced around, her eyes full of happy tears, and then she took my arm and we went down stairs—at least, we tried to go down in that fashion, but soon found it necessary to go one at a time. We wandered over the whole extent of our mansion and found that our carpenter had done his work better than the woman we had engaged to scrub and clean the house. Something akin to despair must have seized upon her, for Euphemia declared that the floors looked dirtier than on the occasion of her first visit, when we rented the boat.

But that did not discourage us. We felt sure that we should get it clean in time.

Early in the afternoon our furniture arrived, together with the other things we had bought, and the men who brought them over from the steamboat landing had the merriest faces I ever noticed among that class of people. Euphemia said it was an excellent omen to have such cheerful fellows come to us on the very first day of our housekeeping.

Then we went to work. I put up the stove, which was not much trouble, as there was a place all ready on the deck for the stove-pipe to be run through. Euphemia was somewhat surprised at the absence of a chimney, but I assured her that canal-boats were very seldom built with chimneys. My dear little wife bustled about and arranged the pots and kettles on nails which I drove into the kitchen walls. Then she made the bed in the bedroom, and I hung up a looking glass and a few little pictures which we had brought in our trunks.

Before four o'clock our house was in order. Then we began to be very hungry.

"My dear," said Euphemia, "we ought to have thought about bringing something to cook."

"That is very true," said I, "but I think we had better walk up to Ginx's and get our supper to-night. You see we are so tired and hungry."

"What!" cried Euphemia, "go to a hotel the very first day? I think it would be dreadful! Why, I have been looking forward to this first meal with the greatest delight. You can go up to the little shop by the hotel and buy some things and I will cook them, and we will have our first dear little supper here all alone by ourselves, at our own table and in our own house."

So this was determined upon and, after a hasty counting of the fund I had reserved for moving and kindred expenses, and which had been sorely depleted during the day, I set out, and in about an hour returned with my first marketing.

I made a fire, using a lot of chips and blocks the carpenters had left, and Euphemia cooked the supper, and we ate it from our little table, with two large towels for a table-cloth.

It was the most delightful meal I ever ate!

And, when we had finished, Euphemia washed the dishes (the thoughtful creature had put some water on the stove to heat for the purpose while we were at supper) and then we went on deck, or on the piazza, as Euphemia thought we had better call it, and there we had our smoke. I say we, for Euphemia always helps me to smoke by sitting by me, and she seems to enjoy it as much as I do.

And when the shades of evening began to gather around us, I hauled in the gang-plank (just like a delightful old draw-bridge, Euphemia said, although I hope for the sake of our ancestors that draw-bridges were easier to haul in) and went to bed.

It is lucky we were tired and wanted to go to bed early, for we had forgotten all about lamps or candle

For the next week we were tw busy and happy people. I rose abo half-past five and made the fire,—w found so much wood on the sho that I thought I should not have t add fuel to my expenses,—and E phemia cooked the breakfast. I the went to a well belonging to a cottag near by, where we had arranged fo water privileges, and filled two buck ets with delicious water and carrie them home for Euphemia's us through the day. Then I hurried o to catch the train, for, as there was station near Ginx's, I ceased to pat ronize the steamboat, the hours o which were not convenient. After day of work and pleasurable anticipa tion at the office, I hastened back t my home, generally laden with a bas ket of provisions and various house hold necessities. Milk was brough to us daily from the above-mentione cottage by a little toddler who seeme just able to carry the small tin bucke which held a lacteal pint. If th urchin had been the child of rich par ents, as Euphemia sometimes ob served, it would have been in hi nurse's arms; but being poor, he wa scarcely weaned before he began t carry milk around to other people.

After I reached home came suppe and the delightful evening hours when over my pipe (I had given u cigars as being too expensive and in appropriate, and took to a tall pip and canaster tobacco) we talked, an planned, and told each other ou day's experiences.

One of our earliest subjects of dis cussion was the name of our home stead. Euphemia insisted that i should have a name. I was quit willing, but we found it no easy matter to select an appropriate title. I proposed a number of appellations intended to suggest the character of the home. Among these were: "Safe Ashore," "Firmly Grounded," and some other names of that style, but Euphemia did not fancy any of them. She wanted a suitable name, of course, she said, but it must be something that would *sound* like a house and *be* like a boat.

"Partitionville," she objected to, and "Gang-plank Terrace," did not suit her because it suggested convicts going out to work, which naturally was unpleasant.

At last, after days of talk and cogitation, we named our house "Rudder Grange."

To be sure, it was not exactly a grange, but then it had such an enormous rudder that the justice of that part of the title seemed to overbalance any little inaccuracy in the other portion.

But we did not spend all our spare time in talking. An hour or two every evening was occupied in what we called "fixing up the house," and gradually the inside of our abode began to look like a conventional dwelling. We put matting on the floors and cheap but very pretty paper on the walls. We added now a couple of chairs, and now a table or something for the kitchen. Frequently, especially of a Sunday, we had company, and our guests were always charmed with Euphemia's cunning little meals. The dear girl loved good eating so much that she could scarcely fail to be a good cook. We removed our bed to the extreme bow-part of the boat, and put up muslin curtains to separate it from the parlor.

We worked hard, and were very happy. And thus the weeks passed on.

In this delightful way of living, only one thing troubled us. We didn't save any money. There were so many little things that we wanted, and so many little things that were so cheap, that I spent pretty much all I made, and that was far from the philosophical plan of living that I wished to follow.

We talked this matter over a great deal after we had lived in our new home for about a month, and we came at last to the conclusion that we would take a boarder.

We had no trouble in getting a boarder, for we had a friend, a young man who was engaged in the flour business, who was very anxious to come and live with us. He had been to see us two or three times, and had expressed himself charmed with our household arrangements.

So we made terms with him. The carpenter partitioned off another room, and our boarder brought his trunk and a large red velvet arm-chair, and took up his abode at "Rudder Grange."

We liked our boarder very much, but he had some peculiarities. I suppose everybody has them. Among other things, he was very fond of telling us what we ought to do. He suggested more improvements in the first three days of his sojourn with us than I had thought of since I commenced housekeeping. And what made the matter worse, his suggestions were generally very good ones. Had it been otherwise I might have borne his remarks more complacently, but to be continually told what you ought to do, and to know that you ought to do it, is extremely annoying.

He was very anxious that I should take off the rudder, which was certainly useless to a boat situated as ours was, and make an ironing-table of it. I persisted that the laws of symmetrical propriety required that the rudder should remain where it was—that the very name of our home would be interfered with by its removal—but he insisted that "Ironing-table Grange" would be just as good a name, and that symmetrical propriety in such a case was not worth "a row of pins."

The result was that we did have the ironing table, and that Euphemia was very much pleased with it. A great many improvements were projected and carried out by him, and I was very much worried. He made a flower-garden for Euphemia on the extreme forward-deck, and having borrowed a wheelbarrow, he wheeled dozens of loads of arable dirt up our gang-plank and dumped them out on the deck. When he had covered the garden with a suitable depth of earth, he smoothed it off and then planted flower-seeds. It was rather late in the season, but most of them came up. I was pleased with the garden, but sorry I had not made it myself.

One afternoon I got away from my office considerably earlier than usual, and I hurried home to enjoy the short period of daylight that I should have before supper. It had been raining the day before, and as the bottom of our garden leaked so that earthy water trickled down at one end of our bedroom, I intended to devote a short time to stuffing up the crack in the ceiling or in the bottom of the deck—whichever seems the most appropriate.

But when I reached a bend in the river road, whence I always had the earliest view of my establishment, didn't have that view. I hurried on The nearer I approached the place where I lived, the more horror stricken I became. There was no mistake.

The boat was not there!

In an instant the truth flashed upon me.

The water was very high—the rain had swollen the river—my house had floated away!

It was Wednesday On Wednesday afternoons our boarder came home early.

I clapped my hat tightly on my head and ground my teeth.

"Confound that boarder!" thought. "He has been fooling with the anchor. He always said it was of no use, and taking advantage of my absence, he has hauled it up, and has floated away, and has gone—gone with my wife and my home!"

Euphemia and "Rudder Grange" had gone off together—where I knew not,—and with them that horrible suggester!

I ran wildly along the bank. called aloud, I shouted and hailed each passing craft—of which there were only two—but their crews must have been very inattentive to the woes of landsmen, or else they did not hear me, for they paid no attention to my cries.

I met a fellow with an axe on his shoulder. I shouted to him before reached him:

"Hello! did you see a boat—a house, I mean—floating up the river?"

"A boat-house?" asked the man.

"No, a house-boat," I gasped.

"Didn't see nuthin' like it," said the man, and he passed on, to his wife and home, no doubt. But me! Oh, where was my wife and my home?

I met several people, but none of them had seen a fugitive canal-boat.

How many thoughts came into my brain as I ran along the river-road! If that wretched boarder had not taken the rudder for an ironing-table he might have steered in shore! Again and again I confounded—as far as mental ejaculations could do it—his suggestions.

I was rapidly becoming frantic when I met a person who hailed me.

"Hello!" he said, "are you after a canal-boat adrift?"

"Yes," I panted.

"I thought you was," he said. "You looked that way. Well, I can tell you where she is. She's stuck fast in the reeds at the lower end o' Peter's Pint."

"Where's that?" said I.

"Oh, it's about a mile furder up. I seed her a-driftin' up with the tide —big flood tide, to-day—and I thought I'd see somebody after her afore long. Anything aboard?"

Anything!

I could not answer the man. Anything, indeed! I hurried on up the river without a word. Was the boat a wreck? I scarcely dared to think of it. I scarcely dared to think at all.

The man called after me and I stopped. I could but stop, no matter what I might hear.

"Hello, mister," he said; "got any tobacco?"

I walked up to him. I took hold of him by the lapel of his coat. It was a dirty lapel, as I remember even now, but I didn't mind that.

"Look here," said I. "Tell me the truth, I can bear it. Was that vessel wrecked?"

The man looked at me a little queerly. I could not exactly interpret his expression.

"You're sure you kin bear it?" said he.

"Yes," said I, my hand trembling as I held his coat.

"Well, then," said he, "it's mor'n I kin," and he jerked his coat out of my hand, and sprang away. When he reached the other side of the road, he turned and shouted at me, as though I had been deaf.

"Do you know what I think?" he yelled. "I think you're a darned lunatic," and with that he went his way.

I hastened on to Peter's Point. Long before I reached it, I saw the boat.

It was apparently deserted. But still I pressed on. I must know the worst. When I reached the Point, I found that the boat had run aground, with her head in among the long reeds and mud, and the rest of her hull lying at an angle from the shore. There was consequently no way for me to get on board, but to wade through the mud and reeds to her bow, and then climb up as well as I could.

This I did, but it was not easy

to do. Twice I sank above my knees in mud and water, and had it not been for reeds, masses of which I frequently clutched when I was going over, I believe I should have fallen down and come to my death in that horrible marsh. When I reached the boat, I stood up to my hips in water and saw no way of climbing up. The gang-plank had undoubtedly floated away, and if it had not, it would have been of no use to me in my position.

But I was desperate. I clasped the post which they put in the bow of canal-boats; I stuck my toes and my finger-nails in the cracks between the boards—how glad I was that the boat was an old one and had cracks!—and so, painfully and slowly, slipping part way down once or twice, and besliming myself from chin to foot, I climbed up that post and scrambled upon deck. In an instant I reached the top of the stairs, and in another instant I rushed below.

There sat my wife and our boarder, one on each side of the dining-room table, complacently playing checkers!

My sudden entrance startled them. My appearance startled them still more.

Euphemia sprang to her feet and tottered toward me.

"Mercy!" she exclaimed; "has anything happened?"

"Happened!" I gasped.

"Look here," cried the boarder, clutching me by the arm, "what a condition you're in. Did you fall in?"

"Fall in!" said I.

Euphemia and the boarder looked at each other. I looked at them.

Then I opened my mouth in earnest

"I suppose you don't know," I yelled, "that you have drifted away!"

"By George!" cried the boarder and in two bounds he was on deck

Dirty as I was, Euphemia fell into my arms. I told her all. She had not known a bit of it!

The boat had so gently drifted off and had so gently grounded among the reeds, that the voyage had never so much as disturbed their games of checkers.

"He plays such a splendid game," Euphemia sobbed, "and just as you came I thought I was going to beat him. I had two kings and two pieces on the next to the last row—and you are nearly drowned. You'll get your death of cold—and—and he had only one king."

She led me away, and I undressed and washed myself and put on my Sunday clothes.

When I reappeared I went out on deck with Euphemia. The boarder was there, standing by the petunia bed. His arms were folded and he was thinking profoundly. As we approached he turned toward us.

"You were right about that anchor," he said, "I ought not to have hauled it in; but it was such a little anchor that I thought it would be of more use on board as a garden hoe."

"A very little anchor will sometimes do very well," said I, cuttingly, "especially when it is hooked around a tree."

"Yes, there is something in that," said he.

It was now growing late, and as our agitation subsided we began to be hungry. Fortunately, we had everything necessary on board, and as it really didn't make any difference in our household economy where we happened to be located, we had supper quite as usual. In fact, the kettle had been put on to boil during the checker-playing.

After supper we went on deck to smoke, as was our custom, but there was a certain coolness between me and our boarder.

Early the next morning I arose and went up-stairs to consider what had better be done, when I saw the boarder standing on shore near by.

"Hello!" he cried, "the tide's down and I got ashore without any trouble. You stay where you are. I've hired a couple of mules to tow the boat back. They'll be here presently. And, hello! I've found the gang-plank. It floated ashore about a quarter of a mile below here."

In about ten minutes the mules and two men with a long rope appeared and then one of the men and the boarder came on board (they didn't seem to have any difficulty in so doing). Then they carried the ironing-table on deck and shipped it into its place as a rudder.

We were then towed back to where we belonged.

And we are there yet. Our boarder remains with us, as the weather is still fine, and the coolness between us is gradually diminishing. But the boat is moored at both ends, and twice a day I look to see if the ropes are all right.

The petunias are growing beautifully, but the geraniums do not seem to flourish. Perhaps there is not a sufficient depth of earth for them.

Several times our boarder has appeared to be on the point of suggesting something in regard to them but, for some reason or other, he says nothing.

1874

III. HELEN HUNT JACKSON
(1830–1885)

From *RAMONA* *

XX

[THE LOT OF THE INDIAN]

One year, and a half of another year, had passed. Sheep-shearings and vintages had been in San Pasquale; and Alessandro's new house, having been beaten on by the heavy spring rains, looked no longer new. It stood on the south side of the valley,—too far, Ramona felt, from the blessed bell; but there had not been land enough for wheat-fields any nearer, and she could see the chapel, and the posts, and, on a clear day, the bell itself. The house was small. "Small to hold so much joy," she said, when Alessandro first led her to it, and said, deprecatingly, "It is small, Majella, —too small;" and he recollected bitterly, as he spoke, the size of Ramona's own room at the Señora's house. "Too small," he repeated.

"Very small to hold so much joy, my Alessandro," she laughed; "but quite large enough to hold two persons."

* From *Ramona*, by Helen Hunt Jackson. Reprinted by permission of Little, Brown & Company.

It looked like a palace to the San Pasquale people, after Ramona had arranged their little possessions in it; and she herself felt rich as she looked around her two small rooms. The old San Luis Rey chairs and the raw-hide bedstead were there, and, most precious of all, the statuette of the Madonna. For this Alessandro had built a niche in the wall, between the head of the bed and the one window. The niche was deep enough to hold small pots in front of the statuette; and Ramona kept constantly growing there wild-cucumber plants, which wreathed and re-wreathed the niche till it looked like a bower. Below it hung her gold rosary and the ivory Christ; and many a woman of the village, when she came to see Ramona, asked permission to go into the bedroom and say her prayers there; so that it finally came to be a sort of shrine for the whole village.

A broad veranda, as broad as the Señora's, ran across the front of the little house. This was the only thing for which Ramona had asked. She could not quite fancy life without a veranda, and linnets in the thatch. But the linnets had not yet come. In vain Ramona strewed food for them, and laid little trains of crumbs to lure them inside the posts; they would not build nests inside. It was not their way in San Pasquale. They lived in the cañons, but this part of the valley was too bare of trees for them. "In a year or two more, when we have orchards, they will come," Alessandro said.

With the money from that first sheep-shearing, and from the sale of part of his cattle Alessandro had bought all he needed in the way of farming implements,—a good wagon and harnesses, and a plough. Baba and Benito, at first restive and indignant, soon made up their mind to work. Ramona had talked to Baba about it as she would have talked to a brother. In fact, except for Ramona's help, it would have been a question whether even Alessandro could have made Baba work in harness. "Good Baba!" Ramona said as she slipped piece after piece of the harness over his neck,—"Good Baba, you must help us; we have so much work to do, and you are so strong! Good Baba, do you love me?" and with one hand in his mane and her cheek, every few steps, laid close to his, she led Baba up and down the first furrows he ploughed.

"My Señorita!" thought Alessandro to himself, half in pain, half in pride, as, running behind with the unevenly jerked plough, he watched her laughing face and blowing hair,—"my Señorita!"

But Ramona would not run with her hand in Baba's mane this winter. There was a new work for her indoors. In a rustic cradle, which Alessandro had made under her directions, of the woven twigs, like the great outdoor acorn-granaries, only closer woven, and of an oval shape and lifted from the floor by four uprights of red manzanita stems,—in this cradle, on soft white wool fleeces, covered with white homespun blankets, lay Ramona's baby, six months old, lusty, strong, and beautiful, as only children born of great love and under healthful conditions can be. This child was a girl, to Alessandro's delight; to Ramona's regret,—so far as a loving mother can

eel regret connected with her first-
orn. Ramona had wished for an
Alessandro; but the disappointed wish
faded out of her thoughts, hour by
hour, as she gazed into her baby-girl's
blue eyes,—eyes so blue that their
color was the first thing noticed by
each person who looked at her.

"Eyes of the sky," exclaimed
Ysidro, when he first saw her.

"Like the mother's," said Alessandro; on which Ysidro turned an
astonished look upon Ramona, and
saw for the first time that her eyes,
too, were blue.

"Wonderful!" he said. "It is so.
never saw it;" and he wondered in
his heart what father it had been,
who had given eyes like those to one
born of an Indian mother.

"Eyes of the sky," became at once
the baby's name in the village; and
Alessandro and Ramona, before they
knew it, had fallen into the way of so
calling her. But when it came to the
christening, they demurred. The
news was brought to the village, one
Saturday, that Father Gaspara would
hold services in the valley the next
day, and that he wished all the
new-born babes to be brought for
christening. Late into the night, Alessandro and Ramona sat by their sleeping baby and discussed what should
be her name. Ramona wondered that
Alessandro did not wish to name her
Majella.

"No! Never but one Majella," he
said, in a tone which gave Ramona a
sense of vague fear, it was so solemn.

They discussed "Ramona," "Isa-
bella." Alessandro suggested Car-
mena. This had been his mother's
name.

At the mention of it Ramona shud-

dered, recollecting the scene in the
Temecula graveyard. "Oh, no, no!
Not that!" she cried. "It is ill-
fated;" and Alessandro blamed himself for having forgotten her only association with the name.

At last Alessandro said: "The people have named her, I think, Majella.
Whatever name we give her in the
chapel, she will never be called anything but 'Eyes of the Sky,' in the
village."

"Let that name be her true one,
then," said Ramona. And so it was
settled; and when Father Gaspara
took the little one in his arms, and
made the sign of the cross on her
brow, he pronounced with some difficulty the syllables of the Indian name,
which meant "Blue Eyes," or "Eyes of
the Sky."

Heretofore, when Father Gaspara
had come to San Pasquale to say
mass, he had slept at Lomax's, the
store and post-office, six miles away,
in the Bernardo valley. But Ysidro,
with great pride, had this time ridden
to meet him, to say that his cousin
Alessandro, who had come to live in
the valley, and had a good new adobe
house, begged that the Father would
do him the honor to stay with him.

"And indeed, Father," added Ysidro,
"you will be far better lodged and fed
than in the house of Lomax. My
cousin's wife knows well how all
should be done."

"Alessandro! Alessandro!" said the
Father, musingly. "Has he been long
married?"

"No, Father," answered Ysidro.
"But little more than two years.
They were married by you, on their
way from Temecula here."

"Ay, ay! I remember," said

Father Gaspara. "I will come;" and it was with no small interest that he looked forward to meeting again the couple that had so strongly impressed him.

Ramona was full of eager interest in her preparations for entertaining the priest. This was like the olden time; and as she busied herself with her cooking and other arrangements, the thought of Father Salvierderra was much in her mind. She could, perhaps, hear news of him from Father Gaspara. It was she who had suggested the idea to Alessandro; and when he said, "But where will you sleep yourself, with the child, Majella, if we give our room to the Father? I can lie on the floor outside; but you?"—"I will go to Ysidro's, and sleep with Juana," she replied. "For two nights, it is no matter; and it is such shame to have the Father sleep in the house of an American, when we have a good bed like this!"

Seldom in his life had Alessandro experienced such a sense of gratification as he did when he led Father Gaspara into his and Ramona's bedroom. The clean whitewashed walls, the bed neatly made, with broad lace on sheets and pillows, hung with curtains and a canopy of bright red calico, the old carved chairs, the Madonna shrine in its bower of green leaves, the shelves on the walls, the white-curtained window,—all made up a picture such as Father Gaspara had never before seen in his pilgrimages among the Indian villages. He could not restrain an ejaculation of surprise. Then his eye falling on the golden rosary, he exclaimed, "Where got you that?"

"It is my wife's," replied Alessandro, proudly. "It was given to her by Father Salvierderra."

"Ah!" said the Father. "He died the other day."

"Dead! Father Salvierderra dead!" cried Alessandro. "That will be a terrible blow. Oh, Father, I implore you not to speak of it in her presence. She must not know it till after the christening. It will make her heart heavy, so that she will have no joy."

Father Gaspara was still scrutinizing the rosary and crucifix. "To be sure, to be sure," he said absently; "I will say nothing of it; but this is a work of art, this crucifix; do you know what you have here? And this,—is this not an altar-cloth?" he added, lifting up the beautiful wrought altar-cloth which Ramona, in honor of his coming, had pinned on the wall below the Madonna's shrine.

"Yes, Father, it was made for that. My wife made it. It was to be a present to Father Salvierderra; but she has not seen him, to give it to him. It will take the light out of the sun for her, when first she hears that he is dead."

Father Gaspara was about to ask another question, when Ramona appeared in the doorway, flushed with running. She had carried the baby over to Juana's and left her there that she might be free to serve the Father's supper.

"I pray you tell her not," said Alessandro, under his breath; but it was too late. Seeing the Father with her rosary in his hand, Ramona exclaimed:—

"That, Father, is my most sacred possession. It once belonged to Father Peyri, of San Luis Rey, and

gave it to Father Salvierderra, who
ave it to me. Know you Father
alvierderra? I was hoping to hear
ews of him through you."

"Yes, I knew him,—not very well;
, is long since I saw him," stam-
ered Father Gaspara. His hesitancy
one would not have told Ramona the
uth; she would have set that down
, the secular priest's indifference, or
ostility, to the Franciscan order; but
oking at Alessandro, she saw terror
nd sadness on his face. No shadow
here ever escaped her eye. "What
, it, Alessandro?" she exclaimed. "Is
something about Father Salvier-
erra? Is he ill?"

Alessandro shook his head. He did
ot know what to say. Looking from
ne to the other, seeing the confused
ain in both their faces, Ramona, lay-
g both her hands on her breast, in
he expressive gesture she had learned
om the Indian women, cried out in
, piteous tone: "You will not tell
e! You do not speak! Then he is
ead!" and she sank on her knees.

"Yes, my daughter, he is dead,"
aid Father Gaspara, more tenderly
han that brusque and warlike priest
ften spoke. "He died a month ago,
t Santa Barbara. I am grieved to
ave brought you tidings to give you
uch sorrow. But you must not
ourn for him. He was very feeble,
nd he longed to die, I heard. He
ould no longer work, and he did
ot wish to live."

Ramona had buried her face in her
ands. The Father's words were only
, confused sound in her ears. She
ad heard nothing after the words, "a
onth ago." She remained silent and
motionless for some moments; then,
ising, without speaking a word, or

looking at either of the men, she
crossed the room and knelt down before the Madonna. By a common impulse, both Alessandro and Father
Gaspara silently left the room. As
they stood together outside the door,
the Father said, "I would go back to
Lomax's if it were not so late. I like
not to be here when your wife is in
such grief." .

"That would be another grief,
Father," said Alessandro. "She has
been full of happiness in making ready
for you. She is very strong of soul.
It is she who makes me strong often,
and not I who give strength to her."

"My faith, but the man is right,"
thought Father Gaspara, a half-hour
later, when, with a calm face Ramona
summoned them to supper. He did
not know, as Alessandro did, how that
face had changed in the half-hour. It
wore a look Alessandro had never seen
upon it. Almost he dreaded to speak
to her.

When he walked by her side, later
in the evening, as she went across the
valley to Fernando's house, he ventured to mention Father Salvierderra's name. Ramona laid her hand
on his lips. "I cannot talk about him,
yet, dear," she said. "I never believed that he would die without giving us his blessing. Do not speak
of him till to-morrow is over."

Ramona's saddened face smote on
all the women's hearts as they met her
the next morning. One by one they
gazed, astonished, then turned away,
and spoke softly among themselves.
They all loved her, and half revered
her too, for her great kindness, and
readiness to teach and to help them.
She had been like a sort of mission-
ary in the valley ever since she came,

and no one had ever seen her face
without a smile. Now she smiled not.
Yet there was the beautiful baby in
its white dress, ready to be christened;
and the sun shone, and the bell had
been ringing for half an hour, and
from every corner of the valley the
people were gathering, and Father
Gaspara, in his gold and green cas-
sock, was praying before the altar;
it was a joyous day in San Pasquale.
Why did Alessandro and Ramona
kneel apart in a corner, with such
heart-stricken countenances, not even
looking glad when their baby laughed,
and reached up her hands? Gradually
it was whispered about what had happened. Some one had got it from
Antonio, of Temecula, Alessandro's
friend. Then all the women's faces
grew sad too. They all had heard of
Father Salvierderra, and many of them
had prayed to the ivory Christ in Ramona's room, and knew that he had
given it to her.

As Ramona passed out of the
chapel, some of them came up to her,
and taking her hand in theirs, laid
it on their hearts, speaking no word.
The gesture was more than any speech
could have been.

When Father Gaspara was taking
leave, Ramona said, with quivering
lips, "Father, if there is anything you
know of Father Salvierderra's last
hours, I would be grateful to you for
telling me."

"I heard very little," replied the
Father, "except that he had been
feeble for some weeks; yet he would
persist in spending most of the night
kneeling on the stone floor in the
church, praying."

"Yes," interrupted Ramona; "that
he always did."

"And the last morning," continu
the Father, "the Brothers found hi
there, still kneeling on the stone floo
but quite powerless to move; and the
lifted him, and carried him to h
room, and there they found, to the
horror, that he had had no bed;
had lain on the stones; and th
they took him to the Superior's ov
room, and laid him in the bed, a
he did not speak any more, and
noon he died."

"Thank you very much, Father
said Ramona, without lifting her ey
from the ground; and in the same lo
tremulous tone, "I am glad that
know that he is dead."

"Strange what a hold those Fra
ciscans got on these Indians!" mus
Father Gaspara, as he rode down t
valley. "There's none of them wou
look like that if I were dead, I wa
rant me! There," he exclaimed,
meant to have asked Alessandro wh
this wife of his is! I don't belie
she is a Temecula Indian. Next tir
I come, I will find out. She's h
some schooling somewhere, that
plain. She's quite superior to the ge
eral run of them. Next time I com
I will find out about her."

"Next time!" In what calendar a
kept the records of those next tim
which never come? Long befo
Father Gaspara visited San Pasqua
again, Alessandro and Ramona we
far away, and strangers were living
their home.

It seemed to Ramona in after yea
as she looked back over this life, th
the news of Father Salvierderr
death was the first note of the kn
of their happiness. It was but a fe
days afterward, when Alessand
came in one noon with an expressi

his face that terrified her; seating imself in a chair, he buried his face his hands, and would neither look p nor speak; not until Ramona was ear crying from his silence, did he tter a word. Then, looking at her ith a ghastly face, he said in a hol-w voice, "It has begun!" and buried is face again. Finally Ramona's tears rung from him the following story: Ysidro, it seemed, had the previous ear rented a cañon, at the head of the alley, to one Doctor Morong. It was mply as bee-pasture that the Doctor anted it, he said. He put his hives ere, and built a sort of hut for the an whom he sent up to look after e honey. Ysidro did not need the nd, and thought it a good chance make a little money. He had taken very precaution to make the transac-on a safe one; had gone to San iego, and got Father Gaspara to act s interpreter for him, in the inter-iew with Morong; it had been a writ-n agreement, and the rent agreed pon had been punctually paid. Now, e time of the lease having expired, sidro had been to San Diego to ask e Doctor if he wished to renew it r another year; and the Doctor had id that the land was his, and he was oming out there to build a house, nd live.

Ysidro had gone to Father Gaspara r help, and Father Gaspara had had angry interview with Doctor Mo-ong; but it had done no good. The octor said the land did not belong Ysidro at all, but to the United tates Government; and that he had id the money for it to the agents Los Angeles, and there would very on come papers from Washington, show that it was his. Father Gas-

para had gone with Ysidro to a law-yer in San Diego, and had shown to this lawyer Ysidro's paper,—the old one from the Mexican Governor of California, establishing the pueblo of San Pasquale, and saying how many leagues of land the Indians were to have; but the lawyer had only laughed at Father Gaspara for believing that such a paper as that was good for anything. He said that was all very well when the country belonged to Mexico, but it was no good now; that the Americans owned it now; and everything was done by the American law now, not by the Mexican law any more.

"Then we do not own any land in San Pasquale at all," said Ysidro. "Is that what it means?"

And the lawyer had said, he did not know how it would be with the cultivated land, and the village where the houses were,—he could not tell about that; but he thought it all be-longed to the men at Washington.

Father Gaspara was in such rage, Ysidro said, that he tore open his gown on his breast, and he smote himself, and he said he wished he were a soldier, and no priest, that he might fight this accursed United States Government; and the lawyer laughed at him, and told him to look after souls,—that was his business,—and let the Indian beggars alone! "Yes, that was what he said,—'the Indian beggars!' and so they would be all beggars, presently."

Alessandro told this by gasps, as it were; at long intervals. His voice was choked; his whole frame shook. He was nearly beside himself with rage and despair.

"You see, it is as I said, Majella.

There is no place safe. We can do nothing! We might better be dead!"

"It is a long way off, that cañon Doctor Morong had," said Ramona, piteously. "It wouldn't do any harm, his living there, if no more came."

"Majella talks like a dove, and not like a woman," said Alessandro, fiercely. "Will there be one to come, and not two? It is the beginning. To-morrow may come ten more, with papers to show that the land is theirs. We can do nothing, any more than the wild beasts. They are better than we."

From this day Alessandro was a changed man. Hope had died in his bosom. In all the village councils,— and they were many and long now, for the little community had been plunged into great anxiety and distress by this Doctor Morong's affair, —Alessandro sat dumb and gloomy. To whatever was proposed, he had but one reply: "It is of no use. We can do nothing."

"Eat your dinners to-day, to-morrow we starve," he said one night, bitterly, as the council broke up. When Ysidro proposed to him that they should journey to Los Angeles, where Father Gaspara had said the headquarters of the Government officers were, and where they could learn all about the new laws in regard to land, Alessandro laughed at him. "What more is it, then, which you wish to know, my brother, about the American laws?" he said. "Is it not enough that you know they have made a law which will take the land from Indians; from us who have owned it longer than any can remember; land that our ancestors are buried in,—

will take that land and give it t themselves, and say it is theirs? it to hear this again said in your fac and to see the man laugh who say it, like the lawyer in San Diego, tha you will journey to Los Angeles? will not go!"

And Ysidro went alone. Fath Gaspara gave him a letter to the L Angeles priest, who went with hi to the land-office, patiently interprete for him all he had to say, and patiently interpreted all that the o ficials had to say in reply. They di not laugh, as Alessandro in his bitte ness had said. They were not i human, and they felt sincere sympath for this man, representative of tw hundred hard-working, industriou people, in danger of being turned ou of house and home. But they we very busy; they had to say curtl and in few words, all there was be said: the San Pasquale distri was certainly the property of th United States Government, and th lands were in market, to be filed o and bought, according to the hom stead laws. These officials had neith authority nor option in the matte They were there simply to carry ou instructions, and obey orders.

Ysidro understood the substance all this, though the details were b yond his comprehension. But he d not regret having taken the journey he had now made his last effort f his people. The Los Angeles prie had promised that he would himse write a letter to Washington, to l the case before the head men the and perhaps something would be do for their relief. It seemed incredib to Ysidro, as, riding along day aft day, on his sad homeward journe

reflected on the subject,—it seemed
credible to him that the Govern-
ent would permit such a village as
eirs to be destroyed. He reached
me just at sunset; and looking
wn, as Alessandro and Ramona had
ne on the morning of their arrival,
m the hill-crests at the west end
the valley, seeing the broad belt
cultivated fields and orchards, the
aceful little hamlet of houses, he
oaned. "If the people who make
ese laws could only see this village,
ey would never turn us out, never!
ey can't know what is being done.
am sure they can't know."

"What did I tell you?" cried Ales-
ndro, galloping up on Benito, and
ining him in so sharply he reared
d plunged. "What did I tell you?
saw by your face, many paces back,
at you had come as you went, or
rse! I have been watching for
u these two days. Another Ameri-
n has come in with Morong in the
ñon; they are making corrals; they
ll keep stock. You will see how
ng we have any pasture-lands in
at end of the valley. I drive all my
ck to San Diego next week. I
ll sell it for what it will bring,—
th the cattle and the sheep. It is
use. You will see."

When Ysidro began to recount his
terview with the land-office authori-
s, Alessandro broke in fiercely:
wish to hear no more of it. Their
mes and their speech are like smoke
my eyes and my nose. I think I
all go mad, Ysidro. Go tell your
ry to the men who are waiting to
ar it, and who yet believe that an
nerican may speak truth!"

Alessandro was as good as his
rd. The very next week he drove

all his cattle and sheep to San Diego,
and sold them at great loss. "It is
better than nothing," he said. "They
will not now be sold by the sheriff,
like my father's in Temecula." The
money he got, he took to Father
Gaspara. "Father," he said huskily,
"I have sold all my stock. I would
not wait for the Americans to sell
it for me, and take the money. I
have not got much, but it is better
than nothing. It will make that we
do not starve for one year. Will you
keep it for me, Father? I dare not
have it in San Pasquale. San Pasquale will be like Temecula,—it may
be to-morrow."

To the Father's suggestion that he
should put the money in a bank in
San Diego, Alessandro cried: "Sooner
would I throw it in the sea yonder!
I trust no man, henceforth; only the
Church I will trust. Keep it for me,
Father, I pray you;" and the Father
could not refuse his imploring tone.

"What are your plans now?" he
asked.

"Plans!" repeated Alessandro,—
"plans, Father! Why should I make
plans? I will stay in my house so
long as the Americans will let me.
You saw our little house, Father!"
His voice broke as he said this. "I
have large wheat-fields; if I can get
one more crop off them, it will be
something; but my land is of the
richest in the valley, and as soon as
the Americans see it, they will want
it. Farewell, Father. I thank you
for keeping my money, and for all
you said to the thief Morong. Ysidro
told me. Farewell." And he was
gone, and out of sight on the swift
galloping Benito, before Father Gaspara bethought himself.

"And I remembered not to ask who his wife was. I will look back at the record," said the Father. Taking down the old volume, he ran his eye back over the year. Marriages were not so many in Father Gaspara's parish, that the list took long to read. The entry of Alessandro's marriage was blotted. The Father had been in haste that night. "Alessandro Assis. Majella Fa—" No more could be read. The name meant nothing to Father Gaspara. "Clearly an Indian name," he said to himself; "yet she seemed superior in every way. I wonder where she got it."

The winter wore along quietly in San Pasquale. The delicious soft rains set in early, promising a good grain year. It seemed a pity not to get in as much wheat as possible; and all the San Pasquale people went early to ploughing new fields,—all but Alessandro.

"If I reap all I have, I will thank the saints," he said. "I will plough no more land for the robbers." But after his fields were all planted, and the beneficent rains still kept on, and the hills all along the valley wall began to turn green earlier than ever before was known, he said to Ramona one morning, "I think I will make one more field of wheat. There will be a great yield this year. Maybe we will be left unmolested till the harvest is over."

"Oh, yes, and for many more harvests, dear Alessandro!" said Ramona, cheerily. "You are always looking on the black side."

"There is no other but the black side, Majella," he replied. "Strain my eyes as I may, on all sides all is black. You will see. Never any more harvests in San Pasquale f[or] us, after this. If we get this, w[e] are lucky. I have seen the whit[e] men riding up and down in the va[l]ley, and I found some of their curse[d] bits of wood with figures on the[m] set up on my land the other day and I pulled them up and burne[d] them to ashes. But I will ploug[h] one more field this week; though, [I] know not why it is, my thoughts g[o] against it even now. But I will d[o] it; and I will not come home t[o] night, Majella, for the field is t[oo] far to go and come twice. I sh[all] be the whole day ploughing." [So] saying, he stooped and kissed t[he] baby, and then kissing Ramona, we[nt] out.

Ramona stood at the door a[nd] watched him as he harnessed Ben[ito] and Baba to the plough. He did n[ot] once look back at her; his fa[ce] seemed full of thought, his hands a[ct]ing as it were mechanically. Af[ter] he had gone a few rods from t[he] house, he stopped, stood still for so[me] minutes, meditating, then went on resolutely, halted again, but fina[lly] went on, and disappeared from sig[ht] among the low foot-hills to the ea[st.] Sighing deeply, Ramona turned ba[ck] to her work. But her heart was [too] disquieted. She could not keep ba[ck] the tears.

"How changed is Alessandro!" s[he] thought. "It terrifies me to see h[im] thus. I will tell the Blessed Vir[gin] about it;" and kneeling before [the] shrine, she prayed fervently and lo[ng.] She rose comforted, and drawing [the] baby's cradle out into the veran[da,] seated herself at her embroidery. [Her] skill with her needle had proved [a] not inconsiderable source of inco[me]

er fine lace-work being always taken
ir San Diego merchants, and at fairly
od prices.

It seemed to her only a short time
at she had been sitting thus, when,
ancing up at the sun, she saw it
as near noon; at the same moment
e saw Alessandro approaching, with
e horses. In dismay, she thought,
There is no dinner! He said he
ould not come!" and springing up,
as about to run to meet him, when
e observed that he was not alone.
short, thick-set man was walking
r his side; they were talking ear-
stly. It was a white man. What
d it bode? Presently they stopped.
e saw Alessandro lift his hand and
int to the house, then to the tool
eds in the rear. He seemed to
talking excitedly; the white man
so; they were both speaking at
ce. Ramona shivered with fear.
otionless she stood, straining eye
d ear; she could hear nothing, but
e gestures told much. Had it come,
the thing Alessandro had said
ould come? Were they to be
iven out,—driven out this very
y, when the Virgin had only just
w seemed to promise her help and
otection?

The baby stirred, waked, began to
y. Catching the child up to her
east, she stilled her by convulsive
resses. Clasping her tight in her
ms, she walked a few steps towards
essandro, who, seeing her, made
imperative gesture to her to re-
rn. Sick at heart, she went back
the veranda and sat down to
it.

In a few moments she saw the
ite man counting out money into
essandro's hand; then he turned and

walked away, Alessandro still standing as if rooted to the spot, gazing
into the palm of his hand, Benito
and Baba slowly walking away from
him unnoticed; at last he seemed to
rouse himself as from a trance, and
picking up the horses' reins, came
slowly toward her. Again she started
to meet him; again he made the same
authoritative gesture to her to return; and again she seated herself,
trembling in every nerve of her body.
Ramona was now sometimes afraid of
Alessandro. When these fierce glooms
seized him, she dreaded, she knew not
what. He seemed no more the Alessandro she had loved.

Deliberately, lingeringly, he unhar-
nessed the horses and put them in
the corral. Then still more deliberately, lingeringly, he walked to the
house; walked, without speaking, past
Ramona, into the door. A lurid spot
on each cheek showed burning red
through the bronze of his skin. His
eyes glittered. In silence Ramona
followed him, and saw him draw from
his pocket a handful of gold-pieces,
fling them on the table, and burst
into a laugh more terrible than any
weeping,—a laugh which wrung from
her instantly, involuntarily, the cry,
"Oh, my Alessandro! my Alessandro!
What is it? Are you mad?"

"No, my sweet Majel," he exclaimed, turning to her, and flinging
his arms round her and the child
together, drawing them so close to
his breast that the embrace hurt,—
"no, I am not mad; but I think I
shall soon be! What is that gold?
The price of this house, Majel, and
of the fields,—of all that was ours
in San Pasquale! To-morrow we will
go out into the world again. I will

see if I can find a place the Americans do not want!"

It did not take many words to tell the story. Alessandro had not been ploughing more than an hour, when, hearing a strange sound, he looked up and saw a man unloading lumber a few rods off. Alessandro stopped midway in the furrow and watched him. The man also watched Alessandro. Presently he came toward him, and said roughly, "Look here! Be off, will you? This is my land. I'm going to build a house here."

Alessandro had replied, "This was my land yesterday. How comes it yours to-day?"

Something in the wording of this answer, or something in Alessandro's tone and bearing, smote the man's conscience, or heart, or what stood to him in the place of conscience and heart, and he said: "Come, now, my good fellow, you look like a reasonable kind of a fellow; you just clear out, will you, and not make me any trouble. You see the land's mine. I've got all this land round here;" and he waved his arm, describing a circle; "three hundred and twenty acres, me and my brother together, and we're coming in here to settle. We got our papers from Washington last week. It's all right, and you may just as well go peaceably, as make a fuss about it. Don't you see?"

Yes, Alessandro saw. He had been seeing this precise thing for months. Many times, in his dreams and in his waking thoughts, he had lived over scenes similar to this. An almost preternatural calm and wisdom seemed to be given him now.

"Yes, I see, Señor," he said. "I

am not surprised. I knew it wou[ld] come; but I hoped it would not [come] till after harvest. I will not give y[ou] any trouble, Señor, because I ca[n] not. If I could, I would. But [I] have heard all about the new la[w] which gives all the Indians' lan[d] to the Americans. We cannot he[lp] ourselves. But it is very har[d], Señor." He paused.

The man, confused and emba[r]rassed, astonished beyond expressi[on] at being met in this way by an I[n]dian, did not find words come rea[dy] to his tongue. "Of course, I kno[w] it does seem a little rough on f[el]lows like you, that are industriou[s] and have done some work on the lan[d]. But you see the land's in the ma[r]ket; I've paid my money for it."

"The Señor is going to build [a] house?" asked Alessandro.

"Yes," the man answered. "I'[ve] got my family in San Diego, and want to get them settled as soon [as] I can. My wife won't feel comfor[t]able till she's in her own hous[e]. We're from the States, and she's be[en] used to having everything comfor[t]able."

"I have a wife and child, Señor[,]" said Alessandro, still in the sam[e] calm, deliberate tone; "and we ha[ve] a very good house of two rooms. [It] would save the Señor's building, if [he] would buy mine."

"How far is it?" said the man. "[I] can't tell exactly where the boun[d]aries of my land are, for the stak[es] we set have been pulled up."

"Yes, Señor, I pulled them up a[nd] burned them. They were on m[y] land," replied Alessandro. "M[y] house is farther west than yo[ur] stakes; and I have large wheat-fiel[ds] here, too,—many acres, Señor, all planted."

Here was a chance, indeed. The man's eyes gleamed. He would do the handsome thing. He would give his fellow something for his house and wheat-crops. First he would see the house, however; and it was for that purpose he had walked back with Alessandro. When he saw the neat whitewashed adobe, with its broad veranda, the sheds and corrals all in good order, he instantly resolved to get possession of them by fair means or foul.

"There will be three hundred dollars' worth of wheat in July, Señor, you can see for yourself; and a house so good as that, you cannot build for less than one hundred dollars. What will you give me for them?"

"I suppose I can have them without paying you for them, if I choose," said the man, insolently.

"No, Señor," replied Alessandro.

"What's to hinder, then, I'd like to know!" in a brutal sneer. "You haven't got any rights here, whatever, according to law."

"I shall hinder, Señor," replied Alessandro. "I shall burn down the sheds and corrals, and tear down the house; and before a blade of the wheat is reaped, I will burn that." Still in the same calm tone.

"What'll you take?" said the man, sullenly.

"Two hundred dollars," replied Alessandro.

"Well, leave your plough and wagon, and I'll give it to you," said the man; "and a big fool I am, too. I'll be laughed at, I'll be, do you know, for buying out an Indian!"

"The wagon, Señor, cost me one hundred and thirty dollars in San Diego. You cannot buy one so good for less. I will not sell it. I need it to take away my things in. The plough you may have. That is worth twenty."

"I'll do it," said the man; and pulling out a heavy buckskin pouch, he counted out into Alessandro's hand two hundred dollars in gold.

"Is that all right?" he said, as he put down the last piece.

"That is the sum I said, Señor," replied Alessandro. "To-morrow, at noon, you can come into the house."

"Where will you go?" asked the man, again slightly touched by Alessandro's manner. "Why don't you stay round here? I expect you could get work enough; there are a lot of farmers coming in here; they'll want hands."

A fierce torrent of words sprang to Alessandro's lips, but he choked them back. "I do not know where I shall go, but I will not stay here," he said; and that ended the interview.

"I don't know as I blame him a mite for feeling that way," thought the man from the States, as he walked slowly back to his pile of lumber. "I expect I should feel just so myself."

Almost before Alessandro had finished this tale, he began to move about the room, taking down, folding up, opening and shutting lids; his restlessness was terrible to see. "By sunrise, I would like to be off," he said. "It is like death, to be in the house which is no longer ours." Ramona had spoken no word since her first cry on hearing that terrible laugh. She was like one stricken dumb. The

shock was greater to her than to
Alessandro. He had lived with it ever
present in his thoughts for a year.
She had always hoped. But far more
dreadful than the loss of her home,
was the anguish of seeing, hearing,
the changed face, changed voice, of
Alessandro. Almost this swallowed up
the other. She obeyed him mechanically, working faster and faster as
he grew more and more feverish in
his haste. Before sundown the little
house was dismantled; everything, except the bed and the stove, packed
in the big wagon.

"Now, we must cook food for the
journey," said Alessandro.

"Where are we going?" said the
weeping Ramona.

"Where?" ejaculated Alessandro, so
scornfully that it sounded like impatience with Ramona, and made her
tears flow afresh. "Where? I know
not, Majella! Into the mountains,
where the white men come not! At
sunrise we will start."

Ramona wished to say good-by to
their friends. There were women in
the village that she tenderly loved.
But Alessandro was unwilling. "There
will be weeping and crying, Majella;
I pray you do not speak to one. Why
should we have more tears? Let us
disappear. I will say all to Ysidro.
He will tell them."

This was a sore grief to Ramona.
In her heart she rebelled against it,
as she had never yet rebelled against
an act of Alessandro's; but she could
not distress him. Was not his burden
heavy enough now?

Without a word of farewell to any
one, they set off in the gray dawn,
before a creature was stirring in the
village,—the wagon piled high; Ramona, her baby in her arms, in front,
Alessandro walking. The load wa
heavy. Benito and Baba walke
slowly. Capitan, unhappy, lookin
first at Ramona's face, then at Ales
sandro's, walked dispiritedly by thei
side. He knew all was wrong.

As Alessandro turned the horses int
a faintly marked road leading in
northeasterly direction, Ramona said
with a sob, "Where does this roa
lead, Alessandro?"

"To San Jacinto," he said. "Sa
Jacinto Mountain. Do not look back
Majella! Do not look back!" h
cried, as he saw Ramona, with stream
ing eyes, gazing back towards Sa
Pasquale. "Do not look back! It i
gone! Pray to the saints now, Ma
jella! Pray! Pray!"

188

IV. FRANCIS MARION CRAWFORD
(1854–1909)

THE UPPER BERTH *

I

Somebody asked for the cigars. W
had talked long, and the conversatio
was beginning to languish; the t
bacco smoke had got into the heav
curtains, the wine had got into tho
brains which were liable to becon
heavy, and it was already perfect
evident that, unless somebody d
something to rouse our oppress
spirits, the meeting would soon con
to its natural conclusion, and we, t
guests, would speedily go home

* Reprinted by permission of The Ma
millan Company.

ed, and most certainly to sleep. No
one had said anything very remark-
ble; it may be that no one had any-
hing very remarkable to say. Jones
had given us every particular of his
last hunting adventure in Yorkshire.
Mr. Tompkins, of Boston, had explained at elaborate length those work-
ng principles, by the due and careful
maintenance of which the Atchison,
Topeka, and Santa Fé Railroad not
nly extended its territory, increased
s departmental influence, and trans-
orted live stock without starving
them to death before the day of
ctual delivery, but also, had for years
ucceeded in deceiving those pas-
engers who bought its tickets into
ae fallacious belief that the corpora-
on aforesaid was really able to trans-
ort human life without destroying it.
ignor Tombola had endeavored to
ersuade us, by arguments which we
ok no trouble to oppose, that the
nity of his country in no way re-
mbled the average modern torpedo,
arefully planned, constructed with all
ae skill of the greatest European
rsenals, but, when constructed, des-
ned to be directed by feeble hands
to a region where it must undoubt-
dly explode, unseen, unfeared, and
aheard, into the illimitable wastes of
olitical chaos.

It is unnecessary to go into further
tails. The conversation had as-
med proportions which would have
red Prometheus on his rock, which
ould have driven Tantalus to dis-
action, and which would have im-
lled Ixion to seek relaxation in the
mple but instructive dialogue of
err Ollendorff, rather than submit to
e greater evil of listening to our
lk. We had sat at table for hours;

we were bored, we were tired, and
nobody showed signs of moving.

Somebody called for cigars. We all
instinctively looked towards the
speaker. Brisbane was a man of five-
and-thirty years of age, and remarkable for those gifts which chiefly attract the attention of men. He was
a strong man. The external proportions of his figure presented nothing
extraordinary to the common eye,
though his size was above the average.
He was a little over six feet in height,
and moderately broad in the shoulder;
he did not appear to be stout, but, on
the other hand, he was certainly not
thin; his small head was supported
by a strong and sinewy neck; his
broad muscular hands appeared to
possess a peculiar skill in breaking
walnuts without the assistance of the
ordinary cracker, and, seeing him in
profile, one could not help remarking
the extraordinary breadth of his
sleeves, and the unusual thickness of
his chest. He was one of those men
who are commonly spoken of among
men as deceptive; that is to say, that
though he looked exceedingly strong
he was in reality very much stronger
than he looked. Of his features I
need say little. His head is small,
his hair is thin, his eyes are blue,
his nose is large, he has a small
mustache, and a square jaw. Everybody knows Brisbane, and when he
asked for a cigar everybody looked at
him.

"It is a very singular thing," said
Brisbane.

Everybody stopped talking. Brisbane's voice was not loud, but possessed a peculiar quality of penetrating general conversation, and cutting
it like a knife. Everybody listened.

Brisbane, perceiving that he had attracted their general attention, lit his cigar with great equanimity.

"It is very singular," he continued, "that thing about ghosts. People are always asking whether anybody has seen a ghost. I have."

"Bosh! What, you? You don't mean to say so, Brisbane? Well, for a man of his intelligence!"

A chorus of exclamations greeted Brisbane's remarkable statement. Everybody called for cigars, and Stubbs the butler suddenly appeared from the depths of nowhere with a fresh bottle of dry champagne. The situation was saved; Brisbane was going to tell a story.

"I am an old sailor," said Brisbane, "and as I have to cross the Atlantic pretty often, I have my favorites. Most men have their favorites. I have seen a man wait in a Broadway bar for three-quarters of an hour for a particular car which he liked. I believe the barkeeper made at least one-third of his living by that man's preference. I have a habit of waiting for certain ships when I am obliged to cross that duck-pond. It may be a prejudice, but I was never cheated out of a good passage but once in my life. I remember it very well; it was a warm morning in June, and the Custom House officials, who were hanging about waiting for a steamer already on her way up from the Quarantine, presented a peculiarly hazy and thoughtful appearance. I had not much luggage—I never have. I mingled with the crowd of passengers, porters, and officious individuals in blue coats and brass buttons, who seem to spring up like mushrooms from the deck of a moored

steamer to obtrude their unnecessary services upon the independent passenger. I have often noticed with a certain interest the spontaneous evolution of these fellows. They are not there when you arrive; five minutes after the pilot has called "Go ahead!" they, or at least their blue coats and brass buttons, have disappeared from deck and gangway as completely as though they had been consigned to that locker which tradition unanimously ascribes to Davy Jones. But, at the moment of starting, they are there, clean-shaved, blue coated, and ravenous for fees. hastened on board. The *Kamtschatka* was one of my favorite ships. I say was, because she emphatically no longer is. I cannot conceive of any inducement which could entice me to make another voyage in her. Yes, I know what you are going to say. She is uncommonly clean in the run aft, she has enough bluffing off in the bows to keep her dry, and the lower berths are most of them double. She has a lot of advantages, but I won't cross in her again. Excuse the digression. I got on board. I hailed a steward, whose red nose and red whiskers were equally familiar to me.

"One hundred and five, lower berth," said I, in the businesslike tone peculiar to men who think no more of crossing the Atlantic than taking a whisky cocktail at downtown Delmonico's.

The steward took my portmanteau, great coat, and rug. I shall never forget the expression of his face. Not that he turned pale. It is maintained by the most eminent divines that even miracles cannot change the course of nature. I have no hesi-

ion in saying that he did not turn pale; but, from his expression, I judged that he was either about to shed tears, to sneeze, or to drop my portmanteau. As the latter contained two bottles of particularly fine old sherry presented to me for my voyage by my old friend Snigginson an Pickyns, I felt extremely nervous. But the steward did none of these things.

"Well, I'm d——d!" said he in a low voice, and led the way.

I supposed my Hermes, as he led me to the lower regions, had had a little grog, but I said nothing, and followed him. One hundred and five was on the port side, well aft. There was nothing remarkable about the state-room. The lower berth, like most of those upon the *Kamtschatka*, was double. There was plenty of room; there was the usual washing apparatus, calculated to convey an idea of luxury to the mind of a North-American Indian; there were the usual inefficient racks of brown wood, in which it is more easy to hang a large-sized umbrella than the common tooth-brush of commerce. Upon the uninviting mattresses were carefully folded together those blankets which a great modern humorist was aptly compared to cold buckwheat cakes. The question of towels was left entirely to the imagination. The glass decanters were filled with a transparent liquid faintly tinged with brown, but from which an odor less faint, but not more pleasing, ascended the nostrils, like a far-off sea-sick reminiscence of oily machinery. Sad-colored curtains half-closed the upper berth. The hazy June daylight shed a faint illumination upon the desolate little scene. Ugh! how I hate that state-room.

The steward deposited my traps and looked at me, as though he wanted to get away—probably in search of more passengers and more fees. It is always a good plan to start in favor with those functionaries, and I accordingly gave him certain coins there and then.

"I'll try and make yer comfortable all I can," he remarked, as he put the coins in his pocket. Nevertheless, there was a doubtful intonation in his voice which surprised me. Possibly his scale of fees had gone up, and he was not satisfied; but on the whole I was inclined to think that, as he himself would have expressed it, he was "the better for a glass." I was wrong, however, and did the man injustice.

II

Nothing especially worthy of mention occurred during that day. We left the pier punctually, and it was very pleasant to be fairly under way, for the weather was warm and sultry, and the motion of the steamer produced a refreshing breeze. Everybody knows what the first day at sea is like. People pace the decks and stare at each other, and occasionally meet acquaintances whom they did not know to be on board. There is the usual uncertainty as to whether the food will be good, bad, or indifferent, until the first two meals have put the matter beyond a doubt; there is the usual uncertainty about the weather, until the ship is fairly off Fire Island. The tables are crowded at first, and then suddenly thinned. Pale-faced people spring from their seats and precipitate themselves towards the door, and each old sailor breathes more freely as his seasick neighbor rushes from his side, leaving him plenty of elbow room and an unlimited command over the mustard.

One passage across the Atlantic is very much like another, and we who cross very often do not make the voyage for the sake of novelty. Whales and icebergs are indeed always objects of interest, but, after all, one whale is very much like another whale, and one rarely sees an iceberg at close quarters. To the majority of us the most delightful moment of the day on board an ocean steamer is when we have taken our last turn on deck, have smoked our last cigar, and having succeeded in tiring ourselves, feel at liberty to turn in with a clear conscience. On that first night of the voyage I felt particularly lazy, and went to bed in one hundred and five rather earlier than I usually do. As I turned in, I was amazed to see that I was to have a companion. A portmanteau, very like my own, lay in the opposite corner, and in the upper berth had been deposited a neatly folded rug with a stick and umbrella. I had hoped to be alone, and I was disappointed; but I wondered who my room-mate was to be, and I determined to have a look at him.

Before I had been long in bed he entered. He was, as far as I could see, a very tall man, very thin, very pale, with sandy hair and whiskers and colorless gray eyes. He had about him, I thought, an air of rather dubious fashion; the sort of man you might see in Wall Street, without being able precisely to say what he was doing there—the sort of man who

frequents the Café Anglais, who al ways seems to be alone and wh drinks champagne; you might mee him on a race-course, but he woul never appear to be doing anythin there either. A little over-dressed— a little odd. There are three or fou of his kind on every ocean steamer I made up my mind that I did no care to make his acquaintance, and went to sleep saying to myself tha I would study his habits in order t avoid him. If he rose early, I woul rise late; if he went to bed late, would go to bed early. I did n care to know him. If you once kno people of that kind they are alway turning up. Poor fellow! I nee not have taken the trouble to com to so many decisions about him, fo I never saw him again after that firs night in one hundred and five.

I was sleeping soundly when I wa suddenly waked by a loud noise. T judge from the sound, my room-mat must have sprung with a single lea from the upper berth to the floor. heard him fumbling with the latc and bolt of the door, which opene almost immediately, and then I hea his footsteps as he ran at full spee down the passage, leaving the do open behind him. The ship was rol ing a little, and I expected to hea him stumble or fall, but he ran though he were running for his lif The door swung on its hinges wi the motion of the vessel, and t sound annoyed me. I got up a shut it, and groped my way back my berth in the darkness. I went sleep again; but I have no idea ho long I slept.

When I awoke it was still qui dark, but I felt a disagreeable sens ion of cold, and it seemed to me that the air was damp. You know he peculiar smell of a cabin which as been wet with sea water. I cov-red myself up as well as I could nd dozed off again, framing com-laints to be made the next day, and electing the most powerful epithets n the language. I could hear my oom-mate turn over in the upper erth. He had probably returned hile I was asleep. Once I thought heard him groan, and I argued that e was sea-sick. That is particularly npleasant when one is below. Nevrtheless I dozed off and slept till arly daylight.

The ship was rolling heavily, much ore than on the previous evening, nd the gray light which came in rough the porthole changed in tint ith every movement according as the ngle of the vessel's side turned the lass seawards or skywards. It was ery cold—unaccountably so for the onth of June. I turned my head nd looked at the porthole, and saw my surprise that it was wide open nd hooked back. I believe I swore dibly. Then I got up and shut it. s I turned back I glanced at the pper berth. The curtains were awn close together; my companion d probably felt cold as well as

It struck me that I had slept ough. The state-room was uncom-rtable, though, strange to say, I uld not smell the dampness which d annoyed me in the night. My om-mate was still asleep—excellent portunity for avoiding him, so I essed at once and went on deck. e day was warm and cloudy, with oily smell on the water. It was ven o'clock as I came out—much

later than I had imagined. I came across the doctor, who was taking his first sniff of the morning air. He was a young man from the West of Ireland—a tremendous fellow, with black hair and blue eyes, already inclined to be stout; he had a happy-go-lucky, healthy look about him which was rather attractive.

"Fine morning," I remarked, by way of introduction.

"Well," said he, eying me with an air of ready interest, "it's a fine morning and it's not a fine morning. I don't think it's much of a morning."

"Well, no—it is not so very fine," said I.

"It's just what I call fuggly weather," replied the doctor.

"It was very cold last night, I thought," I remarked. "However, when I looked about, I found that the porthole was wide open. I had not noticed it when I went to bed. And the state-room was damp, too."

"Damp!" said he. "Whereabouts are you?"

"One hundred and five—"

To my surprise the doctor started visibly, and stared at me.

"What is the matter?" I asked.

"Oh—nothing," he answered; "only everybody has complained of that state-room for the last three trips."

"I shall complain too," I said. "It has certainly not been properly aired. It is a shame!"

"I don't believe it can be helped," answered the doctor. "I believe there is something—well, it is not my business to frighten passengers."

"You need not be afraid of frightening me," I replied. "I can stand any amount of damp. If I should get a bad cold I will come to you."

I offered the doctor a cigar, which he took and examined very critically.

"It is not so much the damp," he remarked. "However, I dare say you will get on very well. Have you a room-mate?"

"Yes; a deuce of a fellow, who bolts out in the middle of the night and leaves the door open."

Again the doctor glanced curiously at me. Then he lit the cigar and looked grave.

"Did he come back?" he asked presently.

"Yes. I was asleep, but I waked up and heard him moving. Then I felt cold and went to sleep again. This morning I found the porthole open."

"Look here," said the doctor, quietly, "I don't care much for this ship. I don't care a rap for her reputation. I tell you what I will do. I have a good-sized place up here. I will share it with you, though I don't know you from Adam."

I was very much surprised at the proposition. I could not imagine why he should take such a sudden interest in my welfare. However, his manner as he spoke of the ship was peculiar.

"You are very good, doctor," I said. "But really, I believe even now the cabin could be aired, or cleaned out, or something. Why do you not care for the ship?"

"We are not superstitious in our profession, sir," replied the doctor. "But the sea makes people so. I don't want to prejudice you, and I don't want to frighten you, but if you will take my advice you will move in here. I would as soon see you overboard," he added, "as know

that you or any other man was t[o] sleep in one hundred and five."

"Good gracious! Why?" I aske[d]

"Just because on the last thre[e] trips the people who have slept ther[e] actually have gone overboard," h[e] answered, gravely.

The intelligence was startling an[d] exceedingly unpleasant, I confess. [I] looked hard at the doctor to se[e] whether he was making game of m[e] but he looked perfectly serious. [I] thanked him warmly for his offe[r] but told him I intended to be th[e] exception to the rule by which ever[y] one who slept in that particular stat[e]room went overboard. He did n[ot] say much, but looked as grave a[s] ever, and hinted that before we g[ot] across I should probably reconsid[er] his proposal. In the course of tim[e] we went to breakfast, at which on[ly] an inconsiderable number of pa[s]sengers assembled. I noticed th[at] one or two of the officers who brea[k]fasted with us looked grave. Aft[er] breakfast I went into my state-roo[m] in order to get a book. The curtai[ns] of the upper berth were still close[ly] drawn. Not a word was to be hear[d] My room-mate was probably st[ill] asleep.

As I came out I met the stewa[rd] whose business it was to look aft[er] me. He whispered that the capta[in] wanted to see me, and then scuttl[ed] away down the passage as if ve[ry] anxious to avoid any questions. [I] went toward the captain's cabin, a[nd] found him waiting for me.

"Sir," said he, "I want to ask [a] favor of you."

I answered that I would do an[y] thing to oblige him.

"Your room-mate has disappeare[d]

said. "He is known to have turned early last night. Did you notice anything extraordinary in his manner?"

The question, coming as it did, in exact confirmation of the fears the doctor had expressed half an hour earlier, staggered me.

"You don't mean to say he has gone overboard?" I asked.

"I fear he has," answered the captain.

"This is the most extraordinary thing—" I began.

"Why?" he asked.

"He is the fourth, then?" I explained. In answer to another question from the captain, I explained, without mentioning the doctor, that I had heard the story concerning one hundred and five. He seemed very much annoyed at hearing that I knew of it. I told him what had occurred in the night.

"What you say," he replied, "coincides almost exactly with what was told me by the room-mates of two of the other three. They bolt out of bed and run down the passage. Two of them were seen to go overboard by the watch; we stopped and lowered boats, but they were not found. Nobody, however, saw or heard the man who was lost last night—if he is really lost. The steward, who is a superstitious fellow, perhaps, and expected something to go wrong, went to look for him this morning, and found his berth empty, but his clothes lying about, just as he had left them. The steward was the only man on board who knew him by sight, and he has been searching everywhere for him. He has disappeared! Now, sir, I want to beg you not to mention the circumstance to any of the passengers; I don't want the ship to get a bad name, and nothing hangs about an ocean-goer like stories of suicides. You shall have your choice of any one of the officers' cabins you like, including my own, for the rest of the passage. Is that a fair bargain?"

"Very," said I; "and I am much obliged to you. But since I am alone, and have the state-room to myself, I would rather not move. If the steward will take out that unfortunate man's things, I would as lief stay where I am. I will not say anything about the matter, and I think I can promise you that I will not follow my room-mate."

The captain tried to dissuade me from my intention, but I preferred having a state-room alone to being the chum of any officer on board. I do not know whether I acted foolishly, but if I had taken his advice I should have had nothing more to tell. There would have remained the disagreeable coincidence of several suicides occurring among men who had slept in the same cabin, but that would have been all.

That was not the end of the matter, however, by any means. I obstinately made up my mind that I would not be disturbed by such tales, and I even went so far as to argue the question with the captain. There was something wrong about the state-room, I said. It was rather damp. The porthole had been left open last night. My room-mate might have been ill when he came on board, and he might have become delirious after he went to bed. He might even now be hiding somewhere on board, and might be found later. The place ought to be aired and the fastening of the port looked to. If the captain would give me leave, I would see that what I thought necessary were done immediately.

"Of course you have a right to stay where you are if you please," he replied, rather petulantly; "but I wish you would turn out and let me lock the place up, and be done with it."

I did not see it in the same light, and left the captain, after promising to be silent concerning the disappearance of my companion. The latter had had no acquaintances on board, and was not missed in the course of the day. Towards evening I met the doctor again, and he asked me whether I had changed my mind. I told him I had not.

"Then you will before long," he said, very gravely.

III

We played whist in the evening, and I went to bed late. I will confess now that I felt a disagreeable sensation when I entered my stateroom. I could not help thinking of the tall man I had seen on the previous night, who was now dead, drowned, tossing about in the long swell, two or three hundred miles astern. His face rose very distinctly before me as I undressed, and I even went so far as to draw back the curtains of the upper berth, as though to persuade myself that he was actually gone. I also bolted the door of the state-room. Suddenly I became aware that the porthole was open, and fastened back. This was more than I could stand. I hastily threw on my dressing-gown and went

in search of Robert, the steward of my passage. I was very angry, remember, and when I found him dragged him roughly to the door of one hundred and five, and pushed him towards the open porthole.

"What the deuce do you mean, you scoundrel, by leaving that port open every night? Don't you know it is against the regulations? Don't you know that if the ship heeled and the water began to come in, ten men could not shut it? I will report you to the captain, you blackguard, for endangering the ship!"

I was exceedingly wroth. The man trembled and turned pale, and then began to shut the round glass plate with the heavy brass fittings.

"Why don't you answer me?" I said, roughly.

"If you please, sir," faltered Robert, "there's nobody on board as can keep this 'ere port shut at night. You can try it yourself, sir. I ain't a-going to stop hany longer on board o this vessel, sir; I ain't, indeed. But if I was you, sir, I'd just clear out and go and sleep with the surgeon, or something, I would. Look 'ere, sir, is that fastened what you may call securely, or not, sir? Try it, sir, see if it will move a hinch."

I tried the port and found it perfectly tight.

"Well, sir," continued Robert, triumphantly, "I wager my reputation as a A 1 steward, that in 'arf an hour it will be open again; fastened back too, sir, that's the horful thing—fastened back!"

I examined the great screw and the looped nut that ran on it.

"If I find it open in the night, Robert, I will give you a sovereign.

It is not possible. You may go."

"Soverin' did you say, sir? Very good, sir. Very good, sir. Thank ye, sir. Good-night, sir. Pleasant ree-pose, sir, and all manner of hinchan-tin' dreams, sir."

Robert scuttled away, delighted at being released. Of course, I thought he was trying to account for his negli-gence by a silly story, intended to frighten me, and I disbelieved him. The consequence was that he got his sovereign, and I spent a very pecul-iarly unpleasant night.

I went to bed, and five minutes after I had rolled myself up in my blankets the inexorable Robert extin-guished the light that burned steadily behind the ground-glass pane near the door. I lay quite still in the dark trying to go to sleep, but I soon found that impossible. It had been some satisfaction to be angry with the stew-ard, and the diversion had banished that unpleasant sensation I had at first experienced when I thought of the drowned man who had been my chum; but I was no longer sleepy, and I lay awake for some time, oc-casionally glancing at the porthole, which I could just see from where I lay, and which, in the darkness, looked like a faintly-luminous soup-plate suspended in blackness. I be-lieved I must have lain there for an hour, and, as I remember, I was just dozing into sleep when I was roused by a draught of cold air and by dis-tinctly feeling the spray of the sea blown upon my face. I started to my feet, and not having allowed in the dark for the motion of the ship, I was instantly thrown violently across the state-room upon the couch which was placed beneath the porthole. I

recovered myself immediately, how-ever, and climbed upon my knees. The porthole was again wide open and fastened back!

Now these things are facts. I was wide awake when I got up, and I should certainly have been waked by the fall had I still been dozing. More-over, I bruised my elbows and knees badly, and the bruises were there on the following morning to testify to the fact, if I myself had doubted it. The porthole was wide open and fas-tened back—a thing so unaccountable that I remember very well feeling astonishment rather than fear when I discovered it. I at once closed the plate again and screwed down the loop nut with all my strength. It was very dark in the state-room. I reflected that the port had certainly been opened within an hour after Robert had at first shut it in my presence, and I determined to watch it and see whether it would open again. Those brass fittings are very heavy and by no means easy to move; I could not believe that the clamp had been turned by the shaking of the screw. I stood peering out through the thick glass at the alter-nate white and gray streaks of the sea that foamed beneath the ship's side. I must have remained there a quarter of an hour.

Suddenly, as I stood, I distinctly heard something moving behind me in one of the berths, and a moment afterwards, just as I turned in-stinctively to look—though I could, of course, see nothing in the darkness—I heard a very faint groan. I sprang across the state-room, and tore the curtains of the upper berth aside, thrusting in my hands to discover if there were any one there. There was some one.

I remember that the sensation as I put my hands forward was as though I were plunging them into the air of a damp cellar, and from behind the curtain came a gust of wind that smelled horribly of stagnant sea-water. I laid hold of something that had the shape of a man's arm, but was smooth, and wet, and icy cold. But suddenly, as I pulled, the creature sprang violently forward against me, a clammy, oozy mass, as it seemed to me, heavy and wet, yet endowed with a sort of supernatural strength. I reeled across the state-room, and in an instant the door opened and the thing rushed out. I had not had time to be frightened, and quickly recovering myself, I sprang through the door and gave chase at the top of my speed, but I was too late. Ten yards before me I could see—I am sure I saw it—a dark shadow moving in the dimly lighted passage, quickly as the shadow of a fast horse thrown before a dog-cart by the lamp on a dark night. But in a moment it had disappeared, and I found myself holding on to the polished rail that ran along the bulkhead where the passage turned towards the companion. My hair stood on end, and the cold perspiration rolled down my face. I am not ashamed of it in the least: I was very badly frightened.

Still I doubted my senses, and pulled myself together. It was absurd, I thought. The Welsh rare-bit I had eaten had disagreed with me. I had been in a nightmare. I made my way back to my state-room, and entered it with an effort. The whole place smelled of stagnant sea-water, as it had when I had waked on the previous evening. It required my utmost strength to go in and grope among my things for a box of wax lights. As I lighted a railway reading lantern which I always carry in case I want to read after the lamps are out, I perceived that the porthole was again open, and a sort of creeping horror began to take possession of me which I never felt before, nor wish to feel again. But I got a light and proceeded to examine the upper berth, expecting to find it drenched with sea-water.

But I was disappointed. The bed had been slept in, and the smell of the sea was strong; but the bedding was as dry as a bone. I fancied that Robert had not had the courage to make the bed after the accident of the previous night—it had all been a hideous dream. I drew the curtain back as far as I could and examined the place very carefully. It was perfectly dry. But the porthole was open again. With a sort of dull bewilderment of horror, I closed it and screwed it down, and thrusting my heavy stick through the brass loop wrenched it with all my might, till the thick metal began to bend under the pressure. Then I hooked my reading lantern into the red velvet at the head of the couch, and sat down to recover my senses if I could. I sat there all night, unable to think of rest—hardly able to think at all. But the porthole remained closed, and I did not believe it would now open again without the application of a considerable force.

The morning dawned at last, and I dressed myself slowly, thinking over all that had happened in the night.

It was a beautiful day and I went on deck, glad to get out in the early, pure sunshine, and to smell the breeze from the blue water, so different from the noisome, stagnant odor from my state-room. Instinctively I turned aft, towards the surgeon's cabin. There he stood, with a pipe in his mouth, taking his morning airing precisely as on the preceding day.

"Good-morning," said he, quietly, but looking at me with evident curiosity.

"Doctor, you were quite right," said I. "There is something wrong about that place."

"I thought you would change your mind," he answered, rather triumphantly. "You have had a bad night, eh? Shall I make you a pick-me-up? I have a capital recipe."

"No, thanks," I cried. "But I would like to tell you what happened."

I then tried to explain as clearly as possible precisely what had occurred, not omitting to state that I had been scared as I had never been scared in my whole life before. I dwelt particularly on the phenomenon of the porthole, which was a fact to which I could testify, even if the rest had been an illusion. I had closed it twice in the night, and the second time I had actually bent the brass in wrenching it with my stick. I believe I insisted a good deal on this point.

"You seem to think I am likely to doubt the story," said the doctor, smiling at the detailed account of the state of the porthole. "I do not doubt it in the least. I renew my invitation to you. Bring your traps here, and take half my cabin."

"Come and take half of mine for one night," I said. "Help me get at the bottom of this thing."

"You will get to the bottom of something else if you try," answered the doctor.

"What?" I asked.

"The bottom of the sea. I am going to leave the ship. It is not canny."

"Then you will not help me to find out—"

"Not I," said the doctor, quickly. "It is my business to keep my wits about me—not to go fiddling about with ghosts and things."

"Do you really believe it is a ghost?" I inquired, rather contemptuously. But as I spoke I remembered very well the horrible sensation of the supernatural which had got possession of me during the night. The doctor turned sharply on me—

"Have you any reasonable explanation of these things to offer?" he asked. "No; you have not. Well, you say you will find an explanation. I say that you won't, sir, simply because there is not any."

"But, my dear sir," I retorted, "do you, a man of science, mean to tell me that such things cannot be explained?"

"I do," he answered, stoutly. "And, if they could, I would not be concerned in the explanation."

I did not care to spend another night alone in the state-room, and yet I was obstinately determined to get at the root of the disturbances. I do not believe there are many men who would have slept there alone, after passing two such nights. But I made up my mind to try it, if I could not get any one to share a watch with me. The doctor was evidently not inclined for such an experiment. He said he was a surgeon, and that in case any accident occurred on board he must always be in readiness. He could not afford to have his nerves unsettled. Perhaps he was quite right, but I am inclined to think that his precaution was prompted by his inclination. On inquiry, he informed me that there was no one on board who would be likely to join me in my investigations, and after a little more conversation I left him. A little later I met the captain, and told him my story. I said that if no one would spend the night with me I would ask leave to have the light burning all night, and would try it alone.

"Look here," said he, "I will tell you what I will do. I will share your watch myself, and we will see what happens. It is my belief that we can find out between us. There may be some fellow skulking on board, who steals a passage by frightening the passengers. It is just possible that there may be something queer in the carpentering of that berth."

I suggested taking the ship's carpenter below and examining the place; but I was overjoyed at the captain's offer to spend the night with me. He accordingly sent for the workman and ordered him to do anything I required. We went below at once. I had all the bedding cleared out of the upper berth, and we examined the place thoroughly to see if there was a board loose anywhere, or a panel which could be opened or pushed aside. We tried the planks everywhere, tapped the flooring, unscrewed the fittings of the lower berth and took it to pieces—in short, there was not a square inch o the state-room which was not searche and tested. Everything was in per fect order, and we put everything bac in its place. As we were finishing ou work, Robert came to the door an looked in.

"Well, sir—find anything, sir?" h asked with a ghastly grin.

"You were right about the port hole, Robert," I said, and I gave hir the promised sovereign. The ca penter did his work silently and ski fully, following my directions. Whe he had done he spoke.

"I'm a plain man, sir," he said "But it's my belief you had bette just turn out your things and let m run half a dozen four inch screw through the door of this cabin. There no good never came o' this cabin ye sir, and that's all about it. There been four lives lost out o' here t my own remembrance, and that i four trips. Better give it up, sir— better give it up!"

"I will try it for one night more, I said.

"Better give it up, sir—better giv it up! It's precious bad job," re peated the workman, putting his too in his bag and leaving the cabin.

But my spirits had risen conside ably at the prospect of having th captain's company, and I made u my mind not to be prevented fro going to the end of the strange bus ness. I abstained from Welsh rar bits and grog that evening, and di not even join in the customary gam of whist. I wanted to be quite su of my nerves, and my vanity ma me anxious to make a good figure i the captain's eyes.

IV

The captain was one of those splendidly tough and cheerful specimens of seafaring humanity whose combined courage, hardihood, and calmness in difficulty leads them naturally into high positions of trust. He was not the man to be led away by an idle tale, and the mere fact that he was willing to join me in the investigation was proof that he thought there was something seriously wrong, which could not be accounted for on ordinary theories, nor laughed down as a common superstition. To some extent, too, his reputation was at stake, as well as the reputation of the ship. It is no light thing to lose passengers overboard, and he knew it.

About ten o'clock that evening, as I was smoking a last cigar, he came up to me and drew me aside from the beat of the other passengers who were patrolling the deck in the warm darkness.

"This is a serious matter, Mr. Brisbane," he said. "We must make up our minds either way—to be disappointed or to have a pretty rough time of it. You see, I cannot afford to laugh at the affair, and I will ask you to sign your name to a statement of whatever occurs. If nothing happens to-night we will try it again to-morrow and next day. Are you ready?"

So we went below, and entered the state-room. As we went in I could see Robert the steward, who stood a little further down the passage, watching us, with his usual grin, as though certain that something dreadful was about to happen. The captain closed the door behind us and bolted it.

"Supposing we put your portmanteau before the door," he suggested. "One of us can sit on it. Nothing can get out then. Is the port screwed down?"

I found it as I had left it in the morning. Indeed, without using a lever, as I had done, no one could have opened it. I drew back the curtains of the upper berth so that I could see well into it. By the captain's advice I lighted my reading-lantern, and placed it so that it shone upon the white sheets above. He insisted upon sitting on the portmanteau, declaring that he wished to be able to swear that he had sat before the door.

Then he requested me to search the state-room thoroughly, an operation very soon accomplished, as it consisted merely in looking beneath the lower berth and under the couch below the porthole. The spaces were quite empty.

"It is impossible for any human being to get in," I said, "or for any human being to open the port."

"Very good," said the captain, calmly. "If we see anything now, it must be either imagination or something supernatural."

I sat down on the edge of the lower berth.

"The first time it happened," said the captain, crossing his legs and leaning back against the door, "was in March. The passenger who slept here, in the upper berth, turned out to have been a lunatic—at all events, he was known to have been a little touched, and he had taken his passage without the knowledge of his friends. He rushed out in the middle of the night, and threw himself overboard, before the officer who had the watch could stop him. We stopped and lowered a boat; it was a quiet night, just before that heavy weather came on; but we could not find him. Of course his suicide was afterwards accounted for on the ground of insanity."

"I suppose that often happens?" I remarked, rather absently.

"Not often—no," said the captain; "never before in my experience, though I have heard of it happening on board of other ships. Well, as I was saying, that occurred in March. On the very next trip—What are you looking at?" he asked, stopping suddenly in his narration.

I believe I gave no answer. My eyes were riveted upon the porthole. It seemed to me that the brass loop-nut was beginning to turn very slowly upon the screw—so slowly, however, that I was not sure it moved at all. I watched it intently, fixing its position in my mind, and trying to ascertain whether it changed. Seeing where I was looking, the captain looked too.

"It moves!" he exclaimed, in a tone of conviction. "No, it does not," he added, after a minute.

"If it were the jarring of the screw," said I, "it would have opened during the day; but I found it this evening jammed tight as I left it this morning."

I rose and tried the nut. It was certainly loosened, for by an effort I could move it with my hands.

"The queer thing," said the captain, "is that the second man who was lost is supposed to have got through that very port. We had a terrible time over it. It was in the middle of the night, and the weather was very heavy; there was an alarm that one of the ports was open and the sea running in. I came below and found everything flooded, the water pouring in every time she rolled, and the whole port swinging from the top bolts—not the porthole in the middle. Well, we managed to shut it, but the water did some damage. Ever since that the place smells of sea-water from time to time. We supposed the passenger had thrown himself out, though the Lord only knows how he did it. The steward kept telling me that he could not keep anything shut here. Upon my word—I can smell it now, cannot you?" he inquired, sniffing the air suspiciously.

"Yes—distinctly," I said, and shuddered as that same odor of stagnant sea-water grew stronger in the cabin. "Now, to smell like this, the place must be damp," I continued, "and yet when I examined it with the carpenter this morning everything was perfectly dry. It is most extraordinary—hallo!"

My reading-lantern, which had been placed in the upper berth, was suddenly extinguished. There was still a good deal of light from the pane of ground glass near the door, behind which loomed the regulation lamp. The ship rolled heavily, and the curtain of the upper berth swung far out into the state-room and back again. I rose quickly from my seat on the edge of the bed, and the captain at the same moment started to his feet with a loud cry of surprise. I had turned with the intention of taking down the lantern to examine it, when I heard his exclamation, and immediately afterwards his call for help.

sprang towards him. He was wrestling with all his might, with the brass loop of the port. It seemed to turn against his hands in spite of all his efforts. I caught up my cane, a heavy oak stick I always used to carry, and thrust it through the ring and bore on it with all my strength. But the strong wood snapped suddenly, and I fell upon the couch. When I rose again the port was wide open, and the captain was standing with his back against the door, pale to the lips.

"There is something in that berth!" he cried, in a strange voice, his eyes almost starting from his head. "Hold the door, while I look—it shall not escape us, whatever it is!"

But instead of taking his place, I sprang upon the lower bed, and seized something which lay in the upper berth.

It was something ghostly, horrible beyond words, and it moved in my grip. It was like the body of a man long drowned, and yet it moved, and had the strength of ten men living; but I gripped it with all my might— the slippery, oozy, horrible thing. The dead white eyes seemed to stare at me out of the dusk; the putrid odor of rank sea-water was about it, and its shiny hair hung in foul wet curls over its dead face. I wrestled with the dead thing; it thrust itself upon me and forced me back and nearly broke my arms; it wound its corpse's arms about my neck, the living death, and overpowered me, so that I, at last, cried aloud and fell, and left my hold.

As I fell the thing sprang across me, and seemed to throw itself upon the captain. When I last saw him on his feet his face was white and his lips set. It seemed to me that he struck a violent blow at the dead being, and then he, too, fell forward upon his face, with an inarticulate cry of horror.

The thing paused an instant, seeming to hover over the prostrate body, and I could have screamed again from very fright, but I had no voice left. The thing vanished suddenly, and it seemed to my disturbed senses that it made its exit through the open port, though how that was possible, considering the smallness of the aperture, is more than any one can tell. I lay a long time upon the floor, and the captain lay beside me. At last I partially recovered my senses and moved, and I instantly knew that my arm was broken—the small bone of the left forearm near the wrist.

I got upon my feet somehow, and with my remaining hand I tried to raise the captain. He groaned and moved, and at last came to himself. He was not hurt, but he seemed badly stunned.

Well, do you want to hear any more? There is nothing more. That is the end of my story. The carpenter carried out his scheme of running half a dozen four-inch screws through the door of one hundred and five; and if ever you take a passage in the *Kamtschatka,* you may ask for a berth in that state-room. You will be told that it is engaged —yes—it is engaged by that dead thing.

I finished the trip in the surgeon's cabin. He doctored my broken arm, and advised me not to "fiddle about with ghosts and things" any more.

The captain was very silent, and never sailed again in that ship, though it is still running. And I will not sail in her either. It was a very disagreeable experience, and I was very badly frightened, which is a thing I do not like. That is all. That is how I saw a ghost—if it was a ghost. It was dead, anyhow.

189-

V. MAURICE THOMPSON
(1844–1901)

WILD HONEY *

Where hints of racy sap and gum
Out of the old dark forest come;

Where birds their beaks like hammers
    wield,
And pith is pierced, and bark is
    peeled;

Where the green walnut's outer rind
Gives precious bitterness to the wind;

There lurks the sweet creative power,
As lurks the honey in the flower.

In winter's bud that bursts in spring,
In nut of autumn's ripening,   10

In acrid bulb beneath the mould,
Sleeps the elixir, strong and old,

That Rosicrucians sought in vain,—
Life that renews itself again!

What bottled perfume is so good
As fragrance of split tulip-wood?

What fabled drink of God or muse
Was rich as purple mulberry juice?

And what school-polished gem of
    thought
Is like the rune from Nature
    caught?   20

* The selections from Thompson are reprinted from *The Poems of Maurice Thompson*, 1892, by permission of Mrs. Austin Long.

He is a poet strong and true
Who loves wild thyme and honey-
    dew;

And like a brown bee works and
    sings
With morning freshness on his wings,

And a gold burden on his thighs,—
The pollen-dust of centuries!
    1892

A CREOLE SLAVE-SONG

(Ah, lo zo-zo chan' dan' branche)

What bird is that, with voice so sweet,
    Sings to the sun from yonder tree?
What girl is that so slim and fleet,
Comes through the cane her love to
    meet?
    Joli zo-zo, sing merrily.
    The pretty girl she comes to me!

What wind is that upon the cane?
    What perfume from a far-off rose
Fills me with dreams? What strange,
    vague pain
Stirs in my heart? What longing
    vain   10
    Is this that through my bosom goes?
Oh, south wind, perfume and desire,
You kiss, you soothe, you burn like
    fire!

Ah, no! Ah, no! It is a cheat.
    There is no bird; my love comes
    not;
The wind chills me from head to
    feet,

And oh, it brings no perfume sweet.
  My slender girl the white man
    bought,
And took her far across the bay—
I cannot cut the cane to-day!   20

I cannot cut the cane to-day—
  O zo-zo, moqueur, come and sing!
O warm wind, through the cane-field
    stray,
Wave the long moss so soft and gray!
  I have no heart for anything;
But life was Heaven and work was
    play
When my love loved me every day!

White man, how I worked for you,
  When I was young and blithe and
    strong!
The earth was green, the sky was
    blue,   30
My love's eyes were as bright as dew;
  And life was like the zo-zo's song!
But you—you sold my love away—
I cannot cut the cane to-day!

I did not dream a slave could be
  A man, and right a grievous wrong.
I writhed and bore your cruelty;
I felt the soul go out of me;
  And yet, I was so lion-strong
I could have torn your heart
    away—   40
I cannot cut the cane to-day!

Freedom! I feel it when too late,
  Like Spring wind on a blasted tree,
A waft of mockery and hate!
Bring back my chains, O cruel Fate!
  Bring youth and slavery back to
    me;
Bring back the lash, the hound, the
    pain,
So that my own love come again!

But hark! A gentle voice afar
  Calls me to go, I know not
    where—   50
Yes, past the sun and past the star,

Into God's land. A golden car
  And milk-white horses—she is
    there!
So sweet—I dream—I float away—
I cannot cut the cane to-day!

                            1892

VI. JAMES WHITCOMB RILEY
(1849–1916)

THE OLD SWIMMIN'-HOLE *

Oh! the old swimmin'-hole! whare the
    crick so still and deep
Looked like a baby-river that was lay-
    ing half asleep,
And the gurgle of the worter round
    the drift jest below
Sounded like the laugh of something
    we onc't ust to know
Before we could remember anything
    but the eyes
Of the angels lookin' out as we left
    Paradise;
But the merry days of youth is be-
    yond our controle,
And it's hard to part ferever with the
    old swimmin'-hole.

Oh! the old swimmin'-hole! In the
    happy days of yore,
When I ust to lean above it on the
    old sickamore,   10
Oh! it showed me a face in its warm
    sunny tide
That gazed back at me so gay and
    glorified,
It made me love myself, as I leaped
    to caress
My shadder smilin' up at me with
    sich tenderness.

---

* From *Neighborly Poems,* by James Whitcomb Riley, copyright 1891 and 1919. Used
by special permission of the publishers, the
Bobbs-Merrill Company.

But them days is past and gone, and
    old Time's tuck his toll
From the old man come back to the
    old swimmin'-hole.

Oh! the old swimmin'-hole! In the
    long, lazy days
When the hum-drum of school made
    so many run-a-ways,
How plesant was the jurney down
    the old dusty lane,
Whare the tracks of our bare feet
    was all printed so plane   20
You could tell by the dent of the
    heel and the sole
They was lots o' fun on hand at
    the old swimmin'-hole.
But the lost joys is past! Let your
    tears in sorrow roll
Like the rain that use to dapple up
    the old swimmin'-hole.

Thare the bullrushes growed, and the
    cat-tails so tall,
And the sunshine and shadder fell
    over it all;
And it mottled the worter with amber
    and gold
Tel the glad lillies rocked in the rip-
    ples that rolled;
And the snake-feeder's four gauzy
    wings fluttered by
Like the ghost of a daisy dropped out
    of the sky,   30
Or a wownded apple-blossom in the
    breeze's controle
As it cut acrost some orchurd to'rds
    the old swimmin'-hole.

Oh! the old swimmin'-hole! When I
    last saw the place,
The scenes was all changed, like the
    change in my face;
The bridge of the railroad now crosses
    the spot
Whare the old divin'-log lays sunk and
    fergot.
And I stray down the banks whare
    the trees ust to be—
But never again will theyr shade shel-
    ter me!

And I wish in my sorrow I could
    strip to the soul,
And dive off in my grave like the
    old swimmin'-hole.   40
(1882)   1882

A LIFE-LESSON *

There! little girl; don't cry!
    They have broken your doll, I
      know;
      And your tea-set blue,
      And your play-house, too,
    Are things of the long ago;
      But childish troubles will soon
        pass by.—
      There! little girl; don't cry!

There! little girl; don't cry!
    They have broken your slate, I
      know;
      And the glad, wild ways   10
      Of your schoolgirl days
    Are things of the long ago;
      But life and love will soon come
        by.—
      There! little girl; don't cry!

There! little girl; don't cry!
    They have broken your heart, I
      know;
      And the rainbow gleams
      Of your youthful dreams
    Are things of the long ago;
      But Heaven holds all for which
        you sigh.—   20
      There! little girl; don't cry!
            1887

THE OLD MAN AND JIM †

Old man never had much to say—
    'Ceptin' to Jim,—

* From *Afterwhiles*, by James Whitcomb
Riley, copyright 1887 and 1915. Used by
special permission of the publishers, the Bobbs-
Merrill Company.
† From *Poems Here at Home*, by James
Whitcomb Riley, copyright 1893 and 1920.
Used by special permission of the publishers,
the Bobbs-Merrill Company.

And Jim was the wildest boy he had—
  And the old man jes' wrapped up
    in him!
Never heerd him speak but once
Er twice in my life,—and first time
    was
When the army broke out, and Jim
    he went,
The old man backin' him, fer three
    months;
And all 'at I heerd the old man say
Was, jes' as we turned to start
    away,—   10
  "Well, good-by, Jim:
  Take keer of yourse'f!"

'Peared like he was more satisfied
  Jes' *lookin'* at Jim
And likin' him all to hisse'f-like,
    see?—
  'Cause he was jes' wrapped up in
    him!
And over and over I mind the day
The old man come and stood round
    in the way
While we was drillin', a-watchin'
    Jim—
And down at the deepot a-heerin' him
    say,   20
  "Well, good-by, Jim:
  Take keer of yourse'f!"

Never was nothin' about the *farm*
  Disting'ished Jim;
Neighbors all ust to wonder why
  The old man 'peared wrapped up
    in him:
But when Cap. Biggler, he writ back
'At Jim was the bravest boy we had
In the whole dern rigiment, white er
    black,
And his fightin' good as his farmin'
    bad—   30
'At he had led, with a bullet clean
Bored through his thigh, and carried
    the flag
Through the bloodiest battle you ever
    seen,—
The old man wound up a letter to him

'At Cap. read to us, 'at said: "Tell
    Jim
  Good-by,
  And take keer of hisse'f!"

Jim come home jes' 'long enough
  To take the whim
'At he'd like to go back in the
    calvery—   40
  And the old man jes' wrapped up
    in him!
Jim 'lowed 'at he'd had sich luck
    afore,
Guessed he'd tackle her three years
    more.
And the old man give him a colt he'd
    raised,
And follered him over to Camp Ben
    Wade,
And laid around fer a week er so,
Watchin' Jim on dress-parade—
'Tel finally he rid away,
And last he heerd was the old man
    say,—
  "Well, good-by, Jim: 50
  Take keer of yourse'f!"

Tuk the papers, the old man did,
  A-watchin' fer Jim,
Fully believin' he'd make his mark
  Some way—jes' wrapped up in
    him!—
And many a time the word 'ud come
'At stirred him up like the tap of a
    drum—
At Petersburg, fer instunce, where
Jim rid right into their cannons there,
And *tuk* 'em and, p'inted 'em t'other
    way,   60
And socked it home to the boys in
    gray,
As they skooted fer timber, and on
    and on—
Jim a lieutenant, and one arm gone,
And the old man's words in his mind
    all day,—
  "Well, good-by, Jim:
  Take keer of yourse'f!"

Think ot a private, now, perhaps,
  We'll say like Jim,

'At's clumb clean up to the shoulder-
    straps—
  And the old man jes' wrapped up
    in him!   70
Think of him—with the war plum'
    through,
And the glorious old Red-White-and-
    Blue
A-laughin' the news down over Jim,
And the old man, bendin' over him—
The surgeon turnin' away with tears
'At hadn't leaked fer years and years,
As the hand of the dyin' boy clung to
His Father's, the old voice in his
    ears,—
  "Well, good-by, Jim:
  Take keer of yourse'f!"   80
                       1888

BEREAVED *

Let me come in where you sit weep-
    ing,—ay,
Let me, who have not any child to die,
Weep with you for the little one whose
    love
    I have known nothing of.

The little arms that slowly, slowly
    loosed
Their pressure round your neck; the
    hands you used
To kiss.—Such arms—such hands I
    never knew.
    May I not weep with you?

Fain would I be of service—say some
    thing,
Between the tears, that would be com-
    forting,—   10
But ah! so sadder than yourselves
    am I,
    Who have no child to die.
                       1890

* From *Poems Here at Home*, by James
Whitcomb Riley, copyright 1893 and 1920.
Used by special permission of the publishers,
the Bobbs-Merrill Company.

VII. EUGENE FIELD
(1850–1895)

LITTLE BOY BLUE *

The little toy dog is covered with dust,
  But sturdy and stanch he stands;
And the little toy soldier is red with
    rust,
  And his musket molds in his hands.
Time was when the little toy dog was
    new
  And the soldier was passing fair,
And that was the time when our Little
    Boy Blue
  Kissed them and put them there

"Now, don't you go till I come," he
    said,
  "And don't you make any noise!" 10
So toddling off to his trundle-bed
  He dreamt of the pretty toys.
And, as he was dreaming, an angel
    song
  Awakened our Little Boy Blue,—
Oh! the years are many, the years are
    long,
  But the little toy friends are true.

Ay, faithful to Little Boy Blue they
    stand,
  Each in the same old place,
Awaiting the touch of a little hand,
  The smile of a little face.   20
And they wonder, as waiting the long
    years through,
  In the dust of that little chair,
What has become of our Little Boy
    Blue
  Since he kissed them and put them
    there.
                       1888

CASEY'S TABLE D'HÔTE

Oh, them days on Red Hoss Moun-
    tain, when the skies wuz fair 'nd
    blue,

* All poems of Field are here reprinted by
permission of Charles Scribner's Sons.

When the money flowed like likker,
   'nd the folks wuz brave 'nd true!
When the nights wuz crisp 'nd balmy,
   'nd the camp wuz all astir,
With the joints all throwed wide open
   'nd no sheriff to demur!
Oh, them times on Red Hoss Moun-
   tain in the Rockies fur away,—
There's no sich place nor times like
   them as I kin find to-day!
What though the camp *hez* busted?
   I seem to see it still
A-lyin', like it loved it, on that big
   'nd warty hill;
And I feel a sort of yearnin' 'nd a
   chokin' in my throat
When I think of Red Hoss Mountain
   'nd of Casey's tabble dote!   10

Wall, yes; it's true I struck it rich,
   but that don't cut a show
When one is old 'nd feeble 'nd it's
   nigh his time to go;
The money that he's got in bonds or
   carries to invest
Don't figger with a codger who has
   lived a life out West;
Us old chaps like to set around, away
   from folks 'nd noise,
'Nd think about the sights we seen
   and things we done when boys;
The which is why *I* love to set 'nd
   think of them old days
When all us Western fellers got the
   Colorado craze,—
And *that* is why I love to set around
   all day 'nd gloat
On thoughts of Red Hoss Mountain
   'nd of Casey's tabble dote.   20

This Casey wuz an Irishman,—you'd
   know it by his name
And by the facial features appertainin'
   to the same.
He'd lived in many places 'nd had
   done a thousand things,
From the noble art of actin' to the
   work of dealin' kings,
But, somehow, hadn't caught on; so,
   driftin' with the rest,

He drifted for a fortune to the undeveloped West,
And he come to Red Hoss Mountain
   when the little camp wuz new,
When the money flowed like likker,
   'nd the folks wuz brave 'nd true;
And, havin' been a stewart on a Mississippi boat,
He opened up a caffy 'nd he run a
   tabble dote.   30

The bar wuz long 'nd rangey, with a
   mirrer on the shelf,
'Nd a pistol, so that Casey, when re-
   quired, could help himself;
Down underneath there wuz a row of
   bottled beer 'nd wine,
'Nd a kag of Burbun whiskey of the
   run of '59;
Upon the walls wuz pictures of hosses
   'nd of girls,—
Not much on dress, perhaps, but
   strong on records 'nd on curls!
The which had been identified with
   Casey in the past,—
The hosses 'nd the girls, I mean,—
   and both wuz mighty fast!
But all these fine attractions wuz of
   precious little note
By the side of what wuz offered at
   Casey's tabble dote.   40

There wuz half-a-dozen tables alto-
   gether in the place,
And the tax you had to pay upon your
   vittles wuz a case;
The boardin'-houses in the camp pro-
   tested 't wuz a shame
To patronize a robber, which this
   Casey wuz the same!
They said a case was robbery to tax
   for ary meal;
But Casey tended strictly to his biz,
   'nd let 'em squeal;
And presently the boardin'-houses all
   began to bust,
While Casey kept on sawin' wood 'nd
   layin' in the dust;
And oncet a trav'lin' editor from Den-
   ver City wrote

A piece back to his paper, puffin'
  Casey's tabble dote.   50

A tabble dote is different from order-
  in' aller cart:
In *one* case you git all there is, in
  t'other, only *part!*
And Casey's tabble dote began in
  French,—as all begin,—
And Casey's ended with the same,
  which is to say, with "vin";
But in between wuz every kind of
  reptile, bird, 'nd beast,
The same like you can git in high-
  toned restauraws down east;
'Nd windin' up wuz cake or pie, with
  coffee demy tass,
Or, sometimes, floatin' Ireland in a
  soothin' kind of sass
That left a sort of pleasant ticklin' in
  a feller's throat,
'Nd made him hanker after more of
  Casey's tabble dote.   60

The very recollection of them puddin's
  'nd them pies
Brings a yearnin' to my buzzum 'nd
  the water to my eyes;
'Nd seems like cookin' nowadays aint
  what it used to be
In camp on Red Hoss Mountain in
  that year of '63;
But, maybe, it is better, 'nd, maybe,
  I'm to blame—
I'd like to be a-livin' in the mountains
  jest the same—
I'd like to live that life again when
  skies wuz fair 'nd blue,
When things wuz run wide open 'nd
  men wuz brave 'nd true;
When brawny arms the flinty ribs of
  Red Hoss Mountain smote
For wherewithal to pay the price of
  Casey's tabble dote.   70

And you, O cherished brother, a-sleep-
  in' way out west,
With Red Hoss Mountain huggin' you
  close to its lovin' breast,—
Oh, do you dream in your last sleep
  of how we used to do,
Of how we worked our little claim
  together, me 'nd you?
Why, when I saw you last a smile
  wuz restin' on your face,
Like you wuz glad to sleep forever
  in that lonely place;
And so you wuz, 'nd I'd be, too, if I
  wuz sleepin' so.
But, bein' how a brother's love aint
  for the world to know,
Whenever I've this heartache 'nd this
  chokin' in my throat,
I lay it all to thinkin' of Casey's
  tabble dote.   80

                                    1889

THE TRUTH ABOUT HORACE

It is very aggravating
To hear the solemn prating
Of the fossils who are stating
    That old Horace was a prude;
When we know that with the ladies
He was always raising Hades,
And with many an escapade his
    Best productions are imbued.

There's really not much harm in a
Large number of his carmina,   10
But these people find alarm in a
    Few records of his acts;
So they'd squelch the muse caloric,
And to students sophomoric
They'd present as metaphoric
    What old Horace meant for facts.

We have always thought 'em lazy;
Now we adjudge 'em crazy!
Why, Horace was a daisy
    That was very much alive!   20
And the wisest of us know him
As his Lydia verses show him,—
Go, read that virile poem,—
    It is No. 25.

He was a very owl, sir,
And starting out to prowl, sir,
You bet he made Rome howl, sir,
    Until he filled his date;

With a massic-laden ditty
And a classic maiden pretty   30
He painted up the city,
    And Mæcenas paid the freight!
                                    1889

THE BIBLIOMANIAC'S PRAYER

Keep me, I pray, in wisdom's way
    That I may truths eternal seek;
I need protecting care to-day.—
    My purse is light, my flesh is weak,
So banish from my erring heart
    All baleful appetites and hints
Of Satan's fascinating art,
    Of first editions, and of prints.
Direct me in some godly walk
    Which leads away from bookish
        strife,   10
That I with pious deed and talk
    May extra-illustrate my life.

But if, O Lord, it pleaseth Thee
    To keep me in temptation's way,
I humbly ask that I may be
    Most notably beset to-day;
Let my temptation be a book,
    Which I shall purchase, hold, and
        keep,
Whereon when other men shall look,
    They'll wail to know I got it
        cheap.   20
Oh, let it such a volume be
    As in rare copperplates abounds,
Large paper, clean, and fair to see,
    Uncut,   unique,   unknown   to
        Lowndes.
                                    1889

THE NEW REALISM

I. EDGAR WATSON HOWE
(1853–   )

From *THE STORY OF A COUNTRY TOWN* *

CHAPTER XXII

A SKELETON IN THE HOUSE AT ERRING'S FORD

More than three years had passed since Jo and Mateel were married, and I was alone on the last night of the year, thinking that the years were slipping away wonderfully fast of late, it seemed so short a time since we had lived in the country; since the Rev. John Westlock so strangely disappeared, and since I was a boy in distress at my own and Jo's misfortunes. The good year was dying, and would soon pass peacefully into the dim past, after the watchers had tired of waiting, and gone to sleep. As is the case when an old man dies, the announcement is speedily followed by the birth of a babe, and so the race and the years are continued. As is now said of the dying year, so it will be said of all of us. At some time in the mysterious future—nobody knows when—the hand that writes this will be picking uneasily at the covering of a death-bed, and it will be whispered in the room, and in all the house, and down the streets, "He is dying; poor

fellow, he is dead." The eye th. reads this—at some time in the future; nobody knows when—will become fixed, and it will be gently sai. "Dying; dead." The front door wi. be black with crape for a few day and the people will pass the hous reverently and silently, but after very little while the token of deat will be removed, the house will b thrown open and aired, and laughte will be heard on the inside. Birds wi sing merrily at the front door, an flowers appear, and happy childre play about the house, and through i as though nothing had happened. Th dead man may have been dearly love but everything and everybody encou. ages his friends to forget him, an they laugh in the room where he die and where his coffin sat through th long nights before the burial.

The relics of departed friend which were at first carefully lai away, are in the course of months c years resurrected, and given to the successors. The hat worn by th pretty boy who died last year, or th year before, is worn to-day by th boy who came after him, and he play with his toys, which were at first s sacred, as though they had bee brought to the house for him. Th mother who put the little hat awa no doubt thought she would keep for years, and look at it to imagin that her first-born was wearin again, but time has softened her grief friends told her he was better o

* Reprinted by permission of the author, Edgar Watson Howe.

d she hoped so, and tried to con-
nce herself that it was all for the
st.

So it will be with the dying year;
was well loved while it lasted, and
ought us many good gifts, but it will
e speedily forgotten, and in twelve
onths we shall be equally indifferent
s to its successor. One dies; an-
her is born; so go the people and the
ars. There will be a birth and a
ath to-night, but it is not an un-
mmon circumstance: there will be a
tle mourning for the death, but a
eat deal of rejoicing and ringing of
lls for the birth.

The fire in the room where I usually
orked had gone out, and I had taken
y papers to an inner room, where
artin had worked late, and which
s yet warm. It must have been ten
clock, and outside the snow was
lling steadily, promising great drifts
the morning, as I could see by the
ys thrown out into the darkness
om the single light which burned
the room. Just after I had set-
d down comfortably in my chair,
ne one opened the front door, and
od on the inside, scraping the snow
om his feet, and brushing it from
s coat, which startled me, for I sup-
sed the door to be locked. Out-
le of the circle of the lamp it
s quite dark, and as the visitor
me slowly toward me, brushing the
ow from his clothing, I was still in
ubt as to who it was, until he stood
most beside me, when I saw with
rprise that it was Jo Erring.

"Of all the men in the world," I
id, getting up, and making a place
r him by the fire, "you are the most
lcome. I think you must be my
w Year's gift, for I am lonely to-

night, and was wishing you were
here."

He held his hands up to the fire to
warm them, but did not reply, and
I noticed, when he looked at me, that
his eyes were bloodshot and swollen.

"Is there anything the matter?" I
asked.

Now that I was looking at him
closely, I saw with alarm that tears
were in his eyes. He made no effort to hide this, but looked at me
as though he would speak, but could
not, and with a face so pitiful that I
became alarmed. He still held his
hands up to the fire to warm them,
and I expected him every moment
to burst out crying.

"Jo, my old friend," I said to him
at last, laying my hand on his shoulder, "tell me the meaning of this.
You distress and alarm me."

Turning his face from the light, he
remained a long while in deep study,
and finally got up and walked to that
part of the room which was the darkest, where he paced up and down a
long time. I added wood to the fire,
expecting him to sit down every moment and tell me his trouble, but he
continued his walk, and wrapped his
great coat about him, as though he
was chilled to the heart. At last he
turned suddenly, and came over into
the light.

"For what I am about to say," he
said, sitting down, "may God forgive
me, for it is a matter that concerns
no one but myself, and should forever
remain a secret with me. But I
have thought of it so much, and am
so distressed from thinking of it, that
I must speak of it to you, or lose
my reason. If I could show you the
wickedness in my thoughts, you would

run away from me in alarm, but if I could show you my heart, you would weep over the misery it contains. It is unmanly for me to tell you what I came here to tell, but I am so wretched that I walked here to-night through the storm for the sympathy I am sure you will give, and which I need so much. I have not slept for weeks, except when nature asserted it- self in spite of my misery, but through all the long nights I have tumbled and tossed about, thinking of the mat- ter in a different light at every turn, hoping to get some comfort out of it, but every new thought of it seems the worst of all. I came out of the house to-night to cool my hot head, and walking towards you caused me to resolve to come on, and freeze my- self into forgetfulness. Mateel does not know where I am, and I must go back as I came, but I would rather walk alone in this storm than trust myself in a darkened room with my thoughts. I am sick to-night, for the first time in my life, but it is from thinking of the matter I came to tell you about, for it has taken such possession of me that even sleep is denied me."

I was so distressed and alarmed that I could not say a word, but tried to appear natural by digging at the fire. After Jo had thought awhile, he continued:—

"I need not rehearse the story of my courtship and marriage—you are familiar with that, and you know that I have been very contented and happy, except that ever since I have known Mateel, I have noticed an indifference which often humiliated me, but which I have excused for a hundred reasons, and tried to think little of. The let-

ter which I will shortly ask you read explains it all, and it is th which has changed me into a wicke worthless man, without hope or amb tion. The letter was written b Mateel to Clinton Bragg, when s was his promised wife, before the came to Fairview, and I received it b mail, addressed in a strange hand, s weeks ago yesterday, on an eveni when I was planning for the futur and when I was in unusual goo spirits. That she had been engaged t Bragg I never knew, nor did I su pect it, for although I knew they we brought up in the same neighborhoo and had been children together, th thought never occurred to me tha they had been lovers, for he is mo fit for a hangman's rope than for a honest woman's regard. I know no that Mateel has never loved me as th letter indicates she loved the mo contemptible man I ever knew; hundred times I have wondered there were no better lovers in th world than Mateel, but I have foun that the trouble was that she ha drained her heart dry in loving m enemy, and that there was none le for me. This is what has wounde my pride, and broken my spirits, an left me a useless wreck."

He took from an inner pocket an handed me an envelope, and takin from it the letter, I began to rea aloud.

"Read it to yourself," he said. ' am familiar with it."

The letter was closely written, an read as follows:—

MY BRAVE LOVER,—I write to-night tell you for the hundredth time ho much I love you. When you are awa from me, I have no other pleasure tha

is, for it brings you to me to receive
y kisses and embraces. Once you came
the middle of the day following the
ght I wrote you, and if you come to-
orrow, and sincerely believe and never
rget what I have to say, this letter
ill have accomplished its mission.

What I want to say is (and I write it
ter a great deal of serious deliberation)
at if by an unlucky chance we should
ver be married, I should still love you 10
I do now, forever. I love you so
uch that I am anxious you should
ow that even though I believed you
d forgotten me, and I became the wife
some one else, because all women are
pected to marry, I should continue to
ink of you as I do now, the only man
orthy of my love in all the world; and
ery night after my husband had gone
sleep, I would put my arms around
m, and imagine that it was you, and 20
at you would waken soon, and love
e as I am sure you do this night.

I want you to believe this, for it is
ritten with absolute sincerity, and if
y hope of the future should never be
alized, please read this over, and over
ain, and feel that I am married only
penance for being unworthy of you.
herever I am, and whatever my con-
tion, I beg of you to remember that
love only you; that I will never love 30
y one else, and that with my last
eath I will tenderly speak your name.
I do not believe God will be so cruel
to separate us, but if He should, the
owledge that you knew I continued
love you would make my loss easier
bear. If I should consent to be mar-
d, it would be to some one who cared
r nothing but my promise to live with
m; and if I could call him up from
e future now to stand beside me, I 40
uld bravely tell him that I love only
inton Bragg, and that though my mind
ay change, my heart never will.

If I should be so unfortunate as to
ve a husband other than you, I would
dutiful and just to him, but my love

I would reserve until I met you in
heaven, when, realizing how perfect it is,
you would accept it. Loving you always.

MATEEL.

I folded the letter, and handed it
back to him, and as it touched his
fingers, he shuddered, as though overtaken by a chill.

"The very touch of it penetrates my
marrow," he said, after putting it
away in his pocket as though it were
red-hot; "but for all my dread of its
infamous contents, I have read it a
hundred times. If I am tossing about
at night, unable to sleep from thinking of it, I cannot help making a light,
and reading it again."

"Did you ever talk to her about
it?" I asked, and I am sure I was
trembling all over; for I felt that
Jo Erring, with all his prospects, was
now a wreck and would never be
himself again.

"Not about this, directly," he answered, "but she has told me that she
was engaged to Bragg. She treated it
so coolly that I thought perhaps such
things are common, and that I am unreasonable to feel as I do. I am not
familiar with the ways of good society; it may be that love is only an
amusement, to be indulged in with
every agreeable person; it may be that
a woman is none the less a true
woman for having been caressed and
fondled by different men, and that it
is no fault for a young girl to spend
half a night with a lover who is liable
to be succeeded in a month by another, but if such is the social creed,
something convinces me that society is
wrong, and that my revolting manhood is right."

He rose from his chair, and walked

up and down in the dark part of the room again, and I could not help thinking of what Mr. Biggs had said: That every one has a private history.

"I do not know who broke the engagement," he said, returning to the fire at last, "but I have evidence in this letter that it was not Mateel, therefore it is fair to suppose that the insolent dog who sent this, tired of the contract, and broke it off. The girl was heart-broken, no doubt, and was brought West with the hope that she would encounter an ignorant fellow with industrious habits, but no sensibility, who could comfortably support her until old age and death came to the relief of her heart, but who could never hope to have her love, for that she had given already, although it was not wanted. Through the cruel neglect of God I became the man who is expected to labor early and late that she may be made as comfortable as possible in her affliction. I receive nothing in return for this except the knowledge that as another man did not want her love, I may have her to care for, as her family is not well-to-do, and somebody must do it.

"Whenever I knock at my heart's door, it is opened by a skeleton hand, and this letter handed out to me; if ambition beckons to me now, the fleshless fingers of an inexorable devil hold me back; and instead of pushing on, I sit down and cry that I have been so disgraced through no fault of my own. They thought I was a rough country boy, lacking so delicate a thing as a heart, and that I would be content with a broken flower because it had once been very beautiful; I doubt if they thought of me at all,

except that I was industrious an healthy, as all the consideration wa for Mateel, who had been wounde and hurt."

I listened to the wind blowing o the outside, and I thought it was mo mournful than I had ever heard before.

"I cannot tell you how much m marriage to Mateel would have do for me had this letter never been wri ten, for I should have divined its e istence though it had never fallen my way. Before I read it I was happy as it is possible for a man be, though the fear often oppresse me that a dark shadow would fa across my path, for I had always bee taught to believe that great sorro followed great happiness. The shado has come, and the devils are probab content with its black intensity. I wa proud that the home I had provide for Mateel was better than any sh had ever lived in before, and was kir and careful of her that she might ble the day we met; I was proud to known as a progressing, growing ma that her father might be proud of m as he knew how hard my boyhood wa but I see now that they all regarde me as a convenience; a trusty pac horse of great endurance, and I kno that my years of work for Mate were not worthy of a man's ambitio I can never tell you, though I wou willingly if I could, how great is t burden I must bear from this tin forward. Hope has been killed with me, except hope to die, and my amb tion has been cruelly trampled up and killed by a man I never wronged

He sat crouching before the fir like a man who had been beaten wit out cause by superior numbers, a

ho felt humiliated because his op-
ressors had escaped, and he could not
e avenged upon them.

"Until six weeks ago, Mateel was
perfect woman in my eyes, and the
ueen of my heart; but since that time
have begun to criticise her (to my-
lf; she does not know it), and if I
ecome an indifferent husband, the
ult is her own. I cannot be the same
s I was before, for I shall be inclined
o look upon her simply as the con-
enience she undertook to become, in-
tead of my wife. If she fails to be
onvenient—and I fear I shall be a
ard critic—I cannot help observing
in my present state of mind, though
shall remark it only to myself. She
as deliberately deceived me, but in
ite of it I love her, and every night-
ind brings me word that it is not
turned. The very wheels in the mill
ve voice to her entreaty to Bragg
 remember that she will never love
e; every sound mocks me that my
ife is proud of her love for another,
d piteously begs that it may never
 forgotten. Since reading the let-
r I have never kissed my wife, or
t my arms about her, and I hope
od may strike me dead if ever I
 either again."

He stood up in great excitement, as
calling on God to witness his oath;
t, as if recalling something, he
eekly sat down again, and continued
a subdued tone.

"I have apologized to her for my
nduct, for she seems distressed
out it, and promised that perhaps I
ould think better of it after a while,
t I never shall; it is growing worse
th me, and I tremble when I think
my future. I talk with her about
e old affair with Bragg over and

over again, hoping it was not so bad
as I think. She is very truthful and
candid, and reluctantly answers every
question, however searching it may
be, but the more I talk of it the worse
it gets. Don't imagine from what I
have said that she was ever anything
but a virtuous girl; but she once loved
that man so madly that she denounced
me before she had seen me. The
fresh and innocent affection which I
should have had was given to Bragg
—he had the fragrance of the rose;
I have the withered leaves, after he
tired of its beauty, and tossed it away.
You can imagine the scenes between
two young people who passionately
love each other, and who only delay
marriage until a convenient time. If
you cannot, I can; and it is this
imagination which never leaves me.
And to add to my wretchedness, Bragg
throws himself in my way as often
as possible, that I may contemplate
the man who was worthy of the
woman I am not. The time may come
when I would give my life to take him
by the throat, and if ever it does,
there will be murder done, for with
my hands once upon him I would
tear him into bits."

I did not know what to say in reply,
for I could think of nothing that
would comfort him; and though I
knew he would never again need my
friendship as he needed it then, this
knowledge only confused me, and
made me stammer when I attempted
to put in a word. He seemed to have
so thoroughly considered the matter
that there was no defence, and stated
it so candidly that I thought he only
expected me to pity him.

"Jo," I said, as the thought occurred to me, "you undoubtedly re-

ceived this letter from Bragg; no one else would be malicious enough to send it. Are you certain he did not write it?"

A new hope sprang into his eyes, though I noticed that his hand paused on its way to the pocket which contained the letter, as though it was of no use to look. But he unfolded the letter with trembling hands, and studied it with great care, spending so much time over it that I hoped we should have occasion to go out and find the scoundrel, and beat him, but after Jo had finished his inspection, I saw that he was satisfied that the letter was written by Mateel.

"That it might be a forgery never occurred to me before," he said, with a long sigh, "but it is genuine; there is no doubt."

"I need not tell you, my dear old friend," I said, "that I am sorry this has happened. I regret it so much that I am powerless to comfort you, if that were possible. Your tears have unmanned me."

"I want to apologize to-night for my future," he said, after a long silence, "for I no longer have ambition. I can never succeed now, and I want you to know why. If I do not advance in the future, I desire that my only friend know that I no longer cared to advance; that I have no reason to wish for success, and that I am not trying. If I become a Fairview man, miserable and silent, without hope or ambition, I want you to know that I am not to blame. I have just such a business, and just such a home, as we pictured together when we were boys. I have proved to you that I did not over-estimate my

strength, and if I do not progress no[w] that I am a man, you will know tha[t] my strength has been broken. Th[e] home I built with so much care [is] distasteful to me, the business I ow[n] after such a struggle, I hate; and [I] want you to know that, while I hav[e] not tired of working, I no longer ca[n] to succeed. The one above all othe[r] who should have helped me has onl[y] brought me disgrace, and broken m[y] heart. There was no contract betwee[n] us, but when Mateel became m[y] promised wife, I made a vow to ac[-] complish what I have; I have su[c-] ceeded, but she has succeeded i[n] nothing except to bring me this le[t-] ter and its humiliating contents. [I] would not be a successful man in th[e] future if I could. Bragg will final[ly] become a beggar, for he is a spen[d-] thrift and loafer, and I believe tha[t] she would use my means to help hi[m] I would rather be poor than rich, f[or] if I should die possessed of propert[y] that scoundrel would overcome h[is] former scruples and marry my widow[.] My ambition in the future will be t[o] live long and die poor. I hope th[e] Devil is satisfied. He has been aft[er] me a long while, and I have passe[d] into his possession body and soul. Bu[t] I must return home," he said, as [if] remembering the hour. "Mateel do[es] not know where I am, though I su[s-] pect she does not care, and is soundl[y] sleeping."

"How are you going?" I asked, a[s] he got up, and began buttoning h[is] great coat around him.

"As I came—on foot."

He started to walk past me, an[d] would have gone away had I not hel[d] him back.

"To-morrow is Saturday, and Ne[w]

year," I said. "It is a holiday, and will go with you. Wait here until come back."

He consented without a word, and at down, and I think did not change his position until I came back with the horses. It was an hour after midnight, and the cold was intense—a miserable night for such a ride, but I willingly undertook it, knowing it was a kindness to Jo, and that we could easily make the distance in an hour. When I told my mother that I was going to Fairview, she was not surprised, nor did she ask me any questions, and I was soon on the way, with Jo by my side.

When we drove up to the house at the mill, which we did after a cold ride without speaking a word, I saw a curtain pulled aside in a room where there was a light, and Mateel's pale and frightened face peering out, but by the time she appeared at the door, and opened it, we had passed on to the stables, and were putting away the horses. I was chilled through with cold, but when we walked back toward the house, I am certain I shivered because I dreaded to see them meet, knowing how unhappy and how helpless both were. I opened the door, and we walked in together, Jo a little behind me, and we went direct to the fire, though I stopped and held out my hand to his frightened wife. She was very pale, and I knew she had been weeping, for her eyes were red and swollen. While she took my hat and coat, Jo took off his, and held his hands out to the fire as he had done when he came to see me in town. He had taken a hasty glance at his wife, and I thought her distress added to his own, as though now both

were wretched, and nobody to blame for it.

"Jo, my husband," she said, in a piteous, hesitating tone, and almost crying, "what has happened? You look so strange. I have been walking the floor since eight o'clock waiting for you. Is there anything the matter?"

As Jo did not reply, she looked at me for an answer, and I said he had business in town which occupied him until late; and that, knowing she would be worried, I had brought him home. But this did not satisfy her, and walking over to Jo, she stood beside him.

"Why don't you speak to me? You have never treated me this way before."

As she stood trembling beside him, I thought that surely Jo's letter was a forgery, and that if she did not love her husband, a woman never did.

Looking up at her as though half ashamed, Jo said:—

"You know why I went out of the house to-night. It is nothing more than that; you say it is not serious."

Mateel walked over to a chair near me—I thought she staggered as she went—and sat down, and her face was so pale and frightened that I felt sure Jo wronged her when he said she did not care. We sat there so long in silence that I began wondering who would first speak, and what would be said, and whether it would clear up this distressing matter. When I glanced at Mateel, I saw despair and helplessness written in her face, and determined to go to bed, and leave them alone, hoping they would talk it over, and forget it. Jo saw my intention, and motioned me back.

"You say it is not serious," he said, glancing hurriedly at his wife, as if afraid that if he looked in her face, and saw its distress, his stubborn heart would relent so much so as to commit the unpardonable offense of taking her in his arms; "therefore you will not care that I have told Ned. I have talked to him more freely than to you. I went to town for that purpose."

Had my life depended upon it, I could not have told which one I pitied most.

"As I know you to be a truthful woman," he went on, after a long pause, "and you say it is not serious, I believe that you think so; but it is all the more unfortunate on that account, for it is a very grave matter to me. I can never explain to you fully why I take it so much to heart, because I should wound your feelings in doing it, but the change in me within six weeks will convince you that if I am unreasonable about it, I cannot help it, and that my pride has been humbled, and my spirit broken, by a circumstance for which you are probably not to blame, when everything is considered. It is unmanly in me to feel as I do, and I apologize to you that I have not manhood sufficient (if that is a reasonable excuse) to shake off a circumstance which will affect my future, but which you regard as trifling. I have loved you—and I do yet; it is nothing to me what those I do not care for have been—I have loved you with my whole heart, and I have never divided my affection with anyone, if I except an honest friendship for my sister's son, and who was the sole companion of my wretched boyhood; but the more I love you, the more unhappy I am. This is my unfortunate dilemma, and I only mention it because the serious truth must be known. Although it nearly killed me I asked you never to show me affection until I felt differently; I did this because I believed you learned to be affectionate with a man I hate, and that you can never show me an act of kindness you did not show him, and which your love for him taught you. No woman's lips ever touched mine—my only sister's alone excepted and hers not frequently—until yours did; my mind was never occupied with thoughts of love until I met you, and now that I know you only consented to marry me because you could not be better suited, my simple affection is hurt. I know that you care for me in a fashion; so you do for every one who is kind to you but I wanted the affection you gave HIM, your first and best. I feel debased that this affair has ruined me for it has completely, and I can no longer look an honest man in the face, for against my will I am an indifferent husband, instead of the worthy one I hoped to become. I was brought up in a community where the women were overworked, imposed upon, and unhappy; I resolved to make my wife a notable exception to this rule, but I cannot now, and I feel the disgrace keenly."

The pale, fretful women of Fairview, who talked in the church of their heavy crosses to bear, and sat down crying, passed before me in procession; and staggering behind them with the heaviest cross of all, was Mateel.

"I was so particular to tell you ow I felt about this matter before 'e were married," Jo went on, still oking into the fire, "though I spoke f it then only to convince you that was a good lover, for I did not uspect that you regarded me as a ictim instead of a man. I talked of seriously that you might know I 'as in earnest, and much as I loved ou, had I known this I would have iven you up at the last moment. 'here might have been a remedy for t then; there is none now. As I have een during the past six weeks, so hall I be as long as I live, except nat I shall grow more bitter and re- entful. It is cruel that I have been nercilessly ruined, and nobody to lame for it. Were I injured in any ther way, there would be some one o punish, and amends to be made, ut in this no wrong has been done; ndeed, I suppose I, who am so griev- usly injured, am more to blame than ny one else for being so absurd. I m certain every one will regard it n this way, although that will not elp the matter so far as I am con- erned."

There were evidences of bitterness n his words now, rather than of sad- ess and regret; and he looked around he room fiercely, as though he would o something desperate to those who ad injured him. But he soon began hinking again, and went on talking:—

"I speak frankly only that we may nderstand each other, for it grieves ne to do it. It is not a pleasure or me to command you never to ouch me again. During the short ime we have lived apart on account of his unfortunate matter, I have prayed very night that you would come to me, though I had locked my door so you could not. When my heart finally breaks it will be because you no longer come to me, though I will not let you. One night I became so dis- tracted thinking of your unhappiness as well as my own that I stole softly into your room intending to kiss away your tears, and ask you to forgive my unintended cruelty; but I found you quietly sleeping, and I will swear that by the light of my lamp I saw you smiling. I will swear that you spoke the name of Clinton; and I went back to my room determined to kill him, and then myself. But my cowardly heart—it was never cowardly before—failed me, and I could only become more ugly and wicked."

From the manner in which Mateel started at this I believed she had only gone to sleep when completely ex- hausted, and that she had only spoken the name because she was familiar with it, as she was familiar with a thousand others; but the circumstance seemed only to convince her that everything was against her, and that explanations would be useless; but, as if trying to avoid the subject, she asked, without looking up:—

"Since you have told Ned, what does he think?"

"I am not a competent judge," I answered hurriedly, sorry that she had appealed to me at all, for I could think of no comfort for either of them. "I can only say that I have so much confidence in your husband that I do not question his sorrow. It is enough for me to know that he is unhappy, though, if I should advise him, it would be to try to forget. The world is full of difficulties which have no other remedy than this though they are seldom forgotten. I have always known that Jo was just such a man as he has shown himself to be to-night; I remember distinctly how gloomy he became in talking about it the evening I first went to your house with him, and how it changed his disposition; and I remember how gayly you laughed at it as if it were of no consequence. I have always been Jo's friend; I always shall be, and am his friend in this."

She did not look up, but kept gazing at the fire, as she had done before.

"It is my most serious fault that I did not tell him of it before we were married; but I was timid, and thought of it only as one of the many little regrets with which every life is filled, and neglected it. I could not love my husband more than I do, and I only failed to tell him of it because I feared it would give him unnecessary pain. I was but sixteen then; a school-girl without serious thought or purpose, and certainly every one of my companions was as guilty as I, if it can be called guilt. It is not necessary for me to make explanations, for he has given me notice that they will not be accepted, but if there is anything I can do to make atonement —no difference what it is; even to going away from him, and dying alone and neglected—I will gladly do it, and humble myself cheerfully if that course will relieve him. I have so much confidence in my husband that I do not question the honesty of his grief, and for his sake I regret my past. In justice to my womanhood I cannot say I am ashamed of it. If I mentioned a name which was obnoxious to my husband in my sleep,

it was because the name had cause me trouble. I do not remember ▮ for since this unhappy change in ou home I have been ill and worn ou I was never strong, but I am so wea now as to be helpless."

Jo seemed to not pay the slightes attention while his wife was talkin for he kept his eyes on the floor, bu that he was listening intently I kne very well. Mateel looked at him tim idly when she had finished, as if ex pecting a reply, but as he made non she too looked at the floor. I watche her face narrowly, and there saw de picted such misery as I can neve forget. She seemed to realize tha she had made her husband unhapp by a thoughtless act, and to realiz her utter inability to supply a rem edy. I think a more ingenious woma could have made a more cautiou statement, though not a more hon est one, and won her husband bac by explanations; but Mateel, as wa the case with her father, gave up a once on the approach of a difficult and prepared for the worst. I sav in her face that she would never b able to effect a reconciliation; for, be lieving it to be hopeless, she woul be dumb in contemplating the lif they would lead in future. I kne she would be kind and attentive, an hope for the best, but in her frigh and consternation she could no gather strength to test her ingenuity I knew that she would accept he husband's increasing obstinacy as evi dence that a great calamity had com upon their house, and meekly submit instead of resolving to conquer an triumph over it. If she had put he arms around his neck then (as h wanted her to do, in spite of hi

mmands to the contrary), and, be-
veen declarations of her love, asked
m to give her a year in which to
ove her devotion, and explain away
e unhappy past, I believe this story
ould never have been written, but
ey misunderstood each other at the
:ginning, and continued it until the
id. I could see, also, that Jo re-
rded what she had said as a sort of
stification of her course, thus wid-
ing and deepening the gulf between
em; and I became so uncomfortable
at I walked the floor to collect my-
lf, but I could not think of any-
ing which, if expressed, would help
em, and I became more uncomfort-
le still when I reflected that they
ould accept my embarrassment as an
idence that I thought there was 20
thing to be done except the worst
at could be done. I sat down then
termined to speak of the matter
htly, but a look at them convinced
e that this would be mockery, there-
re I changed my mind, and said I
ould go to bed. This seemed to
artle them both, as though they
eaded to be left alone, and Jo asked
a favor that I stay with him. 30
"If you leave that chair," he said,
Devil will occupy it, and stare at
e until daylight."

I replied that I only thought of
ing to bed to leave them alone, be-
use I felt like an intruder, and was
t at all sleepy, and in response to
s request I stirred the fire, and sat
wn between them. Occasionally I
zed, but on waking again, I found 40
em sitting on either side of the
e, as far apart as possible, as my
andfather and grandmother had done
fore them. I felt that all had been
id that could be said, and although

once or twice I broke the silence by
some commonplace remark, neither of
them replied further than to look up
as if imploring me not to go to sleep
again, and leave them alone.

I thought the night would never
end, but at last the room began to
grow lighter, and when the sun came
up over the woods, its first rays
looked in upon two faces so haggard
and worn that I wondered whether it
did not pity them. The sun came up
higher yet, but still they sat there;
and the curtains being down, and the
shutters closed, I thought the sunlight
had deserted that house, and given it
over to gloom and despair.

1883

II. JOSEPH KIRKLAND
(1830–1894)

From *ZURY: THE MEANEST
MAN IN SPRING COUNTY* *

CHAPTER V

HOW THE MEANEST MAN GOT
SO MEAN, AND HOW MEAN
HE GOT

Ephraim wanted Zury to marry,
but it was with "a sharp eye to the
main chance." Property and personal
service at no wages might both be
secured by a judicious choice. Girls
were not plenty, but at the Peddi-
combs' there were three of marriage-
able age. Their place was only three
miles from Prouder's, and they were
still the nearest neighbors. Mrs.
Peddicomb had not long survived the

* Reprinted by permission of Louise Kirkland Sanborn.

birth of her three daughters. She died (as was and is common among farmers' wives) at not much over thirty years of age, just when her life ought to have been in its prime.

She was called a "Come-gals kind of a woman" by neighbors; partly in ridicule of her enthusiasm, and partly in admiration of her energy. It was told of her that she would get up before light on Monday, "fly 'raound," uncover the fire, hang on the kettle, and call up the ladder to the loft,—

"Come gals! *Dew* git up 'n' start in! To-day's Monday, to-morrow's Tuesday, 'n' next day's Wednesday; 'n' then comes Thursday, Friday, 'n' Saturday,—the hull week gone 'n' nothin' done."

The two younger girls had been cared for by the oldest, and so had retained some girlish freshness and delicacy, but as for Mary (the caretaker after her mother's death), she was "good-looking" only because she looked good.

On this marriage subject Ephraim took occasion to speak to Zury.

"Mary Peddicomb, she's a likely gal."

"Mary? Why not S'manthy 'n' Flory?"

"Oh, yes; they're all right tew. Th' ol' man he's got th' best part of a section. Some stawk, tew; 'n' th' haouse 'n' barn's fust rate."

"Ya-as. Ef th' haouse 'n' barn worn't so good he'd have more stawk th't 'd pay him right smart better'n th' haouse 'n' barn dooz."

"Peddicomb ain't like t' marry ag'in. Mary she'll have her sheer."

"Any more'n th' others?"

"Oh, no. All same. But I reck' Mary she'd be more of a manage She kin work. I've watched her eve sence she wuz knee-high to a hoppy toad, 'n' *I* tell ye she kin work!"

"Ef ye mean more manageable y mought's well say so."

"Wal, I dew 'llaow she'd be fu 's little likely t' be uppish 's tl others."

"Ye 'llaow 't humbly and humbl goes t'gether?"

"Wal, yes; 'mongst the wimmi folks, substantially. Nothin' sets 'e so bad up 's bein' ha'ans'm. Spile 'em fer use abaout the place. T' humbly ones take t' milkin' mo willin' like; 'n' I don't see but wha the caows give daown tew 'em full well 's tew the ha'ans'm ones. 'N then when ther' looks goes the' 'n apt t' kick."

"What, the caows?"

"No, the wimmin."

("Humbly" in country parlance a corruption of "homely," the o posite of handsome; plain, ungainl "Humbly as a hedge fence.")

Zury pondered on this shrewd cou sel from time to time, but took r step toward marrying.

"Right smart o' things t' think c afore th' 'll be any hurry 'baout gittin' marr'd. Th' feller th't 's an orfle sweat t' marry, he 's li'b t' be the very feller th't 's behin hand with everythin' else. Tak Time by the forelock 'baout gitti a wife; 'n' by the fetlock 'baout g tin' suthin' fer her t' eat."

The boy was wedded to his ido quite as faithfully, if not quite sordidly, as was his father. The dispositions were much alike. N raft on their powers of endurance nd self-denial could be too great.

As to niggardliness, there was a onfessed rivalry between them. Each would tell of the money-making nd money-saving exploits of the ther, and of his efforts to surpass hem.

"Dad's a screamer t' save money!)' ye ever see him withe a plaow-int ontew a plaow? Give him a ickory grub, 'n' he kin dew it so 'll run a good half a day; 'n' then vithe it on agin in noon-spell whilst h' team 's a eatin', 'n' then withe on agin come night so 's t' be ready er nex' morn'n', 'n' keep it up fer week that-a-way, sonner 'n pay th' mith a cent t' rivit it fast."

"Thasso, thasso, Zury. Hickory wigs is cheaper ner iron any day.

"Ya-as, dad; but then I kin make shillin' while ye 're a savin' a cent. ook at it wunst. I upped 'n' sold ie smith a half an acre, 'n' took a iortgage on it, 'n' made him dew all our repairin' b' way of interest on ie mortgage, 'n' then foreclosed th' iortgage when it come dew, 'n' got i' land back, shop 'n' all. Business business!"

Ephraim always wanted to buy at ie shop where they wrapped up the urchases with the largest and rongest paper and twine, and the irnesses on the farm gradually grew be largely composed of twine. ury could buy everything at whole-le, half price, including merchan-se, paper, twine, harnesses, and all. One day Zury came across a poor ttle boy carrying a poorer little ippy and crying bitterly.

"What 's the matter, sonny?"

"Our folks gimme a dime t' draownd this h'yer purp, 'n' I—I—I—hate t' dew it."

"Wal, ne' mind, bub; gimme the dime 'n' I'll draownd him fer ye."

Whereupon he took the cash and the pup and walked to the mill-pond, while the boy ran home. Zury threw the little trembling creature as far as he could into the pond. A few seconds of wildly waving small ears, legs, and tail, and then a splash, and then nothing but widening ripples. But out of one of the ripples is poked a little round object, which directs itself bravely toward the shore. Nearer and nearer struggles the small black nozzle, sometimes under water, and sometimes on top, but always nearer.

"Ye mis'able, ornery little fyce, ye! Lemme ketch ye swimmin' ashore! I'll throw ye furder nex' time."

At last poor little roly-poly drags itself to the land and squats down at the very water's edge, evidently near to the end of its powers. Zury picks it up and swings it for a mighty cast, but stops and studies it a moment.

"Looks fer all the world like a sheep-dawg-purp."

Whereupon he slipped it into his pocket and carried it home, where it grew up to be a fit mate to old Shep, and the ancestress of a line of sheep dogs which ornament Spring County to this day.

Later, when the same boy, grown older, applied to Zury for one of the pups, he charged him the full price fifty cents, took all he had, thirty-six cents, and his note on interest for the balance, the dog being pledged as security. The note being unpaid when due, Zury took back the dog. "Business is business!"

Years passed, and it came time for the old man to be gathered to his fathers and the son to reign in his stead. When Ephraim lay on his deathbed, he whispered to Zury:—

"What day 's to-day?"

"Tuesday, father."

"I hope I'll live ontel Thursday, 'n' then ye kin hev the fun'r'l Sunday, 'n' not lose a day's work with the teams."

He did not die till Saturday night, but Zury had the funeral on Sunday all the same, like a dutiful son as he was, bent on carrying out his father's last request.

After Zury had grown to be a prosperous farmer, Chicago became the great market for the sale of grain. Teams by the score would start out from far down the State, and, driving during the day and camping at night, make the long journey. They would go in pairs or squads so as to be able to double teams over the bad places. Forty or fifty bushels could thus be carried in one load, when the chief parts of the roads were good, and "the ready john" (hard cash), could be got for the grain, at twenty or thirty cents a bushel for corn or wheat. This sum would provide a barrel or two of salt, and perhaps a plow and a bundle of dry goods and knickknacks for the women folks, the arrival of which was a great event in the lonely farm-houses.

Zury had now working for him (beside Jule, who kept house and attended to the live stock), a young

fellow who became a score of yea[rs] afterward private, corporal, sergea[nt] lieutenant, and captain in the —[th] Illinois Volunteer Infantry in th[e] great war. From his stories, told i[n] bivouacs and beside camp fires, t[he] toiling, struggling, suffering "boys i[n] blue," these tales are taken almo[st] verbatim. (Some of them have a[l]ready found their way into print.)

"Zury always wanted to get ont[o] the road with farmers whose hous[e] keeping was good, because his ow[n] was—well, wuss th'n what we g[ot] down here in Dixie, an' there 's n[o] need of *that*. Well, when they'd ha[lt] for noon-spell, Zury he 'd happe[n] along promiscuous-like, an' most gen[n]erally some of 'em would make hi[m] stop an' take a bite. He was goo[d] company if he *was* so near. 'N' the[n] a man's feed warn't counted fer muc[h] unless it was some store-truck o[r] boughten stuff.

"But one day they jest passed th[e] wink and sot it up on him, and com[e] noon-spell nobody asked Zury an' m[e] to eat. Zury left me to take car[e] of both teams while he walked u[p] and down the line of wagins. Every[-] body who hadn't 'jest eat,' warn['t] 'quite ready' yet, an' by the next tim[e] he came to those who hadn't bee[n] 'quite ready,' they'd 'jest eat.'

"Wal, Zury swallered his disap[-] pointment and I swallered all th[e] chawed wheat I could git away wit[h] and the first settlement we passe[d] Zury went and bought a monstrou[s] big bag of sody-crackers, and we ea[t] them for supper and breakfast. An[d] still we were not happy.

"Next noon-spell Zury said, 'Boy[s] s'posin' we kinder whack up 'n' me[ss] ogether.' Wal, the others 'd had nough of their joke, and so they all greed, and chipped in. Ham, pickles, ies, cakes, honey, eggs, apples, and ne thing another. Ye see every nan's o' woman knew that when they ot together, her housekeep would be ompared with everybody else's; so hese long drives were like donation arties, or weddings, or funerals,— ell fed.

"Of course, Zury's sody-crackers vent in with the rest, an' me an' Zury lways ate *some* anyhow for appear- nce sake. I could see the fellers vere all makin' fun of Zury's cute odge of gettin' a dozen good meals or him an' me at the price of a few ounds of sody-crackers. But *then,* hey did n't know Zury so well as hey thought they did. By an' by he trip was done an' settlin'-up-time ame, when each man was called on or his share of pasturage, ferriage, n' one thing another. Zury paid his, ut he deducted out twenty-five cents aid for sody-crackers. Said it was ne of the cash outlays for the com- non good, an' if any of the rest of em spent money an' did n't put it n, more fools they. Business is busi- ess."

So Zury in the soda-cracker episode ame out "top of the heap" as usual. The top of the heap was his accus- omed place, but still he perceived hat he was living under one useless lisability, and, with his quick adap- ation of means to ends and remedies o deficiencies, he simply—married. n doing this, he was guided by his ather's shrewd words; counsel which ad lain fallow in his memory for ears.

Zury's marriageability had, of course, not been unobserved in the household of the three daughters. Peddicomb had remarked what a good "outin'" the Prouders had made in their purchase of swine from him. and cherished the same kind of feel- ing toward them that most of us ex- perience when some other person has done better in a joint transaction than we did.

"Them Praouders, the' 'll skin outer the land all the' kin skin, 'n' then sell offen the place all 't anybody 'll buy, 'n' then feed t' the hawgs all a hawg 'll eat, 'n' then give th' rest t' th' dawg, 'n' then what th' dawg won't tech the' 'll live on theirselves."

"Yew bet," tittered Samantha, the second. "That thar ornery Zury Praouder he'd let a woman starve t' death ef he could. 'N' o' man Praouder wuz th' same way, tew. Th' o' woman she wuz near abaout skin 'n' bone when the' buried her. I seen her in her coffin, 'n' I know."

"Oh, don't *yew* be scaret, S'man- thy. I hain't saw Zury a-lookin' over t' your side o' the meetin'-haouse, no gre't," kindly rejoined Flora, the youngest daughter.

"Who, me? He knows better! Not ef husbands wuz scarcer ner hen's teeth."

"Six hundred 'n' forty acres o' good land, all fenced 'n' paid fer; 'n' a big orchard; 'n' all well stocked, tew." (He added this with a pang, remem- bering once more the pig-purchase, which by this time had grown to a mighty drove, spite of many sales.)

"Don't care ef he owned all ou' doors. Th' more the' 've got, th' more it shows haow stingy the' be."

Then the meek Mary ventured a remark.

"Mebbe ef Zury wuz t' marry a good gal it 'd be the makin' on him."

"Oh, Mary, *yew* hain't no call t' stan' up fer Zury! Th' o' man he 'd a ben more in yewr line."

"No, Zury would n't want *me,* ner no other man, I don't expect," she answered with a laugh—and a sigh.

One Sunday afternoon Zury rode over to Peddicomb's to get a wife. He tried to decide which girl to ask, but his mind would wander off to other subjects,—crops, live stock, bargains, investments. He did n't much think that either girl he asked would say no, but if she did, he could ask the others. When he came near the house he caught sight of one of the girls, in her Sunday clothes, picking a "posy" in the "front garding." It was Mary.

"Good day, Mary. Haow 's all the folks?"

"Good day, Zury—Mr. Praouder, I s'pose I should say. Won't ye 'light?"

"Wal, I guess not. I jes' wanted t' speak abaout a little matter."

"Wal, father he 's raoun' some 'ers. Haow 's the folks t' your 'us?"

"All peart; that is t' say th' ain't no one naow ye know, but me 'n' Jule 'n' Mac. That makes a kind of a bob-tail team, ye know, Mary. Nobody but Jule t' look out fer things. Not b't what he 's a pretty fair of a nigger as niggers go. He c'd stay raoun' 'n' help some aoutside."

"Whatever is he a-drivin' at?" thought Mary, but she said nothing.

"The's three of you gals to hum.

Ye don't none of ye seem t' go o yit, tho' I sh'd a-thought Flory sh 'd a-ben picked up afore this, 'r S'manthy tew fer that matter."

Neither of them saw the unintende slur this rough speech cast upon poo Mary.

"Don't ye think we 'd better g married, Mary?"

"What, *me?*"

"Wal, yes." He answered this i a tone where she might have detecte the suggestion, "Or one of your sis ters," if she had been keen and criti cal. But she was neither. She simpl rested her work-worn hand upon th gate post and her chin upon her hand and looked dreamily off over the prai rie. She pondered the novel proposi tion for some time, but fortunatel not quite long enough to cause Zur to ask if either of her sisters was a home, as he was quite capable o doing.

She looked up at him, the bloo slowly mounting to her face, and con sidered how to say yes. He saw tha she meant yes, so he helped her ou a little. He wanted to have it settle and go.

"Wal, Mary, silence gives consen they say. When shall it be?"

"Oh, yew ain't in no hurry, Zury I don't expect."

He was about to urge prompt ac tion, but the thought occurred to hir that she must want to get her "things ready, and the longer she waited th more "things" she would bring wit her. So he said:—

"Suit yerself, Mary. I'll drop ove 'n' see ye nex' Sunday, 'n' we 'll fi it all up."

Mary had no objection to urg

ough possibly in her secret heart
he wished there had been a little
more sentiment and romance about it.
No woman likes "to be cheated out
of her wooing," but then this might
come later. He called for her with
the wagon on the appointed day, and
they drove to the house of a justice
of the peace who lived a good distance away. This was not for the
sake of making a wedding trip, but
because this particular justice owed
Zury money, as Zury carefully explained.

And so Mary went to work for
Zury very much as Jule did, only it
was for less wages, as Jule got a dollar a month besides his board and
clothes, while Mary did not.

For a year or two or three after
marriage (during which two boys
were born to them) Zury found that
he had gained, by this investment,
something more than mere profit and
economy—that affection and sympathy were realities in life. But
gradually the old dominant mania resumed its course, and involved in its
current the weak wife as well as the
strong husband. The general verdict
was that both Zury and Mary were
jest 'as near 's they could stick 'n'
ive." "They 'd skin a flea fer its
ide 'n' taller."

"He gin an acre o' graound fer the
churh 'n' scule-house, 'n' it raised
he value of his hull farm more 'n'
dollar an acre. 'N' when he got
nto the scule-board *she* 'llaowed she
ad n't released her daower right, 'n'
ut him up t' tax the deestrick fer
he price of that same acre o'
round."

So Zury, claiming the proud position of "the meanest ma-an in Spring
Caounty," would like to hear his
claim disputed. If he had a rival he
would like to have him pointed out,
and would "try pootty hard but what
he 'd match him."

Strange as it may seem, these
grasping characteristics did not make
Zury despised or even disliked among
his associates. His "meanness" was
not underhanded.

"Th' ain't nothin' *mean* abaout
Zury, *mean* 's he is. Gimme a man
as sez aout 'look aout fer yerself,' 'n' I kin git along with him.
It 's these h'yer sneakin' fellers th't
's one thing afore yer face 'n' another
behind yer back th't I can't abide.
Take ye by th' beard with one hand
'n' smite ye under th' fifth rib with
t' other! He pays his way 'n' dooz
's he 'grees every time. When he
buys 'taters o' me, I 'd jest 's live
's hev him measure 'em 's measure
'em myself with him a-lookin' on.
He knows haow t' trade, 'n' ef yew
don't, he don't want ye t' trade with
him, that 's all; ner t' grumble if ye
git holt o' the hot eend o' th' poker
arter he 's give ye fair notice. Better
be shaved with a sharp razor than a
dull one."

On an occasion when the honesty
of a more pretentious citizen was
compared with Zury's to the advantage of the latter, he said:—

"Honest? Me? Wal, I guess so.
Fustly, I would n't be noth'n' else,
nohaow; seck'ndly, I kin 'fford t' be,
seein' 's haow it takes a full bag t'
stand alone; thirdly, I can't 'fford t'
be noth'n' else, coz honesty 's th' best
policy."

He was evidently quoting, unconsciously but by direst inheritance, the aphorisms of his fellow Pennsylvanian, Dr. Franklin.

In peace as in war strong men love "foemen worthy of their steel." Men liked to be with Zury and hear his gay, shrewd talk; to trade with him, and meet his frankly brutal greed. He enjoyed his popularity, and liked

to do good turns to others when cost him nothing. When elected t local posts of trust and confidence h served the public in the same eff cient fashion in which he served him self, and he was therefore continuall elected to school directorships an other like "thank 'ee jobs."

188

EMILY DICKINSON
(1830–1886)

[THIS IS MY LETTER TO THE WORLD] *

This is my letter to the world,
  That never wrote to me,—
The simple news that Nature told,
  With tender majesty.

Her message is committed
  To hands I cannot see;
For love of her, sweet countrymen,
  Judge tenderly of me!

               1924

[I NEVER SAW A MOOR] *

I never saw a moor,
I never saw the sea;
Yet know I how the heather looks,
And what a wave must be.

I never spoke with God,
Nor visited in heaven;
Yet certain am I of the spot
As if the chart were given.

               1890

[THE BUSTLE IN A HOUSE] *

The bustle in a house
The morning after death
Is solemnest of industries
Enacted upon earth,—

The sweeping up the heart,
And putting love away
We shall not want to use again
Until eternity.

               1890

[MY LIFE CLOSED TWICE] *

My life closed twice before its close;
It yet remains to see
If Immortality unveil
A third event to me,

So huge, so hopeless to conceive,
As these that twice befell.
Parting is all we know of heaven,
And all we need of hell.

               1896

[TO FIGHT ALOUD] *

To fight aloud is very brave,
But gallanter, I know,
Who charge within the bosom,
The cavalry of woe.

Who win, and nations do not see,
Who fall, and none observe,
Whose dying eyes no country
Regards with patriot love.

We trust, in plumed procession,
For such the angels go,   10
Rank after rank, with even feet
And uniforms of snow.

               1890

[I LIKE TO SEE IT LAP THE MILES] *

I like to see it lap the miles,
And lick the valleys up,
And stop to feed itself at tanks;
And then, prodigious, step

* From *The Poems of Emily Dickinson*, Centenary Edition, edited by Martha Dickinson Bianchi and Alfred Leete Hampson. Reprinted by permission of Little, Brown & Company.

Around a pile of mountains,
And, supercilious, peer
In shanties by the sides of roads;
And then a quarry pare

To fit its sides, and crawl between,
Complaining all the while   10
In horrid, hooting stanza;
Then chase itself down hill

And neigh like Boanerges;
Then, punctual as a star,
Stop,—docile and omnipotent—
At its own stable door.

                              1891

[THE WAY I READ A LETTER'S
              THIS] *

The way I read a letter's this:
'Tis first I lock the door,
And push it with my fingers next,
For transport it be sure.

And then I go the furthest off
To counteract a knock;
Then draw my little letter forth
And softly pick its lock.

Then, glancing narrow at the wall,
And narrow at the floor,   10
For firm conviction of a mouse
Not exorcised before,

Peruse how infinite I am
To—no one that you know!

LETTERS *

I

TO MR. AND MRS. SAMUEL BOWLES

[1862]

DEAR MR. BOWLES,—Thank you.

    Faith is a fine invention
    When gentlemen can see!

* From The Letters of Emily Dickinson, ed.
by Mabel Loomis Todd, 1894.

And sigh for lack of heaven,—but not
The heaven the creeds bestow.

                              1891

[TITLE DIVINE IS MINE] *

    Title divine is mine—
    The Wife without
    The Sign.
    Acute degree
    Conferred on me—
    Empress of Calvary.
    Royal all but the
    Crown—
    Betrothed, without the swoon
    God gives us women   1
    When two hold
    Garnet to garnet,
    Gold to gold—
    Born—Bridalled—
    Shrouded—

    In a day
    Tri-Victory—
      "My Husband"
    Women say
    Stroking the melody,   2
    Is this the way?

                              1924

* From The Poems of Emily Dickinson
Centenary Edition, edited by Martha Dickin-
son Bianchi and Alfred Leete Hampson
Reprinted by permission of Little, Brown &
Company.

But miscroscopes are prudent
In an emergency! †

You spoke of the "East." I hav
thought about it this winter.

Don't you think you and I shoul
be shrewder to take the mountai
road?

That bareheaded life, under th
grass, worries one like a wasp.

The rose is for Mary.

                              EMILY

† Second Series, page 53.—[Editor's note.

The zeros taught us phosphorus—
We learned to like the fire
By playing glaciers when a boy,
And tinder guessed by power
Of opposite to balance odd,
If white, a red must be!*
Paralysis, our primer dumb
Unto vitality.

I couldn't let Austin's note go,
without a word.

EMILY

[AUGUST, 1862.]

DEAR MR. BOWLES.—Vinnie is trad-
ng with a tin peddler—buying water-
pots for me to sprinkle geraniums with
when you get home next winter, and
she has gone to the war.

Summer isn't so long as it was,
when we stood looking at it before
you went away; and when I finish
August, we'll hop the autumn very
soon, and then 't will be yourself.

I don't know how many will be
glad to see you,—because I never saw
your whole friends, but I have heard
that in large cities noted persons chose
you—though how glad those I know
will be, is easier told.

I tell you, Mr. Bowles, it is a
suffering to have a sea—no care how
blue—between your soul and you.

The hills you used to love when
you were in Northampton, miss their
old lover, could they speak; and the
puzzled look deepens in Carlo's forehead as the days go by and you never
come.

I've learned to read the steamer
place in newspapers now. It's 'most

* The poems enclosed in letters to friends
are often slightly different from her own
copies preserved in the manuscript volumes.
This line, for instance, in another place
reads "Eclipses suns imply."—[Editor's note.]

like shaking hands with you, or more
like your ringing at the door.

We reckon your coming by the
fruit. When the grape gets by, and
the pippin and the chestnut—when the
days are a little short by the clock,
and a little long by the want—when
the sky has new red gowns, and a
purple bonnet—then we say you will
come. I am glad that kind of time
goes by.

It is easier to look behind at a
pain, than to see it coming.

A soldier called, a morning ago, and
asked for a nosegay to take to battle.
I suppose he thought we kept an
aquarium.

How sweet it must be to one to
come home, whose home is in so
many houses, and every heart a 'best
room.' I mean you, Mr. Bowles. . . .
Have not the clovers names to the
bees?

EMILY

Before he comes
We weigh the time,
'T is heavy, and 't is light.
When he departs
An emptiness
Is the superior freight.

EMILY

While asters
On the hill
Their everlasting fashions set,
And covenant gentians frill!

EMILY

[LATE AUTUMN, 1862]

So glad we are, a stranger'd deem
'T was sorry that we were;
For where the holiday should be
There publishes a tear;
Nor how ourselves be justified,
Since grief and joy are done
So similar, an optizan
Could not decide between.

[EARLY WINTER, 1862]

DEAR FRIEND,—Had we the art like you, to endow so many, by just recovering our health, 't would give us tender pride, nor could we keep the news, but carry it to you, who seem to us to own it most.

So few that live have life, it seems of quick importance not one of those escape by death. And since you gave us fear, congratulate us for ourselves —you give us safer peace.

How extraordinary that life's large population contain so few of power to us—and those a vivid species who leave no mode, like Tyrian dye.

Remembering these minorities, permit our gratitude for you. We ask that you be cautious, for many sakes, excelling ours. To recapitulate the stars were useless as supreme. Yourself is yours, dear friend, but ceded, is it not, to here and there a minor life? Do not defraud these, for gold may be bought, and purple may be bought, but the sale of the spirit never did occur.

Do not yet work. No public so exorbitant of any as its friend, and we can wait your health. Besides, there is an idleness more tonic than toil.

The loss of sickness—was it loss?
Or that ethereal gain
You earned by measuring the grave,
Then measuring the sun.

Be sure, dear friend, for want you have estates of lives.

                              EMILY

[WITH FLOWERS]

If she had been the mistletoe,
And I had been the rose,
How gay upon your table
My velvet life to close!

Since I am of the Druid,
And she is of the dew,
I'll deck tradition's buttonhole,
And send the rose to you.
                              E.

DEAR MR. BOWLES,—I can't thank you any more. You are thoughtful so many times you grieve me always; *now* the old words are numb, and there are n't any new ones.

Brooks are useless in freshet time. When you come to Amherst—please God it were to-day—I will tell you about the picture—if I *can*, I will.

Speech is a prank of Parliament,
Tears a trick of the nerve,—
But the heart with the heaviest
    freight on
Does n't always serve.

                              EMILY

Perhaps you think me stooping!
I'm not ashamed of that!
Christ stooped until he touched the
    grave!
Do those at sacrament
Commemorate dishonor—
Or love, annealed of love,
Until it bend as low as death
Re-royalized above?

The juggler's hat her country is,
The mountain gorse the bee's.

I stole them from a bee,
Because—thee!
Sweet plea—
He pardoned me!

                              EMILY

[1863]

DEAR MRS. BOWLES,—Since I have no sweet flower to send you, I enclose my heart. A little one, sunburnt, half broken sometimes, yet close as the spaniel to its friends. Your flowers come from heaven, to

which, if I should ever go, I will pluck
you palms.

My words are far away when I
attempt to thank you, so take the
silver tear instead, from my full eye.

You have so often remembered me.

I have little dominion. Are there
not wiser than I, who, with curious
treasure, could requite your gift?

Angels fill the hand that loaded

EMILY'S

Nature and God, I neither knew,
Yet both, so well knew me
They startled, like executors
Of an identity.
Yet neither told, that I could learn;
My secret as secure
As Herschel's private interest,
Or Mercury's affair.

II

To T. W. HIGGINSON

[APRIL 16, 1862]

MR. HIGGINSON,—Are you too
deeply occupied to say if my verse
is alive?

The mind is so near itself it cannot
see distinctly, and I have none to ask.

Should you think it breathed, and
had you the leisure to tell me, I
should feel quick gratitude.

If I make the mistake, that you
dared to tell me would give me sin-
cerer honor toward you.

I enclose my name, asking you, if
you please, sir, to tell me what is
true?

That you will not betray me it is
needless to ask, since honor is its own
pawn.

[APRIL 26, 1862]

MR. HIGGINSON,—Your kindness
claimed earlier gratitude, but I was

ill, and write to-day from my pillow.

Thank you for the surgery; it was
not so painful as I supposed. I bring
you others, as you ask, though they
might not differ. While my thought
is undressed, I can make the distinction; but when I put them in the
gown, they look alike and numb.

You asked how old I was? I made
no verse, but one or two, until this
winter, sir.

I had a terror since September, I
could tell to none; and so I sing, as
the boy does of the burying ground,
because I am afraid.

You inquire my books. For poets,
I have Keats, and Mr. and Mrs.
Browning. For prose, Mr. Ruskin,
Sir Thomas Browne, and the *Revela-*
tions. I went to school, but in your
manner of the phrase, had no education. When a little girl, I had a
friend who taught me Immortality;
but venturing too near, himself, he
never returned. Soon after my tutor
died, and for several years my lexicon
was my only companion. Then I
found one more, but he was not contented I be his scholar, so he left the
land.

You ask of my companions. Hills,
sir, and the sundown, and a dog large
as myself, that my father bought me.
They are better than beings because
they know, but do not tell; and the
noise in the pool at noon excels my
piano.

I have a brother and sister; my
mother does not care for thought, and
father, too busy with his briefs to
notice what we do. He buys me
many books, but begs me not to read
them, because he fears they joggle
the mind. They are religious, except
me, and address an eclipse, every

morning, whom they call their "Father."

But I fear my story fatigues you. I would like to learn. Could you tell me how to grow, or is it unconveyed, like melody or witchcraft?

You speak of Mr. Whitman. I never read his book, but was told that it was disgraceful.

I read Miss Prescott's *Circumstance,* but it followed me in the dark, so I avoided her.

Two editors of journals came to my father's house this winter, and asked me for my mind, and when I asked them "why" they said I was penurious, and they would use it for the world.

I could not weigh myself, myself. My size felt small to me. I read your chapters in *The Atlantic,* and experienced honor for you. I was sure you would not reject a confiding question.

Is this, sir, what you asked me to tell you?

Your friend,
E. DICKINSON

[JULY, 1862]

Could you believe me without? I had no portrait, now, but am small like the wren; and my hair is bold, like the chestnut burr; and my eyes, like the sherry in the glass that the guest leaves. Would this do just as well?

It often alarms father. He says death might occur, and he has moulds of all the rest, but has no mould of me; but I noticed the quick wore off those things in a few days, and forestall the dishonor. You will think no caprice of me.

You said "dark." I know the but-

terfly, and the lizard, and the orchis. Are not those *your* countrymen?

I am happy to be your scholar, and will deserve the kindness I cannot repay.

If you truly consent, I recite now. Will you tell me my fault, frankly as to yourself, for I had rather wince than die. Men do not call the surgeon to commend the bone, but to set it, sir, and fracture within is more critical. And for this, preceptor, shall bring you obedience, the blossom from my garden, and every gratitude I know.

Perhaps you smile at me. I could not stop for that. My business is circumference. An ignorance, not of customs, but if caught with the dawn, or the sunset see me, myself the only kangaroo among the beauty, sir, if you please, it afflicts me, and I thought that instruction would take it away.

Because you have much business beside the growth of me, you will appoint, yourself, how often I shall come without your inconvenience.

And if at any time you regret you received me, or I prove a different fabric to that you supposed, you must banish me.

When I state myself, as the representative of the verse, it does not mean me, but a supposed person.

You are true about the "perfection." To-day makes yesterday mean.

You spoke of *Pippa Passes.* I never heard anybody speak of *Pippa Passes* before. You see my posture is benighted.

To thank you baffles me. Are you perfectly powerful? Had I a pleasure you had not, I could delight to bring it.

YOUR SCHOLAR

[ACKNOWLEDGING A PHOTOGRAPH,
1876]

DEAR FRIEND,—Except your coming
I know no gift so great, and in one
extent it exceeds that,—it is permanent.

Your face is more joyful when you
speak, and I miss an almost arrogant
look that at times haunts you, but
with that exception, it is so real I
could think it you.

Thank you with delight, and please
to thank your friend for the lovely
suggestion.

I hope she has no suffering now.

Was it Browning's flower that
"ailed till evening"? I shall think of
your "keeping house" at night when
I close the shutter—but to be Mrs.
Higginson's guest is the boon of birds.

Judge Lord was with us a few days
since, and told me that the joy we
most revere we profane in taking. I
wish that was wrong.

Mrs. Jackson has written. It was
not stories she asked of me. But may
I tell her just the same that you
don't prefer it? Thank you if I may,
for it almost seems sordid to refuse
from myself again.

My brother and sister speak of you,
and covet your remembrance, and perhaps you will not reject my own to
Mrs. Higginson?

Summer laid her supple glove
In its sylvan drawer—
Whereso'er, or was she
The demand of awe?

YOUR SCHOLAR

[1877]

Thank you, dear friend, for my
"New Year," but did you not confer

it? Had your scholar permission to
fashion yours, it were perhaps too
fair. I always ran home to awe when
a child, if anything befell me. He
was an awful mother, but I liked him
better than none.

There remained this shelter after
you left me the other day.

Of your flitting coming it is fair to
think, like the bee's coupé, vanishing
in music.

Would you with the bee return,
What a firm of noon!
Death obtains the rose,
But the news of dying goes
No further than the breeze.

The ear is the last face. We hear
after we see, which to tell you first
is still my destiny.

Meeting a bird this morning, I began to flee. He saw it and sung.

Presuming on that lone result,
His infinite disdain,
But vanquished him with my de-
feat—
'T was victory was slain.

I shall read the book.
Thank you for telling me.

[SUMMER, 1878]

DEAR FRIEND,—When you wrote
you would come in November, it
would please me it were November
then—but the time has moved. You
went with the coming of the birds
—they will go with your coming,
but to see you is so much sweeter
than birds, I could excuse the
spring.

With the bloom of the flower your
friend loved, I have wished for her,
but God cannot discontinue Himself.

Mr. Bowles was not willing to die.

When you have lost a friend, Master, you remember you could not begin again, because there was no world. I have thought of you often since the darkness, though we cannot assist another's night.

I have hoped you were saved.

That those have immortality with whom we talked about it, makes it no more mighty but perhaps more sudden. . . .

How brittle are the piers
On which our faith doth tread—
No bridge below doth totter so,
Yet none hath such a crowd.

It is as old as God—
Indeed, 't was built by Him—
He sent His son to test the plank,
And he pronounced it firm.

I hope you have been well. I hope your rambles have been sweet, and your reveries spacious.

To have seen Stratford on Avon, and the Dresden Madonna, must be almost peace.

And perhaps you have spoken with George Eliot. Will you "tell me about it"? Will you come in November, and will November come, or is this the hope that opens and shuts, like the eye of the wax doll?

YOUR SCHOLAR

[IN ACKNOWLEDGMENT OF HIS "SHORT STUDIES OF AMERICAN AUTHORS"]

[1879]

DEAR FRIEND,—Brabantio's gift was not more fair than yours, though I trust without his pathetic inscription, "Which but thou hast already, with all my heart I would keep from thee."

Of Poe, I know too little to think —Hawthorne appalls—entices.

Mrs. Jackson soars to your estimate lawfully as a bird, but of Howells and James, one hesitates. Your relentless music dooms as it redeems.

Remorse for the brevity of a book is a rare emotion, though fair as Lowell's "sweet despair" in the "slipper hymn."

One thing of it we borrow
And promise to return,
The booty and the sorrow
Its sweetness to have known.
One thing of it we covet—
The power to forget,
The anguish of the avarice
Defrays the dross of it.

Had I tried before reading your gift to thank you, it had perhaps been possible, but I waited, and now it disables my lips.

Magic, as it electrifies, also makes decripit. Thank you for thinking of me.

YOUR SCHOLAR
1894

NOTES

In these Notes a concise biographical sketch is provided, followed by a selected list of the author's publications, a selected bibliography, and details of publication (so far as they are known) for each selection. The more difficult passages and allusions are annotated.

Walt Whitman (1819–1892)

Walt Whitman was born May 31, 1819, near Huntington, Long Island. His father, of English stock long settled in Huntington township, was first a farmer and later a house-builder. The poet's mother, of mixed Dutch and Welsh extraction, as deficient as her husband in education, so impressed her son with her commonsense and her unfailing affection as ever to be regarded by him as the "perfect mother." In 1824 the family moved to Brooklyn. Until he was twelve Walt attended the public schools, but his scanty formal education was richly complemented by wide reading, some experience as a school-teacher on Long Island, much intimate contact with nature and the varied experiences of city life (particularly in New York City), and a long association with many newspapers and magazines in Brooklyn and New York City as typesetter, contributor, and editor. During the 1840's Whitman displayed interest in many social problems: he championed idealistic reforms, he espoused a patriotic nationalism, he opposed the extension of slavery, and he even wrote a temperance novel, entitled Franklin Evans; or, the Inebriate, 1842. His verse of this period, however, was conventional, with no suggestion of the freedom of thought or style of Leaves of Grass. His personal appearance, too, was distinctly that of the "dandy." In 1848 he spent a few months in the South, whither he had gone to accept a position on the New Orleans Crescent. The facts regarding this sojourn are not yet entirely clear, but the importance of this experience in the gestation of Leaves of Grass seems unquestionable. Between 1848 and 1855 the new ideas and the new form took shape and resulted in the first edition of Leaves of Grass. The book met a varied reception, but in spite of such occasional praise as that bestowed by Emerson, the opposition to both Whitman's ideas and form persisted with little abatement until the closing years of his life. Yet the poet, undeterred, kept adding to the original twelve poems, in edition after edition, until a volume of considerable bulk had been achieved. The advent of the Civil War transformed Whitman, largely through his long service as a nurse in the war hospitals of Washington, from the singer of the body to a chanter of the soul. In 1873 he was stricken with paralysis and forced to relinquish a government position in Washington in favor of an invalid's retreat in Camden, N. J. Here, in spite of some unhappy years, he began to enjoy the homage of disciples from many parts of the world. He died in Camden March 26, 1892, and was accorded a notable "pagan" funeral.

Leaves of Grass, 1855, 1856, 1860, 1867, 1871, 1876, 1881–82, 1882, 1884, 1889, 1891–92, 1897, 1900, 1908, 1914, 1917, 1919, 1924, 1926, 1932; Drum-Taps, 1865; Democratic Vistas, 1871; After All Not to Create Only, 1871; Passage to India, 1871; As a Strong Bird on Pinions Free and Other Poems, 1872; Memoranda During the War, 1875; Two Rivulets, 1876; Specimen Days and Collect, 1882–83; A Backward Glance O'er Travell'd Roads, 1885; November Boughs, 1888; Good-Bye, My Fancy, 1891; Complete Prose Works, 1892, 1898, 1908; Calamus, 1897; The Wound Dresser, 1898; Notes and Fragments, 1899; The Complete Writings of Walt Whitman (Camden ed., 10 vols.), 1902; An American Primer, 1904; The Gathering of the Forces, 2 vols., 1920; The Uncollected Poetry and Prose of Walt Whitman, 2 vols., 1921; Leaves of Grass (Inclusive ed.), 1926; Walt Whitman's Workshop: A Collection of Unpublished Manuscripts, 1928; I Sit and Look Out, 1932.

For life and criticism, see: John Bailey, Walt Whitman, 1926; Leon Bazalgette, Walt Whitman, L'Homme et Son Oeuvre, 1908 (trans. by Ellen Fitzgerald, 1920); Henry Bryan Binns, A Life of Walt Whitman, 1905; Van Wyck Brooks, America's Coming of Age, 1915; Richard M. Bucke, Walt Whitman, 1883; John Burroughs, *Whitman: a Study*, 1896; Henry S. Canby. *Classic Americans*, 1931; Edward Carpenter, *Days with Walt Whitman*, 1906; G. R. Carpenter, *Walt Whitman* (E. M. of L. series), 1909; Basil de Selincourt, *Walt Whitman: a Critical Study*, 1914; Thomas B. Harned (ed.), *The Letters of Anne Gilchrist and Walt Whitman*, 1918; Emory Holloway, *Whitman: an Interpretation in Narrative*, 1926; Elizabeth L. Keller, *Walt Whitman in Mickle Street*, 1921; Paul Elmer More, *Shelburne Essays*, IV, 1906; Harvey O'Higgins, "Alias Walt Whitman," *Harper's*, May, 1929; Bliss Perry, *Walt Whitman: His Life and Work*, 1906; George Santayana, *Interpretations of Poetry and Religion*, 1900; John A. Symonds, *Walt Whitman: a Study*, 1893; Horace Traubel, *With Walt Whitman in Camden*, 1906, 1908, 1914.

For bibliography, see: *CHAL*, II, 551–81; Frank Shay, *Bibliography of Walt Whitman*, 1920; Carolyn Wells and Alfred E. Goldsmith, *A Concise Bibliography of Walt Whitman*, 1922.

The text for all the selections from Whitman is that of the *Inclusive Edition*, ed. Emory Holloway, 1926, with the exception of that for *Democratic Vistas* where the text of the *Complete Prose Works*, 1897, is followed.

19. PREFACE TO "LEAVES OF GRASS." The original form, as here printed, was considerably altered in subsequent editions, with a consequent toning down of its original fervor and ruggedness.

35. SONG OF MYSELF. The introductory poem of the 1855 edition of *Leaves of Grass*, without title. Subsequent editions carried titles as follows: 1856, "A Poem of Walt Whitman, an American"; 1860 and 1867, "Walt Whitman"; 1881, "Song of Myself." The portrait of Whitman in workman's clothes appeared as the frontispiece of the 1855 edition, but from 1876 on this portrait faced this poem itself. See the *Inclusive Edition*, pp. 553 ff., for variorum readings supplied by O. L. Triggs.

76. THERE WAS A CHILD WENT FORTH. In 1855 edition without title, reprinted in 1860 as, "Poem of the Child That Went Forth, and Always Goes Forth, Forever and Forever," again in 1867. Given present title in 1871. How Whitman reduced the offensive material in his writings is illustrated by line 19 which first read "he that had propelled the fatherstuff at night, and fathered him." For other changes, see variorum readings.

77. CROSSING BROOKLYN FERRY. Compare a passage in Whitman's *Specimen Days* entitled "My Passion for Ferries," in which Whitman tells of his crossing from Brooklyn to New York almost daily from 1850 to 1860 and his

absorption in all he could see from the ferry boat. In *Leaves*, 1856.

81. OUT OF THE CRADLE ENDLESSLY ROCKING. The 1860 version was entitled "A Word Out of the Sea," and the sub-title "Reminiscence" appeared after the first stanza. ¶ 8 "Once Paumanok." Once Long Island, for which Whitman preferred the Indian name.

85. I HEAR AMERICA SINGING. In 1860 edition, "Chants Democratic" section, as "No 20"; present title, 1867.

86. ME IMPERTURBE. In 1860 edition, as "No. 18" of "Chants Democratic." The title illustrates Whitman's fondness for French phrases; the second phrase of the first line explains its meaning.

86. I SAW IN LOUISIANA A LIVE OAK GROWING. In "Calamus," 1860, as "No. 20"; present title, 1867.

87. RECORDERS AGES HENCE. In "Calamus," 1860, as "No. 11"; present title, 1867.

87. I HEAR IT WAS CHARGED AGAINST ME. In "Calamus," 1860, as "No. 24"; present title, 1867.

87. FACING WEST FROM CALIFORNIA'S SHORES. In 1860 edition, the "Enfans d' Adam" section. An imagined experience, as are many such situations in Whitman. The poet travelled as far west as Colorado in 1879 some years after this poem was written.

88. PIONEERS! O PIONEERS! In *Drum-Taps*, 1865. One of the least emended poems.

90. VIGIL STRANGE I KEPT. . . . In 1865 edition; probably composed in 1865.

91. COME UP FROM THE FIELDS FATHER. In 1867 edition.

92. GIVE ME THE SPLENDID SILENT SUN. In 1867 edition.

93. WHEN I HEARD THE LEARN'D ASTRONOMER. In *Drum-Taps*, 1865.

94. SHUT NOT YOUR DOORS. In *Drum-Taps*, 1865; greatly emended in 1867 text here given.

94. WHEN LILACS LAST IN THE DOORYARD BLOOMED. In *Sequel to Drum-Taps*, 1865–66. Sections 5–6 must be read in the light of the facts concerned with the burial of Lincoln. From the morning of his death (April 15) till April 21 the body remained in Washington and was accorded impressive honors in the great procession from the White House to the Capitol where it lay in state. On the 21st began the long procession through many of the main cities of the land, including Baltimore, Harrisburg, Philadelphia (where the body lay in state in Independence Hall), New York City, Albany, Buffalo, Cleveland, Columbus, Indianapolis and Chicago. The final obsequies took place

Springfield May 4, when the body was placed in a vault in Oak Ridge Cemetery along with the remains of Lincoln's son Willie, who had died in Feb., 1862.

100. O CAPTAIN! MY CAPTAIN! In 1867 edition; greatly emended in 1871.

100. BEAT! BEAT! DRUMS! In 1867 edition.

101. RECONCILIATION. In *Sequel to Drum-taps*, 1865–6.

101. ONE'S-SELF I SING. Heads the group of poems entitled "Inscriptions," which Whitman placed first in the later editions of *Leaves of Grass*, 1867, 1871, etc.

101. WHISPERS OF HEAVENLY DEATH. Used as a group title, 1871.

102. A NOISELESS PATIENT SPIDER. In 1871 edition.

102. DAREST THOU NOW O SOUL. In 1871 edition.

103. ETHIOPIA SALUTING THE COLORS. In 1871 edition, with subtitle, "A Reminiscence of 1864."

103. THE BASE OF ALL METAPHYSICS. In 1871 edition.

103. TO A LOCOMOTIVE IN WINTER. In 1876 edition. Compare: "Readers of poetry see the victory-village and the railway, and fancy that the poetry of the landscape is broken up by these,—for these works of art are not yet consecrated in their reading; but the poet sees them fall within the great Order not less than the bee-hive or the spider's geometrical web. . . ." (Emerson, "The Poet.")

104. SPIRIT THAT FORM'D THIS SCENE. In "From Noon to Starry Night" section, 1881 edition.

104. GOOD-BYE MY FANCY! Poem at the end of the section by the same title in 1891 edition. See briefer poem and note in *Inclusive Edition*, p. 444.

105. DEMOCRATIC VISTAS. Based on two essays which Whitman had sent to *The Galaxy*: "Democracy," pub. in Dec., 1867, and "Personalism," pub. in May, 1868. These were incorporated practically *in toto* in the pamphlet entitled *Democratic Vistas*, 1871. The two essays had been called forth by the publication of Thomas Carlyle's attack upon democracy in his article called "Shooting Niagara: And After?" in *Macmillan's Magazine* in the fall of 1867.

Abraham Lincoln (*1809–1865*)

Abraham Lincoln was born on a farm in Kentucky Feb. 12, 1809. His ancestry, both immediate and remote, has been the subject of much controversy. Certain it is that he was reared in the most humble circumstances. His father shifted from farm to farm in Kentucky and finally, in 1816, "took to the road," crossing with his family into southern Indiana, where the family lived till 1830. Extremely scanty schooling, hard work, a passion for reading, and two trips on a flat-boat to New Orleans suggest the character of this period of Lincoln's life. In 1830 the family migrated to Illinois, where Abraham, after an unsuccessful career as a clerk in a general store in New Salem (1831–37), turned to politics, representing New Salem in the Illinois Legislature 1834–37. In 1837 he entered into a law partnership with John T. Stuart in Springfield and married Mary Todd in 1842. Failing at election to Congress in 1843, he served a term in 1847–49. His law partnership with W. H. Herndon (1849–54) proved successful, and Lincoln became prosperous. His debate with Stephen A. Douglas in 1854 on the Kansas-Nebraska Act was the forerunner of the Lincoln-Douglas debates of 1858, which were instrumental in bringing him to the attention of the country at large and eventually in securing his nomination for the Presidency on the Republican ticket at Chicago in May, 1860. On his election, Lincoln bade farewell to Springfield and entered upon his four arduous years as Civil War president, made notable by his many important messages, addresses, and proclamations. He was reëlected in November, 1864, but shortly after entering upon his second term of office (March 4, 1865), he was shot by John Wilkes Booth during the performance of a play at Ford's Theatre, Washington. He died Apr. 15, and was buried in Springfield, Ill., on the 4th of May.

Complete Works of Abraham Lincoln (2 vols., ed. by Nicolay and Hay), Century Co., 1894; "Gettysburg Edition," 12 vols., 1905; *The Complete Works of Abraham Lincoln* (8 vols., ed. by G. H. Putnam and A. B. Lapsley—Constitutional ed.), G. P. Putnam's Sons, 1906; Gilbert A. Tracy (ed.), *Uncollected Letters of Abraham Lincoln*, 1917; *Lincoln Letters at Brown*, Brown Univ., 1927; *New Letters and Papers of Lincoln* (compiled by Paul M. Angle), 1930.

For life and criticism, see: William E. Barton, *The Life of Abraham Lincoln*, 1925; Albert J. Beveridge, *Abraham Lincoln*, 1928 (unfinished, but supersedes everything covering the period included); Lord Charnwood, *Abraham Lincoln*, 1917; W. H. Herndon and J. W. Weik, *The True Story of a Great Life*, 1890; Emanuel Hertz, *Abraham Lincoln: a New Portrait*, 1931; W. H. Lamon, *The Life of Abraham Lincoln*, 1872; Lloyd Lewis, *Myths after Lincoln*, 1929;

Emil Ludwig, *Lincoln*, 1930; J. G. Nicolay and John Hay, *Life of Abraham Lincoln*, 10 vols. 1890 (also an abridgment in one volume by J. G. Nicolay, *Short Life of Lincoln*, 1904); Carl Sandburg, *Abraham Lincoln: the Prairie Years*, 1926; Nathaniel W. Stephenson, *Lincoln*, 1922; Ida M. Tarbell, *Life of Abraham Lincoln*, 1917; J. W. Weik, *The Real Lincoln*, 1922; Brand Whitlock, *Abraham Lincoln*, 1916.

113. FAREWELL REMARKS AT SPRINGFIELD. Made on leaving for Washington, Feb. 11, 1861.

113. REPLY TO GREELEY. Horace Greeley, owner and editor of the New York *Tribune*, had supported Lincoln up to the summer of 1862, when he voiced the objection of many to what they considered Lincoln's temporizing policy in regard to slavery by publishing his "Open Letter" entitled "A Prayer of Twenty Millions."

114. MEDITATION ON THE DIVINE WILL. Compare letter of W. H. Herndon to Edward McPherson, on Feb. 11, 1866 (in N. Y. *Herald Trib. Mag.*, Feb. 10, 1929).

114. ADDRESS AT GETTYSBURG. The orator of the day for the dedication of the Battlefield of Gettysburg was Edward Everett, who delivered a brilliant oration in the accepted manner. Lincoln followed with the few lines that he had scratched on the back of an envelope and when he had finished was convinced that he had been a miserable failure. ¶114. "*Of the people . . .*": Theodore Parker, in an anti-slavery address in 1850, had described democracy as "a government of all the people, by all the people, for all the people."

115. SECOND INAUGURAL. Delivered Mar. 4, 1865.

116. LETTERS. John D. Johnston (Lincoln's step-brother) was the son of Sarah Bush Johnston, the widow whom Tom Lincoln married after the death of his first wife, Nancy Hanks. (117.) Joseph Hooker, who commanded the center in General Burnside's advance on Fredericksburg, was placed in command of the Army of the Potomac when the latter requested to be relieved. (117.) The letter to Grant is addressed after the surrender of Vicksburg on July 4, 1863. (118.) The authenticity of the letter to Mrs. Bixby has been questioned, since the document is not now known to exist. See articles concerning this letter in the N. Y. *Times*, Aug. 6–7, 1925.

Edward Everett Hale (1822–1909)

Edward Everett Hale was born in Boston Apr. 3, 1822, and died there June 10, 1909, after a life of service in the cause of the "New

Civilization"—the improvement of all types of human relationships. Graduating at Harvard College in 1839, he began his long career as a Unitarian minister in 1842, and, reared as he had been in the shadow of his father's newspaper, he devoted himself to journalism of humanitarian character. In addition to forty-three years of service as minister of the South Congregational Church of Boston (from 1856 he identified himself with many social movements, such as the Emigrant Aid Movement and the cause of international peace. His literary product was extensive. Publishing his first volume of fiction in 1868, he became identified with the type of story whose large meaning, if clear and persuasive, was of more importance than its accord with fact or plausibility.

"My Double; and How He Undid Me, 1859; "The Man without a Country," 1863; *If, Yes, and Perhaps*, 1868; *Ten Times One Is Ten*, 1871; *In His Name*, 1873; *A New England Boyhood*, 1893; *James Russell Lowell and His Friends*, 1899; *Memories of a Hundred Years*, 1902.

For life, see: Edward Everett Hale, Jr., *Life and Letters of Edward Everett Hale*, 1917.

118. THE MAN WITHOUT A COUNTRY. *Atlantic*, Dec., 1863. For the explanation of the difference between the true and the fictious Nolan, see: *Miss. Hist. Soc. Pub.*, I (1901), 281–329. ¶119. "*Non mi ricordo*" I do not remember. ¶119. "*Ross burned*" The British General, Robert Ross, captured Washington and burned the public buildings Aug. 24, 1814. ¶119. "*Aaron Burr*": In 1806 Burr was busy in the Southwest with those plots which later caused his arrest for treason. ¶120. "*Clarences of . . . York.*" See Shakespeare's *Richard III*. ¶120. "*Colonel Morgan.*" Not Daniel Morgan, who died in 1802, but fictitious character. ¶121. "*The first Crowning shield.*" Fictitious character. ¶123. "*Innocent as Hesiod.*" Greek didactic poet (*fl.* 750). ¶123. "*Canning*": George Canning, British statesman (1770–1827). ¶124. "*Fléchier.*" Celebrated French bishop and poet, Esprit Fléchier (1632–1710). ¶125. "*Mrs. Graff.*" Fictitious character. ¶125. "*Lady Hamilton.*" Wife of the British diplomat, Sir William, mistress of Lord Nelson. ¶126. "*Contretemps*" mishap. ¶125. "*Iron Mask*": Celebrated unknown prisoner, who, having worn a mask for thirty years, died in the Bastile, 1703. ¶126. "*Junius.*" Reference to an unknown pamphleteer who wrote under the name of the celebrated anonymous author of the British *Letters Junius*. ¶127. "*Essex Porter.*" David Porter

nerican naval officer (1780–1843), as com-
ander of the U. S. *Essex* defeated the *Alert*
1812, but later in the neutral harbor of
lparaiso while commanding the *Essex* and
sex Jr. was defeated by the British frigates,
œbe and *Cherub*, 1814. Porter took posses-
n of the Marquesas Islands in 1813. ¶128.
innæus": Carl von Linné (1707–78), Swed-
botanist. ¶128. *"John Foy."* See Words-
rth's "The Idiot Boy." ¶128. *"Slave-Trade
aty."* Treaty of Ghent (1814) abolished
ve traffic. ¶128. *"Middle Passage."* The
lantic route between Africa and the West
lies. ¶129. *"Parisian of Beledeljereed."*
ench was the commercial language of Beled
Jerid, "the country of dates" in northern
rica. ¶129. *"Deus ex machina"*: The god
m the machine. ¶130. *"Mountains of the
on."* In Central Africa. ¶130. *"Great
hite Desert"*: The Sahara. ¶131. *"Ben
vato"*: well-invented. ¶132. *"Vallandig-
ms and Tatnalls."* Clement Vallandigham
22–71), "Copperhead" candidate for gov-
nor of Ohio, 1863; and Josiah Tattnall who
igned from the U. S. Navy to serve the
te of Georgia; commanded the *Merrimac*.
32. *"Southard."* Fictitious character. ¶134.
hesapeak . . . Barron." In 1807 the Brit-
frigate *Leopard* seized four American sea-
n from Capt. Barron's *Chesapeak* as de-
ters from the British navy. ¶135. *"General
njamin Lincoln."* Revolutionary soldier
733–1810). ¶135. *"The Exploring Expedi-
n."* Under John C. Frémont, 1843–45.
35. *"Order of Cincinnati."* An association
Revolutionary officers.

ongs and Ballads of the Civil War

For texts, see especially: C. G. Eggleston,
nerican War Ballads and Lyrics, 1889; Esther
Ellinger, *Southern Poetry of the Civil War*,
18; Frank Moore, *Songs for the Soldiers*, 1864;
ne, *Lyrics of Loyalty*, 1864; same, *Personal
d Political Ballads*, 1864; same, *Songs and
llads of the Southern People*, 1866; Richard
ant White, *The Poetry of the Civil War*,
56; Jean Broadhurst and Clara Lawton
odes, *Verse for Patriots*, 1919.

For criticism, see (in addition to critical
terial in the above): W. D. Howe, "Poets
the Civil War: The North," *CHAL*, II,
5 ff.; Edwin Mims, "Poets of the Civil War:
e South," *CHAL*, II, 288 ff.

For bibliography, see: *CHAL*, II, 582–588;
ther P. Ellinger, *Southern Poetry of the Civil
ar*, 1918; and T. H. Dickinson, *The Making
American Literature*, 1932, p. 592.

In addition to the Civil War poems given in

this section, see also the war poems in this
volume by Stedman (pp. 215 ff.), Hayne (pp.
150 ff.), Timrod (pp. 144 ff.), and Ryan (pp.
154 ff.), and in *The Romantic Triumph* the following: Whittier's *"Laus Deo"* (p. 500), Lowell's
"Commemoration Ode" (p. 596), and Boker's
"Dirge for a Soldier" (p. 636).

136. JOHN BROWN'S BODY. The origin of
the famous "John Brown" song is unknown,
though it has been suggested that it was first
sung by a quartette. It soon gained popularity
in the army, and many versions resulted, of
which only one is here reproduced, that known
to have been written by Charles Sprague Hall.

136. MARYLAND! MY MARYLAND! In New
Orleans *Delta*, 1861. James R. Randall, the
author of this stirring Southern song, was a
native of Baltimore who was in Louisiana
(professor of English Literature in Poydras
College) when news came of the passage of the
Massachusetts troops through Baltimore.
Among the names referred to (beginning with
line 21) are Charles Carroll, one of the signers
of the Declaration of Independence, John Eager
Howard, a soldier of the War of the Revolution,
and Samuel Ringgold, William Henry Watson,
Enoch Lewis Lowe, and Charles A. May, well-
known soldiers of the Mexican War.

137. DIXIE. This is the best of many versions of this song whose original form is as-
cribed to Daniel Decatur Emmett, one of the
troupe of the "Virginia Minstrels" of 1859.
See J. F. Steele, "How Emmett Wrote 'Dixie,' "
N. Y. *Tribune*, Jan. 28, 1926. Gen. Albert Pike
(1809–91), who revised it, served the South in
the battles of Elkhorn and Pea Ridge.

138. THE PICKET-GUARD. Since this poem
was published in *Harper's Weekly*, Nov. 30,
1861, over the signature "E. L. B." it has been
attributed to the New Englander, Miss Ethel
Lynn Beers (1827–79) who published a volume,
All Quiet Along the Potomac and Other Poems,
1879. But Thaddeus Oliver (1826–64) of
Georgia has recently been credited with its
authorship. See *Sou. Hist. Soc. Papers*, VIII,
255–260.

139. BATTLE-HYMN OF THE REPUBLIC.
Written by Mrs. Julia Ward Howe (1819–
1910) as an improvement on the John Brown
song. Published in *Atlantic*, Feb., 1862.

139. THREE HUNDRED THOUSAND MORE.
In N. Y. *Eve. Post*, July 2, 1862. First attributed to W. C. Bryant, editor of the paper, who
assigned the authorship to James Sloan Gib-
bons, a Quaker editor and abolitionist.

140. STONEWALL JACKSON'S WAY. P. H.
Boynton conjectures that this was written and
published in 1863.

140. TENTING ON THE OLD CAMP GROUND. Date of first publication unknown. Walter Kittredge, New Hampshire ballad singer, composed the song before enlisting, 1861.

141. LITTLE GIFFEN. In *The Land We Love*, 1867. Francis Orrey Ticknor (1822–74) was a poet-physician who based this poem on an actual experience of his with a young Confederate soldier.

141. MARCHING THROUGH GEORGIA. Date of first publication unknown. Sherman's march began Nov. 16, 1864. Henry Clay Work (1832–84), was a Connecticut composer, who frequently used negro melodies.

142. SHERIDAN'S RIDE. Thomas Buchanan Read (1822–72) was the author of several collections of verse, but today only this ballad is remembered. Sheridan's presence did save the day at the battle of Winchester, Sept. 19–20, 1864.

143. THE BLUE AND THE GRAY. When this poem first appeared in the *Atlantic* (Sept., 1867), the following note was prefixed to the poem: "The women of Columbus, Mississippi, animated by nobler sentiments than are many of their sisters, have shown themselves impartial in their offerings in memory of the dead. They strewed flowers alike on the graves of the Confederate and of the National soldiers. —New York *Tribune*."

Henry Timrod (1829–1867)

Born in Charleston, S. C., Dec. 8, 1829, Henry Timrod, after some study at the University of Georgia, first tried tutoring and then, at the outbreak of the Civil War, became war correspondent for the Charleston *Mercury*. In 1864 he was made asst. editor of the *South Carolinian* at Columbia, but the destruction of Columbia ruined his occupation, and the few years left to him were years of frustration. He was associated before the War with the brilliant coterie of Southern literary men, including Paul Hamilton Hayne and W. G. Simms, known as the "Charleston school." Timrod died Oct. 6, 1867, at Columbia, S. C.

Collected Verse (with biog. sketch by P. H. Hayne), 1873; "Memorial" edition of *Poems*, 1901.

For life and criticism, see: Paul Hamilton Hayne's biographical sketch in 1873 edition; H. T. Thompson, *Henry Timrod, Laureate of the Confederacy*, 1929 (a tribute, not a serious study); G. A. Wauchope, *Henry Timrod: Man and Poet. A Critical Study*, 1915.

144. SONNET[s]: I SCARCELY GRIEVE and I KNOW NOT WHY. The text follows that of the *Collected Verse*. The dates for first publication for much of Timrod's poetry are unknown. Prof. G. A. Wauchope, in response to a query, makes the following valuable suggestion: "*Russell's Magazine* (Apr. 1857–Mar. 1860) probably contains some of Timrod's sonnets as he was closely associated with Simms, the editor. The Charleston *Evening News* printed many of Timrod's love poems during his college days. . . . The *Southern Literary Messenger* should also be searched." Professor Charles Anderson advises that "I Scarcely Grieve" was collected in *Poems*, 1860, and "I Know Not Why" in *Poems of Henry Timrod* (ed. P. H. Hayne), 1873.

145. ETHNOGENESIS. "Pub. in the Charleston *Daily Courier*, Jan. 31, 1862; collected in *Poems of Henry Timrod*, 1873" (Anderson). Subtitle furnishes only evidence as regards date of composition.

146. CHARLESTON. H. T. Wynne (*Southern Literature*, 1932) conjectures this was written during the winter of 1861–62, when the Confederates held Forts Sumter and Moultrie. ¶147. "*Calpe*": Greek name for Gibraltar.

147. THE COTTON BOLL. First date of publication unknown; "collected in *Poems of Henry Timrod*, 1873" (Anderson). ¶149. "*Poet the 'Woodlands'*": William Gilmore Simms (1806–70) who lived on his father-in-law's estate, "The Woodlands."

150. ODE. G. P. Voight has recently shown (*Am. Lit.*, Jan., 1933) that this Ode was given in Magnolia Cemetery, June 16, 1866, and first printed in the Charleston *Daily Courier*, June 18, 1866.

Paul Hamilton Hayne (1830–1886)

Paul Hamilton Hayne was born in Charleston, S. C., Jan. 1, 1830. After graduating Charleston College, he turned to the law and soon after to literature as a profession, alternating during the '50's between journalism and poetry. In 1857 he joined W. B. Carlisle in editing the newly launched *Russell's Magazine*, which came to an end with the opening of the Civil War. Having served on Governor Pickens' staff during the War, he attempted a fresh start on the cessation of hostilities, moving his wife and son to Groveton, near Augusta, Ga. Here he lived out his remaining years in practical poverty, though encouraged by many literary friends and maintaining his own courage unfalteringly. At his death in 1886 he left a considerable quantity of verse, notable for its delicacy and sectional fervor.

Poems, 1855; *Sonnets and Other Poems*, 18

volio, a Legend of the Island of Cos, 1860;
egends and Lyrics, 1872; *The Mountain of the
vers*, 1875; *Lives of Robert Young Hayne and
ugh Swinton Legaré*, 1878; *Complete Poems*,
82 (best ed.); *The Broken Battalions*, 1885.

For life and criticism: No adequate life yet
blished, but see: J. T. Brown, Jr., "Paul
amilton Hayne," *Sewanee Rev.*, April, 1906;
. H. Hayne, "Paul H. Hayne's Methods of
omposition," *Lippincott's Mag.*, December,
92; C. W. Hubner, *Representative Southern
ets*, 1906; Sidney Lanier, "Paul H. Hayne's
etry"; S. A. Link, *Pioneers of Southern
terature*, 1903; Margaret J. Preston, biog.
etch in 1882 ed. of *Poems;* Maurice Thomp-
n, "The Last Literary Cavalier," *Critic*, Apr.,
01; W. P. Trent, *Wm. Gilmore Simms*, 1892.

150. VICKSBURG—A BALLAD. In the Charles-
n *Daily Courier*, Jan. 1, 1864; collected in
gends and Lyrics, 1872. Professor Charles
derson, of Duke University, has kindly sup-
ed the editor with dates here given for
ayne's poems. ¶150. *"Sixty days"*: May 18
July 4, 1863.

151. UNDER THE PINE. In *Legends and
rics*, 1872.

152. ASPECTS OF THE PINES. In *So. Lit.
essenger*, Mar., 1858; reprinted in *Atlantic,
pt.*, 1872; collected in *The Mountain of the
vers*, 1875.

153. A LITTLE WHILE I FAIN WOULD
NGER YET. In *Complete Poems*, 1882. Writ-
n shortly before the poet's death, as was the
lowing poem.

153. IN HARBOR. In *Complete Poems*, 1882.

Abram Joseph Ryan (1839–1886)

Abram Joseph Ryan ("Father" Ryan) was
rn in Norfolk, Va., Aug. 15, 1839. Shortly
er his ordination to the Roman Catholic
esthood he became a chaplain in the Con-
derate army, serving till the close of the War.
e then added to his parish duties those of a
rnalist, moving from New Orleans, where
edited the *Star*, to Knoxville, Tenn., thence
Augusta, Ga., where he founded *The Banner
the South*, and then to a parish in Mobile,
. In 1880 he went North, where he was
gaged in lecturing and in publishing his
ems. Returning later to the South, he died
Louisville, Ky., Apr. 22, 1886.

Father Ryan's Poems, 1879; *Poems: Patriotic,
igious, Miscellaneous*, 1880; *Poems: Patri-
, Religious, Miscellaneous . . . Containing
s Posthumous Poems*, 1896.

For life, see: John Moran, "Memoir" in
6 ed. of *Poems*.

154. THE CONQUERED BANNER. In Father
Ryan's paper, *The Banner of the South*, in 1868
(Pattee). Text is from 1879 edition.

155. THE SWORD OF ROBERT LEE. First
place of publication supposed by Boynton to
be *"Richmond Enquirer*, 1865."

Albion Winegar Tourgée (1838–1905)

Born at Williamsfield, Ohio, May 2, 1838,
Albion W. Tourgée graduated at the University
of Rochester, N. Y., and at the outbreak of the
Civil War enlisted as a private in the 27th N. Y.
Volunteers. Wounded at the first battle of
Bull Run, he was discharged and returned to
Ohio to practice law at Painsville. After another period of enlistment he resigned. In 1865
he began professional practice at Greensboro,
N. C. He was a delegate to the Southern
Loyalist Convention at Philadelphia in 1867
and in the same year a delegate to the Constitutional Convention of North Carolina, where
he contributed the article on the judiciary.
During his term as judge of the superior court
of North Carolina (1868–1874) he rendered
efficient aid in breaking up the Ku Klux Klan.
The knowledge thus gained of the activities
of the Ku Klux Klan he later utilized in a
number of works of fiction dealing with Reconstruction problems, of which *A Fool's Errand*
(1879) was the most successful. From 1897
till his death he was in the U. S. Consular
service, dying at Bordeaux on May 21, 1905.

A Fool's Errand, 1879; *Bricks without Straw*,
1880; *John Eax*, 1882; *An Appeal to Caesar*,
1884; *Button's Inn*, 1887; *With Gauge and
Swallow*, 1889; *Murvale Eastman*, 1890; *Out of
the Sunset Sea*, 1892; *The Mortgage on the Hip-
roof House*, 1896.

For life and criticism, see: R. F. Dibble,
Albion W. Tourgée, 1921. See also various reviews of Tourgée's works, especially: *Dial*, I,
110 (excellent review of *Bricks without Straw*
by Joseph Kirkland); *Critic*, I, 51; *Arena*, 28,
333; *Nation*, XXIX, 278; *Critic*, XXIX, 230;
Independent, 50, 693.

155. A NEW INSTITUTION. From *A Fool's
Errand*, 1879, "by One of the Fools," pub. with
no other ascription.

Henry Woodfin Grady (1850–1889)

Henry W. Grady was born May 24, 1850, at
Athens, Ga. After graduating in 1868 at the
University of Georgia, he took a law course at
the University of Virginia and soon after entered the field of journalism. Having edited
the *Courier* of Rome, Ga., and having seen two
of his newspapers fail, he finally bought an

interest in the Atlanta *Constitution* in 1879 and proceeded to make himself a power in the South in the rehabilitation of the agriculture and industries of that section and in dispelling the post-war despair. In 1886 he delivered his most famous and effective oration, that on "The New South," before the New England Club of New York. This was followed by several other orations on the problems of the South. His untimely death in 1889 was mourned throughout the nation as the loss of an accepted leader of unquestioned power and sincerity who was contributing much toward the healing of the nation's wounds.

The Complete Orations and Speeches of Henry W. Grady, 1910.

For life and criticism, see: Anon., *Life and Labors of Henry W. Grady*, 1890; Atlanta *Constitution*, Dec. 23, 24, 1889, and Oct. 21, 22, 1891; Joel Chandler Harris, *Life of Henry W. Grady . . . A Memorial Volume*, 1890; Dudley Miles, *CHAL*, Book III, Chap. IV; W. J. Northen, *Men of Mark in Georgia* (III), 1911; F. H. Richardson, *A Fruitful Life*, 1890; R. F. Terrell, *Study of the Early Journalistic Writings of Henry W. Grady*, 1927; Edna H. L. Turpin, "Henry W. Grady," in *Henry W. Grady's The New South and Other Addresses*, 1904.

162. THE NEW SOUTH. Delivered in New York, Dec. 22, 1886, before the New England Club.

Sidney Lanier (1842–1881)

Sidney Lanier was born Feb. 3, 1842, at Macon, Ga. Of Huguenot descent on his father's side and Scottish-American on his mother's, Lanier early displayed the passion for music that had characterized the Laniers of the seventeenth century. But this passion for music, as well as his rival passion for poetry, was not encouraged by his father, who preferred for his son his own profession of the law. After graduating at Oglethorpe College in 1856, Lanier held a tutorship there for a time. When the Civil War broke out, he enlisted as a private and served throughout the War, returning to his home in broken health. After the publication of his war novel, *Tiger Lilies* (1867), he began to study and practice law with his father. But his ill health forced him to seek a better climate. He went to Texas for this purpose in 1872 but was forced to return. In Dec., 1873, his cherished ambition seemed realized when he secured an engagement as first flute in the Peabody Symphony Orchestra in Baltimore. By doing hackwork he supplemented his slender income somewhat, and his appointment as lecturer on

English literature at Johns Hopkins Universi[ty] was an additional encouragement, both fina[ncially] cially and morally. But his struggle wi[th] poverty and ill health continued a serious o[ne] till his death. His first volume of poems a[p]peared in 1877, from which date his reputatic[on] increased perceptibly. The only importa[nt] fruit of his lectureship at Johns Hopkins appear before his death was *The Science English Verse* (1880). Increasing feeblene[ss] forced him to abandon his work and make [a] last attempt to find a suitable climate. [He] was thus taken to Lynn, N. C. in 1881 to t[ry] camp life, but he died there Sept. 7, 1881, aft[er] having waged a valiant but losing fight.

Tiger Lilies: A Novel, 1867; *Florida: [Its] Scenery, Climate, and History*, 1875; *Poem[s]* 1877; *St. Augustine in April*, 1878; *The Boy['s] Library of Legend and Chivalry (The Boy['s] Froissart; The Boy's King Arthur; Knigh[t] Legends of Wales, or The Boy's Mabinogio[n]; The Boy's Percy)*, 1879–82; *The Science of En[g]lish Verse*, 1880; *The English Novel*, 188[3]; *Poems* (enlarged and final edition, edited [by] Mary Day Lanier), 1884; *Music and Poetr[y]* 1898; *Letters (1866–1881)*, 1899; *Retrospects a[nd] Prospects*, 1899; *Shakespeare and His Forerun[n]ers*, 1902; *Poem Outlines*, 1908.

For life and criticism, see: W. M. Baskerv[ill] *Southern Writers*, 1898; Gamaliel Bradfor[d] *American Portraits 1875–1900*, 1922; F. [L.] Cady, *Sidney Lanier*, 1914; C. C. Carroll, *T[he] Synthesis and Analysis of the Poetry of Sidn[ey] Lanier*, 1910; D. C. Gilman, *A Memorial Sidney Lanier*, 1888; C. W. Kent, "A Study [of] Lanier's Poems," *PMLA*, VII, 2, pp. 33–6[3]; *Letters of Sidney Lanier*, 1899; John Mac[y] *The Spirit of American Literature*, 1913; Dudl[ey] Miles, *CHAL*, II, 331 ff.; Edwin Mims, *Sidn[ey] Lanier*, 1905; M. J. Moses, *The Literature [of] the South*, 1910; V. L. Parrington, *Main Cu[r]rents in American Thought*, III, 334; H. [N.] Snyder, *Modern Poets and Christian Teachi[ng]* 1906; A. H. Strong, *American Poets and The[ir] Theology*, 1916; W. H. Ward, "Memorial" pr[e]fixed to *Poems*, 1884; John W. Wayland, *Sidn[ey] Lanier at Rockingham Springs*, 1912; C. [N.] West, *A Brief Sketch of the Life and Writin[gs] of Sidney Lanier*, 1888; George S. Wills, "Sidn[ey] Lanier—His Life and Writings," *Pub. So[.] Hist. Assn.*, III, 190–211 (July, 1899). A li[fe] of Lanier by Aubrey Harrison Starke was a[n]nounced for publication in Nov., 1932.

For bibliography, see: *CHAL*, II, 600–6[0]0 Morgan Callaway (ed.), *Select Poems* (189[6]) pp. 87–97.

169. NIGHT AND DAY. In *The Independe[nt]* July 3, 1884.

169. Song for "The Jacquerie." Dated
at Macon, Ga., 1868, pub. in the "Unrevised
Early Poems" section of the 1884 edition.
Although 'The Jacquerie' remained a fragment for thirteen years, Mr. Lanier's interest
in the subject never abated. Far on in this
interval he is found planning for leisure to
work out in romance the story of that savage
insurrection of the French peasantry [1358],
which the Chronicles of Froissart had impressed
upon his boyish imagination" (Mrs. Lanier).

169. Corn. In Lippincott's Mag., Feb.,
875. Poem had been previously rejected by
Howells for the Atlantic (See A. H. Starke,
"William Dean Howells and Sidney Lanier,"
Am. Lit., Mar., 1931.) ¶172. "Jason." Leader
of the Argonauts, sent to seek a golden fleece
by his uncle, the temporary regent. ¶172.
"Dives." Parable of the rich man (dives, Lat.
"rich") and Lazarus (Luke xvi, 19–31).

173. The Power of Prayer. "Mr. Clifford
A. Lanier was a younger brother of Sidney,
and though not a writer by profession he was
the author of a number of prose sketches and
poems. The present poem was suggested to
him by a brief newspaper notice. He wrote
the poem and sent it to his brother Sidney,
who revised it and published it under their
joint authorship. A sketch by Mark Twain
called Uncle Daniel's Apparition and Prayer,
which appeared a year or two before The Power
of Prayer, has a very similar plot. The Laniers
did not know of the existence of this sketch,
however, until Doctor Holland, then editor of
Scribner's Monthly [June, 1875], in which the
poem appeared, called Clifford Lanier's attention to the fact." (Henry W. Lanier.)

174. The Symphony. In Lippincott's Mag.,
June, 1875.

180. The Centennial Meditation of Columbia. Bayard Taylor, who was instrumental
in securing the appointment of Lanier as the
writer of the ode for the opening of the Philadelphia Exposition in 1876, wrote as follows
in the New York Daily Tribune, Apr. 12, 1876:

The announcement of the Centennial Commission that the hymn for the opening ceremonies of the Exhibition on May 10, has been
furnished by John G. Whittier, and the text of
Mr. Dudley Buck's cantata by Sidney Lanier
of Georgia, has been received by the press and
people of the United States with entire satisfaction. No voice more earnest than that of
the Psalmist of Amesbury could be found to
breathe the solemn invocation; and Mr. Lanier,
also, if less widely known as a poet, possesses
the qualities which fit him for the more difficult
task. He is a native of Georgia, who, after
fighting in the Southern ranks as a youth,

studied law at Macon, but has at last found his
true field of activity, and devotes himself wholly
to music and literature. His two remarkable
poems entitled Corn and The Symphony, published in Lippincott's Magazine, brought him
suddenly into prominence. They are characterized by a freshness and affluence of thought,
a tropical luxuriance of fancy, and a singular
grace and variety of rhythmical effect, which
justify the anticipations of his friends in regard
to future achievement. Moreover, he has the
additional advantage, exceptionally rare among
poets, of pronounced musical talent. For three
Winters past, he has been a performer in the
Peabody Orchestra, at Baltimore, under Mr.
Asgar Hamerik.

The Cantata is a form of musical composition which was primarily applied to subjects of
a meditative, didactic or devotional character.
It has thus come to be one of the accepted forms
of musical expression for anniversaries, historical commemorations, and other occasions
of a large and stately character. The text
bears the same relation to the music as that
of an oratorio, and must be written with direct
reference to the changes, contrasts, and com-
binations of voices and instruments. It presents a most ungrateful task to the poet who
is not able to call up an attendant musical
inspiration, and persuade his conceptions to
acknowledge the double sway. Mr. Lanier's
verses, therefore, must be read with constant
reference to the inevitable restrictions of his
task. Limited to sixty lines, in which not only
the solos and choruses, but also the violins and
bassoons must have their share; compelled to
tell his story, not in poetic recital, but through
the medium of reflection and contrasted emotions; governed, finally, in the very sounds of
his words by that of the notes to which they
are set, his work is amenable to a separate
law, and may fairly assert its right to a separate judgment.

The verses represent, as largely as the space
allows, the past and present of the Country,
the powers which opposed themselves to settlement, growth, and independence, and the
blended elements which gave success, closing
with rejoicing, an angelic voice of promise, and
a welcome to the world. It is both simple
and original in character. Contrasted with the
Cantata written by Tennyson for the opening
of the International Exhibition in London, its
greater freedom and freshness are very evident,
while in earnestness and absence of self-gratu-
lation it will doubtless harmonize with the
spirit of Whittier's hymn. Mr. Dudley Buck's
music has already been noticed in The Tribune,
and there seems to be no impropriety in also
giving the complete text of Mr. Lanier's share
in the work, especially as the printed copies
are now in the hands of 800 singers.

181. The Revenge of Hamish. In Appleton's Mag., Oct., 1878.

184. The Marshes of Glynn. In The

Masque of Poets, 1879. ¶184. "*Glynn*." A county in southeastern Georgia.

186. SUNRISE. In *The Independent*, Dec., 1882.

191. THE WAR-FLOWER. From *Tiger Lilies: A Novel* (1867), Book II, Ch. I and part of Ch. II. Professor Pattee has called this novel "the transition novel of the decade," in that the first part is "romantic" and the second part "realistic."

193. LETTERS. The text is that of *Letters (1866–1881)*, 1899. ¶194. "*Giuseppe Caponsachi, etc.*" The characters named in order are the lover, the wife (heroine), and the husband (villain) of *The Ring and the Book*. ¶194. "*me judice*": I judge. ¶196. "*Niels Gade.*" Danish composer (1817–1890). ¶197. "*Deucalion.*" A dramatic poem by Bayard Taylor. ¶197. "*Sir Henry Wotton.*" Twenty years a diplomat (1568–1639), wrote essays on diplomacy and "the state of Christendom."

George William Curtis (1824–1892)

George William Curtis was born at Providence, R. I., Feb. 24, 1824. When he was 15 the family moved to New York City, where the young Curtis held a clerkship. Shortly thereafter he spent two years at Brook Farm, where his idealistic strain was deepened; he was later to become "the outstanding example of the man of letters who sets aside the possibility of literary fame because of the inner urge toward what he considers to be the highest duties of citizenship" (George S. Hellman). In 1846 he embarked upon a four years' trip to Europe, which resulted in two travel books. After producing two books of satire on New York society, he became, in 1856, associate editor of *Putnam's Monthly*, which went bankrupt and left Curtis with the strain of a self-assumed financial responsibility. Then followed a notable career as orator, distinguished by such orations as "The Duty of the American Scholar to Politics and the Times" (1856). In 1863, as editor of *Harper's Weekly*, he began a career of great journalistic usefulness on behalf of better understanding between capital and labor, woman suffrage, civil service reform, etc. Later, as editor of the "Easy Chair" department of *Harper's Magazine* he contributed important literary and social criticism, and his commemorative addresses during the latter part of his life attested his sound sense of literary values. He died in 1892.

Nile Notes of a Howadji, 1851; *The Howadji in Syria*, 1852; *Lotus Eating*, 1852; *The Potiphar Papers*, 1853; *Prue and I*, 1857; *Orations and Addresses of George William Curtis* (ed. by C. E. Norton), 1893–94.

For life and criticism, see: Edward Cary, *George William Curtis*, 1894; John W. Chadwick, *George William Curtis*, 1893; E. E. Hale, *Five Prophets of Today*, 1892; Edward M. Merrill, *Jour. Social Science*, Jan., 1894; S. S. Rogers, *Atlantic*, Jan., 1893; Carl Schurz, *McClure's Mag.*, Oct., 1904.

199. [JOSEPH JEFFERSON AS RIP VAN WINKLE.] In *Harper's New Monthly Mag.*, Mar., 1871. ¶199. "*Pieta in St. Peter's.*" Statue of Mary with the body of Christ, by Michelangelo. ¶199. "*Garrick, etc.*" David Garrick, English actor (1717–1779); Mrs. [Nance] Oldfield (1683–1730), and Mrs. Siddons [Sarah Kemble, 1755–1831], both English actresses. The latter was painted by Sir Joshua [Reynolds, 1723–1792], English portrait painter, as the "Muse of Tragedy." ¶202. "*In secul seculorum*": Forever and ever.

Richard Henry Stoddard (1825–1903)

Richard Henry Stoddard was born July 2, 1825, at Hingham, Mass. He evinced an early interest in writing, contributed frequently to magazines, and saved up enough money to publish his first book, *Footprints*, in 1848. He held a position in the New York Custom House from 1853 to 1870. Then, after holding two other positions, he entered the field of journalism, serving as literary editor of the New York *World* (1860–70), and in the same capacity on the *Mail and Express* (1880–1903). He died in New York, May 12, 1903.

Footprints, 1848; *Poems*, 1852; *Songs of Summer*, 1857; *The King's Bell*, 1862; *Abraham Lincoln*, 1865; *The Book of the East*, 1871; *Poems*, 1880; *The Lion's Cub*, 1890.

For life, see Stoddard's *Recollections, Personal and Literary* (ed. by Ripley Hitchcock), 1903.

204. THE WITCH'S WHELP. In *Poems*, 1852. For source and allusions, see Shakespeare's *The Tempest;* also compare Browning's "Caliban upon Setebos."

205. "POEMS OF THE ORIENT." In *Songs of Summer*, 1857. Title taken from Taylor's book (pub. 1850). See also Stoddard's essay, "Reminiscences of Bayard Taylor," *Atlantic*, Feb. 1879.

205. THERE ARE GAINS FOR ALL OUR LOSSES. In *Songs of Summer*, 1857; text from *Poems*, 1880.

206. IMOGEN. In *Songs of Summer*, 1857. See poem by same title in *Century*, Jan., 1894. For allusions, see Shakespeare's *Cymbeline*.

207. WE PARTED IN THE STREETS OF IS-
PAHAN. In *Songs of Summer*, 1857. Originally
entitled "Persia." Compare Aldrich's "When
the Sultan Goes to Ispahan." Ispahan is a
city in West Central Persia.

Bayard Taylor (1825–1878)

Bayard Taylor was born in Chester County,
Pa., Jan. 11, 1825, of mixed English and German stock. He published his first volume of
poems in 1844, receiving generous remunera-
tion therefor and securing an engagement to
write travel letters for the *Saturday Evening
Post* and the *United States Gazette*. In 1844 he
began a two years' trip afoot through various
countries of the Old World, incorporating the
results of this trip in *Views Afoot* (1846). This
was the beginning of a life spent chiefly in
wandering and lecturing or writing about his
wanderings. In 1848 he represented the New
York *Tribune* on a trip to California to report
the story of the gold rush. The result was
El Dorado (1850). After several years of travel
and lecturing, he entered the diplomatic service
as chargé d'affaires at St. Petersburg, but he
left the service because of disappointment over
failure to be advanced. In 1870–71 he brought
out a translation of *Faust* in the original metres.
In 1878 he was appointed minister to Germany,
but he had served only a few months when he
died, Dec. 19, 1878.

Ximena, etc., 1844; *Views Afoot*, 1846; *El
Dorado*, 1850; *Poems of the Orient*, 1854; *A
Journey to Central Africa*, 1854; *Hannah
Thurston* (novel), 1863; *The Picture of St. John*,
1866; *Faust* (translation), 1870–71; *Home
Pastorals*, 1875; *Studies in German Literature*,
1879; *Critical Essays and Literary Notes*, 1880;
Dramatic Works, 1880; *Poetical Works*, 1880.
For life and criticism, see: R. H. Stoddard,
Critic, Oct. 11, 1884; Marie Hansen Taylor
and Lilian Bayard Taylor Kiliani, *On Two
Continents*, 1905; Marie Hansen Taylor and
H. E. Scudder, *Life and Letters of Bayard
Taylor*, 1884; William Winter, *Old Friends*,
1909.

207. SONG. In *Poems of the Orient*, 1854.
207. BEDOUIN SONG. In *Poems of the Orient*,
154.
208. THE QUAKER WIDOW. In *The Poet's
Journal*, 1862. ¶208. "*Hicksite*." Liberal
branch of American Quakers, who take their
name from their leader, Elias Hicks (1748–
1830).
210. WALT WHITMAN. In *The Echo Club*,
176. One of the most effective of the many
parodies of Whitman. See *Parodies on Walt

Whitman, compiled by Henry S. Saunders, 1923.
210. SAN FRANCISCO BY DAY AND NIGHT.
From *El Dorado*, 1850, the book form of Taylor's letters to the N. Y. *Tribune*. He sailed
for California June 28, 1849, and returned to
New York City Mar., 1850.

Edmund Clarence Stedman (1833–1908)

Edmund Clarence Stedman, born in Hartford, Conn., in 1833, was as a boy sensitive and
rebellious. Though he had won several prizes
for composition, he was suspended from Yale
after two years as a student and not allowed
to return; in 1871 Yale conferred upon him
both the B.A. and M.A. degrees. After some
newspaper experience in Connecticut, he went
into business in New York City. Following a
connection with the *Tribune*, he went, in 1860,
to the New York *World* as its editor, later
becoming its war correspondent. His first book
appeared in 1860, but he spent much of his
life as a trader on the New York Stock Exchange. In the 1870's he began that careful
critical study of English and American literature, chiefly poetry, which resulted in his important anthologies and critical works that are
still respected for their insight and their careful
workmanship.

Poems, Lyrical and Idyllic, 1860; *Alice of
Monmouth; an Idyll of the Great War*, 1863;
The Blameless Prince, 1869; edited (with T. B.
Aldrich) *Cameos from Landor*, 1873; *Poetical
Works*, 1873; *Victorian Poets*, 1875; *Commemo-
rative Ode on Hawthorne*, 1877; *Poets of America*,
1885; edited *A Library of American Literature*,
1887–90; *The Nature and Elements of Poetry*,
1892; edited (with G. E. Woodberry) *The
Works of Edgar Allan Poe*, 1894–95; edited
A Victorian Anthology, 1895; *Poems Now First
Collected . . .*, 1897; edited *An American An-
thology*, 1900; *The Poems of Edmund Clarence
Stedman*, 1908.

For life and criticism, see: H. W. Boynton,
Putnam's Mag., June, 1908; W. D. Howells,
Harper's Monthly, Feb., 1911; Laura Stedman
and G. M. Gould, *Life and Letters of Edmund
Clarence Stedman* (with full bibliography), 1910.

215. HÓW OLD BROWN TOOK HARPER'S
FERRY. Pub. in N. Y. *Tribune*, Nov. 12, 1859.
¶215. "*Osawatomie*" John Brown (b. 1800),
abolitionist, won celebrity by his victory at
Ossowattomie, in the fight for "free-soil" in
Kansas. The raid on Harper's Ferry took place
on Oct. 10, 1859; Brown was taken prisoner on
Oct. 18, tried on Oct. 27, and executed on
Dec. 2. ¶217. "*Emperor's coup d'état*." Louis

Napoleon, elected president of the French republic, declared himself Emperor, Dec. 2, 1851.

218. WANTED—A MAN. In N. Y. *Tribune*, Sept. 8, 1862, this poem voices the discontent of the North with the Union Generals—particularly with McClellan.

218. PAN IN WALL STREET. In "The Contributor's Club," *Atlantic*, Jan., 1867. ¶219. "*Trinacrian hills.*" In Sicily. ¶219. "*Ægon, etc.*" For these allusions see C. M. Gayley, *Classical Myths in English: com.* §116.

220. FALSTAFF'S SONG. In *Poems Now First Collected*, 1897.

220. W. W. In *Poems Now First Collected*, 1897.

220. EDGAR ALLAN POE. The essay from which this extract is taken formed one in the volume of studies of American authors published as *Poets of America*, 1885. Originally printed in *Scribner's Monthly*, May, 1880. ¶222. "*John Martin.*" English painter (1789–1854) whose extravagance excited much criticism. ¶225. "*reliquiæ*": remains. ¶226. "*Landor's Pentameron.*" A book of critical prose by Walter Savage Landor (1775–1864), English poet. ¶226. "*Beecher.*" Henry Ward (1813–1887), American preacher. ¶226. "*Dr. Chivers.*" See *The Romantic Triumph*.

Thomas Bailey Aldrich (1836–1907)

Thomas Bailey Aldrich, of New England Colonial ancestry on both sides, was born in Portsmouth, N. H., Nov. 11, 1836. Owing to his father's wandering disposition, he travelled about much, visiting among other places New Orleans, whose influence marked his work and his manner of life by disposing him "to a fondness for subjects touched with a southern sun and . . . a blithe assurance of manner that never grew in a New England air" (W. B. Parker). After his father's death in 1849, young Aldrich returned to his maternal home in Portsmouth, and after three years in New York City as a clerk in his uncle's office, he published in 1855 a volume of poems (*The Bells*). He now resigned his clerkship and upon accepting the position of junior literary critic of the *Evening Mirror* began a 35-year career in the editorial world. After serving successively on the popular *Home Journal* and the *Saturday Press*, and making the acquaintance of Bayard Taylor, Stedman, Stoddard, and others of the New York group of writers, he became a war correspondent at the outbreak of the Civil War and gained an experience that gave reality to much of his verse of this period. In 1865 when he moved to Boston as editor of

Every Saturday and made the acquaintance of the Longfellow group, he turned his back upon New York, returning to his spiritual as well as physical home, New England. The publication of *The Story of a Bad Boy* (1868) began a career in prose as successful as that which he had enjoyed as a poet. From 1874, when *Every Saturday* ceased publication, to 1880 he enjoyed a freedom devoted to the novel and the short story. From 1881 to 1890 Aldrich edited, as successor to Howells, the *Atlantic Monthly*, in which he exerted his most distinctive influence upon American letters. Resigning his editorship in 1890, he enjoyed 17 years of leisure, making several trips to Europe and two journeys around the world, while doing much writing. The death of his son Charles had robbed him of the zest of life, and he died after a brief illness on March 19, 1907.

The Bells, 1855; *The Ballad of Babie Bell*, *Judith and Holofernes*, 1863; *Friar Jerome Beautiful Book*, 1863; *The Story of a Bad Boy*, 1868; *Marjorie Daw*, 1873; *Prudence Palfrey* (novel), 1874; *The Queen of Sheba*, 1877; *The Stillwater Tragedy*, 1880; *The Old Town by the Sea*, 1893; *Two Bites at a Cherry*, 1894; *A Sea Turn and Other Matters*, 1902; *Ponkapog Papers*, 1903; *Mercedes* (dramatic poem for stage), 1894; *Judith of Bethulia* (dramatized version of *Judith and Holofernes*), 1904; *Works* (Riverside ed.) 9 vols.), 1907.

For life, see: Lilian W. Aldrich, *Crowding Memories*, 1920; Ferris Greenslet, *Life of Thomas Bailey Aldrich* (with bibliography) 1908.

227. PALABRAS CARIÑOSAS. In *The Ballad of Babie Bell and Other Poems*, 1859. The Spanish title means "Affectionate Words."

228. IDENTITY. In *Atlantic*, July, 1875.

228. ENAMORED ARCHITECT OF AIRY RHYME. In *Flower and Thorn*, 1876 (dated, 1877).

228. PAULINE PAVLOVNA. In *The Poems* (Household Edition), 1897.

232. UNGUARDED GATES. *Atlantic*, July 1892. In *Unguarded Gates and Other Poems*, 1895. In a letter of May 14, 1892, to Woodberry (cf. Greenslet, 167–169) Aldrich wrote "I went home and wrote a misanthropic poem called 'Unguarded Gates' (July *Atlantic*), in which I mildly protest against America becoming the cesspool of Europe."

233. REALISM. In *The Poems* (Household Edition), 1897. For criticism, see V. L. Parrington, *Main Currents*, III, 55.

233. MEMORY. In *The Works*, Riverside Edition, 1896.

233. MARJORIE DAW. In *Atlantic*, April 1873; collected in *Marjorie Daw and Other*

People, 1873. This is the *Atlantic* text. ¶234.
"*Fidus Achates.*" The "faithful" companion
of Æneas. ¶235. "*Tourguénieff.*" Ivan Ser-
gyeevich (1818–1883), Russian novelist. ¶236.
"*César Birotteau.*" *The Life and Adventures of,*
a novel of bourgeois life by Balzac. ¶236.
"*Cheops.*" Egyptian king and builder of the
largest pyramid. ¶238. "*Galatea in the play.*"
W. S. Gilbert's burlesque drama, *Pygmalion
and Galatea* (?).

Edward Rowland Sill (*1841–1887*)

Puritan in his ancestry, Edward Rowland
Sill was born in Windsor, Conn., Apr. 29, 1841.
Left an orphan at an early age, he went to
Yale, where, though recognized as a genius, he
drifted through college because of his lack of
sympathy with the "Puritanic atmosphere and
academic formalism of Yale at the period,"
graduating in 1861. Ill health and philosophic
unrest were responsible for two sojourns in
California. From 1861 to 1866 California
offered him work in a post-office, on a ranch,
and in a bank, and an opportunity to study
medicine and law. In 1866 he again tried the
East; but after his failure to "conform" in the
Harvard Divinity School, his dissatisfaction
with newspaper work, the disappointing reception of his first book (1868), and a brief experience in teaching at Cuyahoga Falls, Ohio, he
returned to California, where he taught in the
Oakland high school (1871–74) and then served
as professor of English at the University of
California (1874–82). Ill health forced the
resignation of this last position, and he returned
to Cuyahoga Falls in 1882, occupying himself
with literary work until his unexpected death
in Cleveland, Feb., 27, 1887.

The Hermitage and Other Poems, 1868; *The
Venus of Milo and Other Poems,* 1883; *Poems,*
1886; *The Prose of Edward Rowland Sill,* 1900;
The Poetical Works of Edward Rowland Sill,
1906.

For life and criticism, see: N. Arvin, "The
Failure of E. R. Sill," *Bookman,* Feb., 1931;
W. B. Parker, *Edward Rowland Sill, His Life
and Work,* 1915. See also the "Memorial"
volume privately printed by Sill's friends, 1887;
biographical sketches in the collection of Sill's
Prose, 1900; and the biographical sketch in
Poetical Works, 1906.

247. MORNING. In *Yale Lit. Mag.,* June, 1860.
247. THE FOOL'S PRAYER. In *Atlantic,* Apr.,
1879. See comment on this poem by Josiah
Royce in *The Spirit of Modern Philosophy,*
pp. 465–467.
248. AMONG THE REDWOODS. In *Atlantic,*
Dec., 1884; collected in *Poems,* 1886.

249. BEFORE SUNRISE IN WINTER. In *The
Poetical Works,* 1906.
250. ON SECOND THOUGHT. In *Hermione,
and Other Poems,* 1899.

Richard Watson Gilder (*1844–1909*)

Richard Watson Gilder, of English ancestry,
was born at Belle Vue, Bordentown, N. J.,
Feb. 8, 1844. After assisting his father in his
school at Yonkers, N. Y., Gilder saw service
in the Civil War as an army chaplain and as
a member of the 1st Philadelphia Artillery.
Following some newspaper and magazine work,
he became assistant editor of *Scribner's Monthly*
in 1870; becoming editor in 1881, he continued
as editor of the *Century Magazine,* the reborn
Scribner's, for twenty-five years. His sound
taste secured recognition for many new writers
and won a justly high reputation for the *Century.* His home became a center of intellectual
life and an artists' rendezvous. He also gave
notable service in many civic and social movements. He died Nov. 18, 1909.

The New Day, 1876; *Lyrics and Other Poems,*
1885; *Five Books of Song,* 1894; *Poems and Inscriptions,* 1901; *A Book of Music,* 1906; *The
Fire Divine,* 1907; *Complete Poems,* 1908; *Lincoln the Leader, and Lincoln's Genius for Expression,* 1909; *Grover Cleveland, a Record of
Friendship,* 1910.

For life and criticism, see: Rosamund Gilder
(ed.), *Letters of Richard Watson Gilder* (inadequate, but the chief source of information),
1916; Maria H. Lansdale, "Life-Work and
Homes of Richard Watson Gilder," *Century,*
March, 1911. See also list of commemorative
notices in sketch of Gilder in *D.A.B.,* IV, 278.

250. THE SONNET In *Lyrics and Other
Poems,* 1885.
250. THE NIGHT PASTURE. In *Poems and
Inscriptions,* 1901. See *Letters,* p. 416, for
Gilder's views on poetic rhythms.

Emma Lazarus (*1849–1887*)

Of Portuguese Jewish ancestry, Emma
Lazarus was born in New York City July 22,
1849. Educated at home, she began writing
poems at 14 and published her first volume
of poems in 1867, following this with *Admetus
and Other Poems* (1871), inscribed to Emerson.
Much of her subsequent verse appeared in
Lippincott's Magazine. In 1876 she visited
Concord and there made the acquaintance of
the Concord group. Emerson praised her
tragedy, *The Spagnoletto* (1876) as Turgeniev
had commended her prose romance *Alide*
(1874). Following her excellent translations
of Heine, published in 1881, her interest

changed from the more conventional themes she had been handling to the cause of the persecuted Jews and the movement for Jewish nationalism, as evidenced in her *Songs of a Semite* (1882) and her later prose poems, *By the Waters of Babylon* (1887). She visited Europe in 1883 and again in 1885–86. She died in New York Nov. 19, 1887.

Poems and Translations, 1867; *Admetus and Other Poems*, 1871; *Alide*, 1874; *The Spagnoletto*, 1876; *Poems and Ballads of Heine*, 1881; *Songs of a Semite*, 1882; *By the Waters of Babylon*, 1887; *The Poems of Emma Lazarus*, 1889.

For life and criticism, see: E. C. Stedman, *Genius and Other Essays*, 1911; article in *Century Mag.*, new series, Vol. 14, p. 875 (afterwards prefixed as a "Memoir" to *Poems*, 1889). See also reference list in *The Jewish Encyclopedia*, VII, 652.

251. VENUS OF THE LOUVRE. In *The Poems*, 1889. ¶251. "*Heine wept.*" Incident in the exile of the great German-Jewish lyricist, Heinrich Heine (1799–1856).

251. How LONG? From *Admetus and Other Poems*, 1871.

252. THE BANNER OF THE JEW. In *The Critic*, June 3, 1882. ¶252. "*Maccabean rage.*" Led by Judas Maccabeus and other members of his family, the Jews threw off the yoke of Antiochus Epiphanes.

253. THE NEW COLOSSUS. This sonnet is engraved on the base of the Statue of Liberty. For a reproduction of the plate, see the *Jewish Encyclopedia*, VII, 652.

The Western Humorists

For general discussions of the subject, see: Walter Blair, "Burlesque in Nineteenth-Century Humor," *Am. Lit.*, Nov., 1930; same, "The Popularity of Nineteenth-Century American Humorists," *Am. Lit.*, May, 1931; W. D. Howe, "Early Humorists," *CHAL*, II, 148 ff.; F. L. Pattee, "The Laughter of the West," in *Amer. Lit. since 1870*, 1915; Constance Rourke, *American Humor: A Study of the National Character*, 1931.

For the bibliography of the Western Humorists in general, see: *CHAL*, II, 503 ff.

John Phoenix
(George Horatio Derby)
(1823–1861)

George Horatio Derby was born in Dedham, Mass., Apr. 3, 1823. After preparing for an army career at the U. S. Military Academy

(1842–46), he joined the topographical engineers, saw service in the Mexican War, in which he was wounded and received promotion to a first lieutenancy for meritorious conduct and assisted in the exploration of Minnesota Territory (1848–49). His humorous predilections, which had shown themselves at West Point, again were displayed (according to tradition) in his reports, and he was punished for his flippancy by being transferred to California. Except for a brief sojourn in Texas in 1852 he spent the years 1849–56 in California, interlarding his tasks as an engineer with rollicking excursions in humor. His reputation as the state's best wit was made during his residence in San Diego from July, 1853, to the spring of 1855. Sent to that city to change the course of the San Diego River, he was asked by J Judson Ames, editor of the San Diego *Herald* to take over the editorship while Ames went to San Francisco on business. Derby proceeded, under the name of "John Phoenix," to change the politics of the paper and to make it the medium for his riotous humor, notably in his famous "Illustrated Edition" of October 1, 1852. On Ames's return, Derby's delinquencies were goodhumoredly pardoned, and Ames himself collected and published the first volume of Derby's sketches under the title of *Phoenixiana* (1855). The only other volume of Derby's humor to appear was *The Squibob Papers* (1859), a collection of earlier burlesque written under the name of "Squibob," inferior work which Derby's wife later regretted that she was responsible in making known to a wider audience. After suffering a sunstroke in Florida in 1859, Derby went on sick leave. His death occurred shortly after, May 15, 1861.

Phoenixiana; or Sketches and Burlesques 1855, etc. (also special editions by John Vance Cheney, 1897, and J. K. Bangs, 1908); *The Squibob Papers*, 1859.

For life and criticism, see: Walter Blair, "Burlesques in Nineteenth Century Humor, *Am. Lit.*, Nov., 1930; J. V. Cheney, Preface to 1897 edition of *Phoenixiana*; G. W. Cullum *Biog. Reg. U. S. Mil. Acad.*, 3d ed (1891); Charles Johnston, "The First Jester in California," *Harper's Weekly*, May 17, 1913; W. P Trent, "A Retrospect of American Humor," *Century*, Nov., 1901; A. H. Warren, *San Diego Yesterdays*, 1921.

254. MUSICAL REVIEW EXTRAORDINARY. The present text is the complete account as it appeared in *The Pioneer; or, California Monthly Magazine*, August, 1854. The burlesque as printed in *Phoenixiana* omits the interesting explanatory matter of the editor

preceding and following Derby's contribution
proper. Phoenix was the first to attach the
name "Pike" to Westerners in narratives about
them. ¶255. *Il frappe.* . . .": He knocks
everything perfectly cold. ¶256. *"orpheclide":*
This word does not exist, but *ophicleide* denotes
the now obsolete predecessor of the tuba.

Artemus Ward
(Charles Farrar Browne)
(1834–1867)

Charles Farrar Browne, who added the "e"
to his father's name, was born in Waterford,
Me., Apr. 26, 1834. At the age of 13 he lost
his father and, entering the printing trade,
spent three years in Boston, wandered westward, and finally attached himself to the Cleve-
and *Plain Dealer*, using for his pen name
("Artemus Ward") one selected from old family records. His assumption of the rôle of the
quaint travelling showman became the basis
of his literary work. Moving to New York
City in 1859 to work on the new magazine,
Vanity Fair, he created an immense popularity
on the publication of his sketches in 1862, as
well as with his lecture, "Babes in the Wood,"
which he delivered on tour in 1861. He helped
Lincoln's cause during the War; Lincoln's fondness for the humorist's work (his favorite reading) was paralleled by Browne's admiration for
Lincoln and his attachment to the Union. A
Western tour in 1863 was followed by an
Eastern tour the next year, when he gave his
famous lecture on the Mormons illustrated by
a panorama. In 1866 he invaded England,
where he was greeted by a reception which
constituted the crowning triumph of his life.
He died shortly after, of consumption, in
Southampton, March 6, 1867.

Sketches in the Boston *Carpet Bag*, 1852–53;
Cleveland *Plain Dealer*, 1858–59, and *Vanity
Fair*, 1860–62; *Artemus Ward: His Book*, 1862;
Artemus Ward: His Travels, 1865; sketches in
the London *Punch*, Sept. and Nov., 1866;
Artemus Ward: His Works Complete, 1875.

For life and criticism, see: Walter Blair,
"Burlesques in Nineteenth Century American
Humor," *Am. Lit.*, Nov., 1930; M. D. Landow,
biog. sketch in *Complete Works*, 1875; A. S.
Nock, *On Doing the Right Thing*, 1928; D. C.
Seitz, *Artemus Ward*, 1919.

258. THE LONDON PUNCH LETTERS. The
selection in this volume, after having appeared
in *Punch* in 1866, was first published in book
form in *Artemus Ward in London, and
Other Papers*, 1867. ¶259. *"Gloster."* Richard III, who, as Protector, seized the throne

in 1484. He lost his life at the battle of
Bosworth, resisting "Col." [Henry of] Richmond. ¶259. *"Dr. Catlin."* George (1796–
1872), a writer on the Indians.

Josh Billings
(Henry Wheeler Shaw)
(1818–1885)

Henry Wheeler Shaw was born at Lanes-
borough, Mass., Apr. 21, 1818, of Puritan stock.
Leaving Hamilton College to go West, he lived
a varied life as a worker on steamboats, farmer,
and auctioneer. In 1858 he settled in Poughkeepsie, N. Y., as a land agent and auctioneer.
Failing to secure an audience by his conventional writing for the Poughkeepsie *Daily Press*
and other papers, he published in a New York
newspaper in 1860 his "Essa on the Muel bi
Josh Billings," which won him a hearing, and
which he followed by similar contributions to
the *New York Weekly*, the New York *Saturday
Press*, and other papers, and by several volumes that increased his popularity. From 1870
he published for a decade his annual burlesque
of the familiar almanac. He died in Monterey,
Calif., Oct. 14, 1885.

Josh Billings: His Sayings, 1866; *Josh
Billings on Ice and Other Things*, 1868; *Josh
Billings: His Works, Complete*, 1876; *Complete
Comical Writings of Josh Billings* (with biog.
intro.), 1877; *Trump Kards*, 1877; *Old Proba-
bilities*, 1879; *Josh Billings' Spice Box*, 1881;
Josh Billings' Old Farmers' Allminax, 1902.

For life and criticism, see: F. S. Smith, *Life
and Adventures of Josh Billings*, 1883; A. P.
Thompson, "Josh Billings," *New Eng. Mag.*,
New Series, Vol. 19, p. 696. See also biog.
intro. to *Complete Writings*, 1877. A biography
of Shaw is in preparation by Cyril Clemens.

260. GLASS DIMONDS. In *Josh Billings: His
Works, Complete*, 1876.

Petroleum V. Nasby
(David Ross Locke)
(1833–1888)

David Ross Locke was born Sept. 20, 1833,
at Vestal, Broome County, N. Y. Having
learned the printer's trade and having gained
experience on several newspapers, he began his
series of "Nasby" letters in 1860 in the Findlay
Jeffersonian. These letters were continued
throughout the War as satiric comments on
the politics of the time, exercising great influence upon public opinion in support of Lincoln.
At Lincoln's death, Locke's satire was directed

at President Johnson. In book form these letters continued their popularity for many years. In 1865 Locke became editor and owner of the Toledo *Blade*. He later added lecturing to his work as a humorous writer. He died at Toledo, Feb. 15, 1888.

Nasby Papers (intro. by G. A. Sala), 1864; *Divers Views, Opinions and Prophecies of Yours Truly*, 1865; *"Swingin' round the Cirkle,"* 1866; *Ekkoes from Kentucky*, 1867; *The Struggles—Social, Financial and Political—of Petroleum V. Nasby*, 1872; *Hannah Jane*, 1882; *The Moral History of America's Life-Struggle*, 1872; *The Morals of Abou Ben Adhem*, 1875; *A Paper City*, 1878; *Nasby in Exile*, 1882.

For life and criticism, see: G. A. Sala, intro. to *Nasby Papers*, 1866.

262. A FEW LAST WORDS. Final chapter of *"Swingin' round the Cirkle,"* 1866. The satiric purpose of this volume, which it is said was taken seriously by a great many as a support of the cause of Southern Democracy, may be seen from the dedication: "Dedikashun Uv This Book. To Androo Johnson, The Pride and Hope uv Dimocrisy. . . . And to Alex. W. Randall, Postmaster General."

Folk Literature

With the publication in 1910 of John A. Lomax's *Cowboy Songs and Other Frontier Ballads*, the beginning may be said to have been made in a serious and widespread study of the folk literature of America. Previous to this time only two main types of folk literature had received much attention—the traditional ballad, descended from the old English folk ballad, and the negro spiritual. But Professor Lomax inspired, by his collection and publication of the disappearing cowboy ballads, the study of this and many other types of folk material. A few years later Professor Homer A. Watt and his collaborator, Miss Bernice K. Stewart, were to call attention to the lore of the lumberjack in the Paul Bunyan tales. Several collections of these tales and those of the analogous Tony Beaver were to appear within the next fifteen years. Still other groups throughout the country received attention until, as one may observe by running through the table of contents of Carl Sandburg's *American Songbag*, twelve or fifteen different types are now illustrated, representing the city streets, the river-wharf, and the tramp's highway, as well as the mountain cabin, the cattle-range, the plantation, and the lumberjack's shanty. What is of most importance in all this activity of collectors is that the interest denotes, not merely curiosity for the novel, but a serious realization that upon this folk literature as a basis was built much of the literature of realism, Western humor, local color, and the literature of the people—these are the bases of American realism of the Frontier Period.

For general bibliography, see: Louis Untermeyer, *American Poetry from the Beginning to Whitman* (pp. 803–807), 1931; Lucy L. Hazard *In Search of America* (pp. 577–581), 1930.

For general collections, see: *Folk-Say: A Regional Miscellany*, 1930; Lucy L. Hazard *In Search of America*, 1930; Carl Sandburg *The American Songbag*, 1930; Louis Untermeyer, *American Poetry from the Beginning to Whitman*, 1931.

For general criticism (in addition to critical material in the above), see: A. K Davis, "On Collecting and Editing of Ballads," *Amer Speech*, Aug., 1930; L. W. Payne, Jr., "Recent Research in Balladry and Folk Songs," *Pub Texas Folklore Soc.*, VIII, 160–169, 1930; Ruth Suckow, "The Folk Idea in American Life," *Scribner's Mag.*, Sept., 1930.

THE COWBOY AND FRONTIERSMAN: John A. Lomax, *Cowboy Songs and Other Frontier Ballads*, 1910, 1925; same, *Songs of the Cattle Trail and Cow Camp*, 1919.

THE LUMBERJACK: E. C. Beck, "Lumberjack Ballads and Songs," *Eng. Jour.*, Jan., 1932; Charles J. Finger, *A Paul Bunyan Geography*, 1931; Margaret P. Montagu, *Up Eel River*, 1927; Esther Shephard, *Paul Bunyan*, 1924; James Stevens, *Paul Bunyan*, 1924; same, *The Saginaw Paul Bunyan*, 1932; Bernice K. Stewart and Homer A. Watt, "Legends of Paul Bunyan, Lumberjack," *Trans. Wis. Acad. of Sciences, Arts, and Letters*, XVIII, Part II, 639–651; Ida Virginia Turney, *Paul Bunyan Comes West*, 1928.

THE MOUNTAINEER: John Harrington Cox, *Folk-Songs of the South*, 1925; Arthur K. Davis, Jr., *Traditional Ballads of Virginia*, 1929; M. E. Henry, "More Songs from the Southern Highlands," *Jour. Amer. Folk-Lore*, Jan.–Mar., 1931; Reed Smith, *South Carolina Ballads, with a Study of the Traditional Ballad of To-day*, 1928.

THE NEGRO: W. F. Allen and others, *Slave Songs of the United States*, 1867, new ed., 1929; Wm. E. Barton, *Old Plantation Hymns*, 1899; V. F. Calverton, *An Anthology of American Negro Verse*, 1929; T. W. Higginson, "Negro Spirituals," *Atlantic*, June, 1867; same, *Army Life in a Black Regiment* (Chap. IX), 1870; John Huston, *Frankie and Johnnie*, 1930; R. E. Kennedy, *Mellows*, 1925; John H. Nelson, *The Negro Character in American Literature*, 1926; H. W. Odum and Guy B. Johnson, *The Negro and His Songs*, 1925; same, *Negro Workaday*

Songs, 1926; same, *Rainbow round My Shoulder*, 1928; Thos. W. Talley, *Negro Folk-Rhymes*, 1922; Newman I. White, *American Negro Folk-Songs*, 1928. See also *Jour. Amer. Folk-Lore* from 1888 to 1914, esp. articles by E. C. Perrow.

266. THE COWBOY'S DREAM. This and the following three ballads appeared in the 1910 edition of Lomax's *Cowboy Songs and Other Frontier Ballads*. ¶266. *"Dogies."* Yearling runts which trail the herd. ¶267. *"Old Chisholm Trail."* Cattle trail from Texas to Montana. ¶269. *"Jesse James."* American desperado (1847–1882), who, while living in disguise as Thomas Howard, was shot by a member of his own gang, Robert Ford.

270. PAUL BUNYAN PROVIDES FOR HIS CREW. "During the second half of the nineteenth century there came into being in the lumber camps of North America a series of legends dealing with the exploits of a giant lumberjack, Paul Bunyan, who performed, with the help of his mammoth blue ox and his crew of hardened men, such notable feats of swamping, digging, and logging that he changed the face of nature wherever he set up his camp. In their idealization of the hero and their ascription to him of powers and deeds far beyond those of mortal men, these tales are epic in character and scope. Like the epics, too, their unity consists in their centering on the activities of a hero whose interests and occupations are those of the men who created him. They are unlike the epics, however, in having certain elements that are characteristic of pioneer—not to say American—humor, notably a mock-seriousness in the telling and a conscious comic inflation of both characters and episodes. They belong, therefore, definitely within the body of American folklore, and Paul Bunyan's place is by the side of Tony Beaver and John Henry.

"After having been told and retold for decades in the lumber camps from Maine to British Columbia, the legends of Paul Bunyan were introduced to readers in 1914 by Mr. W. B. Laughead in advertising pamphlets of the Red River Lumber Company. Shortly afterwards Douglas Malloch, the Chicago poet, retold some of them in verse, and in 1916 the tales were brought to the notice of students of folklore by Bernice Stewart and Homer A. Watt in an article which appeared in the *Publications* of the Wisconsin Academy of Sciences, Arts, and Letters in that year under the title *Legends of Paul Bunyan, Lumberjack*. Since then a dozen or more volumes of Bunyan tales have been published, among which are the following: Esther Shephard's *Paul Bunyan*,

Seattle, 1924; James Stevens's *Paul Bunyan*, Garden City, 1925, and *The Saginaw Paul Bunyan*, New York, 1931; James Cloyd Bowman's *The Adventures of Paul Bunyan*, New York, 1927; and Charles J. Finger's *A Paul Bunyan Geography*, The Maple Press, York, Pa., 1931. In collections of Paul Bunyan yarns it is not always possible, unfortunately, to separate those which belong to the legitimate Bunyan cycle from those which have been added from other sources or even invented by the compilers. Compilers, moreover, have sometimes destroyed the mood and flavor of the Bunyan tales by sentimentalizing or otherwise distorting them. In the short collection in this volume a few of the most characteristic of the stories have been retold, and an attempt has been made to give some suggestion of the original *milieu* of the tales. Since the crew of a lumber camp represents various races and social strata, there is no lumberjack dialect, and no attempt has been made here to create one" (Homer A. Watt).

273. THE WRECK ON THE C. AND O. Version C of No. 47 in Cox's *Folk-Songs of the South*, pp. 224–225. Eleven versions are recorded by Cox, who says: "This ballad, like that of 'John Hardy,' was made in West Virginia. The wreck referred to, caused by a landslide three miles east of Hinton, occurred Oct. 23, 1890. The F. F. V. was the 'Fast Flying Vestibule,' train No. 4, engine 134, on the Chesapeake and Ohio R. R." For full details, see Cox, p. 221. The brother of the dead engineer thought the ballad was started by a negro who worked in the roundhouse at Hinton. ¶274. *"dome"* means "doom."

274. THE ROWAN COUNTY CREW. This ballad was communicated to Professor Cox, through whose kindness it is here printed, by Mr. Aubrey Goff, of Lenore, Mingo County, W. Va. For a brief statement of the facts after Martin had been sent to jail, see *Folk-Songs of the South*, p. 203. The locale of the piece is Kentucky.

275. ROOM IN THERE. Taken from the article by T. W. Higginson, entitled "Negro Spirituals," *Atlantic*, June, 1867, where the circumstances of his hearing the songs sung by the members of his black regiment may be found.

276. JOHN HENRY. Version H of No. 35, "John Hardy," in Cox, pp. 185–186. This is now recognized as a true negro ballad about a different man from John Hardy. See Guy B. Johnson, *John Henry, Tracking Down a Negro Legend*, 1929. The version here given is the best of the "John Henry" songs. For full

details about the "John Hardy" ballads, see Cox, pp. 175-177.

277. PROMISES OF FREEDOM. This and the following two poems represent, as does "John Henry," the secular as opposed to the spiritual aspects of the negro folk.

Bret Harte
(Francis Brett Harte)
(1836-1902)

Francis Brett Harte, of mixed English, Dutch, and Hebrew descent, was born in Albany, N. Y., Aug. 25, 1836. His childhood was passed in straitened circumstances, and at 16 Harte was self-supporting. In 1853 his mother's second marriage (to Col. Andrews Williams, of Oakland, Calif.) was the occasion for the family's removal to California. Harte himself arrived in San Francisco in 1854. Until 1860 he lived a varied life, as teacher, type-setter, drug-clerk, messenger, and so forth, in different parts of northern California. He had begun to write before he came to California, and he continued to write while engaged in other occupations. But in 1860 he began his association with The Golden Era which led step by step to his discovery of his true forte, the local-color story. Though holding positions of a non-literary character, he turned out numerous poems and sketches, and edited a book of western verse, Outcroppings, in 1865. In 1868 he became the first editor of the Overland Monthly. The second issue contained "The Luck of Roaring Camp," whose success in the East was followed by a similar success for "The Outcasts of Poker Flat" in January, 1869. The publication of his poem familiarly known as "The Heathen Chinee" in 1870 gave him world fame as a humorist. Harte accepted a contract with the Atlantic to write for it for twelve months for $10,000. In 1871, intoxicated with success, Harte returned to the East. He spent the years 1871-78 in New York City, writing steadily but suffering a decline in popularity and running into debt. After the failure of a magazine venture, he entered the consular service, occupying positions at Crefeld (Prussia) and Glasgow until, in 1885, a change of administration forced him out. Harte now turned to his writing again, but though he wrote steadily, his inspiration was gone. His domestic life had not been a happy one for some time when in 1902 he died of cancer in England.

Outcroppings [ed.], 1865; The Lost Galleon and Other Tales, 1867; Condensed Novels and Other Papers, 1867; The Luck of Roaring Camp and Other Sketches, 1870; Mrs. Skaggs's Husbands, and Other Sketches, 1873; Tales of the Argonauts, 1875; Gabriel Conroy, 1876; Two Men of Sandy Bar, 1876; The Writings of Bret Harte (20 vols.), 1896-1903.

For life and criticism, see: Noah Brooks, "Bret Harte in California," Century Mag., July, 1897; H. S. Canby, "Bret Harte's Tragedy," Sat. Rev. Lit., January 30, 1932; Will M. Clemens, "Bret Harte's Country," Bookman, XIII, 224; Geoffrey Bret Harte (ed.), Letters of Bret Harte, 1926; London Times, May 7, 1902; H. C. Merwin, Life of Bret Harte, 1911; Overland Monthly, Sept., 1902; T. E. Pemberton, Life of Bret Harte, 1903; G. R. Stewart, Jr., Bret Harte: Argonaut and Exile, 1931.

For bibliography, see: CHAL, II, 622-625 (A bibliographical study by George R. Stewart, Jr., is in preparation.)

278. THE WORK ON RED MOUNTAIN. Reprinted from The Golden Era, Dec. 9 and 16, 1860. The first version of "Mliss," which went through several changes before it reached its final form. See Stewart's Bret Harte: Argonaut and Exile for a discussion of Harte's early writings. The appearance of this story in 1860 shows that Harte is fully entitled to his place as the beginner of the local color vogue.

297. MUCK-A-MUCK. In Condensed Novels, 1867, published by Harte himself.

301. THE LUCK OF ROARING CAMP. From Overland Monthly, Aug., 1868. ¶301. "ab initio": In the beginning. ¶303. "Romulus and Remus." Mythological founders of Rome who, as babes, were suckled by a wolf.

308. THE ANGELUS. In the Overland Monthly, 1868.

309. IN THE TUNNEL. In the Overland Monthly, 1869; collected in The Heathen Chinee and Other Poems, 1871.

309. HER LETTER. In The Independent, Feb. 2, 1871. ¶310. "By Brady." American photographer who gained fame in the Civil War.

311. PLAIN LANGUAGE FROM TRUTHFUL JAMES. In the Overland Monthly, Sept., 1870, "brought him a popularity . . . that had had no precedent in America, save in the case of Mrs. Stowe and Uncle Tom's Cabin" (Pattee).

312. THE SOCIETY UPON STANISLAUS. Written some time between 1862 and 1867; collected in The Heathen Chinee, 1871. "Stanislaus" is the name of a river southeast of San Francisco, while "Calaveras" is a county east of the city.

312. "CROTALUS." In Works, 1882.

313. RELIEVING GUARD. In Echoes of the Foot-Hills, 1875. Thomas Starr King is credited

with having kept California in the Union by his oratory.

314. THE AGED STRANGER. In *Echoes of the Foot-Hills,* 1875.

Joaquin Miller
(Cincinnatus Hiner Miller)
(1841–1913)

Joaquin Miller said of his birth: "My cradle was a covered wagon, pointed West. I was born in a covered wagon, I am told, at or about the time it crossed the line dividing Indiana from Ohio." His childhood and youth were spent in the midst of pioneer conditions of life. The family kept moving westward until, in 1854, it reached Oregon, where Miller got a kind of higher education at an institution of high-school grade called Columbia College, now extinct. Following some experience in mining and journalism in Idaho and Oregon, he held a judgeship in Grant County, Oregon, from 1866 to 1870, meanwhile having published his first volume of verse, *Specimens* (1868), and another volume, *Joaquin, et al* (1869), from which he derived his pen-name. Disappointed in the lack of encouragement, he went to London in 1870, where in the following year was published the volume that made his reputation, *Songs of the Sierras.* He followed this success with other volumes of verse, as well as plays. In 1885 he returned to California, where, after a varied and picturesque experience, including trips to the Near and Far East, the Klondike, South Africa, and Central America, he died at "The Heights," in Oakland, Feb. 17, 1913.

Specimens, 1868; *Joaquin, et al,* 1869; *Pacific Poems,* 1870; *Songs of the Sierras,* 1871; *Songs of the Sunlands,* 1873; *Unwritten History: Life amongst the Modocs,* 1874; *The Ship in the Desert,* 1875; *Songs of Italy,* 1878; *The Danites in the Sierras,* 1881; *Collected Poems,* 1882; *The Building of the City Beautiful, A Poetic Romance,* 1893; *Chants for the Boer,* 1900; *Light: a Narrative Poem,* 1907; *Joaquin Miller's Poetry* (Bear Edition), 6 vols., 1909, 7 vols., 1917; *The Poetical Works of Joaquin Miller,* ed. by Stuart P. Sherman, 1923.

For life and criticism, see: *American Mercury,* VII, 220–229; *Overland Monthly,* Vol. 63, pp. 109–119, Vol. 75, pp. 93–96; Fred L. Pattee, *American Literature since 1870* (Chap. VI), 1915; S. P. Sherman, intro. to 1923 edition of Miller's poems; *Sunset Mag.,* Vol. 30, pp. 765–770; Harr Wagner, *Joaquin Miller and His Other Self,* 1929.

314. KIT CARSON'S RIDE. Written in London, in 1870, where he saw Browning and re-quested the latter's permission to use the metre of "How They Carried the Good News from Ghent to Aix." Possibly in *Oxford Magazine,* 1870(?); collected in *Songs of the Sierras,* 1871.

316. THE LAST TASCHASTAS. In *Songs of the Sierras,* 1871. "Tc 'hastas; a name given to King John by the French, a corruption of chaste; for he was a pure, just man and a great warrior. He was the king of the Rouge (Red) River Indians of Oregon, and his story is glorious with great deeds in defense of his people" (Miller's note).

318. EXODUS FOR OREGON. In *Songs of the Sunlands,* 1873.

320. DEAD IN THE SIERRAS. In *Songs of the Sunlands,* 1873.

321. ALASKA. In *Joaquin Miller's Poetry,* Bear Edition, 1909.

321. COLUMBUS. In *Songs of the Soul,* 1896.

322. TWILIGHT AT THE HEIGHTS. In *Joaquin Miller's Poetry,* 1909.

322. SHADOWS OF SHASTA. Ch. I of *Life amongst the Modocs,* 1874.

Rebecca Harding Davis (1831–1910)

Rebecca Harding was born in Washington, Pa., June 24, 1831. She spent her childhood in Alabama and Virginia. Guided only by the extensive reading in which she indulged, she was mainly self-educated. She began writing fiction at an early age and got some of it published, but it was in emulation of the popular women writers of the day until, in April, 1861, she published her grimly realistic story "Life in the Iron Mills" in the *Atlantic Monthly.* She soon became famous, but, though she was a constant contributor to the magazines and in 1869 was appointed to the editorial staff of the New York *Tribune,* her later work was too much in the conventional manner to fulfill the promise of her first story in the *Atlantic.* She married a prominent journalist in 1863 and became the mother of two writers of distinction, Richard Harding Davis and Charles Belmont Davis. She died at Mount Kisco, N. Y., Sept. 29, 1910.

"Life in the Iron Mills," *Atlantic,* April, 1861; *Margaret Howth,* 1862; *Dallas Galbraith,* 1868; *Waiting for the Verdict,* 1868; various novels, tales, and sketches, 1872–97; *Bits of Gossip* (autobiographical), 1904.

For life, see: Rebecca Harding Davis, *Bits of Gossip,* 1904; Dalton Dorr, *American,* March 4, 1882; N. Y. *Times,* Sept. 30, 1910; *Who's Who in America,* 1910–11.

327. LIFE IN THE IRON MILLS. From *At-*

lantic, April, 1861. ¶335. *"Farinata."* Farinata degli Uberti, leader of the Ghibelline faction in Florence, whom Dante represents in *Hell,* Canto X. ¶336. *"Kant, Novalis, Humboldt."* Immanuel Kant, German metaphysician (1724–1804); Friedrich von Hardenburg, German poet and philosopher (1772–1801); and Friedrich H. A. von Humboldt, German scientist (1769–1859). ¶338. *"Ce n'est pas . . .":* It's none of my business. ¶339. *"De profundis clamavi":* Out of the depths I called.

Harriet Beecher Stowe (1811–1896)

Harriet Elizabeth Beecher, the seventh child of parents descended from the founders of New Haven, Conn., was born at Litchfield, Conn., one of the most intellectual communities in New England. She was a pupil, and later a teacher, in the school of her sister Catherine, who exercised a great influence over her. In 1832 her father, the Rev. Lyman Beecher, accepted the presidency of the recently established Lane Theological Seminary in Cincinnati, and Catherine and Harriet accompanied him. Here Harriet was active in the literary and school life of the community, contributing sketches and stories to the local journals. In 1836 she was married to a professor in the Seminary, Calvin E. Stowe, whose precarious health made for a life of anxiety and privation. Her eighteen years in Cincinnati, across the river from a slave state, provided her with her chief basis for her later writings on slavery. On the acceptance of a professorship in Bowdoin College in 1850, Professor Stowe moved his family to Brunswick, Me., where Mrs. Stowe wrote *Uncle Tom's Cabin* for serial publication in the anti-slavery journal *The National Era* (Washington, D. C.). The publication of this story in book form two years later not only gave her world-wide fame but introduced a powerful motive for the Civil War. Her activities during the next few years were centered upon slavery. Writing for the *Atlantic Monthly,* the *Independent,* and the *Christian Union* (for the last two of which her brother, Henry Ward Beecher, was successively one of the editors), she gradually shifted her interest to New England life, signalized by such works as *The Minister's Wooing, Pearl of Orr's Island,* and her Sam Lawson sketches in the *Atlantic Monthly.* In her later manner she obtained less renown but a higher permanent position on the ground of literary merit than in her writings on slavery. Moving to Hartford in 1863, Mrs. Stowe made this city her chief home for the remainder of her life, dying there July 1, 1896.

The Mayflower, or Sketches of Scenes and Characters among the Descendants of the Pilgrims, 1843; *Uncle Tom's Cabin; or, Life among the Lowly,* 1852; *A Key to Uncle Tom's Cabin,* 1853; *Dred: A Tale of the Dismal Swamp,* 1856; *The Minister's Wooing,* 1859; *Pearl of Orr's Island,* 1862; *Oldtown Fireside Sketches,* 1871; Riverside edition of *Works,* 1899, 1906.

For life and criticism, see: Annie Fields (ed.), *Life and Letters of Harriet Beecher Stowe,* 1897; C. E. and L. B. Stowe, *Harriet Beecher Stowe: The Story of Her Life,* 1911; John Erskine, *Leading American Novelists,* 1910.

353. THE GHOST IN THE MILL. The first of a series of sketches that appeared in book form as *Sam Lawson's Oldtown Fireside Stories,* 1871; originally in *Atlantic,* June, 1870. Mrs. Stowe was the first to use the New England dialect for the purposes of realism.

John James Piatt (1835–1917)

John James Piatt was born at James' Mill, Dearborn County, Ind., March 1, 1835. Educated at Capitol University and Kenyon College, he served as a clerk in the U. S. Treasury Dept. from 1861 to 1867, as Librarian of the House of Representatives (1871–75), and as U. S. Consul, first at Cork, Ireland (1882–93), and for a few months at Dublin in 1893. He had meanwhile served on two newspapers, the *Chronicle* (1868–69) and the *Commercial* (1869–78), both in Cincinnati, and had attained a considerable reputation through his numerous volumes of verse. He died Feb. 16, 1917, at Cincinnati, Ohio.

Poems by Two Friends (with W. D. Howells), 1860; *The Nests at Washington,* 1864; *Poems in Sunshine and Firelight,* 1866; *Western Windows and Other Poems,* 1869; *The Pioneer's Chimney,* etc., 1871; *Landmarks, The Lost Farm, and Other Poems,* 1872; *Poems of House and Home,* 1879; *Penciled Fly-Leaves,* 1880; *The Children Out-of-Doors* (with S. M. B. Piatt), 1885; *At the Holy Well,* 1887; *Idyls and Lyrics of the Ohio Valley,* 1881; *A Book of Gold,* 1889; *The Lost Hunting Ground,* etc., 1893; *Little New-World Idyls,* 1893; *The Ghost's Entry and Other Poems,* 1895; editor of: *The Poems of George D. Prentice* (1876); *The Union of American Poetry and Art* (1880); *The Hesperian Tree, An Annual of the Ohio Valley* (1900–03).

For criticism, see: W. D. Howells, "John James Piatt," *Harper's Mag.,* CXXXV, 291.

361. RIDING TO VOTE. In *Western Windows and Other Poems,* 1869.

362. TORCH-LIGHT IN AUTUMN. This text, which differs somewhat from that in Stedman's

Anthology, is from a manuscript version signed by Piatt's initials and appearing in a presentation copy of *Idyls and Lyrics of the Ohio Valley,* 1881, in the possession of the editor. He has been unable to locate the poem in any of Piatt's published works.

362. FARTHER. From *Landmarks and Other Poems,* 1871. Stedman and other anthologists have added the sub-title "(The suggested device of a new western state)." The present editor has not been able to locate a version of this poem in any of Piatt's works that employs this sub-title.

Edward Eggleston (1837–1902)

Edward Eggleston was born at Vevay, Ind., Dec. 10, 1837. His father, a lawyer, alumnus of William and Mary College, came of an important Virginia family. His mother was the daughter of a frontiersman and Indian fighter. After a childhood spent on a farm and in the backwoods country of Decatur County, and a thirteen months' visit to Virginia, the young man became a Bible agent. He conquered consumption by work in the open air in Minnesota in 1856, and spent the next ten years in a variety of occupations, including that of a minister in small churches. He began writing in 1866, contributing to various papers, including the N. Y. *Independent* and *Hearth and Home;* on the latter he held an editorial position which led to his publishing therein *The Hoosier Schoolmaster* in serial form. After writing a number of novels and short stories, he turned to history. He contributed many historical articles to the *Century* from 1882 on and delivered several historical lectures at Columbia College in 1893, besides producing school histories and biographical publications. At his death on Sept. 2, 1902, he had completed only two volumes of an ambitious history of life in the United States. His conception of history was significant in that he envisioned it as primarily "the record of the culture of a people" and thought of his novels as a preparation for the writing of that history.

Mr. Blake's Walking-Stick, 1870; *The Hoosier School-master,* 1871; *The End of the World,* 1872; *The Mystery of Metropolisville,* 1873; *The Circuit Rider* (1873–74); *Roxy,* 1878; *The Hoosier Schoolboy,* 1881–82; *The Graysons,* 1887–88; *The Faith Doctor,* 1891; *Duffels,* 1893; *The Beginners of a Nation,* 1896; *The Transit of Civilization,* 1901.

For life and criticism, see: Frances Eggleston, *Edward Eggleston,* 1895; George C. Eggleston, *The First of the Hoosiers: Reminiscences of Edward Eggleston,* 1903; Hamlin Garland, *A Son of the Middle Border* (p. 115), 1917; Wash-ington Gladden, "Edward Eggleston," *Scribner's Monthly,* Sept., 1873; Edward Eggleston, "Books That Have Helped Me," *Forum,* Aug., 1887; same, "Formative Influences," *Forum,* Nov., 1890; "Edward Eggleston," *Outlook,* Feb. 6, 1897. (A biographical and critical study by Harlan Logan is in preparation.)

For bibliography, see: *CHAL,* II, 634; IV, 661, 737.

363. A PRIVATE LESSON FROM A BULLDOG. In *The Hoosier School-master,* 1871, which had been serialized in *Hearth and Home,* a weekly journal edited by Eggleston. In the "Library Edition" of this novel, 1892, Eggleston added some detailed footnotes in explanation of the dialect. Some slight changes in the text were also made, but the original text, with errors, has been printed in this volume.

John Hay (1838–1905)

John Milton Hay was born in Salem, Ind., Oct. 8, 1838. His childhood and youth were spent largely in Warsaw, Ill. He attended the local schools and academies and apparently had plenty of boy's fun. He was graduated from Brown University in 1858 and began the study of law in his uncle's office, next door to the office of Abraham Lincoln in Springfield, Ill. He was admitted to the bar and became closely associated with John G. Nicolay. Hay served as secretary to President Lincoln from 1861 to Lincoln's death. This long and intimate contact gave him a rare basis for his part of the monumental *Life,* written with Nicolay and published in 1890. Hay now entered a long and useful career in national and international affairs, filling various diplomatic positions (1865–70), doing editorial work on the N. Y. *Tribune* for the next five years, and acting as Assistant Secretary of State (1878–81), ambassador to Great Britain (1897), and finally Secretary of State from 1898 till his death. His influence in international relations was distinctly felt. His contributions to poetry and the novel represent that "other self" that is observable to a noteworthy degree among American men of affairs. He died at Newburg, N. H., July 1, 1905.

Pike County Ballads and Other Pieces, 1871; *Castilian Days,* 1871; *The Breadwinners,* 1884; *Poems,* 1890; *Abraham Lincoln: a History* (with John G. Nicolay), 10 vols., 1890; *Complete Works of Abraham Lincoln,* 1894; *Addresses of John Hay,* 1907; *Letters of John Hay and Extracts from His Diary,* 1908; *A Poet in Exile* (early letters), 1910; *Complete Poetical Works* (with intro. by his son), 1916.

For life and criticism, see: *The Education of*

Henry Adams, 1918; J. B. Bishop, "A Friend-ship with John Hay," *Century Mag.*, Mar., 1906; A. S. Chapman, "The Boyhood of John Hay," *Century Mag.*, July, 1909; G. Hicks, "The Conversion of John Hay," *New Repub.*, June 10, 1931; W. D. Howells, "John Hay in Literature," *N. Am. Rev.*, Sept., 1905; Alfred Kreymborg, *Our Singing Strength*, 1929; J. B. Matthews, *Commemorative Tributes*, 1922; V. L. Parrington, *Main Currents in American Thought*, Vol. 3, 1930; Lorenzo Sear, *John Hay, Author and Statesman*, 1914; William Roscoe Thayer, *The Life and Letters of John Hay*, 1916; Sister Saint Ignatius Ward, *The Poetry of John Hay*, 1930. See also article by Alfred L. P. Dennis in *D.A.B.*, VIII, 430–436.

368. LITTLE BREECHES. Pub. in the N. Y. *Weekly Tribune* Dec. 2, 1870 (signed only with Hay's initials). "Jim Bludso" followed soon after in the same paper (Jan. 5, 1871). In March, 1871, Hay writes that he has just sold "Banty Tim" to *Harper's Weekly* for fifty dollars. In the autumn of 1871, these three, with the addition of "The Mystery of Gilgal," were published in *Pike County Ballads and Other Pieces*. In the 1890 edition of Hay's *Poems* two additional ballads were included.

369. JIM BLUDSO. In N. Y. *Weekly Tribune*, Jan. 5, 1871. Collected in *Pike County Ballads*. As evidence of the unconventional tone of these ballads, which appeared first in the N. Y. *Tribune* and later in *Every Saturday*, one may consult the scathing review in *The Southern Magazine*, 9: 504 (1871).

Rose Terry Cooke (1827–1892)

Rose Terry was born on a farm near Hart-ford, Conn., Feb. 17, 1827. Her childhood was filled with the duties of housekeeping and in-struction she received from her father in the lore of the garden and the woods. After gradu-ating from the Hartford Female Seminary at the age of sixteen, she filled three teaching positions, but the death of her sister and the consequent care of this sister's children forced her own literary aspirations to take second place. She published her first volume of poems in 1860 and therein revealed a sensitiveness to beauty but without freedom from the conven-tional forms. She also contributed to *Harper's*, the *Atlantic*, and other periodicals stories which were later collected in several volumes. New England life constituted the subject-matter which she handled best, especially in its more humdrum aspects. In 1873 she married Rollin H. Cooke, an iron manufacturer. An attack of pneumonia in 1889 made her an invalid, and she died of influenza on July 18, 1892.

Poems, 1860; *Happy Dodd; or, She Hath Done What She Could* (short stories), 1878; *Some-body's Neighbors* (short stories), 1881; *Root-Bound and Other Sketches*, 1885; *The Sphinx's Children and Other People's* (short stories), 1886; *Steadfast* (novel), 1889; *Huckleberries Gathered from New England Hills* (short stories), 1891.

For life and criticism, see: F. L. Pattee, *Development of the American Short Story*, 1923; Harriet P. Spofford, sketch in *Our Famous Women*, 1883; Frances Willard and Mary Liver-more (eds.), *American Women*, 1897. See also obituaries in Boston *Herald*, July 20, 1892; Boston *Transcript*, July 19, 1892; *Critic*, July 23, 1892.

370. TOO LATE. In *The Galaxy*, Jan., 1875. ¶382. *"Monk in Hypatia."* Philammon, hero of Charles Kingsley's novel.

Sarah Orne Jewett (1849–1909)

Sarah Orne Jewett was born at South Ber-wick, Me., Sept. 3, 1849. She received most of her preparation for her writings from long drives with her father, a physician, on his visits to country patients. Her formal schooling was obtained chiefly at Berwick Academy. In 1869 her first story was published in the *Atlantic*, but not till the publication of the "Deephaven" sketches in the same magazine, beginning in Sept., 1875, did she strike her true vein—the realistic yet delicately sympathetic description of the people of Maine and their natural en-vironment. Then followed a steady series of collections of tales, whose high worth was in time everywhere recognized. She was awarded the degree of Litt.D. by Bowdoin College in 1901. Her death occurred at South Berwick, Me., June 24, 1909.

Deephaven, 1877; *Old Friends and New*, 1879; *Country By-Ways* (dedicated to her father), 1881; *A Country Doctor* (draws a portrait of her father), 1884; *A Marsh Island* (novel), 1885; *A White Heron and Other Stories*, 1886; *The King of Folly Island and Other People*, 1888; *Strangers and Wayfarers*, 1890; *A Native of Winby and Other Tales*, 1893; *The Country of Pointed Firs*, 1896; *The Queen's Twin and Other Stories*, 1899; *The Tory Lover* (historical novel), 1901; Willa Cather (ed.), *The Best Short Stories of Sarah Orne Jewett*, 1925.

For life and criticism, see: Annie Fields (ed.), *The Letters of Sarah Orne Jewett*, 1911; Francis O. Mathiessen, *Sarah Orne Jewett*, 1929; C. M. Thompson, "The Art of Miss Jewett," *Atlantic*, XCIV, 485–497.

384. DEEPHAVEN CRONIES. In *Atlantic*, Sept., 1875. This and other sketches in peri-

odical form underwent great changes when Miss Jewett got together her materials for the volume called *Deephaven*, 1877. In the Preface to that work she said: "It has so often been asked if Deephaven may not be found on the map of New England under another name, that, to prevent any misunderstanding, I wish to say, while there is a likeness to be traced, few of the sketches are drawn from that town itself, and the characters will in almost every case be looked for there in vain."

Mark Twain
(Samuel Langhorne Clemens)
(1835–1910)

Samuel Langhorne Clemens was born in the village of Florida, Mo., Nov. 30, 1835. His father, who was of Virginia stock, expected to derive great wealth from a tract of land which he owned in Tennessee. This land, with his expectations, he left, on his death in 1847, to his wife (a woman of English descent) and a family of children of whom Samuel was the third son. The boy's childhood and early youth were passed, without regular schooling, chiefly in Hannibal, Mo., a Mississippi river town which provided the setting and the essential characters and incidents of *Tom Sawyer* and *Huckleberry Finn*. His early apprenticeship to a printer, whose trade he mastered, led to his writing for the local newspaper, and in 1853–54 he began his travels as a journeyman printer, visiting St. Louis, New York, Philadelphia, and Keokuk, Iowa. After a false start for South America in 1856 on a fortune-hunting expedition, he became apprenticed to a river pilot on the Mississippi in 1857 and served some four years at this exacting profession at the very height of the prosperity of the great steamboat days. On the outbreak of the Civil War he experienced a brief farcical adventure as a member of a volunteer company that never saw action. He then took the step that led steadily to his recognition as one of the most original of American writers: his departure, in 1861, with his brother Orion for Carson City, Nevada, where Orion was to serve as the newly appointed secretary to the territorial governor of Nevada. After crossing the plains by stage, he spent a brief time in Carson City, then tried prospecting without success, and finally spent two years as a reporter on the Virginia City *Enterprise*. His meeting with Artemus Ward and his entanglement in a duel determined his departure for California in 1864. Thrown with Bret Harte and the leading literary men of the Bay region, he contributed to the newspapers and

magazines of that district and received that schooling in which he acknowledged Harte to have been the main contributor. The publication of his story "The Jumping Frog of Calaveras County" in the N. Y. *Saturday Press*, Nov. 18, 1865, called the attention of the entire country to the distinctive humor of this writer who was henceforward to be known by his recently assumed pen-name of "Mark Twain." Preceding the appearance of his first collection of sketches in 1867, Twain received a commission to report what he might see in the Sandwich Islands for one of the California newspapers. His next venture was his sailing on the *Quaker City* to report the excursion to the Holy Land that gave him the material for *Innocents Abroad* (1867). His reputation was now made, and, following his marriage to Olivia Langdon in 1870, which brought him into contact henceforth with a more conservative group, he proceeded to exploit the new interest in the South and West with *Roughing It*, *The Gilded Age*, *Old Times on the Mississippi*, and *Tom Sawyer* (1872–76). His humorous powers continued at their best till about 1889, with *Huckleberry Finn* probably representing the height of his achievement (1884). He now began to receive the recognition of serious critics and to win such tangible tokens of esteem as the honorary A.M. degree from Yale (1888). The decade of the nineties saw Twain constantly writing and lecturing but displaying less original power. His financial ventures turned out badly, and a steadily growing darkness came over his spirit, culminating in that somber year of 1898 which saw the composition of *The Man that Corrupted Hadleyburg*, *What Is Man?* and *The Mysterious Stranger*. Though he gained in resignation, his remaining years were saddened by the death of his wife (1904) and the death of his daughter Jean (1909). He gradually slackened his pace and began in 1906 to dictate his autobiography. He prized highly the bestowal of the honorary degree of Litt.D. by Oxford University in 1907. He died at "Stormfield," his residence in Redding, Conn., the most genuinely mourned of all American men of letters.

The Adventures of Thomas Jefferson Snodgrass, 1856; *The Celebrated Jumping Frog of Calaveras County, and Other Sketches*, 1867; *The Innocents Abroad*, 1869; *Roughing It*, 1872; *The Gilded Age* (with Charles Dudley Warner), 1873; "Old Times on the Mississippi," *Atlantic*, 1875; *The Adventures of Tom Sawyer*, 1876; *A Tramp Abroad*, 1880; *Life on the Mississippi* (book form of "Old Times on the Mississippi"), 1882; *The Prince and the Pauper*, 1882; *The*

Adventures of Huckleberry Finn, 1884; *A Connecticut Yankee in King Arthur's Court*, 1889; *The American Claimant*, 1892; *Pudd'nhead Wilson*, 1894; *Tom Sawyer Abroad*, 1894; *Personal Recollections of Joan of Arc*, 1896; *Following the Equator*, 1897; *The Man that Corrupted Hadleyburg*, 1900; *What Is Man?* (1906); *Christian Science*, 1907; *Captain Stormfield's Visit to Heaven*, 1909; *The Writings of Mark Twain*, 25 vols., 1910; *The Mysterious Stranger*, 1916; *The Mysterious Stranger, What Is Man, and Other Essays*, 1917; *Mark Twain's Letters*, 1917; *Mark Twain's Autobiography*, 1924.

For life and criticism, see: Minnie M. Brashear, "Mark Twain Juvenilia," *Am. Lit.*, March, 1930; Van Wyck Brooks, *The Ordeal of Mark Twain*, 1920; Clara Clemens, *My Father: Mark Twain*, 1931; same, "Recollections of Mark Twain," *N. Am. Rev.*, Nov. and Dec., 1930, and Jan., 1931; William R. Gillis, *Gold Rush Days with Mark Twain*, 1930; Bernard De Voto, *Mark Twain's America*, 1932; Mildred Howells (ed.), *William Dean Howells, Life in Letters*, 1928; William Dean Howells, *My Mark Twain*, 1910; Mary Lawton, *A Life-Time with Mark Twain*, 1925; F. W. Lorch, "Mark Twain in Iowa," *Iowa Jour. Hist. and Polit.*, XXVII, 408–456 (1929); Edwin Mims, "Mark Twain: Humorist and Pessimist, *Meth. Rev.*, April, 1913; Albert Bigelow Paine, *Mark Twain: A Biography*, 1912 (3 vols.); same, intro. to *Mark Twain's Autobiography*, 1924; same, *Mark Twain's Letters*, 1917; same, *A Short Life of Mark Twain*, 1920; Friedrich Schönemann, *Mark Twain als literarische Persönlichkeit*, 1925; Stuart P. Sherman, "Mark Twain," *CHAL*, III, 1 ff.

For bibliography, see: *CHAL*, IV, 635–639.

401. THE CELEBRATED JUMPING FROG. In N. Y. *Sat. Press*, Nov. 18, 1865.

406. VENICE. In *Innocents Abroad*, which appeared in letters to the N. Y. *Tribune*, in 1867, and in book form, 1869. ¶410. *"Foscari."* Francesca (d. 1457), whose story was told by Byron in *The Two Foscari*.

414. BUCK FANSHAW'S FUNERAL. From *Roughing It*, 1872.

420. COLONEL SELLERS ENTERTAINS. . . . From *The Gilded Age*, 1873, done in collaboration with Charles Dudley Warner (1829–1900) journalist, and Hartford neighbor. Col. Sellers: "My mother's favorite cousin, James Lampton, who figures in *The Gilded Age*, as Colonel Sellers . . ." (*Mark Twain's Autobiography*).

425. A "CUB" PILOT'S EXPERIENCE. From *Old Times on the Mississippi*, in *Atlantic*, Jan.–June, and Aug., 1875; pub. with an account

of a trip on the river in 1882, as *Life on the Mississippi*, 1883, when some changes in text were made, and the chapter headings were altered. ¶426. *"Mr. B——."* Horace Bixby. ¶433. *"M-a-r-k Twain."* Leadsman's cry for two fathoms. Before Twain adopted this as a pseudonym it had been used by a writer in the New Orleans *Picayune*.

434. WE MISS CAIRO and (440) HIS LORDSHIP AND HIS GRACE are from *Huckleberry Finn*. See *Letters of Richard Watson Gilder*, 1916, p. 399, in regard to the editing of this story for *Century*.

446. HUMAN SHEEP. From *The Mysterious Stranger*, 1916, which had been serialized in *Harper's*, May–Nov., 1916.

449. ON BIOGRAPHY AND CRITICISM. From *Mark Twain's Autobiography*, 1924. Chapters from this book had appeared in the *N. Am. Rev.*, Sept., 1906–Dec., 1909.

William Dean Howells (*1837–1920*)

William Dean Howells was born at Martin's Ferry, Ohio, March 1, 1837. The son of a printer, who was largely of Welsh extraction, and of a mother of Irish and German stock, he began setting type at the age of nine. The father had moved to Hamilton, Ohio, in 1840, and there, without high school or college education, the boy began his training as a printer, reporter, and editor, covering a wide range of reading and obtaining a thorough drill in good English. In 1860 he wrote a campaign life of Lincoln and published (with John J. Piatt) a volume of poems which had no success. In the same year he went to New England for his memorable meeting with Lowell and the literati of New England that introduced him into the charmed society that he was henceforth to enjoy for the remainder of his life. After filling a consulship in Venice (1861–65), he served on the staff of the N. Y. *Nation* and the *Atlantic Monthly*, becoming editor of the latter in 1871. During the next ten years, those of his editorship of the *Atlantic* and his residence in Cambridge, he wrote a number of novels and comedies of manners that reflected his double interest in the West of his rearing and the East of his adoption. In 1888 he went to New York City, which he made his home till his death. As conductor of "The Editor's Study" in *Harper's Magazine* from 1886 to 1891 he waged a battle on behalf of realism which created widespread controversy. In 1900 "The Easy Chair" department of *Harper's* was revived (with Howells in the "chair") and became his medium for a vital review of con-

temporary life and letters. In 1912 his 75th
anniversary was celebrated with a distinctive
dinner, and in 1915 he was awarded the gold
medal of the National Institute of Arts and
Letters for achievement in fiction. At his
death in New York City, May 11, 1920, he
had long been recognized as the dean of American letters and the "foremost representative of
the realistic school of indigenous American
fiction."

Poems of Two Friends (with J. J. Piatt),
1860; *Venetian Life*, 1866; *Suburban Sketches*,
1871; *Their Wedding Journey*, 1872; *A Chance
Acquaintance*, 1873; *Poems*, 1873; "Private
Theatricals," *Atlantic*, Nov., 1875–May, 1876,
(issued as *Mrs. Farrell*, 1921); *A Counterfeit
Presentment* (literary comedy), 1877; *The Lady
of the Aroostook*, 1879; *A Modern Instance*, 1882;
The Rise of Silas Lapham, 1885; *Indian Summer*, 1886; *Modern Italian Poets*, 1887; *A
Hazard of New Fortunes*, 1890; *A Boy's Town*,
1890; *Criticism and Fiction*, 1891; *A Letter of
Introduction* (farce), 1892; *An Imperative Duty*,
1893; *The Unexpected Guests* (farce), 1893; *A
Traveler from Altruria*, 1894; *My Literary Passions*, 1895; *Stops of Various Quills* (verse),
1895; *The Landlord at Lion's Head*, 1897;
Heroines of Fiction, 1901; *Literary Friends and
Acquaintance*, 1900; *The Kentons*, 1902; *Through
the Eye of the Needle*, 1907; *My Mark Twain*,
1910; *New Leaf Mills; a Chronicle*, 1913; *The
Leatherwood God*, 1916; *Years of My Youth*,
1916; editor, *The Great Modern American
Stories*, 1920; *Years of My Middle Life* (unfinished at death).

For life and criticism, see: *CHAL*, III, 77–85;
Delmar G. Cooke, *William Dean Howells*,
1922; H. Edwards, "Howells and the Con-
troversy over Realism in American Fiction,"
Amer. Lit., November, 1931; O. W. Firkins,
William Dean Howells, 1924; H. T. and M.
Follett, *Some Modern Novelists*, 1919; Hamlin
Garland, "Meetings with Howells," *Bookman*,
March, 1917; same, in *American Writers on
American Literature*, 1931; C. H. Grattan,
"Howells: Ten Years After," *Am. Mercury*,
May, 1930; Alexander Harvey, *William Dean
Howells*, 1917; Mildred Howells (ed.), *William
Dean Howells; Life in Letters*, 1928; William
Dean Howells, *My Year in a Log Cabin*, 1893;
Ludwig Lewisohn, *Expression in America*, 1932;
John Macy, *The Spirit of American Literature*,
1913; J. M. Robertson, *Essays towards a Critical
Method*, 1889; H. C. Vedder, *American Writers*,
1894. See also various works of Howells con-
taining autobiographic material, including *New
Leaf Mills*, 1913.

For bibliography, see: *CHAL*, IV, 663–666.

454. AN INTERVIEW. Ch. I of *The Rise of
Silas Lapham*, 1885. Bartley Hubbard, the
journalist, was one of the chief characters in
the novel, *A Modern Instance*, 1881.

467. A MUSICALE. Pt. III, Ch. IX of *A
Hazard of New Fortunes*, 1890.

476. THE UNEXPECTED GUESTS. Pub. in
Harper's "Black and White Series," 1893.

491. ON DECENCY. In *Criticism and Fiction*, 1891.

495. TOURGUENIEF, AUERBACH, and (497)
TOLSTOI are the concluding chapters of *My
Literary Passions*. For Tolstoi's opinion of
Howells, see *Life in Letters*, II, 322.

496. MY FIRST VISIT TO NEW ENGLAND.
In *Literary Friends and Acquaintance*, 1900.
¶501. "*Scholar factories.*" See Lowell's "An
Indian-Summer Reverie." ¶501. "*Washington
Elm.*" See Lowell's "Under the Old Elm."
¶503. "*Spoke to me of Heine.*" Lowell earlier
had detected Howell's passion for Heine. ¶503.
"*James Howel.*" Voluminous English writer
(1594–1666).

Henry James, Jr. (1843–1916)

Henry James, Jr., was born in New York
City Apr. 15, 1843. His father, Henry James,
Sr., was a philosopher-clergyman of strong
Swedenborgian leanings. The novelist's elder
brother was William James, the psychologist.
Thus a strong intellectual atmosphere pervaded
the James household, and the father's inheritance of a fortune enabled him to satisfy his
desire that his sons should have a life of speculation and leisure. The education of the future
novelist was a distinctly cosmopolitan one, involving direct or indirect training in such widely
separated places as Geneva, Bonn, Newport,
Paris, Boulogne, Boston, and Cambridge.
Temperament and training combined to encourage in James a growing detachment from
life itself and the increasing importance of his
assumed rôle of spectator. Particularly was
the refined onlooker drawn more and more
away from materialistic America and more
closely to Europe. Beginning his writing with
critical articles for the *Nation* and stories for
the *Atlantic* and the *Galaxy* (1865–69), he
published in 1871 "A Passionate Pilgrim," the
first clear revelation of the call to Europe.
James tried living in Paris but found that
he really could not fit there. So in 1876 he
turned to London, which he became more and
more sure was his real home. In a very real
sense the remainder of James's life is made up
of successive periods that reflect his changing
reactions to this fact of expatriation. He no

doubt paid a distinct penalty for the self-exile, chiefly in his overconsciousness of the fact. But the assumption that James fled to Europe because he could not write in America might better be replaced with the assumption that he went to Europe because he could write better there than he could in America. The novelist's first reaction is seen in the novels written from 1876 to 1881 (from *The American* to *The Portrait of a Lady*), presenting the problem of the American confronted by a more complex civilization. During the next ten years or so James surrendered himself to the appeal of British culture and lost touch with America. Then followed, chiefly in the nineties, an attempt to regain the favor that he had lost by trying other forms of writing: plays, essays, short stories. But his American audience seemed really lost, and he resigned himself to the quiet practice of his art, which flowered in the three great novels that mark the peak of his art: *The Wings of the Dove*, *The Ambassadors*, and *The Golden Bowl*. Homesickness for America was appeased in 1904–05 by an extensive tour of the United States, which ended in his flight from the immensity of American civilization. He spent many of his latter days in careful revision of his works and prefaces for the collected edition published in 1907–17 and in trying once more varied types of work that he had before attempted with indifferent success. The World War stopped his work as an artist. Convinced that the German attack was a menace to our entire civilization, he protested against the neutrality of the United States, finally sealing his protest by becoming a British subject in 1915. Before he could see the actual entrance of his native land into the War, he died in London Feb. 28, 1916.

"A Passionate Pilgrim," *Atlantic*, 1871; *Roderick Hudson*, 1876; *The American*, 1877; *The Europeans*, 1878; *French Poets and Novelists*, 1878; *Daisy Miller*, 1879; *Hawthorne*, 1879; *An International Episode*, 1879; *The Madonna of the Future* (tales), 1879; *The Portrait of a Lady*, 1881; *Washington Square*, 1881; *Novels and Tales*, 1883; *The Author of Beltraffio* (tales), 1885; *The Bostonians*, 1886; *The Princess Casamassima*, 1886; *Partial Portraits* (essays), 1888; *The Tragic Muse*, 1890; *The Lesson of the Master and Other Stories*, 1892; *The Private Life* (tales), 1893; *The Real Thing and Other Tales*, 1893; *Theatricals*, 1894–95; *Termination* (tales), 1895; *Embarrassments* (tales), 1896; *The Spoils of Poynton*, 1897; *What Maisie Knew*, 1897; *The Awkward Age*, 1899; *The Soft Side* (tales), 1900; *The Wings of the Dove*, 1902; *The Ambassadors*, 1903; *The Better Sort* (tales),

1903; *The Golden Bowl*, 1904; *The American Scene*, 1907; *The Altar of the Dead* (tales), 1909; *The Finer Grain* (tales), 1910; *The Ivory Tower*, 1917; *The Middle Years* (fragment), 1917; *Novels and Tales*, 26 vols. (New York ed.), 1907–17; *Novels and Tales* (Uniform ed.), 1915–16.

For life and criticism, see: Joseph W. Beach, *The Method of Henry James*, 1918; Van Wyck Brooks, *The Pilgrimage of Henry James*, 1925; Elisabeth L. Cary, *The Novels of Henry James*, 1905; Sidney Colvin, *Memories and Notes of Persons and Places*, 1921; Edgar Pelham, *Henry James: Man and Author*, 1927; Marie-Reine Garnier, *Henry James et la France*, 1927; C. Hartley Grattan, *The Three James*, 1932; *William Dean Howells: Life in Letters*, 1928; Ford Madox Hueffer, *Henry James: a Critical Study*, 1915; H. L. Hughes, *Theory and Practice in Henry James*, 1926; *The Letters of Henry James*, 1920; *Letters to A. C. Benson and Auguste Monod*, 1930; *The Letters of William James*, 1920; Cornelia P. Kelley, *The Early Development of Henry James*, 1930; Desmond McCarthy, "The World of Henry James," *Living Age*, January, 1931; John Macy, *The Spirit of American Literature*, 1913; *The Letters of Charles Eliot Norton*, 1913; Robert Herrick, in *American Writers on American Literature*, 1931; Morris Roberts, *Henry James's Criticism*, 1928; *The Letters of Robert Louis Stevenson*, 1899; *Theatre and Friendship: Letters from Henry James to Elizabeth Robins*, 1932; H. M. Walbrook, "The Novels of Henry James," *Fort. Rev.*, May, 1930; Rebecca West, *Henry James*, 1916. See also three autobiographic works: *The Middle Years* (1917), *Notes of a Son and Brother* (1914), and *A Small Boy and Others* (1913). (There is no extended or really authoritative biography of James.)

For bibliography, see: *CHAL*, IV, 671–675; LeRoy Phillips, *A Bibliography of the Writings of Henry James*, 1930.

505. THE LITTLE COPYIST. In *The American* which did not appear in book form until 1877, a year after it started as a serial in the *Atlantic* (June, 1876–May, 1877). Only slight changes were made at this time, but when James revised his works for the New York edition he made drastic changes in the diction of this first chapter. This selection was in the June number of the magazine. ¶508. *"Pas beaucoup?"*: Isn't it too much? ¶508. *"Comprenez?"*: Understand? ¶508. *"Bien sûr!"*: Certainly! ¶510. *"Tres-superieure!"*: Exceptional. ¶510. *"Pas de raisons!"*: No excuses!

512. THE LESSON OF THE MASTER. Appeared originally in the *Universal Review* (July

16, 1888, and Aug. 15, 1888). Reprinted in *The Lesson of the Master and Other Stories*, 1892. ¶516. *"Ils' attache . . ."*: He dogs her steps. ¶522. *"À fleur de peau"*: Neatly skinned (slang). ¶530. *"Cela s'est . . ."*: It happened like that? ¶532. *"Père de famille"*: Father of a family. ¶533. *"Mornes"*: sad. ¶537. *"Commen donc?"*: What then? ¶543. *"Carton-pierre"*: Marbled pasteboard. ¶543. *"Lincrusta-Walton."* An embossed wall covering, named from its inventor, Frederick Walton.

556. THE ART OF FICTION. Appeared originally in *Longman's Mag.*, Sept., 1884, as a reply to a lecture, similarly entitled, by Walter Besant. Both Besant's lecture and James's reply were published together in book form in 1885. James's essay then was included in *Partial Portraits*, 1888. ¶556. *"Discutable"*: debatable. ¶561. *"Rapprochement"*: Comparison. ¶563. *"Pasteur"*: pastor. ¶572. *"Émile Zola"*: French novelist (1840–1902), father of Naturalism.

John Lothrop Motley (1814–1877)

John Lothrop Motley was born at Dorchester (now part of Boston), Mass., Apr. 15, 1814. Graduating at Harvard in 1831, he studied at Göttingen and Berlin, and after a period of European travel returned to America in 1834 to continue the study of law. After the publication of an unsuccessful novel in 1839, he entered the diplomatic service in 1841 as secretary of the legation in Russia. He resigned this position, however, after three months and again returned to America to continue definitely a literary career. He published various essays of historical and critical character in the *North American Review* and a second novel in 1849. But his true strength was shown on the publication of *The Rise of the Dutch Republic*, upon which he spent five years of research in various parts of Europe. The book was very successful and Motley followed it with *The United Netherlands* four years later. In 1861 he again entered the diplomatic service as minister to Austria, holding this position till 1867. After a brief term as minister to Great Britain in 1867, Motley visited Holland and thereafter made his residence in England, where the ill-health and death of his wife interrupted his literary work. He died at Frampton Court near Dorchester, England, May 29, 1877. "The merits of Motley as an historian are undeniably great. He has told the story of a stirring period in the history of the world with full attention to the character of the actors and the vivid details of the action, showing as well a most commendable thoroughness in research" (Ency. Brit.).

Morton's Hope (novel), 1839; *Merry Mount, A Romance of the Massachusetts Colony*, 1849; *The Rise of the Dutch Republic*, 1856; *The History of the United Netherlands*, 1860–68; *Life and Death of John Barneveld*, 1874; *Writings* (Netherlands Ed.), 1900; *Historical Works*, 1903–04.

For life and criticism, see: J. S. Bassett, *The Middle Group of American Historians*, 1917; G. W. Curtis (ed.), *Correspondence of John Lothrop Motley*, 2 vols., 1889; M. D. Conway, biog. intro. to *The Rise of the Dutch Republic*, 1896; O. W. Holmes, *John Lothrop Motley, a Memoir*, 1879; Mrs. Susan St. John Mildmay (ed.), *John Lothrop Motley and His Family: Further Letters and Records*, 1910.

573. THE SPANISH ARMADA. From *The History of the United Netherlands*, 1860–68. For understanding the difficulties attendant to the writing of this great work, see: *Correspondence*, I, 207, 317, 318, 329, 348, 355, 363; II, 118, 253, 257.

John Fiske (1842–1901)

John Fiske was born March 30, 1842, at Hartford, Conn. His father was of Quaker ancestry, and his mother of Puritan stock. He was baptised "Edmund Fisk Green," but in 1855 the name was changed by an act of the legislature to "John Fisk," and the "e" was added five years later without legal sanction. As a youth he was extremely precocious, especially in languages. After an education in private schools and under tutors, he entered Harvard, graduating in 1863. He chose the legal profession, but after an unsuccessful attempt at practice changed to writing as a career. From 1869 to 1872 he lectured at Harvard. Then followed a brief experience in library work and the publication in 1872 of his first important volume, *Myths and Myth-Makers*. After a year abroad, embracing meetings with Spencer, Darwin, Huxley, and other scientists, he published *Outlines of Cosmic Philosophy* (1874). His interest in science and philosophy shifted in 1885 to an interest in American history. He was the most popular lecturer on history that America has known, and his writings in this field were numerous and successful. His later years were spent as professor of American history at Washington University, St. Louis. His death from overwork occurred July 4, 1901, after the bestowal of honorary degrees at Pennsylvania and Harvard had testified to the general esteem in which he was held. "Fiske was one of the most important intellectual influences in America in the last quarter of the nineteenth century" (James T. Adams). He was a brilliant defender of evolution and at his best as a popularizer of the conclusions reached by others. But he was not profound in science, history, or philosophy.

Tobacco and Alcohol, 1869; *Myths and Myth-Makers,* 1872; *History of English Literature,* abridged from Taine, 1872; *The Outlines of Cosmic Philosophy,* 1874; *The Unseen World,* 1876; *Darwinism and Other Essays,* 1879; *The Destiny of Man,* etc., 1884; *American Political Ideals,* etc., 1885; *The Critical Period of American History, 1783–89,* 1888; *The Beginnings of New England,* 1889; *The American Revolution,* 1891; *The Discovery of America,* 1892; *Edward Livingston Youmans, Interpreter of Science for the People,* 1894; *Dutch and Quaker Colonies,* 1899; *The Origin of Evil,* 1899; *Life Everlasting,* 1901; *Essays, Historical and Literary.* 1902; *New France and New England,* 1902; *How the United States Became a Nation,* 1904.

For life and criticism, see: Lyman Abbott, "John Fiske, Evolutionist" in *Silhouettes of My Contemporaries,* 1921; G. L. Beer, *Critic,* Aug., 1901; J. S. Clark, *The Life and Letters of John Fiske,* 1917; A. McF. Davis, "John Fiske," *Proc. Am. Acad. Arts and Sciences,* Aug., 1902; W. D. Howells, "John Fiske," *Harper's Weekly,* July 20, 1901; T. S. Perry, *John Fiske,* 1906; F. C. Pierce, *Fiske and the Fisk Family,* 1896; Josiah Royce, "John Fiske," *Unpop. Rev.,* July, Sept., 1918; J. B. Sanders, "John Fiske," *Miss. Valley Hist. Rev.,* Sept., 1930; Mrs. S. Van Rensselaer, "Mr. Fiske and the History of New York," *N. Am. Rev.,* July, 1901.

580. NATURAL SELECTION. From *Outlines of Cosmic Philosophy,* 1874. The writings of Fiske should be compared with those of Herbert Spencer, the British philosopher. ¶580. "*Conversations of Goethe. . . .*" Contain the *obiter dicta* of the great German poet, whom Fiske admired second only to Spencer. ¶580. "*Cuvier . . . Saint-Hilaire.*" Baron Georges L. C. F. D. Cuvier (1769–1832) who quarrelled with Geoffroy Saint-Hilaire (1772–1844) over fossil remains. ¶581. "*Comte.*" Auguste (1798–1857), French philosopher. ¶581. "*Lyell . . . Hooker.*" Sir Charles Lyell (1797–1875), Eng. geologist, and Sir William Hooker (1785–1865), Eng. botanist. ¶582. "*Haeckel.*" Ernst H., German biologist (1834–1919). ¶582. "*Lamarck.*" Jean B. P. A. de M. de, Fr. zoölogist (1744–1829). ¶586. "*Gravelotte.*" A battle of the Franco-Prussian War, 1870.

John Burroughs (*1837–1921*)

John Burroughs, the seventh of ten children and a descendant of early 17th century settlers in New England, was born on a farm near Roxbury, N. Y. The scenery of his native hills made a profound impression on the boy, whose routine schooling was limited. After some experience at study and teaching at the Ashland Collegiate Institute, he began writing essays. In the later fifties he read Emerson, who "got into his blood" and showed his influence in Burroughs' first published work of importance, his essay on "Expression." He had married in 1857 and taken up teaching, but his interest was gradually turned toward the study of science and nature. From 1863 to 1873 he held a position in the Treasury Dept. at Washington and there made his important acquaintance with Walt Whitman, with whom he collaborated in the work entitled *Notes on Walt Whitman,* etc. (1867). *Wake-Robin* (1871) was his first important nature book, to be followed by many others. In 1873 he built "Riverby," 80 miles from New York City on the Hudson, and in 1895 built "Slabsides" in the hills, a mile from his home. In 1908 he began spending his summers at "Woodchuck Lodge," on the old home farm near Roxbury, which was the object of pilgrimage by many visitors. During his later years he spent much of his time in trips to California, Hawaii, Yellowstone, etc. He died en route from California to the East, Mar. 30, 1921. His interests had progressed from Emersonianism, through the study of external nature, followed by a period of careful scientific analysis, to a philosophical period, which saw the strong influence of Bergson until the post-war years in which Burroughs came to accept the rule of the intellect. But his contribution to American literature is no doubt through the nature essay, in which he combined accuracy of observation with poetic appreciation and interpretation.

"Expression," *Atlantic,* Nov., 1860; *Notes on Walt Whitman as Poet and Person,* 1867; *Wake-Robin,* 1871; *Winter Sunshine,* 1875; *Birds and Poets,* 1877; *Locusts and Wild Honey,* 1879; *Fresh Fields,* 1885; *Whitman, a Study,* 1896; *The Light of Day,* 1900; *Far and Near,* 1904; *Leaf and Tendril,* 1908; *Time and Change,* 1912; *The Summit of the Years,* 1913; *Accepting the Universe,* 1920; *The Last Harvest,* 1922; *Collected Works,* 12 vols., 1922.

For life and criticism, see: Clara Barrus (ed.), *The Heart of Burroughs' Journals,* 1928; same, *John Burroughs, Boy and Man,* 1920; same, *The Life and Letters of John Burroughs,* 1925;

same, *Our Friend, John Burroughs*, 1914; same, *Whitman and Burroughs, Comrades*, 1931; Julian Burroughs, "My Father," (concluding chapter to *My Boyhood*, 1922); John Burroughs, *My Boyhood: an Autobiography*, 1922; Norman Foerster, *Nature in American Literature*, 1923; Philip M. Hicks, *The Development of the Natural History Essay in American Literature*, 1924; *John Burroughs and Ludella Peck* (letters), 1925; Clifton Johnson, *John Burroughs Talks: His Reminiscences and Comments*, 1922; Horace Traubel, *With Walt Whitman in Camden*, 1906–14.

586. BIRDS'-NESTS. In *Atlantic*, June, 1869; collected in *Wake-Robin*, 1871.

John Muir (1838–1914)

John Muir was born in Dunbar, Scotland, Apr. 21, 1838. At the age of eleven he migrated with his family to America, where the family settled in Wisconsin. The youth spent four years at the University of Wisconsin, where he displayed his independence and his inventiveness. He then started on "a glorious botanical and geological excursion," which he later said had lasted fifty years and was not yet completed. He visited Florida and Cuba and was then deflected from a projected trip to South America, going instead to California, where he arrived in 1868. He was henceforward chiefly associated with the exploration of the mountains and glaciers of the West. It was largely owing to his influence that Yosemite and other national parks were established. After his marriage in 1877, he devoted himself to horticulture for a number of years. His later years were spent in getting together for publication the great mass of material which he had collected. He had never cared for money nor for reputation. He was a true scientist. His death occurred in Los Angeles, Calif., Dec. 24, 1914.

"Studies in the Sierras," *Scribner's Monthly*, 1878; *The Mountains of California*, 1894; *Our National Parks*, 1901; *My First Summer in the Sierras*, 1911; *Story of My Boyhood and Youth*, 1913; *A Thousand-Mile Walk to the Gulf*, 1916; *The Cruise of the Corwin*, 1917; *Steep Trails*, 1918; *Writings*, (including *Life and Letters of John Muir*, by W. F. Badé), 1916–24.

For life and criticism, see: W. F. Badé, *Life and Letters of John Muir* (in *Writings*, 1916–24); S. H. Young, *Alaska Days with John Muir*, 1915.

596. THE SIERRA NEVADA. First pub. in a series of studies entitled "Studies in the Sierras," contributed to *Scribner's Monthly*, 1878; collected in *The Mountains of California*, 1894.

Irwin Russell (1853–1879)

Irwin Russell was born at Port Gibson, Miss., June 3, 1853. In 1869 he graduated at the University of St. Louis, studied law, and was admitted to the bar at the unusual age of 19. In 1876 he temporarily abandoned the law for literature, writing for the local newspapers. His dialect verse soon gained him a reputation, and in the last year of his life he went to New York City. But he soon returned to New Orleans, where he succumbed to pneumonia Dec. 23, 1879. He was a writer of great promise who did little with his profession. He shares with Sidney and Clifford Lanier the honor of being the pioneer writer of negro dialect verse.

Poems, 1888 (enlarged editions, 1905, 1917).

For life and criticism, see: W. M. Baskervill, *Southern Writers*, 1897; Maurice Garland Fulton, biog. sketch in 1917 edition of *Poems;* Joel Chandler Harris, intro. to edition of 1888; J. S. Kendall, "Irwin Russell in New Orleans," *La. Hist. Quar.*, July, 1931.

For bibliography, see: *Library of Southern Literature*, Vol. 14.

605. NEBUCHADNEZZAR. In *Scribner's*, June, 1876.

605. MAHSR JOHN. In *Scribner's*, May, 1877.

George Washington Cable (1844–1925)

George Washington Cable, whose father was a member of a slave-holding family of Virginia and whose mother was a strict New England Puritan, was born in New Orleans Oct. 12, 1844. The early death of his father made George (the eldest son) the mother's chief support for several years. Having been sent out of the Union lines in 1863 for refusing to take the oath of allegiance, he enlisted with the Mississippi Cavalry and served to the end of the War. After the close of the War, he began reporting for the New Orleans *Picayune* (1869) and started to work on the city archives. Edward King of *Scribner's Monthly* became interested, when visiting New Orleans, in the possibilities of the material which Cable had collected, inducing him to send some papers to *Scribner's*. The first of these to appear was " 'Sieur George" (Oct., 1873), to be followed by several others, a collection of which was published in 1879 as *Old Creole Days*. This book won immediate recognition, and he followed it in 1880 with *The Grandissimes* and other historical romances In 1885 he removed to Northampton, Mass., partly to be nearer his publishers but also to escape the resentment of the South at what it considered an unfair portrayal of the Creole. Cable spent much of his time in the North in lecturing and promoting various social and philanthropic causes. He returned in 1899 to the writing of romances, but he could not recapture the old charm. He died Jan. 31, 1925.

" 'Sieur George," *Scribner's Monthly*, Oct., 1873; *Old Creole Days*, 1879; *The Grandissimes*, 1880; *Madame Delphine*, 1881; *The Creoles of Louisiana*, 1884; *Dr. Sevier*, 1885; *The Silent South*, 1885; *Bonaventure*, 1888; *The Negro Question*, 1888; *The Busy Man's Bible*, etc., 1893; *Strong Hearts*, 1899; *The Cavalier*, 1901; *Bylow Hill*, 1902; *Kincaid's Battery*, 1908; *Posson Jone and Père Raphael*, 1909; *The Amateur Garden*, 1914; *Gideon's Band*, 1914; *Lovers of Louisiana*, 1918.

For life and criticism, see: W. M. Baskervill, *Southern Writers*, 1897; Lucy L. Cable Bikle, *George W. Cable, His Life and Letters*, 1928; M. Bloom, "G. W. Cable: a New Englander of the South," *Bookman*, June, 1931; F. W. Halsey, *American Authors and Their Homes*, 1901; E. F. Harkins, *Famous Authors*, 1906; Joseph Pennell, *Adventures of an Illustrator*, 1925; George S. Wykoff, "The Cable Family in Indiana," *Am. Lit.*, May, 1929.

606. BELLES DEMOISELLES PLANTATION. In *Scribner's Monthly*, Apr., 1874; collected *Old Creole Days*, 1879; reprinted *Century*, June, 1913. ¶610. *"Comm-e-n-t?"*: What? ¶610. *"Qu'est-ce-que . . . !"*: What's that! ¶611. *"C'est vrai, oui!"*: It's true, yes!

Lafcadio Hearn (1850-1904)

Lafcadio Hearn was born in Leucadia (pronounced Lef-cā'di-a), one of the Greek Ionian islands. His father, Charles Hearn, was a surgeon-major, of mixed Irish, English, and Gypsy extraction, who was stationed in Leucadia during the British occupation. His mother, Rosa Tessima, was a Greek girl who was also part Arab and Moorish. Left with an aunt in Dublin at the age of seven, the boy suffered the loss of one eye in 1863 which resulted in both physical and psychological abnormalities. Following his attendance at St. Cuthbert's College, England, he went to America in 1869 to make his own way. Entering the field of journalism, he worked for a time on the Cincinnati *Enquirer* and the Cincinnati *Commercial* and was then (1877) given an editorial position on the *Times Democrat* in New Orleans, with which city he was associated for the next ten years. He spent two years in

the French West Indies and in 1891 was sent by Harper and Brothers to Japan to act as correspondent. But, severing this connection soon, he settled in a small town in Japan as a teacher, married a Japanese girl, Setsuko Koizumi, and adopted Japanese dress. In 1893 he became a Japanese citizen and the following year joined the staff of the Imperial University at Tokio, remaining there till 1903 Four volumes of his lectures, taken from verbatim transcripts by students, revealed the "splendid informative criticism" bestowed upon his classes. An invitation, later withdrawn, to deliver a series of lectures at Cornell University resulted in *Japan: An Attempt at Interpretation* published in the year of his death, which occurred, as the result of a heart attack, in Tokio Sept. 26, 1904. Though Hearn displayed many defects, such as prejudice and a lack of knowledge of human nature, he won a place in the very front rank of the world's "prose poets," unexcelled among writers in English prose for beauty, exotic lyricism, and careful polish.

One of Cleopatra's Nights (trans. of six of Gautier's stories), 1882; *Stray Leaves from Strange Literatures*, 1884; *Gombo Zhèbes* (proverbs in Louisiana French patois), 1885; *La Cuisine Créole*, 1885; *Some Chinese Ghosts*, 1887 *Chita* (short novel), 1887; *Two Years in the French West Indies*, 1890; *Youma*, 1890; *Karma* 1889; *Glimpses of Unfamiliar Japan*, 1894 *Out of the East*, 1895; *Kokoro*, 1896; *Gleanings in Buddha Fields*, 1897; *Exotics and Retrospections*, 1898; *In Ghostly Japan*, 1899; *Shadowings* 1900; *A Japanese Miscellany*, 1901; *Kotto*, 1902 *Japanese Fairy Tales*, 1903; *Kwaidan*, 1903 *Japan: An Attempt at Interpretation*, 1904; *Fantastics and Other Fancies*, 1914; *The Writings of Lafcadio Hearn* (Koizumi ed.), 1922; *An American Miscellany*, 1924; *Creole Sketches*, 1924. *Occidental Gleanings*, 1925.

For life and criticism, see: E. C. Beck, "Letters of Lafcadio Hearn to His Brother," *Am. Lit.*, May, 1932; Elizabeth Bisland, *The Life and Letters of Lafcadio Hearn*, 1906; same *The Japanese Letters of Lafcadio Hearn*, 1910. G. M. Gould, *Concerning Lafcadio Hearn* (with bibliog. by Laura Stedman), 1908; N. H Kennard, *Lafcadio Hearn*, 1911; Oscar Lewis, *Hearn and His Biographers: the Record of a Literary Controversy*, 1930; P. E. More, *Shelburne Essays*, 2nd series, 1905; Yone Noguchi, *Lafcadio Hearn in Japan*, 1911; Albert Mordell, introductions to *An American Miscellany* and *Occidental Gleanings;* Joseph de Smet, *Lafcadio Hearn: l'homme et l'œuvre*, 1911; Jean Temple, *Blue Ghost: a Study of Lafcadio Hearn*, 1931; Edward Thomas, *Lafcadio Hearn*, 1912; E. L.

Tinker, *Lafcadio Hearn's American Days*, 1924; Henry Watkin, *Letters from the Raven*, 1907. See also the review of *Blue Ghost* by R. M. Lawless in *Am. Lit.*, May, 1931.

618. THE GLAMOUR OF NEW ORLEANS, (619) A CREOLE TYPE, and (621) CHAR-COAL are all from *Creole Sketches*, 1924; these pieces originally appeared in New Orleans newspapers in 1878, 1879, and 1880. ¶621. *"Tonnerre de Dieu!"*: Thunder of God! ¶621. *Vingt-cinq"*: Twenty-five.

622. STRANGENESS AND CHARM. Ch. II of *Japan: An Attempt at Interpretation*, 1904. This book was prepared as the result of an invitation, later retracted, to lecture on the Orient at Cornell University.

Charles Egbert Craddock (Mary Noailles Murfree) (1850–1922)

Mary Noailles Murfree, the daughter of a lawyer, was born near Murfreesboro, Tenn., Jan. 24, 1850. Crippled in childhood by paralysis, she was driven to extensive reading and writing for her entertainment. She attended school in Nashville and Philadelphia, and her sojourns in Nashville (1856–73) and St. Louis (1873–82) provided metropolitan associations that balanced her visits to the mountains of eastern Tennessee, where she obtained her knowledge of primitive people that served as the basis for her stories. She wrote very early, under the pen-name of Charles Egbert Craddock, without success. But her first contribution to the *Atlantic Monthly* in 1878 brought her recognition, though not till the publication of her first volume in 1884 was her identity known even to the editors of the *Atlantic*. She followed *In the Tennessee Mountains* with numerous novels and collections of short stories, but her later works proved distinctly inferior to those written at the height of the interest in local color. She died at Murfreesboro, Tenn., July 31, 1922.

"The Dancin' Party at Harrison's Cove," *Atlantic*, May, 1878; *In the Tennessee Mountains*, 1884; *Down the Ravine*, 1885; *The Prophet of the Great Smoky Mountains*, 1885; *The Story of Keedon Bluffs* (for young people), 1887; *In the Clouds*, 1886; *His Vanished Star*, 1894; *The Mystery of Witch Face Mountain* (short stories), 1895; *The Young Mountaineers* (short stories), 1897; *The Fair Mississippian*, 1908; *The Story of Dulciehurst*, 1914.

For life and criticism, see: W. M. Baskervill, *Southern Writers*, 1897; Edd. W. Parks, *Charles E. Craddock* (announced for publication in

1932); F. L. Pattee, *Amer. Lit. since 1870* (pp. 308–316), 1915.

628. THE "HARNT" THAT WALKS CHIL-HOWEE. In *Atlantic*, May, 1883; collected in *In the Tennessee Mountains*, 1884. ¶628. *"Chilhowee."* The lower of two chains of mountains in east Tennessee.

Joel Chandler Harris (1848–1908)

Joel Chandler Harris, the son of Mary Harris and a young Irish laborer, was born near Eatonton, Putnam County, Ga., Dec. 9, 1848. He spent his first fourteen years in Eatonton with his mother, who stirred his literary ambitions. He attended the local academy and in 1862 became a printer's devil on the *Country-man*, for which he began to write. In consequence of the desolation caused by Sherman's march in 1864, he was forced to secure temporary employment on papers in Macon and New Orleans. Returning to Eatonton in 1867, he secured a reputation as a humorist from the time of his association with the Savannah *Morning News* in 1870. In 1876 he joined the staff of the Atlanta *Constitution*, remaining with it for 24 years as a strong force in liberalism. In 1877 Harris began an intensive study of negro folklore and dialect and began to write stories aimed at a faithful reproduction of both. His first tales, later published in book form as his first volume, were immensely popular in both Northern and Southern newspapers. He followed this volume with many similar collections, as well as with children's stories, miscellaneous articles, novels, and especially short stories portraying realistically the life of both mountaineer and negro that give Harris a deservedly high place among the founders of American realism. From 1907 until his death he was editor of *Uncle Remus's Magazine*. He died July 3, 1908. The rare sweetness of his personality has made him one of the most affectionately remembered of recent American writers.

Uncle Remus: His Songs and Sayings, 1880; *Nights with Uncle Remus*, 1883; *Mingo and Other Sketches in Black and White*, 1884; *Free Joe and Other Georgian Sketches*, 1887; *Balaam and His Master* (short stories), 1891; *Daddy Jake the Runaway and Short Stories Told after Dark*, 1889; *Uncle Remus and His Friends*, 1892; *Tales of the Home Place in Peace and War*, 1898; *Gabriel Tolliver, a Story of Reconstruction*, 1902; *The Tar Baby and Other Rhymes of Uncle Remus*, 1904; *Told by Uncle Remus*, 1905; *Uncle Remus and Brer Rabbit*, 1906; *Uncle Remus and the Little Boy*, 1910; *Uncle Remus Returns*, 1918; *Joel Chandler Harris:*

Editor and Essayist (collection of newspaper and magazine writings of Harris, ed. by Julia Collier Harris), 1931.

For life and criticism, see: Ruth I. Cline, "The Tar-Baby Story," *Am. Lit.*, March, 1930; W. M. Baskervill, *Southern Writers*, 1897; F. P. Gaines, *The Southern Plantation*, etc., 1924; Julia Collier Harris, *Life and Letters of Joel Chandler Harris*, 1918; J. H. Nelson, *The Negro Character in American Literature*, 1926; H. W. Odum, *An American Epoch*, 1930; E. C. Parsons, "Joel Chandler Harris and Negro Folklore," *Dial*, May 17, 1919; C. A. Smith, "Dialect Writers," *CHAL*, II; R. L. Wiggins, *The Life of Joel Chandler Harris*, etc., 1918.

For bibliography, see: *CHAL*, II, 611–614.

644. How Mr. Rabbit Was Too Sharp. From *Uncle Remus: His Songs and Sayings*, 1880.

645. Aunt Fountain's Prisoner. In *Scribner's*, March, 1887; collected in *Free Joe and Other Georgian Sketches*, 1887.

Thomas Nelson Page (1853–1922)

Thomas Nelson Page, descendant of two governors of Virginia, was born at Oakland Plantation, Hanover County, Va., Apr. 23, 1853. After a course at Washington College (now Washington and Lee University) when Robert E. Lee was its president, he taught for a year and then proceeded to the study of law, graduating in law at the University of Virginia in 1874. Though practicing his profession, chiefly in Richmond, he became interested in dialect verse through his acquaintance with the verse of Irwin Russell and, in 1877, contributed a dialect poem, "Uncle Gabe's White Folks," to *Scribner's Monthly*. His success in verse led to his attempts at prose dialect, and his first story, "Marse Chan," though reluctantly printed by the editors of the *Century* in 1884, won him an immediate reputation. This and similar stories appeared in his first book, *In Ole Virginia*. It was followed by a volume or dialect pieces, *Befo' de War*, published with A. C. Gordon. In 1893 Page removed to Washington, D. C., to devote himself to writing and lecturing. He became identified with the portrayal of the more romantic aspects of Southern plantation life, especially the life of the gentry as presented through negro characters. From 1913 to 1918 he served as ambassador to Italy. He died at Oakland, Va., Nov. 1, 1922.

"Marse Chan," *Century Mag.*, 1884; *In Ole Virginia*, 1887; *Befo' de War*, 1888; *Two Little Confederates*, 1888; *The Old South*, 1892; *The Old Gentleman of the Black Stock*, 1897; *Red Rock*, 1898; *The Negro; the Southerner's Problem*, 1904; *Novels, Stories, Sketches, and Poems* (Plantation Ed.), 12 vols., 1906; *The Old Dominion; Her Making and Her Manners*, 1908; *Robert E. Lee, Man and Soldier*, 1911; *Italy and the World War*, 1920.

For life and criticism, see: Rosewell Page, *Thomas Nelson Page, a Memoir of a Virginia Gentleman*, 1923; Armistead C. Gordon, *Virginia Portraits*, 1924; Robert Underwood Johnson, commemorative tribute for the Academy of Arts and Letters, 1925; W. M. Baskervill, *Southern Writers*, 1897.

657. "Unc' Edinburg's Drowndin'." In *Harper's*, Jan., 1886; collected, *In Ole Virginia*, 1887.

Grace Elizabeth King (1852–1932)

Grace Elizabeth King, the daughter of a prominent lawyer of New Orleans and possessing a strain of Creole blood, was born in New Orleans in 1852. Except for comparatively brief periods, including her two years' visit to France, she lived all her life in the place of her birth, a member of the élite of that city. She was educated at one of the fashionable schools of New Orleans, and her home was a social and literary center. Sharing with many Southerners the disapproval of the Creole stories of George W. Cable, she determined to do justice to the class of Creoles that she knew so well and that Cable seemed not to know. Her first story, "Monsieur Motte," appeared in magazine form in 1886 and was followed by many others presenting delicate, minute studies of character. Gradually she became interested in the environment of her characters to the extent that her writing shifted from fiction to history. She had just completed a book of her reminiscences when she died, Jan. 14, 1932.

Monsieur Motte, 1888; *Tales of Time and Place*, 1888; *Earthlings*, 1889; *Chevalier Alain de Triton*, 1889; *Jean Baptiste Lemoine, Founder of New Orleans*, 1892; *Balcony Stories*, 1893 *History of Louisiana*, 1893; *New Orleans: the Place and the People*, 1896; *DeSoto and His Men in the Land of Florida*, 1898; *Stories from Louisiana History*, 1905; *Memories of a Southern Woman of Letters*, 1932.

For life and criticism, see: W. M. Baskervill, *Southern Writers*, 1897; Grace E. King, *Memories of a Southern Woman of Letters*, 1932 F. L. Pattee, *American Literature since 1870* (esp. pp. 362–364), 1915.

674. A Drama of Three. From *Balcony Stories*, 1893. ¶675. "*Je ne sais . . .*": I know not what case. ¶677. "*Au de çà . . .*"

To the time of the Flood. ¶677. *"Roturier"*: plebeian.

Lew (Lewis) Wallace (1827–1905)

Lewis Wallace was born at Brookville, Ind., Apr. 10, 1827. After a brief period of study at Wabash College he took up the practice of law in Indianapolis. But on the outbreak of the War with Mexico he abandoned the law to recruit volunteers and served in the Mexican War, 1846–47. The Civil War offered him many opportunities for conspicuous service. As a major-general he assisted in the capture of Fort Donelson, was engaged in the Battle of Shiloh and saved Cincinnati, and commanded the eighth corps at Baltimore. He was credited with having saved the national capital from almost certain capture by delaying the advance of the Confederate general, J. A. Early. He served as president of the courts of inquiry that investigated the conduct of Gen. D. C. Buell and condemned Henry Wirz, commander of the Confederate prison at Andersonville, Ga. He was likewise a member of the court which tried the alleged conspirators against President Lincoln. In 1865 he resigned from the army to return to the practice of law, but in 1878 he was appointed governor of New Mexico Territory. He served in that capacity till 1881, when he was appointed minister to Turkey, where he remained till 1885. The publication of *Ben Hur* in 1880 had won him an immense popularity, which called into higher favor his earlier and better novel *The Fair God*, little regarded when it appeared. Returning to America, he settled in Crawfordsville, where he built a unique Byzantine study on his beautiful beech-covered estate and wrote his third important novel, the fruit of his stay in Turkey, *The Prince of India*. His other writings proved of comparatively little significance. He died in Crawfordsville, Ind., Feb. 15, 1905.

The Fair God, 1873; *Ben Hur*, 1880; *Life of Gen. Benjamin Harrison*, 1888; *The Boyhood of Christ*, 1889; *Commodus; A Tragedy* (blank verse), 1889; dramatization of *Ben Hur* by William Young, 1889; *The Prince of India*, 1893; *The Story of American Heroism*, etc. (Wallace and others), 1896; *The Wooing of Malkatoon* and *Commodus*, 1898; *Lew Wallace: an Autobiography*, 1906.

For life and criticism, see: E. F. Harkins, *Famous Men*, 1906; Lew Wallace, *Autobiography*, 1906; same, Preface to "The First Christmas" (Book I of *Ben Hur*), for explanation of origin of *Ben Hur*.

679. BATTLE IN THE AIR. Climax of *The Fair God*, 1873.

Frank R. (Francis Richard) Stockton (1834–1902)

Francis Richard Stockton (known in literature as Frank R. Stockton) was born in Philadelphia, Apr. 5, 1834. On the completion of his high-school course he studied wood engraving, but his literary tastes induced him to turn to journalism. He contributed to various periodicals and served on the editorial staffs of *Hearth and Home*, the *Century Magazine*, and *St. Nicholas* (assistant editor of the last from 1873). His reputation was established by the new whimsical tone of *Rudder Grange*, appearing first in magazine form and later enlarged in book form (1879). Equally popular were the novels of similar tone, *The Casting Away of Mrs. Lecks and Mrs. Aleshine* and its sequel *The Dusantes*. But the height of his fame was achieved by the unique story "The Lady or the Tiger?" (1884). Stockton was a prolific writer of effective short stories of varied subject-matter but light and entertaining in style and tone. Much of his attention was given, especially in his earlier years, to children's stories. From 1880 he gave up his editorial work for a career of independent authorship. He died in Washington, D. C., Apr. 20, 1902.

Ting-a-ling Stories, 1869; *Tales out of School*, 1875; *Rudder Grange*, 1879; *The Lady or the Tiger? and Other Stories*, 1884; *The Casting Away of Mrs. Lecks and Mrs. Aleshine*, 1886; *A Christmas Wreck and Other Stories*, 1886; *The Late Mrs. Null*, 1886; *The Dusantes*, 1888; *Amos Kilbright and Other Stories*, 1888; *The Merry Chanter*, 1890; *The Squirrel Inn*, 1891; *Rudder Grangers Abroad*, 1891; *Pomona's Travels*, 1894; *A Story-Teller's Pack*, 1897; *The Great Stone of Sardis*, 1898; *Buccaneers and Pirates of Our Coast*, 1898; *A Bicycle of Cathay*, 1900; *The Novels and Stories of Frank R. Stockton* (Shenandoah ed.), 23 vols., 1900.

For life and criticism, see: F. W. Halsey, *Authors of Our Day*, etc., 1901; E. F. Harkins, *Famous Authors*, 1906; F. L. Pattee, *American Literature since 1870* (esp. pp. 358–361), 1915.

687. RUDDER GRANGE. In *Scribner's Monthly*, Nov., 1874. This sketch underwent much polishing before it appeared in book form in 1879.

Helen Hunt Jackson (1830–1885)

Helen Maria Fiske, the daughter of Nathan Welby Fiske, a professor of languages in Amherst College, was born at Amherst, Mass.,

Oct. 15, 1830. She was cared for by an aunt and received her education in a female academy and in New York City. She was a neighbor and schoolmate of Emily Dickinson, and the two were lifelong friends. In 1852 she was married to Edward Bissell Hunt, an army engineer who lived a roaming life in discharge of his duties. Major Hunt was killed in 1863 while working on a submarine invention. Mrs. Hunt now went to Newport, R. I., where, under the stimulus of T. W. Higginson, she began to write poems and prose sketches, which had immediate acceptance in the magazines. After publishing a volume of verse in 1870 and a book of travel sketches in 1872, she visited California (1872) and Colorado (1875), marrying William Sharpless Jackson, a financier, in 1875. In 1879–81 she became a champion of the rights of the American Indian. After the publication of her book *A Century of Dishonor* (1881), she was asked to assist in a government investigation of the Mission Indians of California, and in 1884 published her novel *Ramona* as a protest against the cruelty to the Indians. She died Aug. 12, 1885, after a prolonged illness. She usually wrote over the signature "H. H." But her shyness and predilection for mystery resulted in the publication of much of her prolific output without any identification.

Verses by H. H., 1870; *Bits of Travel*, 1872; *Poems*, 1873; *Saxe Holm's Stories* (anon.), 1874–78; *Bits of Talk, in Verse and Prose, for Young Folks*, 1876; *Mercy Philbrick's Choice* (in No-Name series), 1876; *Hetty's Strange History*, 1877; *Bits of Travel at Home*, 1878; *Nelly's Silver Mine*, 1878; *The Story of Boon* (poem), 1874; *A Century of Dishonor*, 1881; *The Training of Children*, 1882; *Glimpses of California and the Missions*, 1883; *Ramona*, 1884; *Zeph*, 1885; *Glimpses of Three Coasts*, 1886; *Sonnets and Lyrics*, 1886; *Between Whiles*, 1887.

For life and criticism, see: Margaret V. Allen, *Ramona's Homeland*, 1914; anon., "Ramona and Helen Hunt Jackson's Centenary," *Pub. Wkly.*, Oct. 10, 1931; Martha D. Bianchi, *The Life and Letters of Emily Dickinson*, 1924; M. D. Conway, *Autobiography, Memories and Experiences*, 1904; C. C. Davis and W. A. Alderson, *The True Story of Ramona*, 1914; T. W. Higginson, *Contemporaries*, 1899; George Wharton James, *Ramona's Country*, 1909; D. A. Hufford, *The Real Ramona*, 1900; F. C. Peirce, *Fiske and the Fisk Family*, 1896; Josephine Pollitt, *Emily Dickinson, the Human Background of Her Poetry*, 1930; Louise Pound, "Biographical Accuracy and 'H. H.' " *Am. Lit.*, January, 1931: sketch in N. Y. *Tribune*, Aug. 14, 1885; Frances E. Willard and Mary A.

Livermore, *American Women*, Vol. 2 (ed. 1897). See also *The History of the Town of Amherst, Mass.*, 1896.

699. THE LOT OF THE INDIAN. From *Ramona*, 1884.

Francis Marion Crawford
(1854–1909)

Francis Marion Crawford, the son of Thomas Crawford (an American sculptor residing in Italy) and Louisa Cutler Ward (sister of Julia Ward Howe), was born at Bagni-di-Lucca, Italy, Aug. 2, 1854. He spent the first eleven years of his life in Rome. Having been sent to relatives in Virginia, he was for two years a pupil in St. Paul's School, Concord, N. H., and then returned to Europe for a ten-year education in various parts of the Continent and England, including Rome, Essex (England), Trinity College (Cambridge), Karlsruhe, and Heidelberg. He became fluent in most of the languages of Europe, including Russian and Turkish; he later added an acquaintance with several Far Eastern tongues. In 1879, having become interested in the study of Sanskrit, he went to India to continue his studies and, to meet financial difficulties, served as editor of the Allahabad *Indian Herald* for 18 months. In 1880 he was back in Rome but came to America the following year to pursue the study of Sanskrit at Harvard. While uncertain of what career to follow he was urged by his uncle to put into a novel a well-told tale of an Indian happening, with the result that *Mr. Isaacs*, written in six weeks and published in 1882, was the successful opener to a long series of novels that occupied him till his death. In 1885 he settled in Sorrento, Italy, where he occupied the "Villa Crawford" overlooking the Bay of Naples until his death there Apr. 9, 1909. Crawford was a born story-teller, whose creed insisted that the art of the fiction-writer was one of entertainment exclusively. A natural cosmopolite, he was at home in all quarters of the globe, whether in the flesh or in the pages of imagined experience. His "Saracinesca" series has not been excelled in the field of convincing historical romance. He carried the same skill into the realm of the short story, showing special dexterity in the handling of the supernatural, as in the story "The Upper Berth."

Mr. Isaacs, 1882; *A Roman Singer*, 1884; *An American Politician*, 1885; *Zoroaster*, 1885; *Marzio's Crucifix*, 1887; *Paul Patoff*, 1887; *Saracinesca*, 1887; *With the Immortals*, 1888; *Sant' Ilario*, 1889; *A Cigarette Maker's Romance*

1890; *Khaled*, 1891; *The Children of the King*, 1892; *Don Orsino*, 1892; *Pietro Ghisleri*, 1892; *The Novel: What It Is*, 1893; *Constantinople*, 1895; *Adam Johnstone's Son*, 1895; *Corleone*, 1896; *Via Crucis*, 1898; *Ave Roma Immortalis*, 1898; *In the Palace of the King*, 1900; *Francesca da Rimini*, produced 1902; *Whosoever Shall Offend*, 1904; *Salve Venetia; Gleanings from Venetian History*, 1905; *Arethusa*, 1907; *The Primadonna*, 1908; *Stradella*, 1909; *Wandering Ghosts*, 1911; *Collected Works* (Sorrento ed.), 30 vols., 1919.

For life and criticism, see: Anon., "The Novels of F. Marion Crawford," *Edin. Rev.*, July, 1906; Max Beerbohm, "Crawford versus Dante," *Sat. Rev.*, June 21, 1902; F. T. Cooper, "Marion Crawford," *Forum*, May, 1909; M. C. Fraser, "Notes of a Romantic Life," *Collier's*, Apr. 23, 1910; E. F. Haskins, *Little Pilgrimages among the Men Who Have Written Famous Books*, 1902; F. L. Pattee, *Amer. Lit. since 1870*, 1915; Louise de la Ramee ("Ouida"), "The Italian Novels of Marion Crawford," *Nineteenth Cent.*, Nov., 1897; W. P. Trent, "Mr. Crawford's Novels," *Sewanee Rev.*, Feb., 1894.

For bibliography, see: CHAL, IV, 660.

712. THE UPPER BERTH. In the collection, *The Upper Berth* (Vol. I, Antonym Lib.), 1894; again collected in *Wandering Ghosts*, 1911. The publisher notes that this story had appeared in a Christmas annual "issued some years back." Compare Fitz James O'Brien, "What Was It?"

(*James*) *Maurice Thompson* (*1844–1901*)

James Maurice Thompson, known in literature as Maurice Thompson, was born at Fairfield, Ind., Sept. 9, 1844. Educated in Georgia, he served in the Confederate army during the Civil War. He later settled in Indiana and practiced law and civil engineering in Crawfordsville, Ind. From this period dates his interest in Hoosier ways that resulted in his volume of sketches called *Hoosier Mosaics* (1875). He published poems on nature subjects and conventional classic themes in the periodicals, and showed his peculiar interest in archery, of which he was a master, in *The Witchery of Archery* (1878). From 1885 to 1889 he was state geologist of Indiana and chief of the Dept. of Natural History. In 1890 he joined the staff of the N. Y. *Independent*. In his later years he turned to fiction, producing one of the best of the historical romances in vogue at the end of the century,

Alice of Old Vincennes (1900). He died Feb. 15, 1900.

Hoosier Mosaics, 1875; *The Witchery of Archery*, 1878; *His Second Campaign*, 1882; *By-Ways and Bird Notes*, 1885; *The Boy's Book of Sport*, 1886; *Sylvan Secrets*, 1887; *Poems*, 1892; *The Ocala Boy*, 1895; *My Winter Garden*, 1900; *Alice of Old Vincennes*, 1900.

For life and criticism, see: W. M. Baskervill, *Southern Writers*, 1897.

728. WILD HONEY. In *Atlantic*, Jan., 1883. Praised by Frost as one of the few genuine nature poems of this era.

728. A CREOLE SLAVE-SONG. In *Poems*, 1892.

James Whitcomb Riley (*1849–1916*)

James Whitcomb Riley, a product of pioneer stock, was born in Greenfield, Ind., Oct. 7, 1849. He spent the kind of happy boyhood recorded in his poems, and his distaste for his father's profession of the law sent him out on a wandering life of several years, during which he acted as an itinerant sign-painter (at times astonishing onlookers by his feats as a supposedly blind painter of soap-signs on windows), as entertainer, and as assistant to patent-medicine vendors. This experience taught him the art of entertainment and gave him an invaluable knowledge of the real sentiments of all classes of people in Indiana, especially the rural folk. His first reputation came through his poems published in newspapers, enhanced by the notoriety achieved from his hoax of publishing one of his own compositions as a poem of Poe's. His poems in dialect, ostensibly written by a farmer, "Benjamin F. Johnson of Boone," first contributed to the Indianapolis *Daily Journal*, appeared in his first book of verse, *The Old Swimmin' Hole and 'Leven More Poems* (1883). His popularity steadily increased with the publication of the numerous similar volumes that followed. He became in great demand as a reader of his own verse, appearing with his friends, Bill Nye and Eugene Field, on the Chautauqua circuit. He was elected to the American Academy of Arts and Letters, awarded the gold medal of the National Institute of Arts and Letters, and was honored in 1915 with the distinction of having his birthday declared an official holiday in Indiana. Except for a short period when he acted as local editor of the Anderson (Ind.) *Democrat*, he spent the greater part of his later life in Indianapolis, where he died July 22, 1916.

The Old Swimmin' Hole and 'Leven More Poems, 1883; *The Boss Girl*, 1886 (repub. 1891 as *Sketches in Prose*); *Old Fashioned Roses*, 1888; *Pipes o' Pan at Zekesbury*, 1889; *The Flying Islands of the Night*, 1892; *A Child-World*, 1896; *Home Folks*, 1900; *Poems and Prose Sketches* (Homestead Ed.), 16 vols., 1897–1914; "Biographical" edition of works, ed. by E. H. Eitel, 1913; *Complete Works* (Memorial Ed.), 10 vols., 1916; *The Lockerbie Book* (conventional English verse, ed. by Hewitt Howland), 1911; *The Hoosier Book* (dialect verse, ed. by Hewitt Howland), 1916.

For life and criticism, see: Marcus Dickey, *The Youth of James Whitcomb Riley*, 1919; same, *The Maturity of James Whitcomb Riley*, 1922; Clara E. Laughlin, *Reminiscences of James Whitcomb Riley*, 1916; Edgar Lee Masters, "James Whitcomb Riley," *Century Mag.*, Oct., 1927; Meredith Nicholson, *Atlantic*, 116, 503–14; same, *The Hoosiers*, 1900; William Lyon Phelps (ed.), *Letters of James Whitcomb Riley*, 1930.

729. THE OLD SWIMMIN'-HOLE. Contributed to the Indianapolis *Journal* under the name of "Benjamin F. Johnson of Boone"; collected in *The Old Swimmin' Hole*, 1883.

730. A LIFE-LESSON. In *Poems Here at Home*, 1893.

730. THE OLD MAN AND JIM. In *Pipes o' Pan at Zekesbury*, 1889.

732. BEREAVED. In *Century*, Nov., 1890.

Eugene Field (1850–1895)

Eugene Field, whose parents were natives of Vermont, was born in St. Louis, Mo., Sept. 2, or 3, 1850. After the death of his mother in 1856, he spent thirteen years in the East in the care of a cousin, Miss Mary Field French of Amherst, Mass. Following attendance at a private school he spent a year at Williams College (1868–69) and a year at Knox College (Galesburg, Ill.), and was then transferred to the University of Missouri in 1870. But, coming into his inheritance at the age of 21 (his junior year in college), he decided on a trip to Europe, where in 1872 he himself tells us that he spent "six months and patrimony in France, Italy, Ireland, and England." The year 1873 saw his marriage and his entrance into journalism, the field of his activities till his death. Starting as a reporter on the St. Louis *Evening Journal*, he served successively on the St. Joseph (Mo.) *Gazette*, the Kansas City *Times*, and the Denver *Tribune*. During his association with the *Tribune* he published *The Tribune Primer* (1882), which attracted such wide attention that he received various offers on eastern newspapers. He accepted a position on

the Chicago *Morning News* in 1883 and proceeded to make his column, "Sharps and Flats," the most attractive *mélange* of the day. But he did not become known to the permanent reading public till the publication of "Little Boy Blue" in 1887, and it was not until the publication of his *Little Book of Western Verse* five years before his death, that he won a place of general acceptance as a writer. His early death, Nov. 4, 1895, was mourned by a host of those who had been the beneficients of his humor, sentiment, and whimsey.

The Tribune Primer, 1882; *Culture's Garland*, 1887; *A Little Book of Western Verse*, 1889; *A Little Book of Profitable Tales*, 1890; *Echoes from the Sabine Farm*, 1892; *With Trumpet and Drum*, 1892; *Second Book of Verse*, 1892; *The Holy Cross and Other Tales*, 1893; intro. to Stone's *First Editions of American Authors*, 1893; *Collected Works*, 10 vols., 1896; *Sharps and Flats*, 1900.

For life and criticism, see: Charles H. Dennis, *Eugene Field's Creative Years*, 1924; Eugene Field, *Auto Analysis*, 1896; Hamlin Garland, "A Dialogue between Eugene Field and Hamlin Garland," *McClure's Mag.*, August, 1893; E. C. Stedman, *Genius and Other Essays*, 1911; Slason Thompson, *Eugene Field, a Study in Heredity and Contradictions*, 1901; same, *Life of Eugene Field*, 1927; Francis Wilson, *The Eugene Field I Knew*, 1898; same, "Eugene Field, the Humorist," *Century Mag.*, July, 1902.

For bibliography, see: *CHAL*, II, 543 and IV, 641.

732. LITTLE BOY BLUE. In *Culture's Garland*, 1887.

732. CASEY'S TABLE D'HÔTE. "This and 'The Biblomaniac's Prayer' first appeared in Field's column of the Chicago *Daily News* in Jan., 1889" (Dennis).

734. THE TRUTH ABOUT HORACE. In *A Little Book of Western Verse*, 1889. ¶734. "*Carmina* Horace's name for his *Odes*. Field translated many of these. See: *Echoes from the Sabine Farm*, 1892. ¶734. "*No. 25.*" "To Lydia, is hardly amatory, but expresses the poet' pique. ¶735. "*Mæcenas.*" The wealthy patron of Horace.

735. THE BIBLIOMANIAC'S PRAYER. See above. Collected in *A Little Book of Western Verse*, 1889. ¶735. "*Lowndes.*" William Thomas, English bibliographer (1798–1843).

Edgar Watson Howe (1853–   )

Edgar Watson Howe was born in Treaty, Ind., May 3, 1853. He had some education in the common schools but, like Howells an

Twain, obtained most of his training in the printing office, with which he has been connected since the age of twelve. At 19 (1872) he became publisher of the *Golden Globe*, Golden, Colo. From 1877 to 1911 he was editor and proprietor of the Atchison (Kan.) *Daily Globe*, and since 1911 he has been editor and publisher of *E. W. Howe's Monthly*. His home is in Atchison, Kan. Mr. Howe attracted the attention of discriminating critics with his first novel *The Story of a Country Town*, first printed privately in 1883, read widely for a while, and then almost forgotten until the era of the *Spoon River Anthology* revived interest in it as the pioneer book in its field—unadulterated realism. No other works of Mr. Howe have seemed nearly so significant, except perhaps his *Anthology of Another Town* and his autobiographic *Plain People*, though his aphoristic journalism has won him a distinctive place among American newspaper oracles.

The Story of a Country Town, 1883, 1884, etc. (including special editions, 1917, 1926, 1927); *The Mystery of the Locks*, 1885; *A Moonlight Boy*, 1886; *A Man Story*, 1889; *An Ante-Mortem Statement*, 1891; *Daily Notes of a Trip around the World*, 1907; *Country Town Sayings: a Collection of Paragraphs from the Atchison Globe*, 1911; *The Trip to the West Indies*, 1910; *Travel Letters from New Zealand, Australia, and Africa*, 1913; *Ventures in Common Sense*, 1919; *The Anthology of Another Town*, 1920; *Plain People, an Autobiography*, 1929.

For life and criticism, see: Percy H. Boynton, *The Rediscovery of the Frontier*, 94 ff.; E. W. Howe, *Plain People*, 1929; same, Preface to revised editions of *The Story of a Country Town*; W. D. Howells, "Two Notable Novels," *Cent. Mag.*, Aug., 1884; same, intro. to 1917 edition of *The Story of a Country Town*; Carl Van Doren, intro. to 1926 edition of the same.

736. A SKELETON IN THE HOUSE. From the *Story of a Country Town*, 1883.

Joseph Kirkland (1830–1894)

Joseph Kirkland, the son of Caroline M. Kirkland (author of *A New Home: Who'll Follow?* 1839), was born at Geneva, N. Y., Jan. 7, 1830. Educated in the schools of Michigan, he made his home in Illinois after 1856. He served in the Federal army during the Civil War, attaining to the rank of major. Engaged in coal mining in Illinois and Indiana for a time, he later practiced law in Chicago, where he died in 1894. The publication of his novel *Zury* (1887) reenforced the realistic emphasis of E. W. Howe's *Story of a Country Town*

(1883), and Kirkland was, with Eggleston, an important influence in the shaping of the literary career of Hamlin Garland.

Zury, the Meanest Man in Spring County, 1887; *The McVeys*, 1888; *The Captain of Company K*, 1891; *The Chicago Massacre of 1812*, 1893; *The Story of Chicago*, 1892–94, rev. ed., 1904.

For criticism, see: Hamlin Garland, *A Son of the Middle Border*, 1917; W. D. Howells, *Harper's Mag.*, 77, 152; *Leslie's Weekly*, 83, 119. See also *Allibone's Dict. of Eng. Lit.* Supplement, Vol. 2, p. 957, and a review of *The McVeys* in *Lit. World*, 19, 382.

747. HOW THE MEANEST MAN GOT SO MEAN. From *Zury*, 1887.

Emily (Elizabeth) Dickinson (1830–1886)

Emily Elizabeth Dickinson (known in literature as Emily Dickinson) was born Dec. 10, 1830, in Amherst, Mass., the daughter of Emily Norcross and Edward Dickinson, a lawyer, member of Congress and the state legislature, and treasurer of Amherst College. The exact truth regarding some aspects of Emily Dickinson's life seems, amidst the contradictions of her biographers, impossible of determination as yet. But the following seems a fair statement of what we do know. The father demanded a great deal more of his children's presence in his household than was normal. Consequently none of them married until his death, and Emily's childhood seems to have been prolonged beyond the normal term. She received a very good education, attending the public schools, Amherst Academy, and Mount Holyoke Female Seminary (1847–48). She had numerous friends, especially among girls of talent such as Helen Fiske (Helen Hunt Jackson). She seems to have taken an active part in social affairs in Amherst and in the college until her middle twenties, when she began gradually to show her impatience of formal occasions and to withdraw to the seclusion of her own home. This withdrawal finally became a virtual self-imprisonment. Tradition ascribes this retirement to an affair of the heart, but her biographers differ as to the nature of this affair and as to who was the man in question. Certain it is that in 1854 she went to Washington, D. C., with her mother and sister, visiting Philadelphia before her return to Amherst. Whether she met someone on this trip, as some have felt, whose love she was unable to return to the extent of marriage, or whether she was involved in an affair with someone in Amherst, or whether there never was an actual love affair at all still remains undetermined. Her father's death and her mother's invalidism no doubt confirmed her habits of seclusion. She gave herself to the writing of delicate poems which she secreted and refused to publish, and to correspondence with numerous friends to whom she often enclosed her poems. Only two of her poems saw publication before her death, though she received sufficient encouragement from T. W. Higginson and others to warrant her appearing before the public. She suffered a two years' illness before her death, which occurred in Amherst May 15, 1886. The subject-matter of her verse is as incalculable as its form: love, death, immortality, flowers, fruit, sunsets, animals, locomotives, circuses—all these she sums with swift, intuitive delicacy and finality.

Poems, 1890; *Poems*, 1891; *Poems*, 1896; *The Single Hound*, 1914; *Complete Poems of Emily Dickinson* (contains contents of editions of 1890, 1891, 1896, and 1914), 1924; *Further Poems of Emily Dickinson*, 1929; *The Poems of Emily Dickinson* (Centenary Ed.), 1930; "Unfinished Poems of Emily Dickinson" (six hitherto unpublished poems), *New Eng. Quar.*, April, 1932.

For life and criticism, see: Conrad Aiken, preface to *Selected Poems of Emily Dickinson*, 1924; anon., "Two Unpublished Autograph Letters of Emily Dickinson," *Yale Univ. Lib. Gaz.*, Oct., 1931; M. H. Barney, "Fragments from Emily Dickinson to her Brother's Family," *Atlantic*, June, 1927; Martha Dickinson Bianchi, "Selections from the Unpublished Letters of Emily Dickinson," *Atlantic*, Jan., 1915; same, *Life and Letters of Emily Dickinson*, 1924; same, *Emily Dickinson Face to Face*, 1932; Gamaliel Bradford, *Portraits of American Women*, 1919; Katherine Bregy, *Catholic World*, Dec., 1924; Rollo W. Brown, *Lonely Americans*,

1929; T. W. Higginson, "Emily Dickinson's Letters," *Atlantic*, Oct., 1891; MacGregor Jenkins, *Emily Dickinson: Friend and Neighbor*, 1930; Josephine Pollitt, *Emily Dickinson: The Human Background of Her Poetry*, 1930; Genevieve Taggard, *The Life and Mind of Emily Dickinson*, 1930; Mabel Loomis Todd, *The Letters of Emily Dickinson*, 1894, 1906, rev. ed., 1931; Louis Untermeyer, "Thoughts after a Centenary," *Sat. Rev. Lit.*, June 20, 1931; same, "Emily Dickinson," *Sat. Rev. Lit.*, July 5, 1930; Anna M. Wells, "Early Criticism of Emily Dickinson," *Am. Lit.*, Nov. 1929.

For bibliography, see: Alfred Leete Hampson (compiler), *Emily Dickinson: A Bibliography*, 1930; George F. Whicher, *Emily Dickinson: A Bibliography*, 1930, 2nd ed., 1931; *Emily Dickinson* (a catalogue), Yale Univ. Library, 1930. The MS. letters and poems are in the Galatea Collection of the Boston Public Library.

755. THIS IS MY LETTER TO THE WORLD [and other poems here printed]. With the exception of some verses printed without her permission, none of Emily Dickinson's poems appeared in her lifetime. The dates indicated at the end of each selection are those of the different collections which have since appeared. ¶756. *"Boanerges."* Sons of thunder; name applied by Jesus to his disciples James and John (Mark 3:17).

756. LETTERS. From the 1894 edition. The recently published revised edition of these letters collected by Mrs. Todd makes some slight changes in wording and dates, but no changes that seriously alter the significance of the text as here printed. ¶760. *"Miss Prescott's Circumstance."* A short story, describing the encounter of a woman with a catamount, by Harriet Prescott Spofford, in *Atlantic*, May, 1860. ¶762. *"Brabantio's Gift."* Desdemona, yielded by her father to Othello. ¶762. *"Slipper hymn."* "After the Burial."

INDEX

Non-italic numbers refer to pages in text; italic numbers to pages in notes.